American Home All-Purpose Cookbook

Edited by Virginia T. Habeeb
and the Food Staff of American Home

Published by M. Evans and Company, Inc., New York

Library of Congress Catalog Card Number 66–23272
Manufactured in the United States of America

Designed by Edward Gorey
Illustrated by Jerry Schiano

Martha O'Neill

Table of Food Equivalents

Butter or Margarine
¼ pound = ½ cup
½ pound = 1 cup
Note: Measurement of whipped butter or margarine is greater.

Cream
Heavy cream, ½ pint (1 cup) = 2 cups whipped

Cheese
Cream cheese, 8-ounce package = 1 cup
Cottage cheese, ½-pound carton = 1 cup
Grated process American or Cheddar, ¼ pound = 1 cup
½ pound = 2 cups

Flour and Meal
All-purpose flour, 1 pound = 4 cups sifted
Cake flour, 1 pound = 4½ to 5 cups sifted
Cornmeal, 1 pound = 3 cups

Sugar
Granulated, 1 pound = 2¼ to 2½ cups
Superfine, 1 pound = 2⅓ cups
Confectioners' sugar, 1 pound = Approximately 4 cups, unsifted 4½ to 5 cups sifted
Light brown, 1 pound = 2⅓ cups, firmly packed
Dark brown, 1 pound = 2⅛ to 2¼ cups, firmly packed

Fruit
Apples, 1 pound = 3 medium (3 cups sliced)
1 medium, chopped = 1 cup
Bananas, 1 pound = 3 medium (2½ cups sliced)

Strawberries, 1 quart = 3½ cups hulled
Lemon juice, 1 medium lemon = 3 tablespoons
Lemon rind grated, 1 medium lemon = 1 tablespoon
Orange juice, 1 medium orange = ⅓ to ½ cup
Orange rind grated, 1 medium orange = 2 tablespoons
Dates, pitted, 8-ounce package = 1¾ cups, cut up
Raisins, seedless, 15-ounce package = 3 cups

Vegetables
Onions, 1 pound yellow = 5 or 6 medium, 3 large
1 pound small white = 12 to 14
1 medium, chopped = ½ cup
Potatoes, 1 pound white = 3 medium (2⅓ to 2½ cups sliced)
1 pound sweet = 3 medium (2½ to 3 cups sliced)
Green beans, 1 pound = 3 cups cut

Nuts (1 pound)

	In Shell	Shelled
Almond	1 to 1¾ cups nutmeats	3½ cups nutmeats
Peanuts	2 to 2¼ cups nutmeats	3 cups nutmeats
Pecans	2¼ cups nutmeats	4 cups nutmeats
Walnuts	1⅔ cups nutmeats	4 cups nutmeats

Pasta
Macaroni, elbow, 8 ounces = 2 cups uncooked 4 cups cooked
Spaghetti, (1½-inch pieces) 8 ounces = 2 cups uncooked 4 cups cooked
Noodles, 8 ounces = About 3 cups uncooked, 3¾ cups cooked

AMERICAN HOME
ALL-PURPOSE
COOKBOOK

Preface

THE AMERICAN HOME ALL-PURPOSE COOK-BOOK is dedicated to encouraging in every user a greater appreciation of fine foods, good eating, and a desire to become an accomplished, creative cook. It is dedicated to the purposeful thought that eating is one of life's most consistent pleasures.

This is a basic cookbook which sets forth the principles of creating fine foods and explains the whys and hows of good cooking. It is a cookbook for everyone, beginner or expert. It is devoted to:

· *Helping* the busy wife and mother with her day-by-day cooking for the family.
· *Giving* her ideas for adding new spark and imagination to her menu planning.
· *Guiding* her in the planning and preparation of those special occasions and dinner parties.
· *Encouraging* and assisting the young, inexperienced hostess to become a good cook and a confident, gracious party giver.
· *Teaching* the young bride to please her husband with newly acquired culinary skills.
· *Explaining* and analyzing the facts, the know-how, the secrets behind successful cookery.

You'll find here a large selection of favorite recipes developed over the years in our test kitchens. Many are those you have written and asked for to replace "the copy you lost." A very large number of them are brand new, never before published.

More than anything this cookbook is truly a labor of love . . . by a food staff with a special talent for knowing how to mix ingredients into that magic combination we call a *recipe*. It is the result of the cooperation and meticulous care of our associate food editors, Frances Crawford and Jane O'Keefe, who deserve very special accolades. Our thanks too go to Betty Wason, cookbook author and writer who supplied her special talents as consultant; to Renee Prowitt, production editor, to our secretaries . . . and to our editor Hubbard Cobb, whose appreciation for fine food and faith in his staff was an encouragement throughout.

We are grateful to the food industry and their associations for giving us the wonderfully versatile products on our supermarket shelves. Our thanks to their home economists and consumer service departments for supplying us with charts and reference material.

We hope you'll enjoy reading our book as well as cooking from it. There are pleasurable as well as informative hours to be spent here browsing and reading, and you'll derive the most from it by doing just this.

We offer it to you with the words of one of our favorite Frenchmen, Brillat-Savarin, author of the celebrated work on gastronomy, *La Physiologie du Goût*, "the discovery of a new dish does more for human happiness than the discovery of a new star."

Here's to many hours of new discoveries.

VIRGINIA T. HABEEB
Food and Home Equipment Editor

**THIS COOKBOOK IS DEDICATED to our husbands
and families whose patience made it possible.**

Contents

AMERICAN HOME
ALL-PURPOSE
COOKBOOK

Chapter One

Guide to Good Cooking

In this book we have collected what we think are the most delicious, the most succulent, the most memorable of all the thousands of recipes tested week after week, year after year, in our American Home kitchens. We are proud to be able to present them to you in a format which we hope will be foolproof.

But the most perfect of recipes can go wrong. It may be a matter of measuring, or a difference in ingredients, or a question of timing—or some other variable factor. Here, to help you avoid pitfalls, are a few important guide lines to success.

First, read the recipe carefully. Do you have all the ingredients called for? (An experienced cook can make certain substitutions, but the novice had better stick to the rules.) Do you have the proper utensils, including the right size pans? Check all necessary equipment before you start. Will you have time enough to get this particular dish ready on the day you plan to serve it? Read the recipe through once, then again, making sure you understand it. Confidence is a mighty important ingredient in itself.

Follow directions exactly. Keep the book propped up and the page held open so that you can refer to the recipe as many times

as necessary as you go along. We have worked hard to make instructions as clear and concise as possible, and every word is there for a reason. Where there is a specific technique required we have included a "secret" to success. Treat these secrets with respect.

Check the number of servings before you start. Each of our recipes gives a yield, or average number of servings. Remember these are servings—if second or third helpings are the rule in your family, plan accordingly. Also appetites differ greatly, and what is ample for four people in one household may be barely enough for two in another family. The rest of the menu makes a difference too. An entrée that follows a first course of soup or seafood need not be so plentiful as a stew that is a "one dish" meal. Then consider children's ages. Youngsters under six may consume only a third as much as an adult; teen-age boys sometimes require three times as much.

Within the confines of your own family, you will have learned these differences. However, when entertaining guests, it's always better to have too much than too little. If you are having six at a company dinner, choose recipes with a yield of at least eight to ten servings so that you may offer seconds.

1

Always Measure Accurately

You are all set to go, you have every ingredient, all the right utensils, and you are in the proper mood to try something new. To make sure of success, use standard measuring spoons and cups and *measure carefully*.

Measuring spoons should be used for any measurements, liquid or solid, of less than ¼ cup. Standard measuring spoons come in sets of ¼ teaspoon, ½ teaspoon, 1 teaspoon, and 1 tablespoon. All spoon measurements must be level (a "heaping tablespoon" could vary from 1¼ to 1¾ level tablespoons). To measure, fill to the top, level off with edge of table knife or small spatula.

Experienced cooks may be able to gauge ¼ teaspoon of an herb or other condiment by eye—especially when making the kind of sauce or stew that can be "taste-tested" as one goes along, but as a general rule even this small amount should be measured accurately, not by guess.

To measure ⅛ teaspoon, fill the ¼ teaspoon measure, level it, cut lengthwise through the middle, use only one-half. It is not necessary to measure 1/16 teaspoon. When a recipe gives such a measure, it is a way of telling you this is to be a mere pinch, or, as the French say, a *soupçon* (suspicion).

For measuring ½ tablespoon, or for dividing or multiplying spoon measurements, see the *Table of Equivalent Weights and Measures* on the inside front cover.

Cup measurements for *dry* ingredients (flour, sugar, rice, cereals, biscuit mix, etc.) should be made in graduated cups (metal or plastic) which come in nests of ¼ cup, ⅓ cup, ½ cup, and 1 cup sizes.

Flour and some sugars should be sifted before measuring. Fill the cup lightly, gently level off the top with the edge of a knife or spatula. There are three exceptions: the new instant flours, white sugar, unless it is lumpy, and brown sugar.

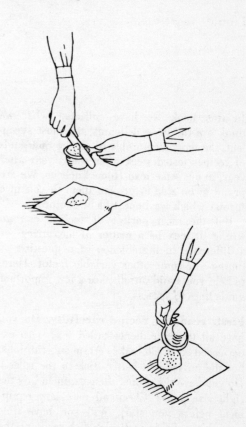

Brown sugar should be pressed down firmly into the measuring cup with the back of a spoon. It should hold its shape when turned out. If it has become dry, hard, or lumpy, brown sugar may have to be crushed with a rolling pin before measuring, or it may be heated in a 250° F. oven until soft. Use immediately. To store brown sugar and keep it soft, put it in a tightly covered container. Should it show signs of lumping, place a dampened bit of a new sponge inside the container for a few days to remoisten the sugar.

The new granulated brown sugar can be poured directly from the spout of the package into the cup. But because it has been processed differently, it is bulkier and drier, and some adjustment in cup measurement will be necessary for most recipes. Check the substitution chart on the package label and in case of doubt, use granulated brown sugar only when so specified in recipes.

Such solid ingredients as fruit, nuts, coconut, breadcrumbs, and grated cheese should also be measured in graduated cups.

Liquid ingredients—water, milk, juices, wine, syrups, and oils, are best measured in a glass measuring cup with a rim above the

1-cup line (to avoid spilling). Fill the cup to the measure indicated on the cup's side. Set cup on the counter and read measure at eye level.

Solid shortenings may be measured in one of several ways. If softened, vegetable shortening, butter, or margarine may be pressed down firmly into a graduated cup and the top leveled off.

For an easier way to measure less than 1 cup solid shortening, use a liquid measuring cup and the "water method." For example, to measure ½ cup shortening, place ½ cup water in the cup; add shortening until the water reaches the 1-cup line. For ⅓ cup shortening, first add water to the ⅔-cup line, then add shortening to raise water level to 1 cup; for ¼ cup shortening, first add water to the ¾-cup line—and so on.

Butter and margarine often come in ¼-pound sticks which have tablespoon measurements indicated on the paper wrappers. These are convenient, but a word of caution: in the process of wrapping, the printed measures sometimes become a little inaccurate. When a tablespoon or two of butter is to be used for sautéing, this slight difference may not matter, but in some recipes it could make considerable difference. Then it is better to press the softened butter into a standard tablespoon or graduated cup measure and level off the top.

A ¼-pound stick of butter or margarine is exactly ½ cup, helpful to remember when a recipe calls for this amount. This means 2 sticks of butter (½ pound) are equivalent to 1 cup, 3 sticks to 1½ cups, and so on. To measure ¼ cup butter, cut the stick in half.

Melted butter or other shortening should be measured by one of the above methods *before* melting. Otherwise, when pouring hot fat into a measuring cup or spoon you might burn your fingers—or break a glass cup.

Be Sure You Use the Right Size Pan

Just as important as accurate measurement of ingredients is using the correct size pan or baking dish in food preparation. Always check the recipe to make sure you have the right size before you start mixing ingredients.

Many manufacturers are now indicating the pan size on the bottom of the pan, but suppose you aren't sure of the size of your pans? It's easy to find out; use a ruler to measure depth, width, and diameter. For casseroles or molds, fill with water, measure the water. A 1½-quart casserole or mold will hold 6 cups of water.

Here is a list of pans generally found on the market with their measurements as manufactured. In some cases, glass and metal ones may be substituted for each other and are so indicated on the chart. Recipes in this book will call for pans by the nearest whole number, omitting fractions. Some recipes call for pans or pan sizes (Turk's head mold, tartlette pans) that may not be generally available. Look for these in specialty gourmet bakeware shops or departments.

	PAN SIZES	
Pan	*Metal*	*Glass*
Round Layer Cake Pans	8 × 1½ inches 9 × 1½ inches	1½ quarts (8¼ × 1¾ inches)
Square Cake Pans	8 × 8 × 2 inches 9 × 9 × 1¾ inches	2 quarts (8 × 8 × 2 inches)
Rectangular Cake Pans and Baking Dishes	12¾ × 9 × 2 inches	1½ quarts (10 × 6 × 1¾ inches) 2 quarts (11¾ × 7½ × 1¾ inches) 3 quarts (13½ × 8¾ × 1¾ inches)
Round Baking Dishes (Deep)		1 quart (6½ × 2½ inches) 1½ quarts (7½ × 2½ inches) 2 quarts (8¼ × 2¾ inches) 3 quarts (9¾ × 3 inches)
Tube Pans (Some have removable bottoms)	8¾ × 3½ inches 9¾ × 4½ inches	
Loaf Pans	7⅜ × 3⅝ × 2¼ inches 9¼ × 5¼ × 2¾ inches 16 × 14½ × 4⅛ inches	1½ quarts (8⅜ × 4½ inches) 2 quarts (9½ × 5⅛ inches)
Pie Pans and Plates	5 inches (tart) 8 inches 9 inches 10 inches	6 inches 8 inches 9 inches 10 inches 11 inches
Tart pans	2½-3½ inches	
Cookie Sheets	12 × 16 inches 14 × 9 inches 14 × 10 inches 15½ × 12 inches 17 × 14 inches	
Jelly-Roll Pan	15½ × 10½ × 1 inch	
Muffin Pans	6 cup: 2¼ and 2½ inch cups 9 cup: 2½ inch cups 12 cup: 2½ inch cups	
Gem Pan (small muffin pan)	12 cup: 1¾ inch cups	
Custard Cups and Deep Pie Dishes		5 ounces (3 × 2 inches) 6 ounces (3½ × 1¾ inches) 10 ounces (4½ × 1¾ inches) 1 pint (5 × 1¾ inches)
Springform Pan	8 × 3 inches 9 × 3 inches 10 × 3 inches	
Turban or Turk's Head Mold	2 quart 3 quart	

PAN SIZES (*Continued*)		
Pan	*Metal*	
Ring Molds	2¾ cups 4½ cups 6 cups (1½ quarts) 6½ cups 11 cups 12 cups (3 quarts)	
Bundt Pan	11 × 4 inches	

How to Divide or Multiply Recipes

Even for the experienced cook, dividing or multiplying recipes can be tricky. The danger is that halfway through you may become confused and forget whether or not you have added half as much (or twice as much, as the case may be) of a particular ingredient.

To be on the safe side, write out the changes in measurements, clip this to the page beside the recipe and use the revised ingredient list, following the same method as in the book. It's a good idea to file away this revised ingredient list, in case you want to use it on a future occasion. Use the *Table of Equivalent Weights and Measures* (see inside front cover) as a mathematical guide.

To divide a recipe in half, use exactly half the amount of each ingredient as listed. With certain ingredients, this may be difficult. If you want to divide a recipe which calls for 1 egg, for example, what do you do? In certain recipes, such as muffins or waffles, the additional amount of egg will make little difference except that the batter will be lighter and slightly thinner. But if you do want to use only half an egg, beat it first, measure, then divide it.

To double a recipe (generally a main dish) use exactly twice as much of each ingredient. However, for best results in making pies, cakes, and desserts, we recommend that you make the recipe exactly as it appears, then repeat it as many times as needed.

Shop for the Best Values

Shopping can be stimulating. The 8,000 or more products in today's supermarket can be both dazzling and confusing. Yet the dish you prepare will be no better than the ingredients that go into it.

How does one know which are the best buys? When are fresh products preferable to frozen—and vice versa? When is a bargain really a bargain?

For flavor and taste, the fresh product may be worth added time and trouble, especially when vegetables or fruits are in the peak of their season. And the creative satisfaction in producing a fragrant loaf of fresh-baked bread or an aromatic stew redolent of herbs is beyond price.

But there are other times when you prefer to take advantage of time-saving convenience foods. Studies have established that the majority of today's convenience foods are real bargains. They save time and trouble, and *most* of them, serving for serving, cost only a little more than the fresh product, prepared the old-fashioned way. There is such a wide variety of convenience foods on the market that you may not be familiar with some of them. To help you with your shopping, check the chart below.

CONVENIENCE FOOD GUIDE

Here are many of the short-cut and instant foods now available at your supermarket— grouped according to the "work" they require once you've opened them. Use this as your buying guide.

Open and Serve

The most convenient of all! The work has been done for you and all you do is open and use.

Meat spreads:
    luncheon meat spread, deviled ham, chicken spread
Canned meats:
    boned chicken or turkey, dried beef, corned beef, Vienna sausages, ham
Canned fish:
    tuna, sardines, anchovies, shrimp, crab-meat, lobster, herring
Canned and frozen fruits

Canned and bottled juices
Dry cereal
Bakery products:
    cakes, pies, breads, rolls, coffee cakes
Crackers, cookies, and chips
Croutons
Dairy products:
    milk and flavored milk, cheeses and cheese
    spreads, butter, margarine, ice cream and
    sherbet
Cold cuts
Refrigerated salads and gelatin salads
Canned and ready-to-use frostings
Refrigerated shrimp cocktail
Mayonnaise and salad dressing
Bottled salad dressings
Prepared mustard
Bottled sauces:
    steak, meat, chili, catsup, Worcestershire,
    Hollandaise, Béarnaise, tartar
Frozen cream cakes and pies
Frozen cake
Canned and bottled beverages
Refrigerated canned milk shakes
Canned liquid diet food
Jellies, jams, preserves
Syrups
Peanut butter
Evaporated and condensed milk
Nondairy creamers

Heat and Serve

*These foods that are already cooked require
only heating to be ready to use.*
Canned vegetables
Frozen dinners and prepared dishes
Canned meats:
    hash, chili, meat balls, beef stew, chicken
    à la king, pickled pigs' feet, whole chicken
Canned and frozen soups
Canned sauces and gravies
Canned steamed clams
Canned puddings
Canned Chinese foods
Canned spaghetti and macaroni
Brown-and-serve rolls and sausages
Frozen main dish and dessert pies
Frozen coffee cakes, doughnuts, rolls
Frozen fish sticks and cakes
Frozen potatoes:
    puffs, patties, French fries, baked
Frozen pizza
Precooked bacon

Mix and Serve

*These are the "instants" that need only the
addition of an ingredient.*
Instant coffee, tea, and instant fruit drinks
Bouillon cubes and granulated bouillon
Packaged salad-dressing mixes
Instant nonfat dry milk
Packaged frosting mixes
Instant oatmeal
Packaged topping mixes
Packaged instant-breakfast mix
Instant mashed potatoes and yams

Cook and Serve

*Though ready in minutes, these do require a
small amount of actual cooking.*
Frozen vegetables
Dehydrated soups
Dehydrated sauces and gravy mixes
Packaged scalloped and au gratin potatoes
Packaged noodle mixes:
    almondine, Romanoff, Italian
Refrigerated biscuits and rolls
Frozen biscuits
Rice, flavored:
    curry, herb, saffron, beef, chicken
Rice, mixes:
    Spanish, wild and white
Refrigerated cookies
Frozen fish and seafood
Prepared pie crusts

Prepare, Cook and Serve

*These require a little more effort as they need
some addition of ingredients and, in some
cases, technique in handling.*
Mixes: cake, cookie, biscuit, muffin, pancake,
    pie crust, cupcake, corn muffin and bread,
    potato pancake or dumpling, pizza, hot roll
Packaged macaroni and cheese dinner
Packaged spaghetti dinner
Packaged pudding and pie-filling mixes

Mix, Chill, and Serve

*Put these together in minutes and the refriger-
ator does the rest of the work.*
Gelatin desserts
Instant puddings
Whipped dessert mix

Use as an Ingredient

Many foods in the preceding listings make perfect recipe ingredients. Here are just some of them.

Canned fish and seafood
Packaged and bottled salad dressings
Canned and dehydrated sauces and gravies
Canned and dehydrated soups
Sliced, shredded, and grated cheese
Canned, dried, and frozen vegetables
Freeze-dried chives, shallots, and mushrooms
Gelatin
Instant flour
Seasoned salt and pepper
Spices, herbs, and condiments
Meat tenderizers and marinades
Shelled nuts
Liquid chocolate products
Bread, cereal, and cracker crumbs and breading mixes

Learn to Read Labels

We can be glad that manufacturers go to so much trouble to let the homemaker know what she is buying. Every can and every packaged food product must state on the label the net contents (weight or liquid measure), list the ingredients, state whether any artificial flavors or coloring matter have been added, and specify any important dietary properties, such as whether the product is sugar- or salt-free. Labels of canned foods specify the variety or style of the product— whether, for example, the can contains pickled sliced beets or small whole beets, or if the peaches are packed in heavy or light syrup or in water. Many canned and packaged products also indicate the number of servings.

The following chart contains a listing of commonly used can sizes. Today we always identify can sizes by weight or fluid measure, but in older recipes you may sometimes find manufacturer's terms used instead, so these are explained in the chart as well.

For those who must prepare food for someone on a special diet, it is particularly important to read the ingredient lists on canned and packaged foods, to make sure "forbidden foods" are not included in the manufactured product.

Labels on packaged mixes and dehydrated foods not only contain step-by-step instructions for use, but often offer extremely helpful recipe variations.

How to Choose the Right Cooking Ingredient

Research laboratories have revolutionized American cooking. Each year sees so many new, easier, more foolproof products on the market, it is hard to keep up with them all. For the consumer, it is often difficult to discriminate between the old and the new, to determine which product is best for a particular use.

We hope the following list will clarify this for you, help you to understand the difference between some of these new wonders of science. Reference to other supermarket products will be found in specific chapters. Since many similar products are manufactured under different brand names, we use generic terms—that is, the terms agreed upon among the various manufacturers.

SUPERMARKET DICTIONARY

Chocolate Products

Unsweetened chocolate is the pure chocolate made from ground cocoa beans. It comes in packages containing 8 separately wrapped 1-ounce squares. Some refer to this as "bitter chocolate."

Semi-sweet chocolate contains some added sugar. It comes both in small nugget-shaped pieces (which can often be used right from the package) and in 1-ounce squares. The former are available in 6-ounce and 12-ounce packages; the latter in 8-ounce packages.

Sweet cooking chocolate has a larger proportion of sugar, but otherwise is pure chocolate. It usually comes in 4-ounce bars marked off in squares.

Milk chocolate has been blended with dried milk as well as sugar before the chocolate is formed into bars or other shapes. This is intended primarily for eating.

COMMON CONTAINER SIZES

Labels on cans or jars of identical size may show a net weight for one product that differs slightly from the net weight of another due to the differences in the density of the foods. An example would be baked beans (1 lb.) and blueberries (14 oz.) in the same size can.

Industry Term	Approx. Net Weight or Fluid Measure (check label)	Approx. Cups	Principal Products
	Consumer Description		
8 oz.	8 oz.	1	Fruits, vegetables, specialties* for small families. 2 servings.
Picnic	10½ to 12 oz.	1¼	Mainly condensed soups. Some fruits, vegetables, meat, fish, specialties.* 3 servings.
12 oz. (vacuum)	12 oz.	1½	Principally for vacuum-pack corn. 3 to 4 servings.
No. 300	14 to 16 oz.	1¾	Pork and beans, baked beans, meat products, cranberry sauce, blueberries, specialties.* 3 to 4 servings.
No. 303	16 to 17 oz.	2	Principal size for fruits and vegetables. Some meat products, ready-to-serve soups, specialties.* 4 servings.
No. 2	1 lb. 4 oz. or 1 pt. 2 fl. oz.	2½	Juices, ready-to-serve soups, some specialties,* pineapple, apple slices. No longer in popular use for most fruits and vegetables. 5 servings.
No. 2½	1 lb. 13 oz.	3½	Fruits, some vegetables (pumpkin, sauerkraut, spinach and other greens, tomatoes). 7 servings.
No. 3 cyl. or 46 fl. oz.	3 lb. 3 oz. or 1 qt. 14 fl. oz.	5¾	"Economy family size" fruit and vegetable juices, pork and beans. Institutional size for condensed soups, some vegetables. 10 to 12 servings.
No. 10	6½ lb. to 7 lb. 5 oz.	12–13	Institutional size for fruits, vegetables, and some other foods. 25 servings.

Meats, fish, and seafood are almost entirely advertised and sold under weight terminology.

Infant and junior foods come in small cans and jars suitable for the smaller servings used. Content is given on label.

*Specialties—Food combinations prepared by special manufacturers' recipes.

Cocoa is a powder processed from cocoa beans with a portion of the fat (cocoa butter) removed.

Dutch cocoa has been treated with a solution to darken the color of the powder and reduce the natural bitterness.

Instant cocoa mix has had sugar and flavorings added to cocoa and is so processed that it dissolves instantly even in cold liquid. Some cocoa mixes also contain instant dry milk.

Unsweetened chocolate-flavored baking product is a blend of cocoa, vegetable oil, and preservatives in liquid form. It is ready to press from its plastic container directly into batters or frostings without previous melting. It may be used in place of unsweetened chocolate squares in most recipes, substituting a 1-ounce packet for a 1-ounce square of unsweetened chocolate.

Dairy Products

Butter

All butter is made by churning sweet or sour pasteurized cream to a smooth, solid consistency, after the cream has been separated from the milk.

Salted creamery butter has had salt added and is usually printed in 1-pound or ¼-pound prints.

Sweet cream butter is made entirely from sweet cream with a small amount of salt added.

Sweet butter has no salt at all.

Whipped butter has had air or gas beaten into the cream while it is being churned to increase the volume and make the butter easier to spread. Usually it is unsalted. Most is sold in 8- or 12-ounce paper containers, some in prints. This is intended primarily for eating. Do not substitute for regular butter in recipes.

Milk

Nearly all milk sold in our markets is pasteurized, meaning that raw (untreated) milk has been subjected to temperatures ranging from 145° to 161° F., then promptly cooled. This is done to reduce the bacterial count.

Grade A pasteurized milk sold in quart, half-gallon, and gallon containers is the whole milk; during storage cream will rise to the top of the bottle.

Certified milk may be raw or pasteurized milk produced and handled under rigid sanitary regulations.

Homogenized milk is pasteurized milk that has been processed to reduce the size of the milk-fat globules so that the cream will not separate.

Skim milk has had most of the milkfat removed.

Fortified milk is whole, skim, or homogenized milk with added vitamins and sometimes added minerals as well.

Chocolate milk is whole milk with sugar and chocolate added. If cocoa has been added instead of chocolate, it is called *chocolate-flavored milk*. If skim milk has been used instead of whole milk, it must be called *chocolate drink*, and if it is a combination of skim milk, sugar, and cocoa, it must be called *chocolate-flavored drink*.

Buttermilk in the old days was the product remaining in the churn after the butter had been removed. Today it is a cultured product made in the dairies by treating pasteurized grade A whole milk, skim, partially-skim milk, or reconstituted nonfat dry milk with a lactic acid culture. Butter granules are sometimes added.

Acidophilus milk has been created by adding lactic acids to pasteurized skim milk, giving it a characteristic tart flavor. It is of the same consistency and nutritive value as skim milk.

Yogurt is a cultured milk product made by fermenting concentrated whole milk or partially-skim milk enriched by the addition of nonfat dry milk with a special lactic acid culture. This gives it a custardlike consistency.

Concentrated milk is a fresh milk product which has had a considerable portion of water removed.

Evaporated milk is a canned product which has had 60 percent of the water removed and has been homogenized before sterilizing and canning.

Sweetened condensed milk is a canned product which has had about half of the water removed and sugar added.

Instant nonfat dry milk has had nearly all milkfat and water removed and has been processed so that it will dissolve readily in water or other liquids.

Dry whole milk is made of whole milk from which water has been removed. With the exception of fat removal, it is processed the same as nonfat dry milk.

Low sodium milk has had 90 percent or more of the sodium removed from fresh whole milk and replaced with an equal amount of potassium. It is available in both canned and fresh forms for use in low-sodium diets.

Cream

Light cream, "coffee cream," or table cream contains between 18% and 30% milkfat.

Heavy cream or "heavy whipping cream" contains between 36% and 40 % milkfat.

Dairy half-and-half is a mixture of milk and cream containing not less than 10% milkfat.

Sour cream, or dairy sour cream as it is properly called, is light cream subjected to a lactic acid culture to give it a creamier consistency and characteristic tart flavor. It usually contains between 18% and 20% milkfat. *Half-and-half sour cream* is a mixture of milk and light cream processed with the same culture, with a milkfat content between 10 and 12 percent. It is lower in calories than sour cream.

Pressurized whipped cream is a mixture of cream, sugar, stabilizers, and emulsifiers packed in aerosol cans. When pressed through a nozzle, the cream emerges in fluffy whipped form.

Cream Substitutes

Dessert topping mix comes in powdered form. A mixture of hydrogenated vegetable oil, sugar, preservatives, and emulsifiers, which,

when mixed with milk and whipped at high speed, produces a product similar in appearance to whipped heavy cream.

Pressurized dessert toppings come in aerosol cans. A mixture of hydrogenated vegetable oil, sugar, preservatives, and emulsifiers which, when pressed out through a nozzle, produce a product similar in appearance to whipped cream.

Nondairy creamers include both powdered products available in jars and liquid products in cartons. The dry product is primarily for use in coffee as a substitute for cream though it can be used in place of milk or cream in many recipes. The liquid form, sometimes found in frozen-food counters, is intended for use in coffee and for certain limited cooking uses for those on special diets. Both products are made with hydrogenated vegetable oils, sugar, preservatives, and emulsifiers.

Ice Cream

Most of our commercial ice creams are made with a mixture of milk, cream, sugar, and stabilizers, with air incorporated into the product by whipping it as it freezes.

French or New York ice cream has eggs or egg yolks added, therefore is richer.

Frozen custard is similar to French or New York ice cream. It also has eggs or egg yolks added.

Ice milk is a frozen dessert similar to regular ice cream but containing less milkfat and milk solids.

Sherbet is a frozen dessert similar to ice milk, but containing less milk and cream. It is made primarily of a water mixture containing fruit juices, sweeteners, flavorings, and stabilizers.

Cheese

There are some 400 varieties of cheese available in our markets today, including hundreds of unusual imported cheeses.

Natural cheeses are made from whole or skim milk, cured or aged to develop their particular flavor and texture. Nearly all our domestic cheeses and most of the imported cheeses are made from cow's milk, but a few imported cheeses are made from sheep or goat milk. The natural cheeses range from very hard, grating cheese such as Parmesan, to firm, such as Cheddar, to semi-soft, such as Roquefort, and soft, such as Neufchatel or Camembert.

Fresh cheeses, such as cottage cheese, farmer's cheese, pot cheese, cream cheese, and ricotta are also natural cheeses which have not been cured or aged.

Processed cheeses are made by blending one or more kinds of fresh cheese into a homogenized mass, adding water and an emulsifier, then pasteurizing. This includes many packaged sliced cheeses and cheeses sold in wrapped wedges or squares.

Cheese spreads and cheese foods are made by blending fresh or processed cheeses with milk solids, salt, and emulsifiers. They have a higher moisture content than the processed cheese.

For more about cheeses, see Chapter 15.

Fats and Oils

Margarine is made with refined vegetable oils or safflower oil, cultured milk, and nonfat milk solids. Some margarines have butter or butter flavoring added. Nearly all are artificially colored. Margarine is usually sold in 1-pound or ¼-pound prints. It is also available as a soft-type margarine, sold in pound cartons or two half-pound tubs; as whipped margarine in pound containers of six sticks; as a no-burn margarine, an unsalted margarine and as a diet table spread. All margarines should be kept under refrigeration.

Vegetable shortening is made of vegetable oils, refined to remove the fatty acids, then bleached to remove color and hydrogenated to change from a liquid to a solid. It is also available with coloring added. It need not be refrigerated.

Lard is rendered pork fat, sometimes hydrogenated. It should be kept under refrigeration.

Vegetable oil may be pressed from cottonseeds, corn, peanuts, soybeans, or safflower seeds. The oil is squeezed out under heavy pressure, then refined, bleached, and deodorized. *Salad oils* are vegetable oils which have been further treated by exposure to low temperatures and filtering so that the oil remains clear at refrigerator temperatures.

Olive oil is pressed from fully ripe olives. *Virgin olive oil* is the pure unrefined oil just as it comes from the first pressing of the fruit. This is the one most prized by connoisseurs. *Refined olive oil* is from later pressings of the same fruit, filtered through layers of felt to remove any impurities. Olive oil need not and should not be stored in the refrigerator as this causes it to cloud and thicken.

Flour

Recipes in this book calling for flour specify the kind of flour to use. Make no substitutions.

All-purpose flour is milled from a selected blend of both "hard" and "soft" wheats. It can be used for all types of baking and general cooking.

Bread flour is milled from hard winter wheats which are higher in protein and it has a higher gluten content than all-purpose flour. This is the type used by commercial bakeries, but in the home, all-purpose flour is perfectly satisfactory.

Cake flour is made from "soft" wheat, highly refined. It is ideal for cakes but not recommended for other baking purposes.

Self-rising flour is all-purpose flour or cake flour to which leavening ingredients and salt have been added in the proper proportions for baking. Follow package directions carefully. This flour should *not* be used in making yeast breads.

Instant-type flours are so new on the market that much still needs to be determined regarding their use. These are all-purpose flours which have been so refined that presifting is not necessary, and for sauces the flour can be added directly to liquids without lumping. For baking purposes, it is best to follow the manufacturer's recipes, as it is not always possible to substitute for all-purpose flour in standard recipes and obtain the same results.

Whole wheat or graham flour is milled from hard-wheat flour with bits of the whole grain retained. It should not be sifted.

Buckwheat flour, soy flour, and rice flour are usually found only in health stores and should be used according to manufacturer's directions.

Rye flour is the finely ground product of sifted rye meal, available in three grades: white, medium, and dark. It is usually combined with wheat flour in making bread at home.

Some flours may be bleached, unbleached, and/or enriched. This is what these terms mean:

Bleached flour has been sifted numerous times to remove all bits of crushed whole grain and has been further processed to whiten the flour and make it more uniform.

Unbleached flour is white flour that has been refined but not put through the bleaching process.

Enriched flour is white flour, bleached or unbleached, which has had those vitamins and minerals replaced which are contained in the whole wheat grain.

Grain Products Other Than Flour

Rice

Regular milled white rice is rice from which the hulls, germ, outer bran layer, and most of the inner bran are removed.

Brown rice has had only the outer hull removed.

Long-grain rice is the best variety for making casseroles or for simple steamed rice. *Short- or medium-grain rice* is suitable for puddings or other dishes which call for a very soft product.

Converted or parboiled rice has been cooked before milling by a special steam-pressure process.

Precooked rice (instant) is packaged long-grain rice which has already been cooked and needs only to steep in boiling water for a few minutes.

Wild rice (not rice at all) is the hulled grain of a reedlike water plant which has not been milled. It requires considerably more cooking time; observe package directions.

For more about rice, see Chapter 16.

Corn Products

Corn meal is made by grinding white or yellow dried field corn.

Cornstarch is the refined starch from the endosperm or heart of the dried corn kernel.

Hominy is corn with the hull and germ removed, usually by soaking in a lye solution. Pearl hominy has had the hulls removed by machinery.

Grits (hominy grits) have been ground, but more coarsely than corn meal

Oat Products

Oatmeal is available as *regular* and *quick-cooking* rolled oats. The only difference is that the latter has been rolled into finer, thinner flakes for quicker cooking. Instant oatmeal, to which you add boiling water, is the newest member of the oatmeal family.

Wheat Products Other Than Flour

Bulgur is whole wheat that has been cooked and dried, with some of the bran removed, then cracked into coarse fragments. It may be used in many rice dishes, and sometimes it is called "wheat pilaf." *Cracked wheat* is similar, but has not had the bran removed.

Farina is a fine meal prepared by grinding and sifting wheat. It has had the bran and most of the germ removed.

Wheat germ is the heart of the wheat kernel. It is high in protein, iron, and vitamins, and has a decided nutlike flavor.

Leavening Agents

Baking soda is pure sodium bicarbonate which, when combined with an acid ingredient, creates a gas which causes breads or cakes to rise. Baking soda is used in recipes containing acid ingredients such as buttermilk, sour cream, molasses, and chocolate. It neutralizes the acidity and helps the leavening.

Baking powders are a mixture of baking soda and dry acids or acid salts and starch. There are three types: tartrate, phosphate, and SAS. The latter two are often called "double acting."

Yeast is available in two forms: *compressed,* a moist mixture of yeast and starch in a firm cake, and *active dry yeast,* which has been dried and packaged in granular form. Both are made with a single-celled microscopic plant which when combined with other ingredients and placed at warm temperature "comes to life" to produce carbon dioxide gas from simple sugars.

For more about leavening, see Chapter 9, Yeast Breads.

Sugars and Syrups

Sugars

Granulated white sugar has been refined from beet sugar or sugar cane and processed to make it pour freely.

Superfine granulated sugar is a uniformly fine-grained sugar, specially screened, in such small granules that it will dissolve almost instantly.

Confectioners' sugar, sometimes called "powdered," has been crushed, screened, and blended with a small amount of cornstarch. It must always be sifted before measuring.

Brown sugar varies in color from light to dark depending on the amount of molasses it contains. It is made from the syrup remaining after the white sugar has been extracted.

Granulated brown sugar is a new product that has been processed to flow freely. It is especially recommended for table use. In baking, follow manufacturer's recommendations in substituting for regular brown sugar.

Cube and tablet sugar, which has been compressed into serving-size pieces, is convenient for special occasions.

Syrups

Molasses is processed from the concentrated sap of sugar cane. *Black strap molasses* is darker, contains a higher percentage of ash (potassium). *Unsulphured molasses* has had the sulphur removed by a special process.

Corn syrup is derived from cornstarch by hydrolysis. *Light corn syrup* has been clarified and bleached. *Dark corn syrup* has been blended with "refiners' syrup"—the product left from refining raw cane or beet sugar.

Maple syrup is made by evaporating the sap from maple trees by boiling; or it may be a solution of maple sugar and water.

Maple-blended syrup is a mixture of syrups, with some syrup made from maple sugar.

Buttered syrup is maple-blended syrup to which butter has been added.

Honey is made only by bees; what we buy in jars has been extracted from the wax honey cone, strained, and clarified.

Vinegar

White Vinegar is a distilled vinegar made from choice corn, rye, and barley malt. It is crystal clear and has a delicate aroma. It is best for pickling and preserving or when the color of the food is important.

Cider Vinegar, made from the juice of apples, is the most popular of vinegars. It imparts a slight fruit flavor to foods and a bit of color. It is an all-purpose vinegar.

Malt Vinegar is a deep russet-colored vinegar brewed from choice barley malt. It has a rich full-bodied flavor which is excellent for hearty salads, seafoods, etc. Use discriminately so as not to overshadow food flavors.

Tarragon Vinegar is a blend of fine distilled and fermented table vinegars in which tarragon leaves have been steeped. It has an herb flavor perfect for many sauces and salads.

Herb Vinegars, like tarragon vinegar, are plain vinegars which have been flavored with spices and herbs. They are generally used in recipes where the herbs themselves might be used, and are particularly popular for salad dressings.

Wine Vinegar is a flavorful vinegar made from either red or white wine. It is generally slightly less acid than other vinegars. Use in fine cookery and salad dressings.

Miscellaneous

Bouillon cubes and concentrates. Most of the bouillon cubes, granulated bouillon, and concentrates are made with a base of plant protein, to which meat by-products, natural and artificial seasonings, spices, starch, and sugar have been added. They dissolve quickly in hot water. As a short cut, bouillon made with one of these may be used in any recipe calling for meat or chicken stock; or they may be used to make a quick cup of clear bouillon.

Gelatin is available in two principal forms. *Unflavored gelatin* comes in boxes containing a number of 1-ounce packets. It must be softened first in cold water, then dissolved in hot water—unless sugar is blended with the gelatin first. *Fruit-flavored gelatins* have already been blended with sugar, natural and artificial flavors; they come in 3-ounce and 6-ounce packages. These are dissolved first in hot water, then cold water is added. If a recipe calls for *unflavored gelatin*, do *not* use a fruit-flavored gelatin—or vice versa.

Dessert mixes keep appearing on the market in such variety and abundance, it is difficult to keep up with them all. One word of caution: avoid confusing instant pudding mixes with those that require cooking. Be sure to read package directions carefully before use, and do not attempt to substitute one dessert mix for another.

DICTIONARY OF COOKING TERMS

Methods of Cooking

bake: to cook by dry heat in an oven.

barbecue: to broil or roast on a grill or a spit; food is very often basted with a highly seasoned sauce.

blanch: to dip quickly in boiling water. For nuts or fruit, to loosen outer skin for easy removal. For vegetables, a step in the preparation for freezing.

boil: to bring water (or any liquid) to 212° F., when bubbles break on the surface; to cook food in liquid that is boiling. See also *simmer*. A rapid boil means an active, rolling boil.

braise: to brown meat or other food in fat, adding a small amount of liquid and cooking, covered, slowly.

broil: to cook over or under direct heat.

caramelize: to melt granulated sugar in a heavy skillet over low heat, stirring constantly, until it forms a golden-brown syrup.

coddle: to cook slowly and gently in water just below the boiling point. Eggs are frequently coddled.

deep fry: to cook in shortening or oil deep enough to cover food completely.

French fry: see *deep fry*.

fricassee: to cook by braising. For chicken it means stewing; the browning process may be omitted.

fry: to cook in hot fat until golden and crisp on all sides. Implies more fat than is used to *sauté*, less than for *deep fry*.

panbroil: to cook meats uncovered in ungreased or very lightly greased skillet, pouring off fat from meat as it accumulates.

panfry (sauté) : to cook in a small amount of fat in skillet.

parboil: to partially cook in water or other liquid before baking or frying.

poach: to cook gently in a small amount of liquid, without permitting it to boil.

pressure-cook: to cook quickly or preserve foods by means of superheated steam under pressure.

roast: to cook by dry heat in the oven or over an open fire; usually refers to meat or poultry.

sauté (panfry) : to cook in a small amount of fat in skillet. Some foods are cooked until soft, but not brown (onions, for example), and others are cooked completely. *The secret of success in sautéeing: have the fat hot, the food dry, and do not crowd pan.*

scald: to heat liquid until tiny bubbles appear around edge.

scallop: to bake in a dish, usually with a sauce, as scalloped potatoes, or topped with crumbs as scalloped tomatoes. *Scallop* also means the edible portion of a mollusk; scallop shells originally were used to hold creamed mixtures for baking, which is the origin of the cookery term. It can also mean thin slices of veal.

scramble: to cook slowly, gently lifting food from bottom and sides as mixtures sets, as in eggs.

sear: to brown the surface of meat quickly over high heat.

shirr: to bake eggs in a dish with cream or crumbs.

simmer: to cook at low heat, below boiling point, so that liquid moves gently with occasional small bubbles.

spit cook: to cook food on a revolving spit (rotisserie).

steam: to cook food on rack above the water level in a covered container.

stew: to cook food in liquid slowly over a long period of time.

stir-fry: a term in Chinese cooking. Food is stirred quickly while it is being sautéed.

toast: to brown by heating.

Methods of Preparation

baste: to spoon liquid, fat, or a sauce over food as it cooks.

beat: to mix with a vigorous, steady motion, by hand with a spoon, or using a rotary beater, electric mixer, or blender.

blend: to mix gently with stirring rather than beating motion. Also to mix in a blender.

bread: as a cookery term, this means to roll meat or other food in fine bread or cracker crumbs; or to dip first in beaten egg, then in the crumbs.

brush with: to apply a thin coating of fat, oil, cream, egg white, etc., over surface of food, using a pastry brush.

chill: to place in refrigerator until thoroughly cold.

chop: to cut into relatively small pieces. See also *cube, dice, grate, grind,* and *mince.*

coat: to cover with a thin film of flour, sugar, batter, crumbs, or crushed nuts. See also *dredge* and *dust.*

cook, stirring constantly: to stir gently but steadily with spoon or wire whisk until mixture thickens.

cool: to let stand until no longer warm to the touch.

cream: as a cookery term, to work one or more foods until soft and creamy, using a spoon or mixer. Applies to fat and sugar most often.

crush: to mash with rolling pin, mortar, or some other utensil until food is granular, powdered, or paste-like.

cube: to cut into ½-inch cubes.

cut in shortening: to cut fat or shortening into flour with a pastry blender or two knives until mixture resembles corn meal.

correct seasoning: to taste as the recipe proceeds to decide whether the taste is satisfactory or would be improved by the addition of, say, a little more salt, a smidgen of pepper, or a squeeze of lemon juice.

deglaze: when meat or poultry (usually) has been roasted or sautéed, there is a rich brown essence in the bottom of the pan. This is an important flavor ingredient. To make use of this essence, pour off all fat, add a small amount of stock, wine, or water to the pan. Stir and scrape over low heat until you have captured all the essence in liquid form (deglazing). This liquid is now the base for a flavorful sauce.

devil: to prepare with a hot seasoning, such as mustard or hot sauce.

dice: to cut into small (about ¼-inch) cubes.

dissolve: to stir a dry or solid substance in liquid to make a solution.

dot: to scatter small pieces of butter or margarine over top of food.

dredge: to cover with flour or a seasoned mixture, but more heavily than the term *coat* implies.

dust: to sprinkle flour or sugar very lightly over food.

flake: when referring to fish, means flesh should come apart easily when touched with a fork. Sometimes means, in reference to other foods, to break lightly into small pieces.

flour: to coat or dust with flour.

fold: to combine two mixtures with an up-and-over gentle motion using a spatula or rubber scraper until ingredients are blended.

fold over: applied to pastry, it means to double over rolled pastry, then roll it out again; applied to omelets, it means to lift the omelet from one side of pan, turn it over like a pocketbook, then slip it out of pan.

glacé: may refer to a food covered with a thin sugar syrup, or to a frozen dessert.

glaze: to coat food to produce a shiny surface.

grate: to rub on a grater to produce fine particles.

grease: to rub with shortening or other fat.

grind: to cut in very small particles by putting through a food grinder.

julienne: to cut into very thin or matchlike pieces.

knead: to work dough with the hands, using a pressing and folding motion until dough is smooth and elastic.

lard: to insert strips of fat through meat to make it more moist.

marinate: to let foods stand in a marinade before cooking or serving.

mash: to make smooth by pressing with a masher or forcing through a ricer.

melt: to reduce a solid food to liquid.

mince: to chop very fine.

pare: to cut off the outer skin of vegetables or fruit with a sharp knife.

peel: may mean same as pare, or may mean to pull off outer skin with fingers, as to peel bananas.

pit: to remove the seeds or stones.

preheat: to turn on oven or broiler long enough before use to make sure it will have reached designated temperature.

purée: to reduce to consistency of mush by forcing through a fine sieve or food mill or whirling in electric blender.

reduce: to cook a liquid until it is reduced in volume. This reduction concentrates flavors and is an essential procedure in making sauces.

render: to free fat from connective tissue over low heat.

score: to cut narrow gashes part way through fat on edge of meat to keep from curling, or to make design on ham.

shred: to cut in very thin pieces.

sift: to force or shake through a fine sieve or flour sifter.

skewer: to thread pieces of food on a long metal or wooden pin for broiling or grilling, as for kabobs.

slice: to cut in flat, thin pieces.

sliver: to cut into narrow, thin pieces (as for *julienne*).

soak: to immerse and let stand in liquid. See *marinate.*

sprinkle: to spread nuts, seasonings, or other ingredients lightly over top of food without blending.

steep: to let stand for about 3 to 5 minutes in water that has just been boiled.

stir: to mix gently with a spoon, with rotary motion.

thicken: to blend flour, cornstarch, or other thickening agent with liquid, then simmer to produce a creamy, smooth sauce.

toss: to mix ingredients lightly.

truss: to close up the cavities of poultry that have been filled with stuffing by fastening with small skewers, then lacing up; to tie any meat, game, or poultry so that it will hold its shape while roasting.

try out: see *render.*

whip: to beat rapidly to incorporate air and increase volume.

General Cooking Terms

à la king: food, such as poultry, tuna, or bland meats, served in a cream sauce with green peppers, pimiento, and mushrooms.

à la mode: pie or cake served with a garnish of ice cream on top; also braised beef with vegetables.

appetizer: a small, savory serving of food served before dinner to stimulate the appetite.

aspic: meat or vegetable jelly, with gelatin, used to coat foods or to enclose foods as in molds or salads.

au gratin: a creamed mixture covered with bread crumbs, grated cheese, and baked until browned.

au jus: meat served in its natural juices.

au lait: beverage made with equal parts of hot milk and coffee or chocolate.

bar-le-duc: fruit preserve made from white or red currants.

bisque: a rich cream soup, usually made from fish or shellfish; also a frozen dessert of cream, macaroons, and nuts.

blanquette: a stew, usually veal, made with a cream or white sauce, enriched with eggs and lemon juice.

bombe: a dessert made by lining a mold with a frozen mixture and filling the center with one or more other frozen mixtures. It may be made with ice cream, sherbet, or mousse.

bouillabaisse: a hearty fish and shellfish stew (soup).

bouillon: a clear broth usually made from beef.

brochette: a small spit or skewer used for broiling meat pieces.

breadcrumbs: fresh breadcrumbs—bread crumbled with fingers or in blender. *Dry, stale bread* crumbs—stale bread crushed with a rolling pin. *Packaged breadcrumbs*—available in supermarkets.

broth: liquid in which meat, poultry, fish, or vegetables have been cooked.

canapé: an appetizer usually served on little pieces of crisp toast or crackers.

charlotte: a molded dessert. Usually a flavored gelatin and whipped cream mixture in a mold lined with ladyfingers.

chaud-froid: a coating sauce made with a white sauce base and gelatin.

chowder: a thick soup made from fish, shellfish, or vegetables.

cobbler: a deep-dish fruit pie topped with rich pastry or biscuit dough.

compote: a mixture of fruit, served in syrup.

consommé: a seasoned, clear soup that jells when chilled. It is made by reducing meat stock.

court bouillon: a flavored and seasoned liquid usually used for cooking fish.

crepe: a thin, rich pancake.

croquette: a mixture of chopped, cooked meat, poultry, fish, rice, etc. in a thick white sauce, usually shaped into individual portions, coated with egg and crumbs, then fried.

croutons: small bread cubes sautéed or toasted in the oven.

demitasse: a small cup of strongly brewed coffee usually served after dinner; also the cup in which it is served.

éclair: a finger-shape pastry, filled with custard, whipped cream, or ice cream. It is related to the cream puff.

en brochette: foods cooked on skewers.

en papillotte: food cooked in parchmentlike paper. Foil can be used for the same purpose.

entrée: the main dish of the meal. Originally the course served before the meat.

filet mignon: an individual steak cut from the tenderloin of beef.

flambé: food laced with flaming brandy, Cognac, or other liqueurs.

fondant: a confection made from a kneaded, cooked sugar-syrup. It is used to make bon bons, cordial cherries, or fondant frosting.

fondue: There are three types: a *Swiss fondue* is a melted cheese and wine mixture into which cubes of bread are dipped; a *cheese fondue* is a casserole of cheese, bread crumbs, and custard; a *beef fondue* (Fondue Bourguignonne) is a dish of cubes of beef cooked in bubbly oil and butter, then dipped in savory sauces.

fritter: batter-coated food which is fried.

frosting: a thick mixture of sugar, liquid, flavoring, and sometimes butter used to coa cakes.

grenadine: a ruby-colored flavoring syrup.

gumbo: a thick soup made of fish, shellfish, or poultry. It is thickened with okra or filé powder.

hors d'oeuvres: a selection of appetizers, usually small pieces of finger food.

icing: a thin mixture of sugar, liquid, and flavoring used to coat cakes, coffee cakes, etc.

macedoine: a mixture of fruits or vegetables.

marzipan: a confection made from almond paste and sugar.

meringue: a mixture of stiffly beaten egg whites and sugar.

monosodium glutamate: a crystalline substance which enhances the natural flavor of foods.

mousse: a fluffy, light mixture which may be chilled or frozen (if made with gelatin), or may be baked (if made with eggs).

parfait: a layered dessert of ice cream, fruit or syrup, and whipped cream, usually served in slender glasses.

pâté: a smooth, richly seasoned mixture usually made from chicken livers, served as an appetizer.

pâté de foie gras: a smooth, richly seasoned mixture made from goose livers.

petit fours: dainty little cakes iced and decorated.

pilaf: rice or cracked wheat cooked in seasoned broth.

rissolé: as applied to potatoes, parboiled and browned in hot fat. *Rissolé* as applied to hors d'oeuvres means small meat, fish, or chicken turnovers, generally fried but may be baked.

smorgasbord: a Scandinavian buffet consisting of a large variety of foods.

soufflé: an entrée or dessert with a base of beaten egg whites.

stock: richly flavored liquid in which meat, fish, fowl, or vegetables have been cooked.

tart: a small individual pie.

timbale: a mixture of finely chopped meat or vegetables, eggs, and milk baked in small molds. Also a fritter batter, deep fried on a timbale iron to form a fluted cup.

torte: a rich cake usually made from crumbs, eggs, and nuts; sometimes a meringue baked in the shape of a cake.

truffles: black fungi of the mushroom family that grow underground, used for garnishing and flavoring.

vinaigrette: a salad dressing or marinade made of oil, vinegar, and seasonings.

Facts on Frying

Panfry: This is one of the simplest methods of cooking and the start of many recipes. It is done in just enough fat or oil to keep the food from sticking or in fat or oil ¼- to ½-inch deep. The fat transfers heat to the food, seals in juices, and helps blend flavors. Put enough fat or oil in a skillet to cover just the bottom. Heat over medium heat until a drop of water sizzles and bounces in the pan. Add food. Cook as recipe directs.

Shallow Fry: This is a kind of deep frying, though on a smaller scale. It is economical, for there is less fat used than in deep frying, and it is ideal for many coated and raw foods that need more fat or oil than foods that are panfried. Put enough fat or oil into a skillet or deep saucepan to make 1 to 1½ inches deep when heated. Heat to temperature required in recipe. Add food. Fry until golden brown and thoroughly cooked. Drain on paper towels.

Deep Fry: Deep, or French frying requires a quantity of fat or oil, for there must be enough to float the foods without crowding them in the pan. The temperature must be high enough to cook the foods quickly.

Cut food into uniform-size pieces and dry on paper towels. Let coated foods stand a few minutes to set coating. Have all foods at room temperature.

Put fat or oil into deep kettle so kettle is no more than ⅓ full when heated. There should be at least 3 inches between top of fat and top of kettle so there is no danger of fat bubbling over during frying.

Clip deep-fat frying thermometer in place. Heat fat or oil to temperature required in recipe.

As soon as temperature is reached, lower food with spoon or tongs, small amounts at a time, into fat. Do it gently to prevent excessive bubbling. Keep temperature as even as possible, adjusting heat if necessary, but don't let fat overheat. Fry until golden brown, turning as recipe directs. Remove from fat and drain on paper towels.

Skim any loose food particles from fat to prevent smoking and bring fat back to desired temperature before adding the next batch of food.

When all food is fried, cool fat and strain through a sieve lined with cleansing tissue or cheesecloth. Cover and store in refrigerator. When reusing, add a little fresh fat or oil to replace that absorbed by foods during frying.

Kitchen Utensils

Here's a list to help you equip your kitchen. It's divided into three groups:

(1) What you need for a basically equipped kitchen (essential utensils that should be in every kitchen).
(2) What a fully equipped kitchen should have (a full complement of utensils that adds the most in cooking convenience).
(3) A completely equipped gourmet kitchen (the extras for gourmet cooking, or specialty items designed to do one job only—but with the greatest of ease).

Of course, what will go into your kitchen to make it fully equipped will depend on the way you cook and the kind of food that you prepare. For instance, if omelets are a favorite of your family, then the omelet pan would be a necessity, not a luxury.

Since this list includes both electric and nonelectric equipment, there are duplications —choose what works best for you.

POTS, PANS, AND UTENSILS

A Basically Equipped Kitchen should have:

Saucepans (with covers):

	1 or 1½ quart	Roast rack	Vegetable peeler
	2 or 2½ quart	French fry basket	Corer
	3 or 4 quart	Coffeepot	Minute timer
Saucepot:	5 quart	Griddle	Flour sifter
Double boiler			Rolling pin
Skillets:	1 small	Kitchen shears	Strainer
	1 large	Can opener	Potato masher
	(with cover)	Bottle opener	Rotary beater
Teakettle		Colander	Pastry blender
Dutch oven		Cutting board	Metal spatula
Roasting pan		Fruit juice extractor	Tongs
Casserole dish:	1 medium	Mary-Ann measuring cups	Ladle
	1 large	Measuring spoons	Pancake turner
Custard cups:	4 to 6	French knife	Grater
Pie plates:	two 9-inch	Paring knife	Long-handled slotted spoon
Cake pans:	two 8-inch	Utility knife	Long-handled basting spoon
	or 9-inch	Serrated slicing knife	Long-handled 2-tine fork
	1 square	Carving knife and fork	Nest of mixing bowls

POTS, PANS, AND UTENSILS (*Continued*)

Cookie sheets: 2
Muffin pan
Loaf pan or dish

Thermometers
    (roast meat, candy and
    deep fat fry)

Pastry brush
Rubber scrapers
Wire cooling racks
Wooden spoons

For a Fully Equipped Kitchen, add:

Chicken fryer
Cook-and-serve utensils
Tube pan
Jelly-roll pan
Additional: saucepans
        skillets
        cake pans
        muffin pans
        cookie sheets
        mixing bowls
        casserole dishes

Egg poacher
Teapot
Roaster (covered)
Springform pan

Wire whisk
Grapefruit knife
Baster
Assorted cutters
    (for cookies, doughnuts,
    biscuits, etc.)
Pressure cooker

For a Completely Equipped Gourmet Kitchen, you may want to add some of these:

Tart pans
Molds and ramekins
Omelet pan
Steamer kettle
Gem pan

Pizza pan
Tiered cake pan set
Corn stick pan
Other specialized utensils,
    such as casserole with
    warmer, beverage server,
    fondue cooker, etc.

Ice cream scoop
Mortar and pestle
Butter ball paddles
Garlic press
Melon ball cutter
Boning knife

PORTABLE APPLIANCES

A Basically Equipped Kitchen should have:

Automatic skillet
Automatic coffee maker

Toaster

Portable Mixer

For a Fully Equipped Kitchen, add:

Automatic griddle
Automatic pressure cooker
Automatic dutch oven
Automatic saucepan or
    saucepot

Toaster-oven
Hot tray
Buffet frypan
Waffle baker

Standard mixer
Blender
Electric knife
Electric can opener
Electric knife sharpener

For a Completely Equipped Gourmet Kitchen, add some of these:

Popcorn popper
Teakettle
Large coffee maker
Deep fat fryer
Roaster-oven
Kabober

Cold tray
Bean pot
Chafing dish
Portable Buffet
    Range

Bun warmer
Pizza warming platter
Coffee grinder
Ice crusher
Juicer
Ice cream freezer
Meat grinder

Table setting for an evening buffe

A SHIP AHOY
CAKE

Chapter Two

Planning Your Meals

Everyone knows well how important nutrition is. We have only to look at the taller younger generations to see the effect of wholesome food in building healthier, more robust bodies. The lengthening average life span too is a testament to the effect of good nutrition on health.

It would be nice to think that the nutrition story has been so well taught that we have no more diet problems. But quite the opposite is true. Many teen-agers fill up on sweets and soft drinks until they have no appetite left for the foods their fast-growing bodies need—then they wonder why they are flabby and overweight, and why their complexions are bad.

Overweight has become a national problem with adults. To a large extent, it can be attributed to poor eating habits. Look at the plates of those dining in restaurants, and it's quite common to see two different fried foods on the same plate, or as many as three starchy foods, no salad or vegetables.

Good eating habits begin at home. The homemaker buying food for her family not only needs to know something about the basics of good nutrition, but how to present well-balanced meals day after day so that her children will learn to *prefer* the right kind of diet.

Required Eating: the Basic Four

A well-balanced diet should include all the following foods *daily* in the amounts indicated.

1. Meat and Meat Substitutes

Eggs, seafood, poultry, cheese, dry beans and *nuts* all belong in this category along with meat because of their high protein content. Each person in the family should have 2 or more servings of foods in this group each day.

2. Milk Products

For very child under 12 years, 3 to 4 glasses of milk or the equivalent.

For teen-agers, 4 or more glasses of milk or the equivalent.

For mothers-to-be, 4 or more glasses daily; for nursing mothers, at least 6 glasses or the equivalent.

Other adults should have 2 glasses of milk daily or an equivalent milk food.

Milk equivalents include *cottage cheese* (½ cup equals ⅓ glass whole milk), *pasteurized process or aged cheese* (1 slice or 1 ounce equals ¾ glass whole milk), *ice cream* (¼ pint or an average portion equals ¼ glass milk), *sour and sweet cream, and yogurt.* Nonfat or skim milk or evaporated milk can be substituted for whole milk. Milk used in cooking, over breakfast cereal, or added to coffee, tea, or cocoa should constitute part of the total.

3. Vegetables and Fruits

The day's meals should include at least one serving *citrus fruit, tomatoes* or other good source of vitamin C, one *green* or *yellow vegetable*, plus two additional servings of other vegetables or fruits.

4. Bread, Cereals, and Other Grains

Whole-grain products (such as whole wheat or rye bread, oatmeal, cornbread) and enriched or fortified white breads, pastas, and rice should be chosen in preference to those refined products to which essential vitamins and minerals have not been added. At least four servings daily of whole-grained or enriched cereal foods belong in the diet.

21

Proteins, Carbohydrates, and Fats

It is easy to oversimplify the nutrition story. Protein foods are essential for growth, energy, and replacement of body tissues. It is because most of us have such an abundance of high-protein foods that we are growing taller and living longer.

It must be recognized, however, that most foods contain all three major food components —proteins, carbohydrates, and fats—in varying proportions. Many of us consume too many foods high in carbohydrate and fat content (fried foods and too many starches and sweets). Yet a certain amount of fats and oils are necessary in each day's diet, and cutting down too drastically on certain of the carbohydrate foods could impair body health.

The challenge is to provide the right balance of protein, carbohydrate, and fat. The Family Menus on the following pages are good examples of how to do this.

Vitamins and Minerals

For those who follow a well-balanced diet, with all the "required eating" foods included in each day's menus, there should be no need to take vitamin or mineral pills, unless your doctor prescribes them.

The following list may serve as a guide to the homemaker conscientious about giving her family all the vital food elements.

Vitamin	Function	Source
Vitamin A	Helps eyes adjust to changes in intensity of light. Helps resist infection. Helps in tooth and bone formation.	Liver, yellow and dark green leafy vegetables, whole milk, cream, egg yolk, butter, margarine.
Vitamin B₁ (*Thiamin*)	Needed for use of food in the body, particularly carbohydrates. Needed for steady nerves and alert mind. Needed to help appetite, digestion, and good muscle tone.	Pork, whole-grain and enriched breads and cereals, milk, dry kidney and lima beans, peanuts.
Vitamin B₂ (*Riboflavin*)	Needed for use of food in the body; for nerves, skin, eyes. Helps resist infection.	Milk, liver, green leafy vegetables, whole-grain and enriched breads and cereals.
Niacin	Needed for use of food in the body; for skin. Helps normal functioning of digestive tract.	Liver, lean meats, whole-grain and enriched breads and cereals, legumes, peanuts, peanut butter.
Vitamin B *Complex* *pantothenic* *acid*	Important as part of enzyme system.	Liver, milk, eggs, whole-grain cereals and breads.
folic acid	Helpful in treatment of special anemia of infancy and pregnancy.	
biotin	Needed for use of fat in body.	
inositol	May be related to fat cholesterol use in body.	
Vitamin B₁₂	Effective in treatment of pernicious anemia. May be related to use of amino acids in the body.	Liver, milk, cheese, meats, egg yolk.

Vitamin	Function	Source
Vitamin C (Ascorbic Acid)	Prevents and cures scurvy. Strengthens capillary walls to prevent easy bleeding. Necessary for sound teeth and gums.	Citrus fruits, cantaloupe, strawberries, tomatoes, green leafy vegetables, apples, potatoes.
Vitamin D	Needed to utilize calcium and phosphorous in building bones and teeth. Helps in absorption of calcium from the blood. Prevents rickets in children.	Sunlight, egg yolk, fish liver oil, fresh and canned oily fish, Vitamin-D-enriched milk.
Vitamin E	Believed to be needed for normal reproduction.	Butter, margarine, oils (wheat germ, cotton seed, corn, soybean), navy beans.
Vitamin K	Needed for normal blood clotting.	Green leafy and root vegetables, cauliflower, fruits, pork liver, soybean oil.

Mineral	Function	Source
Calcium	Needed for building bones and teeth. Helps regulate nerve and muscle action. Helps in absorption of iron and in clotting of blood.	Milk, cheeses made from milk, egg yolk, kale, mustard, and turnip greens.
Phosphorus	Needed for building bones and teeth. Needed for every cell in body. Needed to use proteins, fats, and carbohydrates in the body.	Milk, cheeses made from milk, egg yolk, lean meats, legumes.
Iron	Needed to carry oxygen from lungs to all parts of body. Needed in cells to help provide energy.	Lean meat, liver, egg yolk, green leafy vegetables, enriched breads and cereals, legumes.
Sodium	Helps regulate water balance in body. Helps maintain acid-base balance in body. Needed for muscle contraction.	Table salt, salted meat and fish, cheese, margarine, canned meats, fish, vegetables, breads and cereals.

Special Diets

Until a few years ago, the word cholesterol was not even listed in the dictionary. Today everyone is familiar with it, and with the expression *polyunsaturated fats*. These have become household words because of the growing incidence of heart disease, especially among men over 40.

Most physicians believe there is a definite relation between diet and heart disease, and certain fats, the animal fats in particular, seem to raise the cholesterol level of the blood— one of many factors which may lead to heart attacks. Egg yolk too can raise the cholesterol level. However, it is increasingly recog-nized that what may be an effective diet for one person may be actually harmful for another. Therefore anyone who must follow a special diet, whether it is low-cholesterol, low-sodium, or a severe weight-reducing program, should be under the supervision of a physician at all times.

As a general rule, all those over 40, both men and women, need annual physical check-ups. If your family doctor advises a special diet for you or any member of the family as the result of such an examination, his list is the one to follow. Otherwise, the well-balanced diet which includes all the "required eating" foods and avoids too many fried foods, sweets and starches, is the "safe and sane" way.

PLANNING TASTY MEALS

A Simple Guide to Planning A Dinner Menu

1. Choose the main dish first.
2. Select a starchy food—potato, noodles, spaghetti, rice, etc.
3. Select a vegetable and/or salad.
4. Think about bread or rolls.
5. Decide on dessert.
6. Consider the extras, such as beverages, adding an appetizer, and making a special garnish.

If your main dish is a meal-in-one, all you need is a lovely salad (a green one is delicious), a tempting bread, dessert (if you like), and a beverage.

Keep These Meal-Planning Tips in Mind

1. Remember the daily need for green and yellow vegetables and the importance of contrasts in flavor, color, and texture.
2. If the main course is light, such as salad or soup, choose a heavier dessert.
3. If you are having a hearty main course, serve a light dessert.
4. When planning an entire day's menu, keep all meals in mind for total balance.
5. Consider your food dollar:

Plan meals before you get to the supermarket. Read the food ads thoroughly.
Buy family treats like sirloin steaks when they are on specials.
Go all out on a special meal and cut down on the next.
Keep leftovers in mind (look in the refrigerator when planning meals).

Here is a selection of menus for family dining that keep the rules of nutrition in mind and give you an idea of the infinite variety of possibilities that are yours with the recipes that follow:

A Selection of Family Menus

Breakfasts

Chilled Grapefruit or Apple Juice
Dry or Cooked Cereal
Poached Egg
Crisp Bacon

Muffins   Jam
Coffee   Tea   Milk

Stewed Prunes and Apricots
Scrambled Eggs with Cottage Cheese
(page 265)
Sausage

Hot Biscuits   Jam
Coffee   Tea   Milk

Half Grapefruit
Pancakes   Maple Syrup
Bacon or Sausage
Coffee   Tea   Milk

Chilled Fruit Compote
Fried Eggs
Canadian Bacon

Toast   Jelly
Coffee   Tea   Milk

For the Hearty Appetite

Chilled Tomato Juice
Eggs, Family Style (cooked as you like)
Hashed Brown Potatoes   Fried Ham
Biscuits   Jelly
Coffee   Tea   Milk

Dieter's Breakfast

Half Grapefruit
Soft-cooked Egg
1 Slice Dry Toast
or
Dry Cereal with Skim Milk
Coffee   Tea

Continental Breakfast-on-the-Run

Orange Juice
Raisin Toast or Danish Pastry
Coffee   Tea   Milk

Spanish Omelet   *(page 262)*
Braised Celery   *(page 290)*
Crusty Rolls
Glazed Baked Apple   *(page 309)*
Coffee   Tea   Milk

Lunches or Suppers

Shrimp Quiche Lorraine   *(page 241)*
Cucumber and Endive Salad
Chiffonade Dressing   *(page 343)*
Minted Fruit Cup
Coffee   Tea   Milk

Fish Chowder or Oyster Stew
(pages 129, 130)
Green Salad
French Bread
Applesauce Cake   *(page 440)*
Coffee   Tea   Milk

Cheese and Asparagus Soufflé   *(page 265)*
Herb-Marinated Tomatoes
Drop Biscuits   *(page 89)*
Pineapple Upside-Down Cake   *(page 373)*
Coffee   Tea   Milk

Chili Con Carne   *(page 155)*
Cole Slaw   *(page 329)*
Saltines
Fruit and Sherbet Parfait
Coffee   Tea   Milk

Cream of Tomato Soup
Hearty Supper Salad   *(page 332)*
Corn Bread   *(page 90)*
Lemon Coconut Pudding   *(page 372)*
Coffee   Tea   Milk

Bologna Skillet Supper   *(page 188)*
Lettuce Wedge—French Dressing
with Pimiento
Hard Rolls
Chocolate Blanc Mange   *(page 372)*
Coffee   Tea   Milk

Spaghettini Bake   *(page 277)*
Carrots, Celery, Green Pepper Strips
Garlic Bread
Fresh Fruit Compote
Coffee   Tea   Milk

Tomato Juice
Tuna Salad Rolls
Finger Relishes
French Fries
Coffee   Tea   Milk

Macaroni and Cheese   *(page 276)*
Spinach and Endive Salad   *(page 323)*
Herb Bread
Prune Whip   *(page 357)*
Coffee   Tea   Milk

Cheeseburgers
Mustard   Relish
Rolls
Lettuce   Tomatoes
Potato Chips
Apricot Halves
Coffee   Tea   Milk

Consommé
Tomato-Noodle Bake   *(page 276)*
Green Beans Vinaigrette   *(page 287)*
Finger Rolls
Frozen Lemon Dessert   *(page 392)*
Coffee   Tea   Milk

Dinner Menus

Home-Style Pot Roast   (*page 145*)
Mashed Potatoes
Tossed Green Salad
Stir 'n' Roll Biscuits   (*page 89*)
Jellied Fruit Medley   (*page 362*)
Coffee   Tea   Milk

Roast Veal   (*page 156*)
Herbed Rice
Lettuce and Cucumber Salad
French Dressing   (*page 343*)
Poppy-Seed Rolls
Caramel Custard   (*page 368*)
Coffee   Tea   Milk

Stuffed Braised Pork Chops   (*page 173*)
Baked Sweet Potatoes
Green Beans
Parkerhouse Rolls
Apple Crisp   (*page 356*)
Coffee   Tea   Milk

Chuck-Wagon Steak   (*page 146*)
Parsley Potatoes
Lima Beans with Tomatoes   (*page 293*)
Tossed Green Salad
Biscuits
Peach Crunch Pie   (*page 414*)
Coffee   Tea   Milk

Short Ribs Country Style (*page 147*)
Stuffed Baked Potatoes
Buttered Carrots
Cole Slaw
Apple Pie
Coffee   Tea   Milk

Hungarian Goulash   (*page 150*)
Buttered Noodles
Green Pepper and Onion Salad
Hard Rolls
Fruit Gelatin and Cookies
Coffee   Tea   Milk

Won Ton Soup
Chinese Pepper Steak   (*page 150*)
Boiled Rice
Minted Fruit Bowl   (*page 316*)
Coffee   Tea   Milk

Sirloin Steak, Béarnaise Sauce   (*page 351*)
Herbed Broccoli
Julienne Potatoes
Sliced Tomatoes and Onions
Blueberry Pie
Coffee   Tea   Milk

Beef-Cheese Loaves   (*page 153*)
Baked Potatoes
Old-Fashioned Succotash   (*page 294*)
Carrot Strips
French Bread
Ice Cream and Ginger Cookies
Coffee   Tea   Milk

Corned Beef and Cabbage   (*page 155*)
Boiled Potatoes
Creamy Horseradish Sauce   (*page 352*)
Relish Tray
Pear-Applesauce Upside-Down Cake
(*page 374*)
Coffee   Tea   Milk

Braised Veal Shoulder   (*page 157*)
Buttered Squash   Asparagus
Celery Fingers and Green Pepper Rings
Rolls
Creamy Rice Pudding   (*page 366*)
Coffee   Tea   Milk

Paprika Lamb Shanks   (*page 167*)
Pilaf (*page 274*)
Peas with Water Chestnuts
French Bread
Pineapple Pie   (*page 414*)
Coffee   Tea   Milk

Baked Stuffed Fish
Creamed Potatoes
Brussel Sprouts and Chestnuts (*page 288*)
Beet and Onion Salad
Rolls
Raisin Pound Cake
Peaches
Coffee   Tea   Milk

Frosted Salmon Loaf (*page 238*)
Buttered Boiled Potatoes
Green Peas with Mushrooms
Cucumbers Vinaigrette
Cupcakes
Coffee   Tea   Milk

Southern Fried Chicken (*page 203*)
Mashed Potatoes
Asparagus with Lemon Butter
Fruit Salad
Clover Leaf Rolls
Apple Caramel Pie
Coffee   Tea   Milk

Broiled Ham Steaks
Mashed Sweet Potatoes
Green Beans and Whole Kernel Corn
Celery Curls
Whole Wheat Rolls
Cream Puffs with Chocolate Sauce
Coffee   Tea   Milk

Beef Stew   (*page 148*)
Buttered Noodles
California Slaw (*page 330*)
Tapioca Pudding
Coffee   Tea   Milk

Ham Loaf (*page 178*)
Glazed Carrots
New Potatoes
Lime Gelatin Salad
Rolls
Cherry Pie   (*page 412*)
Coffee   Tea   Milk

Shish Kebob
Broiled Tomatoes
Rice
Spring Garden Green Salad
Hard Rolls
Orange Chiffon Pie   (*page 422*)
Coffee   Tea   Milk

For Weight Watchers

Broiled Veal Chops with Rosemary
Spinach
Sliced Cucumber with Pimiento
Orange Sections
Coffee   Tea   Skim Milk

Broiled Chicken
Asparagus
Green Salad, Low Calorie Dressing
Fruit Gelatin
Coffee   Tea   Skim Milk

Menus from Supermarket Specials

Beef
Pot roast on special? A large one can be company fare or, if some is cut off for stew, two family meals.
Home-Style Pot Roast (*page 145*)
Noodles   Green Salad
Hard Rolls
Apple Tarts   (*page 425*)
Coffee   Tea   Milk

Lamb

Cut off the chops and a leg of lamb is doubly special—a roast and chops.

Herb-Roasted Leg of Lamb   (*page 164*)

Potatoes   Succotash

Spinach and Onion Salad

Patio Party Torte   (*page 457*)

Coffee   Tea   Milk

Ham

Ham and budget go further if you have a steak cut for special eating.

Smothered Ham Steaks   (*page 179*)

Orange Sweet Potatoes   (*page 303*)

Brown 'n' Serve Rolls

Sherbet   Spongecake

Coffee   Tea   Milk

Pork

Cut chops from a whole loin for one meal and roast the center cut.

Fruited Loin of Pork   (*page 172*)

Baked Acorn Squash

Green Beans Vinaigrette   (*page 287*)

Cheesecake

Coffee   Tea   Milk

Turkey

Turkey is special? Instead of roasting, have it cut in parts and try:

Sautéed Turkey, Curry Gravy   (*page 219*)

Green Peas

Mashed Potatoes

Cranberry Sauce

Packaged Refrigerated Biscuits

Chocolate Sundae Pie   (*page 395*)

Coffee Tea Milk

Chicken

Casserole Roasted Chicken (*page 207*)

Pilaf

Herbed-Marinated Tomatoes

Lemon Meringue Pie   (*page 421*)

Coffee   Tea   Milk

EATING TO STAY SLIM

There is an easy way to determine whether you are overweight. With thumb and forefinger, push together the flesh of your midriff. If you find more than an inch of flabby flesh between your fingers, you're too fat.

Doctors and nutritionists are agreed that one should not try to lose more than two pounds a week, so if you are as much as fifteen pounds overweight, you had better become reconciled to a diet you can live with for at least two months. Any diet that promises to take off weight more quickly than this is to be regarded with suspicion. You may lose your health along with the excess pounds. If you are more than fifteen pounds overweight, see your doctor.

For most of us, it's a question of changing eating habits, for even after the unwanted pounds have been eliminated, unless you continue to control the amount of food you eat, you will soon gain back those excess pounds.

Counting calories is a nuisance, and besides, a reduction in calorie intake alone is not the answer. Foods should be chosen as much for their nutritive value as their calorie content. High protein foods, which also may be relatively high in calories, are important because they give *lasting* energy (as compared with the quick energy of sweets). A breakfast that includes eggs, for example, will keep you feeling satisfied and fit until lunchtime, and then, with hunger pangs under control, you will be better able to keep within your diet pattern at the lunch table.

One of the great downfalls of many reducing diets is that the dieter becomes so ravenously hungry, he (or she) furtively gorges between meals on the very snacks that are most to be avoided.

For many people, light between-meal snacks make the diet much easier to take. The emphasis must be on *light:* foods that satisfy the urge to eat (whether psychological or physiological) without adding undue calories. Fruit, carrots, celery, tomatoes, hard-cooked eggs, yogurt, cottage cheese, and certain other cheeses made from skim milk are the best snack foods for the weight-watcher. An eggnog made of instant nonfat dry milk, egg, water, and enough vanilla for flavoring makes an excellent between-meal drink.

There is no magic formula for losing weight quickly, nor any reducing diet that will work with equal success for everyone. Primarily the important thing is to eat less than you have been eating. This may mean simply refusing second helpings, cutting out desserts, giving up the bedtime snacks, eliminating calorie-laden nibble foods.

Two lists follow which should serve as a useful guide in planning meals which will help you and all the family to keep slim, fit, and full of energy. If only the grownups in the family have to worry about overweight, the foods in the "caution" column can be served to the youngsters.

If only five pounds must be taken off, it is usually easy enough to eliminate all or most of the foods in the "caution" column for as brief a time as two weeks. If your dieting regime must last for months, on the other hand, inevitably you will be including many of the forbidden foods in family meals, and offering them to guests when you entertain in your home. Just remember when helping yourself to such foods to take small portions—and absolutely *no* seconds!

If yours is a sweet-tooth family for whom dessert is an important part of the meal, it will help to use artificial sweeteners at least part of the time in place of sugar. If you feel a great yearning for cake, settle for sponge or angel food cake—and a small slice at that. There are many dietetic desserts from which you can choose, including canned fruits and artificially sweetened gelatins. For the topping, use a nondairy topping instead of whipped cream. Sour cream has approximately half as many calories as heavy sweet cream, and yogurt a fourth as many calories as sour cream.

And remember that fruit makes the best of all desserts. A compote of mixed fruit can be delicious, refreshing, and as healthful as it is slimming.

Recommended Foods for Weight-Watchers

Appetizers and snacks
seafood (shrimp, lobsters, crab, mussels, clams, tuna)

small portions of cheese
all vegetable relishes
dips made with cottage cheese, preferably
   skim milk cheeses or yogurt
melba toast
rye wafers
plain crackers
fresh fruits

Main course dishes
seafood of all kinds
chicken or turkey
lean meats
liver
eggs (use sparingly for low-cholesterol diets)

Vegetables, salads and side dishes
all leafy green vegetables
carrots
celery
green peppers
tomatoes
cauliflower
cabbage
broccoli
Brussels sprouts
beets
green beans
baked or boiled white potatoes in small
   portions
rice

Sauces
low calorie salad dressings
small portions of oil and vinegar salad dressings or marinades
tomato sauces
unthickened fat-free gravies

Cheese
cottage cheese
farmer's cheese
pot cheese

Desserts and sweets
all fresh fruits
sherbets
clear or fruit-filled gelatin
small portions sponge or angel cake

Miscellaneous
clear soups or vegetable soups
vegetable oils in small amounts
whole-grain breads and cereals
enriched French or Italian bread
protein or gluten bread

Beverages
fruit juices
tomato juice
sauerkraut juice
black or artificially-sweetened coffee
unsweetened or artifically-sweetened tea
low calorie carbonated beverages
skim or nonfat milk
buttermilk

Foods to Be Used with Caution

Appetizers and snacks
potato chips
corn chips
cheese crackers and nibblers
cream cheese spreads
sour cream dips
nuts
popcorn

Main course dishes
fat meats such as bacon, sausage, pork chops,
    spareribs, corned beef, short ribs
duck or goose
pastas
dried beans (such as baked beans, chili)

Vegetables, salads and side dishes
lima beans
peas
corn
sweet potatoes
dried beans or peas
noodles, spaghetti or macaroni
avocados

Sauces and Toppings
mayonnaise
sour cream
cream sauces (unless made with nonfat milk
    or substitute)
thickened gravies
custard-type sauces
sauces containing nuts
whipped cream

Desserts and sweets
pies
cakes
doughnuts
all chocolate and cocoa products
all candies
ice cream
puddings and pudding sauces

Miscellaneous
butter or margarine (use sparingly in cook-
    ing)
bacon fat or other meat drippings
chicken fat
cream soups
cheese
cheese bread
dinner rolls
coffee cakes
breakfast buns
Danish pastry

Beverages
ice cream sodas
malted milk drinks
cocoa
chocolate-flavored milk
carbonated beverages
sweetened drinks
beer
cocktails, highballs,
    other drinks high in alcoholic content

EATING TO GAIN WEIGHT

While overeating is the great problem with most of us, there are also those who are underweight.

A chief cause of underweight may be emotion. When this is the case, cramming down a lot of calorie-rich foods is not going to help much. It may only lead to increased indigestion and an even poorer appetite than before.

When growing children are too thin it is often simply because they are "shooting up like weeds," and sooner or later they will stop shooting up and start to round out. Yet naturally mothers worry when their youngsters are too thin and, at the same time, have poor appetites. Sometimes mother's fretting only makes the situation worse. A child that is repeatedly urged to eat more and more may want less and less.

Breakfast is an important meal, but there are some individuals who simply have no appetite when they first get up in the morning. For such a child, instead of fussing because he fails to finish breakfast, try tucking into his book bag a snack that can be nibbled during recess, such as nuts, raisins, or oatmeal cookies.

If he has favorite foods, such as pastas,

make a point of serving them often, and besides adding plenty of cheese, stir a little instant nonfat dry milk into the sauce for additional nourishment. Desserts should not replace other important foods, even for the underweight child.

The same basic foods as listed in the "required eating" list given early in this chapter belong in the underweight as well as the overweight diet, but for the underweight there can be a larger proportion of dairy foods, more whole-grain and enriched cereals, and more high-protein foods including the fattier meats.

Here are several ways in which both the caloric level and the nutritional value of everyday foods can be increased.

· Add instant nonfat dry milk to hamburgers or meat loaf, to milk puddings, and such drinks as milk shakes. (With the latter two, this means in effect doubling the milk content per serving.)
· For between-meal drinks, make fruit nogs (with eggs and fruit juice), add egg to chocolate milk shakes, make "sodas" with ice cream and carbonated beverages, such as ginger ale.
· Instead of simple meat sandwiches, make combinations of cheese and meat. Cream cheese is excellent with both bologna and salami, American cheese with tongue as well as ham, Swiss cheese with sliced roast beef.
· Top braised or sautéed veal or pork chops with slices of cheese, slip under the broiler just before serving, until cheese melts.
· For breakfast, offer a selection of cinnamon buns, pecan rolls, or coffee cake, along with scrambled eggs and bacon. Vary scrambled eggs by adding a chopped tomato or a pinch of oregano, or a little grated or shredded cheese.
· Have casseroles frequently, enriching them with cheese, cream sauce, or other nutritious sauces.
· Top puddings with scoops of ice cream for dessert.
· Have cake or pie à la mode with generous scoops of ice cream.

Chapter Three

When You Entertain

Nothing is more exciting than planning and preparing a gala party—a special dinner party with delectable gourmet food, a beautiful table setting . . . or a festive holiday open house with sparkling punch, an array of tempting appetizers, gay decorations. This is when you can let your creativity and imagination run wild in skillfully blending many small elements into a harmonious whole. And there's nothing more satisfying than knowing, in the after-glow of the party, that it's been a great success, that you've created a memorable evening of entertainment.

Good parties like this don't just happen. They *are* work, and though everyone loves to go to one, not everyone loves to give one. You've heard the comment, "I never enjoy my own parties!" Maybe you've even said it yourself. But a party can be fun for *you* as well as for your guests. It's all in knowing how to plan.

There are two secrets of successful entertaining every hostess should know. *First*, invite people who will enjoy one another. The selection of a well-balanced guest list is the best possible way to insure sparkling conversation. *Second*, plan ahead and have most of your work done so you can be relaxed to greet your guests when they arrive.

The food, of course, is important too, and so is the way your house and table look, and there are a dozen other factors which can help

to make your party. But above all, it must be a time of gaiety and relaxation. That's what parties are for. Keep that thought in mind as you read our tips on entertaining. We'll take you through different types of parties, and show you how to make them successful—and enjoy giving them.

Planning and Inviting

How Many Can You Entertain Graciously? Start by taking stock of your facilities for entertaining and decide what kind of party you want to give. (Types of parties are discussed later on in this chapter.) Don't invite more guests than you can entertain graciously. It's better to do it on a small scale, and do it well.

If it's a dinner party, consider the size of your dining area, your supply of china, glassware, and table service. Can you seat everyone around one large table? Or would it be easier to have two tables in adjoining rooms? Or several card tables? Or should you simply serve from a buffet and let people sit where they wish?

Renting Supplies. If you want to invite more people than you have facilities for, think about renting supplies. There are now rental services which will supply you with such things as tables, chairs, punch bowls, glassware, tablecloths, even coat racks. If you give only one large party a year, it is less expensive to rent such things than to buy them—especially as storage in today's compact homes is often a major problem.

The Guest List. Even for a dinner party of six, the choice of guests should be thought out carefully. It is important that they have certain mutual interests, but there should be some good listeners to balance the talkers, and affable, easy-to-meet types to offset the shy ones.

When possible, introduce a new couple to old friends. But be careful about putting too many strangers together—they may have trouble finding things to talk about. To help get conversation going, when making introductions tell something about the background of each person—just enough to start questions.

Inviting. Invite your guests in plenty of time —about two or two-and-a-half weeks ahead for a party (but never more than three weeks, most people don't plan any farther ahead than that). About a week to 10 days may be sufficient for a small, informal dinner party or coffee.

Whether to invite by phone or written invitation is up to you—there are no set rules about it. Written invitations usually suggest a larger, more formal party, unless otherwise specified on the invitation. You may send out invitations for your big once-a-year holiday party, but for all other get-togethers you probably prefer to call your friends to invite them over.

In either case, be specific about the type of party, dress, and time. Tell them: Cocktails from 5 to 7; Dinner at 7:30; or Cocktail-Buffet at 6. If you're serving food, say so, and if it's a cocktail party, tell them what time it's to end. If you send out written invitations, don't forget to put down the date, address, and the R.S.V.P. if you want to know how many to expect.

Tips on Giving a Dinner Party

1. *Plan your menu first.* Write out your complete menu, including all courses, and make your market list from it. Add to the list any equipment or table service needed. Buy your groceries and supplies ahead, because you'll want to do as much cooking as you can in advance.

2. *It's best to serve as the main dish* something you've made before, so you know you can do it well. If you want to make something new, make it a couple of days ahead so you can test it in plenty of time before the party! Develop a few of your own specialities and become an expert with them.

3. *When you've decided on your entrée,* plan your other courses around it. Keep the dishes fairly simple, and make sure they complement and balance each other. For example, if your main course is rich and filling, serve a light dessert. If you're serving seafood as an entrée, don't serve a seafood appetizer. On the other hand, a seafood appetizer is excellent before a meat entrée.

4. *If you don't have help,* it's a good idea to serve simple appetizers as a first course in the living room before dinner.

5. *Have food that can be prepared ahead of time* and heated and served at the last minute. For a barbecue, have the meat ready to place on the grill or spit, and everything else, such as baked beans or scalloped potatoes, precooked or ready to place in the oven.

6. *Get the house in order.* It's best to do your heavy housecleaning a day or two before the party and leave some time for last minute sprucing up. If you own a dishwasher, it can go to work for you before the party as well as after. Your china and crystal will shimmer on the table after a quick, hot-water bath. Be sure there's plenty of room in your refrigerator for the party fixings.

7. *Set your table ahead of time.* Make it pretty and colorful, but don't crowd it. If you have room for a centerpiece, fresh flowers are lovely—make a low arrangement. And always have candles! Candlelight adds a wonderful warm glow, a romantic touch, to any table. Make sure they're high or very low so the flames are above or below eye level. Use them on a buffet table too.

8. *If you're serving cocktails before dinner,* have the liquor, mixes, and glasses out, fill the ice bucket, and have plenty of extra ice cubes on hand.

9. *"Timing" your party:* A meal that must be served promptly at a specified hour is unwise, because even the guests who intend to arrive

exactly on time may be delayed by some unforeseen factor. Your dinner time should be approximate, and your food should be the kind that "waits" well. If you serve cocktails before dinner, let the cocktail hour be long enough for everyone to relax and enjoy their drinks and conversation, but not so long that they lose their appetites. An hour or hour and a half is usually best. A good hostess learns to sense the party's progress and to "time" things properly. Nothing's worse than just starting a cocktail and good conversation and being rushed immediately to the table, or on the other hand, waiting and wondering if dinner will *ever* be served.

10. *Leave yourself time to relax before the party.* We'll say it again because it's important: get most of the work done in advance. No one can relax if the hostess has to work hard during the party.

Dinner Parties

A party can be as informal as crackers and beer on the patio, served to neighbors in slacks and sport shirts, or it can be a formal dinner by candlelight with a maid serving. A dinner party is the most popular and "special" way to entertain, and there are many different ways of doing one.

The small informal dinner party. This is the kind of entertaining you probably do most often—it's our favorite way to entertain. You have a few friends, usually four to six, over to dinner.

This is a dinner you most likely serve without help. You may serve informally, and pass the dishes around the table for everyone to help himself, family-style. Or, for a gracious touch (and smoother serving), the hostess serves. She has all the plates in front of her, serves them, and passes them to each person (ladies first). Condiments and bread or rolls are passed around the table. If you're serving meat that is to be carved at the table, the host might serve as he carves. Or he might serve the meat and pass the plate on to the hostess who will serve the rest of the meal.

It's perfectly proper to use placemats and stainless flatware instead of tablecloth and plated or sterling silver flatware at an informal dinner. Appetizers are usually served before dinner in another room, and just the main course, salad, and dessert at the table.

You may even prefer to serve dessert and coffee later in the living room. The dress for this kind of party is usually jacket and tie for the men, simple dress for the women.

Menu Suggestions for an Informal Dinner Party

Crisp Vegetable Relishes
Carrot Sticks, Radish Roses, Celery Fans
Lamb Stroganoff   (*page 169*)
Pilaf   (*page 274*)
Cucumber and Endive Salad
French Dressing   (*page 342*)
Preserved Ginger
Finger Rolls   Butter Curls
Dry Red Wine
Fresh Fruits in Grand Marnier   (*page 315*)
Coffee or Tea

Consommé
Chicken Marengo, Oven Style   (*page 208*)
Fluffy Buttered Rice
Green Beans and Almonds
Dinner Rolls
White or Rosé Wine
Molded Gelatin Whip
Coffee or Tea

Informal Dinner Table Setting, I

1. Salad plate
2. Napkin (also may be placed under forks or in ring)
3. Salad fork
4. Dinner fork
5. Dinner plate
6. Dinner knife
7. Teaspoon
8. Bread and butter plate and knife (optional)
9. Water goblet
10. Wine glass

Informal Dinner Table Setting, II

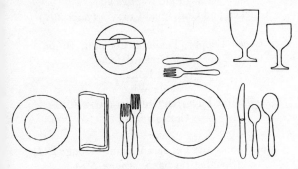

Here is a variation of Setting I, with a continental touch: dessert spoon and/or fork are placed as shown above. If you are serving soup as a first course, the soup spoon goes to right of coffee spoon. The general rule for placement of flatware is outside to inside in order of use.

The semi-formal dinner party. Literally, a formal dinner is a black-tie, five- to seven-course affair, complete with a maid or butler for every six to eight people. Invitations are formal, written in the third person on white cards. The formal dinner is rarely given today. We enjoy more informality, and our homes, with small dining areas and combination dining-family rooms, are not designed for formal entertaining. For this reason we won't discuss the formal dinner party, per se, but rather the kind of party we more often mean when we say "formal"—or a semi-formal dinner.

This is when you bring out your best and "dressiest" china, silverware, crystal, and tablecloth (usually white). You have three or four courses, and hire a maid to serve. (You and the host could manage this kind of dinner for about 12, but it means quite a bit of getting up and down from the table, so you're better off having help to make it go smoothly.) You might have three courses consisting of appetizer, entrée and salad, and dessert; or four courses: appetizer, soup or fish course, entrée and salad, and dessert. If you want to go all out, the five-course menu would include appetizer, soup, fish course, entrée and salad, and dessert. But a word of warning here—don't ever attempt four or five courses without outside help!

Place cards, a traditional must at a formal dinner, are a good idea for this party. It will save the who-sits-where shuffle at the table.

They should read "Miss Brown," "Mr. Smith," etc. If there is a male guest of honor, he should be placed at the hostess's right, a woman guest of honor at the host's right. The dress for this dinner party might be black ties for a special occasion, but more often is jacket and tie for the men, dressy "cocktail" dresses for the women.

You would probably want to extend written invitations for it, but they need not be written in the third person. This is a modern adaptation of a formal dinner party, suited to our more informal way of life and entertaining.

Menu Suggestions for a Semi-Formal Dinner Party

Chicken Liver Paté   (*page 47*)
Rolled Rib Roast   Yorkshire Pudding
        (*page 92*)
Cauliflower and Asparagus Polonaise
        (*page 290*)
Avocado and Mushroom Salad   (*page 324*)
Dry Red Wine
Grand Marnier Soufflé   (*page 366*)
Demitasse

Semi-Formal Dinner Table Setting

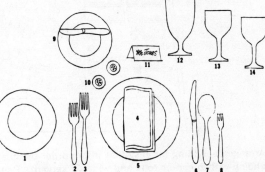

1. Salad plate
2. Salad fork
3. Dinner fork
4. Napkin
5. Dinner plate
6. Dinner knife
7. Soup spoon
8. Cocktail or oyster fork (fish fork would go on left, outside)
9. Bread and butter plate and knife (optional)
10. Individual salt and peppers (optional)
11. Place card (optional)
12. Water goblet
13. First course wine glass
14. Main course wine glass (if you are serving one wine throughout dinner, you need only one glass, of course)

The dessert spoon and/or fork and teaspoon (or demitasse spoon) are brought in with dessert and coffee (or demitasse).

or

French Onion Soup   (*page 127*)
Cheese Matches   (*page 57*)
Fish Filets Normandy   (*page 234*)
Duchess Potatoes   (*page 297*)
Green Peas with Onions
Brioche
Dry White Wine
Cherries Jubilee
Demitasse

Buffets. There are two types of buffet dinners. One is a *"serve yourself—sit where you wish"* buffet. This kind of party is especially good for very large groups, and is often called a cocktail-buffet. It's a good idea at a buffet to serve food that doesn't require a knife, as some people may even stand to eat.

Buffet Table Setting

Menu Suggestions for a Buffet Dinner

Easy Paté   (*page 46*)
Chicken and Crab Meat Curry   (*page 204*)
Rice
Green Pepper, Peanuts, Coconut, Onion
Crisp Green Salad
Hot Rolls
White Wine
Praline Bavarian Cream   (*page 364*)
Coffee or Tea

Mushrooms and Peppers Italiano   (*page 294*)
Spaghettini Bake   (*page 277*)
Vegetable Salad
Garlic Bread
Chianti
Pears Cardinale   (*page 356*)
Coffee or Tea

Arrange everything for easy flow in the order the plates will be filled, beginning with napkin and fork and ending with bread or rolls and wine (if served). Centerpiece and candles should be in center of table.

If table is against a wall, centerpiece and candles should go near wall, with everything else around the table from one side to the other, similar to the above.

Remember, if it is not a seated buffet, it is best to serve something which requires only a fork. If people are to take their plates to a table which has been set, napkins, flatware, and wine glasses will be on that table. Dessert and coffee may be set up on a side table, or if it is a seated buffet you may prefer to serve it.

The other, *a seated buffet*, is one at which everyone serves himself at the buffet table, then goes to another table, already set. (This table setting would be the same as for the informal dinner party). Some hostesses like to set up card tables when their dining table is used for the buffet or is not large enough to seat the group. This seated buffet is more formal than the other.

Menu Suggestions for a Seated Buffet

Party Stuffed Eggs   (*page 55*)
Shrimp, Island Style   (*page 52*)
Apricot Glazed Ham   (*page 177*)
Potato-Cheese Casserole   (*page 299*)
Tomato-Vegetable Soufflé Salad   (*page 339*)
Rosé Wine
Golden Fruitcake   (*page 448*)
Coffee or Tea

Viennese Veal Rolls   (*page 159*)
Buttered Parslied Noodles
Crisp Lettuce Wedges with
Tangy Roquefort Dressing (*page 344*)
Warm Parker House Rolls
Dry White Wine
Frozen Pineapple Chunks with
Crème de Menthe
Coffee or Tea

Cookouts or Barbecues. This is the most informal kind of dinner—becoming more popular all the time in warm climates and everywhere in the summer. Cooking is done on a grill, sometimes with everyone "pitching in," and dress is usually very informal. *For more about barbecues, see Chapter 27.*

Menu Suggestions for a Barbecue

Grilled Steak
Baked Potatoes
Foil-Roasted Corn   (*page 508*)
Tossed Green Salad with Tomatoes
French or Roquefort Dressing
Crispy Club Rolls
Apple Pie à la Mode or with Cheese
Beverages

Grilled Chicken
Frozen Potato Puffs in Foil
Buttered Peas and Onions
Hot Buttermilk Biscuits
Pineapple Coleslaw
Watermelon
Beverages

Luncheons and Brunches

Usually we think of *luncheons* as something for the ladies—a group from the church, fellow members of the PTA, or some friends. Foods are usually light and frivolous, a salad plate plus dessert, or an exotic casserole plus salad and dessert.

Menu Suggestions for a Luncheon

Chicken Divan   (*page 211*)
Salad in High C   (*page 331*)
Butterflake Rolls
Lemon Sherbet with Apricot Liqueur
Old-Fashioned Sugar Cookies   (*page 465*)
Coffee or Tea

Baked Buttered Shrimp   (*page 243*)
Italian Green Beans
Perfection Salad   (*page 340*)
Bread Sticks
Fresh Strawberries
Petits Fours Glacés   (*page 441*)
Coffee or Tea

Brunches have become a popular way to entertain, especially on Sundays or holidays. They are usually held around noon, but can be a little earlier or later. Breakfast foods are served at a brunch, though they're usually a little more elaborate than you'd have at an early-morning breakfast. Table settings are much the same for lunches and brunches as for informal dinners. Luncheon dishes are often included on the menu.

Menu Suggestions for a Brunch

Cranberry–Orange Juice
Welsh Rarebit   (*page 269*)
Toast
Crisp Bacon   Sausages
Peaches and Cream
Coffee

Fresh Blueberries
Scrambled Eggs
Chicken Livers Gourmet   (*page 213*)
Baked Tomatoes   Corn Muffins
Coffee

Coffees, Teas, Showers

Coffees and teas are an easy, simple way of entertaining friends from community groups and committees. Coffee, tea, sandwiches, and cakes are best for this kind of get-together.

Menu Suggestion for a Coffee or Tea

Assorted Tea Sandwiches   (*page 83*)
Pound Cake   (*page 440*)   Petits Fours
Tea   Coffee
Salted Nuts   Mints

For an Evening Dessert Get-Together

French Strawberry Meringue Cake
(*page 383*)
Louisiana Pecan Pie   (*page 418*)
(Guests to take their choice)
Coffee   Tea

Cocktail Parties

Cocktail parties, especially small ones, can be delightful to give as they are relatively little work, leaving you with plenty of time to circulate and talk to your guests without having to check on dinner from time to time.

What time? The most popular time for cocktail parties is about 5 to 7, though it's flexible. Depending on your schedule, you might prefer 4 to 6 or 6 to 8, or a longer party around that time of day. The longer party, often called "open house" may last all afternoon or evening, with people coming and going throughout. This is a wonderful way to entertain at holiday time.

Inviting. As mentioned under the discussion of invitations, do be specific about the time and the kind of party it's to be. Let your guests know if it's just for cocktails or if you're having a buffet of fairly substantial food, so that they know whether or not to make dinner arrangements. If you want the party to be over at 7, say so when you extend the invitation. You'd never expect everyone to be gone at the stroke of 7, but there are those who do have a way of staying on and on at cocktail parties, so it helps if you've specified what time the party's to end.

What drinks to serve. It's best to serve just a few kinds of drinks and keep them simple. If you try to offer an endless variety of cocktails, things may get too confusing—especially if the host is bartending. If you don't know the preferences of the group you might have Scotch, bourbon or rye, vodka or gin, a bottle of dry vermouth, a bottle of an aperitif wine, and plenty of mixes. This way you can offer two types of highballs, martinis, and an aperitif wine. If you have a bartender, and this is a good idea for a party of about 16 or more (almost a must for one of thirty or more)

you might want to add a bottle of sweet vermouth and offer Manhattans, too. If you want to serve a mixed cocktail remember the bottled and frozen mixes that are available. A blender is good for making whiskey sours or daiquiris. Have a couple of batches made up before party time. And don't forget to have soft drinks or tomato juice on hand for the nondrinkers. Here's a list of what you might have for a cocktail party of about 20 to 24:

- 3 quarts of Scotch
- 3 quarts of bourbon or rye
- 2 quarts of gin or vodka
- 1 bottle of dry vermouth
- 1 bottle of an aperitif wine
- 12 small bottles each of carbonated water, ginger ale, cola, and quinine water

We suggest buying the liquor by the quart instead of by the fifth when buying in large quantity, as it is a little more economical. This is probably more liquor and mixers than you'll need, but as with food, it's always better to have too much than too little. Also, it's difficult to judge, because many of the guests might ask for the same thing. (If you don't care to have liquor left over, some liquor stores will take back unopened bottles when you have bought in large quantity for a party.) Also, liquor preferences will vary with sections of the country. You may want to alter the list above to suit your guests' tastes. Some may also prefer beer.

Punches are marvelous for large parties, especially at holiday time. A pretty bowl of punch laced with fruit slices looks so festive on a table! For punch recipes, see *page 67.*

Cocktail party food. You'll want to have a nice variety of hors d'oeuvres, both hot and cold, and have them all prepared before the party—the hot ones keeping warm in a chafing dish, electric skillet, or ready to be heated in the oven.

Menu Suggestions for a Cocktail Party

For a large, gala holiday open house, here's a wide selection of elegant appetizers. See photograph opposite page 52.

Radish and Cauliflower Topiary Tree
Crab Profiteroles   (*page 53*)
Merry Cheese Ball   (*page 57*)
Cherry Tomatoes with Guacomole   (*page 56*)
Miniature Hamburgers   (*page 50*)
Chicken Livers Brochette   (*page 52*)
Salmon and Herring Tidbits
Turkey Amandine   (*page 222*)
with Corn Bread Squares
Lime Angel Tarts   (*page 382*)
Holiday Petits Fours Glacés   (*page 441*)

Here is a simpler selection of appetizers for a small, more informal cocktail party.

Burgundy Meat Balls   (*page 50*)
Stuffed Mushrooms   (*page 56*)
Crisp Vegetable Relish Tray
Dips and Chips   Cheese and Crackers

If it's a large party you might want, in addition to the bartender, a waiter or maid to pass the food. Be sure to have plenty of napkins, coasters, and large ashtrays around.

Have a specific area set aside for the bar, and try not to have all the food in the same area. Have all the bottles, mixes, lots of ice, and a pitcher of water out. And have plenty of glasses—more than the number of people you've invited. People will misplace their glasses and come back for fresh ones. For a party of about 20, figure on at least 30 glasses. (If you don't have enough glasses, you can rent them or buy inexpensive, plain bar glasses at a variety store.) Have a good supply of old-fashioned glasses, as drinks "on the rocks" are now very popular.

Big Parties

When you are having twenty or more guests, whether it's for cocktails or a buffet supper, it is important to consider the line of traffic. Service is smoother when food is served from one part of the room, beverages from another. If you are having outside help, both of these tables should be easily reached from the kitchen, without interfering with the guests. This could mean completely rearranging your dining room. Or you might have the beverage or cocktail table in a study or sunporch, the buffet in the dining room—if both can be reached from the kitchen.

If you are entertaining without outside help, plan some graceful way of removing empty plates from the living room to kitchen, and stacking them out of the way, to clear space for the dessert.

Set up silverware, napkins, plates, and glassware at one end of the buffet. Place foods on the table in the order in which they appear in the menu—hors d'oeuvres first, then the main course, the vegetables and salad next, and so on. A table in the center of the room is far better than a sideboard, so that traffic can move around it in a continuous line.

Handy Party Checklist

Now that we've covered the basic points of party-giving, here are the extras you should not overlook.

Chairs. Avoid a last minute race to the attic to bring out great-grandmother's ladder-back. Be sure that there is comfortable seating arrangement (unless yours is a stand-up cocktail party, of course, then you'd want to clear out some of your furniture).

Cigarettes, lighter (fully filled) or matches. Have them available simply as a nice gesture for the smokers.

Ash trays. Have an assortment scattered in all sitting and eating areas . . . not just decorative, but large, practical ones!

Place for coats. Provide an area for coats. Closets and beds are fine for small parties, but for large ones a coat rack is a better idea.

Tray tables. For buffet entertaining these are especially important for the men. No one is more uncomfortable than a big man balancing a fragile plate on his knee.

Bathroom fixings. Besides having a supply of guest towels, it's thoughtful to supply a tray of convenience items your guests might have forgotten—an extra comb, face powder with individual powder puffs, safety pins, tissues, clothes brush.

So now, go ahead—relax, have fun, and enjoy your party.

Chapter Four

Parties for Children and Teen-Agers

For the little ones, the party begins with the cake, a super-delicious cake to make eyes widen with wonder and sighs of delight fill the air. There will be ice cream, too, and something to drink, and party favors to add to the festive air, but the cake's the thing.

Will it be a Rocket Space Ship to send a junior astronaut into orbit? Or a pretty cake basket sprouting with lemon-cookie flowers? For the nautical minded, there is a cake with a chocolate ship afloat on a blue-frosting sea. Children adore fanciful confections, and to watch mother decorating the cake is often as exciting as the party itself.

Birthdays of course are the chief reason for party-giving for all children up to the age of 12. Child experts advise that for very young children, refreshments should be limited to the birthday cake and ice cream only, and the party should last no more than an hour. If any games are played, they should be simple ones.

Entertainment for five- and six-year-olds should consist mainly of the durable, old-fashioned games such as "Pinning the Tail on the Donkey," "London Bridge," or good old "Hide-and-Seek." If new, complicated games are introduced, the rules will only confuse them. Make sure that by some contrivance every child gets a prize—even if it's only a consolation prize for being last.

By the time they have reached 7 or so, children will expect more elaborate refreshments to supplement the cake and enough games must be planned to keep everyone busy from the time presents have been opened until the candles are lit on the cake. Even at this age, the party should be limited to an hour and a half, and be so specified on the invitations.

With each succeeding year, the games should be more complex and challenging, the refreshments more varied. No child wants the same kind of party as last year. The 8-year-old may demand a say in what games are to be played—and should be encouraged to plan the details. The 9-year-old will probably want to help decorate the cake. Don't be surprised if your 10-year-old decides on an outing instead of a home party, returning to the house for the cake and other refreshments as the finale of a trip to the ball game, museum, theater, or amusement park.

Whatever the occasion or the age group, certain rules apply. The party should be given in a room where it doesn't matter if crumbs and even cake frosting are spilled on the floor, where fragile whatnots have all been removed in advance, and where there is space enough for games. Playing outdoors is preferable when weather permits, but an alternate plan for indoor games must always be ready. An adult should supervise at all times, even for the 11- and 12-year-olds, to settle arguments and suggest activities if the planned games prove to be not enough to keep everyone occupied until refreshment time. Paper plates and cups, of course, can be used for refreshments, and it would be wise to spread a paper cloth over the table, too, for at least one drink is likely to be spilled before the party is over.

Seven Seas Party

(For boys and girls 6 to 10)

It's all hands on deck for rough and tumble shipmates. Their liking for the water can find an outlet in a sea confined to a wading pool in your backyard. Invitations should specify play clothes.

The opening event is a *relay boat race* on the wading-pool sea. Two players face each other on either side of the filled pool in the yard, each with a toy boat. Each player tries to get his boat to the other side by blowing it across the water. The winner of each race wins a compass (costing 10 or 15 cents at toy counters).

Next comes a *fish-blow contest*. A toy whale or any plastic fish or duck that floats can be used. All the toy boats from the preceding game are now in the water. Each child tries to blow the whale or duck through the boats to the other side without knocking over a single boat. Each one who succeeds receives another prize.

And now a *pirate hunt*. By drawing slips or "by appointment" the pirate captain is selected, and he chooses two fellow pirates. The pirates all wear kerchiefs (supplied by the hostess) around their heads. The rest of the children are given sailor's hats or captain's caps. They elect a captain who, after consultation, leads them to a hiding place. Meantime, the pirates have their faces hidden, and the pirate captain counts slowly to ten. If the pirates find their hidden victims in less than 10 minutes, they win a "treasure chest" filled with candy coins. If it takes them longer

than 10 minutes, the sailors get the treasure chest.

Last is the call to eat. A fish net is spread over the table, the centerpiece a Ship Ahoy Cake gleaming with candles. The rest of the menu will consist of Sea Dogs (tuna salad in frankfurter rolls), deviled eggs, carrot sticks, and Long John Sippers (root beer with a scoop of ice cream). For favors, bosun's whistles, to take home with the prizes.

Recipe for the Ship Ahoy Cake is on page 451 and is pictured opposite page 21.

A Tisket, A Tasket Party

(For girls 8 to 12)

This begins with each young lady receiving a basket—decorated with green and yellow ribbons.

First order of the day is to *"find the letter that was dropped"* (according to the words of the song), except that there will be 20 to 30 letters depending on the number of participants, hidden around the house or in the yard.

The letters will contain favorite messages such as "April showers bring May flowers," or a favorite song title. The girl who finds the most letters wins a prize.

Next is a *tisket-tasket flower contest*. Using the same basket, guests and hostess seated around a table or on the floor make flower arrangements from artificial flowers and green modeling clay or plastic foam. Allow 15 minutes for this. The prettiest arrangement wins a real corsage.

After one or two ring games (such as "Farmer in the Dell"), the girls are ready to go to the party table where an enchanting Tisket-Tasket Cake awaits them. There are also little finger-length chicken sandwiches, fruit salad cups, and pink lemonade. Beside each place is a party favor. *Recipe for Tisket-Tasket Cake is on page 450.*

Off-to-the-Moon Trip

(For boys 6 to 9)

The dream costume of all small boys these days is the astronaut's coverall. And their knowledge of rocketry is apt to stun their fathers. So what could be more fun than an off-to-the-moon party? Plan this as an outdoor or playroom party. Pay a visit to the variety store and come home with an assortment of spacecraft toys for competitive games.

Have a *make-it-yourself contest*. Give each boy four or five sheets of construction paper, scissors, a tube of paste, rubber bands, and ten minutes to make his own airborne plane or rocket. The most successful builder gets a prize of a model rocket.

After an hour and a half the astronauts will be ready for the moment all have been waiting for—the arrival of the Rocket Spaceship Cake. *Recipe for Rocket Cake, page 449.*

Besides the cake, the menu may include Orbit-Burgers (two thin beef patties pressed together with a slice of cheese in the middle), carrot, celery, and pickle sticks, milk, and Meteor Sundaes (small scoops of different flavors of ice cream with chocolate sprinkles). The favors? A toy flying saucer for each boy.

Teen Parties

Once they have passed the 12-year-old frontier, young people are likely to rate pizzas of greater importance than a fancifully decorated cake, and the raucous music of a record player as more appropriate than party games. They will not wait for a birthday as an excuse for a party — in fact, may decide to make birthday celebrations family affairs and to give parties on any free Saturday night to celebrate the windup of football season or the end of exams. Though teenagers may think parties just happen — truth of the matter is they don't! They require just as much planning and supervision as any other party.

Teens (both girls and boys) can and should help prepare their own refreshments, accept responsibility for planning the party, for maintaining some semblance of order while the festivities are underway, and for cleaning up afterward. Rules should be established regarding the maximum number of guests to be invited and an agreed-upon closing hour.

Teen parties are easier and more fun if easy-to-operate appliances are set up in a spot where the young people can prepare their own refreshments. Paper plates, cups, and napkins of course are in order, and bottled soda pop may be served from buckets of ice. Be sure a large wastebasket is handy for all the debris that will accumulate.

Teen-agers adore mixing up unlikely combinations, the more weird the better, and a buffet table where the makings of sandwiches, sundaes, or other snacks can be laid out for mixing and matching will suit them just fine. Each guest can make his own sandwich from foods cooked on the spot. Here are a few suggestions:

False-face burgers: Prepare your favorite hamburger mixture. Using olive slices, pimiento, and green-pepper strips, make your own burger funny face before grilling—or top a ready-grilled burger with eyes and mouth cut from slices of process American cheese.

Pickled hot dogs: Split hot dogs vertically down the center, stuff with a pickle strip, wrap with bacon, secure with wooden picks and grill.

Grilled cold cuts: Grill thin slices of assorted cold cuts such as canned luncheon meat, pepperoni sausage, or bologna. Serve with a basket of assorted rolls and plenty of catsup, mustard, and relish.

For sundaes, half a dozen kinds of ice cream plus twice as many toppings will offer a challenge to their way-out imaginations.

Besides the parties that are planned, teen-agers like to bring friends home impulsively for after-school snacks or post-game celebrations, or weekend record sessions, and as all parents of teen-agers know, such friends generally arrive on hollow legs. Mother on such occasions should not allow herself to be trapped into the role of short-order cook. Again, let the youngsters prepare their own food. Make it clear they must not raid the refrigerator without first inquiring what foods are to be left intact for the family dinner, and that when they have satisfied their appetites, the kitchen or family room (or both) must be cleaned up.

Chapter Five

Appetizers

No other foods offer such challenge and such fun as appetizers. The term "appetizers" is used today to include all those foods and beverages served to tempt the appetite—canapés, dips, relishes, juices, first-course salad mixtures, hot hors d'oeuvres.

At a cocktail party, appetizers may be the only food you serve, and then it is important to plan a selection which will complement each other in taste, texture, and appearance, and will be easy to eat with the fingers.

Appetizers also may be the first course of a dinner, served either in the living room with predinner drinks or at the dining table. In this case, the selection will be more simple, something to whet the appetite for the more substantial meal to follow. If serving this course in the living room, you may present a simple tray of assorted vegetable relishes and bite-size chunks of sharp cheese.

Canapés are tiny open-faced sandwiches which can be eaten in one bite. They're usually small fancy shapes of toast or bread topped with a creamy spread and a bit of seafood or a strip of pimiento, or perhaps sieved egg yolk.

Dips are an American invention, created to fill the need of today's servantless homes when it is rarely possible to make elaborate canapés. For example, a mixture of softened, seasoned cream cheese and a can of chopped clams makes a wonderful dip for chips and crackers.

For most functions, one or more of all these may be offered with the beverages: a dip to pass with relishes, crackers, or chips; hot and cold hors d'oeuvres; spreads to use on wafers; and crisp, seasoned nibblers. Some may come ready to serve from cans or jars.

The most exciting appetizers are those you prepare yourself with imaginative, provocative seasoning. But if you are short on time or if you have unexpected guests, there are myriad snacks and appetizer shortcuts available at the supermarket. For example, when tart shells are required for a recipe, you can buy them in several shapes and sizes. There is also a wide variety of frozen hors d'oeuvres, canapés, and puff pastries. Keep a supply on your pantry shelf, or in your freezer.

FRUIT

SERVING FRUIT CUPS

Serve fruit cups in dessert dishes, tall, stemmed glasses, small decorative fruit bowls, or any interesting small glass, crystal, or china dish. If stemmed glasses are used, layer fruits parfait style for a gay rainbow effect. With these use an iced-tea spoon.

Garnish fruit cups with mint leaves, lemon wedges, a twist of candied orange rind, a preserved kumquat, a small scoop of fruit ice or sherbet, a whole strawberry, or frosted grapes. Fruit cups need juice too; add enough to come to ½ inch of the top of the glass or dish.

Whether you use all fresh fruits or a combination of fresh and canned, fruit cups need color as well as flavor contrasts. Serve them icy cold!

Some Favorite Combinations

Fresh Fruits

· Orange sections, grapefruit sections, seedless or pitted grapes, fresh blueberries.
· Orange sections, banana slices, defrosted frozen raspberries, bits of candied ginger.
· Grapefruit sections, diced unpeeled apples, canned Mandarin oranges.
· Peach slices, banana slices, canned or defrosted frozen pineapple chunks, strawberry halves.
· Melon cubes, apple cubes topped with lemon sherbet.
· Melon slices, avocado slices, pineapple juice.

Frozen Fruits
· Thawed frozen sliced peaches and raspberries, sprinkled with orange rind.
· Partially thawed melon balls, thawed strawberry halves, sprinkled with ground cardamom.
· Thawed mixed fruits topped with orange- or lemon-flavored sherbet.

BROILED GRAPEFRUIT

Cut grapefruit in half. Remove core and seeds; loosen each section from membranes. Sprinkle with white or brown sugar and dot with butter. Broil 5 to 10 minutes or until browned and bubbly. Garnish with orange sections and serve hot. For a special treat, spoon a teaspoon of sherry over each half just before sprinkling with sugar. Makes 2 servings.

HONEY BROILED GRAPEFRUIT

2 grapefruit	½ c. honey
2 oranges	2 tsp. sugar
4 maraschino cherries	

Cut grapefruit in half; remove seeds. Insert small knife blade between white inner skin and meat of grapefruit. Cut completely around grapefruit in a sawing motion, freeing meat from shell. Cut down on each side of grapefruit segment to free meat from membranes. Hold center core firmly; cut core at base. Lift out core with membranes attached. Peel and section oranges. Arrange orange sections in pattern between segments of grapefruit. Drop cherry into center of each grapefruit half. Drizzle tops with honey; sprinkle with sugar. Broil 4 to 6 minutes or until honey mixture is bubbly and grapefruit is heated through. Serve hot. Makes 4 servings.

GRAPEFRUIT DELUXE

Cut grapefruit in half; remove seeds. Remove core and membranes as in Honey Broiled Grapefruit. Chill grapefruit sections. Serve with a spoonful of grenadine over the top or remove sections from shell and mix with equal parts of sliced strawberries, sliced seeded grapes, or orange sections. Makes 2 servings.

SHRIMP GRAPEFRUIT APPETIZER

Prepare grapefruit halves as in Grapefruit Deluxe. Fill grapefruit shell with sections of grapefruit and whole cooked shrimp. Serve with Shrimp Cocktail Sauce, *page 48*.

MELON APPETIZERS

Cantaloupe, honeydew, Persian, casaba, in fact any melon makes the easiest possible ap-appetizer to serve. Just cut in wedges and re-move seeds. Chill and serve as is or with fresh berries, orange sections, clusters of seedless white grapes, or sprigs of mint. Serve with wedges of lemon or lime. Good too with a dash of salt. Another popular seasoning for melon is cinnamon sugar.

The size of a melon serving may vary from a narrow wedge or slice to half a melon; it may be peeled or not, although a thin or small slice looks better when peeled.

Melon balls too, fresh or frozen, are refresh-ing appetizers.

FRUIT HORS D'OEUVRES TRAY

Fill a tray with a tempting selection of fruit, and each person can help himself to his favorite. If you're serving it as a first course at the table, at each place setting place a fruit or salad plate with a fruit knife and fork. Then pass the festive tray which may be decorated with fresh green leaves (lemon, violet, peach, or apple), chilled melon sec-tions, pineapple strips, grape clusters, plums, peaches, golden pears, apples—in fact, any fruit in season.

JUICE APPETIZERS

A favorite is the well chilled glass of fruit or vegetable juice served as an appetizer, usually with canapés or crackers.

The kitchen blender can help provide deli-cious fruit and vegetable juices in many combinations. Follow your blender instruc-tion book on just what to add and how long to mix and blend.

Apple Juice. Apple juice is a traditional appetizer with winter holiday dinners. It is not necessary to mix it with other juices. Sprinkle with a dash of nutmeg.

Pineapple Juice. Serve it as is or blend it with orange or grapefruit juice or a little fresh lime or lemon juice. Shake mixture with cracked ice and crushed mint leaves. Pour into frosty glasses.

Cranberry Juice. Shake with cracked ice and a dash of lemon juice, then pour into a glass and top with a spoonful of sherbet. Sprinkle chopped mint leaves on top of sherbet.

Grape Juice. Mix it with equal parts of pine-apple or orange juice. Or serve it plain in a frosty glass.

Loganberry Juice. Like grape, this is a good juice appetizer because the flavor and color add much to the menu. Garnish the logan-berry glass with a thin slice of fresh lime or lemon.

Bottled or Canned Nectars. These make good appetizers if their sweetness is cut with lemon or pineapple juice. Taste as you mix and decide how much zip is needed. Try orange sherbet in an apricot nectar with a little finely cut fresh mint stirred in.

Bottled or Canned Tomato Cocktail. This makes a quick and refreshing appetizer. Serve well chilled with a lemon twist and a dash of hot-pepper sauce or Worcestershire sauce.

CLAM TOMATO COCKTAIL

2 bottles (8 oz.) clam juice, chilled	Several dashes hot-pepper sauce
1 c. tomato juice, chilled	2 tbs. lemon juice ½ tsp. celery salt ¼ tsp. salt

Blend all ingredients together. Makes 6 serv-ings, 4 ounces each.

TOMATO SAUERKRAUT JUICE

Combine equal parts tomato juice and sauer-kraut juice. Add a dash of hot-pepper sauce.

TOMATO REFRESHER

1 can (1 lb. 3 oz.) tomato juice	1 tbs. lemon juice Dairy sour cream
1 can (12½ oz.) chicken broth	Chopped chives

Combine tomato juice, broth, and lemon juice. Chill. Serve topped with a spoonful of sour cream and a sprinkling of chives. Makes 8 servings, 4 ounces each.

COCKTAILS AND FIRST COURSES

EASY PÂTÉ

3 tbs. butter or margarine	¼ lb. soft butter or margarine
¼ c. minced onion	1 tsp. salt
1½ lbs. chicken livers	⅛ tsp. pepper
½ c. Cognac	¼ tsp. nutmeg
½ c. heavy cream	Paprika
	Crisp crackers

Heat butter or margarine in skillet; cook onion until soft, but not browned. Add chicken livers; cook quickly until all pink has disappeared. Put onion and livers through food mill to puree. Add Cognac, cream, butter or margarine, salt, pepper, and nutmeg. Beat at low speed on mixer until creamy and blended. Spoon into serving dish; cover; chill several hours or overnight. For serving, sprinkle with paprika and surround with crisp crackers. Makes about 3½ cups.

LIVER PÂTÉ

1½ lbs. calves liver	¾ c. all-purpose flour
½ c. chopped onion (1 medium)	1½ c. heavy cream
1 can anchovy fillets in oil	7 slices bacon
1 tbs. salt	1 envelope un-flavored gelatin
¼ tsp. ground ginger	¼ c. cold water
⅛ tsp. ground cloves	1 can (10½ oz.) condensed consommé
Dash of cayenne	Truffles or ripe olives
	Watercress

Soak liver in cold water to cover, 6 to 8 hours or overnight; wipe dry. Put liver, onion, anchovy fillets, and oil through food chopper, using fine blade; grind 4 to 5 times more or transfer to blender and mix until smooth. Mix in salt, ginger, cloves, cayenne, and flour; blend in cream; beat well. Line 9 x 5 x 3-inch loaf pan with bacon slices; pour liver mixture carefully into pan; set pan in larger pan of hot water. Bake at 275° F. for 1 hour, 50 minutes or until firm in center. Chill several hours or overnight. Remove thoroughly chilled pâté from pan; discard bacon slices; wash and dry pan. Soften gelatin in cold water; dissolve over hot water; combine with consommé. Spoon ¼-inch layer of gelatin mixture into loaf pan; chill until set; arrange cut pieces of truffles or ripe olives on top; cover with second thin layer of gelatin mixture; chill until set. Place pâté in loaf pan; carefully spoon remaining gelatin mixture around sides; chill until set. When ready to serve, unmold; garnish with watercress. Makes about 18 servings.

PÂTÉ IN ASPIC

2 envelopes un-flavored gelatin	1 pkg. (8 oz.) cream cheese
3 c. chicken broth	1 tube (2 oz.) anchovy paste
1 egg white	2 tbs. dry sherry
1 egg shell	Pimiento
½ c. liverwurst	Parsley sprigs

Soften gelatin in 1 cup chicken broth. Heat remaining broth to boiling; add softened gelatin; stir until dissolved. Beat egg white until frothy; add white and crumbled egg shell to hot broth. Heat slowly to boiling; remove from heat; let settle. Strain through several thicknesses of cheese cloth or clean toweling; cool. Chill until aspic just begins to thicken. Blend liverwurst, cream cheese, and anchovy paste with electric mixer at medium speed; add sherry slowly; beat until fluffy and well blended. Set 6 individual molds firmly on bed of ice; spoon thin layer of aspic into molds; let set. Cut designs from pimiento; place on set aspic layer; spoon thin layer of aspic into each mold; let set.

Press liverwurst mixture through pastry bag into center of each mold, leaving ¼ inch free around edges. Fill mold with aspic; chill until set. Pour any remaining aspic into shallow pan; let set; cut in tiny cubes. Unmold pate; garnish with aspic cubes and parsley sprigs. Makes 6 servings.

CHICKEN LIVER PÂTÉ

2 lbs. chicken livers	3 tbs. anchovy paste
½ c. chopped onion (1 medium)	1 pkg. (3 oz.) cream cheese
2 tbs. butter or margarine	½ c. soft butter or margarine
½ c. Cognac	½ c. finely chopped parsley
½ tsp. salt	2 hard-cooked eggs
½ tsp. powdered thyme	

Sauté chicken livers and onion in butter or margarine until livers are just cooked. Put mixture through a food mill. Heat Cognac until it is reduced to ¼ cup; blend into chicken-liver mixture. Beat in salt, thyme, anchovy paste, cream cheese, and soft butter or margarine, using electric mixer. Continue to beat until smooth and completely blended. Chill until firm. Shape into cylinder; roll in chopped parsley to coat. Peel hard-cooked eggs; cut in half; remove yolks. Sieve egg yolks; sieve egg whites; use to garnish pâté. Serve with melba toast rounds or crisp crackers. Makes 8 servings.

TOMATO SHRIMP FRAPPÉ

¾ c. mixed vegetable or tomato juice	5 or 6 medium-size shrimp, cooked, shelled, and deveined
2 tsp. Worcestershire sauce	⅓ c. lemon juice
¼ tsp. salt	1 can (12½ oz.) jellied madrilene

Place all ingredients in blender; cover; blend well. Pour into shallow pan. Freeze, stirring occasionally, until mixture has frozen to a mush. Spoon into sherbet glasses; garnish with additional shrimp and tomato slice and serve with lemon wedge, if desired. Makes 3 to 4 servings.

SHRIMP COCKTAIL

Use fresh cooked, canned, or frozen shrimp. If shrimp are large, cut in half. Shell and devein fresh shrimp. Sprinkle with lemon juice. Chill until ready to serve. Place shredded lettuce in cocktail glasses; add shrimp. Serve with cocktail sauce and lemon wedges. One pound makes 4 servings.

BAKED CLAMS

12 cherry stone clams	¼ tsp. oregano, crumbled
½ c. packaged bread crumbs	1 tbs. dry white wine
1 tbs. chopped parsley	3 tbs. heavy cream
¼ tsp. garlic powder	2 tbs. packaged bread crumbs
⅛ tsp. pepper	2 tbs. grated Parmesan cheese

Scrub clams well under cold, running water. Open clams; remove them from shells; reserve shells. Chop clams finely. Mix clams, ½ cup bread crumbs, parsley, garlic powder, pepper, oregano, wine, and cream. Spoon about 1 tablespoon mixture into each shell. Sprinkle with mixture of 2 tablespoons bread crumbs and cheese. Bake at 425° F. for 10 to 15 minutes. Makes 4 servings.

OYSTERS ROCKEFELLER

18 large, raw oysters	¼ tsp. salt
2 c. spinach, cooked and well drained	3 drops hot-pepper sauce
¼ c. chopped onion (1 small)	¼ c. soft bread crumbs
1 tbs. chopped parsley	3 tbs. butter or margarine
¼ tsp. celery salt	Lemon slices

Open oysters; remove from shells; drain. Reserve halves of shells. Fill 6 individual heat-proof serving dishes with rock salt (or use a baking pan large enough to hold all the oysters). Place 3 reserved shells in each dish; put an oyster in each shell. Put spinach, onion, and parsley through food grinder using fine blade, or whirl in blender for 1 minute. Add celery salt, salt, hot-pepper sauce, and bread crumbs. Cook in butter or margarine 5 minutes. Spoon about 1 tablespoon of spinach mixture over each oyster. Bake at 400° F. about 10 minutes or until oysters are heated through and sauce bubbles slightly. Serve with lemon slices. Makes 6 servings.

For a special flavor, add 2 tablespoons Pernod or Anisette to spinach mixture before spooning onto oysters.

OYSTERS AND CLAMS ON THE HALF SHELL

If bought in their shells, rinse oysters and clams under running cold water; drain. Pry shells open with oyster shucker or short-blade knife and discard the smaller halves of the shells. Drain the oysters or clams and chill them in a bowl until ready to serve. Rinse the larger halves of shells; drain; replace chilled oysters or clams in shells. Arrange filled shells in a special oyster plate or shallow, round or oval dish, half filled with cracked ice, if desired. Serve at once. Each person seasons them to his own taste. Accompaniments usually served include cocktail sauce, Worcestershire sauce, hot-pepper sauce, freshly ground pepper, celery salt, lemon wedges, or oyster crackers. Usually 4 to 6 oysters or clams make one serving.

ROCK LOBSTER NEWBURG

1 pkg. (9 oz.) frozen rock lobster tails, thawed	¾ c. light cream
	1 egg yolk, slightly beaten
	1 tbs. dry sherry
2 tbs. butter or margarine	¼ tsp. ground nutmeg
2 tbs. flour	½ c. grated Parmesan cheese
½ tsp. salt	
¼ tsp. pepper	

Remove lobster meat carefully from shells; cube meat; reserve shells. Sauté lobster in butter or margarine in skillet for 3 minutes. Remove lobster; reserve. Blend flour, salt, and pepper into butter or margarine remaining in skillet. Stir in cream gradually; cook until mixture comes to boiling. Stir some of hot mixture quickly into egg yolk. Return egg yolk mixture to sauce remaining in skillet; cook 1 minute longer, stirring constantly. Stir in lobster, sherry, and nutmeg. Fill shells with lobster mixture; sprinkle with cheese. Broil until cheese is browned and shells begin to turn red. Makes 4 servings.

LOBSTER COCKTAIL

Use fresh cooked, canned, or frozen lobster meat. Remove meat from shells. Sprinkle with lemon juice. Chill until ready to serve. Place shredded lettuce in cocktail glasses; add lobster. Serve with cocktail sauce and lemon wedges. One pound makes 6 servings.

CRAB MEAT COCKTAIL

Use fresh cooked, canned, or frozen crab meat. Remove bones. Cut into bite-size pieces; sprinkle with lemon juice. Chill until ready to serve. Place shredded lettuce in cocktail glasses; add crab meat. Serve with cocktail sauce and lemon wedges. One pound makes 6 servings.

COCKTAIL SAUCES

AVOCADO COCKTAIL SAUCE

Peel, pit, and sieve 1 small ripe avocado. Add 1 teaspoon grated onion, ½ teaspoon grated lemon rind, 2 tablespoons lemon juice, ⅔ cup mayonnaise or salad dressing, ¼ cup chili sauce, and salt and pepper to taste. Blend well. Cover; chill. Makes about 1½ cups.

NEPTUNE COCKTAIL SAUCE

Combine ¾ cup mayonnaise or salad dressing, ¼ cup chili sauce, 1 tablespoon finely chopped chives, 1 teaspoon prepared horseradish, ¼ teaspoon hot-pepper sauce, salt and pepper to taste. Chill. Makes about 1 cup.

EGG AND CAPER SAUCE

Blend together ¾ cup mayonnaise or salad dressing, 2 tablespoons lemon juice, 1 teaspoon grated onion, 2 finely chopped hard-cooked eggs, 1 to 2 tablespoons drained capers, and salt and pepper to taste. Chill. Makes about 1¼ cups.

CUCUMBER COCKTAIL SAUCE

Blend together ½ cup dairy sour cream, ⅔ cup finely diced cucumber, 1 teaspoon grated onion, ½ teaspoon grated lemon rind, 2 tablespoons mayonnaise or salad dressing, ½ teaspoon dill weed, ⅛ teaspoon hot-pepper sauce, and salt and pepper to taste. Chill. Makes about 1 cup.

SHRIMP COCKTAIL SAUCE

Combine 1 cup catsup, 1 to 2 tablespoons prepared horseradish, few dashes hot-pepper sauce, 1 tablespoon lemon juice, and salt and pepper to taste. Chill. Makes about 1 cup.

CHILI MAYONNAISE DRESSING

Blend 1 cup mayonnaise or salad dressing, ¾ cup chili sauce, and 2 tablespoons lemon juice. Makes about 1¾ cups.

PREPARED COCKTAIL SAUCES

In supermarkets you'll find a wide selection of prepared bottled cocktail sauces and dressings for use with appetizers. Keep a supply on your pantry shelf—they're great time-savers.

SNAILS IN GARLIC BUTTER (Escargots)

Don't be afraid to try snails. They're a truly delightful gourmet experience—you may discover a whole new world of eating!

1 pkg. (4⅖ oz.) extra large snails with shells	1 clove of garlic, minced
¼ c. soft butter or margarine	1 tbs. chopped parsley
1 tbs. finely minced shallots or onion	¼ tsp. salt Dash of pepper

Wash and drain snails. Combine remaining ingredients; put about ¼ teaspoon butter mixture into each shell. Place each snail in a shell; pack remaining mixture into shell to seal in snail. Place in shallow baking dish or snail pan. Bake at 450° F. for 10 minutes. Serve with crusty bread. Makes 3 servings.

APPETIZER PIES

1 small round loaf pumpernickel bread	¼ c. chopped chives
1¼ c. Liverwurst Spread (*page 78*)	3 jars (6 oz. ea.) caviar
2 pkgs. (8 oz. ea.) cream cheese	2 c. Deviled Ham spread (page 78)
¼ c. mayonnaise or salad dressing	½ lb. thinly sliced smoked salmon
	1 large jar stuffed olives

Slice bread into 4 crosswise slices; remove crusts from edges. Spread slices with anchovy butter. Blend cream cheese, mayonnaise or salad dressing, and chives. Spoon small round of caviar in center of slice of bread. Circling the round of caviar, spoon or press through pastry bag alternate circles of ham spread

and cream cheese mixture. Leave a 2-inch border around edge. Cut salmon slices in half lengthwise; roll each strip beginning at narrow end. Arrange around border of bread slice alternately with olives. Repeat pattern with remaining slices of bread. Cover with transparent plastic wrap; refrigerate. For serving, cut into thin wedges. Each pie makes about 12 to 16 wedges.

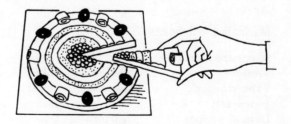

ANTIPASTO PLATTER

1 can (9½ oz.) tuna
1 jar roasted
peppers
1 small head
lettuce, washed
and drained
½ lb. sliced
prosciutto
¼ lb. salami or
pepperoni
¼ lb. provolone
cheese, sliced
1 jar (8 oz.) green
olives

1 can (9 oz.) ripe
olives
1 can (4 oz.) rolled
anchovy fillets
1 fennel, cut into
eighths
Marinated Vege-
tables (below)
Marinated Arti-
chokes (below)
Olive oil
Wine vinegar

Drain tuna; separate into chunks. Drain roasted peppers; cut into strips. Shred lettuce; place on platter. Arrange all ingredients except oil and vinegar in design on lettuce bed. Serve with oil and vinegar to be drizzled over each serving. Makes 4 to 6 servings.

Marinated Vegetables

1 pkg. (⅝ oz.)
onion- or Italian-
flavored
salad dressing
mix
¼ lb. mushrooms

1 pkg. (10 oz.)
frozen artichoke
hearts, cooked
and drained
2 celery stalks
1 large carrot,
pared and cut in
strips

Prepare salad dressing mix according to package directions; heat just to boiling. Put each vegetable in separate bowl. Pour over enough dressing just to cover each vegetable. Refrigerate 4 to 6 hours or overnight.

Marinated Artichokes

½ c. pure vegetable
oil
2 tbs. vinegar
½ tsp. salt
Dash of pepper

1 pkg. (10 oz.)
frozen artichoke
hearts
1 small clove of
garlic
1 bay leaf

Blend oil, vinegar, salt, and pepper. Prepare artichokes according to package directions

adding ¼ cup oil mixture, garlic, and bay leaf to salted water. Drain; remove garlic and bay leaf. Place artichokes in bowl; pour over remaining oil mixture. Refrigerate 4 to 6 hours.

HORS D'OEUVRES

MINIATURE HAMBURGERS

(*Pictured opposite page 52*)

2½ lbs. ground beef
2½ tsp. salt
¼ tsp. pepper
48 two-inch rounds
of bread, toasted

6 tbs. soft butter or
margarine
½ c. finely chopped
parsley
½ c. catsup

Mix beef, salt, and pepper. Shape into small hamburgers using 1½ tablespoons beef mixture for each. Make a depression in center of each hamburger. Place on broiler pan. Spread toast rounds with soft butter or margarine, then sprinkle with chopped parsley. Broil hamburgers in preheated broiler 1½ to 2 minutes on each side. Place hamburgers on toast rounds. Have side of hamburger with depression face up. Place ½ teaspoon catsup in center of each hamburger. Keep warm in very low oven or on electric serving tray, if desired. Makes 4 dozen.

BURGUNDY MEATBALLS

½ lb. ground beef
½ lb. ground pork
1 c. soft bread
crumbs
1 egg
¼ c. grated
Cheddar cheese
1½ tsp. salt
¼ tsp. pepper
¼ tsp. garlic
powder

2 tbs. chopped
parsley
3 tbs. chopped
onion
¼ c. Burgundy
Butter or margarine
2 tbs. flour
1 c. water
½ c. Burgundy

Mix beef, pork, bread crumbs, egg, cheese, salt, pepper, garlic powder, parsley, onion, and ¼ cup wine. Shape into tiny balls. Brown well on all sides in butter or margarine in skillet; remove; reserve. Pour off all but 2 tablespoons fat; stir in flour; add water and ½ cup wine gradually. Bring to boiling; reduce heat; add meatballs; simmer 5 minutes. Makes 4 dozen.

PARISIAN MEATBALLS

1½ lbs. ground round steak	4 oz. (¼ lb.) Roquefort cheese, cubed
Salt	
Pepper	3 to 4 tbs. butter or margarine
	½ c. Burgundy

Season beef with salt and pepper. Flatten rounded tablespoons of mixture. Place cube of cheese in center of each; shape into ball. Brown quickly in butter or margarine; add wine; simmer 3 minutes. Serve hot on wooden picks. Makes about 2 dozen.

TERIYAKI

2 tbs. candied ginger	⅓ c. dry sherry
½ c. brown sugar, firmly packed	2 lbs. chuck or round steak
2 c. soy sauce	Meat tenderizer

Cut candied ginger into small slivers. Mix with brown sugar, soy sauce, and dry sherry. Slice chuck or round steak into thin strips. Strips should be about 1½ inches long, 1 inch wide, and ½ inch thick. Treat with meat tenderizer according to label directions. Thread skewers through strips of beef. Marinate at least ½ hour. Broil 6 inches from heat about 3 minutes on each side. Makes 3 dozen.

MARINATED PORK TIDBITS

½ lb. pork cut in ½-inch cubes	¼ tsp. salt
¼ c. pure vegetable oil	Dash of pepper
1 tbs. wine vinegar	2 tbs. chopped onion

Thread pork cubes on skewers; place in shallow pan. Combine remaining ingredients; pour over pork; refrigerate 4 to 6 hours. Broil 6 inches from heat 10 to 15 minutes or until nicely browned. Makes 4 servings.

PARTY TURNOVERS

5 anchovy fillets, mashed	1 egg
1 tbs. pure vegetable or olive oil	2 tbs. light cream
1 tbs. lemon juice	1 tbs. chopped parsley
½ clove of garlic, mashed	1 tbs. chopped chives
1 c. ground cooked ham	Dash of pepper
	Pastry for 2-crust pie (*page 405*)

Combine anchovy, oil, lemon juice, garlic, ham, egg, cream, parsley, chives, and pepper; mix thoroughly. Roll out pastry thinly on floured surface; cut into 2½-inch circles. Place teaspoon of filling in center of each circle; moisten edges of pastry; fold circles in half; press edges with fork. Prick tops of turnovers; brush with additional cream. Bake at 425° F. for 20 minutes or until golden brown. Serve warm. Turnovers may be made ahead and frozen, then reheated just before serving time. Makes 4 dozen.

FRANKS AND PINEAPPLE CHUNKS ORIENTAL

6 frankfurters	¼ c. brown sugar, firmly packed
1 can (13½ oz.) pineapple chunks	½ tsp. dry mustard
¼ c. soy sauce	

Cut frankfurters into 1-inch pieces; Drain pineapple; reserve ¼ cup juice. Combine frankfurters, pineapple, pineapple juice, and soy sauce in bowl. Marinate 2 to 3 hours. Mix 1 tablespoon marinade, brown sugar, and mustard. Drain pineapple and frankfurters; thread on skewers; brush with sugar mixture. Broil 6 inches from heat, turning to grill all sides. Brush again with sugar mixture and serve. Makes 1½ dozen.

RUMAKI

Cut ½ pound chicken livers into serving-size pieces. Drain 1 can (5 ounces) water chestnuts; cut into thirds. Cut ½ pound bacon into short strips. Wrap livers and chestnuts in bacon strips, thread on long skewers. Broil 6 inches from heat 3 minutes on each side. Makes about 1 dozen.

CHICKEN LIVERS BROCHETTE
(*Pictured opposite page 52*)

1 c. water
1 c. vinegar
½ c. sugar
1 tbs. mixed
  pickling spices
½ c. sliced onion
1 tsp. salt
48 large ½-in. thick
  carrot slices
4 cans (5 oz. ea.)
  water chestnuts,
  drained

24 chicken livers,
  halved
4 tbs. butter or
  margarine
48 slices bacon,
  cooked
3 large green
  peppers, cut in
  squares

Combine water, vinegar, sugar, pickling spice, onion, and salt in saucepan. Cover; simmer 15 minutes. Add carrots; simmer 10 minutes or until carrots are tender. Cool. Add water chestnuts; chill. Before serving, cut carrots with small flower-shaped cutter, if desired. Sauté chicken livers in butter or margarine 5 minutes. Wrap each one in cooked bacon slice; fasten with wooden pick. If made ahead, reheat at 350° F. about 2 minutes before serving. Arrange a square of green pepper, a hot, wrapped chicken liver, a water chestnut, and a carrot slice on each skewer. Serve at once. Makes 4 dozen.

SHRIMP TARTS

1 lb. small fresh
  shrimp, shelled
  and deveined or 1
  pkg. (10 oz.)
  frozen, shelled,
  and deveined
  shrimp
⅔ c. finely chopped
  onion
½ c. finely diced
  celery
3 tbs. butter or
  margarine

1½ tbs. flour
1 tsp. salt
⅛ tsp. pepper
⅛ tsp. powdered
  sage
1 tsp. dill weed
½ c. light cream
6 baked 3-inch tart
  shells, or 20
  baked 1-inch
  shells or pack-
  aged hors
  d'oeuvre shells

Cook fresh shrimp in boiling water 5 to 8 minutes or until tender. Cook frozen shrimp according to package directions. Drain; reserve ½ cup broth. For large tart shells, leave shrimp whole; for small ones, chop shrimp. Sauté onion and celery in butter or margarine until soft; blend in flour, salt, pepper, sage, and dill weed. Add cream and shrimp broth gradually; add shrimp. Cook, stirring constantly, until sauce simmers and thickens. Spoon into tart shells. Makes 6 large or 20 small tarts.

SHRIMP, ISLAND STYLE

2 lbs. fresh jumbo
  shrimp or 2 pkgs.
  (10 oz. ea.)
  frozen, shelled,
  and deveined
  shrimp, thawed
¼ c. soy sauce
¼ c. lemon juice
2 eggs, beaten

2 c. water
2 c. sifted all-
  purpose flour
1 tsp. baking
  powder
2 cans (3½ oz. ea.)
  flaked coconut
Oil for frying

Shell and devein fresh shrimp leaving tails on. Slit shrimp with sharp knife along curved back, cutting not quite through. Spread open. Put shrimp in single layer in large, shallow dish. Mix soy sauce and lemon juice; pour over shrimp. Cover; refrigerate overnight. Combine eggs and water. Add mixture of flour and baking powder slowly; beat until smooth. Put coconut into pie plate. Hold shrimp by tail; dip in batter; let excess drip off. Roll in coconut to coat well. Place on wire racks; let stand 10 to 15 minutes to set coating. Pour oil into heavy saucepan or skillet to depth of 3 inches; heat to 365° F. Add shrimp a few at a time; fry until golden brown, turning once. Serve hot. If making ahead, reheat in 350° F. oven. Makes 8 servings.

SHRIMP IN BEER

1 can (12 oz.) beer
8 peppercorns
½ lemon
1 bay leaf
3 celery tops
2 sprigs parsley

1 lb. fresh shrimp,
  shelled and
  deveined or 1
  pkg. (10 oz.)
  frozen, shelled,
  and deveined
  shrimp
1 tbs. flour
1 tbs. chili sauce
2 tbs. prepared
  horseradish

Combine beer, peppercorns, lemon, bay leaf, celery tops, and parsley in saucepan. Bring to boiling. Add shrimp. Bring to boiling again. Remove from heat; let stand until cool. Remove shrimp; strain liquid; reserve ½ cup. Blend reserved stock and flour in small saucepan; bring to boiling. Boil 1 minute, stirring constantly. Remove from heat; stir in chili sauce and horseradish. Chill. Serve with shrimp. Makes 6 servings.

A selection of taste-tempting party f

FAN-TAN SHRIMP WITH BACON

24 medium-size fresh shrimp or 2 pkgs. (10 oz. ea.) frozen, shelled, and deveined shrimp, thawed	1 c. water
	1 tbs. cornstarch
	⅓ c. sugar
	¼ tsp. monosodium glutamate
	2 tbs. lemon juice
1 lb. bacon	2 tbs. soy sauce

Shell and devein fresh shrimp leaving tails on. Cut bacon slice in half. Wrap each shrimp in ½ bacon slice; secure with wooden pick. Broil, turning once, about 6 minutes or until bacon is crisp. Prepare sauce: Stir water into cornstarch in small saucepan; stir in remaining ingredients; cook over low heat, stirring constantly, until thickened. Arrange shrimp on serving plate; garnish with parsley, if desired. Serve sauce in bowl. Hold shrimp by tail; dip in sauce to eat. Makes 6 servings.

SPICY SHRIMP

3 tbs. pure vegetable oil	1 clove of garlic, crushed
1 lb. fresh shrimp, shelled and deveined or 1 pkg. (10 oz.) frozen, shelled, and deveined shrimp, thawed	3 tbs. chilli sauce
	1 tbs. catsup
	2 tbs. dry white wine
	1½ tbs. soy sauce
	1 tsp. sugar
3 tbs. finely chopped green onion	½ tsp. salt
	¼ tsp. dried crushed red pepper
2 tbs. finely chopped candied ginger	

Heat oil in skillet; add shrimp and onion. Stir-fry 2 minutes. Combine ginger, garlic, chili sauce, catsup, wine, soy sauce, sugar, salt, and red pepper. Pour over shrimp in skillet. Stir rapidly 1 minute. Spear shrimp with wooden picks and serve as appetizers. Makes 6 to 8 servings.

SHRIMP RELISH

¼ c. minced onion	2 tbs. vinegar
¼ c. minced green pepper	½ tsp. salt
	¼ tsp. pepper
¼ c. minced celery	1 lb. fresh shrimp, cooked, shelled, deveined, and chopped
2 tsp. dill weed	
¼ c. pure vegetable oil	

Combine all ingredients; refrigerate 4 to 6 hours. Serve on crisp crackers or toast points. Makes about 1½ cups.

NORWEGIAN FISH PUFFS

½ lb. haddock or cod	½ tsp. sugar
	Dash of pepper
2 eggs	4 tbs. melted butter or margarine
½ c. cream	
½ c. cracker meal	1 tbs. lemon juice
1 tbs. flour	Chopped parsley
1 tbs. anchovy paste	Paprika
½ tsp. salt	

Clean fish; remove bones and skin. Put through food grinder 2 or 3 times; mix with eggs, cream, cracker meal, flour, anchovy paste, salt, sugar, and pepper; shape into small balls. Drop into boiling salted water; cook 8 minutes; drain. Arrange on serving platter; pour over combined melted butter or margarine and lemon juice. Sprinkle with parsley and paprika. Serve hot. Makes 3 dozen.

CRAB MEAT PROFITEROLES
(Pictured opposite page 52)

½ c. hot water	3 pkgs. (6 oz. ea.) frozen crab meat, thawed, or 3 cans (7 oz. ea.) crab meat
4 tbs. butter or margarine	
¼ tsp. salt	
½ c. sifted all-purpose flour	
2 eggs	½ c. mayonnaise or salad dressing
	3 tsp. Worcestershire sauce
	1½ tbs. grated onion

Heat oven to 425° F. Grease cookie sheets lightly. Bring water, butter or margarine, and salt to boiling in saucepan. Add flour all at once; stir rapidly until mixture forms a ball and leaves sides of pan. Remove from heat. Add eggs one at a time, beating very well after each addition. Beat until thick and satiny. Drop by teaspoonfuls onto lightly greased cookie sheets using 1 teaspoon batter for each puff. Bake 18 minutes. Lower heat to 375° F.; bake puffs 15 minutes longer. Remove from cookie sheets. Cool on racks. (Puff shells can be made ahead and frozen. Defrost before filling.) Bone and flake crab meat; add mayonnaise or salad dressing, Worcestershire, and onion. Cut tops off puffs. Spoon in crab-meat mixture. Replace tops. Makes 4 dozen.

CURRIED CRAB MEAT TARTLETS

(Pictured opposite page 53)

2 c. sifted all-purpose flour	1½ tsp. grated onion
¼ tsp. salt	1½ tsp. curry powder
¼ tsp. sugar	
½ c. butter or margarine	¼ c. mayonnaise or salad dressing
¼ c. shortening	Paprika
¼ c. cold water	3 hard-cooked eggs
2 cans (7 oz. ea.) crab meat, boned and finely chopped	

Sift flour, salt, and sugar into bowl. Cut butter or margarine and shortening into small pieces. Blend lightly into flour with fingers. Add water slowly, blending until mixture just clings together. Chill about 1 hour. Roll out ⅛ inch thick. Cut rounds with cookie cutter a little larger than tartlet pans; fit pastry into pans. Fill shells with raw rice to aid shells in holding shape. Bake at 400° F. for 5 minutes. Remove from oven; cool slightly; carefully remove rice. Put shells back into oven to brown, about 5 minutes more. Remove from pans; cool thoroughly. (Shells can be made ahead and frozen. Thaw before filling with crab-meat mixture.) Combine crab meat, onion, curry powder, and mayonnaise or salad dressing. Spoon filling into shells shortly before serving; dust with paprika. Garnish with hard-cooked eggs. Chill. Makes about 6 dozen 1½-inch tartlets.

LOBSTER BARQUETTES

2 c. sifted all-purpose flour	1 tbs. flour
1 c. grated Parmesan cheese	¼ tsp. onion salt
	¼ tsp. garlic salt
1 c. shortening	1½ tsp. lemon juice
½ c. water	2 hard-cooked egg yolks, sieved
1 can (5 oz.) lobster	1 jar or can (4 oz.) shrimp
Milk	
1 tbs. butter or margarine	

Cut paper pattern 1 inch larger in diameter than small tart or barquette pans. Combine flour and cheese in mixing bowl; cut in shortening. Add water gradually, stirring until dough forms a ball. Turn out on floured board; roll out ⅛ inch thick. Trace around paper pattern; cut out; line tart shells with dough; press against bottom and sides; trim even with edge. Fill shells with raw rice to keep them from buckling as they bake. Bake at 425° F. for 12 to 15 minutes or until golden. Cool; carefully remove rice; remove tart shells from pans; cool on wire racks. Drain and flake lobster, reserving liquid; add milk to lobster liquid to make ½ cup. Melt butter or margarine in saucepan; stir in flour, onion salt, and garlic salt. Add liquid slowly; cook, stirring constantly, until thickened; stir in lobster meat and lemon juice. Fill tart shells with lobster mixture; place on cookie sheets; refrigerate until almost ready to serve. Remove from refrigerator; top with egg yolk and shrimp. Bake at 425° F. for 3 to 5 minutes or until piping hot. Serve at once. Makes about 4 dozen.

SCALLOPS FINES HERBS

¼ c. butter or margarine	¼ tsp. chopped parsley
¼ tsp. chopped chives	½ lb. scallops, washed and drained
¼ tsp. leaf tarragon crumbled	

Melt butter or margarine in skillet; add herbs. Heat until mixture bubbles. Add scallops; sauté about 5 minutes. Makes 4 to 6 servings.

SCALLOP WRAP

½ lb. bacon	½ lb. scallops, cut in half

Cut bacon crosswise into three equal pieces. Wrap each piece around piece of scallop; secure with wooden pick. Broil 6 inches from heat 2 to 3 minutes on each side or until bacon is crisp. Makes 6 to 8 servings.

MARINATED MUSSELS

1 pkg. (⅝ oz.) Italian- or onion-flavored salad dressing mix	1 can (9 oz.) mussels, drained
	Toast rounds

Prepare salad-dressing mix according to package directions, substituting 2 tablespoons drained liquid from mussels for 2 tablespoons water. Combine dressing mix and mussels. Chill 4 to 6 hours. Serve on toast rounds or with wooden picks. Makes 6 servings.

CAVIAR

Caviar, the most elegant of appetizers, is the roe (or egg) of the sturgeon. Fresh caviar is usually choice, lightly salted, firm, dark, not-too-ripe, whole eggs of the sturgeon. There are three varieties from three species of sturgeon:

The beluga (large grain) is the most expensive and considered by many to be the best, because of the giant gray grains.

The osetra (medium grain).

The sevruga (small grain) is less expensive. It is considered by many connoisseurs to be more palatable because of its small grain.

Besides the choice caviars from the Caspian Sea, there are those available from the Great Lakes waters and Canada.

Pressed caviar is made from very ripe roe. It has a less salty flavor, because as the roe ripens it becomes sweeter.

Vacuum-packed caviar is available in 1-, 2-, 4-, and 8-ounce jars in gourmet shops and supermarkets. The term "malossol" on some labels means lightly salted. Vacuum-packed caviar usually is more heavily salted than fresh caviar. It is available in whole-grain Caspian Sea caviars, pressed caviar, and whole-grain Great Lakes and Canadian caviars. You can also buy whole-grain varieties of the so-called "caviars" such as the roe of the red salmon, lumpfish, and whitefish.

Red caviar is not strictly a "caviar." It is the roe of the salmon. It is less expensive and much larger grained.

All fresh caviar must be refrigerated. In buying the vacuum-packed type, check the container to see whether it needs refrigeration. Once it is opened it always needs refrigeration. Never freeze caviar. Before recapping, cover the container with transparent plastic wrap to help maintain moisture.

Caviar is usually served as an appetizer. The service is simple. It should be served in its container and the container should always be embedded in a larger dish of crushed ice. Crisp toast fingers are a sufficient accompaniment for the gourmet. Lemon wedges, chopped hard-cooked egg white, sieved hard-cooked egg yolk, and chopped onion are also good accompaniments. Some people like it served with butter. Champagne is the traditional beverage to serve with caviar.

Caviar may also be used as a garnish, an omelet filling, or as an ingredient in a special salad dressing.

CAVIAR THIMBLES
(*Pictured opposite page 53*)

1 loaf unsliced white bread	1 pkg. (8 oz.) process Swiss cheese
½ c. melted butter or margarine	1 jar (6 oz.) red caviar
	Sprigs of parsley

Trim all crusts from loaf of bread. Cut bread into 1-inch cubes. Hollow out center of cubes with small sharp knife. Brush or dip all surfaces in butter or margarine; fill cavity with tiny snips of cheese. Arrange on cookie sheet. Bake at 325° F. until golden brown. Cool. If not using at once, wrap in aluminum foil or transparent plastic wrap and keep at room temperature. Just before serving, top each with tiny spoonful of caviar; add parsley sprig for garnish. Makes about 30.

PARTY STUFFED EGGS

9 hard-cooked eggs, shelled	Dash of cayenne
	Red caviar
½ c. mayonnaise or salad dressing	Green pepper cut in thin, small strips
1 tsp. prepared mustard	

Halve eggs lengthwise; remove yolks. Sieve yolks into bowl; blend in mayonnaise or salad dressing, mustard, and cayenne. Fill whites with yolk mixture. For fancy touch, press yolk mixture through pastry bag. Top each with caviar and green pepper. Place eggs in deep pan; cover top of pan, without touching eggs, with transparent plastic wrap or aluminum foil. Refrigerate. Makes 18.

When eggs are filled and garnished, you may keep them in perfect condition for several hours before the party. Just put them in a deep baking pan; span top with transparent plastic wrap so it does not touch eggs.

STUFFED MUSHROOMS

24 small mush-rooms (about 1 lb.)	¼ tsp. leaf tarragon, crumbled
2 tbs. finely chopped onion	1 egg, beaten
⅓ c. butter or margarine	2 tbs. sherry
1 tbs. chopped parsley	½ tsp. salt
	Dash of pepper
	½ c. packaged bread crumbs

Wash and dry mushrooms. Remove stems; chop stems fine. Sauté stems and onion in 2 tablespoons butter or margarine 5 minutes. Add parsley, tarragon, egg, sherry, salt, pepper, and bread crumbs. Sauté mushroom caps in remaining butter or margarine 10 to 15 minutes or until golden and tender. Fill caps with bread-crumb mixture. Brush caps with butter or margarine remaining in skillet. Broil until lightly browned. Serve hot. Makes 2 dozen.

TOMATO TREATS
(*Pictured opposite page 53*)

1 pt. cherry tomatoes	2 tbs. mayonnaise or salad dressing
4 hard-cooked eggs, shelled	2 cans rolled anchovy fillets
1 tsp. grated onion	1 jar cocktail onions
¼ tsp. salt	
1 tsp. lemon juice	

Cut thin slice off top of tomato; scoop out; turn over to drain. Chop eggs finely; blend in onion, salt, lemon juice, and mayonnaise or salad dressing. Spoon mixture into tomatoes; top each with anchovy fillet. Spear cocktail onions on wooden picks; press upright into top of each tomato. Chill. Makes about 1½ dozen.

CHERRY TOMATOES WITH GUACAMOLE
(*Pictured opposite page 52*)

2 c. mashed avocado (2 large)	1 tsp. Worcestershire sauce
2 tbs. lemon juice	2 tsp. sugar
2 tbs. grated onion	3 tbs. mayonnaise or salad dressing
1 clove of garlic, crushed	1½ tsp. unflavored gelatin
1½ tsp. salt	2 tbs. cold water
Dash of pepper	48 large cherry tomatoes
Dash of cayenne	

Sieve mashed avocado. Add lemon juice, onion, garlic, salt, pepper, cayenne, Worcestershire sauce, sugar, and mayonnaise or salad dressing; mix well. Soak gelatin in cold water, dissolve over hot water. Stir into avocado mixture. Cover tightly with transparent plastic wrap. Chill. Cut tops off cherry tomatoes; scoop out seeds Turn tomatoes upside down on paper towels to drain. Spoon or pipe avocado mixture into tomatoes. If any mixture is left, serve in bowl as a dip. Makes 4 dozen.

CHEESE PINEAPPLE

4 oz. Roquefort cheese	8 oz. Cheddar cheese
2 pkgs. (8 oz. ea.) cream cheese	3 to 4 tbs. milk
1 tsp. onion juice	Sliced stuffed olives
Dash of pepper	Romaine

Have cheeses at room temperature. Cream Roquefort cheese until smooth; blend with cream cheese, onion juice, and pepper; mix thoroughly. Shape mixture into cone on square of wax paper; chill at least ½ hour. (Reshape cone if necessary.) Cut Cheddar cheese into small pieces into bowl; mash with fork until soft and smooth; blend in milk. Spread evenly over Roquefort-cream cheese cone. Wrap wax paper around cone; twist top tightly; chill until serving time. Just before serving, mark diagonal lines on cone with back of knife to simulate a pineapple; decorate with olive slices. Press small inner leaves of romaine into top of cheese to resemble pineapple frond. Makes about 12 servings.

MERRY CHEESE BALL
(*Pictured opposite page 52*)

1 Gouda cheese (about 3½ lbs.)	Assorted crackers, potato chips,
2 cans (4½ oz. ea.) deviled ham	pumpernickel melba toast, or
¼ c. grated onion	party rye bread
1¼ c. dairy sour cream	

Cut top off cheese. Scoop out cheese leaving ¼-inch shell. Cut top edge of cheese shell in scallops. Grate cheese. Combine cheese, deviled ham, onion, and sour cream, mixing well. Fill cheese shell with cheese spread. Chill until serving time. Serve with assorted crackers, potato chips, pumpernickel melba toast, or party rye bread. To make pumpernickel melba toast: Slice pumpernickel very thin; cut into quarters; place on cookie sheets; bake at 300° F. for 30 minutes. Turn bread over after 15 minutes baking. Cool on racks; store in airtight can or jar. Makes about 24 servings.

CHEESE PUFFS

1 loaf firm, unsliced, white bread	½ c. butter or margarine
1 pkg. (3 oz.) cream cheese	2 egg whites, stiffly beaten
¼ lb. sharp Cheddar cheese	

Trim crusts from bread; cut bread into 1-inch cubes. Melt cheeses and butter or margarine in top of double boiler over hot water until of rarebit consistency. Remove from heat; fold in stiffly beaten egg whites. Dip bread cubes into cheese mixture until well coated; place on cookie sheet. Refrigerate overnight. Bake at 400° F. for 12 to 15 minutes or until puffy and golden brown. Makes about 4 dozen.

CHEESE CRISPIES

½ c. soft butter or margarine	½ tsp. Worcestershire sauce
2 c. shredded sharp Cheddar cheese	Dash of cayenne
	1 c. sifted all-purpose flour

Mix butter or margarine, cheese, Worcestershire, and cayenne thoroughly in mixing bowl. Stir in flour; shape into smooth ball. Wrap in wax paper; chill thoroughly. Cut off ¼ of dough; flour hands to make rolling easier. Shape dough into balls about the size of a large marble. Place on ungreased cookie sheet about 2 inches apart. Puffs will spread a bit as they bake. Repeat with rest of dough. Bake at 350° F. for 12 to 15 minutes. Serve piping hot. Makes about 4 dozen.

Dough may be shaped into balls and refrigerated before baking, or it may be frozen and baked as desired.

CHEESE MATCHES

1½ c. sifted all-purpose flour	3 to 4 tbs. water
1 tsp. seasoned salt	1 c. shredded Cheddar cheese
¼ tsp. dry mustard	Paprika
½ c. shortening	

Sift flour, salt, and dry mustard into medium-size bowl; cut in shortening with pastry blender or 2 knives until mixture resembles corn meal. Sprinkle water over; stir until flour is moistened and forms a ball. Turn out onto floured board; roll into rectangle ¼ inch thick. Sprinkle half the surface with ⅓ cup of cheese and 1 teaspoon paprika. Fold plain half onto covered surface; pinch edges to seal. Roll out to rectangle; repeat sprinkling with cheese and paprika and rolling process twice more until all cheese and 3 teaspoons of paprika are used. Roll into rectangle ¼ inch thick. Cut into strips ½ inch wide and 6 inches long. Place on ungreased cookie sheet. Bake at 425° F. for 10 to 12 minutes or until slightly puffed and golden. Cool on wire racks; dip ends in paprika. Makes 3 dozen.

CEREAL NIBBLERS

1 pkg. (9½ oz.) bite-size wheat or corn biscuits	1½ tsp. of one of the following: seasoned salt, garlic powder, onion powder, curry powder, or chili powder

Heat cereal in hot oven; sprinkle with desired flavoring; toss lightly. Cool. Store in tightly covered container.

EGGPLANT WITH PICKLED VEGETABLES

2 medium-size eggplant	1 c. diced celery
½ c. olive oil	2 to 4 tbs. capers
1½ c. sliced onion	¼ c. wine vinegar
1 can (1 lb. 4 oz.) Italian plum tomatoes, strained	2 tbs. sugar
	1 tsp. salt
	¼ tsp. pepper

Wash eggplant; cube but do not pare. Sauté in hot oil in skillet until soft and lightly browned. Remove and reserve. Sauté onion in oil remaining in skillet until golden. Add tomatoes and celery; simmer 15 minutes. Add capers, eggplant, vinegar, sugar, salt, and pepper. Cover; simmer 20 minutes over low heat, stirring occasionally. Chill. This recipe may also be served hot as a vegetable. Makes 4 to 5 cups.

MANDARIN SPARERIBS

2 lbs. spareribs, cracked through center	¼ c. catsup
	½ c. dry white wine
	3 tbs. corn syrup
¼ c. sliced green onions	½ tsp. salt
	½ tsp. monosodium glutamate
1 clove of garlic, mashed	1 tsp. ground ginger
2 tbs. soy sauce	

Cut spareribs into 1-rib portions. Place in shallow dish. Mix onions, garlic, soy sauce, catsup, wine, corn syrup, salt, monosodium glutamate, and ginger together. Pour over ribs. Cover; let marinate for several hours or refrigerate overnight. Place ribs in broiler pan; brush with sauce. Place pan in broiler so tops of ribs are about 4 inches from heat; lower broiler heat to medium. Broil 5 to 7 minutes on one side. Turn and broil 4 to 5 minutes on other side. Makes 10 to 15.

TEMPURA

Tempura, an enchanting type of cookery from the Orient, is perfect for entertaining. Tiny bits of food are dipped in batter, deep fried in bubbly oil, dipped in savory sauce, and eaten piping hot. Tempura foods are artistic to the eye, inviting to the palate, and a great stimulation to conversation. A meal may also be made of Tempura for the whole family to enjoy. Here are directions for Tempura for 6. Use all, or a selection, of the seafood and vegetables.

Seafood

18 fresh shrimp	6 pieces cod filet, 1x1½ in. ea.
6 smelts	
6 pieces flounder filet, 1x1½ in. ea.	6 scallops, halved

Shell shrimp, leaving tail attached. Wash quickly; drain; pat dry. Slit back, cutting almost through; devein. Spread flat; score each side lengthwise with sharp knife. Scale and clean smelts. Wash quickly; pat dry. Remove center bone; split in two lengthwise, leaving tail on. Wash flounder, cod, and scallops quickly; pat dry. Salt all seafood lightly; chill.

Vegetables

6 thin slices peeled sweet potato	6 fresh mushrooms, halved
6 thin slices un-peeled eggplant	12 thin onion rings
6 small strips carrot	6 sprigs parsley
6 small strips green pepper	6 sprigs watercress
6 asparagus spears, parboiled and drained	6 sprigs celery leaves
	18 pieces (1½ in. long ea.) green onion
6 whole green beans, parboiled and drained	

Wash and dry vegetables. Skewer three pieces green onion on each of six wooden picks. Chill.

Tempura Sauce

¼ c. soy sauce	6 tbs. grated white radish
¼ c. sweet wine or 1 tbs. sugar	1 tbs. grated fresh ginger root
1¼ c. soup stock	
1 tsp. salt	
Dash of mono-sodium glutamate	

Combine soy sauce, wine, stock, salt, and monosodium glutamate in saucepan; heat to boiling. Serve hot in individual, small bowls. Stir in radish and ginger root to taste.

Oil

4 c. (1 qt.) pure
  vegetable oil

1 c. sesame oil

Combine oils. Pour into pan to a depth of
about 3 inches. Heat to 350° F.

Batter

½ tsp. baking soda
2 eggs
2 c. cold water

2½ c. sifted all-
  purpose flour
Flour for coating

Add soda and eggs to water; mix well. Add
flour; mix lightly using chopsticks or 2-tine
fork. Coat seafood lightly with flour; do not
flour vegetables. Dip fish and vegetables into
batter one by one; fry in hot oil, a few at a
time. Don't crowd them. Fry until lower side
is crisp; turn and cook other side crisp. Drain
all pieces well on paper towels. Skim any
stray pieces of batter from oil after each
batch is fried. The oil must be kept clean at all
times.

DIPS AND DUNKS

NIPPY CHEESE DIP

1 pkg. (8 oz.)
  cream cheese
6 oz. sharp Cheddar
  cheese
4 tsp. prepared
  mustard

½ c. light cream
½ c. ground cooked
  ham or 3 tbs.
  deviled ham

Combine cream cheese, Cheddar cheese, mustard, and cream in bowl; beat until smooth.
Stir in ham. Chill. Makes 2 cups.

SMOKY DIP

1 jar (5 oz.) smoky
  cheese spread
½ tsp. celery seed
2 tbs. catsup
2 tbs. light cream

1 can (3 oz.)
  chopped
  mushrooms,
  drained

Blend cheese, celery seed, catsup, and light
cream; stir in mushrooms. Refrigerate until
just before serving. Makes about 1 cup.

BLUE CHEESE DIP

½ c. dairy sour
  cream
4 oz. blue cheese,
  crumbled

1 pkg. (3 oz.) cream
  cheese

Blend ingredients together; chill. Serve with
crackers, apple slices, pineapple chunks,
orange sections, grapefruit sections, grapes,
celery sticks, carrot sticks, raw zucchini
sticks, raw cauliflower, broccoli flowerets, or
cherry tomatoes. Makes about 1 cup.

VEGETABLE COTTAGE CHEESE DIP

1 small carrot,
  pared and sliced
½ cucumber, sliced
¼ green pepper,
  cut up

1 small onion,
  peeled and
  halved
½ tsp. salt
Dash of pepper
1 carton (8 oz.)
  cottage cheese

Combine carrot, cucumber, green pepper,
onion, salt, and pepper in blender. Turn
switch on and off to chop fine. (Guide vegetables into blades occasionally while switch
is off.) Stir in cottage cheese. Serve with
crackers or potato chips or use to fill celery
pieces. Makes 3 cups.

SARDINE DIP

2 cans (3¼ oz. ea.)
  sardines
1 pkg. (8 oz.) cream
  cheese
3 tbs. chopped
  onion
½ tsp. seasoned salt

1 tbs. Worcester-
  shire sauce
Few drops hot-
  pepper sauce
1 tbs. lemon juice
¼ c. chopped
  parsley

Mash sardines and cream cheese thoroughly
in bowl. Blend in onion, salt, Worcestershire,
hot-pepper sauce, lemon juice, and parsley.
Chill several hours. Use as dip for chips or
spread on crackers. Makes about 1½ cups.

CRAB DIP

1 can (6½ oz.)
  crab meat,
  drained and
  flaked
¾ c. dairy sour
  cream

1 tbs. mayonnaise
  or salad dressing
1 tbs. chopped
  capers
1 tbs. grated onion
1 tbs. lemon juice

Combine all ingredients in bowl. Chill. Serve
with raw cauliflowerets, celery or carrot sticks
as dippers. Makes about 1 cup.

BLACK BEAN DIP

1 can (10½ oz.)
   condensed black
   bean soup
1 pkg. (3 oz.)
   cream cheese

2 tbs. mayonnaise
   or salad dressing
Several dashes hot-
   pepper sauce

Combine all ingredients and chill. Serve with vegetable sticks, corn chips, or crackers. Makes about 1¾ cups.

CALIFORNIA DIP

1 envelope onion-
   soup mix

1 pt. dairy sour
   cream

Combine ingredients; let stand 1 hour before serving. Serve with vegetable sticks, crackers, or potato chips. Makes 2½ cups.

For variation add one of the following: ¼ cup chopped dill pickle; ¼ cup chopped black olives; ¼ cup crumbled crisp bacon or 1 can (7 ounces) tuna, drained and flaked.

SPICY BARBECUE DUNK

¾ c. chili sauce
1 tsp. dry mustard

¼ c. bottled meat
   sauce

Combine all ingredients; let stand 1 hour. Serve with meat, cheese, or vegetable cubes. Makes about 1 cup.

GUACAMOLE DIP

2 tbs. lemon juice
1 ripe avocado,
   peeled and cut
   into pieces
1 small peeled
   tomato, finely
   chopped
1 small onion,
   peeled and finely
   chopped

1 small clove of
   garlic, peeled
   and crushed
¼ tsp. salt
¼ c. mayonnaise or
   salad dressing
½ tsp. chili powder
Several dashes hot-
   pepper sauce

Sprinkle lemon juice over avocado pieces in small bowl; mash with fork. Add tomato, onion, garlic, salt, 2 tablespoons mayonnaise or salad dressing, chili powder, and pepper sauce. Whip ingredients with fork until thoroughly mixed. Spread remaining 2 tablespoons of mayonnaise or salad dressing over surface to prevent discoloration. Chill. Just before serving, stir layer of mayonnaise or salad dressing into guacamole. Serve with crackers, potato chips, or corn chips. Makes about 1 cup.

Chapter Six

Beverages

The "cup of welcome" you offer those who come to call may hold steaming black coffee, amber-clear tea, or fruit juice tinkling with ice, but whatever it may be, hospitality begins with beverages. And for the family, how nice it is to start off the day with a hot cup of coffee or tea shared across the breakfast table in the family room . . . or to enjoy a moment of relaxation on the patio with a pitcher of punch or ice-cold milk shakes.

COFFEE

Why do Americans drink over 400 million cups of coffee every day? We're a nation of coffee lovers, that's why. The coffee break starts your day or ends it, peps you up or calms you down, stimulates good conversation. How's the coffee at your house? If it falls short of what *you* call perfect, it's time to find out what you're doing wrong.

The coffee itself is the first factor. There are more than 100 kinds of coffee beans grown, and most coffees are a blend of several kinds. Some blends are more flavorful, some more aromatic. Finding the blend and roast you prefer is a matter of trial and error.

Make sure the coffee is fresh. Buy in sizes that can be used within a week, if possible. Heat, air, and moisture rob ground coffee of flavor and aroma, so cover it tightly and keep it cool. It may be kept in your refrigerator.

Select a coffee maker to make your kind of coffee. There are five basic types:

1. A *percolator* is hard to match for aroma; it extracts flavor gradually by spraying hot water over coarsely ground coffee and fills the house with fragrance. Available from 2-cup to 40-cup sizes and in completely automatic styles. Some include adjustable flavor controls to set for desired strength, with "hold" or "reheat" features to keep coffee warm without further brewing. With nonautomatic types, allow 6 to 8 minutes perking on *low* heat—no more.
2. *With a vacuum coffee maker* the water bubbles up into the coffee in the upper container. After 1 to 3 minutes of brewing, the coffee flows down to the bottom bowl. You can't pour without removing the top, and the bowls are easy to clean. Available in sizes up to 12 cups, including automatic electric models.
3. *A drip coffee maker* operates on the law of gravity, and is fine for households where only 1 or 2 cups at a time are needed. Most are made of aluminum, though some have ceramic bottoms that can double as teapots.
4. *Filtered* coffee is the clearest, but takes more time and attention. The equipment consists of a glass flask (in sizes from 1 pint to 3 quarts) and special filter papers. Hot water is poured over regular-grind coffee in the filter paper; it slowly filters into the flask which stands in a low pan of simmering water. Even if water boils, the coffee in the flask won't—the coffee will stay hot indefinitely.
5. *Steeped* coffee made in an old-fashioned-type pot is great for campers, and there are others who insist nothing can compare

with it. Usually an egg shell, sometimes the entire egg, is added with the coffee to keep the brew clear; or a dash of cold water may be thrown in just before the coffee is poured to settle the grounds.

Tips for brewing

· *Buy the right grind for your coffee maker.* Coarse or regular for perked, filtered, or steeped coffee; fine or drip grind for drip coffee makers and most vacuum pots.
· *Start with a clean pot.* The greatest enemy of good coffee is the bitter oil that clings to the inside of the pot or coffee maker. This has ruined more cups of coffee and probably caused more family quarrels than any other kitchen hazard! Just rinsing out the pot is not enough. *Scrub* with a brush, especially around spouts and tubes.
· *Use cold water fresh from the tap.*
· *Measure the same way every time.* How strong or how weak you like your coffee is up to you, of course, but the Coffee Brewing Institute advises two level tablespoons (a standard coffee measure) per 6-ounce cup.
· *Serve coffee freshly brewed.* Always remove grounds when coffee has completed brewing.

Signs of a good cup of coffee

Whether your taste runs to strong, weak, or medium, there are four things a good cup of coffee should be:

1. Clear
2. Full-bodied
3. Aromatic
4. Served at a piping 185° F.

Instant Coffee

The most effective way to make several cups is to place instant coffee in cold water in a small pot, bring it just to boiling, stir briskly, and let it stand another minute or so.

CAFÉ AU LAIT

2 c. hot brewed coffee	2 c. hot milk

Pour equal parts coffee and milk into cups. Sweeten, if desired. Makes 4 servings.

CAFÉ ESPRESSO

Espresso is a special beverage usually served as an after-dinner coffee, made from a dark-roast Italian coffee. It is available both in regular vacuum packed and in instant form.

The espresso pot for home use is similar to a drip pot. However, when the water has reached boiling in the lower pot, the entire coffee maker is quickly and carefully inverted and the water allowed to drip through the grounds over low heat until the coffee brew is ready. You will find specific directions with each espresso maker. The proportions of coffee to water are 1 tablespoon of coffee to 1 demitasse cup of water.

ESPRESSO ROYALE

½ c. Cognac	3 c. hot brewed
¼ c. sugar	espresso coffee

Bring Cognac and sugar to boiling in chafing dish or saucepan. Ignite. Ladle hot coffee into flaming Cognac slowly and carefully, blending well, until flame is extinguished. Serve in demitasse cups. Makes 8 servings.

CAPPUCCINO DELUXE

3 c. espresso or strong brewed coffee	3 in. piece stick cinnamon
	½ c. heavy cream, whipped

Heat coffee and cinnamon stick in saucepan 15 minutes. Remove cinnamon stick. Spoon cream into 6 demitasse cups; add coffee. Serve with additional cream, if desired. Makes 6 servings.

Variation: Pour equal parts hot espresso coffee and hot milk into cups. Top with whipped cream. Sprinkle with ground cinnamon.

CAFÉ BRASILIA

¼ c. instant coffee	¼ c. sugar
1 qt. water	½ c. heavy cream,
¼ c. semi-sweet chocolate pieces	whipped

Combine coffee, water, chocolate pieces, and sugar; heat until chocolate is completely melted. Pour into cups; top with dollop of cream. Makes 5 servings.

IRISH COFFEE

1 tsp. sugar
Strong, hot coffee

3 tbs. Irish whiskey*
Whipped cream

Put sugar into stemmed goblet; add enough coffee to dissolve sugar. Add whiskey. Fill goblet with coffee to within an inch of the top. Float cream on top. The hot, whiskey-laced coffee is sipped through the cool cream. Makes 1 serving.
* Traditionally, this recipe calls for Irish whiskey, but other whiskies may be used.

TURKISH COFFEE

½ tsp. sugar for each cup
1 demitasse c. of water per cup

1 heaping tsp. pulverized (Turkish type) coffee per cup

Mix sugar and water together in saucepan. Bring to boiling. Reduce heat and add coffee; stir until dissolved. Increase heat; let mixture come to boiling slowly. As mixture begins to boil and foam, stir once and remove from heat. Tap saucepan lightly on surface of range and sprinkle a few drops of cold water over coffee to help it settle. Pour into demitasse cups. Allow coffee brew to settle a few minutes before serving.

MOCHA COFFEE

1 tbs. instant coffee
1 tbs. chocolate syrup

1 c. milk
Ice

Blend coffee, chocolate syrup, and milk; pour over ice in tall glass. Makes 1 serving.

CAFÉ BRÛLOT

2 cinnamon sticks, broken
6 whole cloves
Rind of 1 medium-size orange, cut in thin slivers

Rind of ½ lemon, cut in thin slivers
8 lumps sugar
¾ c. Cognac
4 c. strong, hot coffee

Mix cinnamon, cloves, orange and lemon rinds, and sugar in chafing dish. Reserve 2 tablespoons Cognac; add remainder to spice mixture. Warm mixture thoroughly. Put reserved Cognac in large ladle; heat until bubbly. Ignite carefully. Pour at once into chafing dish. Stir gently until flames die. Stir in coffee. When piping hot, ladle at once into demitasse cups or special brûlot cups. Makes 8 servings.

VIENNESE COFFEE

1 qt. vanilla ice cream
5 c. hot brewed coffee

½ c. heavy cream, whipped
Ground nutmeg

Put 1 scoop ice cream in the bottom of 6 tall glasses. Slowly pour in hot coffee to fill glasses half full. Add another scoop ice cream and fill glasses with whipped cream; sprinkle with ground nutmeg. Serve with parfait spoons. Makes 6 servings.

Variation: Chill coffee before pouring over ice cream in glasses. Garnish each serving with stemmed maraschino cherry and a sprig of fresh mint.

COFFEE FOR TWENTY

½ lb. coffee, regular grind

1 gal. cold water

Put coffee on a double thickness of cheesecloth 12 inches square. Tie corners to form bag. Place coffee bag in cold water; bring slowly to boiling. Reduce heat. Simmer gently 3 to 6 minutes. Remove coffee bag; test brew for strength. Cover kettle and let stand 10 minutes over very low heat. Makes 20 servings.

ICED COFFEE

Quick Double Strength

Brew coffee double strength by using half the amount of water to the usual amount of coffee. Pour hot coffee over ice cubes in tall glasses. The extra-strong coffee allows for dilution caused by the melting ice.

Precooled

Make regular strength coffee; refrigerate. (Do not refrigerate for more than three hours or it might lose some of its flavor.) When coffee is chilled, pour over ice in tall glasses. Serve immediately.

Instant

Prepare glass or pitcherful using instant coffee according to label directions.

Coffee Ice Cubes

Brew extra coffee and allow it to cool. When cool, pour into ice-cube tray; freeze. Iced coffee can then be made any time by pouring regular strength hot coffee over the cubes.

COFFEE MIST

Crushed ice
5 c. strong brewed
   coffee, chilled

Confectioners'
   sugar

Fill 6 tall glasses with finely crushed ice. Carefully pour cold coffee over ice. Serve with confectioners' sugar and long spoons. Garnish with lemon rind or orange slices, if desired. Makes 6 servings.

TEA

Few beverages adapt themselves as readily to every occasion as does tea. For centuries con-sidered the correct brew to serve for formal late-afternoon entertaining, tea is enjoyed today with meals from breakfast to dinner. Served hot or cold depending upon the weather, we enjoy it at picnics, as an ingredient in many tasty punches, as a soothing bedtime nightcap.

There are more than 3,000 varieties of tea. They take their names from the districts where they are grown, such as Darjeeling, Assam, Ceylon, Java. The tea we buy is a blend of 20 to 30 different varieties. Though there are three different types of tea—black, green, and oolong—over 97 percent of all tea consumed in the United States is black tea. The familiar word "pekoe" refers only to a size of leaf, not to a type of tea; orange pekoe is the top grade pekoe.

Tea is sold packaged in individual bags, loose or bulk, and processed for instant tea. Whichever tea you prefer and whether you serve it hot or cold, it is one of the easiest beverages to prepare. It retains flavor up to six months, even longer. Just be sure to store it tightly sealed.

HOW TO BREW TEA

1. Use a preheated teapot. This makes the best tea because it holds the water temperature at a high level during the brewing process. Preheat the pot by rinsing it with boiling water. Even for a single cup it is best to use a teapot, but if this is not convenient, convert a cup into a teapot by covering it with a saucer during the brewing.
2. Use enough tea; one teabag or one teaspoon of loose tea per teacup is right.
3. Use freshly drawn cold water. Bring it to a full rolling boil and pour it over the tea in the teapot.
4. Brew tea by the clock—3 to 5 minutes and no guesswork. It takes time for tea leaves to unfold and release their flavor. Some teas brew light and some brew dark so color is no gauge of strength. Only by properly timing can you have good tea every time.
5. Stir tea before pouring to make sure it is uniformly strong.
6. If weaker tea is desired, simply add a little hot water after the brewing period.

Hot tea for a crowd

When serving a large group, solve the problem of keeping enough fresh, hot tea on hand over a period of time by making a tea concentrate ahead of time. Bring 1½ quarts of freshly drawn cold water to a full rolling boil. Remove from the heat and immediately add ¼ pound loose tea. Stir to immerse the leaves; cover. Let stand 5 minutes; strain. This makes enough concentrate to serve 40 to 45 cups of tea. One part concentrate to 7 parts hot water makes the right brew.

Instant tea

There are several brands of instant tea on the market. This product is ready to use with hot water or cold water. The brewing has been done for you.

ICED TEA

To make perfect iced tea

The main thing to remember when making iced tea is to use enough tea. A good rule of thumb is to use half again as much tea as you'd use for hot tea . . . to allow for melting ice. For example, to make 4 glasses of iced tea, use 6 teaspoons of tea or 6 teabags.

Iced tea by the pitcherful

For family service, make iced tea by the pitcherful. Here's an easy way to make 2 quarts or about 10 servings.

Premeasure ⅓ cup loose tea (or use 15 teabags). Bring 1 quart of freshly drawn cold water to a full rolling boil. Remove from heat and immediately add tea. Brew 5 minutes, uncovered. Stir and strain into pitcher holding an additional quart of cold water. Serve in ice-filled glasses with sugar and lemon to taste.

Iced tea for a crowd

When you need iced tea by the gallon, use this easy 1-2-3 formula. For one gallon (20 servings) of iced tea, pour

1 quart boiling water over
2 ounces tea (about ⅔ cup). Brew
   six minutes, stir and strain into
3 quarts cold tap water.

For larger quantities, simply multiply the ingredients above by the number of gallons of iced tea you need.

Iced tea—instantly

Nowadays anyone can conjure up a glass or pitcher of iced tea in seconds—by using instant tea. The youngsters can make their own whenever they feel like it—for it's made with cold tap water. No need to boil water, no need to brew. Just follow directions on the jar, using these general proportions.

By the glass: use 1 rounded teaspoon for each glass (6 ounces) of water.

By the pitcherful: use about 2 tablespoons of instant tea to each quart of cold water.

For a crowd: use 1 small jar of instant tea to 1½ to 2 gallons of water, depending upon the strength desired.

Do not refrigerate iced tea

This will only cause it to cloud. It will keep its fragrance and flavor for several hours at room temperature. Simply pour the tea over ice in tall glasses when ready to serve.

Sometimes, in very hot weather, tea will become cloudy even at room temperature. If this happens, add a little boiling water—it will clear the tea quickly.

Iced tea garnishes

Favorite garnishes with iced tea are lemon slices or wedges or sprigs of mint. Pineapple spears may be used as stirrers. Slices of orange or other fresh fruit, studded with whole cloves, may be added. Spiced tea is pleasantly different: Use cinnamon sticks for stirrers, or cut candied ginger into paper-thin slices and add to the iced tea. Scoops of sherbet are sometimes placed atop each glass of iced tea. Lemon and pineapple sherbet are especially good.

COCOA

Delicious drinks, both hot and cold, may be made instantly with new products that dissolve simply with stirring. When using any recipe that calls for cocoa, be sure to check to see whether it specifies *cocoa* or *sweetened cocoa mix* (which is already blended with sugar and sometimes with dry milk).

COCOA

2 tbs. cocoa	½ c. water
1 tbs. sugar	1½ c. milk
⅛ tsp. salt	

Combine cocoa, sugar, salt, and water. Bring to boiling, stirring constantly. Reduce heat; add milk; heat. Do not allow to boil. Serve with whipped cream or marshmallows, if desired. Makes 2 servings.

To enjoy chocolate drinks for special occasions, serve them from chocolate cups.

HOT COCOA CREAM

2 tbs. cocoa	½ c. water
1 tbs. sugar	1½ c. milk
⅛ tsp. salt	¼ pt. chocolate ice cream
10 cinnamon candies	

Combine cocoa, sugar, salt, cinnamon candies, and water. Bring to boiling, stirring constantly. Reduce heat; add milk; heat. Do not allow to boil. Serve with scoop of ice cream. Makes 2 servings.

INDONESIAN CHOCOLATE

¼ c. cocoa	1 c. water
¼ c. sugar	3 c. milk
⅛ tsp. salt	Whipped cream
¼ tsp. ground cinnamon	6 cinnamon sticks

Combine cocoa, sugar, salt, and cinnamon in saucepan; add water slowly, stirring until smooth. Place over low heat; bring to boiling; boil 2 minutes, stirring constantly. Stir in milk; heat. Do not allow to boil. Serve hot with a spoonful of whipped cream and a cinnamon stick in each cup. Makes 6 servings.

BRAZILIAN CHOCOLATE

¼ c. instant coffee	Dash of salt
2 c. boiling water	2 c. milk
1 sq. unsweetened chocolate	Whipped cream
¼ c. sugar	Grated chocolate

Dissolve coffee in boiling water in top of double boiler; add chocolate; place over low heat, stirring until chocolate is melted and mixture is blended. Add sugar and salt; bring to boiling; boil 4 minutes, stirring constantly. Place over boiling water; add milk gradually, stirring constantly until mixture is hot. Beat until light and frothy. Pour into cups; top with whipped cream and a sprinkling of grated chocolate. Makes 6 to 8 servings.

SPANISH SPICED HOT CHOCOLATE

½ c. semi-sweet chocolate pieces	¼ tsp. ground cinnamon
¾ c. sherry	3 c. milk
Dash of salt	¾ c. heavy cream
	Ground cinnamon

Combine chocolate pieces, sherry, salt, and cinnamon in top of double boiler; cook over hot water, stirring occasionally, until chocolate is melted and mixture is blended. Combine milk and ½ cup of cream in saucepan; heat to scalding. Add to chocolate mixture; beat well with egg beater. Whip remaining ¼ cup of cream. Pour chocolate into cups; top with whipped cream; dust lightly with additional cinnamon. Makes 6 to 8 servings.

FRENCH CHOCOLATE

3 sqs. unsweetened chocolate	Dash of salt
½ c. water	½ c. heavy cream, whipped
¾ c. sugar	6 c. hot milk

Combine chocolate and water in saucepan; cook over low heat, stirring until chocolate is melted and mixture is blended. Add sugar and salt; bring to boiling; boil 4 minutes, stirring constantly. Remove from heat; cool. Fold in whipped cream. Place one tablespoon chocolate mixture in each cup; add hot milk to fill cup; blend. Fold in additional whipped cream, if desired. Makes 8 to 12 servings.

YANKEE COCOA

½ c. instant coffee	4 c. boiling water
½ c. instant chocolate-flavor mix	6 marshmallows
	6 candy sticks

Combine coffee and chocolate-flavor mix in saucepan or heatproof serving pitcher; add boiling water; stir to blend; pour into cups. Serve hot with a marshmallow and candy stick in each. Makes 6 servings.

ACAPULCO CHOCOLATE

2 sqs. unsweetened chocolate	1 tsp. grated orange rind
1 c. water	¼ tsp. almond extract
3 tbs. sugar	
Dash of salt	¼ tsp. vanilla
3 c. milk	Whipped cream

Add chocolate to water in top of double boiler; place over low heat, stirring until chocolate is melted and mixture is blended. Add sugar and salt; bring to boiling; boil 4 minutes, stirring constantly. Place over boiling water; add milk gradually, stirring constantly; stir in orange rind, almond extract, and vanilla; heat through. Just before serving, beat with egg beater until light and frothy. Pour into cups; top with whipped cream. Makes 6 servings.

PUNCHES

Punches, both hot and cold, are a delightful part of any party. What warm summer evening doesn't call for the cool refreshment of a thirst-quenching drink? And when the Merry Christmas season arrives and the tree trimmers have finished their job, bring on the holly trimmed bowl!

Secrets for making punches

· Always chill the ingredients for cold punches before combining them. If the punch is to be served from a punch bowl (and what's more festive at Christmas?), it is best to use a solid block of ice in the bowl because there is less dilution. Ice cubes can be used but the dilution will be greater.
· It is best to make punch in small amounts, renewing the punch bowl with new batches instead of putting too much in at once. The object is to lessen the dilution.

· If a punch recipe calls for sparkling or carbonated beverages, add them at the very last minute so you will retain the sparkle.
· A hot punch should be served in a warm bowl or mugs. Fill the bowl or mug with hot water; let stand. Empty, and quickly dry them. Use only the very best ingredients. Good quality liquor, fresh fruits, and clear, clean ice are the keys to the success of a punch.

Non-Alcoholic Punches

ROSY PUNCH

1½ c. sugar	⅓ c. lime juice
2 c. boiling water	2 c. orange juice
1 bottle (1 qt.) cranberry juice cocktail	1 lime, thinly sliced
	1 bottle (28 oz.) ginger ale

Dissolve sugar in boiling water; cool. Add cranberry, lime, and orange juices; chill thoroughly. At serving time add ginger ale. Serve with slices of lime. Makes 3 quarts.

APPLE BLOSSOM PUNCH

4 c. apple juice	Ice
½ c. lemon juice	1 bottle (28 oz.) ginger ale
2 c. apricot nectar	
¼ c. grenadine	1 pt. lemon sherbet

Combine apple juice, lemon juice, apricot nectar, and grenadine; chill. Just before serving, pour over ice in punch bowl; add ginger ale. Float scoops of lemon sherbet on surface. Makes about 2½ quarts.

GOLDEN APRICOT PUNCH

3 cans (12 oz. ea.) apricot nectar	6 c. fresh or reconstituted frozen orange juice
2 cans (6 oz. ea.) frozen limeade, thawed	Ice
	3 bottles (28 oz. ea.) carbonated water

Combine apricot nectar, limeade, and orange juice; chill until serving time. Pour over ice in punch bowl; add carbonated water; stir slightly. Serve at once. Makes 6 quarts.

TEA PUNCH

2 c. boiling water	1 can (6 oz.)
6 tea bags	undiluted frozen
2½ c. cold water	pineapple juice
1 can (6 oz.)	concentrate,
undiluted frozen	thawed
lemonade	½ c. grenadine
concentrate,	2 bottles (7 oz. ea.)
thawed	ginger ale

Pour boiling water over tea bags; brew 4 to 5 minutes; remove tea bags; combine tea, cold water, lemonade, pineapple juice, and grenadine; chill. Just before serving add ginger ale. Makes about 2 quarts.

PINEAPPLE MINT COOLER

6 sprigs fresh mint	4 bottles (7 oz. ea.)
2 tbs. sugar	lemon-lime-
½ c. lemon juice	flavored carbo-
1 can (46 oz.)	nated beverage
pineapple juice	Pineapple spears
Ice	Mint sprigs

Combine mint and sugar; bruise or crush mint with spoon. Add lemon and pineapple juices. Chill 1 hour or until mint flavor has permeated the mixture; strain. Just before serving, pour over ice in punch bowl; add carbonated beverage. Put a pineapple spear in each punch cup or glass; ladle in punch. Garnish with mint sprigs. Makes about 2½ quarts.

ORANGE CREAM PUNCH

2 c. orange juice	1 bottle (28 oz.)
1 pt. orange sherbet	ginger ale,
1 pt. vanilla ice	chilled
cream	

Beat orange juice with sherbet and ice cream; pour into punch bowl. Stir in ginger ale; serve at once. Makes about 2 quarts.

MULLED CIDER

2 qts. apple cider	2-in. piece stick
½ c. brown sugar,	cinnamon
firmly packed	1 tsp. whole allspice
	1 tsp. whole cloves

Mix cider and sugar in saucepan; add spices. Heat mixture slowly to simmering; cover; simmer 20 minutes. Strain. Serve hot in warm mugs. Makes 2 quarts.

HOLIDAY FRUIT TODDY

1 c. sugar	½ c. lemon juice
1 c. light brown	3½ c. fresh or
sugar, firmly	reconstituted
packed	frozen orange
3-in. piece stick	juice
cinnamon	2 c. water
12 whole cloves	2 lemons, thinly
1½ qts. apple cider	sliced

Combine sugar, brown sugar, cinnamon, cloves, and cider in large saucepan; bring to boiling; simmer 5 minutes. Strain and return to saucepan. Add lemon and orange juices, and water; heat until piping hot. Serve in hot mugs or cups; garnish with lemon slices. Make 3 quarts.

Alcoholic Punches and Nogs

BURGUNDY CHRISTMAS PUNCH

1 c. sugar	½ c. Curaçao
1 c. water	Ice
4 bottles (⅘ qt.	2 bottles (28 oz.
ea.) Burgundy	ea.) carbonated
1 c. lemon juice	water

Cook sugar and water in small saucepan to boiling; boil 5 minutes; remove from heat; cool. Combine cooled sugar syrup, Burgundy, lemon juice, and Curaçao in punch bowl. Chill until serving time. To serve: add large piece of ice to punch bowl; add carbonated water; stir slightly to blend. Makes about 5 quarts.

CARDINAL PUNCH

2 c. sugar
1 bottle (7 oz.) carbonated water
1 bottle (1 pt.) brandy
2 bottles (4/5 qt. ea.) claret or Burgundy, chilled
1/3 c. sweet vermouth
Ice
2 oranges, thinly sliced
2 lemons, thinly sliced
2 bottles (4/5 qt. ea.) sparkling Burgundy

Put sugar in large punch bowl. Add just enough carbonated water to dissolve sugar. Add brandy, claret or Burgundy, and vermouth. Add large block of ice; chill thoroughly. Just before serving, add orange and lemon slices and sparkling Burgundy. Makes about 4 quarts.

CLARET PUNCH

2 lemons
1 bottle (4/5 qt.) claret
2 bottles (7 oz. ea.) carbonated water
2 tbs. sugar
Ice
1 lemon, thinly sliced

Peel lemons; reserve rind; squeeze lemons. Combine lemon rind and juice, claret, carbonated water, and sugar; add ice; stir until thoroughly chilled. Remove rind and ice. Serve punch cold with garnish of thin lemon slices. Makes about 1½ quarts.

FISH HOUSE PUNCH

1 c. sugar
1 c. water
3 c. lemon juice
2 bottles (4/5 qt. ea.) rum
1 bottle (4/5 qt.) Cognac
1/2 c. peach brandy
1½ qts. water
Ice

Mix sugar and water in saucepan. Heat, stirring until sugar is dissolved. Bring to boiling; boil 7 minutes without stirring. Cool. Combine sugar syrup, lemon juice, rum, Cognac, brandy, and water in large punch bowl. Let stand 2 to 3 hours to ripen and blend, stirring occasionally. Add large block of ice to punch in bowl; stir to cool. Makes about 5 quarts.

CHRISTMAS RUM PUNCH

1/2 c. sugar
2 c. orange juice
2/3 c. lemon juice
1/2 c. maraschino cherries and liquid
2 tbs. Curaçao or triple sec
1 bottle (4/5 qt.) light rum
1 orange, thinly sliced
1 lemon, thinly sliced
1 can (1 lb. 4 oz.) pineapple chunks
Ice
1 bottle (28 oz.) carbonated water

Dissolve sugar in orange and lemon juices; add remaining ingredients except ice and carbonated water. Let stand 1 to 2 hours to blend flavors. At party time pour into punch bowl; add ice and carbonated water. Makes about 3 quarts.

CITRUS RUM PUNCH

1 c. sugar
2 c. boiling water
2 c. strong tea, cooled
2 c. orange juice
1/2 c. lemon juice
1½ c. rum
1 bottle (28 oz.) ginger ale
Ice

Dissolve sugar in boiling water; cool. Add remaining ingredients except ice. Serve over ice. Makes about 3 quarts.

SANGRIA

1 bottle (4/5 qt.) dry red wine
1 pkg. (10 oz.) frozen peaches, thawed
4 slices lemon
Ice cubes
Carbonated water

Combine wine, peaches, and lemon slices in large pitcher. Add ice; fill pitcher with carbonated water. Stir well. Serve in wine glasses. Makes about 10 servings.

NOEL PUNCH

2 bottles (⅘ qt. ea.) rosé wine, chilled	2 cans (6 oz. ea.) frozen lemonade concentrate
	Ice
	1 qt. raspberry sherbet

Combine wine and lemonade concentrate; stir until concentrate melts. Pour over ice in small punch bowl. To serve put a spoonful of raspberry sherbet into each punch cup and ladle in punch. Makes about 24 servings.

CHAMPAGNE PUNCH

1 c. maraschino liqueur	1 large orange, thinly sliced
1 c. Cognac or brandy	Ice
1 c. orange juice	3 bottles (1 qt. ea.) champagne, chilled

Combine maraschino liqueur, Cognac or brandy, orange juice, and orange slices in punch bowl; stir well. Chill at least 1 hour. When ready to serve, put a large piece of ice or an ice mold into punch bowl. (If making a mold, it's a good idea to make it part orange juice and part water.) Pour in champagne; stir. Serve at once. Renew the punch bowl with more champagne, if you wish, as the party progresses and the punch becomes diluted from the melting ice. Makes about 3½ quarts.

CHAMPAGNE ORANGE PUNCH

2 c. orange juice	2 bottles (⅘ qt. ea.) Chablis, chilled
Orange bitters	
4 bottles (⅘ qt. ea.) champagne, chilled	1 bottle (28 oz.) carbonated water, chilled
	Orange slices

Combine orange juice and bitters in a large punch bowl. Add champagne, wine, and carbonated water just before serving. Garnish punch cups with orange slices. Makes about 6 quarts.

SYLLABUB

1 qt. dairy eggnog	1 tsp. ground nutmeg
½ c. dry sherry	
½ pt. heavy cream	

Combine eggnog and sherry. Whip cream and nutmeg until cream holds soft peaks; add eggnog mixture; stir through a few times to blend (cream will remain on top). Makes 10 to 12 servings.

EGGNOG

12 eggs, separated	1 qt. whiskey or Cognac
1½ c. sugar	
1 qt. heavy cream, chilled	½ c. Jamaica rum
	Ground nutmeg
1 qt. milk	

Beat egg whites until foamy in large bowl. Add sugar gradually, beating after each addition until sugar is dissolved. Beat egg yolks in second large bowl until thick and lemon colored; fold in egg-white mixture. Add cream, milk, and whiskey or Cognac gradually. Add rum; stir until well mixed. Turn carefully into well chilled punch bowl. Ladle into punch cups. Sprinkle each serving with nutmeg. Makes about 30 servings.

FLUFFY SHERRIED EGGNOG

3 eggs, separated	¼ c. dry sherry
¼ c. sugar	2 tbs. sugar
1½ c. light cream, chilled	Ground nutmeg

Beat egg yolks and ¼ cup sugar together until thick and light yellow in color. Stir in cream; stir in sherry. Whip egg whites until foamy. Add 2 tbs. sugar; continue to beat until soft peaks form. Fold into egg-yolk mixture. Turn carefully into well chilled punch bowl. Sprinkle with nutmeg. Makes 6 servings.

PLANTATION NOG

1 c. bourbon or Southern Comfort	½ c. granulated sugar
	3 egg yolks
	1 pt. heavy cream, whipped

Combine bourbon or Southern Comfort and sugar in a small saucepan; heat just until sugar is dissolved. Cool to lukewarm. Beat egg yolks until thick and pale lemon in color. Slowly add sweetened liquor and let stand 2 to 3 hours. Blend in whipped cream. Chill 1 hour before serving. Makes about 1 quart.

WASSAIL BOWL

1 c. water	1 tsp. whole cloves
2 bottles (⅘ qt. ea.) dry sherry	½ tsp. whole allspice
2 c. sugar	6 eggs, separated
1 tsp. ground ginger	1 c. Cognac or brandy
½ tsp. ground nutmeg	8 small baked apples
4-in. piece stick cinnamon	

Combine water, sherry, sugar, ginger, and nutmeg in large saucepan. Tie cinnamon, cloves, and allspice in small piece of cheesecloth; add to ingredients in saucepan. Bring mixture to boiling, stirring occasionally to blend. Remove from heat; remove cheesecloth bag of spices. Beat egg whites until stiff but not dry; beat egg yolks until thick and light colored. Fold egg whites into egg yolks; add the hot, spiced wine gradually, stirring constantly; stir in Cognac or brandy. Pour into warm punch bowl; float apples in wassail. Makes about 3 quarts.

HOT BUTTERED RUM

½ c. brown sugar, firmly packed	¼ tsp. ground cloves
¼ c. butter or margarine	Rum
	Boiling water
	Cinnamon sticks

Cream sugar, butter or margarine, and cloves together. Put 1 tablespoon of mixture into each mug or glass; add 1 jigger rum to each. Fill mugs or glasses with boiling water to within an inch of top. Put a cinnamon stick in each for a stirrer. Store any leftover sugar mixture in covered jar in refrigerator. Makes about 6 servings.

TOM AND JERRY

12 eggs, separated	Rum
1 c. sugar	Brandy
1 tsp. ground nutmeg	Hot milk or water
	Ground nutmeg

Beat egg yolks until thick and light colored in large bowl; gradually beat in sugar and 1 teaspoon nutmeg; continue beating until very thick. Beat egg whites until stiff but not dry in second bowl; fold into egg-yolk mixture. Chill until serving time. When ready to serve, put ¼ cup of egg mixture into a large, warm mug (Tom-and-Jerry mugs, if you have them); add 2 ounces rum and 1 ounce brandy (or to suit taste) to each mug. Pour hot milk or water into mug to fill it; stir vigorously until it foams. Sprinkle each serving with nutmeg. Makes about 2 quarts.
This recipe can be varied according to personal taste. Bourbon may be used instead of brandy.

JULGLÖGG

10 cardamom seeds	1 c. water
5 whole cloves	1 c. sugar
2 strips (4 in. ea.) orange rind (orange-colored part only)	1 c. seedless raisins
	1 c. whole blanched almonds
3-in. piece stick cinnamon	1 bottle (⅘ qt.) port wine
	1 bottle (⅘ qt.) vodka

Tie cardamom, cloves, orange rind, and cinnamon in cheesecloth bag. Add water and sugar; simmer 5 minutes or until sugar is dissolved. Add raisins and almonds; simmer 2 minutes longer. Stir in port and vodka. Cool; store, covered, overnight. At serving time, remove spice bag; heat julglögg just to boiling. Serve in heated mugs or glasses with a few almonds and raisins in each glass. Makes about 2 quarts.

SMUGGLER'S BREW

2 c. Jamaica rum	1½ qts. brewed tea
½ c. brandy	Sugar
¼ c. butter or margarine	Lemon slices
	Cinnamon sticks

Heat rum, brandy, and butter or margarine over low heat until butter or margarine melts; stir occasionally. Add tea. Sweeten to taste. Add lemon slices. Serve in warm cups or mugs with cinnamon sticks for muddlers. Makes about 3 quarts.

COOLERS AND FRUIT DRINKS

BANANA CRUSH

1 large banana	1 c. ginger ale,
2 c. pineapple juice, chilled	chilled

Mash or puree banana. Beat into pineapple juice. Add ginger ale. Makes 2 servings.

ORANGEADE

1 c. water	1 c. fresh orange
⅓ c. sugar	juice
	Ice cubes
	Orange slices

Heat water and sugar in small saucepan, stirring until sugar is dissolved; boil 5 minutes without stirring. Cool; chill. Combine sugar syrup and orange juice. Pour over ice in glasses. Garnish with orange slices. Makes 3 to 4 servings.

LEMONADE

Prepare recipe for Orangeade, substituting ⅓ cup lemon juice for orange juice. Garnish with lemon slices and mint leaves.

TANGY TANGERINE-GRAPE COOLER

1 can (6 oz.) undiluted frozen tangerine juice concentrate, thawed	½ c. lemon juice
	2½ c. water
	Ice
	1 bottle (28 oz.) ginger ale, chilled
1 can (6 oz.) undiluted frozen grape juice concentrate, thawed	

Combine tangerine juice, grape juice, lemon juice, and water; chill. Just before serving pour over block of ice in punch bowl or over ice cubes in large pitcher; add ginger ale; stir lightly. Makes 1¾ quarts.

QUICKIE COOLERS

Lime Rickey

Combine 2 tablespoons frozen limeade concentrate, thawed, with 1 bottle (7 ounces) chilled carbonated water.

Citrus Cooler

Add a scoop of lemon or orange sherbet to a glass of chilled orange-flavored carbonated beverage.

Brown Cow

Add a scoop of vanilla ice cream to a tall glass of chilled root beer.

GINGER SNAPPER

2 sprigs of fresh mint	1 bottle (10 oz.) ginger beer,
2 tbs. sugar	chilled
2 tbs. lime juice	Mint sprigs
Ice cubes	

Bruise mint with spoon in tall glass; add sugar and lime juice. Add ice cubes; fill glass with ginger beer; garnish with fluff of mint sprigs. Makes 1 serving.

APRICOT SPARKLE

1 can (12 oz.) apricot nectar	1 bottle (12 oz.) lemon-flavored carbonated beverage

Combine apricot nectar and carbonated beverage. Pour over flavored ice cubes (*page 75*). Makes 3 cups.

HAWAIIAN DELIGHT

1 can (6 oz.) undiluted frozen orange-pineapple concentrate, thawed	¼ c. lime juice
	1 pt. lemon sherbet
	2 bottles (28 oz. ea.) carbonated water, chilled
1 can (6 oz.) undiluted frozen lemonade concentrate, thawed	

Mix orange-pineapple concentrate, lemonade concentrate, and lime juice. Divide mixture among 6 tall glasses; add a scoop of lemon sherbet to each. Add carbonated water to fill glasses. Serve with straws. Makes 6 servings.

HONEY ORANGE FIZZ

2 egg whites
¼ c. honey
1 c. water
2 c. orange juice

½ c. lemon juice
3 c. crushed ice
Orange slices
Mint sprigs

Beat egg whites and honey until mixture is peaked and shiny. Add water, orange juice, and lemon juice; blend well. Pour mixture over crushed ice in 4 tall glasses. Garnish with orange slices and mint sprigs. Makes 4 servings.

MILK DRINKS

BANANA MILK SHAKE

1 medium-size banana, peeled
2 tbs. light cream
⅓ c. instant nonfat dry milk

¾ c. ice water
2 tbs. sugar
1 tsp. vanilla
Whipped cream
Ground nutmeg

Mash banana or whirl in blender. Add cream, dry milk, ice water, sugar, and vanilla. Shake in large screw-top jar or shaker or whirl in blender 30 seconds. Pour into tall glass. Garnish with whipped cream and dash of nutmeg. Makes 1 serving.

VANILLA EGGNOG

4 large eggs
3 tbs. sugar
1 qt. cold milk

1 tsp. vanilla
Ground nutmeg

Beat eggs, sugar, milk, and vanilla vigorously in mixer or with beater or whirl in blender. Pour into glasses; sprinkle with nutmeg. Makes 4 servings.

Chocolate: Make as above, using only 1 tablespoon sugar and ¼ cup chocolate syrup.

Strawberry: Make as above, omitting sugar and vanilla; add ¼ cup strawberry preserves.

Coffee: Make as above, adding 4 teaspoons instant coffee.

NEW YORKER SPECIAL

⅓ c. chocolate, vanilla, or strawberry syrup

1 c. milk
1 bottle (12 oz.) carbonated water

Dissolve syrup in milk. Divide evenly among 4 glasses. Add carbonated water to fill glasses; stir and serve. Makes 4 servings.

TUTTI-FRUTTI FLOAT

1 can (8 oz.) sliced peaches, drained and chopped
½ c. chopped maraschino cherries

1 pt. peach or vanilla ice cream
½ c. maraschino cherry juice
1 qt. milk

Combine peaches and maraschino cherries. Alternate spoonfuls of mixture with scoops of ice cream in 4 tall glasses. Mix cherry juice and milk; pour over ice cream in glasses. Top with stemmed maraschino cherries, if desired. Makes 4 servings.

For a pretty and edible garnish for a cold drink, thread bright pieces of canned pineapple and red and green maraschino cherries on long bamboo skewer or drink stirrer.

RASPBERRY MILK SHAKE

1 pkg. (10 oz.) frozen raspberries, partially thawed

1¾ c. milk

Put fruit in blender; puree. Add milk; blend well; strain. Makes 4 servings.

CHOCO-COFFEE SPECIAL

2 bottles (12 oz.
  ea.) chocolate
  flavored milk
  drink, chilled

2 tbs. instant coffee
1 pt. orange sherbet

Blend milk drink and coffee. Serve with scoop of sherbet. Makes 4 servings.

MOCHA FROSTED

2 tbs. chocolate
  syrup
1 c. milk

2 scoops coffee ice
  cream

Combine chocolate syrup, milk, and 1 scoop ice cream. Shake vigorously in shaker or screw-top jar or whirl in blender. Pour into tall glass; top with remaining scoop of ice cream. Garnish with whipped cream and grated chocolate, if desired. Makes 1 serving.

CRANBERRY COW

1 pt. cranberry
  juice, chilled
1 c. milk

1 bottle (7 oz.)
  ginger ale, chilled
1 pt. vanilla ice
  cream

Combine cranberry juice, milk, and ginger ale. Divide evenly among 4 glasses. Serve with scoop of ice cream. Makes 4 servings.

ORANGE BUTTERMILK DRINK

2 c. buttermilk
1 can (6 oz.)
  frozen orange
  concentrate,
  partially thawed

⅛ tsp. ground
  cinnamon
2 tbs. sugar

Blend all ingredients. Chill and serve. Makes 3 to 4 servings.

STRAWBERRY MILK SHAKE

1 tbs. strawberry-
  flavored drink
  mix
1 c. ice water
¼ c. instant nonfat
  dry milk

2 tbs. sliced
  strawberries
1 tbs. sugar
1 whole, sugared
  strawberry

Shake or blend strawberry mix, water, instant dry milk, sliced strawberries, and sugar. Pour into tall glass; press whole strawberry over rim of glass. Makes 1 serving.

ICE CREAM DRINKS

COCOA JAVA FLOAT

1 recipe Cocoa
  (*page 66*)
4 tsp. instant coffee

1 pt. ice cream,
  chocolate or
  vanilla
1 c. carbonated
  water

Combine cocoa and coffee; blend well. To serve: Fill tall glasses half full of cocoa-coffee mixture; add scoop of ice cream; fill with carbonated water. Stir. Makes 4 servings.

ROOT BEER ICE CREAM SODA

1 c. cold milk
1 pt. vanilla ice
  cream

2 bottles (12 oz.
  ea.) root beer,
  chilled

Pour ¼ cup cold milk in each of 4 tall glasses. Add scoop of ice cream. Pour in root beer. Stir and serve. Makes 4 servings.

STRAWBERRY SODA

⅓ c. frozen
  strawberries,
  thawed
¼ c. milk
3 scoops strawberry
  ice cream

2 bottles (7 oz. ea.)
  carbonated water,
  chilled
Whipped cream

Shake or blend strawberries, milk, and 1 scoop ice cream. Pour mixture into 2 tall glasses. Add 1 scoop ice cream to each glass; fill two thirds full with chilled carbonated water; stir; fill with carbonated water. Garnish with whipped cream. Makes 2 servings.

CHOCOLATE MALTED

1 tbs. chocolate
  malted-milk
  drink powder
1 c. milk

2 tbs. light cream
1 scoop chocolate
  ice cream

Shake or blend chocolate malted-milk powder, milk, and cream. Put ice cream into tall glass; pour in chocolate mixture. Makes 1 serving.

BLACK-AND-WHITE SODA

2 tbs. chocolate syrup	1 bottle (7 oz.) carbonated water, chilled
¼ c. milk	
2 or 3 scoops vanilla ice cream	Whipped cream
1 tsp. vanilla	Maraschino cherry

Combine chocolate syrup, milk, 1 scoop vanilla ice cream, and vanilla in tall glass. Stir vigorously with spoon to blend. Fill glass two thirds full with carbonated water; stir. Add 1 or 2 more scoops of ice cream; fill glass with carbonated water. Garnish with whipped cream and cherry. Makes 1 serving.

PINEAPPLE ICE CREAM SODA

1 c. drained, crushed pineapple	1 pt. vanilla ice cream
1 c. milk	2 bottles (12 oz. ea.) ginger ale

Spoon crushed pineapple into 4 tall glasses. Add ¼ cup milk and a scoop of ice cream to each. Stir well. Add ginger ale to fill glasses. Makes 4 servings.

For Calorie Counters

CHERRY O

2 tbs. lime juice	Cherry-flavored low calorie carbonated beverage
Ice cubes	
	Liquid sweetener

Pour lime juice over ice cubes in tall glass. Fill glass with carbonated beverage; add liquid sweetener to taste. Makes 1 serving.

ORANGE VELVET

1 c. fresh orange juice	2 drops liquid sweetener
2 tbs. lemon juice	1 egg white, stiffly beaten

Combine orange and lemon juices and liquid sweetener. Freeze until mushy. Fold in egg white. Freeze until almost firm. Pile into sherbet or champagne glasses. Serve with short straws. Makes 2 servings.

CHOCOLATE SHAKE

1 c. skim milk	1 tbs. chocolate syrup

Combine milk and syrup; shake well. Pour into tall glass. Makes 1 serving.

MINTED PINEAPPLE COOLER

1 c. pineapple juice	Low calorie ginger ale
¼ tsp. mint extract	
Crushed ice	Orange slices
	Mint sprigs

Combine pineapple juice and mint extract. Pour over ice in tall glass. Fill glass with ginger ale. Garnish with orange slice and mint sprigs. Makes 1 serving.

GARNISHES FOR COOL DRINKS

Ice Float
Fill decorative shaped cake pan, loaf pan, metal bowl, or ring mold half full with water. Freeze. Arrange washed strawberries, pineapple slices, maraschino cherries, or grapes on top of ice; freeze until fruit adheres to ice. Fill mold with water; freeze. To unmold, dip pan in hot water until block slips out easily. Float in punch bowl.

Garnished Ice Cubes
For party ice cubes, fill ice cube tray about half full with water; freeze. Place red or green maraschino cherries (halved or sliced), canned pineapple, drained and cut into desired shapes; fresh mint sprigs; orange or lemon slices (quartered, halved, or whole); or washed, unhulled strawberries on top of cubes. Fill ice-cube tray with water; freeze.

Flavored Ice Cubes
Reconstitute 1 can frozen fruit juice, fruit juice combination, ade, or punch concentrate according to label directions. Pour into ice-cube tray; freeze.

Tinted Ice Cubes
Tint water with food coloring, grenadine, or maraschino cherry juice; pour into ice-cube tray; freeze.

Frosty Rims
To frost the rims of glasses, dip top of each glass into fruit juice to a depth of ½ inch; dip into plain or tinted granulated sugar. Refrigerate until sugar is dry.

Chapter Seven

Sandwiches and Snacks

How surprised the Earl of Sandwich would be to see the enticing and elaborate concoctions prepared in his name! The sandwich today can be anything from a bite-size morsel to a full-course meal—from dainty tea sandwiches to mammoth heroes and submarines, bursting with layer upon layer of meat, cheese, tomatoes, and relishes—anything from a mixed grill on toast to open-faced beauties glazed with aspic.

Choosing the Bread

Which kind of bread to use? The decision is important, for the bread must offer the proper flavor and texture to complement the filling.

White bread	Goes with anything
Whole wheat bread Cracked wheat bread Rye bread Pumpernickel Cheese bread	Especially good with cold cuts or cheese
French bread Italian bread	Good with ham, chicken, or tuna salad, bacon, tomato, and lettuce. For hearty heroes.
Hard-crusted rolls Soft buns	Use hollowed-out for salad sandwiches. Best for hot meats: hamburgers, franks, Sloppy Joes, barbecued beef or pork.

Assembly-Line Production

Making sandwiches for a horde of hungry children? Putting a week's supply together for the freezer? Do it this way to speed the process:
· Prepare the fillings.
· Place bread slices two by two in a row. Pair slices as they come from the loaf so they will match at the edges.
· Spread the slices at one time with soft butter or margarine, spreading all the way to the edge.
· Spread filling on half the slices. Spread evenly to the edges and corners. Use a generous amount of filling, but not so much that it will ooze out. Make all sandwiches of one kind of filling at a time.
· Close sandwiches. If crusts are to be removed, trim them off now. (Crusts are best left on all but dainty tea sandwiches, as the crust helps keep the sandwich moist.)
· Cut sandwiches in half, straight across or on the diagonal.
· Wrap each sandwich separately. Set sandwich in center of large square (about 12 inches) of wax paper, transparent plastic wrap, or aluminum foil. Bring opposite ends together over center of sandwich. Fold edges over and over until fold rests on sandwich. Fold ends and tuck under. Or, put each sandwich in a wax paper or plastic sandwich bag and close end.
· Refrigerate sandwiches.

Freezing Sandwiches

· Spread bread with soft butter or margarine.

Mayonnaise or salad dressing and jelly are not recommended as they soak into the bread. Add these after thawing.

· Fill sandwiches with meat or spread. (Lettuce, celery, tomatoes, and hard-cooked egg should be omitted.)

· Wrap sandwiches individually. Unless filling can be seen, label each sandwich.

· Place in freezer in single layer until frozen. Then they may be stacked.

· Sandwiches may be kept frozen up to 3 weeks. Thaw, wrapped, 5 to 6 hours in refrigerator or 2 to 3 hours at room temperature. They may be packed frozen in a lunch box and will be thawed for lunch.

Tips on Making Sandwiches

· Butter or margarine spreads faster and goes farther if it's soft. Spread it generously on the bread right to the edge.

· Use an ice cream scoop to portion out salad-type and other mixed fillings. It's quick, easy, and accurate. Scoops are designated by a number. The number tells you how many scoops you'll get to a quart.

· Fill sandwiches generously—don't skimp. Use several thin slices of meat rather than one thick one. Salad-type fillings should be moist but not soupy.

· When using toast for sandwiches, don't stack the toast slices; this traps steam and makes them soggy.

· Wrap sandwiches individually so there's no transfer of aroma and flavor.

· When sandwiches are made ahead, they should be wrapped in wax paper, transparent plastic wrap, or sandwich bags, and refrigerated until needed. Lunch-box sandwiches particularly should be refrigerator cold before packing.

· For lunch-box or other totable sandwiches, it's best to pack the tomatoes, pickles, and lettuce separately to be added when the sandwich is eaten.

SANDWICH FILLINGS AND SPREADS

BASIC SANDWICH FILLING

1 c. diced cooked meat, poultry, flaked tuna, salmon, or crab meat	1/3 c. chopped celery 1/4 c. mayonnaise or salad dressing

Combine all ingredients; chill until ready to use. Makes about 1 1/3 cups.

CRAB MEAT SALAD

1 can (7 1/2 oz.) crab meat drained, boned, and flaked 2 tbs. chopped green pepper 1/3 c. chopped celery	1 tsp. minced onion 1/4 c. mayonnaise or salad dressing 2 tsp. lemon juice 1/4 tsp. dill weed Salt and pepper to taste

Combine all ingredients; chill until ready to use. Makes about 1 1/3 cups.

EGG SALAD

4 hard-cooked eggs, chopped 3 tbs. chopped stuffed olives	1/4 c. mayonnaise or salad dressing 1/3 c. chopped celery 1/8 tsp. salt Dash of pepper

Combine all ingredients; chill until ready to use. Makes 1 1/4 cups.

CURRIED EGG SALAD

1/4 c. mayonnaise or salad dressing 1 tsp. prepared mustard 1 tsp. grated onion	1/2 tsp. curry powder 1/2 tsp. salt Dash of pepper 3 hard-cooked eggs, chopped

Combine all ingredients; chill until ready to use. Makes about 1 cup.

CHICKEN SALAD

1/3 c. mayonnaise or salad dressing	Dash of pepper
1 tsp. grated onion	1 c. chopped, cooked chicken
1 tsp. lemon juice	3 tbs. finely chopped parsley
1/3 c. chopped celery	
1/2 tsp. salt	

Combine all ingredients; chill until ready to use. Makes about 2 cups.

Curried Chicken Salad: add 1 to 2 teaspoons curry powder to Chicken Salad mixture.

DEVILED HAM

2 cans (2 1/4 oz. ea.) deviled ham	1 tbs. prepared mustard
1/4 c. mayonnaise or salad dressing	1/4 c. pickle relish

Combine all ingredients; chill until ready to use. Makes about 1 cup.

TUNA SALAD

1 can (6 1/2 to 7 oz.) tuna, drained and flaked	2 tbs. pickle relish or chopped sweet pickle
1/2 c. finely chopped celery	1/4 c. mayonnaise or salad dressing
2 tbs. minced onion	1/4 tsp. salt

Combine all ingredients; chill until ready to use. Makes about 2 cups.

TONGUE SPREAD

2 c. ground, cooked beef tongue	2 tbs. prepared horseradish
1/3 c. chopped stuffed olives	2 tbs. prepared mustard
2 tbs. olive juice	1/4 tsp. hot-pepper sauce
1/2 tsp. caraway seeds	1/4 c. mayonnaise or salad dressing

Combine all ingredients; chill until ready to use. Makes 2 cups.

LIVERWURST SPREAD

1 pkg. (6 oz.) Braunschweiger	2 tbs. dairy sour cream
1 pkg. (3 oz.) cream cheese	2 tsp. grated onion
	1 tbs. prepared mustard

Combine all ingredients; chill until ready to use. Makes 1 1/4 cups.

CLAM SPREAD

1 can (10 1/2 oz.) minced clams, drained	1 tbs. finely chopped onion
1 pkg. (3 oz.) cream cheese	1 tbs. capers, finely chopped
1 tbs. lemon juice	1/8 tsp. cayenne pepper
	1/4 tsp. salt

Combine all ingredients; chill until ready to use. Makes 1 1/4 cups.

CLUB SANDWICHES

Toast 3 slices of bread for each sandwich. They may be toasted in the broiler if you're making several sandwiches. Spread each slice with soft butter or margarine, mayonnaise or salad dressing.

Place "lower layer" ingredients on first slice of toast. Top with second slice, spread side up. Add "upper layer" ingredients and top with third slice, spread side down.

Fasten at corners with wooden picks. Cut in 2 or 4 triangles. Garnish with olives, radishes, pickles, or potato chips.

LOWER LAYER	UPPER LAYER
Sliced chicken or turkey, lettuce	Sliced tomato, crisp bacon
Chicken salad, lettuce	Sliced ham, chopped cooked mushrooms
Shrimp salad, lettuce	Sliced hard-cooked egg, sliced tomato
Crab meat salad, lettuce	Sliced avocado, lemon juice, mayonnaise, sliced tomato
Egg salad, lettuce	Chopped ripe olives, sliced ham, sliced tomato
Chicken salad, lettuce	Cream cheese, chopped stuffed olives, sliced tomato

Sliced turkey, sliced
corned beef

Sliced tongue, cole-
slaw, Russian
dressing

Sliced pastrami,
sliced tongue

Sliced salami, India
relish, sliced
tomato

Sliced corned beef,
Swiss cheese

Sliced tongue, cole-
slaw, Russian
dressing

Roast beef, coleslaw

Sliced turkey,
Russian dressing

Roast beef, lettuce

Chopped liver, sliced
Bermuda onion

Chicken liver spread,
crisp bacon

Sliced tomato, lettuce

JUNIOR CLUBS

Make like club sandwiches but omit the center slice of toast. Use one of the following combinations:
· Chicken salad, sliced tomato, crisp bacon, lettuce.
· Tuna salad, Russian dressing (*page 344*), lettuce, sliced hard-cooked egg.
· Sliced chicken, sliced tomato, lettuce, sliced avocado, French Dressing (*page 342*), crisp bacon.
· Sliced tongue, sliced tomato, mayonnaise or salad dressing, crisp bacon.
· Crab meat salad, lettuce, sliced avocado, lemon juice, crisp bacon.
· Sliced sharp Cheddar cheese, sardines, sliced tomato, lettuce.
· Chicken salad, sliced hard-cooked egg, lettuce, sliced tomato, Thousand Island Dressing (*page 343*).
· Spread toast with mixture of Roquefort cheese and butter or margarine. Fill with sliced chicken, sliced tomato, crisp bacon.

HEARTY SANDWICHES

· Sliced tongue, sliced Swiss cheese, sliced tomato, Russian Dressing (*page 344*), on buttered rye bread.
· Lobster salad, tomato, and lettuce in frankfurter roll or hollowed-out club roll.
· Chopped liver, sliced hard-cooked egg, sliced onion, sliced tomato, lettuce, and mayonnaise or salad dressing on pumpernickel.

· Sliced turkey, sliced tomato, mayonnaise or salad dressing on white bread spread with mixture of Roquefort cheese and cream cheese.
· Roast beef, sliced onion, sliced tomato, lettuce, and mayonnaise or salad dressing on whole wheat or rye bread.
· A hero of sliced Swiss cheese, prosciutto, salami, provolone cheese, shredded lettuce, oil and vinegar, sliced tomato, and hot peppers on a split loaf of Italian bread.

OPEN-FACE HEARTIES

A meal in a sandwich—for knife-and-fork eating.
· Lettuce, sliced Swiss cheese, sliced ham, sliced avocado with sour cream and Roquefort dressing, on dark rye bread.
· Sliced Braunschweiger or liver sausage, sliced onion, crisp bacon, sliced tomato, and sliced hard-cooked egg on buttered rye bread. Top with Thousand Island Dressing (*page 343*).
· Spread buttered rye bread with soft cream cheese. Top with thinly sliced smoked salmon and sliced onion.
· Lettuce, pineapple tidbits, chunks of tuna, sliced green onions, Thousand Island Dressing, sliced hard-cooked egg, and sliced tomato on white bread spread with mayonnaise or salad dressing.

SAVORY ROAST BEEF SANDWICHES

1 c. dairy sour cream	2 tsp. prepared horseradish, drained
1 to 2 tsp. seasoned salt or 3 tsp. onion-flavored salad-dressing mix	½ tsp. Worcestershire sauce
1½ tbs. minced onion	16 slices rye or pumpernickel bread
	1 lb. sliced roast beef
	Lettuce leaves

Blend sour cream, seasoned salt or salad-dressing mix, onion, horseradish, and Worcestershire. Spread 1 tablespoon mixture on each of 8 bread slices. Top with roast beef and lettuce leaves; cover with remaining bread slices. Makes 8 servings.

Russian Dressing is a good topper for roast beef.

DOWN-EASTER LOBSTER ROLLS

(*Hot or cold*)

¼ c. mayonnaise or salad dressing	2 tbs. chopped onion
1 tsp. prepared mustard	¼ tsp. salt
½ tsp. parsley flakes	1 can (5 oz.) lobster meat drained, boned, and diced*
½ tsp. leaf tarragon, crumbled	1 tbs. lemon juice
½ tsp. chopped chives	½ c. diced celery
⅛ tsp. cayenne pepper	3 frankfurter rolls, split and buttered

Mix mayonnaise or salad dressing, mustard, parsley, tarragon, chives, cayenne, onion, and salt. Refrigerate. Mix lobster, lemon juice, and celery; refrigerate. Just before serving, mix herbed mayonnaise mixture and lobster mixture; divide evenly among the rolls. If desired, wrap individually in aluminum foil and bake at 350° F. for 15 minutes. Makes 3 sandwiches.

* Fresh or frozen may be substituted.

HOT SANDWICHES

GRILLED

Put one of the following between 2 slices of bread. Spread outside of bread with soft butter or margarine. Grill until golden brown in skillet or sandwich grill.
· Grated Swiss cheese moistened with a little cream, sliced tomato, sliced ham.
· Sliced summer sausage, sliced tomato, sliced onion, sliced American cheese.
· Sliced American or Cheddar cheese. (Serve this one with maple syrup.)
· Sliced American or Cheddar cheese, crisp bacon.

BROILED

Spread toast lightly with butter or margarine. Layer one of the following on toast in order given. Broil until cheese melts and top is golden brown.
· Sliced tomato, crisp bacon, slice of American, Cheddar, or Swiss cheese.
· Slice of ham, slice of American or Swiss cheese, sliced tomato or asparagus spears.

Spoon on *Puffy Topping:* Beat 2 egg whites until stiff; fold in ¾ cup mayonnaise or salad dressing mixed with 1 tablespoon lemon juice. (Enough for 6 sandwiches.)
· Chicken salad, sliced tomato, grated cheese.
· Sautéed sliced mushrooms, sliced tomato, grated American or Cheddar cheese.
· Sliced ham, sliced chicken, sliced American, Swiss, or Cheddar cheese.
· Sliced corned beef, drained hot sauerkraut, sliced Swiss cheese.
· Tuna salad, sliced American cheese. For variation, put a slice of pineapple on tuna before adding cheese.
· Mixture of sautéed sliced mushrooms, sour cream, crab meat; grated Parmesan cheese.
· Crab meat, process cheese spread, sliced avocado, more cheese spread, grated Parmesan.

FRENCH-TOASTED

Make sandwiches using one of the fillings below. For 4 sandwiches, mix 2 beaten eggs, ¼ cup milk, and a dash of salt. Dip sandwiches in mixture. Brown on both sides in hot fat in skillet. Serve hot.
· Chopped ham, moistened with mayonnaise or salad dressing, seasoned with mustard.
· Chopped chicken moistened with chicken gravy.
· Curried crab meat salad.
· Sliced ham, sliced Swiss cheese, mustard, mayonnaise or salad dressing.
· Sliced Swiss cheese, ham, and turkey.

WITH GRAVY

Layer thinly sliced meat, chicken, or turkey on or between buttered toast slices or toasted buns. Spoon over one of the gravies or sauces suggested.
· *Roast Beef* with hot gravy, hot canned or packaged mushroom or beef gravy.
· *Roast Pork* with hot gravy, barbecue sauce, or hot applesauce.
· *Roast Lamb* with hot gravy, hot canned or packaged mushroom gravy, caper sauce, or barbecue sauce.
· *Roast Chicken or Turkey* with hot giblet gravy (left from roast or canned), hot canned chicken gravy, or mushroom sauce.

Sliced meat may also be heated in the gravy or sauce and served over bread, toast, or buns.

OTHER HOT SANDWICHES

· Simmer tiny meatballs in canned marinara sauce. Serve in Italian rolls or toasted frankfurter rolls.

· Sauté onion and green pepper in butter or margarine. Add a can of corned beef hash, and catsup to taste; heat. Serve on toasted buns.

· Panfry minute steaks. Turn; spread top with mixture of Roquefort cheese, butter or margarine, and crushed garlic. Brown second side. Serve on buttered French or Italian bread.

· Layer sliced chicken, crisp bacon, and shredded American cheese on buttered toast. Serve with hot, canned mushroom or chicken gravy.

SLOPPY JOE CHEESEBURGERS

½ c. chopped onion (1 medium)	2 tsp. Worcestershire sauce
½ c. chopped green pepper	1 c. catsup
1 tbs. butter or margarine	½ c. water
1 lb. ground chuck or round	8 hamburger buns, split
1 tsp. salt	1 pkg. (8 oz.) sliced, process American cheese
⅛ tsp. pepper	

Sauté onion and green pepper in butter or margarine until soft. Add ground beef; cook until brown, breaking up with fork as it cooks. Add salt, pepper, Worcestershire, catsup, and water. Simmer, stirring occasionally, 10 to 15 minutes. Spoon on bottom halves of hamburger buns; top each with cheese slice. Broil 6 inches from heat or until cheese begins to melt. Cover with top halves of buns. Makes 8 servings.

WESTERN SANDWICHES

2 eggs, beaten	½ c. finely chopped cooked ham
½ c. finely chopped onion (1 medium)	¼ tsp. salt
¼ c. finely chopped green pepper	Dash of pepper
¼ c. milk	4 tsp. butter or margarine
	4 hard rolls

Mix eggs, onion, green pepper, milk, ham, salt, and pepper together. Melt a teaspoon of butter or margarine in 9-inch skillet. Pour in egg mixture in 2 circles. Cook until set. Turn;

cook 1 minute longer. Repeat with remaining butter or margarine and egg mixture. Serve on rolls. Makes 4 servings.

HOT TOMATO AND CHEESE ROLLS

1 pkg. (8 oz.) brown-and-serve club rolls	⅛ tsp. pepper
¼ c. soft butter or margarine	¼ tsp. leaf basil, crumbled
¼ tsp. garlic powder	12 tomato slices
½ tsp. salt	12 slices Mozzarella or Muenster cheese

Slice rolls in half lengthwise; remove some of the soft center. Mix butter or margarine, garlic powder, salt, pepper, and basil; spread mixture on rolls. Arrange 2 tomato slices and 2 slices of cheese on each roll half; top with other half of roll. Place on cookie sheet. Bake at 400° F. for 15 to 20 minutes or until nicely browned.

CORNED BEEF BURGERS

1 can (12 oz.) corned beef, chopped	¼ c. catsup
	1 egg
½ c. finely chopped onion	2 tbs. prepared mustard
1 c. fresh bread cubes	8 hamburger buns

Mix corned beef, onion, bread cubes, catsup, and egg; form into 8 patties. Broil about 6 inches from heat 5 minutes; turn. Brush with mustard; broil about 5 minutes longer. Serve on hamburger buns. Makes 8 servings.

BAKED TUNA ROLLS

¾ c. mayonnaise or salad dressing	⅓ c. chopped green pepper
2 tbs. lemon juice	¼ c. sliced ripe olives
¼ c. finely chopped onion	2 cans (7 oz. ea.) tuna, drained and flaked
¼ tsp. salt	
Dash of pepper	6 large round or rectangular hard rolls
1 c. finely chopped celery	

Heat oven to 375° F. Combine mayonnaise or salad dressing, lemon juice, onion, salt, and pepper. Stir in celery, green pepper, olives, and tuna. Cut tops off rolls; pull out soft centers. Fill rolls with tuna mixture; replace tops. Wrap each roll in foil. Bake 40 to 45 minutes or until hot.

DELUXE TUNA SANDWICHES WITH PUFFY TOPPING

2 pkgs. (3 oz. ea.) cream cheese	2 tsp. lemon juice
1/4 c. milk	1 can (7 oz.) tuna, drained and flaked
1/2 tsp. parsley flakes	4 club rolls, toasted
1/8 tsp. onion powder	2 tbs. mayonnaise or salad dressing
1 tsp. dry mustard	1 tbs. grated Parmesan cheese
1/4 tsp. pepper	1 egg white
1 egg yolk, slightly beaten	

Blend cream cheese, milk, parsley, onion powder, mustard, and pepper in a saucepan. Cook over medium heat until mixture starts to bubble. Stir some of the hot mixture into the egg yolk, blending rapidly. Return to the remaining hot mixture in the saucepan; cook 1 minute longer or until mixture starts to bubble again. Remove from heat; blend in lemon juice and tuna. Cut thin slices from top of each roll; hollow out rolls; spoon about 1/2 cup tuna mixture into each roll. Blend mayonnaise or salad dressing and Parmesan cheese. Beat egg white until stiff peaks form; blend into mayonnaise mixture. Top each roll with generous amount of egg-white mixture. Broil 6 inches from heat about 3 minutes or until topping is puffed and lightly browned. Makes 4 servings.

PUFF-TOPPED ASPARAGUS SANDWICHES

1 lb. fresh asparagus	3/4 c. mayonnaise or salad dressing
6 slices cooked ham	1 tbs. lemon juice
6 slices buttered toast	2 egg whites
3 medium-size tomatoes, sliced	Dash of salt

Cook asparagus in salted water 13 to 14 minutes or until tender crisp. Drain well. Place 1 slice of ham on each piece of toast; arrange asparagus spears on ham. Place sliced tomatoes on asparagus. Combine mayonnaise or salad dressing and lemon juice. Beat egg whites with salt until stiff; fold in mayonnaise mixture. Spoon over tomatoes. Broil at least 6 inches from heat, 5 minutes or until puffed and brown, or bake at 425° F. about 3 minutes. Makes 6 servings.

EL PASO SPECIALS (Beef 'n' Bean Tacos)

1 can (11 oz.) tortillas	1 can (15½ oz.) chili con carne, heated
Pure vegetable oil	

Remove 8 tortillas (wrap remaining securely and refrigerate for later use). Pour oil to depth of 1/4 inch in skillet; heat oil. Slip tortillas, one at a time, into hot oil. Cook about 15 seconds or until they become pliable. Remove; drain on paper towels. Place 2 tablespoons chili con carne in center of each tortilla; fold over edges; secure with wooden pick. Just before serving, fry quickly in very hot oil to crisp. Drain and serve. Makes 8 tacos.

PIZZA

1 pkg. hot-roll mix	1 can (8 oz.) pizza sauce
1 c. water (105° to 115° F.)	1 pkg. (8 oz.) Mozzarella cheese, sliced
1 tbs. pure vegetable or olive oil	

Heat oven to 450° F. Dissolve packet of yeast from package of hot-roll mix in warm water in bowl. Stir in flour all at once. Pat or roll out dough on lightly floured board to a 12-inch circle or to two 9-inch circles. Place on cookie sheet, or in pizza pan or pie pans. Brush with oil; spread with sauce; top with cheese. Bake about 15 minutes or until crust is nicely browned and cheese is melted and bubbly.

Anchovy Pizza: Make pizza as above. Drain 2 cans (2 ounces each) anchovies; arrange anchovies on sauce; top with cheese.

Mushroom Pizza: Make pizza as above. Drain 2 cans (3 to 4 ounces each) sliced mushrooms; arrange mushrooms on sauce; top with cheese.

Sausage Pizza: Make pizza as above. Arrange slices of sweet Italian sausage, pepperoni, or salami on sauce. Top with cheese.

CALZONE

2 c. (1 lb.) ricotta cheese	1 tsp. salt
1/2 c. (8 oz.) Mozzarella cheese, diced	1/2 tsp. pepper
1/4 c. grated Parmesan cheese	1 pkg. (10 oz.) frozen chopped spinach, cooked and well drained
1 egg	1 pkg. hot-roll mix
	1 c. warm water (105° to 115° F.)

Mix ricotta, Mozzarella, Parmesan cheeses, egg, salt, pepper, and spinach. Dissolve yeast from package of hot-roll mix in warm water; stir in flour; mix until dough forms a ball and cleans sides of bowl. Turn onto lightly floured cookie sheet. Pat out dough into 12-inch circle with floured hands. Spoon filling on half of the circle, leaving a 2-inch edge. Fold other half of dough over cheese filling; press dough together; turn pinched edge over once and pinch again. Bake in 450° F. oven for 30 minutes or until crust is evenly browned. Makes 8 servings.

SANDWICH CASSEROLE

4 hamburger rolls	3 eggs
1 can (12 oz.) luncheon meat	3 c. milk
	1 tbs. instant minced onion
1 c. shredded process American cheese	½ tsp. seasoned salt

Cut rolls in half crosswise, making 8 semi-circles; cut luncheon meat into 8 slices; place 1 slice between halves. Put rolls, cut side down, in two rows in 8x8x2-inch baking dish; sprinkle cheese over top. Beat eggs slightly; add milk, onion, and seasoned salt; pour over rolls. Bake in 350° F. oven for 45 to 50 minutes or until bubbly. Serve at once. Makes 4 servings.

CHICKEN LIVER AND BACON SQUARES

½ lb. chopped chicken liver spread	½ c. (6 to 8 slices) cooked, crumbled bacon
2 to 3 tbs. dairy sour cream, mayonnaise, or salad dressing	8 slices bread, crusts removed
	Melted butter or margarine

Combine chicken liver spread, sour cream, mayonnaise or salad dressing, and bacon. Spread ¼ cup on each of 4 slices of bread. Cover with remaining bread slices. Cut in squares; brush with butter or margarine. Bake at 450° F. for 10 minutes; turn once to brown evenly. Makes 16 squares.

TEA AND PARTY FARE

OPEN-FACE DAINTIES

Trim crusts from bread slices; cut into desired shapes. Or, cut out shapes from slices with fancy cutters. Choose any of the following:
· Spread bread with softened cream cheese. Top with sliced strawberries.
· Spread bread with mayonnaise or salad dressing. Place a cucumber slice in center. Surround with a ring of overlapping thin radish slices. Sprinkle with parsley.
· Press softened cream cheese through pastry bag around edge of bread. Fill center with tart jelly.
· Spread bread with butter or margarine. Cover with sieved hard-cooked egg yolk. Put a small mound of caviar in center. Border edge with chopped hard-cooked egg white.
· Spread bread with mixture of mayonnaise or salad dressing, curry powder, and onion juice. Arrange tiny canned or jarred shrimp on top. Garnish with a sprig of parsley.
· Spread bread with mixture of chopped chicken, chopped toasted almonds, and mayonnaise or salad dressing. Garnish with sliced stuffed olives.
· Spread bread with mixture of softened cream cheese, finely chopped raw mushrooms, and onion juice. Garnish with sprig of watercress.

DAINTY TEA SANDWICHES

Trim crusts from thin-sliced bread. Cut bread, if necessary, to make a perfect square. Spread with softened butter or margarine. Spread half the slices with any of the filling mixtures below. Top with remaining slices. Wrap in aluminum foil or transparent plastic wrap; chill. Cut each sandwich into 4 fingers, triangles, or squares. One loaf of thin-sliced bread will make about 40 sandwiches.
· Chopped cooked chicken, chopped toasted almonds, and drained crushed pineapple moistened with mayonnaise or salad dressing seasoned with curry powder.
· Ground raisins or dates and ground walnuts moistened with spiced peach juice.
· Mashed avocado, cream cheese, chopped onion, lemon juice, Worcestershire sauce, and salt.
· Sliced cucumbers topped with mayonnaise or salad dressing seasoned with onion juice.
· Deviled ham and chopped onion and green pepper moistened with mayonnaise or salad dressing.
· Flaked tuna, chopped chutney, lemon juice, and mayonnaise or salad dressing.
· Ground ham, chopped hard-cooked egg, chopped anchovy, mayonnaise, onion juice, and pepper.

• Chopped pared cucumber, cream cheese, sour cream, salt, celery seed, and dill weed.
• Flaked crab meat, mashed avocado, lemon juice, hot-pepper sauce, and mayonnaise or salad dressing.
• Ground figs and prunes and orange and lemon juices.
• Cream cheese, chopped dried beef, horse-radish, Worcestershire sauce, and cream.
• Cream cheese and chopped strawberries.

CHICKEN-MIMOSA TRIANGLES
(*Pictured opposite page 53*)

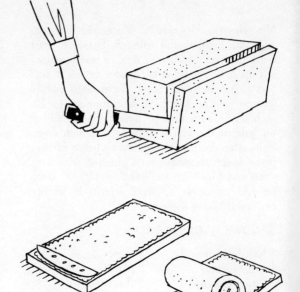

1 loaf thin-sliced whole wheat bread	½ tsp. salt
	⅛ tsp. pepper
1 can (6 oz.) chicken, ground	3 tbs. mayonnaise or salad dressing
2 tbs. minced celery	6 hard-cooked egg yolks
1 tbs. minced chives	½ c. soft butter or margarine
¼ c. stuffed olives, minced	Parsley

Cut triangles from whole wheat bread. Combine chicken, celery, chives, olives, salt, pepper, and mayonnaise or salad dressing. Spread mixture on half the triangles; top with remaining triangles. Sieve egg yolks; cream well with butter or margarine. Press egg-butter mixture through decorating tube with small round tip to form a triangular design like a bunch of grapes. Press parsley sprigs into design for leaf. Makes about 20 sandwiches.

PINWHEELS
(*Pictured opposite page 53*)

Trim crusts from loaf of unsliced bread. Cut loaf lengthwise into ¼-inch-thick slices. Roll each slice with rolling pin to make it more flexible. Spread bread with soft butter or margarine. Spread filling all the way to edge. Roll up like a jelly roll starting from short end. Seal end with soft butter or margarine. Wrap tightly in aluminum foil or transparent plastic wrap. Chill. Cut each roll into 16 slices. One loaf of bread will make 64 sandwiches. Choose any of these fillings:
• Softened cream cheese. Arrange a row of sliced stuffed olives or gherkins at one short end. Roll from that end.
• Mix shredded Cheddar cheese and finely chopped green pepper and onion. Season with Worcestershire sauce; moisten with mayonnaise, salad dressing, or chili sauce.

• Mixture of deviled ham and finely chopped pimiento. Arrange thin spear of dill pickle at one short end. Roll from that end.
• Mixture of mashed avocado and Roquefort cheese.
• Mixture of softened cream cheese, finely chopped raw mushrooms, onion juice, salt, and pepper.
• Mixture of cream cheese, sour cream, chopped watercress, salt and pepper.
• Cream cheese topped with thinly sliced smoked salmon. Arrange green pepper strips along one short end. Roll from that end.
• Mixture of cream cheese, chopped green pepper, onion, pimiento, and salt.
• Mixture of finely chopped cooked shrimp, minced onion, dill, lemon juice, and mayonnaise or salad dressing.
• Mixture of canned deviled ham and pimiento. Arrange dill pickle spears at one end. Roll from that end. Brush roll with softened butter or margarine. Roll in chopped parsley.

ROLL-UPS

Trim crusts from thin slices of fresh bread. Roll slices lightly with rolling pin. Spread slices with soft butter or margarine. Leave plain or spread with softened cream cheese. One loaf of thin-sliced bread will make 20 roll-ups. Prepare one of the following ways:
• Roll up slices. Seal end with soft butter or margarine. Wrap in aluminum foil or trans-

parent plastic wrap. Chill. Before serving tuck sprigs of parsley, watercress, or mint in ends.
· Place sprigs of watercress along one edge so leaves stick out. Roll up, wrap, and chill.
· Place spears of cooked or canned asparagus along one edge. Roll up, wrap, and chill.

CHECKERBOARDS

Stack 2 slices white bread and 2 slices whole wheat bread alternately, filling with one of the soft, creamy fillings for Pinwheels or Dainty Tea Sandwiches. Repeat with remaining bread slices. Press each stack firmly together. Trim crusts from each stack with a sharp knife using a sawing motion. Cut each stack in ½-inch-thick slices.

Put three alternating slices together with filling between. Wrap each separately in transparent plastic wrap or aluminum foil. Chill several hours. Remove from refrigerator; unwrap; cut in ½-inch-thick slices.

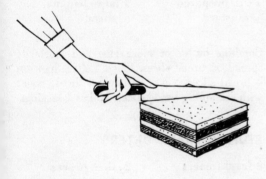

RIBBONS

1 jar (5 oz.) Cheddar cheese spread	1 loaf thin-sliced white bread
½ c. soft butter or margarine	1 loaf thin-sliced whole wheat bread

Blend cheese and butter or margarine together. Trim crusts from 6 slices white and 6 slices whole wheat bread. For each sandwich "block" allow 2 slices of white and 2 slices of whole wheat. Spread 3 slices with filling; stack alternate slices; use fourth slice for top, press firmly. Wrap in transparent plastic wrap or aluminum foil; chill. Slice block in half vertically; slice each half into thin ribbons. Makes 48 sandwiches.

FRUIT-AND-NUT CREAM CHEESE SANDWICHES

1 pkg. (3 oz.) cream cheese	½ tsp. ground cinnamon
½ tsp. grated orange rind	⅛ tsp. ground nutmeg
1 medium-size orange, peeled, sectioned, diced, and drained	8 slices packaged date-nut bread
	¼ c. peanut butter

Blend cream cheese, orange rind, orange, cinnamon, and nutmeg. Spread 4 slices of bread with peanut butter; spread cream cheese mixture on remaining 4 slices. Put together. Makes 4 servings.

STRAWBERRY DAISIES

(*Pictured opposite page 53*)

Thin-sliced white bread	¼ c. chopped strawberries
1 pkg. (8 oz.) cream cheese	

Cut out 72 daisies from bread with daisy-shaped cookie cutter (available at most large department stores). Beat cream cheese until soft; add strawberries; beat until well blended. To spread sandwiches with ease: make cone with triangle of wax paper; fill with strawberry mixture; snip off end of cone; pipe mixture onto 36 of the daisies; cover with remaining daisies. Garnish with additional strawberry-cheese filling if desired. Cover carefully; chill. Makes 36 sandwiches.

CHICKEN SANDWICHES CONTINENTAL

¼ c. mayonnaise or salad dressing	¾ c. quartered, seedless green grapes
½ tsp. curry powder	¼ c. slivered almonds, toasted
⅛ tsp. salt	Soft butter or margarine
⅛ tsp. pepper	8 slices whole wheat or white bread
1 c. diced, cooked chicken	

Blend mayonnaise or salad dressing, curry powder, salt, and pepper. Add chicken, grapes, and almonds. Spread bread slices with butter or margarine; spread 4 slices with chicken mixture; top with remaining bread slices. Makes 4 servings.

CREAM CHEESE PRETTIES

1 pkg. (3 oz.)   ¼ c. jam or jelly
   cream cheese   6 bread slices

Soften cream cheese in small bowl by mashing with fork. Spread on 3 slices of bread. Spread with jam or jelly; top with remaining bread slices. Cut into strips, triangles, squares, or fancy shapes. Makes 12 servings.

FRUITED HAM AND CHICKEN SANDWICHES

2 to 3 tbs. fruit   ½ c. chopped,
   juice   cooked ham or
1 pkg. (3 oz.)   chicken
   cream cheese   6 slices bread

Blend fruit juice into cream cheese. Stir in ham or chicken. Spread on 3 slices of bread; top with remaining bread slices. Cut into strips, triangles, or fancy shapes. Makes 12 servings.

FROSTED SANDWICH LOAF

3 sandwich fillings   2 tbs. mayonnaise
   of your choice   or salad dressing
Peeled tomatoes   2 pkgs. (8 oz. ea.)
1 loaf (about 1 lb.   cream cheese
   13 oz.) unsliced   ¼ c. mayonnaise or
   sandwich bread   salad dressing
Butter or margarine   2 tbs. light cream

Prepare fillings; slice tomatoes; chill. Cut all crusts from bread with sharp knife. Lay loaf on its side; cut into 5 even slices; spread 4 slices with soft butter or margarine. Spread fillings on three slices; arrange tomatoes (halve slices if necessary) on fourth slice; spread tomatoes with 2 tablespoons mayonnaise or salad dressing. Stack slices; top with fifth slice of bread. Combine cream cheese, ¼ cup mayonnaise or salad dressing, and cream. Blend until smooth. Spread mixture on tops and sides of loaf. Chill thoroughly. Garnish with sieved, hard-cooked egg yolks, if desired. Slice to serve. Makes 8 to 10 servings.

SANDWICH TREATS FOR TOTS

• *Window Sandwiches:* Cut out design in slice of bread to be used for top of sandwich. Leave cut-out open to show sandwich filling, or fill it with a cut-out from a different kind of bread.
• *Spooky Cheeseburgers:* Before putting slice of cheese on hamburger, cut eyes, nose, and mouth out of each slice. Broil as usual.
• *Polka-Dot Sandwiches:* Cut out several small circles from slice of bread to be used for top of sandwich. Fill holes with rounds of pickle, pimiento, green pepper, stuffed olive, or radish.

BANANA HAM SANDWICHES

¼ c. soft butter or   8 slices bread
   margarine   8 slices cooked ham
1 tbs. prepared   1 large banana,
   mustard   sliced

Combine butter or margarine and mustard; spread on bread slices. Place 2 slices ham on 4 bread slices, top with banana slices; cover with remaining bread slices. Makes 4 servings.

STUFFED FRANKFURTERS

8 frankfurters   2 slices process
2 tbs. prepared   American cheese,
   mustard   cut in strips
2 tbs. pickle relish   8 split, buttered
                frankfurter rolls

Make a lengthwise cut in each frankfurter, leaving about ¼ inch uncut at either end. Spread with mustard; spoon relish into each cavity; insert cheese strips into cavities. Place in shallow baking dish. Bake at 400° F. for 8 minutes or until cheese is melted. Serve in rolls. Makes 8 servings.

Cottage Cheese Stuffed Frankfurters: Mix ½ cup small curd cottage cheese with 2 tablespoons pickle relish and 2 tablespoons mustard; spoon into cavities. Bake or grill frankfurters and serve in toasted, buttered frankfurter rolls.

TUNA NUT BUTTERWICHES

1 can (7 oz.) tuna	12 slices bread
2 tbs. mayonnaise or salad dressing	6 tbs. peanut butter

Moisten tuna with mayonnaise or salad dressing; spread on 6 slices of bread. Spread peanut butter on other 6 slices; put slices of bread together. Makes 6 servings.

Make it with Peanut Butter

· Spread bread with peanut butter. Top with jelly and sliced bananas.
· Mix peanut butter and drained, crushed pineapple. Spread on one slice of bread. Spread second slice with butter or margarine and marshmallow cream.
· Spread toast with peanut butter mixed with a little horseradish. Top with crisp bacon, sliced tomato, lettuce, and mayonnaise or salad dressing.
· Spread toast with mixture of peanut butter, butter or margarine, and crumbled crisp bacon. Top with slice of tomato and American cheese. Broil.
· Spread bread with mixture of peanut butter, drained crushed pineapple, and grated orange rind. Top with sliced boiled ham and second slice of bread. Spread outside of bread with soft butter or margarine. Brown in skillet or sandwich grill.
· Mix peanut butter with:
  Grated carrot, chopped sweet pickle
  Crumbled cooked bacon
  Raisins, crushed pineapple or diced banana
  Mashed banana, lemon juice
  Drained crushed pineapple, coconut
  Chopped sweet pickle, diced cooked ham, chili sauce
  Grated carrot, diced celery, mayonnaise or salad dressing

SANDWICHES FOR A CROWD

Food	Amount to use for 1 sandwich	Amount needed for 50*
Butter or margarine for spreading	1½ teaspoons for 1 slice	1¼ to 1½ cups for spreading 1 slice of sandwich. Double this amount for spreading both slices.
Bread	2 slices	3 pullman loaves (100 slices); 2-pound pullman loaf, 14 inches long, cuts 35 slices, ⅜ inch thick.
Mayonnaise or salad dressing	2 to 3 teaspoons	2 to 3 cups
Mixed fillings	3 tablespoons (No. 24 ice cream scoop)	2½ to 3 quarts
	2 tablespoons (No. 30 ice cream scoop)	1¾ to 2 quarts
Sliced meat	1½ ounces	5 pounds (10 slices per pound)
Cheese	1 to 1½ ounces	3 to 4 pounds (12–16 slices per pound)
Peanut Butter	2 tablespoons	4 pounds or 7 cups (1 pound equals 1¾ cups)
Lettuce	1 leaf	2½ to 3 heads

* Use half these amounts for 25; double them for 100.

Chapter Eight

Quick Breads

Hot corn bread fresh out of the oven, dripping with butter . . . coffee cake crunchy with nuts or luscious with a baked-on fruit topping . . . blueberry muffins so tender they crumble in the fingers—and melt in the mouth. These are a few of the wonderful breads we call "quick" because the leavening agent which makes them rise is so speedy. They are ready to bake, steam, or fry as soon as they are mixed.

Quick breads are leavened with baking powder, soda, steam, or air, rather than yeast.

Because a similar type batter is used in making pancakes and waffles, fritters and doughnuts, these are also counted as "quick breads," though they are not literally breads at all. Even dumplings steamed in broth or syrup belong to the quick-bread family.

QUICK BREAD SECRETS

· The *secret* in making all quick breads is to avoid overmixing. Use a light hand when handling biscuit dough; pat it only enough to turn out onto a lightly floured board for shaping. Stir the batter for muffins or pancakes just until the flour is well dampened. Overbeating or overmixing may cause toughness, uneven texture, less attractive appearance.
· Plan the cooking of such quick breads as biscuits, muffins, and coffee cakes so that they are ready to serve while piping hot.
· To reheat quick breads, wrap loosely in aluminum foil and heat at 250° F. for 10 to 15 minutes.

BISCUITS

These are one of our great hot breads, in great-grandmother's day a family staple. "Take two and butter 'em while they're hot," is a rule that still applies today.

There are *rolled* biscuits and *drop* biscuits. Here are recipes for both kinds.

BAKING-POWDER BISCUITS

2 c. sifted all-purpose flour	1 tsp. salt
3 tsp. baking powder	¼ c. shortening
	¾ c. milk

Heat oven to 450° F. Sift flour, baking powder, and salt into mixing bowl. Cut in shortening with pastry blender until mixture resembles cornmeal. Make well in center; add milk. Stir quickly and lightly with fork just until dough clings together in a ball. Avoid overhandling. Turn dough out on lightly floured board. Knead gently 10 times. Roll dough or pat out with floured hand to ½-inch thickness. Cut biscuits close together with floured 2-inch cutter. Push leftover pieces together; roll out and cut. Transfer biscuits to ungreased cookie sheet with spatula. For crusty sides, place them 1 inch apart; for soft sides, place them close together. Bake 12 to 15 minutes or until golden brown. Serve hot. Makes about 18 biscuits.

Herb Biscuits. Add ¼ teaspoon dry mustard, ½ teaspoon crumbled sage, and 1¼ teaspoons caraway seeds to flour-shortening mixture.

Bacon Biscuits. Add ⅓ cup crisply cooked, diced bacon to flour-shortening mixture.

Chive Biscuits. Add ¼ cup chopped chives to flour-shortening mixture.

Orange Biscuits. Add 2 tablespoons grated orange rind to flour-shortening mixture. Before baking, press a half piece of lump sugar, dipped in orange juice, into top of each biscuit.

Buttermilk Biscuits. Prepare Baking-Powder Biscuits except use buttermilk for sweet milk. Use only 2 teaspoons baking powder; add ¼ teaspoon baking soda.

DROP BISCUITS

Prepare Baking-Powder Biscuits, increasing milk to 1 cup. Omit kneading and rolling steps. Drop dough by spoonfuls 1 inch apart onto greased cookie sheet or half fill 18 2½-inch greased muffin-pan cups. Bake at 450° F. for 12 to 15 minutes.

Cheese Biscuits. Add ½ cup shredded Cheddar cheese to flour-shortening mixture.

Raisin Biscuits. Add ½ cup seedless raisins to biscuit dough.

Blueberry Biscuits. Add 1 cup washed and very well drained fresh blueberries to biscuit dough.

STIR 'N' ROLL BISCUITS

2 c. sifted all-purpose flour	1 tsp. salt
3 tsp. baking powder	⅓ c. pure vegetable oil
	⅔ c. milk

Heat oven to 475° F. Sift flour, baking powder, and salt into mixing bowl. Put oil and milk into measuring cup (do not stir together). Pour, all at once, onto dry ingredients. Mix with fork until dough rounds into a ball and cleans sides of bowl. Turn out onto sheet of wax paper. Knead lightly without adding additional flour, 10 times. Roll or pat out dough between 2 pieces of wax paper to ½-inch thickness. Remove top piece of paper. Cut with unfloured 2-inch cutter. Transfer to ungreased cookie sheet. Bake 10 to 12 minutes or until golden brown. Makes 16 biscuits.

PINWHEEL BISCUITS

Prepare Baking-Powder Biscuit or Stir'n' Roll Biscuit Dough. Roll or pat out to rectangle about 12 inches long and ¼ inch thick. Spread with one of the fillings below. Roll up from long side as tightly as possible; pinch edge of roll to seal. Cut in 1-inch slices. Place, cut side down, in greased 2½-inch muffin-pan cups. Bake at 425° F. 12 to 15 minutes.

Cinnamon Filling

Spread dough with 2 tablespoons softened butter or margarine. Sprinkle with mixture of ¼ cup sugar and 1 teaspoon cinnamon. Top with raisins, if desired.

Deviled Ham Filling

Spread dough with 2 tablespoons melted butter or margarine, then with mixture of ½ cup deviled ham, 2 tablespoons finely chopped green pepper, and 1 tablespoon chopped pimiento.

Butterscotch Filling

Cream together ⅓ cup butter or margarine and ½ cup brown sugar, firmly packed. Spread in muffin-pan cups; arrange 3 pecan halves in each cup. Spread dough with 2 tablespoons butter or margarine and ½ cup brown sugar, firmly packed.

Cheese Filling

Sprinkle dough with ½ cup shredded Cheddar cheese.

BUTTERBALL BISCUITS

½ c. butter or margarine	1 tsp. salt
2 c. sifted all-purpose flour	⅓ c. soft butter or margarine
3 tsp. baking powder	¾ c. milk

Heat oven to 450° F. Melt ½ cup butter or margarine; put 1 teaspoonful into each of 12 2½-inch muffin-pan cups; reserve remainder. Sift flour, baking powder, and salt into mixing bowl. Add soft butter or margarine; cut in with pastry blender until mixture resembles cornmeal. Stir in milk with fork. Fill each prepared muffin-pan cup almost to top with dough. Bake 10 minutes. Spoon 1 teaspoon melted butter or margarine over each biscuit. Bake 10 minutes longer. Serve piping hot with butter, jam, or honey.

MUFFINS

Back in the Gay Nineties, muffins were called "gems," and when tender, light, and hot from the oven, they are just that.

The *secret* in making muffins is to *stir only until the flour is dampened*. The batter should be lumpy.

It is recommended that you grease just the bottoms of muffin cups. Muffins have better shape when sides are not greased. You may also line muffin cups with paper liners. Fill any empty muffin cups half full with water to prevent grease from browning during baking.

Good muffins will be rounded on top, pebbly in appearance, and have no tunnels or holes inside.

MUFFINS

2 c. sifted all-purpose flour	1 tsp. salt
¼ c. sugar	1 egg
3 tsp. baking powder	1 c. milk
	¼ c. shortening, melted

Heat oven to 400° F. Grease 12 2½-inch muffin-pan cups. Sift flour, sugar, baking powder, and salt into bowl. Make well in center; add egg, milk, and shortening. Stir just to moisten dry ingredients. Batter will be lumpy. Fill muffin-pan cups about two-thirds full. Bake about 20 minutes or until golden brown. Loosen with spatula; remove from pan; cool on wire racks.

Jelly or Jam Muffins. Prepare muffin batter; fill muffin-pan cups half full; add 1 teaspoon jelly or jam; add enough batter to fill cups two-thirds full.

Blueberry Muffins. Prepare muffin batter; fold in 1 cup washed, fresh blueberries.

Crunchy Topped Muffins. Combine ½ cup brown sugar, firmly packed; ⅓ cup coarsely chopped nuts; ¼ teaspoon ground cinnamon; ¼ teaspoon ground nutmeg. Prepare muffin batter; fill muffin-pan cups as directed. Sprinkle with sugar mixture before baking.

CORN MUFFINS

(*Pictured opposite page 116*)

1 c. sifted all-purpose flour	1 tsp. salt
2 c. yellow cornmeal	1 egg
⅓ c. sugar	1 c. milk
4 tsp. baking powder	⅓ c. pure vegetable oil

Grease 12 2½-inch muffin-pan cups lightly. Heat oven to 425° F. Combine flour, cornmeal, sugar, baking powder, and salt in mixing bowl. Beat egg in small bowl; stir in milk and oil. Add liquid ingredients to dry ingredients all at once; stir just until dry ingredients are moistened; do not beat. Fill prepared muffin-pan cups ⅔ full. Bake 20 to 25 minutes or until golden.

CORN BREADS

Corn breads are the gift of our native Indians to American cuisine. They taught early settlers to parch corn, mix it with boiling water, and bake into thin cakes. These cakes were taken on long journeys by hunters and traders over hills and trails and therefore came to be called "journey cakes." This was the origin of "johnnycake." There are many variations of corn bread depending on the region where the recipe originates. Whether you prefer yellow or white cornmeal, the methods of mixing are the same. Whatever your choice, serve corn bread piping hot!

GOLDEN CORN BREAD

1 c. sifted all-purpose flour	4 tsp. baking powder
1 c. yellow cornmeal	2 eggs
½ tsp. salt	⅓ c. melted butter or margarine
⅓ c. sugar	1 c. milk

Heat oven to 425° F. Grease 8x8x2-inch baking pan. Combine flour, cornmeal, salt, sugar, and baking powder in mixing bowl. Add eggs and butter or margarine to milk; beat with rotary beater until blended. Pour liquid ingredients into dry ingredients. Beat with rotary beater until ingredients are just blended. Do not overbeat. Pour into prepared pan. Bake 25 to 30 minutes or until top is golden brown. Makes 16 servings.

CRACKLIN' SKILLET BREAD

½ lb. bacon	3 tsp. baking
1 c. sifted all-	powder
purpose flour	1½ tsp. salt
2 c. cornmeal	1 tsp. baking soda
3 tbs. sugar	2 eggs
	1 c. buttermilk

Cook bacon until very crisp in heavy 10-inch skillet (skillet should have ovenproof handle); drain and reserve drippings; crumble bacon. Do not wash skillet. Heat oven to 375° F. Combine flour, cornmeal, sugar, baking powder, salt, and baking soda in bowl. Beat eggs in small bowl; stir in buttermilk and ¼ cup reserved drippings. Add liquid ingredients to dry ingredients all at once; add crumbled bacon. Beat well; pour into skillet. Bake 20 to 25 minutes or until golden brown. To serve cut into wedges while still warm. (Bread may also be baked in two well-greased 9-inch layer cake pans.)

SPOON BREAD

1 c. cornmeal	2 tbs. melted butter
2 tbs. all-purpose	or margarine
flour	2 eggs
1 tsp. salt	2 tsp. baking
2½ c. milk	powder

Combine cornmeal, flour, and salt in large bowl. Scald milk; stir slowly into cornmeal mixture; beat well to prevent lumping. Add butter or margarine and eggs; beat until smooth. Sprinkle baking powder over surface; beat in quickly. Pour into greased 1½-quart casserole. Bake at 350° F. for 30 to 35 minutes. Serve at once. Makes 6 servings.

GOLDEN JOHNNYCAKES

2½ c. cornmeal	2¼ c. milk
1 tsp. salt	1 egg, beaten

Combine cornmeal, salt, milk, and beaten egg in bowl; beat until blended. Drop by spoonfuls onto hot well-greased griddle. Fry until golden on bottom; turn and brown second side. Serve hot with melted butter or margarine and maple-blended syrup, if desired. Makes 10 to 12.

CORN STICKS

Melted butter or	4 tsp. baking
margarine	powder
⅔ c. sifted all-	1 tsp. salt
purpose flour	1 egg
1⅓ c. cornmeal	1 c. milk
1 tbs. sugar	3 tbs. melted butter
	or margarine

Heat oven to 425° F. Grease 3 corn-stick pans liberally with melted butter or margarine (If you have only one corn-stick pan, bake one batch; rebutter hot pan; fill with batter and bake. Repeat until all batter is used.); place in oven to heat while preparing batter. Combine flour, cornmeal, sugar, baking powder, and salt in bowl. Beat egg in small bowl; add milk and 3 tablespoons melted butter or margarine. Add liquid ingredients to dry ingredients; blend just until dry ingredients are moistened. Do not overbeat. Fill hot corn-stick pans almost full. Bake about 8 minutes; remove pan from oven, turn upside down; tap pan sharply; sticks will fall out. (Batter may be baked in well-greased 8x8x2-inch pan. Bake in 425° F. oven for 12 minutes.) Makes 21 sticks.

HUSH PUPPIES

2 c. cornmeal	1¼ c. milk
2 tsp. baking	½ c. chopped onion
powder	(1 medium)
1 tsp. salt	Fat or pure
1 egg	vegetable oil

Combine cornmeal, baking powder, and salt in bowl. Add egg and milk; beat until smooth; stir in onion. Heat fat or oil in skillet (it should be at least 1 inch deep) to 375° F. Drop batter by spoonfuls into fat; fry until golden brown on both sides. Drain on paper towels. Makes about 20.

PANCAKES AND WAFFLES

Pancakes are much closer to man's original bread than our baked loaves. It was on hot stones set before the hearth fire that simple "ash cakes" of ground cereal and liquid were baked in the days of the cavemen. Today's pancakes are a fluffy, tender, civilized version of this ancient bread, whether they are paper-thin *crepes* that appear at the dessert course, or light buttermilk pancakes served with bacon strips for breakfast.

PANCAKES

1 egg	2 tbs. sugar
1⅓ c. milk	2 tsp. baking
1½ c. sifted all-	powder
purpose flour	¾ tsp. salt
¼ c. melted butter,	
margarine, or	
pure vegetable oil	

Heat griddle; grease lightly. Beat egg; add remaining ingredients; blend until all flour is dampened and mixture is fairly smooth. Pour about ¼ cup batter for each pancake onto griddle. Cook until pancakes are puffed and full of unbroken bubbles; turn to brown other side. Keep hot in warm oven. Serve with butter and syrup. Makes about 12 5-inch pancakes.

Buttermilk Pancakes. Prepare Pancakes substituting buttermilk for milk. Use only 1 teaspoon baking powder; add ¾ teaspoon baking soda.

WAFFLES

2 c. sifted all-	3 eggs
purpose flour	2 c. milk
½ tsp. salt	¼ c. shortening,
4 tsp. baking	butter, or
powder	margarine

Preheat waffle iron. Sift flour, salt, and baking powder into large bowl. Beat eggs until foamy; blend in milk; add shortening. Add liquid ingredients to flour mixture; beat with rotary beater until smooth. Pour batter onto center of waffle iron. Batter should spread to within 1 inch from edge. Bake until steaming stops and waffle is golden brown. Loosen edge with fork; remove from iron. Serve hot with butter, syrup, confectioners' sugar, or ice cream. Makes about 8 waffles.

SOME SPECIAL TOPPINGS FOR PANCAKES AND WAFFLES

1. Blend soft butter or margarine with any of the following:
   > Grated orange rind
   > Well drained crushed pineapple
   > Crushed strawberries
   > Chopped candied ginger
2. Mix melted butter or margarine with any of the following:
   > Maple syrup or honey
   > Crumbled maple sugar
   > Orange juice and grenadine
3. Canned blueberries, seasoned with cinnamon, and thickened with a little cornstarch.

POPOVERS

One of the chief differences between popovers and other quick breads is that they are leavened by steam—no baking powder, no soda.

POPOVERS

1 c. sifted all-	1 c. milk
purpose flour	1 tbs. pure vege-
¾ tsp. salt	table oil
2 eggs, well beaten	

Heat oven to 425° F. Grease 9 6-ounce custard cups or 9 cups of popover pan. Sift flour and salt into mixing bowl. Combine eggs, milk, and oil. Add to flour; beat with rotary beater until well blended. Fill prepared pans half full. Bake 40 to 45 minutes or until golden brown. Remove from pans. Serve immediately.

YORKSHIRE PUDDING FOR ROAST BEEF

Spoon out ½ cup pan drippings from roast beef; pour into 8x8x2-inch pan. Increase oven heat to 425° F. Prepare Popover batter. Heat pan in oven for 2 minutes. Pour Popover batter into pan. Bake 20 minutes. Remove roast from oven; keep warm. Bake pudding 15 to 20 minutes longer. Cut into squares; serve hot with roast. Makes 6 to 8 servings.

DUMPLINGS

These fluffy morsels, so good with savory stews, are at their best steaming hot. Serve them immediately.

The chief difference between dumplings and other quick breads is that they are steamed rather than baked. The dough is dropped from a spoon directly into bubbling broth or other liquid.

DUMPLINGS

1⅓ c. sifted all-purpose flour	½ tsp. salt
2 tsp. baking powder	3 tbs. shortening
	⅔ c. milk

Sift flour, baking powder, and salt together. Cut in shortening with pastry blender. Add milk; stir just until dry ingredients are moistened. Drop by tablespoonfuls onto bubbling stew liquid. Lower heat. Cook uncovered, 10 minutes; cover; cook 10 minutes longer. Remove dumplings; keep warm; thicken liquid if desired. Serve dumplings with stew in casserole or arranged on serving platter. Makes 9 or 10 dumplings.

Flavor secret: Add ¼ cup chopped parsley to sifted flour mixture for tasty Parsley Dumplings.

FRITTERS

The basic batter for making fritters is much like that for making pancakes, but with less liquid and a larger proportion of eggs.

The *secret* of successful fritters is to have the batter of a consistency that will cling evenly to the fruit, vegetable, meat, or fish it covers.

FRITTER BATTER (thick)

1 c. sifted all-purpose flour	2 eggs
1 tsp. baking powder	¼ c. milk
1 tsp. salt	2 tsp. pure vegetable oil

Sift flour, baking powder, and salt into mixing bowl. Beat eggs well; beat in milk and oil. Combine liquid ingredients with dry ingredients; stir until all flour is moistened. Stir in one of the suggested foods below. Drop by tablespoonfuls into hot fat (375° F.). Fry until golden on both sides.

Corn Fritters. Stir 1 can (12 ounces) whole-kernel corn into fritter batter.

Shrimp Fritters. Stir 1 cup chopped, cooked shrimp into fritter batter.

Clam Fritters. Stir 2 cans (7½ ounces each) minced clams, drained, into fritter batter.

FRITTER BATTER (thin)

Prepare thick fritter batter, increasing milk to 1 cup and oil to 2 tablespoons. Dip shelled, deveined shrimp; pineapple slices; quartered bananas; or apple rings or slices into batter, using tongs or fork; let excess drip off. Fry as above.

FRENCH TOAST

This breakfast or dessert delicacy is known in France as *Pain Perdu*, meaning lost bread. Stale bread, "lost" because it could not be eaten, was "recovered" by the simple method of soaking it in egg and milk and then frying it. Good French toast should be puffy. The *secrets* are to have really stale bread, to let the bread soak in the egg-milk mixture until it is well soaked, and to brown it quickly in hot fat.

FRENCH TOAST

2 eggs, beaten	8 slices stale bread
¼ tsp. salt	2 tbs. butter or margarine
⅔ c. milk	

Combine eggs, salt, and milk in flat dish. Soak bread slices in mixture, turning if necessary to moisten both sides. Heat butter or margarine on griddle or in skillet; remove bread, draining slightly. Brown on both sides. Sprinkle with confectioners' sugar and serve with jam, jelly, or maple syrup. Makes 4 servings.

BREADS

PURI

(Indian Bread)

This unusual bread is unleavened and is fried rather than baked.

2¼ c. sifted all-	1 tsp. salt
purpose flour or	1 c. water
whole wheat flour	Pure vegetable oil

Sift flour and salt into bowl; stir in water to make a stiff dough. Turn out on well-floured board; knead as you knead bread dough, about 5 minutes or until dough is smooth and satiny. Pinch off small pieces of dough; let rest on board about 20 minutes. Roll each piece of dough paper-thin to about a 5-inch circle. Pour oil into skillet to a depth of 1 inch; heat to 390° F. Fry circles of dough, one or two at a time, until golden brown on one side; turn and brown other side. Dough will blister and bubble in fat. Drain well on paper towels. Serve warm. Makes about 2 dozen.

DOUGHNUTS

The origin of these favorite fried cakes is surrounded by many legends. One says that they came to us from the Dutch in early Colonial times. Another credits them to a playful Nauset Indian who shot an arrow through a fried cake his squaw was making. Frightened, she dropped the perforated patty into the kettle of hot fat. A Maine sea captain, Hanson Gregory, is also said to have invented the doughnut in 1847. He objected to the soggy center in his mother's fried cakes and suggested she "cut a hole in the middle where it doesn't cook."

The *secrets* of successful doughnuts:
· For easier cutting, roll dough out on a lightly floured board and chill before cutting. The doughnuts are easier to handle and will retain shape while frying.
· If you scoop up the doughnut with a broad spatula or turner and drop it into the hot fat top side down, your doughnuts will be rounder and puffier.
· Be sure fat has reached the specified temperature before adding doughnuts.
· Fry only a few at a time; do not crowd pan. Allow fat to come back to specified temperature before cooking another batch.

DEVIL'S FOOD DOUGHNUTS

2 sqs. unsweetened	3 sqs. unsweetened
chocolate	chocolate
1 tbs. shortening	3 tbs. butter or
2 eggs	margarine
1⅓ c. sugar	2 c. sifted
4 c. sifted all-	confectioners'
purpose flour	sugar
4 tsp. baking	4 to 5 tbs. boiling
powder	water
½ tsp. salt	¼ c. packaged
1 c. milk	grated coconut
Oil or shortening	
for frying	

Melt 2 squares chocolate with shortening over hot water; cool. Beat eggs and sugar until blended; beat in cooled chocolate mixture. Sift flour, baking powder, and salt; add alternately with milk to egg mixture. Roll out dough, ⅓ inch thick, on floured board; cut with floured doughnut cutter. Add enough oil or shortening to skillet or deep, heavy saucepan to have fat 1½ inches deep when heated. Heat to 375° F. Fry about 2 minutes or until golden brown on one side; turn; fry 2 minutes longer to brown other side. Drain on absorbent paper. May be served plain, sugared, or glazed. FOR GLAZE: Melt 3 squares chocolate with butter or margarine over hot water. Stir in confectioners' sugar and enough boiling water to make a thin glaze. Dip doughnuts into glaze; place on wire rack; sprinkle with coconut. Makes 20 doughnuts.

HONEY-NUT DIPS

3 eggs	½ tsp. ground
1 c. brown sugar,	cinnamon
firmly packed	Oil or shortening
½ c. dairy sour	for frying
cream	1 c. honey
3¼ c. sifted all-	1 c. brown sugar,
purpose flour	firmly packed
2 tsp. baking	1 c. finely chopped
powder	nuts
1 tsp. baking soda	

Beat eggs; beat in 1 cup brown sugar and sour cream. Sift flour, baking powder, baking soda, and cinnamon together; add to egg mixture; stir well to blend; chill 1 hour. Roll out chilled dough, 1/3 inch thick, on floured board; cut with floured doughnut cutter. Add enough oil or shortening to large skillet or deep, heavy saucepan to have fat 1½ inches deep when heated. Heat to 375°F. Fry about 2 minutes or until golden brown on one side; turn; fry 2 minutes longer to brown other side. Drain on absorbent paper. Combine honey and 1 cup brown sugar in saucepan; bring to boiling; boil 1 minute. Brush doughnuts with syrup or dip into syrup, allowing excess to run off. Dip each doughnut immediately into nuts; place on wire rack to cool until coating is firm. Makes 24 doughnuts.

OLD-FASHIONED CRULLERS

2 tbs. milk	2½ c. sifted all-
1 c. boiling water	purpose flour
½ pkg. (4 servings)	4 tsp. baking
instant mashed	powder
potatoes	1 tsp. ground mace
3 eggs	Oil or shortening
1 c. sugar	for frying
4 tbs. soft	Cinnamon-sugar
shortening	mix
1 tsp. salt	

Add milk to boiling water; blend in mashed-potato mix; cool slightly. Beat eggs, sugar, and shortening together; stir in potatoes; beat until blended. Sift flour, baking powder, salt, and mace together; blend into egg mixture. until it is ¼ inch thick and 6 inches wide. Cut into ½ inch-wide strips. Form strips into knots or twists. Add enough oil or shortening to skillet or deep, heavy saucepan to have fat 1½ inches deep when heated. Heat to 375° F. Fry about 2 minutes or until golden brown on one side; turn; fry 2 minutes longer to brown other side. Drain on absorbent paper. Place cinnamon-sugar mix in paper bag; drop in crullers a few at a time; shake until well coated. Makes 24 crullers.

CHOCOLATE NUT CHIPPERS

2 eggs	⅔ c. milk
½ c. sugar	1 tsp. vanilla
3 tbs. soft	½ c. semi-sweet
shortening	chocolate pieces
2½ c. sifted all-	¼ c. chopped nuts
purpose flour	Oil or shortening
2½ tsp. baking	for frying
powder	Confectioners'
½ tsp. salt	sugar

Beat eggs; add sugar and shortening; beat until blended. Sift flour, baking powder, and salt together; add alternately with milk to egg mixture; beat well after each addition. Stir in vanilla, chocolate pieces, and nuts. Add enough oil or shortening to skillet or deep, heavy saucepan to have fat 1½ inches deep when heated. Heat to 375° F. Drop dough by rounded teaspoonfuls into hot fat. Fry about 2 minutes or until golden brown on one side; turn; fry 2 minutes longer to brown other side. Drain on absorbent paper. When cool, sprinkle with confectioners' sugar. Makes 3 dozen.

SPICE PUFFS

2¼ c. sifted all-	½ tsp. ground
purpose flour	cinnamon
⅓ c. sugar	¾ c. milk
3 tsp. baking	¼ c. pure vegetable
powder	oil
½ tsp. salt	1 egg
½ tsp. ground mace	Oil or shortening
	for frying

Combine flour, sugar, baking powder, salt, mace, and cinnamon in large bowl. Combine milk, oil, and egg in small bowl; beat lightly with fork until blended; pour into dry ingredients. Stir until well blended. Add enough oil or shortening to skillet or deep, heavy saucepan to have fat 1½ inches deep when heated. Heat to 375° F. Drop dough by scant teaspoonfuls into hot fat; don't crowd pan. Fry about 2 minutes or until golden brown on one side; turn; fry 2 minutes longer to brown other side. Don't make puffs too big or they will not cook in center. Scoop puffs from fat with slotted spoon; drain on paper towels. Serve plain or while still warm, tossed in paper bag with 1 cup sugar mixed with 1 teaspoon cinnamon. Makes about 3 dozen.

ORANGE-BUTTERMILK DOUGHNUTS

2 eggs	1 tsp. baking soda
1 c. sugar	½ tsp. salt
3 tbs. soft shortening	1 c. buttermilk Oil or shortening
1 tbs. grated orange rind	for frying
4¼ c. sifted all-purpose flour	2 c. confectioners' sugar
2 tsp. baking powder	2 to 3 tbs. orange juice

Beat eggs, sugar, and shortening together until blended; stir in orange rind. Sift flour, baking powder, baking soda, and salt together; add alternately with buttermilk to egg mixture; chill 1 hour. Roll out dough ⅓ inch thick, on floured board; cut with floured doughnut cutter. Add enough oil or shortening to skillet or deep, heavy saucepan to have fat 1½ inches deep when heated. Heat to 375° F. Fry about 2 minutes or until golden brown on one side; turn; fry 2 minutes longer to brown other side. Drain on absorbent paper; cool. FOR GLAZE: combine confectioners' sugar with enough orange juice to make thin glaze. Place doughnuts on wire rack; spoon glaze over each, or dip doughnuts; drain on wire rack. Sprinkle with confectioners' sugar, if desired. Makes 28 doughnuts.

When transferring doughnuts to hot fat, use a slotted pancake turner; dip turner; dip turner in hot fat each time so doughnut will slide off turner and into fat.

COFFEE CAKES AND TEA BREADS

Closest relatives to muffins in the quick-bread family are the sweetened nut-fruit breads and the spicy coffee cakes. They may be baked in loaf pans or square cake pans. Wonderful for breakfast, for between-meal snacks, for serving to the ladies at afternoon coffee or tea, or as a simple dessert for the family.

DATE-NUT COFFEE CAKE

2¼ c. sifted all-purpose flour	1 c. finely cut dates
1 c. sugar	½ c. sugar
1½ tsp. baking powder	1 tsp. ground cinnamon
½ tsp. baking soda	½ c. sliced, blanched
1 egg	almonds
1 c. buttermilk	¼ c. butter or margarine, melted
½ c. butter or margarine, melted and cooled	and cooled

Heat oven to 350° F. Grease and flour 11x7x2-inch or 9x9x2-inch pan. Sift flour, 1 cup sugar, baking powder, and baking soda into mixing bowl. Beat egg slightly; blend in buttermilk and ½ cup butter or margarine; stir into dry ingredients until well blended. Stir in dates; pour into prepared pan. Combine ½ cup sugar, cinnamon, and almonds; sprinkle over batter. Drizzle ¼ cup butter or margarine evenly over topping. Bake 35 to 40 minutes or until cake tester inserted in center comes out clean. Cool in pan 10 minutes; remove from pan; cool completely on wire rack. When cool, sprinkle with confectioners' sugar, if desired. Makes 9 to 12 servings.

PINEAPPLE-CHERRY SQUARE

3 tbs. soft butter or margarine	¾ c. sugar
3 tbs. honey	⅓ c. shortening
⅔ c. drained crushed pineapple	2 eggs
6 maraschino cherries, slivered	2¼ c. sifted all-purpose flour
¼ c. flaked coconut	2 tsp. baking powder
	½ tsp. salt
	¾ c. milk

Heat oven to 350° F. Grease and flour 9x9x2-inch pan. Combine butter or margarine, honey, pineapple, cherries, and coconut; reserve. Beat sugar, shortening, and eggs together until light and fluffy. Sift flour, baking powder, and salt together; add alternately with milk to egg mixture, beating until smooth after each addition. Turn into prepared pan;

spread reserved coconut mixture over batter. Bake 35 to 40 minutes or until cake tester inserted in center comes out clean. Cool in pan 10 minutes; remove from pan. Cool completely on wire rack. When cool, drizzle with Easy Confectioners' Sugar Glaze (*page 456*).

PRALINE BRUNCH CAKE

⅓ c. butter or margarine	½ c. shortening
⅓ c. brown sugar, firmly packed	¾ c. sugar
	1 egg
⅓ c. apricot or pineapple preserves	2 c. sifted all-purpose flour
	3 tsp. baking powder
½ c. chopped nuts	½ tsp. salt
½ c. packaged grated coconut	¾ c. milk

Heat oven to 350° F. Grease and flour 9x9x2-inch pan. Combine butter or margarine, brown sugar, preserves, nuts, and coconut; reserve. Beat shortening, sugar, and egg together until fluffy and light. Sift dry ingredients together; add alternately with milk to creamed mixture, beating until well blended. Spoon half the batter into prepared pan. Spoon half the brown sugar mixture evenly over batter; cover with remaining batter. Bake 35 to 40 minutes or until cake tester inserted in center comes out clean. Remove from oven. Carefully spread remaining brown sugar mixture over top of hot cake. Place under broiler 4 to 5 inches from heat; broil until topping bubbles and is nicely browned. Watch carefully to prevent burning. Cut into squares and serve warm. Makes 9 servings.

LEMON CRUNCH COFFEE CAKE

1⅔ c. sifted all-purpose flour	½ c. milk
2 tsp. baking powder	¼ c. brown sugar, firmly packed
½ tsp. salt	¼ c. flour
½ tsp. ground mace	2 tbs. butter or margarine
¼ c. shortening	½ tsp. grated lemon rind
⅔ c. sugar	1 tsp. lemon juice
1 egg	

Heat oven to 350° F. Grease and flour 9x9x2-inch pan. Sift 1⅔ cups flour, baking powder, salt, and mace together. Beat shortening, sugar, and egg at medium speed on mixer for 3 minutes or vigorously by hand. Add sifted dry ingredients alternately with milk, beginning and ending with flour mixture. Spread in prepared pan. Combine brown sugar, ¼ cup flour, butter or margarine, and lemon rind and juice; mix well. Sprinkle evenly over batter. Bake 40 to 45 minutes or until cake tester inserted in center comes out clean. Cut into squares and serve warm. Makes 9 servings.

APRICOT-DATE BREAD

1½ c. sifted all-purpose flour	1 tbs. grated orange rind
2 tsp. baking powder	2 tbs. melted shortening
¼ tsp. baking soda	½ c. finely diced dried apricots
½ tsp. salt	
½ c. sugar	½ c. chopped, pitted dates
¾ c. milk	
1 egg, beaten	½ c. coarsely chopped walnuts

Heat oven to 375° F. Grease and flour 9x5x3-inch loaf pan. Sift 1 cup flour, baking powder, soda, salt, and sugar in mixing bowl. Blend milk, egg, orange rind, and shortening; stir into flour mixture. Stir fruits and nuts into remaining ½ cup flour; toss to coat well; add to batter; mix well. Pour into loaf pan. Bake 50 minutes or until cake tester inserted in center comes out clean. Remove at once from pan; cool completely on wire rack.

Apricot-Date Muffins. Prepare batter as above. Half fill 12 greased 2½-inch muffin-pan cups. Bake 15 to 20 minutes or until muffins are golden brown.

When sprinkling coffee cakes with confectioners' sugar, place a fancy paper doily on top of cake. Sugar will sift through doily pattern onto top of cake in a pretty decoration.

BANANA BREAD

2 c. sifted all- purpose flour	½ c. shortening
2¾ tsp. baking powder	2 eggs
½ tsp. salt	2 to 3 medium-size bananas
¾ c. sugar	½ c. coarsely chopped nuts

Heat oven to 350° F. Grease and flour 9x5x3-inch loaf pan. Sift flour, baking powder, and salt together. Beat sugar, shortening, and eggs 3 minutes at medium speed on mixer or vigorously by hand. Mash bananas. Add sifted dry ingredients alternately with bananas, beginning and ending with flour mixture. Blend well after each addition. Stir in nuts. Turn into loaf pan. Bake 60 to 70 minutes or until cake tester inserted in center comes out clean. Cool 15 minutes in pan. Remove from pan. Cool completely on wire rack. Wrap in aluminum foil or transparent plastic wrap; store overnight at room temperature before slicing to mellow flavor.

CRANBERRY BREAD

3 c. sifted all- purpose flour	2 eggs
3 tsp. baking powder	1¼ c. milk
¾ tsp. baking soda	1 tbs. grated orange rind
1 tsp. salt	½ c. chopped walnuts or pecans
1 c. sugar	1 c. chopped fresh cranberries
½ c. shortening	

Heat oven to 350° F. Grease and flour 9x5x3-inch loaf pan. Sift flour, baking powder, soda, salt, and sugar together. Cut in shortening until mixture resembles cornmeal. Combine eggs and milk; add orange rind. Add liquid to dry ingredients, mixing until just dampened. Stir in nuts and cranberries. Turn into loaf pan. Bake 1 hour or until cake tester inserted in center comes out clean. Remove from pan. Cool. Wrap in aluminum foil or transparent plastic wrap, store overnight for easy slicing.

DATE WALNUT LOAF

2 tsp. grated orange rind	2 eggs
¼ c. orange juice	3 c. sifted all- purpose flour
1¾ c. boiling water	1½ tsp. baking soda
2 c. pitted dates, cut up	½ tsp. salt
2 tbs. shortening	1½ c. chopped walnuts
¾ c. brown sugar, firmly packed	

Heat oven to 350° F. Grease and flour 9x5x3-inch loaf pan. Grate orange rind; reserve. Pour orange juice and boiling water over dates; let stand until cool. Beat shortening, sugar, and eggs together until well blended; add to cooled date mixture. Sift flour, baking soda, and salt together; blend into date mixture. Stir in nuts and reserved orange rind. Pour into prepared pan. Bake 1 hour and 15 minutes, or until cake tester inserted in center comes out clean. Remove from pan; cool completely on wire rack.

IRISH SODA BREAD

Ireland is famous for this bread. It is baked in almost every home, and many say it is one of the finest breads to be found anywhere.

4 c. sifted all- purpose flour	1¾ c. buttermilk
1 tbs. sugar	1 c. raisins
1 tsp. salt	2 tbs. caraway seeds
1½ tsp. baking soda	1 tbs. melted butter or margarine
1 tsp. baking powder	

Heat oven to 350° F. Sift flour, sugar, salt, baking soda, and baking powder together into large mixing bowl. Add buttermilk; stir until all dry ingredients are moistened. Stir in raisins and caraway seeds. Turn dough out onto floured board; knead 10 times. Form dough into round ball; place on greased cookie sheet. With sharp knife, cut shallow cross on top of dough. Bake 50 to 60 minutes or until bread is golden brown. Remove from oven; place on wire rack. Brush top of loaf with melted butter or margarine. Cool.

Made with Biscuit Mix

A biscuit mix on your pantry shelf can be a quick and easy starter for tasty breads and coffee cakes.

CRISPY ONION SQUARES

1½ c. chopped onion
2 tbs. melted butter or margarine
1 egg, slightly beaten
¾ c. dairy sour cream

¼ tsp. salt
Dash of pepper
1 c. milk (about)
3 c. packaged biscuit mix
1 c. crushed potato chips

Heat oven to 450° F. Grease 9x9x2-inch pan. Sauté onion in butter or margarine about 5 minutes or until golden; remove from heat. Combine egg and sour cream in small bowl; mix well; stir in sautéed onion, salt, and pepper. Add milk to biscuit mix in large bowl, stirring with fork until dough is formed. Pat dough into pan; spread sour-cream mixture over top; sprinkle with potato chips. Bake 20 minutes. Cut into squares and serve hot. Makes 9 servings.

QUICK-AND-EASY SCONES

2½ c. packaged biscuit mix
2 tbs. sugar
⅓ c. shortening
⅓ c. milk

2 eggs, slightly beaten
Milk
2 tbs. sugar

Heat oven to 450° F. Combine biscuit mix and sugar in bowl. Cut in shortening. Add ⅓ cup milk and eggs; mix well. Turn out onto floured board; roll or pat into a 9x9x½-inch square. Cut into nine 3-inch squares; cut each square into 2 triangles. Place on greased baking sheet; brush with milk; sprinkle with sugar. Bake 10 to 15 minutes or until golden brown. Serve with jam or jelly. Makes 18 scones.

VELVET CRUNCH BREAKFAST CAKE

1½ c. packaged biscuit mix
¾ c. sugar
2 tbs. shortening
1 tsp. vanilla
1 egg
¾ c. milk

⅓ c. soft butter or margarine
⅔ c. brown sugar, firmly packed
¼ c. heavy cream
½ tsp. vanilla
⅓ c. chopped nuts
⅔ c. flaked coconut

Heat oven to 350° F. Grease and flour 8x8x2-inch pan. Combine biscuit mix, sugar, shortening, 1 teaspoon vanilla, egg, and ½ cup milk in bowl. Beat 1 minute at medium speed on mixer or vigorously by hand. Stir in remaining milk; beat 1 minute. Turn into pan. Bake 35 minutes or until cake tester inserted in center comes out clean. While cake bakes, mix soft butter or margarine, brown sugar, cream, ½ teaspoon vanilla, nuts, and coconut. Spread on warm cake. Broil 3 to 4 inches from heat until bubbly. Cut into squares. Makes 9 servings.

SOUR CREAM COFFEE CAKE

¼ c. shortening
¼ c. sugar
1 egg
1 tsp. vanilla
½ tsp. baking soda
1¾ c. packaged biscuit mix
1 c. dairy sour cream
½ c. brown sugar, firmly packed

½ c. packaged biscuit mix
¼ tsp. ground nutmeg
¼ tsp. ground cinnamon
¼ c. butter or margarine
¼ c. chopped nuts

Heat oven to 375° F. Grease 8x8x2-inch pan. Beat shortening, sugar, eggs, and vanilla 3 minutes at medium speed on mixer or vigorously by hand. Mix baking soda and 1¾ cups biscuit mix together; add alternately with sour cream to shortening mixture. FOR TOPPING: combine brown sugar, ½ cup biscuit mix, nutmeg, cinnamon, butter or margarine, and nuts. Spoon half the batter into prepared pan; sprinkle with half the brown sugar mixture. Cover with remaining batter and sprinkle with remaining brown sugar mixture. Bake 30 to 35 minutes or until cake tester inserted in center comes out clean. Serve warm. Makes 9 servings.

Made with Refrigerated Biscuits and Rolls

Quick breads are quick and easy, but even quicker and easier, of course, are those that come in refrigerated packages ready to place on cookie sheets and pop into the oven.

The following recipes, made with these new short-cuts, are all treasures.

BREAD STICKS

1 pkg. refrigerated
   biscuits
3 tbs. melted butter
   or margarine

1 tbs. sesame or
   caraway seeds

Cut each biscuit in half; roll each half into pencil-thin stick; place on cookie sheet. Brush with butter or margarine; sprinkle with sesame or caraway seeds. Bake at 400° F. for 5 to 8 minutes or until golden. Makes 20 to 24.

PINWHEEL COFFEE CAKE

2 pkgs. refrigerated
   crescent rolls
2 tbs. melted butter
   or margarine
¼ c. granulated
   sugar
½ tsp. ground
   cinnamon

Red jelly, cherry
   preserves, or
   cranberry-orange
   relish
½ c. confectioners'
   sugar
1 tbs. hot milk

Heat oven to 375° F. Separate rolls. Spread each roll with butter or margarine; sprinkle with mixture of granulated sugar and cinnamon. Roll up as directed on package. Arrange 10 rolls in a circle on lightly greased

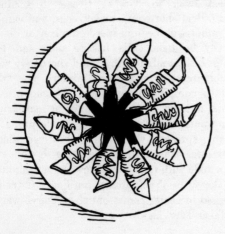

cookie sheet. Arrange remaining 6 rolls on top. Bake 15 minutes or until well browned. Cover tips of rolls with foil if they brown before center of rolls. Spoon jelly, preserves, or relish in center of coffee cake, letting some run between rolls. Combine confectioners' sugar and milk. Drizzle glaze over coffee cake. Serve warm. Makes 8 servings.

CRISPY CHIP BISCUITS

1 pkg. refrigerated
   biscuits
1 tbs. soft butter or
   margarine or 1
   slightly beaten
   egg white

3 tbs. crushed corn
   chips or potato
   chips

Heat oven to 400° F. Separate biscuits. Spread tops with butter or margarine or egg white; place on ungreased cookie sheet. Sprinkle biscuits with crushed chips. Bake 12 to 14 minutes or until browned. Makes 10 to 12.

When measuring molasses, honey, or other sticky liquid, first grease measuring cup or spoon very lightly. Measurement will be accurate and liquid will pour easily.

FRUIT ROLL-UPS

1 pkg. refrigerated
   crescent rolls
1 tbs. melted butter
   or margarine
2 tbs. granulated
   sugar
¼ tsp. ground
   cinnamon
   or mace

8 canned pineapple
   spears or 8 spears
   of banana
⅓ c. confectioners'
   sugar
1 tbs. hot milk

Heat oven to 375° F. Separate rolls; spread each with butter or margarine. Mix granulated sugar and spice; sprinkle on rolls. Place a spear of pineapple or banana on each roll. Roll up; place on ungreased cookie sheet. Bake 15 minutes or until browned. Combine confectioners' sugar and milk; drizzle over hot rolls; serve at once. Makes 8.

HERBED CRESCENTS

2 tbs. melted butter   1 pkg. refrigerated
   or margarine   crescent rolls
¾ tsp. mixed salad
   herbs

Combine butter or margarine and herbs.
Brush on rolls. Shape and bake according
to package directions. Make 8.

QUICK ONION ROLLS

1½ tbs. instant   2 tbs. melted butter
   minced onion   or margarine
1½ tbs. water   1 pkg. refrigerated
                 biscuits

Combine onion and water; let stand for 5
minutes. Add melted butter or margarine;
brush over tops of biscuits. Bake according to
package directions. Makes 10 to 12.

Chapter Nine

Yeast Breads

Perhaps the most soul-satisfying accomplishment a homemaker can master is making homemade bread. Your grandmother probably baked bread every Saturday morning. Maybe your mother did. You'll want to, too, when that heavenly fragrance starts wafting its way through the kitchen . . . when you see the kids gobbling up those still-warm, butter-laden slices . . . and when the whole loaf suddenly disappears. We're all for reviving the age-old art of baking with yeast.

The secret of success in yeast baking is temperature. Yeast needs warmth all the time and temperature is important at every step —the temperature of the water for dissolving yeast, the temperature at which the dough rises, and the baking temperature. It is very important, too, to understand the ingredients and the part each plays in the making of yeast breads.

Flour

Wheat flour is used because it contains that special substance called gluten, so essential to bread making. When flour is kneaded with the liquid, the gluten stretches to form an elasticity that holds the bubbles of gas produced by the yeast. For best results we recommend using regular, sifted all-purpose flour. When flours other than white are used, such as rye, whole wheat, etc., it is best to use them in combination with all-purpose flour with its fine gluten content. In breads calling for a range of flour, add only enough to handle the dough easily. Too much flour will make a heavy dough. Too little flour will make a soft dough, coarser in texture, and more likely to collapse during rising or baking.

Liquid

This may be milk, reconstituted nonfat dry milk, evaporated milk, water, or buttermilk.

Yeast

Yeast makes dough rise and gives bread its porous texture. It is a small plant that "grows" and multiplies under proper conditions. The ideal temperature is 85° F. It feeds on the sugar and starch of the dough and forms gas which makes the dough "rise." It also gives yeast breads that tantalizing aroma and delicious flavor. Yeast is available in two forms. *Compressed yeast* comes in cake form, is perishable and must be refrigerated immediately. It contains a live plant and starts to grow as soon as food, moisture, warmth, and air are present. *Active dry yeast* is granulated and stays fresh for several months without refrigeration. Be sure to check the expiration date on the package. To dissolve either compressed or active dry yeast, crumble or sprinkle it into warm water (105° to 115° F.) in a warm bowl. Let it settle for a few seconds, then stir to dissolve.

Other Ingredients

Salt is essential to give flavor to bread and to control the action of the yeast. *Sugar* provides food for the yeast. It, too, adds flavor and is partly responsible for the nice golden brown crust. *Shortening* improves the flavor, keeping quality, and makes the bread more tender. It also helps contribute to a browner crust. *Eggs* give yeast breads delicate texture and add flavor, color, and richness.

Methods of Making Yeast Breads

Straight-dough method. All the ingredients are mixed together, then the dough is kneaded and allowed to rise.

Sponge method. Part of the flour is combined with the dissolved yeast and the liquid to make a thick batter or sponge. This is allowed to rise until bubbly and spongelike. The remaining flour and other ingredients are then added, and the dough is kneaded and allowed to rise.

Batter method. This is a quick, easy way to bake with yeast. It is a flour-liquid-yeast mixture that has a higher proportion of liquid to flour. It is too soft to be kneaded. Kneading and shaping steps are eliminated and there is only one rising. The rising may take place either in the mixing bowl, baking dish, or bread pan. You can use a standard electric mixer at low to medium speed to blend in half the flour. The rest of the flour may have to be blended by hand if your mixer does not have a special dough-blending attachment.

How to Recognize Good Breads and Rolls

Appearance and Crust: A loaf should have an evenly rounded top and an attractive shape with no bulges, humps, or cracks. Between the sides and top there should be a "break" which should be even and have a well-shredded look. Rolls should be attractively shaped, plump, and all the same size. Crust should be crisp, tender, evenly golden brown, and a bit lighter in color on the sides than on the top.

Interior Color: Interior color will vary with the kind of flour, liquid, sweetening, and other ingredients used. However, it should be uniform without light or dark streaks.

Texture: When fingers are rubbed gently over the cut bread, the interior should feel soft and fine with no crumbliness.

Crumb: The crumb should have many little holes, all about the same size. It should be soft and tender to the touch, moist, and tear or break easily. If the bread contains fruits or nuts, they should be distributed evenly throughout.

Aroma: Freshly baked bread has a deliciously sweet, yeasty fragrance which is most striking when bread is hot, but should be noticeable when it's cold, too.

Flavor: The bread should taste good, whether served warm or cold.

Tips on Baking and Storing Yeast Breads

Baking: Always bake bread and rolls in a pre-heated oven. For two loaves or 2 pans of rolls, place on center shelf in oven with 2 inches between pans to allow for good heat circulation. For more than 2 pans, stagger on 2 shelves and separate for heat circulation.

To test for doneness: Tap the loaf with your knuckles. If it sounds hollow, looks well browned, and shrinks slightly from the sides of the pan it is baked through. Remove from pan immediately to prevent a soggy crust. Place loaves on wire rack. Space them to allow good air circulation but have them free from draft to prevent cracking of the crust. If you want a soft crust, brush the loaves with soft butter or margarine after taking them from the pans. For a crisp crust, do not brush loaves.

To store: Be sure bread is thoroughly cooled before storing. Wrap in wax paper, aluminum foil, or transparent plastic wrap.

BREAD

OLD-FASHIONED HOMEMADE BREAD

1⅔ c. milk	2 pkgs. active dry
3 tbs. sugar	yeast or 2 cakes
1 tbs. salt	compressed yeast
¼ c. shortening	6½ to 7 c. sifted all-
¾ c. warm water	purpose flour
(105° to 115° F.)	

Combine milk, sugar, salt, and shortening in saucepan. Heat until bubbles appear around the edge and shortening is melted; cool to lukewarm. Measure warm water into large mixing bowl; sprinkle or crumble in yeast; stir to dissolve. Add lukewarm milk mixture. Add 3 cups flour; beat until smooth. Add enough remaining flour to make dough easy to handle. Turn out onto floured board. Knead about 5 minutes or until dough is smooth and elastic. Put dough into large, greased bowl; turn over to bring greased side up; cover with damp towel. Let rise in warm place (85° F.), free from draft, about 1 to 1½ hours or until doubled in bulk. Punch dough down; let rise about 30 minutes or until almost double. Grease two 9x5x3-inch loaf pans. Punch dough down; turn out onto board; knead to distribute air bubbles; divide in half. Shape each half into loaf; place in pans; cover. Let rise about 1 hour or until doubled in bulk. Bake at 425° F. for 25 to 30 minutes. Makes 2 loaves. *Even though we urge you to cool bread before eating—we'll wager it will disappear while still warm. It's yummy with butter and jam!*

How to Make Bread

1. Measure warm water into large, warm bowl. Sprinkle or crumble in yeast; stir to dissolve. Add milk as recipe directs.

2. Stir in half the flour; beat until smooth. Mix in enough of the remaining flour until dough pulls away from sides of bowl. It will be sticky.

3. Sprinkle board with some of the remaining measured, sifted flour. Turn dough out onto board.

4. Work flour from board into dough with a spatula, until dough is stiff enough to handle.

5. Dust your hands lightly with flour. Press out dough so it is flat. Pick up the edge of dough farthest from you with fingers of both hands and fold over on top of edge nearest you. Sprinkle flour on board as needed, a little at a time.

6. Push dough away from you with the heels of your hands, using a rocking motion. Press dough lightly as you push. Turn dough one quarter turn around on board. Repeat folding, pushing, and turning until dough is smooth and elastic.

7. Dough is kneaded enough when it looks full and rounded, smooth and elastic. You will see tiny bubbles just under the surface. Dough will not stick to your hands or the board.

8. Place ball of dough in a large, greased bowl. Turn dough over to bring greased side on top. This greases the top lightly so it will stay soft and stretch easily as the dough rises. Cover bowl with a clean towel and let it rise in a warm place (85° F.), free from draft, until doubled in bulk.

9. To test for doubled in bulk: Press the tips of two fingers quickly and lightly about ½ inch into dough. If indentation remains, dough is double. If dent fills in at once, let the dough rise 10 to 15 minutes longer and test again.

10. Punch dough down when it is doubled. Push your fist into center of dough. Pull edges of dough from sides of bowl to the center. Turn ball of dough over.

11. Turn dough out onto lightly floured board. Round it into a ball. Cut in half with a sharp knife. Cover one half with towel while you shape the other half.

12. Flatten dough into a 12x8-inch rectangle. Press out air bubbles with knuckles, heel of hand, or fingertips. Fold in half lengthwise. Press out air again, working from center to edge. Bring ends to center. Overlap; seal by pressing down firmly with knuckles. Press out air. Keep dough 9 inches wide—the same measurement as the length of the bread pan.

COUNTRY-STYLE BUTTERMILK BREAD

2 c. buttermilk	2 pkgs. active dry
¼ c. sugar	yeast or 2 cakes
1 tbs. salt	compressed yeast
¼ c. shortening	½ tsp. baking soda
½ c. warm water	7 to 7½ c. sifted all-
(105° to 115° F.)	purpose flour
	Melted butter or
	margarine

Combine buttermilk, sugar, salt, and shortening in saucepan. Heat until bubbles appear around the edge and shortening is melted; cool to lukewarm. Measure warm water into large mixing bowl; sprinkle or crumble in yeast; stir to dissolve. Add lukewarm milk mixture. Add baking soda and 3 cups flour; beat until smooth. Add enough remaining flour to make a soft dough. Turn out onto floured board. Knead about 5 minutes or until dough is smooth and elastic. Put dough into large, greased bowl; turn over to bring greased side up; cover with damp towel. Let rise in a warm place (85° F.), free from draft, about 1½ hours or until doubled in bulk. Punch dough down; let rise about 30 minutes or until almost double. Grease two 9x5x3-inch loaf pans. Punch dough down; turn out onto board; knead to distribute air bubbles; divide in half. Shape each half into a loaf; place in pans. Brush tops with melted butter or margarine; cover. Let rise 45 to 50 minutes or until doubled in bulk. Bake at 425° F. for 25 to 30 minutes. Makes 2 loaves.

13. Roll dough from narrow end near you. Keep it as tight as you can, sealing after each roll. Pinch edge of finished roll to seal. Roll back and forth to tighten. Press ends with edge of hand to seal. Tuck ends under.

14. Place in greased 9x5x3-inch loaf pan, seam side down. Shape second half of dough. Cover with clean towel and let rise. Bake as recipe directs.

WHOLE WHEAT BREAD

1¾ c. milk	2 pkgs. active dry
1 tbs. sugar	yeast or 2 cakes
1 tbs. salt	compressed yeast
¼ c. honey	4 c. whole wheat
2 tbs. shortening	flour
½ c. warm water	2 to 2½ c. sifted all-
(105° to 115° F.)	purpose flour

Combine milk, sugar, salt, honey, and shortening in saucepan. Heat until bubbles appear around the edge and shortening is melted; cool to lukewarm. Measure warm water into large mixing bowl; sprinkle or crumble in yeast; stir to dissolve. Add lukewarm milk mixture. Stir in whole wheat flour. Add 2 cups all-purpose flour; work in well. Add enough remaining flour, if necessary, to make stiff dough. Turn out onto floured board. Knead about 5 minutes or until dough is smooth and elastic. Dough will not feel as smooth as doughs made with all white flour. Put dough into large greased bowl; turn over to bring greased side up; cover with damp towel. Let rise in warm place (85° F.), free from draft, about 1½ hours or until doubled in bulk. Punch dough down; let rise about 30 minutes or until almost double. Grease two 9x5x3-inch loaf pans. Punch dough down. Turn out onto board; knead to distribute air bubbles; divide in half. Shape each half into a loaf; place in pans; cover. Let rise 50 to 60 minutes or until doubled in bulk. Bake at 375° F. for 25 to 30 minutes. Makes 2 loaves.

CINNAMON RAISIN BREAD

1½ c. milk	2 eggs
¼ c. sugar	7 to 7½ c. sifted all-
1 tbs. salt	purpose flour
¼ c. shortening	1½ tsp. ground
½ c. warm water	cinnamon
(105° to 115° F.)	2 c. seedless raisins
2 pkgs. active dry	1 egg white
yeast or 2 cakes	2 tbs. water
compressed yeast	

Combine milk, sugar, salt, and shortening in saucepan. Heat until bubbles appear around the edge and shortening is melted; cool to lukewarm. Measure warm water into large mixing bowl; sprinkle or crumble in yeast; stir to dissolve. Add lukewarm milk mixture and eggs. Mix 4 cups flour and cinnamon; add to yeast mixture; beat until smooth. Add raisins and enough remaining flour to make soft dough. Turn out onto floured board. Knead about 5 minutes or until dough is smooth and elastic. Put dough into large, greased bowl; turn over to bring greased side up; cover with damp towel. Let rise in warm place (85° F.), free from draft, about 1½ hours or until doubled in bulk. Punch dough down; let rise about 30 minutes or until almost double. Grease two 9x5x3-inch loaf pans. Punch dough down; turn out onto board; knead to distribute air bubbles. Divide dough in half; divide each half into thirds. Shape each third into rope about 12 inches long. Braid 3 together; repeat with other 3. Place in pans; cover. Let rise 50 to 60 minutes or until doubled in bulk. Beat egg white slightly with water; brush on loaves. Bake at 375° F. for 30 to 35 minutes. Makes 2 loaves.

RYE BREAD

1 c. milk	3½ c. rye flour
¼ c. molasses	3½ to 4 c. sifted all-
3 tbs. shortening	purpose flour
2 tsp. salt	2 tbs. caraway seeds
1 c. warm water	Cornmeal
(105° to 115° F.)	1 egg white
2 pkgs. active dry	2 tbs. water
yeast or 2 cakes	
compressed yeast	

Combine milk, molasses, shortening, and salt in saucepan. Heat until bubbles appear around the edge and shortening is melted; cool to lukewarm. Measure warm water into large mixing bowl; sprinkle or crumble in yeast; stir to dissolve. Add lukewarm milk mixture. Stir in 2 cups rye flour, 2 cups all-purpose flour, and caraway seeds; beat until smooth. Mix in 1½ cups more rye flour and 1 cup more all-purpose flour to make a very firm dough. Turn out onto floured board; gradually knead in ½ to 1 cup more all-purpose flour. Continue to knead until dough is smooth and elastic. Put dough into large, greased bowl; turn over to bring greased side up; cover with damp towel. Let rise in warm place (85° F.), free from draft, about 1½ hours or until doubled in bulk. Punch dough down; let rise about 30 minutes or until almost double. Punch dough down; turn out onto board; knead to distribute air bubbles; divide in half. Shape each half into round or oval shape. Place loaves on opposite corners of large cookie sheet which has been greased and sprinkled with cornmeal. Make gash in tops ¼ inch deep. Let rise about 30 minutes or until doubled in bulk. Beat egg white and water just until blended; brush loaves. Bake at 375° F. for 20 minutes. Sprinkle tops with cornmeal or brush again with egg white mixture. Bake 10 to 15 minutes longer. Makes 2 loaves.

FRENCH BREAD

2 c. warm water (105° to 115° F.)	1 tbs. salt
1 pkg. active dry yeast or 1 cake compressed yeast	6 to 6½ c. sifted all-purpose flour
3 tbs. shortening	Cornmeal
	1 egg white
	2 tbs. water

Pour 2 cups warm water into large mixing bowl; sprinkle or crumble in yeast; stir to dissolve. Add shortening, salt, and 4 cups flour. Beat until smooth. Add enough remaining flour to form a stiff dough, mixing in with hands, if necessary. Turn out onto floured board. Knead about 5 minutes or until dough is smooth and elastic. Put dough into large, greased bowl; turn over to bring greased side up; cover with damp towel. Let rise in warm place (85° F.), free from draft, about 1½ hours or until doubled in bulk. Punch dough down; let rise about 30 minutes or until almost double. Punch dough down; turn out onto board; knead to distribute air bubbles; divide in half. Shape into 2 long loaves, tapering ends with hands. Place on cookie sheet which has been greased and sprinkled with cornmeal. Make several gashes in each loaf about ¼ inch deep. Do not cover; let rise about 1 hour or until doubled in bulk. Heat oven to 400° F. Place shallow pan of boiling water on bottom of oven. This will help to create steam for crispy crust. Beat egg white slightly with water; brush on loaves. Bake 20 minutes; brush again; bake 20 minutes longer or until glazed and brown. Cool. Makes 2 loaves.

CHEESE BREAD

1½ c. milk	2 pkgs. active dry yeast or 2 cakes compressed yeast
½ lb. Cheddar cheese, shredded (2 c.)	
	1 egg
2 tsp. salt	6½ to 7 c. sifted all-purpose flour
2 tbs. sugar	
2 tbs. shortening	1 egg yolk
½ c. warm water (105° to 115° F.)	2 tbs. water
	Poppy seeds

Combine milk, cheese, salt, sugar, and shortening in saucepan. Heat until bubbles appear around the edge and cheese and shortening are melted; cool to lukewarm. Measure warm water into large mixing bowl; sprinkle or crumble in yeast; stir to dissolve. Add lukewarm milk mixture and egg. Add 4 cups flour; beat until smooth. Add enough remaining flour to make soft dough. Turn out onto floured board. Knead about 5 minutes or until dough is smooth and elastic. Put dough into large greased bowl; turn over to bring greased side up; cover with damp towel. Let rise in warm place (85° F.), free from draft, about 1½ hours or until doubled in bulk. Punch dough down; let rise about 30 minutes or until almost double. Punch dough down; turn out onto board; knead to distribute air bubbles; divide in half. Shape each half into a 6x20-inch rectangle. Roll up as for a jelly roll starting with long side; seal tightly at each turn. Stretch out to about 24 inches. Coil around on greased cookie sheet, placing one coil on top of the other; tuck end in on top. Repeat with other half of dough. Cover. Let rise 40 to 50 minutes or until doubled in bulk. Beat egg yolk and water together; brush loaves with mixture; sprinkle with poppy seeds. Bake at 375° F. for 25 to 30 minutes. Makes 2 loaves.

ANADAMA CHEESE BREAD

Its name is said to have come from a New England fisherman whose wife, Anna, always served him cornmeal and molasses. He became so bored with this that he mixed it with flour and yeast and baked it, mumbling "Anna damn her."

2⅓ c. water	1 pkg. active dry
½ c. yellow	yeast or 1 cake
cornmeal	compressed yeast
2 tsp. salt	6½ to 7 c. sifted all-
½ c. honey	purpose flour
2 tbs. shortening	2 tbs. soft butter or
½ lb. Cheddar	margarine
cheese, shredded	2 tbs. paprika
(2 c.)	1 tbs. melted butter
½ c. warm water	or margarine
(105° to 115° F.)	Cornmeal

Combine water, ½ cup cornmeal, and salt in saucepan; cook until bubbly and thickened. Add honey, shortening, and cheese; cool to lukewarm. Measure warm water into large mixing bowl; sprinkle or crumble in yeast; stir to dissolve. Stir in lukewarm cornmeal mixture; add 4 cups flour; beat until blended. Add enough remaining flour to form a stiff dough that is easy to handle, mixing in with hands, if necessary. Turn out onto floured board. Knead about 5 minutes or until dough is smooth and elastic. Put dough into large, greased bowl; turn over to bring greased side up; cover with damp towel. Let rise in warm place (85° F.), free from draft, about 1 to 1½ hours or until doubled in bulk. Punch dough down; let rise about 30 minutes or until almost double. Grease two 9x5x3-inch loaf pans. Punch dough down; turn out onto board; knead to distribute air bubbles; divide in half. Roll one half dough into a 9x12-inch rectangle. Spread dough with 1 tablespoon soft butter or margarine; sprinkle with 1 tablespoon paprika. Roll up tightly as for jelly roll, starting with short end; seal each turn and pinch roll to seal. Place sealed side down in pan. Repeat with other half of dough. Brush top with melted butter or margarine; sprinkle with cornmeal. Cover. Let rise about 1 hour or until doubled in bulk. Bake at 350° F. for 45 to 55 minutes. Makes 2 loaves.

SAFFRON BREAD (Saffronsbrod)

¾ c. milk	3 eggs
½ tsp. saffron	5 to 5½ c. sifted al
½ c. sugar	purpose flour
1 tsp. salt	½ c. raisins
½ c. soft butter or	½ c. ground
margarine	almonds
¼ c. warm water	1 egg white, slight
(105° to 115° F.)	beaten
1 pkg. active dry	Slivered almonds
yeast or 1 cake	Sugar
compressed yeast	

Combine milk, saffron, sugar, salt, and butte or margarine in saucepan. Heat until bubble appear around the edge and shortening melted. Strain to remove saffron; cool lukewarm. Measure warm water into larg mixing bowl; sprinkle or crumble in yeast stir to dissolve. Add lukewarm milk mixtur and eggs. Add 2 cups of flour; beat unt smooth. Add raisins, ground almonds, an enough remaining flour to make soft dough Turn out onto floured board. Knead about minutes or until dough is smooth and elastic Put dough into large, greased bowl; turn ove to bring greased side up; cover with damp towel. Let rise in warm place (85° F.), fre from draft, about 1½ hours or until double in bulk. Punch dough down; turn out ont board; knead to distribute air bubbles. Divid two thirds of dough into 3 parts. Shape eac piece into rope 14 inches long; place o greased cookie sheet. Form into braid; pinch ends together; tuck under. Divide remaining third of dough into 3 parts; roll each into 10-inch strip. Braid strips together; pinch ends together; tuck under. Place small braid on top of large braid. Brush top and sides with egg white; sprinkle with slivered almonds and sugar. Let rise 35 minutes or until almos doubled in bulk. Bake at 350° F. for 30 to 40 minutes. Makes 1 braid.

SESAME EGG BRAID (Hallah)

1½ c. milk	2 pkgs. active dry yeast or 2 cakes compressed yeast
¼ c. sugar	3 eggs
1 tbs. salt	7 to 7½ c. sifted all-purpose flour
⅓ c. soft butter or margarine	1 egg yolk
½ c. warm water (105° to 115° F.)	1 tbs. water
	2 tbs. sesame seeds

Combine milk, sugar, salt and butter or margarine in saucepan. Heat until bubbles appear around the edge and shortening is melted; cool to lukewarm. Measure warm water into large mixing bowl; sprinkle or crumble in yeast; stir to dissolve. Add lukewarm milk mixture and eggs. Add 4 cups flour and beat until smooth. Add enough remaining flour to make dough easy to handle, mixing in with hands, if necessary. Turn out onto floured board. Knead about 5 minutes or until dough is smooth and elastic. Put dough into large, greased bowl; turn over to bring greased side up; cover with damp towel. Let rise in warm place (85° F.), free from draft, about 1 to 1½ hours or until doubled in bulk. Punch dough down; let rise about 30 minutes or until almost double. Punch dough down; turn out onto board; knead to distribute air bubbles; divide in half. Cut each half into 3 equal pieces; shape each piece into a rope about 15 inches long. Place 3 ropes on greased cookie sheet; form into braid, fastening securely at both ends. Repeat with second half of dough. Cover; let rise about 1 hour or until doubled in bulk. Mix egg yolk and water; brush tops and sides of braids; sprinkle with sesame seeds. Bake at 350° F. for 30 to 35 minutes. Makes 2 braids.

SALLY LUNN

¾ c. milk	1 pkg. active dry yeast or 1 cake compressed yeast
½ c. butter or margarine	3 eggs, slightly beaten
¼ c. sugar	4 c. sifted all-purpose flour
1 tsp. salt	
¼ c. warm water (105° to 115° F.)	

Combine milk, butter or margarine, sugar, and salt in saucepan. Heat until bubbles appear around the edge and shortening is melted; cool to lukewarm. Measure warm water into a large mixing bowl; sprinkle or crumble in yeast; stir to dissolve. Add lukewarm milk mixture and eggs. Add 3 cups of flour; beat until smooth. Stir in enough remaining flour to make soft dough. Beat until smooth and elastic (dough will begin to pull away from sides of bowl). Scrape down sides of bowl; cover with damp towel. Let rise in warm place (85° F.), free from draft, about 1 hour or until doubled in bulk. Stir dough down; beat until smooth. Spoon dough into greased Turk's head mold or 10-inch tube pan; smooth batter in pan. Cover; let rise about 40 minutes or until doubled in bulk. Bake at 325° F. for 45 minutes. Turn out of pan. Serve warm. Makes 1 cake.

RAISIN BATTER BREAD

½ c. milk	1 tsp. ground cinnamon
1 tbs. sugar	2 tsp. grated orange rind
1½ tsp. salt	3⅓ c. sifted all-purpose flour
¼ c. shortening	1 c. raisins
¾ c. warm water (105° to 115° F.)	Easy Confectioners' Sugar Glaze (*page 456*)
1 pkg. active dry yeast or 1 cake compressed yeast	
1 egg	

Combine milk, sugar, salt, and shortening in saucepan. Heat until bubbles appear around the edge and shortening is melted; cool to lukewarm. Measure warm water into large bowl; sprinkle or crumble in yeast; stir to dissolve. Add lukewarm milk mixture, egg, cinnamon, orange rind, and 2 cups flour. Beat 2 minutes at medium speed on mixer or 300 strokes by hand. Stir in remaining flour and raisins. Spoon batter into greased, 1½-quart casserole; cover with damp towel. Let rise in warm place (85° F.), free from draft, about 1 hour or until doubled in bulk. Bake at 350° F. for 40 to 50 minutes. Remove from casserole; cool on wire rack. Decorate with glaze. Makes 1 loaf.

ONION BATTER BREAD

1½ c. warm water (105° to 115° F.)	½ tsp. leaf oregano, crumbled
1 pkg. active dry yeast or 1 cake compressed yeast	3½ c. sifted all-purpose flour
1 tbs. instant minced onion	1 medium-size onion, peeled, sliced, and separated into rings
2 tbs. sugar	
2 tsp. seasoned salt	
2 tbs. shortening	2 tbs. melted butter or margarine

Measure warm water into large bowl of electric mixer. Sprinkle or crumble in yeast; stir to dissolve. Add instant minced onion, sugar, salt, shortening, oregano, and 2 cups of flour. Beat 2 minutes at medium speed on mixer or 300 strokes by hand. Stir in remaining flour. Let rise in warm place (85° F.), free from draft, about 1 hour or until doubled in bulk. Beat with spoon about 30 seconds. Spread into greased 9x5x3-inch loaf pan. Pat into shape with lightly floured hand. Let rise about 40 minutes or until batter is about ½ inch from top of pan. Dip onion rings into melted butter or margarine; place on top of loaf. Bake at 375° F. for 35 to 40 minutes. Makes 1 loaf.

OATMEAL BATTER BREAD

1⅔ c. boiling water	2 pkgs. active dry yeast or 2 cakes compressed yeast
1¼ c. quick-cooking rolled oats	
¼ c. shortening	2 eggs
½ c. molasses	6 to 6½ c. sifted all-purpose flour
1 tbs. salt	Melted butter or margarine
½ c. warm water (105° to 115° F.)	Quick-cooking rolled oats

Combine boiling water, 1¼ cups rolled oats, shortening, molasses, and salt in large mixing bowl; cool to lukewarm. Measure warm water into small bowl; sprinkle or crumble in yeast; stir to dissolve; stir into lukewarm oat mixture. Add eggs and 3 cups flour; beat until well blended. Mix in enough remaining flour to form a stiff dough that is easy to handle. Divide dough in half; form each half into a

smooth ball; place in greased 9 x 1½-inch layer cake pans. Let rise in warm place (85° F.), free from draft, about 1½ to 2 hours or until doubled in bulk. Brush top of dough with melted butter or margarine; sprinkle with rolled oats. Bake at 350° F. for 45 to 50 minutes. Makes 2 loaves.

ROLLS

BASIC ROLL DOUGH

1⅓ c. milk	2 pkgs. active dry yeast or 2 cakes compressed yeast
⅓ c. sugar	
1½ tsp. salt	
½ c. shortening	2 eggs
½ c. warm water (105° to 115° F.)	7 c. (about) sifted all-purpose flour

Combine milk, sugar, salt, and shortening in saucepan. Heat until bubbles appear around the edge; cool to lukewarm. Measure warm water into large mixing bowl; sprinkle or crumble in yeast; stir to dissolve. Add lukewarm milk mixture and eggs. Add 4 cups flour; beat until smooth. Add enough remaining flour to make a stiff dough. Turn out onto floured board. Knead about 5 minutes or until dough is smooth and elastic. Put dough in large, greased bowl; turn over to bring greased side up; cover with damp towel. Let rise in warm place (85° F.), free from draft, about 1½ hours or until doubled in bulk. Punch dough down; let rise about 30 minutes or until almost double. Punch dough down; turn out onto board; knead to distribute air bubbles. Divide and shape as desired. Cover; let rise about 20 minutes or until doubled in bulk. Bake at 400° F. for 15 to 20 minutes.

To Shape Rolls

Pan rolls: Divide dough into 3 equal pieces. Shape each piece into rope 12 inches long; cut into 12 equal pieces. Shape each piece into smooth ball. Place about ¼ inch apart in greased 9-inch layer-cake pans. Makes 3 dozen.

Knots: Divide dough into 3 equal pieces. Divide each piece into 6 equal pieces. Shape each into rope 6 inches long. Grasp one end; loop; ease other end through hole. Place 2 inches apart on greased cookie sheet. Makes 1½ dozen.

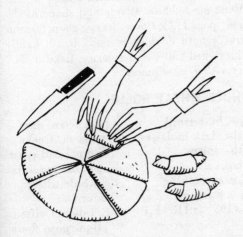

Crescents: Divide dough into 3 equal pieces. Roll out each piece to a 9-inch circle. Brush with melted butter or margarine. Cut into 8 wedges. Roll up tightly, beginning at wide end. Seal points firmly. Place about 2 inches apart on greased cookie sheets, with points underneath. Curve in crescent shapes. Makes 2 dozen.

Cloverleaf Rolls: Divide dough into 3 equal pieces. Shape each piece into rope 12 inches long; cut into 12 equal pieces. Form each piece into 3 small balls. Place 3 balls in each greased muffin-pan cup, brushing each with melted butter or margarine. Makes 3 dozen.

Fan-Tans: Roll dough out ⅛ inch thick to 9-inch-wide rectangle. Spread with soft butter or margarine. Cut into 6 strips 1½ inches wide. Stack strips evenly, one on top of the other. Cut into 1-inch pieces. Place, cut side down, in greased muffin-pan cups. Makes 1½ dozen.

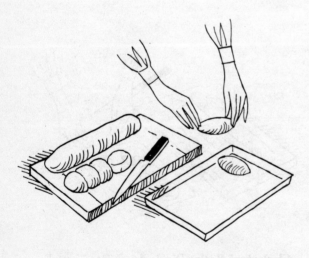

Vienna Rolls: Cut dough in half; divide each half into 6 equal pieces. Shape each piece into a cylinder; taper ends with hands. Place 2 inches apart on greased cookie sheet. Makes 1 dozen.

OLD-FASHIONED POTATO ROLLS

½ c. milk	2 eggs
⅓ c. sugar	¼ c. instant mashed
1 tsp. salt	potatoes
½ c. shortening	(dry mix)
½ c. warm water	3½ to 4 c. sifted all-
(105° to 115° F.)	purpose flour
2 pkgs. active dry	Melted butter or
yeast or 2 cakes	margarine
compressed yeast	

Combine milk, sugar, salt, and shortening in saucepan. Heat until bubbles appear around the edge and shortening is melted; cool to lukewarm. Measure warm water into large mixing bowl; sprinkle or crumble in yeast; stir to dissolve. Add lukewarm milk mixture, eggs, and instant potatoes. Add 2 cups flour; beat until smooth; stir in enough remaining flour to make dough easy to handle. Turn dough out onto floured board. Knead about 5 minutes or until dough is smooth and elastic. Put dough into large, greased bowl; turn over to bring greased side up; cover with damp towel. Let rise in warm place (85° F.), free from draft, about 1½ hours or until doubled in bulk. Punch dough down; let rise about 30 minutes or until almost double. Punch down; turn out onto floured board; knead to distribute air bubbles. Divide and shape as desired (*page 111*). Cover; let rise about 30 minutes or until doubled in bulk. Brush lightly with melted butter or margarine. Bake at 350° F. for 15 to 20 minutes.

WHOLE WHEAT ROLLS

¾ c. buttermilk	1 pkg. active dry
1 tbs. dark molasses	yeast or 1 cake
3 tbs. sugar	compressed yeast
1 tsp. salt	¼ tsp. baking soda
⅓ c. shortening	1 c. whole wheat
¼ c. warm water	flour
(105° to 115° F.)	2 c. (about) sifted
	all-purpose flour

Combine buttermilk, molasses, sugar, salt, and shortening in saucepan. Heat until bubbles appear around the edge and shortening is melted; cool to lukewarm. Measure warm water into large mixing bowl; sprinkle or crumble in yeast; stir to dissolve. Add lukewarm milk mixture. Add soda, whole wheat flour, and 1 cup all-purpose flour; beat until smooth. Add enough remaining all-purpose flour to make soft dough. Turn out onto floured board. Knead about 5 minutes or until dough is smooth and elastic. Put dough into large, greased bowl; turn over to bring greased side up; cover with damp towel. Let rise in warm place (85° F.), free from draft, about 1½ hours or until doubled in bulk. Punch dough down; let rise about 30 minutes or until almost double. Punch dough down; turn out onto board; knead to distribute air bubbles. Divide and shape as desired (*page 111*). Cover; let rise 20 minutes or until doubled in bulk. Bake at 400° F. for 15 minutes.

HOT CROSS BUNS

¾ c. milk
½ c. butter or margarine
¼ c. sugar
1 tsp. salt
¼ c. warm water (105° to 115° F.)
1 pkg. active dry yeast or 1 cake compressed yeast
1 egg

3½ to 4 c. sifted all-purpose flour
½ tsp. ground cinnamon
½ c. currants
½ c. candied citron, finely chopped
1 egg
2 tbs. water
Easy Confectioners' Sugar Glaze (*page 456*)

Combine milk, butter or margarine, sugar, and salt in saucepan. Heat until bubbles appear around the edge and shortening is melted; cool to lukewarm. Measure warm water into large mixing bowl; sprinkle or crumble in yeast; stir to dissolve. Add milk mixture; add 1 egg. Beat in 2 cups flour and cinnamon. Mix in currants and citron. Work in enough remaining flour to form a soft dough. Turn out onto lightly floured board. Knead 5 minutes or until smooth and elastic. Put dough into large, greased bowl; turn over to bring greased side up; cover. Let rise in warm place (85° F.), free from draft, about 1 hour or until doubled in bulk. Punch dough down; knead to distribute air bubbles; divide in half. Cut each half into 9 portions; shape each into smooth round roll. Place ½ inch apart in greased baking dish. Cover; let rise 45 to 55 minutes or until doubled in bulk. Cut shallow cross in top of each with tip of scissors. Brush with mixture of 1 egg and water. Bake at 375° F. for 20 to 25 minutes. Cool on wire racks. Pipe glaze into crosses on tops of buns. Makes 18 buns.

SPECIALTIES

NUT-FILLED COFFEE CAKE (Potica)

1 c. milk
6 tbs. sugar
1½ tsp. salt
¼ c. soft butter or margarine
2 tbs. warm water (105° to 115° F.)
1 pkg. active dry yeast or 1 cake compressed yeast
2 egg yolks
4 to 4½ c. sifted all-purpose flour

2 tbs. fresh bread crumbs
2 tbs. melted butter or margarine
½ c. light cream
½ lb. walnuts, ground
¾ c. sugar
½ tsp. salt
½ tsp. vanilla
2 egg whites, beaten
Easy Confectioners' Sugar Glaze (*page 456*)

Combine milk, 6 tablespoons sugar, 1½ teaspoons salt, and butter or margarine in saucepan. Heat until bubbles appear around the edge and shortening is melted; cool to lukewarm. Measure warm water into large mixing bowl; sprinkle or crumble in yeast; stir to dissolve. Add lukewarm milk mixture and egg yolks. Add 2 cups flour; beat until smooth. Stir in remaining flour. Turn out onto floured board. Knead about 5 minutes or until dough is smooth and elastic. Put dough in large, greased bowl; turn over to bring greased side up; cover with damp towel. Let rise in warm place (85° F.), free from draft, about 1 hour or until doubled in bulk. While dough rises, prepare filling: Heat cream to boiling; remove from heat. Add walnuts, ¾ cup sugar, vanilla, and bread crumbs. Beat egg whites until stiff but not dry; fold into cream mixture. Heat oven to 350° F. Punch dough down; turn out onto floured board; knead to distribute air bubbles; divide in half. Roll out each half to an 18x7-inch rectangle. Spread half the filling mixture on each rectangle of dough. Roll up, jelly-roll fashion, starting from long side. Seal well by pinching edges of roll together. Place, sealed side down, on greased cookie sheet. Shape into ring; pinch ends together. Let rise about 1 hour or until doubled in bulk. Bake 40 to 45 minutes. Glaze while warm. Decorate with candied fruits, if desired. Makes 2.

KUGELHUPF

¼ c. warm water (105° to 115° F.)	1 c. butter or margarine
1 pkg. active dry yeast or 1 cake compressed yeast	⅔ c. sugar
	4 eggs
¾ c. lukewarm milk	3½ c. sifted all-purpose flour
½ c. sifted all-purpose flour	1 tsp. salt
	2 tsp. grated lemon rind
1½ c. blanched, slivered almonds	½ c. raisins

Measure warm water into large mixing bowl; sprinkle or crumble in yeast; stir to dissolve. Stir in lukewarm milk and ½ cup flour; beat until smooth. Let rise in warm place (85° F.), free from draft, 45 to 60 minutes or until bubbly. Butter generously a 3½-quart kugelhupf pan or 10-inch tub pan; sprinkle with ½ cup almonds. Cream butter or margarine in medium-size bowl; beat in sugar. Add eggs, one at a time, beating well after each addition; beat until blended. When yeast mixture is bubbly, stir in egg mixture, remaining ingredients, and 1 cup almonds. Beat until well blended; spoon into pan. Cover; let rise about 1½ hours or until doubled in bulk. Bake at 400° F. for 10 minutes; reduce oven heat to 350° F.; bake 40 minutes longer. Turn out of pan at once; cool completely on wire rack before cutting. Makes 1 cake.

SWISS TWIST

¾ c. milk	2 eggs, beaten
⅓ c. sugar	4½ to 5 c. sifted all-purpose flour
½ tsp. salt	
½ c. butter or margarine	1 tbs. grated lemon rind
¼ c. warm water (105° to 115° F.)	1 tbs. lemon juice
	1 egg yolk
1 pkg. active dry yeast or 1 cake compressed yeast	1 tbs. water

Combine milk, sugar, salt, and butter or margarine in saucepan. Heat until bubbles appear around the edge; cool to lukewarm. Measure warm water into large mixing bowl; sprinkle or crumble in yeast; stir to dissolve. Add lukewarm milk mixture and eggs. Add 2 cups flour; beat until smooth. Add lemon rind and juice and remaining flour; mix well. Turn out onto floured board. Knead 5 minutes or until dough is smooth and elastic. Dough will

be soft. Put dough into large, greased bowl; turn over to bring greased side up; cover with damp towel. Let rise in warm place (85° F.), free from draft, about 1 hour or until doubled in bulk. Punch dough down; turn out onto floured board; knead to distribute air bubbles. Divide dough in 4 equal parts. Shape each part into an 18-inch-long rope. Place ropes side by side on greased cookie sheet; pinch together at one end. Braid by weaving far right strip over and under to the far left. Then weave with the next far right strip; repeat until braid is complete. Pinch ends together and tuck under. Cover. Let rise about 45 minutes or until almost doubled in bulk. Heat oven to 350° F. Brush bread with egg yolk blended with water. Bake 35 to 40 minutes. Makes 1 loaf.

KING'S CAKE

The tradition of this famous cake goes back to medieval times. As the story goes, kings and queens were chosen from among the courtiers to reign for a day. A bean was hidden in the cake and whoever found it in his piece became king and selected his queen. Today in New Orleans, it is traditional to select the king of the carnival this way.

½ c. milk	½ tsp. ground mace or nutmeg
½ c. sugar	
1 tsp. salt	4½ to 5 c. sifted all-purpose flour
⅓ c. warm water (105° to 115° F.)	
	1 jar (4 oz.) candied citron
2 pkgs. active dry yeast or 2 cakes compressed yeast	1 jar (4 oz.) candied orange peel
3 eggs	
½ c. shortening	1 dried bean
1 tsp. grated lemon rind	Easy Confectioners' Sugar Glaze (*page 456*)

Combine milk, sugar, and salt in saucepan. Heat until bubbles appear around the edge; cool to lukewarm. Measure warm water into large mixing bowl; sprinkle or crumble in yeast; stir to dissolve. Add lukewarm milk mixture, eggs, shortening, lemon rind, mace or nutmeg. Add 2 cups flour; beat until smooth. Add citron, orange peel, and enough more flour to make dough easy to handle. Turn out onto floured board. Knead about 5 minutes or until dough is smooth and elastic. Put dough into large, greased bowl; turn over to bring greased side up; cover with damp towel. Let rise in warm place (85° F.), free from draft, 1½ hours, or until doubled in bulk. Punch dough down; turn out onto floured board; knead to distribute air bubbles; divide in thirds. Wrap bean in aluminum foil; put in one portion of dough. Shape each third into rope 28 to 30 inches long; braid; shape in oval on greased cookie sheet. Cover; let rise until doubled in bulk. Bake at 375° F. for 25 minutes; cool. Drizzle glaze over cake. Decorate with colored candies or sugars, if desired. Makes 1 cake.

BASIC YEAST DOUGH FOR CHRISTMAS COFFEE CAKES

¾ c. milk	1 pkg. active dry
½ c. sugar	yeast or 1 cake
1 tsp. salt	compressed yeast
½ c. soft butter or	2 eggs
margarine	5 to 5½ c. sifted all-
¼ c. warm water	purpose flour
(105° to 115° F.)	

Combine milk, sugar, salt, and butter or margarine in saucepan. Heat until bubbles appear around the edge; cool to lukewarm. Measure warm water into large mixing bowl; sprinkle or crumble in yeast; stir to dissolve. Add lukewarm milk mixture and eggs. Add 3 cups flour; beat until smooth. Add 1½ cups flour; dough will be very sticky. Flour board with remaining flour; turn dough out onto floured board. Work just enough flour into dough with spatula or hands until dough handles easily. (*Secret:* this method of adding flour gives a very tender coffee cake.) Knead about 5 minutes or until dough is smooth and elastic. Put dough into large, greased bowl; turn over to bring greased side up; cover with damp towel. Let rise in warm place (85° F.), free from draft, 1 to 1½ hours or until doubled in bulk. Punch dough down; let rise 30 minutes or until double. Shape dough as directed for individual coffee cake.

KULICH

1 recipe Basic	¼ c. chopped,
Yeast Dough	candied orange
(*above*)	peel
½ c. raisins	1 tsp. vanilla
½ c. chopped,	Easy Confectioners'
blanched	Sugar Glaze
almonds	(*page 456*)
	Red food coloring

Prepare Basic Yeast Dough through the step of adding 3 cups flour; beat until smooth. Add raisins, almonds, orange peel, and vanilla. Add 1½ cups flour; work in remaining flour, knead, and let rise in bowl according to basic recipe. When dough has finished rising, punch dough down; turn out onto floured board; knead to distribute air bubbles; divide dough in thirds; shape each third into smooth ball. Press each into a well-greased 1-pound coffee can; cover with clean towel. Let rise 1 hour or until dough rises to top of can. Bake at 375° F. for 30 to 35 minutes. Prepare glaze; tint pastel pink with a few drops of red food coloring. Frost cake. Makes 3.

CHECKERBOARD KUCHEN

½ c. milk	1 can (about 1 lb.)
2 tbs. sugar	apricot halves,
1 tsp. salt	drained
2 tbs. shortening	¾ c. sugar
¼ c. warm water	1 tsp. ground
(105° to 115° F.)	cinnamon
1 pkg. active dry	¼ tsp. ground
yeast or 1 cake	mace or nutmeg
compressed yeast	2 tbs. soft butter or
1 egg	margarine
2½ c. sifted all-	1 egg, slightly
purpose flour	beaten
1 jar (1 lb.) prunes,	⅓ c. light cream
drained and	
pitted	

Combine milk, 2 tablespoons sugar, salt, and shortening in saucepan. Heat until bubbles appear around the edge and shortening is melted; cool to lukewarm. Measure warm water into large mixing bowl; sprinkle or crumble in yeast; stir to dissolve. Add lukewarm milk mixture and 1 egg. Beat in flour gradually. Cover with damp towel; let rise in warm place (85° F.), free from draft, 45 to 60 minutes or until doubled in bulk. Stir down. Spread in greased 13x9x2-inch pan. Place fruits alternately on dough. Mix ¾ cup sugar, spices, and butter or margarine. Sprinkle all but 2 tablespoons on fruits. Cover; let rise 30 minutes or until doubled in bulk. Bake at 375° F. for 20 to 25 minutes. Mix beaten egg and cream; pour over kuchen; sprinkle with reserved sugar mixture. Bake 15 minutes longer. Makes 1.

STOLLEN

1 recipe Basic Yeast Dough (*page 115*)	1 c. raisins
½ c. chopped, blanched almonds	1 tbs. grated lemon rind
½ c. candied cherries, halved	¼ c. melted butter or margarine
½ c. chopped, candied citron	Easy Confectioners' Sugar Glaze (*page 456*)

Prepare Basic Yeast Dough through the step of adding 3 cups flour; beat until smooth. Add almonds, cherries, citron, raisins, and lemon rind. Add 1½ cups flour; work in remaining flour, knead, and let rise in bowl according to basic recipe. When dough has finished rising, punch dough down; turn out onto floured board; knead to distribute air bubbles; divide in half. Shape each half into 7x12-inch oval; brush with melted butter or margarine. Fold long side two thirds across dough (like a Parker House roll). Brush with melted butter or margarine. Place on greased cookie sheets; cover. Let rise 1 hour or until doubled in bulk. Bake at 375° F. for 30 to 35 minutes. Brush with remaining melted butter or margarine halfway through the baking period. Drizzle with glaze. Decorate with additional candied cherries and almonds, if desired. Makes 2.

PANETONE

1 recipe Basic Yeast Dough (*page 115*)	1 c. mixed candied fruits
3 egg yolks, beaten	1½ tsp. anise extract
1 c. golden raisins	2 tbs. melted butter or margarine
½ c. pine nuts (pignoli)	Confectioners' sugar

Prepare Basic Yeast Dough through the step of adding 3 cups flour; beat until smooth. Add beaten egg yolks, raisins, pine nuts, candied fruits, and anise extract. Add 1½ cups flour; work in remaining flour, knead, and let rise according to basic recipe. To make collar to hold dough, tear off piece of heavy aluminum foil large enough to circle 9-inch layer-cake pan. Fold lengthwise until 3 inches wide; form into circle inside pan; secure with paper clip. Grease bottom of pan and inside of foil. When dough has finished rising, punch dough down; turn out onto floured board; knead to distrib-

ute air bubbles. Shape into smooth ball; press into prepared pan. Let rise 1 hour or until doubled in bulk. Cut cross in top with sharp knife; brush with melted butter or margarine. Bake at 400° F. for 10 minutes; reduce oven heat to 325° F.; bake 35 to 40 minutes longer. Sprinkle with confectioners' sugar. Decorate with candied cherries and angelica, if desired. Makes 1.

CHERRY-ALMOND TWIST

1 recipe Basic Yeast Dough (*page 115*)	1 jar (4 oz.) candied cherries, halved
2 egg whites	1 egg yolk
1 can (8 oz.) almond paste	2 tbs. water
2 tbs. sugar	¼ c. sliced, blanched almonds
¼ c. soft butter or margarine	Sugar

Prepare Basic Yeast Dough. Beat egg whites until foamy; crumble in almond paste. Beat at low speed on mixer until all lumps are blended in. Blend in 2 tablespoons sugar and butter or margarine. When dough has finished rising, punch dough down; turn out onto floured board; knead to distribute air bubbles; divide in half. Cut each one-half in half again. Roll each piece out to a 6x15-inch rectangle. Spread each rectangle with a quarter of the almond-paste mixture; dot each with a quarter of the candied cherries. Roll each piece up, jelly-roll fashion, starting from long side. Pinch edge well to seal seam to help keep filling inside dough. Put two filled rolls side by side; twist one roll over the other, forming a fat rope shape. Be sure seam is underneath. Place on greased cookie sheet. Repeat with other two filled rolls. Beat egg yolk with water; brush on top of twists. Scatter almonds over twists; sprinkle with sugar. Cover; let rise about 40 minutes or until doubled in bulk. Bake at 350° F. for 25 to 30 minutes. Remove at once from cookie sheets; place on wire rack. Cool. Decorate with additional candied cherries, if desired. Makes 2.

Corn muffins, light and tender, easy to ma

FRUIT RING

1 recipe Basic Yeast Dough (*page 115*)	2 tsp ground cinnamon
6 tbs. soft butter or margarine	1 c. raisins
4 tbs. grated orange rind	1 c. chopped pecans
⅔ c. sugar	½ c. citron, finely chopped
	Easy Confectioners' Sugar Glaze (*page 456*)

Prepare Basic Yeast Dough. Blend butter or margarine, orange rind, sugar, and cinnamon in small bowl. When dough has finished rising, punch dough down; turn out onto floured board; knead to distribute air bubbles; divide in half. Roll one half out to 9x16-inch rectangle. Spread with butter-orange mixture; sprinkle with raisins, pecans, and citron. Roll up, jelly-roll fashion, starting from long side. Pinch edge to seal. Shape into ring on greased cookie sheet; pinch ends together firmly to seal. Clip roll with scissors from outside about two thirds of the way toward the center. Repeat cut at 2-inch intervals all the way around the ring. Lift each section carefully; turn on side to show filling. Repeat with other half of dough. Cover; let rise about 40 minutes or until doubled in bulk. Bake at 350° F. for 25 to 30 minutes. Remove at once from cookie sheet; place on wire racks. Cool. Drizzle glaze over rings. Sprinkle with whole pecans, if desired. Makes 2.

LITTLE DANISH PASTRIES

1 c. milk	3 eggs, beaten
½ c. sugar	4½ c. sifted all-purpose flour
1½ tsp. salt	
¼ c. butter or margarine	1½ c. butter or margarine
½ c. warm water (105° to 115° F.)	2 egg yolks
	2 tbs. water
2 pkgs. active dry yeast or 2 cakes compressed yeast	

Combine milk, sugar, salt, and ¼ cup butter or margarine in saucepan. Heat until bubbles appear around the edge; cool to lukewarm. Measure warm water into large bowl; sprinkle or crumble in yeast; stir to dissolve. Add lukewarm milk mixture and beaten eggs. Add

1 cup flour; mix well; stir remaining flour into batter just until mixed; chill. Spread 1½ cups butter or margarine out on wax paper to a 10x12-inch rectangle; chill 1 hour. Roll chilled dough out to a 12x16-inch rectangle; place butter or margarine rectangle in center of dough. Fold each side of dough to center, covering butter or margarine. Give dough a quarter turn; roll to a 12 x 16-inch rectangle; fold as above. Turn, roll, and fold once more; chill 1 hour. Repeat procedure of two rollings, foldings, turnings, and chillings two more times. Refrigerate dough overnight. Work with half the dough at a time; keep remainder refrigerated. Shape as below. After shaping, place 2 inches apart on greased cookie sheet. Chill 1 hour. Beat egg yolks and water together; brush over pastries. Bake at 375° F. for 15 to 20 minutes. Makes about 3 dozen.

Twists. Roll half the dough out to a 4x12-inch rectangle. Sprinkle with a mixture of cinnamon and sugar and very finely chopped nuts. Fold dough in half lengthwise. Cut into ½-inch-wide strips. Twist ends in opposite directions.

Pocketbooks. Roll half the dough out to a 4x12-inch rectangle. Cut in half lengthwise. Cut into 2-inch squares; place teaspoon of jelly in center of each square. Bring 2 opposite corners to center; press down to secure.

Elephant Ears. Roll half the dough out to a 4x12-inch rectangle; sprinkle with a mixture of cinnamon and sugar; roll up jelly-roll fashion. Cut into 1-inch pieces; cut each piece in the center almost through to the bottom; spread open.

To help yeast dough rise: if kitchen is cold, place the bowl of dough in a closed cupboard with a pan of hot water; or on a wire rack over a bowl of hot water.

DANISH TWIST

1 c. butter or margarine	1 egg
1/3 c. sifted all-purpose flour	3 to 3 1/2 c. sifted all-purpose flour
2/3 c. milk	Raisin Almond Filling or Apricot Filling
1/4 c. sugar	
1/2 tsp. salt	1 egg yolk
1/3 c. warm water (105° to 115° F.)	2 tbs. water
	Sliced blanched almonds
1 pkg. active dry yeast or 1 cake compressed yeast	Sugar

Cream 1 cup butter or margarine and 1/3 cup flour; shape into 6 x 12-inch rectangle on wax paper; chill. Combine milk, sugar, and salt in saucepan. Heat just until bubbles appear around the edge; cool to lukewarm. Measure warm water into large mixing bowl; sprinkle or crumble in yeast; stir to dissolve. Add lukewarm milk mixture, egg and enough flour to make a soft dough. Turn out onto floured board. Knead about 5 minutes or until dough is smooth and elastic. Roll out to 15-inch square. Place chilled butter rectangle on half the dough; fold other half over; press edges of dough together. Give dough a quarter turn; roll out to 15-inch square. Fold in thirds; give dough a quarter turn to bring long side to front. Repeat rolling, folding, and turning twice more. Chill dough 30 minutes. While dough chills, prepare filling of your choice from recipes below. Roll dough out to a 12x15-inch rectangle; cut in half lengthwise. Spread each strip of dough with half the filling. Roll up each strip, jelly-roll fashion, starting from long side. Press to seal at ends and along seam. Twist each piece into a coil on lightly greased cookie sheets. Blend egg yolk and water; brush over tops of twists. Sprinkle with almonds and sugar. Let rise about 40 minutes or until doubled in bulk. Bake at 375° F. for 25 to 30 minutes. Makes 2.

Raisin Almond Filling

3 tbs. butter or margarine	1/4 c. chopped, blanched almonds
3/4 c. sifted confectioners' sugar	1/4 c. raisins

Blend butter or margarine and sugar. Spread half on each strip of dough. Sprinkle each with half the almonds and raisins.

Apricot Filling

1/2 c. diced, dried apricots	2 tbs. chopped citron
1/2 c. water	2 tbs. chopped candied cherries
2 tbs. sugar	
1/4 c. raisins	

Simmer apricots, water, and sugar in small saucepan until apricots are tender and water is absorbed. Add raisins, citron, and cherries.

RICH COFFEE CAKE DOUGH

1/4 c. milk	1 pkg. active dry yeast or 1 cake compressed yeast
1/4 c. sugar	
1/2 tsp. salt	
1/3 c. shortening	2 eggs
1/4 c. warm water (105° to 115° F.)	2 1/2 to 3 c. sifted all-purpose flour

Combine milk, sugar, salt, and shortening in saucepan. Heat until bubbles appear around the edges; cool to lukewarm. Measure warm water into bowl; sprinkle or crumble in yeast; stir to dissolve. Add lukewarm milk mixture, eggs and 1 1/2 cups flour; beat well until smooth. Add enough remaining flour to make dough easy to handle, mixing in with hands, if necessary. Turn out onto floured board. Knead about 5 minutes or until dough is smooth and elastic. Put dough in large, greased bowl; turn over to bring greased side up; cover with damp towel. Let rise in warm place (85° F.), free from draft, about 1 to 1 1/2 hours or until doubled in bulk. Punch dough down; turn out onto floured board; knead to distribute air bubbles; let rest 5 minutes before shaping one of the recipes below.

PEACHY NUT CRESCENT

1 recipe Rich Coffee Cake Dough (above)	1/2 c. chopped nuts
	3 tbs. soft butter or margarine
1/3 c. sugar	1/2 c. peach preserves
1 tsp. ground cinnamon	
	Easy Confectioners' Sugar Glaze (page 456)
1 tsp. grated lemon rind	

Prepare Rich Coffee Cake Dough. Combine sugar, cinnamon, grated lemon rind, and nuts. Roll dough out to a 6x18-inch rectangle. Spread dough with butter or margarine; sprinkle with sugar mixture. Drop 1/4 cup peach preserves onto dough by teaspoonfuls.

Roll up, jelly-roll fashion, starting from long side; pinch edges firmly to seal seam. Put on well greased cookie sheet seam side down. Curve into crescent shape. Slash top around crescent a third of the way through. Let rise about 1 hour or until doubled in bulk. Carefully spoon remaining ¼ cup peach preserves into slit in crescent. Bake at 375° F. for 30 to 35 minutes. Cool on wire rack. Drizzle glaze over crescent. Makes 1.

BUTTERSCOTCH NUT BUNS

1 recipe Rich Coffee Cake Dough (*page 118*)	½ c. pecan halves
	2 tbs. soft butter or margarine
¾ c. brown sugar, firmly packed	⅓ c. sugar
⅓ c. corn syrup	½ c. raisins
¼ c. butter or margarine	½ tsp. ground cinnamon

Prepare Rich Coffee Cake Dough. Combine brown sugar, corn syrup, and ¼ cup butter or margarine in small saucepan; simmer 2 minutes. Pour into 11x7x2-inch or 9x9x2-inch pan. Sprinkle in the pecan halves. Roll the dough out to a 8x15-inch rectangle. Spread dough with soft butter or margarine. Mix sugar, raisins, and cinnamon; sprinkle over dough. Roll up, jelly-roll fashion, beginning with long side; pinch edges firmly to seal seam. Cut into 12 equal slices. Place slices, cut side down, in prepared pan. Let rise about 1 hour or until doubled in bulk. Bake at 375° F. for 20 to 25 minutes. Turn upside down on serving plate or tray. Leave pan on top of buns about 5 minutes to allow topping to run down over buns. Lift off pan; cool buns. Makes 1 dozen.

MARMALADE UPSIDE-DOWN BUNS

1 recipe Rich Coffee Cake Dough (*page 118*)	2 tbs. butter or margarine
	¼ c. sugar
½ c. orange marmalade	½ c. golden raisins
¼ c. butter or margarine	

Prepare Rich Coffee Cake Dough. Combine marmalade and ¼ cup butter or margarine in small saucepan; simmer 2 minutes. Pour into 9-inch layer-cake pan or 9x9x2-inch pan.

Roll the dough out to 8x15-inch rectangle. Spread dough with 2 tablespoons butter or margarine; sprinkle with sugar and raisins. Roll up, jelly-roll fashion, beginning with long side; pinch edges firmly to seal seam. Cut into 12 equal slices. Place slices, cut side down, in prepared pan. Let rise about 1 hour or until doubled in bulk. Bake at 375° F. for 20 to 25 minutes. Loosen around sides; turn out at once onto serving plate or tray. Leave pan on top of buns 5 minutes to allow topping to run down over buns. Lift off pan; cool buns. Makes 1 dozen.

To freshen rolls that are dry: heat oven to 350°F. Put the rolls in a paper bag and twist closed. Run it quickly under cold water. Heat in oven about 10 to 15 minutes.

CRUNCHY CRUMB CAKE

1 recipe Rich Coffee Cake Dough (*page 118*)	1 c. sifted all-purpose flour
⅓ c. butter or margarine	½ tsp. ground cinnamon
¼ c. brown sugar, firmly packed	Confectioners' sugar

Prepare Rich Coffee Cake Dough. Press dough into 9-inch layer-cake pan or 9x9x2-inch pan. Blend butter or margarine, sugar, flour, and cinnamon in small bowl until crumbly. Sprinkle evenly over dough in pan. Let rise about 1 hour or until doubled in bulk. Bake at 375° F. for 30 to 35 minutes. Remove from pan; cool on wire rack. Sprinkle generously with confectioners' sugar. Makes 1.

RASPBERRY BREAKFAST BREAD

1 c. warm water (105° to 115° F.)	1 egg
1 pkg. active dry yeast or 1 cake compressed yeast	¼ c. shortening
	1 tsp. grated orange rind
⅓ c. sugar	¼ c. chopped nuts
1 tsp. salt	¼ c. raisins
2½ c. sifted all-purpose flour	¼ c. raspberry preserves

Measure warm water into large bowl; sprinkle or crumble in yeast; stir to dissolve. Stir in sugar, salt, and 1½ cups flour; beat about 2 minutes or until batter sheets off spoon. Add egg, shortening, orange rind, nuts, raisins, and remaining 1 cup flour. Grease and flour shallow, 1½-quart oval baking dish or 9x9x2-inch pan; spoon in batter evenly. Let rise in warm place (85° F.), free from draft, about 1½ hours or until doubled in bulk. Gently mark 3 long depressions in dough with floured handle of wooden spoon or tips of fingers; carefully spoon preserves into depressions. Bake at 375° F. for 25 to 30 minutes. Cool in pan 10 minutes; remove from pan; cool on wire rack. Decorate with Easy Confectioners' Sugar Glaze (*page 456*), if desired. Makes 1.

BRIOCHE

3½ c. sifted all-purpose flour	1 pkg. active dry yeast or 1 cake compressed yeast
½ tsp. salt	
2 tbs. sugar	⅔ c. sifted all-purpose flour
4 eggs, beaten	
½ c. soft butter or margarine	Lukewarm water
	1 c. soft butter or margarine
2 to 3 tbs. milk	
¼ c. warm water (105° to 115° F.)	2 eggs
	1 egg yolk
	2 tbs. water

Sift 3½ cups flour, salt, and sugar into large bowl. Beat in 4 eggs and ½ cup butter or margarine. Dough will be quite stiff and too heavy for average mixer; a wooden spoon or your hands will be best. Mix in enough milk to form sticky dough; amount of milk will vary with size of eggs. Pick up dough with a twisting motion of your hand; throw down forcefully onto lightly floured board until dough feels soft and velvety. This will take about 10 minutes and, as you develop the "stretch" in the dough, you will feel all the little lumps smoothing out. Set aside in bowl while you prepare "leaven." Measure warm water into small bowl; sprinkle or crumble in yeast; stir to dissolve. Stir in ⅔ cup flour; knead mixture into a smooth, firm ball. Place leaven in small bowl; pour in lukewarm water to cover leaven; let stand 5 minutes or until ball begins to float and is halfway out of water. Cream 1 cup butter or margarine. Lift leaven from water with fingers; drain. Add to dough with creamed butter or margarine and 2 eggs. Work all together with hands until well blended and no streaks of white leaven are visible. Cover with damp towel; let rise in warm place (85° F.), free from draft, about 1½ hours or until doubled in bulk. Punch dough down; cover; chill 6 hours or overnight. *To shape:* Grease twenty-four 3½-inch brioche pans or 2½-inch muffin-pan cups. Cut dough into quarters; shape each piece into rope 12 inches long. Work with one rope at a time; cover others; chill. Cut a 1½-inch piece for topknots. Cut the rest into sixths. Shape each into a smooth ball between palms; place in pans. Cut reserved piece into six pieces; form each into a ball; pinch into pear shape. Moisten finger; poke dent into center of dough in pans. Set small piece in hole, pointed end down. Repeat with remaining 3 ropes. Cover; let rise 30 to 40 minutes or until increased in bulk by a third. Beat egg yolk and water together; brush over rolls. Bake at 425° F. for 15 to 20 minutes. Makes 2 dozen.

1. Mix just enough milk into flour mixture to form a very soft dough.

2. Because you cannot knead this dough easily the way to work it is to pick it up with a twisting motion and throw it down hard on a floured board until it is smooth and velvety.

3. Make the leaven with the yeast, water, and flour. Knead it into a smooth ball with your fingers, turning out on a board if necessary.

4. To activate the leaven put it in a bowl, cover it with lukewarm water, and let it rise just until it floats.

5. While the leaven is rising, work the butter or margarine in a bowl with a wooden spoon until soft and beat the eggs in another bowl.

6. Work the beaten eggs into the first dough mixture with your hands. Spoon creamed butter or margarine onto the mixture and work it in.

7. Pick up the risen ball of leaven and let it drain. (If a few drops of water remain, it isn't serious.) Work it into the dough completely.

8. Punch down the risen dough and cover the bowl. Chill at least 6 hours. This will resolidify the butter and make the dough easier to handle when you shape it.

9. Petites Brioches: Shape each quarter of the dough into a 12-inch roll on lightly floured board. Try not to work any flour in as it will cause streaks in brioche.

10. Cut off piece for topknots and cut remainder of roll into six pieces. Dust hands with flour. Roll each piece into a smooth ball with palms of hands.

11. Cut topknot piece into sixths. Form each little piece of dough into a pear or teardrop shape.

12. Poke hole in center of dough with moistened finger. Set small piece of dough into hole, pointed end down.

FRENCH MARKET DOUGHNUTS

No visit to New Orleans is complete without a trip to the famous French Market in the wee hours to partake of its heavenly, renowned doughnuts and coffee.

¾ c. milk	1 egg
½ c. sugar	4 to 4½ c. sifted all-
½ c. butter or	purpose flour
margarine	1 tsp. ground mace
1 tsp. salt	Oil or shortening
¼ c. warm water	for frying
(105° to 115° F.)	1 c. sugar
1 pkg. active dry	
yeast or 1 cake	
compressed yeast	

Combine milk, ½ cup sugar, butter or margarine, and salt in saucepan. Heat until bubbles appear around edge and shortening is melted; cool to lukewarm. Measure warm water into large mixing bowl; sprinkle or crumble in yeast; stir to dissolve. Add lukewarm milk mixture and egg. Beat in 2 cups flour and mace. Add enough remaining flour to make a soft dough. Turn dough out onto floured board. Knead about 5 minutes or until dough is smooth and elastic. Put dough in large, greased bowl; cover with damp towel. Let rise in warm place (85° F.), free from draft, about 1 to 1½ hours or until doubled in bulk. Punch dough down; turn out onto floured board; knead to distribute air bubbles. Let rest a few moments if difficult to roll. Roll out to a ¼-inch-thick rectangle. Cut into 2-inch squares; cover. Let rise 30 minutes or until almost double. Heat oil or shortening to 375° F. Fry doughnuts, turning once to brown both sides (about 4 minutes). While warm, shake doughnuts in paper bag with 1 cup sugar. Makes 4 dozen.

DANISH APPLE CAKE

½ c. milk	1 egg, beaten
3 tbs. sugar	¼ c. melted butter
½ tsp. salt	or margarine
2½ to 3 cups sifted	½ c. sugar
all-purpose flour	1 tsp. ground
¾ c. butter or	cinnamon
margarine	Dash of ground
¼ c. warm water	nutmeg
(105° to 115° F.)	3 medium-size
1 pkg. active dry	apples, pared,
yeast or 1 cake	cored, and thinly
compressed yeast	sliced

Heat milk in small saucepan until bubbles appear around the edge; cool to lukewarm. Combine 3 tablespoons sugar, salt, and 2 cups flour in large bowl; cut in ¾ cup butter or margarine with pastry blender until mixture resembles cornmeal. Measure warm water into small bowl; sprinkle or crumble in yeast; stir to dissolve. Add lukewarm milk and egg. Stir into flour mixture; add enough remaining flour to make a stiff dough. Turn out onto floured board. Knead 5 minutes or until dough is smooth and elastic. Put dough into large, greased bowl; turn over to bring greased side up; cover with damp towel. Let rise in warm place, (85° F.), free from draft, about 1 to 1½ hours or until doubled in bulk. Divide dough into two equal parts; press into two greased 8x1½-inch layer pans. Brush surface of each cake with 1 tablespoon melted butter or margarine. Combine ½ cup sugar, cinnamon, and nutmeg; sprinkle evenly over cakes. Arrange apple slices in overlapping ring on each cake; brush slices with remaining melted butter or margarine. Let rise 25 minutes or until doubled in bulk. Cover top of cakes loosely with foil to prevent apples from drying out. Bake at 400° F. for 10 minutes; remove foil; continue baking 15 to 20 minutes or until golden. Remove from pans at once; cool on wire racks. Makes 2.

Made with Hot-Roll Mix

JELLY DOUGHNUTS

¾ c. warm water	1 tsp. vanilla
(105° to 115° F.)	Oil or shortening
1 pkg. hot-roll mix	for frying
1 egg, beaten	1 c. raspberry jam
	or jelly

Measure warm water into large bowl; sprinkle in yeast from package of hot-roll mix; stir to dissolve. Stir in egg and vanilla. Stir in dry mix; dough will be quite stiff. Let rise in warm place (85° F.), free from draft, about 1 hour or until doubled in bulk. Turn out onto lightly floured board; knead 8 to 10 times. Roll out dough ⅓ inch thick; cut rounds with a floured 2- or 2½-inch cutter. Carefully transfer each round to floured cookie sheet or tray. Let rise, uncovered, 30 to 45 minutes or until doubled in bulk. Heat oil or shortening to 375° F. With wide spatula gently transfer doughnuts to hot fat; fry until golden brown. Drain on absorbent paper. When cool, make a deep slit with thin knife in the side of each doughnut; twist to enlarge hole slightly. Fill doughnuts with jam, using pastry bag. Or shape triangle of wax paper into cone; fill with jam; snip about ¼ inch off pointed end; fill doughnuts. Roll in sugar, if desired. Makes 18 doughnuts.

CINNAMON ROLL RING

¾ c. warm water (105° to 115° F.)	½ c. brown sugar, firmly packed
1 pkg. hot-roll mix	1 tsp. ground cinnamon
1 egg	¾ cup raisins
¼ c. honey	½ cup chopped nuts
2 tbs. butter or margarine	Easy Confectioners' Sugar Glaze (*page 456*)
2 tbs. honey	

Measure warm water into large bowl; sprinkle in yeast from package of hot-roll mix; stir to dissolve. Add egg, ¼ cup honey, and dry mix; blend well. Let rise in warm place (85° F.), free from draft, about 1 hour or until doubled in bulk. Roll out onto lightly floured board to a 20x12-inch rectangle. Combine butter or margarine and 2 tablespoons honey; spread evenly on dough. Combine brown sugar, cinnamon, raisins, and nuts; sprinkle over dough. Roll as for jelly roll from long side; cut into 16 slices. Arrange slices, cut side down, in two layers in well greased, 10-inch tube pan. Cover; let rise about 1 hour or until doubled in bulk. Bake at 350° F. for 40 to 45 minutes. Drizzle glaze over ring while still warm. Makes 16 rolls.

LUCIA BUNS

2 tbs. boiling water	1 egg yolk
1 tsp. saffron	2 tbs. water
⅔ c. warm water (105° to 115° F.)	Easy Confectioners' Sugar Glaze (*page 456*)
1 pkg. hot-roll mix	
1 egg	
Raisins	

Pour boiling water over saffron in cup or small bowl; let stand 5 minutes; drain; reserve liquid. Measure warm water into large bowl; sprinkle in yeast from package of hot-roll mix; stir to dissolve. Stir in egg, dry mix, and saffron liquid; mix well; cover with damp towel. Let rise in warm place (85° F.), free from draft, 45 to 60 minutes or until doubled in bulk. Turn out onto floured board; knead 6 to 8 times; divide in half. Roll each piece

¼-inch thick; cut into strips 5½ inches by ½ inch. Cross 2 strips to make an "X"; curl each end into center. Place on greased cookie sheets; insert raisin into each curled end. Let rise about 20 minutes, or until doubled in bulk. Beat egg yolk with 2 tablespoons water; brush over buns. Bake at 400° F. for 12 to 15 minutes. Drizzle buns with glaze while still warm. Makes 1 dozen buns.

Made with Packaged Rolls and Bread

TANGY BREAD

5 tbs. soft butter or margarine	1 tbs. chopped parsley
1 tsp. prepared mustard	1 large loaf French or Italian bread
1 tbs. chopped chives	2 tbs. grated Parmesan cheese

Combine 4 tablespoons butter or margarine, mustard, chives, and parsley; blend well. Slash bread at 1-inch intervals almost through to bottom. Spread butter mixture between slashes. Brush top of bread with remaining tablespoon butter or margarine; sprinkle with cheese. Wrap loaf in aluminum foil. Heat at 400° F. for 8 to 10 minutes or for a barbecue, place on grill until hot, turning frequently.

GLAZED SESAME ROLLS

3 tbs. melted butter or margarine	1 pkg brown 'n serve small dinner rolls
1 tbs. honey	1 tbs. toasted sesame seeds

Combine butter or margarine and honey; brush on tops of rolls; sprinkle with sesame seeds. Bake according to package directions.

SAVORY ROLLS

8 frankfurter rolls	2 tsp. chopped pimiento
2 tbs. chopped parsley	2 tsp. lemon juice
2 tbs. chopped chives or green onion tops	½ c. melted butter or margarine

Slash rolls several times crosswise almost through to bottom. Mix remaining ingredients; spread in cuts and over tops; wrap in aluminum foil. Heat on grill or at 400° F. for 5 to 8 minutes.

Chapter Ten

Soups

On damp, penetrating winter days, nothing warms the bones so quickly as a bowl of steaming soup. And in summer, nothing is more refreshing as a first course to dinner than a chilled soup, deliciously ice cold.

No longer is it necessary to start the soup pot simmering early in the morning to have "good thick soup" to put on the table at night. Today we can keep a variety of *canned soups* on the pantry shelf, or choose from one of dozens of *dried soup mixes* that need nothing more than added water and a few minutes simmering. For clear broth or bouillon, there are the *bouillon cubes and the concentrated beef and chicken stock granules and canned varieties*. Or keep a selection of the tempting *frozen soups* on hand.

It's helpful to keep some of all four kinds on hand at all times. Not only can they be used for quick soups—they're also useful for instant sauces and dips. In this book you will find a number of delectable entreés which use one or more of these soup products as an ingredient.

Soup Tips

· Add a dash of your favorite herb (*Chapter 28*) to canned or frozen soups for an extra flavor touch.
· Lace a bit of wine into an otherwise plain soup to make it a gourmet specialty.
· Make soup elegant by serving from lovely, colored pottery bowls, cups, or mugs.

SOUP STOCKS

Easy as it is to use soup mixes and stock concentrates, for real gourmet flavor there's a pleasant satisfaction in making a stock yourself, with slow, slow simmering to blend flavors perfectly. It's easier than you think, too. The basis of good homemade soup is stock —a flavorful broth made by cooking a bone (with a little meat on it) with vegetables, herbs, and seasonings.

Brown soup stock is made from beef or lamb. Some meat and onion may be browned lightly in the fat before adding to the soup kettle.

Light soup stock is made from veal or poultry bones and bits of meat.

Bouillon is clear brown soup stock seasoned with herbs and vegetables.

Consommé is usually a clear light soup stock which may or may not be made with some beef.

When buying meat for stock, buy shin beef, brisket, or soup meat. Ask for two-thirds lean meat and one-third bone and fat. Have the bones sawed into 4-inch or 5-inch lengths and if desired, lengthwise, to expose the marrow. Remove any bone splinters before adding to pot.

When stock is finished, remove the excess fat from stock by refrigerating until the fat congeals. Then loosen around the edges with a knife and carefully lift fat off. Remove any amount that is left by passing a cloth dipped in hot water around edge and over top of stock.

BEEF STOCK

4 lbs. shin beef, cubed	6 sprigs parsley
4 tbs. butter or margarine	2 medium-size onions
1½ lbs. marrow bone	4 whole cloves
	1 bay leaf
3 qts. water	3 carrots, pared and cut up
1 tbs. salt	2 leeks
3 stalks celery with tops	

Brown beef cubes in butter or margarine in deep kettle; add marrow bone and water; cover. Bring to boiling; boil 5 minutes; skim top of liquid. Reduce heat; simmer 1 hour, skimming top occasionally. Add salt, celery, parsley, onions stuck with cloves, bay leaf, carrots, and leeks. Cover; simmer 2 hours longer; strain; cool; chill.

PRESSURE-COOKER BEEF STOCK

1½ lbs. lean beef, cubed	1 medium-size onion
3 tbs. butter or margarine	2 whole cloves
	3 sprigs parsley
1 knuckle bone	½ tsp. leaf thyme, crumbled
6 c. water	
3 carrots, pared and cut up	1 bay leaf
	1 tbs. salt

Brown beef cubes in butter or margarine in pressure cooker; add remaining ingredients. Cover and secure pressure cooker; cook at 15 pounds for 20 minutes. Cool in pressure cooker; remove cover. Strain; cool; chill.

VEAL OR WHITE STOCK

1 lb. veal neck or lean veal, cut in small pieces	3 small carrots, pared and cut up
	3 stalks celery with tops
3 lbs. veal knuckle	6 sprigs parsley
3 qts. cold water	1 bay leaf
1 medium-size onion	1½ tbs. salt
2 whole cloves	

Put cut-up veal and knuckle in large kettle; add water, onion stuck with cloves, carrots, celery, parsley, and bay leaf. Bring to boiling; skim top as scum forms; cover. Simmer 1 hour; add salt; simmer 2 to 3 hours. Strain; cool; chill.

CHICKEN BROTH

1 stewing chicken (5½ to 6 lbs.)	1 carrot, pared and diced
2 medium-size onions	2 tbs. chopped parsley
3 stalks celery with tops	1 tsp. salt
	¼ tsp. pepper

Wash chicken thoroughly. Put into a large kettle; cover with water. Bring to boiling; reduce heat; skim. Add onions, celery, carrot, parsley, salt, and pepper. Cover; simmer 1½ to 2 hours or until chicken is tender. Remove chicken. Remove meat from bones. Use in recipes calling for cooked chicken. Strain broth; cool; chill. Remove fat from top. Serve hot as broth or use as a base for sauces and gravies. Makes about 4 cups.

HOT SOUPS

Some soups are so thick and hearty they're first cousins to stews—a meal in themselves, and the fragrance of such a soup gently cooking can really whet family appetites. They're inexpensive too.

OLD-FASHIONED VEGETABLE SOUP

What is better than a steaming pot of Old-Fashioned Vegetable Soup? With a marrow bone it tastes just like the one mother used to make!

1 lb. lean beef, cubed	1 c. diced carrots
2 tbs. butter or margarine	2 c. chopped onion (2 large)
2 lbs. marrow bone, cracked	1 c. diced celery
1 bay leaf	3 stalks leek, sliced
½ c. celery leaves	1 c. cubed, pared potatoes
4 sprigs parsley	½ pkg. frozen peas or lima beans
2 tsp. salt	2 cans (1 lb. 3 oz. ea.) tomatoes
6 peppercorns	1 tsp. salt
1 carrot, pared and sliced	2 tbs. chopped parsley
1 onion, sliced	
4 qts. water	

Brown meat in butter or margarine in large heavy pot or kettle. Add bones, bay leaf, celery leaves, parsley, salt, peppercorns, sliced carrot and onion, and water. Cover; bring to boiling; remove scum from top. Reduce heat; simmer 1½ to 2 hours. Strain stock; reserve meat; skim fat from stock or refrigerate overnight, then remove firm layer of fat. Heat stock to boiling; add diced carrots, chopped onions, celery, leek, potatoes, peas or lima beans, tomatoes, salt, and reserved meat. Reduce heat; simmer gently 30 minutes or until vegetables are tender; add parsley. Makes 6 to 8 servings.

CHICKEN SOUP COUNTRY STYLE

The surprise treat in this soup is delicious little chicken balls.

1 stewing chicken (4 lbs.), cut up	½ tsp. salt
1 c. chopped onion (1 large)	½ tsp. poultry seasoning
1 carrot, pared and quartered	1 egg
1 bay leaf	1 tbs. chopped parsley
1 tsp. salt	2 carrots, pared
2 qts. water	2 stalks celery
½ c. fresh bread crumbs	¼ c. chicken fat
	⅓ c. flour
	1 c. milk

Place chicken in large heavy pot or kettle with onion, quartered carrot, bay leaf, 1 teaspoon salt, and water; simmer 1½ to 2 hours or until tender; remove chicken; chill stock. Remove chicken from bones; discard skin; reserve 1 cup chicken for soup. (Chill remainder to use for salad, casserole, or other chicken dish.) Grind 1 cup chicken; add bread crumbs, ½ teaspoon salt, poultry seasoning, egg, and parsley; blend. Form firmly into small balls; set aside. Remove layer of fat from chilled stock; reserve. Heat chicken stock (there should be 4 cups). Cut carrots and celery into matchstick-size pieces; add to stock; cook 10 to 15 minutes or until tender. Melt ¼ cup chicken fat in saucepan; blend in flour; add milk slowly, stirring constantly. Pour mixture slowly into stock; cook, stirring constantly, until mixture is thickened. Drop chicken balls into soup; heat 5 minutes, serve. Makes 8 servings.

GREEN PEA SOUP

1 c. quick-cooking green split peas	½ c. slivered ham pieces
1 ham bone	1 tbs. leaf marjoram, crumbled
5 c. water	
1 small onion, sliced	

Wash peas in cold water; drain. Place ham bone, water, onion, and peas in heavy pot or kettle. Bring to boiling; reduce heat; simmer, stirring occasionally, 1½ hours or until peas are soft. Add more water as necessary. Remove bone; press mixture through sieve or food mill. Add ham pieces and marjoram; reheat until bubbly. Serve at once. Makes 4 to 6 servings.

LENTIL AND SPINACH SOUP

1½ c. lentils	1½ c. diced, pared, potatoes (2 medium)
2½ qts. water	
1 tbs. salt	1 pkg. (10 oz.) frozen chopped spinach
1 c. chopped onion (1 large)	
1 clove of garlic, mashed	2 tbs. lemon juice
4 tbs. olive oil	½ tsp. whole coriander, crushed
	2 tbs. lemon juice

Wash lentils. Put in large saucepan. Add water; bring to boiling. Add salt; reduce heat; simmer about 1 hour or until lentils are almost tender. Sauté onion and garlic in oil until tender. Add potatoes, spinach, 2 tablespoons lemon juice, coriander, onion, and garlic with the olive oil to lentil mixture. Break up block of spinach as it cooks. Simmer soup 15 to 20 minutes or until potatoes are tender. If soup becomes too thick, add a little boiling water to thin. Just before serving, add 2 tablespoons lemon juice. Makes 8 servings.

INDIANA LIMA BEAN SOUP

2 pkgs. (1 lb. ea.) dried lima beans	¼ tsp. pepper
1 c. chopped onion (1 large)	½ tsp. savory
	½ lb. frankfurters, sliced
1 apple, peeled, cored, and chopped	1 tbs. chopped parsley
1 ham bone	1 lb. cooked sauerkraut
2 tsp. salt	

Soak beans several hours or overnight in water to cover in large heavy pot or kettle. Add onion, apple, ham bone, salt, pepper, and savory; add enough more water to bring level 1 inch over beans. Simmer gently 1½ to 2 hours or until beans are mushy; remove ham bone. Put soup mixture through food mill or strainer; taste; season if necessary. Return to soup kettle; add frankfurters; simmer gently until heated through. (If soup is thicker than desired, add milk to thin.) Sprinkle with parsley. Spoon hot sauerkraut into bowls; ladle soup over. Makes 6 to 8 servings.

NAVY BEAN SOUP

1½ lbs. navy beans	1 c. chopped onion (1 large)
2½ qts. boiling water	¼ c. butter or margarine
Ham hock or meaty ham bone	Salt
	Pepper

Wash beans; discard any imperfect ones. Cover with cold water and soak overnight; drain. Put beans in a large kettle; add boiling water and ham. Simmer about 1½ hours or until beans are tender and ham is cooked. Sauté onion in butter or margarine until golden; add to soup. Continue cooking about 1 hour. Remove ham hock or bone. Remove meat; cut into thin slivers. Skim fat from soup. Return meat to kettle; season to taste with salt and pepper. Thin with hot water if soup seems thick. Serve hot, garnished with parsley, if desired. Makes 8 to 10 servings.

POTATO ONION SOUP

1 c. chopped onion (1 large)	1 tsp. salt
	Dash of pepper
3 tbs. butter or margarine	1 c. light cream
3½ c. chicken broth*	3 tbs. chopped parsley
½ pkg. (4 servings) instant mashed potatoes	

Sauté onion in butter or margarine in medium-size saucepan until tender; add broth; simmer 15 minutes. Add potatoes, salt, pepper, and cream; simmer gently until heated through; do not boil. Sprinkle with parsley; serve hot. (Soup may also be chilled and served cold.) Makes 6 servings.

* Or use 3 chicken bouillon cubes, or an equivalent amount of granulated chicken bouillon, dissolved in 3½ cups hot water.

FRENCH ONION SOUP

6 medium-size onions, sliced	Melba toast rounds or French bread, sliced and toasted
2 tbs. butter or margarine	Grated Parmesan cheese
6½ c. beef broth	
½ tsp. salt	

Sauté onions in butter or margarine in large saucepan until lightly brown. Add beef broth; cover; cook about 15 to 20 minutes or until onions are tender. Add salt. To serve, bring soup to boiling; ladle into soup cups or bowls. Top each with melba toast or French bread toast slice and Parmesan cheese. Makes about 8 servings.

EGG DROP SOUP

4 c. chicken broth
  or 3 cans (13½
  oz. ea.) chicken
  broth
1 c. water
½ tsp. salt
⅛ tsp. pepper

2 tbs. sliced green
  onion
1 tbs. cornstarch
¼ c. water
1 tsp. soy sauce
2 eggs

Heat broth, 1 cup water, salt, pepper, and onion 5 minutes over medium heat. Blend cornstarch, ¼ cup water and soy sauce together; add to broth; stir constantly until thickened. If using homemade broth, taste for seasoning at this point. Beat eggs well. Pour into soup in thin stream, stirring constantly. Remove soup from heat at once. Garnish with sprig of watercress, if desired. Makes 6 servings.

CREAM OF POTATO SOUP

⅓ c. chopped onion
3 tbs. butter or
  margarine
2 c. diced, pared
  potato
¾ c. water

1½ tsp. salt
⅛ tsp. pepper
2 c. milk or 1 c.
  milk and 1 c.
  light cream

In saucepan, sauté onion in butter or margarine until golden. Add potato, water, salt, and pepper. Cover and cook slowly until potatoes are tender. Add milk or milk and cream; continue cooking until soup comes to boiling. Correct seasoning. Serve hot, garnished with chopped parsley, if desired. Makes 3 to 4 servings.

BISQUES, CHOWDERS, AND STEWS

A divine bisque thickened with purée . . . a chowder of luscious ingredients simmered together with milk or tomato . . . a lovely oyster stew. Any of these can help turn a family supper or a simple occasion into something special.

LOBSTER BISQUE

1 can (5 oz.) lobster
¼ c. butter or
  margarine
¼ c. flour
1 tsp. salt

1 tsp. paprika
Dash of cayenne
3½ c. milk
¼ c. dry sherry
  (optional)

Bone and flake lobster; reserve liquid. Melt butter or margarine in top of double boiler. Blend in flour, salt, paprika, and cayenne. Stir in milk and reserved lobster liquid. Cook over medium heat, stirring constantly until mixture thickens and comes to boiling. Add lobster meat and sherry; heat through. Keep warm over hot water. Makes 8 servings.

OYSTER BISQUE

1 pt. oysters in
  liquid
4 c. milk
1 slice onion
3 to 4 sprigs parsley
1 bay leaf
½ c. chopped celery

½ c. butter or
  margarine
⅓ c. flour
1½ tsp. salt
⅛ tsp. white
  pepper

Drain oysters; reserve liquid. Chop oysters fine; reserve. Combine milk, onion, parsley, and bay leaf in saucepan; scald; remove from heat. Cook celery in small amount of water until tender; drain; add to milk mixture. Melt butter or margarine in second saucepan; blend in flour, salt, and pepper. Strain milk mixture through fine sieve; stir into flour mixture. Cook over medium heat, stirring constantly, until thickened. Add oysters and liquid. Heat through. Makes 8 to 10 servings.

QUICK CRAB BISQUE

½ lb. (about 1 c.)
  flaked crab meat
½ c. dry sherry
1 can (10½ oz.)
  condensed tomato
  soup

1 can (10½ oz.)
  condensed cream
  of mushroom
  soup
1¼ c. light cream
½ tsp. curry
  powder
Chopped fresh
  parsley

Marinate crab meat in sherry for 1 hour. Blend tomato and mushroom soups, cream, and curry in saucepan. Heat slowly, stirring constantly; do not boil. Add crab meat and sherry; heat through. Serve immediately. Sprinkle lightly with parsley. Makes 4 servings.

NEW ENGLAND CLAM CHOWDER

1½ in. piece salt pork, cut in small cubes	2 c. diced, pared potatoes (about 5)
1 medium-size onion, thinly sliced	1 tsp. salt
	¼ tsp. pepper
2 cans (10½ oz. ea.) minced clams	1 c. water
	1 qt. scalded milk
	2 tbs. butter or margarine

Cook salt pork until crisp and brown; drain on paper towels. Sauté onion in drippings; pour off fat. Drain clams. Combine salt pork bits, onion, clam liquid, potatoes, salt, pepper, and water in large saucepan. Cover; simmer 10 minutes or until potatoes are just tender. Add clams, scalded milk, and butter or margarine. Cover; set aside 1 to 2 hours to blend flavors. Reheat, but do not boil. Serve with soda, pilot, or common crackers that have been soaked in milk or thicken chowder with 3 tablespoons of flour, if desired. Makes 6 servings.

LONG ISLAND CLAM CHOWDER

2 c. chopped onion (2 large)	¼ tsp. pepper
1 clove of garlic, minced	3 qts. water
	1 can (1 lb.) tomatoes
4 medium-size carrots, pared and diced	1 tbs. leaf thyme, crumbled
1 c. diced celery	½ tsp. leaf rosemary, crumbled
1 green pepper, diced	3 doz. large clams with liquid
1 medium-size potato, pared and cubed	3 tbs. cubed salt pork
1 bay leaf	½ c. flour
2 tsp. salt	1 tbs. chopped parsley
½ tsp. monosodium glutamate	

Combine onion, garlic, carrots, celery, green pepper, potato, bay leaf, salt, monosodium glutamate, pepper, and water in large heavy pot or kettle; cook slowly about 30 minutes or until vegetables are tender. Add tomatoes, thyme, and rosemary; simmer 5 minutes. Drain clams; reserve liquid. Remove and discard dark portions from clams; cut clams into

small pieces. Cook salt pork in small saucepan until brown and crispy; remove browned bits. Blend flour into fat remaining in saucepan; add clam liquid; pour into chowder. Simmer, stirring constantly, until thickened. Add clams, parsley, and salt pork bits; simmer 5 minutes longer. Makes 6 to 8 servings.

NEW ENGLAND FISH CHOWDER

½ lb. salt pork, cubed	2 c. diced, pared potatoes (about 5)
1½ c. chopped onion	1 bay leaf
1 c. chopped celery	1 tsp. salt
2 lbs. frozen haddock filets, cut up	⅛ tsp. pepper
	3 c. water
	2½ c. milk
	½ c. light cream

Cook salt pork in large saucepan until crisp and brown; remove; reserve. Pour off all but 2 tablespoons of fat from pan. Add onion and celery; cook until soft. Add fish, potatoes, bay leaf, salt, pepper, and water. Simmer 30 to 35 minutes or until vegetables and fish are tender. Remove bay leaf. Add milk and cream. Heat just to boiling. Sprinkle each serving with salt pork bits. Serve with soda, pilot, or common crackers, if desired. Makes 6 servings.

PRAIRIE CORN CHOWDER

3 tbs. diced salt pork or bacon	2 tsp. salt
	¼ tsp. pepper
½ c. chopped onion (1 medium)	¼ tsp. leaf rosemary, crumbled
2 c. cubed, pared potatoes	¼ c. diced pimiento
2 c. boiling water	¼ c. shredded Cheddar cheese
2 cans (1 lb. ea.) cream-style corn	2 tbs. minced parsley
1 qt. milk	

Cook salt pork in large heavy pot or kettle until crisp and brown; remove browned bits; reserve. Add onion to drippings; sauté until soft, but not browned. Add potatoes and water; simmer about 20 minutes or until potatoes are tender. Add corn, milk, salt, pepper, rosemary, pimiento, and browned pork bits; heat until steaming hot; stir in cheese and parsley. Makes 4 to 6 servings.

CORN CHOWDER

½ c. finely diced salt pork
⅓ c. diced green pepper
⅓ c. chopped onion
1 c. sliced celery
1 c. diced, pared potatoes
2 c. hot water
1 bay leaf
⅛ tsp. leaf sage, crumbled

1 tbs. chopped parsley
1 can (12 oz.) whole-kernel corn
1 qt. scalded half-and-half or light cream
1½ tsp. salt
Dash of pepper
2 tbs. flour
2 tbs. milk

Cook salt pork in a large heavy pot or kettle until crisp and brown; add green pepper and onion; sauté 3 minutes. Add celery, potato, water, bay leaf, sage, and parsley. Simmer about 7 minutes or until potatoes are tender. Remove bay leaf. Add corn, half-and-half or cream, salt, and pepper. Blend flour and milk; add to soup; heat until slightly thickened. Makes about 8 servings.

OYSTER STEW

Serve this as a main course for a special occasion. A green salad and chunks of French bread will round out the meal.

¼ c. butter or margarine
1 qt. oysters in liquid
1 qt. milk
1 c. heavy cream
1 tsp. salt
3 tbs. chopped parsley

¼ tsp. white pepper
2 tsp. Worcestershire sauce
2 dashes hot-pepper sauce
Paprika
2 tbs. butter or margarine

Melt ¼ cup butter or margarine in heavy pan. Add oysters and ½ cup oyster liquid. Heat just until oysters curl around edges. Combine milk, cream, salt, pepper, Worcestershire, and hot-pepper sauce in second pan; heat until bubbles appear around the edge; pour into pan with oysters. Add remaining oyster liquid; heat through. Sprinkle generously with paprika; float 2 tablespoons butter or margarine on top. Serve hot. Makes 8 servings.

BOUILLABAISSE

(*Pictured opposite page 117*)

4 lbs. firm-fleshed fish* (equal parts of any: snapper, bass, cod, haddock, perch)
⅓ c. olive or pure vegetable oil
2 c. sliced onion
3 cloves of garlic, minced
4 carrots, pared and chopped
1 lb. fresh tomatoes, peeled and chopped or 1 can (about 1 lb.) tomatoes
2 bottles (8 oz. ea.) clam juice
1 can (1 pt. 2 oz.) tomato juice
1 tsp. leaf thyme, crumbled

½ tsp. saffron, crumbled
½ tsp. bottled dried orange peel
1½ tsp. salt
¼ tsp. pepper
½ tsp. fennel seeds, crushed
1 bay leaf, crumbled
2 tbs. minced parsley
2 lbs. live lobster
1 lb. fresh shrimp, shelled and deveined
2 doz. clams, scrubbed (optional)
1 doz. mussels, scrubbed (optional)
French bread

Cut fish into serving-size pieces, bone and all. Heat oil in large kettle; add onion, garlic, and carrots; sauté 5 minutes. Add tomatoes, clam juice, tomato juice, thyme, saffron, orange peel, salt, pepper, fennel, bay leaf, and parsley; boil 10 minutes. Cut lobster in serving-size pieces, shell and all; layer onto mixture in kettle; layer cut fish over lobster. Boil hard 10 minutes. Add shrimp; boil 5 minutes. Add clams and mussels; cover; cook 5 minutes or just until shells open. Remove from heat; serve at once with French bread. Soup may be sprinkled with additional parsley, if desired. Makes 6 servings.

* If using frozen fish select a variety in the same total quantity (4 pounds); proceed according to recipe but boil hard for only 5 minutes after adding it to the kettle. Precooked frozen or canned shellfish should be added at the very last and cooked only 5 minutes.

CIOPPINO

This stew, similar to bouillabaisse, is claimed by San Francisco as its very own. One story is that it is the invention of the Portuguese fishermen of Fisherman's Wharf who concocted the stew with whatever the day's catch yielded. They cooked it in a large pot on the wharf, asking each fishing vessel for a contribution to the pot with a cry of "Chip in!"

¾ c. chopped onion	2 tsp. salt
2 cloves of garlic, minced	¼ tsp. pepper
¾ c. chopped green pepper	3 lbs. sea bass (or other firm-fleshed fish), cut in slices
⅓ c. olive oil	1 lobster (2½ lbs.), cut up
1 can (1 lb. 13 oz.) tomatoes, broken up	1 lb. fresh shrimp, shelled and deveined or 1 pkg. (10 oz.) frozen, shelled, and deveined shrimp
1 c. dry red wine	
1 bay leaf	
1 tsp. ground marjoram	
1 tsp. leaf basil, crumbled	1½ doz. littleneck clams, well scrubbed
½ tsp. leaf thyme, crumbled	Toasted Italian bread
3 tbs. chopped parsley	

Sauté onion, garlic, and green pepper in hot oil in large kettle until tender. Add tomatoes, wine, bay leaf, marjoram, basil, thyme, and parsley. Cover; simmer 1 hour. Add salt, pepper, sea bass, lobster, and shrimp. Cook 15 to 20 minutes; do not stir. Add clams; cook 5 minutes or just until shells open. Remove from heat. Serve at once in bowls with toasted Italian bread. Makes 6 servings.

GUMBOS

No soup collection is complete without its gumbo recipes. Whether they contain okra or filé powder for thickening, these hearty soups live up to their Southern heritage. They're a meal in their own right when served with rice.

CREOLE SEAFOOD GUMBO

Gumbo is considered a most distinctive dish in Creole cuisine. Filé powder is this gumbo's secret ingredient. Because gumbo will become stringy if reheated after the filé powder has been added, we suggest you put a bit into each individual bowl, add the gumbo, and stir. This way any leftover gumbo is usable.

4 tbs. pure vegetable oil	1 lb. fresh shrimp, shelled and deveined or 1 pkg. (10 oz.) frozen, shelled, and deveined shrimp
3 tbs. flour	
2 c. chopped onion (2 large)	
1 clove of garlic, chopped	
3 c. water	1 can (7 oz.) crab meat, drained and boned
1 can (1 lb.) tomatoes	
1 tsp. salt	1 can (7 oz.) frozen oysters, thawed
¼ tsp. pepper	
¼ tsp. hot-pepper sauce	3 tbs. chopped parsley
	2 tbs. filé powder
	1 c. hot, cooked rice

Heat oil in Dutch oven or heavy kettle; add flour. Stir constantly over medium heat until flour has turned a warm golden brown. (This is the brown roux or flavor base for the true gumbo.) Add onion and garlic; cook until soft. Add water, tomatoes, salt, pepper, hotpepper sauce, and shrimp; cover; simmer 15 minutes. Add crab meat, oysters, and 2 tablespoons parsley. Simmer 5 minutes. Put 1 teaspoon filé powder and a heaping spoonful of hot, cooked rice into each soup bowl. Ladle the gumbo into each bowl; stir gently until mixture thickens. Sprinkle with remaining parsley. Makes 6 servings.

SEAFOOD GUMBO

3 tbs. butter or margarine	1 pkg. (10 oz.) frozen, shelled, and deveined shrimp
1 c. chopped onion (1 large)	
1 clove of garlic, minced	1 can (1 lb.) tomatoes
2 qts. water	3 tbs. flour
½ c. raw rice	½ tsp. thyme
1 green or red pepper, seeded and diced	2 dashes bottled hot-pepper sauce
1 c. sliced celery	1 tsp. Worcestershire sauce
1 pkg. (10 oz.) frozen okra	1 bottle (8 oz.) clam juice
1 lb. fresh shrimp, shelled and deveined or	1 can (6½ oz.) crab meat, boned
	¼ c. diced pimiento

Melt butter or margarine in large heavy pot or kettle; sauté onion and garlic until lightly browned; add water and rice. Simmer gently 20 minutes. Add green pepper, celery, okra, shrimp, and tomatoes. Simmer 10 minutes or until vegetables and shrimp are tender. Blend flour, thyme, hot-pepper sauce, and Worcestershire sauce with clam juice. Add to gumbo, stirring until smooth. Add crab meat and pimiento; taste for flavor; add additional seasoning if necessary. Makes 6 to 8 servings.

COLD SOUPS

Except for Vichyssoise, the French-inspired chilled potato-and-leek soup, cold soups are Johnny-come-latelies in the American meal pattern. They're worth getting acquainted with—for they can be prepared hours ahead, they're nourishing, and they're refreshing for warm weather.

GAZPACHO

This cold Spanish soup is guaranteed to tempt the appetite. It's zesty! And there are about as many versions of it as there are regions in Spain.

¾ c. finely chopped onion	¼ tsp. pepper
¾ tsp. minced garlic	1 tsp. paprika
1½ c. finely chopped green pepper	2 tbs. chopped chives
	⅓ c. olive oil
2½ c. diced, peeled tomatoes	½ c. lemon juice
	2 c. tomato juice
2½ tsp. salt	½ c. shredded, pared cucumber
½ tsp. sugar	2 tbs. dry sherry

Combine onion, garlic, green pepper, tomatoes, salt, sugar, pepper, paprika, and chives in a large bowl. Stir in oil, lemon juice, and tomato juice. Chill 2 hours. Before serving, blend in cucumber and sherry. Makes 8 servings.

QUICK GAZPACHO

2 cans (10½ oz. ea.) condensed tomato soup	1 tsp. Worcestershire sauce
2 c. water	2 tsp. chopped chives
2 dashes hot-pepper sauce	½ c. finely minced green pepper

Combine soup and water in saucepan; place over medium heat; stir until well blended. Cool. Pour into plastic shaker or large screw-top jar. Add hot-pepper sauce, Worcestershire, chives, and green pepper. Chill. Shake well before serving. Makes 6 servings.

PRESSED CUCUMBER SOUP

Here's a delightful, refreshing soup for a summer day.

2 large cucumbers	2 tsp. chopped chives
1¼ tsp. salt	
¼ tsp. pepper	2 c. dairy sour cream
1 tsp. sugar	
3 tbs. lemon juice	2 c. milk
¾ tsp. leaf chervil, crumbled	Cucumber slices

Pare cucumbers; shred into a bowl. Add salt, pepper, and sugar. Place smaller bowl on top of cucumbers; press out as much juice as possible. Do not drain. Chill at least 2 hours. Stir in lemon juice, chervil, chives, sour cream, and milk. Garnish with cucumber slices. Makes 6 to 8 servings.

PEA SOUP DIABLE

Try this for a cooling first course or as a luncheon or supper main course.

1 can (10½ oz.)
  condensed pea
  soup
2 c. milk
1 can (4½ oz.)
  deviled ham
¼ tsp. hot-pepper
  sauce

2 tsp. chopped
  fresh dill
½ tsp. salt
⅛ tsp. pepper
1 tsp. grated lemon
  rind
Dairy sour cream
Paprika

Blend all ingredients except sour cream and paprika in a large bowl. Chill. Serve in soup cups or bowls topped with sour cream and a sprinkling of paprika. Makes 4 to 6 servings.

AVOCADO SOUP

1 large ripe avocado
1 c. milk
1 c. finely chopped
  peeled tomatoes
¼ tsp. pepper

½ tsp. salt
⅛ tsp. garlic salt
¼ tsp. celery seed
1 c. dairy sour
  cream
1 tbs. chopped
  chives

Peel avocado; remove seed. Cut in small pieces; press through a sieve. Add about half the milk; blend well. Add remaining milk, tomatoes, pepper, salts, and celery seed. Blend. Stir in sour cream. Chill. Thin with a little milk at serving time, if necessary. Garnish with chives. Makes 6 servings.

CREAMED CHICKEN CURRY SOUP

2 cans (10½ oz.
  ea.) condensed
  cream of chicken
  soup
1 tsp. curry
  powder

2 tsp. dried parsley
  flakes
2 tsp. chopped
  chives
1½ c. milk

Combine all ingredients in plastic shaker or large screw-top jar. Shake to blend well. Chill thoroughly. Makes 6 servings.

CHICKEN AND CUCUMBER SOUP

2 cans (10½ oz.
  ea.) condensed
  chicken and rice
  soup

2 soup cans of water
1 c. shredded, pared
  cucumber
½ tsp. dill weed

Combine soup, water, and cucumber. Chill. Sprinkle each serving with dill weed. Makes 6 servings.

VICHYSSOISE

If you've ever tried this while dining out you'll surely want to try it at home.

3 c. washed,
  cleaned, sliced
  leek (about
  1 bunch)
½ c. sliced onion
  (1 medium)
¼ c. butter or
  margarine
5 c. sliced, pared
  potatoes
  (about 6)

2 cans (13¾ oz.
  ea.) chicken
  broth (3½ c.)
1 tsp. salt
2 c. heavy cream
2 c. milk
Chopped chives

Sauté leek and onion in butter or margarine in large saucepan until soft. Add potatoes, chicken broth, and salt. Cook 35 to 40 minutes or until vegetables are very soft. Press through food mill or sieve. Add cream and milk. Chill well. Serve with sprinkling of chives. You may substitute sour cream for the heavy cream, if desired. Makes 8 servings.

SUMMER POTATO SOUP

4 c. pared, diced
  potatoes
¼ c. butter or
  margarine
½ c. chopped green
  onions

3 tbs. flour
1½ tsp. salt
⅛ tsp. cayenne
2 c. milk
1 c. dairy sour
  cream
2 tbs. chopped
  parsley

Cook potatoes in boiling salted water until soft but not mushy; drain. Heat butter or margarine in large saucepan; sauté onions until soft. Stir in flour, salt, and cayenne. Add milk slowly. Cook over medium heat, stirring constantly, until thickened. Reserve 1 cup of cooked potatoes; mash remainder coarsely with fork; beat into milk mixture; stir in reserved potatoes. Cool; chill. Serve cold topped with sour cream and chopped parsley. Makes 4 to 6 servings.

FROSTY CLAM 'N POTATO CHOWDER

1 can (10¼ oz.) frozen cream of potato soup
⅔ c. light cream

¾ c. bottled clam juice
Chopped parsley

Place can of soup in pan of hot water for about 30 minutes. Combine soup with cream and clam juice; beat smooth in electric blender. Chill at least 4 hours. Thin, if desired, with light cream or milk. Serve in chilled bowls. Sprinkle with parsley. Makes 2 or 3 servings.

ICY ASPARAGUS SOUP

2 lbs. fresh asparagus
2 c. chicken broth
3 tbs. flour
¼ c. water
½ tsp. salt

Dash of pepper
1 c. heavy cream
¼ c. dry white wine
Chopped fresh dill or dill weed

Cut off asparagus tips. Cook tips in salted water until just tender. Drain and chill. Cut asparagus stalks in 1-inch pieces. Cook in chicken broth 15 minutes. Make a smooth paste of flour and water; stir into broth; simmer 2 minutes. Strain through sieve or food mill. Add salt, pepper, cream, and wine. Chill several hours. Float asparagus tips on each serving; top with dill. Makes 6 servings.

ASPARAGUS AND CHEESE SOUP

2 cans (10½ oz. ea.) condensed cream of asparagus soup
1 can (10½ oz.) condensed cream of celery soup
¼ tsp. salt

¼ tsp. leaf basil, crumbled
1½ c. water
1 c. tomato juice
⅔ c. crumbled Roquefort or blue cheese
4 slices crisp cooked bacon, crumbled

Blend soups, salt, basil, water, and tomato juice. Stir a small amount of soup mixture into cheese; blend smooth. Stir cheese mixture into remaining soup mixture. Chill. Serve sprinkled with crumbled bacon. Makes 8 servings.

GARNISHES AND GO-WITHS

The sprinkling of minced chives over Vichyssoise is just as important as the puréed potato mixture itself. Soup garnishes should complement the soup in color, texture, and flavor. The go-withs (such as cheese sticks and oyster crackers) do double duty in adding crunchy texture and making the soup itself more filling.

Garnishes

Chopped parsley
Chopped celery leaves
Sliced olives
Lemon slices
Croutons
Sausage slices
Crumbled bacon

Dairy sour cream
Onion rings
Grated cheese
Popcorn
Thin green pepper rings
Minced chives

Go-Withs

Cheese sticks
Oyster crackers
Saltines
Soda crackers
Melba toast
Tiny cheese sandwiches

Cheese roll-ups (Spread soft rolled bread with Cheddar cheese spread. Roll up, skewer, and toast.)

Chapter Eleven

Meats

For most of us, it's the meat that makes the meal, whether it's a succulent roast or a sizzling steak, a bubbling stew, or even the good old American standby, hamburgers.

But meat also accounts for the biggest part of the food budget, and therefore knowing how to buy it wisely is one of the most important of all things for the homemaker to learn.

Buying

Buying meat in today's supermarket is quite different from buying it at the old-fashioned butcher store. A great percentage of meat now is prepackaged. This presents a different set of buying guides.

Are you confused when looking at one packaged cut and the next? You are no different from your next-door neighbor. But there are characteristics that still indicate good quality which you can see and which will help you make a good decision.

· Formerly the most reliable guide to judging good quality was the inspection stamp, which you could see and which told you the grade of meat you were about to purchase. It was most likely to be *Choice* or *Good* since *Prime* is relatively limited in supply. Exclusive hotels, clubs, and restaurants usually bid for this quality. While all meat is still stamped with its federal or state grade, you can seldom see the stamp itself on the smaller cuts of prepackaged meats.

Here are some things to look for:
· Color, firmness, and texture of the lean affects the quality of meat. Bright colored, firm, fine-textured lean is associated with high quality meat.
· Marbleing—flecks of fat within the lean—is an important factor affecting quality in meat. It enhances palatability by increasing juiciness, flavor, and tenderness.

Shopping Tips

· Read the grocery ads in your local newspaper, looking for meat specials. Plan menus around these specials—this can save you dollars. These ads will also frequently tell you what grade of meat is being sold.
· When your favorite cuts are on "special," buy two and store one in the freezer.
· Recently some supermarkets have started packaging their meats in specially designed containers to show both sides of the meat.
· If you have any question about the meat you are about to buy, don't guess. Ask the butcher or the meat manager at the supermarket. Supermarkets will also take care of special requests such as special cuts or boning a roast; but give them enough notice.
· Many supermarket meat managers try to help the shopper by indicating on labels inside the packages how the meat should be used. One cut may bear the label "oven roast," another "pot roast," or a cut-up shoulder of lamb for stew may be marked "lamb for stew."

Storing and Handling Meat

The wise shopper tries to do all or most of her food shopping for a week in one trip, and this usually means bringing home several cuts of meat for the week. Some refrigerators have a special compartment designed for storing fresh meat unwrapped. Follow the manufacturer's instructions.

· Unwrap the prepackaged meats you've brought from the supermarket. Rewrap the meat loosely in transparent plastic wrap, wax paper, or aluminum foil, leaving the ends open for good air circulation. Refrigerate.

· Fresh meat, not prepackaged, should be removed from the market wrapping paper and wrapped as above.

· Variety meats and ground or chopped meats are more perishable than other meats and should be cooked in one or two days or frozen.

· Cured meat, cured and smoked meat, sausages, and ready-to-serve meats should also be stored immediately in the refrigerator. They can be left in their original wrapping.

· Canned hams, picnics, and other perishable canned meats should be stored in the refrigerator unless directions on the can read to the contrary. Do not freeze these meats.

· Frozen meat should be placed in the freezer immediately after purchase. For directions on freezing meat, see page 486.

The Ways of Cooking Meats

There are two general methods of cooking meats:

The Dry Heat Method (for tender cuts)

Roasting: Season with salt and pepper, if desired; place meat, fat side up on rack (unless otherwise directed) in shallow open roasting pan. Insert a meat thermometer so the bulb is in the center of the largest muscle; add no water and do not cover; roast at 325° F. to desired degree of doneness.

Broiling: Set the oven regulator for broiling; place broiler pan in desired position. Place meat on rack of broiler pan; broil, following chart for particular cut. Season with salt and pepper, if desired; turn and cook the other side. Season, if desired, and serve at once.

Panbroiling: Place meat in heavy heated skillet or griddle. Do not add fat or water; do not cover. Cook slowly, turning occasionally; pour off fat as it accumulates. Brown meat on both sides; do not overcook. Season, if desired, and serve at once.

Panfrying: Brown meat on both sides in a small amount of fat over medium heat; season with salt and pepper, if desired. Do not cover the meat. Cook, turning occasionally, until done. Remove from pan and serve at once.

The Moist Heat Method (for less tender cuts)

Braising: Brown meat slowly on all sides in heavy utensil. Pour off drippings after browning. Season with salt, pepper, and other seasonings, if desired. Add a small amount of liquid; cover tightly. Cook over low heat until tender. Make sauce or gravy from the liquid in the pan, if desired. Meat may also be cooked, after browning, in a 300° to 325° F. oven.

Cooking in liquid

(1) *For large cuts:* Brown meat on all sides, if desired. Cover the meat with water or stock; season with salt, pepper, seasonings, and vegetables, if desired. Cover kettle and simmer until tender. When vegetables are to be cooked with the meat, as in "boiled" dinners, add them whole or in pieces, just long enough before the meat is tender to cook them.

(2) *For stews:* Cut meat in uniform pieces, usually 1- to 2-inch cubes. If a brown stew is desired, brown meat cubes on all sides. Add just enough water, vegetable juices, or other liquid to cover the meat. Season with salt, pepper, and other seasonings, if desired. Cover kettle and simmer until tender; add vegetables to stew just long enough before end of cooking time to cook them thoroughly. If desired, thicken the cooking liquid with flour for gravy.

Cooking Frozen Meat

Frozen meat may be cooked satisfactorily either by defrosting prior to or during cooking. Commercially frozen products should be prepared according to package directions.

When defrosting before cooking, the most

STORAGE TIME CHART
Maximum Storage Time Recommendations for Fresh, Cooked, and Processed Meat

Meat	Refrigerator (38° to 40° F.) *	Freezer (at 0° F. or lower)
Beef (fresh)	2 to 4 days	6 to 12 months
Veal (fresh)	2 to 4 days	6 to 9 months
Pork (fresh)	2 to 4 days	3 to 6 months
Lamb (fresh)	2 to 4 days	6 to 9 months
Ground beef, veal, and lamb	1 to 2 days	3 to 4 months
Ground pork	1 to 2 days	1 to 3 months
Variety meats	1 to 2 days	3 to 4 months
Luncheon meats	1 week	not recommended
Sausage, fresh pork	1 week	2 months
Sausage, smoked**	3 to 7 days	
Sausage, dry and semidry (unsliced)**	2 to 3 weeks	
Frankfurters**	4 to 5 days	
Bacon**	5 to 7 days	
Smoked ham, whole	1 week	2 months
Ham slices	3 to 4 days	
Beef, corned	1 week	2 weeks
Leftover cooked meat	4 to 5 days	2 to 3 months
Frozen Combination Foods:		
Meat pies (cooked)	—	3 months
Swiss steak (cooked)	—	3 months
Stews (cooked)	—	3 to 4 months
Prepared meat dinners	—	2 to 6 months

* The range in time reflects recommendations for maximum storage time from several authorities. For top quality, fresh meats should be used in 2 or 3 days, ground meat and variety meats should be used within 24 hours.

** Freezing cured and smoked meats is not recommended as a routine procedure. However, if these meats are frozen, storage should not exceed 60 days.

practical methods are 1) in the refrigerator and 2) at room temperature. The meat should be defrosted in its original wrapping and should not be allowed to remain at room temperature after defrosting. Defrosting in water is recommended only if the meat is to be cooked in liquid. After meat is defrosted, it should be cooked in the same way as other fresh meat.

When cooking meat from the frozen state, it is necessary to allow additional cooking time. Frozen roasts require approximately a third to half again as long for cooking as roasts which have been defrosted. The additional time for cooking steaks and chops varies according to the surface area and thickness of the meat, as well as the broiling temperature.

Thick frozen steaks, chops, and ground meat patties must be broiled farther from the heat than defrosted ones in order that the meat will be cooked to the desired degree of doneness without becoming too brown on the outside. When steaks or chops are to be coated with eggs and crumbs or with batter, the meat should be partially defrosted so the coatings will adhere to the meat.

When panbroiling frozen steaks and chops, a hot skillet should be used so that the meat has a chance to brown before defrosting on the surface, retarding browning. The heat should be reduced after browning and the meat turned occasionally so it will cook through without becoming too brown.

Timetable for Defrosting Frozen Meat

Meat	In Refrigerator	Room Temperature
Large roast	4 to 7 hrs. per lb.	2 to 3 hrs. per lb.
Small roast	3 to 5 hrs. per lb.	1 to 2 hrs. per lb.
1-inch steak	12 to 14 hrs.	2 to 4 hrs.

Refreezing meat is not a recommended practice because of possible variation in the history and treatment of meat before freezing, during freezing, and/or during defrosting prior to refreezing. When refreezing may seem necessary to prevent spoilage, some loss in juiciness can be expected.

Using Tenderizers

You will find on the grocer's shelf several products containing the enzyme from papaya which will tenderize meat without aging. Some are powders, some in liquid form. Use according to label directions. These are particularly useful in treating less tender cuts, to make them tender enough to broil or roast like more costly cuts of meat.

Another method of tenderizing meats is to marinate them in an acid and oil mixture. Many such marinades will be found in chapter 20, Sauces, Marinades, and Bastes.

BROWN PAN GRAVY

When meat has finished roasting, remove from roasting pan to warm platter. Pour off fat from pan; reserve. For each cup of medium-thick gravy desired, return 2 tablespoons fat to roasting pan. Blend in 2 tablespoons flour. Stir in 1 cup water or beef broth (canned broth, beef bouillon, or granulated beef bouillon cube and 1 cup water). Stir to remove all browned meat drippings from pan. Cook over medium heat, stirring constantly, until thickened and bubbly. Taste; add salt and pepper, if necessary.

STEAK

Porterhouse, T-bone, and club steaks are cut from the short loin which contains the tenderloin and is next to the rib section.

Steaks for Broiling

Porterhouse or Large T-Bone: This steak is cut from the large end of the short loin. An average cut is about 3 pounds. It has a T-shape bone and a section of the tenderloin. It makes 3 to 4 servings.

T-Bone Steak: This steak is similar in shape to the Porterhouse, but smaller in size; an average cut weighs about 1½ to 2 pounds. It is cut from the center section of the short loin. It will make 2 to 3 servings.

Club Steak: A small steak cut from the small end of the short loin. There is no tenderloin portion in this steak. An average cut weighs from ½ to ¾ pound. It is a good choice for an individual portion.

Sirloin Steak: Sirloin steaks are cut from the loin end which is between the short loin and the rump. The steaks vary in weight from 3 to 4½ pounds. The smallest sirloin is the pinbone steak, from the end of loin nearest the short loin. The largest sirloin is from the round end of the loin and is sometimes called the wedge bone. It is a full-cut steak. It will make 5 to 6 servings.

Rib Steaks: These are cut from the rib of beef. They have the same shape bone as the standing rib roast.

TIMETABLE FOR BROILING STEAK
(Refrigerated until broiled in preheated broiler)

Cut	Approximate Minutes per side		
	RARE	MEDIUM	WELL DONE
Porterhouse and T-Bone			
1 inch	5	6	7 to 8
1½ inches	9	10	12 to 13
2 inches	16	18	20 to 21
Club			
1 inch	5	6	7 to 8
1½ inches	9	10	12 to 13
2 inches	16	18	20 to 21
Sirloin and Wedge Bone			
1 inch	10	12	14
1½ inches	12	14	16
2 inches	20	22	24
Rib			
1 inch	5	6	7 to 8
1½ inches	9	10	12 to 13
2 inches	16	18	20 to 21

Delmonico Steaks: These are boneless and cut from the eye of the rib roast.

Flank Steak: This is a thin, boneless, less tender steak from the beef flank. It is usually 12 to 14 inches long, 4 to 6 inches wide, 1 inch thick, and weighs 1 to 2 pounds. Top quality flank steak may be broiled and is known as London Broil (see recipe below). It should be cut with a sharp knife at a 90° angle.

How to Broil

1. Preheat broiler.
2. Slash steak through outside fat covering at 1-inch intervals to keep from curling.
3. Place steak on rack of broiler pan 2 to 3 inches from heat.
4. Broil until top side is brown. Use the chart on page 141 only as a guide. Season top with salt and pepper.
5. Turn and brown second side. Steak should be turned only once. To test for doneness, cut small slit in meat close to the bone. Peek to see whether inside color is of desired doneness.

LONDON BROIL

1 flank steak (about 2 lbs.)	¼ tsp. pepper
Instant meat tenderizer	¼ tsp. garlic powder
1 tsp. salt	3 tbs. butter or margarine

Preheat broiler. Sprinkle steak with meat tenderizer according to label instructions. Mix salt, pepper, and garlic powder; rub well into both sides of steak. Place steak on lightly greased broiler rack; dot top with half the butter or margarine. Broil 4 to 5 minutes on one side; turn. Dot surface with remaining butter or margarine; broil 4 to 5 minutes longer. Remove steak to hot platter or board. With very sharp carving knife held almost parallel to top of steak, cut thin diagonal slices across the grain (long fibers) of the steak. Makes 4 servings.

NINO'S STEAK DIANE

2 boneless sirloin steaks (¾-in. thick ea.)	1 tsp. freshly ground pepper
¼ c. butter or margarine	3 tbs. butter or margarine
2 tsp. dry mustard	4 tsp. Worcestershire sauce
½ tsp. onion salt	1 lemon
2 tbs. olive oil	2 tbs. chopped parsley

Cut each steak in half to make 4 pieces. Place steaks between 2 sheets of wax paper; pound with flat of knife or wooden mallet until ½ inch thick. Melt ¼ cup butter or margarine on large griddle (or use two skillets); stir in mustard and salt. Drizzle 1 tablespoon olive oil over steaks. Sprinkle with half the pepper; rub pepper and oil into steaks with bowl of spoon. Cook steaks, oil-pepper side down, for 2 minutes; spoon pan juices over steaks occasionally. Rub remaining oil and pepper on unseasoned side of steaks; turn over; cook 2 minutes. Steaks will be pink inside. Remove from pan; keep warm. Remove pan from heat; add 3 tablespoons butter or margarine and Worcestershire. Cut lemon in quarters, squeeze juice into skillet; spear one quarter on fork and use as a stirrer to blend all juices; add parsley; pour over steaks; serve at once. Makes 4 servings.

Flavor Extras for Steaks

Many steak fanciers agree that perfect steak needs no embellishment. But if you would like to add an extra touch, the following sauces are delicious with steak:

Béarnaise Sauce	page 350
Sautéed Mushrooms	page 294
Maitre d'Hotel Butter	page 350
Roquefort Butter	page 350
Lemon Butter	page 350
Mustard Butter	page 350
Fried Onions	
Bottled Sauces	

FILET OR TENDERLOIN OF BEEF

This is the long section of meat lying in the lower or inner side of the T-bone. It begins in the sirloin and ends at the rib end of the short loin. Because it is a seldom-used muscle, it is very, very tender. The tenderloin is left whole to be roasted or cut into individual steaks and broiled or sautéed quickly in butter. The steaks vary in size because a tenderloin tapers at one end, and the slices are named according to their thickness. There is the *chateaubriand*, cut 2 to 3 inches thick from the widest part of the tenderloin, the *filet mignon*, cut 1½ to 2 inches thick, and the *tournedos*, cut 1 inch thick.

Roast Tenderloin of Beef

Heat oven to 450° F. Remove fat, sinews, and connective tissue from tenderloin. Cover with thin slices of larding pork or beef suet. Tie securely in several places with clean white string. Place in roasting pan; insert meat thermometer so bulb is in center of tenderloin. Roast about 10 minutes per pound or until meat thermometer registers 140° F. Tenderloin is always cooked rare.

Filet Steaks or Filet Mignon

These steaks may be broiled or sautéed. In either case, they are trimmed of all fat and sinews. They need extra fat while cooking, so use plenty of butter or margarine or have a strip of bacon tied around each one. Sauté them quickly, about 3 to 4 minutes per side for 1-inch-thick steaks, about 4 to 5 minutes per side for 1½-inch steaks. To broil, place in preheated broiler.

1-inch steaks	2 to 3 minutes per side
1¼-inch steaks	4 to 5 minutes per side
2-inch steaks	5 to 6 minutes per side

FILET WELLINGTON

1 beef filet (6 lbs.)	2 tbs. tomato paste
Melted butter or	2 c. sifted all-
margarine	purpose flour
½ lb. mushrooms	½ tsp. salt
3 tbs. butter or	¾ c. shortening
margarine	6 tbs. water
1 lb. ground	2 egg yolks
cooked ham	4 tbs. water
¼ c. sherry or	
white wine	

Heat oven to 425° F. Trim fat from filet; place on rack in roasting pan; brush well with melted butter or margarine. Roast 20 to 25 minutes; remove from pan; cool. Chop mushrooms finely; sauté until soft in 3 tablespoons butter or margarine. Combine mushrooms, ham, wine, and tomato paste; reserve. Sift flour and salt into mixing bowl; cut in shortening until mixture resembles cornmeal. Sprinkle 6 tablespoons water over mixture, a tablespoon at a time; toss with fork until mixture clings together. Roll out on floured board to a rectangle 3 inches longer than filet and wide enough to encase it. Heat oven to 450° F. Place filet on pastry 2 inches in from one long side. Pat mushroom mixture firmly onto filet.

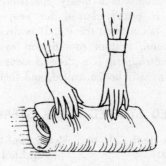

Bring pastry up and over filet to cover it; moisten edges; press firmly to seal. Moisten ends; fold in; seal. Beat egg yolks and 4 tablespoons water; brush over pastry. Cut designs from pastry scraps; arrange on pastry roll; brush with egg mixture. Transfer carefully to baking sheet. Bake 20 to 25 minutes or until golden brown. Makes 12 to 14 servings.

Cuts for Braising

Braising is a method of cooking the less tender large cuts of beef. They are browned and cooked slowly in a small amount of liquid. The slow moist cooking of the meat tenderizes the meat and brings out the best flavor.

Chuck Steak: This steak is usually cut from ½ to 1 inch thick. It is from the shoulder. It has a round bone (arm), a blade bone, or may be boneless.

Round Steak: The round steak is cut ½ to 1 inch thick. It is from the leg and is cut usually as one oval-shaped piece, but may be cut into top or bottom round.

Rump Steak: The rump steak is cut from the hip section. It is part of the larger rump section which is a pot roast cut.

Short Ribs: These are 3-inch lengths cut from the ends of the ribs of beef.

Pot roast: You may not find all these cuts since beef is cut differently in various parts of the country: *Boneless Chuck* has the large blade bone removed and is tied to make a firm piece. *Arm Roast* is a thick-cut flat piece with the round (arm) bone, sometimes called Chuck Roast. *Blade Roast* is a thick-cut flat piece from the larger bone section of the chuck. *Rump* is a meaty cut from the hip which is usually boned for easy carving. *Round* is cut from the leg. It is divided into top round, bottom round, and eye of the round. *Sirloin tip* is a piece of meat from the round usually boned, rolled, and tied.

ROLLED STUFFED FLANK STEAK

1 flank steak (1½ to 2 lbs.)	½ tsp. leaf thyme, crumbled
½ tsp. salt	½ c. hot water
¼ tsp. pepper	½ c. canned whole-kernel corn
½ c. chopped onion (1 medium)	
2 tbs. fat or pure vegetable oil	2 tbs. fat or pure vegetable oil
½ c. soft bread crumbs	1½ c. water
½ tsp. leaf sage, crumbled	2 envelopes granulated beef broth
	1 tbs. flour
	¼ c. water

Heat oven to 300° F. Lay flank steak flat on board; score top side with sharp knife; rub with salt and pepper. Sauté onion in 2 tablespoons hot fat or oil until soft. Combine onion, bread crumbs, sage, and thyme; mix well. Stir in ½ cup hot water and corn. Spread mixture on flank steak; roll up; tie securely in several places with clean white cord. Brown well on all sides in 2 tablespoons hot fat or oil in heavy kettle or Dutch oven. Add 1½ cups water and granulated beef broth; cover. Cook in oven 2 hours or until meat is tender. Transfer meat to heated platter; remove cord. Skim any fat from gravy; mix 1 tablespoon flour and ¼ cup water to a smooth paste; stir into liquid. Cook, stirring constantly, until thickened. Taste gravy. Season to taste with salt, pepper, and bottled meat sauce, if desired. Makes 6 servings.

POT ROAST MILANESE

¼ c. fat or pure vegetable oil	2 tsp. leaf oregano, crumbled
5 lbs. chuck, rump or round	1 tsp. salt
2 stalks celery, finely chopped	⅛ tsp. pepper
1 c. finely chopped, pared carrot	1 can (1 pt. 2 oz.) tomato juice
2 c. chopped onion	2 c. water
1 clove of garlic, halved	8 carrots, pared
2 bay leaves	8 potatoes, pared and halved
½ tsp. leaf basil, crumbled	2 c. celery pieces

Heat fat or oil in large heavy kettle or Dutch oven; brown meat on all sides. Add chopped celery, carrot, and onion; sauté in kettle until golden. Thread garlic on wooden pick; add to kettle with bay leaves, basil, oregano, salt, pepper, tomato juice, and water. Cover; bring to boiling; lower heat; simmer 2½ to 3 hours or until meat is almost tender. Add carrots, potatoes, and celery. Cook 30 minutes longer or until meat and vegetables are tender. Remove meat and vegetables; keep warm. Remove garlic and bay leaves; discard; skim any fat from gravy. *For thicker gravy:* Measure gravy; for each cup, blend 1 tablespoon flour to a smooth paste with water. Stir into gravy; cook, stirring constantly, until thickened. Makes 6 servings.

HOME-STYLE POT ROAST

Take advantage of the "pot roast special." Buy a large roast of the cut featured at your market—chuck, rump, or round. Cooked whole, as below, it can become a company meal. Or cut and freeze part for future eating and pot roast the remainder in your family's favorite way.

6 to 7 lbs. boneless chuck, rolled and tied	1½ c. water
	1 tbs. cornstarch
	2 tbs. cold water
2 tbs. fat or pure vegetable oil	1 c. sliced, cooked carrots
1 c. chopped onion (1 large)	12 small white onions, peeled and cooked
½ c. chopped celery	1 pkg. (10 oz.) frozen lima beans, cooked
1 can (10½ oz.) condensed beef bouillon	

Brown beef in hot fat or oil on all sides in heavy kettle or Dutch oven; remove from pan; keep warm. Sauté chopped onion and celery lightly in fat or oil remaining in pan. Return meat to pan. Add bouillon and water; cover. Bring to boiling; reduce heat. Simmer slowly about 4 hours or until meat is tender. Remove meat. Skim fat from liquid. Blend cornstarch and cold water to a smooth paste. Stir into liquid in pan; cook, stirring constantly, until mixture thickens and boils 1 minute. Add meat and cooked vegetables; heat through. Sprinkle with chopped parsley, if desired. Makes 10 servings.

BOILED BEEF WITH HORSERADISH SAUCE

Handful of parsley	Water
6 peppercorns	3 c. celery pieces
½ tsp. leaf thyme	12 small potatoes, pared
1 bay leaf	
5 to 6 lbs. fresh beef brisket	12 small carrots, pared
2 tsp. salt	3 c. sliced zucchini
1 medium-size onion, sliced	Melted butter or margarine
1 carrot, pared and sliced	Horseradish Sauce (*page 352*)
1 stalk of celery, sliced	

Tie parsley, peppercorns, thyme, and bay leaf in double thickness of cheesecloth. Put in large kettle with beef. Add salt, onion, sliced carrot, and sliced celery. Add enough water so level is 1 inch above top of meat; cover. Simmer 2 to 2½ hours or until meat is tender. While meat cooks, cook each vegetable in separate pot in boiling salted water until tender; drain; toss with melted butter or margarine. Place meat on heated platter. Surround with vegetables. Serve with Horseradish Sauce. Makes 6 servings.

SWISS STEAK

½ c. chopped onion (1 medium)	2 tbs. prepared mustard
3 tbs. fat or pure vegetable oil	1 tbs. Worcestershire sauce
¼ c. flour	Dash of hot-pepper sauce
½ tsp. salt	
⅛ tsp. pepper	1 can (10½ oz.) condensed onion soup
2 to 2½ lbs. round or chuck steak	
	⅓ c. water

Sauté onion in hot fat or oil in heavy skillet or Dutch oven until soft. Mix flour, salt, and pepper; pound into both sides of beef. Brown beef well on both sides in fat or oil remaining in kettle. Add mustard, Worcestershire, hot-pepper sauce, onion soup, and water. Cover; simmer 2 to 2½ hours or until meat is tender when pierced with a two-tined fork. Remove meat to heated platter. Skim fat from broth. Thicken broth, if desired, with flour mixed to a smooth paste with a small amount of water. Makes 6 servings.

DEVILED SWISS STEAK

3 tbs. fat or pure
  vegetable oil
1 medium-size
  onion, sliced
⅓ c. flour
1 tsp. salt
¼ tsp. pepper
2 to 2½ lbs. round
  or chuck steak
2 cans (1 lb. ea.)
  tomatoes

1 tbs. prepared
  mustard
1 tsp. Worcester-
  shire sauce
Dash of hot-pepper
  sauce
½ tsp. garlic
  powder
1 small lemon,
  sliced
1 tbs. brown sugar

Heat fat or oil in heavy skillet or Dutch oven; sauté onion until soft; remove; reserve. Combine flour, salt, and pepper; rub or pound into both sides of meat. Brown meat well on all sides in remaining fat or oil. Add tomatoes, mustard, Worcestershire, hot-pepper sauce, garlic powder, lemon, brown sugar, and sautéed onion; cover. Simmer 2 to 2½ hours or until meat is tender. Remove meat to heated serving platter; keep warm. Thicken gravy if desired; pour over meat. Serve with additional lemon slices and garnish with parsley, if desired. Makes 6 servings.

BRAISED STEAK, INDONESIAN STYLE

2 to 2½ lbs. round
  or chuck steak
⅓ c. flour
1 tsp. salt
¼ tsp. pepper
3 tbs. fat or pure
  vegetable oil
1 can (10½ oz.)
  condensed beef
  broth or
  consommé

½ tsp. garlic salt
½ tsp. ground
  ginger
2 tsp. curry powder
¼ c. chopped onion
  (1 small)
½ c. chutney
¼ c. raisins
2 tomatoes, peeled
  and quartered

Cut meat into serving-size pieces. Mix flour, salt, and pepper together; rub or pound mixture well into all sides of meat. Heat fat or oil in heavy skillet or Dutch oven; brown meat

well. Add beef broth or consommé, garlic salt, ginger, curry powder, onion, chutney, and raisins; cover. Simmer 2 to 2½ hours or until meat is tender; add tomatoes; simmer 5 minutes more. Serve over steaming hot rice, if desired. Makes 6 servings.

CHUCK WAGON STEAK

⅓ c. flour
1 tsp. salt
¼ tsp. pepper
2 to 2½ lbs. round
  or chuck steak
3 tbs. fat
1 can (14½ oz.)
  condensed beef
  broth

½ c. water
½ c. bottled
  barbecue sauce
1 tsp. chili powder
1 green pepper,
  seeded diced
½ c. sliced stuffed
  olives

Mix flour, salt, and pepper together; rub or pound mixture well into both sides of meat. Heat fat in heavy skillet or Dutch oven; brown meat well on all sides. Blend beef broth, water, barbecue sauce, and chili powder; pour over meat; cover. Simmer 1 hour; add green pepper and olives; simmer 1 to 1½ hours longer or until meat is tender. Skim any fat from gravy; thicken gravy, if desired. Makes 6 servings.

SWISS STEAK FOR A CROWD

8 lbs. top round of
  beef, cut in ¾-in.
  slices
2 c. all-purpose
  flour
2 tsp. salt
½ tsp. pepper
1 tbs. paprika
1 c. fat or pure
  vegetable oil

2 c. chopped onion
  (2 large)
2½ qts. hot water
10 beef-bouillon
  cubes
¾ tsp. leaf thyme,
  crumbled
3 bay leaves

Heat oven to 325° F. Cut beef into serving-size pieces. Combine flour, salt, pepper, and paprika. Pound into beef; reserve leftover flour mixture. Brown meat a small amount at a time in hot fat or oil in skillet; put meat in baking pans. Sauté onion in fat or oil remaining in skillet. Add reserved flour mixture; stir well to make a smooth paste. Gradually add hot water. Add bouillon cubes, thyme, and bay leaves. Simmer until gravy thickens. Pour gravy over meat; cover. Bake 1 to 1½ hours or until tender. Remove bay leaves. Makes 25 servings.

SHORT RIBS, COUNTRY STYLE

¼ c. flour	1 can (8 oz.)
1 tsp. salt	tomato sauce
¼ tsp. pepper	2 tsp. Worcester-
4 lbs. beef short ribs,	shire sauce
cut in serving-size	1 tsp. salt
pieces	¼ tsp. pepper
2 tbs. fat	1 can (10½ oz.)
1 c. chopped onion	condensed
(1 large)	consommé
1 c. chopped green	1½ c. water
pepper	12 small white
¼ c. chopped	onions, peeled
parsley	4 carrots, pared and
3 tbs. vinegar	cut in 1½-inch
½ tsp. dry mustard	pieces

Heat oven to 350° F. Combine flour, 1 teaspoon salt, and ¼ teaspoon pepper in paper bag; add ribs; shake gently until well coated. Heat fat or oil in skillet; brown ribs on all sides; place in casserole. Sauté chopped onions and green pepper in fat or oil remaining in skillet about 5 minutes or until soft; add parsley, vinegar, mustard, tomato sauce, Worcestershire, 1 teaspoon salt, ¼ teaspoon pepper, consommé and water; mix well. Add to meat in casserole. Cover; bake 1½ hours, stirring occasionally. Add white onions and carrots; cover; bake 30 minutes or until vegetables and meat are tender. Skim fat; thicken gravy, if desired. Makes 6 servings.

STEWS

Stewing is another method of cooking less tender cuts of meat. The meat is usually cut into cubes, browned or not, and cooked slowly in liquid and seasonings. Cuts for stewing include chuck, round, shank, neck, and plate.

BOEUF À LA MODE

Boeuf à la mode is basic in French cuisine and has been described as being a dish fit for a king. While it is really family fare it will be found everywhere—from the most elegant restaurants to the smallest of homes. It is a dish that is just as good when reheated and excellent when eaten cold with the jellied sauce.

12 strips larding	Pepper
pork	Ground nutmeg
Brandy	1 tbs. fat or pure
4 to 5 lbs. rump of	vegetable oil
beef	1 clove of garlic,
1 medium-size	crushed
onion, sliced	2 calves' feet,
1 carrot, pared and	blanched
thinly sliced	2 c. dry red wine
⅛ tsp. leaf thyme,	3 tbs. brandy
crumbled	1 bay leaf
2 whole cloves	6 sprigs celery
1 bay leaf,	leaves
crumbled	12 small carrots,
¼ tsp. leaf tarragon,	pared
crumbled	12 small white
6 peppercorns	onions, peeled
2 tbs. vinegar	12 small mush-
1 c. dry red wine	rooms
¼ c. water	2 tbs. butter or
Salt	margarine

Marinate pork larding strips in brandy 30 minutes. Insert larding strips into beef with larding needle or make slits in beef with sharp knife and insert strips. Put beef in glass or pottery bowl. Add sliced onion, sliced carrot, thyme, cloves, crumbled bay leaf, tarragon, peppercorns, vinegar, 1 cup wine, and water. Marinate 24 hours, turning meat several times. Next day, remove meat; strain marinade; reserve. Pat meat dry with paper towels. Rub meat with salt, pepper, and nutmeg. Brown meat on all sides in fat or oil in Dutch oven. Pour off most of fat. Sauté garlic in fat or oil remaining in kettle. Add calves' feet, 2 cups wine, 3 tablespoons brandy, bay leaf, celery leaves, and strained marinade; cover. Bring to boiling; simmer 4 hours or bake at 350° F. for 4 hours. Strain liquid; skim off fat. Pour liquid over meat; add carrots and onions. Cover; simmer or bake 45 minutes longer. Sauté mushrooms in butter or margarine; add to meat. Thicken gravy, if desired, with flour mixed to smooth paste with a small amount of water, using 1 tablespoon flour for each cup of gravy. Makes 6 to 8 servings.

OLD-FASHIONED BEEF STEW

1 tbs. fat or pure vegetable oil	2 c. water
1 c. chopped onion (1 large)	1 bay leaf
1 clove of garlic, mashed	1½ tsp. salt
2 tbs. fat or pure vegetable oil	¼ tsp. pepper
2½ lbs. chuck or round, cut in 2-in. cubes	1 tbs. Worcestershire sauce
	6 carrots, pared, cut in 2-inch pieces
	18 small white onions, peeled
1 can (10½ oz.) condensed beef broth	1 c. celery pieces
	1 tbs. flour
	¼ c. water

Heat 1 tablespoon fat or oil in large kettle or Dutch oven. Sauté chopped onion and garlic until soft; remove; reserve. Heat 2 tablespoons fat or oil in kettle; brown meat well on all sides. (This browning gives the gravy its dark, rich color.) Add onion, garlic, beef broth, 2 cups water, bay leaf, salt, pepper, and Worcestershire. Bring to boiling; lower heat; simmer 1½ to 1¾ hours or until meat is almost tender. Add carrots, onions, and celery; simmer 30 to 35 minutes longer or until vegetables and meat are tender. Or vegetables may be cooked separately and added to the stew. Remove bay leaf. Thicken broth with 1 tablespoon flour mixed to a smooth paste with ¼ cup water. Makes 6 to 8 servings.

BELGIAN BEEF STEW
(Carbonnades à la Flamande)

This is the traditional Flemish beef stew which depends on the sorcery of its two special ingredients, beer and onions, for its wonderful flavor.

2 tbs. fat or pure vegetable oil	¼ tsp. leaf thyme, crumbled
2 c. sliced onion (2 large)	1 tsp. salt
2 cloves of garlic, crushed	¼ tsp. pepper
2 tbs. fat or pure vegetable oil	1 bottle or can (12 oz.) beer
3 lbs. chuck or round, cut in 2-in. cubes	1 envelope granulated beef bouillon
2 bay leaves	1 c. water
	Chopped parsley

Heat 2 tablespoons fat or oil in large kettle or Dutch oven. Sauté onion and garlic until soft and lightly browned; remove; reserve. Heat 2 tablespoons fat or oil in kettle; brown meat very well on all sides. This will take 10 to 15 minutes. Add onions, garlic, bay leaves, thyme, salt, pepper, beer, beef bouillon, and water. Bring to boiling; lower heat; simmer 1¾ to 2 hours or until meat is tender. Remove bay leaves. Thicken gravy, if desired, with 1 tablespoon flour blended with ¼ cup water and 1 teaspoon vinegar; add to stew; stir until thickened and bubbly. Sprinkle stew with parsley. Traditionally served with boiled potatoes. Makes 6 to 8 servings.

BEEF RAGOUT

Take a tip from the French and serve Beef Ragout at your buffet party. Make it a day ahead to allow the flavors to mellow and blend to the peak of perfection.

2 tbs. flour	¼ c. chopped parsley
2 tsp. salt	2 bay leaves
¼ tsp. pepper	½ tsp. leaf thyme, crumbled
3 tbs. fat or pure vegetable oil	
3 lbs. chuck or round, cut in 1¼-in. cubes	16 small white onions, peeled
1 clove of garlic, crushed	8 carrots, pared and cut in 1½-inch pieces
1 can (10½ oz.) condensed beef bouillon	¼ c. flour
	½ c. water
1¼ c. dry red wine	

Combine 2 tablespoons flour, salt, and pepper in paper bag; shake beef cubes in mixture, a few at a time, until well coated. Brown beef in fat or oil in large kettle or Dutch oven; add garlic; cook 2 minutes. Add bouillon, wine, parsley, bay leaves, and thyme. Cover; simmer 1½ hours. Add onions and carrots; simmer 30 minutes longer or until meat and vegetables are tender. Remove bay leaves. Blend ¼ cup flour and water to a smooth paste. Stir in ragout; cook, stirring constantly until gravy thickens. Makes 8 servings.

Roast Beef—tender and juicy, everyone's favo

BOEUF BOURGUIGNONNE
(Braised Beef in Burgundy Sauce)

1 lb. salt pork	1 tsp. leaf thyme
4 lbs. round or	2 sprigs parsley
chuck, cut in	6 peppercorns
2-in. cubes	3 tbs. butter or
¼ c. Cognac	margarine
1 c. chopped onion	1 lb. mushrooms,
(1 large)	sliced
2 cloves of garlic,	24 small white
mashed	onions, peeled
1 tsp. salt	4 tbs. flour
1 bottle Burgundy	4 tbs. soft butter
2 tsp. tomato paste	or margarine
1 can (10½ oz.)	1 tsp. grated lemon
condensed beef	rind
broth	2 tbs. chopped
2 bay leaves	parsley

Put salt pork in small saucepan; cover with water. Bring to boiling; simmer 5 minutes. (This blanching step removes much of the salt that might affect flavor.) Drain pork; pat dry; cut into small pieces. Cook pork in large kettle or Dutch oven until crisp and brown; remove; reserve. Brown meat well on all sides in fat remaining in kettle. Add only enough meat to cover bottom of kettle, lest meat might stew and not brown. Remove browned pieces before adding more meat. When meat is browned, pour off any remaining fat. Return meat to kettle. Heat Cognac in small saucepan; ignite carefully; pour over meat. When flames have died, add onion, garlic, salt, wine, tomato paste, and ½ cup of beef broth. Put bay leaves, thyme, parsley, and peppercorns in small piece of clean cheesecloth (a bouquet garni); tie securely; push down into liquid. Bring to boiling; lower heat; cover. Simmer 2 to 2½ hours or until meat is tender. Heat 3 tablespoons butter or margarine in skillet; sauté mushrooms quickly until just tender; remove; reserve. Add onions to fat remaining in skillet; brown well (browning will be spotty). Add remaining beef broth; bring to boiling; cover; lower heat; simmer about 10 minutes or until onions are tender. Blend flour and 4 tablespoons butter or margarine to form a smooth paste. (Called *beurre manié*, this is the thickening for the bourguignonne.) When meat is tender, remove from liquid; keep warm. Remove bouquet garni. Add beurre manié bit by bit to hot liquid until it has reached desired thickness. Stir in lemon

rind. Return meat to kettle; add onions and mushrooms. Add salt pork bits, if desired. Heat until bubbly; sprinkle with parsley. Serve with small boiled potatoes, buttered noodles, or rice. Makes 6 to 8 servings.

DUTCH-STYLE BEEF STEW WITH POTATO DUMPLINGS

¼ c. flour	3 c. water
1 tsp. salt	2 c. sliced celery
¼ tsp. pepper	2 c. diced carrots
3 lbs. beef rump, cut	5 medium-size
in 1¼-inch cubes	potatoes, pared
3 tbs. fat or pure	1½ c. soft bread
vegetable oil	crumbs
2½ c. chopped	1 tbs. flour
onions	1 tbs. chopped
1 envelope dehy-	parsley
drated vegetable	1 tbs. minced onion
broth or beef	1½ tsp. salt
with vegetable	⅛ tsp. pepper
soup mix	2 eggs, beaten
1 tsp. salt	1 tbs. milk
2 tsp. paprika	

Combine ¼ cup flour, 1 teaspoon salt, and ¼ teaspoon pepper in paper bag; add meat; shake to coat well. Heat fat or oil in heavy kettle or Dutch oven; add meat; brown on all sides. Remove meat. Sauté onions in fat or oil remaining in kettle until golden brown. Return meat to kettle. Blend soup mix, 1 teaspoon salt, paprika, and water; pour into kettle. Cover; simmer 1¾ hours or until meat is almost tender. Add celery and carrots; simmer 15 minutes or until tender. While vegetables cook, prepare *Potato Dumplings*. Grate potatoes; squeeze dry in clean towel. Combine with remaining ingredients. Shape into 2-inch balls; coat lightly with flour. Drop onto hot stew; cover. Simmer 15 minutes. Makes 6 servings.

HUNGARIAN GOULASH

¼ c. flour
1 tsp. salt
¼ tsp. pepper
2 tsp. paprika
3 lbs. lean chuck or rump, cut in 1¼-in. cubes
3 tbs. fat or pure vegetable oil
1½ c. chopped onion
1 clove of garlic, mashed
1 can (10½ oz.) condensed beef broth
½ c. water

1 can (1 lb. 4 oz.) tomatoes
½ tsp. salt
¼ tsp. pepper
1 bay leaf
1½ tsp. caraway seeds
½ c. water
1 c. dairy sour cream
1½ pkgs. (12 oz.) medium noodles, cooked and drained
¼ c. butter or margarine, melted

Combine flour, 1 teaspoon salt, ¼ teaspoon pepper, and paprika in paper bag; add meat; shake to coat well. Reserve flour mixture. Heat fat or oil in heavy kettle or Dutch oven; brown meat on all sides; remove meat. Sauté onions and garlic in fat or oil remaining in kettle. Add meat, broth, ½ cup water, tomatoes, ½ teaspoon salt, ¼ teaspoon pepper, bay leaf, and caraway seeds. Cover; simmer 2 hours, stirring occasionally. Remove bay leaf. Blend 3 tablespoons reserved flour mixture and ½ cup water; add to kettle. Stir constantly over low heat until thickened. Stir in sour cream; heat but do not boil. Toss noodles and butter or margarine; serve with goulash. Makes 6 servings.

SPICY BEEF STEW

2 lbs. boneless chuck or round, cut in 1-in. cubes
4 tbs. fat or pure vegetable oil
1 large onion, sliced
2 c. water
1 bay leaf

2 tsp. salt
¼ tsp. pepper
⅛ tsp. ground allspice
¼ c. vinegar
½ c. broken gingersnaps
¼ c. water

Brown beef cubes well on all sides in fat or oil in large heavy kettle or Dutch oven; add sliced onion; brown; add 2 cups water, bay leaf, salt, pepper, and allspice. Cover; simmer over low heat 2 hours or until meat is tender. Add vinegar. Soak gingersnaps in ¼ cup water. Remove meat and bay leaf from stew. Stir gingersnap mixture into remaining stew; cook, stirring constantly, until mixture thickens and comes to boiling. Return meat to pan; stir. Serve with butter noodles, sprinkled with caraway seeds, if desired. Makes 4 to 6 servings.

BEEF STROGANOFF

This a marvelous dish for a buffet or dinner party. You can prepare it almost completely ahead of time.

2 lbs. tenderloin or sirloin
4 tbs. butter or margarine
½ lb. mushrooms, sliced
1 c. sliced onion (1 large)
1 can (10½ oz.) condensed beef broth

½ c. dry white wine or water
¼ tsp. salt
Dash of pepper
1½ c. dairy sour cream
1 tbs. chopped parsley
1 tbs. minced chives
Hot, cooked rice

Slice meat into ½-inch slices; cut slices into ½-inch strips. Heat butter or margarine in large skillet. Brown meat well on all sides; remove; reserve. Sauté mushrooms and onion until tender in fat remaining in skillet. Add meat, beef broth, wine or water, salt, and pepper. Cover; simmer 10 minutes. Stroganoff may be cooked to this stage and reheated. Stir in sour cream; heat just to boiling, stirring constantly. Sprinkle with parsley and chives. Serve with cooked rice. Makes 8 servings.

CHINESE PEPPER STEAK

Here's a dish to prepare in minutes. You could even do it in a chafing dish right in front of your guests. We find men love it, so be forewarned if you have hearty eaters on your guest list.

1½ lbs. sirloin
steak, 1-in. thick
¼ c. fat or pure
vegetable oil
1 clove of garlic,
crushed
1 tsp. salt
1 tsp. ground ginger
½ tsp. pepper
3 large green
peppers, seeded
and sliced
2 large onions,
thinly sliced

¼ c. soy sauce
½ tsp. sugar
½ c. beef bouillon
1 can (6 oz.)
water chestnuts,
drained and
sliced
1 tbs. cornstarch
¼ c. water
4 green onions, cut
in 1-in. pieces
Hot, cooked rice

Freeze steak for one hour (it's easier to slice). When ready to cook, cut into ⅛-inch-thick slices. Heat fat or oil in skillet; add garlic, salt, ginger, and pepper. Sauté until garlic is golden. Add steak slices; brown lightly 2 minutes; remove meat. Add green peppers and onions; cook 3 minutes. Return beef to pan; add soy sauce, sugar, bouillon, water chestnuts, cornstarch dissolved in water, and green onions. Simmer about 2 minutes or until sauce thickens. Serve over hot rice. Makes 6 to 8 servings.

BEEF AND PEPPERS ORIENTAL

¼ c. fat or pure
vegetable oil
1 clove of garlic,
crushed
1 tsp. ground
ginger
Flank steak
(2½ lbs) cut in
very thin
diagonal slices
2 green peppers,
seeded and cut in
julienne strips

¾ c. chopped onion
2 tbs. soy sauce
1 can (8 oz.)
tomato sauce
1 tsp. sugar
Dash of pepper
1 can (about 1 lb.)
bean sprouts,
undrained
Hot cooked rice

Heat fat or oil, garlic, and ginger together in large skillet. Add flank steak slices; cook over high heat 5 minutes, stirring constantly; remove meat. Add peppers and onions to fat or oil remaining in skillet; cook 2 minutes. Add soy sauce, tomato sauce, sugar, and pepper; cook 3 minutes. Add meat and bean sprouts; cook 2 minutes longer or until heated through. Serve over hot rice. Makes 6 servings.

GRILLADES

From their name you would expect these to be grilled or broiled. Actually, in New Orleans "les grillades" are squares of beef or veal browned and combined with a roux, then with the other flavorful ingredients and simmered until tender. You see—no broiler!

2 slices round steak
(½ in. thick)
3 tbs. fat or pure
vegetable oil
1 tbs. flour
1 c. chopped onion
(1 large)
1 clove of garlic,
minced
2 green peppers,
seeded and
chopped

1½ c. peeled,
chopped
tomatoes
½ c. water
2 tbs. chopped
parsley
½ tsp. leaf thyme,
crumbled
1 tsp. salt
¼ tsp. pepper

Cut each round steak into 4 pieces. Brown well in hot fat or oil; remove from pan. Add flour to fat or oil remaining in pan; cook until golden brown. Add onion, garlic, and green pepper; cook until soft. Add remaining ingredients and meat. Cover; simmer over low heat 1½ to 2 hours. Check occasionally. If meat sticks to pan or gravy becomes too thick, add a little hot water. Serve with hot rice, if desired. Makes 8 servings.

INDONESIAN BEEF CURRY

5 tbs. fat or pure
vegetable oil
2 lbs. boneless round
or chuck, cut in
1-in. cubes
1½ c. chopped
onion
2 to 3 cloves of
garlic, mashed
1 tsp. salt
¼ tsp. pepper

½ tsp. monosodium
glutamate
2 tbs. curry powder
2 tbs. granulated
beef bouillon
2 c. hot water
1 can (8 oz.)
tomato sauce
1 tbs. lemon juice
Hot, cooked rice

Heat 3 tablespoons fat or oil in large skillet or Dutch oven; add beef cubes; brown on all sides; remove; reserve. Add 2 tablespoons fat or oil, chopped onion, and garlic to skillet or Dutch oven; cook until soft and lightly browned. Mix together salt, pepper, monosodium glutamate, curry powder, and beef bouillon; stir into fat in pan; cook 2 to 3 minutes, stirring constantly. Add water, tomato sauce, and browned beef cubes. Cover; cook over medium heat 1½ hours. Remove cover; cook 30 minutes longer or until meat is tender and sauce is thickened; stir in lemon juice. Serve with hot, cooked rice. Makes 4 servings.

GROUND BEEF

Top round ground has the least amount of fat, but is the most costly per pound. When used for making hamburgers, it is wise to have a little fat ground with the meat for more tenderness.

Ground chuck contains slightly more fat than top round, and many consider it more flavorful. It is the best buy for the price.

Ground beef, or hamburger meat, as it may be labeled, is the lowest in price per pound but contains much more fat than ground chuck and this means considerable shrinkage during cooking.

Meat loaf mixture is usually a blend of ground beef, veal, and pork. It is intended primarily for baked meat loaves but also may be used in making meatballs, especially Swedish meatballs.

All ground beef should be used within 1 or 2 days after purchase, or stored in the freezer as soon as it has been brought home from market.

HAMBURGERS

The secret of tender, juicy hamburgers is in the handling of the ground beef. Always handle with a light touch.

1 lb. ground chuck or round	Salt Pepper

Shape meat gently into 4 thick or 8 thin patties. Sprinkle generously with salt and pepper. Cook in one of the following ways:

Broiled: Line broiler pan with aluminum foil. Preheat broiler. Place hamburgers on broiler rack. Broil 3 inches from heat about 7 minutes on one side for thick patties, 3 to 4 minutes for thin patties. Turn. Broil second side until done as you like them.

Panbroiled: Heat heavy skillet or griddle sizzling hot. You may rub it lightly with fat or pure vegetable oil or sprinkle with salt if you think patties will stick. Add hamburgers. Brown one side quickly; turn and brown second side. Cook over medium heat 4 to 8 minutes for thick patties, 2 to 6 minutes for thin patties, or until done as you like them.

Cheeseburger: Broil hamburgers on one side. Turn. Broil until almost done; top each with slice of process American cheese. Broil until done and cheese melts. Serve with dill pickle strips and catsup.

Mexican: Add ¼ cup chopped onion to ground beef. Shape patties; cook as desired. Top each with a tomato slice and a mixture of red kidney beans, chopped green pepper, chopped onion, and chopped stuffed olives.

Hawaiian: Season ground beef with soy sauce and ground ginger; cook as desired. Top with drained, canned pineapple chunks and flaked coconut.

French: Skillet-fry patties. Add small amount of dry red wine to skillet; baste patties with mixture of wine and pan juices. Top each with sautéed, sliced mushrooms; pimiento strips; and chopped parsley.

Italian: Mix ¼ cup minced onion and ½ teaspoon leaf oregano, crumbled, into ground beef. Shape into patties; broil; turn. Broil until almost done; top with slices of Mozzarella cheese. Broil until done as you like and the cheese melts. Top with hot, canned pizza sauce.

Swedish: Place thick slice of onion and small wedge of blue cheese on broiled hamburger. Broil one minute. Top with pimiento strips.

Chinese: Season ground beef with soy sauce and grated onion. Shape into patties. Broil. Top with sweet-sour sauce of pineapple chunks, green pepper strips, and orange sections.

Russian: Top broiled hamburger with generous dollop of sour cream. Add a ribbon of red caviar across top.

BURGER IN A BLANKET

1 lb. ground chuck or round	½ c. grated Parmesan cheese
½ c. chopped onion (1 medium)	½ c. grated Swiss cheese
1 small clove of garlic, crushed	2½ c. sifted all-purpose flour
1 tsp. salt	2½ tsp. salt
Dash of pepper	4 tbs. shortening
1 egg, slightly beaten	7 to 8 tbs. water

Combine beef, onion, garlic, salt, pepper, egg, and cheeses; mix well. Shape into 10 patties. Sift flour and salt into mixing bowl; cut in shortening until mixture resembles cornmeal. Add water gradually; mix until dough clings together. Roll out half of dough at a time to 1/8-inch thickness. Cut ten 5-inch circles from each half of dough. Place meat patties on half the circles of dough; moisten edges of dough. Place second circle of dough on top; seal edges; prick top with tines of fork. Place on cookie sheet. Bake at 400° F. for 30 to 35 minutes. Makes 10.

SURPRISE HAMBURGERS

The lowly hamburger goes gourmet with Roquefort cheese and red wine to make an appearance as party fare.

2¼ lbs. ground chuck or round	¾ lb. mushrooms, sliced
1 tsp. salt	6 tbs. butter or margarine
¼ tsp. pepper	1 c. dry red wine
4 oz. Roquefort cheese	

Mix ground beef, salt, and pepper together; divide into 6 portions. Shape each portion into 2 flat patties. Cut cheese into 6 slices; place one slice on each of 6 patties. Top each with second patty; pinch edges together to seal. (If making ahead, wrap in wax paper and refrigerate until ready to cook.) Sauté mushrooms in 3 tablespoons butter or margarine; remove from pan; reserve. Brown beef patties quickly on both sides in remaining 3 tablespoons butter or margarine. Add mushrooms and wine. Simmer 5 minutes for rare, 8 minutes for well done, basting meat constantly. Makes 6 servings.

HOME-STYLE MEAT LOAF

1½ lbs. ground chuck	1/3 c. milk
½ lb. ground veal	1 tbs. minced parsley
¼ lb. ground pork	3 tbs. catsup
2½ c. fresh bread crumbs	2 tsp. prepared mustard
1 c. finely chopped onion (1 large)	1 tsp. Worcestershire sauce
2 tsp. salt	2 eggs
1/8 tsp. pepper	

Combine meats, bread crumbs, onion, salt, pepper, milk, parsley, catsup, mustard, Wor-

cestershire, and eggs in large bowl. Press mixture into greased 9x5x3-inch loaf pan. Meat loaf may be baked in the pan, or if preferred, turned out onto greased baking dish. If baking unmolded, cover meat with several strips of bacon. Bake at 400° F. for 50 to 55 minutes. Makes 8 servings.

NOTE: *You may use 2¼ pounds ground chuck in place of meats above.*

BURGUNDY MEAT LOAVES

1 recipe Home-Style Meat Loaf	1 envelope granulated beef bouillon
3 tbs. butter or margarine	1/3 c. Burgundy
1 c. sliced onion (1 large)	1 c. water
2 tbs. flour	1 can (3 to 4 ozs.) sliced mushrooms, with juice

Shape meat mixture into individual servings by packing into lightly greased custard cup and turning out onto greased baking pan. Bake at 350° F. for 35 minutes. *Sauce:* Melt butter or margarine in skillet; sauté onion until tender. Stir in flour. Add bouillon, wine, water, and mushrooms; stir until thickened and bubbly. Pour over meat loaves. Makes 6 servings.

BEEF-CHEESE LOAVES

¼ c. chopped onion (1 small)	2 tbs. pickle relish, drained
2 tbs. butter or margarine	¼ c. catsup
2 lbs. lean ground chuck or round	2 tsp. salt
½ lb. sharp Cheddar cheese, shredded (2 c.)	1 tsp. Worcestershire sauce

Sauté onion in butter or margarine until soft. Combine beef, 1¾ cups cheese, relish, catsup, salt, Worcestershire, and sautéed onion; mix gently but thoroughly. Shape mixture into 4 to 6 individual loaves. (A small pan or refrigerator dish may be used to shape loaves uniformly.) Turn loaves onto greased baking pan. Bake at 350° F. for 35 to 40 minutes. About 5 minutes before end of baking time, sprinkle tops of loaves with remaining ¼ cup cheese; return to oven until cheese melts. Makes 4 to 6 loaves.

SAVORY SKILLET MEATBALLS

2 lbs. ground chuck
  or round
½ lb. ground pork
¼ c. minced green
  onions
1 c. packaged bread
  crumbs
1½ tsp. salt
¼ tsp. pepper
2 tbs. bottled meat
  sauce
1 egg
⅔ c. milk
4 tbs. butter or
  margarine
2 tbs. flour
¼ tsp. leaf rose-
  mary, crumbled

¼ tsp. leaf basil,
  crumbled
1 can (10½ oz.)
  condensed onion
  soup
⅓ c. water
2 pkgs. (10 oz. ea.)
  frozen whole
  green beans,
  partially
  thawed
2 cans (12 oz. ea.)
  whole-kernel
  corn, drained
½ c. dairy sour
  cream
2 tbs. minced
  parsley

Combine beef, pork, onions, bread crumbs, salt, pepper, meat sauce, egg, and milk in large bowl; mix thoroughly (it's easiest to do it with your hands). Shape into small meatballs (will make about 48). Sauté in butter or margarine in electric skillet or large deep skillet until brown on all sides. Remove from skillet; keep warm. Stir flour, rosemary, basil, onion soup, and water into skillet; cook, stirring constantly, until thickened. Pile meatballs in center of skillet; place green beans on one side, corn on other; cover. Cook over low heat until vegetables are heated through. Spoon meatballs and vegetables onto serving plates. Stir sour cream into skillet; just heat through; spoon over meatballs; sprinkle with parsley. Makes 6 servings.

SWEDISH MEATBALLS

2 lbs. ground chuck
  or round
⅔ c. packaged
  bread crumbs
1 can (10½ oz.)
  condensed
  consommé
4 tsp. minced onion

2 tsp. salt
¼ tsp. pepper
Fat or pure vegeta-
  ble oil for frying
1 tbs. flour
1 c. heavy cream
2 tbs. chopped
  parsley

Combine ground beef, bread crumbs, consommé, onion, salt, and pepper in a large bowl. Mix with spoon or hands until mixture is smooth, spongy mass; let stand at least ½ hour. Shape into small balls; fry in hot fat or oil in skillet until evenly browned. Shake pan during frying to keep balls round. Remove meatballs; keep hot. Blend flour into pan drippings; stir in cream; bring to boiling; simmer about 5 minutes. Pour over meatballs; sprinkle with parsley. Serve at once. Makes 6 servings.

HOT POT

¼ c. milk
2 slices fresh white
  bread, crumbled
½ tsp. garlic salt
¼ tsp. pepper
½ lb. ground chuck
  or round
½ lb. ground lean
  pork
¼ c. butter or
  margarine
2 c. chopped onion
  (2 large)
1 clove of garlic,
  crushed

2 to 3 tsp. chili
  powder
¼ tsp. ground
  cumin
1 c. sliced celery
½ c. chopped green
  pepper
4 cans (8 oz. ea.)
  tomato sauce
1 pkg. (10 oz.)
  frozen baby lima
  beans, thawed
Packaged corn
  chips

Combine milk, crumbled bread, garlic salt, and pepper; mix until all bread is moistened. Add to ground beef and pork; mix well. Form into 18 small meatballs. Sauté in butter or margarine until browned. Remove from pan; set aside. Sauté onion, garlic, chili powder, cumin, celery, and green pepper in fat remaining in pan 10 minutes. Add tomato sauce; mix well. Put a third of the sauce into 2-quart casserole; add half the meatballs and half the lima beans. Repeat layers, ending with the last third of sauce; cover. Bake at 350° F. for 30 minutes. Remove cover; sprinkle with corn chips; bake uncovered 15 minutes longer. Makes 6 servings.

COWBOY STEW

6 slices bacon	1 tsp. salt
1 c. sliced onion (1 large)	¼ tsp. pepper
	1 tbs. chili powder
½ c. chopped green pepper	1 can (12 oz.) whole-kernel corn, drained
1 clove of garlic, crushed	1 can (about 1 lb.) red kidney beans, drained
1½ lbs. ground chuck or round	
2 cans (1 lb. 13 oz. ea.) tomatoes	2 c. cubed, pared potatoes

Cook bacon until crisp; drain on paper towels; crumble; reserve. Sauté onion, green pepper, and garlic in bacon drippings until tender. Add ground beef; cook until well browned, breaking up with fork as it cooks. Add tomatoes, salt, pepper, and chili powder; cover; simmer 30 minutes. Add vegetables; simmer 15 minutes. Sprinkle with bacon. Makes 8 servings.

CHILI CON CARNE

1½ lbs. ground chuck or round	1½ tsp. salt
	¼ tsp. ground cloves
1½ c. chopped onion	1 to 2 tbs. chili powder
1 large green pepper, seeded and chopped	¼ tsp. hot-pepper sauce
2 cans (1 lb. ea.) tomatoes	½ tsp. paprika
1 bay leaf	1 can (about 1 lb.) kidney beans

Brown meat in heavy skillet; break up with spoon or fork as it cooks. Add onion and pepper; cook until soft. Add tomatoes, bay leaf, salt, cloves, chili, hot-pepper sauce, and paprika. Cover; simmer 2 hours; add hot water if necessary to keep mixture from thickening too much. Add beans; heat thoroughly. Remove bay leaf. Serve with corn chips, if desired. Makes 6 servings.

CORNED BEEF

Corned beef is the brisket, plate, or rump that has been mildly cured in a special brine. The brisket is sold as "front cut" which is the round end and has more fat, or as "straight cut" which is leaner and is higher in price.

CORNED BEEF AND CABBAGE

6 lbs. corned beef	2 bay leaves
Water	1 clove of garlic
2 medium-size onions	1 carrot, pared
	1 stalk celery
4 whole cloves	1 large head cabbage
6 peppercorns	

Place corned beef in deep kettle; cover with water. Simmer 1 hour; remove scum. Pour off water; cover with fresh water. Add onions, cloves, peppercorns, bay leaves, garlic, carrot, and celery. Cover; simmer 3 to 4 hours or until tender. Cut cabbage into 6 wedges; place on top of corned beef. Cover; simmer 5 to 15 minutes, depending on crispness of cabbage desired. Serve with mustard, horseradish, Creamy Horseradish Sauce (*page 352*) or Horseradish Cream (*page 352*). Makes 6 servings.

GLAZED CORNED BEEF

5 to 7 lbs. corned beef brisket	1 tbs. prepared mustard
6 peppercorns	1 tsp. prepared horseradish
1 onion, sliced (1 large)	⅓ c. catsup
4 whole cloves	3 tbs. vinegar
1 stalk celery, cut up	2 tbs. butter or margarine
⅓ c. brown sugar, firmly packed	

Cover corned beef with water in deep kettle. Add peppercorns, onion, cloves, and celery. Simmer 4½ to 5 hours or until almost tender; remove from water; place in baking pan. Combine sugar, mustard, horseradish, catsup, vinegar, and butter or margarine in saucepan. Stir over medium heat until blended and bubbly. Spoon some sauce over meat. Bake at 350° F. for 30 minutes or until meat is tender; baste several times with remaining sauce. Makes 8 servings.

Veal

Veal is the meat from young beef. It has a delicious, light, delicate flavor, is grayish pink in color, and has very little fat. Because of this, broiling of veal is not recommended. It is best roasted, braised, or stewed. It should be cooked until thoroughly done with no trace of pink.

Cuts for Roasting or Braising

Loin: The rib and loin (T-Bone) are most often sold as chops, but they also make excellent roasts.

Leg: Meaty roast with a small bone. The leg is often cut into steaks and cutlets.

Rump: This cut is easiest to carve when boned, rolled, and tied.

Shoulder: This cut, too, because of the larger shoulder bone, should be boned, rolled, and tied.

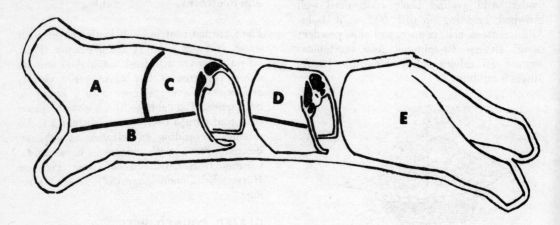

A. Shoulder and Neck
Arm Roast
Rolled Shoulder
Blade Roast
Arm Steak
Blade Steak
Veal for Stew
Neck

B. Breast
Breast
Riblets
Shank

C. Rib
Rib Roast
Crown Rib Roast
Rib Chop

D. Loin
Loin Roast
Loin Chop
Kidney Chop

E. Leg
Standing Rump
Leg Roasts
Cutlets
Veal Scallops (Scallopine)

TIMETABLE FOR ROASTING VEAL

	Pounds	Oven Temperature	Meat Thermometer Temperature	Approximate Cooking Time (Minutes per Pound)
Leg	5 to 8	300°—325° F.	170° F.	25 to 30
Loin	4 to 6	300°—325° F.	170° F.	30 to 35
Rib (rack)	3 to 5	300°—325° F.	170° F.	35 to 40
Rolled shoulder	4 to 6	300°—325° F.	170° F.	40 to 45

How To Roast

Place meat, fat side up, on rack in shallow, open roasting pan. Season with salt and pepper or with herbs as desired. If roast does not have much fat covering, it is advisable to top veal with bacon or salt pork slices. Insert meat thermometer into center of meat, being careful bulb does not touch bone or rest in fat. Do not add water; do not cover. Roast veal to 180° F. When done, take roast from oven; remove from pan and let "rest" for 15 to 20 minutes. This allows the meat to firm up, makes carving easier, helps retain the juices, and allows time to make gravy (*page 141*).

SAVORY STUFFED SHOULDER OF VEAL

1/4 c. butter or margarine
1/4 c. diced celery
2 tbs. chopped onion
1 can (3 to 4 oz.) mushrooms, drained
1 tbs. diced pimiento
1 tsp. grated lemon rind

1 tsp. leaf rosemary, crumbled
2 c. crushed salted crackers
1 c. chicken broth*
1 egg yolk
3 to 4 lbs. veal shoulder, boned
3 tbs. bottled barbecue or meat sauce

Heat butter or margarine in large skillet; add celery and onion; cook until tender. Add mushrooms, pimiento, lemon rind, and rosemary; stir in crackers, chicken broth, and egg yolk. Open veal shoulder, cut side up; spread stuffing almost to edges; roll up veal; tie securely. Insert meat thermometer; brush outside of meat with barbecue or meat sauce. (If roast has little fat covering, lay several thin strips of salt pork or fat bacon on top.) Place on rack in roasting pan; do not cover; do not add water. Roast at 325° F. for 2½ to 3 hours or until meat thermometer registers 180° F. Makes 6 servings.

* Or use 1 chicken bouillon cube or an equivalent amount of granulated chicken bouillon dissolved in 1 cup hot water.

BRAISED VEAL SHOULDER

4 lbs. veal shoulder, boned and rolled
3 tbs. fat or pure vegetable oil
2 c. chopped onion (2 large)
1 c. diced, pared carrots
1 tbs. dry parsley flakes

½ tsp. leaf thyme, crumbled
1 bay leaf
2 tbs. bottled meat sauce
1 c. dry red wine
1 c. water
1 beef bouillon cube

Brown veal on all sides in hot fat or oil in heavy kettle or Dutch oven; remove veal. Sauté onion and carrots in fat or oil remaining in kettle until soft. Add parsley flakes, thyme, bay leaf, meat sauce, wine, water, bouillon cube, and browned veal. Cover; simmer 2½ to 3 hours (allow 35 to 40 minutes per pound of veal) or until veal is tender. Remove bay leaf. Thicken gravy, if desired, with flour that has been mixed to a smooth paste with cold water. Makes 6 servings.

Steaks and Chops

These are best when braised. There are rib and loin chops, blade, arm, and leg or round steaks.

Cutlets and veal for scaloppine: Both these cuts come from the leg. The cutlet is in one piece, usually ½-inch thick. It may make from 2 to 4 servings, depending on what part of the leg it is cut from (the cutlet from the top of the leg will be much larger). Veal for scaloppine is sliced very thin, then pounded to ¼-inch thickness.

VEAL WITH MUSHROOMS
(Natur Schnitzel)

1½ to 2 lbs. veal for scaloppine	1 envelope granulated beef bouillon
½ tsp. onion salt	
⅛ tsp. pepper	⅔ c. water
¼ c. butter or margarine	1 tsp. minced chives
1 can (3 to 4 oz.) sliced mushrooms, drained	

Pound veal slices to ¼-inch thickness. Sprinkle with salt and pepper. Heat butter or margarine in large skillet. Sauté veal until well browned on both sides. Remove; keep warm. Add mushrooms, beef bouillon, and water to fat remaining in pan. Simmer 5 minutes. Return veal to skillet; heat until bubbly. Add chives. Makes 4 to 6 servings.

VEAL SCALLOPS, PROVINCIAL STYLE
(Escalopes De Veau Provençal)

1½ to 2 lbs. veal for scaloppine	½ c. flour
	½ tsp. salt
½ c. minced onion (1 medium)	¼ tsp. pepper
	1 c. tomato juice
1 clove of garlic, mashed	1 c. dry white wine
	¼ tsp. Worcestershire sauce
2 tbs. butter or margarine	¼ tsp. seasoned salt
2 tbs. olive oil	⅛ tsp. seasoned pepper
½ lb. mushrooms, sliced	

Pound veal slices to ¼-inch thickness. Sauté onion and garlic in butter or margarine and olive oil; remove. Sauté mushrooms until soft; remove. Combine flour, salt, and pepper. Dip veal slices into flour mixture; shake off excess; brown in hot fat remaining in skillet, adding more fat if needed to keep meat from sticking; remove from skillet; keep warm. Pour tomato juice into hot skillet; stir well to blend in all brown bits; add wine; cook 5 minutes over low heat. Add veal, onions, mushrooms, Worcestershire, salt, and pepper; cover; simmer gently until heated through. Sprinkle with chopped watercress if desired. Makes 4 to 6 servings.

VEAL SCALOPPINE

1½ to 2 lbs. veal for scaloppine	½ tsp. salt
	¼ tsp. pepper
1 egg slightly beaten	1 tbs. Worcestershire sauce
¾ c. packaged bread crumbs	½ c. beef broth or dry white wine
5 tbs. butter or margarine	2 tbs. chopped parsley
1 tsp. dry mustard	

Pound veal slices to ¼-inch thickness. Dip in beaten egg; coat with bread crumbs. Let stand 10 minutes to dry (this helps keep coating on during cooking). Brown slices on both sides in 3 tablespoons butter or margarine in skillet. Remove veal; keep warm. Add to pan remaining 2 tablespoons butter or margarine, mustard, salt, pepper, Worcestershire, and beef broth or wine. Stir to loosen brown bits on sides and bottom of pan. Heat to boiling. Serve sauce over hot veal; sprinkle with parsley. Makes 4 to 6 servings.

VEAL SCALOPPINE MILANO

½ c. finely chopped onion (1 medium)	1½ tsp. salt
	¼ tsp. pepper
	1 tsp. sugar
2 tbs. olive oil	2 lbs. veal for scaloppine
1 can (6 oz.) tomato paste	
	2 tbs. olive oil
1 can (10½ oz.) condensed consommé	2 tbs. butter or margarine
	½ lb. mushrooms, sliced
1½ c. water	
¾ tsp. leaf thyme, crumbled	1½ c. dry white wine
	½ c. sliced, pitted ripe olives
¼ tsp. leaf rosemary, crumbled	

Sauté onion in 2 tablespoons olive oil. Add tomato paste, consommé, water, thyme, rosemary, salt, pepper, and sugar. Cover; simmer 1½ hours, stirring occasionally. Pound veal slices to ¼-inch thickness. Brown in 2 tablespoons olive oil and butter or margarine; remove from pan. Sauté mushrooms in fat remaining in pan. Add wine, veal, mushrooms, and ripe olives to tomato sauce. Cover; simmer 20 minutes. Makes 4 to 6 servings.

VEAL PARMIGIANA

1 c. packaged bread crumbs	2 cans (8 oz. ea.) tomato sauce
¼ c. grated Parmesan cheese	1½ tsp. leaf basil, crumbled
3 lbs. veal for scaloppine	½ tsp. leaf thyme, crumbled
2 eggs, slightly beaten	½ tsp. salt
1 c. chopped onion (1 large)	½ tsp. onion salt
1 clove of garlic, mashed	¼ tsp. pepper
	2 tbs. olive or pure vegetable oil
2 tbs. olive or pure vegetable oil	2 tbs. butter or margarine
1 can (1 lb.) tomatoes	1 pkg. (8 oz.) mozzarella cheese
	½ c. grated Parmesan cheese

Mix bread crumbs and ¼ cup Parmesan cheese in shallow plate. Pound veal slices to ¼-inch thickness. Dip pieces in beaten eggs; coat well with crumb mixture. Let stand to dry (this helps keep coating on) while preparing sauce. Sauté onion and garlic in 2 tablespoons oil in saucepan until soft. Add tomatoes, tomato sauce, basil, thyme, salts, and pepper. Cover; simmer 15 minutes. Heat oven to 350° F. Heat 2 tablespoons oil and butter or margarine in skillet until mixture foams. Add veal, a few pieces, at a time, and brown on both sides. Add more oil or butter or margarine if needed. Cut mozzarella cheese into 12 slices. Spoon some sauce into shallow baking dish. Arrange alternate, overlapping slices of cheese and veal in dish; spoon on remaining sauce. Sprinkle with ½ cup Parmesan cheese. Bake 15 to 20 minutes or until sauce bubbles and cheese melts. Makes 6 to 8 servings.

VIENNESE VEAL ROLLS

Our Viennese Veal Rolls, along with their vegetables, bake slowly for an hour with no attention or worry on your part, and thus your weekend buffet almost takes care of itself.

½ lb. mushrooms or 2 cans (3 to 4 oz. ea.) mushrooms, drained	1½ c. chicken broth
	1 tsp. salt
	⅛ tsp. pepper
	1 bay leaf
	1 c. dry white wine
½ c. butter or margarine	1½ c. sliced, pared carrots
3 slices bread	1 c. sliced celery
Hot water	1 c. chopped onion (1 large)
¼ tsp. leaf basil, crumbled	
¼ tsp. leaf thyme, crumbled	½ c. diced green pepper
¼ tsp. leaf tarragon, crumbled	½ lb. fresh green beans, tipped, cut, and parboiled or 1 can (1 lb. 4 oz.) cut green beans
3 lbs. veal for scaloppine (12 slices)	
Salt and pepper	2 tbs. cornstarch
	2 tbs. water

Chop mushrooms; sauté in ¼ cup butter or margarine. Soak bread slices in hot water; squeeze dry. Combine basil, thyme, tarragon, and bread; mix well. Sprinkle veal slices lightly with salt and pepper. Place a rounded tablespoon of bread mixture on each veal slice; roll up; fasten with wooden pick. Brown veal rolls in remaining ¼ cup butter or margarine in skillet; place rolls in large casserole. Add chicken broth, salt, pepper, and bay leaf to drippings in skillet; bring to simmering. Stir in wine; pour over veal rolls; arrange vegetables over and around veal; cover. Bake at 350° F. for 1 hour or until tender. Pour liquid into saucepan; thicken with cornstarch blended with water. Pour over veal and vegetables on platter. Makes 6 to 8 servings.

VEAL BIRDS

1½ lbs. veal for scaloppine (6 slices)	1 can (10½ oz.) condensed consommé
4 tbs. butter or margarine	Flour
½ c. minced onion (1 medium)	4 tbs. butter or margarine
2 c. bread cubes (4 slices)	½ tsp. leaf thyme, crumbled
½ tsp. salt	½ tsp. leaf oregano, crumbled
¼ tsp. seasoned pepper	1 tbs. flour
1 tbs. parsley flakes	½ c. water

Pound veal slices to ¼-inch thickness. Melt 4 tablespoons butter or margarine in skillet over medium heat; sauté onion until golden. Add bread cubes; stir quickly until golden. Add salt, pepper, parsley, and ¼ cup consommé; blend well. Divide stuffing among the veal slices; roll up; tie with cord in several places to hold together. Roll in flour; shake off excess. Melt 4 tablespoons butter or margarine in skillet; brown birds on all sides; remove; keep warm. Stir thyme, oregano, and 1 tablespoon flour into fat in skillet; add water and remaining consommé. Stir to loosen brown bits on sides and bottom of pan; stir rapidly until thickened and bubbly. Snip cord carefully from each bird; return birds to skillet; cover; simmer over low heat 10 minutes. Makes 6 servings.

SAUTEED VEAL CUTLET

1 veal cutlet, ½ in. thick (about 1 lb.)	2 tbs. butter or margarine
1 egg, beaten	2 tbs. olive or pure vegetable oil
2 tbs. water	1 can (8 oz.) tomato sauce
½ c. packaged bread crumbs	½ c. water
	½ tsp. salt

Dip cutlet in mixture of egg and water; roll in bread crumbs to coat well. Heat butter or margarine and oil in skillet. Add cutlet; cook slowly until brown on both sides. Combine tomato sauce, water, and salt. Pour over meat. Lower heat; simmer, covered, 20 to 30 minutes or until tender. Makes 2 servings.

WIENER SCHNITZEL

2 veal cutlets (about 2 lbs.), halved	2 tbs. grated Parmesan cheese
Flour	3 tbs. flour
1 egg	4 tbs. butter or margarine
⅔ c. milk	3 tbs. lemon juice
¼ tsp. salt	1 tbs. minced parsley
⅛ tsp. pepper	

Pound cutlets to ¼-inch thickness. Sprinkle with flour. Beat egg with milk. Combine salt, pepper, Parmesan cheese, and flour; add milk mixture; beat until smooth. Dip cutlets into mixture. Melt butter or margarine in large skillet over medium heat. Sauté cutlets until golden brown. Lower heat; cover; cook 5 minutes more or until tender. Add lemon juice to fat remaining in skillet; stir to loosen brown bits on sides and bottom of pan; pour over cutlets. Sprinkle with parsley. Makes 4 servings.

STUFFED VEAL ROLLS

2 veal cutlets (about 2 lbs.)	1 tsp. leaf oregano, crumbled
½ lb. prosciutto or cooked ham, chopped	2 tbs. capers
	4 oz. mozzarella cheese
3 tbs. chopped parsley	Flour
¼ tsp. salt	¼ c. butter or margarine
⅛ tsp. pepper	1 c. chicken broth
	1 c. dry white wine

Pound cutlets to ¼-inch thickness. Combine prosciutto or ham, parsley, salt, pepper, oregano, and capers. Spread over veal. Cut mozzarella into thin strips; place strips over prosciutto mixture. Roll up; tie with cord in several places to hold together. Sprinkle well with flour. Brown in skillet in hot butter or margarine. Add chicken broth and wine. Bring to boiling; turn heat low. Simmer 40 to 45 minutes or until veal is tender. Remove cord; slice veal. Thicken pan juices, with flour mixed to a smooth paste with a small amount of water, if desired. Makes 4 servings.

CITY CHICKEN

2 lbs. veal shoulder,
cut in 2-in. cubes
1 tsp. salt
1/4 tsp. pepper
1 egg, beaten
2 tbs. water

2 c. packaged bread
or cracker
crumbs
1/4 c. fat or pure
vegetable oil
1 can (13 1/2 oz.)
chicken broth

Thread veal cubes on 6 skewers. Sprinkle with salt and pepper. Combine egg and water. Dip veal into egg mixture; roll in crumbs to coat well. Heat fat or oil in large skillet. Brown veal well on all sides. Add chicken broth; lower heat; cover skillet. Simmer 50 to 60 minutes or until tender. Thicken pan juices, if desired. Makes 6 servings.

VEAL CHOPS PAPRIKA

8 rib veal chops
3 tbs. fat or pure
vegetable oil
1 can (10 1/2 oz.)
condensed beef
broth
2 c. (1 pt.) dairy
sour cream

1 1/2 tbs. paprika
1/2 tsp. salt
1 sweet red pepper,
seeded and sliced
1 green pepper,
seeded and sliced
3 tbs. fat or pure
vegetable oil

Brown chops on both sides in 3 tablespoons hot fat or oil in large skillet. Add beef broth; cover. Simmer 1/2 hour or until chops are tender; remove chops; keep warm. Stir sour cream slowly into juices in pan; add paprika and salt; heat but do not boil. Cook red and green peppers in 3 tablespoons hot fat or oil until soft. Spoon gravy over chops; top with peppers. Makes 4 servings.

VEAL RAGOUT

1 1/2 lbs. veal
shoulder, cut in
1-in. cubes
1/4 c. flour
3 tbs. fat or pure
vegetable oil
2 c. water

18 prunes, pitted
2 tbs. sugar
3/4 c. orange juice
2 tbs. vinegar
1/4 tsp. ground
cloves

Coat veal lightly with flour; brown on all sides in hot fat or oil in heavy skillet. Add water; cover; simmer 1 hour. Add prunes, sugar, orange juice, vinegar, and cloves; cover. Simmer 45 minutes or until veal is tender. Taste and add salt, if necessary. Thicken broth, if desired, with flour mixed to a smooth paste with a small amount of water. Makes 6 servings.

BLANQUETTE OF VEAL

4 lbs. breast of veal,
cut in serving-
pieces
1/2 tsp. salt
2 sprigs parsley
1 stalk celery,
cut up
1 bay leaf
1/4 tsp. leaf thyme,
crumbled
2 cloves of garlic
8 peppercorns
2 carrots, pared and
sliced
2 lb. mushrooms,
sliced

2 tbs. butter or
margarine
1 tsp. lemon juice
4 tbs. butter or
margarine
4 tbs. flour
1/2 tsp. salt
2 egg yolks
1 c. light cream
24 small white
onions, peeled,
cooked, and
drained
2 tbs. chopped
parsley

Place veal in large kettle or Dutch oven; cover with cold water. Add salt and "bouquet garni" of parsley, celery, bay leaf, thyme, garlic, peppercorns, and carrots tied in cheesecloth. Simmer 1 1/2 to 2 hours or until tender; remove and discard bouquet garni; remove veal; keep warm. Measure and reserve 2 cups of stock. Cook mushrooms in 2 tablespoons butter or margarine and lemon juice until tender. Melt 4 tablespoons butter or margarine in kettle; blend in flour and salt; stir in reserved 2 cups stock. Cook over medium heat, stirring constantly, until thickened. Beat egg yolks and cream; add to sauce; heat just until it bubbles. Arrange veal, onions, and mushrooms on platter; pour hot sauce over. Sprinkle with parsley. Makes 6 servings.

VEAL RAGOUT MARENGO

2 lbs. veal shoulder,
  cubed
2 tbs. fat or pure
  vegetable oil
1½ c. finely
  chopped onion
1 clove of garlic,
  mashed
2 c. beef broth or
  dry white wine
1 tsp. leaf thyme,
  crumbled

1 bay leaf
2 c. peeled, chopped
  tomatoes (3 to 4
  medium size)
1 tsp. salt
¼ tsp. pepper
2 tbs. diced
  pimiento
1 can (6 oz.) sliced
  mushrooms,
  undrained

Brown veal cubes on all sides in fat or oil in heavy kettle or Dutch oven; remove veal. Sauté onion and garlic in fat or oil in kettle until soft. Add beef broth or wine, thyme, and bay leaf. Simmer until liquid is reduced to half its original volume. Add tomatoes, salt, pepper, and browned veal. Cover; simmer 1¾ to 2 hours or until veal is tender. Add pimiento and mushrooms. Taste for seasoning; add additional salt and pepper, if desired. Heat through. Remove bay leaf. Thicken broth, if desired, with flour mixed to a smooth paste with a small amount of water. Makes 8 servings.

VEAL SHANK RAGOUT

Six 2½-in. veal
  shank crosscuts
¼ c. fat or pure
  vegetable oil
1 c. chopped onion
  (1 large)
½ c. diced celery
½ c. diced carrot
1 can (10½ oz.)
  condensed onion
  soup or beef
  broth

1 c. water
½ tsp. salt
¼ tsp. pepper
1 tsp. grated lemon
  rind
1 tsp. lemon juice
1 tbs. tomato paste
2 tbs. chopped
  parsley

Brown shank pieces in fat or oil in Dutch oven or heavy kettle; remove pieces as they brown. Pour off all but 2 tablespoons fat or oil; add onion, celery, and carrot; sauté until tender. Return shank pieces to pan. Add onion soup or beef broth, water, salt, and pepper. Simmer, covered, 1½ to 2 hours or until meat is tender. Taste; add salt and pepper if needed. Thicken broth, if desired, with flour blended to a smooth paste with a small amount of water. Stir in lemon rind and juice, tomato paste, and parsley. Heat through. Makes 6 servings.

Lamb

Lamb is available all year round though supplies may vary in some areas.

High quality lamb has a smooth covering of clear, white, brittle fat over most of the exterior. The lean is pinkish-red in the yearling lamb and in mutton it is a deeper red. The texture of the lean is fine grained and velvety in appearance.

Cuts for Roasting

Leg: May be purchased as the full leg, weighing 6 to 10 pounds, or a half leg, either the shank end or the sirloin end, weighing 3 to 5 pounds.

Shoulder: This roast may be a cushion shoulder which has the bone removed and is fastened on two sides. One side may be left open for stuffing, then skewered or sewed. Or it may be a rolled shoulder which is a boneless roll made from the square cut shoulder and tied.

Crown Roast: Roast shaped from rib sections. *See recipe on page 166.*

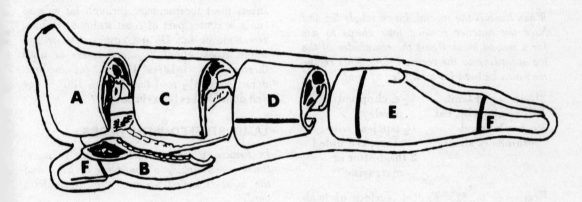

A. **Shoulder**
   Cushion Shoulder
   Rolled Shoulder
   Cubes for Stew
   Neck
   Shoulder Chops

B. **Breast**
   Breast
   Ribs
   Riblets

C. **Rib**
   Rib Roast
   Crown Rib Roast
   Rib Chops

D. **Loin**
   Loin Chops
   Loin Roast

E. **Leg**
   Leg, whole or half
   Leg Chop (Steak)

F. **Shank**
   Shanks

How to Roast

Place meat, fat side up, on rack in shallow, open roasting pan. Season with salt and pepper or as specific recipe directs. Insert meat thermometer into thickest part of muscle, being careful bulb does not touch bone or rest in fat. Do not add water. Do not cover. Place in 300° to 325° F. oven. Roast to 175° F. on meat thermometer for medium done; to 180° F. for well done. When done, take roast from oven; remove from pan and let "rest" on heated platter for 15 to 20 minutes. This allows the meat to firm up, makes carving easier, helps retain the juices, and allows time to make gravy (page 141).

TIMETABLE FOR ROASTING LAMB

Cut	Pounds	Oven Temperature	Meat Thermometer Temperature	Approximate Cooking Time (Minutes per Pound)
Leg	5 to 8	300°–325° F.	175°–180° F.	30 to 35
Cushion Shoulder	3 to 5	300°–325° F.	175°–180° F.	30 to 35
Rolled Shoulder	3 to 5	300°–325° F.	175°–180° F.	40 to 45

HERB ROASTED LEG OF LAMB

When lamb is the special, buy a whole leg and have the butcher remove four chops to use for a second meal. Roast the remainder of the leg according to the recipe below. This recipe may also be used for a half leg of lamb.

3½-lb. leg of lamb	½ c. chopped parsley
1 clove of garlic, cut	½ tsp. leaf rosemary, crumbled
1 c. fresh bread crumbs (2 slices)	2 tbs. butter or margarine

Heat oven to 325° F. Rub surface of lamb with cut clove of garlic. Place, fat side up, on rack in open, shallow roasting pan; do not cover or add water. Roast 1 hour. Combine bread crumbs, parsley, rosemary, and butter or margarine; mix thoroughly. Coat top of leg of lamb with crumb mixture. Continue roasting about 45 minutes or until meat thermometer registers 175° F. for medium done, 180° F. for well done. Makes 8 servings.

ROAST LAMB, MEDITERRANEAN STYLE

6-lb. leg of lamb	½ tsp. pepper
½ lemon	2 tsp. leaf rosemary, crumbled
3 to 4 tbs. olive oil	
2 tsp. garlic salt	

Heat oven to 325° F. Rub surface of lamb well with the cut side of lemon. Drizzle oil over lamb. Sprinkle lamb with garlic salt, pepper, and rosemary. Place roast, fat side up, on rack in open, shallow roasting pan. Insert meat thermometer through fat side so tip is in center part of roast without touching any bone or fat. Do not cover roast or add water. Roast about 2½ to 3 hours or until thermometer registers 175° F. for medium done; roast 3½ to 4 hours or to 180° F. for well done. Makes 8 servings.

LAMB STUFFED WITH HERBS

In France, a savory herb dressing is sometimes spread inside a boned leg of lamb and the meat is rolled up and tied neatly with cord.

½ c. minced parsley	1 tbs. olive or pure vegetable oil
1 clove of garlic, crushed	6-lb. leg of lamb, boned and flattened
½ tsp. leaf basil, crumbled	Soft butter or margarine
1 tsp. salt	Salt
¼ tsp. pepper	
⅛ tsp. ground ginger	

Combine parsley, garlic, basil, 1 teaspoon salt, pepper, ginger, and oil; mix well. Spread evenly over flattened meat; roll up, tucking in ends; tie with clean white cord into even roll. Rub outside of meat with soft butter or margarine; sprinkle with salt. Place, fat side up, on rack in open, shallow roasting pan. Roast at 400° F. for 1½ hours for rare (meat thermometer will register 145° F.), or 1¾ to 2 hours for medium rare (155° F. on meat thermometer). Or, roast at 450° F. for 10 minutes; reduce oven heat to 325° F.; continue roasting 2 hours for rare, 2¼ to 2½ hours for medium rare. Remove roast to heated platter; cut and remove cord before serving. Makes 8 servings.

EXOTIC ORIENTAL LAMB

In the countries of the Near East cinnamon is often used to season lamb, giving the meat and the gravy, too, a subtly different flavor.

¼ to ½ tsp. ground cinnamon	2 tsp. lemon juice
½ tsp. coarsely ground or cracked black pepper	2 tbs. olive or pure vegetable oil
	1 tbs. minced onion
	1 to 1½ tsp. salt
	6-lb. leg of lamb

Combine and mix well all ingredients except lamb. Rub mixture over outside of lamb. Place, fat side up, on rack in open, shallow roasting pan. Roast at 400° F. for 1½ hours for rare (meat thermometer will register 145° F.); 1¾ to 2 hours for medium rare (155° F. on meat thermometer). Or, roast at 450° F. for 10 minutes; reduce heat to 325° F.; continue roasting 2 hours for rare, 2¼ to 2½ hours for medium rare. Makes 8 servings.

NEAPOLITAN LAMB AL VINO

Marinating lamb in wine and herbs for 24 hours before roasting, as they do it in Italy, makes the meat wonderfully tender and fragrant.

1 clove of garlic, slivered	1½ tsp. grated lemon rind
6-lb. leg of lamb	½ tsp. leaf rosemary, crumbled
1 c. dry red or white wine	Olive or pure vegetable oil
¼ c. minced onion	1½ tsp. salt
1 clove of garlic, crushed	2 tbs. flour
	1½ c. water

Insert slivers of garlic around bone in leg of lamb; place in large pan. Combine wine, onion, crushed garlic, lemon rind, and rosemary; pour over lamb. Let stand several hours or overnight, turning meat in marinade several times. Remove meat from marinade; wipe dry. Brush with oil; sprinkle with salt.

Place, fat side up, on rack in open, shallow roasting pan. Roast at 450° F. for 10 minutes; reduce oven heat to 325° F.; roast 2 hours for rare (meat thermometer will register 145° F.); 2½ hours for medium rare (155° F. on meat thermometer). Baste with strained marinade several times during roasting. Remove meat to heated platter; keep warm. Skim fat from pan; mix flour to a smooth paste with a small amount of water; stir into liquid in pan; blend until smooth. Add remaining water; bring to boiling over high heat; continue to boil until reduced and slightly thickened. A boned, rolled leg of lamb may be marinated as above, placed on spit, and spit-roasted at 450° F. for 1 to 1¼ hours, basting with marinade during cooking. Makes 8 servings.

STUFFED SHOULDER OF LAMB

3 tbs. butter or margarine	1 beef bouillon cube
½ c. chopped onion (1 medium)	¾ c. boiling water
2 tbs. diced green pepper	1 boned shoulder of lamb (3½ to 4½ lbs.), with pocket
2 tbs. diced pimiento	Salt and pepper
2 c. fresh bread crumbs (4 slices)	4 tbs. flour
½ tsp. leaf rosemary, crumbled	½ tsp. salt
½ tsp. leaf thyme, crumbled	2 c. hot water
	1 tsp. bottled gravy coloring
	1 c. currant jelly

Melt butter or margarine in skillet; sauté onion and green pepper until soft. Add pimiento, bread crumbs, rosemary, and thyme. Dissolve bouillon cube in boiling water; add to skillet; mix well. Press filling into pocket in shoulder of lamb; roll up. Tie meat securely with clean white string in several places around roll. Place in roasting pan; sprinkle lightly with salt and pepper. Roast at 300° F. allowing 40 to 45 minutes per pound or until meat thermometer, registers 175° F. for medium done, 180° F. for well done. Remove lamb to warm platter; keep warm. Pour off all but 4 tablespoons fat from roasting pan. Place pan over medium heat. Stir in flour and salt until it is smooth and just begins to brown. Add hot water and gravy coloring slowly. Cook, stirring constantly, until thickened. Add jelly; stir until smooth. Serve hot with lamb. Makes 6 servings.

CROWN ROAST OF LAMB

Crown roast of lamb, a gala party roast, is made from the rib sections of lamb, using both sides. Two ribs or chops are allowed per serving, so you would need to order a crown made from 12 to 16 ribs (6 to 8 pounds) to serve 6 to 8 people. Have the butcher prepare the roast. He will separate the ribs at the backbone, but leave them together so that when serving it will be easy for you to cut down between each two ribs or chops and lift them out with stuffing. Crown may be stuffed or unstuffed.

Stuffed Crown Roast of Lamb

For stuffing, have trimmings ground. Measure; mix with half as much packaged bread stuffing prepared according to package directions.

Place crown, rib bones up, on rack in roasting pan; spoon stuffing lightly in center. Cover top of each rib bone with aluminum foil to prevent charring during roasting. Insert meat thermometer between ribs into center of thickest part of meat. Make sure bulb of thermometer does not rest in fat or on bone. Roast at 325° F. or until thermometer registers 175° F. for medium done or 180° F. for well done (it will take about 35 to 40 minutes per pound), or 170° F. or less if you like lamb a little pink. Baste top of stuffing occasionally with pan juices.

When roast is done, place on heated platter; remove aluminum foil from ribs; top each rib with a paper chop frill.

Unstuffed Crown Roast of Lamb

Place crown upside down in roasting pan without a rack, so fat from roast bastes end of rib bones. Roast as above. Unstuffed crown takes a little less time than stuffed crown to reach desired temperature. Fill center with mashed potatoes, creamed mushrooms, or peas with small white onions, if desired.

LAMB CHOPS

Loin Chop: Chop has a T-shaped bone, is quite meaty, and is usually 1 to 2 inches thick. It is the most costly of the lamb chops.

Rib Chop: Smaller than loin chop. It contains an "eye" of tender meat and a rib bone.

Double Rib Chop: Exactly like the rib chop, except it is twice as thick and has 2 rib bones.

French Chop: A rib chop with the meat removed from the end of the rib bone. The chop is often served with a paper frill covering the end.

Sirloin Chop: A heavy chop cut from sirloin section of the leg. The amount of bone will vary depending on where in the sirloin section it is cut.

English Chop: Two-inch thick chop cut from the unsplit loin. The backbone is removed and the chop is skewered together. It may contain the kidney fastened in the middle of the chop.

Shoulder Chop: Larger than loin or rib chops and less expensive. These include:

Arm Shoulder Chop: This chop contains a small bone, the arm bone, and a cross section of the first rib.

Blade Shoulder Chop: This chop contains the backbone and a rib bone.

Leg Steak: Cut from large leg of lamb. Contains round bone.

Timetable for Broiling Lamb Chops

Cut	Minutes per Side
Shoulder Chops	
1 inch	6
1½ inch	9
2 inch	11
Rib Chops	
1 inch	6
1½ inch	9
2 inch	11
Loin Chops	
1 inch	6
1½ inch	9
2 inch	11

Times given are for medium done

SKEWERED LAMB

2 lbs. lamb,
shoulder or leg
1 c. dry red wine
¼ c. tarragon
vinegar
⅔ c. olive or pure
vegetable oil
1 tsp. salt
½ c. sliced onion
(1 medium)

1 tsp. leaf mar-
joram, crumbled
1 tsp. leaf basil,
crumbled
4 small white
onions, peeled
and parboiled
1 green pepper,
cut up
1 tomato, quartered

Cut lamb into pieces about 1½ inches square. Combine wine, vinegar, oil, salt, onion, marjoram, and basil. Pour marinade over lamb; cover; refrigerate several hours or overnight. On each of four skewers, thread 2 pieces of lamb, one onion, one piece of pepper, and one section of tomato. Brush vegetables with marinade. Preheat broiler; broil 12 to 15 minutes, turning to brown all sides. Baste with remaining marinade during broiling. Makes 4 servings.

LAMB STEWS

Stews may be made from the leg, shoulder, shank, or breast of lamb.

LAMB SHANKS WITH DIXIE BARBECUE SAUCE

6 large or 8 small
lamb shanks
3 tbs. fat or pure
vegetable oil
2 c. water
1½ c. orange juice
¼ c. vinegar
2 tsp. Worcester-
shire sauce
1 tsp. bottled meat
sauce

1 tsp. salt
Dash of pepper
Dash of paprika
½ tsp. celery seed
½ tsp. leaf basil,
crumbled
½ tsp. leaf oregano,
crumbled
¼ tsp. dry mustard
5 whole cloves
2 tsp. sugar

Brown lamb shanks in hot fat or oil in large heavy skillet or Dutch oven; add water; cover; simmer 1 hour. Combine remaining ingredients in small saucepan; simmer 10 minutes. Pour off all but 1 cup broth from lamb shanks; pour barbecue sauce over lamb; stir well. Cover; simmer 45 minutes or until lamb is tender. Makes 6 servings.

PAPRIKA LAMB SHANKS

½ c. flour
1 tsp. salt
¼ tsp. pepper
4 lamb shanks
(about 1½ lbs.
ea.)
4 tbs. fat or pure
vegetable oil
3 c. boiling water

1 can (10½ oz.)
condensed onion
soup
⅓ c. flour
1 tbs. paprika
1 c. cold water
1 can (3 to 4 oz.)
sliced mushrooms
1 c. dairy sour
cream

Put ½ cup flour, salt, and pepper in paper bag. Add shanks; shake until well coated. Heat fat or oil in Dutch oven or heavy kettle; add lamb shanks; brown well on all sides. Add boiling water and onion soup; cover. Simmer 1½ to 2 hours or until lamb is tender. Remove from heat; remove lamb shanks; keep warm. Skim all fat from liquid in kettle. Blend ⅓ cup flour, paprika, and cold water until smooth. Stir slowly into liquid in kettle. Cook over medium heat, stirring constantly, until thickened. Add lamb, mushrooms, and mushroom liquid. Just before serving, stir in sour cream. Taste; adjust seasoning, if necessary. Heat through; do not boil. Makes 4 servings.

ARMENIAN LAMB STEW WITH ARTICHOKES

2 lbs. lamb
shoulder, cubed
2 tbs. fat or pure
vegetable oil
1 c. finely chopped
onion (1 large)
1 tsp. salt
1 tsp. anise seeds,
crushed

1 pkg. (10 oz.)
frozen artichoke
hearts
8 oz. medium
noodles, cooked
and drained
1 tbs. flour
¼ c. water
2 tbs. lemon juice

Brown lamb in hot fat or oil in heavy kettle or Dutch oven; add onion; sauté 3 minutes. Add salt, anise seeds, and water to cover. Cover; simmer about 1 hour and 20 minutes or until meat is tender. Add artichokes; simmer 5 to 8 minutes or until artichokes are done. Place hot cooked noodles on platter. Spoon meat and artichokes over. Mix flour and water to smooth paste; stir into broth; cook until thickened. Add lemon juice; pour gravy over meat. Makes 6 servings.

SCOTCH LAMB STEW

2 lbs. lamb shoulder, cubed	½ tsp. salt
1 tbs. fat or pure vegetable oil	Dash of pepper
	Dash of hot-pepper sauce
3 c. water	4 medium-size potatoes, pared and halved
1 can (10½-oz.) condensed beef broth	
¼ c. barley	1 tbs. flour
½ c. sliced onion (1 medium)	½ c. water
	1 pkg. (10 oz.) frozen green beans, cooked, or
2 tbs. minced parsley	1 can (1 lb.) drained green beans, heated
½ c. chopped celery tops	

Brown lamb pieces well on all sides in hot fat or oil in heavy kettle or Dutch oven; add 3 cups water, broth, barley, onion, parsley, celery tops, salt, pepper, and hot-pepper sauce. Cover; simmer 35 minutes. Add potatoes; simmer 30 minutes or until lamb and potatoes are tender. Combine flour and ½ cup water to make a smooth paste; stir into stew; cook until thickened. Just before serving arrange hot green beans on top of stew. Makes 6 servings.

LAMB STEW WITH WINE

2 tbs. fat or pure vegetable oil	¼ tsp. pepper
	3 c. dry red wine
3 lbs. lamb shoulder, cubed	2 c. pared, sliced carrots
1 c. chopped onion (1 large)	18 small white onions, peeled, or
1 carrot, pared and finely chopped	1 can (1 lb.) whole onions, drained
1½ tsp. salt	
½ tsp. leaf rosemary, crumbled	½ lb. mushrooms, sliced
1 tsp. leaf basil, crumbled	2 tbs. butter or margarine
½ tsp. leaf thyme, crumbled	2 tbs. flour
	2 tbs. chopped parsley

Heat fat or oil in kettle or Dutch oven; brown lamb well on all sides; remove meat from kettle; reserve. Add chopped onion and chopped carrot to kettle; cook until soft. Return meat to kettle; add salt, rosemary, basil, thyme, pepper, and red wine. Bring to boiling; turn heat to simmer; cover. Cooking time for lamb will be from 1½ to 2 hours. Sliced carrots and onions will take 30 minutes to cook, mushrooms 15 minutes. Judge the time you should add them to the stew according to the tenderness of the meat. Blend butter or margarine and flour together (called *beurre manié*) in small bowl for thickening stew. When meat and vegetables are tender, spoon enough of the *beurre manié* into the stew to thicken as desired. Taste; add additional seasonings, if desired. Sprinkle with chopped parsley. Makes 6 servings.

LAMB STEW

½ c. flour	1 tsp. leaf rosemary, crumbled
1 tsp. salt	
¼ tsp. pepper	4 c. hot water
2 lbs. lamb shoulder, cubed	12 small white onions, peeled
3 tbs. fat or pure vegetable oil	6 carrots, pared and sliced
1 c. sliced onion (1 large)	2 medium-size potatoes, pared and cubed
2 tsp. salt	
¼ tsp. seasoned pepper	1 c. sliced celery
	⅓ c. flour
1 bay leaf	½ c. water

Put ½ cup flour, 1 teaspoon salt, and pepper in paper bag. Add cubed lamb, a few pieces at a time; shake until well coated. Heat fat or oil in Dutch oven or heavy kettle; add lamb; brown well on all sides. Remove lamb; keep warm. Sauté onion in fat or oil remaining in kettle until soft. Add lamb, 2 teaspoons salt, ¼ teaspoon seasoned pepper, bay leaf, rosemary, and 4 cups water. Cover; simmer 1½ hours or until lamb is tender. While stew cooks, cook vegetables in boiling salted water until just tender. Skim fat from stew. Mix ⅓ cup flour and ½ cup water to a smooth paste; stir into broth. Cook over low heat, stirring constantly, until thickened. Add vegetables. Taste; adjust seasonings, if necessary. Makes 6 servings.

LAMB STROGANOFF

6 tbs. butter or margarine	½ tsp. pepper
½ lb. mushrooms, sliced	1½ lbs. lamb shoulder, thinly sliced
½ c. chopped onion (1 medium)	1½ c. water
	¼ c. dry sherry
1 small clove of garlic, minced	1½ c. yogurt
	1 tsp. salt
½ c. flour	1 tbs. chopped parsley
1 tsp. salt	

Heat 2 tablespoons butter or margarine in large skillet. Sauté mushrooms, onions, and garlic over medium heat until soft but not brown. Remove; reserve. Combine flour, 1 teaspoon salt, and pepper in paper bag. Cut lamb into strips ½ inch wide and 1½ inches long. Shake lamb pieces in mixture to coat lightly; shake off all excess flour. Brown one third of lamb in one third remaining butter or margarine; remove. Repeat with lamb and butter or margarine until all lamb is browned. Add water to hot skillet. Stir and scrape all browned meat glaze from bottom and sides of skillet. Strain, if desired. Add sherry and lamb. Cover; simmer 15 to 20 minutes or until lamb is tender. Stir frequently to prevent sticking. Add mushrooms, onion, garlic, and yogurt, and 1 teaspoon salt.* Heat slowly until piping hot. Sprinkle with parsley. Serve with Pilaf (*page 274*). Makes 4 to 6 servings.
* If making ahead, add everything except yogurt. Just before serving, stir in yogurt and reheat.

LAMB CURRY

3 tbs. fat or pure vegetable oil	¼ tsp. pepper
	¼ tsp. ground cumin
2 lbs. leg or shoulder lamb, cut in 1-in. cubes	1 to 2 tbs. curry powder
	1 tsp. flour
1 c. chopped onion (1 large)	1 can (10½ oz.) condensed beef broth
2 cloves of garlic, crushed	1 c. water
½ tsp. salt	
½ tsp. ground ginger	

Heat fat or oil in large skillet. Add meat; brown well; remove; reserve. Sauté onion and garlic until soft in fat or oil remaining in skillet. Add salt, ginger, pepper, cumin, curry powder, and flour; cook 2 minutes, stirring constantly. Return lamb to skillet. Add beef broth and water. Reduce heat; cover; cook, stirring occasionally, about 45 minutes or until lamb is tender. Serve with hot rice and chutney, if desired. Makes 6 servings.

DEVILED LAMB RIBLETS

¾ c. flour	2 cans (8 oz. ea.) tomato sauce
1 tsp. salt	
¼ tsp. pepper	3 c. water
3½ lbs. breast of lamb, cut in serving-size pieces	1 tbs. Worcestershire sauce
	1 tbs. prepared horseradish
¼ c. fat or pure vegetable oil	1 tbs. prepared mustard
	1 lemon, sliced
1 clove of garlic, mashed	¼ c. flour
	½ c. water
1 c. chopped onion (1 large)	1 can (3 to 4 oz.) sliced mushrooms

Put ¾ cup flour, salt, and pepper in paper bag. Add lamb, a few pieces at a time; shake until coated. Heat fat or oil in Dutch oven or heavy kettle; add lamb; brown well. Remove lamb; keep warm. Sauté garlic and onion in fat or oil remaining in kettle until soft. Add lamb, tomato sauce, water, Worcestershire, horseradish, mustard, and lemon. Cover; cook over low heat or at 350° F. for 1½ hours or until lamb is tender. Remove from heat; skim all fat from liquid. Mix ¼ cup flour and ½ cup water to a smooth paste; stir into broth. Cook over low heat, stirring constantly, until thickened. Add mushrooms. Makes 6 servings.

SHEPHERD'S PIE

3 tbs. butter or margarine	1 can (10¾ oz.) beef gravy
¼ c. minced onion (1 small)	¼ c. water
3 c. cubed, cooked lamb	¼ tsp. salt
1 c. cooked vegetables	½ pkg. (4 servings) instant mashed potatoes

Melt butter or margarine in skillet. Sauté onion until soft. Add lamb; cook 5 minutes; add vegetables. Combine beef gravy, water, and salt; add to skillet. Pour into 1½-quart casserole. Heat oven to 450° F. Prepare potatoes according to package directions; spread carefully over meat mixture. Bake 20 minutes or until potatoes are brown and pie is bubbly. Makes 4 servings.

MADE WITH COOKED LAMB

Lamb patties are often sold in the markets, and many delicious dishes can be made with them. They are usually sold with a slice of bacon wrapped around the edge to incorporate some fat for cooking, since they are comprised mostly of lean meat.

LAMB-HERB LOAF

½ c. catsup	1 pkg. (8 oz.) herb-flavored bread-stuffing mix
1 can (10½ oz.) condensed beef broth	½ c. grated, pared carrot
1 tsp. Worcestershire sauce	¼ c. diced green pepper
½ tsp. sugar	¼ c. water
2 tbs. butter or margarine	1½ lbs. lean lamb, ground
½ c. chopped onion (1 medium)	1 egg
¼ c. butter or margarine	½ tsp. salt

Combine catsup, beef broth, Worcestershire, sugar, and 2 tablespoons butter or margarine in small saucepan; cook over medium heat until mixture comes to boiling; remove from heat; reserve. Sauté onion in ¼ cup butter or margarine in skillet until soft; mix well with ½ package of stuffing mix, carrot, green pepper, and water. Combine lamb, remaining ½ package of stuffing mix, egg, salt, and ½ cup of reserved catsup mixture in bowl; mix well. Press half the meat mixture into 9x5x3-inch loaf pan. Press stuffing mixture firmly over meat layer; press remaining meat mixture carefully over stuffing layer; turn loaf out onto baking pan. Bake at 350° F. for 60 to 70 minutes, brushing loaf with catsup mixture several times during baking. Serve with any remaining sauce. Makes 6 servings.

CURRIED LAMB LOAF

2½ c. cooked lamb	1¼ c. water
1 small green pepper, seeded	1 tsp. salt
1 c. fresh bread crumbs (2 slices)	⅛ tsp. pepper
1 c. cooked green beans	1 to 1½ tsp. curry powder
1 envelope dehydrated onion soup mix	2 eggs, beaten

Heat oven to 350° F. Grease 9x5x3-inch loaf pan. Put lamb and green pepper through food grinder, using medium blade; combine with bread crumbs and green beans. Blend onion soup mix, water, salt, pepper, and curry powder in saucepan. Cover; simmer 5 minutes; cool slightly. Combine soup mixture, lamb mixture, and eggs; blend well. Turn into prepared pan. Bake 50 minutes or until meat is firm and well browned on top. Makes 6 servings.

Pork

There are so many dishes which depend on pork for their goodness. Imagine Boston Baked Beans without chunks of salt pork buried in the molasses-sweetened brown sauce, or sauerkraut without one or another pork product, and what would we do without bacon for breakfast?

Roast loin of pork with its tender white meat and rich brown gravy is always a family favorite. Barbecued spareribs delight old and young alike. And for exotic dishes, think of the lovely oriental uses of pork: in teriyaki, chop suey, or combined with crisp celery and almonds to be simmered in a sweet-sour soy flavored sauce.

The exterior of good quality pork is well covered with a layer of fairly firm white fat. The lean, which is marbled with fat, is grayish-pink in the younger animal, a deeper pink in the older animal. Since all pork is tender, the larger cuts may be cooked by roasting.

Cuts for Roasting

Loin is available as whole loin, rib end, loin end, or center cut which has 7 chops.

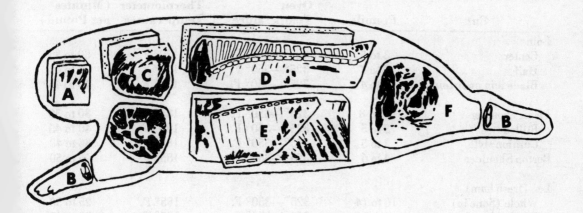

A. **Jowl**
  Jowl Bacon

B. **Feet**
  Fresh and Pickled pig's feet

C. **Shoulder**
  Fresh and Smoked Picnic
  Fresh and Smoked Hock
  Fresh and Smoked Butt
  Sausage

D. **Loin**
  Loin Roasts
  Loin Chops
  Rib Chop
  Blade Chop
  Tenderloin
  Canadian style Bacon
  Back Ribs

E. **Bacon (Belly)**
  Bacon
  Spare Ribs
  Salt Pork

F. **Leg**
  Fresh and Smoked Ham
  Ham Steaks

Shoulder is sold as:

Boston Butt: The upper half of the shoulder that contains part of the blade bone.

Picnic Shoulder: This includes the arm and shank sections of the shoulder. It is sometimes boned, rolled, and tied.

Cushion Shoulder: The arm section of a fresh picnic, boned and with a pocket for stuffing.

Leg (fresh ham): This large, meaty cut is sold whole, boneless, with bone in, or as half ham, bone in.

Crown Roast: Roast made from rib section's "frenched" and formed in shape of crown.

How to Roast

Place meat, fat side up, on rack in shallow, open roasting pan. Season with salt and pepper or as specific recipe directs. Insert meat thermometer in center of pork, being careful bulb does not touch bone or rest in fat. (For a crown roast insert thermometer into meaty part of a chop.) Do not add water; do not cover. Roast to temperature designated on chart for particular cut. Pork should be cooked well done with no tinge of pink. When done, take roast from oven and let "rest" on heated platter for 15 to 20 minutes. This allows meat to firm up, makes carving easier, helps retain the juices, and allows time to make gravy (*page 141*).

TIMETABLE FOR ROASTING FRESH PORK

Cut	Pounds	Oven Temperature	Meat Thermometer Temperature	Approximate Cooking Time (Minutes per Pound)
Loin				
Center	3 to 5	325°—350° F.	170° F.	30 to 35
Half	5 to 7	325°—350° F.	170° F.	35 to 40
Blade loin or sirloin	3 to 4	325°—350° F.	170° F.	40 to 45
Picnic shoulder	5 to 8	325°—350° F.	185° F.	30 to 35
Rolled	3 to 5	325°—350° F.	185° F.	40 to 45
Cushion style	3 to 5	325°—350° F.	185° F.	35 to 40
Boston Shoulder	4 to 6	325°—350° F.	185° F.	45 to 50
Leg (fresh ham)				
Whole (bone in)	10 to 14	325°—350° F.	185° F.	25 to 30
Whole (boneless)	7 to 10	325°—350° F.	185° F.	35 to 40
Half (bone in)	5 to 7	325°—350° F.	185° F.	40 to 45

GLAZED ROAST PORK WITH CORN BREAD STUFFING

5 to 7 lb. loin of pork
½ c. chopped onion (1 medium)
½ c. butter or margarine
½ tsp. fennel seed, crushed
½ tsp. salt
3 tbs. chopped celery leaves
2 c. crumbled corn bread
1 can (8 oz.) whole cranberry sauce

Have butcher crack backbone of pork loin. Make a deep slit in center back of each chop. Sauté onion in butter or margarine until soft; mix in fennel seed, salt, and celery leaves. Combine with corn bread in bowl. Stuff mixture into slits in pork (any leftover may be baked in covered dish during last 30 minutes of roasting). Place pork in roasting pan. Roast at 325° F., allowing 35 to 40 minutes per pound, or until meat thermometer registers 170° F. Break up cranberry sauce in bowl with fork. Thirty minutes before roast is done spoon cranberry sauce over top; baste with remaining sauce 2 or 3 times. Makes 8 servings.

FRUITED LOIN OF PORK

1 c. dried apricots
½ c. dry sherry
1 center cut loin of pork, with backbone cracked
½ c. dark corn syrup
1 tsp. grated orange rind
¼ c. orange juice
½ tsp. soy sauce

Heat oven to 325° F. Cook apricots in sherry in saucepan 3 minutes. Cut deep slit between each pork chop. Insert 2 or 3 apricots into each slit. Place pork in roasting pan. Roast about 2 hours and 20 minutes allowing 30 to 35 minutes per pound or until meat thermometer registers 170° F. While pork roasts, cook corn syrup, orange rind and juice, and soy sauce in small saucepan until mixture bubbles; cook 3 minutes longer. Brush on pork several times during last 30 minutes of roasting. Makes 4 to 6 servings.

PRUNE-STUFFED LOIN OF PORK

2 center cuts loin of pork	½ tsp. pepper
18 to 24 large prunes	1 can (10½-oz.) condensed beef broth
1 tsp. salt	

Make four 1-inch deep cuts lengthwise in each loin. Rinse prunes in warm water; cut in half; remove pits. Insert halves, cut side down, into slits; tie meat securely at intervals with clean white string; rub meat with salt and pepper. Place pork in roasting pan. Roast at 325° F., allowing 30 to 35 minutes per pound or until meat thermometer registers 170° F. Baste pork occasionally during roasting with beef broth. Remove meat to heated platter; cut and remove string. Make gravy (*page 141*). Makes 10 to 12 servings.

PORK CHOPS AND STEAKS

Pork chops are best when braised. They may also be panfried. Broiling is not recommended. Available are loin, rib, and shoulder or blade chops; and arm, blade, and leg steaks.

BAKED PORK CHOPS

6 loin or shoulder pork chops, 1-in. thick	1½ c. cooked rice
3 tbs. fat or pure vegetable oil	6 thick slices tomato
½ tsp. salt	1 can (10½ oz.) condensed vegetable-beef soup
⅛ tsp. pepper	1 c. water
6 thick slices large onion	1 bay leaf
	¼ tsp. celery seed

Heat oven to 350° F. Trim fat on chops; heat fat or oil in skillet; brown chops well on both sides. Transfer chops to baking pan; sprinkle with salt and pepper. Place a slice of onion on each chop; place a mound of rice on onion slice. Top with a slice of tomato. Simmer soup, water, bay leaf, and celery seed 5 minutes; remove bay leaf. Pour soup mixture around pork chops; cover. Bake 1½ hours or until chops are tender. Makes 6 servings.

ORANGE BAKED PORK CHOPS

6 loin pork chops, 1 to 1½ in. thick	¼ tsp. pepper
½ c. orange juice	½ tsp. dry mustard
1 tsp. salt	¼ c. brown sugar, firmly packed

Cut fat from pork chops, if necessary. Place chops in large shallow baking dish; they don't need to be browned. Combine remaining ingredients; pour over chops; cover. Bake at 350° F. for 1 hour or until chops are tender. Makes 6 servings.

STUFFED BRAISED PORK CHOPS

½ c. chopped onion (1 medium)	1 c. packaged herb bread stuffing mix
¼ c. chopped celery	6 double pork chops with pockets
2 tbs. butter or margarine	¼ c. fat or pure vegetable oil
½ c. water	½ c. water

Heat oven to 350° F. Sauté onion and celery in butter or margarine until soft. Add ½ cup water. Stir in stuffing mix; mix well. Stuff pockets in chops loosely with stuffing mixture. Fasten pockets securely with wooden picks; lace closed with clean white string. Heat fat or oil in skillet. Add chops; brown on both sides. Transfer to baking dish; add ½ cup water; cover. Bake 1½ hours, or until chops are tender. Makes 6 servings.

CREOLE PORK CHOPS

4 rib or loin pork chops (½ to ¾ in. thick)	1 can (10½ oz.) condensed vegetable soup
1 tsp. fat or pure vegetable oil	2 tbs. catsup
¼ c. sliced onion (1 small)	⅓ c. water
	1 tsp. vinegar

Brown chops on both sides in hot fat or oil in skillet; remove; reserve. Sauté onion in fat or oil remaining in skillet; return chops to skillet; add soup, catsup, water, and vinegar; mix well. Cover; simmer 15 minutes. Turn chops; simmer 15 minutes longer. Makes 2 servings.

SPICY PORK CHOPS CASSEROLE STYLE

2 tbs. fat or pure
   vegetable oil
4 rib or loin pork
   chops (½ to ¾
   in. thick)
1 large onion,
   peeled and sliced

½ c. bottled
   barbecue sauce
½ c. water
¼ tsp. seasoned salt

Heat fat or oil in skillet; brown chops well on both sides. Heat oven to 350° F. Put a layer of sliced onion in greased 2-quart casserole; arrange chops over onions; cover with remaining onions. Combine barbecue sauce, water, and seasoned salt; pour over chops. Cover; bake 45 to 50 minutes. Makes 4 servings.

PORK TENDERLOIN

The pork tenderloin is similar to the tenderloin of beef. It is a long, tapering piece that weighs ½ to 1 pound. It is very tender. Whole. it may be roasted or braised, sliced, it may be sautéed. It will take approximately 1½ hours to roast at 350° F.

SPARERIBS

Spareribs are the ribs and breast bone cut from the side of fresh pork. Select and buy ribs with a good proportion of lean meat over bones that will be easy to separate in carving. Allow ¾ to 1 pound per serving.

Country-style spareribs are cut with part of the backbone. These contain more meat than the back ribs and must be cooked longer.

GOLDEN GLAZED RIBS

3 lbs. spareribs, cut
   into serving-size
   pieces
1 clove of garlic,
   minced
1½ tsp. salt
½ tsp. pepper
1½ c. dried
   apricots, chopped

¾ c. water
2 tbs. vinegar
¼ tsp. ground
   cloves
1 tsp. ground ginger
3 tbs. sugar
1 tsp. grated lemon
   rind
½ tsp. salt

Heat oven to 325° F. Arrange ribs in large roasting pan. Sprinkle with garlic, 1½ teaspoons salt, and pepper. Bake 45 minutes; pour off fat. Combine remaining ingredients in small saucepan; bring to boiling. Reduce heat;

simmer 5 minutes. Beat mixture with electric mixer or whirl in blender until smooth. Baste ribs with sauce. Bake ½ hour longer, basting frequently. Makes 6 servings.

TANGY STUFFED SPARERIBS

1 c. diced celery
½ c. chopped onion
   (1 medium)
3 tbs. butter or
   margarine
2 tsp. salt
Dash of pepper
¼ tsp. leaf thyme,
   crumbled

1 can (1 lb.) jellied
   cranberry sauce
6 c. bread cubes
   (12 slices)
2 strips spareribs
   (about 2¼ lbs.
   ea.)
2 tbs. brown sugar

Sauté celery and onion in butter or margarine 3 minutes or until tender. Add salt, pepper, thyme, and ½ can of cranberry sauce; mix well. Pour mixture over bread cubes; mix thoroughly. Roast spareribs in shallow pans at 450° F. for 30 minutes; pour off fat. Reduce oven heat to 325° F. Turn one strip of spareribs hollow side up in pan; spoon on bread-cube mixture. Top with second strip of spareribs; secure with wooden picks. Roast for 1½ hours. Heat remaining ½ can of cranberry sauce and brown sugar until melted. Use to glaze spareribs several times during last half hour of roasting. Makes 8 servings.

OTHER PORK DISHES

BAKED PORK SHISH KEBABS WITH DRIED FRUITS

1½ tsp. salt
½ tsp. pepper
2 tsp. grated lemon
   rind
3 tbs. lemon juice
½ c. honey
⅓ c. water
2 tbs. catsup
¼ tsp. ground
   cinnamon

½ tsp. ground
   ginger
¼ c. finely chopped
   onion (1 small)
2½ to 3 lbs. boneless pork shoulder
1 pkg. (1 lb.)
   mixed dried
   fruits

Combine salt, pepper, lemon rind and juice, honey, water, catsup, cinnamon, ginger, and onion in large bowl. Cut pork into 1- or 1½-inch cubes. Add to marinade. Let stand 4 hours, turning often. Heat oven to 350° F. Arrange pork in a shallow roasting pan. Baste with marinade. Bake for 1 hour, basting frequently. Bring fruits to boiling in water to cover. Drain. String fruits on a long skewer or 6 individual skewers. Thread pork on long skewers. (Or string pork and fruit alternately on the skewers.) Arrange skewers in roasting pan. Brush with marinade; continue to bake 15 minutes or until lightly browned. Makes 6 servings.

SWEET AND PUNGENT PORK

6 loin pork chops	1 small onion,
2 eggs, beaten	sliced
½ c. cornstarch	1 can (14 oz.)
Fat or pure	pineapple chunks
vegetable oil	2 tbs. soy sauce
1 carrot, pared and	½ c. wine vinegar
sliced	¼ c. brown sugar,
2 tbs. fat or pure	firmly packed
vegetable oil	½ tsp. garlic
1 green pepper, cut	powder
in strips	2 tbs. cornstarch
	½ c. water

Cut meat from chops; remove as much fat as possible. Cut meat into 1-inch cubes. Dip cubes in beaten egg; roll in ½ cup cornstarch. Put enough fat or oil in heavy skillet or saucepan to make a 2-inch depth when heated. Heat to 375° F. Shallow-fry pork cubes, a few at a time, in hot fat or oil about 5 minutes or until crisp and cooked. Parboil carrot. Heat 2 tablespoons fat or oil in skillet. Stir-fry pepper and onion 2 minutes. Drain pineapple; add enough water to juice to make 1 cup. Combine pineapple, pineapple juice and water, soy sauce, vinegar, brown sugar, garlic powder, browned pork, and carrot in skillet; heat to boiling. Blend 2 tablespoons cornstarch with water until smooth; stir into skillet. Cook over medium heat until bubbly and clear. Serve over crisp noodles or fluffy hot rice, if desired. Makes 6 servings.

TAMALE PIE

1 lb. bulk sausage	½ c. sliced pitted
½ c. chopped onion	ripe olives
(1 medium)	¾ c. yellow corn
1 clove of garlic,	meal
crushed	3 c. boiling water
1 can (8 oz.)	1 tsp. salt
tomato sauce	3 eggs, well beaten
1 tsp. chili powder	1 tbs. melted butter
	or margarine

Cook sausage in skillet until well browned, breaking up with fork as it cooks; pour off all fat. Add onion and garlic; cook 3 minutes.

Add tomato sauce, chili powder, and olives; simmer 5 minutes. Add corn meal slowly to boiling salted water while stirring vigorously. Cook, stirring constantly, 10 minutes or until very thick. Add cooked corn meal to beaten eggs; mix thoroughly. Spread thick layer of corn meal in lightly greased pie plate; spread sausage mixture evenly on top. Spoon remaining corn-meal mixture over sausage; brush top with melted butter or margarine. Bake at 375° F. for 45 minutes or until lightly brown. Garnish with ripe olives, pimiento, and parsley, if desired. Makes 6 servings.

FRUITED PORK WHEEL

¼ c. minced onion	¼ c. water
(1 small)	2 lbs. fresh lean
3 tbs. butter or	pork, ground
margarine	2 eggs
2 c. bread cubes	1 c. fresh bread
(4 slices)	crumbs (2 slices)
1 can (8½ oz.)	1 tsp. seasoned salt
sliced pineapple	¼ tsp. pepper
½ c. diced, dried	1 tbs. butter or
apricots	margarine
¼ c. diced celery	⅓ c. brown sugar,
2 tbs. chopped	firmly packed
parsley	1 tsp. vinegar
½ tsp. salt	

Sauté onion in butter or margarine in large skillet until soft. Add bread cubes; stir over low heat until lightly browned; remove from heat. Drain pineapple; reserve 2 slices and juice; dice 2 remaining slices. Combine diced pineapple, apricots, celery, parsley, salt, and water with bread mixture. Blend pork, eggs, bread crumbs, salt, and pepper. Pat meat mixture evenly and lightly on wax paper, to a 12x15-inch rectangle. Spread stuffing mixture over meat surface. Roll up, starting with short side, pressing firmly at each turn. Lift with wax paper; place, seam side down, in shallow baking pan; remove paper. Bake at 350° F. for 1 hour, 20 minutes. Combine reserved pineapple liquid, butter or margarine, brown sugar, and vinegar in saucepan; bring to boiling; baste pork roll several times during baking. Garnish with reserved pineapple slices and whole dried apricots. Makes 6 servings.

Ham

Buying

The label should designate the kind of ham. Hams are available as:

Fully cooked: The ham is completely cooked, ready to use without further cooking, though it is most often heated and served hot.

Cook-before-Eating: The ham must be completely cooked before it is eaten.

Hams are available in several styles: Bone in, whole or shank or butt end; skinless shankless (the shank removed, the meat skinned and trimmed of excess fat); semi-boneless; boneless; boneless-skinless (shaped into rolls); and canned hams (also boneless and skinless). All are available in various sizes.

Canned Hams: Ready to use as taken from the can or may be reheated. There are also fruited and glazed canned hams available. These should not be reheated.

Smoked Picnics (Shoulder): The lower half of the pork shoulder that contains the arm bone. It is very like ham in appearance and flavor and is available both as cook-before-eating and fully-cooked picnic.

Smoked Shoulder Butt: A boneless cut from the upper half of the shoulder.

Country-Cured Ham: Smithfield, Virginia, and Tennessee style have had a long cure, or cure and smoke, and some need to be soaked and boiled to remove excess salt. Follow label for directions or see recipe for Baked Country Ham on *page 177.* Some country hams are sold already cooked and are available only at specialty shops.

Prosciutto: Italian style ham which has been boned, pressed, and cured in spices to achieve special zesty flavor. It is always sliced paper-thin, may be purchased in sealed packages already sliced.

TIMETABLE FOR ROASTING SMOKED PORK

Cut	Pounds	Oven Temperature	Meat Thermometer Temperature	Approximate Cooking Time (Minutes per Pound)
Ham (cook before eating)				
Whole	10 to 14	300°—325° F.	160° F.	18 to 20
Half	5 to 7	300°—325° F.	160° F.	22 to 25
Shank or butt portion	3 to 4	300°—325° F.	160° F.	35 to 40
Ham (fully cooked)				
Whole (bone in)	12 to 15	325° F.	130° F.	14 to 17
Half	5 to 7	325° F.	130° F.	18 to 24
Picnic shoulder	5 to 8	300°—325° F.	130° F.	35
Shoulder roll	2 to 3	300°—325° F.	170° F.	35 to 40
Canadian style bacon	2 to 4	300°—325° F.	170° F.	35 to 40

How to Bake Ham

If there are directions on wrapper, follow them exactly. If not, bake as follows: Place whole ham, fat side up, or half ham, cut side down, on rack in open, shallow baking pan. Insert meat thermometer into center of thickest part of ham. Do not let it touch the bone. Do not add water; do not cover. Bake according to timetable, allowing an extra 15 minutes for removing skin and scoring ham. If you plan to glaze ham, follow directions below.

Glazes for Baked Ham

· To glaze a ham: Remove ham from oven 20 minutes before end of cooking time. Carefully remove rind with sharp knife. Score ham fat in diamond or square pattern. Stud ham with whole cloves. Spoon on honey, maple syrup, corn syrup, or heated, strained apricot or pineapple preserves. Pat on brown sugar. Return to oven. Continue baking until thermometer registers temperature indicated in chart.
· Heat 1 cup orange marmalade with 3 tablespoons orange juice and ½ cup brown sugar, firmly packed. Spoon over ham. Finish baking as above.
· Add ½ cup dry sherry to pineapple, peach or apricot preserves; heat to boiling. Spoon over ham; sprinkle with brown sugar. Finish baking as above.
· Heat 1 tablespoon prepared mustard with 1 cup red currant jelly, ½ teaspoon ground cloves, ½ teaspoon ground cinnamon, and ½ cup brown sugar, firmly packed. Spoon over ham. Finish baking as above.

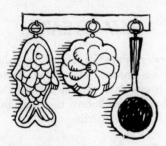

WINE-GLAZED BAKED HAM

1 fully-cooked ham (12 to 14 lbs.)
c. brown sugar, firmly packed
c. dry red wine

4 tsp. grated orange rind
1 tsp. ground allspice
1 tsp. ground cloves

Carefully remove rind from ham with sharp knife. Score ham fat in diamond pattern. Place ham in shallow roasting pan. Combine brown sugar, wine, orange rind, and spices in a small saucepan. Bring to boiling; simmer 5 minutes. Heat oven to 325° F. Drizzle half the wine syrup over ham. Bake, basting frequently with remaining syrup, until meat thermometer registers 130° F., allowing about 14 to 17 minutes per pound. Remove ham from oven. Transfer ham to heated platter. Garnish with cranberry relish in orange cups, if desired.

BAKED COUNTRY HAM

1 country-cured ham (12 to 14 lbs.)

Dark corn syrup
Brown sugar

Remove ham from wrapping and scrub thoroughly with stiff brush to remove excess pepper and any mold. Put ham in large kettle; cover with water. Let soak overnight. Remove ham; discard water. Place ham in clean kettle; cover with cold water. Simmer for approximately 20 minutes per pound or until ham is tender. Cool ham in water. Drain. Remove rind from ham; score fat in large diamonds or desired design. Place ham in shallow, open roasting pan. Bake at 350° F. for 15 to 20 minutes. Coat ham generously with corn syrup; pat on brown sugar. Bake 30 minutes. Drizzle with more corn syrup and sprinkle with brown sugar halfway through baking time if a heavy glaze is desired. Cool completely. Chill.

APRICOT GLAZED HAM

1 fully-cooked ham (about 12 lbs.)
1 c. apricot preserves

3 tbs. vinegar
¼ c. corn syrup
1 tsp. ground ginger

Heat oven to 325° F. Place ham in open, shallow roasting pan. Bake until meat thermometer registers 130° F., allowing about 15 minutes per pound. Combine preserves, vinegar, corn syrup, and ginger in saucepan; heat 5 minutes. Strain, if desired. Remove ham from oven 30 minutes before end of baking time. Remove any rind; trim and smooth fat; score in diamond pattern. Brush ham with glaze; return to oven. Bake 30 minutes or until nicely glazed, brushing several times during baking with remaining glaze.

HAM IN ASPIC

1 canned ham (5 lbs.)	2 hard-cooked eggs
2 envelopes un-flavored gelatin	Green onion tops
2 cans (10½ oz. ea.) condensed consommé	⅓ c. fresh or frozen peas
	3 carrots, pared and sliced
	Watercress

Remove ham from can; chill well. Soften gelatin in ½ cup consommé. Heat remaining consommé to boiling; add to gelatin; stir until dissolved; cool; chill over bowl of ice just until syrupy; remove from ice. Pour cold aspic gently over cold ham until all surfaces except bottom have been covered with a light coat. At once, place cutouts of egg white and yolk, onion tops, peas and carrot rounds on top surface; chill briefly. Flow another coat of aspic over decorations and down sides. Chill. For additional coats of aspic, chill ham briefly just until each coat sets. Aspic may be kept fluid by placing alternately in warm water and then in bowl of ice. Garnish with watercress.

HAM LOAVES

GLAZED HAM LOAF

2 lbs. cook-before-eating ham, ground	2 tbs. cornstarch
1 lb. pork, ground	1 tsp. prepared mustard
1 tbs. prepared mustard	½ c. brown sugar, firmly packed
¾ c. milk	¼ c. vinegar
2 eggs	1 c. water
2 c. fresh bread crumbs (4 slices bread)	¾ c. currant jelly
	½ c. raisins

Mix ham, pork, 1 tablespoon prepared mustard, milk, eggs, and bread crumbs thoroughly in bowl. Pack into 9x5x3-inch loaf pan; turn out onto lightly greased baking pan (or shape into loaf on pan by hand). Bake at 350° F. for 1 hour. While loaf cooks, prepare glaze. Combine cornstarch, 1 teaspoon prepared mustard, and brown sugar in saucepan; stir in vinegar, water, and currant jelly. Cook over

medium heat until thickened and bubbly. Stir in raisins. Spoon a third of mixture over ham loaf at end of hour's baking. Bake loaf 30 minutes longer. Keep remaining sauce hot and serve with ham loaf. Makes 8 servings.

ORANGE-GLAZED HAM LOAF

3 lbs. cook-before-eating ham, ground	1¼ c. buttermilk
2 eggs, slightly beaten	¼ c. brown sugar, firmly packed
3 c. fresh bread crumbs (6 slices)	3 tbs. prepared horseradish
	⅓ c. orange marmalade

Heat oven to 350° F. Mix ham, eggs, bread crumbs, buttermilk, brown sugar, and horseradish thoroughly. Press ham mixture firmly into greased 2-quart baking dish. Bake 1½ hours. Loosen sides with spatula; invert carefully from baking dish onto greased heat-proof serving dish. Spread top of loaf with orange marmalade, letting excess run down sides of loaf. Place under broiler with top of loaf 3 to 4 inches from heat. Broil about 3 to 5 minutes or until topping bubbles. Makes 8 to 10 servings.

HAM STEAKS

These tender, flavorful center cut slices of ham may be broiled, panbroiled, braised, or baked. Always slash the fat around the edge with a sharp knife before cooking; this prevents the meat from curling up.

To broil: Place 3 to 4 inches from the heat; brush with melted butter or margarine, cook until lightly browned; then turn to brown lightly on the other side. If a glaze is to be added, spoon or brush it on during last few minutes.

Timetable for Broiling Ham Slices

Thickness of Slice	Distance from Heat	Approximate Cooking Time (Minutes Per Side)
Fully-cooked ham		
½ inch	3 inches	3 to 5 (do not turn)
1 inch	4 inches	5
Cook-before-eating ham		
½ inch	3 inches	4
1 inch	4 inches	9
1½ inch	4 inches	10

To Panbroil or Braise Ham Slices: Slash fat around edges (as for broiling); heat 1 to 2 tablespoons butter or margarine in skillet; sauté ham until lightly browned on each side. Serve this way or add liquid, such as wine, orange or pineapple juice, or a basting sauce; simmer uncovered at low heat 5 to 10 minutes.

HAM STEAK WITH ORANGE RICE STUFFING

2 c. cooked rice	Few grains of ground nutmeg
½ c. raisins	1 egg, well beaten
3 tbs. undiluted frozen concentrated orange juice	2 fully-cooked ham slices (1 in. thick ea.)
Few grains of pepper	2 tbs. brown sugar

Combine rice, raisins, orange juice, pepper, nutmeg, and beaten egg in large bowl. Place ham slice in baking pan; spoon rice stuffing evenly onto slice; top with second ham slice; sprinkle with brown sugar. Bake at 350° F. for 35 to 40 minutes. Makes 6 servings.

HAM WITH ONION GRAVY

1 ham steak, (1½ in. thick.)	1 c. dairy sour cream
2 c. thinly sliced onions (2 large)	¼ c. milk

Trim all but ¼ inch of fat from ham. Render trimmed fat in heavy skillet. Panbroil steak over low heat until golden brown (3 to 4 minutes each side for fully-cooked ham; 6 to 8 minutes each side for cook-before-eating type); remove from pan. Panfry sliced onions in pan drippings until tender and delicately browned; stir in sour cream and milk; heat thoroughly. Pour over ham steak on platter. Makes 4 servings.

SMOTHERED HAM STEAKS

1 fully cooked ham steak, (1 in. thick)	1 tsp. leaf oregano, crumbled
¼ c. fat or pure vegetable oil	2 cans (8 oz. ea.) tomato sauce with mushrooms
2 c. chopped onion (2 large)	
1 large green pepper, seeded and cut into rings	

Heat oven to 350° F. Cut steak in half for easier handling. Brown pieces quickly on both sides in hot fat or oil in skillet. Remove steak. Sauté onion and green pepper in fat or oil remaining in skillet until soft. Put onion and green pepper in baking dish; place ham steaks on top. Sprinkle with oregano; pour tomato sauce over steaks. Bake 25 minutes or until sauce bubbles. Makes 4 servings.

MADE WITH COOKED HAM

HAM-AND-CHEESE PIE

½ c. chopped onion
 (1 medium)
¼ c. diced celery
2 tbs. butter or
 margarine
2 c. ground cooked
 ham
1 can (3 to 4 oz.)
 chopped mush-
 rooms, drained
¼ tsp. dry mustard
¼ tsp. prepared
 horseradish

1 9-in. baked pastry
 shell (*page 406*)
1 medium-size, firm,
 ripe tomato,
 peeled and sliced
1 pkg. (8 oz.)
 process American
 cheese slices
1 pkg. (8 oz.)
 process Swiss
 cheese slices

Heat oven to 350° F. Sauté onion and celery in butter or margarine in skillet until soft; stir in ham, mushrooms, mustard, and horseradish. Spoon half the mixture into baked pastry shell; top with tomato slices. Cut 4 slices American and 4 slices Swiss cheese; sprinkle over tomatoes; top with remaining ham mixture. Cut remaining 4 slices American and 4 slices Swiss cheese diagonally to form triangles; arrange on top of pie. Bake about 30 minutes or until ham mixture is heated through and cheese is melted. Makes 6 servings.

CREAMED HAM

1 c. water
1 can (11¼ oz.)
 condensed green
 pea soup
1 c. dairy sour
 cream
¼ tsp. leaf marjo-
 ram, crumbled
2 c. slivered, cooked
 ham

2 tbs. diced
 pimiento
⅓ c. sliced, pitted
 ripe olives
2 tbs. chopped
 watercress
1 pkg. (10 oz.)
 frozen patty
 shells, baked and
 cooled

Add water gradually to soup in medium-size saucepan, stirring until blended. Cook over medium heat, stirring constantly, until thickened and bubbly. Blend in sour cream and marjoram; add ham, pimiento, and olives. Cook over low heat, stirring constantly, until heated through. Do not boil. Remove from heat; stir in watercress; spoon into patty shells. Makes 6 servings.

GLAZED HAM AND FRUIT ROLLS

6 medium-size
 green-tipped
 bananas, peeled
1 can (8½ oz.)
 sliced pineapple

2 pkgs. (6 oz. ea.)
 sliced ham
½ c. currant jelly
3 to 4 tbs. prepared
 mustard

Heat oven to 350° F. Cut bananas in half lengthwise. Drain pineapple; reserve syrup. Cut pineapple slices in quarters; put three quarters between each two banana slices. Wrap each banana in 2 slices ham; secure with wooden picks; place in shallow casserole. Combine jelly and mustard; spread evenly over ham rolls; spoon 3 tablespoons reserved pineapple syrup into casserole. Bake 20 to 25 minutes, basting several times. Serve ham rolls with sauce in casserole. Makes 6 servings.

HAM DIVAN

1 tbs. butter or
 margarine
1 tbs. flour
1 c. milk
2 egg yolks, beaten
½ c. grated
 Parmesan cheese

1 pkg. (10 oz.)
 frozen broccoli
 or 1 lb. fresh
 broccoli, cooked
 and drained
4 slices cooked
 ham
 Paprika

Melt butter or margarine in small saucepan; blend in flour. Stir in milk slowly. Cook over low heat, stirring constantly, until sauce is thickened and bubbly. Remove from heat; blend a small amount of sauce into egg yolks. Stir into sauce in pan; stir in cheese. Arrange cooked broccoli in 4 buttered individual heat-proof baking dishes. Place a slice of ham in each dish over broccoli. Pour hot cheese sauce carefully over broccoli and ham; sprinkle with paprika. Broil until sauce is golden and bubbly. Makes 4 servings.

HAM AND ASPARAGUS ROLLS MORNAY

2 boxes (10 oz. ea.)
 frozen asparagus
 spears or 3 cans
 (1 lb. 3 oz. ea.)
 asparagus spears

12 thin slices
 cooked ham
 (about 1½ lbs.)
½ c. chicken broth
 Mornay Sauce
 (*page 348*)

Heat oven to 350° F. Cook and drain frozen asparagus or drain canned asparagus. Arrange 4 spears on each slice of ham; roll up. Place in shallow pan; pour ½ cup of chicken broth over rolls; cover pan with foil. Bake 15 minutes. While ham rolls are baking, prepare Mornay Sauce. Place ham rolls on serving plates; pour hot sauce over each. Makes 6 servings.

HAM AND POTATO SCALLOP

2 tbs. butter or margarine	1½ c. milk
1 tbs. chopped onion	4 c. sliced, pared potatoes
2 tbs. flour	1 c. ground, cooked ham
1½ tsp. salt	⅔ c. grated
⅛ tsp. pepper	Cheddar cheese

Melt butter or margarine in small saucepan; sauté onion until soft; stir in flour, salt, and pepper. Stir in milk slowly. Cook over low heat, stirring constantly, until thickened. Layer half the potatoes, half the ham, and half the cheese in greased 1½-quart baking dish; pour over half the sauce. Repeat this layering with the remaining potatoes, ham, cheese, and sauce. Bake at 350° F. for 1¼ hours or until potatoes are soft. Makes 4 servings.

HAM AND CABBAGE ROLLS

1 c. ground cooked ham	¼ tsp. salt
1 c. cooked rice	1 tbs. water
1 tbs. chopped green pepper	1 medium-size head of cabbage
1 egg	1 tbs. butter or margarine
½ tsp. leaf thyme, crumbled	1 can (10½ oz.) condensed beef broth
¼ tsp. leaf savory, crumbled	2 tbs. cornstarch
	½ c. water

Combine ham, rice, green pepper, egg, thyme, savory, salt, and 1 tablespoon water; mix well. Trim cabbage; remove core; place in boiling water; simmer gently until leaves separate easily; remove from water; cool. Trim thick center vein from eight large cabbage leaves; fill each leaf with 2 tablespoons ham mixture; roll leaves into a tight roll; tuck in ends to enclose filling. Melt butter or margarine in skillet; brown cabbage rolls; add beef broth. Cover and cook gently 30 to 35 minutes. Remove cabbage rolls from skillet; place on serving dish; keep warm. Blend cornstarch and ½ cup water; pour into liquid in skillet, stirring constantly; simmer until thickened. Pour gravy over cabbage rolls. Makes 4 servings.

PINEAPPLE HAM BAKE

2 eggs, slightly beaten	4 c. ground cooked ham
½ c. mayonnaise or salad dressing	1 c. fresh bread crumbs (2 slices)
2 tsp. prepared mustard	6 slices drained canned pineapple
¼ tsp. pepper	1 tbs. brown sugar

Heat oven to 375° F. Combine eggs, mayonnaise or salad dressing, mustard, and pepper. Add ham and bread crumbs; mix thoroughly. Shape into 6 mounds (use a custard cup to shape them). Arrange pineapple slices in lightly greased shallow baking pan; sprinkle slices with brown sugar. Place a ham mound on each pineapple slice. Bake 40 to 45 minutes or until lightly browned and firm. Makes 6 servings.

Bacon

Bacon to be good must have fat, for fat contributes to the flavor and texture. Bacon that has too much lean can lack that wonderful flavor and texture typical of bacon at it best.

In the top or first selection, the slices are uniform, have the best ratio of fat to lean, and are selected for size and location of fat and lean streaks. There are usually more slices per pound and they meet rigid specifications as to width and thickness.

In the lower selections of bacon, the slices have the same flavor as the first selection, but are less uniform and may be slightly less tender and more coarse in texture. The distribution of fat and lean may be less even. Because the slices may be wider and heavier, there are, in some cases, fewer slices per pound.

Kinds of Bacon

Thin-sliced bacon: usually packaged in half-pound (8 ounces), 12-ounce, and 1-pound packages. May have up to 35 slices per pound.

Regular-sliced bacon: usually packaged in half-pound, 1-pound, and 2-pound packages. Will average about 22 slices per pound.

Thick-sliced bacon: packaged both stacked and shingled in 1-pound, 1½-pound, and 2-pound packages. Up to 18 slices per pound.

Ends and pieces: sold in 1-pound packages and boxes, 3-pound cartons, 4- and 5-pound boxes.

Slab bacon: sold by the piece. Has the rind on. You slice as needed.

Precooked bacon: in cans that do not require refrigeration. Contains 18 to 20 slices, equivalent to 1 pound of uncooked bacon. Requires heating for 3 to 5 minutes. New is the precooked bacon in foil packets ready to drop in the toaster to heat.

Bacon crumbles or bits: completely cooked and crumbled, ready to add to salad, casseroles, etc.

Buying and Storing

Buy only enough bacon for one week as it begins to lose flavor if held longer. Store bacon in the refrigerator in its original wrapper. To separate the slices easily, take bacon from the refrigerator 5 to 10 minutes before using it. Bacon may be frozen for short periods, but freezing is not recommended for best flavor.

Cooking

To panfry: Put bacon slices just as they come from the package in a cold skillet. Cook over low heat, separating the slices carefully with a fork so they lie flat. Turn the slices often during cooking. Do not allow the fat to smoke or the flavor will be affected. Remove each slice as it browns and drain on paper towels.

To bake: Arrange bacon slices on a wire rack in a shallow pan. Bake at 400° F. 10 to 15 minutes. No turning or draining is needed.

To broil: Put slices on broiler rack. Broil 3 inches from heat 3 to 4 minutes per side. Turn once.

Canadian Bacon and Smoked Pork Chops

Canadian style bacon is cured pork tenderloin which is sold sometimes in one piece, but more often already sliced. It is virtually free from fat. Panfry, cooking at moderate to low temperatures, until delicately browned on both sides. Or it may be broiled—delicious atop open-faced grilled cheese sandwiches. Allow 2 to 4 slices per serving.

Cured pork chops are frequently found in supermarket counters, packaged, with cooking directions on the label. These are much like center slices of ham in flavor, but more delicate.

Sausage, Frankfurters, and Luncheon Meats

The word sausage has a slightly different meaning to the meat packers than to most homemakers. It's an all-inclusive term covering all those spiced, ready-to-use meats that may come in links, rolls, or loaves; some are already sliced and sold wrapped in sealed packets, the meat ready to slip into sandwiches; others are fully cooked, still others must be cooked before eating.

Frankfurters technically are sausages, as are liverwurst and bologna. The luncheon meats, such as chopped ham, souse, and blood pudding, also belong to the sausage family.

Sausage Glossary

Fresh Uncooked Sausages

(Use within 3 days of purchase; cook thoroughly before serving.)

Fresh pork sausage. Made mostly of lean, fresh pork with added spices and herbs. May be sold in 1-pound bulk packages, in patties, or in links.

Fresh sausage meat. Usually made of pork and spices but sometimes also contains beef and tripe.

Scrapple. A mixture of ground pork scraps and cornmeal, usually sold in loaves or thick slices. Fry or sauté and serve for breakfast.

Fresh, Partly-cooked Sausage

Brown-and-serve sausages. Sausages have been cooked until most of the fat has been rendered. Need only browning.

Smoked Uncooked Sausages

(Use within a week of purchase; cook before serving.)

Smoked country style. Same as fresh sausage but has been cured and smoked; usually sold in links.

Mettwurst. A mixture of cured beef and cured pork, spiced with pepper and coriander; in casings or links.

Polish sausage or kielbasa. Lean pork and beef, garlic flavored, in long, thick links.

Teawurst. A mixture of pork and beef in links.

Cooked Smoked Sausages

Frankfurters, wieners. American adaptations of sausages which originated in Frankfurt, Germany, and Vienna. May be a blend of beef and pork, or beef, pork and veal, or pure beef. Use within a week unless frozen.

Cocktail franks. Same as frankfurters but smaller.

Bologna. Cured beef and pork, seasoned, smoked, cooked, ready to serve.

Ham-style Bologna. Contains large cubes of lean pork. Ready to serve.

Knockwurst. Similar to frankfurters but in bulkier links; contains garlic. Must be cooked before serving.

Bauernwurst. A mixture of pork and beef, fully cooked, needs brief heating.

Blutwurst or blood sausage. Diced cooked fat pork with other meat, gelatin, beef blood, and spices. Ready to serve.

Braunschweiger. Smoked liver sausage.

Liver sausage or liverwurst. Mildly seasoned mixture of cooked ground pork and liver, usually smoked and cured. Ready to serve.

Liver cheese. A mixture of ground cooked liver, veal, and gelatin, delicately spiced.

Thuringer. Made of ground pork, sometimes veal and beef as well. Sold sometimes fresh, sometimes cooked.

Salami. A mixture of pork and beef with spices; cured for 48 hours, put in casings, smoked at high temperature, then air-dried.

Kosher salami. All beef, produced under rabbinical supervision.

Dry and Semidry Sausages

May be stored 2 to 3 weeks; ready to serve.

Lebanon bologna. Coarsely ground beef heavily smoked; sold prepackaged in slices.

Mortadella. Italian style mixture of chopped cured pork and beef with fat, delicately spiced, smoked at high temperatures, air-dried.

Cervelat. Mildly spiced, medium-dry sausage with tangy flavor.

Chorizo. Spanish style semi-dry sausage made of pork, flavored with garlic and paprika. Comes in long links.

Pepperoni. Italian style highly-spiced sausage, smoked, and air-dried.

Luncheon Meats

Some of the following should be used within one week after purchase (unless frozen in sealed packets); others will keep 2 weeks. It's best, if in doubt, to store sliced meats in the freezer.

Head cheese or souse. Chunks of meat, beef, veal, or pork, or a combination, in gelatin.

Blood and tongue pudding. Made with chunks of cooked tongue and beef blood in a gelatinized loaf.

Pickle and pimiento loaf. Similar to bologna, with bits of pickle and pimiento in the gray-pink loaf.

Olive loaf. Also much like bologna, but with sliced stuffed olives.

All-pork luncheon meat. Cooked pork, ground and pressed in a gelatinized mixture.

FRANKFURTERS

Buying

You'll find these kinds of frankfurters: skinless and in natural casings, all-meat franks, all-beef franks, kosher franks.

Frankfurters may be bought in bulk or packaged. The latter come in ½-pound and 1-pound cellophane-wrapped packages, 2- or 3-pound cartons with cellophane windows, in cans and jars.

They come in three sizes: regular franks that average 9 to 10 to the pound, dinner size about 5 to the pound, and cocktail franks 26 to 28 to the pound.

Heating

Frankfurters do not require cooking, only heating through. This can be done by any one of the following methods.

Steamed. Place frankfurters in pan of boiling water to cover. Remove pan from heat. Cover; let stand 7 to 8 minutes to heat through. Or place franks on rack in kettle containing about 1 cup water. Bring water to boiling; reduce heat slightly. Cover; steam franks about 8 minutes. Do not pierce skins; handle with tongs.

Simmered. Drop franks into boiling water. Cover; let water simmer—do not boil—5 to 10 minutes, depending on size until franks are heated through.

Panbroiled or griddle broiled. Heat small amount of fat in heavy skillet or on griddle. Sauté whole franks just until brown, turning occasionally with tongs. Do not pierce with fork. For split franks, sauté cut sides first, turn, and brown skin side.

Broiled. Brush each frankfurter with butter, margarine, or other fat. Broil about 3 inches from heat about 5 minutes on each side.

Grilled. Grill franks on green sticks, in frank roaster, or on grill over glowing coals until brown. Turn to brown evenly. Cook slowly to avoid having a hard, charred outside and tough cold inside. Or, wrap franks in aluminum foil and heat over glowing coals 1(minutes.

To heat rolls. Place rolls on cookie sheet Heat at 250° F. about 5 minutes. To heat o grill, place rolls on edge of grill over glowin; coals for just a few minutes until heate through. Or, wrap in aluminum foil and hea on grill.

To toast rolls. Split frankfurter rolls. Sprea cut sides with soft butter or margarine. Plac in shallow pan or on cookie sheet. Bake 425° F. about 5 minutes. Or toast under th broiler about 2 minutes.

Storing

Frankfurters may be kept in the coldest part of the refrigerator for 4 to 5 days. Wrap bulk franks loosely in wax paper, transparent plastic wrap, or aluminum foil. Store packaged ones in their original wrappings.

HOAGIE FRANKFURTERS

3 c. shredded
  lettuce
6 frankfurter rolls,
  split
Oil
Vinegar
6 slices provolone
  cheese, cut in
  half

12 slices tomato
6 frankfurters,
  heated and split
12 slices
  Bermuda onion
6 slices Swiss
  cheese
½ c. shredded
  hot peppers

Arrange layer of lettuce on bottom of each roll. Drizzle with oil and vinegar. Layer onto each 2 pieces provolone, 2 slices tomato, frankfurter, 2 slices onion, 1 slice Swiss cheese, and some peppers. Add roll tops.

TEEN CLUB FRANKFURTERS

6 frankfurters,
  heated and split
6 frankfurter rolls,
  split and lightly
  toasted

12 small slices
  tomato
12 slices cooked
  bacon
6 slices process
  American cheese,
  cut in half

Place frankfurters on toasted bottom halves of rolls. Top each with 2 slices tomato; add 2 slices bacon. Cover with 2 half-slices cheese. Broil just until cheese starts to melt. Add roll tops.

SWEET 'N SOUR FRANKS

¼ c. chopped
  onion (1 small)
⅓ c. chopped green
  pepper
1 tbs. fat or pure
  vegetable oil
1 tbs. cornstarch
2 tbs. brown sugar
2 tbs. vinegar

2 tsp. soy sauce
½ tsp. salt
1 can (8¾ oz.)
  crushed pine-
  apple
6 frankfurters,
  heated
6 frankfurter rolls,
  toasted

Sauté onion and green pepper in fat or oil 2 minutes. Add cornstarch, sugar, vinegar, soy sauce, salt, and crushed pineapple. Simmer about 2 minutes, stirring constantly. Put a cooked frankfurter in each toasted roll. Spoon on sauce.

ZIPPY FRANKFURTERS

1 c. shredded, sharp
  Cheddar cheese
¼ c. chopped
  onion (1 small)
¼ c. chopped green
  pepper

⅓ c. chili sauce
6 frankfurters,
  heated
6 frankfurter rolls

Combine cheese, onion, green pepper, and chili sauce. Put a cooked frankfurter in each roll. Spread frankfurters with cheese mixture.

PIZZA FRANKFURTERS

6 frankfurters,
  heated and split
6 frankfurter rolls,
  split and toasted
6 tbs. tomato sauce
Oregano

½ c. shredded
  mozzarella
  cheese
2 tbs. grated
  Parmesan cheese

Place frankfurters on bottom halves of toasted rolls. Spread tomato sauce on frankfurters; sprinkle with oregano. Top with mozzarella and Parmesan cheeses. Broil until cheese melts. Add roll tops.

CON CARNE FRANKS

½ c. chopped onion
  (1 medium)
1 tbs. fat or pure
  vegetable oil
½ lb. ground chuck
  or round
1 can (8 oz.)
  tomato sauce
1 tsp. chili powder

½ tsp. salt
Dash of pepper
6 frankfurters,
  heated
6 frankfurter rolls,
  toasted
½ c. chopped onion
  (1 medium)

Sauté ½ cup onion in fat or oil 2 minutes. Add beef; cook until browned, breaking up with fork as it cooks. Add tomato sauce, chili powder, salt, and pepper. Cover; simmer 30 minutes. Uncover for last 5 minutes of cooking. Spoon over frankfurters in rolls. Serve chopped onion to sprinkle on franks.

WOODSY FRANKS

1 jar (5 oz.)
  smoky cheese
6 slices bacon,
  cooked and
  crumbled

6 frankfurters,
  heated
6 frankfurter rolls,
  toasted

Combine cheese and bacon. Put frankfurters in toasted rolls. Spread with cheese mixture.

BROADWAY FRANKS

¼ c. mayonnaise
  or salad dressing
½ tbs. minced
  onion
2 tbs. finely
  chopped green
  pepper
1 tbs. vinegar
½ tsp. salt
Dash of pepper

½ tsp. sugar
2 c. shredded
  cabbage
Prepared mustard
6 frankfurter rolls
6 frankfurters,
  heated
6 slices dill or
  sour pickles

Combine mayonnaise or salad dressing, onion, green pepper, vinegar, salt, pepper, and sugar in bowl. Add cabbage; mix well. Spread mustard on rolls. Put a frankfurter in each roll. Spoon coleslaw over frankfurters; top with pickle slice.

BEANS AND FRANKS

½ c. chopped onion
  (1 medium)
½ c. chopped green
  pepper
1 tbs. fat or pure
  vegetable oil
1 can (1 lb.) pork
  and beans

½ c. chili sauce
1 tbs. prepared
  mustard
6 frankfurters,
  heated
6 frankfurter rolls,
  toasted

Sauté onion and green pepper in fat or oil 3 minutes. Add baked beans, chili sauce, and mustard. Simmer 10 to 15 minutes, stirring frequently. Put a frankfurter in each roll. Spoon beans over frankfurters.

GLAZED TANGY FRANKFURTERS

½ c. currant jelly
3 tbs. prepared
  mustard

6 frankfurters
6 frankfurter rolls,
  toasted

Melt currant jelly; add mustard; mix well. Brush frankfurters with jelly mixture. Broil or grill until lightly browned. Serve in toasted rolls.

SCANDINAVIAN FRANKS

¼ c. soft butter or
  margarine
3 tbs. blue cheese
6 frankfurters,
  heated

6 frankfurter rolls
½ c. chopped
  Bermuda onion

Blend butter or margarine and cheese. Put a frankfurter in each roll. Spread cheese mixture on frankfurter. Sprinkle with onion.

FAVORITE FRANKFURTERS

6 frankfurters,
  heated
6 frankfurter rolls

Bottled hot-dog
  relish
6 tbs. chopped
  onion

Put a frankfurter in each roll. Spread with hot-dog relish; sprinkle with onion. Top with mustard, if desired.

FRANKFURTERS AND ONIONS

6 frankfurters,
  heated
6 frankfurter rolls

Prepared mustard
2 c. fried onions

Put a frankfurter in each roll. Spread with mustard; top with fried onions.

RED AND GREEN FRANKS

6 frankfurters,
  heated
6 frankfurter rolls

6 tbs. catsup
6 tbs. pickle relish

Put a frankfurter in each roll. Spread frankfurter with catsup. Top with pickle relish.

PUSHCART FRANKFURTERS

6 frankfurters,
  heated
6 frankfurter rolls
Prepared mustard

1 can (1 lb. 4 oz.)
  sauerkraut
  cooked and
  drained

Put frankfurter in each roll. Spread frankfurter with mustard. Spoon on sauerkraut.

TEXAS FRANKFURTERS

½ c. finely chopped onion (1 medium)	1 tsp. chili powder
1 clove of garlic, crushed	2 tsp. Worcestershire sauce
2 tbs. butter or margarine	½ tsp. dry mustard
½ c. catsup	¼ c. water
2 tbs. wine vinegar	6 strips bacon
	6 frankfurters
	6 frankfurter rolls, toasted

Sauté onion and garlic in butter or margarine until tender. Add catsup, vinegar, chili powder, Worcestershire, mustard, and water. Cover; simmer 15 minutes. Remove sauce from heat; reserve. Wrap a bacon strip, spiral fashion, around each frankfurter; secure with wooden picks. Grill or broil until bacon is lightly browned. Remove picks. Brush with sauce; broil until browned. Serve on toasted rolls with remaining sauce.

Hot-Dog Go-Withs

A frankfurter by any other name may familiarly be called the "hot-dog" or "red-hots." Besides all the new and tasty twists you've seen above, don't forget those famous hot-dog partners: hot-dog relish, chopped onions, pickle relish, mustard, catsup, bacon, and sauerkraut.

QUICK BARBECUED FRANKFURTERS

½ c. chopped onion (1 medium)	2 cans (8 oz. ea.) tomato sauce
¼ c. chopped green pepper	1 tbs. prepared horseradish
¼ c. chopped celery	2 tbs. brown sugar
2 tbs. butter or margarine	1 tbs. vinegar
¾ c. hot water	8 frankfurters (about 1 lb.)
1 envelope granulated beef broth mix or 1 beef-bouillon cube	1 large dill pickle

Sauté onion, green pepper, and celery in butter or margarine in skillet until tender; add hot water and beef broth mix or bouillon cube; stir to dissolve. Stir in tomato sauce, horseradish, brown sugar, and vinegar; simmer 5 minutes. Split frankfurters lengthwise almost through to bottom. Cut dill pickle lengthwise into eighths; insert one piece in each frankfurter; place frankfurters carefully into sauce; simmer 10 minutes. Serve with additional chopped onion, if desired. Makes 8 servings.

SWEET-SOUR FRANKFURTERS

2 tbs. butter or margarine	1 can (1 lb. 4 oz.) sliced pineapple
1 lb. frankfurters, sliced	2 tbs. diced pimiento
1 small onion, sliced	2 tbs. soy sauce
1 c. sliced celery	2 tbs. vinegar
	2 tbs. cornstarch

Melt butter or margarine in skillet; brown frankfurters lightly; add onion and celery, sauté until soft. Drain pineapple; measure juice: add water to make 1¾ cups. Reserve several slices for garnish; dice remaining slices. Add diced pineapple and pimiento to mixture in skillet. Combine pineapple juice mixture, soy sauce, vinegar, and cornstarch; pour into skillet; stir gently until thickened and bubbly. Garnish with reserved pineapple slices. Makes 6 servings.

CREOLE FRANKS ON CHIPS

8 frankfurters (1 lb.), cut in ½-inch pieces	2 cans (1 lb. ea.) tomatoes
3 tbs. fat or pure vegetable oil	1 tsp. chili powder
1 c. chopped onion (1 large)	1 tsp. salt
½ c. chopped green pepper	2 tsp. sugar
	Dash of pepper
	Potato chips

Brown frankfurters in hot fat or oil in skillet; remove. Sauté onion and green pepper in fat or oil remaining in skillet until tender; add tomatoes, chili powder, salt, sugar, and pepper; cover. Simmer 25 minutes; add frankfurters; simmer 5 minutes longer. Serve hot on potato chips. Makes 6 servings.

RANCH-STYLE FRANKFURTER STEW

8 frankfurters (1
 lb.), cut in 1-in.
 pieces
3 tbs. fat or pure
 vegetable oil
1 clove of garlic,
 mashed
1 c. chopped onion
 (1 large)
½ c. chopped green
 pepper

2 cans (1 lb. ea.)
 tomatoes
2 pkgs. (10 oz. ea.)
 frozen mixed
 vegetables
2 tsp. sugar
1½ tsp. salt
1 tsp. paprika
⅛ tsp. pepper

Brown frankfurter pieces lightly in fat or oil in
large saucepan; remove and reserve. Add
garlic, onion, and green pepper to fat or oil remaining in pan; sauté 3 minutes. Add tomatoes, frozen mixed vegetables, sugar, salt,
paprika, and pepper; cover; simmer 10 minutes. Add frankfurters; simmer 5 minutes.
Makes 6 servings.

HAM AND RICE ORIENTAL

1 pkg. (6 oz.) sliced
 spiced ham,
 bologna, or ham,
 cut in squares
5 tbs. fat or pure
 vegetable oil
2 eggs, beaten
3 c. cold cooked rice

¼ c. thinly sliced
 green onions
1 can (3 to 4 oz.)
 chopped mush-
 rooms
Dash of pepper
1 to 2 tbs. soy sauce

Sauté meat lightly in 1 tablespoon hot fat or
oil; remove and reserve. Add 1 tablespoon fat
or oil and beaten eggs to pan; cook eggs, turning to cook both sides; remove eggs; cut in

strips and reserve. Put remaining 3 tablespoons fat or oil in pan; add rice; sauté 5
minutes, stirring frequently. Add meat, eggs,
green onions, mushrooms, and pepper; cook
3 minutes to heat thoroughly. Add soy sauce;
mix well; serve. Makes 4 servings.

KNOCKWURST BOILED DINNER

2 lbs. knockwurst
6 c. boiling water
3 beef bouillon
 cubes
1½ tsp. salt
4 medium-size
 potatoes, pared
 and cut up

4 carrots, pared and
 cut in pieces
4 white turnips,
 pared and cut up
1½ lbs. head of
 green cabbage,
 cut in 6 wedges

Put knockwurst in boiling water; cover; let
stand 12 minutes. Remove knockwurst; cover;
keep warm. Add bouillon cubes and salt to
water remaining in saucepan; heat until cubes
dissolve. Add vegetables; cover; bring to boiling; boil gently 20 minutes. Drain and serve
with knockwurst. (Knockwurst may be reheated, if necessary, in hot liquid for 2 minutes.) Serve with horseradish or mustard
pickle, if desired. Makes 6 servings.

BOLOGNA SKILLET SUPPER

1 pkg. (6 oz.)
 bologna, cut in
 strips
2 tbs. butter or
 margarine
1 large onion, sliced
 and separated
 into rings
1 can (1 lb. 13 oz.)
 tomatoes, drained
1 pkg. (10 oz.)
 frozen peas

¾ tsp. salt
½ tsp. leaf oregano,
 crumbled
Dash of pepper
½ pkg. (4 servings)
 instant mashed
 potatoes
½ c. shredded
 sharp Cheddar
 cheese

Heat oven to 350° F. Sauté bologna strips in
butter or margarine about 3 minutes; add
onion rings; sauté 3 minutes longer. Add tomatoes, peas, salt, oregano, and pepper; bring
to boiling; lower heat; simmer 5 minutes.
Turn into 1½-quart casserole (mixture may
be prepared and baked in heat-proof skillet).
Prepare mashed potatoes according to package directions; spoon around edge of bologna
mixture; sprinkle with cheese. Bake 25 to
30 minutes or until potatoes are lightly
browned. Makes 4 servings.

Variety Meats

Unusual, interesting dishes can be made with the variety meats which often are available at bargain prices. Many shoppers pass them by only because they don't know what to do with them. Others shy away from them out of pure prejudice. Try using some of these bonus meats in the ways suggested on the following pages, and we predict you'll be delightfully surprised. All the variety meats are quite perishable and should be used within a day or two after purchase.

Liver

Calves' Liver is the most tender and delicately flavored of the livers and also the most costly. It comes from young calves, and is sometimes called veal . liver. It may be sautéed or broiled, and should be cooked gently.

Baby Beef Liver is the next most tender. It is from young beef animals and when of high quality and cooked with care, it is almost as good as calves' liver and much less expensive. Sauté or broil it gently.

Beef Liver is from older beef and is best when braised.

Lamb Liver is mild flavored and tender. Sauté or broil it.

Pork Liver is often used in making pâté; the French rate it next after goose liver. It should be braised.

Sweetbreads

These are considered a gourmet delicacy. They are taken from veal, young beef, or lamb. They may be bought fresh or frozen. Sweetbreads are parboiled before using. This helps to keep them white and firm.

Brains

Brains are a very delicate, perishable meat. They are as delicious as sweetbreads and almost identical in flavor. If frozen, they should be completely thawed before cooking. If purchased fresh, they should be cooked immediately or frozen. Like sweetbreads, they should be parboiled before using.

Kidneys

Kidneys are considered a great delicacy and are served in a variety of gourmet dishes. Veal or lamb kidneys may be bought separately or as part of a kidney chop. They may be broiled or sautéed. Beef kidney is less tender and should be braised.

Heart

The heart is less tender than other variety meats and requires longer cooking in a larger amount of liquid. Beef heart, the least expensive, is usually cut into cubes and used in stews, combined with vegetables. Veal or calves' heart is more delicate and often is cooked whole in flavored broth.

Tripe

Tripe, the lining of the beef stomach, is one of the less tender of the variety meats, requiring long, slow cooking in liquid.

Tongue

Most of the tongue in our markets is either beef or veal. Occasionally pork or lamb tongue is available already cooked, ready to serve. Tongue is available fresh, smoked, pickled, or corned. Fresh tongue is simmered in water with spices and other seasonings for 3 or 4 hours, then cooled, skinned and sliced.

Smoked tongue can be cooked in a shorter length of time but is also simmered in water to cover. It may be soaked in cold water a few hours before cooking.

BRAISED LIVER DELMONICO

1 lb. beef liver	3 tbs. butter or
1 c. flour	margarine
1 tsp. salt	½ c. boiling water
¼ tsp. pepper	½ c. sliced green
	onions

Cut liver into thin slices; remove veins and any fat; cut each slice into strips, about ½-inch wide. Combine flour, salt, and pepper; sprinkle mixture over liver; toss to coat well. Melt butter or margarine in skillet; brown liver quickly on all sides. Add boiling water; reduce heat; simmer 5 minutes, stirring gently, until all liquid is absorbed; add onions. Serve atop scrambled eggs, accompanied by crisp bacon and tomato wedges, if desired. Makes 4 servings.

SWEETBREADS IN CREAM

2 pairs sweetbreads	1 lb mushrooms,
1 tsp. salt	sliced
1 tbs. vinegar or	1 tsp. salt
lemon juice	¼ tsp. pepper
4 tbs. butter or	1 tbs. flour
margarine	1 c. heavy cream
	¼ c. dry sherry

Soak sweetbreads in cold water 30 minutes; drain. Put in saucepan; cover with water; add 1 teaspoon salt and vinegar or lemon juice. Parboil 15 minutes; drain; cover with cold water; chill. Hold under cold running water and slip thin membrane off with fingers; cut out dark veins and thick connective tissue with paring knife. Cut sweetbreads in cubes; sauté in skillet in 2 tablespoons butter or margarine until brown on all sides. Remove; reserve. Sauté mushrooms in remaining 2 tablespoons butter or margarine; add salt and pepper; blend in flour; stir in cream and wine. Bring to boiling; add sweetbreads; simmer 2 to 3 minutes. Serve on toast points sprinkled with chopped parsley, if desired. Makes 4 to 6 servings.

CALF'S BRAINS SAUTÉ

1 lb. calf or beef	½ tsp. salt
brains	⅛ tsp. pepper
1 tbs. vinegar	Fat or pure
1 tsp. salt	vegetable oil for
1 egg	frying
½ c. packaged	
cracker crumbs	

Soak brains in cold water 30 minutes. Drop into boiling water; add vinegar and 1 teaspoon salt; simmer 15 minutes. Drain; cover with cold water; chill. Remove membrane with tip of paring knife; cut brains in cubes. Dip in beaten egg; roll in combined cracker crumbs, ½ teaspoon salt, and pepper. Put enough fat or oil into deep saucepan so it is 2 inches deep when heated. Heat to 400° F. Fry brains 4 to 5 minutes or until crisp and brown. Drain on paper towels. Serve garnished with lemon quarters and parsley, if desired. Makes 4 servings.

SAUTÉED KIDNEY, VINTNER'S STYLE

1 beef kidney	1 beef bouillon
3 tbs. vinegar	cube
4 c. water	1½ c. boiling water
1 c. flour	½ tsp. salt
3 tbs. butter or	⅛ tsp. pepper
margarine	½ tsp. Worcester-
½ cup chopped	shire sauce
onion (1	2 tbs. diced
medium)	pimiento
¼ lb. mushrooms,	¼ c. dry red wine
sliced	2 tbs. chopped
	parsley

Soak kidney in vinegar and water about 2 hours. Rinse; remove fat and tubes with a sharp knife; slice kidney thinly. Coat thoroughly with flour. Melt butter or margarine in skillet or chafing dish; sauté onion and mushrooms; remove and reserve. Add kidney to fat remaining in skillet; brown quickly on both sides. Add bouillon cube to boiling water; pour over kidney. Add salt, pepper, Worcestershire, pimiento, onion, mushrooms, and wine. Cover skillet; reduce heat; simmer 10 minutes. Sprinkle with parsley just before serving. Makes 4 servings.

KIDNEY SAUTÉ

2 veal kidneys	1 can (10½ oz.)
(about 1 lb. ea.)	condensed
4 tbs. butter or	consommé
margarine	¼ c. dry sherry
1 lb. mushrooms,	1 c. heavy cream
sliced	Salt
2 tbs. flour	Pepper
	Chopped parsley

Remove fat and heavy vein from kidneys; cube kidneys. Heat butter or margarine in large skillet; add cubed kidneys; brown evenly on all sides. Add mushrooms; cook 5 minutes. Sprinkle with flour; stir until blended. Add consommé, wine, and cream slowly, stirring constantly. Cook over low heat 10 to 15 minutes; season to taste with salt and pepper; sprinkle with chopped parsley. Serve hot. Makes 4 servings.

BEEF AND KIDNEY PIE

1 c. chopped onion (1 large)	1 c. water
3 tbs. fat or pure vegetable oil	1 tbs. flour
	¼ c. water
2 lbs. beef round, cut in 1-in. cubes	Salt
	Pepper
1 beef kidney, cleaned, trimmed, and cut in pieces	½ pkg. pie-crust mix
	1 egg yolk
	2 tbs. water
1 can (10½ oz.) condensed beef broth	

Sauté onion in hot fat or oil in heavy saucepan until soft; remove; reserve. Brown beef and kidney on all sides in fat or oil remaining in pan. Add beef broth, 1 cup water, and sautéed onion; simmer about 1½ hours or until meat is tender. Mix flour and ¼ cup water to smooth paste; stir into beef mixture. Cook, stirring constantly, until thickened. Taste; season with salt and pepper to taste. Turn into 1½-quart casserole. Heat oven to 425° F. Prepare pie-crust mix according to package directions. Roll out on lightly floured board 1 inch larger than top of casserole. Place on casserole; turn edge under; flute. Make slits in top of pastry to allow steam to escape during baking (use pastry scraps to make design on top, if desired). Beat egg yolk and 2 tablespoons water; brush pastry with mixture; bake 30 to 40 minutes or until pastry is golden and beef gravy is bubbly. Makes 6 servings.

TRIPE CREOLE

1 to 1½ lbs. fresh tripe	1 can (1 lb.) tomatoes
1 tbs. salt	1 can (6 oz.) tomato paste
3 tbs. butter or margarine	1 tsp. salt
½ cup chopped onion (one medium)	½ tsp. garlic salt
	¼ tsp. pepper
¼ c. chopped green pepper	1 tsp. leaf oregano, crumbled

Place tripe in large kettle; cover with cold water; add 1 tablespoon salt; bring to boiling; reduce heat. Simmer 3 hours or until tender; drain; cut in cubes. Melt butter or margarine in large pan; add onion and green pepper; sauté until golden. Add tomatoes, tomato paste, salts, pepper, and oregano; simmer 10 minutes. Add cubed tripe; simmer 5 minutes longer. Makes 4 to 6 servings.

TONGUE WITH SWEET-SOUR RAISIN SAUCE

1 smoked beef tongue (3 to 4 lbs.)	2 tbs. vinegar
	¾ c. water
1 tbs. cornstarch	⅓ c. currant jelly
¼ tsp. dry mustard	¾ c. raisins
¼ c. brown sugar, firmly packed	2 tbs. slivered orange rind

Place tongue in large kettle; cover with cold water; bring to boiling; reduce heat; simmer 3 to 3½ hours or until tender. Remove tongue from water; slit skin on underside with sharp knife; pull off carefully. Remove small bones and excess fat. Slice slightly on the diagonal, to give longer slices. Blend cornstarch, mustard, and brown sugar; stir in vinegar and water; add currant jelly. Cook, stirring constantly, until mixture thickens and is bubbly; add raisins. Just before serving add orange rind. Makes 10 to 12 servings.

OXTAIL RAGOUT

2½ lbs. disjointed oxtails	1 stalk celery, cut up
3 tbs. butter or margarine	1 small onion, sliced
1 tsp. salt	1½ c. water
¼ tsp. pepper	1 c. dry red wine
8 whole allspice	1 tbs. cornstarch
1 bay leaf	Water

Wash and dry oxtails; brown in butter or margarine on all sides in heavy pan. Add salt, pepper, allspice, bay leaf, celery, onion, and 1½ cups water; cover; simmer 2 hours or until meat leaves bone readily. Add red wine; simmer 5 to 10 minutes longer. Remove meat from liquid; strain liquid; skim off fat. Blend cornstarch to a smooth paste with a little water. Stir into liquid; cook, stirring constantly, until thickened and bubbly. Return meat to gravy, or pour gravy over meat on serving platter. Makes 4 servings.

Canned Meats

A selection of canned meats tucked away on the pantry shelf can be a form of meal insurance. On the spur of the moment, you can always be ready with the makings of everything from appetizers to entrees to salads.

Canned luncheon meats include some made of pure pork, others of ham, others of a mixture of beef and pork. There also are jars of dried beef, tiny cans of deviled ham spread, Vienna sausages, corned beef, and canned hamburgers or meat balls in a sauce ready to heat and serve. So many new meat products are introduced all the time, it is impossible for us to mention them all here, but the following recipes may help you to see how versatile these ready-to-serve meat products can be.

DEVILED HAM AND CHEESE BAKE

¼ c. minced onion	4 c. milk
1 clove of garlic, crushed	1 pkg. (8 oz.) process American cheese slices
¼ c. butter or margarine	1 pkg. (8 oz.) process Swiss cheese slices
2 tsp. Worcestershire sauce	
¼ tsp. hot-pepper sauce	1 pkg. (8 oz.) elbow macaroni, cooked and drained
½ tsp. dry mustard	
1 tsp. salt	2 cans (4½ oz. ea.) deviled ham
¼ tsp. pepper	
4 tbs. flour	

Sauté onion and garlic in butter or margarine 5 minutes. Stir in Worcestershire, pepper sauce, mustard, salt, and pepper. Cook 2 or 3 minutes longer. Blend in flour. Stir in milk. Cook over medium heat, stirring constantly, until sauce thickens and boils 1 minute. Reserve 1 or 2 slices of cheese for garnish. Cut up remaining cheese; add half to cream sauce; stir until melted. Spoon half the cooked macaroni into 2-quart greased casserole. Top with remaining half of cut up cheese. Spoon deviled ham over cheese. Pour on half the cheese sauce. Top with the rest of the cooked macaroni; pour remaining cheese sauce over. Garnish with reserved cheese slices cut into strips. Bake at 350° F. for 25 to 30 minutes. Makes 6 servings.

To prepare ahead, cook and drain macaroni and prepare sauce. Keep separate and assemble casserole just before baking.

CORNED BEEF AND BEAN CASSEROLE

1 can (12 oz.) corned beef, chopped	2 cans (1 lb. ea.) pork and beans
⅓ c. chopped onion	¼ c. catsup
	2 tbs. prepared mustard
Dash of pepper	1 tsp. Worcestershire sauce
¼ c. light cream	

Heat oven to 350° F. Combine chopped corned beef, onion, pepper, and cream in medium-size bowl. Mix pork and beans, catsup, mustard, and Worcestershire in 1½-quart casserole; spoon corned beef mixture on top. Bake 30 minutes or until lightly browned. Makes 6 servings.

APPLE-GLAZED SUPPER LOAF WITH YAMS

2 cans (12 oz. ea.) luncheon meat	1 tsp. dry mustard
1½ c. packaged bread crumbs	1 can (1 lb. 10 oz.) syrup-packed yams
1 egg	¼ c. melted butter or margarine
½ c. milk	½ c. apple jelly
¼ c. pickle relish	

Heat oven to 350° F. Chop luncheon meat very fine; add bread crumbs, egg, milk, pickle relish, and mustard; mix well. Press mixture firmly into greased 9x5x3-inch loaf pan; turn out into baking pan. Drain yams; place in baking pan around meat loaf. Brush loaf and potatoes with melted butter or margarine; bake 30 minutes. Beat apple jelly with a fork; spoon over loaf; bake loaf 10 minutes or until nicely glazed. Makes 4 servings.

HAM AND MUSHROOM TURNOVERS

1 can (3 to 4 oz.) chopped mushrooms, drained	2 c. sifted all-purpose flour
3 cans (2¼ oz. ea.) deviled ham	3 tsp. baking powder
2 tbs. dairy sour cream	1 tsp. salt
2 tbs. chopped parsley	⅓ c. shortening
	⅔ c. milk
	Cheese Sauce (*page 348*)

Heat oven to 450° F. Combine mushrooms, deviled ham, sour cream, and parsley. Set aside. Sift flour, baking powder, and salt together. Cut in shortening until mixture resembles cornmeal. Add milk, stirring until soft dough forms. Knead on floured board 10 strokes. Roll dough out on floured board to a rectangle 10x5 inches. Cut into six 5-inch squares. Place filling in center of each square; moisten edges; fold over to form a triangle. Seal edges; crimp with fork. Cut a small gash in top of each turnover. Place on cookie sheet. Bake 10 to 12 minutes until golden brown. Serve with Cheese Sauce. Makes 6 servings.

SWEET AND SOUR HAM

2 cans (12 oz. ea.) luncheon meat, cubed	¼ c. vinegar
2 tbs. fat or pure vegetable oil	⅓ c. light brown sugar, firmly packed
¾ c. sliced onion	2 tbs. cornstarch
¾ c. slivered green pepper	1 tbs. soy sauce
1 can (1 lb. 4 oz.) pineapple chunks	½ tsp. ground ginger (optional)
	4 c. hot, cooked rice

Brown luncheon meat in hot fat or oil in skillet; remove. Sauté onion and green pepper in fat or oil remaining in skillet until almost tender. Return meat to skillet. Drain syrup from pineapple; add enough water to make 1½ cups liquid. Add pineapple to skillet. Combine pineapple liquid, vinegar, sugar, cornstarch, soy sauce, and ginger; add to skillet. Simmer until sauce thickens, stirring constantly. Simmer 3 minutes. Serve on rice. Makes 6 servings.

Carving

Traditionally carving has been a man's prerogative. Today, carving is easier than ever for him, thanks to pretrimmed meats which make bones easier to separate, to specialization of knives to fit the particular job, and of course to the electric knife.

Carving Tools

There is an excellent assortment of carving knives available, some of them designed for slicing specific cuts of meat.

The standard carving knife: Usually used for roasts, it has a blade of medium width, seven to nine inches long. *For slicing steak or poultry,* the blade is narrower and curved, making it easier to maneuver around bones, and usually a little shorter (seven to eight inches long).

The ham slicer with a long (nine- to ten-inch) narrow, blunt-tipped blade is excellent for cold meats which will tend to cling to the wider blade.

A two-tined fork: This is a must to steady the meat as you carve.

A sharpening-honing steel (or electric knife sharpener) will keep blades slicing sharp.

Electric Carving Knife: This new automatic slicing knife (activated by a motor in the handle) is a great boon to carving. It gives one more control of the thinness or thickness of the slice and simplifies carving of all kinds. Always use a wooden cutting board with this knife.

How to Care for Carving Knives: Proper care of a knife is important—whether it be electric or regular. Wash the blades in warm sudsy water by hand, rinse well, dry, and store in a protective case. (This is important both for your safety and for the long life of the blade.)

Carving Tips

Whether you carve at the dining room table or in the kitchen, here are some tips you'll want to keep in mind:
· Let the meat "rest" for ten to twenty minutes (till juices set) before carving. The meat will be firmer and easier to carve, and the slices neater.
· Carve all meats across the grain and fowl with the grain.
· After the first cut is made, the angle at which the knife is held should never be changed. Each cut should be direct, sharp, and incisive, with long sweeping strokes to insure smooth, even slices.

To Carve a Standing Rib Roast of Beef

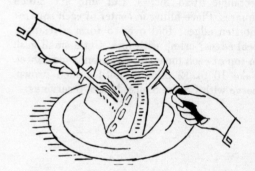

1. Use a large, flat platter. Place roast with flat side down, ribs to the **left** of the carver. The rib ends should be toward the carver. Insert carving fork, tines down, between top and second rib. Slice across roast from right to left, cutting thin slices for better flavor. Beef cut thin is known in restaurants as "English cut."

2. Remove the knife and, with the tip, cut along the side of the rib bone to free the slice.

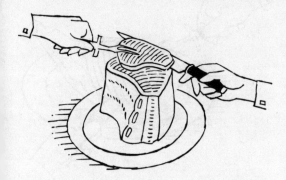

3. With the fork and knife, remove the slice to the platter. If the platter is not large enough to accommodate the slices of beef, use an additional plate or small platter.

To Carve a Rolled Rib Roast

1. Place the roast on platter, largest side down. Leave cord in place. Insert carving fork securely into left side of roast, about 1 inch below top.
2. Slice across top of roast from far side toward the fork. As each cord is reached, cut and remove it. Lift each slice to plate at side.

Carving Steaks

A shorter carving knife is best for this.

Porterhouse Steak

Sirloin Steak. Remove the bone by cutting around it on both sides. Cut steak at a slight angle across the grain.

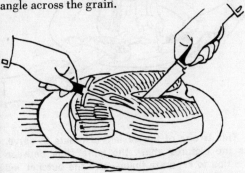

1. Hold steak firmly with fork. Cut around bone closely with tip of knife. Lift bone out and set aside.

2. Carve across full width of steak, cutting through top loin and tenderloin. If steak is thick, cut slices on the diagonal, that is, at a slight angle.

3. Cut end piece of steak as shown.

Sirloin Steak. Remove the bone by cutting around it on both sides. Cut steak at a slight angle across the grain.

To Carve a Roast Leg of Lamb

1. Place roast on platter with leg bone to the right of carver. Cut two or three lengthwise slices from thin side of leg facing you. Turn roast up to rest on flat, just-cut surface.

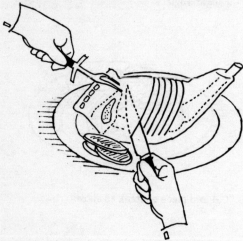

2. Beginning where shank joins leg, cut slices about ¼-inch thick, perpendicular to leg bone.

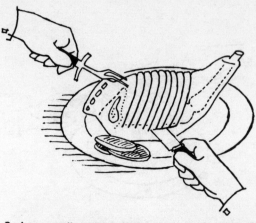

3. Loosen slices by cutting under them, following closely along top of leg bone. Lift slices to serving dishes or separate small platter.

To Carve a Crown Roast

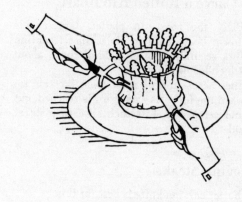

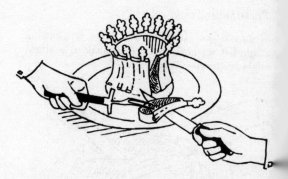

This is one of the easiest of roasts to carve. As the pictures show, the knife slips between the ribs to separate them—and the butcher will have trimmed it in advance so the lower bones are separated. Hold the tines of the fork in the sides, pointed downward, to keep the roast firmly in place.

To Carve a Roast Loin of Pork

Ask the butcher to saw across the base of the ribs, parallel to the backbone, to make it easier to loosen the backbone.

1. Place loin, ribside up, on cutting board.

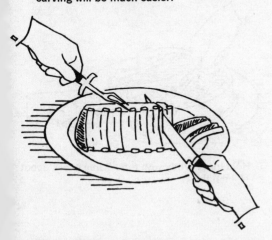

2. Remove backbone, leaving as little meat on it as possible. To do this, place fork astride rib bones, run blade or knife along backbone, close and parallel to it. Once this is done, carving will be much easier.

3. Place roast on platter with rib side facing carver so he can see angle of ribs and slice accordingly. Insert fork in top of roast. Slice by cutting closely along each side of rib bone. One slice will contain the rib, the next will be boneless.

To Carve a Whole Ham

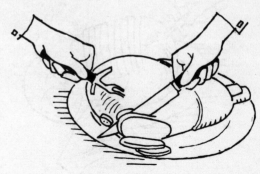

1. Place ham on platter with decorated or fat side up and shank to carver's right. Remove two or three thin slices from thin side of ham. The thin side will face the carver if ham is a left leg and will face away from ham if it is a right leg.

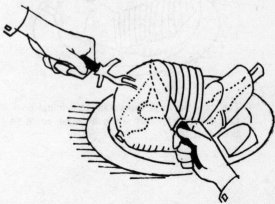

2. Turn ham up on just-cut surface. To make slicing easier, make a straight cut to the leg bone about 6 inches from shank end. Make a second cut at an angle close to shank end. Remove wedge of meat to platter. Cut thin, perpendicular slices down to leg bone.

To Carve a Beef Blade Pot Roast

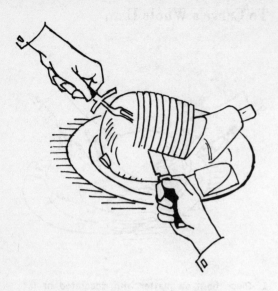

3. Cut along leg bone to release slices.

4. For more servings, turn ham to original position (sketch 1). Cut slices at right angle to the bone.

1. Cut between muscles and around bones to remove one solid section of meat at a time.

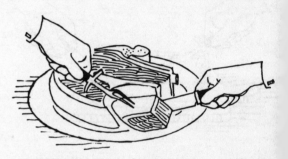

2. Turn piece of meat so fibers are parallel to platter, so you can carve across the grain.

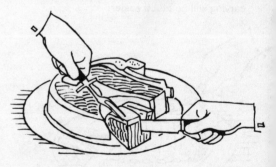

3. Hold meat firmly with fork. Carve slices about ¼-inch thick.

Chapter Twelve

Poultry

Remember when it was "chicken every Sunday" and when turkey was roasted only on Thanksgiving and Christmas? Today, with poultry so plentiful, low in cost, and so versatile for cooking, it is no longer a special-day dinner.

Kinds of Chicken

Broiler-Fryer: The all-purpose chicken, a young, meaty bird that weighs 1½ to 4 pounds. Don't be deceived by its name; a broiler-fryer may be roasted, simmered, or sautéed as successfully as broiled or fried for chicken dishes with moist, succulent meat.

Roaster: A little older and larger than the broiler-fryer, the roaster weighs 3½ to 5 pounds and has tender meat.

Capon: A larger bird, weighing about 4 to 7 pounds, with a fine flavor and a generous quantity of white meat. It is most often roasted.

Bro-Hen: A plump, meaty laying hen, 4½ to 6 pounds in weight, that makes an excellent soup and is good for dishes that cook leisurely, such as stews and fricassees. Provides ample tender meat for dishes made with "cooked chicken."

Rock Cornish Hen: The smallest, newest member of the chicken family, suitable for roasting. May also be baked, broiled, or fried. It usually weighs 1½ pounds or less; many people serve an individual bird to each person.

Buying

Nearly all chickens today are sold ready to cook, meaning they have been fully drawn, cleaned inside and out, and carefully pin-feathered, with head and feet removed.

Ready-to-cook chickens may be fresh or frozen and are government-inspected for wholesomeness. They may be purchased whole, halved, quartered, disjointed, or by the piece. Buying by the piece allows the purchase of any part of the chicken in any amount.

Look for plump birds with pale creamy-pink, moist skin, and fresh, clear yellow fat.

Amounts To Buy Per Serving

Frying:	¾–1 lb.
Roasting:	¾–1 lb.
Stewing:	¾–1 lb.
Broiling:	¼–½ chicken
Rock Cornish Hen:	1 bird

Storing and Handling

Storing

Uncooked, fresh: Remove chicken from original wrappings. Wrap loosely in wax paper or other wrap. Store in coldest, nonfreezing part of refrigerator. It may be kept 1 to 3 days.

Uncooked, frozen: Keep chicken frozen until ready to use—allowing sufficient time for thawing before cooking. Follow package directions for thawing.

Cooked: Always refrigerate leftover chicken and gravy separately in covered containers. Remove any stuffing from stuffed birds and refrigerate it in covered container. Meal-size portions, properly wrapped, may be frozen and held up to 1 month before serving.

Preparation for Cooking

Fresh or Thawed: Clean and wash giblets and chicken. Drain and pat dry.

Frozen: Thaw before cooking. Prompt cooking after thawing is preferable. Follow package directions or thaw by one of the following methods:
　　Place chicken in refrigerator in its original wrap, 12 to 24 hours.
　　Place chicken in pan under running cool water in its original wrap, ½ to 1 hour.

Thawing at room temperature is not recommended.

ROAST CHICKEN

Chickens of any size may be roasted, either in an open pan, in the oven, or on the rotisserie spit. When computing roasting time, plan to remove the chicken 20 minutes before dinner is to be served in order to have time to make gravy, remove the trussing cord, etc. It will be easier to carve after standing 15 to 20 minutes, too.

・ Rinse chicken under cold water; drain; pat dry.
・ Sprinkle chicken with salt and pepper inside and out.
・ If bird is to be stuffed, prepare stuffing just before roasting. (Stuffed birds take longer to roast; see Timetable.)
・ Smaller chickens are delicious without stuffing: place half an orange, a quartered onion, or a handful of chopped parsley in the cavity instead.

To Stuff and Truss:

・ Fill neck cavity with stuffing. Pack lightly, as stuffing will swell during roasting. Fasten flap of neck skin to back with skewer. Force wing tips up and back under body. This forms a cradle for bird to rest on in pan.
・ Stuff body cavity loosely. Close cavity with skewers and string and tie legs together, or, if you have a tuck-type chicken, retuck legs under band of skin.

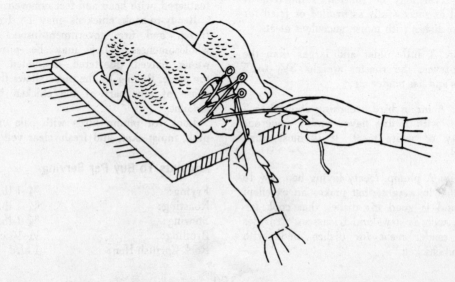

To Roast:

· Brush chicken with butter or margarine.
· Place chicken, breast side up, on rack in shallow, open roasting pan.
· Place in preheated oven. Roast, using Timetable below as a guide.
· Baste several times during roasting.
· Roast until done. To test for doneness: About 20 to 25 minutes before bird should be done grasp end of drumstick. The drumstick-thigh joint moves easily when chicken is done. Or press drumstick meat with fingers protected by paper towels. If meat feels soft, chicken is done.
· Remove from oven. Remove skewers and string. Place chicken on heated platter.

PAN GRAVY

Gravy is best when made in the pan in which the poultry was roasted or cooked, as you want to use all those savory brown bits in the pan.

Proportions for Pan Gravy

	Thin	Medium	Thick
Fat	1 tbs.	2 tbs.	3 tbs.
Flour	1 tbs.	2 tbs.	3 tbs.
Liquid	1 c.	1 c.	1 c.

1. Remove the poultry to a heated platter and keep warm.
2. Pour the fat in the pan into a bowl or jar. Measure back into the pan the amount of fat needed.
3. Blend flour into the fat until smooth. Cook over low heat, stirring constantly, until bubbly. Remove from heat.
4. Add the liquid slowly. The liquid may be water, consommé, stock, or part may be wine. Return pan to heat and cook, stirring and scraping all the brown bits from the pan into the gravy. Continue stirring until mixture comes to boiling. Boil one minute. Taste and season as needed.

Variations for Pan Gravy

Giblet Gravy: Put the neck and giblets (except the liver) in a saucepan with a sliced onion, a handful of celery tops, a teaspoon of salt, and a dash of pepper (or a few peppercorns). Cover with water and simmer 30 minutes for chicken neck and giblets and 1 hour for turkey. Add liver twenty minutes before end of cooking time. Strain and reserve stock. Chop giblets. Use the stock for gravy liquid. Add giblets with stock.

Cream Gravy: Use milk or cream for all or part of the liquid.

Timetable for Roasting Chicken

Name	Purchased Ready-to-Cook Weight	Oven Temperature	Approximate Time* (hours) if unstuffed	if stuffed
Broiler-Fryer**	1½ to 2 lbs.	400° F.	¾ to 1	1 to 1¼
"	2 to 2½ lbs.	400° F.	1 to 1½	1¼ to 1½
"	2½ to 3 lbs.	375° F.	1¼ to 1¾	1½ to 2
"	3 to 4 lbs.	375° F.	1¾ to 2¼	2 to 2½
Roaster	3½ to 6 lbs.	375° F.	3 to 3½	3½ to 4
Cornish Hen	1 to 2 lbs.	400° F. to 450° F.	1	1 to 1¼
Capon	6 to 8 lbs.	350° F.	3 to 3½	3½ to 4½

* Since time periods are only approximate, be sure to test chicken for doneness.

** If preferred, you may roast all broiler-fryers over 1½ pounds in weight at 350° F. for about 30 minutes per pound. For a 1½-pound bird, allow 40 to 45 minutes per pound. Omit wire rack.

For instructions on how to carve chicken, see illustrations, *page 217.*

GLAZED STUFFED CHICKEN

2 broiler-fryers (1½ to 2 lbs. ea.)	2 c. bite-size, shredded-wheat biscuits, crumbled
Chicken giblets	
1½ c. water	
¼ c. butter or margarine	½ c. raisins
	½ tsp. salt
½ c. chopped onion (1 medium)	½ c. currant jelly
	2 tbs. butter or margarine
½ c. chopped celery	

Wash chickens; wipe dry. Simmer giblets in water; drain; reserve broth; chop giblets very fine. Melt ¼ cup butter or margarine in skillet. Sauté onion and celery until soft; add cereal, raisins, salt, and ⅓ cup of giblet broth; toss lightly to blend. Stuff body cavities lightly with stuffing. Truss chicken (*page 200*). Place on rack in shallow roasting pan. Heat jelly and 2 tablespoons butter or margarine in small saucepan until melted; brush over birds. Roast at 325° F. for 40 to 50 minutes or until tender; brush with glaze 2 or 3 times during roasting. Cut each chicken in half to serve. Makes 4 servings.

HERB BAKED CHICKEN

1 broiler-fryer (2½ to 3 lbs.)	⅓ c. dry white wine
1 tsp. garlic salt	1 tsp. leaf rosemary, crumbled
1 tsp. leaf rosemary, crumbled	½ tsp. leaf basil, crumbled
⅓ c. butter or margarine, melted	½ tsp. salt
	¼ tsp. pepper

Heat oven to 400° F. Wash and dry chicken. Sprinkle neck and body cavities with garlic salt and 1 teaspoon rosemary. Combine butter or margarine, wine, 1 teaspoon rosemary, basil, salt, and pepper. Truss chicken (*page 200*). Place on rack in roasting pan. Brush with butter-wine sauce. Bake 1½ to 2 hours or until tender. Brush with sauce several times during baking for a moist, flavorful chicken. When tender, remove from baking pan; remove trussing. Carve chicken or cut into serving pieces with knife and poultry shears. Makes 4 to 6 servings.

BROILED CHICKEN

Young chickens of any weight may be broiled; the popular size is 2½ pounds and under. Follow range directions for use of broiler.

Chicken may be split in half lengthwise or quartered.
· Remove rack from broiler pan. Line pan with aluminum foil, if desired.
· Place chicken, skin side down, on foil. Brush with butter or margarine. Sprinkle with salt and pepper, or herb of your choice.
· Place pan in broiler so surface of chicken is 7 to 9 inches from heat and chicken can broil slowly. Broil 25 to 30 minutes.
· Turn chicken skin side up; brush with melted butter or margarine. Broil 20 minutes or until chicken is well-done, golden brown, and crisp. Brush with butter or margarine or pan drippings several times during broiling to brown and cook evenly. Total cooking time varies from 45 to 50 minutes.
· Test for doneness: The drumstick and wing joints should move readily, and the thickest part of the chicken should yield easily to pressure from fork.

BARBECUE BROILED CHICKEN

¾ c. pure vegetable oil	¾ tsp. leaf oregano, crumbled
¼ c. white wine vinegar	1 tsp. salt
	¼ tsp. pepper
1 large clove of garlic, crushed	2 broiler-fryers, (1½ to 2 lbs. ea.), cut in quarters
1 tbs. minced onion	

Combine oil, vinegar, garlic, and seasonings. Add chicken; marinate at room temperature 2 hours. Broil, skin side down, 7 to 8 inches from heat, 30 minutes. Turn; broil 15 to 30 minutes or until tender; brush often with marinade. Makes 8 servings.

FRIED CHICKEN

BATTER FRIED CHICKEN

2 broiler-fryers (1½ lbs. ea.), cut up	¼ tsp. pepper
	½ tsp. paprika
1 c. sifted all-purpose flour	1 egg, slightly beaten
2 tsp. salt	1 c. milk
1 tsp. sugar	¼ c. fat or pure vegetable oil

Wash and dry chicken. Combine flour, salt, sugar, pepper, and paprika in mixing bowl. Stir egg into milk; blend into dry ingredients. Heat fat or oil in skillet. Dip chicken in batter;

drain off excess. Brown chicken in hot fat or oil in skillet. You may have to cook chicken in 2 batches or use 2 skillets. Turn chicken over to brown both sides. When all chicken is browned, lower heat; cover; cook gently 25 minutes or until chicken is tender. Makes 6 to 8 servings.

SOUTHERN FRIED CHICKEN I
(*Pictured opposite page 149*)

1 broiler-fryer (2½ to 3 lbs.), cut up	½ tsp. Worcestershire sauce
1 tsp. grated lemon rind	1 c. sifted all-purpose flour
⅓ c. lemon juice	1 tsp. salt
⅔ c. pure vegetable oil	1 tsp. paprika
¼ tsp. pepper	½ c. butter or margarine
	1½ c. milk
	1 c. light cream

Place chicken in shallow dish. Combine lemon rind, juice, oil, pepper, and Worcestershire sauce; pour over chicken; allow to marinate for at least 2 hours. Drain chicken; shake in paper bag with flour, salt, and paprika until well coated; save remaining seasoned flour for thickening gravy. Melt butter or margarine in large skillet over medium heat; sauté chicken about 30 to 40 minutes or until golden brown and tender, turning several times. Remove chicken from skillet; keep warm. Pour off drippings; return 3 tablespoons drippings to skillet; stir in ¼ cup reserved seasoned flour; add milk slowly, stirring to scrape up all crusty brown flecks on bottom of skillet. Cook over medium heat, stirring constantly, until thickened and bubbly. Turn heat to low; stir in cream. Taste gravy; add seasoning, if necessary. Add chicken to gravy, or serve gravy in separate container. Makes 4 servings.

SOUTHERN FRIED CHICKEN II

1 broiler-fryer (1½ to 2 lbs.), cut up	1 tsp. paprika
½ c. flour	¼ c. butter or margarine
1 tsp. salt	2 tbs. flour
⅛ tsp. ground cinnamon	1 c. canned chicken broth
¼ tsp. pepper	1 c. light cream
	½ tsp. salt

Wash chicken; do not dry. Mix ½ cup flour, teaspoon salt, cinnamon, pepper, and paprika together. Dip moist chicken in flour mix-

ture to form a thick coating. Heat butter or margarine in skillet; add chicken. Brown well on all sides, turning often. It will take about 30 minutes over medium heat for crisp, well-cooked chicken. When chicken is tender, remove from skillet; keep warm. For Cream Gravy: Stir 2 tablespoons flour into pan drippings; add broth, cream, and ½ teaspoon salt. Cook, stirring constantly, until gravy bubbles and is thickened. Serve with chicken. Makes 4 servings.

CURRIES, SKILLET CHICKEN

MURGHI CURRY
(Indian Chicken Curry)

3 broiler-fryers (1½ to 2 lbs. ea.), cut up	1 c. chopped onion (1 large)
Chicken giblets	2 cloves of garlic, mashed
4 c. water	2 tbs. curry powder
1 onion, sliced	1 tsp. salt
1 tsp. salt	½ tsp. ground ginger
6 peppercorns	¼ tsp. ground cinnamon
Flour	¼ tsp. onion salt
½ c. fat or pure vegetable oil	¼ tsp. pepper
4 tbs. butter or margarine	2 tbs. lime juice
	Cooked rice

Put necks, backs, and wings of chicken in large saucepan (reserve rest of chicken pieces); add giblets, water, sliced onion, 1 teaspoon salt, and peppercorns. Bring to boiling; lower heat; simmer 40 minutes. Drain; add water, if necessary to make 3 cups broth. Coat remaining chicken pieces with flour. Heat fat or oil in large skillet or Dutch oven; sauté chicken until brown; remove from pan. Drain off any fat or oil remaining in pan. Heat butter or margarine in same pan; sauté chopped onion and garlic until lightly browned. Combine curry powder, 1 teaspoon salt, ginger, cinnamon, onion salt, and pepper; stir into fat in pan; cook 2 to 3 minutes, stirring constantly. Add chicken broth and chicken. Cover; simmer 30 minutes or until chicken is tender. Remove chicken; keep warm. Simmer sauce, uncovered, 10 to 15 minutes or until thickened; stir in lime juice. Return chicken; simmer until heated through. Arrange chicken on platter; surround with cooked rice; spoon some sauce over chicken; serve remainder in small bowl. Makes 6 servings.

CHICKEN AND CRAB MEAT CURRY

2 broiler-fryers (2 lbs. ea.), cut up	1½ tbs. curry powder
5 c. water	½ tsp. salt
1 tbs. salt	½ tsp. ground ginger
½ c. flour	¼ tsp. dry mustard
6 tbs. fat or pure vegetable oil	3 tbs. flour
1 clove of garlic, mashed	½ c. heavy cream
1 c. minced onion (1 large)	1 can (6 to 7 oz.) crab meat, drained, boned, and flaked
1 tart apple, pared, cored, and chopped	1 tsp. grated lemon rind
	Hot, cooked rice

Cook necks, giblets, wings, and backs of chickens in water with 1 tablespoon salt until tender; drain. Measure broth; reserve 3 cups. Coat remaining chicken pieces with ½ cup flour. Heat 3 tablespoons fat or oil in large skillet. Sauté chicken until golden, putting in only as many pieces at a time as you can without crowding. Remove browned chicken. Put remaining fat in skillet; heat; brown rest of chicken. Put browned chicken pieces in Dutch oven or heavy kettle. Add garlic, onion, and apple to fat remaining in skillet (there should be about 3 tablespoons); cook until soft. Add curry powder, ½ teaspoon salt, ginger, mustard, and 3 tablespoons flour. Cook, stirring constantly, 2 to 3 minutes. Remove from heat; stir in reserved 3 cups chicken broth slowly. Cook over medium heat, stirring constantly, until thickened and bubbly. Stir in cream and crab meat; pour over chicken; cover. Simmer over low heat 30 to 35 minutes until chicken is quite tender. Just before serving, stir in lemon rind. Serve with steaming hot rice. Makes 8 to 10 servings.

CHICKEN WITH RED WINE
(Coq au Vin)

¼ lb. bacon, diced	½ tsp. leaf tarragon, crumbled
1 c. chopped onion (1 large)	4 peppercorns
¼ lb. mushrooms, sliced	Few sprigs parsley
	1 tsp. salt
2 broiler-fryers (1½ to 2 lbs. ea.), cut up	2 c. dry red wine
	1 tbs. flour
3 tbs. butter or margarine	1 tbs. butter or margarine
1 bay leaf	2 tbs. chopped parsley

Cook bacon in skillet until brown and crispy; remove and reserve bacon. In hot bacon fat, cook onion and mushrooms until soft; remove and reserve. Wash and dry chicken. Add 3 tablespoons butter or margarine to any remaining bacon fat in skillet; add chicken; brown. Return bacon, onions, and mushrooms to skillet. Tie bay leaf, tarragon, peppercorns, and parsley in small piece of clean cheesecloth (a bouquet garni); add to skillet. Add salt to wine; pour over chicken in skillet. Simmer, covered, 25 minutes or until chicken is tender. Remove bouquet garni. Blend flour and 1 tablespoon butter or margarine together (beurre mánie); add to hot liquid bit by bit until sauce is bubbly and thickened as you like. Sprinkle with 2 tablespoons parsley. Makes 6 servings.

SKILLET APRICOT CHICKEN AND RICE

1 broiler-fryer (3 lbs.), cut up	2 tbs. fat or pure vegetable oil
2 tbs. flour	3 c. water
2 tsp. salt	1½ c. rice
¼ tsp. pepper	1 medium-size onion, sliced
½ tsp. leaf rosemary, crumbled	1½ tsp. grated orange rind
¼ tsp. ground ginger	1½ c. dried apricots

Wash and dry chicken pieces. Combine flour, salt, pepper, rosemary, and ginger; dredge chicken in flour mixture. Heat fat or oil in skillet. Brown chicken pieces, turning to brown well on all sides. Pour ½ cup water around chicken; cover and cook for 15 minutes, adding a little more water, if necessary, to keep chicken moist. Push chicken to one side of skillet. Pour rice into pan; stir 1 minute to brown slightly. Add remaining water, onion, orange rind, and apricots; mix. Cover; continue to cook 20 to 25 minutes or until rice is tender and liquid is absorbed. Makes 6 servings.

CHICKEN PAPRIKA WITH SPÄTZLE

½ c. chopped onion (1 medium)	2 tsp. salt
	¼ tsp. pepper
½ c. butter or margarine	1¼ c. water
	2 tbs. paprika
1 broiler-fryer (2½ to 3 lbs.), cut up	1 c. milk
	1 pt. dairy sour cream
⅔ c. sifted all-purpose flour	Spätzle

Sauté onion in butter or margarine; remove and reserve. Shake chicken in paper bag with flour, 1 teaspoon salt, and pepper until coated; save 2 tablespoons of this seasoned flour. Brown chicken in remaining fat. Add 1 cup water and the onions; cook, covered, over low heat, 30 minutes or until tender. Remove chicken; keep warm. Make a paste of 2 tablespoons seasoned flour, paprika, 1 teaspoon salt, and ¼ cup water. Stir into skillet; add milk; cook, stirring constantly, until thickened; cook 10 minutes longer. Add sour cream, very slowly, to avoid curdling; add chicken. Serve on heated platter with spätzle. Makes 4 servings.

Spätzle: Beat 1 egg, 1 cup water, and 1 teaspoon salt; blend in 2½ cups sifted all-purpose flour slowly. Heat 3 quarts water to boiling; add 3 teaspoons salt. Drop dough by ½ teaspoonfuls into water until noodles are 1 layer thick when they rise to surface; cook 10 minutes or until tender. Remove noodles; keep warm. Repeat until all dough is used. Drizzle melted butter or margarine generously over noodles.

CHICKEN HUNTER STYLE
(Poulet Chasseur)

2 tbs. butter or margarine	1 small clove of garlic, mashed
1 tbs. pure vegetable oil	½ c. chopped onion (1 medium)
1 carrot, pared and chopped	½ c. dry white wine
½ c. chopped onion (1 medium)	¼ tsp. leaf tarragon, crumbled
2 broiler-fryers (2 to 2½ lbs. ea.), cut up	¼ tsp. leaf thyme, crumbled
4 c. water	1 tbs. cornstarch
½ tsp. salt	¼ c. dry white wine
3 tbs. butter or margarine	3 firm, ripe, tomatoes, peeled and chopped or 1 can (1 lb.) tomatoes, drained
2 tbs. pure vegetable oil	2 tbs. chopped parsley
½ lb. mushrooms, sliced	

Heat butter or margarine and 1 tablespoon oil in heavy pan. Cook carrot and ½ cup onion in hot fat until soft but not brown. Add necks, wings, backs, and giblets from the two chickens; brown lightly. Add water and salt. Cook slowly about 1 hour or until broth is reduced to 2 cups. Strain and reserve broth. Heat 3 tablespoons butter or margarine and 2 tablespoons oil in skillet. Cook mushrooms, garlic, and ½ cup chopped onion until soft; remove and reserve. Brown chicken legs, breasts, and thighs in fat remaining in skillet (there should be about 3 tablespoons). Do not crowd chicken; if necessary use two skillets. (If using two skillets, be sure to divide ingredients between them.) When chicken is brown, cover skillet; lower heat. Cook 30 to 35 minutes or until chicken is tender. Remove chicken; pour off all fat from pan. Deglaze hot skillet with ½ cup wine. Stir in 2 cups reserved chicken broth; add tarragon and thyme. Blend cornstarch with ¼ cup wine until smooth; beat into hot liquid. Cook over low heat, stirring constantly, until bubbly and thickened. Taste and correct seasonings. Add tomatoes, reserved vegetables, and chicken; cook 5 minutes. Sprinkle with parsley. Makes 6 servings.

POLYNESIAN CHICKEN

1 broiler-fryer (2 to 2½ lbs.), cut up	½ c. flour
¼ c. soy sauce	3 tbs. pure vegetable oil
3 tbs. pure vegetable oil	1 can (8¾ oz.) pineapple tidbits
1 tsp. ground ginger	½ c. orange juice
½ tsp. onion salt	2 tsp. cornstarch
¼ tsp. pepper	¼ c. water
2 tbs. instant minced onion	½ c. orange sections
	¼ c. toasted slivered almonds

Wash and dry chicken; arrange in single layer in shallow pan. Combine soy sauce, 3 tablespoons oil, ginger, onion salt, pepper, and onion; pour over chicken. Let stand 1 hour, turning once. Drain chicken; reserve liquid. Shake chicken with flour in paper bag until well coated. Heat 3 tablespoons oil in skillet; add chicken; brown on all sides. Chicken will be quite dark. Drain pineapple; add juice to reserved soy mixture; add orange juice. Pour over chicken in skillet; lower heat; cover; simmer 30 minutes or until chicken is tender. Remove chicken while making sauce. Combine cornstarch and water; stir into liquid in skillet. Heat until thickened and bubbly. Add orange sections, pineapple tidbits, and chicken; heat until piping hot. Sprinkle with almonds. Makes 4 to 6 servings.

CHICKEN CACCIATORE

2 broiler-fryers (1½ to 2 lbs. ea.), cut up	1 tsp. leaf oregano, crumbled
⅔ c. flour	1 tbs. parsley flakes
1 tbs. paprika	1 bay leaf
6 tbs. olive oil	1 can (2 lbs. 3 oz.) Italian plum tomatoes
1 c. diced, sweet red or green peppers	1 can (8 oz.) tomato sauce
1 c. sliced green onions	½ c. dry red wine
¼ tsp. garlic powder	1½ tsp. salt
	¼ tsp. seasoned pepper

Wash and dry chicken; shake in paper bag with flour and paprika until well coated. Heat oil in large skillet or Dutch oven; brown chicken, a few pieces at a time. Remove chicken; keep warm. Cook red or green peppers and onions in remaining oil until soft but not brown. Discard any remaining oil. Combine chicken, red or green peppers, onions, garlic powder, oregano, parsley flakes, bay leaf, tomatoes, tomato sauce, wine, salt, and pepper in skillet. Simmer, covered, 35 minutes or until chicken is tender. Remove bay leaf. If thicker sauce is desired, blend small amount of flour to a paste with water; stir into sauce and cook until of desired consistency. Makes 6 servings.

PAELLA

2 broiler fryers (3 to 3½ lbs. ea.), cut up	2 c. water
	1 pimiento, sliced
½ c. olive or pure vegetable oil	½ lb. chorizo (Spanish sausage)
3½ tsp. salt	1 dozen small clams, scrubbed
1½ c. rice	
2 cloves of garlic, minced	1 lb. shrimp, shelled, deveined, and cooked
1 bay leaf	
⅛ tsp. saffron	1 pkg. (9 oz.) frozen rock lobster tails, cooked, shelled, and cubed
¼ tasp. pepper	
Dash hot-pepper sauce	
1 can (about 1 lb.) tomatoes	
	1 c. cooked peas

Sauté chicken, a few pieces at a time, in oil in large skillet, adding oil as needed. Put chicken in 3-quart casserole. Sprinkle with 1 teaspoon salt. Cook rice and garlic in oil remaining in skillet until lightly browned. Add remaining 2½ teaspoons salt, bay leaf, saffron, pepper, hot-pepper sauce, tomatoes, water, and pimiento. Bring to boiling; pour over chicken; cover. Bake at 425° F. for 25 minutes. Cut sausage in 1-inch pieces. Sauté until browned. Add clams, shrimp, lobster, peas, and sausage to casserole. Stir lightly. Reduce oven heat to 375° F. Bake casserole, covered, 15 minutes. Remove bay leaf. Makes 8 to 10 servings.

COUNTRY CAPTAIN

2 broiler-fryers (1½ lbs. ea.), cut up	1 large green pepper, seeded and chopped
2 tsp. salt	1 tbs. curry powder
2 tbs. flour	1 tbs. flour
4 tbs. fat or pure vegetable oil	1 tsp. salt
	¼ tsp. pepper
1½ c. chopped onion	1 can (1 lb. 13 oz.) tomatoes
1 clove of garlic, finely chopped	½ c. raisins
	Hot, cooked rice

Wash and dry chicken. Spread out on paper towels. Sprinkle with 2 teaspoons salt and 2 tablespoons flour. Heat fat or oil in skillet. Add chicken; cook until golden on both sides. Remove from skillet; keep warm. Add onion, garlic, and green pepper to fat remaining in skillet; cook until soft. Stir in curry powder, 1 tablespoon flour, 1 teaspoon salt, and pepper. Add tomatoes and raisins; simmer mixture until thickened and bubbly. Return chicken to skillet; cover. Cook gently 25 minutes or until chicken is tender. Stir occasionally to prevent sticking. Serve with hot, cooked rice. Makes 6 servings.

CHICKEN PARMESAN

1 broiler-fryer (2½ to 3 lbs.), cut up	1 c. heavy cream
	1 tsp. grated lemon rind
¼ c. butter or margarine	1 tbs. lemon juice
1 tbs. flour	6 tbs. grated Parmesan cheese
½ c. dry sherry	
½ tsp. salt	1 tbs. butter or margarine
⅛ tsp. pepper	

Wash and dry chicken. Heat ¼ cup butter or margarine in skillet; brown chicken well. Cover skillet; lower heat. Cook chicken about 10 minutes or until tender; remove from pan. Blend flour into fat remaining in skillet. Stir in sherry, salt, pepper, and heavy cream. Return chicken to skillet; cook gently 10 minutes. Stir in lemon rind and juice. Arrange chicken in shallow serving dish; pour sauce over. Sprinkle with Parmesan cheese; dot with 1 tablespoon butter or margarine. Brown under broiler. Makes 4 to 6 servings.

OVEN CHICKEN

CASSEROLE ROASTED CHICKEN

broiler fryers (2½ to 3 lbs. ea.)	24 medium-size whole mushrooms
salt	
Pepper	2 c. 1-in. celery pieces
½ c. butter or margarine	¼ c. chopped parsley
tsp. leaf tarragon, crumbled	

Heat oven to 325° F. Wash and dry chickens. Sprinkle cavities lightly with salt and pepper. Truss chickens (*page 200*). Melt butter or margarine in Dutch oven or large, heatproof casserole. Brown chickens on all sides. Sprinkle with tarragon. Cover. Roast 30 minutes. Add mushrooms and celery. Roast 30 minutes longer or until chicken is tender. Thicken pan juices, if desired, with 1 tablespoon cornstarch blended to a smooth paste with a small amount of cold water. Just before serving, sprinkle chickens with chopped parsley. Makes 8 servings.

SUNDAY CHICKEN BAKE

broiler-fryer (3 to 3½ lbs.), cut up	¼ tsp. pepper ¼ c. melted butter or margarine
½ tsp. salt	1 c. slivered almonds
tsp. paprika	
tsp. curry powder	1½ c. light cream or half-and-half
tsp. leaf oregano, crumbled	

Heat oven to 350° F. Wash and dry chicken; arrange in shallow baking dish. Combine seasonings and melted butter or margarine; brush over chicken, coating well. Sprinkle with almonds; pour cream around pieces. Cover dish. Bake 45 minutes; uncover; bake 10 to 15 minutes or until chicken is tender. Makes 6 servings.

OVEN BARBECUED CHICKEN

2 tbs. instant minced onion	¼ tsp. garlic salt 1 tsp. grated lemon rind
1 c. water	
½ c. catsup	2 tbs. lemon juice
2 tbs. brown sugar	2 broiler-fryers
¼ tsp. hot-pepper sauce	(1½ to 2 lbs. ea.), quartered
1 tsp. Worcester-shire sauce	

Heat oven to 425° F. Combine onion, water, catsup, brown sugar, pepper sauce, Worcestershire, garlic salt, lemon rind and juice in saucepan; simmer 5 minutes. Wash and dry chicken. Brush chicken pieces on both sides with sauce; arrange in greased baking pan, skin side down. Bake 20 minutes; reduce oven heat to 375° F. Turn chicken; brush with remaining sauce; bake 20 minutes or until tender. Makes 6 servings.

GOLDEN CHICKEN AND RICE

1 broiler-fryer (3 lbs.), cut up	1 tsp. salt ⅛ tsp. pepper
¼ c. butter or margarine	1 can (10½ oz.) condensed chicken gravy
1 c. chopped onion (1 large)	1 c. light cream
1 c. sliced celery	½ c. water
1 c. rice	2 pimientos, cut into strips
1 can (3 to 4 oz.) sliced mushrooms and liquid	

Sauté chicken in butter or margarine until golden brown. Remove; reserve. Add onion and celery to fat remaining in pan; sauté 5 minutes. Add rice; cook, stirring constantly, 5 minutes longer. Add remaining ingredients; mix well. Cover; simmer 10 minutes. Heat oven to 350° F. Turn rice mixture into 2-quart casserole. Arrange chicken parts on top of rice mixture; cover. Bake 30 minutes or until chicken is tender. Makes 6 servings.

DEVILED CHICKEN

2 broiler-fryers
(1½ to 2 lbs. ea.),
cut up
3 c. water
1 tsp. salt
1 c. flour
1 tsp. paprika
1 tsp. salt
¼ tsp. pepper

½ c. butter or
margarine
2 tsp. prepared
mustard
1 tbs. Worcester-
shire sauce
1 tbs. instant
minced onion
½ tsp. salt

Wash chicken; pat dry. Simmer wings, necks, and giblets in water and 1 teaspoon salt 30 minutes or until tender; drain; reserve broth; chop giblets. Combine flour, paprika, 1 teaspoon salt, and pepper in paper or plastic bag; add chicken; shake until well coated. Reserve any remaining flour mixture. Melt butter or margarine in large skillet; sauté chicken until golden on all sides; place in 2½- to 3-quart casserole; add chopped giblets. Stir 2 tablespoons of reserved flour mixture into butter or margarine remaining in skillet; add mustard, Worcestershire, onion, ½ teaspoon salt, and 2 cups broth. Stir until thickened and bubbly; pour over chicken; cover. Bake at 350° F. for 40 to 45 minutes. Makes 6 to 8 servings.

BAKED CHICKEN IN WINE

1 clove of garlic,
crushed
3 tbs. lemon juice
2 tbs. olive oil
¾ c. Chablis, Sau-
terne, or dry
sherry

1 tsp. salt
1 broiler-fryer
(2½ to 3 lbs.),
cut up
Paprika

Combine garlic, lemon juice, oil, wine, and salt. Pour over chicken in shallow baking pan. Marinate at least 3 hours, turning frequently. Heat oven to 375° F. Sprinkle chicken generously with paprika. Bake 45 to 55 minutes or until tender. Arrange chicken on heated platter. Serve sauce separately. If a thicker sauce is desired, after removing chicken, blend 1 tablespoon soft butter or margarine and 1 tablespoon flour together thoroughly; heat sauce in baking pan; stir in flour mixture. Continue stirring until sauce thickens and bubbles. Makes 4 servings.

SOUTH-OF-THE-BORDER CHICKEN

1 broiler-fryer
(2½–3 lbs.),
cut up
1½ c. water
½ tsp. salt
⅔ c. sifted, all-
purpose flour
¼ c. grated
Parmesan cheese
1 tsp. paprika
¼ tsp. pepper
½ c. butter or
margarine

1 c. sliced onion
(1 large)
2 tomatoes, peeled
and quartered
2 green peppers,
seeded and diced
8 pitted ripe olives,
sliced
1 tsp. leaf oregano,
crumbled
1 tsp. salt
2 tbs. grated Par-
mesan cheese

Wash chicken; pat dry. Simmer wings, neck, and giblets in water and ½ teaspoon salt 30 minutes or until tender. Drain; reserve broth, chop giblets. Combine flour, ¼ cup cheese, paprika, and pepper in paper or plastic bag. Shake chicken pieces, a few at a time, until well coated; reserve remaining seasoned flour for thickening gravy. Sauté chicken in butter or margarine in large skillet until golden on all sides. Remove from skillet; place in 2½- to 3-quart casserole; add onion, tomatoes, green pepper, and olives. Heat oven to 350° F. Stir oregano, 1 teaspoon salt, and 1 tablespoon of reserved seasoned flour into butter or margarine remaining in skillet. Measure giblet broth; add water if necessary to make one cup; stir into flour mixture. Cook over medium heat, stirring constantly, until thickened; add giblets and 2 tablespoons cheese. Pour gravy over chicken and vegetables in casserole; cover. Bake 40 minutes or until chicken is tender. Makes 4 servings.

CHICKEN MARENGO, OVEN STYLE

2 broiler-fryers
(2½ to 3 lbs. ea.),
cut up
2 c. water
½ tsp. salt
1 c. sifted all-
purpose flour
3 tbs. butter or
margarine
20 small white
onions, peeled
½ lb. mushrooms,
sliced

¼ c. fat or pure
vegetable oil
2 tbs. flour
1 tsp. salt
⅛ tsp. pepper
1 tsp. leaf rose-
mary, crumbled
½ tsp. leaf thyme,
crumbled
2 tomatoes, peeled,
seeded, and diced

Wash chicken; pat dry. Simmer wings, neck, and giblets in water with ½ teaspoon salt 30 minutes or until tender; drain; reserve broth; chop giblets very fine. Shake chicken pieces in 1 cup flour in paper or plastic bag a few at a time until well coated. Melt butter or margarine in large skillet; sauté onions 5 minutes or until well browned and almost tender; remove; reserve. Sauté mushrooms 5 minutes; remove; reserve. Add ¼ cup fat or oil to skillet; sauté chicken until golden on all sides. (If skillet is small, chicken may be sautéed in several batches.) Remove chicken; put in 2½-quart casserole. Pour off all but 2 tablespoons of fat from skillet; stir in 2 tablespoons flour, 1 teaspoon salt, pepper, rosemary, and thyme. Add 1 cup giblet broth; cook over medium heat, stirring constantly, until thickened; stir in giblets. Heat oven to 350° F. Add onions, mushrooms, and tomatoes to chicken in casserole; pour gravy over chicken; cover. Bake 50 to 60 minutes or until chicken is tender. Makes 8 servings.

OVEN-FRIED CHICKEN AND BUTTERMILK BISCUITS

½ c. flour	3 chicken legs and
1 tsp. salt	thighs*
¼ tsp. pepper	½ c. melted butter
1 tsp. paprika	or margarine
2 chicken breasts,*	2 c. biscuit mix
halved	⅔ c. buttermilk

Heat oven to 425° F. Combine flour, salt, pepper, and paprika in paper or plastic bag. Shake chicken, a few pieces at a time, in flour mixture to coat them. Pour melted butter or margarine into a baking pan large enough to hold chicken in single layer. Place chicken, skin side down, in pan. Bake 30 minutes. While chicken bakes, combine biscuit mix and milk; stir until well mixed. Turn dough out on floured board; knead 8 to 10 times. Roll out ½-inch thick. Cut with floured 2-inch cutter; place in baking pan that will fit in oven with chicken. When chicken has cooked 30 minutes, turn. Put biscuits in oven. Bake chicken and biscuits 15 minutes or until biscuits are lightly browned and chicken is tender. Makes 6 servings.

* Or use 2 broiler-fryers about 2 pounds each, cut up, in place of breasts, legs, and thighs.

COUNTRY CHICKEN PIE

2 broiler-fryers	1 c. light cream
(3 lbs. ea.),	¼ c. butter or
cut up	margarine
Water	2 c. biscuit mix
2 tsp. salt	⅔ c. milk
⅓ c. butter or	1 can (about 1 lb.)
margarine	diced carrots,
⅓ c. flour	drained
1½ tsp. salt	1 can (about 1 lb.)
¼ tsp. pepper	onions, drained
½ tsp. leaf thyme,	1 c. cooked, sliced
crumbled	celery
¼ tsp. leaf rosemary, crumbled	

Cook chicken in water to cover with 2 teaspoons salt 45 minutes or until tender. Drain and reserve stock. Add water to stock, if necessary, to make 5 cups. Remove chicken from bones; cut in large pieces. Melt ⅓ cup butter or margarine in large saucepan; stir in flour, 1½ teaspoons salt, pepper, thyme, and rosemary. Add 5 cups of reserved chicken stock and cream gradually. Cook over medium heat, stirring constantly, until thickened and bubbly; keep warm. Heat oven to 450° F. Cut ¼ cup butter or margarine into biscuit mix with pastry blender; stir in milk; beat 15 strokes (mixture will be soft). Turn dough out on floured board; knead several times; roll out; cut in strips. Add chicken, carrots, onions, and celery to warm sauce; heat until piping hot. Pour into shallow 2-quart casserole; arrange strips of biscuit dough in lattice on top. Bake 15 minutes or until sauce bubbles and strips are golden brown. Makes 8 servings.

CHICKEN TETRAZZINI

This recipe was created at the Caruso Restaurant in New York City in honor of the great Italian opera star Luisa Tetrazzini. She was not only the queen of coloraturas but also "an expert in the mysteries of the kitchen range, bake ovens, and chafing dish." Madame Tetrazzini loved to eat and became very plump. She wanted everyone to be healthy and happy and thought that 200 pounds was the right weight for everyone. She was especially fond of spaghetti and pancakes. She gave her recipe for pancakes to the chef of every hotel on her arrival and ate five of them every day.

1 roasting chicken
(3½ to 4 lbs.),
cut up
4 c. water
1 tsp. salt
½ lb. mushrooms,
sliced
3 tbs. butter or
margarine
2 tbs. flour
1 c. heavy cream
3 tbs. dry sherry
1 tsp. salt

Dash of pepper
Dash of ground
nutmeg
1 truffle, finely
chopped or
2 tbs. chopped,
pitted ripe olives
1 pkg. (8 oz.) thin
spaghetti, cooked
and drained
½ c. grated Par-
mesan cheese

Simmer chicken in water with 1 teaspoon salt about 1 hour or until tender. Remove chicken; reserve broth. Remove chicken from bones. Return bones to broth; simmer 30 minutes. Cool and skim off fat. Cut chicken meat into strips or cubes. You should have 2 cups. Sauté mushrooms in butter or margarine 5 minutes. Add flour; mix well. Add ½ cup chicken broth, cream, and sherry. Cook over low heat, stirring constantly, until sauce thickens. Add 1 teaspoon salt, pepper, nutmeg, and truffle or olives; mix well. Combine sauce, chicken, and drained spaghetti. Turn into 2-quart casserole. Sprinkle with Parmesan cheese. Bake at 350° F. for 30 minutes. Makes 6 servings.

CHICKEN BREASTS

CHICKEN IN WHITE WINE
(Suprêmes au Vin Blanc)

4 whole chicken
breasts
⅓ c. butter or
margarine
⅓ c. flour
1 c. canned chicken
broth

½ tsp. leaf rose-
mary, crumbled
½ tsp. salt
⅛ tsp. freshly
ground pepper
½ c. dry white wine

Skin and bone chicken breasts; cut each in half (each half or filet is a suprême). Melt ⅓ cup butter or margarine in large skillet. Dip suprêmes in flour; shake off excess. Sauté suprêmes in melted butter or margarine until golden brown on both sides; remove; keep warm. Pour broth into skillet; stir over medium heat until all brown bits are melted. Add rosemary to skillet with salt, pepper, and wine. Return suprêmes to skillet; lower heat; cover; simmer 5 minutes. Arrange suprêmes on platter. Serve pan juices in sauceboat.

Makes 4 servings. Serve with Duchess Potatoes (*page 297*), if desired.

CHICKEN TAHITIAN

3 chicken breasts,
split
⅓ c. fat or pure
vegetable oil
1 can (6 oz.) frozen
pineapple-orange
concentrate,
undiluted
¼ c. butter or
margarine

1 tsp. ground
ginger
1 tsp. soy sauce
1 avocado, peeled
and sliced
1 tbs. lime juice
6 c. hot, cooked rice
½ c. coarsely
chopped maca-
damia nuts

Sauté chicken in hot fat or oil, turning several times, until lightly browned; place in shallow baking pan in single layer. Heat oven to 350° F. Heat concentrate, butter or margarine, ginger, and soy sauce until blended; brush over chicken. Bake 35 to 40 minutes, basting every 15 minutes with fruit sauce, until chicken is glazed and tender. Brush avocado slices with lime juice. Arrange chicken and avocado on rice; sprinkle nuts over rice; serve with any remaining sauce. Makes 6 servings.

CHICKEN-IN-A-BLANKET

4 chicken breasts,
boned and cut in
half
3½ c. water
1 tsp. salt
5 whole pepper-
corns
½ tsp. rosemary,
crumbled
1 small onion,
sliced

4 tbs. melted
butter or
margarine
4 tbs. flour
2 tbs. lemon juice
1½ tsp. minced
onion
¾ tsp. salt
⅛ tsp. pepper
2 pkgs. refrigerated
crescent rolls
2 tbs. chopped
parsley

Simmer chicken breasts in water with 1 tea-spoon salt, peppercorns, rosemary, and sliced onion 25 to 35 minutes or until tender. Remove breasts from broth. Strain broth; skim off fat. Measure broth; add water, if neces-sary, to make 3 cups. Skin breasts. Combine butter or margarine and flour; add chicken broth. Simmer 3 minutes or until thickened. Add lemon juice, minced onion, ¾ teaspoon salt, and ⅛ teaspoon pepper. Remove from heat; reserve. Heat oven to 375° F. Open crescent rolls. Put 2 triangles together; pinch perforations to make a solid oblong piece of dough. Repeat with remaining rolls. Sprinkle parsley on each oblong of dough. Place chicken breast in center of each piece of dough; fold dough over; seal with water. Bake on cookie sheet, seam side down, about 15 minutes or until well browned. Reheat lemon-chicken gravy. Serve with chicken. Makes 8 servings.

SESAME CHICKEN

4 whole chicken breasts	¼ c. butter or margarine
½ lb. thinly sliced ham	2 tbs. melted butter or margarine
½ lb. sliced Swiss cheese	1 tbs. soy sauce
1 egg	½ c. canned chicken broth
1 tbs. water	2 tbs. sesame seeds
¾ c. packaged bread crumbs	

Skin and bone chicken breasts. For each, cut a thin strip of ham about 1-inch wide and 2 strips of Swiss cheese the same size. Fill chicken breasts with strips; press edges firmly together. Edges may be secured with pieces of wooden picks and strong white thread. Beat egg with water. Measure bread crumbs into pie plate. Dip chicken in egg, then in crumbs, coating well. Sauté chicken in ¼ cup butter or margarine until golden brown; place in baking dish. Heat oven to 350° F. Combine 2 tablespoons melted butter or margarine, soy sauce, and chicken broth; brush chicken with sauce; sprinkle with sesame seeds. Bake 35 to 40 minutes or until tender, basting with remaining sauce. Garnish with kumquats and pineapple, if desired. Makes 4 servings.

MOO GOO GAI PAN
(Chicken and Vegetables)

2 whole chicken breasts	1 can (3 to 4 oz.) sliced mushrooms
½ tsp. salt	2 tbs. sliced pimiento
⅛ tsp. pepper	2 tbs. finely chopped preserved ginger
1 tsp. cornstarch	
2 tbs. pure vegetable oil	
3 tbs. thinly sliced green onions	½ c. canned chicken broth
pkg. (10 oz.) frozen snow peas	1 tsp. cornstarch
	1 tbs. water

Skin and bone chicken breasts; slice them into 1x1x¼-inch pieces. Sprinkle chicken pieces with salt, pepper, and 1 teaspoon cornstarch; let stand a few minutes. Heat oil in skillet; add chicken, a small amount at a time; stir-fry until chicken has turned white all the way through. Chicken will be done, as small pieces cook quickly. Remove; repeat until all chicken has been cooked and removed from skillet. Add onions to skillet; stir-fry one minute. Add peas, mushrooms, pimiento, and ginger; stir rapidly until peas are crisp-tender. Add broth; heat to boiling. Stir 1 teaspoon cornstarch and water together until smooth. Stir quickly into liquid in skillet. Cook over medium heat until bubbly and clear. Add chicken; heat until piping hot. May be served with or over rice. Makes 6 servings.

CHICKEN DIVAN

2 chicken breasts, halved	2 tbs. flour
6 tbs. butter or margarine	½ tsp. salt
	¼ tsp. pepper
½ c. water	1 c. light cream
16 spears fresh or frozen asparagus	¼ c. dry white wine
	¼ c. grated Parmesan cheese
3 green onions, thinly sliced	

Skin and bone the chicken breasts. Brown in 3 tablespoons butter or margarine in skillet; add water; cover. Lower heat; cook slowly until tender. While chicken cooks, cook asparagus until barely tender in small amount of boiling, salted water; drain. Heat oven to 350° F. Melt remaining 3 tablespoons butter or margarine in small saucepan; add green onions; sauté about 2 minutes. Blend in flour, salt, and pepper. Stir in cream gradually, whipping constantly with wire whisk or fork to keep mixture smooth. Add wine; bring to boiling. Remove from heat. Add 2 tablespoons Parmesan cheese; stir until cheese melts. Arrange asparagus in four portions of four spears each in shallow, greased baking dish or in four individual baking dishes. Place a half chicken breast on each portion. Pour sauce over. Sprinkle with remaining cheese. Bake 15 minutes or until bubbly and slightly browned. Serve in individual dishes or transfer portions from large baking dish with broad spatula to heated luncheon plates. Makes 4 servings.

CHICKEN STEWS

CHICKEN STEW

2 broiler-fryers (2 lbs. ea.), cut up	12 small white onions, peeled
½ c. flour	½ tsp. leaf thyme, crumbled
½ tsp. salt	¼ tsp. leaf basil, crumbled
¼ tsp. pepper	
6 tbs. pure vegetable oil	¼ tsp. leaf marjoram, crumbled
½ c. diced celery	½ lb. mushrooms, sliced
½ c. diced carrots	
3 c. canned chicken broth	1 pkg. (10 oz.) frozen green peas
1 can (about 1 lb.) tomatoes	½ c. dry red wine
	2 tbs. flour
Chicken liver, finely chopped	Water

Shake chicken in paper or plastic bag with ½ cup flour, salt, and pepper. Heat oil in heavy kettle; sauté chicken until golden brown; remove; keep warm. Sauté celery and carrots in remaining oil until tender. Add chicken, broth, tomatoes, liver, onions, and herbs. Cover; simmer 45 minutes or until chicken is tender. Skim off fat. Add mushrooms, peas, and wine; cook 15 minutes or until vegetables are tender. Combine 2 tablespoons flour with enough water to make a smooth paste; stir into stew; cook until thickened. Makes 6 servings.

CREOLE CHICKEN

⅓ c. flour	1 can (1 lb. 13 oz.) tomatoes
1 tsp. salt	
Dash of pepper	1 bay leaf
2 broiler-fryers (2½ to 3 lbs. ea.), cut up	¼ tsp. leaf thyme, crumbled
	2 tbs. chopped parsley
2 tbs. fat or pure vegetable oil	1½ tsp. salt
1 c. chopped onion (1 large)	¼ tsp. pepper
	2 tsp. chili powder
½ c. chopped green pepper	1 c. diced celery
	1 c. rice
1 clove of garlic, mashed	1½ c. cooked green beans
2 c. water	

Combine flour, salt, and pepper in paper bag. Add chicken; shake with flour mixture until well coated. Brown chicken in fat or oil in kettle; remove. Sauté onion, green pepper, and garlic in remaining fat. Add water, tomatoes, and seasonings; mix well. Add chicken. Cover; simmer 30 to 40 minutes or until chicken is tender. Stir in celery and rice. Simmer 25 minutes or until rice is tender. Add water, if necessary, while rice is cooking. Add beans. Makes 6 servings.

COOKED CHICKEN

SOUTHERN DEVILED CHICKEN

¼ c. chopped onion (1 small)	1 tsp. Worcestershire sauce
3 tbs. butter or margarine	1 tbs. prepared mustard
¼ c. flour	4 c. diced, cooked chicken
2 envelopes instant chicken broth mix or 2 chicken-bouillon cubes	1 c. cooked vegetables
	1 pkg. corn bread mix
1 tsp. onion salt	
1½ c. milk	

Sauté onion in butter or margarine until soft; blend in flour, chicken broth mix or bouillon cubes, and onion salt. Stir in milk slowly; add Worcestershire sauce and mustard. Cook over medium heat, stirring constantly, until mixture thickens and boils 1 minute. Add chicken and vegetables; turn into 2½-quart casserole. Prepare corn bread mix according to package directions. Spoon corn bread mixture over chicken. (If your casserole is not large enough to take all the corn bread mixture, bake any remaining as muffins.) Bake at 400° F. for 25 to 30 minutes or until corn bread is golden brown and chicken mixture is bubbly. Makes 6 servings.

CHICKEN ORIENTAL

1 c. sliced onion (1 large)	1½ c. sliced celery
	2½ c. canned chicken broth
1 large green pepper, seeded and cut in strips	4 tbs. cornstarch
	⅛ tsp. pepper
4 tbs. butter or margarine	3 tbs. soy sauce
2 cans (3 to 4 oz. ea.) mushrooms	4 firm, ripe tomatoes, cut in wedges
3 c. cubed, cooked chicken	2 cans (3 oz. ea.) Chinese noodles

Sauté onion and green pepper in butter or margarine in skillet 3 minutes. Drain mushrooms, reserve liquid; add mushrooms and chicken to skillet. Cook over low heat about 10 minutes; add celery. Mix ¼ cup chicken broth with cornstarch to make a smooth paste. Add remaining chicken broth and reserved mushroom liquid to chicken mixture; cook until hot; stir in cornstarch mixture. Cook, stirring constantly, until sauce is bubbling and looks clear. Stir in pepper and soy sauce; add tomatoes. Cook slowly 5 to 10 minutes or until slightly thickened. Serve with Chinese noodles. Makes 8 servings.

CHICKEN PIE WITH CURRIED POTATOES

½ c. melted butter or margarine	1 can (3 to 4 oz.) sliced mush-
3 tbs. flour	rooms
½ tsp. seasoned salt	¾ c. cooked peas
½ tsp. leaf rose-mary, crumbled	½ pkg. (4 servings) instant mashed
1½ c. canned chicken broth	potatoes
½ c. light cream	1 egg, beaten
2 c. diced, cooked chicken	1 tsp. curry powder

Heat 3 tablespoons butter or margarine in saucepan; stir in flour, salt, and rosemary; gradually stir in chicken broth. Cook, stirring constantly, until mixture thickens. Stir in cream, chicken, mushrooms, and peas; spoon into baking dishes. Prepare potatoes according to package directions; beat in egg, curry, and 3 tablespoons melted butter or margarine. Spoon around edges of dishes; drizzle remaining butter or margarine over potatoes. Bake at 350° F. for 15 to 20 minutes or until potatoes are browned. Makes 6 servings.

CHICKEN AMANDINE

½ lb. mushrooms, sliced	1 tsp. salt
⅓ c. diced green pepper	Dash of pepper
	2 c. diced, cooked chicken
4 tbs. butter or margarine	3 tbs. dry sherry
⅓ c. flour	⅓ c. diced pimiento
2 c. canned chicken broth	½ c. blanched almonds, toasted
1 c. light cream	Patty shells or toast points
⅛ tsp. nutmeg	

Sauté mushrooms and green pepper in butter or margarine 5 minutes. Add flour; blend until smooth. Stir in chicken broth and cream slowly. Add nutmeg, salt, pepper, and chicken; simmer 5 minutes. Add sherry and pimiento; sprinkle with almonds. Garnish with additional pimiento, if desired. Serve in patty shells or on toast points. Makes 6 to 8 servings.

CHICKEN LIVERS

CHICKEN LIVERS MADEIRA

½ c. flour	3 tbs. butter or margarine
½ tsp. salt	
⅛ tsp. pepper	¼ c. Madeira
1 lb. chicken livers	1 c. heavy cream
	2 egg yolks

Combine flour, salt, and pepper in paper bag. Add livers; shake with flour mixture until well coated. Heat butter or margarine in skillet over medium heat; add chicken livers; sauté until well browned. Add Madeira; turn heat to low. Beat cream with egg yolks until blended; add to skillet. Stir constantly until bubbly and thickened. Makes 4 servings.

CHICKEN LIVERS GOURMET

1 lb. chicken livers	3 tbs. flour
⅓ c. butter or margarine	1 tsp. salt
	Dash of pepper
½ lb. mushrooms, sliced	2 c. canned chicken broth
1 small green pepper, seeded and sliced in short strips	1 bay leaf
	2 whole cloves
	2 tbs. chopped parsley
¼ c. thinly sliced onion (1 small)	

Pat livers dry with paper towels; cut in half. Sauté livers in half the butter or margarine until browned on all sides; remove from skillet. Add remaining butter or margarine to skillet. Sauté mushrooms, green pepper, and onion 5 minutes. Add flour, salt, and pepper; stir until smooth. Add chicken broth, stirring constantly. Add bay leaf, cloves, and sautéed chicken livers. Cover; simmer 15 minutes. Remove bay leaf and cloves. Sprinkle with parsley. Makes 6 servings.

CHICKEN LIVER SAUTÉ WITH GREEN RICE

¼ c. butter or margarine	½ tsp. leaf marjoram, crumbled
½ c. chopped onion (1 medium)	3 tbs. butter or margarine
¼ c. diced celery	1½ c. canned chicken broth
¼ c. blanched, sliced almonds	4 c. hot, cooked rice
2 pkgs. (8 oz. ea.) frozen chicken livers, thawed	¼ c. sliced, stuffed olives
½ c. flour	⅓ c. chopped parsley
1 tsp. seasoned salt	1 large tomato, cut in wedges

Melt ¼ cup butter or margarine in heavy saucepan. Sauté onion, celery, and almonds until vegetables are soft; keep warm. Shake chicken livers in paper bag with flour, salt, and marjoram; reserve remaining flour mixture. Melt 3 tablespoons butter or margarine in skillet; sauté chicken livers over medium heat until browned; remove; keep warm. Stir 2 teaspoons reserved flour mixture into skillet; add broth; stir to scrape up crusty flecks on bottom. Cook over low heat, stirring constantly, until thickened. Return chicken livers to skillet to heat through. Add hot rice, olives, and parsley to vegetables and almonds in saucepan; stir over low heat until hot; turn into serving dish. Top with chicken livers; garnish with tomato wedges. Serve with any remaining gravy. Makes 4 servings.

FRIED NOODLES WITH CHICKEN LIVERS

¾ lb. fine noodles	⅓ c. finely chopped onion
3 qts. boiling water	
1 tbs. salt	2 tbs. chopped parsley
3 tbs. pure vegetable oil	1½ tbs. cornstarch
1½ lbs. chicken livers	1½ c. canned chicken broth
4 tbs. butter or margarine	1 tbs. soy sauce
⅓ c. finely chopped celery	1 tsp. Worcestershire sauce

Cook noodles in boiling, salted water 10 minutes. Drain; rinse with cold water. Dry well on paper towels. Heat oil in 8-inch skillet; brown half the noodles, turning to brown both sides. Drain on paper towels. Place on hot platter. Repeat with remaining noodles. Quarter chicken livers; sauté in butter or margarine with celery and onion 5 minutes, stirring constantly. Add parsley, cornstarch dissolved in chicken broth, soy sauce, Worcestershire. Simmer until thickened. Serve on noodles. Makes 6 servings.

ROCK CORNISH HENS

ROAST ROCK CORNISH HENS

8 Rock Cornish hens (about 1 lb. ea.), thawed	Parsley sprigs
	1 tsp. leaf rosemary, crumbled
Lemon juice	½ c. butter or margarine
Salt	
Pepper	½ lb. bacon

Wash Rock Cornish hens; pat dry. Sprinkle cavities with lemon juice and salt and pepper. Put 1 or 2 sprigs of parsley, a pinch of crushed rosemary, and 1 tablespoon butter or margarine in each bird. Place, breast side up, in roasting pan. Cover breasts with bacon slices; roast at 425° F. 45 to 50 minutes or until fork-tender. Remove to heated platter and serve immediately. Garnish with apricot halves, stemmed cherries, and parsley, if desired. Serve with Pilaf (*page 274*), if desired. Makes 8 servings.

ROCK CORNISH HENS WITH CHIP STUFFING

½ lb. mushrooms, chopped	½ tsp. salt
	Dash of pepper
¼ c. butter or margarine	2 c. crushed potato chips
¾ c. finely chopped celery	2 c. small bread cubes (4 slices)
¼ c. chopped onion (1 small)	6 Rock Cornish game hens
½ tsp. leaf rosemary, crumbled	⅓ c. soft butter or margarine

Heat oven to 425° F. Sauté mushrooms in ¼ cup butter or margarine until tender; add celery and onion; sauté 3 minutes; remove from heat. Add rosemary, salt, pepper, potato chips, and bread cubes; mix well. Stuff hens with mixture; fasten with wooden picks or skewers; lace closed with string. Brush hens with ⅓ cup softened butter or margarine; wrap each hen in single piece of heavy aluminum foil; place hens on cookie sheet or in shallow pan. Roast 35 minutes. Open foil; brush hens with drippings; roast 25 minutes or until hens are golden brown. Prepare and serve with extra stuffing, if desired. Makes 6 servings.

Turkey

Kinds of Turkey

Ready-to-cook turkeys, trimmed, fully drawn, and with the giblets neatly packaged inside the breast cavity, are sold both fresh and frozen. They are available in sizes from 6 pounds all the way up to 24 pounds in oven-ready weight.

Frozen stuffed turkeys should be roasted while still solidly frozen, and this is a point to consider when purchasing them. However, it is safe to store them in a refrigerator overnight. (If this is done, the roasting time will be shorter.) Follow label directions on turkey *exactly* for roasting.

Fryer-roaster turkey is a young, delicately flavored small bird that tips the scale at 4 to 8 pounds, ready-to-cook weight. Fryer-roasters are available fresh or fresh-frozen; in some markets, 4- to 6-pound sizes may be purchased cut up, or by the piece. Fryer-roasters are delicious prepared by any basic cooking method.

Turkey breasts and *turkey legs* are available in many markets, both fresh and frozen.

Frozen boned turkey in roll or loaf shapes, some with gravy, may now be found in all parts of the country. These should be cooked as directed on the label. Frozen turkey slices in gravy are also available.

Smoked turkey is a specialty item, found mostly in gourmet departments. Many are ready to eat; others require further cooking. Follow label directions.

Buying

When buying turkeys under 12 pounds, allow ¾ to 1 pound *per serving* (ready-to-cook weight). When buying medium or heavy birds, 12 pounds and over, allow ½ to ¾ pound *per serving*. The actual number of servings depends on the quality of the turkey, correct cooking, and carving skill. The table below suggests the *number of servings*.

Ready-to-Cook Turkey (pounds)	Number of Servings
6 to 8	6 to 10
8 to 12	10 to 20
12 to 16	20 to 32
16 to 20	32 to 40
20 to 24	40 to 50

In most instances, large turkeys are more economical and excellent for use in future meals.

Storing

Fresh, ready-to-cook turkeys: Remove giblets and neck. Wrap turkey loosely in original wrapper, wax paper, or aluminum foil and refrigerate. Cook within 2 days.

Frozen, ready-to-cook turkeys: Store in freezer until ready to thaw for cooking.

Frozen stuffed turkeys: Follow the label directions exactly.

Thawing frozen turkey: The best way is to move it from freezer to refrigerator 3 days before cooking and let it thaw slowly. But if you can't do this, place it in a large pan on the counter at room temperature the night before you plan to cook it and let it thaw at room temperature overnight.

ROAST TURKEY

ROAST STUFFED TURKEY

To Stuff and Truss

Turkey should be stuffed just before roasting. Allow one cup large bread crumbs for each pound ready-to-cook weight. Pull the bread apart or cut it into cubes. When measuring, pile it lightly into the cup. Two regular-size slices of bread will give one cup of bread crumbs. Heat oven to 325° F. Rinse the bird with cold water; drain and pat dry with paper towels. Rub cavity with salt, if desired, though your stuffing may not need this extra salt and it is sometimes better to leave the cavity unsalted. Fill the neck (wishbone) cavity with stuffing and skewer neck skin to back. Tuck wing tips behind shoulder joints. Spoon stuffing into body cavity lightly; do not pack it. If opening has a band of skin across it, push drumsticks under it. Otherwise, close the openings by placing skewers across it and lacing closed with cord, then tie drumsticks securely to the tail.

To Roast

Place turkey on rack in shallow, open roasting pan, breast side up. Brush the skin with soft fat. If you are using a roast-meat thermometer, insert it so the bulb is in the center of the inside thigh muscle or in the thickest part of the breast meat. Be sure the bulb is not touching bone. Put the turkey in the pre-

heated oven and roast, using the chart below as a guide or follow directions that come with turkey. (Times are only approximate as differences in individual turkeys may require a slight increase or decrease in cooking time.) Baste or brush the turkey occasionally during roasting with pan drippings. When turkey is about two thirds done, cut cord or band of skin at drumsticks so heat can reach inside of thighs.

To test for doneness when not using a meat thermometer, about 20 minutes before roasting time is up, press the thick part of the drumstick between fingers protected with paper towels. Meat should feel very soft. Move the drumstick up and down. It should move easily or twist out of joint. Remove the turkey to a heated platter. Let bird rest 20 minutes before carving.

Timetable for Roasting Turkey

Purchased Ready-to-cook Weight	Oven Temperature	Internal Temperature	Approximate Time (hours)
6 to 8 lbs.	325° F.	185° F.	3 to 3½
8 to 12 lbs.	325° F.	185° F.	3½ to 4
12 to 16 lbs.	325° F.	185° F.	4½ to 5½
16 to 20 lbs.	325° F.	185° F.	5½ to 6½
20 to 24 lbs.	325° F.	185° F.	6½ to 7

TURKEY ROASTED IN FOIL

Any size turkey may be roasted in foil. It is particularly good when roasting the large (16 to 24 pounds) birds. Two advantages of the method are the shorter cooking time and the fact that there is no spattering in the oven. There are two ways to do it—wrapping or tenting. For the wrapping method, heat the oven to 450° F. Stuff and truss the turkey exactly as in Roast Stuffed Turkey. Brush skin with soft fat. Use heavy, wide aluminum foil. Place the turkey, breast side up, in center of piece of foil 12 inches longer than the bird. If one 18-inch width is not large enough,

put two pieces together with a double fold pressed flat to make leakproof joining. To prevent puncture, wrap small pieces of foil around drumsticks and wings. Bring ends of foil together over breast of turkey. Fasten tightly, using drugstore fold. Bring sides up high enough to prevent drippings from escaping into pan. Package should not be airtight. Put the turkey in shallow, open roasting pan. Roast to within 30 to 40 minutes of total time in chart below. Open foil carefully and fold back from bird to edges of pan. If using a meat thermometer, insert it now in center of inside thigh muscle or thickest part of breast. Continue roasting turkey until done.

Purchased Ready-to-cook Weight	Oven Temperature	Internal Temperature	Approximate Time (hours)
6 to 8 lbs.	450° F.	185° F.	1½ to 2
8 to 12 lbs.	450° F.	185° F.	2 to 2½
12 to 16 lbs.	450° F.	185° F.	2½ to 3
16 to 20 lbs.	450° F.	185° F.	3 to 3½
20 to 24 lbs.	450° F.	185° F.	3½ to 4

The *tenting method* is simple. Heat the oven to 325° F. Stuff and truss the turkey as above. Tear off a piece of aluminum foil four to five inches longer than the turkey and crease it lengthwise through the center. Rub the turkey with soft fat and place it on a rack in a shallow, open roasting pan. Place the foil, tent style, over the turkey. Pinch the foil lightly at the drumsticks and breasts to anchor it. If the legs or breast begin to brown too rapidly, press the foil tent down over these parts to prevent overbrowning. Roast according to chart for Roast Stuffed Turkey on page 216.

For directions for making Pan Gravy, see *page 201*.

To Carve Chicken or Turkey

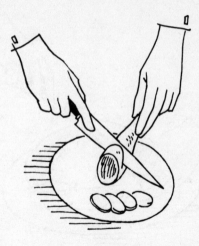

1. To remove leg (drumstick and thigh): hold the drumstick firmly with fingers, pulling gently away from turkey body. At the same time cut through skin between leg and body. Continue as follows:

2. Press leg away from body with flat side of knife. Then cut through joint joining leg to backbone and skin on the back. Hold leg on service plate with drumstick at a convenient angle to plate. Separate drumstick and thigh by cutting down through the joint to the plate.

3. Slice drumstick meat. Hold drumstick upright at a convenient angle to plate and cut down, turning drumstick to get uniform slices. Drumsticks and thighs from smaller turkeys are usually served without slicing.

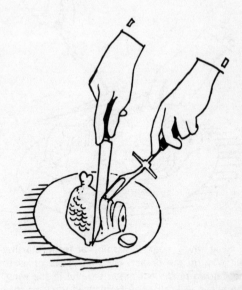

4. Slice thigh meat. Hold thigh firmly on plate with a fork. Cut slices of meat parallel to the bone.

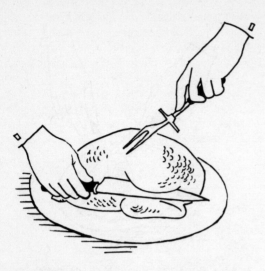

5. Cut into white meat parallel to wing. Make a cut deep into the breast to the body frame parallel to and as close to the wing as possible.

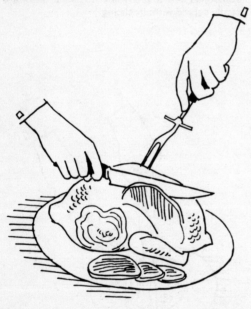

6. Slice white meat. Beginning at front, starting half way up the breast, cut thin slices of white meat down to the cut made parallel to the wing. The slices will fall away from the turkey as they are cut to this line. Continue carving until enough meat has been carved for first servings. Additional turkey may be carved as needed.

BROILED TURKEY

Split a 4- to 6-pound turkey in half lengthwise. Follow range directions for using broiler.

· Fold wing tips onto back (cut side).

· Place turkey in broiler pan (do not use the rack) or any shallow pan, skin side down. Turkey should fill the pan, in one layer, without crowding.

· Brush well with melted fat or oil. Season each half with 1 teaspoon salt, ½ teaspoon sugar; sprinkle with pepper.

· Place pan in broiler about 9 inches from heat, regulating the distance or the heat so that surface of turkey *just begins* to brown after 20 minutes of cooking. Broil slowly until nicely browned, about 40 minutes.

· Turn skin side up. Baste with pan drippings, and additional fat if necessary. Continue broiling until turkey is brown, crisp, and well-done, 40 to 50 minutes. Baste with pan drippings or fat several times during broiling to brown and cook evenly. Total cooking time: 1¼ to 1½ hours.

· To test doneness: The drumstick twists easily in the thigh joint, and breast meat near shoulder joint is fork-tender.

· Divide halves into quarters for serving. Serve on heated platter.

FRIED TURKEY

Select a whole, 4- to 6-pound turkey, cut up to yield 2 drumsticks, 2 thighs, 4 breast pieces, 2 wings, 3 back pieces, neck, giblets. Or, select by the piece, for choice of favorite parts.

PANFRIED TURKEY

· For each 5 pounds of cut-up turkey blend together ¾ cup flour, 1 teaspoon paprika, 4 teaspoons salt, and ½ teaspoon pepper in a bag. Shake turkey, 2 or 3 pieces at a time, in flour mixture in bag to coat evenly. Save any leftover mixture for gravy.

· Heat ½ inch of fat or oil in a heavy skillet until a drop of water just sizzles.

· Start browning meaty pieces first, slipping less meaty pieces in between as turkey browns.

· Turn as necessary with kitchen tongs or two spoons to brown and cook evenly.

· When pieces are *lightly* and *evenly* browned, about 20 minutes, reduce heat; add 2 tablespoons water; cover tightly.

• Cook slowly until thickest pieces are fork-tender, 45 to 60 minutes. Turn pieces 2 or 3 times to assure even cooking and browning. Uncover pan the last 10 minutes of frying to recrisp skin. Total cooking time: 1 to 1¼ hours.

• When done, drain pieces on absorbent paper, if desired, then arrange on heated platter. Pan gravy (*page 201*) may be prepared with pan drippings.

OVEN FRIED TURKEY

• Heat oven to 350° F. Coat turkey with seasoned flour (see Panfried Turkey). Melt 1 cup butter or margarine (for 5 pounds of turkey) in a shallow baking pan in oven.

• Place coated pieces in pan; turn to coat both sides with the butter or margarine, then leave skin side down. Turkey should fill pan, one layer deep, without crowding.

• Bake turkey 45 minutes. Turn turkey skin side up and bake until fork-tender, about 45 minutes. Total cooking time: about 1½ hours.

SAUTÉED TURKEY, CURRY GRAVY

1 turkey (6 to 8 lbs.), cut up	Water
1 c. flour	2 tbs. butter or margarine
1 tbs. paprika	2 tbs. flour
2 tsp. salt	1 tbs. curry powder
½ tsp. pepper	½ c. light cream
Fat or pure vegetable oil	

Cook back, neck, wing tips, and giblets from turkey in water to cover 45 minutes. Strain and reserve broth. Combine 1 cup flour, paprika, salt, and pepper in large paper bag. Shake turkey pieces, a few at a time, in mixture to coat well. Heat ¼ inch of fat or oil in heavy skillet. (For larger turkey you may need to use 2 skillets. If so, put fat in each.) Brown turkey pieces in hot fat, turning to brown all sides evenly. When all pieces are browned, reduce heat; add 1 tablespoon water to each skillet. Cover; cook slowly 50 to 60 minutes or until turkey is fork-tender. Turn pieces 2 or 3 times so they cook evenly. Uncover skillet for last 10 minutes of cooking to crisp skin. Remove turkey to heated platter; keep warm.

Pour all fat from pan, retaining any brown bits in pan. Melt butter or margarine in pan; blend in 2 tablespoons flour and curry powder; cook 1 to 2 minutes. Stir in 2 cups broth from giblets. Cook, stirring constantly, until gravy comes to boiling and is thickened. Boil 1 minute. Stir in cream; heat through. Serve with turkey. Makes 6 servings.

COOKED TURKEY

SAVORY TURKEY HASH

2 cans (3 to 4 oz. ea.) chopped mushrooms	2 tsp. salt
	½ tsp. pepper
	⅓ c. butter or margarine
4 c. cut-up, cooked turkey	2 tbs. flour
	½ tsp. salt
4 c. cut-up, pared potatoes	⅛ tsp. pepper
1 large onion, cut up	¼ tsp. poultry seasoning
1 green pepper, seeded and cut up	1 c. canned chicken broth
1 tsp. poultry seasoning	1 c. milk

Drain mushrooms; measure and reserve 4 tablespoons; discard liquid. Put remaining mushrooms, turkey, potatoes, onion and green pepper through food chopper using medium blade. Stir in 1 teaspoon poultry seasoning, 2 teaspoons salt, and ½ teaspoon pepper. Form mixture into 16 patties. Heat butter or margarine in large skillet (or use 2 skillets). Cook patties over low heat about 10 minutes or until potatoes are cooked and patties are crusty on bottom. Turn and brown second side. Remove to heated platter; keep warm. Blend flour into fat remaining in skillet; add ½ teaspoon salt, ⅛ teaspoon pepper, and ¼ teaspoon poultry seasoning. Stir in chicken broth and milk slowly. Cook over medium heat, stirring constantly, until thickened and bubbly. Reduce heat; add reserved mushrooms; simmer 2 to 3 minutes. Serve sauce over patties. Makes 8 servings.

Skillet Hash: Prepare hash mixture (as above). Heat butter or margarine in large skillet with heat-proof handle. Place hash in skillet; press to cover bottom completely. Cook covered, about 15 minutes or until brown on bottom. Uncover; broil about 3 minutes or until top is browned. Loosen edges with spatula; turn one half onto other half. Turn out on serving platter. To make sauce, melt 2 tablespoons butter or margarine in medium-size saucepan and proceed as in Savory Turkey Hash.

Baked Hash: Prepare hash mixture (*page 219*). Turn into buttered, 2-quart shallow baking dish. Sprinkle with ½ cup grated Cheddar cheese, if desired. Bake at 350° F. for 30 minutes or until nicely browned. Prepare sauce as in Skillet Hash.

TURKEY FAR EAST

½ c. finely chopped onion (1 medium)	8 whole cardamom seeds
2 tbs. butter or margarine	1 tbs. whole coriander
2 tbs. quick-cooking tapioca	1 tsp. whole peppercorns
½ tsp. salt	2 medium-size oranges
½ tsp. ground cinnamon	3 c. diced, cooked turkey
½ tsp. ground ginger	1 large apple, pared, cored, and diced
⅛ tsp. ground cloves	Hot, cooked rice
2½ c. canned chicken broth	

Sauté onion in butter or margarine in large skillet until tender but not browned. Combine tapioca, salt, cinnamon, ginger, and cloves; add to skillet. Add broth and whole spices tied in cheesecloth. Bring to boiling; simmer 15 minutes; remove spice bag. Peel and section oranges, being careful to save all juice; stir into spice mixture; add turkey and apple; simmer 10 minutes longer. Serve over hot, cooked rice. Makes 4 to 6 servings.

HASHED CREAMED TURKEY

1 tbs. butter or margarine	½ c. heavy cream
1 tbs. flour	2 egg yolks, slightly beaten
1 tsp. minced onion	¼ c. dry sherry
Dash of ground nutmeg	2 c. diced cooked turkey
1 tsp. salt	3 tbs. chopped parsley
⅛ tps. pepper	
½ c. milk	

Melt butter or margarine in saucepan; blend in flour, onion, nutmeg, salt, and pepper. Stir in milk and cream. Cook over medium heat until thickened and bubbly. Blend half of hot mixture into egg yolks; stir into mixture in saucepan. Add sherry, turkey, and parsley. Heat over low heat until mixture is thoroughly hot. Serve over buttered hot toast, if desired. Makes 4 servings.

TURKEY MACARONI CASSEROLE

3 tbs. butter or margarine	Canned chicken broth
4 tbs. flour	1½ c. milk
1 tsp. salt	2 c. diced, cooked turkey
1 tsp. dry mustard	
½ tsp. paprika	2 c. cooked macaroni shells
⅛ tsp. pepper	
Dash of cayenne	¼ c. sliced, pitted ripe olives
1 tsp. Worcestershire sauce	
Dash of hot-pepper sauce	4 slices (4 oz.) process American cheese
1 can (3 to 4 oz.) sliced mushrooms	

Melt butter or margarine in saucepan; blend in flour, seasonings, Worcestershire sauce, and hot-pepper sauce. Drain and reserve mushrooms; measure liquid; add sufficient chicken broth to make 1½ cups; gradually stir into flour mixture; add milk. Cook over medium heat, stirring constantly, until mixture thickens and comes to boiling; remove from heat. Add turkey, macaroni, olives, and reserved mushrooms; turn half the mixture into greased 1½-quart casserole; dice and add two slices of cheese; top with remaining macaroni mixture. Cut remaining cheese slices into triangles; arrange in pattern on top of casserole. Bake at 425° F. for 15 to 20 minutes or until browned and bubbly. Makes 6 servings.

GLAZED STUFFED TURKEY SLICES

½ pkg. (4 servings) instant mashed potatoes or 2 c. leftover mashed potatoes	4 tbs. butter or margarine
	½ c. chopped onion (1 medium)
1 egg, slightly beaten	½ c. chopped celery
½ c. packaged herb-seasoned bread stuffing	8 to 10 large slices of cooked turkey
¼ c. chopped parsley	½ c. canned chicken broth
½ tsp. salt	½ c. canned whole cranberry sauce
Dash of pepper	¼ c. sugar

Prepare mashed potatoes according to package directions; beat in egg. Add bread stuffing, parsley, salt, and pepper. Melt butter or margarine in small skillet; sauté onion and celery until tender; add to potato mixture. Spread stuffing on 4 or 5 large turkey slices; place in shallow baking dish with broth; top with remaining turkey slices; cover. Bake at 425° F. for 10 to 15 minutes to heat thoroughly. Remove from oven; uncover. Combine cranberry sauce and sugar; spoon onto top of turkey slices. Broil 2 to 3 minutes to glaze. Makes 6 servings.

TURKEY OYSTER SCALLOP

1 tbs. instant minced onion	Canned chicken broth
2 tbs. minced celery	¾ c. milk
3 tbs. butter or margarine	2 c. diced, cooked turkey
3 tbs. flour	¼ c. packaged bread crumbs
½ tsp. leaf marjoram, crumbled	2 tbs. melted butter or margarine
½ tsp. salt	2 tbs. grated Romano or Parmesan cheese
Dash of pepper	
½ tsp. Worcestershire sauce	
1 can (12 oz.) or 2 cans (7 oz. ea.) frozen oysters, thawed	

Sauté onion and celery in butter or margarine in saucepan until tender but not browned. Blend in flour, marjoram, salt, pepper, and Worcestershire sauce. Drain oysters; reserve and measure liquid; add sufficient broth to make ¾ cup; stir into flour mixture; add milk. Cook over medium heat, stirring constantly, until mixture thickens and comes to boiling. Add oysters and turkey. Turn into greased 1-quart casserole. Combine bread crumbs, melted butter or margarine, and cheese; sprinkle over turkey mixture. Bake at 350° F. for 20 to 25 minutes or until crumbs are browned. Makes 4 servings.

TURKEY AND AVOCADO NEWBURG

4 tbs. butter or margarine	1½ c. canned chicken broth
4 tbs. flour	1 tbs. lemon juice
1 tsp. salt	3 tbs. dry sherry
Dash of ground nutmeg	2 c. diced, cooked turkey
Dash of cayenne	1 medium-size avocado, peeled
1 egg yolk, slightly beaten	Patty shells or toast points

Melt butter or margarine in medium-size saucepan; blend in flour and seasonings. Combine egg yolk and broth; add to flour mixture gradually. Cook over medium heat, stirring constantly, until mixture thickens and comes to boiling. Carefully stir in lemon juice, sherry, and turkey. Just before serving, scoop out avocado with melon-ball cutter; dice remaining avocado. Add avocado to sauce; heat through. Serve in patty shells or on toast points. Makes 4 servings.

TURKEY STUFFED ONIONS

6 large red Italian onions or Spanish onions	1 egg, slightly beaten
Salt	½ c. herb-seasoned bread stuffing
2 slices bacon, diced	2 tbs. water
1 c. finely minced, cooked turkey	1 tsp. salt
	Dash of pepper

Peel onions; cut slice off tops. Parboil onions in boiling, salted water 20 to 30 minutes or until tender. Cut out centers to make shells about ½-inch thick; sprinkle insides with salt. Chop enough of centers to make ½ cup. Fry bacon; set aside. Sauté chopped onion in bacon fat until lightly browned. Combine minced turkey, egg, bread stuffing, water, salt, pepper, sautéed onion, and diced bacon. Stuff onions; place in shallow baking dish with small amount of water. Bake at 375° F. for 30 minutes or until lightly browned. Makes 6 servings.

HOT TURKEY SALAD

1½ c. diced or slivered, cooked turkey	2 tbs. lemon juice
1 c. diced celery	2 tsp. minced onion
½ c. chopped walnuts	½ tsp. salt
¼ c. chopped watercress	Dash of pepper
1 pimiento, chopped	½ c. mayonnaise or salad dressing
	¼ c. milk
	2 tbs. grated Parmesan cheese

Combine all ingredients except cheese; spoon into 4 individual baking dishes or one 9-inch pie plate; sprinkle with cheese. Bake at 450° F. for 15 minutes, or until lightly browned. Serve hot. Makes 4 servings.

CHINESE TURKEY PIE IN ALMOND CRUST

2½ c. canned chicken broth
1 c. slivered celery
2 tbs. cornstarch
2 tbs. soy sauce
¼ c. water
½ tsp. ground ginger
½ tsp. salt
Dash of pepper
2 c. diced, cooked turkey

1 can (1 lb., 4 oz.) pineapple chunks, drained
1 c. cooked small white onions
¼ c. sliced water chestnuts
⅓ c. finely chopped or ground blanched almonds
½ pkg. pie crust mix

Heat broth to boiling in saucepan; add celery; simmer about 5 to 8 minutes or until just tender. Combine cornstarch, soy sauce, water, ginger, salt, and pepper; stir into hot mixture; cook, stirring constantly, until clear and slightly thickened. Add turkey, pineapple, onions, and water chestnuts; heat thoroughly. Turn into 1½-quart casserole. Add almonds to pie crust mix; prepare mix according to package directions. Roll to fit top of casserole; cut vents in pastry to allow steam to escape during baking; place over hot turkey mixture. Bake at 425° F. for 20 to 25 minutes or until crust is browned. Makes 4 servings.

TURKEY AMANDINE
(Pictured opposite page 52)

3 pkgs. corn bread mix
1 lb. mushrooms, sliced
6 tbs. butter or margarine
¾ c. flour
3 tsp. salt
¼ tsp. pepper

½ tsp. leaf thyme, crumbled
2 qts. turkey broth* or canned chicken broth
5 c. diced, cooked turkey
¾ c. dry sherry
1 c. blanched almonds, toasted

Prepare corn bread according to package directions. Sauté mushrooms in butter or margarine 5 minutes or until tender. Add flour, salt, pepper, and thyme; mix well. Gradually add turkey or chicken broth. Cook until sauce thickens and simmers 5 minutes, stirring constantly. Add turkey and sherry; heat well. Taste for seasoning, adding salt and pepper as needed. Dish may be prepared to this point and frozen. Thaw and reheat. Add almonds. Serve on squares of corn bread. Makes 3 quarts or 20 servings.
* To make turkey broth, cook turkey bones and neck in 3 quarts water with 1 sliced onion, 2 stalks celery, 1 carrot, 2 teaspoons salt, and 5 peppercorns. Cover; simmer 1½ hours. Strain. Skim off fat.

Duckling and Goose

Buying Duckling:

· Ducklings may be purchased whole, or cut up and packaged. They usually weigh about 5 pounds and are available fresh, but more often are frozen.

To Thaw Duckling:

Thaw in original wrapper. Thaw in refrigerator 24 to 36 hours. Or, thaw at room temperature for about 12 to 18 hours. Cook immediately after thawing.

ROAST DUCKLING

· Duckling may be roasted stuffed or unstuffed.
· Prepare for roasting; stuff and truss according to directions for roasting chicken (*page 200*).
· Duckling may be roasted by one of the following methods:

Roast ducking, breast side up, on rack in shallow pan at 325° F. about 2 to 2½ hours.

For a very crisp skin and very well-done meat, increase oven heat to 425° F. for the last 15 minutes of roasting.

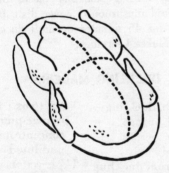

One duckling makes 4 servings, all of which are dark meat. The easiest way to portion it is to use poultry shears.

Cut duckling in half lengthwise through the breast, then continue cutting along the backbone. Cut duckling crosswise just under the ribs. Duckling may also be carved with a steak knife and fork. Remove leg and thigh from each side as in carving roast turkey **(page 217)**. Cut breast meat along ridge of breast bone and lift full half of breast meat from the bone. Serve a wing with the breast meat, if desired.

DUCKLING WITH ORANGE SAUCE
(Caneton à l'Orange)

5 to 6 lb. duckling	3 c. water
1 carrot, pared and chopped	4 tbs. sugar
¼ c. chopped onion (1 small)	¼ c. vinegar
2 tbs. pure vegetable oil	¼ c. dry white wine
1 tsp. salt	3 tbs. cornstarch
4 c. water	1 to 2 tbs. Grand Marnier
3 navel oranges	Watercress

Remove giblets from duckling and reserve. Place duckling on rack in shallow roasting pan. Roast, uncovered, at 450° F. for 15 minutes or until lightly browned. Pour off fat from pan. Lower heat to 350° F.; roast duckling about 1 to 1½ hours longer or until done. (When done, the juices that appear when duckling is pierced with a fork will be colorless.) While duckling roasts, sauté carrot, onion, and giblets in oil until browned. Pour off fat; add salt and 4 cups water. Simmer 1 to 1½ hours or until liquid is reduced to 2 cups; strain and reserve. Cut off just the orange part of skin of 2 oranges in thin strips with vegetable parer. Cut strips into thin slivers. Cook slivers in 3 cups water in saucepan 20 minutes; drain. Remove all white membrane from the 2 oranges; section oranges. Cut third orange into thin slices; cut slices in half; save for garnish. Cook sugar and vinegar slowly until liquid is golden brown and reduced to 2 tablespoons. Remove finished duckling from pan. (If there are any brown drippings in pan, pour off all fat and deglaze pan with a little wine; pour liquid into reserved duckling stock.) Blend wine and cornstarch until smooth in saucepan; add duckling stock and sugar-vinegar mixture. Cook over low heat, stirring constantly, until bubbly and thickened. Add orange slivers and Grand Marnier. Taste and correct seasonings. Put duckling on a heated platter; arrange some orange sections over duckling; heat remainder in sauce. Spoon part of sauce over duckling; garnish with orange slices and watercress. Serve remaining sauce with each serving. Makes 6 servings.

IMPERIAL DUCK

4 to 5 lb. duckling	3 tbs. sugar
1 tbs. honey	¼ c. wine vinegar
1 tsp. soy sauce	1 tbs. soy sauce
2 tbs. pure vege-	1 tbs. cornstarch
table oil	2 tbs. water
1 c. sliced celery	1 can (11 oz.)
¼ c. sliced onion	mandarin
(1 small)	oranges, drained
¼ c. sliced water	2 tbs. chopped
chestnuts	parsley
1 c. canned chicken	¼ c. blanched
broth	almonds, toasted

Place duck, breast side up, on rack in shallow roasting pan. Roast 2½ to 3 hours at 325° F. About ½ hour before duck is done, rub skin well with mixture of honey and 1 teaspoon soy sauce. Increase heat to 400° F. Continue to roast until duck is golden brown. If leg can be moved up and down easily, duck is done. Duck may be roasted day before and reheated in sauce. Quarter duck; keep warm. Heat oil in skillet; quickly stir-fry celery, onion, and water chestnuts for 2 minutes. Add chicken broth, sugar, vinegar, and 1 tablespoon soy sauce. Stir cornstarch and water together until smooth; stir into liquid in skillet. Cook over medium heat until bubbly and clear. Return pieces of duckling to skillet; add mandarin oranges; cover; heat until piping hot; add parsley. Transfer to serving dish; sprinkle with almonds. Makes 4 servings.

ROAST DUCKLING WITH PEACH SAUCE

4 to 5 lb. duckling,	½ c. orange juice
quartered	1 tbs. lemon juice
1 c. water	2 pkgs. (10 oz. ea.)
⅓ c. sugar	frozen peach
3 tbs. cornstarch	slices, slightly
½ tsp. salt	thawed
2 tsp. grated orange	
rind	

Place duckling on rack in roasting pan. Roast at 325° F. for 2½ hours or until tender. Transfer duck to platter; keep warm. Pour off all fat from roasting pan. Add 1 cup water to pan; heat and stir to dissolve all brown particles; reserve. Combine sugar, cornstarch, salt, and orange rind in saucepan; gradually stir in stock from roasting pan, and orange

and lemon juices. Add peaches. Cook over medium heat, stirring constantly, until mixture thickens and comes to boiling. Serve warm over duck. Makes 4 servings.

CASSEROLE OF ORIENTAL DUCK

4 to 5 lb. duckling,	½ tsp. ground
cut up	cinnamon
Flour	½ tsp. ground
2 tbs. pure vege-	nutmeg
table oil	¼ tsp. ground
¾ c. water	cloves
1 tbs. cornstarch	1 large clove of
1½ tsp. salt	garlic, mashed
¼ tsp. pepper	1¾ c. pineapple
1 tbs. brown sugar	juice
½ tsp. ground	3 tbs. lemon juice
allspice	1 can (3 to 4 oz.)
½ tsp. ground	mushroom
ginger	crowns

Coat duckling pieces lightly with flour; sauté in oil until golden; transfer to baking pan; add water; cover. Bake at 350° F. for 1 hour. Combine cornstarch, salt, pepper, brown sugar, spices, and garlic in saucepan; stir in pineapple juice. Cook over medium heat, stirring constantly, until thickened; remove from heat; stir in lemon juice. Place duckling in shallow casserole; pour sauce over; let stand 2 hours, turning duckling pieces once or twice. Add mushrooms; cover dish. Bake at 350° F. for 45 minutes or until duckling is tender. Makes 4 servings.

ROAST DUCKLING MADEIRA

4 to 5 lb. duckling	1 can (6 oz.) frozen
1 navel orange	orange-pineapple
Parsley	concentrate,
Bay leaf	undiluted
Liver from duckling	1¼ c. water
2 tbs. butter or	½ c. currant jelly
margarine	1 tbs. cornstarch
	½ c. dry Madeira

Heat oven to 425° F. Place duckling on rack in roasting pan. Shred rind from orange, being careful not to include any white; reserve for sauce. Cut orange into quarters; put in cavity of duckling with handful of parsley and a bay leaf. Roast duckling 1½ to 2 hours or until golden brown. Sauté duckling liver in butter or margarine in skillet until brown; remove; chop and reserve. Pour orange-pineapple concentrate and 1 cup water into skillet. Cook over medium heat, stirring constantly, until all brown bits are blended with juice. Add currant jelly; heat until melted. Mix cornstarch and ¼ cup water; stir into jelly mixture. Cook, stirring constantly, until thickened and bubbly. Add wine and reserved liver and orange rind; keep warm. Remove duckling to heated platter; spoon some sauce over duckling. Serve remainder of sauce in sauceboat. Makes 4 servings.

GOOSE

Goose is now available in many markets the year round, frozen and ready-to-cook. At Christmastime it may often be bought fresh on order.

Goose, like duck, is fatty. Remove as much fat as possible before cooking, both from inside the bird and from under the skin.

To thaw frozen goose: Follow directions for thawing frozen turkey (*page 215*).

To roast goose: Prepare for roasting, stuff and truss according to directions for roasting chicken (*page 200*). Do *not* rub outside with butter or margarine.

Goose may be roasted stuffed or unstuffed. Place goose on rack in a shallow open pan. Follow roasting chart.

Timetable for Roasting Goose

Because of the variation among geese, allow an extra half hour in case more cooking is needed—especially if the meal is planned for a set time.

Purchased Ready-to-Cook Weight	Oven Temp.	Approximate Time hours
4 to 6 lbs.	325° F.	2¾ to 3
6 to 8 lbs.	325° F.	3 to 3½
8 to 10 lbs.	325° F.	3½ to 3¾
10 to 12 lbs.	325° F.	3¾ to 4¼
12 to 14 lbs.	325° F.	4 to 4¾

Game Birds

QUAIL

Braising is a good way to cook these small birds since they tend to be dry unless kept moist during cooking period. The full, delicate flavor is preserved by care in browning and simmering the bird.

BRAISED QUAIL WITH GRAPES

6 quail
½ c. flour
1 tsp. salt
¼ tsp. pepper
¼ c. butter or
 margarine
1¼ c. canned
 chicken broth
1 tsp. chopped
 parsley

⅛ tsp. leaf thyme
 crumbled
1 bay leaf
Dash of pepper
1 tsp. slivered
 orange rind
1 c. seedless green
 grapes, halved
6 slices buttered
 toast

Coat quail lightly with combined flour, salt, and ¼ tsp. pepper; brown in butter or margarine in large skillet; remove. Combine chicken broth, parsley, thyme, bay leaf, and dash of pepper; pour into skillet. Cover; simmer sauce 10 minutes; remove bay leaf. Add browned quail; cover; simmer 15 minutes. Add orange rind and grapes; simmer 5 minutes longer or until quail are tender. Place a quail on each toast slice. Serve with sauce. Garnish with grapes and orange slices, if desired. Makes 6 servings.

PARTRIDGE

The flavor of partridge, like quail, is greatly enhanced by the moist cooking method. These birds do not have the natural fat covering that water birds have, so it is necessary to keep the meat moist by cooking with liquid.

PARTRIDGE PIE

3 partridge, cut in
 serving-size pieces
½ c. flour
1 tsp. salt
¼ tsp. pepper
2 tbs. butter or
 margarine
½ lb mushrooms,
 sliced
½ c. chopped
 onion (1
 medium)

½ c. diced celery
2 c. canned chicken
 broth
½ tsp. salt
Dash of pepper
½ lb. cooked ham,
 diced
1½ tbs. flour
3 tbs. water
Pastry for 1-crust
 pie (*page 406*)

Coat partridge pieces with combined ½ cup flour, 1 teaspoon salt, and ¼ teaspoon pepper; brown in butter or margarine in skillet; remove partridge. Sauté mushrooms and onion in remaining fat 5 minutes. Return partridge to skillet; add celery, chicken broth, ½ teaspoon salt, and dash of pepper. Cover; simmer 10 minutes. Place partridge pieces and ham in 2-quart casserole. Mix 1½ tablespoons flour and 3 tablespoons water to a smooth paste; stir into mixture in skillet; cook until thickened; pour into casserole. Roll out pastry; fit over casserole; flute edge; cut vents to allow steam to escape. Bake at 350° F. for 40 to 50 minutes or until pastry is browned. Makes 6 servings.

WILD DUCK

Wild duck has a pleasant gamey flavor, but the flavor can be ruined by overcooking. The best method of cooking is with high heat for a short time. The meat should be juicy and just a little pink.

ROAST WILD DUCK WITH APRICOT STUFFING

3 wild ducks (about
  1½ lbs. ea.)
¾ c. chopped onion
1½ c. diced celery
3 tbs. butter or
  margarine
1¼ c. toasted bread
  cubes
⅓ c. finely chopped
  dried apricots

1 tbs. brandy
½ tsp. salt
Dash of pepper
¾ c. dry red
  wine
⅓ c. water
2 tsp. cornstarch
1 tbs. cold water

Heat oven to 450° F. Wash and dry ducks thoroughly; salt insides. Sauté onion and celery in butter or margarine 5 minutes; combine with toasted bread cubes and apricots. Sprinkle with brandy, salt, and pepper; mix well. Fill ducks loosely with stuffing; fasten opening with skewers; lace closed; place ducks in open roasting pan. Combine wine and water; pour over ducks. Roast 30 minutes, basting frequently. Remove ducks to hot platter. Skim fat from drippings in pan. Dissolve cornstarch in 1 tablespoon cold water; stir into drippings in pan; cook, stirring constantly, until thickened. Serve gravy with ducks. Makes 6 servings.

PHEASANT

Pheasant has very little fat to keep it moist while roasting. For this reason, the bird should be roasted at the moderate temperature indicated and basted frequently.

ROAST PHEASANT WITH WILD RICE

1 c. wild rice
5 c. boiling water
1 tsp. salt
½ lb. mushrooms,
  sliced
3 tbs. butter or
  margarine
½ c. chopped
  pecans

2 pheasants (2 to
  3 lbs. ea.,
  dressed weight)
Melted butter or
  margarine
1 c. dry white wine
½ c. canned
  chicken broth

Add well-washed wild rice to rapidly boiling, salted water; boil 35 to 40 minutes or until just tender. Drain; rinse with hot water. Dry out over low heat (or place rice in colander, cover with cloth, and place over steaming water; or place in shallow pan in 325° F. oven for 15 to 30 minutes). Sauté mushrooms in butter or margarine until tender; add pecans and wild rice. Heat oven to 350° F. Salt insides of pheasants; stuff with rice mixture. (Or roast pheasants unstuffed and serve wild-rice mixture with them.) Brush pheasants with melted butter or margarine; place in open roasting pan. Roast, allowing 30 minutes per pound. Baste frequently during roasting with combined white wine and chicken broth. Makes 6 servings.

Chapter Thirteen

Fish and Shellfish

The wondrous variety of shrimp, lobster, swordfish, mackerel, halibut, salmon, cod, and pompano found in abundance in our markets are often called the "fruits of the sea."

In our great port cities, the fishing boats bring in their glistening loads daily to be delivered at wharfside markets. In inland regions, lakes and rivers yield such treasures as trout, striped bass, yellow perch, and pickerel. But for most American families, it's the miracle of quick-freezing and canning that has made possible a year-round variety of fish. And keep this thought in mind: fish or shellfish should be served at least once a week for its nutritive value.

Kinds of Fish

Fish is often described as "lean" or "fat" fish. The amount of fat will vary according to the season. Included among the lean fish are: black, white, and sea bass; bluefish; catfish; cod; crappie; croaker; flounder; haddock; hake; mullet; perch; pickerel; pike; pollock; red snapper; swordfish; weakfish; and whiting. The fat fish include: butterfish; eel; halibut; lake trout; lingcod; mackerel; pompano; porgy; salmon; shad; smelt; tuna; and white fish.

Here are some of the most popular fish found on the market.

Fresh Water Fish

Carp. Found in the East and West, but most comes from the Great Lakes and the Mississippi and its tributaries. Available all year but the best season is from October through March. Sold whole, and as filets and steaks. It may be fresh, frozen, and smoked.

Pike. Found from the Great Lakes area north to Alaska. In season all year. Average market weight is 1½ to 10 pounds. Smaller ones are marketed whole, larger ones are fileted. Pike is available fresh and frozen.

Smelt. These are found in great abundance in the Great Lakes region. They are a transplant from New England that adapted themselves to fresh water. (Salt water smelt are found in New England and Columbia River waters.) They are in season from September to May. They are about 7 to 8 inches long and it takes about 10 to make a pound. They are marketed fresh and frozen.

Trout. There are many varieties of trout. The brook trout, also known as speckled and mountain trout, is one of the best known. Trout are found in rapid streams and lakes and cold torrents. Most trout is marketed frozen and each weighs about 1 pound.

Whitefish. This fish is found in abundance in many of the lakes of the East and North and most particularly in the Great Lakes. It is in season all year and weighs 2 to 6 pounds. It is marketed whole and in filets, fresh, frozen, and smoked.

Yellow Perch. A native of the Great Lakes, yellow perch has been transplanted so it is now found in lakes in the West. It is in season all year. It is marketed whole and fileted, fresh and frozen, and rarely weighs more than 1 pound.

Salt Water Fish

Bass. This is found in both the Atlantic and Pacific. The black sea bass found in both oceans is in season all year and weighs 1 to 4 pounds. White sea bass, caught off the California coast, is in season from May to November and is also 1 to 4 pounds. Striped bass, from the Atlantic, is in season all year, and is marketed in sizes up to 20 pounds, whole and fileted.

Bluefish. Found in the Atlantic from Florida to Massachusetts. It is primarily a warm water fish and the season varies with localities from December through May as the fish migrate from Florida through the warm waters to the north. Average weight is 10 pounds, though it is usually marketed whole in sizes from 1 to 7 pounds.

Cod. A native of the North Atlantic and Pacific. Most comes from the North Atlantic— the Grand Banks of Newfoundland and the other banks from Cape Sable to Nantucket. It is in season all year. Average market size is 10 pounds. Larger cod are marketed as filets, steaks, sticks. Cod is marketed fresh, frozen, salted, pickled, smoked, flaked, and shredded. Scrod is the young cod, weighing 1½ to 2½ pounds.

Flounder. This is a native of the North and South Atlantic and of the South Pacific. It is in season all year. Included in the flounder family are gray sole, winter flounder (black backs), summer flounder (fluke), lemon sole, yellowtails, and dabs. Flounder is in season all year. It is marketed whole and as filets, fresh and frozen, and the average weight is about 2 pounds.

Haddock. A native of the North Atlantic from Nova Scotia to Cape Hatteras. It is closely related to the cod though it is smaller, weighing 2 to 6 pounds. It is in season all year and is marketed whole and as filets, fresh, frozen, salted, flaked, and smoked. The smoked is known as Finnan Haddie.

Halibut. This fish is found in all Northern seas. It is in season all year, on the West coast from July to December while the greatest catch on the East coast is from March to September. The average halibut weighs 50 to 100 pounds, though many are from 500 to 600 pounds. It is marketed dressed and as steaks, fresh, frozen, and smoked.

Mackerel. Found in the North and South Atlantic and in the Pacific. It is in season from April to December and averages about 2 pounds in weight. It is marketed whole and as steaks and filets, fresh, frozen, smoked, salted, and canned.

Pompano. A native of the South Atlantic and Gulf of Mexico, the pompano is in season all year, with the peak of the season from January to April. It is marketed whole and as filets, fresh and frozen. The average weight is 1 to 1½ pounds.

Red Snapper. A native of the South Atlantic and Gulf of Mexico. It is in season all year. It averages 4 to 5 pounds in weight though it can weigh as much as 30 pounds. It is sometimes marketed whole, but more often as steaks and filets, fresh and frozen.

Salmon. Native to the Atlantic and Pacific. The Atlantic salmon is not so abundant as it once was, though it is still found in some abundance in Maine. There are several varieties of Pacific salmon. Chinook is probably the best known. The meat of the different salmon varies from pale pink to reddish. Salmon from either the Pacific or Atlantic is available all year. Salmon may be bought whole, in steaks or chunks. It is also available canned.

Shad. A native of the Atlantic Coast, shad is also found in the Pacific because it was transplanted. It is a seasonal fish that travels up the coast to spawn in coastal rivers. Shad is caught off Florida in December, and the "shad runs" start in North Carolina in late February and early March, in the Chesapeake in March, and along the Jersey coast and in the Hudson River in April. It weighs from 1½ to 8 pounds and is usually marketed fresh, whole, and as filets. Gourmets prize the shad roe.

Swordfish. Swordfish is found in the Atlantic and in southern California waters. It is caught in the Atlantic from April to September, in the Pacific from September to December and weighs from 200 to 600 pounds. Swordfish is marketed mainly as steaks, sometimes as filets, fresh and frozen.

Tuna. A native of the Atlantic and Pacific oceans. It is in season in the Atlantic from July to October, in the Pacific from May to December. The Atlantic tuna can weigh 1600 pounds. The Pacific tuna is much smaller. The albacore, a small tuna, is the only white-meat tuna. It is marketed whole and as steaks and filets. A great percentage of the catch is canned.

FRESH FISH

Where you live will make a difference as to the kind of fresh fish you find in local markets. Florida has its pompano; Boston its scrod; the Northwest, salmon; the South, near the Gulf of Mexico, its red snapper; and in California the sand dabs.

Buying Fresh Fish

You will find fresh fish in the market in various forms for different uses. The best-known forms fish are sold in are:

Whole: Fish just as they come from the water. Before cooking they must be scaled, have the insides removed, and often the head, tail, and fins removed. Your fish-market man will do this for you.

Drawn: Whole fish with insides removed. They must be scaled before cooking. The head, tail, and fins may be removed.

Dressed or Pan-Dressed: Whole fish with scales and insides removed and usually with head, tail, and fins removed. Ready to cook as purchased.

Steaks: Cross-section slices cut from dressed fish. Ready to cook.

Filets: Sides of fish, cut lengthwise away from backbone. Practically boneless and ready to cook as purchased.

Sticks: Pieces cut from filets or steaks into portions of uniform size.

How To Choose Fresh Fish

A whole fresh fish should have bright, bulging eyes, reddish pink gills, and firm elastic flesh which springs back when pressed. All fish should be fresh smelling.

How Much to Buy

A serving of fish is generally one-third to one-half pound of edible fish. Use the following as a guide for fresh or frozen:

Whole Fish: 1 pound—1 serving

Dressed Fish or Fish Steaks: 1 pound—2 servings

Fish Filets or Fish Sticks: 1 pound—3 servings.

How to Handle and Store Fresh Fish

If fish is not to be cooked immediately, remove from wrapper, wipe with a damp cloth. Wrap in transparent plastic wrap or aluminum foil or store in a tightly covered container and keep in refrigerator until time to cook. Cook as soon as possible after purchase. If you are not going to use fresh fish within 24 hours, freeze it (*see page 487*).

FROZEN FISH

Buying Frozen Fish

An infinite variety of frozen fresh- and salt-water fish may be purchased ready to cook. They may be purchased either *whole*, as *steaks* or *filets*, and in *prepared portions*, such as fish sticks. Some may be partially cooked while others are breaded or prepared for baking or frying. They may be prepared in the same way as fresh fish after thawing. Check the package label for directions. Ready-to-heat-and-serve fish are also available. Besides those that are breaded, many are in a sauce in aluminum packets, ready to place in the oven, and others come in transparent plastic bags, to be heated, immersed in boiling water.

How to Store Frozen Fish

Place immediately after purchase in the freezer until ready to cook. Thaw it slowly in the refrigerator rather than at room temperature.

How to Cook Fresh and Frozen Fish

To Bake: Dressed whole fish, steaks, or filets may be baked. Season fish with salt and pepper. Place in shallow, greased baking dish; brush with melted butter or margarine. Bake whole fish, uncovered at 400° F. allowing 8 to 10 minutes per pound dressed weight, though time will vary with kind and size of fish. Baste lean fish frequently with melted butter or margarine. Fish is done when flesh loses its translucency and flakes easily when tested with fork. Steaks will usually bake the same length of time as whole fish; filets will take less time. Test for doneness as with whole fish.

To Bake Stuffed Whole Fish: Cut several gashes through skin of fish to keep it from bursting. Season fish cavity and outside with salt and pepper. Fill cavity two-thirds full with stuffing (see *page 254*); secure with skewers or wooden picks to hold stuffing. Place fish in greased, shallow baking dish; brush with melted butter or margarine. Bake as above. Serve baked fish with lemon wedges, Lemon

Butter (*page 350*), or Curry Butter (*page 350*).

To Broil: Steaks, filets, split dressed whole fish, and whole fish may be broiled. Preheat broiler and broiler pan. Grease broiler pan or line pan with aluminum foil and grease foil. Place fish in pan. Filets and split fish should be placed skin side down and should not be turned. Steaks and whole fish should be cooked on one side and turned to cook second side. Baste lean fish with melted butter or margarine during broiling. Broil filets, split fish, and steaks about 2 inches from heat. Filets and split fish will take 5 to 8 minutes. Broil steaks, about 1 inch thick, 3 minutes on first side; turn; broil second side 5 minutes. Broil whole fish 4 to 6 inches from heat, about 5 minutes on each side. Fish is done when it flakes easily. Season all broiled fish at end of cooking time.

To Panfry (Sauté): Small whole fish, filets, and steaks are suitable for panfrying. Flour fish or dip in cornmeal. Fat or butter or margarine should be ¼ to ½ inch deep depending on thickness of fish. Heat fat; add fish. Cook until golden on one side; turn; repeat, removing as soon as crisp on both sides. It should take about 3 minutes on each side.

To Deep Fry: Filets, small whole fish, batter-dipped fish, and fish sticks may be deep fried. Fry in deep, hot fat (365° to 375° F.) until golden brown (see directions *page 14*). Drain on paper towels. Serve fish with Tartar Sauce (*page 352*) or Cucumber Sauce (*page 349*).

To Poach: Thick filets, steaks, and whole fish may be poached. Thin filets, when rolled, are often done by this method of cooking. It may be done on top of range or in the oven.

Fish may be poached in seasoned water to which a small amount of vinegar has been added. It is more often poached in a seasoned, wine-water combination. These liquids are known as "court bouillons" and during cooking must be kept at simmering and never allowed to boil.

Secrets of Fish Cookery

· Avoid overcooking fish. Fish is done when it has changed to a cream color, can be easily pierced with a fork, and the flakes are easily separated but still juicy.
· Handle fish as little as possible during and after cooking. Fish flesh is tender and delicate.
· Before frying fish, dry it thoroughly so you won't have spattering when it is placed in the hot fat.
· Lean fish need more fat added during cooking to keep them moist and flavorful. Baste frequently with melted butter or margarine.

BASS WITH MINT DRESSING

½ c. packaged bread crumbs	½ c. olive or pure vegetable oil
2 tbs. chopped parsley	1 small clove of garlic, minced
2 tbs. chopped fresh mint	1 striped bass (about 4 lbs.) cleaned, split, and boned
½ tsp. seasoned salt	
⅛ tsp. pepper	½ c. dry white wine
¼ tsp. leaf oregano, crumbled	

Combine bread crumbs, parsley, mint, salt, pepper, and oregano in bowl; blend in 2 tablespoons oil and garlic. Place half the bass in buttered baking dish; top with bread-crumb mixture. Pour over ¼ cup wine; top with second half of bass; tie fish at ends. Pour remaining oil over fish. Bake at 400° F. for 30 to 40 minutes or until fish flakes easily. Baste fish occasionally with remaining ¼ cup wine as it bakes. Remove fish to heated platter; untie. Pour any remaining wine mixture over. Garnish with additional mint, if desired. Serve piping hot. Makes 4 servings.

YELLOW OR WHITE PERCH MACKINAC

6 yellow or white perch	1 tsp. chili powder
½ c. packaged bread crumbs	½ tsp. salt
	⅛ tsp. leaf thyme, crumbled
¼ c. minced onion (1 small)	⅛ tsp. leaf marjoram, crumbled
4 tbs. butter or margarine	⅛ tsp. pepper
	Watercress

Have the market man cut the perch butterfly fashion and remove the backbone. Preheat broiler pan. Wipe fish with damp cloth; place in greased shallow baking dish. Combine remaining ingredients, except watercress, in small bowl; blend well; spread mixture over fish. Broil fish slowly 15 to 20 minutes or until it flakes easily. Arrange on heated platter; garnish with watercress. Serve with Tartar Sauce (*page 352*), if desired. Makes 6 servings.

CAPER-STUFFED BLUEFISH

2 c. soft bread
  crumbs (4 slices)
2 tbs. capers
2 tbs. chopped dill
  pickle
2 tbs. chopped
  parsley
¼ c. chopped onion
  (1 small)
1 tsp. salt

¼ tsp. pepper
1 c. dairy sour
  cream
1 bluefish (about
  5 lbs.), dressed
Salt and pepper
1 tbs. melted butter
  or margarine
½ c. hot water
1 onion, sliced

Combine bread crumbs, capers, pickle, parsley, chopped onion, 1 teaspoon salt, and ¼ teaspoon pepper in large bowl; blend in sour cream. Wipe fish with damp cloth; sprinkle inside and out lightly with salt and pepper. Stuff fish loosely with caper mixture; skewer closed. Place fish in greased baking pan; brush with melted butter or margarine; add hot water and sliced onion. Bake at 400° F. for 40 or 50 minutes or until fish flakes easily. Remove skewers. Place on heated platter. Makes 4 to 5 servings.

FISHERMAN'S PIE

1 qt. water
1 small carrot,
  pared
4 peppercorns
1 strip lemon rind
3 sprigs parsley
1 bay leaf
1 lb. flounder or
  haddock, cut in
  1-in. cubes
1½ lbs. shrimp,
  shelled and
  deveined
½ c. chopped onion
  (1 medium)
¾ c. sliced celery

3 tbs. butter or
  margarine
⅓ c. flour
1 c. light cream
½ tsp. dill weed
1 can (3 to 4 oz.)
  chopped
  mushrooms,
  drained
3 c. hot mashed
  potatoes
2 egg yolks
2 tbs. butter or
  margarine
2 to 4 tbs. milk
Melted butter or
  margarine

Simmer water, carrot, peppercorns, lemon rind, parsley, and bay leaf 10 minutes. Strain; return to saucepan; add fish and shrimp; simmer 5 minutes. Drain; reserve 1¾ cups broth. Sauté onion and celery in 3 tablespoons butter or margarine; blend in flour; add broth slowly; add cream and dill. Cook over medium heat, stirring constantly, until thickened; stir in fish, shrimp, and ½ can mushrooms. Turn into 1½-quart greased casserole. Heat oven to 375° F. Mix potatoes, egg yolks, 2 table-spoons butter or margarine, enough milk to make smooth, and remaining mushrooms. Spoon potato mixture onto fish mixture; brush with melted butter or margarine. Bake 25 minutes or until lightly browned. Makes 6 servings.

SHRIMP AND HADDOCK STEW

½ lb. salt pork,
  diced
2 pkgs. (1 lb. ea.)
  frozen haddock
  filets, thawed
5 medium-size
  potatoes, pared
  and thinly sliced
3 medium-size
  onions, thinly
  sliced
4 tbs. chopped
  parsley

1½ tsp. salt
½ tsp. pepper
1 can (46 oz.)
  tomato juice
1 lb. fresh shrimp,
  shelled and de-
  veined, or 1 pkg.
  (about 10 oz.)
  frozen, shelled,
  and deveined
  shrimp

Sauté salt pork in small skillet until crisp and golden; remove from pan; drain on paper towels; place in large heavy kettle. Cut haddock into 2-inch-wide strips. Arrange alternate layers of haddock, potatoes, and onions in kettle; sprinkle each layer with parsley, salt, and pepper. Pour tomato juice over. Cover; simmer about 40 minutes or until tender. Add shrimp; cook about 5 minutes or until shrimp are cooked through. Sprinkle with extra chopped parsley, if desired. Makes 6 servings.

STRIPED BASS EN GELÉE

1 striped bass
  (about 4 lbs.),
  dressed
1 carrot, pared and
  sliced
1 stalk celery
3 slices onion
2 sprigs parsley
10 peppercorns

2 tsp. salt
1 envelope
  unflavored gelatin
¼ c. cold water
2 tsp. soy sauce
2 tsp. vinegar
Parsley
Watercress

Wrap fish in cheesecloth; place on rack in large kettle; fill kettle with water to depth of about 2 inches. Add carrot, celery, onion, parsley, peppercorns, and salt. Cover; bring to boiling; reduce heat; simmer 20 to 25 minutes or until tender. Remove fish; unwrap; carefully take off skin. Cool fish completely; chill. Strain liquid in kettle; reserve 1 cup. Soften gelatin in cold water; dissolve over hot water; stir into reserved fish liquid; add soy sauce and vinegar. Place chilled fish on serving platter. Spoon gelatin over fish; let set. Repeat spooning gelatin in layers over fish until fish is glazed and all gelatin is used. Garnish with parsley and watercress. Makes 4 servings.

FILETS OF POMPANO SUPREME

1 orange	1 c. White Sauce
4 pompano filets	(*page 347*)
½ tsp. salt	¼ c. dry sherry
Dash of pepper	½ tsp. ground
1 tbs. butter or	ginger
margarine	Fresh dill,
1 tbs. chopped	(optional)
onion	Paprika
½ c. dry white wine	

Remove rind from orange in thin strips, using vegetable peeler; cut into slivers; measure 2 tablespoons. Slice orange and reserve for garnish. Season filets with salt and pepper; put into shallow pan with butter or margarine, onion, white wine, and orange slivers. Bring to boiling; reduce heat; simmer gently 8 to 10 minutes or until fish flakes easily. Remove fish to heated serving dish; keep warm. Strain liquid remaining in pan; stir into white sauce; add sherry and ginger; heat through. Pour sauce over and around filets; garnish with orange slices and dill. Sprinkle with paprika. Makes 4 servings.

POACHED SALMON WITH SHRIMP SAUCE

5 lbs. salmon	½ tsp. whole
4 bay leaves	allspice
4 slices onion	1 qt. water
2 tsp. salt	Shrimp Sauce
	(*page 352*)

Wrap salmon in cheesecloth; place on rack in fish cooker or large kettle. Add 4 bay leaves, onion, salt, allspice, and water. Cover; simmer gently, allowing 8 to 10 minutes per pound. Lift out carefully; remove cheesecloth; trim away and discard skin. Place fish on heated platter. Serve with Shrimp Sauce. Makes 6 servings.

POACHED SALMON STEAKS WITH MUSTARD-DILL SAUCE

6 salmon steaks,	1 tsp. salt
(1¼-in. thick	1 slice lemon
ea.)	Hot water
1 bay leaf	Mustard-Dill Sauce
1 small onion, sliced	(*page 351*)

Arrange steaks in a large skillet. Add bay leaf, onion, salt, and lemon. Pour in enough hot water to almost cover steaks. Bring to boiling. Reduce heat; simmer 8 to 10 minutes or until fish flakes easily when tested with a fork. Remove steaks to heated platter and serve with Mustard-Dill Sauce. Makes 6 servings.

SWORDFISH OLIVETTE

2 swordfish steaks,	1 can (8 oz.)
(about 1½ in.	tomato sauce
thick)	1 can or bottle
4 tbs. butter or	(12 oz.) beer
margarine	½ c. chopped
2 tbs. pure vege-	stuffed olives
table oil	1 tsp. salt
¼ c. flour	Dash of pepper
½ c. chopped	
onion (1	
medium)	

Dot swordfish steaks with half the butter or margarine; place on greased broiler rack 3 inches from heat. Broil about 4 minutes or until browned; turn; dot with remaining butter or margarine. Broil second side 4 or 5 minutes or until fish flakes easily. While fish broils, heat oil in saucepan; blend in flour; add onion, tomato sauce, beer, olives, salt, and pepper; simmer 15 minutes. Arrange fish in heated serving dish; pour sauce over. Garnish with olives and lemon, if desired. Makes 4 servings.

OVEN-FRIED FILETS

1 c. milk	2 pkgs. (1 lb. ea.)
2 tbs. salt	frozen fish
1½ c. packaged	filets, thawed or
bread crumbs	2 lbs. fresh filets
1 tbs. paprika	2 tbs. melted butter
	or margarine

Heat oven to 525° F. Combine milk and salt in shallow dish; mix bread crumbs and paprika in second shallow dish. Dip fish filets into milk mixture, then into bread-crumb mixture, coating them well. Place in lightly oiled shallow baking pan; sprinkle lightly with melted butter or margarine. Bake 12 to 15 minutes or until fish is brown and crisp. Serve with Tartar Sauce (*page 352*), if desired. Makes 4 servings.

FISH FILETS, NORMANDY STYLE

(Filets de Poisson à la Normande)

1 tbs. minced onion	1 tbs. lemon juice
1½ lbs. fish filets	1 c. water
(flounder, lemon	¼ tsp. salt
sole)	2 tbs. lemon juice
1 tbs. butter or	¼ c. butter or
margarine	margarine
2 c. dry white wine	1 lb. shrimp,
½ lb. mushrooms	cooked, shelled,
3 tbs. butter or	and deveined
margarine	Thin bread
4 tbs. flour	triangles
¾ c. milk	Butter or
2 egg yolks	margarine
½ c. heavy cream	

Heat oven to 350° F. Sprinkle buttered baking dish with minced onion. Arrange filets on dish, overlapping them slightly. Dot with 1 tablespoon butter or margarine. Pour wine over filets; cover filets completely with piece of wax paper. Poach in oven 15 to 20 minutes or until filets are just tender. Transfer filets to heatproof platter. Turn off heat. Keep filets warm in oven. Remove stems from mushrooms; slice; reserve caps and stems. Carefully pour poaching liquid (fish stock) into a saucepan; boil rapidly until it is reduced to 1 cup. Melt 3 tablespoons butter or margarine in another saucepan; stir in flour. Cook over low heat, stirring constantly, until mixture bubbles and foams 3 minutes. It should not brown. Remove from heat. Add reduced fish stock and milk. Stir rapidly with wooden spoon or beat with wire whisk. Cook over low heat, stirring constantly, until mixture bubbles; cook 1 minute. Beat egg yolks and cream together. Stir at least half the hot sauce slowly into egg-yolk mixture; blend into sauce in saucepan. Cook 1 minute. Add 1 tablespoon lemon juice. Taste and correct seasonings. Combine water, salt, 2 tablespoons lemon juice, and ¼ cup butter or margarine in small saucepan. Cook over low heat until bubbling; add mushroom caps and stems; cover; cook gently 5 minutes. Remove from heat. Add shrimp; let stand in hot liquid to heat through. Drain; arrange half the shrimp and mushrooms on filets. Spoon layer of sauce over filets with large spoon. Garnish with remaining shrimp and mushroom caps, and toast triangles that have been sauteed in butter or margarine until brown. Serve at once.

Sauced filets may be placed under broiler to brown, if desired, before garnishing. Makes 6 servings.

FILETS OF SOLE JACQUELINE

½ c. finely chopped	2 tbs. butter or
green onions	margarine
1½ lbs. fish filets	2 tbs. flour
(flounder, lemon	2 egg yolks
sole)	½ c. heavy cream
1 c. dry white wine	3 tbs. lemon juice
½ c. water	2 tbs. melted butter
¼ tsp. salt	or margarine
⅛ tsp. pepper	Chopped parsley

Heat oven to 350° F. Sprinkle onions in bottom of baking pan large enough to accommodate fish. The filets may overlap, but should be in a single layer as much as possible. Pour wine and water over filets; sprinkle with salt and pepper. Cover filets with a piece of buttered wax paper. Poach in oven 12 to 15 minutes or until fish is translucent and flakes easily; do not overcook. Transfer carefully to an ovenproof serving dish. Pour off poaching liquid carefully into saucepan; cook until it is reduced to 1 cup; skim and discard foam from top; reserve liquid. Melt butter or margarine in saucepan; stir in flour; add poaching liquid. Cook over medium heat, stirring constantly, until thickened and bubbly. Combine egg yolks with cream; pour mixture slowly into sauce, stirring constantly; cook 1 minute longer; add lemon juice. Preheat broiler. With large spoon, coat filets evenly with sauce; drizzle with melted butter or margarine. Broil until top is bubbly and brown. Sprinkle generously with chopped parsley. Makes 6 servings.

SOLE AND SALMON ROULETTES

1½ lbs. salmon	2 tbs. butter or
6 thin filets of sole	margarine
1½ c. water	1 tbs. flour
9 whole allspice	3 hard-cooked eggs,
1 bay leaf	chopped
1 tsp. salt	1 tbs. chopped
3 slices lemon	parsley

Cut salmon into six chunks; fold fish filets in half lengthwise; wrap one filet around each salmon chunk; secure with wooden picks. Combine water, allspice, bay leaf, salt, and lemon slices in greased shallow pan; bring to boiling; reduce heat to simmering. Poach fish in liquid 8 to 10 minutes or until fish flakes easily. Remove to hot platter; keep warm. Strain liquid in pan; reserve 1 cup. Melt butter or margarine in saucepan; blend in flour; add reserved liquid. Cook over medium heat, stirring constantly, until thickened. Add chopped hard-cooked eggs; heat through. Sprinkle chopped parsley on filets around salmon; spoon sauce onto platter around fish. Garnish with lemon wedges dipped in paprika, if desired. Makes 6 servings.

TROUT PARMESAN

4 fresh or frozen trout (about 1 lb. ea.)	2 tbs. flour
	½ tsp. salt
	Dash of pepper
½ c. milk	1 c. milk
½ c. cornmeal	1 tbs. capers
6 tbs. butter or margarine	½ c. grated Parmesan cheese

Wash trout; pat dry with paper towel. Pour ½ cup milk into shallow dish; put cornmeal into second shallow dish or on wax paper. Dip trout in milk; roll in cornmeal to coat. Sauté in 4 tablespoons butter or margarine until golden brown on both sides, adding more butter or margarine, if necessary. Transfer to heat-proof serving dish; keep warm. Melt 2 tablespoons butter or margarine in saucepan; blend in flour, salt, and pepper; add 1 cup milk gradually; stir in capers and Parmesan cheese. Cook, stirring constantly, until sauce comes to boiling and is thickened; pour over trout. Broil until sauce is lightly browned and bubbly. Makes 4 servings.

CANNED FISH

We can't always pluck fish fresh from a fisherman's boat, but their delectable flavors have been captured in the can. Just check your supermarket shelf for the countless varieties of canned fish available. Recipes from a can of seafood are limitless. Serve them as gourmet dishes, quick luncheons, family dinners. They can be delicious time-savers from your pantry shelf.

Tuna is one of the most popular of canned seafood. It is available as albacore, white meat; yellowfin; skipjack; and bluefin. It is packed in several ways:

Solid pack—Large pieces from choice cuts
Chunk style—Bite-size pieces
Grated or Flaked—Small pieces

The most popular can size of tuna is 6½ to 7 ounces. It also comes in 3¼ to 3½ ounces; 9¼ ounce and 12½ to 13 ounce cans.

Most tuna is packed in corn oil, cottonseed, or soy oil. Some are packed in vegetable broth and dietetic tuna is packed salt-free in distilled water.

Salmon varies from light pink to red. The red is most in demand and brings the highest price, though the pink salmon is equally nutritious and excellent for casseroles or salads. It is available in 1-pound, 7¾-ounce, and 3¼-ounce cans.

Sardines come in various shapes and sizes. Actually there is no one fish answering to this name; it refers to almost any tiny fish with rich flesh and weak bones. In the Mediterranean, the "sardine" is actually a pilchard. Off Norway, the fish caught and canned as a sardine is the bristling or the sprat. Maine sardines are small herrings. Sardines are packed in 3¾- or 4-ounce and 1-pound cans.

Codfish flakes, *herring*, and *anchovies* are also available canned.

TUNA BISCUIT ROLL

1 can (6½ to 7 oz.) tuna, drained and flaked	1 can (10½ oz.) condensed cream of mushroom soup
1 can (3 to 4 oz.) sliced mushrooms, drained	2 c. biscuit mix
	1 tsp. onion powder
2 tbs. diced pimiento	½ tsp. seasoned salt
2 tbs. parsley flakes	1⅓ c. milk

Combine tuna, mushrooms, pimiento, parsley, and 2 tablespoons undiluted soup in small bowl. Combine biscuit mix, onion powder, and salt in medium-size bowl; add ⅔ cup milk; stir until moistened. Turn out on lightly floured surface; knead 5 or 6 times. Roll dough out to 9x12-inch rectangle. Spread tuna mixture on dough; roll up, jelly-roll fashion, starting at short side; place on greased cookie sheet. Bake at 425° F. for 20 to 25 minutes or until golden brown. Serve with sauce made by combining remaining cream of mushroom soup with ⅔ cup milk. Heat slowly, stirring until smooth. Makes 8 servings.

TUNA SUPREME

2 c. half-and-half or light cream	Dash of pepper
1 bay leaf	1 tbs. chopped parsley
1/4 c. sliced onion	2 tbs. diced pimiento
5 sprigs parsley	1 can (12½ to 13 oz.) tuna, drained and flaked
½ clove of garlic	
2 whole cloves	
3 tbs. melted butter or margarine	
3 tbs. flour	6 French rolls, scooped out and toasted or 6 baked potatoes
½ tsp. celery salt	
½ tsp. salt	

Heat half-and-half or light cream, bay leaf, onion, parsley, garlic, and cloves to scalding. Remove from heat; strain. Blend butter or margarine and flour; add scalded mixture gradually, stirring constantly. Heat until sauce thickens, stirring constantly. Add celery salt, salt, pepper, parsley, pimiento, and tuna; heat. Serve in toasted French rolls or over baked potatoes. Makes 6 servings.

TUNA TAMALE PIE

4½ c. water	1 tsp. chili powder
1½ tsp. salt	1 can (8 oz.) tomato sauce
1½ c. cornmeal	
1 c. chopped ripe olives	1 tsp. salt
½ c. chopped onion (1 medium)	¼ tsp. leaf basil, crumbled
½ clove of garlic, crushed	½ tsp. Worcestershire sauce
½ c. chopped green pepper	1 can (12½ to 13 oz.) tuna, drained and flaked
¼ c. chopped celery	
3 tbs. butter or margarine	2 tbs. melted butter or margarine

Bring water and 1½ teaspoons salt to boiling. Add cornmeal slowly, stirring constantly. Cover; cook slowly 20 minutes, stirring occasionally. Add olives. Cover; set aside to cool. Sauté onions, garlic, green pepper, and celery in 3 tablespoons butter or margarine until tender. Add chili powder, tomato sauce, 1 teaspoon salt, basil, and Worcestershire; simmer. Add tuna; remove from heat. Spread two thirds of cornmeal mixture on bottom and sides of buttered 2-quart casserole or 9x9x2-

inch pan. Add tuna mixture. Spoon remaining cornmeal mixture on top. Brush with 2 tablespoons butter or margarine. Bake at 400° F. for 30 minutes. Place under broiler a few minutes for a crispy top. Makes 6 servings.

TUNA SOUFFLÉ SUPREME

2 cans (10½ oz. ea.) condensed cream of celery or mushroom soup	4 egg yolks, well beaten
	1 can (6½ to 7 oz.) tuna, drained and chopped
1 tbs. chopped parsley	4 egg whites
	¼ tsp. salt
¼ tsp. leaf thyme, crumbled	¼ tsp. cream of tartar
Dash of pepper	½ c. milk

Heat 1 cup of soup; remove from heat; add parsley, thyme, pepper, and egg yolks; stir in tuna. Heat oven to 325° F. Beat egg whites, salt, and cream of tartar until stiff but not dry. Fold into tuna mixture. Turn into greased 1½-quart casserole; place in pan of hot water. Bake about 1 hour or until puffy and brown. Heat remaining soup and ½ cup milk for a sauce to serve with soufflé. Makes 6 servings.

ORIENTAL TUNA FISH

¾ c. thinly sliced onion	Dash of pepper
	½ tsp. ground ginger
2 tbs. butter or margarine	
1 can (13 oz.) chicken broth	1 pkg. frozen snow peas*
	2 cans (6½ to 7 oz. ea.) tuna, drained and flaked
¼ c. sliced water chestnuts	
1 can (3 to 4 oz.) sliced mushrooms	2 tbs. cornstarch
	2 tbs. water
½ tsp. salt	Hot, buttered rice

Sauté onion in butter or margarine until tender; add chicken broth, water chestnuts, mushrooms, salt, pepper, and ginger; mix well. Add snow peas and tuna; cover; simmer 2 minutes. Dissolve cornstarch in water; add to tuna mixture; cook until sauce thickens. Serve on hot, buttered rice. Makes about 6 servings.
* If snow peas are not available, use Italian green beans and simmer for 6 minutes.

TUNA MARINER

½ of 8-oz. pkg. medium noodles	1 can (3 to 4 oz.) mushroom crowns, drained
1 can (10 oz.) frozen cream of shrimp soup	1 can (4 oz.) pimiento, drained and diced
1 c. milk	
Dash hot-pepper sauce	
2 cans (6½ to 7 oz. ea.) tuna, drained	1 pkg. (3¾ oz.) corn chips, crushed

Cook noodles in boiling, salted water according to package directions; drain. Combine soup, milk, and hot-pepper sauce in saucepan; cook over low heat until bubbly. Break tuna into bite-size pieces. Mix noodles, soup mixture, tuna, mushrooms, and pimiento gently. Heat oven to 350° F. Spoon half the tuna mixture into buttered 2-quart casserole; sprinkle with half the crushed corn chips. Repeat with remaining tuna mixture and corn chips. Bake 35 minutes or until bubbly. Makes 4 servings.

TUNA FLORENTINE

1 pkg. (10 oz.) fresh, washed spinach or 2 pkgs. (about 9 oz. ea.) frozen spinach	¾ c. milk 4 tbs. grated Parmesan cheese
	2 cans (6½ to 7 oz. ea.) tuna, drained and flaked
1 can (10 oz.) frozen cream of potato soup	2 tbs. melted butter or margarine

Cook spinach; drain well. Combine soup and milk in top of double boiler; heat over simmering water until blended and heated through. Add cheese; stir until cheese melts. Divide spinach among 4 individual ramekins or baking dishes; top with flaked tuna. Pour sauce over tuna; drizzle with melted butter or margarine. Broil about 5 minutes or until sauce bubbles. Garnish with lemon slices, if desired. Makes 4 servings.

TUNA CASSEROLE

3 tbs. chopped onion	1 can (10½ oz.) condensed cream of celery soup
3 tbs. chopped green pepper	⅔ c. milk
1 tbs. melted butter or margarine	1 tbs. lemon juice
2 tbs. diced pimiento	2 cans (6½ to 7 oz. ea.) tuna, drained and flaked
1 can (10½ oz.) condensed cream of chicken soup	2 c. coarsely crushed potato chips

Heat oven to 350° F. Sauté onion and green pepper in butter or margarine 3 minutes or until tender; remove from heat. Combine sautéed onion and green pepper, pimiento, soups, milk, lemon juice, and tuna; mix well. Place 1 cup crushed potato chips in bottom of lightly buttered 1½-quart casserole; add tuna mixture. Sprinkle remaining 1 cup potato chips on top. Bake 30 minutes. Makes 6 servings.

TUNABURGERS

1 egg, beaten	1 can (12½ to 13 oz.) tuna, drained and flaked
½ c. mayonnaise or salad dressing	
1 tbs. lemon juice	Fat or pure vegetable oil
2 tbs. finely chopped onion	6 to 7 toasted buns
Dash of pepper	

Combine egg, mayonnaise or salad dressing, lemon juice, onion, and pepper; mix well. Stir in tuna. Drop tuna mixture by large spoonfuls into small amount of hot fat or oil in skillet. Flatten tuna mixture with back of spoon to form a patty. Brown on both sides. If desired, place a slice of American or Swiss cheese on browned tunaburger and broil until cheese melts. Serve on toasted buns. Makes 6 to 7 servings.

TUNA CROQUETTES

1 can (9¼ oz.)
  tuna
2 tbs. butter or
  margarine
3 tbs. flour
½ tsp. salt
1 tsp. instant
  minced onion
1 c. milk
1 tbs. lemon juice
2 tsp. Worcester-
  shire sauce

1 egg yolk
1½ c. soft bread
  crumbs (3 slices)
1 c. packaged bread
  crumbs
1 egg white
1 tbs. water
Fat or pure
  vegetable oil
1 jar (8 oz.) process
  cheese spread,
  heated

Drain tuna; reserve oil; chop tuna fine. Melt butter or margarine in saucepan; blend in flour, salt, and reserved tuna and oil; add onion. Add milk gradually; cook over medium heat, stirring constantly, until sauce thickens and comes to boiling; add lemon juice and Worcestershire. Stir a small amount into slightly beaten egg yolk; stir into mixture in saucepan; add tuna and soft bread crumbs; blend well. Chill several hours. Shape into 8 croquettes or patties; dust lightly with packaged bread crumbs. Combine slightly beaten egg white and water in shallow dish. Dip croquettes in mixture; roll in remaining packaged bread crumbs. Let dry a few minutes. Put enough fat or oil into skillet to make 1 to 1½ inches deep when heated; heat to 375° F. Fry croquettes until brown; drain on paper towels. Arrange on platter; serve with heated cheese spread. Makes 4 servings.

POTATO SALMON PUFF

½ pkg. (4 servings)
  instant mashed
  potatoes
3 egg yolks, beaten
2 tbs. minced
  parsley
1 can (7¾ oz.)
  salmon, drained,
  boned, and
  flaked

1 tbs. minced onion
1 tbs. lemon juice
1 tsp. seasoned salt
⅛ tsp. pepper
3 egg whites, stiffly
  beaten

Heat oven to 325° F. Prepare potatoes according to package directions. Stir in egg yolks, parsley, salmon, onion, lemon juice, seasoned salt, and pepper; blend well. Gently fold in egg whites; turn mixture into lightly buttered 2-quart casserole. Bake about 1 hour or until puffy and golden brown. Makes 4 servings.

FROSTED SALMON LOAF

2 cans (1 lb. ea.)
  salmon, drained,
  boned, and flaked
2½ c. fresh bread
  crumbs (5 slices)
2 eggs
1 egg white
⅓ c. milk
2 tbs. dried parsley
  flakes
2 tbs. instant
  minced onion

1 tsp. salt
⅛ tsp. seasoned
  pepper
½ pkg. (4 servings)
  instant mashed
  potatoes
1 egg yolk
Melted butter or
  margarine
Dill Sauce
  (page 351)

Heat oven to 350° F. Line 9x5x3-inch loaf pan lengthwise with strip of foil; make the strip long enough to extend slightly beyond the pan at both ends for ease in lifting finished loaf from pan. Grease pan and foil. Combine salmon, bread crumbs, eggs, egg white, milk, parsley, onion, salt, and pepper in large bowl; mix thoroughly. Turn into prepared pan. Bake 45 to 50 minutes or until firm. While loaf bakes, prepare instant mashed potatoes according to package directions; beat in egg yolk. Increase oven to 425° F. Remove loaf from pan; place on cookie sheet. Spread mashed potatoes on top and sides of loaf; brush with melted butter or margarine. Bake until potatoes are tipped with brown. Serve with Dill Sauce. Makes 8 servings.

SALMON CROQUETTES

¼ c. butter or
  margarine
¼ c. flour
½ tsp. salt
⅛ tsp. pepper
1 c. milk
1 c. soft bread
  crumbs (2 slices)
1 can (1 lb.)
  salmon, drained,
  boned, and flaked
Flour

1 egg, beaten
1½ c. packaged
  bread crumbs
Fat or pure
  vegetable oil
1 can (10½ oz.)
  condensed cream
  of mushroom
  soup
1 tbs. lemon juice
1 c. light cream
½ tsp. curry
  powder

Melt butter or margarine in saucepan over medium heat; stir in flour, salt, and pepper. Add milk slowly; cook over medium heat, stirring constantly, until thick; remove from heat. Blend in bread crumbs and salmon; chill several hours. Shape mixture into 8 croquettes or patties. Roll each lightly in flour; dip in beaten egg; roll in bread crumbs. Put enough fat or oil into skillet to make 1 to 1½ inches deep when heated; heat to 375° F. Fry croquettes until golden (1½ to 2 minutes), turning once; drain on paper towels; keep warm. Combine soup, lemon juice, cream, and curry powder; heat until bubbly; serve with croquettes. Makes 8 servings.

DEEP SEA SALMON BAKE

1½ c. packaged precooked rice	2 tbs. instant minced onion
1½ c. boiling water	2 egg whites
1 can (1 lb.) salmon, drained, boned, and flaked	1 egg
	2 tbs. melted butter or margarine
2 tsp. salt	Lemon Cucumber
¼ tsp. pepper	Sauce (*page 349*)

Add rice to boiling water; cover; remove from heat; let stand 5 minutes. Heat oven to 375° F. Combine salmon, rice, salt, pepper, and onion. Beat egg whites and egg; add to salmon mixture; blend well. Press into well-buttered 9x5x3-inch loaf pan. Brush top with melted butter or margarine. Bake 30 minutes or until firm and golden. Serve with sauce. Makes 4 servings.

DEVILED CODFISH CAKES OR BALLS

1 egg, beaten	1 tsp. prepared horseradish
1 tsp. prepared mustard	Dash of pepper
Few grains cayenne	1 can (10½ oz.) codfish cakes
¼ tsp. curry powder	Fat or pure vegetable oil
¼ tsp. paprika	
¼ tsp. garlic powder	

Combine egg, mustard, cayenne, curry powder, paprika, garlic powder, horseradish, and pepper. Add codfish cakes; mix well. Shape mixture into 4 cakes or 20 balls. Fry cakes in shallow fat until crispy on both sides. To fry codfish balls, put enough fat or oil into skillet or deep saucepan to make 2 inches deep when heated. Heat to 375° F. Fry codfish balls about 2 minutes or until golden brown. Makes 4 servings.

Shellfish

What delightful gourmet treats come to us in shells from the sea! "Shellfish" is the general name given to the crustaceans (lobster, crab, and shrimp) and mollusks (oysters, clams, and mussels). They can be used in limitless ways to add variety to menus.

SHRIMP

Shrimp are available in many forms, fresh, frozen, and canned.

Buying Shrimp

When buying shrimp, keep in mind that 1 pound fresh or frozen shrimp in the shell is equivalent to ½ pound shelled, cooked shrimp. A 10-ounce package of frozen, shelled, and deveined shrimp may be substituted for a pound of fresh shrimp, shelled and deveined.

Shrimp is sold according to size. Here are the number of shrimp per pound:

Large:	15 and under per pound
Medium large:	16 to 20 per pound
Medium:	21 to 25 per pound
Small:	26 to 30 per pound
Very small:	31 to 42 per pound
	And on up

The color of the uncooked shrimp you see piled on ice in fish markets may vary from gray to pink to red, depending on the variety. The most common is the gray-shelled, which fishermen call "white." All shrimp, regardless of shell color in the natural state, turn pink when cooked.

Frozen shrimp are found in the following forms: Raw—in shell; deveined in shell; shelled and deveined; shelled, deveined, and breaded. Cooked—in shell; shelled and deveined; shelled, deveined, and breaded; shelled, deveined, stuffed, and breaded.

Canned shrimp are packed shelled and sometimes deveined in 4½- and 5-ounce cans. They are packed in brine (wet pack) or are vacuum packed (dry pack).

Handling and Storing Shrimp

If *frozen* when purchased, place in freezer immediately and keep frozen until needed. Frozen shrimp is often cooked from the frozen state. If it is to be thawed, it's preferable to thaw them slowly, on the refrigerator shelf; though when they are to be cooked soon after, it's perfectly safe to thaw them at room temperature.

If *fresh* when purchased, shrimp should be used within 24 hours—or frozen for future use.

How To Shell and Devein Shrimp

Whether to shell before or after cooking is a matter of personal preference. If shelled before cooking, place the shells in the water with the shrimp during cooking, for the shells add flavor. (When shrimp are cooked, discard shells.)

To Remove Shells: Hold the tail end of the shrimp in the left hand, slip the thumb of the right hand under the shell between the feelers and lift off two or three segments. Still holding firmly to the tail, pull out the shrimp from the remaining tail section.

To Devein: Though it is not really necessary, most people prefer to remove the black sand veins. Cut along the back of shelled, raw shrimp with a small sharp knife and lift out vein. For cooked shrimp, cut as for raw shrimp and scrape out vein with knife, rinsing under cold water, if necessary.

How to Cook Shrimp

To "Boil": Shell and devein shrimp. Bring seasoned water to boiling, with parsley, a few peppercorns, 2 bay leaves, and a sprinkling of salt. Add the shrimp; bring water back to boiling and cook 2 to 3 minutes until shrimp is delicately pink. Drain and chill. The secret in cooking shrimp is to avoid overcooking and *never* use high heat. A minute too long in too hot water can make tender shrimp tough. To cook shrimp in shells, follow th same directions. Cool quickly. Shell and de-vein.

To Poach: An excellent way is to let the sea-soned water simmer for two minutes, then turn off the heat and leave the shrimp in the water, covered, another 6 or 7 minutes. If not shelled before cooking, let them cool com-pletely before removing shells. If they are not to be served immediately, let the cooked shrimp stand in their broth, covered, in the refrigerator until needed. This helps to keep them moist.

To Sauté: It is not necessary to boil raw shrimp before sautéeing; in fact, many peo-ple think shrimp are more flavorful if *not* boiled first. Shell and devein; heat butter, margarine, or oil in skillet; add shrimp; cook over medium heat 2 to 4 minutes just until pink on both sides. If a sauce is to be added, such as a wine or tomato sauce, let the shrimp cook in this *very gently* for no more than 5 minutes.

To Deep-fry: If purchased frozen and already breaded (but not cooked), place shrimp (still frozen) in deep fat, at 375° F., and fry about 4 minutes just until golden on each side. If raw and not frozen, but dipped in batter or breaded, frying time may be cut to 3 minutes, depending on the size of the shrimp.

SHRIMP JAMBALAYA

1 c. chopped onion (1 large)	2 tsp. Worcester-shire sauce
1 clove of garlic, minced	1 tsp. salt
1 green pepper, seeded and chopped	Dash of hot-pepper sauce
1 lb. cooked ham, diced	2 bottles (7 oz. ea.) clam broth
3 tbs. butter or margarine	2¼ c. water
1 can (1 lb. 13 oz.) tomatoes	2 c. rice
	2 lbs. shrimp, shelled and deveined

Sauté onion, garlic, green pepper, and ham in butter or margarine in large heavy skillet until golden. Add tomatoes, Worcestershire, salt, hot-pepper sauce, clam broth, and water. Bring to boiling. Add rice and shrimp. Cover; simmer 30 to 40 minutes or until rice is tender and most of the liquid is absorbed.

Jambalaya may be cooked as a casserole. After adding seasoning and liquids, stir in rice

and shrimp and turn mixture into greased casserole. Cover and bake at 350° F. for 45 to 50 minutes or until rice is tender. Makes 8 servings.

SHRIMP PIE

1 envelope dehy-drated leek soup mix	2 lbs. shrimp, shelled and deveined, or 2 pkgs. (10 oz. ea.) frozen, shelled, and deveined shrimp
1¾ c. water	
2 tbs. lemon juice	
1 small bay leaf	
¼ tsp. leaf thyme, crumbled	½ c. light cream
1 tsp. salt	1 pkg. (about 9 oz.) frozen peas, cooked and drained
⅛ tsp. pepper	
2 tbs. chopped parsley	
	2 c. diced, cooked potatoes
	1 pkg. refrigerated biscuits

Heat oven to 450° F. Butter 2½-quart cas-serole. Combine soup mix, water, lemon juice, bay leaf, thyme, salt, pepper, and parsley in saucepan; heat to simmering. Add shrimp; simmer 5 minutes. Remove bay leaf. Add cream, peas, and potatoes. Turn into prepared casserole. Separate biscuits; arrange on top of casserole. Bake 15 minutes or until biscuits are golden brown. Makes 6 servings.

SHRIMP QUICHE LORRAINE

1 unbaked 9-inch pastry shell (*page 406*)	2 c. light cream
	1 tsp. salt
	Dash of pepper
¼ c. chopped onion (1 small)	Dash of cayenne
	2 cans (5 oz. ea.) shrimp
1 tbs. butter or margarine	¼ lb. Gruyère cheese, shredded
4 eggs, slightly beaten	

Heat oven to 425° F. Line pastry with wax paper. Fill half full with raw rice or dried beans. Bake 7 minutes. Remove from oven. Remove wax paper and rice or beans. Reduce oven heat to 400° F. Sauté onion in butter or margarine. Combine eggs, cream, salt, pepper, cayenne, and sautéed onion. Drain shrimp; rinse; pat dry. Scatter shrimp and cheese in pastry shell. Pour in egg mixture. Bake on bottom rack of oven 35 to 40 minutes or until top browns and puffs. Cool 5 minutes before serving. Makes 6 servings.

PEPPERED SHRIMP

2 tbs. pure vege-
 table oil
1½ lbs. shrimp,
 shelled and
 deveined or
 1 pkg. (10 oz.)
 frozen, shelled,
 and deveined
 shrimp, thawed
1 clove of garlic
½ c. sliced green
 onions

1 c. slivered green
 pepper
1 bottle (7 oz.)
 clam juice
½ tsp. salt
⅛ tsp. pepper
1 tsp. sugar
½ tsp. monosodium
 glutamate
1 can (3 to 4 oz.)
 sliced mush-
 rooms, drained
1 tbs. cornstarch
2 tbs. water

Heat oil in skillet; add shrimp and garlic clove; quickly stir-fry about 3 to 5 minutes or until shrimp turns pink; remove garlic. Add green onions and green pepper; stir-fry rapidly until vegetables are tender-crisp. Add clam juice, salt, pepper, sugar, and monosodium glutamate; heat to boiling; add mushrooms. Blend cornstarch and water until smooth; quickly stir into hot liquid in skillet. Cook over medium heat until clear and bubbly. Serve with or over fluffy, hot rice, if desired. Makes 4 servings.

SOUTHERN SHRIMP STEW

4 slices bacon, diced
½ c. chopped onion
 (1 medium)
1 green pepper,
 seeded and
 chopped
1 can (about 1 lb.)
 tomatoes
2 tbs. chili sauce

Dash of hot-pepper
 sauce
2 tsp. salt
½ tsp. pepper
8 medium-size
 potatoes, pared
 and cut in large
 cubes
2 cans (5 oz. ea.)
 shrimp

Fry bacon until crisp in large, heavy skillet or Dutch oven; remove and reserve. Add onion and green pepper to bacon fat remaining in pan; cook until onion is transparent. Add tomatoes, chili sauce, hot-pepper sauce, salt, and pepper; bring to boiling. Add potatoes; cover; cook slowly about 35 minutes or until potatoes are tender. Add shrimp during last 5 minutes of cooking. Add a little water, if needed, during cooking. Serve sprinkled with bacon bits. Makes 8 servings.

MALAYAN SHRIMP CURRY

⅓ c. butter or
 margarine
½ c. chopped onion
 (1 medium)
1 clove of garlic,
 mashed
1 tsp. salt
1 tbs. curry powder

1 tbs. flour
1 tbs. granulated
 chicken bouillon
2 c. yogurt
3 lbs. shrimp,
 shelled, deveined,
 and cooked
Hot, cooked rice

Heat butter or margarine in skillet; sauté onion and garlic until soft and lightly browned. Combine salt, curry powder, flour, and chicken bouillon; stir into fat in pan; cook 2 to 3 minutes, stirring constantly. Stir in yogurt and shrimp; cook over low heat, stirring occasionally, until bubbly and heated through. Serve over hot, fluffy rice. Makes 6 servings.

CANTONESE SHRIMP AND BEANS

3 tbs. pure vege-
 table oil
1½ lbs. shrimp,
 shelled and
 deveined
1 clove of garlic,
 mashed
¼ c. thinly sliced
 green onions
½ tsp. ground
 ginger
1 tsp. salt

Dash of pepper
1 c. canned chicken
 broth or 1
 chicken bouillon
 cube dissolved
 in 1 c. boiling
 water
1 pkg. (10 oz.)
 frozen Italian
 green beans
1 tbs. cornstarch
1 tbs. cold water

Heat oil in skillet; sauté shrimp, garlic, and green onions 5 minutes; stir in ginger, salt, pepper, chicken broth, and beans; cover; simmer 6 minutes. Combine cornstarch with cold water; stir into shrimp mixture; simmer 1 minute longer. Serve on bed of steaming hot rice, if desired. Makes 6 servings.

CREPES CREVETTE

1 recipe Crepes
 (page 383)
4 egg yolks
⅓ c. lemon juice
1 c. butter or
 margarine
2 pkgs. (10 oz. ea.)
 frozen, shelled,
 and deveined
 shrimp, thawed

1 tbs. minced onion
2 tbs. butter or
 margarine
1 pkg. (10 oz.)
 spinach, cooked,
 drained, and
 chopped

Prepare Crepes according to recipe. Keep warm. Combine egg yolks and lemon juice in double boiler over hot water. Add ½ cup butter or margarine; stir until melted. Add remaining ½ cup butter or margarine; stir until melted and sauce is thick. Cut up shrimp. Sauté onion in 2 tablespoons butter or margarine; mix in shrimp, spinach, and ⅓ cup sauce. Spoon filling on crepes; roll up. Place in baking dish; cover with sauce. Broil until browned and bubbly. Makes 6 servings.

ASPARAGUS AND SHRIMP AU GRATIN

2 lbs. asparagus, cut in 2-in. pieces	¼ c. shredded Swiss cheese
¼ c. thinly sliced green onions	¼ c. grated Parmesan cheese
4 tbs. melted butter or margarine	1 tbs. lemon juice
4 tbs. flour	1 lb. shrimp, shelled, deveined, and cooked
½ tsp. salt	
Dash of pepper	2 tbs. grated Parmesan cheese
2 c. light cream	

Cook asparagus in salted water 13 to 14 minutes or until tender-crisp. Drain well. Sauté green onions in butter or margarine 2 minutes; add flour, salt, and pepper; mix well. Stir in cream slowly. Cook, stirring constantly, until sauce thickens; simmer 1 minute. Add Swiss cheese and ¼ cup Parmesan cheese; stir until melted. Add lemon juice and shrimp. Place asparagus in greased, shallow 1½-quart baking dish. Pour in shrimp sauce. Sprinkle with 2 tablespoons cheese. Bake at 400° F. for 15 to 20 minutes or until lightly browned. Makes 6 servings.

BAKED BUTTERED SHRIMP

2 cloves of garlic	1½ tsp. salt
1 c. butter or margarine	¼ tsp. pepper
	½ c. dry sherry
1 c. packaged bread crumbs	3 lbs. shrimp, shelled, deveined, and cooked
1 tbs. minced onion	
1 tbs. minced parsley	3 pkgs. (10 oz. ea.) frozen Italian green beans, cooked
¼ tsp. leaf tarragon, crumbled	
¼ tsp. leaf basil, crumbled	

Heat oven to 400° F. Cook garlic in butter or margarine until it browns; remove; discard. Add bread crumbs, onion, parsley, tarragon, basil, salt, pepper, and sherry to butter or margarine. Reserve ¼ cup of mixture; divide remainder among 8 individual baking dishes. Arrange shrimp over mixture in each dish. Sprinkle shrimp with reserved crumb mixture. Bake 15 minutes or until crumbs are golden. Edge each dish with hot, seasoned green beans. Makes 8 servings.

LOBSTER

Of all the crustaceans, lobster is probably the most elegant, the most luxurious.

The two main types of lobster sold in our markets are the *Maine lobsters*, sold either alive or cooked in the shell, or as fresh, frozen, or canned lobster meat; and *rock* and *spiny lobster*, of which only the tail section is sold, usually frozen.

Rock lobster tails may come from tropical waters (quite a number from the Caribbean), or from the colder waters of South Africa and New Zealand. The rock lobster tails from colder water are more tender and succulent than those from the tropic seas.

Buying Lobster

Maine lobsters, when purchased alive, have the most delicate sweet flesh of any crustacean in the world, but the proportion of meat to overall weight is small. A 1- to 1¼-pound lobster will serve just one person. There are a few lobsters which weigh as much as 2 pounds each, but any larger than this are rarely sold commercially. Maine lobsters are in season during the spring and summer months. Frozen rock lobster tails are available throughout the year. A 9-ounce box will contain three or four tiny lobster tails, weighing 2 to 3 ounces each. Large ones weighing about 8 ounces each come two to a package.

Canned lobster is available in 5-ounce cans.

How To Boil a Live Lobster

Allow 1 small or ½ large lobster per person. Fill a large pot two thirds full with water and season with a few peppercorns, onion, bay leaf, celery tops, parsley, lemon, and 3 tablespoons salt to 3 quarts of water. Bring water to rapid boil. Grasp live lobster by the body with the claws away from you or with a pair of tongs. Plunge it head first into boiling water; cover and bring water back to boiling. Cook 12 to 15 minutes.

If you can't bring yourself to place a live lobster in a pot of boiling water, ask the man in the fish market to do it for you. It's best to have them cooked only a short time before using, though, for much of the delicate flavor of the meat disappears when the cooked lobster is kept under refrigeration for more than 24 hours.

To serve: After removing from water, place lobster on back. Slit center of undershell from head to tail with kitchen shears or sharp knife. Spread open and remove dark sand vein and stomach sac just below the head. Leave in the green liver or tomalley and red roe or "coral." Crack large claws for easier eating. Serve hot with lemon, small dishes of melted butter, and garnish with parsley. It is good to have cocktail forks and nutcrackers or lobster shears handy so every delicious little morsel is easy to eat.

To serve cold: Chill boiled lobster in the refrigerator. When ready to eat, split as above for serving boiled lobster. Serve tartar sauce or seasoned mayonnaise and a lemon wedge with it for added zest.

To remove lobster meat from shell for use in recipes: With lobster on its back, twist claws close to body; slit center of undershell from head to tail with kitchen shears or sharp knife. Spread lobster apart and pull meat up from tail, slipping it out in one piece. Slit center of meat (white side) to remove dark sand vein. Red roe or "coral" in female lobsters can be used for garnish or mixed with a cold salad; the green liver is also good. Separate tail from body; remove meat from body and discard stomach sac back of the head. Crack claws with nutcracker and remove meat.

How To Broil a Live Lobster

Allow 1 small or ½ large lobster per person. Lay lobster on chopping block, back shell down. At point where body and tail meet, insert sharp pick or point of knife through to back shell. Split lobster down the middle with a sharp knife; remove the stomach sac back of the head and discard it along with the dark intestinal vein that runs down the center. Crack claws. Preheat broiler for 10 minutes. Place lobster on broiler pan, shell side down. Brush with melted butter or margarine; season with salt and pepper, sprinkle with paprika. Broil 3 to 4 inches from heat about 15 to 18 minutes, depending on size, until lightly browned. Serve with lemon and melted butter or margarine. Garnish with parsley.

How To Cook Rock Lobster Tails

To Boil: Drop frozen tails into boiling, salted water (about 1 teaspoon salt per 1 quart of water). Bring water back to boiling; reduce heat; simmer tails 7 to 8 minutes for 4-ounce size. For larger tails increase simmering time. Follow package directions. When done, drain; cut thin membrane surrounding meat. Serve hot with melted butter or margarine or chilled with Tartar Sauce (*page 352*) or mayonnaise.

To Broil: Thaw in refrigerator or at room temperature if you plan to cook them immediately. Cut thin membrane surrounding the meat. Bend tail backwards, away from curled side, to crack slightly and to prevent curling; or insert skewer lengthwise through tail to keep tail flat. Preheat broiler for 10 minutes. Place tails on broiler rack, shell side up, about 5 inches away from heat. Broil about 2 minutes; turn and brush with butter or margarine. Broil 3 minutes or until lightly flecked with brown. Serve in shell with melted butter or margarine.

STUFFED LOBSTER TAILS

6 frozen lobster tails (8 to 10 oz. ea.)	2 tbs. chopped parsley
3 tbs. butter or margarine	½ tsp. salt
¼ lb. mushrooms, finely chopped	¼ tsp. pepper
¼ c. thinly sliced green onions	½ c. packaged bread crumbs
3 tbs. lemon juice or ¼ c. dry sherry	3 tbs. melted butter or margarine
	¼ tsp. leaf tarragon, crumbled
	Hot, cooked rice or Pilaf (*page 274*)

Mushroom-Cheese Pie—a delightful main dish, accompaniment, or app

THIS IS MUSHROOM CHEESE PIE!

Cook lobster tails according to directions on package; drain; cool. Remove meat from shell, taking care to keep shell intact; cube lobster meat. Melt 3 tablespoons butter or margarine in skillet; sauté mushrooms, onions, and lobster meat until vegetables are soft. Add lemon juice or sherry, parsley, salt, and pepper. Fill shells; sprinkle with bread crumbs which have been mixed with 3 tablespoons melted butter or margarine and tarragon. Bake at 450° F. for 12 to 15 minutes or until golden brown. Serve over hot, cooked rice or Pilaf. Makes 6 servings.

LOBSTER THERMIDOR
(Pictured opposite)

Chef Bailley at Very's Restaurant in Paris created this recipe and named it Lobster Napoleon in honor of the emperor. However, Napoleon thought that this recipe was so exceptional that it should be called Lobster Thermidor. Thermidor was the name given during the French Revolution to the eleventh month of the year in the Republican calendar.

3 lobsters* (2 lbs. ea.)	Dash of white pepper
3 shallots or green onions, chopped	Dash of ground nutmeg
2 tbs. butter or margarine	4 tbs. flour
1 tsp. dry mustard	2 c. milk, scalded
1 tsp. chopped parsley	¼ c. heavy cream
½ c. dry white wine	3 egg yolks, slightly beaten
4 tsp. minced onion	2 tbs. grated Parmesan cheese
4 tbs. melted butter or margarine	¾ tsp. salt
Dash of powdered thyme	2 tbs. whipped cream
	Grated Parmesan cheese

Boil lobsters in salted water 10 minutes; drain. Cool. Cut off claws. Crack claws. Cut lobsters in half lengthwise. Remove lobster meat from body and claws; cut into cubes. Clean out shells; reserve. Sauté shallots or green onions in 2 tablespoons butter or margarine; add mustard, parsley, and wine. Heat until wine is reduced to ¼ cup. Cook onion in 4 tablespoons butter or margarine 3 minutes; do not brown. Add thyme, pepper, nutmeg, and flour. Add scalded milk gradually. Simmer gently 5 minutes; strain. Add wine mixture. Combine heavy cream and egg yolks; add to sauce. Add 2 tablespoons Parmesan cheese and salt.

Heat 2 minutes. Reserve a third of sauce. Add lobster meat to remaining sauce. Heat gently. Place a spoonful of reserved sauce in each lobster shell. Fill shells with lobster mixture. Add whipped cream to remaining reserved sauce; spoon over lobsters. Sprinkle with additional cheese. Broil until lightly browned. Makes 6 servings.
* Or use 6 frozen lobster tails (8 to 10 oz. ea.). Boil the lobster tails in salted water according to the directions on the package. Drain. Cool. Remove membrane from tails; remove lobster meat; cut into cubes. Clean out shells; reserve. Prepare lobster mixture; fill shells, and broil as above.

CLAMS

Littlenecks, cherrystones, razor clams, quahogs, soft-shell clams—to the clam lover, each has its own special succulence. Clams offer their own variety of good eating for, in addition to the sumptuous recipes for clam dishes, they are also baked in pits under seaweed, as for clambakes, and stewed in chowders.

Kinds of Clams

Soft-shell Clams: These are found mainly in northern New England and Cape Cod waters. They are somewhat oval in shape with a long neck. There are two sizes, the smaller is known as "steamers," the larger known as "in-shells." They are especially good when steamed or fried.

Hard-shell Clams: They are found on the Atlantic Coast south of Cape Cod. They are also found in many varieties along the West Coast. The favorite hard-shell clams of the Northern Atlantic waters are known by the old Indian name *quahog*. They have a smooth, rounded shell and are usually found in three sizes: The smallest, the littleneck, and the medium, the cherrystone, are eaten raw on the half shell, and the largest, the chowder clam, is used for making the many kinds of chowder. The favorite West Coast clams are the razor clam, the littleneck (different from the Eastern variety), and the Pismo clam.

Buying Clams

Hard-shell clams can be purchased shucked or in the shell. If you buy them in the shell, make sure the shells are tightly closed, or if they are open slightly, that they close immediately when touched. Discard any that are broken. When steamed, the shells must all come wide open. If they do not, discard them.

For steamers, allow about one quart of unshucked clams per person. For eating them on the half shell, allow a minimum of 6 per person if they are to be served as a cocktail. Otherwise, hearty clam lovers know no limit!

How To Shuck, Serve, and Cook Clams

To Steam: Soft-shell clams are best for steaming. Wash and scrub clams under cold, running water until all sand disappears. Place clams in large kettle with 1 to 1½ inches water for about 4 quarts of clams. Cover and steam just until shells open. Serve each person about 1 quart, heaped in a bowl; add cups of strained clam broth and melted butter. *To eat:* Shell clam, dip into broth and then into butter. Eat all but the neck of the clam.

To Serve on the Half Shell: Wash and scrub clams under running cold water until all sand disappears. Drain. Place in refrigerator to let them "rest." This makes them easier to open. Shuck clams by inserting a sharp, thin knife or clam shucker between shells, cutting around the entire clam. Twist knife to pry open. Separate halves. Run knife under clam to loosen. Arrange on half shell.

To Fry: Drain shucked soft-shell clams, removing bits of shell. Dip each clam into beaten egg, then in packaged bread crumbs or fine cracker crumbs. Fry in deep fat at 375° F. until golden brown. Drain on paper towel.

CLAMS LICATA

4 dozen small hard-shell clams	1 can (2 lbs. 3 oz.) Italian plum tomatoes
8 cloves of garlic	
½ c. olive oil	Italian bread
1 bunch Italian parsley, chopped	

Scrub clams thoroughly with brush; reserve. Peel cloves of garlic; cut in half. Heat oil in large saucepan; add garlic. Cook just until garlic starts to brown; remove; discard. Add

parsley and tomatoes to oil. Bring to boiling, breaking tomatoes up with fork. Add clams; cover. Cook about 5 minutes or just until clams open. Serve in large soup plates with chunks of Italian bread. Makes 4 servings.

CRABS

Hard-Shell Crabs

If you live on the Pacific Coast, crab probably means *Dungeness* to you; if you live somewhere in the vicinity of the Chesapeake shore, it's *blue crab*. Or crab can be *king crab* from Alaska, available frozen and canned. The meat of all three is delicious, and in recipes calling for crab meat they can be used interchangeably.

Blue Crab: They are found along the Atlantic Coast, from North to South, though their chief habitat is the Chesapeake Bay. They are called "blue" because this is the color of the shell before they are cooked (when it turns bright red). They weigh from ¼ to 1 pound. Depending on size, 6 to 8 crabs will yield about 1 pound of cooked meat. Blue crab is packed and cooked in *lump* meat, *flake* meat, *lump and flake combined*, and *claw meat*.

King Crab: From Alaska, most of them are frozen or canned. The meat, in chunks, comes in 6-ounce packages, and leg portions in 12-ounce packages. Store in freezer unless you plan to use immediately.

Dungeness Crab: They are named for a town in the state of Washington that is on a strait where a large portion of the crabs breed. They weigh from 1¾ to 3½ pounds and are sold by the pound. The meat is sweet and delicate, more pinkish in color than the blue crab.

Japanese King Crab: Available canned only in 6½- to 7-ounce cans. It is meat from the claws of the Northern Pacific crabs.

To Cook Hard-Shell Crabs: Wash, scrub, and rinse thoroughly in cold water until crabs are clean. Grasping crabs by tongs, put them head first into seasoned boiling water to cover. (For every quart of water, use 1 tablespoon salt, 1 onion, sliced, 1 bay leaf, 1 tablespoon vinegar—or use "Crab Boil" seasoning available in your supermarket.) Return to boiling; cook 15 to 20 minutes until red. Drain and rinse with cold water; cool on board or tray.

To Remove the Meat: When cool, scrub under running, cold water. Twist off claws and legs; crack claws with mallet or hammer. Remove meat with pick or sharp paring knife. Slip knife under "apron" on back shell; break off. Pull body shells apart and discard top shell; rinse crab under running, cold water to remove spongy matter. Break body in half and cut off membranes around edges. Remove meat with pick or sharp knife, keeping it in as large pieces as possible.

Soft-Shell Crabs

These are blue crabs which have been caught just after they have shed their old shell and before the new shell has hardened.

Buying Soft-Shell Crabs: They are available during warm months from June until September. Allow about two per person.

To Prepare: Remove head of crab. Lay on back shell and pull shell from point on back about halfway to remove spongy matter and lungs. Repeat on other side. Remove "apron," as for hard-shell crabs. Rinse under running, cold water to remove all excess spongy matter.

How To Cook Soft-Shell Crabs

To Boil: Put cleaned crabs into boiling, salted water (1 teaspoon for each quart) to cover. Cover and return to boiling; boil for 15 minutes. Drain and serve, hot or cold with Tartar Sauce (*page 352*), lemon, or mayonnaise.

To Broil: Dip crab into seasoned butter or margarine mixture, then in flour. Broil under medium heat 8 to 10 minutes, turning once. Baste as they broil with rest of seasoned butter or margarine mixture. Serve with lemon wedges on toast points.

To Sauté: Season crabs with salt and pepper. Sauté in about 6 to 8 tablespoons of butter or margarine in skillet for about 2 to 3 minutes on each side or until golden brown. Season butter or margarine that remains in skillet with Worcestershire sauce, lemon juice, and parsley. Serve, topped with sauce, on toast points.

DEVILED CRAB

½ c. finely chopped onion (1 medium)	2 tsp. Worcestershire sauce
¼ c. finely chopped green pepper	1 tbs. prepared mustard
3 tbs. butter or margarine	1 tbs. finely chopped chives
3 tbs. flour	2 cans (7½ oz. ea.) crab meat, drained, boned, and flaked
1½ c. light cream	
2 egg yolks, slightly beaten	1 c. soft bread crumbs (2 slices)
Dash of cayenne	2 tbs. melted butter or margarine
½ tsp. salt	

Heat oven to 375° F. Sauté onion and green pepper in 3 tablespoons butter or margarine in saucepan until tender. Add flour; mix until smooth. Stir in cream gradually. Cook over medium heat, stirring constantly, until sauce thickens. Stir a small amount of hot sauce into egg yolks; add to sauce remaining in pan; heat 2 minutes. Remove from heat; add cayenne, salt, Worcestershire, mustard, and chives; mix well. Stir in crab meat. Spoon crab mixture in 6 buttered ramekins, custard cups, or 1-quart casserole. Combine bread crumbs and 2 tablespoons melted butter or margarine; sprinkle on crab mixture. Bake 20 to 25 minutes or until crumbs are golden brown. Makes 6 servings.

CRAB CREPES

1 recipe Crepes (*page 383*)	¾ c. milk
3 tbs. butter or margarine	2 egg yolks, beaten
3 tbs. flour	2 c. cooked fresh, thawed frozen, or drained canned crab meat
½ tsp. leaf thyme, crumbled	
2 tsp. minced onion	⅓ c. heavy cream, whipped
½ tsp. salt	
Dash of pepper	2 tbs. grated Parmesan cheese
¾ c. canned chicken broth	

Prepare Crepes according to recipe. Keep warm. Melt butter or margarine; blend in flour, thyme, onion, salt, and pepper. Mix in broth and milk gradually. Heat to simmering, stirring constantly. Lower heat; barely simmer 5 minutes. Stir half the mixture into egg yolks; stir into mixture in saucepan; cook 2 minutes. Add crab meat to 1 cup sauce. Fold whipped cream into remaining sauce. Place a spoonful of crab-meat mixture on each crepe; roll up. Place in single layer in shallow baking dish. Spoon whipped-cream mixture over crepes. Sprinkle with cheese. Broil until lightly browned. Makes 6 serivngs.

CRAB IMPERIAL

1 c. mayonnaise or salad dressing	2 c. cooked fresh, thawed frozen, or drained, canned crab meat
¼ c. finely chopped green pepper	
¼ c. finely chopped onion (1 small)	2 hard-cooked eggs, chopped
½ tsp. dry mustard	4 medium-size avocados
2 tbs. lemon juice	
½ tsp. salt	1 tbs. lemon juice
Dash of pepper	1 c. soft bread crumbs (2 slices)
	2 tbs. melted butter or margarine

Combine mayonnaise or salad dressing, green pepper, onion, mustard, 2 tablespoons lemon juice, salt, and pepper. Mix in crab meat and eggs. Cut avocados in half; remove seed. Cut a thin slice off bottom of each so avocado will stand. Brush cut surfaces with 1 tablespoon lemon juice. Mound crab-meat mixture on avocado halves. Combine bread crumbs and melted butter or margarine; sprinkle over

crab meat. Bake at 350° F. for 10 to 15 minutes or until crumbs are lightly browned. Serve at once. Makes 8 servings.

OYSTERS

In the Gay Nineties when oyster suppers were the rage, young people gathered in "oyster parlors" instead of sweet shops or drug stores. The renowned bivalve is not so plentiful now and no longer a raging fashion, but an Oyster Stew (*page 130*), when properly prepared is still a great American dish, and the "Peacemakers" (*below*) of New Orleans are as renowned as the gastronomic reputation of the old French Quarter itself.

Oysters are grown in shallow waters, bays, and the mouths of rivers, most of them on the Eastern seaboard, with Chesapeake Bay a major oyster-bed area. They range in size from very small to very large. On the Pacific Coast oysters range from the tiny Olympia oysters, that are no bigger than your thumbnail, to the giant-sized Japanese oysters.

Buying Oysters

They are sold alive in shells; shucked, in quart, pint, and ½-pint containers; canned; and frozen. Fresh oysters are available from September to May. When in the shell, buy only those with tightly closed shells. Allow about 6 oysters per person for a first course. Smoked oysters are available in cans to be served as hors d'ouevres.

Oysters come canned (about 5 ounces) and frozen (about 7-ounce cans).

How To Shuck, Serve, and Cook Oysters

To Serve on the Half-Shell: Wash, scrub, and rinse thoroughly in cold water. Shuck and serve as clams (*page 246*).

To Fry: See Peacemaker.

Pacemaker (Hot Oyster Loaf)

This hot, crispy, oyster-filled loaf, called the Peacemaker or La Médiatrice, is a well-known tradition in New Orleans. It is said that years ago husbands arriving home late at night would bring one of these to appease their waiting wives.

1 loaf French bread
¼ c. melted butter
  or margarine
2 cans (7 oz. ea.)
  frozen oysters,
  thawed or 3 doz.
  fresh oysters,
  shucked

Flour
2 eggs, slightly
  beaten
Packaged bread
  crumbs
Fat or pure vege-
  table oil

Cut top off loaf. Hollow out inside, leaving a ½-inch-thick shell. Brush inside and outside with melted butter or margarine. Place on baking sheet. Bake at 400° F. for 10 to 12 minutes or until loaf is nicely toasted. Drain oysters; coat with flour; dip in beaten eggs; roll in bread crumbs. Put enough fat or oil into skillet or deep saucepan to make it 2 inches deep when heated. Heat to 375° F. Fry oysters 3 to 4 minutes or until golden; drain on paper towels. Fill hot, toasted loaf with hot oysters; replace top. Slice or break into pieces. Makes 6 to 8 servings.

ESCALLOPED OYSTERS

1 c. soft bread
  crumbs (2 slices)
1 c. coarsely
  crumbled saltine
  crackers
⅓ c. melted butter
  or margarine
2 doz. raw oysters,
  shucked and
  drained (about
  1 qt.)

¼ c. oyster liquid
½ tsp. salt
⅛ tsp. pepper
2 tbs. light cream
1 tsp. Worcester-
  shire sauce
Dash cayenne
2 tbs. dry sherry

Sauté bread and cracker crumbs in butter or margarine in skillet over medium heat until golden. Sprinkle ⅓ crumb mixture on bottom of shallow 1½-quart casserole. Arrange half the oysters over crumbs. Combine oyster liquid and remaining ingredients. Sprinkle half the mixture over oysters. Repeat. Top with remaining crumbs. Bake at 425° F. for 30 minutes. Makes 6 servings.

MUSSELS

For those who live in port cities, the mussels are a favorite, inexpensive shellfish. Their meat is tender and delicious and they add dashing appearance to a paella or a bouilla-baisse.

Buying Mussels: Mussels are available all year. Buy them alive. Keep them covered in a cool, dark place but use as quickly as possible. They are usually sold by the peck or quart. A quart is enough to serve 2.

To Prepare: Mussels have a purple-black shell and each has a straggling "beard" which must be pulled away. Scrub them thoroughly before using to get rid of all the sand. Cook as for clams or oysters. Make sure the shell opens wide when cooked; otherwise discard.

SCALLOPS

There are *sea scallops* and *bay scallops:* the sea scallops come from the depths of the North Atlantic, the bay scallops are found in inshore waters from New England to the Gulf of Mexico. Many people believe the tiny bay scallops are sweeter and more tender than the larger, more economical sea scallops.

The name was said to have been given to these mollusks because the shell is daintily scalloped around the edges. In France, they are called "Coquilles Saint Jacques" (Shell of St. James), an emblem of one of the Crusader knights of the Middle Ages. The same name is given to a dish of creamed scallops baked in the shell.

Buying Scallops

Only the inside muscle or "eye" of the scallop is sold. Both types of scallops are at their best from November to April, though frozen sea scallops are now in our markets throughout the year, both in the natural state and breaded, ready to heat and serve.

Buy one pound of scallops for 3 or 4 persons.

How to Cook Scallops

To Sauté: Dip scallops into milk, then into flour seasoned with salt and pepper. Sauté in hot butter or margarine in skillet over low heat for 7 or 8 minutes until lightly browned but still moist. Serve with lemon wedges, garnish with chopped parsley.

To Broil: Preheat broiler for 10 minutes. Place scallops in a shallow pan. Brush with butter or margarine and season with salt, pepper, and paprika. Broil about 4 or 5 minutes, turning and basting often. Serve on toast points with melted butter seasoned with lemon juice.

COQUILLES ST. JACQUES MORNAY

1 c. dry white wine	3 tbs. flour
1½ c. water	½ c. shredded Swiss
½ tsp. salt	cheese
⅛ tsp. pepper	2 tbs. grated Par-
1 tbs. minced onion	mesan cheese
2 lbs. fresh or	¼ c. heavy cream,
frozen scallops	whipped
(sliced if large)	¼ c. melted butter
½ lb. mushrooms,	or margarine
sliced	3 tbs. chopped
1 c. milk	parsley
2 tbs. butter or	
margarine	

Combine wine, water, salt, pepper, and onion in large saucepan; simmer 5 minutes. Add scallops and mushrooms; cover; simmer 5 minutes. Remove scallops and mushrooms from pan and reserve. Cook liquid remaining in pan (the fish stock) until it is reduced to 1 cup. Heat milk just to boiling. Melt butter or margarine in saucepan; stir in flour (the roux). Cook over low heat, stirring constantly, until roux bubbles and foams for 3 minutes. It should not brown. Remove from heat. Stir in fish stock and milk. Stir rapidly with a wooden spoon or beat with wire whisk. Cook over low heat, stirring constantly, until mixture bubbles. Cook 1 minute longer. Stir in ¼ cup shredded Swiss cheese and the Parmesan cheese. Taste; correct seasonings. Remove from heat. Remove and reserve two-thirds cup

of sauce. Heat oven to 375° F. Add scallops and mushrooms to remaining sauce. Spoon mixture into each of six large buttered scallop shells or individual casseroles. Add whipped cream to reserved sauce. Spread layer of sauce with large spoon over scallop mixture. Sprinkle with remaining ¼ cup Swiss cheese. Drizzle the tops with butter or margarine. Bake until sauce bubbles and top is lightly brown. Sprinkle tops with parsley. Makes 6 servings.

SKILLET SCALLOPS ITALIENNE

¼ c. flour	1 envelope (1 tbs.)
1 tsp. paprika	instant chicken
1 tsp. salt	bouillon mix
1 lb. fresh or frozen	1 tsp. salt
scallops	¼ tsp. pepper
¼ c. olive oil	2 tbs. diced
1 clove of garlic	pimiento
1 pkg. (10 oz.)	2 tbs. lemon juice
frozen Italian	1 tbs. chopped
green beans	parsley
1 c. boiling water	

Combine flour, paprika, and 1 teaspoon salt. Toss scallops in mixture to coat evenly. Heat oil in skillet; add scallops with garlic clove; sauté about 5 minutes or until golden. Remove scallops from skillet; keep warm. Remove and discard garlic clove. Add green beans, boiling water, instant chicken bouillon, 1 teaspoon salt, pepper, and pimiento to oil remaining in skillet; cover; simmer 10 minutes. Add scallops and lemon juice; cook 5 minutes. Sprinkle with parsley. Makes 4 servings.

Chapter Fourteen

Stuffings

The stuffing is the extra dividend—an aromatic, taste-tingling ingredient—whether it's in the Thanksgiving turkey, a Cornish hen, a breast of veal, a flank steak, or a whole fish.

The ingredients that go into a stuffing are endless. Begin with white bread, corn bread, or rice. Then add tasty morsels such as mushrooms, celery, parsley, cranberries, chestnuts, nuts, oysters, sausage, potatoes, or onions. For seasonings, try thyme or sage, rosemary or celery seed, or already-blended poultry seasoning herbs.

Tips for Making Stuffing

· Bread stuffing should start with bread two to three days old. An easy way to make crumbs is to stack several slices of bread evenly, cut off the crusts, then cut the bread into cubes. (Our favorite way of doing it is to toast the bread first before cutting it into cubes.) Or you can pull the bread apart with your fingers into any size you like.
· How much bread? A 1-pound loaf of white bread will yield about 8 cups (2 quarts) of crumbs. You need 1 cup of stuffing for each pound of dressed bird. But have too much rather than too little and bake any extra in a covered casserole during the last hour the bird roasts.
· *Rice, potatoes, and corn bread* make marvelous stuffings, too.
· *Two kinds of stuffing* are better than one for a holiday bird; one in the neck, the other in the breast cavity. Put a plain bread stuffing in one for those who like things simple; in

the other put something imaginative and different like oyster or sausage stuffing, or a crunchy mixture of nuts and fruit with the bread.
· Always pack stuffing loosely; remember it swells with the moist juices of the bird during roasting.
· If you prefer your stuffing light and dry, no liquid need be added at all. If a moist stuffing is your preference, add about 2 tablespoons liquid to each cup of stuffing.
· Never place stuffing inside the bird until shortly before time to put it in the oven. You can have all the ingredients ready a day ahead. To do so:
1. Break the bread into crumbs; mix with dried herbs, salt, and other nonperishable seasonings.
2. Cook rice or potatoes ahead; keep covered in the refrigerator until needed.
3. Cook chestnuts at least a day ahead. They can be boiled, cooled, shelled, and chopped. Keep covered in the refrigerator.
4. Chop nuts and other ingredients such as dried fruits ahead of time.
5. Don't add ingredients such as meats, giblets, or fish in advance.
6. Cook onion and celery just before adding to the stuffing—the flavor will be much better that way.

Tips for Stuffing Birds

· Rinse bird with cold water. Drain and pat dry with paper towels.
· It's easier to stuff the neck cavity first. Put

in just enough stuffing to fill it lightly. Skewer the neck skin to the back.

· Now turn the bird over on its back and fill the body cavity lightly. Skewer, tuck, or sew closed. (See illustration *page 200*).

OLD-FASHIONED BREAD STUFFING

½ c. butter or margarine
2 c. finely chopped onion (2 large)
1½ c. chopped celery
1 c. butter or margarine

4 qts. cubed bread (about 32 slices), toasted if desired
1 to 1½ tsp. salt
1 tbs. poultry seasoning
2 tbs. chopped parsley
½ c. turkey broth or water

Melt ½ cup butter or margarine in skillet. Cook onion and celery until soft but not brown; add and melt 1 cup butter or margarine. Combine onion, celery, and butter or margarine, bread cubes, salt, poultry seasoning, parsley, and broth or water in large bowl; mix well. Stuff lightly into turkey. Enough for neck and body cavities of 16-to 18-pound turkey.

Moist Stuffing. Add an additional ½ cup turkey broth or water to Old-Fashioned Bread Stuffing.

Giblet Stuffing. Chop cooked giblets; add to Moist Stuffing.

You may want to add your own flavor variation such as sautéed sliced mushrooms or roasted chestnuts to this basic stuffing.

SAUSAGE STUFFING

2 lbs. sausage meat
5 qts. cubed day-old bread (about 40 slices)
2 lbs. chestnuts, roasted and halved
2 c. chopped onion (2 large)

1 c. chopped celery
1 c. chopped green olives
½ c. chopped parsley
2 tbs. leaf thyme, crumbled
2 tbs. leaf marjoram, crumbled
1 tsp. pepper
Turkey broth or water

Cook sausage meat in large skillet over medium heat, breaking meat up with fork as it cooks; drain. Combine all remaining ingredients, except broth or water, with sausage meat in large bowl; toss lightly to mix. Add only enough broth or water to moisten stuffing lightly. Sufficient to stuff neck and body cavities of a 20-pound turkey.

CORN BREAD STUFFING

1 c. minced onion (1 large)
½ c. chopped celery
½ c. butter or margarine
4 c. soft white bread crumbs (8 slices)
6 c. crumbled Corn Bread (*page 90*)

1 tsp. salt
1 tsp. thyme
½ tsp. sage
¼ tsp. pepper
¼ c. chopped parsley
1 c. chopped pecans (optional)
2 eggs, beaten

Sauté onion and celery in butter or margarine until soft. Combine white and corn bread crumbs, seasonings, and parsley. Stir in sautéed vegetables and pecans. Add eggs; mix well. Enough for neck and body cavities of a 10- to 12-pound turkey.

Mushroom Stuffing. Sauté 2 cups chopped mushrooms with onion and celery. Add to bread mixture.

CORN-BREAD SAUSAGE STUFFING

1 lb. sausage meat
1½ c. chopped onion
2 qts. cubed white bread (16 slices)
2 qts. cubed Corn Bread (*page 90*)
2 tsp. salt
¼ tsp. pepper

2 tsp. powdered sage
1 tsp. powdered thyme
1 tsp. leaf rosemary, crumbled
2½ c. turkey or chicken broth
1 egg, beaten

Brown sausage meat lightly over medium heat, breaking up with spoon as it cooks; remove meat; reserve. Sauté onion in sausage drippings until soft. Combine sausage, onion and drippings, white bread, corn bread, salt, pepper, sage, thyme, rosemary, broth, and egg; mix well. Stuff lightly into turkey. Enough for neck and body cavities of 16- to 18-pound turkey.

SAVORY RICE STUFFING

5 c. raw rice
Water
5 chicken-bouillon
  cubes
1 c. butter or
  margarine
2 c. chopped onion
  (2 large)

1 tsp. salt
¼ tsp. pepper
1 tsp. powdered
  thyme
1 tsp. powdered
  sage
1 tbs. chopped
  parsley

Cook rice in water according to package directions omitting salt and adding bouillon cubes. While rice cooks, melt butter or margarine in skillet; cook onion until soft. Combine cooked rice, onion and butter or margarine, salt, pepper, thyme, sage, and parsley; mix well. Stuff lightly into turkey. Enough for neck and body cavities of 16- to 18-pound turkey.

BRAZIL-NUT STUFFING

1 c. butter or
  margarine
2 c. sliced Brazil
  nuts
2 c. finely chopped
  onion (2 large)
3½ qts. cubed
  bread (about 28
  slices)

2 tsp. poultry
  seasoning
2 tsp. salt
¼ tsp. pepper
1 tsp. celery salt
1½ c. turkey broth
  or water

Melt butter or margarine in skillet. Sauté nuts and onion until onion is soft. Combine with bread cubes, poultry seasoning, salt, pepper, celery salt, and liquid; mix well. Stuff lightly into turkey. Enough for neck and body cavities of 16- to 18-pound turkey.

OYSTER STUFFING

4 qts. toasted bread
  cubes (about 32
  slices)
½ c. butter or
  margarine
1 c. chopped celery
1½ c. chopped
  onion
½ c. butter or
  margarine

1 qt. oysters with
  liquid or 4 cans
  (7 oz. ea.)
  frozen oysters
  with liquid,
  thawed
½ c. milk
1 tsp. powdered
  sage
2 tsp. salt
⅛ tsp. pepper

Measure bread cubes into large bowl. Melt ½ cup butter or margarine in skillet; cook celery and onion until soft. Pour over bread cubes. Heat ½ cup butter or margarine in skillet; add oysters and liquid; heat a few minutes until edges curl; remove oysters. Pour liquid from skillet over bread cubes. Chop oysters coarsely; add to bread mixture. Add milk, sage, salt, and pepper; mix well. Stuff lightly into turkey. Enough for neck and body cavities of 16- to 18-pound turkey.

WILD RICE — MUSHROOM STUFFING

1 pkg. wild and
  white rice mix
2 tbs. butter or
  margarine
2 tbs. chopped
  onion

1 can (3 to 4 oz.)
  mushrooms,
  stems and pieces
1 tbs. chopped
  parsley

Cook rice mix according to package directions. Melt butter or margarine in small skillet; cook onion until soft. Drain and chop mushrooms. Combine cooked wild rice mixture, onion, mushrooms, and parsley; Mix well. Stuff lightly into neck cavity of 16- to 18-pound turkey.

PENNSYLVANIA-DUTCH POTATO STUFFING

1 pkg. (8 servings)
  instant mashed
  potatoes
7 c. toasted bread
  cubes (14 to 16
  slices)
¼ c. butter or
  margarine
1 c. minced onion
  (1 large)

½ c. minced celery
1 tsp. leaf rose-
  mary, crumbled
1 tsp. powdered
  sage
½ tsp. powdered
  thyme
1 tsp. salt
¼ tsp. pepper

Prepare instant potatoes according to package directions. Measure bread cubes into large bowl. Heat butter or margarine in skillet; cook onion and celery until soft. Add potatoes, onion, celery, rosemary, sage, thyme, salt, and pepper to bread cubes; mix well. Stuff lightly into turkey. Enough for neck and body cavities of 16- to 18-pound turkey.

STUFFING BALLS

3 qts. cubed bread
  (about 24 slices)
1 tsp. powdered
  sage
2 tbs. chopped
  parsley
¼ c. minced onion
  (1 small)

1 tsp. celery seed
1 tsp. salt
¼ tsp. pepper
½ c. butter or
  margarine,
  melted
½ c. turkey broth
  or water
2 egg whites,
  slightly beaten

Combine all ingredients in large bowl; mix well. Form into 12 balls. Place on greased cookie sheet. Bake at 325° F. for 35 to 45 minutes. Makes 1 dozen.

CRANBERRY-PECAN STUFFING

½ c. cranberry-
  orange relish
  (from 14 oz. jar)
½ c. chopped
  pecans
2 c. cubed bread
  (4 slices)

½ tsp. powdered
  sage
¼ tsp. salt
⅛ tsp. pepper
2 tbs. melted butter
  or margarine
2 tbs. turkey broth
  or water

Mix all ingredients well. Stuff lightly into neck cavity of 16- to 18-pound turkey.

CHESTNUT STUFFING

1 lb. chestnuts
4 c. soft bread
  crumbs (8 slices)
¼ c. butter or
  margarine
¼ c. finely chopped
  onion (1 small)

1 tsp. powdered
  sage
1 tsp. salt
⅛ tsp. pepper
1 c. turkey broth
  or water

Cut long slits in chestnuts. Roast at 450° F. for 20 minutes. Put crumbs on baking sheet; toast lightly in oven while roasting chestnuts. Shell and remove inner skin of chestnuts. Cook in boiling salted water 15 to 20 minutes or until tender; drain; chop. Melt butter or margarine in skillet; cook onion until soft. Add toasted crumbs, sage, salt, pepper, broth or water, and chestnuts; mix well. Stuff lightly into neck cavity of 16- to 18-pound turkey.

FISH STUFFING I

2 tbs. finely
  chopped onion
2 tbs. butter or
  margarine
1½ c. diced bread
½ c. cottage cheese
1 tsp. finely
  chopped fresh
  dill or dried dill

1 tbs. finely
  chopped dill
  pickle
½ tsp. salt
Dash of pepper
2 tsp. lemon juice

Sauté onion in butter or margarine; add bread; mix well; add cottage cheese, dill, dill pickle, salt, pepper, and lemon juice; mix thoroughly. Sufficient to stuff 3-pound fish.

FISH STUFFING II

½ c. diced celery
½ c. chopped onion
  (1 medium)
⅓ c. butter or
  margarine
½ tsp. salt
⅛ tsp. pepper

½ tsp. leaf
  tarragon,
  crumbled
3 c. soft bread
  crumbs (6 slices)
Milk

Sauté celery and onion in butter or margarine 5 minutes or until soft. Add salt, pepper, and tarragon; remove from heat. Measure bread crumbs into large mixing bowl; add celery mixture; toss to mix well. Add just enough milk to moisten stuffing lightly. Sufficient for 4-pound fish.

Chapter Fifteen

Eggs and Cheese

How To Buy Eggs

Fresh fancy, grade A, large, extra large, jumbo,—aren't the labels on an egg carton bewildering? And yet they are very simple to understand once you know that one set of terms denotes the quality of the egg, the other the size.

Grade

Eggs of all sizes, brown or white, are graded *fresh fancy* or *grade AA, grade A, grade B,* and *grade C.* What is the difference? You can't tell by the shell. The best eggs bear a U.S. *fresh fancy* or *grade AA* label. They have a small spread when broken. The white is thick and high, the yolk firm and high. The egg marked *grade A* has a little more spread and a white that's not so thick and high. *Grade B* and *C* eggs have a widely spreading white and a flat, large yolk. They are fine for general cooking and baking. All the other grades are perfect for any use but are especially good for frying, poaching, and boiling where the appearance of the egg is important.

Size

How large is a large egg? Government standards say a dozen *large eggs* must weigh at least 24 ounces, so a large egg should average about 2 ounces. *Extra-large* eggs and *jumbo* eggs are somewhat heavier and *medium* and *small* eggs lighter. Most standard recipes have been developed using large and medium eggs. Homemakers generally prefer large eggs for breakfast, luncheon, and dinner main dishes. Medium and small are excellent hard-cooked or deviled.

Color

Shell color may vary from white to deep brown, but the egg is still the same. There is no reason to pay a higher price for a particular shell color. In areas where white eggs are in greater demand you can save money buying the brown ones—and vice versa.

Temperature

It is best to buy eggs from a refrigerated counter. Heat and abrupt changes in temperature destroy quality.

How To Handle and Store Eggs

Eggs are delicate and their shells porous. Treat them gently.

Place eggs in the refrigerator as soon as possible after you buy them. Store them small side down and away from strong-smelling food. If any have cracked shells, use them first. If there are several cracked eggs in the box and if the shells are soiled, better return them to the store. Use the eggs you buy as soon as possible.

Leftover yolks may be kept two or three days if covered with water in a covered jar and refrigerated.

Store *leftover egg whites* in a tightly-covered jar. They will keep fresh for a week to ten days.

Tips on Egg Cooking

· *Eggs beat up faster* and give their greatest volume at room temperature, so take them out of the refrigerator 30 to 45 minutes before using. This is particularly true of the whites of the eggs.

· *When eggs are to be beaten separately*, it's practical to beat the whites first, then the yolks, to save washing the beaters. If you must beat the yolks first, be sure to wash off all the yolk from the beaters carefully in sudsy water, then rinse well and dry thoroughly before beating the whites.

· *To combine beaten egg whites with other ingredients*, fold—don't stir—using a light under-and-over motion. Follow your recipe; often it's best to fold the heavy mixture into the beaten egg whites, rather than the whites into the other mixture. Overmixing will cause loss of some of the air you've so carefully incorporated into the whites—so take it easy.

· *When combining hot mixtures and beaten eggs or yolks*, always stir the hot mixture into the beaten eggs a little at a time. Keep stirring constantly. When half the hot mixture has been added to the eggs, return this mixture to the saucepan and continue with the recipe.

· *Always cook eggs at low temperature.* Whether frying, scrambling, boiling, or baking eggs, keep the heat low. (Eggs should never literally be "boiled"; the water should simmer ever so gently—that's why they are often referred to as "hard-cooked eggs.") When heat is too high, the eggs become tough and harder to digest—as well as less flavorful.

· *To separate yolks from whites:* They separate better when at room temperature. Crack the shell right in the middle, by giving the egg a quick, sharp tap on the edge of a sharp object. Then pull apart gently, and with a juggling motion, move the yolk from one-half the shell to the other, letting the white dribble down into a clean bowl. (Be sure the bowl is clean—not a trace of grease.)

· *What to do if a bit of yolk gets into the white?* Carefully lift it out by scooping up with a half-shell or with a corner of torn paper towel.

How Many Eggs to a Cup: Four to six whole eggs, 8 to 10 egg whites, or 12 to 14 egg yolks are the equivalent of one standard measuring cup.

Uses for Leftover Yolks and Whites

When a recipe calls for only yolks, or only whites, what do you do with the leftovers? There are many recipes in this book that call for either egg yolks or egg whites. The following are just some suggestions of things you can make to use up those leftover yolks and whites.

EGG YOLKS

Two Egg Yolks

Mayonnaise (*page 344*)
Old-Fashioned Boiled Dressing (*page 345*)
Fish Filets Normandy Style (*page 234*)
Filets of Sole Jacqueline (*page 234*)
De Luxe Chocolate Frosting (*page 453*)
Chocolate Cream Filling (*page 455*)
Orange-Pineapple Filling (*page 455*)
Lemon Filling (*page 455*)
Eggnog Sauce (*page 399*)
Butterscotch Crème Sauce (*page 399*)
Peach Brandy Bavarian Cream (*page 364*)

Three Egg Yolks

Gold Cake (*page 438*)
Hungarian Chocolate Frosting (*page 453*)
Custard Sauce Royale (*page 399*)

Four Egg Yolks

French Velvet Chocolate Frosting (*page 453*)
Custard Rum Sauce (*page 399*)
Old-Fashioned Lemon Ice Cream (*page 391*)
Orange Rice Imperial (*page 367*)
Apricot Bavarian Cream (*page 365*)

Five Egg Yolks

Royal Gold Cake (*page 438*)

Six Egg Yolks

Zabaglione (*page 369*)
Pots de Crème au Chocolat (*page 369*)

EGG WHITES

Two Egg Whites

Fluffy Orange Frosting (454)
Jelly Frosting (*page 454*)
Peppermint Candy Charlotte (*page 392*)
Raspberry Velvet Soufflé (*page 365*)
Frozen Lemon Dessert (*page 392*)

Three Egg Whites

Fluffy 7-Minute Frosting (*page 454*)
White Mountain Cream Frosting (*page 454*)
Seafoam Frosting (*page 454*)
Royal Frosting (*page 454*)
Prune Whip (*page 357*)
Snowberry Cake (*page 435*)

Four Egg Whites

Raspberry Alaska (*page 397*)
Poppy Seed Cake (*page 436*)

Five Egg Whites

White Cloud Cake (*page 436*)

Six Egg Whites

Baby Angel Food Cake (*page 445*)
Meringues (*page 381*)

BASIC WAYS OF COOKING EGGS

It's hard to change cooking terms that have been used for generations—but there should be no such thing as a "boiled" egg. The correct term is soft- or hard-cooked because they should cook by heat, not boiling water.

To Soft-Cook

Cold Water Method: Put eggs in saucepan. Add water so it comes at least 1 inch above the eggs. Bring rapidly to boiling. Turn off heat. If necessary, remove pan from burner or unit to prevent further cooking. Cover; let stand 2 to 4 minutes, depending on how done you wish your eggs. Cool eggs at once in cold water for several seconds to prevent further cooking and to make them easier to handle.

Boiling Water Method: To avoid cracked shells, place cold eggs in warm water. Transfer eggs to boiling water in saucepan with spoon (there should be enough water to cover eggs); turn off heat. If necessary, remove pan from burner or unit to prevent further boiling. Cover and let stand 6 to 8 minutes. Cool as above.

To Hard-Cook

Cold Water Method: Follow directions for Soft-Cooked Eggs—Cold Water Method. Let stand 15 minutes. Cool promptly and thoroughly in cold water. This makes the shells easier to remove and helps prevent dark surface on yolks.

Boiling Water Method: Follow directions for Soft-Cooked Eggs—Boiling Water Method, but after placing eggs in boiling water, reduce heat to keep water below *simmering* and hold 20 minutes. Cool as above.

To Remove the Shell: Crackle the shell by rolling egg on counter top. Roll egg between hands to loosen shell, then start the peeling at the large end of the egg. Dipping in a bowl of water helps to ease the shell off.

To Fry, Method 1

Heat 1 to 2 tablespoons fat in a skillet that is just hot enough to sizzle a drop of water. Break and slip eggs into skillet—from a sauce dish, if preferred. Reduce heat immediately. Cook slowly to desired doneness, 3 to 4 minutes. Baste with fat during cooking. Instead of basting, skillet may be covered, or eggs may be turned over.

To Fry, Method 2

Use just enough fat to grease a skillet. Proceed as above. Cook over low heat until edges turn white, about 1 minute. Add ½ teaspoon water for one egg, decreasing proportion slightly for each additional egg. Cover skillet tightly to hold in steam which bastes the egg. Cook to desired doneness.

To Poach

Put water in a shallow pan; bring to boiling— there should be about two inches of water. Reduce heat to hold temperature at simmering. Break each egg into a sauce dish and slip egg into water quickly at the surface. Cook 3 to 5 minutes depending on the firmness desired. Remove eggs with slotted pancake turner or spoon, and drain.

Salt and vinegar are unnecessary to poaching. Milk or broth may be used instead of water.

There are egg poachers in all housewares departments which many people feel are much easier to use. Follow manufacturer's directions.

To Scramble

Success in scrambling eggs depends to a large degree on the pan or skillet you use. An omelet pan with sloping sides is ideal or a Teflon-coated skillet (these usually have sloping sides). The pan should be the right size for the number of eggs you plan to scramble. If too large, the beaten egg spreads out too thin. If too small, the beaten egg mixture is too thick and does not cook quickly enough to be still soft, yet firm when cooked through.

A 7- to 8-inch omelet pan or skillet is just right for three or four eggs. For 5 to 6 eggs, you should use a 10-inch skillet. Don't try to scramble more than six eggs at a time. It's better to cook two or more batches in succession.

Allow at least 2 eggs to a serving. Six eggs will serve two or three persons—scrambled eggs somehow never seem to go as far as other egg dishes.

Beat the eggs so that they are well blended but not foamy. Use a whisk or fork, or for fluffier eggs a rotary beater or hand mixer.

Add 1 tablespoon liquid (milk, cream, or evaporated milk), salt (¼ teaspoon for 3 or 4 eggs, ½ teaspoon for 6 eggs), a dash of pepper, and any other seasonings you happen to like.

Melt 1 to 1½ tablespoons butter or margarine in the skillet over *low heat*. Do not let butter sizzle; it should be merely liquid when eggs are added. Keep heat *very* low as eggs cook. Lift from bottom and sides as mixture thickens. As cooked mixture is lifted, the thin, uncooked part should flow to bottom. Cook until eggs are thickened throughout but still moist, about 5 to 8 minutes.

To Bake or Shirr

In France eggs prepared this way are called *oeufs aux plat*, and they make not only superb fare for brunch, but are marvelous for lunch or supper dishes, too.

Preheat oven to 325° F. Break and slip 1 or 2 eggs into buttered individual shallow baking dishes or shirred-egg dishes. Bake 12 to 18 minutes, depending upon firmness desired. Serve from baking dishes.

SHIRRED EGGS WITH HAM

8 thin slices cooked ham, cut in triangles	Dash of salt Dash of pepper Dash of paprika
½ c. light cream	1 tbs. chopped
8 eggs	parsley

Heat oven to 325° F. Arrange 4 triangles of ham around sides of each of 4 buttered shirred-egg dishes. Pour a tablespoon of cream into each dish. Carefully break 2 eggs into each dish; sprinkle with salt, pepper, and paprika. Bake 12 to 18 minutes or until just set. Sprinkle with chopped parsley. Makes 4 servings.

CREOLE EGGS

½ c. finely chopped onion (1 medium)	1 tsp. salt Dash of pepper 1 tsp. sugar
½ c. finely chopped green pepper	1 tsp. Worcestershire sauce
½ c. finely diced celery	½ tsp. leaf basil, crumbled
2 tbs. butter or margarine	8 eggs ⅓ c. shredded
1 can (1 lb. 4 oz.) tomatoes	Cheddar cheese

Sauté onion, green pepper, and celery in butter or margarine until tender. Add tomatoes; break tomatoes up with fork. Stir in salt, pepper, sugar, Worcestershire, and basil. Simmer, uncovered, 15 minutes. Heat oven to 325° F. Pour ¼ cup tomato mixture into each of 8 shirred-egg dishes or small custard cups. Carefully break an egg into each dish; sprinkle with cheese. Bake about 12 to 18 minutes or until eggs are just set. Makes 8 servings.

OMELETS

The French Omelet

Say "omelet," and you immediately visualize a delectable oval of egg, cooked to such perfection that it is firm on the outside, yet soft and creamy inside. The omelet, when properly prepared, is a culinary triumph and can establish a reputation for the one who masters its techniques. This technique, once learned, is never forgotten. And, consider the omelet's versatility. It can be the main course for any meal of the day, whether served plain or filled. In its sweet version, filled with jelly or fruit it becomes a most impressive dessert.

Start

Secrets of Making Successful Omelets

· To make an omelet you need the proper skillet, fresh eggs, butter, a willing hand, and *practice, practice, practice*. First choose your skillet. It may be of cast aluminum, stainless steel, or cast iron. Be sure it is rounded where the bottom and sides meet. A 10-inch skillet is ideal for a four-egg omelet, a 7-inch one for an omelet made with two or three eggs. We recommend that you do not attempt to make an omelet of more than four eggs as it becomes too difficult to handle. They take so little time to make, it is better to make smaller ones, one after another, than a large one.

· Before using your skillet, it must be seasoned. Experts and purists maintain that once this is done, you should reserve this skillet solely for omelets, wiping—not washing—after each use. This is fine if you plan to make omelets often. On the other hand, if the skillet is one you must use for everyday cooking and omelets are a sometimes thing, remember that you must season the skillet each time before making an omelet.

· Clean the skillet to a glistening brightness with a soapy steel-wool pad, then wash and dry it. Pour in pure vegetable oil to a depth of one inch and place over medium heat for 20 minutes. Pour off the oil (you can use it for other cooking), wipe the skillet with paper towels and it is ready.

· Take the eggs from the refrigerator about an hour ahead of time. Have everything ready before you begin. If you are going to make a filled omelet, always prepare the filling mixture first.

· With these secrets, the recipe below, and the step-by-step illustrations you are ready to make an omelet. One last caution—it is a quick process, taking only about two minutes from start to finish, so study all the steps carefully before you begin. There won't be an opportunity to stop and consult them once you start.

BASIC FRENCH OMELET

4 eggs	1 tbs. butter or
1/4 tsp. salt	margarine
Dash of pepper	

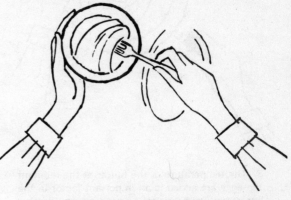

1. Break the eggs into a bowl and add the seasonings. Beat them briskly with a fork just until the yolks and whites are mixed. Don't overbeat! They will look stringy and will actually form a string on the fork as you lift.

2. Place the seasoned skillet over high heat. When it is sizzling hot, put in the butter. Stir it around quickly with the fork to coat the bottom and sides of pan.

3. The temperature of the butter at the moment the eggs are added is an important factor in the success of your omelet. As soon as the foaming subsides, quickly pour in the eggs all at once. If the butter has turned brown, discard it and wipe out the skillet with a paper towel. Then begin again.

5. Shake the pan. The omelet should move freely and is ready to roll. If it is to be a filled omelet, spoon or sprinkle on filling as individual omelet recipe directs.

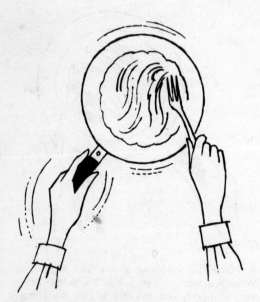

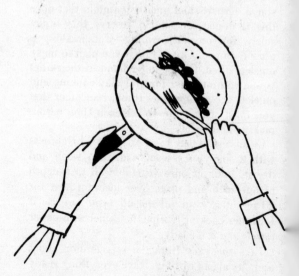

4. Now you must work quickly. Stir the eggs rapidly with a circular motion with the flat of the fork, and, at the same time, shake the pan vigorously to and fro over the heat. Stir just until all the free liquid begins to set. Pat the omelet with the back of fork so it is even in the pan, and let it stand about two or three seconds.

6. Take the fork and start rolling the omelet gently. Lift the side nearest the skillet handle and fold one third of the omelet over the center. Always use a light and delicate touch so you will preserve the omelet's fluffiness.

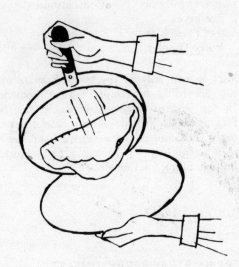

7. Hold the heated serving plate in your left hand and grasp the pan handle with your right, palm up. As you tilt the pan over the plate let the omelet roll out onto it. Rub top of omelet with butter or margarine to give it a shine, if desired. Makes 2 servings.

Sweet French Omelet: Add 1 tbs. sugar to eggs with salt and pepper before beating. Proceed as for Basic French Omelet.

The Puffy Omelet

This member of the omelet family has been praised as "a most heavenly bit of air." The air you beat into the eggs gives the puff to your omelet. *Secret:* To get the most air in your omelet, you must always beat the whites to stiff peaks and then carefully and thoroughly fold in the yolks. It has two steps in its cooking—on the range and in the oven. Because of this second phase, choose a skillet that has a heatproof or removable handle.

BASIC PUFFY OMELET

4 egg whites	Dash of pepper
4 egg yolks	2 tbs. butter or
¼ c. milk or cream	margarine
⅛ tsp. salt	

Heat oven to 350° F. Beat egg whites until stiff peaks form. Beat egg yolks in second bowl until thick and lemon colored; beat in milk or cream, salt, and pepper. Fold into beaten egg whites. Heat butter or margarine in heavy skillet with heatproof or removable handle until sizzling. Pour in egg mixture. Cook slowly, about 10 minutes or until brown underneath. (Bubbles will appear through uncooked puffy top and mixture will look moist.) Transfer to oven. Bake 10 to 15 minutes or until light brown on top and no imprint remains when it is lightly touched with finger. With spatula, cut a deep gash through center of omelet being careful not to cut through to bottom. (Omelet can be filled at this point.) Slip broad spatula or pancake turner under one side, tip skillet to loosen omelet and fold carefully in half without breaking. Slip omelet onto heated platter with spatula. Serve at once. Makes 2 servings.

HERB OMELET
(Omelette aux Fines Herbes)

2 tbs. chopped parsley	¼ tsp. leaf basil, crumbled
1 tsp. chopped chives	Basic French Omelet
¼ tsp. leaf tarragon, crumbled	

Beat herbs into eggs with salt and pepper in preparing the Basic French Omelet. Cook as for omelet. Makes 1.

OMELET WITH CROUTONS
(Omelette aux Croutons)

2 tbs. butter or margarine	2 slices day-old bread, cut in
½ clove of garlic	¼-inch cubes
	Basic French or Puffy Omelet

Melt butter or margarine in skillet. Spear garlic with fork; rub all around hot fat in skillet; remove and discard. Sauté bread cubes in garlic-flavored fat until golden and toasted. Prepare omelet according to recipe; scatter croutons over omelet just before folding. Enough filling for 1 omelet.

SPANISH OMELET

(Omelette à l'Espagnole)

1 c. sliced onion (1 large)
1 green pepper, seeded and cut in strips
2 tbs. butter or margarine

1 can (about 1 lb.) Italian plum tomatoes
1 tsp. salt
⅛ tsp. pepper
1 tsp. leaf basil, crumbled
Basic French or Puffy Omelet

Sauté onion and green pepper in butter or margarine until soft; add tomatoes, salt, pepper, and basil. Cook over medium heat, stirring occasionally, about 20 minutes or until mixture is quite thick. Keep warm. Prepare omelet according to recipe. Spoon ¼ cup tomato mixture onto omelet just before folding. Spoon second ¼ cup over folded omelet. Enough filling for 2 omelets.

OMELET, PEASANT STYLE

(Omelette Paysanne)

4 slices bacon
1 tbs. minced onion
2 medium-size potatoes, pared and cut in ¼-inch cubes

1 tbs. chopped parsley
Basic French or Puffy Omelet

Cook bacon until crisp; crumble. Sauté onion and potatoes in 2 tablespoons of bacon fat until soft and brown; sprinkle with parsley; stir in bacon; keep warm. Prepare omelet according to recipe; sprinkle with half the potato mixture just before folding. Enough filling for 2 omelets.

CHEESE OMELET

(Omelette au Fromage)

Cheddar, Swiss, or Provolone cheese
Basic French or Puffy Omelet

1 tsp. softened butter or margarine
1 tbs. grated Parmesan cheese

Shred or cube enough cheese to make ¼ cup. Prepare omelet according to recipe. Sprinkle cheese over omelet just before folding. Rub top of folded omelet with butter or margarine; sprinkle with Parmesan cheese. Enough filling for 1 omelet.

JELLY OMELET

(Omelette aux Confiture)

½ c. tart jelly or preserves
Sweet French or Puffy Omelet

Confectioners' sugar

Melt ¼ cup jelly or preserves. Prepare omelet according to recipe. Spread unmelted ¼ cup jelly or preserves on omelet just before folding. Sprinkle folded omelet generously with confectioners' sugar; pour melted jelly or preserves over and around omelet. Enough filling for 1 omelet.

FRESH STRAWBERRY OMELET

(Omelette Parisienne aux Fraises)

½ c. strawberries, washed, hulled, and sliced
2 tbs. sugar

1 tbs. orange curaçao
Sweet French or Puffy Omelet
Dairy sour cream

Combine sliced strawberries, sugar, and curaçao in small bowl; refrigerate 15 minutes. Prepare omelet according to recipe. Spoon strawberry mixture on omelet just before folding. Top folded omelet with a generous dollop of sour cream. Garnish with whole, unhulled strawberry and a sprig of mint, if desired. Enough filling for 1 omelet.

NORMANDY APPLE OMELET

(Omelette à la Normande)

1 c. water
1 c. sugar
2 apples, pared, cored, and sliced
2 tbs. butter or margarine

½ tsp. ground cinnamon
Sweet French or Puffy Omelet
2 tbs. sugar

Cook water and 1 cup of sugar to boiling. Add apple slices; simmer gently until slices are soft and slightly translucent, but still whole. Drain (use syrup for other desserts). Add butter or margarine and cinnamon to apple slices; stir gently to coat evenly. Prepare omelet according to recipe. Arrange half the apple slices on omelet just before folding. Place on heatproof plate. Sprinkle top with 2 tablespoons sugar. Slip omelet under hot broiler for 1½ to 2 minutes or until sugar forms a crusty shell. Enough filling for 2 omelets.

LOBSTER OMELET

(Omelette d'Homard)

1 tbs. butter or margarine	1 can (3 to 4 oz.) sliced mush- rooms, drained
2 tsp. flour	
¼ tsp. seasoned salt	2 tbs. dry sherry
⅛ tsp. pepper	Basic French or
1 c. light cream	Puffy Omelet
1 can (5 oz.) lobster, drained and boned	1 tbs. chopped parsley

Melt butter or margarine in saucepan; stir in flour, salt, and pepper. Add cream slowly. Cook, stirring constantly until thickened and bubbly. Stir in lobster, mushrooms, and sherry. Simmer 2 minutes; keep warm. Prepare omelet according to recipe. Spoon on half the lobster mixture just before folding. Fold; sprinkle with parsley. Enough filling for 2 omelets.

CHICKEN LIVER OMELET

(Omelette aux Foie de Volailles)

1 pkg. (8 oz.) frozen chicken livers, thawed	½ c. dry white wine
¼ c. flour	1 tsp. finely chopped chives
2 tbs. minced green onions	1 tbs. chopped parsley
2 tbs. butter or margarine	Basic French or Puffy Omelet

Separate chicken livers; coat lightly with flour. Sauté onions in butter or margarine in medium-size skillet until soft. Add chicken livers; cook until brown on all sides. Remove livers from skillet; chop coarsely. Pour wine into hot skillet; stir with spoon to loosen all brown bits on bottom of pan. Add chopped livers, chives, and parsley; simmer 5 minutes, stirring occasionally; keep warm. Prepare omelet according to recipe. Spoon half the chicken liver mixture on omelet just before folding. Enough filling for 2 omelets.

COTTAGE CHEESE OMELET

¼ c. diced celery	1 can (3 to 4 oz.) sliced mush- rooms, drained
1 tbs. minced onion	
¼ c. diced cooked ham	1 carton (8 oz.) cottage cheese
2 tbs. butter or margarine	Puffy Omelet

Sauté celery, onion, and ham in butter or margarine in skillet 5 minutes or until vegetables are tender. Stir in mushrooms and cottage cheese. Cook just until heated through; remove from heat. Prepare omelet according to recipe. Spoon cottage cheese mixture onto omelet just before folding. Enough filling for 1 omelet.

THE BASQUE PIPÉRADE

Basque pipérade is a specialty of that region of France that borders on Spain. Because of the proximity of the two countries, many recipes of the region show a definite Spanish flavor. The pipérade is an open-faced omelet with a tomato topping and it is served in wedges. Since it does not have to be folded, there is no cause for alarm if it sticks a bit.

½ c. sliced onion (1 medium)	1 firm, ripe tomato, peeled and diced
½ c. diced green pepper	8 eggs
3 tbs. butter or margarine	½ tsp. salt
1 c. slivered, cooked ham	⅛ tsp. pepper
	2 tbs. butter or margarine

Sauté onion and green pepper in 3 tablespoons butter or margarine until soft; remove from pan. Sauté ham in fat remaining in pan until nicely browned. Combine onion mixture, ham, and tomato; keep warm. Beat eggs, salt, and pepper until blended. Melt 2 tablespoons butter or margarine in 10-inch skillet. Pour in eggs; stir quickly with flat of fork until eggs are beginning to set. Stir warm tomato mixture into soft top layer of eggs. Cook 1 minute longer. Cut in wedges to serve. Makes 6 servings.

SOUFFLÉS

Why is it so many women never dream of serving a puffy soufflé? Just because you had a devastating experience that left both you and the soufflé deflated? Or you think a soufflé is expensive, overly difficult, a dish only for the gourmet chef? A soufflé is none of these. There's nothing expensive about a few eggs, white sauce, a cup of diced or pureed food—*and air*. There's nothing difficult if you know a few simple *secrets*.

· First, the thick sauce is combined with the beaten egg yolks, then with the chosen cheese, meat, or vegetable.

· Next come the egg whites on which the success and glory of your soufflé depend. Whites should be stiff but not dry, folded, never stirred or beaten, into the sauce mixture.

· The sauce mixture can be made a little ahead of time but the whites should be beaten and added to the warm, not hot, sauce, just before baking time.

· And just one more secret—the guests must wait for the soufflé, the soufflé must *never, never* wait for the guests.

TUNA SOUFFLÉ

4 tbs. butter or margarine	1 can (6½ to 7 oz.) tuna, drained and finely chopped
4 tbs. flour	
⅛ tsp. pepper	¼ c. diced (¼ in. pieces) Swiss cheese
½ tsp. onion salt	
¼ tsp. salt	
1 c. milk	4 egg whites
4 egg yolks, well beaten	¼ tsp. cream of tartar

Melt butter or margarine in saucepan; stir in flour, pepper, onion salt, and salt. Cook over medium heat, stirring constantly, until mixture bubbles. Remove from heat; blend in milk slowly. Cook over medium heat, stirring constantly, until mixture thickens and bubbles (sauce will be quite thick). Remove from heat; beat mixture slowly into egg yolks; stir in tuna and Swiss cheese; cool. Heat oven to 350° F. Beat egg whites with cream of tartar until stiff but not dry. Gently fold tuna mixture into egg whites. Pour into an ungreased 1½-quart soufflé dish. Bake 50 to 60 minutes or until soufflé is puffed and golden and fairly firm to touch. Serve at once. Makes 6 servings.

Salmon Soufflé: Use 1 can (about 7¾ oz.) salmon, drained, boned, and finely chopped in place of tuna.

Seafood Soufflé: Use 1 can (5 oz.) lobster or 1 can (7½ oz.) crab meat, drained, boned, and finely chopped in place of tuna.

HAM-MUSHROOM SOUFFLÉ

4 tbs. butter or margarine	⅔ c. ground, cooked ham (lightly packed)
4 tbs. flour	
¼ to ½ tsp. salt	1 can (3 to 4 oz.) mushrooms, drained and finely chopped
⅛ tsp. pepper	
Dash of hot-pepper sauce	
1 c. milk	2 tbs. minced chives
4 egg yolks, well beaten	4 egg whites
	¼ tsp. cream of tartar

Melt butter or margarine in saucepan; stir in flour, salt (amount will vary depending on saltiness of ham), pepper, and hot-pepper sauce. Cook over medium heat, stirring constantly, until mixture bubbles. Remove from heat; blend in milk slowly. Cook over medium heat, stirring constantly, until mixture thickens and bubbles (sauce will be quite thick). Remove from heat; beat mixture slowly into egg yolks; stir in ham, mushrooms, and chives; cool. Heat oven to 350° F. Beat egg whites with cream of tartar until stiff but not dry. Gently fold ham mixture into egg whites. Pour into ungreased 1½-quart soufflé dish. Bake 50 to 60 minutes or until soufflé is puffed and golden and fairly firm to the touch. Serve at once. Makes 6 servings.

Cheese-Topped Soufflé: Sprinkle top of Ham-Mushroom Soufflé with grated Parmesan cheese before baking.

Chicken or Turkey Soufflé: Substitute ⅔ cup ground, cooked chicken or turkey for ham.

CHEESE-ASPARAGUS SOUFFLÉ

4 tbs. butter or margarine
4 tbs. flour
½ tsp. salt
⅛ tsp. pepper
¼ tsp. dry mustard
⅛ tsp. ground nutmeg
1 c. milk
4 egg yolks, well beaten

1 c. shredded sharp Cheddar cheese (¼ lb.)
2 tbs. grated Parmesan cheese
4 egg whites
¼ tsp. cream of tartar
1 c. chopped, cooked asparagus

Melt butter or margarine in saucepan; stir in flour, salt, pepper, mustard, and nutmeg. Cook over medium heat, stirring constantly, until mixture bubbles. Remove from heat; blend in milk slowly. Cook over medium heat, stirring constantly, until mixture thickens and bubbles (sauce will be quite thick). Remove from heat; beat mixture slowly into egg yolks; beat in cheeses; cool. Heat oven to 350° F. Beat egg whites with cream of tartar until stiff but not dry. Gently fold cheese mixture into egg whites. Pour a small amount of mixture into an ungreased 1½-quart soufflé dish; spoon on asparagus in even layer; top with remaining soufflé mixture. Run spoon around top, 1 inch from edge, for a top-hat effect. Bake 45 to 55 minutes or until soufflé is puffed and golden and fairly firm to the touch. Serve at once. Makes 6 servings.

Cheese Soufflé: Prepare as above omitting the asparagus.

Vegetables Cheese Soufflé: Substitute 1 cup cooked, chopped broccoli, cauliflower, or French green beans, or 1 cup cooked green peas for asparagus.

SPECIALTY EGG DISHES

SCRAMBLED EGGS WITH COTTAGE CHEESE

9 eggs
¼ c. milk
1 carton (8 oz.) cream-style cottage cheese
⅛ tsp. pepper

2 tbs. butter or margarine
6 strips cooked bacon, crumbled, or ½ c. diced, cooked ham

Beat eggs slightly; add milk, cottage cheese, and pepper. Heat butter or margarine in skil-

let; add egg mixture; cook over low heat, lifting mixture from bottom and sides of pan until eggs are just set. Add crumbled bacon or diced ham as eggs begin to set. Makes 6 servings.

EGG FOO YUNG

6 eggs
½ c. chopped onion (1 medium)
1 small green pepper, seeded and diced

1 can (about 1 lb.) bean sprouts, drained
¾ tsp. salt

Beat eggs in large bowl. Add remaining ingredients. Ladle about ½ cup of mixture for each pancake onto lightly greased griddle. Cook until golden on bottom; turn and brown other side. Serve hot with Foo Yung gravy. Makes 6 servings.

Foo Yung Gravy

1½ c. chicken broth
1½ tbs. cornstarch
1 tsp. soy sauce

½ tsp. salt
Dash of pepper
¼ tsp. sugar

Blend chicken broth into cornstarch in small saucepan. Stir in soy sauce, salt, pepper, and sugar. Cook over medium heat, stirring constantly, until mixture thickens and boils 1 minute. Serve hot.

EGGS BENEDICT

4 English muffins
Butter or margarine
8 slices Canadian-style bacon or ham

8 poached eggs
Hollandaise Sauce (*page 349*)

Split and toast English muffins; spread with butter or margarine. Sauté bacon or ham slices slightly in a small amount of butter or margarine; place one slice on each muffin half; top each with a poached egg. Cover with Hollandaise Sauce. Makes 4 servings.

EGGS GOLDENROD

4 hard-cooked eggs, shelled
2 tbs. butter or margarine
2 tbs. flour
¼ tsp. salt

⅛ tsp. pepper
1 c. milk
4 slices of toast or 2 English muffins, split and toasted

Cut eggs in half; remove yolks; press through fine sieve; reserve. Chop egg whites; reserve. Melt butter or margarine in small saucepan; blend in flour; salt, and pepper. Cook over low heat, stirring constantly, until bubbly; remove from heat. Stir in milk gradually. Cook over medium heat, stirring constantly, until mixture comes to boiling; boil 1 minute. Stir in chopped egg whites. Spoon over toast or English muffins; sprinkle with sieved egg yolks. Serve hot. Makes 4 servings.

HAM AND EGGS AU GRATIN

4 tbs. butter or margarine	1 c. shredded Cheddar cheese (¼ lb.)
4 tbs. flour	
2 c. milk	½ lb. cooked ham, cut in ½-inch cubes
1½ tsp. prepared mustard	
1½ tsp. Worcestershire sauce	6 hard-cooked eggs, halved

Melt butter or margarine in saucepan; stir in flour. Add milk slowly; cook, stirring constantly, until thickened and bubbly. Add mustard, Worcestershire, and cheese; heat until cheese melts. Add ham and eggs; heat through. Turn into serving dish; garnish with buttered crumbs, if desired. Or, mixture may be turned into shallow baking dish, covered with buttered crumbs and broiled just until lightly browned. Makes 6 servings.

EGGS FLORENTINE

6 hard-cooked eggs	2 lbs. fresh spinach, washed
2 tsp. vinegar	
1 tsp. prepared mustard	½ tsp. salt
	1 can (10½ oz.) condensed cream of mushroom soup
2 tbs. mayonnaise or salad dressing	
½ tsp. Worcestershire sauce	
	1 soup can of water
½ tsp. salt	¼ tsp. ground nutmeg
Dash of pepper	
1 tbs. milk	

Halve eggs lengthwise. Mash yolks; mix in vinegar, mustard, mayonnaise or salad dressing, Worcestershire, ½ teaspoon salt, pepper, and milk. Fill egg whites with mixture. Cook spinach with ½ teaspoon salt and water that clings to leaves until just tender; drain. Chop. Turn into shallow baking dish. Place eggs on spinach. Combine soup, water, and nutmeg. Pour over eggs. Heat at 350° F. for 20 minutes. Makes 6 servings.

Cheese

Cheese has been a universal favorite ever since man can remember—savored with reverence in its own true state or used as a versatile ingredient in the heartiest of dishes and the most delicate of desserts.

CLASSIFICATIONS OF CHEESE

The more than 400 varieties of natural cheese available in American markets today can be grouped in three broad classifications: *hard*, *semisoft* and *soft*. Natural cheese is made directly from milk, or, sometimes, whey. Process cheese is a combination of natural cheeses heated to melting temperature to blend, then poured into shapes to mold.

Hard Cheeses

Cheddar (sometimes called American or store) is far and away the favorite American cheese, the most versatile too. Whether you like it mild or sharp is a matter of taste, but the sharp has the more authentic Cheddar flavor and is generally preferred, especially in cooking. (The color of the cheese, incidentally, has nothing to do with the flavor.) New York and Vermont are famous for theirs, but you're a wizard if you can distinguish them from the fine Cheddars made in Wisconsin, Kentucky, and other major cheese-producing states.

Several delightful cheeses similar to Cheddar, but with characteristics of their own, include: *Cheshire*, which is somewhat crumbly and has a salty tang; *Colby* is a mild cheese with a somewhat softer, more open texture; *Coon* is crumbly and very sharp; *Derby* and *Gloucester* are milder, slightly flakier varieties; *Sage* has a mottled green appearance and a sage flavor.

Swiss. This is the one cheese that you might have to go to a specialty shop or a cheese store to find if you want a wide choice. And if you want to taste Swiss at its best, buy it by the chunk. You can buy both domestic and imported Swiss.

Gruyère (pronounced groo-yehr) is like Swiss cheese but has smaller eyes and a sharper, nutlike flavor. It's a grand munching variety; also makes an unusually tasty fondue.

Edam and *Gouda* are close cousins from Holland. They are yellowish; firm to semisoft; with a mellow but hearty "real cheese" flavor. Edam is usually shaped like a cannonball and covered with red paraffin. Gouda is usually a flattened ball which may or may not have a red wax covering. If you yearn to be an authentic gourmet, eat them for breakfast as the Dutch do.

Provolone (proh-voh-loh-neh). In both appearance and flavor Provolone is quite different from most of the popular hard cheeses. It is shaped like a large pear, sausage, or ball, and has grooves where the strings of the net in which it is hung press into the surface. The cream-colored body has a sharp, salty, smoky flavor. Good to eat by itself or as a pizza topping.

Caciocavallo (kah-choh-kah-val-luh) is much like Provolone except that it is not smoked, is a little whiter inside, and is tenpin shaped. When it grows hard with age, it's perfect for grating.

Parmesan (pahr-muh-zahn). Freshly grated Parmesan has a zesty flavor that adds a special touch to many dishes.

Sapsago is a rocklike green cheese with a delectable flavor. Mixed into cream cheese, Sapsago makes a superlative spread or dip with a pecanlike flavor.

Semisoft Cheeses

Roquefort. Many of the tangy, white cheeses veined with blue or blue-green mold are called Roquefort. The ones legally entitled to this name are those that are produced from ewes' milk in the vicinity of Roquefort, France. These are among the world's truly noble food products. But don't overlook other blue-veined cheeses. They're good too. Included in this outstanding assemblage are *blue* (or bleu) cheese made in many parts of the world, but especially in Denmark, France, and the United States; *Gorgonzola* from Italy; and *Stilton* from England. The last—a little milder than the others—is considered to be one of the great dessert cheeses.

Bel Paese (bell pah-aye-seh) is a smooth, creamy-yellow, mild, sweet cheese which lives up to its name—"beautiful country."

Brick, appropriately called, is brick-shaped. The elastic, creamy-yellow body has a mild but fairly pungent flavor.

Münster (mun-ztir) is like Brick but usually cylindrical, milder, and creamy-white inside.

Port du Salut (por do sah-loo), *Trappist* and *Oka* are smooth, creamy-yellow cheeses made by Trappist monks in various parts of the world. Some of the cheeses are mild, others deliciously stronger.

Chantelle is a Midwestern cheese similar to Port du Salut and covered with red wax.

Caerphilly (car-fil-lee) is a white, smooth but granular, delicately flavored cheese. People who have sampled it often rate it as one of England's best. It should be eaten soon after it comes on the market because it is perishable.

Fontina is a smooth, yellowish, gently tangy cheese that originated in Italy but has been largely taken over by Danish producers.

Soft Cheeses

Camembert (kam-em-bare) is another classic cheese. The creamy-yellow body, which is very soft when the cheese is fully ripe, has a rich, mild, but very definite flavor that is beautifully complemented by fruit. The grayish rind should be eaten too.

Brie (bree) and *Coulommiers* (koo-lawm-me-ehr) are much like Camembert but firmer. *Pont l'Evêque* (pawn lay-veck) is also similar to Camembert but yellow and firm enough sometimes to be classified as a semisoft cheese.

Limburger is so famous for its aroma that many people have undoubtedly been discouraged from sampling its robust, pungent goodness. But if you will try it just once on crackers or dark bread, you'll become a fan.

Liederkranz was invented accidentally by a New York delicatessen keeper who was attempting to imitate a favorite old German cheese that didn't keep well in transit to this country. The new concoction, which turned out to be superior to the original, is like a mild, yellow Limburger.

Feta is a white, crumbly Greek cheese with a briny flavor. Eat it with grapes or melons.

Vacherin. Depending on how it is made, this resembles either a zesty Camembert or a nutty Swiss. It is runny enough to be eaten with a spoon. Wonderful with berries or a light claret.

Mozzarella (moh-tsuh-rel-luh). A creamy-white, slightly firm, delicately flavored cheese used in cooking. *Scamorze* is quite similar. Try toasting it on bread. Other soft, white, mild cheeses that are used in cooking and for salads, dips, snacks, etc., are *cottage; cream; Neufchâtel* (nuh-shah-tell), which has a slightly acid taste; and sweet, nutlike *ricotta*.

Two unusually rich, creamy, white cheeses are *Crèma Danica* and *Petit Suisse*.

Serving Cheese

Here are four tips that will increase your enjoyment of cheese:

· Don't ever let tradition limit the way you use, serve, or eat a particular variety of cheese. Remember that all cheeses can be eaten in a number of ways and at any time of day you like. For example, Roquefort is just as good before dinner as after, just as delicious melted on top of a hamburger as it is in a salad dressing.

· Don't camouflage the flavor of cheese by serving it with highly seasoned cocktail crackers or breads. It should be eaten either by itself, with soda crackers, water biscuits, plain breads, or with fruit or wine.

· Serve the soft, white cheeses, such as Neufchâtel, within a few days after buying them. They are perishable. Other soft cheeses are best to eat when they are quite soft and creamy inside. (Semisoft and hard cheeses should also be allowed to reach a definite stage of ripeness before they are served. If you cannot tell when this is, depend on the good judgment of your cheese dealer.)

· Serve the soft white cheeses while they are slightly chilled. All other varieties should be served at room temperature. This means that they should be removed from the refrigerator 30 minutes to an hour or more before serving.

Experimenting with serving different cheeses in unusual ways and keeping an open mind will add immeasurably to your enjoyment.

Storing Cheese

All cheeses should be kept in the fresh-food compartment of your refrigerator. To keep them from drying out and transmitting or picking up odors, wrap them in aluminum foil or transparent plastic wrap or store small pieces in tightly covered jars or plastic bags. If mold forms on a cheese, cut it off; it is not harmful.

Cottage Cheese

Types Available: You can usually buy small curd or large curd, either creamed or un-creamed. *Creamed cottage cheese* is the curd of the coagulated protein of skimmed milk, with fresh sweet cream added. The curd is cooked in its own whey, drained, and washed. *Uncreamed cottage cheese* is drained curd without the cream added. A third variety, called *bakers' cheese,* may be found in some markets. It is also known as *pot or hoop cheese* and is mostly used by bakeries, hotels, etc. It is curd drained dry of whey but without cooking or washing.

You will also find cottage cheese with vege-tables, or pineapple, or fruit salad added.

How to Store Cottage Cheese: Cottage cheese, a delicate-flavored product, should be kept cold and covered for it readily picks up per-meating odors. Under these conditions it will stay at its peak for about a week. Do not freeze cottage cheese.

QUICHE LORRAINE

1 unbaked 9-in. pastry shell (*page 406*)	4 eggs, beaten
	1 c. milk
	1 c. heavy cream
5 slices bacon	1 tsp. salt
½ c. sliced onion (1 medium)	⅛ tsp. pepper
	¼ tsp. ground
¼ lb. Swiss cheese, diced	nutmeg

Prepare pastry shell. Heat oven to 450° F. Cover inside of shell with piece of wax paper; fill shell with dry rice or beans (to keep shell from buckling as it bakes). Bake 10 minutes; remove rice or beans and paper; cool shell. Fry bacon until crisp; drain and crumble. Sauté onion in 1 tablespoon bacon fat just until transparent. Put diced cheese, crumbled bacon, and onion in pastry shell. Combine beaten eggs, milk, cream, salt, pepper, and nutmeg; pour into shell. Bake 15 minutes; re-duce oven heat to 350° F.; bake 10 to 15 min-utes or until thin-bladed knife or spatula in-serted halfway between center and edge comes out clean. Let stand 10 to 15 minutes before cutting. Makes 6 servings.

WELSH RAREBIT

½ c. beer or ale	1 lb. Cheddar cheese, shredded
1 tsp. Worcester-shire sauce	1 egg, slightly beaten
1 tsp. dry mustard	
½ tsp. paprika	Toast, pilot crackers, or
Dash of cayenne	English muffins

Combine beer, Worcestershire, mustard, pa-prika, and cayenne in top of double boiler. Heat over simmering water until warm. Add cheese; cook, stirring constantly, until cheese is melted. Add small amount of hot mixture to beaten egg; stir into mixture in double boiler; stir until smooth and hot. Serve over toast, crackers, or English muffins. Makes 4 servings.

CHEESE TUNA CASSEROLE

3 c. cooked rice	½ c. dairy sour cream
1 c. milk	
1 can (10½ oz.) condensed cream of mushroom soup	1 can (6½ to 7 oz.) tuna, drained and flaked
	1 pkg. (10 oz.) frozen asparagus spears, cooked
2 tbs. instant onion flakes	
¼ c. sliced stuffed olives	½ c. packaged bread crumbs
1 carton (8 oz.) cottage cheese	2 tbs. melted butter or margarine

Combine rice, milk, soup, onion, sliced olives, cottage cheese, sour cream, and tuna in me-dium-size bowl. Cut asparagus into 1-inch pieces; stir into rice mixture; turn into but-tered 2-quart casserole. Combine bread crumbs and melted butter or margarine; sprinkle over top of casserole. Bake at 350° F. for 35 to 40 minutes or until mixture is heated through and crumbs are golden brown. Makes 6 serv-ings.

MUSHROOM CHEESE PIE
(*Pictured opposite page 244*)

1½ lbs. mushrooms, sliced
1 c. thinly sliced onion (1 large)
4 tbs. butter or margarine
⅓ c. flour
1 carton (8 oz.) cream-style cottage cheese
¼ c. chopped parsley
¼ c. dry sherry
1 tsp. salt
⅛ tsp. pepper
Pastry for 2-crust pie (*page 405*)
1 egg yolk
2 tbs. water

Sauté mushrooms and onion in butter or margarine about 10 minutes or until tender; remove from heat. Mix in flour. Add cottage cheese, parsley, sherry, salt, and pepper; mix thoroughly; reserve. Prepare pastry. Heat oven to 425° F. Roll out half the pastry on lightly floured board to a 12-inch circle. Line a 9-inch pie plate allowing 1-inch overhang. Roll out remaining pastry; cut into ½-inch strips. Pour mushroom-cheese mixture into pastry-lined pie plate. Arrange pastry strips lattice-fashion (*page 406*) on top of filling. Trim ends even with edge. Moisten and fold overhang up over ends. Flute edge. Beat egg yolk and water; brush on pastry strips. Bake 40 to 45 minutes or until browned. Cover edge of pie with strip of aluminum foil after 20 minutes to prevent overbrowning. Cool 5 minutes. Makes 6 servings as a luncheon entrée or 8 servings as accompaniment with meat.

CHEESE-STUFFED TOMATOES

6 large, ripe tomatoes
Salt
1½ c. small bread cubes (3 slices)
1 tbs. melted butter or margarine
1 tbs. minced onion
¼ tsp. leaf oregano, crumbled
¼ tsp. leaf basil, crumbled
¼ tsp. salt
Dash of pepper
1 c. pot cheese
1 tbs. grated Parmesan cheese

Heat oven to 350° F. Cut tops off tomatoes; scoop out pulp; chop and reserve ½ cup firm pulp. Sprinkle inside of tomatoes lightly with salt; invert on paper towels for 20 minutes to drain. Combine bread cubes, butter or margarine, onion, oregano, basil, ¼ teaspoon salt, and pepper. Add pot cheese and ½ cup tomato pulp; mix well. Spoon filling into tomatoes. Sprinkle Parmesan cheese over tops. Bake in shallow pan in a small amount of water about 30 minutes. Makes 6 servings.

ONION CHEESE CASSEROLE

1 c. soft bread crumbs (2 slices)
1 tbs. melted butter or margarine
½ lb. bulk sausage meat
3 tbs. flour
¼ tsp. leaf thyme, crumbled
½ c. light cream
1 carton (8 oz.) cream-style cottage cheese
2 lbs. small white onions, peeled, cooked, and drained

Combine bread crumbs and butter or margarine in small bowl; set aside. Brown sausage in large skillet, breaking meat up with fork as it cooks; add flour and thyme; mix well. Add cream gradually; simmer until thickened. Stir in cottage cheese and onions; heat until mixture simmers. Pour mixture into greased 1½-quart baking dish; sprinkle with buttered crumbs. Place under broiler 2 to 3 minutes or until crumbs are browned. Serve at once. Makes 6 servings.

EASY CHEESE FONDUE

2 c. soft bread crumbs (4 slices)
1 c. shredded sharp Cheddar cheese (¼ lb.)
2 c. milk, scalded
Dash of pepper
1 tsp. prepared mustard
1 tsp. Worcestershire sauce
4 eggs, slightly beaten
½ c. cooked, crumbled bacon

Heat oven to 350° F. Place bread crumbs and cheese in shallow 1½-quart baking dish. Combine milk, pepper, mustard, Worcestershire and eggs; pour over bread crumbs and cheese add bacon. Bake 25 minutes or until set and lightly browned. Makes 6 servings.

HAM AND CHEESE FONDUE

12 slices white bread
3 cans (2¼ oz. ea.) deviled ham
1 c. shredded Cheddar cheese (¼ lb.)
4 eggs, slightly beaten
2 c. milk
Few grains cayenne
1 tsp. salt

Heat oven to 350° F. Remove crusts from bread. Spread 6 slices with deviled ham; top with remaining 6 slices. Cut sandwiches into quarters. Place sandwiches in single layer in buttered 9x9x2-inch pan. Sprinkle with cheese. Combine eggs, milk, cayenne, and salt. Pour milk mixture over sandwiches. Bake 25 to 30 minutes or until a thin-bladed knife or spatula inserted one-inch from edge comes out clean. Makes 6 servings.

SWISS FONDUE

½ lb. Swiss cheese, shredded	⅛ tsp. pepper
1½ tbs. flour	Dash of nutmeg
1 clove of garlic, cut	3 tbs. kirsch
1 c. dry white wine	French bread, cut
½ tsp. salt	or broken into bite-size pieces

Dredge cheese with flour. Rub pan of chafing dish or earthenware casserole well with clove of garlic. Pour wine into pan; set over low flame. When air bubbles rise to surface (before boiling point) stir with fork and add cheese by handfuls; dissolve each handful before adding the next. Stir until mixture starts bubbling lightly; add salt, pepper, and nutmeg. Stir in Kirsch; mix thoroughly. *To serve:* Keep fondue bubbling lightly. Spear bite-size piece of French bread with fork, going through soft part first and securing tines in crust. Each guest dunks his own bread in fondue with a stirring motion. If fondue becomes too thick stir in a little preheated (never cold) wine. Keep heat low when, towards the end, the melted cheese forms a brown crust (a special delicacy) at bottom of utensil. Makes 4 servings.

Tips with Cheese

Try crisp cheese croutons in green salads, as a garnish for soup, or sprinkled over cooked vegetables. Sauté 1 cup small bread cubes in 4 tablespoons fat or pure vegetable oil, stirring occasionally, until they are golden. Remove from heat and sprinkle with grated Parmesan cheese.

Like popcorn? Next time you pop some, toss it with grated American or Parmesan cheese. This is a good garnish for soups, too.

Sesame Cheese Biscuits are a perfect accompaniment for a salad luncheon. Combine ¾ cup grated Parmesan cheese and 3 tablespoons sesame seeds in a shallow dish. Melt ¼ cup butter or margarine in saucepan. Open and separate a package of refrigerated biscuits. Dip each in melted butter or margarine, then roll in cheese mixture to coat. Place on ungreased baking sheet. Bake at 500° F. for 8 minutes.

Cheese Straws add a tangy note to a fruit or vegetable juice first course. Prepare ½ package pie crust mix according to package directions, adding ½ cup grated sharp Cheddar cheese with water. Roll out on lightly floured board to ⅛-inch thickness. Cut into narrow strips about 4 inches long; dust with paprika. Place on baking sheet. Bake at 450° F. for 10 to 12 minutes or until brown. Makes about 4 dozen.

For cocktail nibbles, combine equal parts of Roquefort or blue cheese and cream cheese and whip until smooth. Put pecan or walnut halves together sandwich-fashion with cheese mixture between. Chill.

Dress up frozen chicken à la king with the addition of some grated Cheddar or Parmesan cheese before heating.

A tray of cheese, fruit, and crisp unsweetened crackers is a simple, decorative, and tempting way to end a meal. Coffee or wine is usually served with it. Here are some suggestions of fruits and cheeses that go well together.

Red apples or fresh pineapple	Cheddar, Camembert, Liederkranz
Fresh pears	Blue or Roquefort, Provolone, Cream
Fresh strawberries	Sweetened Cream cheese
Tokay grapes	Mild Brick or Cheddar
Melon wedges, Bing cherries	Gouda or Edam

Chapter Sixteen

Rice, Pasta, and Cereal

From Hong Kong to Houston, everybody loves rice. Think of the countless ways we use it: as a vegetable . . . the basis for exotic curries . . . cooked with herbs and chicken broth as a pilaf . . . quick fried rice for a family supper . . . creamy rice pudding for a dessert youngsters always love.

Pasta is the Italian word for all the wonderful products made with spaghetti dough: it includes macaroni, lasagne, vermicelli, flat noodles, amusing shapes like shells, hats, bow ties, and rings, ravioli stuffed with a meat or cheese mixture, canneloni filled with smooth ricotta—to name a few!

Rice and pasta have much in common. Both start out as cereals (yes, rice too is a cereal grain and pastas are made with wheat flour), both are marvelous convenience foods which can be kept handy on the shelf until needed, and both are delightfully versatile.

Rice

Kinds of Rice

Regular *milled white rice* is the inner core of the rice grain from which hulls, germ, outer bran layers, and most of the inner bran have been removed. When a recipe calls for "rice" without specifying any particular kind, this is the kind it means. The rice we buy in packages today has already been washed and graded in the milling process and needs no further rinsing or cleaning. It is available in long-, medium-, and short-grain type rice. *Long-grain* is the variety most prized for making casseroles or for simple steamed rice. *Short- or medium-grain* is preferable for puddings or other dishes in which a soft product is desired.

Parboiled rice (also called processed or converted) is white rice that has been processed before milling under steam pressure in such a way that natural vitamins and minerals are retained and the rice starch itself becomes fluffier and plumper when cooked.

Precooked rice (instant) is milled rice that has been completely cooked and the water extracted. It needs only to stand in boiling water a few minutes to reconstitute the cooked white grains.

Brown rice is the unpolished grain—only the outer, inedible fibrous hull is removed with milling. Brown rice is richer in natural salts and vitamins than polished rice, but it has a shorter shelf life and must be cooked two to two-and-a-half times as long.

Wild rice is not a true rice. It is the hulled grain or seed of a reedlike shallow-water plant. Most of it grows in Minnesota, some in Wisconsin and Canada. By Minnesota law, it may be harvested only by Indians and is bought from them by the large processing companies. A gourmet treat, it is more expensive than the other kinds of rice. The kernels vary in length, thickness, and hardness. Be sure to follow package directions when cooking.

How Much Rice to Cook

The usual amount of *cooked* rice to allow for each serving is ¾ cup.

Yield Chart for Rice

Uncooked Measure	Approximate Yield
1 cup regular milled white rice	3 cups cooked
1 cup parboiled rice	4 cups cooked
1 cup precooked rice	3 cups cooked
1 cup brown rice	4 cups cooked

FLUFFY RICE

1 c. rice	1 tsp. salt
2 c. water	

Combine rice, water, and salt in 3-quart saucepan with tight-fitting lid. Bring to boiling, stirring once or twice. Lower heat. Cover pan. Cook, without removing lid or stirring, about 14 minutes or until liquid is absorbed and rice is fluffy. Makes 3 cups (4 servings).

· If you wish drier rice, fluff lightly with fork and let stand, covered, 5 to 10 minutes to steam dry.
· For extra tender rice, use 2⅓ cups water and cook 4 to 5 minutes longer.
· Parboiled and brown rice require more liquid and longer cooking time. Follow the package directions.
· Prepare precooked rice according to package directions.

Oven-baked Rice: Put ingredients for Fluffy Rice in baking dish; cover. Bake at 350° F. for 25 to 30 minutes or until rice is tender.

To Cook Rice in Other Liquids. Follow directions for Fluffy Rice, except:

· Substitute chicken broth, beef broth, or consommé for water.
· Substitute orange, tangerine, or apple juice for water. Cook 15 to 20 minutes.
· Substitute 1 cup tomato or mixed vegetable juice for 1 cup of the water. Cook 15 minutes.

Tips on Cooking and Serving Rice

· Don't stir rice after it comes to boiling. This can mash the grains, causing rice to become mushy.
· If rice is left in the pan for more than 5 or 10 minutes after it is cooked, it will pack.
· Store leftover cooked rice, covered, in the refrigerator. It can be kept about a week.
· To reheat rice, place enough liquid in pan to cover the bottom (about 2 tablespoons per cup of rice). Bring to boiling; add rice; cover. Lower heat; simmer about 5 minutes.
· Use leftover cooked rice in any of these ways:
  In desserts: Combine with fruits, nuts, dairy foods, custards or gelatin.
  In main dishes: Combine with meats, poultry, sea food, game, or wild fowl.
  As a vegetable: Combine with vegetables, nuts, herbs, or cheese.
  As a salad: Combine with crisp greens, fruits, vegetables, meat, poultry, cheese, or fish. Or, marinate in wine or French Dressing.

Seasoned Rice Mixes

Any number of seasoned, ready-to-cook rice mixes are now to be found on supermarket shelves, including saffron rice, mixes for making Spanish rice, rice blended with herbs and meat stock concentrate, and combined parboiled rice and wild rice.

SAVORY RICE

4 tbs. butter or margarine	2 tbs. instant minced onion
2 c. packaged precooked rice	Pinch of powdered saffron
2½ c. chicken broth	Salt
	Pepper

Heat oven to 425° F. Melt butter or margarine in large skillet until golden. Add precooked rice; cook, stirring constantly, until rice takes on color. Add chicken broth, instant minced onion, saffron, salt and pepper to taste; mix thoroughly. Turn into 2-quart baking dish; cover. Bake 20 to 25 minutes or until liquid is absorbed and rice is tender. (To use raw rice, use 1½ cups rice and 3½ cups chicken broth.) Makes 4 to 6 servings.

PILAF

2/3 c. chopped onion
3 tbs. butter or
   margarine
1 c. rice
1 tsp. leaf marjo-
   ram, crumbled

1 tsp. leaf rosemary,
   crumbled
1/2 tsp. leaf savory,
   crumbled
3 c. chicken broth

Sauté onion in butter or margarine in skillet until soft. Add rice, marjoram, rosemary, and savory; cook, stirring constantly, until rice starts to brown. Add chicken broth; simmer until rice is tender and liquid is absorbed. Makes 4 to 6 servings.

FRIED RICE

6 tbs. fat or pure
   vegetable oil
3 eggs, beaten
Dash of salt
1/2 c. chopped onion
   (1 medium)
1 can (5 oz.)
   bamboo shoots,
   drained and
   slivered

1/4 lb. mushrooms,
   sliced
6 c. cold, cooked
   rice
1 tbs. soy sauce

Heat 1 tablespoon fat or oil in skillet. Add eggs and salt. Fry until eggs are firm; remove to plate; cut into strips and reserve. Heat remaining 5 tablespoons fat or oil in skillet. Add onion, bamboo shoots, and mushrooms. Sauté just until tender and crisp. Add rice; cook over low heat, stirring constantly, until heated through. Stir in soy sauce and eggs. Taste and add more soy sauce, if desired. Makes 6 servings.

SINGAPORE RICE

1/2 c. chopped onion
   (1 medium)
3 tbs. butter or
   margarine
2 c. chicken broth
1/4 tsp. ground
   cardamom
1/4 tsp. ground
   nutmeg

1/4 tsp. ground
   ginger
1/2 tsp. ground
   cinnamon
1 tsp. salt
1/8 tsp. pepper
1 tbs. grated orange
   rind
2 c. packaged
   precooked rice

Sauté onion in butter or margarine in skillet or saucepan 3 minutes; add chicken broth, cardamom, nutmeg, ginger, cinnamon, salt, pepper, and orange rind. Cover; bring to boiling. Add rice; mix well. Cover; remove from heat. Let stand 10 minutes. Serve with chicken,

pork, ham, or broiled white fish. Makes 6 servings.

RAISIN RICE MOLDS

4 c. hot, cooked rice
1/2 c. raisins

1/4 c. melted butter
   or margarine

Toss rice, raisins, and butter or margarine together gently. Press into molds or custard cups. Turn out onto serving plate. Serve immediately. Makes 4 servings.

COTTAGE CHEESE AND RICE CROQUETTES

1/4 c. finely chopped
   onion (1 small)
1/4 c. finely chopped
   green pepper
3 tbs. butter or
   margarine
3 tbs. flour
3/4 c. milk
1/4 tsp. leaf thyme,
   crumbled
1 tsp. salt
1/8 tsp. pepper
1 carton (8 oz.)
   cream-style
   cottage cheese

2 c. cooked rice
1 c. soft bread
   crumbs (2 slices)
2 eggs, beaten
2 tbs. water
1/4 tsp. salt
Fat or pure vege-
   table oil for
   frying
1/2 lb. mushrooms,
   sliced
1/4 c. butter or
   margarine

Sauté onion and green pepper in 3 tablespoons butter or margarine; add flour; mix well. Add milk slowly, stirring constantly; cook until very thick. Remove from heat; stir in thyme, 1 teaspoon salt, and pepper; add cottage cheese and rice; mix well. Spread mixture in shallow pan; cover with aluminum foil; chill 2 hours. Shape into 6 flat cakes. Coat with crumbs; dip in mixture of eggs, water, and 1/4 teaspoon salt; coat again in crumbs. Fry in hot, shallow fat or oil until well browned on both sides. Sauté mushrooms in 1/4 cup butter or margarine; serve over the croquettes. Makes 6 servings.

RICE AND PEAS ROMANO

3 slices bacon
1/2 c. finely chopped
   onion (1
   medium)
3/4 c. canned
   consommé
3/4 c. water
1 pkg. (10 oz.)
   frozen peas

2 tbs. chopped
   parsley
1/2 tsp. salt
1/8 tsp. pepper
1/4 tsp. leaf thyme,
   crumbled
1 1/2 c. packaged
   precooked rice
3 tbs. grated
   Parmesan cheese

Cook bacon until crisp; remove; crumble. Sauté onion in bacon drippings. Add consommé, water, peas, parsley, salt, pepper, and thyme. Cover; simmer 3 minutes. Add rice; mix well; cover; set aside for 10 minutes. Add cheese and bacon; mix well. Makes 6 servings.

FEATHERED RICE

The rice puffs up to a light fluffiness with a wonderful toasted flavor.

1 c. rice   2½ c. boiling water
1½ tsp. salt

Spread rice in shallow pan. Bake at 375° F. stirring occasionally, until rice grains are golden brown. Remove from oven. Increase heat of oven to 400° F. Put toasted rice into a 1½-quart casserole that has a tight-fitting cover. Stir in salt and boiling water. Bake, covered, for 20 minutes. A pound or so of rice may be browned at one time and stored in a tightly covered jar for future use.

Pasta

How do you like your spaghetti? Smothered in spicy tomato sauce, topped with a mound of grated cheese? Or have you tried it tossed simply with butter and cheese and a sprinkling of parsley, served like a vegetable? You don't have to serve tomato sauce with Italian pastas, you know—in fact, if this is the only kind of sauce you use, you're missing some mighty exciting dishes!

Kinds of Pasta

Macaroni is tube-shaped, and comes in two-inch lengths, or the regulation 8-inch length. Included are manicotti (very large in diameter), tufoli, rigatoni, ziti, and occhi di lupo.

Spaghetti is technically a member of the macaroni family. It is solid, rodlike in shape, comes in several sizes from medium to very thin, and is always at least 8 inches long.

Noodles come in fine, medium, and broad flat strands of dough and in bows, alphabets, and rings. They are made with durum flour, salt, and water. *Egg noodles* must contain a definite percentage of egg solids.

Secrets for Perfect Pasta

Always use plenty of salted water—the rule is six quarts of water and 2 tablespoons salt for a pound of pasta, not less than four quarts of water for a pound of egg noodles. The water should fill no more than three-fourths of the kettle, which means you should have an 8-quart kettle in your kitchen if you serve pasta often.

· The salted water should be boiling rapidly before the pasta is added, and should be kept boiling hard throughout the cooking period.

· Add all the pasta at once. If the strands are long, push them down with a long-handled spoon, stirring to separate the strands. Cook uncovered, stirring several times during cooking, to make sure strands are separated. Some people add a little olive oil to the water to prevent the strands from sticking together.

· The size and shape of your pasta will determine the cooking time. Very thin spaghetti will cook in 10 minutes; lasagne may require 15 to 18 minutes. Check the package label to see if it gives cooking time. If not, remove a strand or small piece of pasta from time to time and bite it. If it's firm all the way through, not hard in the center, not soft, then it is *al dente*, the way Italians like their pasta. If you prefer spaghetti and macaroni softer, cook it until of desired doneness.

· Egg noodles cook much more quickly. Six to eight minutes is usually enough. Make the same test: Bite a small piece to see when the noodles are soft enough to serve.

· As soon as the pasta is cooked, remove from heat and add a cup of cold water to stop the cooking.

· Drain pasta or noodles in a large colander or sieve. Do *not* rinse with cold water. This will only cool off the pasta. Shake until all the water is drained.

· When thoroughly drained, return pasta to the pan in which it cooked or place in a serving dish and add butter or a mixture of butter and cheese, and seasonings. Serve immediately with or without sauce.

· Casseroles can be prepared for baking hours ahead, placed in the baking dish with cheese or crumb topping, and refrigerated until baking time.

BAKED MACARONI AND CHEESE

1 pkg. (8 oz.) elbow macaroni
2 c. Medium White Sauce (*page 348*)
1½ to 2 c. shredded sharp Cheddar cheese
½ c. packaged bread crumbs
2 tbs. melted butter or margarine

Heat oven to 375° F. Cook macaroni as label directs. Layer macaroni, sauce, and cheese alternately into greased 1½-quart casserole, ending with layer of cheese. Toss bread crumbs with melted butter or margarine. Sprinkle over casserole. Bake 25 to 30 minutes or until sauce is bubbly and crumbs are browned. Makes 6 servings.

NEPTUNE'S DELIGHT NOODLE CASSEROLE

1 pkg. (8 oz.) cream cheese
1 c. dairy sour cream
¼ c. milk
1 can (6½ to 7 oz.) tuna, drained and flaked
2 tbs. finely chopped onion
1 tsp. prepared horseradish
2 tbs. chopped pimiento
¼ tsp. seasoned salt
1 pkg. (8 oz.) broad noodles, cooked and drained
⅓ c. toasted, sliced almonds

Heat oven to 375° F. Blend cream cheese and sour cream in large bowl. Stir in milk, tuna, onion, horseradish, pimiento, and seasoned salt. Add noodles; mix well. Turn into 1½-quart greased casserole. Sprinkle with almonds. Bake 20 to 30 minutes or until top is slightly brown. Makes 6 servings.

TOMATO-NOODLE BAKE

1 pkg. (8 oz.) cream cheese
¾ c. milk
1 can (8 oz.) tomato sauce
½ c. minced onion (1 medium)
1 clove of garlic, minced
2 tsp. Worcestershire sauce
½ tsp. salt
⅛ tsp. pepper
¼ tsp. paprika
1 pkg. (8 oz.) noodles, cooked and drained
2 cans (4 oz. ea.) Vienna sausage, cut in ½-inch slices
¼ c. grated Parmesan cheese
3 tbs. packaged bread crumbs
1 tbs. butter or margarine

Heat oven to 350° F. Beat cream cheese until soft. Add milk gradually, beating until smooth and creamy. Beat in tomato sauce, onion, garlic, Worcestershire, salt, pepper, and paprika. Pour over cooked, drained noodles in large bowl; add sausages; mix or toss well. Turn into greased, shallow 2-quart baking dish. Combine Parmesan cheese, bread crumbs, and butter or margarine. Sprinkle over noodle mixture. Bake 20 minutes or until top is brown and mixture is bubbly. Makes 6 to 8 servings.

FETTUCINI ROMANO

1 egg yolk
½ c. heavy cream
½ c. melted butter or margarine
1 pkg. (8 oz.) medium noodles, cooked and drained
½ c. freshly grated Romano or Parmesan cheese
1 tbs. chopped parsley

Beat egg yolk with cream; add melted butter or margarine. Pour mixture over hot, steaming noodles; sprinkle with cheese; toss gently to coat well. Sprinkle with parsley. Serve at once. Makes 4 servings.

NOODLES ALFREDO
(Fettucini al Burro Alfredo)

A famous dish from Italy—outstanding in its simplicity.

1 pkg. (8 oz.) thin noodles, cooked and drained
½ c. melted, unsalted butter or margarine
½ c. freshly grated Parmesan cheese

Toss hot noodles gently with butter or margarine. Sprinkle with cheese; toss lightly. Serve at once. Makes 4 servings.

SPAGHETTI AND MEATBALLS

1 lb. ground chuck or round	1 tsp. leaf oregano, crumbled
½ c. packaged bread crumbs	½ tsp. leaf basil, crumbled
½ tsp. salt	1½ tsp. salt
¼ tsp. pepper	3 cans (8 oz. ea.) tomato sauce
1 tsp. Worcestershire sauce	1 c. water
⅓ c. milk	¼ c. grated Parmesan cheese
⅓ c. fat or pure vegetable oil	1 pkg. (8 oz.) thin spaghetti, cooked and drained
½ c. chopped onion (1 medium)	Grated Parmesan cheese
½ green pepper, chopped	

Mix ground beef, bread crumbs, ½ teaspoon salt, pepper, Worcestershire, and milk in bowl. Shape into 20 medium-size meatballs. Heat fat or oil in skillet. Sauté meatballs until brown on all sides; remove from skillet and reserve. Sauté onion and green pepper in fat or oil remaining in skillet just until soft. Add oregano, basil, 1½ teaspoons salt, tomato sauce, and water. Bring to boiling; reduce heat; simmer 20 minutes. Add meatballs; simmer 10 minutes. Stir in Parmesan cheese just before serving. Serve over hot, cooked spaghetti; sprinkle with cheese. Makes 4 servings.

SPAGHETTINI BAKE

3 tbs. olive oil, butter, or margarine	1½ c. dry red wine
	1 c. water
	2 tsp. salt
¼ c. grated carrot	½ tsp. sugar
¼ c. finely chopped celery	2 tsp. leaf basil, crumbled
¼ c. finely chopped green pepper	¼ tsp. pepper
1 c. minced onion (1 large)	1 lb. spaghettini cooked and drained
1 lb. ground chuck	4 tbs. grated Parmesan cheese
1 can (1 lb. 13 oz.) Italian plum tomatoes	2 tbs. melted butter or margarine
3 cans (8 oz. ea.) tomato sauce	

Heat oil, butter, or margarine in Dutch oven. Sauté carrot, celery, green pepper, and onion until soft, but not brown. Add meat; break up with spoon or fork; stir until all pink has disappeared. Add tomatoes, tomato sauce, wine, water, salt, sugar, basil, and pepper. Heat until bubbly; turn heat low; cook, uncovered, 45 minutes or until sauce is thickened. Heat oven to 350° F. Combine sauce, spaghettini, and 2 tablespoons Parmesan cheese in large casserole. Sprinkle with remaining Parmesan cheese. Drizzle top with melted butter or margarine. Bake 25 minutes or until bubbly. Makes 10 to 12 servings.

SPAGHETTI AND MEATBALLS FOR A CROWD

Sauce	Meatballs
2 c. minced onions (2 large)	6 lbs. ground lean chuck
4 cloves of garlic, mashed	2 c. soft bread crumbs (4 slices)
½ c. fat or pure vegetable oil	1 c. minced onion (1 large)
4 cans (1 lb. 13 oz. ea.) tomatoes	½ c. finely chopped parsley
8 cans (6 oz. ea.) tomato paste	1 can (10½ oz.) condensed tomato soup
4 qts. water	3 tbs. water
¼ c. sugar	6 eggs, beaten
3 to 4 tbs. salt	2 tbs. salt
2 tsp. pepper	½ tsp. pepper
2 tsp. leaf oregano, crumbled	1 c. fat or pure vegetable oil
3 bay leaves	5 lbs. spaghetti, cooked and drained

Prepare sauce: Sauté onions and garlic in fat or oil in large pot until soft. Add remaining sauce ingredients. Cover, simmer 1½ hours. While sauce cooks, prepare meatballs: Mix ground chuck, bread crumbs, onion, and parsley in large bowl. Combine soup, water, eggs, salt, and pepper. Add to meat mixture; mix thoroughly. Shape into 1½-inch balls. Brown in fat or oil. When sauce has simmered 1½ hours, add meatballs. Simmer for 30 minutes. Serve over hot spaghetti. Makes 20 to 25 servings.

wberry Torte—a beautiful, impressive, and luscious dessert

SPAGHETTINI WITH EGGPLANT

2 medium-size unpared eggplant	¼ c. chopped parsley
⅔ c. olive oil (about)	1 tsp. leaf basil, crumbled
1 clove of garlic, crushed	2 tsp. salt
	¼ tsp. pepper
1 c. chopped onion (1 large)	2 tbs. chopped capers
1 can (1 lb. 13 oz.) Italian plum tomatoes	⅔ c. sliced, pitted green olives
1 can (8 oz.) tomato sauce	1 lb. spaghettini, cooked and drained
2 c. diced celery	Grated Romano or Pecorino cheese

Wash eggplant; cut into 1-inch cubes. Brown one quarter at a time in hot oil, using about 2 tablespoons of oil each time. Drain on paper towels. Sauté garlic and onion in oil, adding 1 tablespoon of oil if necessary. Add tomatoes, tomato sauce, celery, parsley, basil, salt, and pepper. Cover; simmer 15 minutes. Add eggplant, capers, and olives; cover. Simmer 20 to 25 minutes or until eggplant is tender, stirring occasionally. Serve on hot spaghettini, sprinkle with cheese. Makes 6 to 8 servings.

BAKED STUFFED LASAGNE

¼ c. olive or pure vegetable oil	1 lb. ground beef
	1 egg
2 cloves of garlic, minced	¼ tsp. garlic salt
	½ tsp. salt
2 c. chopped onions (2 large)	¼ tsp. pepper
	½ tsp. leaf basil, crumbled
1 can (2 lbs. 3 oz.) Italian plum tomatoes	6 tbs. chopped parsley
1 can (6 oz.) tomato paste	Fat or pure vegetable oil
2 tsp. salt	1 lb. lasagne, cooked and drained
1 tsp. sugar	
1 tsp. leaf oregano, crumbled	1 lb. ricotta
½ tsp. leaf basil, crumbled	½ lb. mozzarella, thinly sliced
Few dried red pepper seeds	½ c. grated Parmesan cheese
½ c. water	

Heat oil in large saucepan; add garlic and onions; cook over low heat 10 minutes. Add tomatoes, tomato paste, 2 teaspoons salt, sugar, oregano, ½ teaspoon basil, red pepper seeds, and water. Cover; cook over low heat 1½ hours, stirring occasionally. Mix beef, egg, garlic salt, ½ teaspoon salt, pepper, ½ teaspoon basil, and 2 tablespoons chopped parsley. Drop by spoonfuls into fat or oil in skillet; brown lightly. Add to sauce; cook uncovered ½ hour. Spoon some sauce in bottom of 13x9x2-inch baking pan. Arrange drained lasagne in layer in pan, overlapping them slightly. Spoon over about one quarter meat sauce and ricotta; top with one quarter of mozzarella, grated Parmesan, and remaining chopped parsley. Repeat until all ingredients are used, making top layer sauce and mozzarella. Bake at 375° F. for 40 to 45 minutes or until hot and bubbling. Garnish with parsley sprigs, if desired. Makes 8 servings.

ROLLINI WITH MUSHROOM AND MEAT SAUCE

3 slices bacon	1 tsp. salt
2 Spanish sausages or ½ lb. hot Italian sausage,*	¼ tsp. pepper
	1 c. finely chopped mushrooms
½ c. chopped onion (1 medium)	1 can (10½ oz.) condensed beef broth
¼ lb. cooked ham, cut in julienne strips	¾ lb. rollini (wagon wheels), cooked and drained
1 can (8 oz.) tomato sauce	
1 tomato, chopped	1 c. shredded Cheddar cheese

Fry bacon until crisp; drain on paper towel; crumble. Remove casings from sausage; cut up sausage. Add onions, ham, and sausage to bacon drippings; sauté lightly. Add tomato sauce, tomato, salt, and pepper; cover; simmer 20 minutes. Add mushrooms, bacon, and broth; simmer 15 minutes longer. Arrange layers of cooked rollini, sauce, and cheese in 2-quart casserole ending with sauce and cheese. Bake at 350° F. for 25 minutes or until lightly browned. Makes 6 servings.

* For less hot flavor, use half sweet sausage.

STUFFED SHELLS

1 c. finely chopped
   onion (1 large)
3 tbs. olive oil
2 cans (6 oz. ea.)
   tomato paste
1 can (1 lb. 13 oz.)
   Italian plum
   tomatoes
4 c. water
1 tbs. sugar
1 tbs. salt
1 bay leaf

½ tsp. leaf oregano,
   crumbled
1 lb. ricotta cheese
2 eggs, beaten
2 tbs. chopped
   parsley
¾ c. grated
   Parmesan cheese
1 tsp. salt
⅛ tsp. pepper
¾ lb. large shells or
   rigatoni, cooked
   and drained

Sauté onion in hot oil until soft. Add tomato paste, tomatoes, 4 cups water, sugar, 1 tablespoon salt, bay leaf, and oregano. Cover; simmer 1 hour. Heat oven to 350° F. Combine ricotta, eggs, parsley, ¼ cup Parmesan cheese, 1 teaspoon salt, and pepper. Stuff shells with cheese mixture. Layer stuffed shells and sauce in 13x9x2-inch casserole. Sprinkle with remaining ½ cup Parmesan cheese. Bake 40 to 45 minutes. Makes 6 to 8 servings.

MANICOTTI WITH RED CLAM SAUCE

1 pkg. (8 oz.)
   manicotti
5 qts. boiling water
   tbs. salt
   lbs. ricotta cheese
⅓ c. grated
   Parmesan cheese
   egg yolks
½ tsp. salt

1 pkg. (6 oz.)
   process garlic
   cheese roll, cubed
1 recipe Red Clam
   Sauce (*page 281*)
Grated Parmesan
   cheese
Chopped parsley

Parboil manicotti in salted water 5 minutes; drain thoroughly. Combine ricotta, Parmesan, egg yolks, ½ teaspoon salt, and garlic cheese; mix well. Spoon mixture into drained manicotti; arrange in single layer in shallow baking dish. Prepare clam sauce according to recipe. Pour over manicotti in baking dish. Sprinkle with Parmesan cheese and parsley.

Bake at 350° F. for 35 to 40 minutes or until cheese melts and sauce bubbles. Makes 8 servings.

STUFFED RIGATONI

1 c. finely chopped
   onion (1 large)
3 tbs. olive or pure
   vegetable oil
2 cans (6 oz. ea.)
   tomato paste
1 can (1 lb. 13 oz.)
   Italian plum
   tomatoes
4 c. water
1 tbs. sugar
1 tbs. salt
½ tsp. pepper
1 bay leaf

½ tsp. leaf oregano,
   crumbled
1 lb. hot Italian
   sausage*
¾ c. packaged
   bread crumbs
⅓ c. milk
1 egg
¾ lb. rigatoni,
   cooked and
   drained
⅓ c. grated
   Parmesan cheese

Sauté onion in hot oil until soft; add tomato paste, tomatoes, and water; stir well. Add seasonings; cover; simmer 1 hour, stirring occasionally. Remove casing from sausage; break up meat; brown well. Add bread crumbs, milk, and egg; mix well. Stuff rigatoni with sausage mixture. Layer sauce and rigatoni into large casserole. Sprinkle with cheese. Bake at 350° F. for 35 to 45 minutes. Serve at once. Makes 6 servings.
*For less hot flavor, use half sweet sausage.

BACON-MACARONI-CHEESE CASSEROLE

1 can (14½ oz.)
   evaporated milk
   (1⅔ c.)
½ c. water
1 can (10½ oz.)
   condensed cream
   of mushroom
   soup
½ lb. process
   American cheese,
   cubed

2 tbs. grated
   Parmesan or
   Romano cheese
1 tsp. prepared
   mustard
½ lb. bacon
1 pkg. (8 oz.)
   elbow macaroni,
   cooked and
   drained

Combine milk, water, soup, cheeses, and mustard in medium-size saucepan; cook over low heat, stirring constantly, until cheese is melted. Cook bacon until crisp; drain; crumble. Combine macaroni, crumbled bacon, and cheese sauce; turn into buttered 2-quart casserole. Bake at 350° F. for 25 to 30 minutes. Makes 6 servings.

FRIED NOODLES WITH CHICKEN LIVERS

¾ lb. fine noodles, cooked and drained
3 tbs. fat or pure vegetable oil
1½ lbs. chicken livers
4 tbs. butter or margarine
⅓ c. finely chopped celery
⅓ c. finely chopped onion
2 tbs. chopped parsley
1½ tbs. cornstarch
1½ c. chicken broth
1 tbs. soy sauce
1 tsp. Worcestershire sauce

Dry cooked noodles on paper towels. Heat fat or oil in 8-inch skillet; brown half the noodles, turning to brown both sides. Drain on paper towels. Place on hot platter. Repeat with remaining noodles. Quarter chicken livers; sauté in butter or margarine with celery and onion 5 minutes, stirring constantly. Add parsley, cornstarch mixed with chicken broth, soy sauce, and Worcestershire. Simmer until thickened. Serve on noodles. Makes 6 servings.

NOODLES DANDY

1 clove of garlic, crushed
½ c. chopped onion (1 medium)
2 tbs. butter or margarine
½ lb. cooked ham, cubed
1 carton (8 oz.) large-curd cottage cheese
1 can (10½ oz.) condensed cream of mushroom soup
½ c. milk
½ lb. green noodles, cooked and drained
¼ c. grated Parmesan cheese

Heat oven to 350° F. Sauté garlic and onion in butter or margarine. Add ham; brown lightly. Add cottage cheese, mushroom soup, and milk; mix well. Combine ham mixture

with noodles. Pour mixture into buttered 2-quart casserole. Sprinkle with Parmesan cheese. Bake 40 to 45 minutes or until lightly browned. Makes 6 servings.

NOODLE-ALMOND CASSEROLE

2 tbs. butter or margarine
½ lb. mushrooms, thinly sliced
2 tbs. minced onion
½ tsp. salt
1 pkg. (8 oz.) noodles, cooked and drained
1½ c. chicken broth or consommé
4 tbs. butter or margarine
½ c. slivered almonds
3 tbs. flour
2 tbs. chopped parsley

Melt 2 tablespoons butter or margarine in skillet; add mushrooms; cook, stirring occasionally, until lightly browned. Add onion and salt; cook 1 minute. Combine noodles and mushroom mixture; pour into 1½-quart buttered casserole. Pour chicken broth or consommé over. Refrigerate until 30 minutes before serving time. Heat oven to 375° F. Cover casserole; bake 25 minutes. Combine 4 tablespoons butter or margarine, almonds, and flour in small saucepan. Heat, stirring, until mixture is a deep golden brown. Stir mixture through noodles. Sprinkle with parsley. Serve at once. Makes 6 servings.

PASTA SAUCES

MEAT SAUCE FOR PASTA

2 tbs. olive oil
2 cloves of garlic, crushed
1 c. chopped onion (1 large)
1 green pepper, seeded and chopped
1 sweet or hot Italian sausage
½ lb. ground chuck or round
1 tbs. salt
¼ tsp. pepper
1 tsp. sugar
1 can (6 oz.) tomato paste
1 can (1 lb. 13 oz.) Italian plum tomatoes
2 tsp. leaf oregano, crumbled
½ c. grated Parmesan cheese
2 tbs. chopped parsley

Heat oil in large skillet or saucepan. Sauté garlic, onion, and pepper until soft; remove, reserve. Remove casing from sausage; break up. Add sausage and meat to oil remaining skillet; cook until well browned. Pour off much oil as possible. Return garlic, onion, and pepper to skillet. Add salt, pepper, sugar, tomato paste, tomatoes, and oregano. Simmer 40 minutes, stirring occasionally. Stir in cheese and parsley just before serving. Makes about 2 quarts.

MARINARA SAUCE

2 tbs. olive oil	1½ tsp. salt
2 cloves of garlic, chopped	1 tsp. leaf basil, crumbled
2 c. chopped onion (2 large)	½ tsp. leaf oregano, crumbled
1 can (1 lb. 13 oz.) Italian plum tomatoes	½ c. water Few dried red pepper seeds
1 can (6 oz.) tomato paste	

Heat oil in large saucepan. Add garlic and onion; cook over low heat 10 minutes. Stir in tomatoes, tomato paste, salt, basil, oregano, water, and red pepper seeds. Cook, covered, over low heat 1½ hours, stirring occasionally. Uncover; cook ½ hour or until as thick as desired. Makes about 1½ quarts.

RED CLAM SAUCE

1 c. chopped onion (1 large)	½ tsp. salt
3 tbs. olive oil, butter, or margarine	2 tbs. chopped parsley
1 tsp. leaf oregano, crumbled	2 cans (8 oz. ea.) tomato sauce
1 tsp. leaf basil, crumbled	2 cans (7½ oz. ea.) minced clams

Sauté onion in oil, butter, or margarine until tender. Stir in oregano, basil, salt, parsley, and tomato sauce. Drain clams; reserve clams. Add juice to tomato mixture; simmer 15 minutes. Remove from heat. Stir in clams; heat through. Makes about 1 quart.

WHITE CLAM SAUCE

2 doz. clams	1 c. chopped Italian parsley
½ c. olive oil	
3 cloves of garlic, crushed	

Open clams; remove from shells, saving all liquid. (Or have fish-market man do it for you.) Put clams through food grinder, using coarse blade or chop coarsely with sharp knife. Drain off any liquid from ground clams and add to liquid above. Reserve clams and liquid in separate bowls. Heat oil in saucepan. Add garlic; cook gently about 3 minutes. Watch carefully; do not let garlic brown. Add parsley and clam liquid. Simmer 3 to 5 minutes. Add clams; heat through. Serve over hot, cooked linguine or spaghettini. Makes about 1 quart.

SALSA NAPOLI

½ lb. ground beef	½ tsp. garlic powder
1 c. chopped onion (1 large)	½ tsp. sugar
¼ c. pure vegetable or olive oil	1 tbs. leaf oregano, crumbled
1 can (1 lb. 4 oz.) tomato purée	½ tsp. seasoned pepper
1½ c. water	¼ c. grated Parmesan cheese
1 tbs. salt	

Brown beef and onion in hot oil in large skillet. Add tomato purée, water, salt, garlic powder, sugar, oregano, and pepper. Simmer, uncovered, 30 minutes; stir occasionally. Add cheese; cook 5 minutes. Makes about 1½ quarts.

SALSA VERDE

2 pkgs. (3 oz. ea.) cream cheese	½ tsp. salt
1 clove of garlic, minced	¼ c. olive oil
¼ c. grated Parmesan cheese	¼ c. hot water ¼ c. finely chopped parsley

Mash cream cheese; stir until smooth. Blend in garlic, Parmesan cheese, salt, and olive oil. Add hot water; beat until smooth. Stir in parsley. Makes about 1¼ cups.

Cereals

Next to rice and wheat, corn is the favorite cereal in the American cuisine, though oats, buckwheat, rye, and barley all have their place.

The word "cereal" to most of us means breakfast food—crisp cornflakes, shredded wheat squares or biscuits, or steaming oatmeal. The choice is so wide in both ready-to-eat breakfast cereals and those which require brief cooking that you can have a different kind on the table every day.

Cereal Grains

Barley we use mainly in soups. *Pearl barley* looks like little transparent seeds. *Rye* we know mostly in bread because the grain is made into flour. *Buckwheat* groats are popular with Americans of Russian or Polish background, who call this brown, flavorful cereal *kasha*. When cooked, kasha tastes much like brown rice.

Cracked wheat, sometimes called "wheat pilaf" is a gourmet item found in specialty stores. This is the heart of the wheat, rich in flavor and food value, delightful when cooked in meat broth with the addition of raisins, nuts, and bits of meat. It is used extensively in Near Eastern cookery.

Cornmeal. The type you prefer probably depends on where you grew up. In the South, white cornmeal is considered the only proper kind. Northerners, especially New England Yankees, consider yellow cornmeal more flavorful. The two may be used interchangeably in most recipes.

Hominy grits are very popular throughout the South where this white product of hulled corn is served as a vegetable, in place of potatoes. To cook, stir 1 cup hominy grits slowly into 5 cups boiling, salted water (using 1 teaspoon salt). Cover; cook 20 to 25 minutes, stirring frequently.

Storing Cereals

All cereals should be kept in a dry place away from heat. The ready-to-eat cereals should always be resealed after use, the inner cellophane wrapper folded over. Use as soon as possible after purchase, for once they lose crispness, these cereals also lose flavor.

Cereals that are to be cooked, including rice, cornmeal, and hominy grits, should also be kept tightly closed and away from heat, though their shelf life is much longer than that of the ready-to-eat type.

POLENTA

1 envelope dehydrated onion soup mix	1½ c. cornmeal
	3 tbs. melted butter or margarine
4½ c. water	½ c. grated
1 tsp. salt	Parmesan cheese

Combine onion soup mix, water, and salt in large saucepan; bring to boiling. Add cornmeal slowly, stirring constantly. Cook over low heat, stirring often, about 10 minutes or until mixture is very thick. Cool. Heat oven to 375° F. Brush shallow 1½-quart baking dish with half the melted butter or margarine; sprinkle with half the Parmesan cheese. Drop polenta by spoonfuls into dish (or shape polenta into large balls between palms of hands). Brush with remaining melted butter or margarine; sprinkle with remaining Parmesan cheese. Bake 15 minutes. Serve with *Savory Sauce:* Combine 1 envelope dehydrated tomato or chicken soup mix and 1¾ cups water in saucepan; simmer 5 minutes. Stir in ½ cup milk; heat slowly until piping hot. Makes 6 servings.

GNOCCHI PARMESAN

1 c. quick-cooking farina	2 eggs, beaten
	1½ c. grated Parmesan cheese
3½ c. milk	
1 tsp. salt	¼ c. melted butter or margarine
¼ c. butter or margarine	

Combine farina and 1 cup milk in small bowl; stir until smooth. Heat remaining 2½ cups milk, salt, and ¼ cup butter or margarine to boiling in medium-size saucepan; stir in farina mixture quickly. Cook, stirring constantly, 5 minutes or until very thick; remove from heat. Stir in beaten eggs and 1 cup grated Parmesan cheese; beat until blended. Pour into 9x9x2-inch pan; cool; chill several hours or overnight. Cut into squares or rectangles; arrange in shallow baking dish; brush with melted butter or margarine; sprinkle with remaining ½ cup Parmesan cheese. Bake at 425° F. for 20 to 25 minutes or until golden. Makes 4 servings.

Chapter Seventeen

Vegetables

It's always a pleasure to serve colorful, flavor-rich vegetables—cooked till just tender and crisp. Even in the market these luscious garden gems almost beckon you to take them home. And there are so many imaginative ways to cook vegetables. Crumb or cream them, try them scalloped, au gratin, or with any number of mouth-watering sauces.

Vegetables have a very generous supply of vitamins and minerals, but unfortunately much of it is lost—along with their good flavor—because of careless cooking and over-cooking. Only when cooked properly can vegetables be as wonderfully delicious and nutritious as they should be. Sometimes imaginative cooking can even make a vegetable enthusiast of the toughest antivegetable rebel in the family! Follow a few simple rules for cooking, season with a deft hand, serve piping hot—and just watch your family sit up and take notice.

Buying Vegetables

• Read your weekly food ads and check for specials.
• Select carefully. Look for vegetables that are fresh and crisp looking. They may not be displayed on ice, but if the vegetable dealer has a quick turnover, this will not affect quality.
• Become familiar with the season of the year when each is most plentiful and of peak quality.

Storing and Handling Vegetables

• Store onions, potatoes, garlic, and winter squash in containers where air can circulate round them. Refrigeration is not necessary. Do not wash before storing.

• Remove excessive soil from vegetables to be stored in the refrigerator. Take off wilted outer leaves from salad greens, cauliflower, and cabbage.
• It is better not to wash lettuce unless you plan to use within 2 days. If you are going to use it immediately, wash, core, and drain. Store, wrapped in transparent plastic wrap or plastic bags in the vegetable drawer or bin.

Ways of Cooking Vegetables

To Boil: Cook vegetables, covered, in ½ to 1 inch boiling, salted water except where otherwise directed. Try them at the crisp, tender stage, slightly undercooked. You may like them even more.

To Steam: Place vegetables in the perforated compartment of a steamer over rapidly boiling water. Cover and steam just until tender.

To Oven Steam: Place in a covered casserole with a small amount of water. This is particularly good when cooking oven meals. When done in a 350° F. oven allow the vegetables to cook about three times longer than for boiled vegetables.

To Bake: Place vegetables on the oven rack, on a baking sheet, or in a shallow casserole.

To Braise: Put vegetables in a covered skillet with about two tablespoons butter, margarine, or drippings and one or two tablespoons water. These are also known as "panned vegetables."

To Broil: Use tender, raw vegetables such as tomatoes and mushrooms or use this method to reheat cooked vegetables (first brush with butter or margarine).

To Fry: Sauté in small amount of fat in skillet over medium heat, or shallow fry in ½ to 1 inch hot fat, or French fry in hot fat deep enough to cover or float vegetables. Cook small amount at a time. Never crowd the pan.

To Pressure Cook: Follow the manufacturer's directions for your pressure cooker.

Cooking Frozen Vegetables

Cook frozen vegetables in as little water as possible; follow package directions for amount. Whether you use the packaged frozen vegetables or the larger family size, it is possible to use as much or as little as you wish to cook and return the remainder to the freezer. When cooking vegetables that are in a frozen block, break up the block as it cooks. Corn on the cob should be thawed before cooking or the corn kernels will be cooked and the cob will remain cold.

Frozen vegetables can be baked in a covered casserole with one to two tablespoons butter or margarine and a quarter teaspoon salt. The cooking time in a 350° F. oven varies from 40 to 60 minutes according to the vegetables. Frozen vegetables are also available in pliofilm bags in butter and special sauces. Follow package directions for cooking.

Cooking Canned Vegetables

To retain the best fresh flavor of canned vegetables, drain the liquid from the can into a saucepan. Boil it until it is reduced down to one half. Add the vegetables and heat quickly. Do not boil. Season to taste with salt, pepper, and butter or margarine.

Add a Touch of Glamour to Vegetables

Most frequently vegetables are served buttered but there are so many extra touches to make the vegetable of the day more interesting and glamorous. Seasoning added to melted butter or margarine is the simplest, but consider creamed, scalloped, au gratin, and crumbed as well as the many sauces that go so well with vegetables. Here are some hints on how to add these touches.

Seasoned Butters: Heat a quarter cup butter or margarine to a golden brown. Add one of the following: one teaspoon celery seed, one tablespoon horseradish, two tablespoons lemon juice and one teaspoon grated lemon rind, or two tablespoons grated Parmesan cheese.

Creamed Vegetables: To two cups cooked vegetables add one cup Medium White Sauce (*page 348*) and reheat. Or place hot vegetables in serving dish and pour hot sauce over. A second and quick way to cream vegetables is done by heating light cream seasoned with salt, pepper, and butter or margarine, then pouring it over the vegetable.

Scalloped Vegetables: Arrange cooked vegetables and White Sauce in alternate layers in a casserole. Top with buttered bread crumbs and bake at 350° F. for 20 minutes or until browned.

Vegetables au Gratin: This may be done one of two ways. Layer the vegetables and a cheese sauce in a greased casserole and top with buttered crumbs, or follow the directions for Scalloped Vegetables, sprinkling each layer with cheese.

Vegetables with Crumbs: Cook a half cup dry bread crumbs in a quarter cup butter or margarine until golden brown. Sprinkle over hot cooked vegetable and serve immediately.

ARTICHOKES

Buying: Available September to May. Look for compact, uniformly green heads with tightly adhering leaves. Allow one per serving.

Preparing: Cut 1 inch off top, straight across. Cut off stem 1 inch from base, leaving a stub. With scissors, cut off tip of each leaf.

Cooking: Drop artichokes into boiling, salted water. Add garlic clove, 2 lemon slices, and 1 tablespoon olive or pure vegetable oil fo each artichoke. Cover; cook 20 to 45 minutes, depending on size, until stub can be pierced easily with a fork. Drain; cut off stub.

How to Eat: Pull off leaves one by one. Dip the base of the leaves (the thick part) in Drawn Butter Sauce (*page 350*) or Hollandaise Sauce (*page 349*). Eat only the tender part of the leaf by drawing it between the teeth; continue eating, leaf after leaf, until you reach the fuzzy center or "choke." Remove with knife and fork; discard. Cut the thick heart or bottom into cubes with knife and fork; dip in sauce. Well-chilled artichokes may be eaten the same way with Vinaigrette Dressing (*page 343*).

ARTICHOKES SAUTÉ

3 large artichokes   ¼ c. melted butter
1 tsp. salt   or margarine
¼ tsp. pepper

Cut artichokes in quarters; remove chokes; clip off any thorny tips on leaves with scissors. Parboil 5 minutes in salted water; drain; place in shallow baking dish. Blend salt and pepper with melted butter or margarine; pour over artichokes; cover dish. Bake at 350° F. for 20 to 25 minutes or until artichokes are tender. Garnish with strips of pimiento and serve with Hollandaise Sauce (*page 349*), if desired. Makes 4 servings.

ARTICHOKES PARMESAN

1 pkg. (9 oz.)   ½ tsp. salt
  frozen artichoke   ¼ tsp. pepper
  hearts   2 tbs. grated
2 tbs. lemon juice   Parmesan cheese
3 tbs. butter or   Paprika
  margarine

Cook artichoke hearts according to package directions. Drain. Combine lemon juice, butter or margarine, salt, and pepper in small saucepan. Heat until butter or margarine is melted and mixture blended. Pour over artichoke hearts; toss lightly to coat well. Turn into serving dish; sprinkle with cheese and paprika. Makes 3 to 4 servings.

ASPARAGUS

Buying: Available February to June (peak in March and April). Look for stalks that are green and tender almost the entire length. The tips should be well formed and tightly closed. Buy stalks that are as nearly uniform in size as possible since varying sizes will cook in different times. Allow 2 pounds for 4 servings.

Preparing: To prepare, break off each stalk as far down as it snaps easily. Wash it thoroughly in warm water to release any sand. Pare the stalk thinly with a vegetable parer.

Cooking: Cook in a large, shallow skillet. Lay stalks flat in skillet. Add 1 inch boiling, salted water. Cover and cook 10 to 13 minutes or until the lower parts of the stalks are tender and firm.

SPRINGTIME ASPARAGUS

2 lbs. asparagus   ⅓ c. butter or
¼ c. packaged   margarine
  bread crumbs   1 tbs. chopped
                                   parsley

Snap off asparagus stalks as far down as they break easily. Cook in boiling, salted water 10 to 12 minutes or until just tender. Sauté bread crumbs in butter or margarine until golden; add parsley. Drain asparagus; **top** with crumbs. Makes 4 servings.

ASPARAGUS WITH MUSHROOM SAUCE

2 lbs. fresh   2 tbs. flour
  asparagus   ½ tsp. salt
¾ lb. fresh mush-   Dash of pepper
  rooms, sliced   2 c. half-and-half
3 tbs. butter or   or light cream
  margarine

Prepare asparagus; cook in boiling, salted water 10 to 12 minutes or until tender. Sauté mushrooms in butter or margarine 5 minutes. Add flour, salt, and pepper. Stir in cream; simmer 1 minute. Pour sauce over hot asparagus. Makes 6 servings.

ASPARAGUS, CHINESE STYLE

2 lbs. asparagus	2 tbs. pure vege-
1 tbs. cornstarch	table oil
1 c. chicken broth	⅓ c. thinly sliced
1 tbs. soy sauce	water chestnuts
2 tsp. onion juice	2 tbs. slivered,
Dash of pepper	toasted almonds

Snap off ends of asparagus stalks. Cut asparagus in very thin diagonal slices. Combine cornstarch, chicken broth, soy sauce, onion juice, and pepper. Cook, stirring constantly, until thickened; simmer 2 minutes. Cook asparagus in hot oil in large skillet 2 minutes, stirring constantly. Add sauce; cook 2 minutes longer. Stir in water chestnuts and almonds. Makes 6 servings.

ASPARAGUS VINAIGRETTE

2 lbs. asparagus	½ tsp. leaf chervil,
6 tbs. pure	crumbled
vegetable oil	½ tsp. leaf
3 tbs. wine vinegar	tarragon,
1 tsp. dry mustard	crumbled
1 tsp. finely	¼ clove of garlic,
chopped parsley	mashed
1 tsp. finely	1 tbs. finely
chopped chives	chopped hard-
½ tsp. salt	cooked egg white
⅛ tsp. pepper	

Prepare asparagus; cook in boiling, salted water 10 to 12 minutes or until tender. Drain well. Chill in glass or pottery dish. Combine remaining ingredients. Chill. Pour dressing over asparagus. Chill 30 minutes. Serve on lettuce, if desired. Makes 6 servings.

ASPARAGUS LOAF

1 c. coarsely	½ tsp. salt
crumbled saltine	Dash of pepper
crackers	2 tsp. grated onion
4 tbs. melted butter	2 pkgs. (10 oz. ea.)
or margarine	frozen asparagus
2 eggs, slightly	cuts, cooked and
beaten	drained
2 c. hot milk	

Heat oven to 350° F. Line 9x5x3-inch loaf pan with strip of aluminum foil; butter well. Sauté crackers in butter or margarine until golden brown. Combine eggs, milk, salt, pepper, and onion; mix well; add cooked asparagus and sautéed crackers; turn into prepared pan. Bake 30 minutes or until knife inserted 1 inch from edge of pan comes out clean. Serve with hot canned chicken gravy, or canned mushroom soup diluted with ⅓ cup of milk, if desired. Makes 6 servings.

GREEN OR SNAP BEANS AND WAX BEANS

Buying: Available all year. Buy fresh, crispy pods that snap easily when bent. Allow 1½ pounds for 4 servings.

Preparing: Nip off ends of pods; string if necessary, but most beans marketed today are stringless. They may be cut crosswise, slivered lengthwise (French cut) or cooked whole.

Cooking: Cook, covered, in about ½ inch boiling, salted water about 5 minutes. Lower heat; uncover; simmer 15 to 20 minutes or until just tender.

GOURMET BEANS

1½ lbs. green beans,	2 tbs. chopped
tipped and cut in	chives
pieces	1 c. dairy sour
3 tbs. butter or	cream
margarine	1 tsp. dill weed

Prepare beans; cook in boiling, salted water until tender; drain. Melt butter or margarine in small saucepan; stir in chives, sour cream, and dill weed. Pour over hot green beans. Makes 6 servings.

WAX BEANS AND TOMATOES

3 tbs. butter or	1 lb. wax beans,
margarine	sliced
¼ c. chopped onion	1½ c. water
(1 small)	½ tsp. salt
¼ c. chopped	½ tsp. leaf basil,
celery	crumbled
2 tomatoes, peeled	
and chopped	

Melt butter or margarine in saucepan or skillet. Add onion, celery, and tomatoes; cook 10 minutes over low heat or until vegetable are soft but not browned. Cook beans in water with salt and basil 20 minutes or until tender; drain. Add hot beans to tomato mixture; heat 1 minute. Makes 6 servings.

GREEN BEANS IN TOMATOES

8 large firm, ripe tomatoes	1 envelope Italian-style salad dressing mix
2 pkgs. (10 oz. ea.) frozen, cut green beans	Pimiento strips
	Crisp salad greens

Drop tomatoes into boiling water for a few minutes until skins loosen. Peel; core; remove seeds and pulp carefully. Turn upside down on tray to drain; chill. Cook green beans; drain; spoon into shallow dish. Prepare salad dressing mix according to package directions; pour over beans; refrigerate several hours or overnight. An hour or so before serving, fill tomatoes with green beans and dressing. Top each with a pimiento strip. Arrange on a platter of crisp greens. Makes 8 servings.

GREEN BEANS VINAIGRETTE

½ lb. bacon	2 cans (1 lb. ea.) whole green beans
2 eggs	
⅓ c. vinegar	
½ c. water	1 tbs. diced pimiento
3 tbs. sugar	
¼ tsp. salt	

Cook bacon until crisp; drain; crumble. Reserve ¼ cup bacon drippings. Beat eggs, vinegar, water, sugar, and salt together until well blended. Return ¼ cup bacon drippings to skillet; add egg mixture. Cook over low heat, stirring constantly, until mixture is thickened. Heat beans in can liquid; drain. Put beans in serving dish. Pour hot dressing over beans. Sprinkle with pimiento and crumbled bacon. Makes 8 servings.

BEETS

Buying: Available all year. Select bunches that are smooth, clean, and firm. Tops may or may not be left on. Allow 2 bunches for 4 servings.

Preparing: Wash. Cut off all but 2 inches of tops. Leave root end on.

Cooking: Cook, covered, in boiling, salted water to cover, about 35 to 45 minutes until tender.

ORANGE-GLAZED BEETS

3 bunches medium-size to small beets	1½ tsp. grated orange rind
1 tbs. chopped onion	1½ c. orange juice
3 tbs. butter or margarine	2 tbs. sugar
	1 tbs. lemon juice
1 tbs. cornstarch	½ tsp. salt
	Dash of pepper

Wash beets; cut off tops, leaving 1-inch stems. Cook beets in boiling, salted water 35 to 45 minutes or until tender. Rinse beets in cold water; peel off skin. Slice medium-size beets, leave small ones whole. Sauté onion in butter or margarine; add cornstarch, orange rind and juice, sugar, lemon juice, salt, and pepper. Simmer until sauce thickens. Add beets; simmer, covered, 10 minutes. Makes 8 servings.

HARVARD BEETS

2 bunches beets, cooked and drained	1 tbs. cornstarch
	½ c. vinegar
¼ c. sugar	3 tbs. butter or margarine
¼ tsp. salt	

Slip skins off beets; trim; slice or dice. Combine sugar, salt, and cornstarch in saucepan. Blend in vinegar. Cook, over low heat, stirring constantly until thickened and bubbly. Add beets and butter or margarine. Heat 10 minutes over low heat. Makes 4 servings.

BROCCOLI

Buying: Available all year except the hottest summer months. Look for bright green, crisp stems with compact flower heads. There should be no yellow color in heads. Allow 1½ pounds for 4 servings.

Preparing: Cut off bottom of stem. Remove any large leaves. If stalks are thicker than 1 inch, make lengthwise gashes through them to insure quick cooking. Pare stalks thinly just through to bright green.

Cooking: Lay stalks in large skillet; add 1 inch boiling, salted water; cover; cook 10 to 15 minutes until just tender.

BROCCOLI AMANDINE

2 bunches broccoli
½ c. blanched
  slivered almonds
½ c. butter or
  margarine

2 tbs. lemon juice
¼ tsp. salt
Dash of pepper

Wash broccoli well; drain. Remove and discard large coarse outer leaves; cut off tough lower parts of the stalks. Cut large stalks lengthwise into quarters or halves. Put in 1 inch boiling, salted water in large skillet. Cook 10 to 15 minutes or until just tender. Sauté almonds in butter or margarine in small saucepan or skillet until golden. Add lemon juice, salt, and pepper; heat through. Serve over broccoli. Makes 8 servings.

HERBED BROCCOLI

2 bunches broccoli
3 chicken bouillon
  cubes
2 c. boiling water
¼ c. choppen onion
  (1 small)

1 tsp. leaf marjo-
  ram, crumbled
1 tsp. leaf basil,
  crumbled
3 tbs. melted butter
  or margarine

Wash broccoli well; remove large leaves and cut off ends of stalks. Cut large stalks in half lengthwise. Dissolve bouillon cubes in water in large skillet. Add onion, marjoram, basil, and broccoli. Cover; cook quickly about 10 minutes or until just tender. Drain. Add butter or margarine. Make 8 servings.

BRUSSELS SPROUTS

Buying: Available fall and winter. Buy compact, bright green heads. Allow 1 quart (about 1 pound) for 4 servings.

Preparing: Remove any loose or yellowed leaves. Cut thin slice off stem end. Wash well in cold water.

Cooking: Cook, covered, in 1 inch boiling, salted water about 8 to 10 minutes or until just tender.

CREAMED BRUSSELS SPROUTS AND CELERY

1 qt. Brussels
  sprouts
1½ c. chopped
  celery
1½ c. boiling water
1 tsp. salt
2 tbs. melted butter
  or margarine

4 tbs. flour
Milk
Dash of ground
  nutmeg
½ c. shredded
  Cheddar cheese

Wash sprouts well; remove wilted leaves. Cut off ends. Cook sprouts and celery in boiling water with salt in covered pan about 8 minutes or until just tender. Drain; save vegetable liquid. Blend butter or margarine and flour in small saucepan. Measure vegetable liquid; add enough milk to make 1¾ cups. Stir gradually into flour mixture. Cook over medium heat, stirring constantly, until sauce thickens; add nutmeg. Combine vegetables and sauce in heatproof, 1½-quart shallow casserole. Sprinkle with cheese. Broil until lightly browned. Makes 6 servings.

BRUSSELS SPROUTS AND CHESTNUTS

½ c. butter or
  margarine
½ lb. chestnuts,
  shelled, skinned,
  and sliced
2 c. water
2 tbs. instant
  minced onion

2 envelopes or 2 tbs.
  granulated beef
  or chicken
  bouillon
1½ qts. fresh
  Brussels sprouts
  or 4 pkgs. (8 oz.
  ea.) frozen
  Brussels sprouts
Butter or margarine

Melt ½ cup butter or margarine in large skillet; add chestnuts; sauté until golden. Remove and keep warm. Combine water, onion, and bouillon in skillet; bring to boiling. Add Brussels sprouts; cook until tender; drain. Add warm chestnuts and butter or margarine; toss gently. Makes 8 servings.

CABBAGE

Green Cabbage

Buying: Available all year. Select solid, heav' heads. Cabbage held in storage will not be s green and leafy as the new cabbage. Allow 1½ pounds for 4 servings.

Preparing: Wash; cut into wedges; remove core.

Cooking: Cook, covered, in ½ inch boiling, salted water for about 5 minutes or until just crisp-tender; do not overcook.

Red Cabbage

Buying: Available all year. Look for solid, heavy heads and a clear red color. Allow 1½ pounds for 4 servings.

Preparing: Wash; cut into wedges; remove core. Or cabbage may be shredded to be cooked for certain recipes.

Cooking: Cook, covered, in ½ inch boiling, salted water to which 2 tablespoons of vinegar or lemon juice have been added to keep the warm red color.

SAUTEED RED CABBAGE

1 c. chopped onion (1 large)	3 medium-size tart apples, cored, pared, and chopped
⅓ c. pure vegetable oil or bacon drippings	1 bay leaf
1 medium-size head red cabbage (2 to 2½ lbs.), cored and shredded	1½ tsp. salt
	Dash of pepper
	¼ c. red wine vinegar
	1 tbs. sugar

Sauté onion in oil or bacon drippings 5 minutes or until tender. Add cabbage, apples, bay leaf, salt, and pepper; mix well. Cover; cook over low heat 20 minutes, stirring occasionally. Combine vinegar and sugar; add to cabbage mixture. Cook 5 minutes. Makes 6 servings.

Chinese Cabbage

Buying: Available all year. Select tender, green compact heads. Allow 1½ pounds for 4 servings.

Preparing: Remove any bruised outer leaves. Cut thin slice off bottom. Shred.

Cooking: Cook, covered, in 1 inch boiling, salted water for 3 to 4 minutes until just crisp-tender.

CARROTS

Buying: Available all year. Select firm, bright orange carrots; tops should be crispy and fresh, but most carrots in supermarkets have tops removed. Allow 1 bunch or package for 4 servings.

Preparing: Scape or pare carrots with vegetable peeler. Cut into slices or strips, dice, or leave whole.

Cooking: Cook, covered, in 1 inch boiling, salted water for 10 to 20 minutes if sliced or 15 to 20 minutes if whole.

LEMON BUTTERED CARROTS

24 small carrots	2 tsp. grated lemon rind
½ c. butter or margarine	1 tbs. lemon juice
½ c. sugar	

Pare carrots; trim tops. Cook, covered, in a small amount of boiling, salted water in a large skillet 15 to 20 minutes or until tender. Drain; remove carrots from skillet. Melt butter or margarine and sugar in skillet; stir in lemon rind and juice. Add carrots; cook over low heat, turning carrots slowly and often until they are glazed. Garnish with parsley, if desired. Makes 8 servings.

CARROT PUDDING

12 medium-size carrots	1 tbs. sugar
1 tbs. minced onion	½ tsp. salt
⅓ c. finely diced green pepper	Dash of pepper
2 tbs. butter or margarine	1 c. milk
1 tbs. flour	1 tbs. melted butter or margarine
	½ c. soft bread crumbs (1 slice)

Pare carrots; cut in 1-inch pieces. Cook, covered, in boiling, salted water 10 to 18 minutes or until tender. Drain; mash. Heat oven to 350° F. Sauté onion and green pepper in 2 tablespoons butter or margarine about 3 minutes or until tender. Add flour, sugar, salt, and pepper. Add milk gradually, stirring until smooth. Cook over medium heat, stirring constantly, until sauce thickens. Add carrots; mix well. Turn into 9-inch pie plate or 1-quart casserole. Combine 1 tablespoon melted butter or margarine and bread crumbs. Sprinkle over carrot mixture. Bake 30 to 35 minutes or until lightly browned. Makes 6 servings.

CAULIFLOWER

Buying: Available all year except during hottest summer months. Select heavy, compact heads with creamy white *flowerets* and crisp green outer leaves. Do not buy if bruised or discolored. Allow 1 large head for 4 servings.

Preparing: Remove green leaves; cut slice off root end; cut or separate head into flowerets; or head may be cooked whole.

Cooking: Cook, covered, in 1 inch boiling, salted water for 8 to 15 minutes for flowerets or 20 to 30 minutes for whole head.

CAULIFLOWER AND ASPARAGUS POLONAISE

1 large head cauliflower	½ c. soft bread crumbs
3 pkgs. (10 oz. ea.) frozen asparagus spears	Chopped pimiento or chopped hard-cooked egg
1 c. butter or margarine	

Remove outer leaves and stalks from cauliflower. Trim off any blemishes on flowerets; wash well. Carefully cut out as much of center core as possible, keeping head whole and in shape. Cook in boiling, salted water 20 to 30 minutes or until tender. Drain. Cook asparagus according to package directions; drain. Melt butter or margarine; add bread crumbs. Cook slowly until crumbs are brown. Arrange vegetables in serving dish. Top with crumbs. Sprinkle with chopped pimiento or chopped hard-cooked egg. Makes 8 servings.

CELERY

Buying: Available all year. Select celery that is clean and crispy with fresh green leaves. There are two types available, Pascal or green celery and golden or bleached celery. Allow 1 bunch for 4 servings.

Preparing: Trim root; remove leaves (which make a good soup ingredient). Scrub with vegetable brush to remove sand and dirt. Use outer stalks for dicing, slicing, and cooking. Reserve inner and most tender stalks to cut for celery hearts.

Cooking: Cook diced or sliced celery, covered, in 1 inch boiling, salted water for 12 to 15 minutes or until just tender.

BRAISED CELERY

3 tbs. butter or margarine	¼ tsp. salt
	⅛ tsp. pepper
3 c. sliced celery	1 c. chicken broth

Melt butter or margarine in large saucepan or skillet. Add celery, salt, and pepper; cook 3 minutes, stirring occasionally. Add chicken broth; cover; cook 5 to 8 minutes or until celery is tender-crisp. Makes 4 servings.

HERBED CELERY AND TOMATOES

1 can (about 1 lb.) whole, peeled tomatoes	1 tsp. salt
	⅛ tsp. seasoned pepper
3 tbs. butter or margarine	1 tsp. leaf basil, crumbled
3 c. sliced celery	1 tsp. sugar

Drain tomatoes; reserve liquid. Melt butter or margarine in medium-size saucepan. Add celery, tomato liquid, salt, pepper, basil, and sugar. Cover; simmer over medium heat about 15 minutes or until celery is tender. Add tomatoes; stir to blend; simmer 5 minutes. Makes 4 servings.

Celery Root (Celeriac)

Buying: Available October through April. Look for firm, crisp roots that are fairly heavy. Allow 1½ pounds for 4 servings.

Preparing: Remove leaves and fibrous roots. Scrub well.

Cooking: Cook, covered, in boiling, salted water to cover for 40 to 55 minutes or until tender. Peel root; slice.

CORN

Buying: Available fresh, on the cob May through December. Select ears of corn with fresh green husks and plump milky kernels. Keep refrigerated until ready to cook. Allow 1 to 2 ears per serving.

Preparation: Remove husks and silk and snap off ends of stalks just before cooking.

Cooking: Cook, covered, in boiling, salted water to cover for 5 to 7 minutes.

To Roast: Brush with butter or margarine; sprinkle with salt and pepper. Wrap ears in aluminum foil. Roast over hot coals for 10 to 15 minutes on each side.

SQUAW CORN

½ to 1 c. cubed, cooked ham	1 can (1 lb.) cream-style corn
2 tbs. fat or pure vegetable oil	Salt and pepper to taste
	2 eggs, beaten

Brown ham in fat or oil; add corn, seasonings, and eggs. Mix. Cook over low heat, stirring constantly until eggs are set. Makes 6 servings.

CREOLE CORN PUDDING

1 lb. bacon	1 can (12 oz.) whole-kernel corn
¾ c. chopped onion	
½ c. diced green pepper	2 eggs, beaten
3 tbs. bacon drippings	2½ c. milk
	½ c. cornmeal
	Dash of pepper

Heat oven to 350° F. Cook bacon until crisp; drain and crumble. Sauté onion and green pepper in 3 tablespoons of bacon drippings. Mix with corn, eggs, milk, cornmeal, and pepper; add bacon. Turn into 2-quart casserole. Bake 45 minutes. Makes 6 servings.

CUCUMBER

Buying: Available all year. Select firm, bright green, evenly shaped cucumbers. Allow 2 cucumbers for 4 servings.

Preparing: Pare thinly; cut into thick slices.

Cooking: Cook, covered, in 1 inch boiling, salted water 12 to 15 minutes or until tender.

EGGPLANT

Buying: Available all year. Select firm, smooth skinned, heavy eggplant with rich purple color. Allow 1 medium eggplant for 4 servings.

Preparing: Peel, if desired or if skin is a bit tough. Cut into thick slices for panfrying.

Cooking: Dredge slices in flour; dip in egg beaten with 2 tablespoons milk; coat with packaged bread crumbs. Sauté in small amount of hot fat or oil until browned on one side and slightly transparent. Turn; brown on other side.

Optional Note: To remove excess moisture from eggplant, salt slices; let set for 1 hour; pat dry with a paper towel, then prepare for frying, sautéeing, or for use in a casserole.

BAKED EGGPLANT PARMIGIANA

1 large eggplant	Dash of pepper
3 to 4 tbs. fat or pure vegetable oil	1 can (3 to 4 oz.) mushroom crowns, drained
1 can (about 1 lb.) tomatoes	½ c. grated Parmesan cheese
1 can (6 oz.) tomato paste	2 c. soft bread crumbs (4 slices)
2 cloves of garlic, mashed	½ lb. mozzarella cheese, thinly sliced
1 tsp. salt	

Cut eggplant in half lengthwise; scoop out interior, leaving ¼-inch shell; cut scooped-out portion into 1-inch cubes; sauté in fat or oil 5 minutes or until tender; reserve. Combine tomatoes, tomato paste, garlic, salt, and pepper in saucepan; simmer 15 minutes; stir in mushrooms, Parmesan cheese, and bread crumbs; mix well. Add eggplant; heat through. Heat oven to 375° F. Spoon one fourth the tomato mixture into each eggplant shell; top with mozzarella cheese slices; add remaining tomato mixture; top with remaining cheese slices. Bake 15 to 20 minutes or until cheese melts and is lightly browned. Makes 6 servings.

STUFFED EGGPLANT

1 large eggplant or 2 small eggplant	1 tsp. leaf basil, crumbled
¼ c. butter or margarine	1 can (1 lb. 4 oz.) tomatoes, drained
½ c. chopped onion (1 medium)	½ pkg. (4 oz.) process Swiss cheese, cubed
1 green pepper, seeded and cubed	½ c. pine nuts or pignoli
½ tsp. salt	
⅛ tsp. pepper	

Cut slice off eggplant lengthwise. Cut around eggplant ¼ inch in from edge; carefully cut and scoop out interior, leaving ¼-inch shell; cube scooped-out portion; reserve. Parboil eggplant shell in boiling, salted water 5 minutes; drain. Melt butter or margarine in skillet; add onion, green pepper, and cubed eggplant; sauté until tender. Add salt, pepper, basil, tomatoes, cheese, and pine nuts or pignoli; mix well. Spoon mixture into eggplant shell; place in greased baking dish. Cover (if dish has no cover, you can use aluminum foil). Bake at 350° F. for 30 minutes or until eggplant is tender. Cut to serve. Makes 4 servings.

EGGPLANT PROVINCIAL

1 medium-size eggplant, peeled and cubed	2 tbs. chopped parsley
5 tbs. fat or pure vegetable oil	¼ tsp. leaf thyme, crumbled
1 c. sliced onion	1 tsp. salt
1 clove of garlic, crushed	⅛ tsp. pepper
4 medium-size tomatoes, peeled and chopped	¼ c. packaged bread crumbs
	2 tbs. grated Parmesan cheese

Sauté cubed eggplant in 3 tablespoons fat or oil 5 minutes or until tender. Remove and reserve eggplant. Sauté onion and garlic in remaining 2 tablespoons fat or oil 5 minutes. Add tomatoes; simmer, covered, 10 minutes. Add eggplant, parsley, thyme, salt, and pepper; simmer 5 minutes. Turn into heatproof

1½-quart casserole. Combine bread crumbs and cheese. Sprinkle over eggplant mixture. Broil until crumbs are browned. Makes 6 servings.

FENNEL, ANISE OR FINOCCHI

Buying: Available October through January. Look for bulbs with bright green color and crisp texture like celery.

Preparing: Scrape bulb; cut bulb into 1-inch slices. For preparing for salads, cut into dice.

Cooking: Cook, covered, in small amount of boiling, salted water about 15 to 20 minutes or until just tender.

GREENS

(Mustard greens, kale, Swiss chard, dandelion greens, turnip greens, collards, beet tops)

Buying: Available all year. Select fresh, crisp greens with tender stems. Allow 2 pounds for 4 servings.

Preparing: Remove root ends and bruised leaves. Wash well in several changes of water to remove sand. When greens are packaged, wash only once.

Cooking: Cook, covered, with water which clings to leaves after washing. Allow 15 to 20 minutes for kale and turnip greens; 5 to 15 minutes for beet tops; 15 to 20 minutes for Swiss chard, mustard greens, and dandelion greens; 10 to 15 minutes for collards.

KOHLRABI

Buying: Available summer and fall. Look for small or medium-size bulbs, with fresh green tops if they have been left on. Allow 1 medium-size kohlrabi for each serving.

Preparing: Pare thinly, slice, or dice.

Cooking: Cook, covered, in 1 inch boiling, salted water about 20 to 25 minutes or until just tender.

LEEK

Buying: Available all year. Select firm stalks with white to pale green color. Leaves should be crisp and dark green. Allow 2 bunches for 4 servings.

Preparing: Wash; remove root fibers, green leafy tops, and any tough outer layer. Cut into 2-inch lengths or leave whole.

Cooking: Cook, covered, in boiling, salted water about 15 minutes or until just tender.

BRAISED LEEK

1 bunch leek	1 can (10½ oz.)
2 tbs. butter or	condensed beef
margarine	broth
1 small onion,	¼ tsp. leaf thyme,
peeled and	crumbled
thinly sliced	1 bay leaf

Wash leek; remove root and tough outer layer. Cut into short lengths. Melt butter or margarine in skillet. Add leek and onion; cook until lightly browned. Add beef broth, thyme, and bay leaf. Cover; simmer 15 minutes or until tender. Makes 3 servings.

LIMA BEANS

Buying: Peak of season July through November, but sometimes found all year in certain localities. Look for full, green pods. Yellowish pods indicate mature beans. Allow 3 pounds for 4 servings.

Preparing: Wash pods; shell beans just before cooking. For easy shelling, cut off thin outer edge of pod with sharp knife or scissors; beans will slip out easily.

Cooking: Cook, covered, in 1 inch boiling, salted water about 20 to 25 minutes until lima beans are just tender.

LIMA BEANS WITH TOMATOES

1 c. sliced celery	¾ tsp. salt
⅓ c. chopped onion	½ tsp. sugar
3 tbs. fat or pure	⅛ tsp. pepper
vegetable oil	2 pkgs. (10 oz. ea.)
1 can (about 1 lb.)	frozen Fordhook
tomatoes, broken	lima beans
up	

Sauté celery and onion in hot fat or oil in saucepan 3 minutes. Add tomatoes, salt, sugar, and pepper. Bring to boiling; lower heat; simmer, uncovered, 10 minutes. Add lima beans; cover; simmer 10 to 12 minutes or until beans are tender. Makes 6 servings.

LIMA BEANS IN SQUASH RING

2 pkgs. (10 oz. ea.)	3 eggs, well beaten
frozen winter	1 pkg. (10 oz.)
squash	frozen baby lima
¼ c. butter or	beans
margarine	3 slices bacon
1 tsp. salt	

Heat oven to 350° F. Cut block of frozen squash into chunks or defrost completely. Combine butter or margarine, salt, and squash in medium-size saucepan; heat until piping hot, stirring often. Blend hot squash mixture slowly into beaten eggs. Pour into greased 1-quart ring mold; place mold in pan of hot water. Bake 1 hour or until firm. While squash is baking, cook lima beans according to package directions; drain; keep warm. Cook bacon until crisp; crumble; reserve drippings. Loosen top edge of ring with small knife or spatula; turn out onto hot serving plate. Add bacon and drippings to lima beans; spoon into center of squash ring. Makes 6 servings.

THREE-TONE BEAN CASSEROLE

1 can (1 lb. 4 oz.)	¼ tsp. pepper
red kidney beans	1 tbs. dried parsley
1 pkg. (10 oz.)	flakes
frozen lima beans	1 can (10½ oz.)
1 pkg. (10 oz.)	condensed
frozen cut green	tomato soup
beans	1 tbs. butter or
2 tbs. minced onion	margarine
1 tsp. prepared	½ c. soft bread
mustard	crumbs (1 slice)
1 tsp. salt	

Heat oven to 375° F. Drain kidney beans. Cook limas and green beans as packages direct; drain. Blend together onion, mustard, salt, pepper, parsley flakes, and soup. Stir in beans; turn into 1½-quart casserole. Melt butter or margarine in small saucepan; stir in crumbs. Sprinkle over beans. Bake 20 minutes, or until crumbs are golden brown and mixture bubbling. Makes 8 servings.

SUCCOTASH

2 pkgs. (10 oz. ea.) frozen whole-kernel corn	¼ c. butter or margarine
1 pkg. (10 oz.) frozen lima beans	1 c. light cream
	1 tsp. salt
	¼ tsp. pepper

Cook corn and lima beans according to package directions. Drain. Combine corn, lima beans, butter or margarine, cream, salt, and pepper in saucepan. Heat 5 minutes over low heat. Makes 6 servings.

MUSHROOMS

Buying: Available all year. Select firm, white mushrooms, free of discolorations or blemishes. The sizes will vary from very small to medium to large. Allow 1 pound for 4 servings.

Preparing: Do not wash unless sandy; it is best to wipe with damp cloth. Small mushrooms are cooked whole; slice medium mushrooms down through cap and stem. Large mushrooms are usually stuffed with a simple herb bread dressing and broiled.

SAUTÉED MUSHROOMS

1 lb. firm, medium-size mushrooms	½ tsp. salt
¼ c. butter or margarine	⅛ tsp. pepper

Wash mushrooms; dry with paper towels. Slice lengthwise through cap and stem, or snap off stem and slice cap and stem separately. Melt butter or margarine in large skillet over medium heat. Add mushrooms. Cook quickly, stirring briskly, about 5 minutes, until mushrooms are just translucent and tender. Do not overcook. Sprinkle with salt and pepper. Makes 4 servings.

Creamed Mushrooms: Add ½ cup heavy cream to mushrooms when cooked; heat 1 minute longer.

MUSHROOMS AND PEPPERS ITALIANO

1 lb. mushrooms, sliced	1 tsp. sugar
2 large green peppers, cut in ¼-inch strips	2 tbs. capers (optional)
¼ c. olive oil	¼ c. sliced, pitted ripe olives
1 tbs. red wine vinegar	¼ tsp. leaf oregano, crumbled
	1 tsp. salt
	Dash of pepper

Sauté mushrooms and peppers in oil 5 minutes. Add vinegar, sugar, capers, olives, oregano, salt, and pepper. Simmer 15 minutes. Chill until serving time. Makes 8 servings.

OKRA

Buying: Available June through November. Select young, crisp, tender pods about 2 to 4 inches in length. Allow 1 pound for 4 servings.

Preparing: Wash; cut off stem end. Small pods may be left whole; large pods may be sliced or halved.

Cooking: Cook, covered, in 1 inch boiling, salted water about 10 minutes or until just tender.

OKRA PIQUANT

1 lb. fresh okra or 1 pkg. (10 oz.) frozen okra	2 tbs. butter or margarine
¼ c. chopped green onions	2 tbs. lemon juice

Cook okra, covered, in 1 inch boiling, salted water 10 minutes or until just tender; drain. Sauté onions in butter or margarine until soft but not brown; add lemon juice. Toss lightly with okra. Makes 4 servings.

ONIONS

Green Onions or Scallions

Buying: Available all year. Sold in bunches. Onions should be creamy white with crisp green tops. Allow 2 bunches for 4 servings.

Preparing: Cut off root fibers. Remove tops and any tough outer layers.

Cooking: Cook in 1 inch boiling, salted water for 8 to 10 minutes until just tender. Onions are chopped and cooked with other vegetables, meats, poultry, and fish. They are also served raw as a relish or salad accompaniment.

Yellow and White Onions

Buying: Available all year. Look for unsprouted, firm, clean, well-shaped onions with dry skins. Allow 1½ pounds for 4 servings.

Preparing: Onions are peeled, cut up, and used as an ingredient in many recipes. For cooked whole onions, peel; cut out core or cut across at root end. Onions may also be skinned by pouring boiling water over them, rinsing in cold water, then slipping off the skins. Very large onions may be parboiled, stuffed, and baked.

Cooking: Cook in boiling, salted water to cover. Cook large onions 30 to 35 minutes; small silverskins or white onions 15 to 20 minutes.

CREAMED ONIONS

1½ lbs. small white onions, peeled	¼ c. butter or margarine
1 c. milk or cream	½ tsp. salt
	⅛ tsp. pepper

Cook onions in boiling, salted water 20 minutes or until tender. Drain. Add milk or cream, butter or margarine, salt, and pepper. Heat over low heat until piping hot. Makes 4 servings.

BROWN BRAISED ONIONS

1½ tbs. butter or margarine	½ tsp. salt
	Dash of pepper
1½ tbs. olive oil	Few parsley sprigs
18 to 24 peeled, small white onions	1 small bay leaf
	¼ tsp. leaf thyme, crumbled
½ c. beef bouillon, consommé, or white wine	

Heat butter or margarine and olive oil in large skillet until bubbling. Add onions. Cook over moderate heat about 10 minutes. Keep rolling the onions in the fat so they will brown as

evenly as possible. Take care not to break the skins. Add bouillon, consommé, or white wine, salt, pepper, and remaining ingredients tied in a piece of cheesecloth. Cover; simmer slowly over low heat 40 to 50 minutes or until the onions are tender but still hold their shape and the liquid has been completely absorbed. Makes 6 servings.

GLAZED ONIONS

1 lb. small white onions (about 20)	⅓ c. sugar
	1 tbs. water
	Paprika
3 tbs. butter or margarine	

Peel onions. Cook in boiling, salted water 12 to 15 minutes until almost tender; drain. Blend butter or margarine, sugar, and water in large skillet over low heat. Add onions. Cook, turning occasionally, until glazed and slightly brown. Sprinkle with paprika. Makes 6 servings.

SPINACH-STUFFED ONIONS

8 large onions, peeled	1 pkg. (10 oz.) frozen chopped spinach
1 c. mayonnaise or salad dressing	1 tsp. seasoned salt
¼ c. lemon juice	2 pimientos, cut in strips
⅓ c. milk	

Cook onions in boiling, salted water 20 minutes or until tender (do not overcook). Combine mayonnaise or salad dressing, lemon juice, and milk in small bowl. Cook spinach according to package directions; drain very well. Remove centers from onions; chop; mix with spinach, seasoned salt, and 2 tablespoons mayonnaise mixture. Stuff onions with spinach mixture; garnish with pimiento strips. Place onions in baking dish; pour remaining mayonnaise mixture into dish. Bake at 350° F. for 20 minutes or until heated through. Makes 8 servings.

CHEESE TOPPED BAKED ONIONS

2 lbs. small white onions, peeled
½ c. shredded Cheddar cheese
2 c. Thin White Sauce (*page 348*)
3 tbs. melted butter or margarine
½ c. packaged bread crumbs

Cook onions in boiling, salted water about 20 to 25 minutes or until tender; drain. Prepare White Sauce. Place onions in greased 1½-quart baking dish; pour sauce over onions. Combine bread crumbs, cheese, and butter or margarine; sprinkle over top. Bake at 400° F. for 15 minutes or until sauce is bubbly and crumbs are golden brown. Makes 4 to 6 servings.

BAKED STUFFED ONIONS

6 medium-size onions
Salt
3 tbs. butter or margarine
2 tbs. chopped parsley
½ tsp. leaf marjoram, crumbled
1 c. soft bread crumbs (2 slices)
1 tbs. finely diced pimiento
½ tsp. salt
2 tbs. grated Parmesan cheese

Heat oven to 425° F. Cut tops off onions; peel. Remove centers, leaving a shell ½- to ¾-inch thick. Sprinkle insides of onions with salt. Chop half the onion removed from centers; sauté in 2 tablespoons butter or margarine. Add parsley, marjoram, bread crumbs, pimiento, ½ teaspoon salt, and cheese. Spoon into onion shells. Brush with remaining butter or margarine. Place in casserole; cover. Bake 45 to 50 minutes or until tender. Makes 6 servings.

PARSNIPS

Buying: Available all year. Select smooth, firm, well-shaped roots that are small to medium in size. Allow 1½ pounds for 4 servings.

Preparing: Scrape or pare with vegetable parer. Leave whole or cut into halves, quarters, or slices.

Cooking: Cook, covered, in 1 inch boiling, salted water about 25 to 30 minutes or until tender.

PARSNIPS DELUXE

1 lb. parsnips, washed and pared
½ tsp. salt
2 tbs. butter or margarine
1 c. water
¼ c. light cream
Chopped parsley

Halve parsnips; remove core; slice parsnips. Bring water and salt to boiling; add parsnips; cook 15 minutes or until tender. Drain. Add butter or margarine and cream to parsnips; heat over low heat for 5 minutes. Sprinkle with parsley. Makes 4 servings.

POTATOES

Buying: Available all year. *Irish* or *Long Island* are the best all-around cooking potato. Look for firm, well-shaped, medium-size potatoes that have no blemishes or sprouts. Texture is mealy. Allow 1½ pounds for 4 servings. *Idaho* or *baking*—Select clean, long, firm tubers that have no blemishes. Texture is more waxy. Allow 1 potato per serving. *Russet* or *new*—Best when used whole for boiling. Allow 1½ to 2 pounds for 4 servings.

Preparing: Irish potatoes: Scrub; pare very thinly with knife or vegetable parer; remove any eyes or spots; cut up or leave whole. Potatoes may also be cooked in jackets and the skin peeled off after cooking. *Idaho potatoes:* Scrub well; prick with fork in several places to prevent them from bursting in oven as they bake. *Russet* or *new potatoes:* Scrub; remove a thin strip of skin around the center with vegetable parer or sharp knife.

Cooking: Irish potatoes: Cook, covered, in boiling, salted water to cover for 20 to 25 minutes or until just tender. Cook whole potatoes about 35 to 40 minutes. *Idaho potatoes:* Bake at 400° F. for 55 to 60 minutes or until tender. *Russet* or *new potatoes:* Cook, covered, in boiling, salted water to cover for 30 to 35 minutes or until tender.

MASHED POTATOES

10 medium-size   ¾ c. warm milk
  potatoes   Salt
¼ c. butter or   Pepper
  margarine

Scrub potatoes well: remove eyes and blemishes. Cook in boiling, salted water 35 to 40 minutes or until tender. Drain; peel. Mash potatoes in large bowl with potato masher or electric mixer until no lumps remain. Beat in butter or margarine. Add just enough warm milk gradually to potatoes, beating constantly, until potatoes are fluffy and creamy. Season to taste with salt and pepper. Makes 8 servings.

DUCHESS POTATOES

3 lbs. potatoes   ½ tsp. salt
  (9 to 10 medium),   ⅛ tsp. pepper
  pared   ¼ c. warm milk
½ c. melted butter   3 tbs. melted butter
  or margarine   or margarine
3 egg yolks, beaten

Cook, drain, and mash potatoes. Beat in ½ cup butter or margarine, egg yolks, salt, and pepper. Beat in just enough warm milk to make smooth and fluffy. Shape 8 portions by mounding with spoon or pressing through pastry bag onto lightly greased cookie sheet. Spoon butter or margarine over each. Brown at 450° F. or under broiler. Makes 8 servings.

COUNTRY FRIED POTATOES

3 tbs. butter or   1 tsp. salt
  margarine   ⅛ tsp. pepper
4 c. sliced, pared
  potatoes, ¼ inch
  thick

Heat butter or margarine in skillet. Add potatoes; sprinkle with salt and pepper. Cook, covered, over low heat 10 minutes. Remove cover; increase heat to medium; cook until golden brown on underside. Turn to brown other side. Makes 4 servings.

Lyonnaise Potatoes: Sauté ½ cup chopped onion in butter or margarine before adding potatoes. Cook as above.

COTTAGE FRIED POTATOES

3 tbs. butter or   ½ tsp. salt
  margarine   ⅛ tsp. pepper
3 c. cold, cooked,   1 tbs. chopped
  cubed potatoes   parsley

Heat butter or margarine in large skillet. Add potatoes; cook about 10 minutes or until browned on one side; turn and brown second side. Season with salt and pepper; sprinkle with parsley. Makes 4 to 6 servings.

Potatoes O'Brien: Sauté ¼ cup chopped onion and 3 tablespoons chopped green pepper in butter or margarine until soft. Add potatoes and 2 tablespoons chopped pimiento. Cook until potatoes are browned, shaking pan occasionally. Season with salt and pepper. Makes 6 servings.

HASHED BROWN POTATOES

4 c. cold, cooked   ¼ tsp. pepper
  diced potatoes   ¼ c. milk
¼ c. minced onion   2 tbs. flour
  (1 small)   ⅓ c. butter or
2 tsp. salt   margarine

Combine potatoes, onion, salt, pepper, and milk. Shape into 6 patties; dust lightly with flour. Heat butter or margarine in large skillet; add patties. Cook until golden brown on one side; turn and brown second side. Makes 6 servings.

FRENCH FRIED POTATOES

(*Two-step method*)

6 medium-size   Fat or oil for frying
  potatoes

Wash and pare potatoes. Cut into ½-inch slices, then cut slices into ½-inch strips. Wash in cold water; drain; pat dry with paper towels. Precook potatoes (blanch) in fat or oil heated to 370° F. until tender, but not brown. Follow Deep Frying directions (*page 19*) or Shallow Frying directions (*page 18*). Drain on paper towels. Potatoes may be held for several hours in this manner before their final cooking. Just before serving, heat fat or oil to 390° F. Fry potatoes until golden brown.

Drain well on paper towels; sprinkle with salt. Potatoes may be kept warm in a 300° F. oven if a large amount is to be fried.

AMBASSADOR POTATOES

12 medium-size potatoes, pared and cubed (6 c.)	Dash of ground nutmeg
¼ c. melted butter or margarine	½ c. all-purpose flour
3 egg yolks	1 c. blanched, slivered almonds
2 tsp. salt	3 egg whites
¼ tsp. pepper	Fat or oil for frying

Cook potatoes in boiling, salted water until tender. Drain; mash. Add ¼ cup butter or margarine; blend in egg yolks, salt, pepper, and nutmeg. Form mixture into 12 rolls or patties, using about ⅓ cup of mixture for each. Measure flour into a shallow dish; put slivered blanched almonds in second shallow dish; lightly beat whites in a third. Dip each roll into flour, then into egg white, and then roll in almonds. Put enough fat or oil into large skillet or heavy saucepan to fill pan two-thirds full when melted; heat to 360° F. Carefully place rolls in fat; fry until crispy golden brown, turning once. Drain on paper towels. Makes 12 rolls.

BAKED POTATOES

Scrub large potatoes well; dry; prick with fork. Potatoes may be baked separately at 400° F. for one hour or along with meat that is roasting or baking. At 325° F. they will take about 1½ hours; at 350° F. about 1¼ hours. Place potatoes on oven rack or in shallow pan. Bake until tender when tested with a two-tined fork. When potatoes are done, cut a cross in the top of each, hold with towel and press gently to allow steam to escape and potato to come through cross. Top with butter or margarine or one of the following:

• Mixture of ½ cup dairy sour cream; 4 tablespoons finely chopped, pared cucumber; and ⅛ teaspoon salt.
• Butter or margarine and caraway, sesame, or poppy seeds.
• Sprinkle with seasoned salt; add a pat of butter or margarine; top with dairy sour cream, chopped chives, and crumbled bacon.
• Butter or margarine and minced green onions or chopped chives.
• Mixture of ½ cup dairy sour cream, 2 tablespoons vinegar, and 1½ tablespoons blue cheese salad-dressing mix.

STUFFED BAKED POTATOES

Heat oven to 325° F. Wash and dry 9 medium-size unpared baking potatoes. Rub with fat; prick with fork. Arrange on oven rack. Bake about 1½ hours or until tender when tested with a two-tined fork. Cut slice from top of each potato. Scoop out potato, taking care not to break the skins; mash well in medium-size bowl. Beat in enough milk or light cream to make potatoes smooth and fluffy; add butter or margarine and salt and pepper to taste. Pile whipped potatoes back into 8 of the shells, mounding slightly. Return to oven to heat through. Makes 8 servings.

FRANCONIA POTATOES

About 1½ hours before roast is done, cook 8 medium-size pared and halved potatoes in boiling, salted water 10 minutes; drain. Arrange around roast in roasting pan. Roast 45 to 60 minutes or until tender and nicely browned, turning often and basting with fat drippings in pan. Remove from pan with slotted spoon and transfer to paper towels to drain. Makes 8 servings.

POTATO PANCAKES

6 medium-size potatoes, pared	¼ tsp. pepper
	3 tbs. flour
1 medium-size onion, grated	2 tbs. chopped parsley
2 eggs	Butter or margarine
1 tsp. salt	

Grate potatoes on fine grater into bowl; drain very well. Add onion, eggs, salt, pepper, flour, and parsley; mix well. Heat 2 to 3 tablespoons butter or margarine in large skillet. Drop potato mixture by heaping tablespoonfuls into hot fat. Fry until golden brown on bottom; turn and brown second side, adding more fat as needed. Drain on paper towels. Pancakes may be served as a vegetable with meats or as a luncheon or supper dish accompanied with applesauce or dairy sour cream. Makes 12 to 14.

SCALLOPED POTATOES

4 c. thinly sliced, pared potatoes	1 tsp. salt
½ c. minced onion (1 medium)	⅛ tsp. pepper
2 to 3 tbs. flour	3 tbs. butter or margarine
	1½ c. scalded milk

Heat oven to 375° F. Arrange layer of potatoes in greased 2-quart casserole. Top with some of the onion. Sprinkle with part of the flour, salt, and pepper. Dot with some butter or margarine. Repeat layers until all are used, ending with butter or margarine. Pour milk over layers. Cover. Bake 45 minutes; uncover; bake 15 minutes or until potatoes are tender. Makes 4 servings.

POTATO PUFF

2 c. thick mashed potatoes	2 tbs. chopped parsley
½ c. light cream	4 egg yolks
1 tsp. salt	4 egg whites
Dash of ground nutmeg	¼ tsp. cream of tartar
2 tbs. grated Parmesan cheese	

Heat oven to 375° F. Grease 1½-quart casserole. Combine mashed potatoes, cream, salt, nutmeg, Parmesan cheese, and parsley. Beat egg yolks until thick and lemon colored; beat into potato mixture. Beat egg whites until foamy; add cream of tartar; beat until stiff peaks form. Fold egg whites into potato mixture. Turn into prepared casserole. Bake 30 minutes or until puffy and golden. Serve at once. Makes 6 servings.

POTATO-CHEESE CASSEROLE

½ c. finely chopped onion (1 medium)	1½ c. shredded process American cheese
4 tbs. butter or margarine	2½ c. milk
3 tbs. flour	8 c. sliced, cooked potatoes
½ tsp. salt	1 pkg. (8 oz.) sliced process American cheese
⅛ tsp. pepper	
1 tsp. dry mustard	
1 tsp. Worcestershire sauce	

Sauté onion in butter or margarine in medium-size saucepan until soft but not brown. Stir in flour, salt, pepper, and mustard; cook about 2 minutes or until bubbly. Remove from heat; stir in Worcestershire, shredded cheese, and milk. Cook over low heat, stirring constantly, until cheese is melted and sauce is bubbly. Pour over potatoes in large bowl; mix thoroughly. Turn into 2-quart casserole. Heat oven to 350° F. Arrange cheese slices on potatoes. Bake 30 minutes or until hot and bubbly. Makes 8 servings.

COUNTRY-STYLE POTATOES AND MUSHROOMS

½ lb. mushrooms, chopped	1 tsp. salt
½ c. chopped onion (1 medium)	Dash of pepper
	4 c. hot, seasoned, mashed potatoes
3 tbs. butter or margarine	1 tbs. chopped parsley

Sauté mushrooms and onion in butter or margarine about 8 minutes or until tender. Add salt and pepper; stir into mashed potatoes. Serve, sprinkled with parsley. Makes 6 servings.

CHEESE SPUDNIKS

½ pkg. (4 servings) instant mashed potatoes	1 pkg. (8 oz.) process American cheese
2 tbs. minced parsley	½ c. melted butter or margarine
	1 c. crushed cornflakes

Prepare instant potatoes according to package directions. Beat in parsley. Heat oven to 400° F. Cut six ½-inch cubes of cheese (use remainder another time). Divide potato mixture into six equal portions; press a cheese cube into each; shape into balls. Dip potato balls into melted butter or margarine; roll in cornflake crumbs; place in shallow baking dish. Bake 10 minutes or until brown. Makes 6 servings.

PEAS

Buying: Available September to June; peak season in April and May. Select bright green, well-filled, crispy pods. Use as soon as possible after purchase for sweetest flavor. Allow 3 pounds for 4 servings.

Preparing: Shell just before cooking.

Cooking: Cook, covered, in 1 inch boiling, salted water for 8 to 10 minutes or until just tender.

PEPPERS

Buying: Available April through December. Look for firm, bright-colored, thick-walled peppers with no bruises or discolorations. Allow 1 pepper per serving.

Preparing: For stuffing, cut slice off top; remove seeds and white membranes. For cooking, cut up; cut in half; remove seeds and membranes; cut in slices or dice.

Cooking: To parboil for stuffing, cook, covered, in boiling, salted water to cover for 3 minutes; drain; stuff; bake as directed in recipes. To sauté, cook sliced or diced pepper in hot fat until just tender and slightly browned.

STUFFED PEPPERS

4 large green peppers	1 tsp. salt
½ lb. bulk sausage	¼ tsp. pepper
1 lb. ground chuck	1 tsp. leaf basil, crumbled
½ c. chopped onion (1 medium)	½ tsp. leaf oregano, crumbled
½ c. chopped celery	2 cans (8 oz. ea.) tomato sauce
1½ c. soft bread crumbs (3 slices)	

Wash peppers; cut slice off tops; remove seeds. Drop into boiling, salted water; parboil for 3 minutes; drain. Cook sausage and chuck in skillet over medium heat until all pink disappears; remove; reserve. Pour off all but 2 tablespoons of fat from skillet. Add onion and celery; cook over medium heat until soft. Add meat, bread crumbs, salt, pepper, basil, oregano, and ¼ cup tomato sauce. Spoon lightly into peppers. Stand peppers upright, close together, in baking dish. Pour remaining tomato sauce around peppers. Bake at 350° F. for 35 to 40 minutes. Makes 4 servings.

Cheese Topped Peppers: Top each pepper with 2 tablespoons grated process American cheese before baking.

HAM-AND-CHEESE STUFFED PEPPERS

4 large red or green peppers	2 tbs. dried parsley flakes
¼ c. chopped onion (1 small)	¼ tsp. pepper
2 tbs. butter or margarine	1 can (about 1 lb.) tomatoes
½ lb. ready-to-eat ham, ground*	1 pkg. (8 oz.) sliced process Swiss cheese
1 c. packaged herb-flavored bread stuffing	

Cut slice from stem ends of peppers; remove seeds. Cook peppers and slices in boiling, salted water 3 minutes; drain. Heat oven to 350° F. Sauté onion in butter or margarine until tender. Combine ham, bread stuffing, parsley, pepper, tomatoes, and sautéed onion. Take 2 slices of cheese from package without separating them; cut into 6 strips. Repeat with 2 more slices. Place 3 strips upright in each pepper. Cube remaining cheese; stir into ham mixture. Pile mixture into peppers; replace top slices; arrange peppers in shallow baking pan. Bake 20 minutes or until peppers are tender. Makes 4 servings.

*Buy ½ pound ready-to-eat ham, ground or use leftover ham.

RADISHES

Buying: Available all year. Look for bright red, crispy radishes that have no blemishes. Leaves should be fresh and green if they have been left attached. Allow 2 bunches for 4 servings.

Preparing: Wash; remove roots and leaves. Raw radishes are served crisp and cold for salads and as relishes.

Cooking: Cook, covered, in 1 inch boiling, salted water about 6 to 8 minutes or until just tender.

RUTABAGA
(YELLOW TURNIPS)

Buying: Available all year; peak supply October through March. Select firm, heavy roots. They are marketed loose. Allow 2 pounds for 4 servings.

Preparing: Scrub; pare thinly with vegetable parer. Cut into thin slices or dice.

Cooking: Cook in 1 inch boiling, salted water for 15 to 20 minutes or until just tender.

MASHED TURNIPS AND CARROTS

1 large yellow turnip, pared and cubed	¼ c. melted butter or margarine
1 bunch carrots, pared	1 tsp. salt
	¼ tsp. pepper
	¼ tsp. ground nutmeg

Cook and drain turnips and carrots; mash. Beat in butter or margarine, salt, pepper, and nutmeg. Makes 6 servings.

SAVORY TURNIPS

3 c. cooked, cubed yellow turnips	½ c. packaged bread crumbs
½ c. bottled French dressing	

Combine turnips and all but 2 tablespoons of dressing; toss to blend. Turn into shallow, lightly greased 1-quart baking dish. Combine bread crumbs and reserved dressing; sprinkle over turnips. Bake at 400° F. for 15 to 20 minutes or until crumbs are golden brown. Makes 4 servings.

SALSIFY OR OYSTER PLANT

Buying: Available October through November. Select firm, medium-length roots that have no blemishes. Allow 1½ pounds for 4 servings.

Preparing: Scrub; scrape or pare with vegetable parer. Slice thinly or cut into slivers.

Cooking: Cook, covered, in boiling, salted water to cover to which a teaspoon of vinegar has been added to keep salsify white. Cook 15 to 20 minutes or until tender.

SAUERKRAUT

Buying: Available all year. Sauerkraut may be purchased canned, in several size cans, or fresh in 1 pound bags in grocer's cold case.

Cooking: Cook canned sauerkraut, covered, in can liquid for 20 to 30 minutes. Cook fresh sauerkraut, covered, in water to cover about 35 to 40 minutes or until tender. You may add caraway seeds, chopped onion or apple.

SAUERKRAUT WITH APPLE

4 slices bacon	1 tsp. caraway seeds
2 tbs. chopped onion	1 apple, pared, cored, and chopped
1 lb. sauerkraut, fresh or canned	

Fry bacon in skillet until crisp. Drain bacon; crumble; reserve. Sauté onion in 1 tablespoon bacon fat until soft. Add sauerkraut and caraway seeds. Add water just to cover. Simmer 20 minutes. Add apple; simmer 10 minutes. Serve topped with reserved bacon. Makes 4 servings.

SWEET POTATOES AND YAMS

Buying: Available all year. Select tubers with firm, smooth skins and bright color. Sweet potatoes have light yellowish skins and meat and are dry and mealy; yams have reddish-orange skins and have more moist, deep orange meat. Allow 1½ to 2 pounds for 4 servings.

Preparing: Scrub well. Potatoes are best if cooked in jackets.

Cooking: Cook, covered, in boiling, salted water to cover for 35 to 40 minutes or until just tender. For baking, rub skins with butter or margarine; prick well with fork; bake at 325° F. for 45 to 55 minutes or until just tender.

PUFFY BAKED SWEET POTATOES

6 medium- to large-size sweet potatoes	½ c. crunch-style peanut butter
3 tbs. butter or margarine	2 tsp. salt
1 tbs. brandy extract	½ tsp. ground allspice
	Dash of pepper
	½ c. milk

Heat oven to 425° F. Scrub sweet potatoes; dry. Bake 45 to 55 minutes or until tender. Cut slice from top of each potato; scoop out insides, being careful not to break shells; mash thoroughly. Add butter or margarine, brandy extract, peanut butter, salt, allspice, pepper, and milk; beat until light and fluffy. Add more milk if necessary. Spoon into shells. Bake 15 to 20 minutes or until tops are lightly browned. Makes 6 servings.

SWEET POTATO SURPRISE

6 sweet potatoes or yams	2 tsp. grated orange rind
4 tbs. butter or margarine	6 marshmallows
1 tsp. salt	Cornflake crumbs
2 tbs. light brown sugar	6 slices canned pineapple
	Melted butter or margarine

Cook unpared sweet potatoes or yams in boiling, salted water 30 to 35 minutes or until tender. Heat oven to 375° F. Peel and mash potatoes. Beat in 4 tablespoons butter or margarine, salt, brown sugar, and orange rind. Divide into 6 portions. Press a marshmallow into each portion; mold potato around marshmallow into a ball. Roll in cornflake crumbs to coat. Arrange pineapple slices in shallow baking pan; top each with sweet potato ball. Brush with melted butter or margarine. Bake 20 to 25 minutes or until lightly browned. Makes 6 servings.

HONEY-SPICED SWEET POTATOES

6 or 7 medium-size sweet potatoes or yams	1 c. honey or maple-blended syrup
¼ c. melted butter or margarine	½ tsp. ground cinnamon
	¼ tsp. ground nutmeg

Cook sweet potatoes or yams in boiling, salted water 30 to 35 minutes or until tender. Heat oven to 350° F. Peel potatoes; cut in ½-inch slices. Combine butter or margarine, honey or maple-blended syrup, cinnamon, and nutmeg. Place potatoes in buttered, shallow 1½-quart casserole in layers, pouring honey or maple-blended syrup mixture over each layer. Bake 35 to 40 minutes or until glazed, basting several times with syrup in casserole. Makes 6 servings.

SWEET POTATOES RHUMBA

4 c. hot, boiled sweet potatoes or yams	½ tsp. salt
	¼ c. sugar
	1 tsp. rum extract
¼ c. melted butter or margarine	1 tbs. melted butter or margarine
½ c. heavy cream	1 tbs. grated orange rind
½ tsp. ground nutmeg	

Heat oven to 400° F. Press sweet potatoes or yams through food mill or ricer. Add ¼ cup butter or margarine, cream, nutmeg, salt, sugar, and rum extract. Beat until fluffy. Turn into buttered 1-quart casserole. Drizzle with 1 tablespoon melted butter or margarine. Sprinkle with orange rind. Bake 30 minutes or until lightly browned. Makes 6 servings.

HAWAIIAN SWEET POTATOES

3 medium-size sweet potatoes or yams	3 tbs. butter or margarine
⅔ c. light brown sugar, firmly packed	3 bananas, peeled and sliced
1 tsp. salt	⅓ c. orange juice
	¼ c. shredded coconut

Cook sweet potatoes or yams in boiling water to cover about 25 minutes or until tender but firm. Cool; pare; cut into ¼-inch-thick slices. Heat oven to 350° F. Arrange layer of potatoes in buttered 1-quart casserole. Sprinkle with sugar mixed with salt. Dot with butter or margarine. Top with layer of bananas. Repeat layers. Pour orange juice over layers. Sprinkle with coconut. Bake 20 minutes or until top is lightly browned. Makes 6 servings.

CRANBERRY-STUFFED SWEET POTATOES

6 medium-size sweet potatoes or yams	3 tbs. cranberry sauce
¼ c. butter or margarine	1 tsp. sugar
	¼ tsp. salt
	⅛ tsp. pepper

Heat oven to 425° F. Scrub potatoes well; dry on paper towels. Bake about 40 minutes or until done. Increase oven heat to 450° F. Cut a slice from the top of each potato. Scoop out insides, being careful not to break shells. Combine potato, 2 tablespoons butter or margarine, cranberry sauce, sugar, salt, and pepper. Whip until well blended; spoon into shells; dot with remaining butter or margarine. Heat about 15 minutes or until lightly browned. Makes 6 servings.

ORANGE-GLAZED SWEET POTATOES

2 lbs. sweet potatoes or 2 cans (1 lb. 13 oz. ea.) sweet potatoes	½ c. butter or margarine
½ c. dark corn syrup	½ c. orange juice
	½ tsp. salt

Cook fresh potatoes in jackets in boiling, salted water until tender; drain; peel. If using canned potatoes, drain. Cut potatoes in halves. Mix corn syrup, butter or margarine, orange juice, and salt in large skillet. Cook until mixture comes to boiling; boil 3 minutes. Add potatoes. Cook slowly, turning occasionally, about 12 to 15 minutes or until potatoes are well glazed. Makes 8 servings.

ORANGE SWEET POTATOES

2 cans (about 1 lb. ea.) yams or sweet potatoes, drained	⅓ c. soft butter or margarine
1 tbs. grated orange rind	2 navel oranges, peeled and sectioned
½ c. orange juice	Miniature marshmallows

Heat oven to 350° F. Beat yams or sweet potatoes until smooth. Beat in orange rind and juice and butter or margarine. Turn into 1-quart casserole; top with orange sections. Bake 10 minutes. Cover top with marshmallows. Bake 20 minutes. Makes 6 servings.

SPINACH

Buying: Available all year. Look for bright green, crisp, crinkly leaves. Spinach which has been cleaned and washed is often sold in plastic bags in 10- and 16-ounce sizes. Allow 2 to 2½ pounds for 4 servings.

Preparing: When spinach is purchased with roots attached, remove. Pick over spinach to remove any bruised and discolored leaves. Fill sink with cold water; wash spinach in 3 changes of water. Lift spinach out of water each time to allow sand to fall to bottom. Wash packaged spinach once; remove any thick stems and discolored leaves.

Cooking: Raw, cleaned, crispy spinach is wonderful in green salads. Cook spinach, covered, in large pot in water that clings to leaves; you may press leaves firmly into pot. Do not add water. Sprinkle lightly with salt. Cook over medium heat until wilted and tender but still bright green, about 3 to 5 minutes.

CREAMED SPINACH WITH ONION

3 lbs. spinach, cooked and drained	½ c. chopped onion (1 medium)
2 tbs. butter or margarine	2 tsp. flour
	½ tsp. salt
	½ c. light cream

Chop spinach very fine or force through a coarse sieve. Melt butter or margarine in saucepan; cook onion until soft. Stir in flour; cook, stirring, until it turns a golden brown. Stir in spinach; cook a few minutes until it is quite dry; add salt. Stir in cream; bring to boiling; cook 2 minutes. Makes 8 servings.

SPINACH AND CELERY CASSEROLE

2 pkgs. (10 oz. ea.) frozen chopped spinach	¼ tsp. salt
	¼ tsp. pepper
	1 tbs. flour
2½ c. thinly sliced celery	½ c. light cream
	2 tsp. prepared horseradish
1 c. water	
1 tsp. salt	1 tbs. grated Parmesan cheese
3 tbs. butter or margarine	

Cook spinach as package directs; drain well. Combine celery, water, and 1 teaspoon salt in saucepan. Cover; cook rapidly 5 minutes. Remove cover; cook until liquid is almost absorbed. Add butter or margarine, ¼ teaspoon salt, and pepper. Blend flour and cream until smooth; add to celery. Stir until sauce is thick and just begins to bubble; stir in horseradish and drained spinach. Turn into buttered 1½-quart casserole; sprinkle with cheese. Bake at 375° F. for 20 minutes. Makes 6 servings.

SQUASH–SUMMER

Buying: Available all year. Four varieties are available: *yellow,* which may be straight neck or crookneck; *white,* cymling or patty pan; *green,* zucchini and cocozelle (striped); and *light green* or chayote. Select summer squash (all varieties) for its immaturity, firmness, and heaviness for its size. The skin may be smooth or warty (as crookneck), but should be tender. Allow 2 pounds for 4 servings.

Preparing: Wash; do not pare—skin is edible. Cut into slices or cubes depending on recipe. Squash may also be used whole.

Cooking: Cook, covered, in small amount of boiling, salted water 10 to 15 minutes or until tender.

ZUCCHINI A L'ORANGE

1½ lbs. zucchini	¼ tsp. pepper
¼ c. butter or margarine	2 tbs. undiluted frozen orange juice concentrate
½ tsp. salt	

Wash squash; slice thinly in rounds if small; cut slices into fourths if larger. Melt butter or margarine in skillet; sauté squash until just tender. Sprinkle with salt and pepper; add orange juice concentrate; stir gently until blended. Cover; simmer 3 to 4 minutes or until steaming hot. Makes 4 servings.

ZUCCHINI SKILLET CASSEROLE

1 c. green pepper strips	¾ tsp. leaf basil, crumbled
1 c. sliced onion (1 large)	1 tsp. salt
	Dash of pepper
3 tbs. butter or margarine	1 tbs. cornstarch
	1 tbs. water
1½ lbs. zucchini, sliced	¼ c. grated Parmesan cheese
3 medium-size firm, ripe tomatoes, peeled and chopped, or 1 can (1 lb. 4 oz.) Italian plum tomatoes	

Sauté green pepper and onion in butter or margarine until soft. Add zucchini, tomatoes, basil, salt, and pepper. Cover; simmer 15 minutes. Blend cornstarch and water to a smooth paste; stir into mixture in skillet. Cook until thickened. Sprinkle with cheese. Broil just until cheese melts. Makes 6 servings.

ZUCCHINI ITALIAN STYLE

6 small zucchini (about 1½ lbs.)	½ tsp. leaf oregano, crumbled
3 tbs. flour	½ c. fine bread or cracker crumbs
½ tsp. salt	
⅛ tsp. pepper	½ c. pure vegetable oil
1 egg, slightly beaten	6 large lemon wedges
1 tbs. water	
2 tsp. onion juice	

Wash zucchini well; do not pare. Cut each zucchini into 6 or 8 strips, ½ inch wide. Combine flour, salt, and pepper in shallow pan. Combine egg, water, onion juice, and oregano in second pan. Coat each strip of zucchini in flour mixture; dip in egg mixture; coat with crumbs. Fry zucchini in hot oil, using about 3 tablespoons of oil at a time, until golden brown on all sides. Drain on paper towels. Serve with lemon wedges. Makes 6 servings.

SWEET-SOUR ZUCCHINI

2 lbs. medium-size zucchini	1 tsp. salt
½ c. fat or pure vegetable oil	⅛ tsp. pepper
	1 clove of garlic, crushed
2 tsp. leaf basil, crumbled	½ c. wine vinegar
	1½ tbs. sugar

Wash zucchini; remove ends; cut in ½-inch slices. Fry in hot fat or oil until lightly browned. Remove; put in glass or pottery bowl. Add remaining ingredients to fat or oil remaining in pan. Simmer 2 to 3 minutes; pour over zucchini. Cover; refrigerate. Let stand at room temperature before serving. Makes 6 servings.

SQUASH—WINTER

Buying: Available all year. Varieties are Hubbard, acorn, butternut, banana, buttercup (or turban). Select heavy, firm squash with thick rind that has no large blemishes.

Preparing: Wash. Cut the larger squash into individual pieces; remove seeds. Halve the acorn squash; remove seeds and fibers. Pare butternut. Remove seeds and cube banana.

Cooking: Bake Hubbard squash at 400° F. for about 1 hour or until tender. Bake acorn squash halves, cut side down, about 25 minutes; turn cut side up; season; bake 30 to 35 minutes more. Cook butternut or banana squash in 2 inches boiling, salted water for 25 to 30 minutes or until tender.

BAKED ACORN SQUASH

2 medium-size acorn squash	¼ c. honey, maple, or corn syrup
1 tsp. salt	2 tbs. brown sugar
¼ c. melted butter or margarine	

Wash squash; halve lengthwise. Remove seeds and stringy portion. Scrape cavities with tea-spoon if very stringy. Sprinkle cut surfaces with salt; place, cut side down, in greased baking dish. Bake at 400° F. for 25 minutes. Combine butter or margarine, syrup, and brown sugar. Turn squash cut side up; spoon butter-syrup mixture into each cavity. Bake 30 to 35 minutes or until tender. Makes 4 servings.

STUFFED ACORN SQUASH

3 medium-size acorn squash	½ tsp. poultry seasoning
2 c. coarse day-old bread crumbs	1 tsp. salt
	¼ tsp. pepper
⅓ c. dried apricots, coarsely cut	2 tbs. butter or margarine
¼ c. chopped, pitted dates	½ c. minced onion
	1 c. ground, cooked lamb*

Cut squash in half; remove seeds and stringy portion. Combine crumbs, apricots, dates, poultry seasoning, salt, and pepper in large bowl. Combine butter or margarine, onion, and lamb in a small saucepan. Cook slowly until lamb is lightly browned, stirring often to break it into small bits. Blend lamb and crumb mixtures. Heat oven to 375° F. Arrange squash, cut sides down, in shallow roasting pan. Bake 20 to 25 minutes or until almost tender. Turn squash hollow sides up; fill with stuffing. Bake 35 to 40 minutes or until lightly brown.

* If desired, substitute diced, ready-to-eat ham for lamb. If ham is salty, use only ½ teaspoon salt. Makes 6 servings.

PINEAPPLE STUFFED SQUASH

3 medium-size acorn squash	½ tsp. ground cinnamon
1 can (8½ oz.) crushed pine-apple, drained	¼ c. chopped walnuts or pecans
	3 tbs. soft butter or margarine
⅓ c. brown sugar, firmly packed	¾ c. water

Heat oven to 375° F. Cut squash in half; remove seeds and stringy portion. Place in baking pan. Combine pineapple, sugar, cinnamon, nuts, and butter or margarine. Spoon into squash halves. Pour water into pan; cover. Bake 45 minutes. Uncover; bake 15 minutes or until tender. Makes 6 servings.

CRISP SQUASH SLICES

1 egg, slightly
  beaten
1 tbs. water
1 tsp. salt
⅛ tsp. pepper
1 tsp. onion powder
2 lbs. yellow squash,
  cut in ½-in.
  slices

¾ c. packaged
  bread crumbs
½ c. fat or pure
  vegetable oil
2 tbs. grated Par-
  mesan cheese
1 tbs. chopped
  parsley

Combine egg, water, salt, pepper, and onion powder in shallow dish. Dip squash slices in egg mixture; coat with crumbs. Heat fat or oil in skillet; fry squash slowly until golden brown on both sides. Layer in serving dish; sprinkle layers with cheese and parsley. Makes 6 servings.

TOMATOES

Buying: Hothouse tomatoes are available all year. Vine-ripened tomatoes are available at the peak of the outdoor growing season, June through September, from local farms. Allow 2 pounds for 4 servings.

Varieties found in most markets are the large pink Ponderosa tomato; the medium-size red Rutgers; the yellow; the cherry-red; and the yellow and red plum tomatoes. Look for firm, heavy tomatoes, well formed and not overripe.

Preparing: Tomatoes need only to be washed, cored, and skinned if the skin is not tender. To skin: dip in boiling water for 30 to 40 seconds; chill quickly in cold water. Skin will peel off easily. Chill tomatoes before using.

Cooking: Cut peeled tomato in quarters. Simmer gently, uncovered, for about 10 minutes.

Add a slice of onion and a bay leaf, if desired. Green tomatoes from the garden may be dipped in dry bread crumbs and fried in butter or margarine.

TOMATOES STUFFED WITH CORN

6 medium-size, firm,
  ripe tomatoes
¼ c. minced onion
  (1 small)
¼ c. butter or
  margarine
2 c. fresh or canned
  whole-kernel
  corn, drained

¼ c. shredded
  Cheddar cheese
2 tbs. chopped
  parsley
1 tsp. salt
¼ tsp. pepper

Scoop pulp and juice from tomatoes; arrange in baking pan. (Use pulp and juice another time.) Heat oven to 350° F. Sauté onion in butter or margarine until golden. Stir in corn, cheese, parsley, salt, and pepper. Spoon mixture into tomatoes. Bake 15 to 20 minutes or until heated through. Makes 6 servings.

HERBED TOMATOES

¼ c. chopped onion
  (1 small)
¼ c. chopped green
  pepper
2 tbs. butter or
  margarine
1 can (1 lb. 13 oz.)
  tomatoes

1 tsp. salt
⅛ tsp. pepper
½ tsp. leaf oregano,
  crumbled
¼ tsp. leaf basil,
  crumbled
1½ tsp. sugar

Sauté onion and green pepper in butter or margarine 3 minutes or until tender. Add remaining ingredients; simmer 15 minutes. Makes 4 servings.

Scalloped Tomatoes: Toast 2 slices day-old bread; cube; stir into mixture just before serving.

TOMATO VEGETABLE PIE

¾ c. chopped onion
1 clove of garlic,
  crushed
1 tbs. fat or pure
  vegetable oil
1 can (1 lb. 3 oz.)
  tomatoes
½ lb. zucchini,
  thinly sliced
2 tbs. chopped
  parsley

¼ tsp. leaf basil,
  crumbled
¾ tsp. salt
⅛ tsp. pepper
Pastry for 9-inch
  pastry shell
  (*page 406*)
2 eggs, well beaten
½ c. shredded
  Cheddar cheese

Sauté onion and garlic in hot fat or oil until tender. Add tomatoes; break up with fork. Add zucchini, parsley, basil, salt, and pepper. Simmer, uncovered, 15 minutes. Cool. Heat oven to 425° F. Roll out pastry to a 12-inch circle; fit into 9-inch pie plate; flute edge. Cut wax paper to fit into pie shell; place in shell; fill with raw rice or dried beans. Bake 8 minutes. Remove from oven; remove rice or beans and wax paper. Stir eggs into cooled tomato mixture. Pour into pie shell. Sprinkle with cheese. Bake 20 minutes. Makes 6 servings.

TURNIPS–WHITE

Buying: Available all year. Look for firm, smooth turnips without discoloration and with some fresh green top attached. Allow 2 pounds for 4 servings.

Preparing: Scrub; pare thinly with knife or vegetable parer. Dice or slice.

Cooking: Cook, covered, in 2 inches boiling salted water for 30 to 40 minutes or until tender.

DRIED BEANS

BOSTON BAKED BEANS

1 lb. dried pea or navy beans	1 tsp. salt
1 c. diced onion (1 large)	1 tsp. dry mustard
½ c. molasses	1 c. boiling water
¼ c. brown sugar, firmly packed	¼ lb. salt pork

Wash beans; soak overnight in water to cover.* Drain; place beans in large saucepan; cover with water; add onion; simmer 1 hour or until tender. Drain; turn into 2-quart bean pot or casserole. Combine molasses, brown sugar, salt, and dry mustard; add boiling water; pour over beans; add additional water to cover, if necessary. Place salt pork on top; cover. Bake at 300° F. for 6 hours, adding

water if top seems dry. Uncover for last half hour of baking. Makes 6 servings.

* Quick Cooking Method: To shorten soaking time of beans, the United States Department of Agriculture suggests this method. Boil beans in 3 quarts water for two minutes. Remove from heat; cover; soak 1 hour; cook as directed.

CARAMEL BAKED BEANS

1 lb. dried lima beans	1 c. brown sugar, firmly packed
1 tsp. salt	¼ c. butter or margarine

Wash beans well; soak beans overnight in water to cover. Drain; add fresh water to cover; add salt. Cover; simmer about 1 hour or until beans are tender. Drain, reserving 1 cup of bean broth. Heat oven to 325° F. Combine 1 cup bean broth, brown sugar, and butter or margarine. Place beans in 2-quart casserole; pour sugar mixture over beans. Cover; bake 1½ hours. Uncover; bake 30 minutes. Makes 6 to 8 servings.

GOURMET BLACK BEANS

1 lb. dried black beans	1 tbs. chopped parsley
5 bouillon cubes	4 tbs. butter or margarine
2 qts. hot water	
1 c. chopped onion (1 large)	¼ c. dark rum
	1 tsp. basil
1 c. chopped celery and leaves	¼ tsp. pepper
	Dairy sour cream

Wash beans well; soak overnight in water to cover; drain. Dissolve bouillon cubes in hot water; add beans. Cover; simmer about 1 hour or until tender. Drain, reserving 1½ cups bean broth. Heat oven to 350° F. Sauté onion, celery, and parsley in butter or margarine 5 minutes. Add reserved 1½ cups bean broth, rum, basil, pepper, and beans. Turn into greased 2-quart casserole; cover. Bake 1 hour. Uncover; bake 15 minutes longer. Serve hot or cold with sour cream. Makes 6 to 8 servings.

Chapter Eighteen

Fruits

Luscious is the word for fruit, whether it's iced watermelon or crunchy tart apples, golden sweet pears, or red-purple grapes. Arrange fruit in a bowl, ripe bananas atop apricots and oranges with a cluster of grapes, and you have a centerpiece pretty to look at, delightful to eat. And don't forget—fruits are high in vitamins, low in calories.

Whatever the time of year, there are many kinds of fresh fruit to chose from in our markets (thanks to modern refrigerated transportation), plus all those wonderful canned and frozen fruits. Throughout this book you'll find fruit used in desserts, pies, salads, and many other recipes.

Which Fruit to Buy When

The sooner fruit is eaten after picking, the more flavor and nutritive value it has. It's wise to buy fruit during the peak of its season and to eat it as soon as possible after purchasing. Prices are lowest whenever a particular fruit is most plentiful too—a factor a wise shopper should not overlook.

Spring is the best season for strawberries, rhubarb, and pineapple, while bananas, grapefruit, and oranges which have been gracing winter counters are still in plentiful supply.

Summer is the bountiful season, when counters are piled with many wonderful fruits: cherries (both sweet black and tart red); berries of all kinds (blackberries, blueberries, loganberries, raspberries, boysenberries and gooseberries); figs and mangoes for those in southern states; nectarines, plums, peaches, plus seedless white grapes for all of us. The melon season begins in May and builds to a peak in September with cantaloupes, honeydews, honeyballs, and watermelons in profusion.

Fall is the best season for apples and pears, with plenty of peaches for canning. Persian, Casaba, and Cranshaw melons become plentiful as the cantaloupe supply dwindles. And grapes of all sizes and colors tempt us, from the white-green Thompson seedless and jet black Ribier grapes to the American varieties, including blue Concords and sweet white Niagaras.

Winter is the time for exotic fruits: coconuts, persimmons, pomegranates, tangerines, as well as the other year-round citrus standbys—grapefruit and oranges. Cranberries, of course, appear in plenty of time for Thanksgiving and Christmas though they are now available frozen all year. Emperor grapes, the favorite for holiday fruit bowls, are at their peak in November along with red Tokays and white Malagas.

Many seasonal fruits may be enjoyed all year round, thanks to freezing. You may freeze your own fruit (*Chapter 26*) or buy frozen fruit at the supermarket.

APPLES

Buying: Apples may be purchased fresh, processed (canned), or dried. *Fresh apples* are available all year round. They are at their peak from October to March. Three medium-size apples equal one pound. One pound of unpared apples yields about 3 cups of pared, diced, or sliced apples. Store fresh apples in a cold, dry place.

Processed apples are available in cans and jars sliced, in rings, as baked apples and apple sauce, and as sweetened pie filling, and in bottles and cans as apple juice. Cider and apple juice are also available as frozen concentrates

Variety	All-Purpose*	Pie	Sauce	Salad	Eating Raw	Baking	Months Available	Flavor and Texture
Wealthy	●						Aug—Oct	tart, spicy
Jonathan	●	●	●	●	●	●	Sept—Jan	spicy, juicy
Delicious	●				●	●	Sept—April	firm, sweet
Grimes Golden	●		●	●	●	●	Sept—Dec	bland, sweet
McIntosh		●	●	●	●		Oct—Feb	mild, spicy
Cortland		●	●	●	●	●	Oct—Jan	mild, spicy
Golden Delicious	●	●	●	●	●	●	Oct—April	rich, sweet, firm
R.I. Greening		●				●	Oct—Feb	aromatic, crisp
Stayman	●	●	●	●	●	●	Oct—Feb	rich, winy
York	●	●	●	●	●	●	Oct—Feb	tart, firm
Baldwin	●	●	●	●	●	●	Nov—April	mild, firm
Rome Beauty						●	Nov—April	bland, firm
Northern Spy	●	●	●				Dec—Mar	tender, spicy
Newtown Pippin	●	●	●	●	●	●	Nov—May	tart, crisp
Winesap		●		●	●		Dec—May	spicy, sweet

Apples in this column are good for all uses. Those in other columns are superior for the specific purposes indicated.

GLAZED BAKED APPLES

Serve baked apples more often, they're so good and so often forgotten!

6 large or 8 small   ¼ c. sugar
  cooking apples   ½ tsp. ground
Raisins, dates, or   cinnamon
  cooked dried   1½ c. water
  apricots   1¼ c. sugar
                  Sugar

Core apples; pare halfway down apple; reserve some parings. Place apples in baking dish so that they just fit, if possible. Too large a baking dish will evaporate too much syrup. Fill centers with raisins, dates, or apricots. Combine ¼ cup sugar and cinnamon; sprinkle over fruits in centers of apples. Heat oven to 350° F. Combine water, 1¼ cups sugar, and a few of the apple parings in saucepan. Bring to boiling over medium heat; lower heat; simmer 10 minutes; remove parings. Pour syrup over and around apples. Bake, basting frequently, 45 to 60 minutes or until apples are tender. Remove from oven; baste again. Sprinkle tops of apples with sugar; place under broiler until tops are bubbly and glazed. Serve warm or chilled with cream, if desired. Makes 6 to 8 servings.

Rosy Baked Apples: Reduce sugar to 1 cup in syrup recipe above; add ½ cup grenadine.

Cinnamon Baked Apples: Reduce sugar to 1 cup in syrup recipe above; add 1 jar (1¾ ounces) red cinnamon candies.

APPLESAUCE

8 medium-size   ½ c. water
  cooking apples,   ½ c. sugar (about)
  pared, quartered, 1 tsp. ground
  and cored   cinnamon

Put apples and water in saucepan; cover. Simmer 15 to 20 minutes or until apples are tender. Remove from heat. Stir in sugar (use enough to make applesauce desired sweetness) and cinnamon. If a smooth applesauce is desired, press through sieve or food mill. Serve warm or cold. Makes about 4 cups.

APRICOTS

Buying: Apricots may be purchased fresh, canned, or dried. *Fresh* apricots are available from May through August. They are at their peak in June and July.

Buy apricots that are orange yellow, plump, and juicy. One pound will contain 8 to 16 depending on size.

Storing: Store apricots in the refrigerator.

Preparing: Prepare by peeling: Let stand in boiling water to cover, 1 to 2 minutes. Remove and plunge into cold water. Slip off skins.

Canned apricots are available as unpeeled halves, and peeled or unpeeled whole. They may be packed in water, syrup, or apricot juice.

APRICOT AMBROSIA

1 c. cooked, dried apricots	¼ c. confectioners' sugar
2 bananas, peeled and sliced	¾ c. flaked coconut
2 large oranges, peeled and sliced	½ c. orange juice
2 tbs. slivered, candied or preserved ginger or ground ginger to taste	

Arrange layers of apricots, bananas, and oranges in serving bowl, sprinkling each layer with ginger, sugar, and coconut. Pour orange juice over fruits. Chill at least 1 hour. Makes 4 servings.

CREAMY SPIKED APRICOTS

12 fresh apricots	Dairy sour cream
6 tbs. Grand Marnier	Ground nutmeg

Halve and pit apricots. Put 4 halves in each of 6 serving dishes. Spoon a tablespoon of Grand Marnier over each serving. Top with a generous dollop of sour cream. Sprinkle with nutmeg. Makes 6 servings.

AVOCADOS

Buying: This pear-shaped dark green fruit is available all year round. California avocados are at their peak from February through April; Florida avocados from September through November. A ripe avocado is mellow and soft and yields readily to gentle pressure.

Storing: Keep refrigerated until ready to use. A firm avocado should be allowed to soften in a warm room before refrigerating. It may take 2, 3, or 4 days.

Preparing: Cut avocado in half, lengthwise or crosswise. Hold in palms of hands; twist halves in opposite direction. Lift out seed with tip of knife; discard. Halves may be used unpeeled or may be peeled and sliced or diced.

Brush cut surfaces with lemon juice to prevent darkening if avocado must stand before serving. Wrap leftover avocado in aluminum foil or transparent plastic wrap or bags and refrigerate.

BANANAS

Buying: Bananas are available all year round. Buy them by the hand, the cluster, or by the pound at the stage of ripeness you find them in the market and finish ripening at home. Three or four bananas equal one pound. Bananas tipped with green are partially ripe, ready to bake, broil, or fry. When they are all yellow, they are ready to eat, cook, or use as an ingredient in baking. Bananas that are flecked with brown are fully ripe, best for eating, infant feeding, and as a baking ingredient.

Storing: Keep bananas at room temperature until they reach the desired stage of ripeness. They may then be refrigerated for 2 or 3 days. The peel will darken but the fruit will hold at the same stage of ripeness.

BAKED BANANAS, WAIKIKI

6 firm, green-tipped bananas	¼ c. butter or margarine
1 c. orange juice	¼ c. brown sugar, firmly packed

Heat oven to 350° F. Butter a shallow baking dish large enough to fit bananas. Heat orange juice, butter or margarine, and brown sugar until mixture just comes to boiling. Pour over bananas. Bake 15 to 18 minutes or until bananas are tender. Makes 6 servings.

BERRIES

Buying: Berries are available fresh, frozen, or canned.

Blackberries: May–August. At peak in June, July, and August.
Blueberries: May–September. Most plentiful in July.
Gooseberries: June–July.
Loganberries: April–September. Peak season in June.

Raspberries: June, July, and August. Small amounts available in September, October, and November.
Strawberries: Some available all year round. At their peak April through July.

Buy berries that are ripe, have good color, and are free from off-color spots. One quart of berries will yield about 3½ cups.

Storing: Before storing, pick over berries to remove any bruised or spoiled ones. Spread unwashed and unhulled in shallow pan. Refrigerate uncovered.

Preparing: Wash before eating. Put berries in colander or large sieve and run water over them gently. Drain well. Hull or remove stems where necessary.

Canned berries come packed in water or syrup or in canned pie fillings. Frozen berries: Blueberries are usually unsweetened. Raspberries are sweetened. Strawberries may be whole, sweetened or unsweetened; or sliced, sweetened.

FRUIT AND SHERBET PARFAIT

1 pt. strawberries, washed, hulled, and sliced	2 tbs. kirsch
	1 tbs. chopped mint
	1 pt. orange sherbet
1 small pineapple, cored, peeled, and diced	Mint sprigs

Combine strawberries, pineapple, and Kirsch in bowl. Chill at least 1 hour. Stir in mint. Layer fruit mixture and sherbet in parfait glasses. Garnish with mint sprigs. Makes 6 servings.

CHERRIES

Buying: Available fresh and canned. Fresh red, light, white, and black sweet cherries are available from May through August. Red sour cherries may be found from late June to mid-August.
Buy cherries that are firm, shiny, plump, of fully ripe color, and free from spots.

Storing: Refrigerate cherries after washing, draining, and drying.

Preparing: Pit cherries with tip of vegetable parer, or a new wire paper clip.

Canned cherries include light and dark sweet cherries, water-packed sour red cherries, and cherry-pie filling.

COCONUT

Buying: When you buy a *fresh*, ripe coconut, choose one that sounds full of liquid when you shake it and is heavy with the weight of the liquid. Avoid any with a cracked outer shell. Canned or packaged flaked or grated coconut is also available.

Preparing: Pierce the three indentations at the end of the husky shell (the "eyes") with a long nail or ice pick, then allow the liquid to drain out. Put the whole coconut on a shallow pan and bake it at 350° F. for 15 minutes. This will crack the shell and you can complete the cracking with a hammer.

To remove the meat, force a firm, thin-bladed knife between the shell and the meat and pry up in as large pieces as possible. Rinse the coconut in cold water and drain on paper towels. Peel off the outer brown skin or leave it on according to your preference or the recipe you're using.

Grate coconut by cutting it into small pieces and whirling them, a few at a time, in a blender, or by hand using the medium-fine blade of a hand grater. Be sure to rub each piece the full length of the grater. One medium-size coconut yields about 3 to 4 cups grated coconut.

CRANBERRIES

Buying: Available fresh and frozen and in canned forms. *Fresh* cranberries are available from September through March and are most plentiful October through December. Buy berries that are firm, plump, fresh appearing, and with high luster.

Storing: Refrigerate or freeze cranberries.

Preparing: Use *fresh* cranberries after picking over, washing, and draining. Frozen cranberries may be used unthawed.

Canned cranberries are available as whole or jellied cranberry sauce.

CURRANTS

Buying: Available fresh in July. Buy bright, plump currants. They should not be so ripe as to fall off stems.

Storing: Refrigerate on shallow trays. Use red or white currants in salads, fruit cups, or desserts; black currants for jelly or jam.

Preparing: Wash and dry currants before using.

FIGS

Buying: Available fresh, canned, or dried. *Fresh* figs are in season from June through November and are most plentiful in August, September, and October.

Buy figs that are soft. Kadota figs should be greenish yellow; Black Mission figs, purplish. Buy them when slightly underripe.

Storing: Store in refrigerator until fully ripe. Then they are ready to eat.

Preparing: Wash and pare off skin.

Canned figs are available whole or split in water, juice, or syrup.

GRAPEFRUIT

Buying: Available fresh and as canned, chilled, or frozen sections. *Fresh* grapefruit from California and Arizona are shipped the year round. Florida grapefruit are at their best from October through June.

Buy grapefruit that are firm, well shaped, heavy for their size, and thin skinned. In color, grapefruit varies from pale yellow to reddish brown. Inner quality is not affected by rust spots or green tinges. Grapefruit meat may be pink or white, with or without seeds though the "seedless" grapefruit may contain a few seeds.

Canned grapefruit is sold as sections or segments or in combination with orange sections. Chilled sections are sold in 32-ounce jars. Frozen grapefruit sections are available in cans. Grapefruit juice is available canned and as frozen concentrate. It comes plain and combined with other fruit juices.

To Peel and Section a Grapefruit

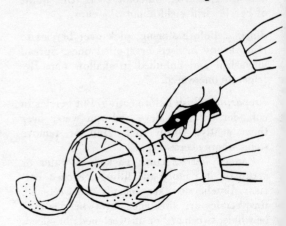

1. Hold fruit firmly in left hand. Cut a thin slice from the top. Cut off peel round and round in one long spiraling cut. Cut deep enough to remove all the white membrance.

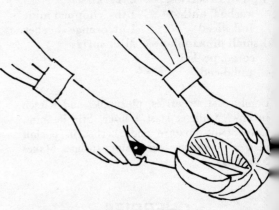

2. Hold fruit over a bowl or pie plate to catch any juice. Cut along membrane of each section from outer edge to the core. Tip knife outward and roll out the whole section. Repeat until all sections have been removed.

GRAPES

Buying: Fresh grapes are available from June through December. Select bunches that are well formed and good looking. Color is a good guide to ripeness: darker varieties should have no green tinge; white grapes, which actually appear green, should have a decided amber cast when completely matured. Fully ripened grapes are fairly soft to the touch and tender to the taste.

Most of the early grapes come from California, the later crops from the Eastern states.

California grapes have skins that adhere tightly to the pulp and the seeds are easily removed. The opposite is true of Eastern grapes.

California and Arizona Grapes

Cardinal. A cross of Flame Tokay and Ribier with more of the characteristics of the Ribier. They are heavy and sweet in flavor when fully mature. The bunch and grapes are somewhat similar in size and shape to Ribier. Cardinal matures 3 to 4 weeks ahead of Thompson.

Perlettes. A white, rather small, round to olive shaped grape. Fairly small to medium-size, rather compact, tight bunches. Available in June and July.

Thompson Seedless. White, small, olive-shaped grapes, practically seedless. Bunches are large. Available July to October. Also available canned in light and heavy syrup.

Malaga. White Malaga are round, white, medium-size grapes. Bunches are medium-size. Available August through November. Red Malaga are larger, round red grapes. Available August to September.

Flame Tokay. Red, large oval grapes. Medium to large bunches. Available September through November.

Cornichon. Blue, long, olive-shaped grapes. Bunches are large. Fruit is rather soft. Available September to November.

Emperor. The latest California variety. Red, rather like the Tokays in appearance. Quite firm; even when ripe. Available in November and December, sometimes longer.

Ribier. Black, large round grapes. Small to large bunches. Available August to October.

Eastern Grapes

Concord. The standard Eastern variety. Blue, round grapes, unexcelled for grape juice, jelly, or table use. Available from August to early November.

Niagara. Leading Eastern table variety. White grapes. Available from September to early November.

KUMQUATS

Buying: Kumquats are available fresh and preserved. *Fresh* kumquats are in season from November through February. They are a small orangelike fruit similar to unshelled pecans in shape. Select firm fruit, heavy for its size.

Storing: Refrigerate.

Preparing: Wash. Cut in thin slices or quarters. The entire fruit is edible. The rind is sweet, the juice tart.

Preserved kumquats are available in jars or cans in heavy syrup.

LEMONS

Buying: Fresh lemons are available all year round and come mostly from California and Arizona. Select lemons that are fine textured, heavy for their size, and moderately firm. These characteristics indicate juiciness. Lemon juice is available bottled and frozen.

Storing: Refrigerate.

LIMES

Buying: Limes from Florida are available between June and September; those from California between October and December. There are two common varieties: Persian limes, which are similar to lemons in size and shape; and Key limes, which are small and round.

Select limes that are green (they lose flavor and acidity as they turn yellow) and heavy for their size.

Storing: Refrigerate.

MANGOES

Buying: Available May to September. Look for smooth yellow-orange to red skin, speckled with black. They vary in size, the largest about the size of an apple. Their taste is quite distinctive, a combination resembling pineapple and apricot.

Storing: Refrigerate before eating.

Preparing: May be peeled and sectioned for fruit cups. They are usually eaten by peeling skin back in sections and eating the pulp with a spoon. Have a little fresh lime juice handy for sprinkling on fruit. Green mangoes are used for chutney.

MELONS

You may enjoy melons through a long season because of the many varieties available. The season is May to December. However, some melons may be available in certain areas in late January.

Cantaloupe: These open the melon season. They are available May to November. They are sweet and meaty with a salmon-color flesh and fragrant aroma. Look for a clean scar at the stem end which indicates the melon has ripened on the vine. The netting on a ripe melon is well raised, coarse, and grayish in color. The rind under the netting has a yellowish cast.

Casaba: A late variety available from August through November. They are large and somewhat pointed at one end. The yellowish rind is rough and ridged. The flesh is creamy and soft but with little fragrance and aroma.

Persian: In the market July to October. Larger than the cantaloupe and with finer netting. The flesh is deep pink orange, mild, and sweet with a pleasant aroma.

Honeydew: Overlap the cantaloupe season— usually June to November. A large, creamy, yellow white, smooth-skinned melon. It is bluntly oval in shape. The flesh is a delicate pale green with great aroma and sweetness. These melons are not usually ripened to maturity on the vine because of their high sugar content.

Honeyball: Follow the cantaloupes into the market, June through November. They are smaller than the honeydews and are covered with fine netting. They are slightly soft and fragrant when ripe. Some varieties have pink flesh.

Cranshaw: A fairly new melon to the market. Available July through October. It is a cross between the casaba and the Persian. It is a large green and gold melon pointed at the stem end and rounded at the base. The outside is smooth and the flesh is yellow orange, sweet, and spicy.

Santa Claus or Christmas Melon: An elongated oval, somewhat like a football in shape, with a mottled green and gold rind. The flesh is light green, mild and sweet.

Watermelon: Big watermelons are plentiful from June through August. There is another variety which has come into the market in the last few years—the New Hampshire midget, a tiny melon not quite as large as a honeydew. Watermelons may be dark green or green with a lighter stripe. The underside should be yellowish. Look for symmetrical shape. Thump it if you wish—a ripe melon chimes a deep hollow note. The flesh is a deep, pink red.

Spanish: Large, slightly elongated melon with dark green, ridged, very firm skin. The flesh is pale green, sweet and delicate.

Storing: Refrigerate all melons. Wrap cantaloupes, honeydews, honeyballs, and Persians in transparent plastic-wrap or aluminum foil before storing in refrigerator. Otherwise, they are so fragrant they will perfume other foods in the refrigerator.

If melon is not quite ripe, leave at room temperature for a few days. You will be able to judge, by the increasing aroma just when to refrigerate.

Frozen melon balls (cantaloupe, honeydew) are found in your grocer's frozen food case. For best taste do not defrost fully.

Serving Tips: Serve cantaloupe and honeyball melons as halves or quarters, à la mode or with a wedge of lemon, or as a salad with cottage cheese. Serve honeydews in thin wedges. The big, juicy watermelon is usually cut in thick slices, then in half circles.

FRUIT-FILLED WATERMELON

½ medium-size watermelon (cut crosswise)	Seedless grapes
	1 c. sliced, fresh strawberries
1 cantaloupe	Mint sprigs
1 honeydew	

Cut a thin slice from end of watermelon so it stands without tipping. Cut edge of melon in saw-tooth design with sharp knife. Scoop out center with melon-ball scoop, leaving about an inch shell. Cut cantaloupe and honeydew melons in half. Remove seeds; scoop out with melon-ball scoop. Fill the watermelon half with melon balls. Decorate with grapes, strawberries, and mint. Wrap in transparent plastic wrap or aluminum foil. Chill. Makes 10 servings.

HONEYDEW AND LIME RING

1 pt. strawberries, washed, hulled, and sliced	1 honeydew
	1 pt. lime sherbet
½ c. sugar	Lime wedges

Combine strawberries and sugar in bowl. Chill at least 1 hour. Cut honeydew crosswise into 6 slices; remove seeds and rind. Place a scoop of sherbet on each melon slice. Spoon strawberries over. Serve with lime wedges. Makes 6 servings.

FRESH FRUITS IN GRAND MARNIER

This recipe is positively delicious and so simple to make and easy to serve.

4 large navel oranges	1 pt. strawberries, washed, hulled, and sliced
1 c. sugar	
¼ c. Grand Marnier	2 c. melon balls

Remove just the zest (the very outside rind) from one orange with a vegetable peeler. Sliver enough to make 2 tablespoons; reserve. Peel the other 3 oranges; remove all white membrane from all oranges. Section oranges over a bowl to catch all juice. Drain juice from sections. You should have ½ cup. Combine orange juice, sugar, and zest in saucepan. Bring to boiling; boil 3 minutes. Cool; stir in Grand Marnier. Combine orange sections, strawberries, and melon balls in bowl. Pour syrup over. Refrigerate several hours to blend all the flavors. Serve garnished with mint, if desired. Makes 6 servings.

NECTARINES

Buying: Available in midsummer, June through August. Look for firm, but not hard fruit with a characteristic "peach" fragrance. The nectarine resembles a peach without the fuzz; it is a crossbreed between the plum and the peach.

Storing: Refrigerate if fully ripe, otherwise leave at room temperature for 12 hours, then refrigerate.

Serving: Delicious eaten out of hand or sliced in fruit compote.

ORANGES

Buying: Available all year. As with many other fruits, the weight of an orange is a good indication of its juiciness. All oranges are mature when they reach market. Color is not always a guide to quality. Some oranges from Florida and Texas, which are pale in color, are sprayed with a harmless dye. This does not affect the fruit in any way; it merely gives it the bright orange appearance, which has become an accepted standard among consumers.

California and Arizona Oranges

Navels. Seedless, thick-skinned oranges, easy to peel and separate into segments. In season December to May.

Valencias. These have more juice than navels, but have a few seeds. In season May to November.

Florida Oranges

Parson Browns. These oranges are thin-skinned with a paler orange color. In season October through December.

Hamlins. These oranges have a slightly rough peel, few seeds, but an abundance of juice. In season October through December.

Pineapple oranges. These oranges have a brilliant smooth orange skin, are full of juice and almost seedless. In season December through February.

Valencias. These oranges are ideal for sectioning as well as squeezing for juice. They have a few seeds. In season October through January.

Navels. These large seedless oranges are easy to peel and section. Their thick pebbly skin is a brilliant clear orange. In season October through January.

Temples. Though they are called oranges, these are actually part of the tangerine family. See *page 318*.

Preparing: To section an orange: Remove peel from orange with sharp knife, cutting through and removing the white membrane too. Cut in spiral, sawing fashion as you would pare an apple. Hold orange over bowl to save juice. With knife, cut on either side of membrane between segments; lift out segments.

MINTED FRUIT BOWL

2 cans (13¼ oz. ea.) frozen pineapple chunks

1 c. mint leaves, coarsely chopped

¼ c. sugar

1 qt. strawberries, washed and hulled

8 navel oranges, peeled and sectioned

Let cans of pineapple stand in warm water ½ hour to thaw partially. Mix mint and sugar in large serving bowl; let stand ½ hour. Add strawberries, orange sections, and pineapple to mint mixture. Toss gently to mix. Chill until serving time. Garnish with mint sprigs, if desired. Makes 8 servings.

PAPAYAS

Buying: Available in limited areas, usually in the South and in California where they are grown.

The papaya is shaped like a melon. It is 5 to 10 inches long. It is ready to eat when the green rind has turned yellow. The flesh is deep yellow and the fruit has many black seeds. It is usually eaten raw as a fruit or in a salad.

Storing: Refrigerate.

Preparing: Cut in half or in wedges. Remove seeds.

PASSION FRUIT

Buying: Also known as granadilla, it is grown in California and is not nationally available. The name is thought to be given to the fruit by the early missionaries who thought the flower resembled the crown and nails of the Crucifixion.

It is a small, purple, egg-shaped fruit with a tough skin. The flesh is yellow.

Storing: Refrigerate.

Preparing: The fruit is usually eaten fresh with a spoon, or cooked for cakes and pies.

PEACHES

Buying: The peach season begins in June, reaches a peak in August, and tapers off in October. Look for plump, smooth-skinned, and well filled-out fruit. They should be creamy white or yellow with a rosy blush. Most of the early peaches are clingstone; the midseason and late peaches are freestone. Peaches, whether they are yellow fleshed or white fleshed, are splendid for eating out of hand or for use in any number of ways.

Storing: If you buy fruit that has a slight green tinge, ripen at room temperature for a few days before refrigerating.

Preparing: Skin may be peeled off thinly. Or you may remove it by plunging the peaches into boiling water for 1 minute; then into cold water. Skin slips off easily.

Frozen Peaches come sliced and sweetened, ready to use after thawing. Thaw in package, unopened.

Canned Peaches are found in clingstone and freestone varieties. The clingstone is a firmer peach than the freestone. The freestone is much like home-canned fruit in flavor and texture. Both kinds are available halved and sliced.

CURRIED FRUIT

⅓ c. butter or margarine

¾ c. light brown sugar, firmly packed

4 tsp. curry powder

1 can (about 1 lb.) pineapple chunks

1 can (about 1 lb.) pear halves, drained

1 can (about 1 lb.) peach halves, drained

10 maraschino cherries

Melt butter or margarine in skillet. Add sugar and curry powder. Drain pineapple; add ¼ cup syrup to skillet; simmer until sugar is melted. Put drained fruits in buttered, shallow 1½-quart baking dish; pour sauce over. Bake at 325° F. for 1 hour. Serve in sauce dishes. Makes 8 servings.

PEARS

Buying: Available fresh, canned, and dried. Fresh pears are available most months of the year with the peak season August through October.

Bartletts. These pears start the season and are available July through October. A large pear with creamy yellow skin and a rosy-red blush, these sweet juicy fruits are excellent for all purposes.

Seckel. This late summer fruit is small, sweet, and russet colored.

Bosc. A long-necked pear appearing in September, with brownish mottling turning to russet at base.

Winter Nelis. Medium size, with brown mottling over green. February through June.

Du Comice. One of the most luscious. A large fruit with greenish skin. Available October through February.

D'Anjou. Medium to large in size with smooth light-green or creamy-yellow skin when ripe. Available October through May.

Storing: Pears are usually picked and shipped when green, as it is characteristic that they develop a finer flavor and texture when ripened off the tree. If they are not fully ripe when purchased, allow to mellow at room temperature.

Canned pears are available in halves in syrup or whole in spicy pickling syrup. Pear nectar may also be found in some markets.

PEARS WITH ROSÉ WINE

1 c. rosé wine	1 pt. vanilla ice
1 c. water	cream
2 c. sugar	½ c. heavy cream,
8 pears, pared,	whipped
halved, and cored	Mint sprigs
1 c. strawberries,	
washed and	
hulled	

Combine wine, water, and sugar; bring to boiling; turn heat down; cook 2 minutes. Add pear halves a few at a time; poach until tender; do not overcook. Cool pears in syrup; chill. Purée strawberries; stir in 2 tablespoons of wine syrup. Place scoop of ice cream in individual serving dish; arrange two pear halves on ice cream. With spoon, coat completely with purée. Garnish with whipped cream and mint sprigs. Makes 8 servings.

PERSIMMONS

Buying: Available October to February. A bright orange-colored fruit with smooth skin resembling a tomato.

Storing: Persimmons are ready to eat when soft. Use whole or in halves.

PINEAPPLE

Buying: Available fresh all year, with the peak period April through June. May also be found canned and frozen. Pineapples come mainly from Hawaii and Puerto Rico. A fully ripe pineapple will have a characteristic aroma and will be heavy for its size. If the leaflike center leaves pull easily, the pineapple is ripe.

Storing: Wrap in transparent plastic wrap or aluminum foil for storing in refrigerator.

Preparing: To prepare pineapple, twist or cut off top. For slicing or dicing, cut pineapple into thick slices; remove core and rind (including eyes) from each slice. For spears, cut pineapple in quarters, core each quarter, slice off rind, cut into spears.

Canned pineapple is available in slices, spears, tidbits, chunks, crushed, and as juice. The juice is also available in combination with other fruit juices.

Frozen pineapple is available in chunks in syrup, and as pineapple juice concentrate.

CELESTIAL PINEAPPLE

1 large pineapple	½ pt. strawberries,
1 cantaloupe	washed, hulled,
2 oranges, peeled	and sliced
and sectioned	Mint sprigs

Cut pineapple into sixths; core each piece. Remove pineapple from shells in one piece with sharp knife. Reserve shells; cut pineapple into thin slices. Peel, quarter, and remove seeds from cantaloupe; slice thinly. Arrange pineapple slices, cantaloupe slices, orange sections, and strawberries in layers in pineapple shells. Top with mint sprigs. Cover with transparent plastic wrap. Chill until serving time. Makes 6 servings.

PLUMS AND FRESH PRUNES

Buying: May be found fresh and canned. *Fresh plums* available June to October. *Fresh prunes,* a variety of plums suited to drying, are plentiful August to late October.

Plums range in color from purple to red to green. The prune plum is a small, oval, dark purple free-pitted fruit of unusual sweetness. The red plum, sweet and juicy, is a clingstone. The green plum, known as greengage, is a freestone with a mealy flesh. Look for plump fruit, full color, and softness that yields to pressure.

Storing: Refrigerate.

POMEGRANATE

Buying: These colorful apple-size fruits with a hard yellow-orange rind are available October to January. The juicy meat and the seeds are edible. The juice is often used for drinks. (Do you know the Spanish word Granada means pomegranate?)

Storing: Refrigerate.

Preparing: Cut in half. Eat with a spoon.

QUINCE

Buying: This bright-yellow, hard fruit comes into the market in October. Quinces are not edible raw, but make wonderful jelly.

Storing: Refrigerate.

Preparing: Baked quinces are a beautiful ruby red. Just pare, core, and cut in quarters. Sprinkle with sugar; add water or orange juice to come ½ inch up in baking dish. Bake at 300° F. for 2 hours. Cool; serve with cream.

RHUBARB

Buying: May be purchased fresh and frozen. Available fresh January through July with the peak in May and June. Look for crisp, long, rosy-red stalks. Leaves are not edible.

Preparing: To cook: wash 2 pounds rhubarb; cut into 1-inch pieces. Put in heavy saucepan; add ¼ cup water and 1 cup sugar. Bring to boiling; cover; cook over low heat until rhubarb is tender.

Frozen rhubarb is available cut up, in syrup.

TANGERINES

Buying: This family of citrus fruits is generally agreed to include all those loose-skinned or "kid glove" fruits. The tangerine, mandarin orange, tangelo, and temple orange are included in this group. The first tangerines are available in late November and conclude their season in May. Although there is seldom a choice of fruits in the market, each variety comes along in close order.

Tangerine. Small to medium-size, it has a deep orange color with many seeds and loose, easily peeled skin. A puffy skin indicates overripeness. Available November through March, their peak is during the holidays.

Mandarin oranges. Usually found canned, in syrup. They are ready to use for salads, desserts, fruit garnishes, or just good eating.

Tangelo. A cross between the tangerine and grapefruit, with the taste of an orange. Available November through February.

Temple Orange (or tangor). This delicious sweet fruit is as large as an orange and looks like an orange on the exterior, except for a slight rounded top. It is easy to peel as are all fruits in this family, and has an average of one seed to a segment. Available December through February.

Tangerine juice is available as a frozen concentrate.

Chapter Nineteen

Salads and Salad Dressing

Before we get into the whole cool, crisp, crunchy subject of salads, we'd like to remind you that the supermarket is your garden and it's in bloom the whole year round. No longer do you have to go rushing down to a garden plot to gather lettuce and fresh spinach while the dew is still on them, or watch anxiously for the tomatoes to ripen on the vines.

Tender lettuce and crinkly chicory are rushed in refrigerated cars from thousands of miles away; arrive washed, crisped, wrapped in transparent covers and still so garden-like they crackle when you pull the leaves apart. And did you ever count the shades of green that "greens" come in? An all-greens salad can be a masterpiece of fascinating shades and tints, textures and flavors.

Salad Dressing

A good salad may often become a superb salad with a wise choice of salad dressings. Your grocer's shelves offer an infinite variety, from the bottled dressings to the make-it-from-a-package kind. When you have a less busy moment in your hectic day, try some of our make-it-all-yourself recipes. You'll like them.

The Salad Starts with the Greens

Whatever your definition of salad may be, and it can go from A to Z, there's bound to be a lettuce leaf or its equivalent somewhere in the sentence.

In the section *Greens to Know and Enjoy* is a description of each.

Selecting Greens

Keep in mind the words—fresh, crisp, bright, tender. Buy greens in a market where the vegetable area is refrigerated or properly cooled and where the turnover is rapid. When selecting a crisp-type lettuce, such as iceberg, look for firm, hard heads. Lift them in your hands and pick those heavy for their size. (One exception—if they are to be used as lettuce cups, choose loose heads.) Watch out for and avoid any brown, so-called "rust" edges. While this "rust" is not harmful as a food, it is unpalatable in appearance and, moreover, may go deep enough to spoil the whole head. When buying the escarole-endive-chicory type of greens, be sure you examine the heads carefully for bruises. These will be evident as browning on the outer leaves. Select those plants that have relatively few tough, dark green outer leaves, as the tender inside ones will have the best flavor and are more likely to stay crisp longer.

Washing and Storing Greens

Once you have arrived home from the market with the greens, they should be washed and dried, then refrigerated as quickly as possible. This will insure the retaining of their crisp texture, pleasing color, and very best flavor.

Here are some tips for handling certain greens:

· Remove any bruised outer leaves from a head of lettuce. Cut out the core with a sharp knife, then hold the head, core cavity up, under running, cold water. Leave the root ends on such greens as escarole, chicory, and romaine, and wash the heads thoroughly under running cold water.

· Drain all greens after washing them. Shake off as much water as possible, then blot them dry with paper towels.

· Store washed heads in a vegetable hydrator in the refrigerator. If you find it necessary to keep greens any length of time, put them in pliofilm bags or in transparent plastic wrap.

· For small leaves such as spinach, cut off roots and remove any bruised leaves. Swish leaves in a sinkful of cold water, changing the water several times until it remains clear and the leaves are clean. Blot them dry between paper towels.

Greens with small whole leaves like watercress and parsley are best stored in tightly covered jars, pliofilm bags, or transparent plastic wrap in the refrigerator after washing and drying.

Preparing Greens for Serving

· An hour or so before using, remove crisped greens from the refrigerator. Tear into bite-size pieces, removing any tough stem portions if necessary. We say "tear," not because flavor suffers if greens are cut, but because we believe torn greens make a more handsome salad and are less apt to wilt or discolor.

· Use one, two, three, or more greens in your salads to give them contrast in color, flavor, and texture.

· Be sparing of dressing! Too much will make your salad wilt. As a guide, use ¼ cup of dressing for each 1½ quarts of greens. Keep tossing gently just until all the leaves are just coated—never dripping. When the salad is served there should be no more than a teaspoon of dressing in the bottom of the salad bowl.

· Always toss chilled greens and dressing at serving time.

When To Serve the Salad

Except for a main course or a dessert salad, it's entirely up to you whether you serve your salad as a first-course appetizer, with the main course, or as a separate salad course following the main part of the meal. Perhaps we should say that when you serve a salad depends to a degree on where you live. West Coasters tend to prefer serving salads first, while Easterners, following the European custom, often serve them as a separate salad course. However, the choice of most Midwesterners is to eat them right along with the meat, potatoes, and vegetables.

Greens To Know and Enjoy

Crisphead—For all practical purposes, most of us call all crisp lettuce iceberg, for though it is but one variety of crisphead, it is the best known and most available. Heads are heavy, firm, and crisp-textured, and have a small core. Leaves are a medium green on the outside, shading to a pale green in the center.

Boston lettuce, technically a member of the Butterhead family, is loosely headed with leaves that have an oily feeling and is not especially crisp. Outer leaves are a deep dark green, the inner leaves shade almost to white. It is more perishable than crisphead types and should be used the day it is purchased. The leaves are prized for dainty cups when making individual salads.

Bibb lettuce was generally unknown until rapid transportation took the tiny heads from their Kentucky homelands, where it was developed by Major John Bibb. It is a small cup-shaped lettuce with a distinct color, flavor, and crispness. The leaves are a deep rich green, blending to a whitish green toward the core. It is prized for tiny individual salads.

Leaf is a non-heading type of lettuce and has light green, loosely bunched leaves with raggedy edges. It is very seasonal. Did you ever grow a crop yourself and serve it as wilted lettuce? Oh what you've missed if you haven't! For a few weeks leaf lettuce is in most markets—from March through June depending on your locale.

Chicory should, to be botanically correct, be called curly endive. It is a large head with long ragged-edged leaves that have a slight bitter flavor. It, like romaine, is one of the greens invariably found in tossed salads.

Cos or Romaine is a lettuce with an elongated head and stiff leaves. The leaves are coarse though sweet with good keeping quality. Dark green outer leaves shade to almost white at the root end. The lighter inner leaves are particularly tender and flavorful and are considered by many salad lovers a stand-by in tossed green salads.

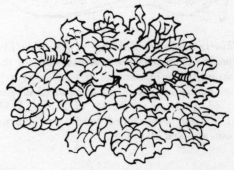

Escarole is actually another variety of endive. Its large, broad leaves shade from deep green on the outside to butter yellow in the center and have edges with a ruffled appearance. Sturdy and crisp, escarole adds a slightly bitter flavor to tossed salads and is particularly good in combination with sweeter leaves of lettuce and romaine.

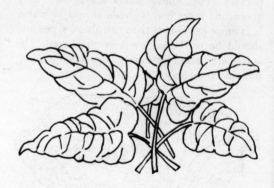

Spinach leaves—who doesn't recognize these? The tiny inside leaves add color variety to tossed salads. Tangy, slightly tart, spinach is gaining in popularity as an ingredient in salads and as a dark green garnish, frequently being substituted for watercress.

French or Belgian Endive is a member of the chicory family, really called witloof chicory. We recognize it by its light green, almost white head tightly packed into a shape resembling a fat cigar. The compact heads, 5 to 6 inches long, have small leaves that are slightly bitter in taste. They are usually left whole, adding texture, flavor, color, and shape to other torn greens in a salad.

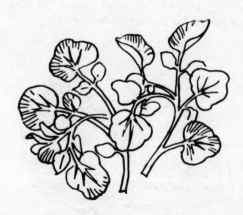

Chinese or Celery Cabbage is somewhat like romaine in appearance and has some of the characteristics of romaine and cabbage. It is used mostly in slaws and salads, or sliced and served much as are hearts of lettuce. Look for a long, oval-shaped head that is firm, fresh, and well blanched.

Watercress is an aquatic plant sold in bunches and the small, oval mildly pungent leaves are used as a garnish or a salad ingredient.

Other greens are regional favorites—kale, beet, and turnip greens, mustard greens, dandelion greens—their names are legion. Herbs, such as fresh dill, are available in large city markets in the summer months. Many salad fans grow their own herbs in their gardens. And, don't forget the tender celery leaves —they are so common that they are often discarded without a thought to their use as a pungent salad ingredient.

GREEN SALADS

CHEF'S SALAD

2 heads lettuce or
   chicory
4 hard-cooked eggs
4 medium-size
   tomatoes
1 cucumber
1 lb. unsliced salami

1 whole, cooked
   chicken breast
½ lb. Cheddar
   cheese
½ lb. Swiss cheese
1 bunch radishes
French Dressing
   (*page 342*)

Wash and dry salad greens; separate leaves; wrap in aluminum foil or transparent plastic wrap; chill overnight if possible. Shell eggs; cool; slice. Wash tomatoes; cut in eighths. Cut unpared cucumber in thin slices. Cut salami in ½-inch-thick slices; slice into julienne strips. Cut chicken breast, Cheddar cheese, and Swiss cheese into julienne strips. Trim and wash radishes; cut into slices. Line salad bowl with greens. Arrange ingredients in groups on greens. Before serving, toss gently with French Dressing. Makes 4 to 6 servings.

CAESAR SALAD

3 heads romaine
1 head lettuce
¼ c. olive oil
2 cloves garlic,
   halved
2 slices bread, cubed
6 anchovy fillets
1½ tsp. Worcester-
   shire sauce

6 tbs. French
   Dressing
   (*page 342*)
1 clove of garlic
1 egg
2 tbs. lemon juice
¼ tsp. salt
¼ tsp. pepper
4 tbs. grated
   Parmesan cheese

Wash salad greens; break into bite-size pieces. Wrap; chill. Heat 2 tablespoons oil. Add halved garlic cloves and bread cubes. Sauté until croutons are golden brown. Remove garlic; discard. Drain croutons on paper towels. Make paste of anchovy fillets, remaining 2 tablespoons oil, Worcestershire, and French Dressing in small bowl. Rub salad bowl with cut clove of garlic. Put egg, lemon juice, salt, pepper, and anchovy mixture in salad bowl. Beat with fork until well blended. Add salad greens. Toss gently until all greens are glistening. Sprinkle with croutons and Parmesan cheese. Makes 4 to 6 servings.

CALIFORNIA SALAD BOWL

1 small head Boston
   lettuce
½ bunch watercress
1 c. small spinach
   leaves
2 oranges, peeled
   and sectioned

½ mild onion,
   sliced and sepa-
   rated into rings
¼ c. toasted
   slivered almonds
Bottled Italian-style
   dressing

Wash and dry greens. Break into bite-size pieces. Combine greens, orange sections, onion rings, and almonds in bowl. To serve, toss lightly with dressing. Makes 4 servings.

CUCUMBER AND CHICORY SALAD

½ medium-size
   head chicory
4 Belgian endive

2 medium-size
   cucumbers
Tangy Roquefort
   Dressing
   (*page 344*)

Wash and trim chicory. Separate Belgian endive. Break both into bite-size pieces into bowl. Chill to crisp. Just before serving, pare cucumbers. Score lengthwise with fork; slice. Mix with chicory and endive. Toss with dressing and serve. Makes 6 servings.

SPINACH AND ENDIVE SALAD WITH CRISP BACON CURLS

1 small clove of
   garlic, sliced
¼ c. olive or pure
   vegetable oil
1 tsp. sugar
1 tsp. leaf oregano,
   crumbled
1 tsp. salt
⅛ tsp. pepper
1 tbs. wine vinegar

2 tbs. lemon juice
8 slices bacon
2 Belgian endive
1 small head
   chicory
¼ lb. crisp raw
   spinach
1 small onion, sliced
   and separated
   into rings

Combine garlic, oil, sugar, oregano, salt, pepper, vinegar, and lemon juice in small bowl; let stand ½ hour; remove garlic. Fry bacon until crisp. Roll 6 slices bacon around a 4-tined fork to make curls; drain on paper towels. Crumble remaining 2 slices bacon into dressing mixture. Slice off root end of endive; separate leaves. Break chicory into bite-size pieces. Toss all greens and dressing in salad bowl; sprinkle onion rings and bacon curls on top. Makes 6 servings.

CHINESE SALAD

2 qts. crisp raw spinach leaves	1 tbs. cider vinegar
2 cucumbers, pared and thinly sliced	1½ tsp. soy sauce
½ c. thinly sliced green onions	½ tsp. salt
¼ c. pure vegetable oil	1 small clove of garlic, crushed
	½ c. chopped, cooked ham

Place spinach, cucumbers, and green onions in salad bowl. Combine oil, vinegar, soy sauce, salt, and garlic; beat well. Pour over salad. Toss until spinach leaves are lightly coated. Sprinkle with chopped ham. Makes 6 servings.

SPINACH AND BEANSPROUT SALAD

½ of 10 oz. package washed spinach	1 tsp. seasoned salt
1 can (1 lb.) bean sprouts, drained	¼ c. French Dressing (*page 342*)

Rinse and pick over spinach; break into small pieces in salad bowl. Add bean sprouts; refrigerate. Just before serving, sprinkle with seasoned salt. Add dressing; toss gently until ingredients are well coated. Makes 4 servings.

WILTED LETTUCE SALAD

1 head lettuce or romaine	2 tbs. chopped green onion
4 slices bacon	½ tsp. salt
2 tbs. vinegar	⅛ tsp. pepper
¼ tsp. sugar	

Break lettuce into salad bowl; cover; refrigerate. Cook bacon; drain; crumble; reserve bacon fat. Combine bacon fat with vinegar, sugar, onion, salt and pepper. Pour over lettuce; toss to blend. Sprinkle with crumbled bacon. Serve at once. Makes 6 servings.

VEGETABLE SALADS

AVOCADO AND MUSHROOM SALAD

2 avocados	½ c. Golden French Dressing (*page 343*)
2 cans (3 to 4 oz. ea.) mushroom crowns, drained	8 lettuce cups

Peel and seed avocados; cut into quarters. Put avocado quarters and drained mushrooms in bowl; pour dressing over. Let stand 1 to 2 hours. To serve, place avocado quarter in each lettuce cup; spoon mushrooms onto avocado. Makes 8 servings.

GOURMET SALAD

2 pkgs. (9 oz. ea.) frozen artichoke hearts	½ tsp. leaf oregano, crumbled
⅓ c. olive or pure vegetable oil	1 head romaine
3 tbs. lemon juice	1 large Belgian endive
½ tsp. salt	1 small head of cauliflower, cut into flowerets
Dash of pepper	3 tomatoes, cut in wedges
1 clove of garlic, mashed	Pitted ripe olives

Cook artichoke hearts according to package directions; drain and place in shallow dish. Combine oil, lemon juice, salt, pepper, garlic, and oregano; mix well. Pour over artichoke hearts; let stand several hours or overnight. To serve, arrange several leaves romaine and endive on each salad plate. Place artichoke hearts, cauliflowerets, tomato wedges, and olives on leaves. Drizzle with any remaining dressing. Makes 6 servings.

LAYERED VEGETABLE SALAD

1½ c. pure vegetable or olive oil	3 medium-size carrots, pared and slivered
½ c. wine vinegar	1 can (1 lb.) sliced beets, drained
1 tsp. Worcestershire sauce	¾ lb. mushrooms, sliced
½ tsp. salt	1 large cucumber, scored and sliced
½ tsp. dry mustard	1 head chicory, washed
½ tsp. celery seed	
¼ tsp. garlic salt	
¼ tsp. pepper	

Combine oil, vinegar, Worcestershire, salt, dry mustard, celery seed, garlic salt, and pepper in screw-top jar; shake well. Cook carrots in boiling salted water until tender; drain; cool. Place beets, mushrooms, carrots, and cucumber in separate bowls; pour dressing over each. Let stand in refrigerator 2 to 3 hours to marinate. Just before serving, arrange vegetables and chicory in layers in salad bowl. Makes 6 servings.

BUFFET SALAD

2 pkgs. (9 oz. ea.)
  frozen artichoke
  hearts
2 tbs. vinegar
2 qts. salad greens,
  washed and
  coarsely shredded
1 can (8 oz.) pitted
  olives, sliced
1 pt. cherry
  tomatoes

1 pkg. (8 oz.) sharp
  Cheddar cheese,
  cubed
1 pkg. (8 oz.)
  Muenster cheese,
  cubed
2 tbs. chopped
  pimiento
2 tbs. chopped
  green pepper
Golden French
  Dressing
  (*page 343*)

Cook artichoke hearts according to package directions, adding vinegar to salted water. Drain and chill. Have all ingredients well chilled. Arrange salad greens on platter; arrange artichokes, olives, tomatoes, and cheeses in strips on top of greens. Sprinkle pimiento and green pepper over artichokes. Serve with Golden French Dressing. To serve: Sprinkle small amount of dressing on a cross-section of ingredients; mix lightly and serve that section. Salad can then be dressed and served as needed by portion and the remainder will stay fresh and crisp until the last serving. Makes 6 to 8 servings.

GADO-GADO
(Indonesian Salad)

2 c. shredded
  cabbage
1 pkg. (10 oz.)
  frozen French-
  style green beans
1 pkg. (10 oz.)
  frozen peas and
  carrots

1 can (1 lb.) bean
  sprouts
1 cucumber, thinly
  sliced
2 hard-cooked eggs
Peanut Butter
  Dressing
  (*page 343*)

Simmer cabbage in boiling salted water 2 minutes; drain. Cook green beans and peas and carrots according to package directions; drain. Simmer bean sprouts in can liquid 2 minutes; drain. Chill vegetables until serving time. Arrange vegetables on large serving plate in layers as follows: cabbage, green beans, bean sprouts, peas and carrots, and cucumbers. Garnish with sections of hard-cooked eggs. Serve with Peanut Butter Dressing. Salad may be served on cooked rice if a heartier salad is desired. Makes 6 servings.

CARROT AND RAISIN SALAD

4 c. grated or
  shredded, pared
  carrots
1 c. raisins
½ c. mayonnaise or
  salad dressing

1 tsp. lemon juice
2 tbs. light cream
Lettuce
½ c. toasted,
  blanched
  almonds

Combine carrots and raisins. Blend mayonnaise or salad dressing, lemon juice and cream; mix with carrots and raisins. Spoon into lettuce cups or over shredded lettuce. Sprinkle with almonds. Makes 6 servings.

TOMATO STUFFED WITH CURRIED CHICKEN

8 large tomatoes,
  cored and peeled
1¼ c. mayonnaise
  or salad dressing
1½ tsp. curry
  powder
1 tsp. salt
¼ tsp. pepper
1½ tbs. lemon juice

2 c. cooked rice
2 c. diced, cooked
  chicken
1 c. diced celery
⅓ c. sliced green
  onions
1½ c. cooked peas
2 tbs. diced
  pimiento

Prepare tomatoes: scoop out centers; turn upside down to drain; chill. Combine mayonnaise or salad dressing, curry powder, salt, pepper, and lemon juice. Add rice, chicken, celery, green onions, peas, and pimiento; mix well. Fill tomatoes; chill. Makes 8 servings.

SALAD BEATRICE

Lettuce leaves
3 large tomatoes,
  sliced
2 pkgs. (10 oz. ea.)
  frozen asparagus
  or 2 lbs. fresh
  asparagus spears,
  cooked
1 can (15 oz.) arti-
  choke bottoms,
  drained and cut
  in julienne strips

1 hard-cooked egg,
  finely chopped
½ c. pure vege-
  table oil
¼ c. wine vinegar
1 tsp. finely
  chopped chives
1 tsp. finely
  chopped parsley
½ tsp. mixed salad
  herbs
½ tsp. salt
⅛ tsp. pepper

Arrange lettuce on serving plate. Place tomatoes in a ring around edge of plate. Place asparagus in center with artichoke bottoms on either side. Sprinkle asparagus with egg. Combine oil, vinegar, chives, parsley, salad herbs, salt, and pepper; beat well. Pour over salad. Makes 6 servings.

HEARTY ITALIAN SALAD

1 tbs. mayonnaise or salad dressing	1 celery heart, diced
2 tbs. wine vinegar	1 fennel (finocchio), pared and diced
1/2 c. olive or pure vegetable oil	1 pkg. (9 oz.) frozen artichoke hearts, cooked and chilled
1 tsp. salt	
1/4 tsp. seasoned pepper	4 anchovy fillets, minced
2 c. hot, cubed, boiled potatoes	
1 head romaine	1 tbs. capers, drained
1 head chicory	
1/4 c. cubed Swiss cheese	2 hard-cooked eggs, sliced

Combine mayonnaise or salad dressing, vinegar, oil, salt, and pepper; beat well. Marinate hot potatoes in 2 tablespoons dressing mixture several hours. Break romaine and chicory into bite-size pieces; place in large salad bowl. Add cheese, celery, fennel, artichokes, anchovies, capers, and marinated potatoes; mix well. Add just enough salad dressing to coat leaves; toss. Garnish with a ring of hard-cooked egg slices. Makes 6 to 8 servings.

TOSSED GREENS ANTIPASTO
(*Pictured opposite page 276*)

1/3 c. olive oil	1/2 medium-size head cauliflower
1 small clove of garlic, sliced	3 to 4 mushrooms, sliced
2 tbs. lemon juice	2 firm, ripe tomatoes, quartered
2 tbs. wine vinegar	
1 tsp. leaf tarragon, crumbled	6 thin slices Italian salami, slivered
1 tsp. dry mustard	
1 tsp. salt	2 qts. crisp salad greens
2 large carrots, pared	
1 medium-size zucchini	1/4 c. thinly sliced green onions
2 stalks celery	1/3 c. thinly sliced radishes

Combine olive oil, garlic, lemon juice, vinegar, tarragon, mustard, and salt; let stand at room temperature 1/2 hour. Cut carrots and zucchini into slices. Cut celery in slices. Cook carrots, zucchini, celery, and cauliflower in boiling salted water 5 minutes (vegetables should be crunchy); drain. Separate cauliflower into florets. Remove garlic from oilvinegar mixture; pour mixture over cooked vegetables in large bowl; chill several hours. At serving time, drain cooked vegetables; reserve dressing. Combine vegetables, mushrooms, and tomatoes, salami, and greens in large salad bowl; sprinkle green onions and radishes on top. Pour over reserved dressing; toss well. Makes 6 servings.

To arrange salad as pictured: Leave salami slices whole and fold in quarters. String salami and pieces of vegetables on wooden skewers; arrange around inside of salad bowl; fill bowl with greens. At serving time, pull out skewers, leaving salami and vegetables in bowl. Pour over reserved dressing. Toss well.

GREEK SALAD

1 head iceberg lettuce	1/2 c. cubed, cooked beets
1 unpared cucumber, thinly sliced	1/2 c. sliced radishes
	6 anchovies, chopped
2 ripe tomatoes, cubed	1 tbs. capers, drained
1 c. crumbled Feta cheese	1 tsp. leaf oregano, crumbled
12 Greek black olives	1/2 c. olive or pure vegetable oil
1 medium-size onion, thinly sliced	2 tbs. vinegar
	1 tsp. dry mustard
	1/2 tsp. salt
	1/8 tsp. pepper

Break lettuce into bite-size pieces; place in large salad bowl. Add cucumber, tomatoes, cheese, olives, onion, beets, radishes, anchovies, capers and oregano; mix well. Chill at least 1 hour. Combine oil, vinegar, mustard, salt, and pepper; beat well. At serving time add just enough salad dressing to coat leaves. Toss. Serve immediately. Makes 6 servings.

POTATO SALADS

GARDEN POTATO SALAD

1 pkg. (10 oz.) frozen mixed vegetables	1 tsp. salt
	1 tbs. sugar
	1/2 tsp. paprika
1/4 c. diced pimiento	1/8 tsp. pepper
2/3 c. pure vegetable oil	6 c. sliced, cooked, potatoes
1/3 c. vinegar	1 c. diced celery
1 tsp. dry mustard	Crisp greens
1 tsp. Worcestershire sauce	

Cook mixed vegetables according to package directions; drain; add pimiento. Combine oil, vinegar, mustard, Worcestershire, salt, sugar, paprika, and pepper in a blender or screw-top jar; whirl or shake well. Combine potatoes, cooked vegetables, and celery in salad bowl; pour dressing over all; allow to marinate in refrigerator for 1 to 2 hours. Toss salad lightly just before serving to blend all ingredients. Serve on crisp greens. Makes 8 servings.

POTATO SALAD CORNUCOPIAS

4 c. mashed potatoes	¼ c. minced cucumber
⅔ c. mayonnaise or salad dressing	2 tsp. paprika
	1 tsp. prepared mustard
2 tbs. minced onion	
1 tbs. prepared horseradish	Dash hot-pepper sauce
½ tsp. salt	24 thin slices salami or other thinly sliced, round cold cuts
¼ tsp. pepper	
2 tbs. minced parsley	
¼ c. minced celery	Crisp greens

Blend potatoes, mayonnaise or salad dressing, and onion; divide mixture in half. To one half add horseradish, salt, pepper, and parsley. To the other half add celery, cucumber, paprika, mustard, and hot-pepper sauce. Roll each slice of salami into a cornucopia shape; fasten with wooden pick. Press parsley filling into half the cornucopias, using a pastry bag and star tube, or carefully fill with spoon, swirling the mixture slightly. Fill remaining cornucopias with cucumber filling; chill. Arrange on crisp greens on serving platter; garnish with parsley, ripe olives, and tomato wedges, if desired. Makes 12 servings.

SOUR CREAM POTATO SALAD

4 c. sliced, cooked potatoes	¼ c. vinegar
1 c. diced celery	1 tbs. bleu cheese salad dressing mix
¼ c. sliced green onions	
¼ c. sliced radishes	Thinly sliced radishes for garnish
1 c. (½ pt.) dairy sour cream	Parsley

Combine potatoes, celery, green onions, and radishes. Blend sour cream, vinegar, and bleu cheese dressing mix; pour over vegetables; toss gently to blend. Spoon salad into an 8-inch ring mold, pressing down well with spoon. Cover with aluminum foil or transparent plastic wrap; chill several hours. To unmold, loosen top edges carefully with spatula or thin-bladed knife; place serving plate over mold; invert; shake hard once; salad will drop out. Garnish with sliced radishes; surround salad and fill center with parsley sprigs. Makes 6 servings.

BAKED POTATO SALAD

½ c. chopped onion (1 medium)	½ c. water
	¼ c. vinegar
¼ c. pure vegetable oil	6 c. cubed, cooked potatoes
1 tbs. flour	½ c. diced celery
1 tsp. sugar	¼ c. diced green pepper
¼ tsp. paprika	
½ tsp. dry mustard	½ lb. sliced process American cheese
1 tsp. salt	
½ tsp. seasoned salt	

Sauté onion in oil 10 minutes or until soft. Stir in flour, sugar, paprika, mustard, and salts; add water and vinegar slowly. Cook over medium heat, stirring constantly, until thickened and bubbly. Combine potatoes, celery, green pepper, and sauce; spoon half of mixture into buttered 1½-quart casserole. Arrange cheese slices over potato layer; top with rest of potato mixture. Bake at 350° F. for 15 to 20 minutes or until salad is hot. Serve at once. Makes 8 servings.

GERMAN POTATO SALAD

8 c. sliced, cooked warm potatoes	3 tsp. salt
	¼ tsp. pepper
6 tbs. pure vegetable oil	2 tbs. minced onion
1 can (10½ oz.) condensed beef broth	¼ c. chopped parsley
	1 medium-size onion, thinly sliced
½ c. vinegar	

Put potatoes in large bowl; sprinkle with oil. Combine broth, vinegar, salt, pepper, and onion in saucepan; heat to boiling. Pour over potatoes; toss carefully until all potatoes are coated; add parsley. Garnish with onions. Makes 12 servings.

PIQUANT POTATO SALAD

2 hard-cooked eggs	½ c. vinegar
4 slices bacon	2 tbs. diced
½ c. chopped onion	pimiento
(1 medium)	2 tbs. diced green
1½ tbs. flour	pepper
2 tbs. sugar	¼ c. sliced celery
½ tsp. salt	6 c. sliced, cooked
1 tsp. dry mustard	potatoes
1½ c. water	

Dice egg whites; sieve yolks. Cook bacon slowly; drain; reserve bacon. Add onion to bacon drippings; cook until golden. Combine flour, sugar, salt and dry mustard; stir into skillet. Add water and vinegar. Cook, stirring constantly, until mixture bubbles and is thickened. Add pimiento, green pepper, celery, bacon, and egg whites; cook 1 minute longer. Pour mixture over potatoes in large bowl; toss gently to blend. Garnish with sieved egg yolks. Makes 6 to 8 servings.

SPRING POTATO SALAD

6 c. sliced, cooked	2 tbs. vinegar
warm potatoes	6 tbs. olive or pure
2 tbs. finely	vegetable oil
chopped green	1 carton (1 lb.)
onions	cottage cheese
½ tsp. dry mustard	½ c. mayonnaise or
½ tsp. salt	salad dressing
¼ tsp. garlic salt	2 hard-cooked egg
¼ tsp. sugar	yolks, sieved
Dash of pepper	Crisp greens
¼ tsp. Worcester-	
shire sauce	

Put potatoes into large bowl; add onions. Combine mustard, salts, sugar, pepper, Worcestershire, vinegar, and oil in bottle or jar; cover tightly; shake well. Pour over warm potatoes; toss gently to blend; refrigerate several hours. Thirty minutes before serving, combine cot-

tage cheese and mayonnaise or salad dressing; add to potatoes; toss until blended. Mound on platter; sprinkle top with sieved egg yolk. Serve on crisp greens. Makes 8 servings.

CURRIED POTATO SALAD

6 c. cubed, cooked	1 to 1½ tbs. curry
potatoes	powder
½ c. diced green	2 tbs. finely
pepper	chopped onion
1 c. diced celery	3 tbs. lemon juice
2 hard-cooked eggs,	1 tsp. salt
diced	¼ tsp. pepper
1 c. mayonnaise or	Crisp greens
salad dressing	

Mix potatoes, green pepper, celery, and hard-cooked eggs in large bowl. Combine mayonnaise or salad dressing, curry, onion, lemon juice, salt, and pepper; pour over potato mixture. Toss gently until potatoes are coated. Chill several hours. Serve on crisp greens. Makes 8 servings.

SWEET AND WHITE POTATO SALAD

¼ c. orange juice	2½ c. sliced, cooked
¼ c. vinegar	sweet potatoes or
1 tbs. lemon juice	yams, fresh or
⅔ c. pure vegetable	canned
oil	2½ c. sliced, cooked
½ tsp. dry mustard	white potatoes
1 tsp. paprika	Romaine
1 tsp. celery seed	

Combine orange juice, vinegar, lemon juice, oil, mustard, paprika, and celery seed in blender or screw-top jar; whirl or shake well. Combine potatoes in a large bowl; pour dressing over all; chill 1 to 2 hours. When ready to serve, line salad bowl with crisp romaine; drain potatoes, reserving dressing; spoon potatoes onto greens. Serve with reserved dressing. Makes 6 servings.

HOT SWEET POTATO SALAD

6 slices bacon	¼ tsp. salt
½ c. raisins	1 large red-skinned
1 tsp. grated orange	apple, cored and
rind	diced
¼ c. orange juice	4 c. hot, cooked
2 tbs. vinegar	sweet potatoes or
2 tbs. brown sugar	yams, diced
¼ tsp. ground	
cinnamon	

Fry bacon crisp; drain; crumble. Return ⅓ cup drippings to skillet. Stir in raisins, orange rind and juice, vinegar, sugar, cinnamon, and salt. Cook, stirring, until sugar is dissolved and mixture hot. Combine apple and sweet potatoes or yams in bowl. Pour on orange mixture. Toss. Sprinkle with bacon. Serve hot. Makes 6 servings.

POTATO CHEF'S SALAD

4 c. hot, cubed, cooked potatoes	½ c. chopped onion (1 medium)
½ c. bottled garlic or onion French dressing	½ c. green pepper strips
1 c. cubed Swiss cheese	2 tomatoes, cubed
	Crisp greens
¼ lb. salami, slivered	Mayonnaise or salad dressing
	2 tbs. chopped parsley

Marinate hot potatoes in ¼ cup French dressing several hours. Combine Swiss cheese, salami, onion, green pepper, and tomatoes. Add remaining French dressing; chill 1 hour. At serving time, drain French dressing from cheese-salami mixture. Add potatoes; mix well. Serve salad on crisp salad greens. Top with mayonnaise or salad dressing and chopped parsley. Makes 6 servings.

LOBSTER AND EGG POTATO SALAD

2 pkgs. (9 oz. ea.) frozen lobster tails, cooked	¼ tsp. paprika
	⅔ c. milk
	1 egg yolk
3 hard-cooked eggs	¼ c. vinegar
2 tbs. butter or margarine	4 c. sliced, cooked potatoes
1 tbs. flour	¼ c. minced onion (1 small)
¾ tsp. salt	
1 tsp. dry mustard	1 c. sliced celery
2 tsp. sugar	Lettuce

Shell lobster tails; cut into cubes. Shell eggs; cut in half; remove and sieve yolks; chop whites. Melt butter or margarine in saucepan; blend in dry ingredients; stir in milk slowly. Cook over medium heat, stirring constantly, until thickened. Beat egg yolk slightly; stir a small amount of hot mixture into egg yolk; blend into hot mixture in saucepan. Cook one minute more; stir in vinegar; cool. Combine potatoes, onion, celery, lobster, egg whites, and dressing; toss gently to blend; chill well.

When ready to serve, line salad bowl with lettuce; spoon salad mixture into bowl; garnish top with sieved egg yolk. Makes 6 servings.

COLESLAWS

OLD-FASHIONED CABBAGE SLAW

6 c. finely shredded green cabbage	⅔ c. Old-Fashioned Boiled Dressing
½ tsp. salt	(page 344)

Measure cabbage into large bowl; sprinkle with salt. Add dressing; toss thoroughly until cabbage is well coated. Chill. Makes 6 servings.

Green and Red Cabbage Slaw: Use 3 cups finely shredded green cabbage and 3 cups finely shredded red cabbage. Proceed as for Old-Fashioned Cabbage Slaw.

Harlequin Slaw: Use 5 cups finely shredded green cabbage, ½ cup coarsely grated raw carrot, ½ cup thinly sliced radishes, and ¼ cup diced green pepper. Proceed as for Old-Fashioned Cabbage Slaw.

HAM COLESLAW

1 c. slivered or diced cooked ham	1 tsp. sugar
	1 tsp. dry mustard
	1 tsp. celery seed
2 c. finely shredded cabbage (½ small head)	½ tsp. salt
	¼ tsp. pepper
	¼ tsp. paprika
¼ c. chopped green pepper	¼ c. pure vegetable oil
2 tbs. chopped pimiento	2 tbs. vinegar

Place ham, cabbage, green pepper, and pimiento in serving bowl. Combine seasonings, oil, and vinegar. Just before serving, pour on dressing; toss lightly. Makes 4 to 6 servings.

COLESLAW WITH BLUE CHEESE DRESSING

1 c. mayonnaise or salad dressing	⅓ c. crumbled blue cheese
¼ c. milk	3 c. shredded cabbage
½ tsp. salt	
¼ tsp. seasoned pepper	½ c. shredded, pared carrot
Dash of hot-pepper sauce	¼ c. chopped green pepper

Blend mayonnaise or salad dressing, milk, salt, pepper, and hot-pepper sauce in small bowl; stir in blue cheese. Combine cabbage, carrot, and green pepper in large bowl. Add blue cheese mixture; toss gently until vegetables are coated. Chill. Makes 4 servings.

HOT CURRIED SLAW

1 can (10½ oz.) condensed consommé	1 clove of garlic, crushed
1 c. water	4 tbs. butter or margarine
1 bay leaf	2 tbs. flour
3 whole cloves	1 tbs. curry powder
½ tsp. salt	
3 to 3½ lb. head cabbage, shredded	1 tsp. salt
	Dash of pepper
½ c. finely chopped onion (1 medium)	1½ c. dairy sour cream
	¼ c. packaged bread crumbs

Simmer consommé, water, bay leaf, cloves, and ½ teaspoon salt in large saucepan 5 minutes; remove bay leaf and cloves. Add cabbage; cover; simmer 10 minutes, stirring occasionally. Drain; reserve ½ cup broth. Sauté onion and garlic in butter or margarine 3 minutes; blend in flour, curry powder, 1 teaspoon salt, and pepper. Stir in sour cream and reserved broth. Cook over low heat, stirring constantly, until sauce simmers and thickens. Combine sauce and cabbage; turn into 2-quart casserole; sprinkle with crumbs. Bake at 425° F. for 15 to 20 minutes or until crumbs are lightly browned. Makes 8 servings.

SAUERKRAUT SLAW

3 c. fresh sauerkraut	1 c. dairy sour cream
2 cloves of garlic, mashed	

Combine sauerkraut and garlic in large bowl. Chill at least 2 hours. Just before serving, stir in sour cream. For extra flavor, add 1 teaspoon caraway seeds, if desired. Makes 6 servings.

CALIFORNIA SLAW

1 can (11 oz.) mandarin oranges	1 tbs. vinegar
	1 tbs. sugar
½ c. mayonnaise or salad dressing	6 c. finely shredded cabbage
¾ tsp. salt	½ c. coarsely chopped walnuts
¾ tsp. ground ginger	

Drain oranges well; reserve juice and orange sections. Blend mayonnaise or salad dressing, salt, ginger, 1 tablespoon juice from oranges, vinegar, and sugar. Place cabbage in a large bowl. Pour dressing over; toss thoroughly. Add oranges and nuts. Toss lightly. Chill. Makes about 4 or 5 servings.

SWEET-AND-SOUR RED CABBAGE SLAW

6 slices bacon	⅓ c. vinegar
2 tbs. finely chopped onion	¼ c. water
	6 c. finely shredded red cabbage
½ c. brown sugar, firmly packed	
1 tsp. cornstarch	1 tsp. caraway seeds (optional)
1 tsp. salt	

Cook bacon until crisp; drain on paper towels; crumble. Measure 3 tablespoons bacon drippings into skillet. Stir in onion, brown sugar, cornstarch, salt, vinegar, and water. Cook over medium heat, stirring constantly, until mixture is smooth and clear. Cool to room temperature; pour over cabbage in large bowl. Stir in caraway seeds. Toss. Chill. Makes 6 servings.

SPICY APPLE SLAW

¾ c. mayonnaise or salad dressing	⅛ tsp. ground cloves
1 tsp. grated orange rind	¾ tsp. salt
	1 tbs. sugar
1 tbs. orange juice	6 c. finely shredded cabbage
⅛ tsp. ground cinnamon	1 large red-skinned apple

Blend mayonnaise or salad dressing, orange rind and juice, cinnamon, cloves, salt, and sugar. Place cabbage in large bowl. Stir in dressing mixture. Chill. Before serving, dice unpared apple or slice it very thin. Add to slaw; toss lightly. Makes 6 to 8 servings.

FRUIT SALADS

SALAD IN HIGH C

3 tbs. olive oil
1½ tbs. vinegar
1 tbs. sugar
½ tsp. salt
Few drops hot-
    pepper sauce
2 dashes paprika
2 cloves of garlic
Romaine

1 can (11 oz.)
    mandarin
    oranges, drained
1 can (13½ oz.)
    pineapple
    chunks, drained
½ c. golden
    raisins
¼ c. coarsely
    chopped pecans

Combine olive oil, vinegar, sugar, salt, hot-pepper sauce, paprika, and the whole garlic cloves in small screw-top jar. Shake well; refrigerate. Wash romaine; dry. Chill. When ready to make salad, tear romaine into bite-size pieces. Combine in salad bowl with remaining ingredients and 3 tablespoons dressing. Toss gently. Makes 4 servings.

CALIFORNIA FRUIT SALAD

2 eggs
¼ cup honey
¼ cup lemon juice
1 cup heavy cream,
    whipped
9 large cooked
    prunes, pitted
½ c. cottage cheese
Crisp greens
1 pt. strawberries,
    washed and
    hulled

½ fresh pineapple,
    peeled, cored,
    and cut in wedges
3 oranges, peeled
    and sliced
1½ c. watermelon
    balls
1½ cups honeydew
    melon balls
1½ c. cantaloupe
    balls
2 large bananas,
    peeled and sliced

Beat eggs until light in top of double boiler; add honey and lemon juice. Cook over hot, not boiling, water, stirring constantly, until thick. Cool. Fold in whipped cream; chill. Stuff prunes with cottage cheese; chill. Line large, flat serving plate with salad greens. Arrange mounds of each fruit on greens. Serve with honey-cream mixture. Makes 6 servings.

AVOCADO-ORANGE-GRAPEFRUIT SALAD

2 grapefruit
2 navel oranges
3 avocados
Lettuce

Polynesian Fruit
    Dressing (page
    343) or French
    Dressing (page
    342)

Peel and section grapefruit and oranges; reserve juice. Halve avocados; pit; peel. Brush avocados with combined grapefruit and orange juices to prevent darkening. Arrange avocados on lettuce. Arrange sections of grapefruit and orange on avocado. Serve with Polynesian Fruit Dressing or French Dressing. Makes 6 servings.

RAISIN WALDORF SALAD

3 c. diced, pared or
    unpared apples
2 tsp. lemon juice
¾ c. diced celery
½ c. raisins or
    chopped pitted
    dates
¼ tsp. salt

½ c. mayonnaise or
    salad dressing
2 tsp. confectioners'
    sugar
¼ c. dairy sour
    cream
Lettuce cups
⅓ c. coarsely
    broken walnuts

Sprinkle apples with lemon juice. Combine apples, celery, raisins or dates, and salt. Blend mayonnaise or salad dressing, sugar, and sour cream together; pour over apple mixture; toss lightly with fork until apple pieces are well coated. Arrange salad in lettuce cups. Sprinkle with walnuts. Makes 4 to 6 servings.

FROZEN FRUIT SALAD

1 pkg. (3 oz.)
    cream cheese
⅓ c. mayonnaise or
    salad dressing
2 tbs. lemon juice
Dash of salt
½ c. heavy cream,
    whipped
1 can (1 lb. 14 oz.)
    fruit cocktail,
    drained

1 c. diced bananas
¼ c. chopped
    pecans or walnuts
2 tbs. diced mara-
    schino cherries
Lettuce
Honey-Lime
    Dressing
    (page 344)

Combine cream cheese, mayonnaise or salad dressing, lemon juice, and salt in large bowl. Fold in whipped cream. Add fruit cocktail, bananas, nuts, and cherries; mix well. Pour into 9x5x3-inch loaf pan or shallow pan that will fit your freezing compartment. Freeze 3 to 4 hours or until firm. Cut in slices and serve on lettuce with Honey-Lime Dressing. Makes 6 to 8 servings.

MAIN DISH SALADS

HEARTY SUPPER SALAD

3 c. cooked elbow
  macaroni
1 can (12 oz.)
  luncheon meat,
  cut into strips
¾ c. diced green
  pepper
¾ c. thinly sliced
  green onions
½ c. chopped dill
  pickle

1 c. diced celery
1½ c. cottage
  cheese
¼ c. diced pimiento
1½ c. mayonnaise
  or salad dressing
2½ tbs. vinegar
¼ tsp. salt
¼ tsp. pepper
Lettuce cups

Combine macaroni, luncheon meat, green pepper, green onions, pickle, celery, cottage cheese, and pimiento in large bowl. Combine mayonnaise or salad dressing, vinegar, salt, and pepper. Add to macaroni mixture; mix well. Chill. Serve in lettuce cups. Makes 6 to 8 servings.

MEDITERRANEAN SALAD

1 can (about 1 lb.)
  cut green beans
1 can (1 lb. 4 oz.)
  garbanzos or
  chick peas
1 small head
  cauliflower
1 pkg. (9 oz.)
  frozen artichoke
  hearts
1 c. olive oil
½ c. wine vinegar
2 large cloves of
  garlic, crushed
1 tsp. salt

¼ tsp. pepper
½ tsp. leaf oregano,
  crumbled
2½ qts. salad greens
  (lettuce, romaine,
  escarole, chicory)
1 can (4 oz.) pitted,
  ripe olives, sliced
1 red onion, sliced
  and separated
  into rings
3 tomatoes, diced
4 hard-cooked eggs,
  sliced
2 c. slivered, cooked
  ham

Drain and rinse green beans and garbanzos or chick peas. Cut cauliflower into flowerets and cook in boiling salted water 3 minutes or until almost tender. Cook artichoke hearts as directed on package. Combine oil, vinegar, garlic, salt, pepper, and oregano. Marinate green beans, garbanzos or chick peas, cauliflower, and artichokes in separate bowls in 3 to 4 tablespoons dressing mixture each. Chill at least 1 hour. Break salad greens into bite-size pieces. Place greens in large salad bowl; toss with remaining dressing. Arrange marinated vegetables, olives, onion rings, tomatoes,

eggs, and ham in rows on top of greens. Serve at once. Makes 8 servings.

PARTY MACARONI SALAD

½ c. Roquefort
  cheese
½ c. olive or pure
  vegetable oil
4 tbs. wine vinegar
¼ tsp. salt
Dash of pepper
1 pkg. (8 oz.) elbow
  macaroni, cooked
  and drained

½ c. sliced green
  onions
¾ c. diced celery
¼ c. diced green
  pepper
2 hard-cooked eggs,
  sliced
3 firm, ripe
  tomatoes, cut in
  wedges

Cream Roquefort cheese in salad bowl. Stir in oil gradually, keeping mixture smooth. Add vinegar, salt, and pepper; mix well. Add macaroni, green onions, celery, and green pepper. Toss until well coated with dressing. Chill. When ready to serve, garnish with hard-cooked eggs and tomato wedges. Makes 8 servings.

BEAN SUPPER SALAD

1 c. diced celery
½ c. sliced green
  onions
⅓ c. chopped green
  pepper
¼ c. pickle relish
½ c. cubed Cheddar
  or process
  American cheese

1 can (12 oz.)
  luncheon meat,
  cubed
⅓ c. bottled French
  dressing
1 can (1 lb.) beans
  in tomato sauce

Combine celery, onion, green pepper, pickle relish, cheese, luncheon meat, and French dressing. Add beans; mix well. Chill. Makes 6 servings.

EGG SALAD

8 hard-cooked eggs,
  shelled
1 c. chopped celery
2 tbs. chopped
  chives
1 tbs. chopped
  parsley

½ c. mayonnaise or
  salad dressing
1 tbs. lemon juice
3 tbs. cream
¼ tsp. salt
Lettuce

Slice eggs. Combine celery, chives, parsley, mayonnaise or salad dressing, lemon juice, cream, and salt. Line small bowl with lettuce. Arrange sliced eggs and celery mixture in layers in bowl. Cover; chill. Just before serving, toss to mix. Makes 6 servings.

COBB SALAD

This is a spectacular salad, suitable for special occasions. It takes a little extra care to shape the layered ingredients into a cone.

1½ c. bottled French Dressing	Lettuce leaves
½ c. crumbled Roquefort cheese	1½ c. finely chopped, cooked chicken
½ head iceberg lettuce	6 strips cooked bacon, finely chopped
½ head romaine	1 hard-cooked egg white, finely chopped
½ bunch water-cress	1 hard-cooked egg yolk, sieved
1 small head chicory	2 tbs. finely chopped chives
2 hard-cooked eggs, chopped	3 medium-size avocados, diced or sliced
2 tomatoes, peeled, seeded, and chopped	

Combine French dressing and Roquefort cheese; chill. Chop ½ head lettuce, romaine, watercress, and chicory. Add chopped eggs and tomatoes. Line flat serving plate with lettuce leaves. Mound chopped greens mixture in center. Top with layer of chicken; top with bacon. Make each layer slightly smaller in diameter than preceding one, so salad becomes cone shaped. Sprinkle bacon with chopped egg white and sieved egg yolk. Sprinkle with chives. Place avocado around base of salad. Serve with Roquefort-French dressing mixture. Makes 8 servings.

CHICKEN SALAD IN CURRIED RING

2 envelopes un-flavored gelatin	4 hard-cooked eggs, chopped
3⅓ c. canned chicken broth	½ c. mayonnaise or salad dressing
1 tbs. curry powder	1 tbs. minced onion
1 c. mayonnaise or salad dressing	1 tbs. lemon juice
2½ tbs. minced onion	½ tsp. salt
1 tsp. salt	Dash of pepper
Dash of pepper	3 c. diced, cooked chicken
1 c. thinly sliced celery	1 c. diced celery
¼ c. finely diced pimiento	1 c. seedless green grapes, halved
	½ c. slivered toasted almonds
	Crisp greens

Soften gelatin in 1 cup chicken broth 5 minutes. Add curry powder; heat until mixture simmers and gelatin is dissolved. Remove from heat. Add remaining chicken broth, 1 cup mayonnaise or salad dressing, 2½ tablespoons onion, 1 teaspoon salt, and dash of pepper; beat slightly until smooth. Chill until mixture begins to set. Fold in sliced celery, pimiento, and hard-cooked eggs. Pour into 6-cup ring mold. Chill about 3 hours or until firm. Combine ½ cup mayonnaise or salad dressing, 1 tablespoon onion, lemon juice, ½ teaspoon salt, and dash of pepper. Add chicken, diced celery, grapes, and all but 1 tablespoon almonds. Mix lightly. Unmold curry ring onto serving plate. Fill center of curry ring mold with chicken salad. Sprinkle with reserved almonds. Garnish with crisp salad greens. Makes 6 servings.

CURRIED CHICKEN AND VEGETABLE SALAD

2 tbs. bottled French dressing or French Dressing (*page 342*)	¼ c. thinly sliced radishes
½ tsp. grated lemon rind	1 can (5 oz.) water chestnuts, drained and thinly sliced
2 c. diced, cooked chicken	¾ tsp. salt
1 c. thinly sliced celery	⅔ c. mayonnaise or salad dressing
1 c. cooked, chilled peas	1 to 2 tsp. curry powder
	Lettuce cups
	Watercress

Combine French dressing and lemon rind. Pour over chicken in large bowl, stirring to coat chicken pieces well. Add celery, peas, radishes, water chestnuts, and salt. Blend together mayonnaise or salad dressing and curry powder; toss with chicken and vegetables. Chill 15 to 20 minutes. To serve, shape lettuce into cups on salad plates; spoon chicken mixture into each; garnish with watercress. Makes 4 servings.

SURPRISE CHICKEN SALAD

4 c. diced, cooked chicken	1 c. mayonnaise or salad dressing
1½ c. sliced celery	1 tsp. curry powder
¾ c. green pepper strips	1 tbs. minced onion
1 c. diced cucumber	1 tbs. chopped parsley
1 pink grapefruit, peeled, sectioned, and cubed	Crisp greens
	1 tsp. chopped chives
⅓ c. bottled French dressing	1 tbs. capers, drained

Combine chicken, celery, green pepper, cucumber, and grapefruit in large bowl. Add French dressing; chill at least 1 hour. Combine mayonnaise or salad dressing, curry powder, onion, and parsley. At serving time, drain French dressing from chicken mixture. Line large serving plate with crisp salad greens. Spoon chicken mixture onto greens. Pour curry-mayonnaise dressing over salad. Sprinkle with chives and capers. Makes 8 servings.

FISH AND SHELLFISH SALADS

EMERALD SALAD

1 pkg. garlic-flavored salad dressing mix	2 avocados, peeled and cut in half
1 c. boiling water	1 lb. small shrimp, cooked, shelled, and deveined or 1 pkg. (10 oz.) frozen, shelled, and deveined shrimp, cooked
1 pkg. (3 oz.) lime-flavored gelatin	
¾ c. cold water	
1 tbs. vinegar	
1 tsp. minced onion	
Crisp greens	

Prepare salad dressing mix as directed on package. Add boiling water to gelatin; stir until dissolved. Add cold water, vinegar, onion, and 2 tablespoons of garlic salad dressing. Pour mixture into 8x8x2-inch pan; chill about 2 hours or until firm. Cut into ½-inch squares. Line serving plate with salad greens. Brush avocados with salad dressing. Fill centers with shrimp and cubed gelatin. Place on serving plate. Pile remaining gelatin cubes in center. Serve with remaining salad dressing. Makes 6 servings.

SALAD BOUTIQUE

1 c. pure vegetable oil	1 pkg. (9 oz.) frozen artichoke hearts, cooked and chilled
½ c. wine vinegar	
1 large clove of garlic, crushed	1 small head or 2 pkgs. (10 oz. ea.) frozen cauliflower, cooked and chilled
1½ tbs. minced onion	
1 tsp. salt	
¼ tsp. pepper	1½ c. sliced carrots, cooked and chilled
1 pkg. (10 oz.) frozen peas or 1½ c. fresh peas, cooked and chilled	
	Crisp greens
	2 cans (about 6 oz. ea.) lobster, drained
1 pkg. (9 oz.) frozen cut green beans or 1½ c. fresh cut green beans, cooked and chilled	2 cans (6½ to 7½ oz. ea.) crab meat, drained
	3 can (about 5 oz. ea.) shrimp, drained

Combine oil, vinegar, garlic, onion, salt, and pepper; beat well. Put peas, beans, artichoke hearts, cauliflower, and carrots in separate shallow dishes. Add 2 tablespoons of dressing mixture to each. Chill. At serving time, line large serving plate with crisp greens. Place lobster in center of salad plate. Arrange crab around lobster, and place shrimp in a ring around crab. Arrange vegetables in mounds around edge of serving plate. Serve with remaining dressing. Makes 10 to 12 servings.

ASPARAGUS AND SHRIMP SALAD

½ c. pure vegetable oil	2 pkgs. (10 oz. ea.) frozen asparagus or 2 lbs. fresh asparagus, cooked and drained
¼ c. lemon juice	
½ tsp. salt	
⅛ tsp. pepper	
1 tsp. chopped chives	1 can (5 oz.) water chestnuts, sliced
½ tsp. mixed salad herbs	Crisp greens
2 lbs. shrimp, cooked, shelled, and deveined or 2 pkgs. (10 oz. ea.) frozen, shelled, and deveined shrimp, cooked	

Combine oil, lemon juice, salt, pepper, chives, and salad herbs; beat well. Pour half the mixture over shrimp in bowl; pour remainder over asparagus in shallow dish. Chill both at least 1 hour. When ready to serve, mix water chestnuts with shrimp; line serving plate with greens. Mound shrimp in center. Arrange asparagus in six bundles around shrimp. Makes 6 servings.

ITALIAN SHRIMP AND RICE SALAD

⅛ tsp. garlic powder	1 c. coarsely grated raw cauliflower
½ tsp. salt	½ c. sliced pitted ripe olives
¼ tsp. pepper	
⅓ c. bottled Italian-style dressing	⅓ c. thinly sliced green onions
½ tsp. leaf basil, crumbled	Crisp chicory or romaine
2 tbs. chili sauce	1 firm, ripe tomato, cut in wedges
2 c. diced, cleaned and cooked shrimp	
3 c. chilled, cooked rice	1 to 2 tbs. grated Parmesan cheese

Blend garlic powder, salt, pepper, dressing, basil, and chili sauce in small bowl. Combine shrimp, rice, cauliflower, olives, and green onions in large bowl. Pour dressing mixture over shrimp mixture; toss well. Serve in salad bowl lined with greens; garnish with tomato wedges; sprinkle with Parmesan cheese. Makes 4 servings.

CRAB AND AVOCADO SALAD

½ c. mayonnaise or salad dressing	2 tbs. chopped chives
⅓ c. dairy sour cream	2 cans (6½ to 7½ oz. ea.) crab meat, drained and boned
2 tbs. lemon juice	
2 tbs. prepared horseradish	
1 tsp. salt	1 large head lettuce
2 tbs. capers	2 medium-size avocados
2 hard-cooked eggs, finely chopped	

Blend together mayonnaise or salad dressing, sour cream, 1 tablespoon lemon juice, horseradish, salt, capers, eggs, and chives; chill.

Place crab meat in large salad bowl. Break lettuce into bite-size pieces; add to crab meat. Peel avocados; slice them into salad bowl; sprinkle with remaining 1 tablespoon lemon juice. Toss salad with half the dressing; pass remaining dressing for a creamy, tasty salad topping. Makes 6 servings.

TUNA SUPREME

½ c. mayonnaise or salad dressing	½ c. diced green pepper
1 tbs. vinegar	1 can (5 oz.) water chestnuts, sliced
2 tbs. light cream	
1 small clove of garlic, crushed	⅓ c. thinly sliced green onions
2 cans (6½ to 7 oz. ea.) tuna, drained and broken in chunks	¼ c. diced pimiento
	½ c. sliced, pitted, ripe olives
1 c. sliced celery	1 can (3 oz.) Chinese noodles
	Crisp greens

Combine mayonnaise or salad dressing, vinegar, cream, and garlic; mix well. Add tuna, celery, green pepper, water chestnuts, green onions, pimiento, and olives. Mix lightly until salad is coated with dressing. Chill. Just before serving, add noodles; mix quickly. Serve immediately on crisp greens. Makes 6 servings.

TUNA SALAD IMPERIAL

1 tsp. leaf thyme, crumbled	3 cans (6½ to 7 oz. ea.) tuna, drained and flaked
1 tsp. dill seeds	
1 tsp. salt	¾ c. thinly sliced green onions
⅓ c. French Dressing (page 342)	2 c. torn spinach leaves
½ head chicory	
½ head romaine	1 large firm, ripe tomato
½ head escarole	1 lemon, cut in wedges

Blend together thyme, dill, salt, and French Dressing. Line salad bowl with greens. Combine tuna, green onions, spinach, and dressing mixture; toss. Spoon into prepared salad bowl; garnish with tomato and lemon wedges. Makes 6 servings.

CALIFORNIA TUNA SALAD

1 c. dairy sour cream	Crisp greens, washed and dried
1 tsp. salt	1 medium-size avocado, peeled and sliced
⅛ tsp. cayenne	
3 tbs. lemon juice	
2 tbs. capers	1 can (13½ oz.) pineapple chunks, drained
2 cans (6½ to 7 oz. ea.) tuna, drained	
1 c. diced celery	

Combine sour cream, salt, cayenne, lemon juice, and capers; mix well. Toss tuna and celery with half the sour cream mixture. Mound tuna mixture on bed of greens in salad bowl. Surround with avocado and pineapple. Serve remaining dressing with salad. Makes 6 servings.

HERRING SALAD

1 salt herring	½ c. chopped dill pickle
2 c. diced, cooked potatoes	1 tbs. salt
2 c. diced, cooked beets	3 tbs. vinegar
	2 tbs. water
¼ c. chopped onion (1 small)	2 tbs. sugar
	Hard-cooked egg
	Parsley

Clean herring; remove head; soak in cold water 6 to 8 hours or overnight. Drain; skin; bone; chop. Mix chopped herring, potatoes, beets, onion, and pickle. Blend carefully with salt, vinegar, water, and sugar. Pack herring mixture firmly into 1½-quart mold. Chill several hours; unmold onto serving plate; garnish with hard-cooked egg and parsley. Makes 4 servings.

MOLDED SALADS

Success in making a refreshingly cool, molded salad is not difficult—once you understand the *secrets* of handling gelatin in all its phases, from the dissolving all the way through to the unmolding of the finished salad.

Layering: When a salad is to be set in layers, the first portion is put into the mold and chilled "just until set." You can best determine if it has reached this stage by touching it with your fingertip. The top of the layer should be set, but sticky to the touch, not smooth as a finished, set gelatin would be. The "stickiness" is needed to make the next layer cling to the first layer. If they don't stick together during the final chilling, they will slide apart when you unmold the salad.

Folding: Fruits, vegetables, and meat when part of a gelatin salad should be distributed all through the mixture. They should neither sink to the bottom nor float to the top. To accomplish this, the gelatin mixture is, as the recipe describes, chilled until it is syrupy (about the consistency of honey) before the food is folded in. If, by chance, you allow the gelatin to become too set, place the bowl in a bowl or pan of hot water and stir until the gelatin is liquid. Then rechill to the syrupy stage.

Whipping: Salads of the soufflé type, such as our Tomato-Vegetable Soufflé Salad (*page 339*), contain mayonnaise or salad dressing as part of the mixture (you could say the dressing is built in) and a slightly different technique is used to achieve the right consistency for folding in the solid foods. The gelatin mixture is chilled quickly in the freezer until it is firm about an inch from the edges; then it is beaten until fluffy. The other ingredients are then quickly folded in, and the salad turned into its mold and chilled until firm.

Coating: When you wish to have a pretty design set in gelatin or in a layer of contrasting gelatin at the top of a finished salad, here is what to do. Spoon enough of your liquid gelatin into the bottom of the mold to form a thin layer. Chill until just set, either in the refrigerator or, to do it more quickly, by setting the mold firmly in a bed of cracked ice. Arrange your vegetables or fancily-cut pieces of vegetables on the just-set gelatin, spoon over another layer of gelatin, and chill again. Then proceed with the rest of the salad according to the directions in the recipe.

All gelatin salads must be chilled until firm. Allow several hours or overnight for this. This quality of gelatin salads makes them perfect make-aheads for special occasions.

Unmolding: This is easy as one, two, three, as you will see in the illustrations on *page 361*. But, a few *secrets:*
· Select a plate large enough for the salad and its garnish.

· Rinse the plate in cold water so you will be able to move the salad if it is not centered when unmolded.

· Run tip of small knife or spatula carefully around top of gelatin to loosen from sides of mold.

· Dip mold into warm, not hot, water. If water is too hot, it will melt the gelatin.

· Dip mold into water until water comes as high as level of gelatin. Leave mold in water only a few seconds—work quickly.

· Place plate over mold; invert. Hold plate and mold together and shake gently to release gelatin. Lift off mold.

· If gelatin does not release at once, either redip quickly in warm water or tip mold up slightly at one side so air will help to release gelatin.

FRUIT NECTAR SALAD

1 can (12 oz.) apricot nectar	1 can (1 lb. 4 oz.) crushed pine-
½ c. water	apple
2 pkgs. (3 oz. ea.) orange-flavored gelatin	1 can (1 lb. 14 oz.) whole apricots
	Crisp greens

Heat apricot nectar and water to boiling; pour over orange gelatin; stir to dissolve. Drain and reserve pineapple; measure syrup (there should be 1 cup; add water, if necessary). Add syrup to orange gelatin mixture; chill until syrupy. Drain apricots (save syrup to use another time); remove pits. Cut enough apricots into eighths to make 1 cup; reserve remaining whole apricots. Fold crushed pineapple and apricot pieces into chilled, syrupy gelatin. Turn into 1½-quart mold; chill until firm. Unmold onto serving plate; garnish with reserved whole apricots and crisp greens. Makes 6 servings.

GRAPE ASPIC WITH MELON BALLS

1¾ c. bottled grape juice	2½ c. melon balls (honeydew or
1 tsp. grated lemon or lime rind	cantaloupe) Mint
1 pkg. (3 oz.) lemon-flavored gelatin	Chicory Spice and Honey Cream Dressing (*page 344*)

Combine grape juice and lemon or lime rind in saucepan; bring to boiling. Pour over gelatin in bowl; stir until gelatin is dissolved. Chill just until mixture begins to thicken. Stir in 1½ cups melon balls (chill remainder); pour into 3-cup mold or into 6 individual molds. Chill until firm. Unmold; garnish with melon balls, mint leaves, and chicory. Serve with dressing. Makes 6 servings.

MELON BALL COOLER

1 envelope un- flavored gelatin	2 tbs. boiling water ¼ c. mint, chopped
2 c. canned grape- fruit, orange, or grapefruit-orange juice	1½ c. melon balls (cantaloupe, honeydew, water- melon, etc.)
¼ c. sugar	Crisp greens

Soften gelatin in ¼ cup grapefruit, orange, or grapefruit-orange juice. Combine remaining juice and sugar in small saucepan; bring to boiling; remove from heat. Add softened gelatin mixture; stir until dissolved. Pour boiling water over mint leaves in cup or small bowl; press leaves with back of spoon to extract flavor. Strain; discard leaves; add liquid to gelatin mixture; chill until mixture begins to set. Fold in melon balls; pour into 6 individual molds or into 4-cup mold. Chill until firm. Unmold onto serving plate; garnish with crisp greens. Makes 6 servings.

MOLDED SPINACH SALAD

1 pkg. (3 oz.) lemon- or lime-flavored gelatin	½ tsp. salt Dash of pepper 1 carton (8 oz.) cream-style
1 c. boiling water	cottage cheese
½ c. cold water	⅓ c. chopped
2 tbs. vinegar	celery
½ c. mayonnaise or salad dressing	1 c. raw, chopped spinach
4 tsp. minced onion	Crisp greens

Dissolve gelatin in boiling water. Add cold water, vinegar, mayonnaise or salad dressing, minced onion, salt, and pepper. Beat slightly to blend. Chill until mixture begins to set. Fold in cottage cheese, celery, and spinach. Pour into 4-cup mold or six 5-ounce molds. Chill about 2 hours or until firm. Unmold. Serve with crisp greens. Makes 6 servings.

JELLIED STUFFED-PRUNE-AND-CHEESE SALAD

2 large navel oranges	½ c. slivered, blanched almonds
12 prunes, cooked and pitted	⅛ tsp. ground ginger
3½ c. water	1 tsp. grated orange rind
2 pkgs. (3 oz. ea.) orange-flavored gelatin	¾ c. finely chopped celery
1 pkg. (8 oz.) cream cheese	1 c. heavy cream, whipped
	Crisp greens

Peel and section oranges, removing all white membrane; stuff prunes with orange sections. Heat 2 cups water to boiling; pour over gelatin; stir until dissolved; stir in remaining 1½ cups cold water. Pour about ½ cup gelatin into 6-cup mold. Chill until firm. Arrange stuffed prunes, orange side down, on gelatin layer. Chill remaining gelatin until it just begins to thicken; pour half over prunes; chill until firm. Meanwhile, blend cream cheese, almonds, ginger, orange rind, celery, and remaining gelatin in a large bowl. Fold in whipped cream. Spoon over jellied prune layer in mold. Chill until firm. Unmold and garnish with crisp greens. Makes 8 to 10 servings.

MOLDED CABBAGE SALAD

1 pkg. (3 oz.) lemon- or lime-flavored gelatin	2 tsp. finely chopped onion
1 c. hot water	¼ c. finely diced green pepper
¾ c. cold water	1 c. finely chopped cabbage
2 tbs. vinegar	½ c. diced celery
¾ tsp. salt	¼ c. sliced radishes
Dash of pepper	

Dissolve gelatin in hot water; stir in cold water, vinegar, salt, and pepper. Chill until

slightly thickened. Fold in remaining ingredients. Turn into 4-cup mold. Chill several hours or until firm. Unmold. Makes 6 servings.

TOMATO-AVOCADO MOUSSE

6 medium-size firm, ripe tomatoes	Dash of pepper
	2 tbs. lemon juice
	2 tsp. minced onion
Salt	1 cup mashed avocado (1 large)
1 envelope unflavored gelatin	½ c. dairy sour cream
¼ c. cold water	½ c. mayonnaise or salad dressing
¾ c. hot water	
½ tsp. salt	

Cut tops from stem ends of tomatoes; scoop out pulp and seeds (they can be used in other recipes). Salt insides of tomato shells; invert on paper towels. Soften gelatin in cold water; dissolve in hot water; add ½ teaspoon salt and pepper. Chill just until mixture begins to thicken. Combine lemon juice, onion, mashed avocado, sour cream, and mayonnaise or salad dressing. Fold into thickened gelatin. Spoon into tomato shells. (If you wish, you can omit tomatoes and mold salad in individual molds.) Chill until avocado mixture is firm. Makes 6 servings.

MOLDED GAZPACHO SALAD

2 envelopes unflavored gelatin	¾ c. finely chopped green pepper
3 c. tomato juice	¾ c. finely chopped cucumber, well drained
¼ c. wine vinegar	
1 clove of garlic, crushed	¼ c. finely diced pimiento
2 tsp. salt	1 small avocado
¼ tsp. pepper	1 tbs. lemon juice
Dash of cayenne	½ c. dairy sour cream
2 large tomatoes, peeled, seeded, chopped, and drained	½ tsp. salt
	Dash of cayenne
	Crisp greens
½ c. finely chopped onion (1 medium)	

Soften gelatin in 1 cup tomato juice 5 minutes. Heat until mixture simmers and gelatin is dissolved. Remove from heat; add remain ing tomato juice, vinegar, garlic, 2 teaspoons salt, pepper, and dash of cayenne. Chill until mixture begins to set; fold in tomatoes, onion, green pepper, cucumber, and pimiento. Pour into 6-cup mold. Chill about 3 hours or until firm. Unmold onto serving plate. Mash avocado with lemon juice in small bowl. Stir in sour cream, ½ teaspoon salt, and dash of cayenne. Spread on top of unmolded salad. Garnish with crisp greens. Makes 6 to 8 servings.

TOMATO-VEGETABLE SOUFFLÉ SALAD

2 pkgs. (3 oz. ea.) lemon-flavored gelatin	2 tsp. lemon juice
	1 c. mayonnaise or salad dressing
2 c. hot tomato juice	1½ c. cooked vegetables
¼ c. cold tomato juice	½ c. diced celery
¼ c. vinegar	¼ c. diced green pepper
1 tsp. grated lemon rind	¼ c. diced pimiento
	Crisp greens

Dissolve gelatin in hot tomato juice. Stir in cold tomato juice, vinegar, lemon rind, and lemon juice. Add mayonnaise or salad dressing; blend mixture thoroughly with rotary beater. Pour into shallow pan; chill in freezer 15 to 20 minutes or until firm 1 inch from edge all around sides but still liquid in center. Turn into bowl. Beat with rotary or electric beater until light and fluffy. Fold in cooked vegetables, celery, green pepper, and pimiento. Pour into 6-cup mold. Chill several hours or until firm. Unmold onto serving plate; garnish with crisp greens. Makes 4 to 6 servings.

THREE-LAYERED VEGETABLE SALAD

3 envelopes unflavored gelatin	2½ c. water
	1 c. shredded green pepper
½ c. sugar	
½ tsp. salt	1 c. shredded, pared carrot
1½ c. water	
½ c. lemon juice	1 c. shredded cabbage
½ c. vinegar	Crisp greens

Combine gelatin, sugar, and salt in saucepan; add 1½ cups water. Stir over low heat until gelatin mixture is dissolved. Stir in lemon juice, vinegar, and 2½ cups water. Divide into three parts; chill each third, one at a time,

until syrupy. Fold green pepper into one third. Spoon into 6-cup mold; chill until almost set. Fold carrots into second third; spoon carefully over green pepper layer; chill until almost set. Fold cabbage into remaining third; spoon carefully over carrot layer. Chill several hours or until firm. Unmold onto serving plate; garnish with crisp greens. This will give you a salad that is equally layered. *Secret:* If your mold has unequal divisions, measure the amount of water each section holds. This will be the amount of gelatin-vegetable mixture to spoon into each section of the mold. Makes 6 servings.

TOMATO ASPIC RIBBON SALAD

2 pkgs. (3 oz. ea.) lemon-flavored gelatin	½ c. finely chopped celery
	½ c. finely chopped green pepper
1¾ c. boiling water	½ c. finely chopped cucumber
1 tsp. salt	
Dash of pepper	
3 tbs. vinegar	1 carton (8 oz.) cottage cheese
1 tbs. minced onion	
2 cans (8 oz. ea.) tomato sauce	Chicory

Dissolve gelatin in boiling water; stir in salt, pepper, vinegar, and minced onion. Remove and reserve ¼ cup gelatin mixture; add tomato sauce to remainder. Measure 1½ cups tomato-gelatin mixture into small bowl; chill until it begins to thicken (keep remainder at room temperature). Combine vegetables; stir ⅓ of mixture into slightly thickened tomato gelatin; pour into 6-cup mold or loaf pan; chill until almost set. Mix reserved ¼ cup lemon gelatin with cottage cheese; spoon evenly over tomato layer in mold or loaf pan; chill. Chill remaining tomato-gelatin mixture until slightly thickened; stir in remaining vegetables; pour over cheese layer in pan. Chill several hours or overnight. Unmold on serving plate; garnish with chicory. Makes 8 servings.

PERFECTION SALAD

4 c. boiling water
3 pkgs. (3 oz. ea.)
  lemon-flavored
  gelatin
½ c. vinegar
2 c. finely shredded
  cabbage

1 c. shredded, pared
  carrot
¼ c. diced green
  pepper
Chicory
French Dressing
  (*page 342*)

Add boiling water to gelatin; stir until completely dissolved; add vinegar; cool. Chill until mixture begins to thicken. Fold cabbage, carrot, and green pepper into thickened gelatin mixture; pour into 6-cup mold; chill until set. Unmold onto serving plate. Garnish with chicory; serve with French Dressing. Makes 8 servings.

CRAB AND CUCUMBER MOUSSE

2 envelopes un-
  flavored gelatin
½ c. cold water
2 c. boiling water
Few drops green
  food coloring
1 pkg. (8 oz.)
  cream cheese
½ c. mayonnaise
  or salad dressing
1 c. dairy sour
  cream
⅓ c. vinegar
2 tbs. sugar
1 tsp. grated lemon
  rind

2 tbs. lemon juice
2 medium-size
  cucumbers, pared
  and diced
1 c. minced celery
1½ tsp. salt
1 tsp. leaf thyme,
  crumbled
⅓ c. thinly sliced
  green onions
2 cans (6½ to 7½
  oz. ea.) crab
  meat, drained
  and boned
Crisp greens

Soften gelatin in cold water; dissolve in boiling water; stir in food coloring. Chill just until mixture begins to thicken. Mix cream cheese, mayonnaise or salad dressing, sour cream, vinegar, sugar, and lemon rind and juice in medium-size bowl; beat until smooth. Blend slightly thickened gelatin mixture into cream cheese mixture; add cucumbers, celery, salt, thyme, green onions, and crab meat.

Pour into 8-cup mold. Chill several hours or overnight. Just before serving, unmold onto serving platter. Garnish with crisp greens. Makes 8 servings.

SHRIMP AND CUCUMBER MOLD

2 pkgs. (3 oz. ea.)
  lime-flavored
  gelatin
1 tsp. unflavored
  gelatin
2 c. hot water
¼ c. lemon juice
½ c. cold water
1 small cucumber,
  sliced
2 c. dairy sour
  cream

2 tsp. minced onion
1½ c. finely
  chopped
  cucumber
1 pkg. (10 oz.)
  frozen, shelled,
  and deveined
  shrimp, cooked
½ tsp. salt
Crisp greens

Blend flavored gelatin with unflavored gelatin; dissolve in hot water; stir in lemon juice. Measure ½ cup mixture into small bowl; chill remainder until syrupy. Stir cold water into the ½ cup gelatin mixture. Cover bottom of 6-cup mold with half the mixture; chill until almost set. Overlap cucumber slices on gelatin. Carefully cover with second half of gelatin mixture; chill until almost set. Fold sour cream, onion, chopped cucumber, shrimp, and salt into syrupy gelatin. Spoon mixture carefully into mold over cucumber layer. Chill until firm. Unmold onto serving plate; garnish with crisp greens. Makes 6 servings.

CUCUMBER TUNA MOLD

1 pkg. (3 oz.) lime-
  flavored gelatin
1 c. boiling water
1½ tsp. minced
  onion
1 tsp. salt
2 tbs. vinegar
1 c. dairy sour
  cream
¼ c. mayonnaise or
  salad dressing
2 large cucumbers,
  pared, grated,
  and drained
  (1 c.)

1 can (6½ to 7 oz.)
  tuna, drained and
  flaked
2 tbs. bottled
  French dressing
1 pkg. (3 oz.)
  lemon-flavored
  gelatin
1 c. boiling water
⅔ c. cold water
1½ tsp. minced
  onion
¾ tsp. salt
Dash of pepper
1½ tbs. vinegar
⅓ c. diced celery
Chicory

Dissolve lime gelatin in 1 cup boiling water; add 1½ teaspoons onion, 1 teaspoon salt, and 2 tablespoons vinegar. Chill until slightly thickened. Fold in sour cream, mayonnaise or salad dressing, and cucumber. Turn into 6-cup mold; chill. Combine tuna and French dressing; let stand. Dissolve lemon gelatin in 1 cup boiling water; add cold water, 1½ teaspoons onion, ¾ teaspoon salt, pepper, and 1½ tablespoons vinegar. Chill until mixture begins to set; fold in tuna mixture and celery. Turn into mold on top of cucumber layer. Chill 4 hours or overnight. Unmold onto serving plate; garnish with chicory. Makes 8 servings.

TUNA SALAD MOLD

1 pkg. (3 oz.) lemon-flavored gelatin	½ tsp. salt
	⅛ tsp. pepper
	1 can (6½ to 7 oz.)
1½ c. boiling water	tuna, drained
½ c. mayonnaise or salad dressing	and flaked
	¼ c. chopped ripe olives
1 tbs. onion juice	
2 tbs. vinegar or lemon juice	½ c. diced celery
	2 tbs. diced pimiento
1½ tsp. Worcestershire sauce	2 tbs. chopped green pepper
Few drops hot-pepper sauce	Crisp greens

Dissolve gelatin in boiling water. Add mayonnaise or salad dressing, onion juice, vinegar or lemon juice, Worcestershire, hot-pepper sauce, salt, and pepper; mix well. Chill until mixture begins to set. Stir in tuna, olives, celery, pimiento, and green pepper. Pour salad mixture into 6 individual molds or 4-cup mold. Chill 2 to 3 hours or until firm. Serve on crisp greens. Makes 6 servings.

SALMON MOUSSE

2 cans (7¾ oz. ea.) salmon	1 tsp. minced onion
	½ c. mayonnaise or salad dressing
2 envelopes unflavored gelatin	
	2 egg whites, stiffly beaten
⅓ c. cold water	
1 c. boiling water	Crisp greens
3 tbs. vinegar	

Drain salmon; remove skin and bones; mash very fine or whirl in blender. Soften gelatin in cold water; add boiling water, stirring well to dissolve; cool. Add salmon, vinegar, minced onion, and mayonnaise or salad dressing; chill until mixture begins to thicken. Fold in beaten egg whites; spoon into 5-cup mold; chill 3 to 4 hours or until set. Unmold; garnish with crisp greens. Makes 6 servings.

CREAMY CHICKEN MOLD

2 broiler-fryers (about 2½ lbs. ea.), cut up	4 tsp. minced onion
	2 tbs. lemon juice
	1 c. mayonnaise or salad dressing
2 tsp. salt	
5 peppercorns	1 tsp. dry mustard
1 small onion, sliced	2 tsp. salt
	½ tsp. pepper
3 sprigs celery leaves	1 c. diced celery
	2 tbs. chopped parsley
2 envelopes un-flavored gelatin	Crisp greens

Put chicken, 2 teaspoons salt, peppercorns, sliced onion, and celery leaves in large kettle. Add water to cover. Simmer until tender. Remove cooked chicken from bones; return bones and skin to broth. Cook until broth is reduced to 1 quart; strain; cool; remove fat. Cube chicken (you should have 4 cups); reserve. Soften gelatin in ½ cup chicken broth. Heat 2½ cups chicken broth; add gelatin mixture; stir until dissolved. Combine minced onion, lemon juice, mayonnaise or salad dressing, mustard, 2 teaspoons salt, and pepper. Add to gelatin mixture; mix well. Chill until mixture begins to set. Fold in celery, parsley, and cubed chicken. Turn into 7-cup mold. Chill several hours or until firm. Unmold onto serving plate. Garnish with crisp greens. Makes 6 to 8 servings.

BUFFET CHICKEN IN ASPIC

6 whole chicken
  breasts (broiler-
  fryers)
2 tsp. salt
6 peppercorns
1 bay leaf
1 small onion,
  sliced
Water

2 pkgs. (10 oz. ea.)
  frozen peas,
  cooked according
  to package
  directions
3 egg whites
6 envelopes un-
  flavored gelatin
Pimiento
Black olives
Crisp greens

Place chicken, salt, peppercorns, bay leaf, and onion in large kettle; add just enough water to cover chicken. Bring to boiling; lower heat. Simmer gently 40 to 50 minutes or until chicken is tender. Remove chicken; strain broth; there should be 8 cups. (If you don't have this much, add water to make 8 cups.) Cool broth and chicken. Skin and bone chicken; cut chicken into thick slices; discard skin and bones. Chill broth, chicken slices, and peas. To prepare and clarify aspic: Remove all fat from broth. Beat egg whites in the kettle until frothy. Add chicken broth and gelatin; stir thoroughly. Bring slowly to boiling; lower heat; simmer gently about 5 minutes or until cooked egg whites rise to surface. Remove from heat; let stand for 10 minutes. Line a sieve or colander with a clean, damp towel; place over large bowl. Pour gelatin-chicken broth mixture (aspic) carefully through cloth; allow to drip undisturbed. The clarified aspic will drain through clear, leaving all the cloudy particles in the cooked egg whites. Cool aspic; chill until syrupy. Make cut-outs from pimiento and olives for decorating top of mold. Set 10-cup mold firmly in bed of cracked ice. Pour a small amount of syrupy aspic into the mold to form a thin layer on the bottom; chill until just set. Arrange pimiento and olive pieces in design on aspic. Spoon over just enough aspic to cover design; chill until set. Arrange layer of chicken slices on aspic; spoon gelatin over and around chicken; chill until set. Arrange green peas over set chicken layer; spoon aspic over peas; chill until set. Continue in this manner until mold is filled, ending with aspic layer. Chill at least 4 hours or overnight. Unmold; serve with crisp greens. Recipe may be halved and molded in a 6-cup mold for family-size salad. Makes 10 servings.

HAM MADRILENE MOLD

1 envelope un-
  flavored gelatin
1 c. water
1 can (13 oz.)
  madrilene
2 tbs. vinegar
Ripe olives

½ c. heavy cream,
  whipped
2 c. finely chopped,
  cooked ham
½ c. diced Swiss
  cheese
2 tbs. pickle relish
Crisp greens

Soften gelatin in water in saucepan; let stand 5 minutes; place over low heat; stir until dissolved. Remove from heat; stir in madrilene and vinegar. Measure 2 cups of gelatin mixture into medium-size bowl; chill until syrupy. Cover bottom of 6-cup mold with half the remaining gelatin mixture; chill until almost set. Cut ripe olives into fancy shapes with sharp knife or small hors d'oeuvre cutters. Arrange in design on almost-set gelatin. Carefully cover with second half of gelatin mixture. Chill until just set. Fold whipped cream, ham, Swiss cheese, and pickle relish into syrupy gelatin mixture. Turn into mold on top of just-set madrilene layer. Chill several hours or overnight until firm. Unmold onto serving plate; garnish with crisp greens. Makes 6 servings.

Salad Dressings

FRENCH DRESSING

⅔ c. pure vegetable
  or olive oil
⅓ c. wine, tarragon,
  or cider vinegar

1 tsp. salt
¼ tsp. pepper
¼ tsp. sugar

Combine ingredients in screw-top jar or blender. Shake or whirl to blend. Makes 1 cup.

French Dressing Variations

To French Dressing or bottled French dressing add your choice of any one of the following.

Watercress: ⅓ cup chili sauce; ½ teaspoon dry mustard; 2 teaspoons Worcestershire sauce; dash hot-pepper sauce; 1 cup chopped watercress. For fruit, seafood, and egg salads

Cucumber: ½ cup grated cucumber; ½ teaspoon sugar; 1 teaspoon minced onion. For seafood salads.

Peanut Butter: Blend in 2 tablespoons cream-style peanut butter. For vegetable salads.

Cream: 1 medium-size potato, boiled and mashed; ¼ cup chopped, pitted green olives; 2 tablespoons chopped chives. For green salads.

Bar-Le-Duc: ¼ cup Bar-Le-Duc; 2 tablespoons dry sherry. For fruit, cottage and cream cheese, and chicken salads.

Blue Cheese: ½ cup crumbled blue cheese. For green salads.

Vinaigrette: 1 hard-cooked egg, chopped; 1 tablespoon chopped pimiento; 1 tablespoon pickle relish; 1 tablespoon minced onion; 1 tablespoon minced parsley. For green and seafood salads.

Chiffonade: ⅓ cup chopped, cooked beets; 2 tablespoons chopped parsley; 2 hard-cooked eggs, chopped; 1 tablespoon minced chives. For seafood and green salads.

Creamy French: 1 tablespoon paprika; 1 egg; ½ teaspoon sugar; dash hot-pepper sauce. For vegetable and meat salads.

GOLDEN FRENCH DRESSING

¾ c. pure vegetable oil	¼ tsp. pepper
⅓ c. tarragon vinegar	½ tsp. sugar
1 tsp. Worcestershire sauce	1 tsp. prepared mustard
1 tsp. salt	1 clove garlic, halved

Combine all ingredients in screw-top jar. Shake until blended. Makes 1 cup. For vegetable, green, and seafood salads.

TOMATO FRENCH DRESSING

1 can (10½ oz.) condensed tomato soup	¼ tsp. pepper
⅔ c. vinegar	1 clove of garlic, minced
2 tbs. sugar	1 tsp. prepared mustard
1⅓ c. pure vegetable oil	1 tbs. Worcestershire sauce
½ tsp. salt	

Combine all ingredients in screw-top jar or blender. Shake or whirl to blend. Makes 3½ cups. For vegetable, green, and seafood salads.

POLYNESIAN FRUIT DRESSING

½ c. pineapple juice	1½ tbs. sugar
½ tsp. grated lime rind	¼ tsp. salt
¼ c. lime juice	2 tbs. honey
	½ c. pure vegetable oil

Combine all ingredients in screw-top jar or blender. Shake or whirl to blend. Makes 1½ cups. For fruit salads.

POPPY SEED DRESSING

¼ c. orange juice	⅓ c. light corn syrup
¼ c. lemon juice	1 tbs. poppy seeds
⅓ c. pure vegetable oil	

Combine all ingredients in screw-top jar or blender. Shake or whirl to blend. Makes 1 cup. For fruit salads.

THOUSAND ISLAND DRESSING

½ c. pure vegetable oil	1 tsp. Worcestershire sauce
1 tbs. lemon juice	6 pitted green olives, sliced
3 tbs. orange juice	½ tsp. salt
1 tsp. minced onion	¼ tsp. paprika
2 tsp. chopped parsley	½ tsp. dry mustard

Combine all ingredients in screw-top jar or blender. Shake or whirl to blend. Makes 1 cup. For vegetable and seafood salads.

AVOCADO CHEESE DRESSING

1 large ripe avocado	½ tsp. salt
4 tbs. lemon juice	1 tsp. prepared mustard
¼ c. blue cheese	½ tsp. Worcestershire sauce
⅓ c. light cream	

Peel and dice avocado. Combine avocado, lemon juice, cheese, cream, salt, mustard, and Worcestershire in blender. Whirl to blend. Or mash avocado and cheese; add remaining ingredients. Makes about 2 cups. For vegetable salads.

HONEY FRUIT DRESSING

1 pkg. (3 oz.) cream cheese	2 tsp. grated orange rind
2 tbs. honey	¼ c. orange juice
1 tbs. lime juice	¼ tsp. salt
	¼ tsp. paprika

Soften cheese. Blend in honey, lime juice, orange rind and juice, salt and paprika. Makes about 1 cup. For fruit salads.

SPICE AND HONEY CREAM DRESSING

1 c. dairy sour cream	½ tsp. ground cinnamon
1 tbs. honey	½ tsp. grated lemon or lime rind

Combine all ingredients; chill. Makes 1 cup. For fruit salads.

MAYONNAISE

1 tsp. sugar	1½ tbs. vinegar
1 tsp. salt	2 c. pure vegetable oil
½ tsp. dry mustard	
Dash of cayenne	2 tbs. lemon juice
2 egg yolks	

Combine sugar, salt, mustard, and cayenne in deep bowl; add egg yolks; blend. Add vinegar slowly, stirring constantly. Slowly beat in ¼ cup oil, a teaspoon at a time, with rotary beater or electric mixer at medium speed. Beat in remaining oil a small amount at a time until mixture thickens. Be sure mixture is smooth before making next addition of oil. Stir in lemon juice. Store, covered, in refrigerator. Makes 2 cups.

Mayonnaise Variations

To 1 cup Mayonnaise, or bottled mayonnaise or salad dressing blend in your choice of any of the following:

Caper: 2 tablespoons chopped ripe olives; 2 tablespoons chopped pimiento; 2 teaspoons chopped capers; 2 teaspoons wine vinegar. For seafood and green salads.

Curry: 1 teaspoon curry powder; 2 tablespoons drained, chopped chutney. For chicken, meat, and egg salads.

Russian: ½ cup chili sauce; 2 tablespoons chopped green pepper; 2 tablespoons chopped pimiento; 1 teaspoon chopped chives; 2 tablespoons caviar (optional). For meat and seafood salads.

Honey Lime: ½ cup honey; ¼ cup lime juice; 1 cup heavy cream, whipped. For fruit salads.

Horseradish: 2 tablespoons prepared horseradish; 2 tablespoons dairy sour cream; 2 tablespoons chopped radishes. For meat and seafood salads.

Anchovy: 1 teaspoon anchovy paste; 2 tablespoons chopped parsley. For meat and green salads.

Creamy Blue Cheese: 1 cup dairy sour cream; 2 tablespoons finely chopped onion; ½ cup blue cheese, crumbled; ½ cup milk; ¼ teaspoon salt; ⅛ teaspoon pepper. For green salads.

Green Goddess: ½ cup dairy sour cream; ⅓ cup chopped parsley; 2 tablespoons chopped chives or green onions; 2 tablespoons anchovy paste; 3 tablespoons tarragon vinegar; 1 teaspoon Worcestershire sauce; ½ teaspoon dry mustard; ¼ teaspoon pepper; 1 clove of garlic, minced. For seafood salads.

Helen's Fruit Dressing: 3 tablespoons juice from jar of maraschino cherries; 2 tablespoons cream; ½ teaspoon grated orange rind; 2 tablespoons chopped maraschino cherries. For fruit salads.

Tangy Roquefort: ½ cup crumbled Roquefort or Blue cheese; ⅔ cup French Dressing (*page 342*); ½ teaspoon Worcestershire sauce. For green and vegetable salads.

OLD-FASHIONED BOILED DRESSING

2 tbs. flour	¼ c. vinegar
1 tsp. dry mustard	1 tbs. butter or margarine
½ tsp. salt	
¼ tsp. paprika	¼ c. light cream or evaporated milk
2 tbs. sugar	
½ c. cold water	
2 egg yolks, beaten	

Combine flour, mustard, salt, paprika, and sugar in small saucepan; stir in water, egg yolks, and vinegar. Cook over very low heat or over hot, not boiling, water, stirring constantly, until smooth and thick enough to mound slightly. Stir in butter or margarine and cream or milk; chill. When ready to use thin, if necessary, with more cream or milk.

Dressing should be about as thick as heavy cream. Keep stored in refrigerator in covered container. Makes about 1½ cups.

Boiled Dressing Variations

To 1 cup Old-Fashioned Boiled Dressing blend in your choice of any one of the following:

Egg: 1 hard-cooked egg, chopped; 1 tablespoon parsley. For meat, vegetable, and seafood salads.

Onion: 3 tablespoons pickled onions, chopped; 1 teaspoon Worcestershire sauce. For seafood and green salads.

Dill: 2 tablespoons chopped fresh dill. For seafood salads.

Chapter Twenty

Sauces, Marinades, and Bastes

In the fine restaurants of the world, the saucier or chef in charge of sauces is second only to the master chef himself. To achieve this lofty position the saucier has served a long apprenticeship, for it is upon the mastery of his art that the reputation of the restaurant often depends. Perhaps that's why so many homemakers are hesitant about making sauces— they feel sauces are mysterious and should exist only in the world of haute cuisine. Not so! There is little mystery to making them even though they take time, patience, and watching. The three most important basic sauces for meat, fish, and vegetables are *White* (cream sauce or Béchamel), *Brown*, and *Egg-and-Butter*.

Each is made in its own special way. By simply changing or adding ingredients you get countless variations—each with a different name.

Secrets of Sauces

· To have the best sauce, cook with the very best ingredients.
· White and Brown Sauces start with a roux. The method of making the roux is described in each of the sauce families and you'll also find it along with a description of other methods needed to make good sauces in our glossary of terms.
· When egg yolks are used, beat them slightly and warm them by mixing in at least half of the hot sauce. If you add the egg to the hot sauce, it coagulates instead of blending in and the sauce curdles.

· When a recipe calls for egg yolks and cream, they may be beaten together and added to the sauce without danger of curdling.

Glossary of Terms in Sauce Cookery

Correct Seasoning. A smart cook will always taste as the recipe proceeds to decide whether the taste is satisfactory or would be improved by the addition of a little more salt, a smidgen of pepper, or a squeeze of lemon juice.

Deglaze. When meat or poultry (usually) has been roasted or sautéed, there is a rich brown essence in the bottom of the pan. This is an important flavor ingredient. To make use of this essence, pour off all grease, add a small amount of stock, wine, or water to the pan. Stir and scrape over low heat until you have captured all the essence in liquid form (deglazing). This liquid is now the base for a flavorful sauce.

Enrich. In the art of sauce making; this is the addition of cream, eggs, or butter to a basic sauce, which will change taste, consistency, and appearance. Usually a sauce is made thick enough so that the enrichment will not thin it too much.

Glaze. As applied to entrées, a process of coating cooked food with a rich sauce and browning in a very hot oven or broiler.

Poach. A method of cooking used especially for delicate fish or other foods whose appearance and consistency would be ruined by vi orous boiling. The food is just covered with cold liquid, usually wine or water, then placed in a moderate oven or very gently simmered in a skillet on top of the range until just cooked. The food is removed from the liquid, then the poaching liquid is reduced to form a concentrated flavor base for the sauce.

Reduce. To cook a liquid until it is reduced in volume. This reduction concentrates flavors and is an essential procedure in making sauces.

Roux. In French cooking, the flour and butter, which begin your sauce and thicken it, are cooked together for several minutes before adding the liquid. The cooking eliminates the raw taste of flour and allows the flour particles to absorb the liquid smoothly. In a brown roux, the butter and flour are cooked until they are amber brown, which imparts a delightfully different taste to the sauce.

Sauté. To brown and cook foods in a small quantity of hot fat. Some foods are merely browned, others are cooked completely. For success in sautéeing, have fat hot, food dry, and do not crowd pan.

WHITE SAUCE FAMILY

White sauces are made with a white roux and milk or a white stock such as chicken, veal, or fish. The roux, that is the flour and butter or margarine, is cooked several minutes to eliminate any raw flour taste and to get the flour ready to absorb liquid. The basic sauce is known as Béchamel.

BÉCHAMEL (*White Sauce*)

2 tbs. butter or margarine	Dash of cayenne (optional)
3 tbs. flour	2 c. hot milk
¼ tsp. salt	

Melt butter or margarine in saucepan; stir in flour. Cook slowly over low heat, stirring constantly, until the roux bubbles and foams for about 3 minutes. It will be slightly golden but should not brown. Remove from heat. Add salt, cayenne, and milk. Stir rapidly with a wooden spoon or beat vigorously with a wire whisk. Cook over medium heat, stirring constantly, until sauce bubbles. Cook 1 minute longer. Use as a base for other sauces, for creamed soups, vegetables, and soufflés. Makes 2 cups.

Velouté Sauce (*Velvet Sauce*)

This is a variant of Béchamel and may be a fish, chicken, or veal stock velouté depending on the stock used. To make Velouté Sauce, substitute 2 cups hot fish stock, chicken stock, or veal stock for hot milk in Béchamel Sauce. Uses of this sauce depend upon the source of the liquid. Fish stock velouté will sauce a fish dish.

Soubise Sauce (*Onion Sauce*)

This is a smooth onion sauce based on either the Béchamel or Velouté Sauce, depending on its use and your preference. Use it for au gratin dishes, chicken, eggs, or vegetables. Cook 1 cup chopped onion in 3 tablespoons butter or margarine over low heat until very tender. Do not allow them to brown. Press onions through fine sieve or food mill. Prepare Béchamel or Velouté Sauce; stir in onion mixture.

Cari Sauce (*Curry Sauce*)

Mild or hot, this is one of the most useful sauces in the White Sauce family. It is good with chicken, seafood, vegetables, and eggs. Cook ½ cup minced onion in 2 tablespoons butter or margarine over low heat until soft. Stir in 1 to 2 tablespoons curry powder, 3 tablespoons flour, and ¼ teaspoon salt. Cook, stirring constantly, 3 minutes. Add 2 cups hot milk, or fish or meat stock. Stir rapidly until thickened and bubbly. Cook 1 minute longer.

Parisienne Sauce

Also a variant of Béchamel Sauce. Prepare sauce, using 1 cup hot milk and 1 cup fish stock. Beat 2 egg yolks and ½ cup heavy cream. Stir at least half the hot sauce slowly into egg yolk mixture; blend into sauce in saucepan. Cook 1 minute. Add 1 tablespoon lemon juice. A classic example of its use is Fish Filets, Normandy Style (*page 234*).

Mornay Sauce

A variant of Béchamel or Velouté Sauce. Either Swiss or Parmesan cheese or a combination of the two may be used. Stir ¼ to ⅓ cup grated Swiss cheese and 2 tablespoons grated Parmesan cheese into the Béchamel or Velouté Sauce. It must not be allowed to boil after the cheese is added. It is used with vegetables, spaghetti, eggs, fish, or shellfish.

Caper Sauce

A variant of Velouté Sauce, a piquant sauce ideally suited for broiled fish or poached fish. Stir 2 tablespoons lemon juice into hot Velouté Sauce made with fish stock (chicken stock may be substituted). Beat 2 egg yolks with 2 tablespoons heavy cream; blend in a small amount of hot sauce; blend into mixture in saucepan. Stir in ¼ cup drained capers.

Egg Sauce

A welcome topping for fish, croquettes, or vegetables. Prepare Béchamel Sauce. Stir in 2 chopped hard-cooked eggs, 1 tablespoon chopped parsley, and ¼ teaspoon ground nutmeg.

Mustard Dill Sauce

Prepare Béchamel Sauce. Stir in 2 teaspoons prepared mustard, ½ teaspoon dill seed, and ½ teaspoon grated lemon rind. Beat 2 egg yolks slightly. Blend in half the hot sauce; blend into mixture in saucepan. Cook 1 minute. Stir in 2 tablespoons lemon juice. Serve with salmon steaks, ham loaf, or vegetables.

Cheese Sauce

Prepare Béchamel Sauce. Add 2 cups shredded process American cheese, 1 tablespoon Worcestershire sauce, and 1 teaspoon dry mustard.

Mushroom-Cheese Sauce

A sauce to dress up a meat loaf or a soufflé, and quick to make. Prepare Béchamel Sauce. Add ½ cup shredded process American cheese and 1 can (3 to 4 ounces) sliced mushrooms, drained.

White Sauce for Special Uses

To use White Sauce as a binder for croquettes or in casserole dishes or vegetable dishes, several consistencies or thicknesses may be required. Prepare as directed in Béchamel Sauce using proportions below.

	Thin	Medium	Thick
Butter	1 tbs.	2 tbs.	4 tbs.
Flour	1 tbs.	2 tbs.	4 tbs.
Salt	¼ tsp.	¼ tsp.	¼ tsp.
Pepper	Dash	Dash	Dash
Milk	1 c.	1 c.	1 c.

BROWN SAUCE FAMILY

French cuisine considers the Sauce Espagnole the basic Brown Sauce. As it requires long, long cooking we are including a simplified Brown Sauce recipe. Brown Sauces are thickened with a brown roux. The flour and fat are cooked slowly until amber colored and care must be taken to prevent scorching which will impair the flavor and thickening of the sauce.

BROWN SAUCE

¼ c. minced onion (1 small)
¼ c. minced carrot
¼ c. minced celery
¼ c. butter or margarine
3 tbs. flour

2 cans (10½ oz. ea.) condensed beef bouillon, heated or 3 c. hot beef stock
2 tbs. tomato paste

Cook onion, carrot, and celery in butter or margarine in saucepan until soft but not brown. Stir in flour; cook over low heat, stirring constantly, until mixture is amber brown (be careful not to burn). This is a brown roux. Remove from heat. Add beef bouillon or stock. Stir rapidly with a wooden spoon or beat vigorously with a wire whisk. Cook over low heat, stirring constantly, until mixture bubbles and is thickened. Beat in tomato paste. Strain, if desired. Cook over low heat 30 minutes, stirring occasionally. Taste and correct seasoning. Makes about 2 cups.

SAUCE ROBERT

A brown mustard sauce, especially good with pork (roasts or chops), boiled beef, hamburgers, and broiled chicken.

½ c. minced onion
(1 medium)
¼ c. chopped
carrot
¼ c. chopped
celery
2 tbs. butter or
margarine
1 c. dry white wine
4 tbs. butter or
margarine

3 tbs. flour
2 cans (10½ oz.
ea.) condensed
beef bouillon or
3 c. hot beef stock
2 tbs. prepared
mustard
2 tbs. chopped
parsley

Sauté onion, carrot, and celery in 2 tablespoons butter or margarine in saucepan until soft, but not brown. Add wine; simmer over low heat until mixture is reduced to about ½ cup. Cook 4 tablespoons butter or margarine and flour in saucepan over medium heat, stirring constantly until mixture is amber brown (brown roux). Add bouillon or stock; cook until bubbly; add reduced wine mixture. Continue cooking over low heat, 25 to 30 minutes, stirring occasionally. Mixture will thicken to a sauce consistency as it reduces. Press sauce through sieve. Add mustard and parsley. Reheat just to boiling. Makes about 2 cups.

HUNTER'S SAUCE
(Chasseur Sauce)

¼ c. butter or
margarine
½ lb. mushrooms,
sliced
1 clove of garlic,
crushed
½ c. chopped
onion
(1 medium)
2 tbs. flour

¼ tsp. leaf thyme,
crumbled
¼ tsp. leaf tarragon, crumbled
1 tsp. bottled meat
glaze
1 can (13½ oz.)
chicken broth
1 c. dry white wine
1 can (1 lb.) tomatoes

Heat butter or margarine in large saucepan. Sauté mushrooms, garlic, and onion until soft. Stir in flour, thyme, and tarragon; cook 1 minute, stirring constantly. Add meat glaze, chicken broth, wine, and tomatoes. Cook over low heat, stirring constantly, until bubbly and thickened; cook 1 minute longer. Taste; correct seasonings. Makes about 4½ cups.

EGG AND BUTTER SAUCE FAMILY

This group of sauces is sometimes called the Hollandaise family for all the variants stem from this one sauce. It is probably the best-known sauce of all and the one many people hesitate to try. These sauces, with their high concentration of egg yolks, are usually cooked in a double boiler rather than over direct heat because it is easier to control the cooking of the egg yolks. Follow the directions carefully and you'll find it's not difficult to make a good Hollandaise.

HOLLANDAISE SAUCE

3 egg yolks
¼ c. lemon juice

12 tbs. butter or
margarine (¾ c.)

Beat egg yolks and lemon juice together in top of double boiler. Add 6 tablespoons butter or margarine. Place over hot, not boiling, water. Stir rapidly until butter or margarine melts. Add remaining 6 tablespoons butter or margarine. Continue stirring until it is melted and sauce is thickened. Leftover sauce may be kept in the refrigerator. Use Hollandaise with vegetables, fish, or eggs. Makes about 1½ cups.

Mousseline Sauce

A variant of Hollandaise, excellent with fish and vegetables. Fold ½ cup heavy cream, whipped, into 1½ cups Hollandaise Sauce just before serving. Makes about 2½ cups.

EASY HOLLANDAISE

2 egg yolks
3 tbs. lemon juice

½ c. butter or
margarine
Dash of cayenne

Stir egg yolks and lemon juice in saucepan until blended. Add one half the butter or margarine. Stir briskly over low heat until butter is melted. Add remaining butter or margarine and cayenne; continue to stir briskly until butter or margarine is melted and sauce is thickened. Serve at once. Leftover sauce may be kept in refrigerator in tightly covered jar. Makes about ⅔ cup.

Cucumber Sauce

Stir ⅓ cup well-drained grated cucumber into Easy Hollandaise Sauce. Just right for salmon loaf, or hot cooked shrimp.

BÉARNAISE SAUCE

Related to Hollandaise though it uses wine, vinegar, and tarragon for its distinctive flavor. It is recommended for use with steaks, broiled chicken, and fish.

¼ c. vinegar
⅓ c. dry white wine
1 tbs. minced onion
1 tsp. leaf tarragon, crumbled
¼ tsp. salt
3 egg yolks
3 tbs. cold butter or margarine
½ c. melted butter or margarine
2 tbs. minced parsley

Combine vinegar, wine, onion, tarragon, and salt in saucepan. Boil rapidly until reduced to 2 tablespoons; strain. Beat egg yolks in top of double boiler until thick; beat in vinegar mixture. Place over hot, not boiling, water. Add cold butter or margarine, a tablespoon at a time, beating rapidly after each addition. Add melted butter or margarine slowly; continue to beat until quite thick. Stir in parsley. Keep warm over hot water. Makes about 1½ cups.

MOCK HOLLANDAISE SAUCE

2 tbs. butter or margarine
1 c. mayonnaise or salad dressing
2 to 4 tbs. lemon juice

Melt butter or margarine in small saucepan. Stir in mayonnaise or salad dressing and lemon juice. Cook over low heat just until hot. Do not boil. Makes 1 cup.

BUTTER SAUCES

DRAWN BUTTER

Melt ½ cup butter or margarine in small saucepan over low heat; do not brown. For lobster, vegetables, and steaks.

Lemon Butter

Stir 1 tablespoon lemon juice into melted butter or margarine. Good with green vegetables and lobster.

Mustard Butter

Add 2 teaspoons prepared mustard gradually to melted butter or margarine. Serve with steaks, hamburgers, and fish.

Curry Butter

Melt butter or margarine with 1 teaspoon curry powder. Add 1 tablespoon lemon juice. Nice with shellfish.

BROWN BUTTER

Heat ½ cup butter or margarine over low heat until amber brown. Good with fish filets.

GARLIC BUTTER

Cream ½ cup butter or margarine with 2 finely chopped cloves of garlic. Add ¼ teaspoon salt and a dash of pepper. Chill. Use as topping for steaks and for making garlic bread.

ROQUEFORT BUTTER

Cream ½ cup butter or margarine, ¼ cup crumbled Roquefort cheese, ½ teaspoon Worcestershire sauce, and 1 teaspoon lemon juice. Chill. Use as topping for steaks, chops, and hamburgers.

MAÎTRE D'HÔTEL BUTTER

½ c. butter or margarine
1 tsp. chopped green onions
1 tsp. chopped parsley
1 tbs. lemon juice

Cream butter or margarine. Blend in onions, parsley, and lemon juice. Serve with steaks, chops, and broiled chicken.

ALMOND SAUCE

⅓ c. butter or margarine
½ c. slivered, blanched almonds
¼ c. dry sherry
2 tbs. lemon juice
2 tbs. chopped parsley

Melt butter or margarine in saucepan. Add almonds; cook 3 minutes or until lightly browned. Stir in sherry, lemon juice, and parsley. Heat through. Makes about ¾ cup.

OTHER SAUCES

DILL SAUCE

Good on lima beans, spinach, green beans, Brussels sprouts, or broccoli.

2 tbs. butter or margarine	1 tsp. dill weed or 2 tsp. finely chopped fresh dill
1 c. dairy sour cream	

Melt butter or margarine in small saucepan. Stir in sour cream and dill. Cook over low heat just until hot. Do not boil. Makes 1 cup.

MUSTARD-DILL SAUCE

¼ c. butter or margarine	½ tsp. grated lemon rind
⅛ tsp. pepper	2 tbs. flour
1½ tsp. salt	1½ c. milk
2 tsp. prepared mustard	2 egg yolks
½ tsp. dill seed	2 tbs. lemon juice

Melt butter or margarine in saucepan. Stir in pepper, salt, mustard, dill, lemon rind, and flour. Add milk slowly. Cook, stirring, until sauce is smooth and just beginning to bubble around the edges. Beat egg yolks; stir about half the sauce into yolks. Stir into sauce in pan; cook, stirring, 1 minute. Add lemon juice. Strain. Makes about 1½ cups.

TOMATO SAUCE

1 can (1 lb.) tomatoes	1 tsp. sugar
½ c. chopped onion (1 medium)	¼ tsp. ground cloves
½ tsp. salt	2 tbs. butter or margarine
¼ tsp. pepper	2 tbs. flour

Combine tomatoes, onion, salt, pepper, sugar, and cloves in saucepan. Bring to boiling over medium heat. Cook 10 minutes, stirring occasionally. Press through sieve or food mill. Melt butter or margarine in saucepan; stir in flour; cook 1 minute, stirring constantly. Add tomato mixture. Cook, stirring constantly, until thickened and bubbly. Makes 1½ cups.

SPANISH SAUCE

¾ c. finely chopped onion	2 tbs. chopped parsley
1 clove of garlic, crushed	¼ c. chopped green olives
2 tbs. pure vegetable or olive oil	¼ tsp. leaf marjoram, crumbled
2 tbs. butter or margarine	2 tsp. chili powder
1 can (1 lb. 13 oz.) tomatoes	1 small bay leaf
	½ tsp. sugar
	¾ tsp. salt
	⅛ tsp. pepper

Sauté onion and garlic in oil and butter or margarine until soft. Add tomatoes; break up with a fork. Add parsley, olives, and seasonings. Simmer, uncovered, 15 minutes or until slightly thickened. Remove bay leaf. Makes about 3 cups.

SWEET-SOUR RAISIN SAUCE

This sauce is nice with tongue and ham.

1 tbs. cornstarch	¾ c. water
¼ tsp. dry mustard	⅓ c. currant jelly
¼ c. brown sugar, firmly packed	¾ c. raisins
2 tbs. vinegar	2 tbs. slivered orange rind

Blend cornstarch, mustard, and brown sugar; stir in vinegar and water; add currant jelly. Cook, stirring constantly, until mixture thickens and is bubbly; add raisins. Just before serving add orange rind. Makes about 1½ cups.

MUSHROOM-WINE SAUCE

½ lb. mushrooms, sliced	½ tsp. salt
¼ c. chopped green onions	Dash of pepper
	1 c. chicken broth
¼ c. butter or margarine	½ c. dry red wine
2 tbs. flour	2 tbs. chopped parsley

Sauté mushrooms and onions in butter or margarine in saucepan over medium heat until soft. Stir in flour, salt, and pepper; cook 1 minute. Stir in broth and wine. Cook, stirring constantly, until thickened and bubbly. Add parsley. Makes about 2 cups.

HORSERADISH SAUCE

4 tbs. butter or margarine	2 c. milk
4 tbs. flour	½ c. prepared horseradish
1 tsp. salt	1 tbs. lemon juice

Melt butter or margarine in saucepan; blend in flour and salt. Stir in milk gradually. Cook over medium heat, stirring constantly, until mixture thickens and comes to boiling. Remove from heat; stir in horseradish and lemon juice. Makes 2 cups.

Creamy Horseradish Sauce

2 tsp. minced onion	1 c. light cream
2 tbs. butter or margarine	1 to 2 tbs. prepared horseradish
2 tbs. flour	

Sauté onion in butter or margarine until soft. Stir in flour. Add cream slowly. Cook over medium heat, stirring constantly, until thickened and bubbly. Stir in horseradish. Makes 1 cup.

Horseradish Cream

½ c. heavy cream	1 to 2 tbs. prepared horseradish

Whip cream; fold in horseradish. Chill. Makes 1 cup.

SHRIMP SAUCE

2 tbs. butter or margarine	1½ c. milk or fish stock
2 tbs. flour	1 tbs. lemon juice
½ tsp. salt	2 tbs. dry sherry
½ tsp. dry mustard	2 egg yolks, beaten
Pinch of cayenne	1 can (4½ to 5 oz.) shrimp, drained

Melt butter or margarine in small saucepan. Blend in flour, salt, mustard, and cayenne. Add milk or stock gradually. Cook over medium heat, stirring constantly, until mixture comes to boiling. Remove from heat; add lemon juice and sherry. Stir half the mixture into beaten egg yolks; return to saucepan. Add shrimp; heat through. Makes about 2 cups.

TARTAR SAUCE

A favorite accompaniment for all fish and seafood.

2 tbs. finely chopped sweet or sour pickle	1 tbs. minced parsley
1 tbs. minced onion	2 tbs. lemon juice
	1 c. mayonnaise or salad dressing

Blend pickle, onion, parsley, and lemon juice into mayonnaise or salad dressing. Makes 1½ cups.

Marinades and Bastes

Just what is a marinade or a baste? Actually, a marinade is a thin sauce, usually with a wine, vinegar, or lemon-juice base, seasoned with condiments and herbs, in which food is soaked before it's cooked. It penetrates the food to flavor and tenderize it. A baste is a sauce, sometimes thin, sometimes thick, brushed on the food to give it a special flavor on the outside and at the same time keep it moist. Both may be served as a sauce with the cooked foods.

Secrets of Marinades and Bastes

· If you wish a marinade to tenderize as well as flavor meat, allow plenty of time for the process—a minimum of one hour.
· Unless the temperature is in the nineties the marinade will penetrate more effectively at room temperature than in the refrigerator
· In very hot weather, when the meat must be refrigerated, cover it with the marinad the night before, leave in the refrigerator un

til an hour before time to cook, then remove to allow it to come to room temperature before cooking.

· Turn the food being marinated several times so that all surfaces will be penetrated.

· Some marinades are also used as basting sauces. If any ingredients are in the marinade that might burn (such as onion slices), strain the marinade before using it to baste.

· A long-handled barbecue brush is best for applying basting sauces to foods roasting over an open fire.

· A kitchen syringe is sometimes better for basting foods roasting in an oven. The syringe is also useful in drawing up sauce from the roasting pan to baste the food with its own drippings.

· If the broiler rack is lined with aluminum foil, punch holes in the foil to allow the fat or oil to drip through.

QUICK-AND-EASY MARINADE

Marinate chicken, flank steak, beef or lamb cubes for shish kebabs in homemade or bottled French dressing or in bottled Italian-style dressing at least 2 hours. Grill or broil, brushing meat with marinade as it cooks.

MARINADE FOR BEEF, LAMB, OR CHICKEN

1 tbs. salt	2 tbs. sugar
3/4 tsp. ground cinnamon	2 tbs. soy sauce
	2 tbs. dry sherry

Combine all ingredients; mix well. Spread mixture on both sides of meat. Marinate 1 to 2 hours. Grill over coals until tender. This marinade is particularly good with flank steak. Enough for 2 to 3 pounds of meat.

ZESTY BEEF MARINADE

3/4 c. Burgundy or Bordeaux wine	1 tsp. salt
3/4 c. olive or pure vegetable oil	1/4 tsp. pepper
	1/2 tsp. leaf oregano, crumbled
1 clove of garlic, mashed	1/2 tsp. leaf basil, crumbled
1 tbs. grated onion	

Combine all ingredients in flat glass or enamel pan; mix well. Add beef; cover; refrigerate overnight. When ready to cook, place beef on greased grill rack; baste with marinade. Grill meat, turning often and basting fre-

quently with marinade. Heat any remaining marinade and serve with beef. Enough for 6 to 7 pounds of beef.

BARBECUE MARINADE FOR LAMB OR PORK

1 can (10½-oz.) condensed beef bouillon or 1 beef-bouillon cube dissolved in 1 c. water	1/2 tsp. dried mint leaves
	Dash of hot-pepper sauce
	1/4 tsp. pepper
2 c. cider vinegar	1 tbs. mixed whole pickling spices
2 tbs. Worcestershire sauce	3 slices orange
	2 slices lemon
1 tbs. bottled meat sauce	1 tbs. catsup
1 tsp. salt	1/2 tsp. leaf basil, crumbled
1 tbs. sugar	1/2 tsp. leaf oregano, crumbled

Combine all ingredients; simmer 30 minutes; strain. Pour over meat in shallow glass or enamel pan. Marinate at least 2 hours, turning frequently. Baste meat often with marinade as it cooks. Sufficient for 5 to 7 pounds of meat.

TERIYAKI MARINADE

1 large clove of garlic, crushed	1 tbs. sugar
	1 tbs. vinegar
2 tsp. ground ginger	1/2 c. soy sauce
	1/4 c. dry white wine

Combine all ingredients; mix well. Use to marinate 2 pounds of cubed beef, pork, or fish. Beef and pork should marinate 3 hours, fish 1 hour. Thread cubes on skewers and broil, turning to cook all sides.

LAMB BASTING SAUCE

3/4 c. dry sherry	1 tsp. salt
1 tbs. chopped parsley	1/4 tsp. pepper
2 tbs. lemon juice	1/2 tsp. leaf rosemary, crumbled
1 tbs. pure vegetable oil	1/2 tsp. leaf oregano, crumbled
1 tsp. grated onion	

Combine all ingredients in bowl; let stand several hours to blend flavors. Brush frequently over meat as it grills or roasts. Enough for 5 pounds of lamb.

ZIPPY BEEF BASTING SAUCE

¼ lb. butter or margarine	¼ c. chili sauce
¾ c. vinegar	1 tbs. brown sugar
1 tbs. prepared mustard	½ tsp. crushed dried red peppers
2 tbs. Worcestershire sauce	2 tbs. grated onion

Combine all ingredients in saucepan; simmer 15 minutes. Brush frequently on meat as it cooks on grill. Enough for 5-pound roast or steak.

LEMON BASTING SAUCE (FOR TURKEY OR CHICKEN)

¾ c. butter or margarine	½ tsp. pepper
2 tsp. paprika	½ c. lemon juice
1 tsp. sugar	½ c. water
1 tsp. salt	Few drops hot-pepper sauce
½ tsp. dry mustard	

Melt butter or margarine. Add paprika, sugar, salt, mustard, pepper, lemon juice, water, and hot-pepper sauce. Baste chicken or turkey frequently with sauce during grilling. If you wish, add 2 tablespoons minced or grated onion to the sauce. Makes about 1½ cups.

SWEET AND TANGY BASTING SAUCE FOR PORK

1 c. apricot preserves	¼ tsp. ground cloves
½ c. orange or pineapple juice	¼ tsp. ground ginger
1½ tbs. prepared mustard	

Combine apricot preserves, fruit juice, mustard, cloves, and ginger in small saucepan; simmer 5 minutes. Use to baste loin of pork, ham, or spareribs. Thin remaining glaze with additional fruit juice and serve as a sauce with meat. Makes 1⅓ cups.

PINEAPPLE BASTE FOR HAM STEAK

1 c. pineapple juice	¼ c. vinegar
½ c. brown sugar, firmly packed	2 tsp. dry mustard

Blend pineapple juice, sugar, vinegar, and mustard. Baste ham steak several times during grilling. Makes about 1⅓ cups.

FRUIT BARBECUE BASTE FOR SPARERIBS

1 can (1 lb. 1 oz.) apricot halves, drained	1 tsp. hot-pepper sauce
1 can (1 lb. 14 oz.) freestone peaches, drained	2 tbs. tomato paste
	1 tsp. dry mustard
	¼ tsp. seasoned pepper
¾ c. vinegar	¼ tsp. seasoned salt
¾ c. brown sugar, firmly packed	1 tbs. butter or margarine

Chop apricots and peaches very finely; sieve or whirl in blender. Combine with vinegar, brown sugar, hot-pepper sauce, tomato paste, dry mustard, pepper, salt, and butter or margarine in saucepan. Simmer 25 minutes, stirring occasionally. Bake or spit-cook spareribs. Brush ribs with sauce 30 minutes before end of cooking time; finish cooking. Makes 2 cups.

Chapter Twenty-One

Desserts

Desserts are the perfect ending to a meal—the pièce de résistance for a very special occasion—a delectable dish to satisfy a "sweet tooth." Desserts can be traditional classics that will remind you of bygone days when grandmother's specialty was Snow Pudding or Floating Island. Or they can be brand new—made from one of the latest packaged puddings and cake mixes. Their variety is endless: Fruits, Gelatins, Rices, Custards, Old-Fashioned Short Cakes, Puddings, Tortes, Cream Puffs, Meringues, Dessert Pancakes, fancy and plain, Soufflés, Cheesecakes, Refrigerator and Frozen Desserts, Ice Creams, and Dessert Sauces. Each one is guaranteed to fill everyone with anticipation as they hear that sweet word, dessert.

FRUIT DESSERTS

APPLE-THAT-TOPS-ALL

1 c. sugar
1 c. water
¾ c. red cinnamon candies (3 jars)
6 medium-size red apples
½ pt. vanilla ice cream
2 egg whites
¼ c. sugar

Combine sugar, water, and cinnamon candies in 10-inch skillet with cover; simmer syrup until candies are dissolved. Wash apples; core; pare skin 1 inch down from top; place in syrup. Cover; simmer, turning once or twice, until apples are soft but still hold their shape. Place in baking dish; pour syrup over; cool; chill. Shape tiny balls of ice cream to fit tops of apples; keep hard in freezer. Just before serving, preheat broiler; turn heat down halfway. Beat egg whites until foamy. Beat in sugar gradually at low speed; increase speed; continue beating until meringue stands in stiff, glossy peaks. Place ice cream on chilled apples; cover thickly and quickly with meringue, using spoon or pastry bag and tube. Place under broiler 2 to 3 minutes or until meringue is lightly touched with brown. Serve at once. Makes 6 servings.

APPLE BETTY À LA MODE

½ c. melted butter or margarine
3 c. fresh bread cubes (6 slices)
6 c. sliced, pared, cored, cooking apples
½ c. brown sugar, firmly packed
1 tsp. ground cinnamon
½ tsp. ground allspice
⅓ c. water
1 pt. vanilla ice cream

Heat oven to 375° F. Mix melted butter or margarine and bread cubes together; reserve ½ cup for topping. Combine remainder with apples, brown sugar, cinnamon, and allspice; stir in water. Turn into greased 1½-quart casserole; sprinkle with reserved bread cubes; cover. Bake 30 minutes; remove cover; bake 30 minutes longer. Serve warm with ice cream. Makes 6 servings.

APPLE CRISP

This is a wonderfully nostalgic dish that reminds us of home.

4 c. sliced, pared,
and cored
cooking apples
1 c. flour
¾ c. brown sugar,
firmly packed

1 tsp. ground
cinnamon
¼ tsp. ground
nutmeg
½ c. butter or
margarine

Heat oven to 375° F. Put apples into a greased 1½-quart baking dish. Blend flour, sugar, cinnamon, nutmeg, and butter or margarine; sprinkle over the apples. Bake 30 to 35 minutes or until the apples are tender and the topping is slightly crusty and brown. Serve warm with cream or whipped cream, if desired. Makes 6 to 8 servings.

APPLE DUMPLINGS

2 c. water
1 c. sugar
½ c. grenadine
Pastry for 2-crust
pie (*page 405*)
6 pared and cored
medium-sized
cooking apples

½ c. brown sugar,
firmly packed
¼ tsp. ground
cinnamon
2 tbs. butter or
margarine

Heat oven to 425° F. Combine water, sugar, and grenadine in saucepan; bring to boiling; lower heat; simmer 5 minutes. Divide pastry into 6 equal portions. Roll each portion to a 7-inch square. Place apples on centers of squares. Combine brown sugar, cinnamon, and butter or margarine; spoon mixture into centers of apples. Moisten edges of pastry squares. Bring pastry up and over apples; pinch to seal. Place in baking pan. Pour syrup around apples. Bake 30 to 35 minutes or until pastry is golden and apples are tender. Makes 6 dumplings.

Baked Dumplings: Heat oven to 425° F. Place apple-filled pastries on greased cookie sheet. Bake 30 to 35 minutes until golden brown. Serve warm with Holiday Hard Sauce (*page 400*).

STRAWBERRY RHUBARB BAKE

1 lb. rhubarb
1 pt. strawberries,
washed and
hulled
1 tbs. lemon juice
½ c. sugar
½ c. flour

½ c. brown sugar,
firmly packed
½ tsp. salt
¼ c. butter or
margarine
Heavy cream

Cut rhubarb into ½-inch pieces; mix with strawberries. Place in shallow 9-inch baking dish; sprinkle with lemon juice and sugar. Combine flour, brown sugar, and salt. Cut butter or margarine into flour mixture with pastry blender or two knives until it resembles cornmeal. Spoon over fruit in baking dish. Bake at 375° F. for 25 minutes. Serve warm or cold with heavy cream. Makes 6 servings.

STEWED PEARS WITH MINTED CUSTARD

1½ c. sugar
¼ tsp. ground
cardamom
2 whole cloves
1 c. water

6 pears, peeled,
halved, and cored
3 eggs
¼ tsp. salt
2 c. milk
½ tsp. mint extract

Combine 1 cup sugar, cardamom, cloves, and water. Add pears; bring to boiling. Reduce heat; cover; simmer 10 minutes or until pears are just tender. Remove from heat; remove and discard cloves. Beat eggs, ½ cup sugar, and salt in top of double boiler. Stir in milk. Cook over hot water, stirring constantly, until mixture coats spoon. Remove from heat; add mint extract. Cool; chill. Serve pears warm or cold with minted custard. Makes 6 servings.

PEARS CARDINALE

2 cans (1 lb. 14 oz.
ea.) pear halves,
drained
1 qt. vanilla ice
cream

2 pkgs. (10 oz. ea.)
frozen rasp-
berries, thawed
2 tsp. cornstarch
¼ c. sugar

Place pear halves, cut sides down, on wax paper on cookie sheet or flat dish. Scoop ice cream into balls or shape with large spoon into serving-size portions; place on foil; return to freezer to keep firm. Put raspberries with juice through a fine sieve, rubbing through as much pulp as possible. Combine cornstarch and sugar; add raspberry purée slowly; blend well. Cook over medium heat until thickened and bubbly; cool; chill. Spoon a small amount of raspberry sauce over each pear to coat. Arrange ice cream balls in serving dish; leave space around edge for pear halves. Carefully place pears around ice cream. Spoon remaining sauce over pears. Sprinkle with nuts, if desired. Assembled dish may be returned to freezer, but not for more than 1 hour. Makes 8 to 12 servings.

FLAMING STRAWBERRIES À L'ORANGE

3 pts. large ripe strawberries	2 tbs. butter or margarine
1 large thin-skinned orange	¼ c. sugar
	¼ c. Cognac
	2 tbs. kirsch

Wash, hull, and drain strawberries. Peel orange with sharp knife or vegetable peeler. Remove any white from inside of rind; cut rind into thin strips; simmer in small amount of water 5 minutes. Squeeze orange; reserve juice. Melt butter or margarine in blazer pan of chafing dish or in skillet, over low heat. Add sugar, rind, and strawberries. Cook, stirring constantly, 1 minute. Add Cognac; cook until mixture just bubbles. Heat kirsch in small pan until it is hot but does not boil. Carefully ignite kirsch with long match; pour quickly over strawberries. Stir gently until flames die. Add orange juice. Serve at once as is or over vanilla ice cream. Makes 8 servings.

MELON EN SURPRISE

2 cantaloupes	Sauterne
1 honeydew melon	1 pt. lemon sherbet
Confectioners' sugar	½ lb. seedless green grapes

Cut a V-shaped plug from top of each cantaloupe; remove seeds; stand each melon securely in small bowl. Sprinkle melon cavities with confectioners' sugar. Scoop enough melon balls from honeydew to fill cavities of cantaloupes. Pour sauterne into cantaloupes to completely fill all spaces; replace plugs. Chill several hours. To serve: drain wine from melons; reserve; cut melons into serving pieces; arrange honeydew on each serving; spoon wine over. Top with a tiny scoop of sherbet and a small bunch of green grapes. Makes 8 servings.

GOOSEBERRY FOOL

3 c. gooseberries	2 c. heavy cream
½ c. brown sugar, firmly packed	½ c. sifted confectioners' sugar
½ c. water	

Wash gooseberries; remove any blossoms and stems. Put into saucepan with brown sugar and water. Bring to boiling; reduce heat; simmer, uncovered, until gooseberries become soft and mushy. Remove from heat; press through sieve or food mill. Chill gooseberry purée. Whip cream until it begins to thicken; add confectioners' sugar; continue beating until thick. Fold in chilled gooseberry purée. Pile into sherbet or parfait glasses; chill. Makes 6 servings.

PRUNE WHIP

1½ c. sieved, cooked prunes	Dash of nutmeg
½ tsp. grated lemon rind	¼ c. chopped nuts
	3 egg whites
1 tbs. lemon juice	½ c. sugar

Combine prunes, lemon rind, lemon juice, nutmeg, and nuts. Beat egg whites until foamy; beat in sugar gradually; continue beating until mixture stands in stiff, glossy peaks. Fold in prune mixture. Chill. Serve with cream or with Custard Sauce Royale (*page 399*). Makes 6 servings.

Baked Prune Whip: Heat oven to 350° F. Prepare Prune Whip. Turn mixture into lightly buttered 1½- to 2-quart baking dish. Set in pan of hot water 1-inch deep. Bake 30 to 35 minutes until whip is puffed and a thin coating has formed on top. Makes 6 servings.

VIENNESE APPLE STRUDEL

3 c. sifted all-
purpose flour
¼ tsp. salt
1 egg
1 tbs. pure vegetable
oil
1 c. lukewarm water
1 c. fresh bread
crumbs (2 slices)
½ c. butter or
margarine
½ c. raisins

4 c. chopped, pared,
and cored
cooking apples
½ c. chopped
walnuts
1 tsp. grated lemon
rind
½ c. sugar
1 tsp. ground
cinnamon
5 tbs. melted butter
or margarine
Confectioners'
sugar

Measure flour and salt into bowl; add egg, oil, and water. Work ingredients with hands until dough clings together (it will be soft and sticky); knead on floured board a few times until it can be picked up. Throw ball of dough quickly down on lightly floured board; pick up; throw down again. Continue this process 10 minutes or until dough is silky and pliable. (This is necessary to develop the stretch needed in the dough for delicate paper-thin pastry.) Place dough on lightly floured surface; cover with bowl; let rest 30 minutes.

Prepare filling: fry crumbs in ½ cup butter or margarine until golden; add raisins, apples, walnuts, lemon rind, sugar, and cinnamon. Cover kitchen or card table with clean cloth (an old sheet will do); sprinkle lightly with flour. Roll dough to rectangle as thin as possible. (Remove rings which might tear dough.) Place backs of hands under dough; stretch very, very gently toward you, using a hand-over-hand motion. Continue pulling and stretching in all directions until dough covers table top, and thicker edges hang down. Dough should be extremely thin and semi-transparent. Clip off thick edges with scissors; brush dough with 4 tablespoons melted butter or margarine. Mound filling evenly along one short side an inch from edge leaving about 2 inches uncovered at either side. Fold corners up over filling. Starting from filling end, lift cloth to start strudel rolling; roll, jelly-roll fashion, stopping when end of strudel is underneath. Slide onto buttered cookie sheet, placing diagonally on sheet or bending into a horseshoe to fit. Brush entire surface of strudel with 1 tablespoon melted butter or margarine. Bake at 400° F. for 35 to 40 minutes

or until golden brown. Remove from cookie sheet; sprinkle with confectioners' sugar. Serve warm with whipped cream if desired. Makes 10 servings.

GLAZED FRUIT TOWERS

1 jar (12 oz.)
raspberry,
currant, or apple
jelly
1 tbs. water

1 can (4 oz.)
shredded coconut
6 packaged dessert
shells
Drained canned
fruit

Melt jelly in water in small saucepan over medium heat, stirring constantly. (Use raspberry or currant jelly for red fruits, apple jelly for light-colored fruits.) Cool jelly mixture until it begins to thicken. Spread coconut out on wax paper. Brush sides of dessert shells with jelly mixture; roll in coconut; press coconut in place where necessary to coat sides well. Spoon drained fruit into shells, piling fruit high where possible. Spoon jelly carefully over fruit, glazing all surfaces. Chill.

To fill 6 dessert shells, use any one of the following:
1 can (about 1 lb.) red tart pitted cherries, drained
1 can (1 lb. 14 oz.) unpeeled apricot halves, drained
1 can (1 lb. 13 oz.) whole figs, drained
1 can (1 lb. 14 oz.) fruit cocktail, drained
1 can (1 lb. 15 oz.) dark sweet cherries and 1 can (11 oz.) mandarin oranges, drained
1 can (8½ oz.) sliced pineapple and 1 can (11 oz.) mandarin oranges, drained.

Makes 6 servings.

How to Make Apple Strudel

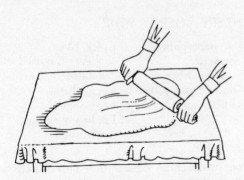

1. Prepare dough according to recipe. Roll out, as thin as possible, on floured cloth on kitchen table or card table to large rectangle or square.

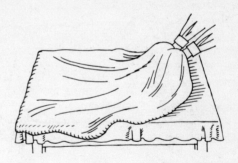

4. Stretch dough until it covers table top. It will be very thin and semitransparent.

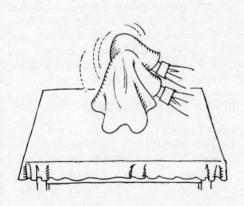

2. Lift dough on back of hands. Let hang. This helps start stretching of dough.

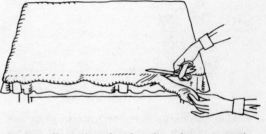

5. Cut off overhanging heavier edges as neatly as possible on all sides, using regular kitchen scissors.

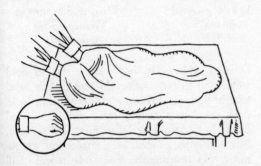

3. Stretch dough in all directions with backs of fists, using a gentle hand-over-hand motion.

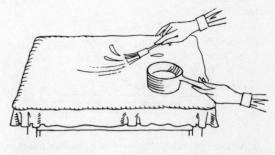

6. Cover surface of dough generously with melted butter or margarine, using a pastry brush.

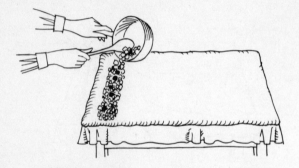

7. Mound filling evenly along one short side an inch in from edge, leaving about 2 inches uncovered at either side.

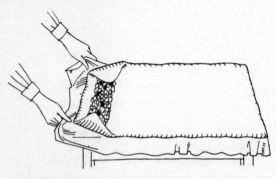

8. Fold corners up over filling. Grasp cloth and dough with both hands and carefully lift end up from table. Continue to lift making dough roll over and over itself.

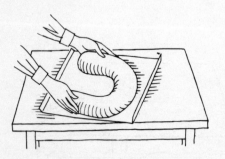

9. Lift roll carefully. Place on large cookie sheet. Shape gently into horseshoe.

GELATIN DESSERTS

CHEERY CHERRY WHIP

¼ c. maraschino liqueur	1 pkg. (3 oz.) cherry-flavored gelatin
2 c. Bing cherries, halved and pitted	2 egg whites
1 c. hot water	4 tbs. sugar
	1 c. heavy cream, whipped

Pour maraschino liqueur over cherry halves. Let stand at room temperature ½ hour. Drain; reserve cherries. Measure liquid; add water if necessary to make ½ cup. Pour hot water over gelatin; stir until thoroughly dissolved. Add maraschino mixture. Chill until consistency of thick syrup. Beat egg whites until stiff. Gradually beat in sugar until meringue forms stiff, glossy peaks. Fold in whippped cream. Beat gelatin until it is light and fluffy and will mound when stirred with a spoon. Quickly fold in cream-meringue mixture and cherries. Spoon into sherbet or parfait glasses; chill several hours. Makes 6 servings.

SURPRISE PLUM PUDDING

2 pkgs. (3 oz. ea.) cherry-flavored gelatin	1 c. finely cut raisins
2 c. hot water	1 c. finely cut cooked prunes
½ c. cold water	1 c. finely cut nuts (walnuts or pecans)
½ c. brandy	
1 can (1 lb.) jellied cranberry sauce	⅓ c. finely cut citron
Dash of salt	1 c. grapenuts cereal
¾ tsp. ground cinnamon	Whipped cream or Foamy Sauce (*page 400*)
¼ tsp. ground cloves	

Dissolve gelatin in hot water; stir in cold water and brandy; place ⅓ cup of this mixture in bottom of 6-cup mold; chill until firm. Add cranberry sauce, salt, cinnamon, and cloves to remaining gelatin; mix until smooth. Stir in raisins, prunes, nuts, citron, and grapenuts; mix thoroughly. Pour into mold; chill 4 hours or more. Unmold; serve with whipped cream or Foamy Sauce. Makes 10 servings.

FRUIT JEWELS

2 pkgs. (3 oz. ea.)
  lime-flavored
  gelatin
1 pkg. (3 oz.)
  lemon-flavored
  gelatin
1 pkg. (3 oz.)
  orange-flavored
  gelatin

4 c. hot water
2 c. cold water
2 egg whites
¼ c. sugar
½ c. heavy cream,
  whipped

Empty the four packages of gelatin into separate bowls. Use 1 cup of hot water to dissolve each flavor; add ½ cup cold water to each. Pour 1 of the lime mixtures and the lemon and orange mixtures into 3 shallow pans to depth of ½ inch; chill until firm; cut into squares. These are the "jewels." Chill remaining package of prepared lime gelatin until thick and syrupy. Beat egg whites until foamy; beat in sugar gradually; continue beating until meringue forms stiff, glossy peaks. Fold meringue, whipped cream, and gelatin jewels into syrupy lime gelatin. Spoon into 9x5x3-inch loaf pan; chill until set, about 3 hours. Unmold; slice to serve. Top with additional whipped cream, if desired. Makes 8 servings.

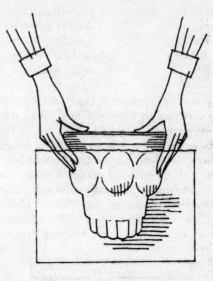

2. Dip mold into warm, not hot, water, just to the depth of gelatin. Remove quickly. Shake gently to loosen gelatin.

To Unmold Gelatin

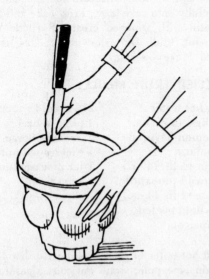

1. Loosen gelatin by running tip of small spatula or paring knife between gelatin and mold.

3. Rinse plate in cold water. Place on top of mold. Hold tightly and invert quickly. Shake holding dish tightly to mold; lift off mold. If gelatin doesn't unmold readily, repeat steps.

CHERRY MOUSSE PARFAIT

1 can (1 lb.) pitted
  dark, sweet
  cherries
¼ c. brandy
Water

1 pkg. (3 oz.)
  cherry-flavored
  gelatin
½ c. heavy cream,
  whipped

Drain cherries; reserve syrup. Cut cherries in half; marinate in brandy 1 hour. Add water to cherry syrup to make 1½ cups liquid. Heat to simmering; remove from heat. Add gelatin; stir until dissolved. Chill until mixture begins to set. Fold in whipped cream. Fold in cherries and brandy. Chill until mousse begins to set. Spoon into six parfait glasses. Chill 2 hours or until firm. Top with additional whipped cream, if desired. Makes 6 servings.

PARTY RIBBON LOAF

1 envelope un-
  flavored gelatin
1½ c. pineapple
  juice
¼ c. granulated
  sugar
Dash of salt
1 tsp. grated lemon
  rind

5 drops red food
  coloring
3 drops yellow food
  coloring
2 c. heavy cream
12 ladyfingers, split
2 tbs. confectioners'
  sugar
4 drops green food
  coloring

Soften gelatin in ¼ cup pineapple juice. Combine remaining 1¼ cups pineapple juice, granulated sugar, and salt in small saucepan; heat to boiling; remove from heat. Add softened gelatin and lemon rind; stir until gelatin is dissolved; divide in half. Tint one half with red food coloring; other half with yellow food coloring. Chill until slightly thickened. Whip ½ cup cream until stiff; fold half into each gelatin mixture; chill until mixtures just begin to set. Line 9x5x3-inch loaf pan with strip of wax paper; place layer of lady-

fingers in pan. Spread yellow gelatin mixture on ladyfingers; top with layer of ladyfingers; spread with pink gelatin mixture; top with remaining ladyfingers. Chill about 2 hours or until firm. Unmold onto serving dish. Whip remaining 1½ cups cream and confectioners' sugar until stiff; tint with green food coloring. Spread on top and sides of loaf; chill 1 hour before serving. Makes 6 servings.

HAWAIIAN DREAM DESSERT

1 pkg. white cake
  mix
1 pkg. (3 oz.) lime-
  flavored gelatin
1½ c. hot water
¼ c. sugar
2 tsp. grated lime
  rind
2 tbs. lime juice
3 egg whites

¼ c. sugar
1 can (1 lb.)
  crushed pine-
  apple, well
  drained
1 c. heavy cream,
  whipped
¾ c. canned flaked
  coconut

Prepare, bake and cool one 8-inch layer from half the package of cake mix according to package directions. Dissolve gelatin in hot water. Add ¼ cup sugar, lime rind and juice. Chill until it begins to thicken. Beat egg whites until foamy; beat in remaining ¼ cup sugar gradually; continue to beat until stiff peaks form. Fold in gelatin mixture. Chill, stirring occasionally, until mixture begins to set. Fold in pineapple. Pour into 1½-quart bowl. Chill about 4 hours or until firm. Loosen edges from side of bowl with thin spatula. Unmold carefully onto cake layer. Frost cake and fruit gelatin with whipped cream. Sprinkle with coconut. Chill. Garnish with oranges, if desired. Makes 8 servings.

JELLIED FRUIT MEDLEY

4 c. hot water
4 pkgs. (3 oz. ea.)
  lemon-flavored
  gelatin
1 can (1 lb. 14 oz.)
  sliced pineapple
1 can (1 lb. 14 oz.)
  whole peeled
  apricots

2½ c. cold water
1 pkg. (8 oz.)
  cream cheese
1 c. chopped nuts
1 jar maraschino
  cherries

Add hot water to gelatin; stir until dissolved. Drain pineapple; drain apricots. Measure ½ cup of each syrup (1 cup total); combine with cold water; stir into gelatin. Cool; chill until syrupy. Cut cheese into 1-inch cubes; roll in nuts; shape firmly into balls. Set a 2½-quart mold firmly in bowl of ice cubes. Spoon thin layer of gelatin into bottom of mold; let set. Remove pits from apricots; cut in half; arrange half the apricots in pattern on set layer of gelatin. Pour thickened gelatin carefully around apricots; chill until set. Proceed in this manner adding cream cheese–nut balls, quartered slices of pineapple, maraschino cherries, and remaining apricot halves in layered design. Allow each layer to set before adding next. Chill mold 4 to 6 hours or overnight. Unmold on serving plate; garnish with fresh mint, if desired. Makes 10 servings.

LEMON SNOW PUDDING

2 envelopes un- flavored gelatin	3 egg whites ¼ tsp. cream of
⅔ c. sugar	tartar
⅛ tsp. salt	¼ c. sugar
3 c. boiling water	1 tsp. grated lemon
⅔ c. lemon juice	rind
Yellow food coloring	

Combine gelatin, ⅔ cup sugar, and salt in mixing bowl. Add water; stir until all ingredients are dissolved; cool. Add lemon juice. For sparkling lemon top, measure about ½ cup of gelatin mixture into small bowl (amount you use will depend on design of your mold, but use no more than ½ cup). Add a drop of yellow food coloring to make a bright lemon-yellow. Pour into 6-cup mold; chill until almost set. Chill remaining gelatin mixture until syrupy. Set bowl in a larger bowl with ice cubes for quick chilling. When gelatin is syrupy, quickly beat egg whites and cream of tartar until soft peaks form; beat in ¼ cup sugar slowly; continue to beat until meringue forms stiff, glossy peaks. Fold syrupy gelatin mixture and grated lemon rind gently into meringue. Spoon carefully into mold. Chill several hours or until firm. Unmold; garnish with fresh, frozen, or canned fruits, as desired. Makes 6 servings.

LEMON FROMAGE

2 envelopes un- flavored gelatin	1 tbs. grated lemon rind
½ c. cold water	½ c. lemon juice
6 egg yolks	6 egg whites
½ c. sugar	¼ c. sugar

Soften gelatin in cold water; dissolve over hot water; cool. Beat egg yolks with ½ cup sugar until light and thick. Fold in lemon rind and juice. Beat egg whites until foamy; beat in ¼ cup sugar slowly; continue to beat until meringue forms stiff glossy peaks. Fold egg-yolk mixture into meringue. Chill slightly until mixture thickens and mounds when spooned. Pour into 1½-quart mold. Chill several hours or overnight. Nice with topping of just-thawed frozen strawberries, raspberries, or peaches. Makes 6 to 8 servings.

When grating citrus fruits, stop when you reach the white part, for it is only the bright-colored skin that has the rich flavoring oils. Use a pastry brush to remove all of the grated rind from the teeth of the grater.

STRAWBERRY CHARLOTTE RUSSE

1 envelope un- flavored gelatin	¼ c. sugar 2 c. heavy cream
¼ c. water	1 pkg. ladyfingers,
2 pkgs. (10 oz. ea.) frozen straw- berries, thawed	split

Soften gelatin in water; dissolve over hot water. Empty strawberries into bowl; beat until well broken up. Stir in sugar and dissolved gelatin. Cool until mixture just begins to thicken. Whip 1½ cups cream; fold into gelatin mixture. Line sides of 1½-quart mold with ladyfingers, rounded sides outward. Spoon gelatin mixture into mold; chill until firm. To serve, carefully loosen around sides with small spatula; shake mold gently; invert; turn out onto serving plate. Whip remaining ½ cup cream; decorate charlotte. Garnish with strawberries, if desired. Makes 6 servings.

SPANISH CREAM

1 envelope un-	2½ c. milk
flavored gelatin	1 tsp. vanilla
¼ c. sugar	3 egg whites
⅛ tsp. salt	¼ c. sugar
3 egg yolks	

Blend gelatin, ¼ cup sugar, and salt in top of double boiler. Beat egg yolks with milk until blended; stir into gelatin mixture. Cook over simmering, not boiling, water, stirring constantly, until gelatin and sugar are dissolved, about 10 minutes. Remove from heat; stir in vanilla; cool; chill until mixture mounds slightly when spooned. Beat whites until soft peaks form. Beat in ¼ cup sugar slowly; continue to beat until meringue forms stiff, glossy peaks. Fold thickened egg yolk mixture into meringue. Pour into 1-quart mold. Chill several hours or overnight. Serve with Double Chocolate Sauce (*page 399*), Raspberry Sauce (*page 401*), or whipped cream, if desired. Makes 6 servings.

LIME BAVARIAN CHARLOTTE

2 doz. ladyfingers	½ tsp. cream of
2 envelopes un-	tartar
flavored gelatin	½ c. sugar
½ c. sugar	1 tsp. grated lime
¾ c. lime juice	rind
¼ c. water	1 c. heavy cream,
4 egg yolks, slightly	whipped
beaten	Green food coloring
4 egg whites	

Separate ladyfingers. Line an 8-inch spring-form pan with split ladyfingers, cutting to fit pan so all spaces are filled. Combine gelatin, ½ cup sugar, lime juice, water, and egg yolks in top of double boiler. Cook over simmering, not boiling, water until gelatin and sugar are dissolved and mixture thickens slightly. Cool; chill until mixture mounds slightly when spooned. Beat egg whites with cream of tartar until soft peaks form. Beat in ½ cup sugar slowly. Continue to beat until meringue forms stiff, glossy peaks. Fold chilled lime mixture and lime rind gently into meringue; fold in whipped cream and enough food coloring to tint a delicate green. Pour into prepared pan. Chill several hours or until set. Garnish with chopped pistachio nuts and additional whipped cream, if desired. Makes 10 to 12 servings.

PEACH BRANDY BAVARIAN CREAM

1 envelope un-	½ c. sugar
flavored gelatin	1 c. heavy cream
½ c. water	3 peaches, peeled,
¼ c. peach brandy	pitted, and diced
2 egg yolks	

Soften gelatin in water; stir over hot water until gelatin is dissolved. Cool slightly; stir in peach brandy. Beat egg yolks until light; add sugar gradually, beating constantly until thick and very light. Add gelatin mixture; mix well. Chill until it starts to thicken. Whip cream until very thick. Fold into chilled gelatin mixture; add peaches; mix well. Pour into 1-quart mold; chill at least 4 hours. Unmold; garnish with additional peaches, if desired. Makes 8 servings.

PRALINE BAVARIAN CREAM

½ c. sliced,	¼ tsp. salt
blanched	6 egg yolks, slightly
almonds	beaten
½ c. sugar	3½ c. milk
2 tbs. water	½ tsp. almond
½ c. sugar	extract
2 envelopes un-	1½ c. heavy cream,
flavored gelatin	whipped

Make praline powder: Toast almonds at 350° F. for 6 to 10 minutes or until golden. Grease cookie sheet lightly. Heat ½ cup sugar and water in small saucepan until mixture turns golden. Add almonds; stir quickly into syrup until well coated. Pour out at once onto cookie sheet; cool completely. Crush to powder with rolling pin; reserve. Blend ½ cup sugar, gelatin, and salt in saucepan. Combine egg yolks and milk; stir slowly into gelatin mixture. Cook over medium heat, stirring constantly, until mixture thickens slightly and just coats spoon. Remove from heat; add almond extract and reserved praline powder. Chill until mixture thickens and mounds when spooned. Fold in whipped cream. Turn into 6-cup mold. Chill 3 to 4 hours or overnight until firm. Unmold onto serving plate (this may be done an hour before serving and dessert returned to refrigerator). Garnish with additional whipped cream or serve with Double Chocolate Sauce (*page 399*), if desired. Makes 8 to 10 servings.

APRICOT BAVARIAN CREAM

1 pkg. (11 oz.) dried apricots	2½ c. milk
2½ c. water	4 egg yolks, slightly beaten
2 envelopes un-flavored gelatin	1 c. heavy cream, whipped
½ c. sugar	1 c. water
⅛ tsp. salt	½ c. sugar

Chop apricots coarsely; simmer in 2½ cups water 20 to 25 minutes or until quite soft. Press through sieve or food mill; there should be 2 cups of purée; if not add water to make 2 cups. Combine gelatin, ½ cup sugar, and salt in saucepan; slowly add milk and egg yolks. Cook over medium heat, stirring constantly, until mixture just comes to boiling; do not boil. Remove from heat; stir in 1½ cups apricot purée; chill mixture until it begins to thicken. Fold in whipped cream; pour into 6-cup mold; chill until set. For sauce, combine remaining ½ cup of purée with 1 cup water and ½ cup sugar. Cook over medium heat, stirring constantly, 5 minutes; cool; chill. Unmold dessert onto serving plate; spoon some sauce on top; serve with remaining sauce. Makes 6 to 8 servings.

MOCHA BAVARIAN CREAM

1 envelope un-flavored gelatin	3 egg yolks
¼ c. sugar	1 tsp. vanilla
¼ tsp. salt	3 egg whites
2 tbs. instant coffee	¼ c. sugar
1½ c. milk	½ c. heavy cream, whipped
1 pkg. (6 oz.) semi-sweet chocolate pieces	

Combine gelatin, ¼ cup sugar, salt, coffee, milk, and chocolate in saucepan; mix well. Cook over low heat, stirring constantly, until gelatin dissolves and chocolate melts. Beat with egg beater to blend. Beat egg yolks until blended; slowly stir in half the chocolate mixture. Return mixture to saucepan; cook, stirring constantly, 3 minutes. Remove from heat; stir in vanilla; cool 10 to 15 minutes. Beat egg whites until foamy, add remaining ¼ cup sugar gradually; continue to beat until meringue forms stiff, glossy peaks. Fold in chocolate mixture; spoon into 5-cup mold. Chill about 3 hours or until firm. Unmold onto serving plate; garnish with whipped cream. Makes 6 servings.

RASPBERRY VELVET SOUFFLÉ

1 pkg. (10 oz.) frozen rasp-berries, thawed	¼ tsp. cream of tartar
1 envelope un-flavored gelatin	2 egg whites
¼ c. water	¼ c. sugar
	½ c. heavy cream, whipped

Put raspberries through sieve, pressing pulp and juice through. Measure purée; add water to make 1½ cups; heat to boiling. Soften gelatin in ¼ cup water; add to hot purée; stir until dissolved; cool; chill until slightly thickened. Add cream of tartar to egg whites; beat until foamy. Beat in sugar gradually; continue beating until meringue forms stiff glossy peaks. Fold cream and thickened purée mixture into meringue; pour into 1½-quart mold. Chill until set. Unmold onto serving plate; garnish with sieved raspberry preserves and additional whipped cream, if desired. Makes 6 servings.

LEMONADE SOUFFLÉ

⅔ c. sugar	2 tsp. grated lemon rind
3 envelopes un-flavored gelatin	½ c. lemon juice
6 egg yolks, slightly beaten	6 egg whites
1½ c. water	⅓ c. sugar
	2 c. heavy cream, whipped

Fold long strip of wax paper in half lengthwise. Tie securely around 1 quart soufflé dish, to form collar and hold soufflé mixture above dish until it sets. Combine ⅔ cup sugar and gelatin in saucepan. Blend egg yolks and water; stir into gelatin mixture. Cook over medium heat, stirring constantly, until mixture just comes to boiling; do not boil. Cool; add lemon rind and juice; chill until mixture mounds slightly when spooned. Beat egg whites until foamy; add ⅓ cup sugar slowly; continue to beat until meringue forms stiff, glossy peaks. Fold meringue into chilled gelatin mixture; fold in whipped cream. Pour into prepared dish; chill 3 to 4 hours or until set. Carefully peel off wax paper. Garnish with additional whipped cream, if desired. Makes 8 servings.

GRAND MARNIER SOUFFLÉ

½ c. sugar	1 c. orange juice
2 envelopes un-flavored gelatin	6 egg whites
	½ tsp. cream of tartar
1 c. milk	
6 egg yolks, slightly beaten	½ c. sugar
	¼ c. Grand Marnier
1 tbs. grated orange rind	1 c. heavy cream, whipped

Fold long piece of wax paper in half lengthwise. Tie securely around 1-quart soufflé dish to form collar and hold soufflé mixture above dish until it sets. Combine ½ cup sugar, gelatin, milk, and egg yolks in saucepan. Cook over medium heat, stirring constantly, until mixture just comes to boiling; do not boil. Remove from heat; cool. Add orange rind and juice. Chill until mixture mounds slightly when spooned. Beat egg whites and cream of tartar until foamy; gradually beat in ½ cup sugar; continue beating until meringue forms stiff, glossy peaks. Fold meringue into chilled gelatin mixture; fold in Grand Marnier and whipped cream. Turn into prepared dish; chill 3 to 4 hours or until set. Before serving, carefully peel off wax paper. Decorate soufflé with additional whipped cream and orange sections, if desired. Makes 8 servings.

RICE DESSERTS

CREAMY RICE PUDDING

½ c. rice	¼ tsp. ground cinnamon
3 c. milk	
¼ c. sugar	⅓ c. raisins
¼ tsp. salt	

Combine rice, milk, sugar, salt, cinnamon, and raisins in top of double boiler. Cover; cook over hot, not boiling, water 1 hour or until rice is tender. Stir frequently during cooking. Serve warm or cold, with cream if desired. Makes 6 servings.

RICE CUSTARD PUDDING

4 eggs, beaten	1 tsp. vanilla
1 c. sugar	1 c. raisins
⅛ tsp. salt	2 c. cooked rice
1 qt. milk, scalded	

Heat oven to 350° F. Combine eggs, sugar, and salt. Stir in scalded milk; add vanilla. Add raisins and cooked rice. Pour into a 2-quart baking dish; set dish in pan of hot water (water should be 1 inch deep). Bake 45 to 50 minutes. Makes 6 servings.

FRUITED RICE RING

1 envelope un-flavored gelatin	1 tsp. vanilla
	¾ c. mixed candied fruit, chopped
¼ c. cold water	
2 c. scalded milk	2 c. cooked rice
2 eggs, slightly beaten	½ c. heavy cream, whipped
½ c. sugar	

Soften gelatin in water. Add scalded milk to eggs, mixing quickly; add sugar. Cook over low heat, stirring constantly, until custard coats spoon. Remove from heat; add gelatin and vanilla, mixing well. Chill just until custard begins to thicken and jell. Fold in candied fruit, rice, and whipped cream. Pour pudding into 8-inch (5-cup) ring mold. Chill until firm. Unmold and serve with additional whipped cream, if desired. Makes 6 servings.

CHOCO-MINT CREAM RICE

1 envelope unflavored gelatin	1¼ c. milk
	2 c. cooked rice
	½ c. heavy cream
¼ c. sugar	2 egg whites
⅛ tsp. salt	2 tbs. sugar
1 pkg. (6 oz.) semi-sweet chocolate pieces	⅓ c. mint jelly
	½ c. heavy cream
2 egg yolks	1 tbs. mint jelly

Combine gelatin, ¼ cup sugar, salt, and chocolate pieces in top of double boiler. Beat egg yolks slightly with milk; stir into gelatin mixture. Cook over hot, not boiling water, stirring constantly, until chocolate is melted and mixture is slightly thickened. Remove from heat; stir in rice; chill until mixture is quite cold and has begun to set. Beat ½ cup heavy cream until stiff. Beat egg whites until foamy; add 2 tablespoons sugar and continue to beat until meringue forms stiff, glossy peaks. Break up ⅓ cup mint jelly with a fork; fold into chocolate mixture with cream and egg whites. Chill until mixture begins to set. Spoon into 6 sherbet glasses. Whip ½ cup heavy cream; beat in 1 tablespoon mint jelly; spoon over pudding in sherbets. Top with additional mint jelly, if desired. Makes 6 servings.

APRICOT-RICE MERINGUE

1 c. rice	⅓ c. toasted
1 qt. milk, scalded	slivered almonds
½ c. sugar	1 can (1 lb. 13 oz.)
½ tsp. salt	whole apricots,
1 tsp. vanilla	drained and
½ tsp. ground mace	pitted
1 tbs. butter or	3 egg whites
margarine	¼ tsp. cream of
3 egg yolks	tartar
2 tbs. milk	¼ tsp. salt
	6 tbs. sugar

Cover rice with water in saucepan; bring to boiling; let stand 5 minutes; drain. Combine rice, scalded milk, ½ cup sugar, ½ teaspoon salt, vanilla, mace, and butter or margarine. Cover; simmer 30 minutes, stirring occasionally. Combine egg yolks and 2 tablespoons milk; add to rice mixture, stirring quickly.

Add almonds. Pour pudding into buttered 2-quart casserole. Let stand 5 minutes. Arrange apricots over top. Beat egg whites, cream of tartar, and ¼ teaspoon salt until foamy. Gradually add 6 tablespoons sugar; beat until meringue forms stiff, glossy peaks. Swirl meringue on top of pudding. Bake at 350° F. for 12 to 15 minutes or until meringue is browned. Makes 6 to 8 servings.

GLORIFIED RICE

2 c. cooked rice*	¼ c. quartered
¼ c. sugar	maraschino
1 can (8¾ oz.)	cherries
crushed pine-	2 tbs. grenadine or
apple, drained	maraschino
1 c. miniature	cherry juice
marshmallows	1 c. heavy cream,
	whipped

Combine rice, sugar, pineapple, marshmallows, cherries, and grenadine or cherry juice; mix well. Fold in whipped cream. Chill until firm. Makes 4 servings.
* Do not use chilled rice. Warm rice will absorb flavors best. If using leftover rice, put it in a sieve and run it under hot water.

ORANGE RICE IMPERIAL

2 c. cooked rice*	1 c. sugar
1½ c. milk	½ c. milk
2 envelopes	4 egg yolks, slightly
unflavored	beaten
gelatin	1 c. heavy cream,
1 c. orange juice	whipped
1 tbs. grated orange	
rind	

Combine rice and 1½ cups milk in saucepan; cook over medium heat about 20 minutes, or until all milk is absorbed. Soften gelatin in orange juice; stir in orange rind. Combine sugar, ½ cup milk, and egg yolks in top of double boiler. Cook over hot, not boiling, water until sugar is dissolved and mixture coats a spoon. Add gelatin mixture and rice; cool; chill. Fold whipped cream into chilled mixture. Turn into 6-cup mold. Chill several hours or until firm. Unmold on serving plate; garnish with orange slices and whipped cream, if desired. Makes 6 to 8 servings.
* Use only regular or converted rice, not precooked rice.

CUSTARDS

BAKED CUSTARD

2 eggs	2 c. milk, scalded
½ c. sugar	1 tsp. vanilla
¼ tsp. salt	Nutmeg

Heat oven to 350° F. Beat eggs, sugar, and salt until just blended. Stir in scalded milk and vanilla. Pour into 1½-quart ovenproof baking dish. Set dish in larger pan. Pour hot water into larger pan so level of water is even with level of custard. *This is the secret of perfect baked custards.* The water bath protects the custard during baking and keeps it from overcooking. The levels of the water and custard should be even because all the custard needs protection. Sprinkle top with nutmeg. Bake 40 to 45 minutes or until thin-bladed knife inserted 1 inch from edge comes out clean. Center will be soft, but will set when cool. Cool; chill. Custard may also be baked in 6 custard cups and unmolded when chilled, if desired. Serve with fruit or cream. Makes 6 servings.

Baked Coconut Custard: Stir 1 cup flaked or shredded coconut into custard before baking.

CARAMEL CUSTARD

⅓ c. sugar	⅛ tsp. salt
¼ c. water	1 c. heavy cream
4 eggs	1½ c. milk
⅓ c. sugar	

Melt ⅓ cup sugar in large skillet over medium heat until golden; add water slowly and care-

fully, stirring constantly (take care steam does not burn hand). Heat slowly until caramel is entirely dissolved in water. Pour caramel into 1-quart ring mold; rotate to coat all surfaces as caramel thickens and cools. Heat oven to 300° F. Beat eggs, ⅓ cup sugar, and salt until blended; add cream and milk; stir to blend. Pour into prepared mold; set mold in larger pan. Pour hot water into larger pan so level of water is even with level of custard. Bake 1 hour, 20 minutes or until thin-bladed knife inserted 1 inch from edge of custard comes out clean. Cool, chill; loosen edges; unmold; caramel will form sauce. Fill center with peaches or other fruits, if desired. Makes 6 servings.

FLOATING ISLAND

4 egg whites	4 egg yolks
½ c. sugar	⅓ c. sugar
1 tsp. vanilla	2 tsp. flour
1½ c. milk	

Heat oven to 275° F. Butter and sugar a 1-quart ovenproof mixing bowl. Beat egg whites until foamy; beat in ½ cup sugar, a small amount at a time, beating after each addition until sugar is dissolved. Beat in vanilla; continue beating until meringue forms stiff, glossy peaks. Spoon small amount into prepared bowl; spread with back of spoon against bowl to form smooth lining. Spoon in remaining meringue evenly. Bake 25 to 30 minutes or until firm. Cool. Unmold carefully into serving bowl; cover lightly with transparent plastic wrap. Chill. Scald milk in top of double boiler. Beat egg yolks; add ⅓ cup sugar and flour. Stir hot milk slowly into egg yolk mixture; return to top of double boiler. Cook over hot, not boiling, water until custard coats spoon; remove from heat; cool; cover with piece of wax paper to prevent skin forming on top; chill. When ready to serve, carefully pour chilled custard around meringue in serving bowl until meringue "island" floats. Garnish by drizzling maple-blended syrup over island and sprinkling with toasted, sliced almonds, if desired. Makes 6 servings.

CRÈME BRÛLEE

This elegant dessert often thought of as French is really Creole. The rich, chilled custard is topped with brown sugar which is caramelized under the broiler.

2 c. heavy cream	Pinch of salt
4 eggs	1 tsp. vanilla
¼ c. sugar	Brown sugar

Heat cream in top of double boiler over simmering water until bubbles appear around the edge. Beat eggs, ¼ cup sugar, and salt together until blended. Pour scalded cream over egg mixture, stirring constantly. Return mixture to top of double boiler; cook over simmering, not boiling, water until mixture coats spoon quite heavily and is as thick as a medium white sauce. Soft custards do not become too thick, so do not overcook or the custard may curdle. Stir constantly; scrape mixture from sides and bottom. Mixture will thicken in about 10 to 12 minutes. Remove from heat; stir in vanilla. Pour into heatproof bowl or baking dish so mixture will be about 1 inch from top. Cool, stirring several times to keep skin from forming; chill well. One hour before serving place bowl of chilled custard in larger heatproof bowl filled with crushed ice. This precaution will keep the custard from cooking and curdling. Sprinkle an even coat of brown sugar over the top of the custard about ½ inch thick. Place under broiler, about 3 to 4 inches from heat. Broil until sugar is melted and bubbly, taking care not to burn. Cool slightly. To serve, tap crisp sugar top lightly with spoon to crack surface. Each guest should have crisp sugary top and creamy cold custard. Nice too with sliced fresh or frozen strawberries or peaches. Makes 4 to 6 servings.

ZABAGLIONE

6 egg yolks	½ c. Marsala
½ c. sugar	

Beat egg yolks in bowl with rotary beater or electric mixer until thick and pale in color. Beat in sugar gradually. Beat in Marsala slowly. Pour into top pan of chafing dish or double boiler. Place over simmering water; continue beating until mixture foams up and begins to thicken. Do not overcook. Serve warm in sherbet glasses. Glasses may be lined with ladyfingers. Or serve over fresh fruit. Makes 4 servings.

POTS DE CRÈME AU CHOCOLAT

1 pkg. (6 oz.) semisweet chocolate pieces	3 egg yolks, slightly beaten
2 tbs. sugar	½ c. heavy cream, whipped
½ c. heavy cream	

Melt chocolate pieces over hot water; blend in sugar and cream; cook, stirring occasionally, until smooth. Pour hot chocolate mixture slowly over beaten egg yolks, beating constantly until well blended and thickened; cool. Fold in whipped cream; spoon into special pot de crème cups, demitasse cups, or custard cups. Makes 4 servings.

When beating egg whites, if the recipe says: **foamy** —the entire mass forms bubbles; **rounded peaks**— peaks turn over slightly when the beater is lifted; **stiff peaks**—peaks remain standing when beater is lifted.

SHORTCAKES AND COBBLERS

OLD-FASHIONED STRAWBERRY SHORTCAKE

1 qt. fresh straw-berries or 2 pkgs. (10 oz. ea.) frozen straw-berries, thawed	1 tsp. salt
	½ c. shortening
	1 c. milk
	¼ c. soft butter or margarine
½ c. sugar	1 c. sifted confectioners' sugar
2 c. sifted all-purpose flour	
3 tsp. baking powder	1 c. heavy cream, whipped
2 tbs. sugar	

Wash and hull berries; reserve ½ cup whole berries for garnish. Crush remaining berries; sprinkle with ½ cup sugar; let stand 30 minutes. For frozen berries, omit sugar. Heat oven to 450° F. Sift flour, baking powder, 2 table-spoons sugar, and salt into mixing bowl. Cut in shortening with pastry blender until mixture resembles cornmeal. Add milk; stir quickly and lightly together with fork until all dry ingredients are moistened and dough clings together. Turn dough onto floured board; knead 10 times. Divide dough in half. Pat each half into a greased 8x1½-inch layer cake pan. Bake 12 to 15 minutes or until golden brown. Blend butter or margarine with confectioners' sugar; spread over top of one baked shortcake layer. Spoon half the crushed strawberries over layer; top with second layer. Spoon remaining strawberries over top layer. Cover stawberries with whipped cream. Decorate with reserved whole strawberries. Serve warm. Cream may be left unwhipped, if desired. Makes 6 servings.

Kansas Strawberry Sweet Cake (Sponge cake layers): Bake and cool 1 recipe Golden Sponge Cake (*page 443*). Assemble cake as above. Omit butter-confectioners' sugar mixture.

Fresh Berry Shortcake: Sprinkle 1 quart fresh raspberries or blueberries with ¾ cup sugar. Let stand 30 minutes. Proceed with shortcake as above.

Fresh Peach Shortcake: Peel and slice 6 large ripe peaches; sprinkle with 1 cup sugar;

let stand 30 minutes. Proceed with shortcake as above.

Individual Shortcakes: Make shortcake dough as in Strawberry Shortcake. Pat or roll dough to a ½-inch thickness. Cut into 6 to 8 squares. Or cut in rounds with floured 3-inch biscuit cutter. Place on greased cookie sheet. Bake at 450° F. for 10 to 12 minutes. Break apart while hot. Assemble as in Strawberry Shortcake. Makes 6 to 8 servings.

STRAWBERRY RHUBARB COBBLER

4 c. sliced rhubarb (½-in. pieces)	3 tbs. water
	1 pt. strawberries, washed, hulled, and halved
3 tbs. water	
1 c. sugar	
3 tbs. cornstarch	1 pkg. refrigerated biscuits
¼ c. sugar	
¼ tsp. salt	Sugar

Combine rhubarb, water, and 1 cup sugar in saucepan. Cook, covered, over low heat, stirring occasionally, until rhubarb softens but is not mushy. Combine cornstarch, remaining ¼ cup sugar, salt, and water. Stir quickly into hot rhubarb mixture. Continue cooking until mixture bubbles and is thickened. Add strawberries; pour into lightly buttered 8x8x2-inch baking dish. Heat oven to 400° F. Separate refrigerated biscuits; arrange on *hot* mixture. *This is the secret. If mixture is not bubbling hot when you put the biscuits on, the bottoms may be soggy.* Sprinkle lightly with sugar. Bake 20 to 25 minutes until filling bubbles and topping is golden brown. Serve with cream, if desired. Makes 6 servings.

PLUM COBBLER

1 can (1 lb. 14 oz.) purple plums	1 c. sifted all-purpose flour
2 tbs. sugar	1¼ tsp. baking powder
1 tbs. cornstarch	½ tsp. salt
¼ tsp. ground cinnamon	2 tbs. brown sugar
2 tbs. grated orange rind	3 tbs. butter or margarine
¼ c. orange juice	½ c. milk

Heat oven to 400° F. Drain plums; reserve syrup. Pit plums; place in 1½-quart baking dish. Combine sugar, cornstarch, cinnamon, and orange rind in saucepan. Stir in orange juice and plum syrup. Cook over medium heat, stirring constantly, until thickened and bubbly. Pour over plums. Heat in oven until bubbly while making topping. Sift flour, baking powder, and salt into bowl. Stir in brown sugar; cut in butter or margarine until mixture resembles cornmeal; stir in milk. Drop by spoonfuls onto *hot* fruit. Bake 15 to 20 minutes or until golden brown. Serve warm. Makes 4 servings.

PUDDINGS AND CAKE DESSERTS

BREAD PUDDING

2 c. milk	¼ tsp. salt
4 tbs. butter or margarine	1 tsp. ground cinnamon
2 eggs	3 c. soft bread cubes
½ c. sugar	½ c. raisins

Heat oven to 350° F. Scald milk; add butter or margarine. Beat eggs slightly in bowl; stir in milk mixture, sugar, salt, and cinnamon. Put bread cubes and raisins in 1½-quart baking dish; pour milk mixture over; stir gently. Place in pan of hot water. Bake 40 to 45 minutes or until thin-bladed knife inserted 1 inch from edge comes out clean. Serve warm or cold with cream, whipped cream, or Hard Sauce (*page 400*). Makes 6 servings.

CHOCOLATE BREAD PUDDING

3 c. milk	2 eggs
3 sqs. unsweetened chocolate	1 tsp. vanilla
½ c. sugar	2 c. day-old bread cubes
⅛ tsp. salt	

Heat milk and chocolate together in double boiler until chocolate is melted. Beat sugar, salt, and eggs together just until blended; add vanilla. Pour chocolate mixture slowly into egg mixture, stirring constantly. Pour over bread cubes in greased 1½-quart baking dish. Let stand 20 minutes. Heat oven to 350° F. Stir pudding well; set dish in pan of hot water (water should be 1 inch deep). Bake 45 to 50 minutes or until thin-bladed knife inserted 1 inch from edge comes out clean. Makes 6 servings.

QUEEN'S PUDDING

2 eggs, beaten	3 tbs. melted butter or margarine
2 egg yolks, beaten	1 qt. milk, scalded
⅓ c. sugar	2 c. day-old bread cubes
¼ tsp. salt	½ c. tart jelly
¼ tsp. ground cinnamon	2 egg whites
2 tsp. vanilla	¼ c. sugar

Heat oven to 350° F. Combine eggs, egg yolks, ⅓ cup sugar, salt, cinnamon, vanilla, and butter or margarine. Add milk; blend. Pour over bread cubes in a 1½-quart casserole. Let stand 20 minutes for bread to soak up custard mixture; stir. Set in pan of hot water to depth of 1 inch. Bake 1 hour and 15 minutes or until thin-bladed knife inserted 1 inch from edge comes out clean. Remove from oven. Spread jelly over hot pudding. Beat egg whites until foamy; beat in ¼ cup sugar; beat until meringue stands in stiff peaks. Cover pudding with meringue. Bake 15 minutes or until meringue is golden. Cool. Makes 6 servings.

NORWEGIAN PRUNE PUDDING

½ lb. prunes	⅓ c. cold water
1 c. sugar	¼ c. cornstarch
¼ tsp. ground cinnamon	2 tbs. lemon juice

Cook prunes according to package directions; drain, reserving liquid. Pit prunes. Combine prune pulp, sugar, and cinnamon in saucepan. Measure reserved juice; add water, if necessary, to make 1½ cups liquid; stir into pulp mixture. Cook over medium heat, stirring constantly, 10 minutes or until sugar is dissolved. Stir ⅓ cup water into cornstarch, blending well; stir into prune mixture. Cook over low heat, stirring rapidly, until mixture is very thick and transparent. Add lemon juice. Chill. Serve with light cream, Lemon Sauce, (*page 400*), or Custard Sauce Royale (*page 399*), if desired. Makes 5 to 6 servings.

VANILLA BLANC MANGE
(Cornstarch Pudding)

¾ c. sugar	2¼ c. milk
¼ c. cornstarch	1 tsp. vanilla
¼ tsp. salt	

Combine sugar, cornstarch, and salt in top of double boiler; add milk. Cook over hot, not boiling, water, stirring constantly until thickened. Cook 10 minutes, stirring occasionally. Remove from heat; stir in vanilla. Pour into 3-cup mold or 4 individual molds. Chill for 2 to 3 hours or until pudding is firm. Unmold; serve with Raspberry Sauce (*page 401*), Double Chocolate Sauce (*page 399*), or poured cream. Makes 4 servings.

Chocolate Blanc Mange: Add 2 squares chocolate, cut up, to sugar mixture above. Serve with poured cream. Makes 4 servings.

CRANBERRY COTTAGE PUDDING

2 c. sifted all-purpose flour	½ c. sugar
3 tsp. baking powder	1 egg, beaten
¼ tsp. salt	¾ c. milk
½ c. shortening	2 c. cranberries, chopped

Sift flour, baking powder, and salt together. Cream shortening and sugar together; add egg. Add flour mixture alternately with milk, beating well after each addition. Stir in cranberries. Turn into greased 8x8x2-inch baking pan. Bake at 350° F. for 1 hour or until cake tests done. Cut in squares; serve in bowls with Spiced Cream: Mix 1 pint half-and-half or light cream, 2 tablespoon sugar, 1 teaspoon ground cinnamon, and ½ teaspoon ground nutmeg. Makes 9 servings.

LEMON-COCONUT PUDDING

3 tbs. butter or margarine	3 tbs. flour
1 c. sugar	1½ c. milk
3 egg yolks	1 c. fine grated coconut
2 tsp. grated lemon rind	3 egg whites
¼ c. lemon juice	¼ tsp. salt

Heat oven to 375° F. Cream butter or margarine; add sugar; mix well. Beat egg yolks till thick; add to sugar mixture. Add lemon rind and juice; fold in flour; stir in milk and coconut. Beat egg whites and salt until stiff peaks form; fold into egg yolk mixture. Pour mixture into lightly greased 1½-quart baking dish; place in pan of hot water to depth of 1 inch. Bake 40 to 45 minutes or until firm. Cool; chill until serving time. Makes 6 servings.

ORANGE CAKE-TOP PUDDING

¼ c. sifted all-purpose flour	½ c. orange juice
1 c. sugar	2 egg yolks
¼ tsp. salt	¾ c. milk
1 tbs. grated orange rind	2 egg whites

Heat oven to 350° F. Sift flour, sugar, and salt together. Stir in orange rind and juice, egg yolks, and milk; blend well. Beat egg whites until stiff but not dry. Pour orange mixture onto beaten whites; fold gently to blend. Pour into greased 1-quart baking dish. Set dish in pan of hot water to depth of 1 inch. Bake 50 minutes. Makes 6 servings.

Lemon Cake-Top Pudding: Substitute ¼ cup lemon juice and 1 tablespoon lemon rind for orange juice and orange rind. Increase milk to 1 cup. Follow directions for Orange Cake-Top Pudding.

DUTCH APPLE CAKE

1½ c. sifted all-purpose flour	2 c. sliced, pared, cored, cooking apples
2 tsp. baking powder	¼ c. sugar
½ tsp. salt	1 tsp. ground cinnamon
¼ c. sugar	3 tbs. melted butter or margarine
½ c. shortening	
1 egg	
½ c. milk	

Heat oven to 400° F. Sift flour, baking powder, salt, and ¼ cup sugar into bowl. Cut in shortening with pastry blender. Beat egg and milk together until blended; add to dry ingredients; stir just to blend well. Spread dough in greased 9x9x2-inch pan. Arrange apple slices on dough. Sprinkle with ¼ cup sugar mixed with cinnamon. Drizzle with butter or margarine. Bake 30 to 35 minutes or until cake tester inserted in center of cake comes out clean. Serve with Vanilla Sauce (*page 398*), Lemon Sauce (*page 400*), or whipped cream. Makes 9 servings.

OLD-FASHIONED GINGERBREAD

2 c. sifted all-purpose flour	½ tsp. ground cinnamon
1 tsp. baking soda	½ c. shortening
½ tsp. salt	¼ c. sugar
1½ tsp. ground ginger	1 egg
	½ c. molasses
	1 c. boiling water

Heat oven to 325° F. Sift flour, baking soda, salt, ginger, and cinnamon together. Blend shortening, sugar, and egg thoroughly in mixing bowl. Combine molasses and boiling water. Add sifted dry ingredients and molasses mixture alternately to shortening mixture, beating well after each addition. Turn into greased 9x9x2-inch pan. Bake 40 to 45 minutes or until gingerbread springs back when lightly touched with finger tip. Cool slightly; remove from pan. Cut into squares. Serve with Lemon Sauce (*page 400*). Makes 9 servings.

CHOCOLATE NUT UPSIDE-DOWN CAKE

¼ c. butter or margarine	¼ tsp. salt
¼ c. brown sugar, firmly packed	¼ c. butter or margarine
¾ c. light corn syrup	1 c. sugar
¾ c. broken walnuts	1 egg yolk
1¼ c. sifted cake flour	2 sqs. unsweetened chocolate, melted
1 tsp. baking powder	¾ c. milk
	1 tsp. vanilla
	1 egg white, stiffly beaten

Prepare topping: Cream ¼ cup butter or margarine and brown sugar together in small bowl; stir in syrup and nuts. Spread in bottom of buttered 9-inch tube pan or 1½-quart ring mold. Prepare cake: Sift flour, baking powder, and salt together. Cream ¼ cup butter or margarine until soft in medium-size bowl; add sugar gradually, creaming after each addition until mixture is light and fluffy. Add egg yolk; beat well; add melted chocolate. Add sifted dry ingredients alternately with milk; add vanilla; fold in stiffly beaten egg white. Carefully pour into prepared pan. Bake at 350° F. for 45 minutes or until cake tester comes out clean. Cool in pan 10 minutes. Loosen cake from sides of pan; invert onto large cake plate. Serve warm or let cool before serving. Makes 8 to 10 servings.

PINEAPPLE UPSIDE-DOWN CAKE

¼ c. butter or margarine	2 tsp. baking powder
¼ c. brown sugar, firmly packed	¼ tsp. salt
1 can (1 lb. 4½ oz.) sliced pineapple	1 c. sugar
Maraschino cherries	¼ c. shortening
1¼ c. sifted all-purpose flour	¾ c. milk
	1 tsp. vanilla
	1 egg

Melt butter or margarine in 9x9x2-inch pan. Sprinkle brown sugar evenly over melted butter. Drain pineapple; reserve syrup; arrange 9 slices evenly in pan; press maraschino cherry in center of each. Heat oven to 350° F. Sift flour, baking powder, and salt into mixing bowl; stir in sugar. Add shortening and milk. Beat 2 minutes at medium speed on mixer; scrape bowl frequently. Add vanilla and egg. Beat 2 minutes at medium speed on mixer. Pour carefully over pineapple slices in pan. Bake 50 to 60 minutes or until cake springs back when top is lightly touched with finger. Remove from oven; place serving plate face down over cake; turn upside down at once. Leave pan in place 1 to 2 minutes so topping will not stick to pan; remove pan. Cake may be served warm or cold, with whipped cream or with Fruit Sauce. Makes 9 servings.

Fruit Sauce

1 tbs. cornstarch	1 pineapple slice, chopped
2 tbs. brown sugar	1 tbs. chopped maraschino cherries
¾ c. reserved pineapple syrup	
2 tsp. lemon juice	
1 tsp. butter or margarine	

Combine cornstarch and brown sugar in saucepan; add pineapple syrup. Cook over medium heat, stirring constantly, until thickened and clear. Remove from heat; add lemon juice, butter or margarine, pineapple, and cherries. Serve warm.

PEAR-APPLESAUCE UPSIDE-DOWN CAKE

⅓ c. melted butter or margarine
½ c. light brown sugar, firmly packed
1 can (1 lb. 13 oz.) pear halves
Maraschino cherries
2½ c. sifted all-purpose flour
2 c. sugar
¼ tsp. baking powder
1½ tsp. baking soda
1 tsp. ground ginger
½ tsp. ground cinnamon
½ c. shortening
½ c. water
1½ c. canned applesauce
2 eggs

Melt butter or margarine in 10-inch skillet with heatproof handle, or 13x9x2-inch baking dish. Sprinkle evenly with brown sugar. Drain pears; arrange, cut side down, with a cherry in each pear half in pan. Heat oven to 350° F. Sift flour, sugar, baking powder, baking soda, ginger, and cinnamon in bowl. Add shortening, water, and applesauce; beat 2 minutes at medium speed on mixer or 300 strokes by hand; scrape bowl frequently. Add eggs; beat 2 minutes more. Pour carefully over pears. Bake 55 to 65 minutes or until cake springs back when lightly touched with finger. Loosen edges, turn quickly upside down on large serving plate; leave pan in place 1 minute to allow syrup to run down. Serve warm or cool, with whipped cream, if desired. Makes 12 servings.

APPLE TOPSY-TURVY CAKE

3 tbs. butter or margarine
⅔ c. apricot preserves
3 to 4 medium-size apples, pared and cored
¼ c. raisins
1¾ c. sifted cake flour
1 c. sugar
2½ tsp. baking powder
¼ tsp. salt
1 tsp. ground cinnamon
¼ tsp. ground cloves
¼ tsp. ground nutmeg
⅓ c. shortening
¾ c. milk
1 egg

Combine butter or margarine and apricot preserves in small saucepan; stir over low heat until butter is melted and mixture is bubbly; pour into 9x9x2-inch pan. Cut apples into ¼-inch-thick rings; chop end slices finely (there should be 1 cup); reserve. Place 1 apple ring in center of pan; cut remaining rings in half; arrange around center ring; press raisins in centers of apple rings. Heat oven to 350° F. Sift flour, sugar, baking powder, salt, cinnamon, cloves, and nutmeg into mixing bowl. Add shortening and milk; blend; beat 2 minutes at medium speed of mixer (or 300 strokes by hand); scrape bowl frequently. Add egg; beat an additional 2 minutes; fold in reserved 1 cup chopped apples. Spoon batter carefully over apple rings in pan, so design is not disturbed. Bake 45 to 50 minutes or until cake springs back when lightly touched with finger. Loosen sides of cake with spatula; invert cake on plate; leave pan over cake for 5 minutes so topping will run down over cake; remove pan. Serve warm. Makes 9 servings.

BABA AU RHUM

According to French culinary history this delicacy was the invention of King Stanislas Leczinski, the exiled king of Poland. He is said to have invented a new way of eating the kugelhopf of eastern France by saturating it in rum and setting it ablaze. As he was an ardent reader of the Thousand and One Nights, he named it for one of the heroes of the book, Ali Baba.

¼ c. milk
¼ c. warm water (105°–115° F.)
1 pkg. active dry yeast or 1 cake compressed yeast
1 egg
2 egg yolks
¼ c. sugar
¼ tsp. vanilla
¼ c. melted butter or margarine
2¼ c. sifted all-purpose flour
Hot water
1 tbs. sultana raisins
1 tbs. currants
1 c. sugar
1 can (12 oz.) apricot nectar
1½ tsp. lemon juice
⅓ c. dark rum

Scald milk; cool to lukewarm. Measure warm water into large, warm bowl; sprinkle or crumble in yeast; stir until dissolved. Stir in milk. Beat egg and egg yolks until thick; add ¼ cup sugar; beat well. Add vanilla and butter or margarine. Stir egg mixture into yeast mixture. Add flour; beat until smooth. The dough will be soft. Cover; let rise in warm place (85° F.), free from draft, about 1 hour or until doubled in bulk. Pour hot water over raisins and currants; let stand 2 minutes to soften; drain well. Beat dough well. Add raisins and currants. Fill greased 2½-inch muffin-pan cups a scant half full. Cover; let rise in warm place, free from draft, about 45 minutes or until doubled in bulk. Bake at 350° F. for 20 minutes or until golden brown. While babas bake, combine 1 cup sugar and apricot nectar in large skillet. Heat until sugar dissolves. Remove from heat; add lemon juice and rum. When babas are baked, remove from pans and place in hot syrup in skillet. Baste babas with syrup. Let stand in syrup several hours before serving. Serve with whipped cream, if desired. Makes 18 babas.

APRICOT SAVARIN

⅓ c. warm water (105° 115° F.)	½ tsp. salt
1 pkg. active dry yeast or 1 cake compressed yeast	3 eggs
	2 tsp. grated lemon rind
1¾ c. sifted all-purpose flour	1 can (12 oz.) apricot nectar
½ c. sugar	1 c. sugar
½ c. soft butter or margarine	¼ c. light or dark rum

Measure warm water into medium-size bowl; sprinkle or crumble in yeast; stir to dissolve. Add ½ cup flour and 1 tablespoon sugar to yeast mixture; blend. Let rise in warm place (85° F.), free from draft, about 1 hour or until very light and bubbly. Cream butter or margarine, 7 tablespoons sugar, and salt; beat in eggs. Stir in yeast mixture, lemon rind, and remaining flour. Beat 2 minutes at medium speed with electric mixer. Turn into well-buttered 1½-quart ring mold. Let rise 45 to 50 minutes or until doubled in bulk. Bake at 350° F. for 35 to 40 minutes. Remove from mold; cool on wire rack. Wash and dry mold. Simmer apricot nectar and 1 cup sugar 5 minutes; stir in rum. Pour half into mold; put cooled cake into mold; pour remaining sauce slowly over cake. Let stand several hours. Unmold onto plate; decorate with fruits and nuts, if desired. Makes 8 servings.

STEAMED PUDDINGS

CRANBERRY PUDDING

4 c. cranberries, coarsely chopped	3 c. sifted all-purpose flour
1 c. raisins	3¼ tsp. baking soda
1 jar (4 oz.) candied lemon peel (½ c.)	1 c. molasses
	¾ c. hot water

Butter and sugar a 2-quart mold. Mix cranberries, raisins, and lemon peel in large bowl. Sift flour and baking soda over fruit mixture. Blend molasses and hot water; stir into fruit-flour mixture until thoroughly mixed. Pour into prepared mold; cover (if mold does not have cover, use buttered aluminum foil and tie securely). Steam on rack in large kettle half filled with boiling water 1½ hours or until done. Let stand in mold 5 minutes; unmold onto serving plate. Serve with Foamy Sauce (*page 400*) or Holiday Hard Sauce (*page 400*). Makes 8 servings.

STEAMED CHOCOLATE PUDDING

3 c. sifted all-purpose flour	3 sqs. unsweetened chocolate
½ tsp. salt	3 eggs
½ tsp. cream of tartar	1½ c. brown sugar, firmly packed
¼ tsp. baking soda	1½ c. milk
4 tbs. butter or margarine	

Butter and sugar 1½-quart mold or 12 custard cups. Sift flour, salt, cream of tartar, and baking soda together. Melt butter or margarine and chocolate in small saucepan over low heat; cool slightly. Beat eggs in medium-size bowl; stir in brown sugar and melted butter or margarine and chocolate. Add sifted dry ingredients alternately with milk to chocolate mixture. Pour into prepared mold or custard cups, filling only two-thirds full; cover (use lightly buttered aluminum foil; tie it securely). Place on rack or trivet in kettle; add enough boiling water to come halfway up sides of mold or custard cups. Steam, covered, about 1½ hours for large mold or 1 hour for custard cups. Unmold onto serving plate. Serve with Foamy Sauce (*page 400*) or Hard Sauce (*page 400*). Makes 12 servings.

To Butter and Sugar Mold

Brush softened butter or margarine generously on inside of mold. Sprinkle surface with sugar. Shake out any excess sugar.

GLAZED DATE-ORANGE PUDDING

½ c. brown sugar, firmly packed
1 tbs. cornstarch
¾ c. water
1½ c. (8 oz. pkg.) pitted dates, cut up
½ c. orange sections
1½ c. sifted all-purpose flour
1 tsp. salt
2¼ tsp. baking soda
½ tsp. ground cinnamon
½ tsp. ground ginger
¼ tsp. ground cloves
1½ c. packaged bread crumbs
1½ c. orange marmalade
½ c. pure vegetable oil
1 c. milk

Butter and sugar a 2-quart mold. Blend brown sugar and cornstarch; add water. Cook over medium heat, stirring constantly, until clear and thickened. Add ½ cup cut-up dates; pour into prepared mold; place orange sections in sauce in mold. Combine flour, salt, soda, spices, bread crumbs, marmalade, oil, milk, and remaining dates; stir until well blended. Pour carefully into mold; cover (if mold does not have cover, use lightly buttered aluminum foil and tie securely). Steam 2 hours on rack in large kettle half filled with boiling water. Let pudding stand in mold 5 minutes; unmold onto serving plate. Serve warm with whipped cream, if desired. Makes 8 servings.

ORANGE-FIG PUDDING

1 c. finely cut dried figs
½ c. shortening
1 c. light brown sugar, firmly packed
2 eggs
2 tbs. grated orange rind
2 c. sifted all-purpose flour
1½ tsp. baking powder
½ tsp. baking soda
½ tsp. ground cinnamon
½ tsp. salt
¼ c. orange juice

Simmer figs in water to cover for 3 minutes; drain; cool. Butter and dust 6-cup mold with sugar. Beat shortening, brown sugar, eggs and orange rind until fluffy. Sift flour, baking powder, baking soda, cinnamon, and salt together. Add dry ingredients alternately with orange juice to the shortening-sugar mixture. Stir figs into batter. Spoon into mold. Cover with lightly greased aluminum foil, leaving loose pouch on top to allow pudding to ex-

HARD SAUCE

⅔ cup soft butter

1½ cups sifted confectioners sugar

1½ teaspoons vanilla

Cream butter until soft. Gradually beat in sugar until light and fluffy. Beat in vanilla. Pile in serving dish and chill until firm. Serve about two tablespoons on each serving of warm plum pudding. Yield: about 10 servings.

... and sugar a 6-cup pudding mold. Combine all fruits, nuts, and orange juice in large bowl; mix well. Beat eggs in medium-size bowl; beat in sugar; stir in orange rind, corn syrup, suet, and bread crumbs. Sift flour, spices, and salt together; blend into egg mixture. Pour over fruit-nut mixture; mix thoroughly. Fill mold ¾ full; cover (if mold does not have cover, use lightly buttered aluminum foil and tie securely). Steam on rack in large kettle half filled with boiling water 6 hours. Add more water to the kettle during steaming if necessary. Let pudding stand in mold 10 minutes; unmold. Let cool. Wrap in aluminum foil or transparent plastic wrap to store. Baste occasionally with brandy and rewrap, if desired. To reheat for serving, steam in top of double boiler. Serve with Foamy Sauce (*page 400*) or Holiday Hard Sauce (*page 400*). Makes 8 servings.

When combining hot mixtures with whole eggs or egg yolks, always add part of the hot mixture to eggs, stirring constantly with a wooden spoon. Stir this back into the mixture remaining in saucepan and then proceed with the recipe.

PRUNE-APRICOT DUFF

½ c. chopped dried apricots	2 c. sifted all-purpose flour
1 c. drained cooked prunes	1½ tsp. baking powder
½ c. shortening	½ tsp. baking soda
1¼ c. light brown sugar, firmly packed	½ tsp. salt
2 eggs	1 tsp. ground cinnamon

Simmer chopped apricots in water to cover 5 minutes; drain. Remove pits from prunes; cut up. Butter and sugar a 6-cup mold. Beat shortening, brown sugar, and eggs in medium-size bowl until fluffy and well blended. Sift flour, baking powder, baking soda, and salt together. Beat into shortening mixture. Turn ⅓ of batter into small bowl; stir in apricots; spoon into prepared mold. Stir prunes and cinnamon into remaining batter; spoon carefully into mold on top of apricot batter. Cover (if mold does not have cover, use lightly buttered aluminum foil and tie securely). Steam on rack in large kettle half filled with boiling water 2 hours or until done. Let stand in mold 5 minutes; unmold onto serving plate. Serve warm with Holiday Hard Sauce (*page 400*), if desired. Makes 8 servings.

TORTES

CHOCOLATE CREAM TORTE

4 egg whites	¼ c. slivered
1 c. sugar	almonds
1¾ c. sifted cake	¾ c. dairy sour
flour	cream
2¼ tsp. baking	4 egg yolks
powder	½ c. sugar
¾ tsp. salt	¾ c. semi-sweet
½ c. butter or	chocolate pieces
margarine	1 tsp. vanilla
1 c. plus 2 tbs. sugar	1 c. heavy cream,
1 tsp. vanilla	sweetened and
2 eggs	whipped
¾ c. milk	Maraschino cherries

Make meringue: Beat egg whites until foamy; add 1 cup sugar gradually; beat well after each addition; continue beating until meringue forms stiff, glossy peaks.
Make cake: Line two 9-inch layer pans with wax paper. Sift flour, baking powder, and salt together. Cream butter or margarine, 1 cup plus 2 tablespoons sugar, and vanilla until fluffy; beat in eggs one at a time. Add dry ingredients alternately with milk; beat smooth after each addition. Pour into pans; spread meringue evenly over batter; sprinkle with almonds. Bake at 350° F. for 35 to 40 minutes. Cool in pans 5 minutes. Loosen edges; turn out of pans; remove paper; cool on wire racks, meringue side up. *Make filling:* Combine sour cream, egg yolks, ½ cup sugar, and chocolate pieces in saucepan. Cook over medium heat, stirring constantly, until thick; remove from heat; cool. Add vanilla; chill. Place 1 layer on plate, meringue side up; spread with filling; top with second layer. Frost sides with whipped cream; garnish with cherries. Chill 1 to 2 hours before serving.

DOBOS TORTE

6 egg whites	1 c. soft butter or
½ c. sugar	margarine
6 egg yolks	2 egg yolks
⅓ c. sugar	½ c. light cream or
1 c. sifted cake	milk
flour	2 pkgs. (1 lb. ea.)
4 sqs. unsweetened	confectioners'
chocolate	sugar
4 tbs. butter or	½ c. sugar
margarine	1 can (8 oz.) sliced
1 tbs. instant coffee	almonds
2 tbs. hot water	Candied cherries

Heat oven to 350° F. Trace seven 8-inch circles on large pieces of heavy aluminum foil; grease and flour area within circles. Beat egg whites until foamy; gradually beat in ½ cup sugar; continue beating until meringue forms stiff, glossy peaks. Beat 6 egg yolks and ⅓ cup sugar until thick and lemon colored; fold in meringue mixture. Fold in sifted flour. Spread batter as thinly as possible in circles on prepared foil. Bake 12 to 15 minutes or until golden. Remove from foil with spatula; cool thoroughly on wire racks. Melt chocolate and 4 tablespoons butter or margarine together; cool. Dissolve coffee in hot water; cool. Beat soft butter or margarine and 2 egg yolks at low speed on mixer or by hand just until blended. Combine coffee and cream or milk; add alternately with confectioners' sugar to egg yolk mixture; beat until well blended and smooth. Add cooled chocolate slowly; beat just until blended. Melt ½ cup sugar in large, heavy skillet, stirring constantly, until syrup turns golden brown. Pour immediately onto 1 layer, spreading evenly to edge with knife; mark at once with buttered knife into radiating lines for serving portions. Spread 6 layers with chocolate mixture; stack; place glazed layer on top; frost sides and top edge. Sprinkle sides with almonds; decorate edge with cherries.

VIENNESE CHOCOLATE TORTE

1 pkg. (6 oz.) semi-	1½ c. apricot
sweet chocolate	preserves
pieces	1 pkg. (6 oz.) semi-
¼ c. coffee or water	sweet chocolate
6 eggs	pieces
⅔ c. sugar	3 tbs. light corn
⅔ c. sifted all-	syrup
purpose flour	2 tsp. coffee

Melt 1 package chocolate pieces with ¼ cup coffee or water in top of double boiler over hot water; stir to blend; cool. Grease 8-inch springform pan; line bottom with wax paper; grease wax paper. Beat eggs and sugar together in large bowl of electric mixer at high speed about 10 minutes or until soft peaks form. Heat oven to 350° F. Fold cooled chocolate mixture carefully into beaten egg mixture. Sift flour a tablespoon at a time over batter; carefully fold each addition into batter. Pour batter into prepared pan. Bake 55 to 60 minutes. Cool on wire rack 10 min.

utes; loosen and remove sides of cake pan; cool cake completely. Loosen and remove bottom of cake pan; turn cake upside down; peel off wax paper. With sharp knife split cake in half. Spread bottom half with 3/4 cup of apricot preserves; replace top. Spread remaining preserves smoothly over top of cake; chill. Melt 1 package chocolate pieces with corn syrup and 2 teaspoons coffee in top of double boiler over hot water; stir well until mixture is smooth and glossy. Pour over cake while hot; spread with spatula to cover top and sides with thin glaze. Chill well before serving.

STRAWBERRY TORTE

(*Pictured opposite page 277*)

1/2 c. shortening
1/2 c. sugar
4 egg yolks
1/2 tsp. vanilla
1 1/4 c. sifted cake flour
1 1/4 tsp. baking powder
1/4 tsp. salt
1/4 c. milk
4 egg whites
2/3 c. sugar
1/2 c. sliced, blanched almonds
2 tbs. sugar
3 pts. strawberries
1/4 c. sugar
1 tbs. cornstarch
1/2 c. currant jelly
1 tbs. water

Grease and flour two 9x1 1/2-inch layer pans. Heat oven to 350° F. Beat shortening, 1/2 cup sugar, egg yolks, and vanilla at high speed on mixer until light and fluffy. Sift flour, baking powder, and salt together; add alternately with milk to egg mixture. Spread batter evenly in prepared pans. Beat egg whites until foamy; gradually add 2/3 cup sugar; continue beating until meringue forms stiff, glossy peaks. Spread meringue over batter in pans; sprinkle almonds and 2 tablespoons of sugar evenly over meringue. Bake 30 to 35 minutes or until meringue is delicately browned. Remove from oven; cool on wire racks 10 minutes. Carefully remove from pans. Place layers on wire racks, meringue side up; cool thoroughly. Wash, hull, and crush 1 pint of strawberries. Mix with 1/4 cup sugar; let stand 1 hour. Add cornstarch to strawberries; cook over medium heat until thickened and clear. Cool. Spread filling on top of one layer; place second layer on top. Heat currant jelly with water until melted; cool slightly. Wash and hull 2 pints of strawberries. Dip in melted jelly to glaze; arrange on top of torte, pointed ends up. Chill. Makes 10 to 12 servings.

SEVEN-LAYER DATE LEMON TORTE

4 egg whites
1 c. sugar
4 egg yolks
2 tbs. shortening, melted and cooled
1 tsp. vanilla
1 c. sifted cake flour
1 tsp. baking powder
1/8 tsp. salt
1/4 tsp. ground cloves
1/4 tsp. ground cinnamon
2 c. chopped, pitted dates
1/2 c. chopped walnuts
2/3 c. sugar
4 tbs. cornstarch
1/8 tsp. salt
2 c. water
1 tsp. grated lemon rind
1/3 c. lemon juice
1/2 c. heavy cream, whipped

Heat oven to 350° F. Grease seven 6-inch disposable foil pans or four 8-inch layer cake pans. Beat egg whites until foamy; beat in 1/2 cup sugar gradually. Continue beating until meringue forms stiff, glossy peaks. Measure remaining 1/2 cup sugar into bowl. Beat in 3 egg yolks, one at a time (save fourth egg yolk for filling). Stir in shortening and vanilla. Sift flour, baking powder, 1/8 teaspoon salt, and spices into large bowl. Stir dates and nuts into flour mixture. Stir in egg yolk mixture (batter will be very stiff). Fold in meringue. Spread batter evenly in prepared pans. Bake 15 to 20 minutes or until well browned on top. Remove layers from pans at once; place on wire racks; cool thoroughly. Mix 2/3 cup sugar, cornstarch, and 1/8 teaspoon salt in small saucepan; beat in reserved egg yolk. Stir in water. Cook over medium heat, stirring constantly, until thick and clear. Remove from heat; stir in lemon rind and juice; cool. Spread on cooled cake layers; stack layers. Chill overnight. Just before serving, spread top of torte with whipped cream. Makes 8 to 10 servings.

QUICK MOCHA TORTE

1 packaged angel food cake	½ tsp. vanilla
1 tbs. instant coffee	1 tsp. grated, unsweetened chocolate
1 tsp. hot water	
1 jar (6½ to 7 oz.) marshmallow cream	12 ladyfingers
	Chopped toasted almonds
¾ c. heavy cream, whipped	

Cut angel food cake crosswise in 3 layers. Dissolve instant coffee in hot water. Mix with marshmallow; fold in whipped cream, vanilla, and chocolate. Spread one third of mixture between layers; stack layers. Spread one third of mixture on sides of cake. Split ladyfingers. Press against side of cake, rounded sides out. Spread top of cake with remaining mixture; sprinkle with almonds. Chill. Makes 6 to 8 servings.

CREAM PUFFS

CREAM PUFFS AND ÉCLAIRS
(Pâte à choux)

1 c. water	1 c. sifted all-purpose flour
½ c. butter or margarine	4 eggs
⅛ tsp. salt	

Combine water, butter or margarine, and salt; bring to boiling. Add flour all at once; stir rapidly over heat until mixture forms ball and follows spoon around pan. Cool slightly. Beat in eggs, one at a time; beat well until mixture is smooth and each egg is blended in. Mixture will be slippery and separated, but the beating will smooth it. Heat oven to 400° F.

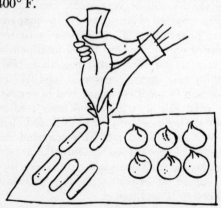

Cream Puffs: Press mixture through pastry bag (without metal tip) or spoon in 8 even mounds about 3 inches apart onto ungreased cookie sheet.

Éclairs: Press mixture through pastry bag (without metal tip) into 4x1-inch strips onto ungreased cookie sheet. Makes about 12.

Bake Puffs and Eclairs 45 to 50 minutes or until puffed, brown, and there are no tiny bubbles of moisture on surface. Cool; cut off tops; remove moist centers, if desired. Fill with Rich Pastry Cream (*page 455*). Ice tops with Chocolate Glaze (*page 456*). Puffs and Eclairs may be filled with whipped cream and fresh berries or ice cream and served with Double Chocolate Sauce (*page 399*) or Butterscotch Crème Sauce (*page 399*).

Profiteroles au Chocolat: Prepare half Cream Puff and Éclair mixture. Drop mixture from spoon or press through pastry bag into 24 small mounds about 2 inches apart onto ungreased cookie sheet. Bake 30 minutes or until puffed, brown, and there are no tiny bubbles of moisture on surface. Cool on wire rack. Make small slit in each puff with knife. Fill with Chocolate Cream filling (*page 455*) or Rich Pastry Cream (*page 455*). Chill. Arrange in pyramid on serving dish or allow 4 per serving and arrange individual servings. Serve with Double Chocolate Sauce (*page 399*).

Ice Cream Puffs: Prepare Cream Puff and Éclair mixture. Shape into 8 puffs as for Cream Puffs. Bake; cool. Cut off tops of puffs; fill with softened ice cream; replace tops. Wrap puffs in transparent plastic wrap or aluminum foil; freeze. Keep in freezer until 20 minutes before serving. Serve with Hot Chocolate Sauce (*page 399*) or Butterscotch Crème Sauce (*page 399*). Makes 8 servings.

MOCHA CREAM PUFFS

½ recipe Cream Puffs and Éclairs	1 pkg. (14 oz.) chocolate fudge frosting mix
1 pkg. (2 oz.) dessert topping mix	3 tbs. milk
1 tbs. instant coffee	Sifted confectioners' sugar
½ c. milk	

Prepare Cream Puff and Éclair mixture; shape into 6 puffs; bake; cool. Blend dessert topping mix, instant coffee, and ½ cup milk in small bowl of electric mixer; beat at high speed until soft peaks form. Slowly beat in frosting mix alternately with remaining 3 tablespoons milk until mixture is smooth and blended. Cut tops off puffs; spoon in filling; replace tops; chill. Just before serving, dust tops with sifted confectioners' sugar. Makes 6 servings.

GÂTEAU ST. HONORÉ

½ pkg. pie crust mix	4 egg yolks, slightly beaten
1 egg yolk	¼ c. Cointreau or curaçao
2 tbs. water	
1 recipe Cream Puffs and Éclairs	4 egg whites
	⅓ c. sugar
1 envelope un-flavored gelatin	1 c. sugar
	¼ tsp. cream of tartar
¾ c. sugar	
½ c. sifted all-purpose flour	⅓ c. water
	Confectioners' sugar
½ tsp. salt	
3 c. milk	1 c. heavy cream, whipped

Prepare pie crust mix according to package directions; roll out to 8-inch circle; transfer to cookie sheet; brush with egg yolk beaten with water; prick well with fork. Prepare cream puff mixture. Press through pastry bag (without metal tip) in circle, onto edge of pie crust circle. Form second circle of cream puff mixture, same size, on second cookie sheet. Form remaining mixture into 8 small cream puffs. Bake at 400° F. for 30 to 35 minutes or until done; cool. Prepare *Crème St. Honoré Filling:* Combine gelatin, ¾ cup sugar, flour, and salt in saucepan; stir in milk. Cook over medium heat, stirring constantly until thickened and bubbly. Stir ½ of mixture into egg yolks. Return mixture to saucepan; cook 1 minute longer. Remove from heat; cool; stir in Cointreau or curaçao; chill until mixture begins to thicken. Beat egg whites until foamy; add ⅓ cup sugar gradually; continue beating until meringue forms stiff, glossy peaks. Fold meringue into chilled custard. Make slit in side of each puff. Fill with Crème St. Honoré Filling; chill. *Caramel Glaze:* Combine 1 cup sugar, cream of tartar, and water in saucepan; cook over low heat until golden, and caramelized, about 25 minutes. Brush bottom of separate puff ring with caramel glaze; press onto ring formed on pastry circle. Dip each puff into caramel; arrange on top of top ring of Gâteau. Fill center of Gâteau with remaining Crème St. Honoré. Just before serving, dust Gâteau with confectioners' sugar; decorate with whipped cream. Makes 8 servings.

MERINGUES

The secret of success in making meringues is to beat the egg whites until foamy, then to beat in the sugar gradually, beating after each addition until the sugar is dissolved, and to continue beating until stiff, glossy peaks form.

MERINGUE SHELLS

6 egg whites	1½ c. sugar
¼ tsp. salt	1 tsp. vanilla or almond extract
¼ tsp. cream of tartar	

Beat egg whites with salt and cream of tartar until foamy. They will beat to greater volume if they have been out of the refrigerator for a few hours. Add sugar very slowly; continue to beat until meringue forms stiff, glossy peaks and is very stiff. Beat in vanilla or almond extract. Shape meringue mixture into any one of the following forms. Heat oven to 275° F. Bake 55 to 60 minutes or until crisp. Remove from cookie sheet; cool on wire rack.

Pistachio Meringue Basket: Grease and flour cookie sheet. Make a guideline in shape of 9-inch circle or oval or heart in coating on cookie sheet. Prepare meringue according to recipe. Shape meringue with back of spoon within guideline. Build up sides higher than center to form a shell. Bake; cool. Form 1 quart of pistachio ice cream into balls; fill meringue shell with ice cream. Top with Hot Chocolate Sauce (*page 399*). Makes 6 to 8 servings.

Meringue Nut Nests: Prepare meringue according to recipe. Fold in ½ cup finely chopped walnuts or pecans. Shape into 12 individual nests. Bake; cool. Fill with tiny ice cream balls in a variety of flavors. Makes 12 servings.

Swan Ice Cream Boats: Prepare meringue according to recipe. Grease and flour cookie sheet. Shape two thirds of meringue into ten 4-inch ovals about 1¼ inches high; shape one end into point for swan's body. Put remaining meringue into pastry bag, fitted with round metal tip. Shape ten 4-inch narrow S's for swan's neck and head. Bake. Scoop out centers of ovals; return to oven right side up; bake 10 minutes longer, or until they are dry and crisp. Cool. Fill with tiny balls of ice cream; press S's into ice cream to hold upright. Makes 10 servings.

Melba Nut Meringues:

½ recipe Meringue Nut Nests
4 ripe peaches or 1 pkg. (10 oz.) frozen peaches, thawed
¼ c. sugar

2 c. raspberries or 1 pkg. (10 oz.) frozen raspberries, thawed
¼ c. sugar
1 pt. vanilla ice cream

Prepare Meringue Nut Nests; bake; cool. Peel and slice peaches; combine with ¼ cup sugar. Wash and drain raspberries; combine with ¼ cup sugar. Let fruits stand 20 minutes. If using frozen fruits, drain; omit sugar. Spoon peaches into meringue nests; add scoop of vanilla ice cream; top with raspberries. Makes 6 servings.

Lime Angel Tarts
(*Pictured opposite page 52*)

½ recipe Meringue Shells
3 tbs. cornstarch
1 c. sugar
⅛ tsp. salt
1⅓ c. water

2 tsp. grated lime rind
⅓ c. lime juice
½ c. heavy cream, whipped
Few drops green food coloring

Heat oven to 250° F. Grease and flour cookie sheets. Prepare ½ Meringue Shells recipe. Shape meringue mixture with spoon or pastry bag into small nests 1½ inches wide and 1 inch high on prepared cookie sheets. Bake 50 to 55 minutes or until dry. Remove from cookie sheets with spatula. Cool on wire racks. Meringues can be prepared ahead and stored in covered containers. Combine cornstarch, sugar, salt, and water in saucepan. Cook over medium heat, stirring constantly, until mixture simmers. Simmer 5 minutes. Remove from heat; add lime rind and juice. Cool, stirring occasionally. Chill. Before serving, fold in whipped cream and green food coloring. Spoon into meringue nests. Makes 3 dozen.

LEMON ANGEL PIE
(Schaum Torte)

This delicious dessert is truly a make-ahead. It needs that overnight mellowing to develop full flavor.

4 egg whites
¼ tsp. cream of tartar
1 c. sugar
4 egg yolks
½ c. sugar

2 tbs. grated lemon rind
¼ c. lemon juice
1 c. heavy cream, whipped

Meringue Shell: Heat oven to 275° F. Grease 9-inch pie plate. Beat egg whites and cream of tartar until foamy. Beat in 1 cup sugar gradually. Continue beating until meringue forms stiff, glossy peaks. Spread over bottom and sides of prepared pie plate; shape with back of spoon so bottom is ¼ inch thick and sides 1 inch thick. Bake 60 minutes. Turn off oven; leave meringue shell in oven until cool. Beat egg yolks in top of double boiler until thick and lemon colored. Beat in ½ cup sugar gradually. Blend in lemon rind and juice. Cook over hot water, stirring constantly, 5 to 8 minutes or until thick. Cool. Turn into cooled meringue shell. Chill at least 12 hours. Top with whipped cream before serving. Makes 8 servings.

Lime Angel Pie: Substitute ½ teaspoon of lime rind for lemon rind and ⅓ cup of lime juice for lemon juice in above recipe.

PINEAPPLE ANGEL PIE

1 meringue shell
1 can (1 lb. 4½ oz.) crushed pineapple
1 envelope unflavored gelatin
¼ c. sugar

4 egg yolks, slightly beaten
1 tsp. grated lemon rind
½ c. instant nonfat dry milk
½ c. ice water
2 tbs. lemon juice

Prepare, bake, and cool meringue shell as in Lemon Angel Pie. Mix pineapple, gelatin, and sugar in saucepan. Let stand 3 to 5 minutes. Add egg yolks. Cook over low heat, stirring constantly, until mixture thickens and just begins to simmer. Remove from heat; add lemon rind. Chill until mixture will mound when spooned. Beat nonfat dry milk and ice water 3 to 4 minutes or until soft peaks form. Add lemon juice; beat until stiff. Fold into pineapple mixture. Turn into cooled meringue shell. Chill at least 12 hours. Makes 8 servings.

FRENCH STRAWBERRY MERINGUE CAKE

Here's a cake from New Orleans with a very French touch—almond meringue layers are filled and topped with whipped cream and strawberries.

6 egg whites	⅔ c. sifted corn-
¼ tsp. cream of	starch
tartar	1 qt. strawberries
1½ c. sugar	1½ pts. heavy
½ c. ground,	cream
blanched	
almonds	

Grease and dust with flour six cookie sheets or the bottoms of six 8-inch cake pans. (Or if you do not have that many, use heavy-duty aluminum foil. Be sure to keep foil smooth.) Mark an 8-inch circle on each sheet, pan, or piece of foil. Heat oven to 300° F. Beat egg whites with cream of tartar at high speed on mixer until foamy. Beat in sugar, a little at a time; continue beating at high speed for about 5 minutes until meringue forms stiff, glossy peaks (most of the sugar will be dissolved in the egg whites). Combine almonds and cornstarch; fold gently into meringue mixture. Divide mixture evenly among the 6 circles; spread smoothly within circular markings; take care that you do not have any thin spots which would overbrown. Bake 30 to 35 minutes or until meringues are dry and golden. Cool slightly on wire racks; gently loosen and remove with broad spatula. *Caution:* meringue layers are brittle and will not bend, so be sure to slide the spatula straight under the layers to free them. (Meringues may be kept in loosely covered container at room temperature for several days. Slip sheets of wax paper between each

layer of meringue.) Reserve prettiest strawberries for garnish; crush remainder; you may add sugar, if desired. Whip 2 cups (1 pint) cream. Spread 5 layers with cream; top with crushed strawberries. Stack layers; top with 6th layer. Whip remaining 1 cup of cream; spread over top layer. Halve the reserved strawberries; press cut side up into the cream. Chill two to three hours to allow meringue layers to soften and mellow. Makes 8 to 10 servings.

DESSERT PANCAKES

CREPES

1 c. plus 2 tbs. sifted	1½ c. milk
all-purpose flour	1 tbs. melted butter
¼ c. sugar	or margarine
¼ tsp. salt	1 tbs. Cognac or
3 eggs, beaten	brandy

Sift flour, sugar, and salt together. Combine eggs, milk, butter or margarine, and Cognac or brandy; add to flour mixture, beating until smooth. Cover bowl; let batter stand at room temperature for 2 hours. Bake in hot, greased 6- to 7-inch skillet, using 2 tablespoons batter for each crepe, tilting pan to make a very thin crepe. When crepe is delicately brown on underside, turn to brown other side. Repeat with remaining batter. If making crepes ahead, wrap loosely in aluminum foil until ready to use.

Crepes Suzette

1 recipe Crepes	½ tsp. lemon juice
3 tbs. butter or	½ c. Cointreau,
margarine	curaçao, Bene-
4 tsp. sugar	dictine, or Grand
1 tsp. grated orange	Marnier
rind	½ c. warm brandy
⅔ c. orange juice	

Prepare crepes according to recipe. Melt butter or margarine in skillet or chafing dish; add sugar, orange rind, orange and lemon juices; heat until sugar dissolves; add liqueur; heat; add crepes folded in quarters; baste with sauce. Remove pan from heat (or turn off heat if using electric skillet). Add warm brandy; ignite; when flames die, serve. Makes about 6 to 7 servings.

Crepes Maltaise Flambé

1 recipe Crepes
1 tbs. slivered
  orange rind
½ c. orange juice
½ c. butter or
  margarine
2 tsp. lemon juice
¼ c. sugar

2 large oranges,
  peeled and
  sectioned
⅓ c. Grand Marnier
  or Cointreau
¼ c. Maraschino
  liqueur

Prepare crepes according to recipe. Reserve orange rind. Combine orange juice, butter or margarine, lemon juice, and sugar in small saucepan; simmer 2 to 3 minutes; add orange sections; heat 1 minute. Arrange orange sections and crepes in chafing dish; pour hot sauce over; add orange rind. Place over chafing-dish burner. Combine Grand Marnier or Cointreau and Maraschino; stir half into bubbling sauce; float half on top. When hot, ignite and serve flaming. Makes 4 servings.

Crepes Jubilee

1 recipe Crepes
1 pkg. (8 oz.)
  cream cheese
¾ c. dairy sour
  cream
1 can (1 lb. 5 oz.)
  cherry pie filling

2 tbs. water
2 tbs. butter or
  margarine
2 tbs. Cointreau
3 tbs. Cognac

Prepare crepes according to recipe. Blend cream cheese and sour cream until smooth. Place spoonful of mixture on each baked crepe; roll up; place in single layer in shallow, flat pan. Cover with aluminum foil, bake at 350° F. for 15 minutes. Heat cherry pie filling, water, and butter or margarine. Add Cointreau and cognac. Serve over warm crepes. Makes 20 crepes or 6 to 7 servings.

Crepes New Orleans

1 recipe Crepes
¼ c. sugar
3 tbs. flour
⅔ c. milk, scalded
2 egg yolks, beaten
½ tsp. vanilla

¾ c. heavy cream,
  whipped
1 c. apricot jam
⅓ c. orange juice
1 tbs. butter or
  margarine
¼ c. rum

Prepare crepes according to recipe. Combine sugar and flour in saucepan; stir in milk. Cook over medium heat, stirring constantly, until thickened. Stir one half the hot mixture into beaten yolks; blend into remaining mixture in saucepan. Cook over low heat 2 minutes, stirring constantly. Cool, stirring occasionally; chill. When cold, fold in vanilla and whipped cream. Mash apricot jam in saucepan with fork to break up large pieces of fruit; add orange juice and butter or margarine; heat until bubbly. Place spoonful of whipped cream mixture on each baked crepe; roll up. Place in single layer in shallow pan. Brush ⅓ cup apricot sauce over crepes. Place under broiler 1 minute. Add rum to remaining sauce; heat until bubbly; serve hot over crepes. To flame, pour additional warm rum over crepes and ignite. Makes 6 to 7 servings.

BLINTZES

3 egg yolks, beaten
2 tbs. melted butter
  or margarine
¾ tsp. salt
2 tsp. sugar

¾ c. sifted all-
  purpose flour
1½ c. milk
3 egg whites

Beat egg yolks, butter or margarine, salt, sugar, flour, and milk until smooth; fold in egg whites beaten to soft peaks. Cover bowl; let batter stand at room temperature 1 hour. Bake on hot, greased skillet, using 2 tablespoons batter for each pancake, tilting pan to make very thin blintzes. Brown on one side only; stack, browned side up, between squares of wax paper. Makes 20 to 21 blintzes.

Strawberry Blintzes

1 recipe Blintzes
1 carton (8 oz.)
  cottage cheese,
  sieved
1 egg yolk
2 tbs. dairy sour
  cream

1 tbs. sugar
Dash of salt
½ tsp. grated lemon
  rind
1 c. sliced straw-
  berries
Butter or margarine

Prepare Blintzes according to recipe. Combine cottage cheese, egg yolk, sour cream, sugar, salt, and lemon rind; fold in strawberries. Place heaping tablespoon of cheese mixture in center of browned side of each blintz; fold sides over filling like an envelope, pressing to seal. Brown in butter or margarine; serve with sour cream and additional sliced strawberries, if desired. Makes 6 to 7 servings.

Cherry Blintzes

1 recipe Blintzes
1 can (1 lb. 5 oz.)
   cherry pie filling
Butter or margarine
Dairy sour cream

Prepare Blintzes according to recipe. Place spoonful of cherry pie filling on browned side of each blintz; fold sides over filling and press to seal. Brown in butter or margarine. Serve with sour cream. Makes 6 to 7 servings.

Cheese Blintzes

1 recipe Blintzes
2 cartons (1 lb. ea.)
   cream style
   cottage cheese
2 egg yolks, beaten
¼ c. sugar
¼ tsp. salt
2 tsp. grated lemon
   rind
Butter or margarine

Prepare Blintzes according to recipe. Combine cottage cheese, egg yolks, sugar, salt, and lemon rind in bowl; mix thoroughly. Place a blintz, browned side up, on wax paper; put ¼ cup cottage cheese mixture in center. Fold over from both sides, then from top and bottom to form a small envelope; seal edges with a little batter. Repeat until all blintzes and filling have been used. Brown blintzes on both sides in butter or margarine in skillet. Serve hot with sour cream and brown sugar, or sour cream and sliced strawberries, or sour cream and canned cherry pie filling, if desired. Makes 20 blintzes or 10 servings.

AMERICAN DESSERT PANCAKES

1½ c. sifted all-
   purpose flour
2 tsp. baking
   powder
1 tsp. salt
3 tbs. sugar
2 egg yolks
1¼ c. milk
3 tbs. melted butter
   or margarine
2 egg whites, stiffly
   beaten

Sift flour, baking powder, salt, and sugar together. Combine egg yolks, milk, and butter or margarine. Add liquid mixture to flour mixture, mix until flour is damp. Fold in egg whites. Use ¼ cup batter per pancake. Bake on hot, greased griddle. Makes 12 to 14 four-inch pancakes. Serve stacked with butter or margarine and maple or brown sugar. For parties, make 6 large pancakes using ½ cup batter per pancake. Make a stack of 6 pancakes; cut in wedges to make 6 servings.

Fruited Pancakes

Prepare American Dessert Pancake batter according to recipe. Use 3 tablespoons of batter for each pancake. Pour about 1½ tablespoons of batter on griddle; place a thin slice of pared apple ring or 4 slices of banana on top of batter. Immediately pour remaining 1½ tablespoons of batter on top of fruit. When brown on bottom, turn and brown other side. Serve with butter, cinnamon and sugar, or with Lemon Sauce (*page 400*). Makes 18 to 20 three-and-a-half-inch pancakes.

HUNGARIAN MERINGUE PANCAKES

3 egg yolks
1 egg white
¾ c. light cream
¾ c. carbonated
   water
1½ c. sifted all-
   purpose flour
¾ tsp. salt

Combine egg yolks, egg white, cream, carbonated water, flour, and salt; beat until smooth. Use ¼ cup batter for each pancake. Bake on greased 9-inch skillet, tilting pan to make thin pancake. When pancake is lightly browned, brown other side. Repeat with remaining batter. Stack pancakes between squares of wax paper while making filling. Makes 10 eight-inch pancakes.

Filling

1 carton (8 oz.)
   cottage cheese,
   sieved
1 egg yolk
⅓ c. raisins
3 tbs. sugar
½ c. ground
   walnuts
1 sq. semi-sweet
   chocolate, grated
¾ c. apricot or
   orange jam
3 egg whites
6 tbs. sugar

Combine cottage cheese, egg yolk, raisins, and 2 tablespoons sugar. Combine 1 tablespoon sugar, ground walnuts, and grated chocolate. Place one pancake on ovenproof plate; spread with ⅓ cottage cheese mixture; place second pancake on top; sprinkle with ⅓ chocolate-nut mixture; place third pancake on top, spread with ¼ cup jam. Repeat layering twice. Place tenth pancake on top. Beat egg whites until foamy; slowly add 6 tablespoons sugar; beat until stiff, glossy peaks form. Spread meringue on top of pancakes. Bake at 325° F. for 15 to 20 minutes or until delicately browned. Serve cut in wedges. Makes 6 to 8 servings. Serve at once.

VIENNESE CHOCOLATE PANCAKES

¾ c. sifted all-
 purpose flour
⅓ c. sugar
1 tsp. salt
2 eggs, beaten
1 c. milk

½ c. light cream
1½ sqs. unsweet-
 ened chocolate,
 melted
1 tsp. vanilla

Sift flour, sugar, and salt together. Combine eggs, milk, cream, melted chocolate, and vanilla; beat until blended. Add flour mixture; beat until smooth. Cover bowl; let batter stand half hour. Bake on greased skillet or griddle using 2 tablespoons of batter for each pancake. Keep pancakes warm in a towel (or reheat in oven) while preparing filling.

Coffee Cream Filling

1½ c. heavy cream
3 tbs. confectioners'
 sugar
2½ tsp. instant
 coffee

Confectioners'
 sugar
Chocolate curls

Combine heavy cream, 3 tablespoons confectioners' sugar, and coffee; beat until soft peaks form. Place spoonful on each pancake; fold pancake in half. Sprinkle with confectioners' sugar and a few chocolate curls. Makes 6 to 7 servings.

Franz Pancakes

1 recipe Viennese
 Chocolate Pan-
 cakes
¼ c. sugar
3 tbs. flour

⅔ c. milk
2 egg yolks, beaten
½ tsp. vanilla
¾ c. heavy cream,
 whipped

Prepare pancakes according to recipe. Combine sugar and flour in saucepan; stir in milk. Cook over medium heat, stirring constantly until thickened. Stir half the hot mixture into beaten yolks; blend into mixture in saucepan. Cook over low heat two minutes, stirring constantly. Cool, stirring occasionally; chill. When cold, fold in vanilla and whipped cream. Place spoonful of cream mixture on each pancake; fold in half. Serve with Orange Sauce (*page 401*) or Double Chocolate Sauce (*page 399*), if desired.

DUTCH BABY

3 eggs
½ c. sifted all-
 purpose flour
½ tsp. salt
½ c. milk
2 tbs. melted butter
 or margarine

1 tbs. lemon juice
1½ pts. straw-
 berries, washed
 and hulled
Confectioners'
 sugar
Dairy sour cream

Heat oven to 450° F. Beat eggs until blended. Sift flour and salt together. Add sifted dry ingredients and milk to eggs; beat until smooth. Stir in melted butter or margarine. Pour into greased 9-inch skillet with oven-proof handle. Bake on bottom shelf of oven 20 minutes. Reduce oven heat to 350° F. Prick shell well with tines of fork; bake 10 minutes longer. Remove from oven; sprinkle with lemon juice. Fill with strawberries; sprinkle with confectioners' sugar. Cut in wedges; top with a dollop of sour cream. Serve at once. Makes 6 servings.

DANISH THIN PANCAKES

1½ c. sifted all-
 purpose flour
2 tbs. sugar
1 tsp. salt
½ tsp. ground
 cardamom
4 egg yolks, beaten
1⅔ c. milk

7 tbs. melted butter
 or margarine
4 egg whites, stiffly
 beaten
Lingonberries or
 whole cranberry
 sauce

Sift flour, sugar, salt, and cardamom together. Combine egg yolks and milk; add gradually to flour mixture, mixing until smooth. Stir in butter or margarine; fold in egg whites. Bake on ungreased skillet, using 3 to 4 tablespoons batter for each pancake; tilt pan to make 6- to 7-inch pancakes. Fold in quarters, serve with lingonberries or whole cranberry sauce. Makes about 16 pancakes.

SWEDISH PLÄTTAR

1¼ c. sifted all-
 purpose flour
2 tbs. sugar
½ tsp. salt
3 eggs
1 c. light cream

2 c. milk
Lingonberries or
 applesauce
Confectioners'
 sugar

Sift flour, sugar, and salt together. Beat eggs and cream; add flour mixture; beat until smooth. Stir in milk gradually; cover bowl. Let batter stand at room temperature 1 hour. Heat plättar pan (plättpanna) or use a heavy iron skillet or griddle. Butter each section of plättar pan or griddle. Use 1 tablespoon batter for each pancake; turn pancakes when golden brown. Stack pancakes on top of each other; cover with towel to keep warm. Use 6 to 8 pancakes per serving. Layer with lingonberries or applesauce and sprinkle with confectioners' sugar. Makes 8 to 10 servings.

Baked Plättar: Melt 1 tablespoon butter or margarine in 12x9x2-inch pan. Pour batter into pan. Bake at 425° F. for 40 to 45 minutes or until puffed and browned. Cut into squares. Serve as above. Makes 8 servings.

DESSERT SOUFFLÉS

TOASTED ALMOND SOUFFLÉ

3 tbs. cornstarch	½ tsp. almond
½ c. sugar	extract
⅛ tsp. salt	1 tsp. vanilla
¾ c. milk	3 egg whites
3 egg yolks, well	¼ tsp. cream of
beaten	tartar
½ c. finely chopped	
toasted, blanched	
almonds	

Butter a 1½-quart soufflé dish; sprinkle liberally with granulated sugar; tap out excess. This mixture will form a sweet, crispy crust on your soufflé. Combine cornstarch, sugar, and salt in saucepan. Add milk; stir until mixture is smooth. Cook over medium heat, stirring constantly, until mixture thickens and bubbles (mixture will be quite thick). Remove from heat; beat mixture slowly into egg yolks; stir in almonds and almond and vanilla extracts; cool. Heat oven to 300° F. Beat egg whites with cream of tartar until stiff but not dry. Gently fold almond mixture into egg whites. Pour into prepared soufflé dish. Set dish in pan of hot water 1 inch deep. Bake 50 to 60 minutes or until puffed and golden and fairly firm to the touch. Serve at once. Makes 6 servings.

Note: Soufflé may be baked in six individual soufflé dishes. Bake at 300° F. 25 to 30 minutes; serve at once.

CHOCOLATE SOUFFLÉ

2 sqs. unsweetened	2 tbs. milk
chocolate	3 egg yolks, well
¾ c. milk	beaten
3 tbs. cornstarch	3 egg whites
½ c. sugar	¼ tsp. cream of
¼ tsp. salt	tartar

Butter a 1½-quart soufflé dish; sprinkle liberally with granulated sugar; tap out excess. This mixture will form a sweet, crispy crust in your soufflé. Melt chocolate in ¾ cup milk in top of double boiler over hot, not boiling water. Combine cornstarch, sugar, and salt in saucepan. Slowly add 2 tablespoons milk, stirring until mixture is smooth. Stir in hot chocolate mixture. Cook over medium heat, stirring constantly, until mixture thickens and bubbles. Remove from heat; beat mixture slowly into egg yolks; cool. Heat oven to 350° F. Beat egg whites with cream of tartar until stiff but not dry. Gently fold in chocolate mixture. Pour into prepared soufflé dish. Set dish in pan of hot water 1 inch deep. Bake 45 to 55 minutes or until puffed and fairly firm to the touch. Serve at once. Makes 6 servings.

APRICOT SOUFFLÉ

3 tbs. cornstarch	1 tsp. grated lemon
½ c. sugar	rind
⅛ tsp. salt	3 egg whites
¾ c. milk	¼ tsp. cream of
½ c. apricot purée*	tartar
3 egg yolks, well	
beaten	

Butter a 1½-quart soufflé dish; sprinkle liberally with granulated sugar; tap out excess. This mixture will form a sweet, crispy crust on your soufflé. Combine cornstarch, sugar, and salt in saucepan. Slowly add milk, stirring until mixture is smooth. Stir in apricot purée.* (To make purée, drain 1 can [1 lb. 13 oz.] apricots; pat dry on paper towels. Press through sieve or food mill.) Cook over medium heat, stirring constantly, until mixture thickens and bubbles. Remove from heat; beat mixture slowly into egg yolks; stir in lemon rind; cool. Heat oven to 300° F. Beat egg whites with cream of tartar until stiff but not dry. Gently fold apricot mixture into egg whites. Pour into prepared soufflé dish. Set dish in pan of hot water 1 inch deep. Bake 50 to 60 minutes or until soufflé is puffed and golden and fairly firm to the touch. Serve at once. Makes 6 servings.

CHEESECAKES

PERFECT CHEESECAKE

Pastry

1 c. sifted all-purpose flour
¼ c. sugar
1 tsp. grated lemon rind
¼ tsp. vanilla
¼ c. butter or margarine
1 egg yolk

Filling

5 pkgs. (8 oz. ea.) cream cheese (2½ lbs.)

1¾ c. sifted granulated sugar
3 tbs. all-purpose flour
¼ tsp. salt
½ tsp. grated orange rind
½ tsp. grated lemon rind
¼ tsp. vanilla
5 whole eggs, unbeaten
2 egg yolks
¼ c. heavy cream

Pastry: Mix flour, sugar, lemon rind, and vanilla with pastry blender in medium-size bowl; cut in butter or margarine; stir in egg yolk. Shape into mound; wrap in wax paper. Chill at least 1 hour. Heat oven to 400° F. Remove side from 9-inch springform pan. Place ⅓ of dough on ungreased bottom of pan; cover with floured wax paper. Roll or pat dough to fit pan bottom; remove paper. Bake 10 minutes or until golden. Remove from oven; turn oven temperature to 500° F. Cool pastry, leaving it on pan bottom. Grease side of springform pan; fit over cooled base. Form remaining dough into thick rectangle; cut in half lengthwise; line side of pan, patting and stretching dough to fit. (Patching won't hurt, but dough must be paper thin and cover side completely.)

Filling: Soften cream cheese in large bowl; beat until fluffy. Mix sugar, flour, salt, orange and lemon rinds, and vanilla; add very slowly to cheese; beat until smooth. Add eggs and egg yolks, one at a time, beating well after each addition; stir in cream. Turn into pastry-lined pan. Bake at 500° F. for 12 minutes. Do not open oven door; reduce oven temperature to 200° F.; bake cake 1 hour longer. Remove from oven; cool on wire rack, away from draft. Cake will shrink slightly as it cools. When cool, loosen cake from pan with spatula; remove side of pan; chill cake.

CREAMY CHEESECAKE

2 c. graham-cracker crumbs (about 24 crackers)
1 tbs. sugar
½ c. melted butter or margarine
4 egg yolks
¼ c. sugar
¼ c. sifted all-purpose flour
2 cartons (1 lb. ea.) cottage cheese, sieved
1 tsp. grated lemon rind
1 tbs. lemon juice
2 tsp. vanilla
½ c. heavy cream
4 egg whites
¼ c. sugar

Combine cracker crumbs and 1 tablespoon sugar in small bowl; stir in melted butter or margarine; press evenly on bottom and sides of buttered 8-inch springform pan; chill. Beat egg yolks in large bowl; beat in ¼ cup sugar; continue beating until thick and light. Stir in flour, cottage cheese, lemon rind and juice, and vanilla; blend in cream. Beat egg whites in medium-size bowl until frothy; beat in ¼ cup sugar, a tablespoon at a time; continue beating until meringue forms stiff, glossy peaks; carefully fold into cheese mixture; pour into crumb-lined pan. Bake at 325° F. for 1 hour and 15 minutes or until browned on top. Turn off oven heat; open oven door, let cake cool in oven 1 hour. Cake will shrink slightly as it cools. Remove from oven; cool thoroughly on wire cake rack before removing from pan.

CRANBERRY CHEESECAKE

1¼ c. fine zwieback crumbs
¼ c. sugar
¼ c. melted butter or margarine
2 pkgs. (8 oz. ea.) cream cheese
½ c. sugar
½ tsp. ground cinnamon
1 tsp. vanilla
3 eggs, beaten
½ envelope (1½ tsp.) unflavored gelatin
3 tbs. cold water
1 can (about 1 lb.) whole cranberry sauce
1 c. dairy sour cream
2 tbs. chopped walnuts or pecans

Heat oven to 350° F. Combine zwieback crumbs, ¼ cup sugar, and butter or margarine; mix well. Press crumbs firmly on bottom and sides of an 8-inch springform pan. Bake 10 minutes. Cool. Beat cream cheese until fluffy; add ½ cup sugar, cinnamon, and vanilla; beat well. Blend in eggs. Pour cheese mixture into crust-lined pan. Bake 35 to 40 minutes or until cheesecake is firm in center. Cool. Soak gelatin in cold water; melt over hot water; stir into cranberry sauce. Chill until mixture begins to set; spread over cooled cheesecake. Spread sour cream on top of cranberry layer. Sprinkle with nuts. Chill.

EASY PEACH CHEESECAKE

¾ c. graham-cracker crumbs	3 cartons (8 oz. ea.) cottage cheese, sieved
2 tbs. melted butter or margarine	1 can (1 lb. 13 oz.) sliced cling peaches, well drained
2 tbs. sugar	
1 tbs. grated orange rind	
2 envelopes unflavored gelatin	2 egg whites
	¼ c. sugar
⅔ c. sugar	1 tbs. lime or lemon juice
½ c. orange juice	1 c. dairy sour cream
2 egg yolks, slightly beaten	

Blend cracker crumbs, butter or margarine, and 2 tablespoons sugar together; press on bottom of 8-inch springform pan; chill. Grate and reserve orange rind. Mix gelatin and ⅔ cup sugar; stir in orange juice and egg yolks. Cook over medium heat, stirring constantly, until mixture just comes to boiling; cool. Stir in cottage cheese; chill until it begins to set. Dice enough peaches to make 1 cup; reserve remainder. Beat egg whites until foamy; beat in ¼ cup sugar slowly; continue beating until stiff. Fold egg whites, orange rind, lime or lemon juice, sour cream, and diced peaches into cheese mixture. Pour into pan; chill 3 hours or until set. Top with reserved peaches.

STRAWBERRY CHEESECAKE

1⅓ c. graham-cracker crumbs	2 egg whites
	¼ c. sugar
¼ c. sugar	1 carton (1 lb.) cottage cheese
¼ c. soft butter or margarine	
	½ c. dairy sour cream
2 c. crushed strawberries	
	Few drops red food coloring
½ c. sugar	
2 envelopes unflavored gelatin	

Heat oven to 375° F. Blend graham-cracker crumbs, ¼ cup sugar, and butter or marga-

rine. Press firmly on bottom and sides of 8-inch springform pan. Bake 8 minutes; remove from oven; cool. Mix strawberries and ½ cup sugar; let stand 15 minutes. Put through sieve or food mill to purée; put in top of double boiler. Sprinkle gelatin on purée; heat over simmering water until gelatin is dissolved; remove from heat; cool. Beat egg whites until foamy; gradually beat in ¼ cup sugar; continue beating until stiff meringue forms. Fold cottage cheese, sour cream, and meringue into strawberry mixture. Fold in red food coloring to make a slightly deeper pink. Turn into prepared pan. Chill several hours or until firm. Release clip to open springform pan; lift ring straight up to remove.

PINEAPPLE CHEESECAKE

1 c. graham-cracker crumbs	1 tbs. lemon juice
	2 pkgs. (8 oz. ea.) cream cheese
¼ c. sugar	
¼ c. softened butter or margarine	¾ c. sugar
	3 egg yolks
3 tbs. cornstarch	1 pt. (2 c.) dairy sour cream
¼ c. sugar	
2 cans (8¾ oz. ea.) crushed pineapple	½ tsp. grated lemon rind
	3 egg whites

Heat oven to 375° F. Blend graham-cracker crumbs, ¼ cup sugar, and butter or margarine. Press firmly on bottom and sides of 8- or 9-inch springform pan; bake 8 minutes; cool. Combine cornstarch and ¼ cup sugar; stir in pineapple with juice. Cook over medium heat, stirring briskly, until thickened and clear; cool; stir in lemon juice. Spread pineapple mixture evenly over bottom of crumb crust. Heat oven to 325° F. Beat cheese, ¾ cup sugar, and egg yolks in electric mixer until blended and smooth. Beat in 1½ cups sour cream (reserve ½ cup for garnish) and lemon rind. Beat egg whites until stiff but not dry; blend into cheese mixture; pour mixture carefully on top of pineapple layer. Bake 1 hour and 30 minutes or until set and brown. Turn off oven heat; open oven door; let cake cool in oven ½ hour. Top of cake will crack during baking but will settle as cake cools. Remove from oven; cool thoroughly; chill. Before serving, remove from pan; spoon reserved sour cream on top. Garnish with pineapple slices and maraschino cherries, if desired.

CHEESE PIE

12 ladyfingers, split
  lengthwise and
  cut in half
  crosswise
2 envelopes un-
  flavored gelatin
1/4 c. sugar
1 1/2 c. orange juice
2 egg yolks
1 can (8 1/2 oz.)
  sliced pineapple

1 carton (1 lb.)
  cottage cheese,
  sieved
2 egg whites
1/4 c. sugar
1/2 c. heavy cream,
  whipped
4 maraschino
  cherries
1 small orange,
  peeled and
  sectioned

Stand ladyfinger halves, rounded end up, around edge of 9-inch pie plate; fill bottom with remaining ladyfingers. Combine gelatin and 1/4 cup sugar in top of double boiler; add orange juice and egg yolks. Cook over hot water, stirring constantly, about 5 minutes or until gelatin dissolves; remove from heat; cool. Drain pineapple; reserve 2 slices for garnish; chop remaining 2 slices; stir into cooled gelatin mixture. Beat in sieved cheese; chill until almost set. Beat egg whites until foamy in medium-size bowl; beat in 1/4 cup sugar gradually, a tablespoon at a time; continue beating until meringue forms stiff, glossy peaks. Fold into gelatin mixture; fold in whipped cream. Turn into ladyfinger-lined pie plate; chill until firm. Just before serving, garnish top of pie with reserved pineapple slices, halved; cherries; and orange sections.

CHOCOLATE CHEESE PIE

1 1/3 c. chocolate
  wafer crumbs
3 tbs. soft butter
  or margarine
2 envelopes un-
  flavored gelatin
1/4 c. sugar
2 egg yolks
2 1/2 c. milk

1 pkg. (6 oz.) semi-
  sweet chocolate
  pieces
1 carton (8 oz.)
  cottage cheese
1/3 c. mint jelly
2 egg whites
1/4 c. sugar

Blend chocolate wafer crumbs and butter or margarine in bowl with fork until crumbly. Press firmly on bottom and sides of 9-inch pie pan with back of spoon; form a small rim. Bake at 375° F. for 8 minutes; cool. Combine gelatin and 1/4 cup sugar in top of a double boiler. Beat egg yolks and milk; add to gela-tin mixture. Cook over hot water, stirring constantly, about 5 minutes or until gelatin is dissolved and mixture thickens slightly. Remove from heat; add chocolate pieces; stir until well blended. Cool. Chill until mixture thickens and mounds when spooned. Sieve cottage cheese into large bowl. Whip mint jelly with fork until foamy; beat into cottage cheese; beat in chocolate-gelatin mixture. Chill until thickened. Beat egg whites until foamy; beat in 1/4 cup sugar gradually; continue beating until meringue forms stiff, glossy peaks. Fold into cottage cheese-chocolate mixture. Pile gently into prepared pie shell. Chill.

REFRIGERATOR DESSERTS

COEUR À LA CRÈME

1 carton (1 lb.)
  cottage cheese
2 pkgs. (8 oz. ea.)
  cream cheese,
  softened

Dash of salt
2 c. heavy cream
1 qt. strawberries
Sugar

Beat cottage cheese, cream cheese, and salt until smooth. Add cream gradually, beating constantly; continue beating until mixture is smooth. Line a traditional heart-shaped basket with cheesecloth; pack cheese mixture into basket. Place on plate; refrigerate overnight to let liquid (whey) drain off. (If heart-shaped basket is not available, line fine-meshed sieve with dampened cheesecloth, pack with cheese mixture and let stand over a bowl in the refrigerator overnight. Next day, cheese can be packed in cheesecloth-lined, heart-shaped metal mold, if desired.) Reserve a few whole strawberries for garnish; hull and crush remainder; sweeten with sugar to taste. To serve, unmold cheese heart onto serving plate; remove cheesecloth; garnish with reserved strawberries; serve with crushed strawberries. Makes 6 servings.

CHARLOTTE AU CHOCOLAT

2 pkgs. (6 oz. ea.)
  semi-sweet
  chocolate pieces
6 egg yolks
6 egg whites

2 tbs. sugar
2 c. heavy cream,
  whipped
4 doz. ladyfingers,
  split

Melt chocolate pieces in top of double boiler over hot water; cool; beat in egg yolks one at a time, beating well after each addition. Beat egg whites until foamy; gradually beat in sugar until stiff peaks form. Beat one quarter of egg white mixture into chocolate; fold in remaining mixture; fold in whipped cream. Line bottom and sides of 9-inch springform pan with ladyfingers; spoon one third chocolate mixture into pan; top with layer of ladyfingers. Repeat layers, ending with chocolate mixture. Chill until firm, about 4 hours. Garnish with whipped cream and chocolate candy wafers, if desired. Cut in thin wedges to serve. Makes 16 servings.

TRAFALGAR SQUARE TRIFLE

4 eggs	¼ c. sherry
⅓ c. sugar	½ c. heavy cream,
2½ c. milk	whipped
⅛ tsp. salt	Candied or
1 recipe Jelly Roll	maraschino
(*page 444*) or	cherries
1 baker's jelly roll	

Beat eggs slightly; combine with sugar, milk, and salt in top of double boiler. Cook over hot, not boiling, water, stirring constantly until mixture thickens slightly and coats spoon; cool. Cut jelly roll into 6 to 8 equal slices. Line your prettiest glass bowl with slices of jelly roll; fit one slice into the bottom of bowl; sprinkle with sherry. Pour cooked custard carefully into bowl so jelly-roll slices are not dislodged; chill several hours. Just before serving, decorate top with whipped cream and candied or maraschino cherries. Makes 6 servings.

CHOCOLATE ICEBOX CAKE

4 sqs. unsweetened	1 tsp. vanilla
chocolate	3 egg whites
⅓ c. sugar	⅓ c. sugar
⅛ tsp. salt	1 c. heavy cream,
2 tsp. unflavored	whipped
gelatin	2 doz. ladyfingers
⅓ c. water	(about 2 pkgs.)
3 egg yolks, slightly	
beaten	

Melt chocolate in top of double boiler over hot, not boiling, water. Combine ⅓ cup sugar, salt, and gelatin; add to chocolate; stir until sugar is dissolved. Blend in water; cook until mixture is smooth and thickened. Remove from heat; stir half of hot mixture into egg yolks. Return to mixture in double boiler; cook 2 minutes, stirring constantly. Cool; add vanilla. Beat egg whites until foamy; add ⅓ cup sugar slowly. Continue beating until meringue forms stiff, glossy peaks. Fold meringue and cream into chocolate mixture. Cut a long strip of aluminum foil or wax paper to fit along bottom and up sides of a 9x5x3-inch loaf pan; leave ends long enough so you can lift cake from pan to serve. Split ladyfingers; line pan across bottom and along sides. Pour in a layer of chocolate mixture; add a layer of ladyfingers. Alternate chocolate and ladyfingers in pan, ending with chocolate. Cover loosely; refrigerate 6 to 8 hours or overnight. Lift from pan onto serving plate; remove paper or foil. Cut into thick slices for serving; top with additional whipped cream, if desired. Makes 8 servings.

FROZEN DESSERTS AND ICE CREAM

OLD-FASHIONED LEMON ICE CREAM

⅔ c. sugar	1 tsp. grated lemon
⅛ tsp. salt	rind
1 tbs. flour	½ c. lemon juice
1 c. milk	1 c. heavy cream,
4 egg yolks, slightly	whipped
beaten	

Combine sugar, salt, and flour in saucepan; add milk gradually. Cook over medium heat, stirring constantly, until mixture thickens and comes to boiling. Stir half of mixture slowly into beaten egg yolks; stir into mixture in saucepan; cook 1 minute. Remove from heat; cool. Add lemon rind and juice; chill. Pour into loaf pan; freeze 1 hour. Turn mixture into bowl; beat until light and frothy; fold in cream. Freeze 3 to 4 hours or until firm.

For crank freezer: Pour chilled lemon mixture into freezer can; add heavy cream, unwhipped. Adjust dasher; set cover in place. Fill around sides with cracked ice and salt in an 8 to 1 ratio. Turn until resistance is felt; remove dasher. Repack freezer can in ice and salt; allow to ripen 2 hours. Makes 1 quart.

AVOCADO-LIME ICE CREAM

1 medium-size ripe avocado, mashed (¾ c.)	3½ tbs. lime juice
	1 c. pineapple juice
⅔ c. sugar	½ tsp. salt
	1½ c. light cream

Combine mashed avocado, sugar, lime juice, pineapple juice, salt, and cream in bowl; mix until completely blended. Place in freezer; freeze about 3 hours or until almost firm. Break up mixture with spoon; whip until fluffy. Leave in bowl or pour into 1-quart mold; freeze 1 to 2 hours or until completely firm. Makes 1 quart.

STRAWBERRY ICE CREAM

1 qt. strawberries, washed and hulled	¼ tsp. salt
	2 c. sugar
⅓ c. sugar	2 c. milk, scalded
⅓ c. sifted all-purpose flour	6 eggs
	3 tsp. vanilla
	4 c. heavy cream

Mash strawberries with ⅓ cup sugar; let stand while preparing custard mixture. Mix flour, salt, and 2 cups sugar in top of double boiler; blend in milk. Cook over simmering water, stirring constantly, about 5 minutes or until thickened; cover; cook 5 minutes longer. Beat eggs slightly; stir in hot mixture; return to double boiler; cook 1 minute longer. Cool; add vanilla. Blend in cream and strawberry mixture. Freeze according to directions of manufacturer of your ice-cream freezer. After ice cream is frozen, the paddle can be removed and freezer packed with salt and ice. Ice cream will keep for three to four hours with this packing. Makes 1 gallon.

FROZEN STRAWBERRY MOUSSE

2 c. heavy cream	1 qt. strawberries, washed, hulled, and crushed
1 c. sugar	
½ tsp. salt	
	½ c. chopped, toasted almonds

Whip cream until it begins to thicken. Gradually add sugar, beating constantly. Add salt; beat until cream is stiff. Fold in strawberries and almonds. Turn into 2-quart mold. Freeze until firm. Unmold onto serving plate. Garnish with whole strawberries and mint sprigs, if desired. Makes 6 to 8 servings.

LIME MALLOW

2½ c. miniature marshmallows or 24 large marshmallows, cut in quarters	½ tsp. grated lime rind
	2 tbs. lime juice
	Few drops of green food coloring
1 c. orange juice	1 c. heavy cream, whipped

Combine marshmallows and orange juice in top of double boiler; cook over boiling water until marshmallows melt. Cool; chill until almost thickened. Add lime rind and juice and a few drops of green food coloring. Fold whipped cream into lime mixture; turn into 1-quart mold. Freeze several hours. Unmold or spoon into serving dishes; garnish with fresh mint sprigs and lime slices, if desired. Makes 6 servings.

FROZEN LEMON DESSERT

1 c. finely crushed vanilla wafers or graham crackers	Dash of salt
	⅓ c. sugar
	2 tsp. grated lemon rind
¼ c. melted butter or margarine	2 tbs. lemon juice
2 tbs. sugar	1 c. heavy cream, whipped
2 egg whites	

Combine crumbs, butter or margarine, and 2 tablespoons sugar. Reserve 1 tablespoon of mixture; press remainder firmly on bottom and sides of 9x5x3-inch pan. Beat egg whites and salt until foamy; gradually beat in ⅓ cup sugar; continue beating until meringue forms stiff, glossy peaks. Fold in lemon rind and juice; fold in whipped cream. Pour into crumb-lined pan; sprinkle with reserved crumbs. Freeze 2 to 3 hours or until firm. Slice. Makes 6 servings.

PEPPERMINT CANDY CHARLOTTE

2 egg whites	1 tsp. vanilla
¼ c. sifted confectioners' sugar	Few drops red food coloring
2 c. heavy cream	½ pkg. ladyfingers
½ c. crushed hard peppermint candies (about 16 round candies)	

Beat egg whites until foamy; gradually beat in sugar; continue beating until meringue forms stiff, glossy peaks. Whip cream until thick but not stiff; fold in candy, vanilla, and food coloring. Fold cream mixture into meringue. Line 1-quart mold with ladyfingers; spoon peppermint mixture into mold. Cover with aluminum foil or plastic wrap; freeze several hours or until firm. Carefully unmold onto serving plate: loosen around edges with knife; dip mold quickly in and out of warm water. Invert on serving plate; lift mold off carefully. Garnish with additional peppermint candies and whipped cream, if desired. Makes 6 servings.

FROSTED APRICOT CREAM

1 can (8 oz.) apricot halves, drained	½ c. milk ⅓ c. sugar 1 tsp. lemon juice
1 pkg. (2 oz.) dessert-topping mix	

Drain apricots; press through sieve or whirl in blender. Whip topping mix with milk according to package directions. Add apricot purée, sugar, and lemon juice; continue beating until mixture is smooth and forms soft peaks. Spoon into 6 small paper soufflé cups; sprinkle with finely crumbled macaroons or vanilla wafers, if desired. Freeze 3 to 4 hours or until firm. Or freeze until partly frozen, about 2 hours, and serve at once. Makes 6 servings.

LEMON MILK SHERBET

1½ tsp. un-flavored gelatin	2 tsp. grated lemon rind
1 c. sugar	¾ c. lemon juice
1 c. milk	1 egg white
	2 tbs. sugar

Combine gelatin and 1 cup sugar in saucepan; stir in milk. Cook over low heat until gelatin and sugar are dissolved, about 5 minutes. Cool; add lemon rind and juice. Pour into shallow pan; freeze about 1 hour or until partly frozen and mushy. Scrape mixture into bowl; beat quickly with rotary beater or electric mixer until smooth. Beat egg white with 2 tablespoons sugar until stiff; fold into lemon mixture. Freeze several hours or until firm. Makes 6 servings.

STRAWBERRY ICE

1 qt. strawberries	¾ c. sugar
1½ c. water	2 tbs. lemon juice

Wash, hull, and purée strawberries. Combine strawberries, water, sugar, and lemon juice; stir occasionally until sugar dissolves, about 10 minutes. Pour into shallow pan. Freeze about 1 hour or until mixture is frozen a half inch around edges. Place mixture in a bowl and beat with electric mixer until fluffy. Freeze another hour; beat again. Return strawberry ice to freezer. Freeze until firm. Makes 6 servings.

PINEAPPLE MINT FRAPPÉ

2 cans (13½ oz. ea.) frozen pineapple chunks	½ c. flaked coconut ¼ c. heavy cream Green food coloring (optional)
¼ c. green crème de menthe	Mint

Thaw pineapple just enough to separate chunks. Reserve ½ cup for garnish. Put remaining pineapple and crème de menthe in electric blender. Blend until mixture is frothy and light; pour into shallow pan; freeze 30 minutes to 2 hours depending on your preference of firmness. Toast coconut at 350° F. for 10 minutes or until golden brown. Whip heavy cream; tint delicate green with food coloring, if desired. When serving, scoop frappé generously into sherbet glasses; top with reserved pineapple, a sprinkling of toasted coconut, a swirl of whipped cream, and a sprig of mint. Makes 4 to 6 servings.

FRESH STRAWBERRY FRAPPÉ

1 pt. strawberries, washed and hulled	¾ c. sugar 1¾ c. hot water ¾ c. orange juice
1 pkg. (3 oz.) strawberry-flavored gelatin	¼ c. lemon juice

Purée berries by whirling in blender or putting through sieve or food mill. Combine gelatin and sugar; add hot water; stir until dissolved. Combine berries, gelatin mixture, and fruit juices. Turn into shallow pan; freeze until almost firm. Turn into chilled mixing bowl; beat until thoroughly blended; return to pan. Freeze several hours until firm. Makes 6 servings.

TROPICAL FRAPPÉ

½ c. sugar
¾ c. water
1 can (1 pt. 2 oz.) pineapple juice or 2½ c. grape juice
1 tsp. grated lemon rind
1 tsp. grated lime rind

Combine sugar and water in medium-size saucepan; cook 5 minutes; cool slightly. Add pineapple or grape juice, lemon rind, and lime rind; mix well. Pour into shallow pan; freeze just until firm; beat until fluffy. Serve over fresh fruit. If desired, ½ cup grated coconut may be added before freezing. Makes 6 servings.

CRANBERRY FRUIT FRAPPÉ

1½ c. cranberry juice
¾ c. sugar
1 c. orange juice
¾ c. pineapple juice
1 tsp. grated lemon rind

Simmer cranberry juice and sugar 3 minutes; cool. Add orange juice, pineapple juice, and lemon rind. Pour into 9x5x3-inch pan. Freeze until just firm. Spoon into bowl; beat with electric mixer until fluffy. Makes 1 quart.

STRAWBERRY BOMBE

1 c. sliced strawberries
¼ c. sugar
2 c. heavy cream, whipped
1½ pts. vanilla ice cream

Line a 6-cup bowl with heavy foil; smooth out as evenly as possible. Combine strawberries and sugar in medium-size bowl; crush. Let stand 15 minutes; sieve or purée. Fold into whipped cream. Soften ice cream but do not allow to melt. Spread ice cream quickly in thick layer over bottom and sides of foil-lined bowl to form shell for strawberry mixture. Make sure it comes all the way to the top. If it softens during this operation, cover the bowl and set in freezer to harden. Spoon strawberry mixture into center of ice cream shell. Cover with a piece of foil. Freeze several hours or overnight until firm. Peel off foil used as cover. Invert bowl onto chilled serving plate; lift off bowl. Peel foil off bombe. Any marks or wrinkles on bombe may be smoothed by quickly running a warm spatula over them. Return bombe to freezer

to harden, if necessary. Garnish, if desired, with crushed strawberries. Makes 8 servings.

ORANGE BLOSSOMS

6 large navel oranges
1 qt. vanilla ice cream
4 tbs. Cointreau
4 egg whites
½ c. sugar

Cut tops off oranges; scoop out pulp (use at another meal). Combine ice cream and Cointreau; fill orange shells with mixture. Keep frozen if making ahead; beat egg whites until foamy; add sugar gradually, beating well after each addition. Continue beating until meringue stands in stiff, glossy peaks. Swirl meringue on top of each orange with pastry tube or spoon, making sure meringue comes to edge of orange and ice cream is covered. Bake at 450° F. for 3 to 5 minutes, or until lightly browned. Serve at once. Makes 6 servings.

GINGER PEACH MELBA

1½ qts. peach ice cream
¼ c. slivered candied ginger
½ pt. red raspberries
½ c. currant jelly
2 tsp. cornstarch
2 tbs. cold water
3 peaches, peeled and sliced
½ pt. blueberries

Soften ice cream; blend in ginger. Pack into 6-cup mold; cover with mold top or aluminum foil. Freeze several hours or until firm. Mash raspberries in small saucepan; add jelly; bring to boiling. Blend cornstarch and water; stir into raspberry mixture; cook, stirring constantly, until thickened and clear. Strain sauce; cool and chill. At dessert time, unmold ice cream: loosen around sides with knife; dip mold quickly in and out of warm water. Invert on serving plate; lift mold off carefully. Arrange peaches and blueberries over ice cream; spoon sauce over fruit and ice cream. Makes 8 servings.

RAINBOW PARFAIT

2 pkgs. (10 oz. ea.) frozen raspberries, thawed
4 tsp. cornstarch
¼ c. sugar
1 pt. vanilla ice cream
1 pt. strawberry ice cream
1 pt. pistachio ice cream

Drain raspberries; save juice. Combine cornstarch and sugar in small saucepan; add raspberry juice. Cook until sauce thickens and bubbles, stirring constantly. Simmer 1 minute. Remove from heat; cool, stirring occasionally. Add raspberries; chill. Place small balls of ice creams in parfait or sherbet glasses; add raspberry sauce to each layer and on top. Top with whipped cream, if desired. Makes 6 servings.

TIPSY ICE CREAM CAKE

1 qt. vanilla ice cream	1/3 c. chopped toasted almonds
2 c. heavy cream	Strawberries and fresh mint
16 ladyfingers, split	
3 tbs. rum	

Soften ice cream. Whip 1 cup heavy cream; mix thoroughly with ice cream. Line a 9-inch ring mold with ladyfingers; sprinkle with 1 tablespoon rum; spoon in half the ice cream; sprinkle with 2 tablespoons almonds. Repeat layers; top with ladyfingers; sprinkle with remaining rum. Freeze until firm. Unmold onto serving plate. Whip remaining 1 cup heavy cream. Spread on top and sides of cake. Sprinkle with remaining almonds. Freeze until serving time, if desired. Garnish with strawberries and mint. Makes 12 servings.

CHOCOLATE SUNDAE PIE

4 oz. (2/3 c.) semi-sweet chocolate pieces	2 c. shredded coconut
4 tbs. butter or margarine	1 qt. vanilla ice cream
	Butterscotch Sundae Sauce

Melt chocolate and butter or margarine over hot water; remove from heat. Place coconut in shallow pan; toast at 350° F. for 5 to 8 minutes or until golden. Remove and reserve 1 tablespoon coconut; mix remainder into chocolate. Spread mixture evenly on bottom and sides of 9-inch pie plate; chill until firm. Remove from refrigerator; let stand at room temperature 5 to 10 minutes. Fill shell with ice cream balls; drizzle with Butterscotch Sundae Sauce; sprinkle with reserved 1 tablespoon coconut. Serve with remaining sauce. Makes 8 servings.

Butterscotch Sundae Sauce: Cook 4 tablespoons butter or margarine; 1/2 cup dark brown sugar, firmly packed; and 2 tablespoons light corn syrup over low heat, stirring constantly, until mixture bubbles. Add 3 tablespoons water; bring to boiling; boil 1 1/2 minutes; remove from heat; stir in 1/2 teaspoon vanilla. Makes 3/4 cup.

BAKED ALASKA

1 packaged sponge layer (1/2 pkg.)	4 egg whites
1 qt. ice cream, firmly frozen	1/2 c. sugar

Cut piece of heavy brown paper to fit small cookie sheet. Place sponge layer on lined cookie sheet. Split ice cream carton with sharp knife; remove ice cream in one piece. Place ice cream in center of sponge layer. If ice cream is cylindrical in shape, place it on its side. Trim cake, allowing 1/2 inch to extend beyond ice cream all the way around. Keep in freezer while making meringue. Heat oven to 400° F. Beat egg whites until foamy; beat in sugar gradually. Continue beating until meringue forms stiff, glossy peaks. Swirl meringue quickly over ice cream and cake with spatula. Ice cream and cake must be covered completely to protect them from heat of oven. Bake 3 to 5 minutes or until peaks of meringue are golden brown. Cut into slices to serve. Makes 6 servings.

CHOCOLATE ALASKAS

1 pt. chocolate ice cream	4 egg whites
1 pkg. sponge dessert shells	1/2 c. sugar
	Double Chocolate Sauce (*page 399*)

Divide ice cream into 6 portions. Spoon into individual shells; keep frozen until near serving time. Beat egg whites until foamy; beat in sugar gradually. Continue beating at high speed until meringue forms stiff, glossy peaks. Heat oven to 400° F. Place frozen filled shells on cookie sheet. With small spatula or spoon, quickly swirl meringue completely over ice cream and sides of cake. Bake 3 to 5 minutes or until peaks of meringue are golden. Remove from oven; drizzle Chocolate Sauce over tops; serve at once. Makes 6 servings.

FRUITED MELON ALASKA

3 cantaloupes	6 egg whites
1 c. strawberries, washed, hulled and halved	½ tsp. salt
	1 c. sugar
	1 pt. lemon sherbet
1 c. blueberries	

Have all fruits ice cold. Cut cantaloupes in half; remove seeds. With melon ball cutter scoop out flesh of melon to within half inch of rind. Invert melon shells on cookie sheet lined with paper towels. Allow to drain at least 1 hour in the refrigerator. Mix melon balls with strawberries and blueberries. Heat oven to 500° F. Beat egg whites and salt until foamy. Gradually beat in ¾ cup sugar; continue to beat until meringue forms stiff glossy peaks. Cut a piece of rind off bottom of each cantaloupe half so it will stand straight. Fill hollows with mixed fruits; top with a scoop of lemon sherbet. Quickly spread meringue over all, bringing it out to very edge of melon rind. Sprinkle meringue with remaining ¼ cup sugar. Bake 2 or 3 minutes or until meringue is lightly browned. Serve immediately. Makes 6 servings.

RASPBERRY ALASKA

1 pt. raspberry sherbet	4 peach halves, drained
1 packaged sponge layer cake (½ pkg.)	4 egg whites
	½ c. sugar
	4 tbs. raspberry preserves

Split sherbet carton lengthwise at opposite sides with sharp knife; remove sherbet in one piece. Place sponge layer on small baking sheet or small cutting board. Center sherbet vertically on sponge layer. Cut a thin sliver from end of each peach half; stand peach halves on end all around sherbet. Put in freezer till ready to bake. Heat oven to 400° F. Beat egg whites until foamy. Add sugar gradually. Continue beating until meringue forms stiff, glossy peaks. Cover sherbet, peaches, and cake quickly with swirls of meringue. Bake 3 to 5 minutes or until peaks of meringue are golden brown. Remove from oven; spoon preserves over top; serve at once. Makes 4 servings.

STRAWBERRIES ROMANOFF

1 qt. strawberries, washed and hulled	1 pt. vanilla ice cream
¼ c. Grand Marnier	½ pt. heavy cream, whipped
2 tbs. confectioners' sugar	Fresh mint

Save a few whole strawberries for garnish. Halve remainder. Combine halved strawberries, Grand Marnier, and sugar; cover; refrigerate several hours to develop flavor. Just before serving, soften vanilla ice cream, but do not melt. Whip cream; combine with ice cream and strawberry mixture. Spoon into chilled serving dishes. Garnish with whole strawberries and mint. Makes 8 servings.

CHOCOLATE CUPS (Colettes)

These dainty little chocolate cups to be filled with ice cream are perfect choices for that special tea or dinner party. We are using semi-sweet chocolate; a true colette is made from sweet chocolate, omitting the butter.

1 pkg. (6 oz.) semi-sweet chocolate pieces	1½ tbs. butter or margarine
	1 pt. ice cream

Melt chocolate and butter or margarine in top of double boiler over hot, not boiling, water until chocolate is just melted; stir to blend. With teaspoon or small spatula, spread chocolate mixture around insides of pleated paper baking cups, coating evenly. Set cups in muffin-pan cups; chill until firm. Just before serving, peel off paper. Fill cups with ice cream. Garnish as desired. Makes about 10 cups.

QUICK CHERRY TORTONI

1 pt. vanilla ice cream	¼ c. drained, chopped maraschino cherries
½ c. crushed vanilla wafers (12 wafers)	1 tsp. almond extract

Scoop ice cream from package into mixing bowl; let stand while preparing remaining ingredients. Reserve 2 tablespoons crushed vanilla wafers for topping. Stir ice cream until softened, but not melted. Blend cherries, wafers, and almond extract into ice cream; quickly spoon into four 4-ounce paper or foil soufflé cups. Sprinkle reserved crumbs over top. Place filled cups directly on freezing surface of freezer or freezer compartment of refrigerator to quick-freeze. Decorate with whipped cream and additional maraschino cherries, if desired. Makes 4 servings.

COUPE GOURMET

1 can (11 oz.) mandarin oranges, drained	2 tbs. brandy
	1 qt. vanilla ice cream
2 bottles preserved marrons	

Combine mandarin oranges, marrons, and brandy. Spoon small amount into each of 8 sherbet glasses. Top with scoops of vanilla ice cream. Spoon remaining marron mixture over. Garnish with whipped cream and mint, if desired. Makes 8 servings.

PINEAPPLE COUPE

3 small, ripe pineapples	½ pt. heavy cream
6 large, ripe peaches	1 pt. vanilla ice cream
2 tbs. sugar	1 pt. strawberry ice cream
½ c. curaçao or ½ c. orange juice	

Halve pineapples; carefully remove pineapple meat with sharp knife, leaving ½-inch shell. Wrap shells in transparent plastic wrap or aluminum foil; chill. Core and cube pineapple meat. Peel and cut up 4 peaches; combine with pineapple; add sugar and curaçao or orange juice; cover; chill several hours or overnight. Just before serving, whip cream. Pile cut-up fruit in shells; top each with scoops of vanilla and strawberry ice cream. Peel and slice 2 peaches; garnish each serving with peach slices and whipped cream. Makes 6 servings.

Ways to Serve Ice Cream

Ice Cream in many flavors is a versatile ingredient for unusual quickie dessert variations. Here are a few:

Warm Indian Pudding topped with vanilla ice cream.

Brownie topped with vanilla, coffee, or peppermint ice cream, and Double Chocolate Sauce (*page 399*).

Apple Pie with cinnamon ice cream. Add ½ teaspoon ground cinnamon to 1 quart softened vanilla ice cream. Freeze until firm.

Sponge Cake Square topped with vanilla or coffee ice cream and Butterscotch Sundae Sauce (*page 395*).

Cantaloupe Alaska: Fill cantaloupe halves with ice cream, cover with meringue, and bake at 450° F. for 3 to 5 minutes.

Pears Heléne: Chill canned or fresh pears; top with vanilla ice cream and Hot Chocolate Sauce (*page 399*).

DESSERTS FROM PUDDING MIXES

PINEAPPLE CREAM CAKE

1 can (8½ oz.) crushed pineapple	1 c. heavy cream, whipped
1½ c. milk	1 pkg. (2 layers) 7 to 8 in.-sponge layers
1 pkg. (4 oz.) vanilla-flavored pudding and pie filling	3 tbs. raspberry preserves

Drain and reserve pineapple. Blend pineapple juice and milk with pudding mix in saucepan. Cook over medium heat, stirring constantly, until mixture thickens and comes to boiling. Remove from heat; cool; chill. Add crushed pineapple and half the whipped cream to pudding. Split layers crosswise, making 4 layers. Spread pudding mixture on three layers; stack; top with fourth layer, pressing lightly together. Spread remaining whipped cream smoothly on top of cake. Drizzle preserves from tip of spoon in circle on cream. Draw knife in alternate directions through preserves and cream to form design. Chill well. Makes 8 servings.

MOCHA CREAM DESSERT

2 pkgs. (3 oz. ea.)
  chocolate-
  flavored pudding
  and pie filling
¼ c. sugar

¼ tsp. salt
2 tsp. instant coffee
1½ c. water
1 c. dairy sour
  cream

Combine pudding, sugar, salt, and coffee in
saucepan; stir in water. Cook, stirring constantly, until mixture comes to boiling. Cool
10 minutes, stirring occasionally. Blend in
sour cream; chill well. Makes 6 servings.

TRIPLE-LAYER CRANBERRY DESSERT

2 c. milk
1 pkg. (4 oz.)
  vanilla-flavored
  pudding and pie
  filling
¾ c. flaked coconut
9 ladyfingers, split
½ envelope (about
  1½ tsp.) un-
  flavored gelatin

3 tbs. cold water
1 can (1 lb.) whole
  cranberry sauce
¼ tsp. ground
  cinnamon
1 tsp. grated orange
  rind

Stir milk into pudding mix; cook over medium heat, stirring constantly, until mixture
comes to boiling. Remove from heat; add
coconut; cool 5 minutes. Arrange ladyfingers in bottom of 8x8x2-inch pan. Pour
pudding over ladyfingers. Cover with aluminum foil; chill. Soften gelatin in cold water;
dissolve over hot water. Add to cranberry
sauce; add cinnamon and orange rind. Pour
sauce over top of coconut pudding. Chill until
firm. Makes 8 to 9 servings.

COFFEE POTS DE CRÈME

1 pkg. (4 oz.)
  vanilla-flavored
  pudding and pie
  filling
¼ c. sugar
1 tbs. instant coffee
1½ c. milk
2 egg yolks, slightly
  beaten

1 c. heavy cream,
  whipped
½ c. crushed nut
  brittle (pecan,
  walnut, or pea-
  nut) or ½ c.
  crushed ginger-
  snap crumbs

Blend pudding, sugar, and coffee with milk
in saucepan. Cook, stirring constantly, until
mixture thickens and is bubbly. Quickly
blend one half of hot mixture into egg yolks;
return mixture to saucepan. Cook, stirring

constantly, until mixture comes to a full boil.
Cool, stirring often. Place piece of wax paper
or transparent plastic wrap directly on surface
of pudding to prevent tough top layer; chill.
Beat pudding until smooth; fold in whipped
cream. Spoon into tiny pots de crème cups,
demitasse cups, or custard cups. Chill 2 to 3
hours. Sprinkle tops with nut brittle or gingersnap crumbs. Makes 6 servings.

HASTY PUDDING WHIP

1 pkg. (3 oz.)
  cherry-flavored
  gelatin
1 c. boiling water
½ c. cold water

1 pkg. (3¾ oz.)
  vanilla-flavored
  instant pudding
½ c. toasted
  slivered almonds

Dissolve gelatin in boiling water; add cold
water. Chill until very thick. Prepare instant
pudding according to package directions; let
stand 5 minutes. Whip gelatin until it is
light and fluffy and about double in volume.
Fold gelatin into pudding; blend thoroughly.
Turn into serving bowl or 8 individual
dishes. Chill until firm. Top with almonds.
Makes 8 servings.

FRUIT TAPIOCA PUDDING

3 large cooking
  apples, pared,
  cored, and thinly
  sliced
2¼ c. canned
  apricot-orange
  drink
1 tbs. lemon juice

Dash of salt
1 pkg. (3¼ oz.)
  vanilla-flavored
  tapioca pudding
2 tbs. butter or
  margarine
¼ tsp. ground
  nutmeg

Combine apple slices and fruit juices in
saucepan. Bring to boiling; lower heat;
cover; simmer 10 minutes or until apples are
almost tender. Blend in salt and pudding
mix; cook, stirring constantly, until tapioca
is clear. Stir in butter or margarine and nutmeg. Serve warm. Makes 6 servings.

DESSERT SAUCES

VANILLA SAUCE

⅓ c. sugar
1½ tbs. cornstarch
¼ tsp. salt
1⅔ c. boiling water

3 tbs. butter or
  margarine
2 tsp. vanilla

Combine sugar, cornstarch, and salt in sauce-pan. Stir in boiling water. Cook over medium heat, stirring constantly, until thickened and clear. Cook 3 minutes longer. Remove from heat; add butter or margarine and vanilla. Serve warm. Makes 2 cups.

BUTTERSCOTCH CRÈME SAUCE

¼ c. butter or margarine	1 tbs. hot water
¾ c. brown sugar, firmly packed	2 egg yolks, beaten
	1 c. heavy cream, whipped

Combine butter or margarine, brown sugar, hot water, and egg yolks in top of double boiler; cook over hot water, stirring constantly, until sauce thickens slightly. Cool; fold in whipped cream. Makes 2 cups.

QUICK CARAMEL SAUCE

2 egg yolks, beaten	½ c. water
½ c. brown sugar, firmly packed	¼ c. butter or margarine
½ c. granulated sugar	1½ tsp. vanilla
	⅛ tsp. salt

Combine all ingredients in saucepan. Cook over medium heat, stirring constantly, until sauce boils. Boil gently 1 minute. Serve warm or cold. Makes about 1⅓ cups.

DOUBLE CHOCOLATE SAUCE

4 sqs. unsweetened chocolate	2 tbs. light corn syrup
1 pkg. (6 oz.) semi-sweet chocolate pieces	½ c. sugar
	1 c. milk
2 tbs. butter or margarine	Dash of salt

Combine chocolates and butter or margarine in top of double boiler; melt over hot water. Blend in remaining ingredients. Cook, stirring constantly, about 8 minutes or until thickened and smooth. Makes 2 cups.

HOT CHOCOLATE SAUCE

4 sqs. unsweetened chocolate	1 c. sugar
⅔ c. water	1 tsp. vanilla

Melt chocolate with water in saucepan over medium heat; stir in sugar. Cook over low

heat, stirring constantly until thickened. Stir in vanilla. Serve warm. Makes 1½ cups.

QUICK CHOCOLATE MINT SAUCE

1 pkg. (6 oz.) semi-sweet chocolate pieces	Dash of salt
	½ tsp. peppermint flavoring or 2 drops oil of peppermint
⅔ c. (1 small can) evaporated milk	

Melt chocolate pieces in top of double boiler over hot water. Beat in milk. Stir in salt and flavoring. Serve hot or cold. Makes about 1½ cups.

CUSTARD RUM SAUCE

1½ c. milk	1 tbs. flour
½ c. heavy cream	⅛ tsp. salt
4 egg yolks	½ tsp. rum extract
¼ c. sugar	

Scald milk and cream in top of double boiler. Beat yolks slightly; combine sugar, flour, and salt; stir into egg yolks. Pour hot milk and cream slowly into egg mixture, stirring briskly. Return mixture to double boiler. Cook over hot, not boiling, water until sauce thickens. Stir in rum extract. Chill. Makes about 2½ cups.

CUSTARD SAUCE ROYALE

1 c. milk	⅛ tsp. salt
3 egg yolks	1 tsp. vanilla
3 tbs. sugar	

Heat milk in top of double boiler until bubbles appear around edge. Beat egg yolks in small bowl with sugar and salt until blended. Stir in milk slowly. Return mixture to double boiler. Cook over hot, not boiling, water, until mixture just coats spoon. Pour into bowl; add vanilla. Cover; cool; chill. Serve with Prune Whip (*page 357*), fruit desserts, cake, or ice cream. Makes 1½ cups.

EGGNOG SAUCE

2 egg yolks, slightly beaten	Dash of salt
¼ c. sugar	1 c. heavy cream, whipped
1 tsp. vanilla	

Combine egg yolks, sugar, vanilla, and salt; blend well. Fold mixture into whipped cream. Serve over fruit or fruit puddings. Makes 2 cups.

HARD SAUCE

½ c. soft butter or margarine
2 c. sifted confectioners' sugar

2 tbs. rum or 1 tsp. rum extract

Cream butter or margarine, sugar, and rum or rum extract until smooth. Chill. For special occasions, when you may want individual servings, drop by teaspoonfuls or press through pastry bag onto wax paper or cookie sheet; chill or freeze until serving time. Makes about 1 cup.

Pinwheels: Prepare Hard Sauce. Divide in half. Tint one half with enough red food coloring to make a delicate pink. Leave other half plain; chill. Roll each half of hard sauce between squares of wax paper, to rectangles. Place one on top of the other; roll up tightly. Wrap in transparent plastic wrap or aluminum foil; chill. Slice.

HOLIDAY HARD SAUCE

½ c. butter or margarine, softened
1½ c. sifted confectioners' sugar

2 to 3 tbs. brandy
¼ c. almonds, blanched and grated (optional)
Dash of salt

Cream butter or margarine until light; gradually beat in sugar and brandy. Stir in almonds and salt; chill well. Serve with steamed puddings or warm cake. Makes about 2 cups.

WARM BRANDY SAUCE

½ c. butter or margarine
1 egg, well beaten

1 c. sifted confectioners' sugar
2 tbs. brandy

Beat butter or margarine until creamy; add egg. Beat in sugar gradually; continue to beat until light and fluffy. Put mixture in top of double boiler over hot, not boiling, water. Beat until light and creamy. Stir in brandy. Serve with steamed puddings or fruit desserts. Makes about 1 cup.

FOAMY SAUCE

1 egg
¼ c. melted butter or margarine
1¼ c. sifted confectioners' sugar

2 tbs. sherry or 1 tsp. vanilla or 1 tsp. rum
1 c. heavy cream, whipped

Beat egg until light and thick. Blend in butter or margarine, confectioners' sugar, and sherry, vanilla, or rum. Fold in whipped cream. Makes 2⅓ cups.

HONEY-RUM SAUCE

2 tbs. butter or margarine
3 tbs. light rum

⅓ c. coarsely chopped nuts
1 c. honey

Combine all ingredients in small saucepan; cook slowly 8 to 10 minutes, stirring constantly. Cool slightly. Serve warm. Makes 1¼ cups.

HOT LEMON SAUCE

⅔ c. sugar
¼ c. cornstarch
Dash of salt
1⅓ c. water

1 tbs. grated lemon rind
⅓ c. lemon juice
2 egg yolks
2 egg whites

Combine sugar, cornstarch, and salt in small saucepan; gradually stir in water and lemon rind and juice. Cook, stirring constantly, until mixture thickens and boils 1 minute. Beat egg yolks slightly; stir a little hot lemon mixture into egg yolks; return mixture to saucepan and cook, stirring constantly, about 1 minute. Beat egg whites until stiff but not dry; fold into sauce. Serve hot. Makes about 3 cups.

LEMON SAUCE

½ c. sugar
1 tbs. cornstarch
1 c. boiling water
3 tbs. butter or margarine

1 tsp. grated lemon rind
3 tbs. lemon juice

Combine sugar, cornstarch, and boiling water in saucepan. Cook over medium heat, stirring constantly, until thickened and bubbly. Remove from heat. Stir in butter or margarine, lemon rind, and lemon juice. Cool. Makes 1⅔ cups.

ORANGE SAUCE

¾ c. sugar	2 tbs. butter or
¼ tsp. salt	margarine
2 tbs. cornstarch	2 tsp. grated orange
1 c. orange juice	rind
3 tbs. lemon juice	½ tsp. grated lemon
¾ c. boiling water	rind

Mix sugar, salt, and cornstarch in saucepan. Stir in orange juice, lemon juice, and water. Bring to boiling; boil 1 minute, stirring constantly. Stir in butter or margarine and orange and lemon rinds. Makes 2½ cups.

QUICK MELBA SAUCE

1 c. raspberry	½ c. currant jelly
preserves	

Combine raspberry preserves and currant jelly in small saucepan; heat slowly until melted, stirring constantly. Remove from heat; strain through fine sieve; chill. Makes 1 cup.

RASPBERRY SAUCE

2 tbs. cornstarch	⅓ c. wine (rosé,
¼ c. sugar	sherry, or
1 c. water	muscatel)
1 pkg. (10 oz.)	
frozen rasp-	
berries, thawed	
and not drained	

Combine cornstarch and sugar in saucepan; stir in water; Cook, stirring constantly, until thickened and clear. Stir in raspberries; cool. Add wine; chill, covered, 1 to 2 hours. Makes 2⅓ cups.

QUICK SUNDAE SAUCE

1 pkg. (4 oz.)	2 tbs. butter or
chocolate fudge-	margarine
flavored pudding	½ tsp. mint extract
and pie filling	or few drops oil
½ c. sugar	of peppermint
1 c. water	

Blend pudding and sugar with water in saucepan. Cook over low heat, stirring constantly, until sugar dissolves. Continue cooking until mixture comes to a full boil; add butter or margarine and mint extract or oil of peppermint. Serve warm or cold on ice cream, pound cake, or pudding. Makes 1 cup.

SEVEN SUNDAE SAUCES

Taffy Peanut Butter Sauce: Blend together 1 cup evaporated milk or light cream, ¾ cup plain or chunk-style peanut butter, and ½ cup molasses. Serve warm or cold. Makes 2 cups.

Chocolate Honey Sauce: Combine 1 package (6 oz.) semi-sweet chocolate pieces and ⅔ cup evaporated milk or light cream in top of double boiler. Heat over hot water until chocolate is melted. Stir in ½ cup honey. Serve warm. Makes 1⅔ cups.

Maple Walnut Sauce: Pour ¾ cup cold evaporated milk or light cream into mixing bowl. Add 1 package (4 oz.) butterscotch instant pudding and dash of salt. Beat with egg beater just to mix, about 1 minute (do not overbeat). Stir in ⅔ cup maple-blended syrup and ½ cup chopped walnuts. Makes 1¾ cups.

Pineapple Sauce: Combine 1½ tablespoons cornstarch and ½ cup sugar in saucepan; add 1 can (8½ oz.) crushed pineapple with juice and ½ cup water. Bring to boiling, stirring constantly; boil 2 to 3 minutes or until clear and slightly thickened. Chill; add 1 tablespoon lemon juice. Makes 1¾ cups.

Cherry Sauce: Substitute syrup-packed pitted bing cherries and juice for the pineapple and water in the above recipe.

Mocha Marshmallow Sauce: Dissolve 2 tablespoons instant coffee in 1 tablespoon hot water; add to 1 can (1 lb.) chocolate syrup (1½ cups); blend in 1 jar (7 oz.) prepared marshmallow topping. Makes 2½ cups.

Raspberry Jam Sauce: Combine 1 cup raspberry jam, ¼ cup red currant jelly, 2 tablespoons lemon juice, and a dash of salt; heat together until smooth and blended. Makes 1¼ cups.

Chapter Twenty-Two

Pies and Pastry

Ask any family to name their favorite dessert, and pie is sure to stand high on the list. Like many other New World foods, pie as we know it today is an All-American invention. Pastries from the Old World were adapted by our Colonial ancestors to meet the sparse food supplies. Fillings for the pies—shiny tart apples, mellow, golden pumpkin, and tart rhubarb—were gathered from the surrounding countryside. Today's pie, with improvements in flour, shortening, and other ingredients has evolved into a culinary delight. And the modern supermarket offers a wealth of ready-to-use fruit fillings, quick-trick combinations for fillings, and easy-to-use pastry mixes.

Pastry

Keep in mind that pies are dependent on that special ingredient—*pastry*. It is the fond desire of all good cooks to achieve divinely tender pastry. Follow our step-by-step directions to make you the best pie maker in the neighborhood.

Secrets for Successful Pie Making

· Always measure ingredients for pastry with an accurate hand. Too much or too little of any one of the three main ingredients (flour, shortening, and water) will bring disappointing results.
· Use a light hand with your pastry. Too much handling toughens pastry.
· For a sparkling, extra-flaky top crust on fruit pies, brush with milk or cream, then sprinkle with sugar.
· If you wish to reroll scraps of pastry, do not squeeze the bits together and reroll for a pastry crust. Instead, roll the scraps separately; cut into little shapes; sprinkle with sugar and cinnamon or shredded cheese; bake. These little goodies are a happy treat for the children.

· Use a pastry wheel for cutting pretty strips for lattice-top pies.
· To prevent pie meringue from weeping (little droplets of moisture over surface); be sure to spread meringue over *hot* filling; bake at once.
· To prevent pie meringue from shrinking, spread meringue over filling, making sure it touches crust all the way around.
· Cook fillings for cream pies in a heavy saucepan and stir constantly to prevent scorching.
· Don't overcook fillings with a cornstarch base. Overcooking tends to thin cornstarch fillings.
· When two-crust pies are browning a little too quickly, cover top crust with a circle of aluminum foil.
· Cream, custard, and chiffon pies and pies with whipped-cream decorations should be kept refrigerated.
· To quicken the chilling of chiffon pies, place saucepan of filling in large bowl with ice cubes and water. Stir frequently until mixture begins to thicken and mounds when spooned. Remove from ice at once. Have remaining ingredients ready to fold in. Do this too when finished fillings are not quite

stiffened enough to mound high in the pastry shell.

· To crush graham crackers or cookies neatly, wrap loosely in large piece of transparent plastic wrap or aluminum foil; fold edges to seal; crush with rolling pin. There are packaged graham cracker crumbs now available in most markets.

· For better bottom crusts on custard and pumpkin pies, try this. Beat eggs for filling; remove 1 teaspoonful; brush over pastry crust; chill while preparing filling. This will help seal pastry so filling will not soak in too much.

· To reheat baked two-crust fruit pies the next day for that "just baked" taste, wrap loosely in aluminum foil; place in 350° F. oven for 10 minutes.

· Pastry and crumb crusts may be made one to two weeks ahead of a festive occasion if kept wrapped in transparent plastic wrap or aluminum foil in freezer.

· To keep fruit pies from dripping onto oven bottom, place large piece of aluminum foil on oven rack directly below rack on which pie is baking. Turn up edges of foil all around to form rim and prevent spills from rolling off.

2. Sprinkle water, a small amount at a time, over flour mixture. Mix lightly with fork, using a tossing motion, until all flour is moistened.

How to Make Basic Pastry

3. Gather dough together with fingers so it cleans the bowl. Press gently into a ball.

1. Cut shortening into sifted flour and salt with a pastry blender until mixture resembles cornmeal.

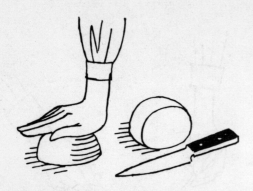

4. Place ball of dough on lightly floured surface. Cut in half. Turn one half over onto cut surface. Flatten with hand.

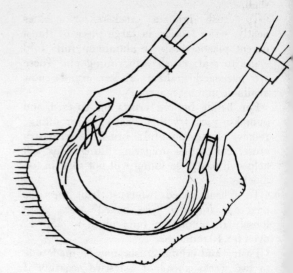

6. Roll dough out to a 12-inch circle for a 9-inch pie, or an 11-inch circle for an 8-inch pie. Hold inverted pie plate over dough to check size of circle.

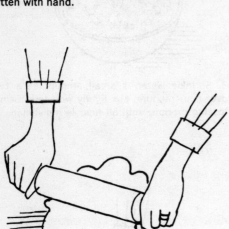

5. Flour rolling pin lightly. Place on center of dough. Roll dough from center to edge with quick, light strokes. Lift rolling pin near edge to keep it from becoming too thin.

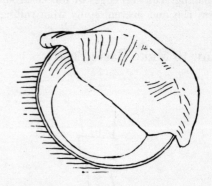

7. Fold pastry in half. Place in pie plate with fold at center.

Pumpkin Chiffon, Glazed Apple-Mince, Apple Cheese Crumb — beautiful, taste-tempting

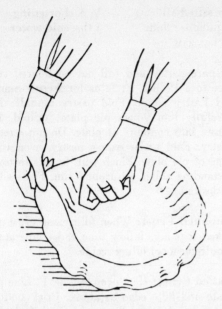

STANDARD PASTRY (*for 2-crust pie*)

2 c. sifted all- purpose flour ½ tsp. salt	¾ c. shortening 6 tbs. cold water

Sift flour and salt into mixing bowl. Cut in shortening with pastry blender until mixture resembles corn meal. Sprinkle cold water evenly over surface; stir with fork until all dry particles are moistened and pastry clings together. Shape into ball; divide in half. Roll out one half to 12-inch circle on floured surface, using a light motion from center to edge. Be sure pastry is free moving at all times. If it sticks, loosen with spatula and sprinkle a little flour underneath. To make it 12 inches round, invert pie plate over pastry; mark 1½ inches larger all around plate. Cut through mark with sharp knife; remove plate. Fold pastry in half; lift into 9-inch pie plate; unfold. Fit gently into contours of plate. Do not stretch. Spoon or pour in filling.

Top Crust: Roll out second half of pastry to 12-inch circle; cut vents for steam to escape.

8. Unfold pastry. Ease into plate loosely without stretching. Fit pastry into plate by pressing lightly with knuckle of index finger. Hold outer edge with other hand but do not stretch.

9. Trim overhanging edge with scissors, leaving ½ to 1 inch of pastry.

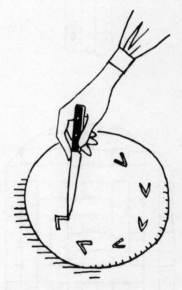

Fold in half; place on filling. Fold under excess pastry, even with edge of plate. Pinch with fingers to form a high standing collar around rim. Flute edge. For flat edge trim both crusts even with edge of plate; crimp with tines of floured fork (see illustrations, *pages 408–9*).

Banana Spice Cake—a delicious combination of flavors

Lattice-Top Crust: Prepare pastry for 2-crust pie; line pan with half of pastry. Trim, leaving 1-inch overhang. Roll rest of pastry; cut into ½-inch strips. Use pastry wheel or paring knife for this. Fill pie; moisten edge of bottom crust with water. Place 2 strips of pastry across top of pie, forming a cross (strips 1 and 2). Work from center outward, adding a strip at a time across each arm of cross (strips 3 and 4); allow ¼ to ½ inch between strips. Continue adding strips until top is complete. Press strips to bottom crust. Fold crust over strips; form standing rim; flute.

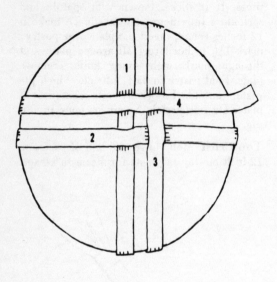

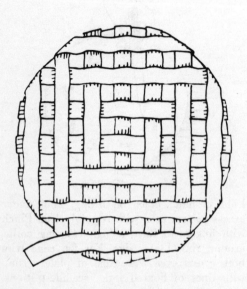

STANDARD PASTRY (for 1-crust pie)

1 c. sifted all-purpose flour	⅓ c. shortening
½ tsp. salt	3 tbs. cold water

Prepare pastry and roll out on floured surface to a 12-inch circle as for 2-crust Standard Pastry recipe. Fold pastry in half; lift carefully into 9-inch pie plate; unfold. Fit gently into contours of plate. Do not stretch pastry. Fold under excess pastry, even with edge of pie plate. Pinch with fingers to form a standing collar all around rim. Flute edge as desired.

Unbaked Crust: When filling and crust are baked together, follow time and temperature requirements of filling recipe.

Baked Crust: Heat oven to 450° F. Line pie plate and flute edge as above. Prick bottom and sides of pastry thoroughly with fork. Fit a piece of wax paper into pastry shell; fill with raw rice or beans. This will weigh pastry down until it sets and prevent bubbles and shrinkage. Bake 8 to 10 minutes; remove rice or beans and paper. Bake shell 8 to 10 minutes longer or until golden brown. Cool before filling.

Cheese Pastry (for 1-crust pie)

1 c. sifted all-purpose flour	½ c. shredded Cheddar cheese
½ tsp. salt	4 tbs. cold water
⅓ c. shortening	

Make as for 1-crust Standard Pastry; cut in cheese with shortening.

PIE PLATE PASTRY (for 1-crust pie)

1½ c. sifted all-purpose flour	½ c. pure vegetable oil
1½ tsp. sugar	2 tbs. milk
1 tsp. salt	

Sift flour, sugar, and salt into 9-inch pie plate. Combine oil and milk in measuring cup; beat with fork until blended. Pour over flour mixture; mix with fork until all flour is moistened. With fingers, press mixture firmly against bottom and sides of pie plate. Make small edge on rim of plate; flute. Do no form a high edge. Spoon or pour in filling and bake according to time and temperature requirements of filling recipe.

Baked Crust: Heat oven to 425° F. Make crust and flute edge as above. Prick crust thoroughly with fork. Bake 12 to 15 minutes or until golden brown. Cool and fill as desired.

HOT-WATER PASTRY (for 2-crust pie)

⅔ c. shortening	½ tsp. salt
6 tbs. boiling water	½ tsp. baking
2 c. sifted all-	powder
purpose flour	

Combine shortening and water in mixing bowl; beat with fork until mixture is smooth and creamy. Sift in flour, salt, and baking powder; stir with fork until dough clings together and cleans bowl. Shape pastry into a ball; divide into two equal parts. Roll out and line 9-inch pie plate as in directions for Standard Pastry (*page 405*).

Single Crust: Use half the recipe for Hot Water Pastry. Roll out and line pie plate as in directions for 1-crust Standard Pastry (*page 406*).

EASY STIRRED PASTRY (for 2-crust pie)

2½ c. sifted all-	⅔ c. pure vegetable
purpose flour	oil
1½ tsp. salt	⅓ c. milk

Sift flour and salt into mixing bowl. Pour oil and milk into measuring cup; do not stir. Add to flour mixture all at once. Stir with fork until all flour is moistened. Form pastry into ball; divide in half. Tear off two pieces of wax paper, each 12 inches long, so you have two 12-inch squares. Moisten a small area of the table top with damp cloth; press one square of paper on moistened surface to keep pastry in place when rolling. Place portion of pastry on paper; press flat; cover with remaining paper. Roll out gently between squares of paper, from center to edge, until round of pastry reaches edges of paper. Peel off top paper; pick up bottom paper with pastry attached. Place, pastry side down, on 9-inch pie plate. Peel off paper; ease pastry into plate. Spoon or pour in filling. For top crust, repeat procedure for rolling and handling; invert pastry over filling; peel off paper. Make slits for steam to escape. Fold under excess pastry, even with edge of plate. Pinch with fingers to form a standing collar all around rim. Flute edge.

Lattice Top: Roll out second half of pastry; peel off top paper. Make strips by cutting through remaining paper and pastry with scissors. Invert each strip over filling; peel off paper. Flute edge.

EASY STIRRED PASTRY (for 1-crust pie)

1⅓ c. sifted all-	⅓ c. pure vegetable
purpose flour	oil
1 tsp. salt	3 tbs. milk

Unbaked Crust: Follow directions for 2-crust pie for rolling pastry, lining pie plate, and shaping edge. Spoon or pour in filling and bake according to time and temperature requirements of filling recipe.

Baked Crust: Line pie plate; prick crust thoroughly with fork. Bake at 475° F. for 8 to 10 minutes or until golden brown.

BAKED CRUMB CRUST (for 1-crust pie)

1⅓ c. crushed	¼ c. soft butter or
graham cracker	margarine
crumbs	¼ c. sugar
(about 18) or	
1⅓ c. packaged	
graham cracker	
crumbs	

Heat oven to 350° F. Mix crumbs, butter or margarine, and sugar in bowl thoroughly. Press firmly on bottom and sides of lightly buttered 9-inch pie plate. Bake 8 minutes. Cool before filling.

Unbaked Crumb Crust: Prepare crumb crust. Line pie plate.

Vanilla Crumb Crust: Substitute equal amount of vanilla wafer crumbs for graham cracker crumbs. Use only 2 tablespoons sugar.

Chocolate Crumb Crust: Substitute equal amount of chocolate wafer crumbs for graham cracker crumbs. Use only 2 tablespoons sugar.

Gingersnap Crumb Crust: Substitute equal amount of gingersnap crumbs for graham cracker crumbs. Use only 2 tablespoons sugar.

Nut Crumb Crust: Add ¼ cup finely chopped walnuts or pecans to graham cracker crumb mixture.

NUT BROWN CRUST (*for 1-crust pie*)

1½ c. ground almonds, walnuts, Brazil nuts, or pecans	3 tbs. sugar 2 tbs. soft butter or margarine

Blend nuts, sugar, and butter or margarine together with fingers. Press firmly on bottom and sides of lightly buttered 9-inch pie plate. Bake at 400° F. for 6 to 8 minutes. Cool before filling.

COCONUT CRUST

1 can (7 oz.) flaked coconut	½ c. butter or margarine, melted

Blend coconut and butter or margarine. Press into 9-inch pie plate. Bake at 300° F. for 25 to 30 minutes or until golden brown.

Pie Crust Mixes and Prepared Crusts

There are many excellent products in the supermarket for those times you don't wish to make a crust from scratch. You will find packaged pie crust mix that will make an 8- or 9-inch 2-crust pie or two 8- or 9-inch pastry shells. There are packaged graham cracker crumbs and graham cracker crumb mix. Prepared, ready-to-use pastry and crumb crusts are also available.

How to Make Decorative Edgings

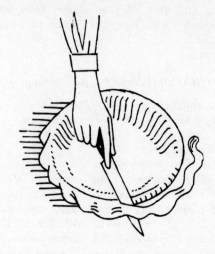

Trim pastry even with edge of pie plate. Make:

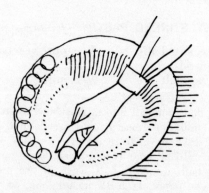

Coin edge. Cut pastry rounds the size of a penny from pastry trimmings. You'll need about 4 dozen for a nine inch pie. Brush rim lightly with water. Place "coins" on rim, overlapping them slightly. Press lightly with fingertips.

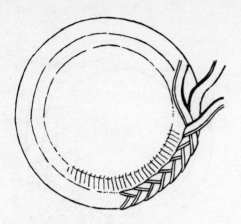

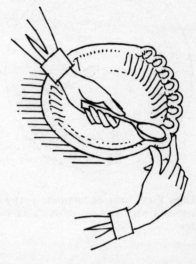

Braid edge. Roll out second half of pastry to rectangle ⅛-inch thick. Cut into ¼-inch wide strips. Braid three strips. Piece three more strips to end and braid. Repeat until braid is long enough to go around pie. Brush rim with water. Place braid carefully on rim. Cut to fit; join ends. Press in place.

Scalloped edge. Place bowl of small spoon (a measuring teaspoon is excellent) on inside of rim and thumb and index finger on outside of pastry. Shape pastry around spoon. Repeat all around edge.

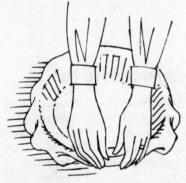

For a stand-up rim, fold overhand under so the edge stands up on pie plate. Press between fingers so it's smooth and stands up. Make:

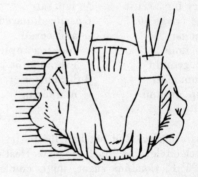

Fold edge of pastry under, even with edge of pie plate. Make:

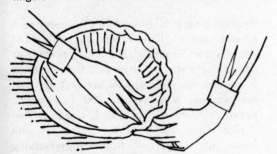

Fluted edge. Place index finger of one hand on inside of rim and thumb and index finger of other hand on outside of pastry at the same point. Pinch pastry. Repeat all around edge. Sharpen points by pinching each firmly a second time.

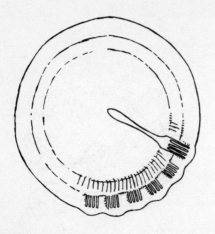

Tine Edge. Press tines of fork onto pastry from inside toward edge at even intervals all around the edge.

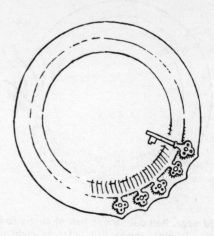

Key Edge. Press the top of a fancy key onto edge of pastry at even intervals all around the edge.

Pies

FRUIT PIES

COUNTRY APPLE PIE

Pastry for 2-crust pie (*page 405*)	¼ tsp. salt
1 c. sugar	6 c. sliced, pared, and cored cooking apples (about 2 lbs.)
2 tbs. flour	
1 tsp. ground cinnamon	
½ tsp. ground nutmeg	3 tbs. butter or margarine

Prepare pastry. Roll out half the pastry to a 12-inch circle; line 9-inch pie plate. Heat oven to 425° F. Combine sugar, flour, cinnamon, nutmeg, and salt in bowl. Arrange half the apple slices in pastry-lined pie plate. Sprinkle with half the sugar mixture. Repeat with remaining apples and sugar mixture. Dot with butter or margarine. Roll out remaining pastry for top crust; cut vents to allow steam to escape during baking. Place over filling; seal; flute. For a sparkly top, brush pie lightly with milk; sprinkle with sugar. Bake 40 to 45 minutes or until pie is golden brown. Serve with wedges of Cheddar cheese, if desired.

SNOW-CAPPED APPLE PIE

Pastry for 2-crust pie (*page 405*)	1½ tsp. ground cinnamon
8 c. sliced, pared, and cored cooking apples (about 3 lbs.)	1½ tbs. cornstarch
	2 tbs. butter or margarine
1 c. sugar	1 c. sifted confectioners' sugar
	2 to 3 tbs. water

Prepare pastry. Roll out half the pastry to a 12-inch circle; line 9-inch pie plate. Put sliced apples in colander or sieve; place over simmering water in large pot. Cover; steam 5 minutes or until apples are soft but not mushy; cool. Heat oven to 400° F. Combine sugar, cinnamon, cornstarch, and cooled apples. Turn into lined pie plate; dot with butter or margarine. Roll out remaining pastry for top crust; cut vents to allow steam to escape during baking. Place over filling; seal; flute. Bake 40 to 50 minutes or until pie is golden brown. Remove from oven; cool. Blend confectioners' sugar and water. Drizzle onto pie.

APPLE CHEESE CRUMB PIE

(Pictured opposite page 404)

1 unbaked 9-inch Cheese Pastry Crust (*page 406*)	½ c. shredded Cheddar cheese
2 cans (1 lb. 4 oz. ea.) sliced pie apples	½ c. butter or margarine
1 tbs. flour	⅓ c. brown sugar, firmly packed
⅔ c. sugar	1¼ c. sifted all-purpose flour
1½ tsp. ground cinnamon	Confectioners' sugar
½ tsp. ground nutmeg	

Prepare pastry crust according to recipe. Heat oven to 400° F. Combine apples, 1 tablespoon flour, sugar, cinnamon, and nutmeg. Turn filling into pastry crust; press down gently; sprinkle with cheese. Blend butter or margarine, brown sugar, and 1¼ cups flour with fingers until crumbs are formed. Sprinkle apples evenly with crumbs. Bake 35 to 40 minutes or until pastry and crumbs are golden brown. If crumbs brown too rapidly, cover with a circle of aluminum foil. Cool; dust generously with confectioners' sugar.

APPLE CRISP PIE

1 unbaked 9-inch pastry crust (*page 406*)	½ tsp. ground cinnamon
6 c. sliced, pared, and cored cooking apples (about 2 lbs.)	1 c. bran flakes
	¼ c. flaked coconut
	⅓ c. chopped pecans
¾ c. sugar	¼ c. brown sugar, firmly packed
⅛ tsp. salt	¼ c. melted butter or margarine
2 tbs. flour	

Prepare pastry crust according to recipe. Heat oven to 400° F. Combine apples, sugar, salt, flour, and cinnamon; turn into prepared pastry shell. Cut a circle of aluminum foil just large enough to cover filling but not pastry edge; fit over filling. Bake 30 minutes. Remove foil. Mix bran flakes, coconut, pecans, brown sugar, and butter or margarine. Sprinkle over top of hot pie. Bake 10 to 15 minutes or until pastry is golden brown and filling is bubbly. Topping may have to be protected from over-browning with aluminum foil during last few minutes of baking.

ROSY APPLE PIE

1 baked 9-inch Pastry Crust (*page 406*)	6 c. sliced, pared, and cored cooking apples (about 2 lbs.)
2 c. sugar	
1½ c. water	½ c. heavy cream, whipped
1 jar (1¾ oz.) red cinnamon candies	

Prepare pastry crust according to recipe. Combine sugar, water, and cinnamon candies in skillet. Cook over low heat, stirring until candies dissolve; bring to simmering. Poach apple slices, a few at a time, in simmering syrup until tender. Cool slices. Arrange slices in circular pattern in pastry shell. Cook remaining syrup until thickened; cool. Spoon over apple slices to glaze. Chill pie several hours. Just before serving, rim edge of pie with whipped cream.

HARVEST APPLE PIE

1 unbaked 9-inch Cheese Pastry Crust (*page 406*)	¼ tsp. ground nutmeg
	⅛ tsp. salt
½ c. sugar	¼ c. butter or margarine
½ c. brown sugar, firmly packed	6 c. sliced, pared, and cored cooking apples (about 2 lbs.)
¼ c. sifted all-purpose flour	
½ tsp. ground cinnamon	2 tsp. lemon juice
	¼ c. heavy cream

Prepare pastry crust according to recipe. Heat oven to 450° F. Mix together sugars, flour, cinnamon, nutmeg, and salt in small bowl; cut in butter or margarine. Sprinkle apples with lemon juice in large bowl; add 1 cup of sugar mixture; toss gently to coat apples evenly. Arrange apples in pastry shell; sprinkle with remaining mixture. Bake at 450° F. 10 minutes; reduce oven heat to 350° F.; bake 25 minutes or until apples are just tender. Carefully pour cream over apples; bake 10 minutes longer. Serve warm.

APRICOT CHEESE TORTE

1 baked 9-inch
  Pastry Crust
  (*page 406*)
1 can (1 lb. 14 oz.)
  peeled, whole
  apricots

2 pkgs. (8 oz. ea.)
  cream cheese
2 tbs. sugar
2 tsp. grated lemon
  rind
1/3 c. currant jelly
1 tbs. water

Prepare pastry crust according to recipe. Drain apricots; reserve 1/2 cup syrup. Remove pits from apricots carefully, leaving fruit whole. Soften cream cheese in small bowl; blend in reserved 1/2 cup apricot syrup, sugar, and lemon rind. Spread evenly in baked pastry shell. Arrange well-drained whole apricots on top. Heat jelly with water until smooth and syrupy; spoon over apricots. Garnish with chopped pistachio nuts, if desired. Chill 2 to 3 hours or until jelly glaze thickens.

FRESH BERRY PIE

Pastry for 2-crust
  pie (*page 405*)
2 qts. fresh blue-
  berries, black-
  berries, or
  raspberries

1 1/3 c. sugar
1/3 c. sifted all-
  purpose flour
2 tbs. butter or
  margarine

Prepare pastry. Roll out half the dough to a 12-inch circle; line 9-inch pie plate. Heat oven to 400° F. Wash berries; dry on paper towels. Combine berries with sugar and flour; turn into lined pie plate. Dot filling with butter or margarine. Roll out remaining pastry for top crust; cut vents to allow steam to escape during baking. Place over filling; seal; flute. Bake 35 to 45 minutes or until pie is golden brown or juices bubble through vents.

BLUEBERRY PIE

Pastry for 2-crust
  pie (*page 405*)
2 cans (14 oz. ea.)
  blueberries
1/3 c. sugar
1/4 tsp. salt

2 tbs. quick-cooking
  tapioca
2 tsp. lemon juice
2 tbs. butter or
  margarine

Prepare pastry. Roll out half the pastry to a 12-inch circle; line 9-inch pie plate. Drain blueberries; reserve 1/4 cup syrup. Combine blueberries, syrup, sugar, salt, tapioca, and lemon juice in bowl. Let stand 15 minutes. Heat oven to 425° F. Turn filling into lined pie plate; dot with butter or margarine. Roll out remaining pastry for top crust; cut vents to allow steam to escape during baking. Place over filling; seal; flute. Bake 35 to 40 minutes or until pie is golden brown or juices bubble through vents.

CHERRY PIE

Pastry for 2-crust
  pie (*page 405*)
2 cans (about 1 lb.
  ea.) red tart
  pitted cherries
1 c. sugar
1/8 tsp. salt
2 tbs. quick-cooking
  tapioca

1/4 tsp. almond
  extract
1/2 tsp. red food
  coloring
1 tbs. butter or
  margarine
Milk or cream
Sugar

Prepare pastry. Roll out half the pastry to a 12-inch circle; line a 9-inch pie plate. Drain cherries. Combine cherries, sugar, salt, tapioca, almond extract, and food coloring; let stand 15 minutes. Heat oven to 425° F. Turn filling into lined pie plate; dot with butter or margarine. Roll out remaining pastry for top crust; cut vents to allow steam to escape during baking. Place over filling; seal; flute. Brush top with milk or cream; sprinkle with sugar. Bake 35 to 45 minutes or until pie is golden brown or juices bubble through vents.

CRANBERRY PEAR PIE

1 unbaked 9-inch
  Pastry Crust
  (*page 406*)
2 c. sugar
1/4 tsp. salt
3/4 c. water
3 c. cranberries
4 tbs. cornstarch

2 tbs. cold water
2 tbs. butter or
  margarine
1 tbs. lemon juice
2 medium-size
  pears, peeled,
  cored, and diced
  (about 2 c.)

Prepare pastry crust according to recipe. Combine sugar, salt, and water in large saucepan; bring to boiling; add cranberries. Cook over low heat, without stirring, until all cranberries pop. Combine cornstarch and cold water to make smooth paste; stir into cranberry mixture and continue cooking, stirring constantly, until clear and slightly thickened. Remove from heat; add butter or margarine and lemon juice. Cool about 20 minutes. Heat oven to 425° F. Add pears to cranberry mixture; turn into pastry shell. Reroll pastry trimmings; cut into star shapes. Place on top of filling. Bake 25 to 30 minutes or until browned and bubbly.

GLAZED APPLE-MINCE PIE

(*Pictured opposite page 404*)

1 unbaked 9-inch Pastry Crust (*page 406*)	½ c. (4 oz. jar) candied diced citron
2 jars (1 lb. 12 oz. ea.) prepared mincemeat	½ c. (4 oz. jar) candied cherries, halved
1 medium-size apple, pared, cored, and chopped	1 tbs. brandy
	2 medium-size apples, pared, cored, and sliced
	½ c. apricot preserves

Prepare pastry crust according to recipe. Heat oven to 400° F. Combine mincemeat, chopped apple, citron, ¼ cup of cherries, and brandy; turn into unbaked pastry shell. Arrange sliced apples in overlapping ring on top of mincemeat. Heat apricot preserves until bubbly; brush or spoon generously over apple slices. Bake 30 to 35 minutes or until pastry is golden brown. If apples are browning too quickly, cover with circle of aluminum foil until pastry browns. Garnish with remaining ¼ cup cherries.

CRANBERRY MINCE PIE

Pastry for 2-crust pie (*page 405*)	¼ c. cornstarch
2 c. sugar	⅓ c. orange juice
⅔ c. water	1 c. prepared mincemeat
4 c. fresh cranberries	

Prepare pastry. Roll out half the pastry to a 12-inch circle; line 9-inch pie plate. Bring sugar and water to boiling in large saucepan; add cranberries; cook until skins pop. Combine cornstarch and orange juice; add quickly to cranberry mixture, stirring con-

stantly to prevent lumping. Cook until thickened and bubbly; add mincemeat; cool. Turn into pastry-lined pie plate. Heat oven to 400° F. Cut strips from remaining pastry; arrange on top of pie in design or lattice fashion (*page 406*); form edge; flute. Bake 35 to 40 minutes or until pastry is brown and filling is bubbly. Serve with Hard Sauce (*page 400*).

For a garnish for the top of a 1 crust pie, roll out leftover scraps and cut with a fancy cookie cutter. Place on cookie sheet. Bake at 400° F. just until golden.

MINCEMEAT PIE

Pastry for 2-crust pie (*page 405*)	1 large apple, pared, cored, and chopped
1 jar (1 lb., 12 oz.) prepared mincemeat or 1 pkg. (9 oz.) condensed mincemeat	

Prepare pastry; roll out half the pastry to a 12-inch circle; line 9-inch pie plate. If using condensed mincemeat, prepare according to package directions. Heat oven to 425° F. Combine mincemeat and apple; turn filling into lined pie plate. Roll out remaining pastry for top crust; cut vents to allow steam to escape during baking. Place over filling; seal; flute. Bake 30 to 35 minutes or until pie is golden brown.

RAISIN PIE

Pastry for 2-crust
 pie (*page 405*)
2 c. raisins
2¼ c. boiling water
⅔ c. sugar

2 tbs. flour
2 tsp. grated lemon
 rind
3 tbs. lemon juice

Prepare pastry crust according to recipe. Roll out half the pastry to a 12-inch circle; line 9-inch pie plate. Roll out second half; cut into ½-inch strips; reserve. Heat oven to 425° F. Cook raisins in water in covered saucepan 6 to 8 minutes or until tender. Combine sugar and flour; stir into raisins. Cook over low heat, stirring constantly, until mixture comes to boiling; remove from heat. Stir in lemon rind and juice; turn into pastry-lined pie plate. Arrange pastry strips lattice fashion (*page 406*) on top of filling; seal strips to edge; flute. Bake 35 to 40 minutes or until pie is golden brown.

PEACH CRUNCH PIE

1 unbaked 9-inch
 Pastry Crust
 (*page 406*)
¾ c. sugar
¼ c. flour
½ tsp. ground
 cinnamon
¼ tsp. ground
 nutmeg
½ tsp. salt
5 c. sliced, peeled,
 and pitted
 peaches

1 tbs. lemon juice
1 c. sifted all-
 purpose flour
½ c. brown sugar,
 firmly packed
½ c. butter or
 margarine
½ c. chopped
 pecans
2 tbs. butter or
 margarine

Prepare pastry crust according to recipe. Mix ¾ cup sugar, ¼ cup flour, cinnamon, nutmeg, and salt. Mix lightly with peaches; stir in lemon juice. Let stand while preparing topping. Heat oven to 400° F. Combine 1 cup flour, brown sugar, and ½ cup butter or margarine in bowl; mix with fingers until crumbly. Stir in nuts. Turn peach mixture into pastry-lined pie plate. Dot with 2 tablespoons butter or margarine. Sprinkle topping mixture over peaches. Because nuts brown quickly, cut an aluminum foil circle to fit top of pie; place on pie. Bake 25 minutes. Remove foil; bake 15 minutes.

PEACHES AND CREAM PIE

1 unbaked 9-inch
 Pastry Crust
 (*page 406*)
4 c. sliced, peeled,
 and pitted
 peaches
2 tbs. lemon juice
2 eggs
⅓ c. brown sugar,
 firmly packed

1 tbs. flour
¼ tsp. ground
 nutmeg
½ c. dairy sour
 cream
2 tbs. soft butter or
 margarine
2 tbs. brown sugar
⅓ c. flour

Prepare pastry crust according to recipe. Heat oven to 450° F. Pile peaches into pastry shell; sprinkle with lemon juice. Beat eggs; add ⅓ cup brown sugar, 1 tablespoon flour, nutmeg, and sour cream; mix until well blended; pour over peaches. Combine butter or margarine, 2 tablespoons brown sugar, and ⅓ cup flour; blend with fingers until crumbs form. Sprinkle over top of pie. Bake 15 minutes; reduce heat to 350° F.; bake 25 minutes or until filling is firm.

PEACH SOUR CREAM PIE

Pastry for 2-crust
 pie (*page 405*)
⅓ c. sifted all-
 purpose flour
⅔ c. sugar
¼ tsp. ground
 cinnamon
¼ tsp. ground
 nutmeg
⅛ tsp. salt

1 c. dairy sour
 cream
5 c. sliced, peeled,
 and pitted
 peaches
Milk
1 tbs. sugar
⅛ tsp. ground
 cinnamon

Prepare pastry. Roll out half the pastry to a 12-inch circle; line 9-inch pie plate. Combine flour, sugar, ¼ teaspoon cinnamon, nutmeg, salt, and sour cream; fold in peaches. Turn into lined pie plate. Heat oven to 400° F. Roll out remaining pastry for top crust; cut vents to allow steam to escape during baking. Place over filling; seal; flute. Brush pie with milk. Mix 1 tablespoon sugar and ⅛ teaspoon cinnamon; sprinkle over pie. Bake 30 minutes or until pie is golden brown.

PINEAPPLE PIE DELUXE

Pastry for 2-crust
   pie (*page 405*)
1 c. sugar
3 tbs. cornstarch
¼ tsp. salt
1 can (1 lb. 14 oz.)
   crushed pine-
   apple (3½ c.)

¼ c. chopped
   maraschino
   cherries
1 tsp. grated orange
   rind
Milk
Sugar

Prepare pastry. Roll out half the pastry to a 12-inch circle; line 9-inch pie plate. Heat oven to 425° F. Combine sugar, cornstarch, and salt in saucepan; add crushed pineapple with juice and maraschino cherries. Cook over medium heat, stirring constantly, until mixture thickens and boils; boil 1 minute longer. Remove from heat; stir in orange rind. Pour into pastry-lined pie plate. Roll out remaining pastry for top crust; cut vents to allow steam to escape during baking. Place over filling; seal; flute. Brush crust lightly with milk; sprinkle with sugar. Bake 30 to 35 minutes or until pie is golden brown.

ROSY PEAR PIE

Pastry for 2-crust
   pie (*page 405*)
6 c. sliced, pared,
   and cored pears
   (about 6 large
   pears)
3 c. water

2 tbs. lemon juice
1 jar (1¾ oz.) red
   cinnamon candies
3 tbs. cornstarch
¼ c. cold water
1 c. sugar

Prepare pastry. Roll out half the pastry to a 12-inch circle; line 9-inch pie plate. Simmer pears in water and lemon juice just until tender but not mushy. Drain; measure 1 cup pear liquid; reserve pear slices. Add cinnamon candies to measured pear liquid; simmer until candies have dissolved. Blend cornstarch and cold water until smooth; stir into cinnamon mixture. Cook over low heat, stirring constantly, until thickened and clear. Remove from heat. Stir in sugar; stir until dissolved. Add pears; cool. Heat oven to 400° F. Turn filling into lined pie plate. Roll out remaining pastry; cut into ½-inch-wide strips. Arrange strips lattice fashion (*page 406*) over pears; form edge; flute. For a sugary crust brush strips with milk and sprinkle with sugar. Bake 35 to 40 minutes or until pie is golden brown.

RHUBARB CHERRY PIE

Pastry for 2-crust
   pie (*page 405*)
4 c. (2 lbs.)
   rhubarb, diced
1 can (1 lb.) red
   tart pitted
   cherries, drained

1 c. sugar
¼ c. quick-cooking
   tapioca
Few drops red food
   coloring

Prepare pastry. Roll out half the pastry to a 12-inch circle; line 9-inch pie plate. Combine rhubarb, cherries, sugar, tapioca, and food coloring; let stand 15 minutes. Heat oven to 425° F. Turn rhubarb-cherry mixture into lined pie plate. Roll out remaining pastry for top crust; cut vents to allow steam to escape during baking. Place over filling; seal; flute. For sparkling top, brush top of pie with milk; sprinkle with sugar. Bake 45 to 50 minutes or until pie is golden brown or juices bubble through vents.

STRAWBERRY PIE

1 qt. strawberries,
   washed, hulled,
   and halved
1 c. sugar
3½ tbs. quick-
   cooking tapioca
¼ tsp. salt

1 tsp. grated orange
   rind
Pastry for 2-crust
   pie (*page 405*)
2 tbs. butter or
   margarine

Combine strawberries, sugar, tapioca, salt, and orange rind in large bowl. Let stand 20 to 25 minutes until sugar draws some juice from the berries. Heat oven to 425° F. Prepare pastry. Roll out half the pastry to a 12-inch circle; line 9-inch pie plate. Turn strawberry mixture into pastry-lined pie plate; dot with butter or margarine. Roll out remaining pastry for top crust; cut vents to allow steam to escape during baking. Place over strawberry filling; seal; flute. For a sparkling crust, brush top with milk and sprinkle with sugar. Bake 40 to 50 minutes or until pie is golden brown or juices bubble through vents.

COLONIAL GRAPE PIE

Pastry for 2-crust
pie (*page 405*)
5 c. Concord grapes
(about 2½ lbs.)
1 c. sugar

1½ tbs. quick-
cooking tapioca
¼ tsp. salt
1 tbs. grated orange
rind
2 tbs. lemon juice

Prepare pastry. Roll out half the pastry to a
12-inch circle; line a 9-inch pie plate. Wash
and stem grapes; slip pulp from skins; reserve skins. Cook pulp 5 minutes or until
seeds loosen. Press through coarse sieve to
remove seeds. Combine pulp, skins, sugar,
tapioca, salt, orange rind, and lemon juice;
let stand 15 minutes. Heat oven to 450° F.
Turn filling into lined pie plate. Roll out remaining pastry; cut into ½-inch-wide strips.
Arrange strips lattice fashion (*page 406*) over
filling; form edge; flute. Bake 10 minutes; reduce oven heat to 350° F. Bake 20 to 25 minutes or until juices bubble through vents.

DEEP-DISH PLUM PIE

6 c. halved, pitted
purple plums
⅓ c. quick-cooking
tapioca
1½ c. sugar
⅛ tsp. salt

½ tsp. ground
cinnamon
¼ tsp. ground
allspice
Pastry for 1-crust
pie (*page 406*)

Combine plums, tapioca, sugar, salt, cinnamon, and allspice. Turn into 1½-quart
baking dish. Let stand 20 minutes. Heat oven
to 425° F. Prepare pastry. Roll out to fit top
of baking dish. Cut vents to allow steam to
escape during baking. Place over filling;
press pastry to rim of baking dish; flute.
Bake 40 to 50 minutes or until crust is golden
brown and juices bubble through vents. If
a sugary crust is desired, brush with milk
and sprinkle with sugar before baking.

Deep-Dish Fruit Pies

Double recipe for
filling for Snow
Capped Apple
Pie (*page 410*),
Blueberry Pie
(*page 412*),

Cherry Pie
(*page 412*), or
Strawberry Pie
(*page 415*)
Pastry for 1-crust
pie (*page 406*)

Heat oven to 425° F. Prepare filling; pour

into 2-quart baking dish. Prepare pastry; roll
out to fit top of baking dish; cut vents to
allow steam to escape during baking. Place
over filling; seal; flute. Bake 45 to 50 minutes or until golden brown.

PLUM TART

Pastry for 2-crust
pie (*page 405*)
2 lbs. purple plums,
halved and pitted
1 c. sugar

1 tsp. ground
cinnamon
½ c. red currant
jelly
1 tbs. water
Whipped cream

Heat oven to 425° F. Prepare pastry. Roll out
pastry to 18x12-inch rectangle. Line 15x10x
1-inch jelly-roll pan. Flute edge, if desired. Arrange plums, rounded side down, on pastry.
Sprinkle with sugar mixed with cinnamon.
Bake 20 to 25 minutes. Heat jelly and water
over low heat, stirring constantly, until jelly
is melted. Spoon over plums. Cut into squares
or rectangles. Serve warm or cold with whipped
cream. Makes 15 to 18 servings.

PARTY FRUIT TART

Pastry for 2-crust
pie (*page 405*)
2 cans (about 1 lb.
ea.) red tart
pitted cherries
1 c. sugar
2 cans (14 oz. ea.)
blueberries,
drained
2 cans (about 1 lb.
ea.) pineapple
chunks, drained
2 cans (about 1 lb.
ea.) apricot
halves, drained

6 tbs. cornstarch
1 c. sugar
Dash of salt
4 c. water
2 tbs. grated lemon
rind
¼ c. lemon juice
½ tsp. almond
extract
¼ tsp. mint extract
½ tsp. ground
cinnamon
¼ tsp. ground mace

Heat oven to 425° F. Prepare pastry. Roll
out to 18x12-inch rectangle. Line 15x10x1-
inch pan; prick well; flute edge. Bake 12 to
15 minutes or until golden brown. Remove
from oven; cool. Drain cherries. Put juice
and 1 cup sugar in saucepan; simmer 5 minutes. Add cherries; simmer 5 minutes; drain;
discard juice. Put each fruit in separate bowl.
Combine cornstarch, 1 cup sugar, and salt in

saucepan; stir in water. Simmer 3 minutes. Remove from heat; add lemon rind and juice. Pour 1 cup mixture over each fruit. Add almond extract to cherries, mint extract to pineapple, cinnamon to blueberries, and mace to apricots. Arrange fruits in rows in tart shell. Chill. Makes 16 to 20 servings.

CUSTARD PIES

CUSTARD PIE

1 unbaked 9-inch	⅔ c. sugar
Pastry Crust	½ tsp. salt
(*page 406*)	2½ c. milk
4 eggs, slightly	1 tsp. vanilla
beaten	Ground nutmeg

Prepare pastry crust according to recipe. Heat oven to 425° F. Combine eggs, sugar, salt, milk, and vanilla. To have full pie without spilling, take pastry shell and custard filling over to oven. Pull out oven rack;

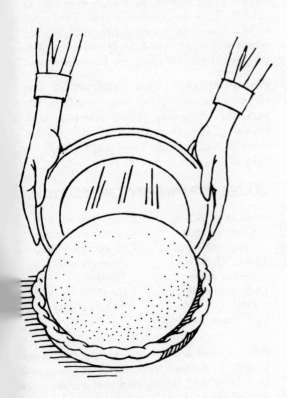

place pastry shell on rack. Pour filling into pastry shell. Sprinkle with nutmeg. Push shelf and filled shell carefully back into oven. Bake 30 minutes or until thin-bladed knife or spatula inserted 1-inch from edge will come out clean. Center will look soft, but will set later. Do not overbake.

Coconut Custard Pie: Add ½ cup shredded or flaked canned coconut to Custard Pie Filling. Fill pastry shell; sprinkle top with additional ¼ cup coconut.

Slipped Custard Pie: Bake and cool 9-inch pastry shell. Heat oven to 350° F. Prepare filling for Custard Pie. Place pie plate in shallow pan; pour in filling. Pour hot water in outer pan to depth of 1 inch. Bake 30 minutes or until thin-bladed knife or spatula inserted 1-inch from edge will come out clean. Cool to room temperature. Carefully loosen custard around edge; shake gently to be sure it is loose in plate. Tilt plate over baked pastry shell; gently coax custard into shell. Let settle a few moments before serving.

PEAR CUSTARD PIE

Pastry for 2-crust	½ tsp. grated lemon
pie (*page 405*)	rind
8 c. sliced, pared,	1 tbs. lemon juice
and cored pears	⅓ c. sugar
(about 8 large	½ tsp. ground
pears)	cinnamon
2 eggs	1 tbs. melted butter
½ c. heavy cream	or margarine
¼ c. milk	

Prepare pastry. Roll out half the pastry to a 12-inch circle; line 9-inch pie plate. Put sliced pears into colander or sieve; place over simmering water in large pot. Cover; steam 5 minutes or until pears are soft but not mushy; cool. Heat oven to 400° F. Beat eggs slightly in large bowl. Add cream, milk, lemon rind and juice, sugar, cinnamon, and melted butter or margarine. Fold in cooled pears; turn into pastry-lined pie plate. Roll out remaining pastry for top crust; cut vents to allow steam to escape during baking. Place over filling; seal; flute. For a sugary top, brush top of pie with milk and sprinkle with sugar. Bake 40 minutes or until pie is golden brown.

LOUISIANA PECAN PIE

1 unbaked 9-inch
Pastry Crust
(*page 406*)
¼ c. butter or
margarine
3 eggs
¾ c. sugar

¼ tsp. salt
1 c. dark corn
syrup
1 tsp. vanilla
1½ c. chopped
pecans

Prepare pastry crust according to recipe. Heat oven to 350° F. Melt butter or margarine; cool. Beat eggs with sugar and salt until foamy and well blended. Add corn syrup, vanilla, and cooled butter or margarine; blend. Stir in pecans. Pour into pastry shell. Bake 40 to 50 minutes or until filling is set at edges but is still slightly soft in center. Overbaking will curdle the filling. Cool. Serve with puffs of whipped cream and whole toasted pecans, if desired.

FUDGE NUT PIE

1 unbaked 9-inch
Pastry Crust
(*page 406*)
½ c. butter or
margarine
1 c. sugar
2 egg yolks
1 tsp. vanilla

2 sqs. unsweetened
chocolate, melted
⅓ c. sifted all-
purpose flour
2 egg whites
Dash of salt
¾ c. coarsely
chopped walnuts

Prepare pastry crust according to recipe. Cream butter or margarine in bowl; beat in sugar gradually; continue beating until light and fluffy. Add egg yolks and vanilla; blend well. Add melted chocolate and flour. Beat egg whites and salt in second bowl until

stiff but not dry; fold into chocolate mixture. Add walnuts; turn into pastry shell. Bake at 375° F. for 30 to 35 minutes or until puffed. Cool. Serve with vanilla or coffee ice cream or with whipped cream, if desired.

PUMPKIN PIE

1 unbaked 9-inch
Pastry Crust
(*page 406*)
2 eggs
¾ c. brown sugar,
firmly packed
1 can (about 1 lb.)
pumpkin
½ tsp. salt
1 tsp. ground
cinnamon

½ tsp. ground
ginger
½ tsp. ground
nutmeg
¼ tsp. ground
cloves
1 can (14½ oz.)
evaporated milk
(1⅔ c.)

Prepare pastry crust according to recipe. Beat eggs slightly in large bowl; add brown sugar, pumpkin, salt, and spices; mix well. Stir in evaporated milk; pour into pastry shell. Bake at 425° F. for 15 minutes. Reduce oven heat to 375° F.; bake 30 minutes or until thin-bladed knife or spatula inserted 1-inch from edge comes out clean. Cool Serve plain or with whipped cream, ice cream, or Cheddar cheese.

Pecan-Pumpkin Pie: Combine ½ cup chopped pecans; ¼ cup brown sugar, firmly packed; and ¼ cup melted butter or margarine. Bake Pumpkin Pie 20 minutes. Sprinkle nut mixture over pie. Continue to bake as directed.

GLAZED STRAWBERRY CHEESE PIE

1 unbaked 9-inch
Crumb Crust
(*page 407*)
2 pkgs. (8 oz. ea.)
cream cheese
1 tsp. grated lemon
rind
½ c. sugar

3 eggs
¼ c. heavy cream
1 qt. strawberries,
washed and
hulled
1 jar (8 oz.)
currant jelly

Prepare crust according to recipe. Heat oven to 350° F. Soften cream cheese at low speed on mixer. Add lemon rind and sugar; continue beating until blended. Blend in eggs one at a time; stir in cream. Pour into prepared crumb crust. Bake 30 to 35 minutes or until cheese-custard filling is firm at edges but still soft in center. It will become firm when cool. Arrange strawberries, points up, on top of pie. Melt currant jelly over low heat; cool; spoon over strawberries. Chill about 1 hour.

APPLE CUSTARD PIE

1 unbaked 9-inch Pastry Crust (*page 406*)	¼ tsp. salt
	½ tsp. grated lemon rind
1 can (about 1 lb.) applesauce	2 tbs. lemon juice
½ c. sugar	4 eggs, slightly beaten
¼ tsp. ground nutmeg	½ c. heavy cream

Prepare pastry crust according to recipe. Heat oven to 450° F. Blend applesauce, sugar, nutmeg, salt, lemon rind, lemon juice, eggs, and cream in mixing bowl. Pour into pastry shell. Bake 15 minutes. Reduce oven heat to 275° F.; bake 55 to 65 minutes or until a thin-bladed knife or spatula inserted 1-inch from edge comes out clean. Cool.

SWEET POTATO PECAN PIE

1 unbaked 9-inch Pastry Crust (*page 406*)	½ c. brown sugar, firmly packed
½ c. chopped pecans	1 tsp. ground ginger
2 tbs. butter or margarine	¼ tsp. ground cloves
¼ c. brown sugar, firmly packed	1½ tsp. ground cinnamon
1 can (1 lb. 14 oz.) sweet potatoes or yams, drained	¼ tsp. salt
	2 eggs, beaten
	1½ c. milk

Prepare pastry crust according to recipe. Heat oven to 450° F. Combine pecans, butter or margarine, and ¼ cup brown sugar; spread evenly on bottom of pastry shell. Bake 10 minutes; cool. Reduce oven heat to 350° F. Beat sweet potatoes or yams with electric mixer until smooth. Add ½ cup brown sugar, ginger, cloves, cinnamon, salt, and eggs; beat until blended. Add milk slowly; continue beating until mixture is quite smooth. Pour into cooled pastry shell. Bake 35 to 40 minutes or until thin-bladed knife or spatula inserted 1-inch from edge comes out clean. Cool before serving. Serve with whipped cream, if desired.

CREAM PIES

VANILLA CREAM PIE

1 baked 9-inch Pastry Crust (*page 406*)	2½ c. milk
	3 egg yolks, slightly beaten
¼ c. cornstarch	1 tbs. butter or margarine
¾ c. sugar	2 tsp. vanilla
½ tsp. salt	

Prepare pastry crust according to recipe. Combine cornstarch, sugar, and salt in saucepan. Stir in milk gradually. Cook over medium heat, stirring constantly, until mixture thickens and comes to boiling. Boil 1 minute. Blend one half the mixture into egg yolks; stir into mixture in saucepan; cook 1 minute, stirring constantly. Remove from heat; stir in butter or margarine and vanilla; cool slightly. Pour filling into pastry shell. Top with meringue and bake (*page 420*) or chill pie thoroughly and top with whipped cream.

Banana Cream Pie: Prepare Vanilla Cream Pie Filling; place piece of wax paper directly on surface of filling to keep filling soft; cool. Slice 3 medium-size peeled bananas into baked 9-inch pastry shell. Pour filling over bananas. Chill thoroughly. Top with 1 cup heavy cream, whipped. Decorate if desired, with additional banana slices which have been dipped in orange or lemon juice to keep their color.

Coconut Cream Pie: Prepare Vanilla Cream Pie Filling. Fold 1 cup flaked or grated coconut into filling. Pour into pastry shell. Top with meringue and bake (*page 420*) or chill pie thoroughly and top with whipped cream.

CHOCOLATE CREAM PIE

1 baked 9-inch
Pastry Crust
(*page 406*)
4 tbs. cornstarch
1 c. sugar
½ tsp. salt
3 sqs. unsweetened
chocolate, cut up

2½ c. milk
3 egg yolks, slightly
beaten
1 tbs. butter or
margarine
2 tsp. vanilla

Prepare pastry crust according to recipe. Combine cornstarch, sugar, salt, and chocolate in saucepan. Stir in milk gradually. Cook over medium heat, stirring constantly, until mixture thickens and comes to boiling. Boil 1 minute. Blend half the mixture into egg yolks; stir into mixture in saucepan; cook 1 minute, stirring constantly. Remove from heat; stir in butter or margarine and vanilla; cool slightly. Pour filling into pastry shell. Top with meringue and bake (*below*) or chill pie thoroughly and top with whipped cream.

BUTTERSCOTCH CREAM PIE

1 baked 9-inch
Pastry Crust
(*page 406*)
⅓ c. butter or
margarine
1 c. brown sugar,
firmly packed

1 c. boiling water
5 tbs. cornstarch
¼ tsp. salt
1½ c. milk
3 egg yolks, slightly
beaten
2 tsp. vanilla

Prepare pastry crust according to recipe. Heat butter or margarine in skillet over low heat until it foams and becomes amber brown. Add brown sugar; cook, stirring constantly, until mixture liquefies slightly and just begins to bubble. Add boiling water slowly and carefully. Cook, stirring constantly, until sugar mixture is dissolved. Blend cornstarch, salt, and ¼ cup of milk in saucepan until smooth. Add remaining milk and brown-sugar syrup. Cook over medium heat, stirring constantly, until mixture thickens and comes to boiling. Boil 1 minute. Blend half the mixture into egg yolks; stir into mixture in saucepan. Boil one minute. Remove from heat; stir in vanilla. Place piece of wax paper directly on surface of filling to keep filling soft; cool. Fill pie shell. Top with meringue and bake (*below*) or chill pie thoroughly and top with whipped cream.

Meringue Topped Cream Pie

Prepare Vanilla, Chocolate, Butterscotch, or Coconut Cream Pie.

Beat 3 egg whites and ¼ teaspoon cream of tartar until foamy. Add 6 tablespoons sugar gradually. Continue beating until meringue forms stiff, glossy peaks. Spread meringue over filling, making sure it touches crust all the way around. Bake at 350° F. for 15 to 20 minutes or until meringue is tipped with brown. Cool at room temperature.

FRENCH RASPBERRY CREAM TART

1½ c. sifted all-
purpose flour
2 tbs. sugar
½ c. butter or
margarine
1 egg
1 pkg. (4 oz.)
vanilla pudding
and pie filling

1 envelope
unflavored
gelatin
1½ c. milk
½ c. heavy cream,
whipped
1 tsp. vanilla
1 pt. raspberries
¼ c. raspberry
jelly
1 tbs. water

Blend flour, sugar, butter or margarine, and egg; chill. Roll out onto floured board to a 12-inch circle. Press into 9-inch pie plate. Cut pastry even with edge of plate. (Pastry is short, but will patch easily.) Prick pastry with fork. Bake at 400° F. for 10 minutes; reduce oven heat to 350° F.; bake 15 minutes or until golden. Cool. Combine pudding mix and gelatin; stir in milk. Cook over medium heat, stirring constantly, until thickened. Cool. Chill until mixture begins to set; fold in whipped cream and vanilla; pour into pastry shell. Wash and drain raspberries; place, stem end down, on filling. Melt jelly with water; cool; spoon over berries to glaze. Chill until set. Decorate with whipped cream, if desired.

PEACH BLOSSOM PIE

1 baked 9-inch Pastry Crust (*page 406*)	1 tsp. butter or margarine
⅔ c. sugar	1 tsp. almond extract
3 tbs. cornstarch	½ tsp. vanilla
1 tsp. unflavored gelatin	4 large peaches, peeled, pitted, and sliced
¼ tsp. salt	2 tbs. lemon juice
3 c. milk	½ c. apricot preserves
3 egg yolks, slightly beaten	1 tbs. water

Prepare pastry crust according to recipe. Combine sugar, cornstarch, gelatin, salt, and milk in saucepan. Cook over medium heat, stirring constantly, until mixture thickens and boils 1 minute. Stir more than half the mixture into egg yolks; stir into mixture in saucepan. Cook 1 minute; remove from heat. Add butter or margarine, almond extract, and vanilla. Cool. Pour into pastry shell. Chill 1 hour or until firm. Brush peach slices with lemon juice to keep them from darkening. Heat apricot preserves and water just until melted; press through sieve. Arrange peach slices on firm custard in pie shell; brush with sieved preserves.

RASPBERRY AND APRICOT GLACÉ PIE

1 baked 9-inch Pastry Crust (*page 406*)	3½ tbs. cornstarch
	4 egg yolks
	2 c. milk, scalded
1 pt. raspberries	1 tsp. vanilla
1 c. sugar	6 apricots, peeled, halved, and pitted
2 tbs. water	
½ tsp. ground ginger	

Prepare pastry crust according to recipe. Crush 1 cup raspberries; add ¼ cup sugar and water. Set aside. Combine remaining ¾ cup sugar, ginger, and 3 tablespoons cornstarch. Beat egg yolks until thick. Gradually add sugar mixture, beating constantly, until mixture is thick and light. Add scalded milk slowly, stirring briskly. Cook over very low heat, stirring constantly, until smooth and thickened. Remove from heat; let stand 5 minutes. Stir in vanilla. Pour into pastry shell. Chill at least one hour. Strain crushed raspberry mixture through fine sieve, pressing through as much juice as possible. Add water, if necessary, to make 1 cup. Mix with remaining ½ tablespoon cornstarch. Cook over low heat until mixture is thickened and clear. Arrange apricot halves and remaining 1 cup of raspberries on chilled pie. Spoon thickened raspberry glaze over. Chill at least ½ hour.

MERINGUE PIES

LEMON MERINGUE PIE

1 baked 9-inch Pastry Crust (*page 406*)	2 tbs. butter or margarine
½ c. cornstarch	1 tbs. grated lemon rind
1½ c. sugar	½ c. lemon juice
¼ tsp. salt	4 egg whites
1¾ c. water	¼ tsp. cream of tartar
4 egg yolks, slightly beaten	½ c. sugar

Prepare pastry crust according to recipe. Blend cornstarch, 1½ cups sugar, and salt in saucepan; stir in water gradually. Cook over medium heat, stirring constantly, until mixture comes to boiling. Boil 1 minute. Stir half the mixture slowly into egg yolks; stir into mixture in saucepan. Cook over low heat, stirring constantly, 2 minutes; remove from heat. Add butter or margarine, lemon rind, and juice; cool slightly. Pour into baked pastry shell. Beat egg whites and cream of tartar until foamy; beat in ½ cup sugar gradually; continue beating until meringue forms stiff, glossy peaks. Swirl meringue onto filling with spoon or spatula. Be sure meringue touches crust all the way around to prevent shrinkage. Bake at 350 F. for 15 to 20 minutes or until meringue is tipped with brown. Cool to room temperature before serving.

Key Lime Pie: Follow recipe for Lemon Meringue Pie substituting 2 teaspoons grated lime rind for the lemon rind and ½ cup lime juice for the lemon juice. You may add a few drops of green food coloring, if desired. Pour cooled mixture into baked pastry shell. Omit meringue; chill pie. Just before serving, whip 1 cup heavy cream; spread over filling. Garnish with chopped pistachio nuts, if desired.

CHIFFON AND GELATIN PIES

ORANGE CHIFFON PIE

1 baked 9-inch Pastry Crust (*page 406*)	4 egg yolks, slightly beaten
1 envelope un-flavored gelatin	4 egg whites
½ c. sugar	½ tsp. cream of tartar
¾ c. orange juice	½ c. sugar
2 tbs. lemon juice	1 tbs. grated orange rind

Prepare pastry crust according to recipe. Combine gelatin, ½ cup sugar, orange juice, lemon juice, and egg yolks in top of double boiler. Cook over simmering, not boiling, water until gelatin and sugar are dissolved and mixture slightly coats spoon. Cool; chill until mixture mounds when spooned. Beat egg whites and cream of tartar until foamy. Add ½ cup sugar gradually; continue beating until meringue forms stiff, glossy peaks. Fold thickened gelatin mixture and orange rind gently into meringue. Pour into pastry shell. Chill 1 to 2 hours. Garnish with fresh orange sections and whipped cream, if desired.

LEMON CHIFFON PIE

1 baked 9-inch Pastry Crust (*page 406*)	4 egg yolks, slightly beaten
1 envelope un-flavored gelatin	1 tbs. grated lemon rind
⅔ c. sugar	4 egg whites
¾ c. water	¼ tsp. cream of tartar
¼ c. lemon juice	4 tbs. sugar

Prepare pastry crust according to recipe. Combine gelatin, ⅔ cup sugar, water, lemon juice, and egg yolks in saucepan; cook over medium heat, stirring constantly, until mix-

ture just comes to boiling. Remove from heat; stir in lemon rind; cool. Chill until mixture mounds when spooned. Beat egg whites and cream of tartar in large bowl until foamy; beat in 4 tablespoons sugar gradually. Continue beating until meringue forms stiff, glossy peaks. Fold lemon mixture into meringue; spoon into pastry shell. Chill 1 to 2 hours. Garnish as desired.

STRAWBERRY CHIFFON PIE

1 baked 9-inch Vanilla Crumb Crust (*page 408*)	¼ c. water
1 pt. strawberries	2 egg whites
⅓ c. sugar	¼ c. sugar
1 envelope un-flavored gelatin	½ c. heavy cream, whipped
	14 to 15 whole vanilla wafers

Prepare crumb crust according to recipe. Wash strawberries; save several nicely shaped ones for garnish; hull and slice remainder. Combine sliced strawberries and ⅓ cup sugar; let stand 15 minutes until juices run freely; strain juice into saucepan. Soften gelatin in water 5 minutes; add to strawberry juice; heat until gelatin is dissolved; cool. Add sliced strawberries to cooled mixture; chill until mixture mounds when spooned. Beat egg whites until foamy; beat in ¼ cup of sugar gradually. Continue beating until meringue forms stiff, glossy peaks. Fold thickened strawberry mixture into meringue; fold in whipped cream; pour into cooled crust. Press whole vanilla wafers into filling all around pie to form scalloped edge. Garnish with reserved whole strawberries.

PEACH MELBA CHIFFON PIE

1 baked 9-inch Pastry Crust (*page 406*)	1 tbs. lemon juice
⅓ c. sugar	4 egg whites
1 envelope un-flavored gelatin	⅓ c. sugar
¼ tsp. salt	1 pkg. (10 oz.) frozen rasp-berries, thawed
4 egg yolks, slightly beaten	2 tsp. cornstarch
⅔ c. milk	½ c. heavy cream, whipped
1 pkg. (10 oz.) frozen peaches, thawed and drained	

Prepare pastry crust according to recipe. Combine ⅓ cup sugar, gelatin, and salt in top of double boiler. Add egg yolks and milk to sugar mixture. Stir over hot, not boiling, water until custard thickens and coats spoon; remove from heat; cool. Combine peaches with lemon juice; press through sieve or purée in blender; add to cooled custard; chill until mixture mounds when spooned. Beat whites until foamy; add ⅓ cup sugar gradually. Continue beating until meringue forms stiff, glossy peaks. Fold in yolk mixture. Pour into prepared pastry shell; chill until set. Drain raspberries; reserve syrup. Combine cornstarch and ½ cup reserved syrup in saucepan. Cook until bubbly and thickened; cool; add raspberries. Spoon cooled raspberry mixture over peach filling. Decorate with whipped cream.

BLACK BOTTOM PIE

1 baked 9-inch crumb crust (*page 407*)	3 sqs. unsweetened chocolate, melted and cooled
1 envelope un-flavored gelatin	2 tbs. light rum
¼ c. cold water	3 egg whites
⅔ c. sugar	¼ tsp. cream of tartar
2 tbs. cornstarch	⅓ c. sugar
¼ tsp. salt	½ c. heavy cream, whipped
2½ c. milk	
3 egg yolks, slightly beaten	

Prepare crumb crust according to recipe. Soften gelatin in cold water. Mix ⅔ cup sugar, cornstarch, and salt in top of double boiler. Combine milk and egg yolks; stir into cornstarch mixture. Cook over hot, not boiling, water until custard coats spoon; remove from heat. Measure 1½ cups custard mixture into bowl; blend in melted chocolate. Pour into prepared crumb crust; chill until firm.

Add softened gelatin to remaining custard; stir until dissolved; chill just until it begins to set; stir in rum. Beat egg whites and cream of tartar until foamy; beat in ⅓ cup sugar gradually. Continue beating until meringue forms stiff, glossy peaks; fold custard mixture into meringue; fold in whipped cream. Spoon onto chocolate layer in crumb crust. Chill until set. Garnish with grated chocolate, if desired.

CRANBERRY CHIFFON PIE

1 baked 9-inch crumb crust (*page 407*)	1 bottle (1 pt.) cranberry juice cocktail
½ c. sugar	3 egg whites
¼ c. flour	⅓ c. sugar
1 envelope un-flavored gelatin	½ c. heavy cream, whipped
½ tsp. salt	

Prepare crumb crust according to recipe. Combine ½ cup sugar, flour, gelatin, and salt in saucepan. Add cranberry juice; stir to blend. Cook over medium heat, stirring constantly, until thickened and bubbly. Cool; chill until mixture mounds when spooned. Beat egg whites until foamy; add ⅓ cup sugar gradually. Continue beating until meringue forms stiff, glossy peaks. Fold into cranberry mixture; fold in whipped cream. Spoon into crumb crust; chill several hours or until set. Garnish with additional whipped cream, if desired.

APRICOT VELVET PIE

1 baked 9-inch Pastry Crust (*page 406*)	1½ c. boiling water
2 pkgs. (3 oz. ea.) orange-flavored gelatin	1 can (12 oz.) apricot nectar
¼ c. sugar	1 pkg. (2 oz.) dessert-topping mix

Prepare pastry crust according to recipe. Mix gelatin and sugar; add boiling water; stir to dissolve. Add nectar. Chill until mixture mounds when spooned. Prepare topping mix according to package directions. Stir about 1 cup thickened gelatin into topping; fold in remaining gelatin mixture. Chill mixture until it mounds slightly when spooned. Pour into pastry shell; chill until set. Garnish as desired.

PUMPKIN CHIFFON PIE

(*Pictured opposite page 404*)

1 baked 9-inch Nut Crumb Crust (*page 408*)	¼ tsp. ground cloves
1 envelope un-flavored gelatin	1 can (about 1 lb.) pumpkin
¾ c. brown sugar, firmly packed	2 egg yolks
½ tsp. salt	½ c. milk
1 tsp. ground cinnamon	2 egg whites
½ tsp. ground ginger	⅓ c. sugar
	1 tsp. grated orange rind
	½ c. dairy sour cream

Prepare crumb crust according to recipe. Combine gelatin, brown sugar, salt, cinnamon, ginger, cloves, pumpkin, egg yolks, and milk in saucepan. Cook over medium heat, stirring constantly, until mixture comes to boiling. Do not boil. Cool; chill until mixture mounds when spooned. Beat egg whites until foamy; add sugar gradually. Continue beating until meringue forms stiff, glossy peaks. Fold pumpkin mixture into meringue; fold in orange rind and sour cream. Spoon into crumb crust; chill several hours or until set. Garnish with orange sections and additional sour cream, if desired.

NESSELRODE PIE

1 baked 9-inch Nut Brown Crust (*page 408*)	1½ c. milk
1 envelope un-flavored gelatin	3 egg whites
¼ c. sugar	¼ c. sugar
3 egg yolks, slightly beaten	½ c. heavy cream, whipped
	1 jar (10 oz.) Nesselrode mixture

Prepare nut crust according to recipe. Blend gelatin and ¼ cup sugar in top of double boiler. Add egg yolks and milk. Cook over hot, not boiling, water until custard thickens and coats spoon. Cool; chill until mixture mounds when spooned. Beat egg whites until foamy; add ¼ cup sugar gradually. Continue beating until meringue forms stiff, glossy peaks. Fold custard mixture into meringue; fold in whipped cream and Nesselrode mixture. Spoon into crumb crust; chill several hours or until set.

CRANBERRY PINEAPPLE PIE

1 baked 9-inch crumb crust (*page 407*)	⅓ c. sugar
1 envelope un-flavored gelatin	1 can (8½ oz.) crushed pine-apple, well drained
¼ c. bottled cran-berry juice cocktail	2 tsp. grated orange rind
2 egg yolks	½ c. heavy cream, whipped
1¼ c. bottled cran-berry juice cocktail	2 egg whites
	¼ tsp. salt
	¼ c. sugar

Prepare crumb crust according to recipe. Soften gelatin in ¼ cup cranberry juice. Combine egg yolks, 1¼ cups cranberry juice, and ⅓ cup sugar in saucepan. Cook, stirring constantly, until mixture comes to boiling. Remove from heat; add gelatin; stir to dissolve. Chill until mixture mounds when spooned. Fold in pineapple, orange rind, and whipped cream. Beat egg whites and salt until foamy; add ¼ cup sugar gradually. Continue beating until meringue forms stiff, glossy peaks. Fold cranberry mixture into meringue. Pour into crumb crust. Chill until firm. Serve topped with sweetened whipped cream, if desired.

FROZEN PIES

MOCHA CRUNCH ANGEL PIE

1 baked 9-inch Chocolate Crumb Crust (*page 408*)	Dash of salt
1 c. sugar	2 c. heavy cream, whipped
½ c. water	½ c. slivered almonds
3 egg whites, stiffly beaten	Chocolate curls
1 tbs. instant coffee	

Prepare crumb crust according to recipe. Combine 1 cup sugar and water in saucepan; bring to boiling; cook rapidly until candy thermometer registers 242° F. or syrup spins a thread. Pour syrup in fine stream over beaten egg whites, beating constantly. Continue beating until meringue is thick and cool. Beat in coffee and salt; fold in whipped cream and slivered almonds. Turn into crumb crust; garnish with chocolate curls. Freeze several hours or until firm.

FROZEN TUTTI-FRUTTI PIE

1 baked 9-inch Pastry Crust (*page 406*)	½ c. heavy cream, whipped
½ c. sliced, blanched almonds	½ c. macaroon crumbs or vanilla wafer crumbs
1 tbs. butter or margarine	1 tsp. almond extract
3 pts. vanilla ice cream	¼ c. maraschino cherries, drained and chopped
	Red food coloring

Prepare pastry crust according to recipe. Brown almonds in butter or margarine in skillet until light brown; cool. Soften ice cream in bowl. Do not allow to melt. Working quickly, fold in almonds, cream, macaroon or vanilla wafer crumbs, almond extract, maraschino cherries, and a few drops of red food coloring to tint a delicate pink. Spoon mixture into pastry shell; freeze several hours or overnight. Wrap with transparent plastic wrap or aluminum foil if keeping longer than a day. Decorate with additional whipped cream, if desired.

TARTS

APPLE PETAL TARTS

Pastry for 2-crust pie (*page 405*)	3 c. sliced, pared, and cored, cooking apples
2 c. sugar	1 c. apricot preserves
1½ c. water	1 tbs. lemon juice

Heat oven to 425° F. Prepare pastry; roll out. For each tart, cut six 2¼-inch rounds. Fit 1 round in bottom of 2½-inch muffin-pan cups; moisten edge. Press 5 rounds onto sides of cup and bottom round, overlapping them slightly. Bake 15 to 20 minutes or until golden. Cool. Remove from pan carefully. Combine sugar and water in skillet; bring to boiling. Add apple slices (do not crowd pan); poach 3 to 5 minutes or until translucent. Remove carefully; cool. Arrange slices in cooled tart shells. Heat preserves and lemon juice until bubbly; sieve. Spoon over apples to glaze. Chill until serving time. Garnish as desired. Makes 12 tarts.

STRAWBERRY TARTS

2 c. sifted all-purpose flour	3 pts. strawberries, washed and hulled
2 tbs. sugar	½ c. water
½ tsp. salt	2 tbs. cornstarch
½ c. soft butter or margarine	1 tsp. lemon juice
¼ c. shortening	½ c. heavy cream, whipped
6 tbs. water	Chopped pistachio nuts
1 recipe Rich Pastry Cream (*page 455*)	

Sift flour, sugar, and salt into large bowl. Cut in butter or margarine and shortening with pastry blender until mixture resembles cornmeal. Sprinkle mixture with water. Mix in with fingers and rub with palm of hand until pastry is smooth and blended; divide into twelve pieces. Press each piece into a 2½- to 3-inch tart pan; prick each well with fork. Heat oven to 400° F. Cut piece of wax paper to fit each tart; press into tart; fill with dry rice or beans to keep shape of tart while baking. Bake 10 minutes; remove paper and rice or beans. Bake tarts 10 to 15 minutes longer or until golden; cool. Prepare Rich Pastry Cream according to recipe; cool. Fill tarts. Crush enough stawberries to make ½ cup; reserve remainder. Combine crushed strawberries, water, cornstarch, and lemon juice in saucepan. Cook over medium heat, stirring constantly, until thickened and bubbly; sieve; cool. Arrange reserved whole strawberries on tarts, about 3 to each tart. Spoon cooled strawberry glaze over strawberries; chill. To serve, garnish with whipped cream and a sprinkling of pistachio nuts. Makes 12 tarts.

LIME CHEESE TARTS

½ c. butter or margarine	1 pkg. (8 oz.) cream cheese
⅓ c. sugar	⅓ c. sugar
2 egg yolks	2 eggs
1¼ c. sifted all-purpose flour	1 tsp. grated lime rind
2 tsp. milk	1 tbs. lime juice
¾ c. finely chopped nuts	Green food coloring

Cream butter or margarine and ⅓ cup sugar in medium-size bowl; add egg yolks; beat until well blended. Stir in flour, milk, and nuts. Divide dough into eight pieces; press each evenly on bottom and sides of a 3-inch tart pan; prick dough well with fork. Bake at 350° F. for 10 minutes or until golden. Cool. Soften cream cheese; blend in ⅓ cup sugar; add eggs, one at a time, beating until smooth after each addition. Stir in lime rind and juice. Tint pastel green with food coloring. Pour into cooled tart shells. Bake at 350° F. for 20 minutes or until filling is firm. Cool; chill several hours. Garnish with whipped cream and grated lime rind, if desired. Makes 8 tarts.

CHESS TARTS

Pastry for 2-crust pie (*page 405*)	½ c. dairy sour cream
½ c. butter or margarine	1½ c. chopped pecans
1 c. sugar	1 c. raisins
2 eggs	Pecan halves
2 tsp. grated orange rind	

Prepare pastry according to recipe. Roll out on floured board; cut into eight 5-inch circles; fit circles into 3-inch tart pans. Flute edge. Heat oven to 425° F. Cream butter or margarine and sugar in bowl; beat in eggs, one at a time, beating well after each addition. Stir in orange rind, sour cream, chopped pecans, and raisins; fill tart shells ¾ full with mixture; arrange pecan halves on top. Bake 10 minutes; reduce oven heat to 350° F.; bake 30 minutes or until filling is firm. Cool on wire racks; remove carefully from tart pans. Garnish with additional sour cream and chopped pistachio nuts, if desired. Makes 8 tarts.

PECAN TARTS

⅔ c. butter or margarine	⅔ c. sugar
½ c. sugar	⅔ c. dark corn syrup
2 egg yolks	4 tsp. melted butter or margarine
2 c. sifted all-purpose flour	1 tsp. vanilla
2 eggs, beaten	1⅓ c. pecan halves

Blend ⅔ cup butter or margarine, ½ cup sugar, egg yolks, and flour together. (Dough will be stiff.) Divide dough into 12 pieces; press each piece into a 2-inch tart pan. Flute edge. Chill while preparing filling. Combine eggs, ⅔ cup sugar, corn syrup, melted butter or margarine, and vanilla. Divide pecans among twelve tart shells; carefully pour egg mixture into shells. Place tarts on cookie sheets so that they will not tip in oven. Bake at 350° F. for 20 to 25 minutes. Makes 12 tarts.

Chapter Twenty-Three

Cakes

At any time of the year, a cake is a wonderful thing, to please the eye and delight the palate. And for special occasions, there's nothing more exciting than a lavishly frosted cake, whether it's a birthday or anniversary celebration, or a holiday that's brought the family together for a reunion.

A cake is a work of art. But it doesn't require any special trick to produce one—not today when every step of cake making has been worked out to simple step-by-step directions. Only one thing is necessary: follow the rules.

Cake-making is not a time for improvisation. Ingredients must be exact, the right pans must be used, the method followed to the last "dotting of i's and crossing of t's." When your cake has cooled and is ready to frost and decorate, then let your imagination run riot. Until that moment, follow the recipe.

Secrets for Successful Cake Baking

· *Select your recipe* and read it carefully.
· *Assemble all the utensils.* Use standard measuring cups and spoons. Decide whether you are going to make your cake on the electric mixer or by hand, then follow these specific directions. Cake recipes are a delicate balance of ingredients. For this reason always follow directions faithfully.
· *Use fresh, good-quality ingredients.* Be sure baking powder, baking soda, and cream of tartar, especially, are fresh. All our recipes have been tested with large eggs and double-action baking powder. Shortening should be soft enough to blend with other ingredients. All our recipes use sifted cake or all-purpose flour. If you are using flour which calls for no sifting, follow manufacturer's instructions.
· *Always preheat the oven.* Time and tem-

perature directions are based on preheating.
· *Use the exact size pan called for in the recipe.* Too small a pan will result in runover, while too large a pan will result in a compactness and underbrowning. Bright, shiny pans will brown more evenly than dull pans. When glass ovenproof baking dishes are used, the cakes will brown faster, so decrease oven temperatures by 25 degrees.
· *To fill special-shaped or odd-size pans,* such as Valentine or Christmas cake pans, which are not the same size as standard layer cake pans, fill them two-thirds full for the Modern Creaming Method and one-half full for the One-Bowl Method. Make small cakes or cupcakes with leftover batter.

Preparation of Pans

Butter Cakes. For golden-brown bottoms and sides, grease pans with shortening; sprinkle evenly with flour. Tap pans, face down, over wax paper to catch excess flour and leave a smooth dusting of flour on pans. With some delicate cakes, it may be necessary to give the cake support by greasing the pans and lining the bottom with wax paper, then greasing the paper.

Sponge, Angel, and Chiffon Cakes. Tube pans should *not* be greased. The foamy batter should cling to sides of pan and bake to a high, fluffy perfection. Some recipes for smaller sponge and chiffon cakes will direct you to grease the pan. Follow specific directions for each. Jelly-roll pans, an exception to the rule, are always greased and lined with paper. The hot baked cake is turned out at once onto a sugar-sprinkled towel.

Fruitcakes. These pans may be greased and lined with paper, or only greased.

Tips on Cake Pans

The cake pan suggested in a recipe is the ideal pan for that particular cake, though sometimes a cake will bake in other pans with almost as good results. The one exception is pound cake which should always be done in a loaf or tube pan. The following chart gives suggested pan substitutions. Use it only as a guide, for every cake has a character of its own. Remember in all cases to fill a cake pan only half full. If you have batter left use it for cupcakes. Bake as directed for Cupcakes (*page 442*).

If a cake bakes as:	It will also bake as:
two 8-inch layers	two thin 8x8x2-inch squares eighteen to twenty-four 2½-inch cupcakes
three 8-inch layers	two 9x9x2-inch squares
two 9-inch layers	two 8x8x2-inch squares three thin 8-inch layers one 15x10x1-inch rectangle thirty 2½-inch cupcakes
one 8x8x2-inch square	one 9-inch layer
two 8x8x2-inch squares	two 9-inch layers one 13x9x2-inch rectangle
one 9x9x2-inch square	two thin 8-inch layers
two 9x9x2-inch squares	three 8-inch layers
one 13x9x2-inch rectangle	two 9-inch layers two 8x8x2-inch squares
one 9x5x3-inch loaf pan	one 9x9x2-inch square twenty-four to thirty 2½-inch cupcakes
one 8x4x3-inch loaf pan	one 8x8x2-inch square
one 9x3½-inch tube pan	two 9-inch layers twenty-four to thirty 2½-inch cupcakes
one 10x4-inch tube pan	two 9x5x3-inch loaf pans one 13x9x2-inch rectangle two 15x10x1-inch rectangles

Placement of Pans in the Oven

Place oven rack in center of oven. When placing pans on racks, keep pans from touching the sides of the oven and each other.

Single Cake: Place pan in center of rack.

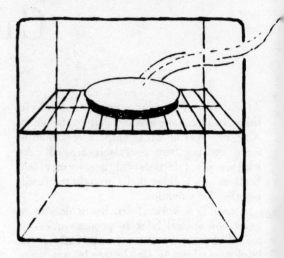

Two Layers: Place pans in opposite corners.

Three or Four Layers: Two oven racks are needed. Arrange racks in center third of oven, allowing space for cakes to rise in pans. Place pans in opposite staggered pattern.

Loaf or Tube Pan: Place rack in lower third of oven. Place pan in center of rack.

To Test for Doneness

Touch center of baked cake lightly with finger. Cake will spring back if done. If it needs longer baking, an imprint will remain. Cake will also shrink from sides of pan when done. You may use cake tester or a wooden pick to test for doneness: insert tester into center of cake. A clean, dry tester means cake is done. If batter or soft crumbs cling to tester, bake cake longer; retest.

Cooling Cakes and Removing From Pans

Use wire racks to cool cakes to allow circulation of air.

Butter Cakes: Allow cake to remain in pan on wire rack for 10 minutes. Loosen sides with thin-bladed knife or spatula; shake gently to free from pan. Invert cake on wire rack or flat plate. Peel off paper if the pan was lined. Quickly turn right side up on wire rack to finish cooling. Cool completely before frosting.

Angel, Sponge, and Chiffon Cakes: All tube-pan foam cakes should remain in pan, with pan inverted, until thoroughly cool. When cake tests done, remove from oven, invert. If tube pan does not have high center tube or little feet around rim of pan, put tube over neck of bottle, or balance rim of pan on inverted cups to keep top of cake from touching tabletop.

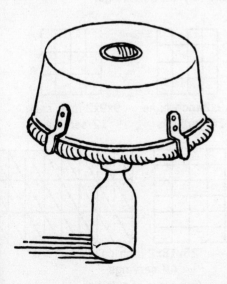

Adjustments for High Altitude Baking

If you live where the altitude is 3000 or more feet above sea level, you should make certain adjustments in the recipe itself and in baking temperatures.

For complete information write to one of these sources:

General Foods Corporation
250 North Street,
White Plains, N.Y.

Colorado Agricultural Experiment Station
Colorado State University
Fort Collins, Colorado

University of Wyoming
Agricultural Experiment Station
University Station
Box 3354, Laramie, Wyoming

Or you can call your local extension agent or the home economist at your local utility company.

Storing Cakes

If a cake is not eaten entirely the day it is made, it will taste just as good the second or third day, if properly stored. *Store frosted cakes* in a covered cake keeper, or cover cake with a large inverted pan or bowl. Cake may then be stored in refrigerator, if desired. *Unfrosted cakes* may be wrapped in transparent plastic wrap, wax paper, or aluminum foil, and stored at room temperature. Always keep *cream-filled cakes*, or cakes frosted with whipped cream in refrigerator. For directions on freezing cakes see *page 490*.

How to Frost a Cake

1. Brush loose crumbs from cooled cake.
2. Select a plate or tray for the cake which is at least one to two inches larger all around than the cake.
3. To keep serving plate clean while frosting cake, arrange 4 strips of wax paper on edges of plate and extending beyond plate, to form a square. After cake is frosted and set, carefully pull out papers.
4. When frosting cakes, place single layer top side up. Place tube cake bottom side up. For layer cakes, place first layer bottom side up.

5. To frost layer cakes, spread bottom layer with one third of frosting, or if using filling, with all the filling. Bring frosting or filling to within one-quarter inch of the edge. Place second layer on filling, bottom side down. With these two flat sides of the layers together, the cake will be even.

6. It is easier to frost a cake that can rotate freely. Place cake plate on rim of large mixing bowl, so cake will be up off the tabletop and may be turned easily as you frost. Large department stores have rotating cake stands available.

7. Spread thin layer of frosting over top and sides of filled cake. Allow about 10 minutes for it to set. This will form a firm base for the remaining frosting and trap any crumbs that might pull off cake and spoil the frosting.

8. Spread frosting with broad spatula around sides of cake. Bring frosting up to top of cake to form rim. This will help to "square off" top of cake, which otherwise might slope downward. Pile remaining frosting on top of cake. Spread frosting out to meet rim, swirling with spatula to make pretty top.

9. To "ice" angel food, sponge, or chiffon cakes, spoon glaze over top and allow to drip down sides. Or frost entire cake with whipped cream or frosting.

How to Cut a Cake

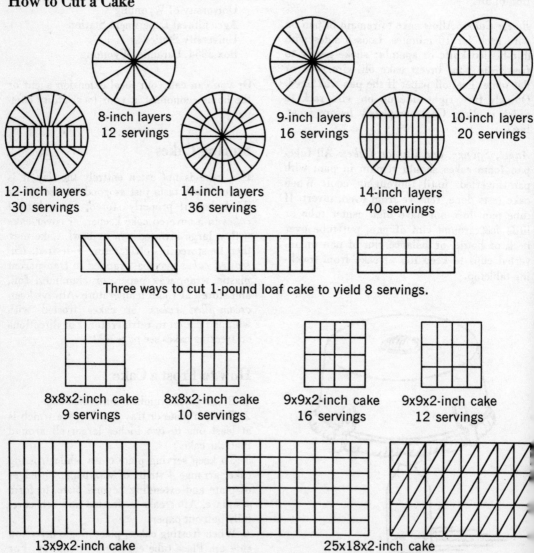

8-inch layers
12 servings

9-inch layers
16 servings

10-inch layers
20 servings

12-inch layers
30 servings

14-inch layers
36 servings

14-inch layers
40 servings

Three ways to cut 1-pound loaf cake to yield 8 servings.

8x8x2-inch cake
9 servings

8x8x2-inch cake
10 servings

9x9x2-inch cake
16 servings

9x9x2-inch cake
12 servings

13x9x2-inch cake
30 servings

25x18x2-inch cake
48 servings
(two ways of cutting)

For butter cakes use thin-pointed, sharp knife and a sawing motion to cut through cake. *For angel food, chiffon, or spongecakes* (foam cakes) use 2 forks to pull pieces apart or use a cake breaker. Or use a sawing motion with a serrated, long-blade knife. Wipe off crumbs after each cutting as they accumulate or rinse knife in hot water.

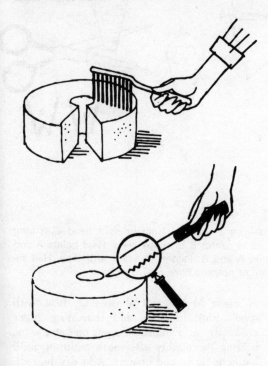

To cut a jelly roll, use a 15-inch long piece of heavy white thread. Place it under the jelly roll where you wish to slice it. Bring the ends of the thread up over the top, cross them, and pull down quickly to cut through the cake.

Tips on Cake Decorating

You don't have to be a professional pastry chef to make a cake look pretty. With all the wonderful cake-decorating aids at your fingertips in the supermarket—tiny candles, sprinkles, sparkles, cake and cookie decorators that make a professional out of an amateur—it's fun to decorate a cake.

With a good recipe for butter frosting *(page 452)* and an investment in a small cake-decorating set with fancy tips you can make a cake look beautiful. If you don't have a cake-decorating set you can make a paper decorating cone. It is particularly useful when you are working with several different colors of frosting, as you can make one for each color, and after each use, toss them away. To make them, see page 432.

It's easy to color frosting with the food colorings available. They come in two forms —liquid and paste. Liquid food coloring is available in supermarkets in bottles or plastic tubes and comes in red, blue, yellow, and green. There is a blending chart on the package showing how to make other colors from these basic four. Paste food colors are more expensive but come in a wider range of colors. (They may be obtained from Kitchen Glamor, 15300 Fenkell Ave., Detroit, Michigan 48227, or Maid of Scandinavia Co., 3245 Raleigh Avenue, Minneapolis, Minnesota 55416.) Colored frosting in plastic tubes and in pressurized cans can also be found in supermarkets.

The *secret* in using food coloring is to use only a small amount, for it goes a long way, and it is always easy to add a little more if needed. Add liquid food coloring to your white frosting very slowly, one drop at a time from the tip of a teaspoon, and blend it in thoroughly before adding the next drop.

To add paste food coloring to the white frosting, take a very tiny bit on the tip of a wooden pick, add to the frosting, and blend it in completely. Continue until the frosting is the desired shade.

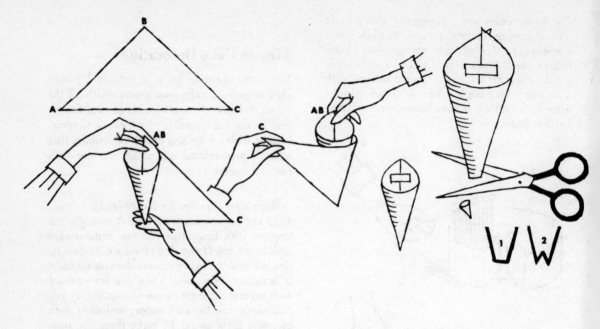

How to Make a Paper Decorating Cone

Fold a 12-inch square of wax paper on the diagonal to form a triangle. Hold in right hand with long side at bottom and thumb at center. Bring corner A up to center B to shape cone. Hold points A and B together. Bring corner C around cone to meet point A and B. Fasten at seam with tape. Half fill cone with frosting. Fold top down. Snip off end in straight or notched line.

BUTTER CAKES

Butter cakes are so named because originally butter was the shortening most frequently used in making these cakes. With the perfecting of margarine and vegetable shortenings, their use in cake making became accepted, and we refer to those cakes, too, as "butter" cakes. Butter cakes may be mixed by the *Modern Creaming Method* or by the *One-Bowl Method.*

Modern Creaming Method. This is the up-to-date version of the time-honored *creaming* method. Using an *electric mixer:* The creaming of the shortening is simplified to a quick beating process. Beat the shortening (butter, margarine, or vegetable shortening), sugar, and eggs together in the mixer at high speed for 3 minutes. This creamy, fluffy mixture is the basis for fine-textured, velvety cakes. Add the sifted dry ingredients and liquid alternately to the creamed mixture, with mixer at low speed, beginning and ending with flour. Scrape the bowl frequently to keep batter blended. *For Hand Mixing:* If you wish to make your cake by hand, add a small amount of sugar to the soft shortening. Beat with spoon until creamy; add remaining sugar gradually. Add unbeaten eggs, one at a time, beating thoroughly after each addition, until batter is fluffy and creamy. Add dry ingredients and liquid ingredients alternately, beginning and ending with flour.

One-Bowl Method. This popular, quick method is the result of great improvements in the blending qualities of vegetable shortenings. Cakes made with this method are made principally with vegetable shortening, although a small percentage of shortening may be replaced with butter or margarine for flavor, if desired. Sift dry ingredients into the mixing bowl. Add the shortening and part of the liquid. *Using an electric mixer:* Beat mixture for 2 minutes at medium speed (middle of the dial on mixer). Add remaining liquid, eggs, and flavoring. Beat mixture 2 minutes at medium speed on mixer. Scrape the bowl frequently to blend batter. *Hand mixing:* Sift dry ingredients into bowl, add shortening and part of liquid. Beat vigorously with spoon for 300 strokes. Add remaining liquid, eggs, and flavoring; beat another 300 strokes.

Secret: For both methods of mixing butter cakes, be careful not to overbeat once the flour is added. For Modern Creaming Method, beat just enough to blend ingredients. For One-Bowl Method, beat at the time and speed specified.

YELLOW CAKES

BONANZA CAKE
(*Modern Creaming—1 Egg*)

1¾ c. sifted cake flour	¼ c. shortening
2¼ tsp. baking powder	1 c. sugar
	1 egg
½ tsp. salt	1 tsp. vanilla
	1 c. milk

Heat oven to 350° F. Grease and flour two 8x1½-inch layer-cake pans or one 8x8x2-inch pan. Sift flour, baking powder, and salt together; set aside. Beat shortening, sugar, egg, and vanilla at high speed on electric mixer* about 3 minutes or until light and fluffy. Add flour mixture alternately with the milk, at low speed, beginning and ending with the flour. Scrape bowl frequently. Pour into prepared pans. Bake layers 30 to 35 minutes, square 35 to 40 minutes or until cake tests done (*page 429*). Fill and frost layers with Cherry-Almond Frosting (*page 452*). Serve square cake with Cherry Sauce (*page 401*).
* For hand mixing, see directions *above.*

Crunchy-Top Cake

1 recipe Bonanza Cake	¼ c. heavy cream
⅓ c. soft butter or margarine	½ tsp. vanilla
	⅓ c. chopped nuts
⅔ c. brown sugar, firmly packed	⅔ c. flaked coconut

Prepare cake batter; bake in 8x8x2-inch pan. Combine butter or margarine, brown sugar, heavy cream, vanilla, nuts, and coconut. Spread evenly over warm cake. Broil about 5 inches from heat about 3 minutes or until top surface is bubbly and begins to brown. Watch carefully to prevent scorching.

BUSY DAY CAKE
(*One Bowl—2 Eggs*)

2¼ c. sifted cake flour	½ c. shortening
	¾ c. milk
1½ c. sugar	1½ tsp. vanilla
3 tsp. baking powder	¼ c. milk
1 tsp. salt	2 eggs

Heat oven to 350° F. Grease and flour two 9x1½-inch layer-cake pans. Sift flour, sugar, baking powder, and salt into mixing bowl. Add shortening and ¾ cup milk. Beat 2 minutes at medium speed on electric mixer or 300 strokes by hand. Add vanilla, ¼ cup milk, and eggs. Beat 2 minutes. Scrape bowl frequently. Pour into prepared pans. Bake 30 to 35 minutes or until cake tests done (*page 429*).

Ice Cream Party Cake

1 recipe Busy Day Cake	1 pt. chocolate ice cream
1 pt. pistachio ice cream	1 pt. heavy cream
	4 tbs. confectioners' sugar
1 pt. strawberry ice cream	Few drops red food coloring

Prepare, bake, and cool cake as directed. Split each layer through center to make 4 thin layers. Spread each flavor of softened (not melted) ice cream into foil-lined 9-inch layer cake pan. (If you don't have 3 pans, freeze one flavor, lift out firm ice cream with foil; reline pan.) Freeze about 40 minutes or until firm. Remove from pans; peel off foil; put cake layers together with ice cream between. Place on foil-covered 10-inch square of cardboard. Freeze several hours or until very firm. Cake may be made several days ahead and kept frozen. For freezer storage over one day, wrap firm frozen cake in transparent plastic wrap or aluminum foil. Several hours before serving, whip 1½ cups cream; fold in confectioners' sugar; spread thinly and smoothly over entire cake. Whip remaining ½ cup of cream; tint a pastel pink with food coloring. Press through pastry bag to form decorative edging around cake. Return cake to freezer until about 20 minutes before serving.

WASHINGTON PIE

(One bowl—1 egg)

2 c. sifted cake flour	1 tsp. vanilla
1¼ c. sugar	1 egg
2½ tsp. baking powder	Raspberry preserves
1 tsp. salt	Confectioners' sugar
⅓ c. shortening	
1 c. milk	

Heat oven to 350° F. Grease and flour two 8x1½-inch layer-cake pans. Sift flour, sugar, baking powder, and salt together into mixing bowl. Add shortening, ⅔ cup milk, and vanilla. Beat 2 minutes at medium speed on electric mixer or 300 strokes by hand. Add remaining milk and egg. Beat 2 minutes more. Scrape bowl frequently. Pour into prepared pans. Bake about 30 minutes or until cake tests done (*page 429*). Remove from pans; cool on wire racks. Spread preserves between layers; sprinkle top with confectioners' sugar.

SUNFLOWER CAKE

(Modern Creaming—2 Eggs)

2¼ c. sifted cake flour	½ c. shortening
3 tsp. baking powder	1½ c. sugar
1 tsp. salt	2 eggs
	1½ tsp. vanilla
	1 c. milk

Heat oven to 350° F. Grease and flour two 9x1½-inch layer-cake pans. Sift flour, baking powder, and salt together. Beat shortening, sugar, eggs, and vanilla at high speed on electric mixer* about 3 minutes or until light and fluffy. Add flour mixture alternately with milk, at low speed, beginning and ending with flour. Pour into prepared pans. Bake 30 minutes or until cake tests done (*page 429*). Fill with whipped cream, jam, or marmalade. Frost with Hungarian Chocolate Frosting (*page 453*).
* For hand mixing, see directions *page 432*.

Marble Cake

1 recipe Sunflower Cake	2 tbs. water
1 sq. unsweetened chocolate	1 tbs. sugar
	¼ tsp. baking soda

Prepare Sunflower Cake batter. Measure 1 cup batter into separate bowl. Melt chocolate.

Blend in water, sugar, and baking soda. Blend into 1 cup of batter. Spoon chocolate batter and plain batter by alternate spoonfuls into layer cake pans. Marble batters by zigzagging through with spatula several times. Bake as directed. Frost with Favorite Chocolate Frosting (*page 453*).

FAVORITE LAYER CAKE

(Modern Creaming—3 Eggs)

3 c. sifted cake flour	¾ c. shortening
2½ tsp. baking powder	1½ c. sugar
½ tsp. salt	3 eggs
	1½ tsp. vanilla
	1 c. milk

Heat oven to 350° F. Grease and flour two 9x1½-inch layer-cake pans. Sift flour, baking powder, and salt together. Beat shortening, sugar, eggs, and vanilla at high speed on electric mixer* about 3 minutes or until light and fluffy. Add flour mixture alternately with milk, at low speed, beginning and ending with flour. Scrape bowl frequently. Pour into prepared pans. Bake 30 to 35 minutes or until cake tests done (*page 429*). Fill and frost with Deluxe Chocolate Frosting (*page 453*).
* For hand mixing, see directions *page 432*.

DELICATE FRESH ORANGE CAKE

(Modern Creaming—2 Eggs)

3 c. sifted cake flour	1¾ c. sugar
3 tsp. baking powder	1 tbs. grated orange rind
½ tsp. salt	2 eggs
¼ tsp. baking soda	¾ c. milk
⅔ c. shortening	¾ c. orange juice

Heat oven to 350° F. Grease and flour two 9x9x2-inch pans or two 9x1½-inch layer-cake pans. Sift flour, baking powder, salt, and baking soda together. Beat shortening, sugar, orange rind, and eggs at high speed on electric mixer* about 3 minutes or until light and fluffy. Add flour mixture alternately with milk and orange juice, at low speed, beginning and ending with flour. Scrape bowl frequently. Pour into prepared pans. Bake 30 to 35 minutes or until cake tests done (*page 429*). Fill and frost with Fresh Orange Frosting (*page 452*) or Fluffy 7-Minute Frosting (*page 454*).
* For hand mixing see directions *page 432*.

BROWN SUGAR CAKE

(One Bowl—2 Eggs)

2⅓ c. sifted all- purpose flour	1⅔ c. brown sugar, firmly packed
3 tbs. baking powder	½ c. shortening
½ tsp. salt	1 c. milk
	1½ tsp. vanilla
	2 eggs

Heat oven to 350° F. Grease and flour two 9x1½-inch layer-cake pans. Sift flour, baking powder, and salt together into mixing bowl. Add brown sugar, shortening, and milk. Beat 2 minutes at medium speed on electric mixer or 300 strokes by hand. Add vanilla and eggs. Beat 2 minutes. Scrape bowl frequently. Pour into prepared pans. Bake 30 to 35 minutes or until cake tests done (*page 429*). Fill and frost with Burnt Sugar Frosting (*page 452*) or Seafoam Frosting (*page 454*).

VELVET CREAM CAKE

(Modern Creaming—3 Eggs)

2½ c. sifted cake flour	3 eggs
3 tsp. baking powder	1½ c. sugar
1 tsp. salt	1½ tsp. vanilla
	1⅓ c. heavy cream

Heat oven to 350° F. Grease and flour two 9x1½-inch layer-cake pans. Sift flour, baking powder, and salt together. Beat eggs, sugar, and vanilla at high speed on electric mixer* about 3 minutes or until light and fluffy. Add flour mixture alternately with heavy cream, beginning and ending with flour. Scrape bowl frequently. Pour into prepared pans. Bake 25 to 30 minutes or until cake tests done (*page 429*). Fill and frost with Lemon Butter Cream (*page 452*) or Pineapple Butter Cream (*page 452*).

* For hand mixing, see directions *page 432*.

LEMON CAKE

(Modern Creaming—2 Eggs)

3 c. sifted cake flour	1⅔ c. sugar
3¼ tsp. baking powder	1 tbs. grated lemon rind
¼ tsp. salt	2 tbs. lemon juice
½ tsp. baking soda	2 eggs
⅓ c. shortening	1¼ c. milk

Heat oven to 375° F. Grease and flour two 9x1½-inch layer-cake pans. Sift flour, baking powder, salt, and soda together. Beat shortening, sugar, lemon rind, juice, and eggs at high speed on electric mixer* about 3 minutes or until light and fluffy. Add flour mixture and milk alternately, at low speed, beginning and ending with flour. Scrape bowl frequently. Pour batter into prepared pans. Bake 25 minutes or until cake tests done (*page 429*). Fill and frost with Lemon Butter Cream Frosting (*page 452*).

* For hand mixing, see directions *page 432*.

WHITE CAKES

SNOWBERRY CAKE

(Modern Creaming—3 Egg Whites)

2 c. sifted cake flour	½ c. shortening
2 tsp. baking powder	1 c. sugar
½ tsp. salt	1 tsp. vanilla
3 egg whites	½ tsp. almond extract
¼ c. sugar	1 c. milk

Heat oven to 350° F. Grease and flour two 8x1½-inch layer-cake pans. Sift flour, baking powder, and salt together. Beat egg whites until foamy. Add ¼ cup sugar gradually; continue beating until meringue forms stiff, glossy peaks. Beat shortening, 1 cup sugar, vanilla, and almond extract at high speed on electric mixer* about 3 minutes or until light and fluffy. Add flour mixture alternately with milk, at low speed, beginning and ending with the flour. Scrape bowl frequently. Fold in meringue. Pour into prepared pans. Bakes 25 to 30 minutes or until cake tests done (*page 429*). Fill and frost with Jelly Frosting (*page 454*).

* For hand mixing, see directions *page 432*.

Tropical Coconut Cake

Prepare, bake, and cool Snowberry Cake. Fill with Lime Filling (*page 455*). Frost top and sides with White Mountain Cream Frosting (*page 454*). Sprinkle cake generously with canned, flaked coconut.

POPPY SEED CAKE

(Modern Creaming—4 egg whites)

⅔ c. poppy seeds	4 tsp. baking
½ c. water	powder
4 egg whites	¾ c. shortening
½ c. sugar	1 c. sugar
2¾ c. sifted cake	1 tsp. vanilla
flour	1 c. milk

Heat oven to 350° F. Grease and flour two 9x1½-inch layer-cake pans. Pour poppy seeds onto double thickness of wax paper; fold paper over seeds; secure ends. Crush with rolling pin. Combine seeds with water in small saucepan; simmer until all the liquid is absorbed, stirring occasionally. Cool. Beat egg whites until foamy. Add ½ cup sugar gradually. Continue beating until meringue forms stiff, glossy peaks. Sift flour and baking powder together. Beat shortening, 1 cup sugar, and vanilla at high speed on electric mixer* about 3 minutes until light and fluffy. Add flour mixture alternately with milk, at low speed, beginning and ending with flour. Scrape bowl frequently. Stir in poppy seeds. Fold in meringue. Pour into prepared pans. Bake 30 to 35 minutes or until cake tests done (*page 429*). Fill and frost with Butter Cream Frosting (*page 452*) or Lemon Butter Cream Frosting (*page 452*).

* For hand mixing, see directions *page 432.*

WHITE CLOUD CAKE

(One Bowl—5 Egg Whites)

2¾ c. sifted cake	¾ c. milk
flour	1 tsp. grated orange
1¾ c. sugar	rind
4½ tsp. baking	1 tsp. vanilla
powder	½ c. milk
1 tsp. salt	5 egg whites
⅔ c. shortening	

Heat oven to 350° F. Grease and flour three 8x1½-inch layer-cake pans or two 9x1½-inch layer-cake pans. Sift flour, sugar, baking powder, and salt into mixing bowl. Add shortening and ¾ cup milk; beat 2 minutes at medium speed on electric mixer or 300 strokes by hand. Scrape bowl frequently. Add orange rind, vanilla, ½ cup milk, and egg whites; beat 2 minutes. Pour into prepared pans. Bake 25 to 30 minutes or until cake tests done (*page 429*). Fill with Lemon Filling (*page 455*). Frost with Fluffy 7-Minute Frosting (*page 454*).

Lady Baltimore Cake

1 recipe White	½ c. raisins,
Cloud Cake	chopped
1 recipe Pink	½ c. chopped
Mountain Cream	walnuts
Frosting	2 tbs. chopped
(*page 454*)	maraschino
¼ c. cut-up dried	cherries
figs	1 tsp. grated orange
	rind

Prepare, bake, and cool cake. Prepare frosting. Mix figs, raisins, walnuts, cherries, and orange rind into one third of frosting. Spread between layers. Frost cake with remaining frosting.

CARIOCA CAKE

(One Bowl—4 Egg Whites)

2 c. sifted all-	1 c. milk
purpose flour	1 tsp. vanilla
1⅓ c. sugar	4 egg whites
3½ tsp. baking	1 c. finely chopped
powder	Brazil nuts or
½ tsp. salt	walnuts
½ c. shortening	

Heat oven to 350° F. Grease and flour two 9x1½-inch layer-cake pans. Sift flour, sugar, baking powder, and salt into mixing bowl. Add shortening, milk, and vanilla; beat 2 minutes at medium speed on electric mixer or 300 strokes by hand. Scrape bowl frequently. Add egg whites; beat 1 minute. Fold in nuts. Pour into prepared pans. Bake 2 to 30 minutes or until cake tests done (*page 429*). Fill and frost with Seafoam Frosting (*page 454*). Decorate with additional chopped nuts, if desired.

Chicken-on-a-Spit—roasted to perfection, it always makes

CHOCOLATE CAKES

AMERICAN HOME CHOCOLATE CAKE

(Modern Creaming—3 Eggs)

3 sqs. unsweetened chocolate, melted	1 tsp. salt
½ c. boiling water	¼ tsp. baking soda
2⅓ c. sifted cake flour	½ c. shortening
	1¾ c. sugar
2¼ tsp. baking powder	3 eggs
	1 c. buttermilk

Heat oven to 350° F. Grease and flour two 9x1½-inch layer-cake pans or one 13x9x2-inch pan. Stir melted chocolate and boiling water together until thickened and smooth; cool. Sift flour, baking powder, salt, and soda together. Beat shortening, sugar, and eggs at high speed on electric mixer* about 3 minutes or until light and fluffy. Blend in chocolate mixture. Add flour mixture alternately with buttermilk, at low speed, beginning and ending with flour. Scrape bowl frequently. Pour into prepared pans. Bake 35 to 40 minutes or until cakes tests done (*page 429*). Fill and frost with Favorite Chocolate Frosting (*page 453*).
* For hand mixing, see directions *page 432*.

CANDY STRIPED CHOCOLATE CAKE

(One-bowl—2 Eggs)

4 sqs. unsweetened chocolate	½ tsp. salt
1½ c. sifted all-purpose flour	¼ tsp. baking soda
	1 tsp. instant coffee
1¾ c. sugar	¼ c. shortening
2 tsp. baking powder	1⅓ c. milk
	2 eggs
	1 tsp. vanilla

Heat oven to 350° F. Grease and flour 13x9x2-inch baking pan. Melt chocolate over hot water; cool. Sift flour, sugar, baking powder, salt, baking soda, and instant coffee into mixing bowl. Add shortening and milk; beat 2 minutes at medium speed on electric mixer or 300 strokes by hand. Add eggs, vanilla, and chocolate. Beat 2 minutes. Scrape bowl frequently. Pour into prepared pan. Bake 40 to 45 minutes or until cake tests done (*page 429*). Frost with Peppermint Stripe Frosting (*page 453*).

DEVIL'S FOOD CAKE

(Modern Creaming—3 Eggs)

2⅓ c. sifted cake flour	1 tsp. salt
	¾ c. shortening
⅔ c. cocoa	1¾ c. sugar
¼ tsp. baking powder	3 eggs
	1½ c. water
1¼ tsp. baking soda	1½ tsp. vanilla

Heat oven to 350° F. Grease and flour two 9x1½-inch layer-cake pans. Sift flour, cocoa, baking powder, baking soda, and salt together. Beat shortening, sugar, and eggs at high speed on electric mixer* about 3 minutes or until mixture is light and fluffy. Add flour mixture alternately with water and vanilla, at low speed, beginning and ending with flour. Scrape bowl frequently. Pour batter into prepared pans. Bake 30 to 35 minutes or until cake tests done (*page 429*). Fill with whipped cream. Frost with French Velvet Chocolate Frosting (*page 453*).
* For hand mixing, see directions *page 432*.

CREOLE FUDGE CAKE

(Modern Creaming—3 Eggs)

4 sqs. unsweetened chocolate	2 tsp. baking powder
1 tbs. instant coffee	½ tsp. baking soda
½ c. water	¼ tsp. salt
1 c. brown sugar, firmly packed	½ c. shortening
	1 c. sugar
2½ c. sifted cake flour	3 eggs
	1 c. milk

Heat oven to 350° F. Grease and flour three 8x1½-inch layer-cake pans. Combine chocolate, coffee, water, and brown sugar in top of double boiler. Heat over hot, not boiling, water, stirring until chocolate is melted. Sift flour, baking powder, soda, and salt together. Beat shortening, sugar, and eggs at high speed on electric mixer* about 3 minutes or until light and fluffy. Blend in chocolate mixture. Add flour mixture alternately with milk, at low speed, beginning and ending with flour. Scrape bowl frequently. Pour into prepared pans. Bake 25 to 30 minutes or until cake tests done (*page 429*). Fill and frost with Coffee Butter Cream Frosting (*page 452*).
* For hand mixing, see directions *page 432*.

GOLD CAKES

GOLD CAKE
(Modern Creaming—3 Egg Yolks)

2 c. sifted cake flour	½ c. shortening
2½ tsp. baking powder	1 c. sugar
	3 egg yolks
½ tsp. salt	1 c. milk
	1½ tsp. vanilla

Heat oven to 350° F. Grease and flour two 8x1½-inch layer-cake pans. Sift flour, baking powder, and salt together. Beat shortening, sugar, and egg yolks at high speed on electric mixer* about 3 minutes or until light and fluffy. Add flour mixture alternately with milk and vanilla, at low speed, beginning and ending with flour. Scrape bowl frequently. Pour into prepared pans. Bake 30 to 35 minutes or until cake tests done (*page 429*). Fill and frost with Fluffy Orange Frosting (*page 454*).
* For hand mixing, see directions *page 432*.

ROYAL GOLD CAKE
(One Bowl—5 Egg Yolks)

2½ c. sifted cake flour	1 c. milk
1⅔ c. sugar	½ tsp. almond extract
3½ tsp. baking powder	1 tsp. orange extract
1 tsp. salt	5 egg yolks
⅔ c. shortening	¼ c. milk

Heat oven to 350° F. Grease and flour two 8x8x2-inch pans or two 9x1½-inch layer-cake pans. Sift flour, sugar, baking powder, and salt into mixing bowl. Add shortening and 1 cup milk; beat 2 minutes at medium speed on electric mixer or 300 strokes by hand. Add extracts, egg yolks, and ¼ cup milk; beat 2 minutes. Scrape bowl frequently. Pour into prepared pans. Bake 30 to 35 minutes or until cake tests done (*page 429*).

Lord Baltimore Cake

1 recipe Gold Cake	¼ c. chopped pecans
1 recipe White Mountain Cream Frosting (*page 454*)	1 tsp. grated orange rind
¼ c. flaked or fine-grated coconut	¼ c. candied cherries, halved

Prepare, bake, and cool cake. Prepare frosting. Combine coconut and pecans in shallow pan. Toast at 350° F. for 6 to 8 minutes; cool. Mix coconut, pecans, orange rind, and cherries into one third of frosting. Spread between layers. Frost cake with remaining frosting.

SPICE CAKES

FLUFFY SPICE CAKE
(Modern Creaming—2 Eggs)

2 c. sifted cake flour	½ tsp. ground allspice
1¼ tsp. baking powder	½ c. shortening
½ tsp. baking soda	1 c. sugar
¼ tsp. salt	½ c. light brown sugar, firmly packed
1 tsp. ground cinnamon	
½ tsp. ground cloves	2 eggs
½ tsp. ground nutmeg	1 c. dairy sour cream

Heat oven to 350° F. Grease and flour 13x9x2-inch pan or two 9x1½-inch layer-cake pans. Sift flour, baking powder, baking soda, salt, and spices together. Beat shortening, sugars, and eggs at high speed on electric mixer* about 3 minutes or until light and fluffy. Add flour mixture alternately with the sour cream, at low speed, beginning and ending with flour. Scrape bowl frequently. Pour into prepared pans. Bake 35 to 40 minutes for 13x9x2-inch pan, 25 to 30 minutes for the layers or until cake tests done (*page 429*). Fill and frost with Lemon Butter Cream Frosting (*page 452*).
* For hand mixing, see directions *page 432*

Crunchy Topped Spice Cake

Grease and flour 12-cup Bundt mold. Combine 3 tablespoons soft butter or margarine, 3 tablespoons brown sugar, 1 tablespoon light corn syrup, and ¼ cup chopped nuts. Spread in bottom of pan. Prepare Fluffy Spice Cake batter; pour into pan. Bake at 350° F. for 40 to 45 minutes or until cake tests done (*page 429*). Loosen sides of cake with spatula; loosen cake around tube. Invert on wire rack; leave mold in place 5 minutes. Remove mold; cool cake completely.

BANANA SPICE CAKE

(One Bowl—2 Eggs)

(pictured opposite page 405)

2¼ c. sifted cake flour	⅔ c. buttermilk
1⅔ c. sugar	1¼ c. mashed bananas (3 medium)
1¼ tsp. baking powder	
1 tsp. salt	2 eggs
1¼ tsp. baking soda	½ c. semi-sweet chocolate pieces
1½ tsp. ground cinnamon	1 tsp. butter or margarine
¾ tsp. ground nutmeg	Seafoam Frosting (*page 454*)
¾ tsp. ground cloves	1 large banana, sliced
⅔ c. shortening	

Heat oven to 350° F. Grease and flour three 8x1½-inch or two 9x1½-inch layer-cake pans. Sift flour, sugar, baking powder, salt, baking soda, cinnamon, nutmeg, and cloves into mixing bowl. Add shortening, buttermilk, and mashed bananas. Beat 2 minutes at medium speed on electric mixer or 300 strokes by hand. Add eggs; beat 1 minute. Scrape bowl frequently. Pour into prepared pans. Bake 30 minutes or until cake tests done (*page 429*). Melt chocolate and butter or margarine; cool. Spread one layer with frosting; cover with banana slices; top with second layer. Frost sides and top of cake with remaining frosting. Dip back of teaspoon into cooled chocolate; make deep swirls in frosting.

DIXIE MARBLE SPICE CAKE

(Modern Creaming—2 Eggs)

2¼ c. sifted cake flour	¾ c. milk
2½ tsp. baking powder	2 tbs. molasses
½ tsp. salt	1½ tsp. ground cinnamon
⅔ c. shortening	½ tsp. ground cloves
1 c. sugar	½ tsp. ground nutmeg
2 eggs	

Heat oven to 350° F. Grease and flour 9x5x3-inch loaf pan or 9x9x2-inch pan. Sift flour, baking powder, and salt together. Beat shortening, sugar, and eggs at high speed on electric mixer* about 3 minutes or until light and fluffy. Add flour mixture alternately with milk, at low speed, beginning and ending with flour. Scrape bowl frequently. Divide batter in half; add molasses and spices to one half. Spoon spice batter and plain batter into prepared pan by alternate spoonfuls. Cut through batter several times with a knife to create marble effect. Bake 60 to 65 minutes for loaf, 35 to 40 minutes for square cake, or until cake tests done (*page 429*). Frost with Lemon Butter Cream Frosting (*page 452*) or Caramel Frosting (*page 453*).

* For hand mixing, see directions *page 432*.

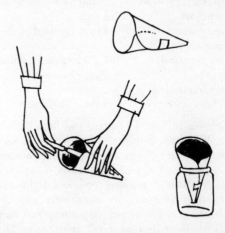

Chocolate Cornucopias. Melt 1 pkg. (6 oz.) semi-sweet chocolate pieces in top of double boiler over hot water; cool. Cut 3-in. circles of wax paper; curl into cornucopias; fasten with cellophane tape. Spread cooled chocolate thinly on inside of cornucopias with small spatula or thin knife. Set upright in small bottles; chill until firm. Peel off paper; fill chocolate cornucopias with whipped cream. Use to decorate a cake.

RAISIN SPICE CAKE

(One Bowl—3 Eggs)

2⅓ c. sifted cake flour	½ tsp. ground cloves
1 c. sugar	½ c. shortening
1½ tsp. baking powder	⅔ c. brown sugar, firmly packed
½ tsp. baking soda	1 c. buttermilk
½ tsp. salt	3 eggs
1 tsp. ground cinnamon	½ c. chopped nuts
	½ c. chopped raisins

Heat oven to 350° F. Grease and flour two 9x1½-inch layer-cake pans. Sift flour, sugar, baking powder, baking soda, salt, cinnamon, and cloves into mixing bowl. Add shortening, brown sugar, and buttermilk. Beat 2 minutes at medium speed on electric mixer or 300 strokes by hand. Add eggs. Beat 2 minutes. Scrape bowl frequently. Stir in nuts and raisins. Turn into prepared pans. Bake 30 to 35 minutes or until cake tests done (*page 429*). Fill and frost with Cream Cheese Frosting (*page 453*).

APPLESAUCE CAKE

(Modern Creaming—1 Egg)

1¾ c. sifted cake flour	¾ c. light brown sugar, firmly packed
1 tsp. baking soda	1 egg
⅛ tsp. salt	1¼ c. canned applesauce
1 tsp. ground cinnamon	1 c. chopped raisins
½ tsp. ground cloves	½ c. chopped pecans
½ c. shortening	1 tbs. cake flour

Heat oven to 350° F. Grease and flour 9x5x3-inch loaf pan. Sift flour, baking soda, salt, cinnamon, and cloves together. Beat shortening, sugar, and egg at high speed on electric mixer* about 3 minutes or until light and fluffy. Add flour mixture alternately with the applesauce, at low speed, beginning and ending with flour. Scrape bowl frequently. Mix raisins, nuts, and 1 tablespoon flour; fold into batter. Pour into prepared pan. Bake 55 to 60 minutes or until cake tests done (*page 429*). Wrap cooled cake in aluminum foil or transparent plastic wrap; store overnight at room temperature before serving. (This mellows flavor and enhances texture.)
* For hand mixing, see directions *page 432*.

POUND CAKES

STARDUST POUND CAKE

(Modern Creaming—3 Eggs)

2⅓ c. sifted cake flour	¾ c. milk
1 tsp. baking powder	1 tbs. grated orange rind
½ tsp. salt	1 tsp. grated lemon rind
⅔ c. shortening	1 tsp. lemon juice
1⅓ c. sugar	Confectioners' sugar
3 eggs	

Heat oven to 350° F. Grease and flour a 2-quart fancy tube pan or 9x5x3-inch loaf pan. Sift flour, baking powder, and salt together. Beat shortening, sugar, and eggs at high speed on electric mixer* about 3 minutes or until light and fluffy. Add flour mixture alternately with milk, rinds, and juice at low speed; beginning and ending with flour. Scrape bowl frequently. Pour into prepared pan. Bake 55 to 60 minutes for tube pan, 1 hour, 20 minutes for loaf pan or until cake tests done (*page 429*). When thoroughly cool, dust lightly with confectioners' sugar. Cut in thin slices for serving.
* For hand mixing, see directions *page 432*.

Raisin Stardust Pound Cake: Prepare Stardust Pound Cake batter. Fold ⅔ cup raisins into batter before pouring into pan.

1-2-3-4 CAKE

(Modern Creaming—4 Eggs)

3 c. sifted cake flour	1 tsp. grated lemon rind
2 tsp. baking powder	4 eggs
½ tsp. salt	1 c. milk
1 c. shortening	2 tbs. lemon juice
2 c. sugar	

Heat oven to 350° F. Grease and flour 10x4-inch tube pan or two 15x10x1-inch jelly-roll pans. Sift flour, baking powder and salt together. Beat shortening, sugar, lemon rind and eggs at high speed on electric mixer* about 3 minutes or until light and fluffy. Add flour mixture alternately with milk and lemon juice; at low speed, beginning and ending with flour. Scrape bowl frequently. Pour into prepared pans. Bake tube pan about 1 hour, jelly-roll pans about 15 minutes or until cake tests done (*page 429*).

* For hand mixing, see directions *page 432*.

PETITS FOURS GLACÉ

1 recipe 1-2-3-4 Cake	½ c. water
2 c. apricot preserves	½ c. light corn syrup
½ c. water	Food coloring, as desired
9 c. sifted confectioners' sugar (about three 1-lb. packages)	

Prepare 1-2-3-4 Cake batter. Bake in two greased and floured 15x10x1-inch pans; cool. Cut out small fancy shapes from sheet cake. Cake shapes may be split and sandwiched together with apricot or raspberry preserves, if desired. Heat apricot preserves and ½ cup water over medium heat until bubbly. Cook 2 to 3 minutes; remove from heat; sieve; cool. Spear each little cake with 2-tined fork;

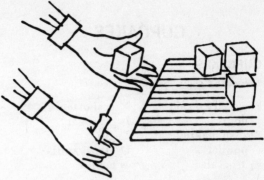

boiling, water. Stir occasionally until frosting is fluid and pourable. Tint with food coloring, if desired. Pour frosting over row of little cakes, letting excess drip down onto paper.

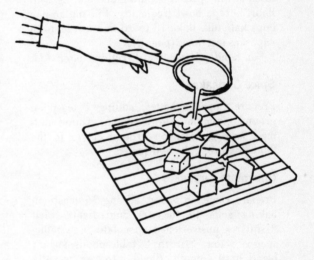

dip in glaze; place right side up on wire rack, over wax paper, to set glaze. This glaze will set the crumbs on the cakes so they may be managed more easily. When glaze is just set, heat sugar, ½ cup water, and corn syrup together in top of double boiler over hot, not

Cakes may be frosted by spearing and dipping into frosting until coated. This may require more frosting. After cakes are frosted, allow frosting to set. Decorate as desired. Makes about 4 dozen.

Holiday Petits Fours Glacé

(*pictured opposite page 52*)

Prepare, bake, cool, and cut cakes as above. Prepare frosting; tint pastel green with a few drops green food coloring. Frost cakes. Prepare 1 recipe Butter Cream Frosting (*page 452*). Tint two thirds deep green, one third red. Decorate cakes to resemble holly.

CUPCAKES

CUPCAKES

(Modern Creaming—2 Eggs)

2½ c. sifted cake flour	½ c. shortening
2¼ tsp. baking powder	1¼ c. sugar
¾ tsp. salt	2 eggs
	1½ tsp. vanilla
	¾ c. milk

Heat oven to 400° F. Line twenty-four 2½-inch muffin-pan cups with fluted paper liners or grease and flour pans. Sift flour, baking powder, and salt together. Beat shortening, sugar, eggs, and vanilla at high speed on electric mixer* about 3 minutes or until light and fluffy. Add flour mixture alternately with milk, at low speed, beginning and ending with flour. Scrape bowl frequently. Fill muffin-pan cups half full. Bake 18 to 20 minutes or until cupcakes test done (*page 429*).
* For hand mixing, see directions *page 432*.

Spice Cupcakes

Prepare Cupcake batter, adding 1 teaspoon ground cinnamon, ¼ teaspoon ground nutmeg, and ¼ teaspoon ground cloves to the flour mixture. Bake as directed.

Chocolate Cupcakes

Prepare Cupcake batter, adding ¼ teaspoon baking soda to the dry ingredients. Melt 2 squares unsweetened chocolate in 3 tablespoons water. Stir in 2 tablespoons sugar; blend until smooth. Blend into egg mixture before adding flour. Bake as directed.

Lemon Cupcakes

Prepare Cupcake batter, reducing milk to ½ cup and omitting vanilla. Add 1 teaspoon grated lemon rind and ¼ cup lemon juice to shortening mixture. Bake as directed.

MOLASSES GEMS

(Modern Creaming—1 Egg)

2 c. sifted cake flour	½ c. shortening
2 tsp. baking powder	¼ c. sugar
½ tsp. baking soda	½ c. molasses
½ tsp. salt	1 egg
1½ tsp. ground cinnamon	½ c. milk

Heat oven to 400° F. Line twenty-four 2½-inch muffin-pan cups with fluted paper liners, or grease and flour well. Sift flour, baking powder, baking soda, salt, and cinnamon together. Beat shortening, sugar, molasses, and egg at high speed on electric mixer* about 3 minutes or until light and fluffy (batter will look curdled). Add flour mixture alternately with the milk, at low speed, beginning and ending with the flour. Scrape bowl frequently. Fill cupcake pans ½ full. Bake 15 to 18 minutes or until cupcakes test done (*page 429*).
* For hand mixing, see directions *page 432*.

FOAM CAKES

The family of Foam Cakes gets its name from the light, fluffy texture of the batter—the result of beating egg whites. Eggs will beat to their highest foam if removed from the refrigerator several hours before using. If using egg whites or egg yolks, separate eggs right out of the refrigerator; let them warm to room temperature. When folding mixtures into egg-white meringue, a rubber scraper is helpful.

The True Sponge Cake is leavened with air alone. The air that is carefully beaten into the egg whites and egg yolks expands in the heat of the oven, making the cake rise high and light. That is why great care should be taken to beat the eggs properly. Other sponge cakes and angel cakes are aided by the addition of a leavening agent, sometimes cream of tartar, sometimes baking powder.

Angel Food Cakes are made with egg whites alone. The measurement of whites is always given in cup measure to provide an accurate guide for the amount of whites needed.

The Chiffon Cake is the newest member of the Foam Cake family. It uses both egg yolks and egg white and has vegetable oil for the shortening. It has a texture between the Sponge Cake and the Butter Cake. The method of combining the ingredients is unique and the results are superlative. Sift the dry ingredients into the mixing bowl; make a "well" in the center. Add the remaining ingredients, except the egg whites and part of the sugar; blend the mixture. Beat the egg whites with sugar to form the meringue; carefully fold meringue into the first mixture.

TRUE SPONGE CAKE

(6 Eggs)

6 egg whites	1 tsp. lemon rind
½ c. sugar	1 tbs. lemon juice
6 egg yolks	1 c. sifted cake flour
½ c. sugar	¼ tsp. salt

Heat oven to 325° F. Beat egg whites in large bowl until foamy. Add ½ cup sugar gradually. Continue beating until meringue forms stiff glossy peaks. Beat egg yolks, ½ cup sugar, and lemon rind and juice in small bowl until thick and light. Fold egg yolk mixture gently into meringue. Combine flour and salt. Sift flour mixture, one quarter at a time, over egg mixture. Fold in. Pour into ungreased 10x4-inch tube pan. Cut through batter gently with knife or spatula to prevent air pockets. Bake 55 to 65 minutes or until cake tests done *(page 429)*. Invert pan; let stand until cold. Remove cake from pan. Dust cake with confectioners' sugar on glaze with Chocolate Glaze *(page 456)* or Raspberry Glaze *(page 456)*.

CALIFORNIA SPONGE CAKE

(6 Eggs)

6 egg whites	1 tsp. baking
½ tsp. cream of	powder
tartar	1 tsp. salt
¾ c. sugar	2 tsp. grated lemon
6 egg yolks	rind
¾ c. sugar	1 tbs. lemon juice
1½ c. sifted cake	¼ c. water
flour	

Heat oven to 325° F. Beat whites and cream of tartar until foamy; add ¾ cup sugar gradually. Continue beating until meringue forms stiff, glossy peaks. Beat egg yolks until thick; beat in ¾ cup sugar until light and fluffy. Sift flour, baking powder, and salt to-

gether; add alternately with combined lemon rind, juice, and water to yolk mixture. Fold yolk mixture gently into meringue mixture. Pour into ungreased 10x4-inch tube pan. Cut through batter gently with knife or spatula to prevent air pockets. Bake 60 to 65 minutes or until cake tests done *(page 429)*. Invert pan: let stand until cold. Remove cake from pan.

GOLDEN SPONGE CAKE

(6 Egg Yolks)

1½ c. sifted cake	6 egg yolks
flour	1 c. sugar
2 tsp. baking	⅓ c. boiling water
powder	1½ tsp. vanilla
½ tsp. salt	

Heat oven to 350° F. Grease and flour two 8x1½-inch layer-cake pans or 9x5x3-inch loaf pan. Sift flour, baking powder, and salt together. Beat egg yolks at high speed on electric mixer until thick. Add sugar gradually, beating well after each addition. Continue beating until mixture is very thick and light colored. Stir in boiling water and vanilla. Fold in flour mixture. Turn into prepared pans. Bake 25 minutes for layers, 30 to 35 minutes for loaf or until cake tests done *(page 429)*. Cool in pans 8 to 10 minutes. Remove from pans to wire racks (this cake should not be inverted to cool). Cool cake completely.

HOT MILK SPONGE CAKE

(3 Eggs)

1 c. sifted cake flour	1 c. sugar
1 tsp. baking	1 tsp. lemon juice
powder	⅓ c. hot milk
3 eggs	

Heat oven to 350° F. Grease and flour 9x9x2-inch cake pan or two 8x1½-inch layer-cake pans. Sift flour and baking powder together. Beat eggs at high speed on electric mixer until thick and light colored. Add sugar gradually, beating well after each addition. Continue beating until mixture is very thick. Add lemon juice and hot milk. Fold in flour mixture. Turn into prepared pan. Bake 25 to 30 minutes or until cake tests done *(page 429)*. Cool in pans 8 to 10 minutes. Remove from pans to wire racks (this cake should not be inverted to cool). Cool cake completely.

Boston Cream Pie

1 recipe Hot Milk
Sponge Cake
1 pkg. (4 oz.)
vanilla pudding
and pie filling
1½ c. milk

½ c. heavy cream,
whipped
1 recipe Dark
Chocolate Glaze
(*page 456*)

Prepare, bake, and cool Hot Milk Sponge Cake, using two 8x1½-inch layer-cake pans. Prepare pudding according to package directions, using 1½ cups milk; cool; fold in whipped cream. Prepare Dark Chocolate Glaze. Spread one layer with cooled pudding; add second layer. Ice top with Dark Chocolate Glaze.

JELLY ROLL

(*3 Eggs*)

1 c. sifted cake flour
1 tsp. baking
powder
¼ tsp. salt
3 eggs
1 c. sugar
¼ c. water

1 tsp. grated lemon
rind
1 tbs. lemon juice
Confectioners'
sugar
1 c. currant or
raspberry jelly

Heat oven to 375° F. Grease 15x10x1-inch jelly roll pan; line with wax paper cut to fit bottom only; grease lightly. Sift flour, baking powder, and salt together. Beat eggs at high speed on electric mixer about 3 minutes or until thick and light. Add 1 cup sugar gradually. Continue beating until mixture is very thick. Blend in water and lemon rind and juice. Gently fold in dry ingredients, a little at a time, taking care not to break down the lightness of the batter; spread batter evenly in prepared pan. Bake 12 to 14 minutes or until cake tests done (*page 429*). Sift confectioners' sugar over clean towel. Loosen edges of cake; turn out on towel. Peel off paper carefully. Trim off dry crisp edges of cake.

Roll up cake and towel, starting with long or short side. Cool on wire rack. Unroll; remove towel. Whip jelly slightly; spread to within one inch of edges of cake. Reroll. Sprinkle with sugar again, if desired.

Chocolate Cream Roll

Prepare Jelly Roll but substitute ¼ cup of cocoa for ¼ cup of flour and sift with other dry ingredients. Substitute 1 teaspoon vanilla for lemon rind and juice. Bake and roll as directed. Unroll cooled cake. Spread with 1 cup heavy cream, whipped and slightly sweetened; reroll. May be frosted with Chocolate Glaze (*page 456*) or dusted with confectioners' sugar, if desired. Chill.

Strawberry Cream Roll

Prepare Jelly Roll. Bake and roll as directed. Unroll cooled cake. Spread with 1 cup heavy cream, whipped; sprinkle with 1½ cups sliced strawberries; reroll. Wrap snugly in aluminum foil or transparent plastic wrap. Chill.

LADYFINGERS

(*3 Eggs*)

3 egg yolks
⅓ c. sugar
1 tsp. vanilla
½ tsp. lemon
extract
⅔ c. sifted cake
flour

3 egg whites
Dash of salt
3 tbs. sugar
Confectioners'
sugar

Heat oven to 300° F. Grease and flour two large cookie sheets. Beat egg yolks, ⅓ cup sugar, vanilla, and lemon extract in mixing bowl until very thick and light. Fold in flour. Beat egg whites and salt in second bowl until foamy. Add 3 tablespoons of sugar gradually. Continue beating until meringue forms stiff, glossy peaks. Stir one-quarter of meringue into the egg-yolk mixture; fold in remainder gently. Spoon batter into pastry bag with large, plain tip. Press onto greased and floured cookie sheets into strips ½ inch wide and 3½ inches long. Sprinkle with confectioners' sugar. Bake 20 to 25 minutes or until a delicate golden brown. Remove from oven. Transfer to wire racks. Cool slightly. Sprinkle again with confectioners' sugar. Cool completely. Makes 2 dozen ladyfingers. Delicious when two are put together with tart jam or jelly.

DAFFODIL CAKE

(10 to 12 Egg Whites, 4 Egg Yolks)

1¼ c. sifted cake flour	½ tsp. vanilla
½ c. sugar	1 c. sugar
1¼ c. (10 to 12) egg whites, at room temperature	4 egg yolks
¼ tsp. salt	1 tsp. grated orange rind
1½ tsp. cream of tartar	2 tbs. orange juice
	2 tbs. sugar
	Confectioners' sugar

Heat oven to 375° F. Sift flour and ½ cup sugar together. Beat egg whites, salt, cream of tartar, and vanilla until foamy. Add 1 cup sugar gradually. Continue beating until meringue forms stiff, glossy peaks. Sift flour mixture one quarter at a time, over meringue; fold in. Beat egg yolks, orange rind and juice, and 2 tablespoons sugar until very thick and light. Add one third of meringue mixture to yolk mixture; fold in gently; spoon batters alternately into ungreased 10x4-inch tube pan. Bake 35 to 40 minutes or until cake tests done *(page 429)*. Invert pan; let stand until cold. Remove cake from pan. Sprinkle with confectioners' sugar or frost with Lemon Butter Cream Frosting *(page 452)*, if desired.

ANGEL SPONGE CAKE

(6 Eggs)

½ c. sifted cake flour	1½ c. sifted cake flour
¼ c. sugar	2 tsp. baking powder
6 egg whites	6 egg yolks
¾ tsp. cream of tartar	1 c. sugar
½ c. sugar	½ c. boiling water
½ tsp. almond extract	1 tsp. lemon extract

Heat oven to 350° F. Sift ½ cup cake flour and ¼ cup sugar together. Beat egg whites and cream of tartar until foamy. Add ½ cup sugar gradually. Add almond extract. Continue beating until meringue forms stiff, glossy peaks. Sift flour mixture, one quarter at a time, over meringue; fold in. Push mixture into ungreased 10x4-inch tube pan. Cut through batter gently with knife or spatula to prevent air pockets. Sift 1½ cups cake flour and baking powder together. Beat egg yolks

until thick and light. Add 1 cup sugar; beat until very thick. Stir in boiling water and lemon extract. Fold in sifted flour mixture. Spoon over egg white mixture in tube pan. Bake 50 to 60 minutes or until cake tests done *(page 429)*. Invert pan; let stand until cold. Remove cake from pan.

ANGEL FOOD CAKE

(10 to 12 Egg Whites)

1 c. sifted cake flour	¼ tsp. salt
1½ c. sifted confectioners' sugar	1 c. sugar
1½ c. egg whites (10 to 12)	1½ tsp. vanilla
1½ tsp. cream of tartar	½ tsp. almond extract

Heat oven to 375° F. Sift flour and confectioners' sugar together. Combine egg whites, cream of tartar, and salt in large bowl; beat until foamy. Add sugar gradually. Continue beating until meringue forms stiff, glossy peaks. Fold in vanilla and almond extract. Sift flour mixture, one quarter at a time, over meringue; fold in. Push batter into ungreased 10x4-inch tube pan. Cut through batter gently with knife or spatula to prevent air pockets. Bake 30 to 35 minutes or until cake tests done *(page 429)*. Invert pan; let stand until cold. Remove cake from pan.

BABY ANGEL FOOD CAKE

(6 Egg Whites)

½ c. sifted cake flour	¾ tsp. cream of tartar
¼ c. sugar	1 tsp. almond extract
6 egg whites	½ c. sugar

Heat oven to 350° F. Sift flour and ¼ cup sugar together. Beat egg whites, cream of tartar, and almond extract until foamy. Add ½ cup sugar gradually. Continue beating until meringue forms stiff, glossy peaks. Sift flour mixture, one quarter at a time, over meringue; fold in. Push batter into ungreased 9x5x3-inch loaf pan. Cut through batter with knife or spatula to prevent air pockets. Bake 30 to 35 minutes or until cake tests done *(page 429)*. Invert pan by setting corners on other pans or custard cups; cool completely. Remove from pan.

SUNNY CHIFFON CAKE

(2 Eggs)

2¼ c. sifted cake flour	½ c. milk
1 c. sugar	2 tsp. vanilla
3 tsp. baking powder	2 egg yolks
½ tsp. salt	½ c. milk
⅓ c. pure vegetable oil	2 egg whites
	½ c. sugar

Heat oven to 350° F. Grease and flour two 8x1½- or 9x1½-inch layer-cake pans. Sift flour, 1 cup sugar, baking powder, and salt into bowl. Make a well in center; add in order oil, ½ cup milk, and vanilla. Beat 1 minute at medium speed on electric mixer or 150 strokes by hand. Add egg yolks and ½ cup milk. Beat 1 minute or another 150 strokes. Beat egg whites in large bowl until foamy. Add ½ cup sugar gradually. Continue beating until meringue forms stiff, glossy peaks. Pour egg-yolk mixture gradually over meringue; fold in. Pour into prepared pans. Bake 30 to 35 minutes or until cake tests done(*page 429*). Cool in pans 8 to 10 minutes. Remove from pans to wire racks. Cool cake completely. Fill with Orange Pineapple Filling (*page 455*). Frost with Fluffy Orange Frosting (*page 454*).

ORANGE CHIFFON CAKE

(5 Egg Yolks, 7 to 8 Egg Whites)

2¼ c. sifted cake flour	¾ c. orange juice
1 c. sugar	2 tsp. grated lemon rind
3 tsp. baking powder	1 c. egg whites (7 to 8)
1 tsp. salt	½ tsp. cream of tartar
½ c. pure vegetable oil	½ c. sugar
5 egg yolks	

Heat oven to 325° F. Sift flour, 1 cup sugar, baking powder, and salt into large bowl. Make a well in center; add in order oil, egg yolks, orange juice, and lemon rind. Beat until smooth. Beat egg whites and cream of tartar until foamy. Add ½ cup sugar gradually. Continue beating until meringue forms stiff, glossy peaks. Pour egg-yolk mixture gradually over meringue; fold in. Pour into un-

greased 10x4-inch tube pan. Bake 55 minutes; increase oven heat to 350° F. Bake 10 to 15 minutes or until cake tests done (*page 429*). Invert pan; let stand until cold. Remove cake from pan. Sprinkle with confectioners' sugar or spread with Raspberry Glaze (*page 456*).

MEXICAN CHOCOLATE CHIFFON CAKE

(7 eggs)

¾ c. hot coffee	½ c. pure vegetable oil
⅓ c. cocoa	
1¾ c. sifted cake flour	7 egg yolks
1⅓ c. sugar	2 tsp. vanilla
1½ tsp. baking soda	7 egg whites
½ tsp. salt	½ tsp. cream of tartar
	⅓ c. sugar

Heat oven to 325° F. Blend hot coffee and cocoa together; set aside to cool. Sift flour, 1⅓ cups sugar, baking soda, and salt into bowl. Make a well in center; add in order oil, egg yolks, vanilla, and cooled coffee mixture. Beat until smooth. Beat egg whites and cream of tartar in large bowl until foamy. Add ⅓ cup sugar gradually. Continue beating until meringue forms stiff, glossy peaks. Pour chocolate mixture gradually over meringue; fold in. Pour into ungreased 10x4-inch tube pan. Bake 55 minutes. Increase oven heat to 350° F. Bake 10 to 15 minutes or until cake tests done (*page 429*). Invert pan; let stand until cold. Remove cake from pan.

FRUITCAKES

CHEDDAR CHEESE DATE CAKE

¾ c. butter or margarine	¼ tsp. ground cloves
1½ c. light brown sugar, firmly packed	1 c. milk
4 eggs	2 pkgs. (8 oz. ea.) pitted dates, cut up
1 c. shredded Cheddar cheese	2 c. chopped pecans
3½ c. sifted all-purpose flour	1 jar (4 oz.) candied cherries, halved
½ tsp. baking soda	2 c. raisins
1 tsp. salt	
1 tsp. ground cinnamon	

Heat oven to 300° F. Grease and flour 10x4-inch tube pan. Beat butter or margarine and sugar in large bowl until blended. Add eggs, one at a time, beating well after each addition. Beat in cheese. Sift flour, soda, salt, cinnamon, and cloves together; add alternately with milk to butter-sugar mixture. Beat until smooth and blended. Stir in dates, pecans, cherries, and raisins. Pour into prepared pan. Bake 2 to 2½ hours or until cake tests done (*page 429*). Cool cake; remove from pan. Store cooled cake several weeks in covered container to mellow flavors. Decorate with candied fruits, if desired.

NOEL FRUITCAKE

3½ c. sifted all-purpose flour	1 jar (4 oz.) candied lemon peel
1¼ tsp. baking powder	1 jar (4 oz.) candied citron
1 tsp. salt	1 tbs. grated orange rind
2 tsp. ground cinnamon	½ c. orange juice
¼ tsp. ground cloves	1 c. currant or grape jelly
1¼ c. raisins	1½ c. shortening
1 c. chopped nuts	2½ c. brown sugar, firmly packed
1 pkg. (about 12 oz.) dried apricots, chopped	5 eggs
2 jars (4 oz. ea.) candied cherries, halved	

Heat oven to 300° F. Line 10x4-inch tube pan or two 9x5x3-inch loaf pans with heavy brown paper; grease paper. Sift flour, baking powder, salt, cinnamon, and cloves together. Combine raisins, nuts, apricots, cherries, lemon peel, and citron in bowl; reserve. Beat orange rind, juice, and jelly together with a fork in small bowl. Reserve. Beat shortening, sugar, and eggs in large bowl until fluffy. Add flour mixture alternately with reserved orange-juice mixture, beginning and ending with flour. Stir in reserved fruit mixture. Turn batter into prepared pans. Bake 3½ to 4 hours for tube cake, 2½ to 3 hours for loaf cakes or until cake tests done (*page 429*). Cover cake with brown paper during last hour of baking to keep top from darkening too much. Cool cake; remove from pan. Store cooled cake several weeks in covered container to mellow flavors.

EASY HOLIDAY FRUITCAKE

1 c. seedless raisins	2 c. walnuts, chopped
1 c. seeded raisins	4 eggs, beaten
1 can (about 1 lb.) cling peaches, drained and chopped	2½ c. sifted all-purpose flour
1 c. shortening	1 tsp. baking powder
1 c. brown sugar, firmly packed	1½ tsp. salt
½ c. orange juice	1 tsp. ground cinnamon
2 jars (1 lb. ea.) mixed candied fruits	1 tsp. ground nutmeg
	½ tsp. ground cloves

Heat oven to 300° F. Grease two 9x5x3-inch loaf pans. Combine raisins, peaches, shortening, sugar, and orange juice in saucepan; heat just to boiling. Remove from heat; pour into large bowl; cool. Add candied fruits and nuts to cooled mixture; stir in beaten eggs. Sift flour, baking powder, salt, cinnamon, nutmeg, and cloves together; beat into fruit mixture. Spoon into prepared pans. Bake 2 hours or until cake tests done (*page 429*). Cool cake; remove from pans. Store cooled cake several weeks in covered container to mellow flavors.

DUNDEE CAKE

2½ c. sifted all-purpose flour	½ c. currants
1 tsp. baking powder	½ c. candied lemon peel
¾ c. butter or margarine	½ c. candied cherries, halved
1 tsp. grated orange rind	¼ c. chopped, blanched almonds
1 c. sugar	Whole blanched almonds
4 eggs	Candied cherries
2 tbs. orange juice	
½ c. golden raisins	

Heat oven to 275° F. Line 9x5x3-inch loaf pan with aluminum foil; grease foil. Sift flour and baking powder together. Beat butter or margarine, orange rind, sugar, and eggs together until well blended. Add flour mixture alternately with orange juice, beginning and ending with flour. Stir in raisins, currants, lemon peel, cherries, and almonds. Spread evenly in prepared pan. Bake 1 hour and 50 minutes or until cake tests done (*page 429*). Cool cake; remove from pan; peel off foil. Cool completely. Decorate cake with additional whole almonds and cherries.

GOLDEN FRUITCAKE

1 pkg. (8 oz.) pitted
dates, cut up
2 c. walnuts,
chopped
2 jars (4 oz. ea.)
candied cherries,
halved
1 c. raisins
2 jars (4 oz. ea.)
candied citron
¾ c. soft butter or
margarine

1½ c. sugar
4 eggs
3½ c. sifted all-
purpose flour
½ tsp. baking soda
1½ tsp. salt
1½ tsp. ground
nutmeg
1 c. dairy sour
cream

Heat oven to 300° F. Grease and flour a 10x4-inch tube pan or two 9x5x3-inch loaf pans. Combine dates, walnuts, cherries, raisins, and citron. Beat butter or margarine with sugar in large bowl until blended; add eggs. Beat at high speed on electric mixer about 10 minutes or until light and fluffy. Sift flour, soda, salt, and nutmeg together; add alternately with sour cream to butter mixture; beat until well blended. Add fruit mixture; mix thoroughly. Spoon into prepared pans. Bake 3 to 3½ hours for tube cake, 2 to 2½ hours for loaf cakes or until cake tests done (*page 429*). Cool cake. Remove from pan. Cake is best if allowed to ripen at least 24 hours.

ORIENTAL FRUITCAKE

2 c. sifted all-
purpose flour
½ tsp. baking soda
½ tsp. salt
½ tsp. ground
allspice
¼ tsp. ground
cloves
½ tsp. ground
mace
1 tsp. ground
cinnamon
½ c. shortening
1¼ c. sugar
3 eggs

⅓ c. molasses
½ c. milk
1 c. chopped
walnuts or
pecans
1 c. raisins
2 c. mixed candied
fruits
1 pkg. white cake
mix
Lemon Coconut
Filling
(*page 455*)
Fluffy 7-Minute
Frosting
(*page 454*)

Heat oven to 275° F. Grease two 9-inch layer-cake pans; line bottoms with wax paper; grease paper. Sift flour, soda, salt, allspice, cloves, mace, and cinnamon together. Beat shortening, sugar, eggs, and molasses until well blended. Add flour mixture alternately with milk; beginning and ending with flour. Stir in nuts, raisins, and candied fruits. Pour batter into prepared pans. Bake 1 hour and 15 minutes or until cake tests done (*page 429*). Cool in pans 10 minutes; remove from pans; peel off paper; cool completely. Prepare, bake, and cool one 9-inch layer from half the package of white cake mix according to package directions. Put 3 cooled layers together, with white layer in middle, with Lemon Coconut Filling. Frost with Fluffy 7-Minute Frosting.

WEXFORD CHRISTMAS FRUITCAKE

3 c. sifted all-
purpose flour
½ tsp. baking
powder
½ tsp. ground
cinnamon
1 c. butter or
margarine
1 c. plus 2 tbs. light
brown sugar,
firmly packed
6 eggs
⅓ c. Irish whiskey
½ lb. raisins
½ lb. golden raisins
½ lb. currants

2 jars (4 oz. ea.)
mixed candied
fruits, chopped
¼ c. candied
cherries, chopped
1 tsp. grated lemon
rind
½ c. blanched
almonds, ground
½ c. chopped,
blanched
almonds
½ c. Irish whiskey
Glaze*

Heat oven to 275° F. Line 9x3-inch tube pan with brown paper; grease paper. Sift flour, baking powder, and cinnamon together. Cream butter or margarine; add brown sugar gradually, beating until fluffy. Add eggs, one at a time, beating well after each addition. Add flour mixture and ⅓ cup whiskey; mix until blended. Fold in fruits and nuts. Turn into prepared pan. Bake 3 hours or until cake tests done (*page 429*). Brush hot cake with ¼ cup whiskey. Cool cake in pan. Remove from pan; peel off paper. Brush with remaining ¼ cup whiskey. Wrap in aluminum foil or store in covered container. Before serving, brush cake with glaze.* Garnish with cherries, almonds and citron or angelica cut into leaves, if desired.

* *Glaze:* Combine ¼ cup light brown sugar, firmly packed; 3 tablespoons light corn syrup; and 3 tablespoons water in saucepan. Bring slowly to boiling; boil 2 minutes; remove from heat. Add 1 tablespoon lemon juice.

SPECIAL PARTY CAKES

Every child loves a special cake for a birthday. These cakes have been created for the occasion. They are all made with convenience foods to short-cut the preparation time for a busy mother and leave time for her to make the elaborate decorations.

ROCKET SPACE SHIP

1 pkg. angel or chiffon cake mix
1 pkg. (18 oz.) refrigerated slice-and-bake sugar cookies
Fin pattern (*page 451*)
Cardboard tube from wax paper or aluminum foil roll
1 pkg. (6½ oz.) fluffy white frosting mix

2 pkgs. (6½ oz. ea.) creamy white frosting mix
Blue food coloring
Red food coloring
1 thin 14-inch-long knitting needle
1 ice cream cone
3 red gumdrops
Candles

1. Prepare and bake cake in 10x4-inch tube pan according to package directions. Remove from pan and cool as directed.
2. Roll out packaged refrigerated cookies to ¼-inch thickness.
3. Cut out about 12 cookies with a 1½-inch floured, plain cookie cutter. Cut small hole in center of each cookie with end of pencil from which the eraser has been removed.
4. Cut out three fins from cookie dough using pattern.
5. Transfer cookies and fins to cookie sheet.

Bake according to package directions. Cool on wire racks.
6. Cut cardboard tube one inch higher than cake. Stuff with crumpled foil. Place in center hole of baked cake.
7. Prepare packaged fluffy white frosting mix. Frost top and sides of the cake and exposed portion of the cardboard tube.
8. Prepare creamy white frosting mix. Leave a third white, tint a third deep blue, tint a third red.
9. Stack cookies with a dab of white frosting between to hold them together. Frost top cookie thickly. Thread stack on knitting needle. Press needle down through foil in cardboard tube. Frost complete outside of cookies.

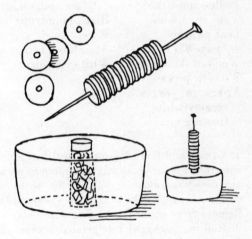

10. Frost ice cream cone with blue frosting. Put a small favor, such as a tiny plastic spaceman, in the cone to be discovered by the child who "wins" the cone. Invert the cone and press firmly into frosting on stack of cookies to form the nose cone of rocket.
11. Frost one side of fins with blue frosting. Press fins in place equidistant around bottom of rocket. Frost other side of fins.

12. Pipe band of white frosting where cone joins rocket body, using paper cone with end snipped off. Pipe second band to separate first and second stages of rocket.

13. Spoon red frosting into paper cone; snip off tiny tip of cone to make a very thin line of frosting. Letter rocket U.S.A.F.; stripe fins; band rocket.

14. Cut gumdrops in half; press 2 halves into each of the spaces between the fins.

15. Spoon blue frosting into paper cone, pipe edging around bottom of cake. Decorate sides of cakes with free-form stars.

16. Press small mounds of frosting around top of cake to form candleholders; insert candles.

A TISKET A TASKET CAKE

1 pkg. yellow cake mix	Yellow food coloring
1 pkg. (18 oz.) refrigerated slice-and-bake sugar cookies	Green food coloring
	1 recipe Sugar Glaze (*page 456*)
Leaf pattern (*page 451*)	Black gumdrops
	Wire
Wooden skewers	Aluminum foil
Wooden picks	White ribbon
3 pkgs. (6½ oz. ea.) creamy white frosting mix	

1. Grease and flour 2½-quart oval heatproof casserole. Prepare cake mix according to package directions. Bake at 325° F. for 45 to 50 minutes or until cake tests done (*page 429*). Remove from casserole; cool on wire rack.

2. Roll out packaged refrigerated cookies on floured surface to ¼-inch thickness. Cut leaf cookies with pattern. Cut 1½-inch-round cookies with floured, plain cutter. (Be sure you cut enough rounds so each child has a "daisy pop.") Transfer cookies and leaves to cookie sheet. Press wooden skewer into each round. Press wooden pick into each leaf. Bake according to package directions; cool on wire racks.

3. Prepare creamy white frosting mix. Measure 1 cup; leave white and reserve. Measure second cup; tint pastel yellow. Tint remaining frosting light green.

4. Frost cooled cake thinly with green frosting.

5. Spoon white frosting into decorating tube

with plain tip (No. 9). Pipe vertical lines, 1 inch apart, all around cake. Be sure to make

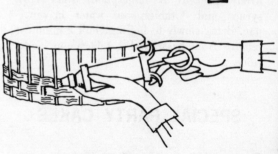

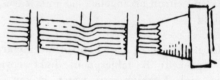

an even number of white lines, so "basketwork" will come out evenly.

6. Spoon green frosting into decorating tube with serrated ribbon tip (No. 48). Pipe a band around bottom of cake, covering only every other white line. Repeat bands one on top of the other, covering the alternate white lines in each row with green frosting so cake resembles a woven basket.

7. Prepare Sugar Glaze. Dip one side of each daisy pop and leaf in glaze. Set, unglazed side down, on wire rack to let glaze drip.

8. Spoon yellow frosting into paper cone; cut off tip. Pipe yellow daisy onto each dry, glazed pop. Cut gumdrops in thirds crosswise with scissors; press a slice in center of each daisy.

9. Add additional green food coloring to light green frosting to make it leaf green in color. Pipe outlines onto leaves.

10. Press daisy pops and leaves into top of cake.

11. Cover wire with crumpled foil, leaving one inch at each end uncovered; bend into handle shape. Wind ribbon securely around foil. Make bow; tie to handle. Press ends of handle into cake.

SHIP AHOY CAKE
(Pictured opposite page 21)

1 pkg. white or yellow cake mix	1 pkg. (14 oz.) fudge frosting mix
1 pkg. (18 oz.) refrigerated slice-and-bake sugar cookies	2 pkgs. (6½ oz. ea.) creamy white frosting mix
Patterns for sail, pennant, and hull	1 pkg. (6½ oz.) fluffy white frosting mix
2 bamboo or wooden skewers, 7½ in. long	Blue food coloring
Wooden picks	Red food coloring

1. Prepare and bake cake in two 9x1½-inch layer-cake pans according to package directions. Remove from pans and cool as directed.
2. Roll out packaged refrigerator cookie dough on floured surface to ¼-inch thickness.

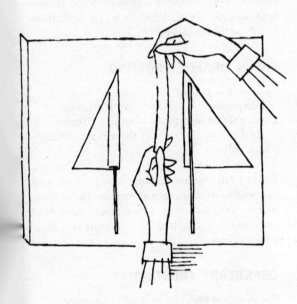

3. Cut out two sails using patterns. Transfer to cookie sheet. Press skewer along edge of each sail to hold sail erect. Cut narrow strip of dough the same length as the sail. Moisten edges; cover skewer. Press edges firmly to sail to enclose skewer completely.
4. Cut out pennant. Transfer to cookie sheet. Press wooden pick securely into pennant.
5. Cut out four hulls; transfer to cookie sheet. Make holes in hulls as shown on pattern.

These are to hold sails later. Bake and cool as directed.
6. Prepare fudge frosting mix; prepare creamy white frosting mix.
7. Stack four hull pieces with fudge frosting. Frost sides. Insert a wooden pick in each hole in top.
8. Frost top of hull section (deck) with fudge frosting. Pipe white frosting around top edge.
9. Frost sails and pennant with white frosting.
10. Prepare fluffy white frosting mix. Tint a delicate blue. Fill and frost cake, reserving a half cup for waves.
11. Place hull in center of cake. Make waves, with reserved blue frosting, all around hull with back of spoon.
12. Spoon fudge frosting into paper cone. Cut off just enough of tip to make small hole. Pipe anchors on sides of cake.
13. Spoon white frosting into paper cone. Cut off tip. Join anchors with continuous line of rope.
14. Remove wooden picks from hull. Insert skewers of sails into holes. Fill in space between two sails with white frosting. Pipe thin chocolate mast between sails.
15. Decorate top of cake with white frosting rope.
16. Tint small amount of white frosting red; pipe lines or write child's name on pennant. Insert into frosting between sails.

Patterns for Special Party Cake Decorating
(½ actual size)

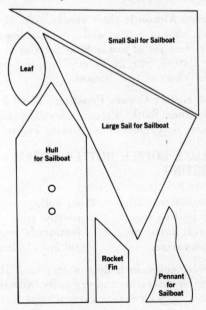

Frostings and Fillings

BUTTER CREAM FROSTING

½ c. butter or margarine
1 tsp. vanilla

1 pkg. (1 lb.) confectioners' sugar, sifted
3 to 4 tbs. milk or cream

Blend butter or margarine, vanilla, and half the sugar. Beat in remaining sugar. Add milk or cream gradually, adding just enough to make a smooth frosting of good spreading consistency. Enough to fill and frost two 8- or 9-inch layers or about 2 dozen cupcakes.

Lemon: Add 1 teaspoon grated lemon rind and 3 to 4 tablespoons lemon juice in place of vanilla and milk or cream.

Chocolate: Add 2 squares unsweetened chocolate, melted and cooled, to butter or margarine.

Coffee: Add 2 teaspoons instant coffee to milk; blend; add to sugar mixture.

Pineapple: Drain 1 can (8¾ oz.) crushed pineapple; reserve syrup. Add 3 tablespoons syrup in place of milk or cream. Stir in ¼ cup drained, crushed pineapple and 1 teaspoon grated lemon rind.

Cherry Almond: Omit vanilla. Add ½ teaspoon almond extract and 3 to 4 tablespoons juice from jar of maraschino cherries to butter mixture. Stir in ¼ cup chopped maraschino cherries, well drained.

Rich Butter Cream Frosting: Blend 2 egg yolks into Butter Cream, Chocolate Butter Cream, or Lemon Butter Cream Frosting.

DELUXE COFFEE BUTTER CREAM FROSTING

2 tbs. instant coffee
¼ c. boiling water
1 c. soft butter or margarine

2 egg yolks
6 c. sifted confectioners' sugar (about 1½ lbs.)

Dissolve coffee in boiling water; cool. Blend butter or margarine and egg yolks. Add sugar alternately with coffee mixture until frosting is of good spreading consistency. Enough to fill and frost three 8- or 9-inch layers.

BURNT SUGAR FROSTING

⅓ c. sugar
⅓ c. water
½ c. soft butter or margarine

2 egg yolks
1 pkg. (1 lb.) confectioners' sugar, sifted

Heat sugar in heavy skillet over low heat, until it melts and turns golden brown. Add water, a small amount at a time, stirring constantly. Boil syrup for 1 minute; cool. Cream butter or margarine; blend in egg yolks. Add confectioners' sugar alternately with syrup; beat well to blend. Enough to fill and frost two 8- or 9-inch layers.

FRESH ORANGE FROSTING

½ c. soft butter or margarine
2 tsp. grated orange rind
2 egg yolks

1 pkg. (1 lb.) confectioners' sugar, sifted
2 tbs. orange juice

Blend butter or margarine, orange rind, and egg yolks. Add sugar and orange juice alternately until mixture is of good spreading consistency. Enough to fill and frost two 8- or 9-inch layers.

CRANBERRY FROSTING

2½ c. sifted confectioners' sugar
¼ c. ground cranberries
1½ tbs. lemon juice

4 tbs. butter or margarine
1 tsp grated lemon rind
Dash of salt

Combine ½ cup of sugar, cranberries, and lemon juice; let stand about 30 minutes to dissolve sugar. Cream butter or margarine; add grated lemon rind and salt. Add remaining sugar alternately with cranberry mixture, beating well after each addition. Enough to frost top and sides of two 8- or 9-inch layers.

PEPPERMINT STRIPE FROSTING

½ c. soft butter or margarine
1 pkg. (1 lb.) confectioners' sugar, sifted
1 c. after-dinner mints, crushed
4 to 5 tbs. cream or milk
Red food coloring

Blend butter or margarine, sugar, and crushed mints. Add cream or milk gradually until frosting is of good spreading consistency. Remove one third; tint with a few drops of red food coloring to make a bright pink. Frost cooled cake with white frosting. Put pink frosting in pastry bag and pipe strips of frosting diagonally across cake. Enough to frost one 13x9x2-inch cake.

CREAM CHEESE FROSTING

2 pkgs. (3 oz. ea.) cream cheese
⅛ tsp. salt
1 pkg. (1 lb.) confectioners' sugar, sifted
1 tsp. vanilla
1 tbs. milk

Beat cream cheese and salt until softened; add confectioners' sugar gradually, blending well after each addition. Stir in vanilla. Blend in milk until of good spreading consistency. Enough to fill and frost two 8- or 9-inch layers.

CARAMEL FROSTING

½ c. soft butter or margarine
1 c. brown sugar, firmly packed
⅓ c. milk
1 pkg. (1 lb.) confectioners' sugar, sifted

Combine butter or margarine and brown sugar in saucepan. Cook over medium heat, stirring constantly, until mixture bubbles. Cook 1 minute. Pour into mixing bowl; cool 10 minutes; stir in milk; cool completely. When caramel mixture is cool, add confectioners' sugar gradually, beating well after each addition. Enough to fill and frost two 8- or 9-inch layers.

FAVORITE CHOCOLATE FROSTING

4 sqs. unsweetened chocolate
½ c. butter or margarine
1 pkg. (1 lb.) confectioners' sugar, sifted
½ c. milk
1 tsp. vanilla

Melt chocolate and butter or margarine over hot, not boiling, water. Combine sugar, milk, and vanilla in bowl. Add chocolate mixture. Beat until thick enough to spread. Enough to fill and frost two 8- or 9-inch layers.

HUNGARIAN CHOCOLATE FROSTING

3 sqs. unsweetened chocolate
1½ c. sifted confectioners' sugar
2½ tbs. hot water
3 egg yolks
4 tbs. butter or margarine

Melt chocolate in top of double boiler over hot, not boiling, water. Remove from heat; blend in sugar and water. Add egg yolks, one at a time, beating well after each addition. Add butter or margarine, 1 tablespoon at a time, beating well. Chill, if necessary, until thick enough to spread. Enough to frost top and sides of two 8- or 9x1½-inch layers or about 1 dozen cupcakes.

DELUXE CHOCOLATE FROSTING

½ c. soft butter or margarine
4 sqs. unsweetened chocolate, melted and cooled
1 pkg. (1 lb.) confectioners' sugar, sifted
2 egg yolks
4 tbs. milk

Combine butter or margarine, melted chocolate, and half the sugar. Add yolks, remaining sugar, and enough milk to make a smooth frosting of good spreading consistency. Enough to fill and frost two 8- or 9-inch layers.

FRENCH VELVET CHOCOLATE FROSTING

1 pkg. (6 oz.) semi-sweet chocolate pieces
¼ c. strong, brewed coffee
1 c. soft butter or margarine
¾ c. light corn syrup
4 egg yolks

Melt chocolate with coffee over hot, not boiling, water; cool. Cream butter or margarine; beat in chocolate mixture. Bring corn syrup to boiling in small saucepan; boil about 2 minutes, or until it spins a thread. Beat egg yolks until thick; beat in corn syrup; cool. Combine cooled chocolate and cooled egg mixtures; beat well. Chill. Enough to frost top and sides of two 8- or 9-inch layers.

CREAMY CHOCOLATE FROSTING

1 small can (⅔ c.)   2 pkgs. (6 oz. ea.)
    evaporated milk   semi-sweet choco-
⅔ c. sugar   late pieces
3 tbs. butter or   2 tbs. light corn
    margarine   syrup
⅛ tsp. salt

Combine evaporated milk, sugar, butter or margarine, and salt in saucepan. Cook rapidly over medium heat 5 minutes, stirring occasionally. Add chocolate pieces and corn syrup; beat until blended. Cool until of spreading consistency. Enough to frost top and sides of two 8- or 9-inch layers or 1½ dozen cupcakes.

FLUFFY 7-MINUTE FROSTING

3 egg whites   3 tbs. water
1 c. sugar   ¼ tsp. cream of
⅓ c. light corn   tartar
    syrup   1 tsp. vanilla

Blend egg whites, sugar, corn syrup, water, and cream of tartar in top of double boiler. Beat rapidly with rotary beater over boiling water until mixture stands in stiff peaks. Remove from heat; beat in vanilla. Enough to fill and frost two 8- or 9-inch layers.

FLUFFY ORANGE FROSTING

2 egg whites   3 tbs. orange juice
1½ c. sugar   2 tbs. water
1 tbs. light corn
    syrup

Blend egg whites, sugar, corn syrup, orange juice, and water in top of double boiler. Beat rapidly with rotary beater over boiling water until stiff peaks form. Enough to fill and frost two 8- or 9-inch layers.

WHITE MOUNTAIN CREAM FROSTING

¾ c. sugar   3 egg whites
¼ c. water   1 tsp. vanilla or
¼ c. light corn   almond extract
    syrup

Combine sugar, water, and corn syrup in small saucepan. Cook over medium heat until sugar is dissolved and mixture begins to boil. Boil,

without stirring, until mixture reaches 242° F. on candy thermometer or until syrup spins a 6- to 8-inch long thread from tip of spoon. Just before syrup reaches temperature, beat egg whites until stiff, but not dry. Pour syrup in thin stream over egg whites, while beating at high speed. Beat until mixture is stiff and glossy and holds shape nicely. Beat in flavoring. Enough to frost and fill 8- or 9-inch cake or from 24 to 30 cupcakes.

Pink Mountain Cream Frosting. Substitute ¼ cup syrup from jar of maraschino cherries for water in above recipe.

SEAFOAM FROSTING

¾ c. brown sugar,   ⅓ c. dark corn
    firmly packed   syrup
3 tbs. water   3 egg whites
                                 1 tsp. vanilla

Combine brown sugar, water, and corn syrup in saucepan. Cook over medium heat until sugar is dissolved and mixture begins to boil. Boil, without stirring, until mixture reaches 242° F. on candy thermometer or until syrup spins 6- to 8-inch long thread from tip of spoon. Just before syrup reaches temperature, beat egg whites until stiff, but not dry. Pour hot syrup slowly in thin, steady stream over beaten egg whites. Continue beating until frosting holds peaks. Fold in 1 teaspoon vanilla. Enough to fill and frost two 8- or 9x1½-inch layers.

JELLY FROSTING

2 egg whites   1 c. tart jelly (mint,
⅛ tsp. salt   currant, apple)

Beat egg whites and salt at high speed on electric mixer until soft peaks form. Add jelly gradually; continue to beat until mixture forms stiff, glossy peaks. Enough to fill and frost two 8- or 9-inch layers.

ROYAL FROSTING
(Ornamental Frosting)

This special decorating frosting will hold its shape well. Since it hardens quickly, decorations made from it are quite durable.

3 egg whites   1 pkg. (1 lb.)
½ tsp. cream of   confectioners'
    tartar   sugar, sifted

Beat egg whites and cream of tartar until foamy. Beat in confectioners' sugar slowly until well blended. Beat at high speed until mixture holds its shape and knife drawn through frosting leaves sharp, clean path. Frosting will harden quickly, so keep it covered with a damp towel to prevent drying out. If frosting loses stiffness, beat hard to restiffen. Used for frosting and decorating cakes.

RICH PASTRY CREAM

½ c. sifted all- purpose flour	1½ tsp. vanilla 1 tsp. butter or
½ c. sugar	margarine
¼ tsp. salt	½ c. heavy cream,
2 c. milk	whipped
3 eggs, slightly beaten	

Combine flour, sugar, and salt in saucepan. Add milk slowly; stir until blended. Cook over medium heat, stirring constantly, until thickened and bubbly; cook 2 minutes longer. Beat half the hot mixture into eggs; stir into mixture in saucepan; cook 1 minute longer or until bubbly, stirring constantly. Remove from heat; stir in vanilla and butter or margarine. Place piece of wax paper directly on top of hot pastry cream to prevent skin from forming; cool. Fold in whipped cream; chill. Makes about 4 cups.

CHOCOLATE CREAM FILLING

½ c. sugar	1 tsp. unflavored
2 sqs. unsweetened chocolate	gelatin 1½ c. milk
2 tbs. cornstarch	2 egg yolks, slightly beaten

Combine sugar, chocolate, cornstarch, and gelatin in saucepan. Stir in milk. Cook over medium heat, stirring constantly, until mixture comes to boiling; boil 1 minute. Pour half the hot mixture slowly into egg yolks; stir into mixture in saucepan; cook 1 minute longer, stirring constantly. Remove from heat. Place piece of wax paper directly on top of hot filling to prevent skin from forming. Cool; chill. Makes about 2½ cups.

ORANGE-PINEAPPLE FILLING

⅔ c. sugar	2 egg yolks, slightly
3 tbs. cornstarch	beaten
⅔ c. orange juice	2 tsp. grated orange
1 can (8½ oz.) crushed pine- apple, drained	rind 1 tbs. butter or margarine

Combine sugar, cornstarch, orange juice, and pineapple in saucepan. Cook over medium heat, stirring constantly, until mixture bubbles and is thickened. Stir half of hot mixture into egg yolks; stir into mixture in saucepan; cook 1 minute. Remove from heat; add orange rind and butter or margarine. Cool; chill. Makes about 2½ cups.

LEMON FILLING

½ c. sugar	1 tsp. butter or
3 tbs. cornstarch	margarine
⅛ tsp. salt	1 tbs. grated lemon
¾ c. water	rind
1 egg yolk, slightly beaten	2 tbs. lemon juice

Combine sugar, cornstarch, and salt in saucepan; add water. Cook over medium heat, stirring constantly, until thickened and bubbly. Continue cooking 1 minute longer. Blend half the hot mixture into egg yolk. Blend into mixture remaining in saucepan. Cook 1 minute, stirring rapidly. Remove from heat; add butter or margarine and lemon rind and juice; cool. Spread between cooled cake layers. Makes about 1 cup.

Lime Filling

Substitute lime rind and juice for lemon rind and juice in above recipe. Add a few drops of green food coloring, if desired.

LEMON COCONUT FILLING

¾ c. sugar	2 tbs. grated lemon
3 tbs. cornstarch	rind
¾ c. water	¼ c. lemon juice
1 tbs. butter or margarine	½ c. flaked coconut

Mix sugar and cornstarch in saucepan; add water. Cook over medium heat, stirring constantly, until thickened and clear. Remove from heat; add butter or margarine. Cool. Stir in lemon rind and juice and coconut. Makes about 2½ cups.

RASPBERRY GLAZE

½ of 10 oz. pkg.   1½ c. sifted con-
  frozen rasp-   fectioners' sugar
  berries, thawed
  and drained

Press raspberries through sieve to purée and
remove seeds. Stir enough of the puréed mixture into sugar to make of pouring consistency. Spoon over baked cooled cake, allowing glaze to run down sides. Enough for 10-
inch tube cake.

DARK CHOCOLATE GLAZE

2 sqs. unsweetened   1 c. sifted con-
  chocolate   fectioners' sugar
1 tsp. butter or   3 tbs. water
  margarine

Melt chocolate with butter or margarine over
hot water. Stir in confectioners' sugar; beat
in water until mixture is smooth. Spoon over
tops of éclairs or cream puffs at once. May
also be used as glaze for Boston Cream Pie,
chiffon and sponge cakes.

CHOCOLATE GLAZE

1 pkg. (6 oz.) semi-   3 tbs. light corn
  sweet chocolate   syrup
  pieces   2 tsp. strong,
                    brewed coffee

Melt chocolate with corn syrup and coffee in
top of double boiler over hot, not boiling,
water. Stir until smooth and glossy. Pour,
while hot, over cake. Spread with spatula to
cover top and sides with thin glaze. Chill.
Enough for 10-inch tube cake.

EASY CONFECTIONERS' SUGAR GLAZE

Milk or water   1 c. sifted con-
                    fectioners' sugar

Stir enough milk or water into sugar to make
of good pouring consistency. Drizzle or spoon
over cake or coffee cake.

SUGAR GLAZE

3½ c. sifted con-   ⅓ c. boiling water
  fectioners' sugar

Combine sugar and water; stir until smooth.

Made with Cake Mixes

FUDGE MACAROON TORTE

1 pkg. (2-layer)   1 pkg. (about 4 oz.)
  yellow cake mix   chocolate pud-
¼ c. shortening   ding and pie
1 egg   filling mix
2 tbs. water   1¾ c. milk
1 c. flaked coconut   1 c. heavy cream,
                    whipped

Heat oven to 350° F. Blend cake mix, shortening, egg, water, and coconut thoroughly with
spoon or hand, mixing until dough holds together. Pat out in even layer in greased
13x9x2-inch pan. Bake 12 to 18 minutes or
until golden; cool in pan. Prepare pudding
mix with milk according to package directions; cool; fold in whipped cream. Spread
over baked crust. Top with additional whipped
cream, if desired. Cut into squares.

SUNSHINE COBBLER

1 pkg. (4 oz.)   ¾ tsp. ground
  lemon pudding   nutmeg
  and pie filling   1 pkg. (2-layer)
  mix   white cake mix
2 egg yolks   2 egg whites
1 can (1 lb.) fruit   1 tsp. almond
  cocktail, drained   extract

Heat oven to 350° F. Cook lemon pie filling
according to package directions, using 2 egg
yolks. Pour filling into ungreased 13x9x2-
inch pan; spoon drained fruit cocktail and
nutmeg over top. Make cake batter according
to directions, using egg whites and almond
extract. Pour batter carefully over fruit.
Bake 45 to 50 minutes. Cut in squares and
serve warm in dessert or fruit dishes.

PATIO PARTY TORTE

1 pkg. (2-layer) yellow cake mix	2 tbs. sugar
2 eggs	1 c. chopped pecans or toasted, slivered almonds
1 pkg. (6½ oz.) fluffy white frosting mix	

Heat oven to 350° F. Prepare cake batter according to package directions, using 2 eggs. Bake in 2 greased and floured 9x1½-inch layer-cake pans as directed. Cool cakes about 15 minutes; place layers on cookie sheets. Prepare frosting mix as directed on package. Swirl on top of layers; sprinkle with sugar and nuts. Bake at 375° F. for 10 minutes or until lightly browned. Cool on wire racks. Cut in wedges and serve with soft whipped cream, if desired.

KIDDY CAKE CONES

1 pkg. (1-layer) chocolate or yellow cake mix	1 pkg. (6½ oz.) fluffy frosting mix (vanilla or lemon)
1 egg	
16 ice cream cone cups	

Heat oven to 350° F. Prepare cake batter according to package directions, using egg. Line sixteen 2½-inch muffin-pan cups with paper baking cups; spoon batter into cups, filling halfway; invert a cone cup on each. Bake 15 to 20 minutes or until done. Cool cupcake cones; carefully peel off paper baking cups. Prepare frosting according to package directions; tint with food coloring, if desired. Frost cones. Decorate with coconut, candy sprinkles, chopped nuts, or chocolate pieces, if desired.

PARTY BARS

½ c. butter or margarine	1 pkg. (6½ oz.) lemon-flavored fluffy frosting mix
1 pkg. (2-layer) lemon cake mix	1½ c. chopped, blanched almonds
	1 c. flaked or shredded coconut

Heat oven to 350° F. With pastry blender or two knives cut butter or margarine into dry cake mix until evenly blended. Press mixture into ungreased 15x10x1-inch jelly-roll pan. Bake 5 to 7 minutes or until surface is set. Prepare frosting mix according to package directions; fold in 1 cup nuts and coconut. Spread over crust. Sprinkle with remaining nuts. Bake 25 minutes or until golden; cool in pan. Cut into bars.

PRALINE CAKE

1 pkg. (2-layer) chocolate cake mix	2 tsp. maple flavoring
2 eggs	⅔ c. chopped pecans
1 pkg. (6½ oz.) fluffy white frosting mix	

Heat oven to 350° F. Prepare cake batter according to package directions, using eggs; turn into greased 13x9x2-inch pan. Bake 30 to 35 minutes. Just before cake is done, prepare frosting according to package directions; fold in flavoring. Spread frosting over top of warm cake; sprinkle with nuts. Bake 5 minutes or until lightly browned.

COCONUT WHIPPED CREAM CAKE

½ pkg. yellow cake mix	1 pkg. (6½ oz.) fluffy white frosting mix
⅔ c. heavy cream, whipped and sweetened	2 c. flaked coconut

Heat oven to 350° F. Prepare ½ package of cake mix following directions on package. Turn into greased and floured 9-inch pie plate. Bake 20 to 25 minutes or until done. Cool 10 minutes; remove cake from pie plate. Cool thoroughly. Split cold cake in half, making 2 layers. Spread whipped cream between layers. Prepare frosting according to package directions. Frost top and sides of cake generously. Sprinkle with coconut; chill.

Chapter Twenty-Four

Cookies

Looking for cookies to fill the cookie jar? Want to mail a package of goodies to a homesick soldier, or to a daughter away at college? Having a tea for the bride? Or have the warm, wonderful Christmas holidays arrived? Whatever your need, that special recipe you are looking for will probably be here in our little treasury of cookies. Here are nut-filled brownies, golden toasty oatmeal cookies, tiny doughnuts, crisp lemony wafers, elfin meringue mushrooms, and so many more!

Secrets for Successful Cookies

Baking

· Use shiny cookie sheets. Dark cookie sheets absorb heat and may over-brown bottoms of cookies.

· Cookies bake best if you bake one sheet at a time. Bake on oven rack placed in upper third of oven. If you wish to bake two sheets of cookies at a time, add another rack in the oven close to the first rack. Place one cookie sheet on each rack; reverse sheets from top to bottom racks part way through baking, for more even browning.

· Cool sheets before baking more cookies to prevent shortening in cookies from melting while you are filling the sheet—this would spoil the shape of your cookies.

· For a quick trick when baking a quantity of cookies, place unbaked cookies on heavy-duty aluminum foil cut to fit cookie sheet. You will then be able to slide the foil onto the warm cookie sheet and pop the whole thing right in the oven.

· Cookies should always be thoroughly cooled before storing. It is best to transfer them to wire racks for quick cooling. Do not overlap cookies as this could cause them to stick together and lose their shape.

Storing

· Bar cookies may be cooled, then covered and stored in the pan in which they were baked. However, if there are only a few left, it is best to remove them from the baking pan and wrap in transparent plastic wrap or aluminum foil. Soft cookies should be stored in a container with a tight-fitting cover. Crisp cookies store well in a container with a loose-fitting cover.

· Store fragile or specially frosted cookies in a roasting or baking pan. Cover with transparent plastic wrap or aluminum foil. It will form a little "tent" over the cookies.

· To mail cookies, select your recipe with care. Most bar cookies, including brownies, will travel well, as will sugar cookies, chocolate chip cookies, and other firm drop cookies. Choose a sturdy carton for mailing. Wrap the cookies, a few at a time, in transparent plastic wrap or aluminum foil. Fill corners and in-between spaces of carton with popcorn or shredded newspapers to cushion cookies. If you save coffee cans or large shortening cans with the plastic snap-off covers, these cans make ideal containers for sending cookies through the mail. Place cans in sturdy carton, cushion with shredded paper.

BAR COOKIES

DATE-NUT BARS

1 pkg. (8 oz.) dates, cut up	½ c. brown sugar, firmly packed
2 tbs. sugar	1 c. sifted all-purpose flour
⅓ c. water	¼ tsp. baking soda
¼ c. chopped nuts	½ tsp. salt
⅓ c. butter or margarine	¾ c. rolled oats

Cook dates, 2 tablespoons sugar, and water over low heat, stirring constantly about 10 minutes, or until thickened. Cool. Stir in nuts. Grease 9x9x2-inch baking pan. Heat oven to 400° F. Blend butter or margarine and brown sugar. Sift flour, soda, and salt together; stir into butter mixture; stir in oats. Press two thirds of mixture over bottom of prepared pan. Spread date filling evenly over surface. Sprinkle with remaining one third mixture, patting slightly onto filling. Bake 25 minutes or until lightly browned. Cut into bars while still warm. Makes 2 dozen.

DOUBLE CHOCOLATE BROWNIES

1½ c. sifted all-purpose flour	½ c. butter or margarine
½ tsp. baking powder	1½ c. sugar
½ tsp. salt	2 eggs, slightly beaten
3 sqs. unsweetened chocolate	½ c. semi-sweet chocolate pieces
	¾ c. chopped nuts

Heat oven to 350° F. Grease 8x8x2-inch pan. Sift flour, baking powder, and salt together. Melt chocolate and butter or margarine in top of double boiler over hot, not boiling, water; remove from heat. Gradually beat in sugar. Blend in eggs. Add dry ingredients, semi-sweet chocolate pieces, and nuts. Spread batter evenly in prepared pan. Bake 30 to 35 minutes or until top has dull crust. Cool on wire rack. Makes 16.

TWO-TONED BROWNIES

1 c. butter or margarine	½ tsp. salt
2 c. brown sugar, firmly packed	1½ tsp. baking powder
3 eggs	1 c. coarsely chopped walnuts or pecans
2 tsp. vanilla	
2 c. sifted all-purpose flour	2 sqs. unsweetened chocolate, melted

Heat oven to 350° F. Grease 11x7x2-inch baking dish. Melt butter or margarine; beat in sugar; cool slightly; beat in eggs and vanilla. Sift flour, salt, and baking powder together; stir into sugar mixture; add nuts. Divide batter in half; blend melted chocolate into one half. Spread chocolate mixture in pan. Spread remaining half of batter carefully on top of chocolate layer. Bake 30 to 35 minutes or until done. Cool on wire rack. Makes 16.

NEW ORLEANS PECAN BARS

1 c. sifted all-purpose flour	2 eggs
¼ tsp. baking powder	¾ c. dark corn syrup
½ c. soft butter or margarine	⅓ c. brown sugar, firmly packed
⅓ c. brown sugar, firmly packed	3 tbs. all-purpose flour
½ c. finely chopped pecans	½ tsp. salt
	1 tsp. vanilla
	1 c. coarsely broken pecans

Heat oven to 350° F. Grease 11x7x2-inch baking dish. Combine 1 cup flour, baking powder, butter or margarine, ⅓ cup brown sugar, and ½ cup chopped pecans. Work mixture until it is crumbly; press into pan. Bake 10 minutes. Beat eggs well; add corn syrup, ⅓ cup brown sugar, 3 tablespoons flour, salt, and vanilla. Pour over baked layer in pan; sprinkle with remaining 1 cup pecans; bake an additional 25 minutes. Cool on wire rack. Makes 16.

PERSIAN SWEETS

1 c. sifted all-purpose flour	1 tsp. grated orange rind
1 c. sugar	2 tbs. orange juice
1 tsp. baking powder	1 c. chopped dates
¼ tsp. salt	1 c. chopped walnuts
3 eggs	Sugar

Heat oven to 350° F. Grease 11x7x2-inch baking dish. Sift flour, sugar, baking powder, and salt together. Beat eggs until thick and lemon-colored; stir in sifted dry ingredients, orange rind and juice, dates, and nuts. Pour into baking pan. Bake 30 minutes. Cool slightly on wire rack. Cut into finger-length pieces; roll in sugar. Makes about 3 dozen.

APRICOT MERINGUE BARS

½ c. soft butter or margarine	1 c. apricot preserves
½ c. sugar	2 egg whites
2 egg yolks	⅓ c. sugar
1¼ c. sifted all-purpose flour	1 c. finely chopped walnuts

Heat oven to 350° F. Grease 11x7x2-inch baking dish. Blend butter or margarine, ½ cup sugar, and egg yolks together; work in flour. Lightly flour hands; pat mixture into baking dish. Bake 15 minutes; remove from oven; spread evenly with preserves. Beat egg whites until foamy; gradually beat in ⅓ cup sugar; continue beating until meringue forms stiff, glossy peaks; fold in nuts. Spread carefully over preserves. Return to oven; bake 25 minutes. Cool on wire rack. Makes about 16.

WALNUT MERINGUE BARS
(Walnuss Meringe)

½ lb. unsalted butter or margarine	1 c. currant jelly
	4 egg whites
½ c. sugar	1 c. sugar
1 egg yolk	1 tsp. lemon extract
½ tsp. salt	¾ c. finely ground walnuts
2½ c. sifted all-purpose flour	1 c. chopped walnuts

Heat oven to 350° F. Cream butter or margarine with ½ cup sugar. Blend in egg yolk and salt. Add flour. Pat into 10x15-inch rectangle on cookie sheet. Spread jelly over dough to within ¼ inch of edge of dough. Beat egg whites until foamy. Gradually beat in 1 cup sugar; continue beating until meringue forms stiff, glossy peaks. Fold in lemon extract and ground walnuts. Spread meringue over jelly layer, sealing to edge of dough. Sprinkle chopped walnuts over meringue. Bake 35 to 40 minutes or until browned. Cut into squares while warm. Makes 3 dozen.

NUT BARS (Frystekaka)

2½ c. sifted all-purpose flour	1 egg
2 tsp. baking powder	1¼ c. blanched almonds, finely chopped
1 c. butter or margarine	2 c. sifted confectioners' sugar
½ c. granulated sugar	3 tbs. sherry
	1 egg white

Sift flour and baking powder into bowl; cut in butter or margarine with pastry blender. Add ½ cup sugar and egg; blend well. Chill dough at least 2 hours. Combine remaining ingredients in small bowl. Heat oven to 375° F. Place half the chilled dough in 13x9x2-inch baking pan; pat out evenly to cover pan; spread almond mixture over dough. Roll remaining half of dough between two pieces of wax paper to 13x9-inch rectangle; carefully peel off top paper. Invert dough and paper onto filling in pan; peel off paper; pat dough gently to fit. Bake 30 to 35 minutes or until lightly browned. Cool on wire rack. Makes about 4 dozen.

DROP COOKIES

CHOCOLATE CHIP COOKIES

¾ c. butter or margarine	1⅔ c. sifted all-purpose flour
⅓ c. granulated sugar	½ tsp. baking soda
⅓ c. brown sugar, firmly packed	½ tsp. salt
	½ c. chopped nuts
1 egg	1 pkg. (6 oz.) semi-sweet chocolate pieces
1 tsp. vanilla	

Heat oven to 375° F. Beat butter or margarine, sugars, egg, and vanilla in large bowl until fluffy. Sift flour, baking soda, and salt together; blend into butter mixture. Stir in nuts and chocolate. Drop by rounded teaspoonfuls, about 2 inches apart, onto lightly greased cookie sheets. Bake 8 to 10 minutes or until golden brown. Cool slightly before removing from cookie sheets. Transfer to wire racks; cool. Makes about 4 dozen.

SOFT MOLASSES COOKIES

2½ c. sifted all-purpose flour	½ c. sugar
1 tsp. ground ginger	½ c. molasses
1 tsp. ground cinnamon	1 egg
¼ tsp. salt	2 tsp. baking soda
½ c. soft butter or margarine	2 tsp. hot water
	¼ c. cold water
	½ c. raisins

Heat oven to 400° F. Sift flour, ginger, cinnamon, and salt together. Beat butter or margarine, sugar, molasses, and egg together in bowl until light and fluffy. Dissolve baking soda in hot water; stir into creamed mixture. Add sifted dry ingredients alternately with cold water; beat until blended; stir in raisins. Drop by rounded teaspoonfuls, about 3 inches apart, onto lightly greased cookie sheets. Bake 10 minutes. Transfer to wire racks; cool. Makes about 3 dozen.

HIGHLAND OATMEAL COOKIES

1 c. sifted all-purpose flour	½ c. granulated sugar
½ tsp. salt	1 egg
½ tsp. baking soda	2 tsp. vanilla
1 c. soft butter or margarine	¼ c. water
	½ c. chopped nuts
1 c. brown sugar, firmly packed	½ c. raisins
	3 c. rolled oats
	Pecan halves

Heat oven to 350° F. Sift flour, salt, and baking soda together. Beat butter or margarine, sugars, egg, and vanilla until light and fluffy. Add sifted dry ingredients alternately with water, blending thoroughly after each addition. Stir in nuts and raisins; stir in rolled oats 1 cup at a time; mix well. Drop by rounded teaspoonfuls, about 2 inches apart, onto lightly greased cookie sheets. Press a pecan half into the top of each cookie. Bake 12 to 15 minutes. Transfer to wire racks; cool. Makes about 4 dozen.

BUTTERSCOTCH DROPS

¼ c. soft butter or margarine	¼ tsp. salt
	½ tsp. vanilla
1¼ c. brown sugar, firmly packed	½ c. coarsely chopped nuts
1 egg	¾ c. golden raisins, washed, drained, and coarsely chopped
⅔ c. sifted all-purpose flour	
1 tsp. baking powder	

Heat oven to 325° F. Beat butter or margarine, brown sugar, and egg in bowl until light and fluffy. Sift flour, baking powder, and salt together; stir into creamed mixture; blend in vanilla, nuts, and raisins. Drop by rounded teaspoonfuls, about 2 inches apart,

onto greased cookie sheets. Bake 15 minutes. Let stand 1 to 2 minutes; transfer to wire racks; cool. If cookies become difficult to remove from cookie sheet, return to oven for one minute. Makes about 3½ dozen.

GUMDROP COOKIES

½ c. butter or margarine	1⅔ c. sifted all-purpose flour
½ c. brown sugar, firmly packed	½ tsp. baking soda
	¼ tsp. salt
¼ c. granulated sugar	¼ c. buttermilk
1 egg	2 c. tiny multi-colored gumdrops, halved

Heat oven to 400° F. Beat butter or margarine, sugars, and egg until light and fluffy. Sift flour, baking soda, and salt together; add alternately with buttermilk to creamed mixture. Stir in gumdrops. Drop mixture by rounded teaspoonfuls about 2 inches apart, onto greased cookie sheets. Bake 8 to 10 minutes or until lightly browned. Transfer to wire racks; cool. Makes about 3½ dozen.

FUDGIES

3½ c. sifted all-purpose flour	1 c. brown sugar, firmly packed
½ tsp. baking powder	½ c. granulated sugar
½ tsp. baking soda	2 eggs
½ tsp. salt	2 tsp. vanilla
¾ c. soft butter or margarine	4 sqs. unsweetened chocolate, melted
	¼ c. milk

Heat oven to 350° F. Sift flour, baking powder, baking soda, and salt together. Beat butter or margarine, sugars, eggs, and vanilla in bowl until light and fluffy; stir in chocolate. Add sifted dry ingredients alternately with milk, blending thoroughly after each addition. Drop dough by rounded teaspoonfuls, about 2 inches apart, onto greased cookie sheets. Bake 10 to 12 minutes. Transfer to wire racks; cool. Makes about 3 dozen.

Nut Fudgies

Stir 1 cup finely chopped walnuts or pecans into Fudgies dough. Drop by rounded teaspoonfuls, about 2 inches apart, onto cookie sheets, and bake and cool as above.

Peppermint Chocolate Sandwiches

Pinch off pieces of Fudgies dough; roll into balls and place on cookie sheets about 2 inches apart. Press cookie dough down with buttered, sugared tumbler until about ⅛ inch thick. Bake and cool as above. Put two together with Pink Peppermint Frosting: Blend ¼ cup soft butter or margarine, 2 cups sifted confectioners' sugar, 2 tablespoons milk, ¼ teaspoon peppermint extract, and a few drops red food coloring until of good spreading consistency.

HOLIDAY NUGGETS

¾ c. butter or margarine	½ tsp. salt
¾ c. sugar	1 c. flaked coconut
1 egg	¾ c. golden or dark raisins
1 tsp. grated lemon rind	¼ c. candied cherries, coarsely chopped
2 c. sifted all-purpose flour	

Heat oven to 350° F. Cream butter or margarine in large bowl until soft; add sugar gradually, creaming well after each addition; continue creaming until light and fluffy. Stir in egg and lemon rind. Sift flour and salt into creamed mixture; mix to form stiff dough; stir in coconut, raisins, and cherries. Drop by teaspoonfuls, about 2 inches apart, onto greased cookie sheets. Bake 15 to 18 minutes or until golden. Transfer to wire racks; cool. Makes about 3 dozen.

MERINGUES

4 egg whites	1¼ c. sugar
¼ tsp. cream of tartar	1 tsp. almond extract

Heat oven to 250° F. Grease and flour cookie sheets or cut brown wrapping paper to fit. Beat egg whites with cream of tartar until foamy. Gradually add sugar and almond extract. Continue beating until meringue forms stiff, glossy peaks. Press mixture through pastry bag or drop by heaping teaspoonfuls, about 2 inches apart, onto prepared cookie sheets. Bake 30 to 40 minutes or until set but not brown. Transfer to wire racks; cool. Makes about 2½ dozen.

Peppermint Meringues

Prepare Meringues, substituting ½ teaspoon peppermint extract for the almond extract. Divide mixture in half. Tint one half pale pink with red food coloring; tint remaining half pale green with green food coloring. Bake and cool as Meringues.

Cherry Meringues

Prepare Meringues. Fold in ¼ cup chopped maraschino cherries. Bake and cool as Meringues.

Meringue Jewels

Prepare Meringues. Fold in ¾ cup diced candied fruits. Bake and cool as Meringues.

Meringue Mushrooms

Prepare Meringues. Drop large round tip into pastry bag, or you may use just the pastry bag. Spoon a portion of meringue into pastry bag. Do not fill bag too full, as it may be hard to manage. Form mushroom crowns by holding pastry bag fairly close to surface and pressing mixture out into cap shape; release

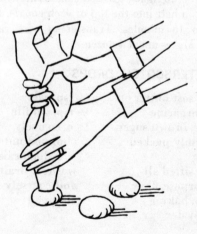

pressure. Smooth top with finger if peaked. To make stems, hold bag in vertical position; press mixture onto cookie sheet; pull straight up until short stem forms; release pressure.

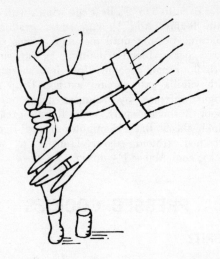

Bake 30 to 40 minutes until dry and ivory colored. Do not allow to brown. Cool slightly on cookie sheets. Loosen with spatula; transfer to wire racks; cool. Melt ½ cup semi-sweet chocolate pieces over hot, not boiling, water. Press indentation in bottom of crown with finger or rounded tip of wooden spoon handle. Paint indented portions of crowns with liquid chocolate; press stems into crowns at once; allow chocolate to set. Store in tightly covered container in a cool, dry place. Do not refrigerate. Will keep well two weeks. Makes about 2 dozen meringues.

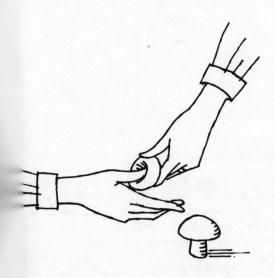

ALMOND WAFER CONES
(Cornets Amandine)

3 egg whites	⅓ c. butter or
Dash of salt	margarine,
½ c. sugar	melted and
⅓ c. sifted all-	cooled
purpose flour	½ tsp. almond
⅓ c. finely ground	extract
almonds	

Heat oven to 400° F. Beat egg whites with salt until stiff but not dry. Fold in sugar, flour, and almonds. Gently fold in cooled butter or margarine and almond extract. Drop by teaspoonfuls about 3 inches apart, (do only 3 at a time) on greased cookie sheet; spread with back of spoon. Bake 3 to 4 minutes or until edges are lightly browned. Cool a few seconds. Remove with thin spatula; quickly shape into cornucopias. Cool on wire racks; store in airtight container. Fill with *Cocoa Butter Cream:* Cream ⅓ cup soft butter or margarine, dash of salt, 1 pound sifted confectioners' sugar, ½ cup cocoa, and 2 teaspoons instant coffee. Blend in ⅓ cup light cream and ½ teaspoon vanilla. Makes 4 dozen.

CHOCOLATE ALMOND MACAROONS
(Schokaladenmakronen Mit Mandeln)

3 egg whites	1 pkg. (6 oz.) semi-
1 tbs. vinegar	sweet chocolate
½ tsp. salt	pieces
1 c. sugar	1 tbs. shortening
1 c. finely chopped,	Finely chopped
blanched	pistachio nuts
almonds	
4 sqs. unsweetened	
chocolate,	
coarsely grated	

Heat oven to 275° F. Beat egg whites, vinegar, and salt in large bowl until foamy. Add sugar gradually. Continue beating until meringue forms stiff, glossy peaks. (This takes about 10 minutes.) Fold in almonds and grated chocolate very gently. Drop by teaspoonfuls, about 1 inch apart, on lightly greased cookie sheets. Bake 20 to 25 minutes or until set. Transfer to wire racks; cool. Melt semi-sweet chocolate pieces and shortening in top of double boiler over hot, not boiling, water. Swirl on tops of cookies from tip of spoon. Sprinkle with chopped pistachio nuts. Makes 10 to 11 dozen.

BRANDY SNAPS

2 tbs. corn syrup
⅓ c. molasses
½ c. butter or margarine
1 c. sifted all-purpose flour

¾ c. sugar
1 tsp. ground ginger (No brandy is required)

Heat oven to 300° F. Heat corn syrup and molasses just to boiling. Remove from heat; add butter or margarine. Sift flour, sugar, and ginger together; stir gradually into molasses mixture; mix well. Drop by teaspoonfuls, about 3 inches apart, onto greased cookie sheet. Bake 10 to 12 minutes. Let stand about 2 minutes to cool slightly. Loosen one cookie at a time; roll over cornucopia form or handle of wooden spoon; let cool, slip off carefully when firm. Serve plain or fill with *Whipped Apricot Cream:* Fold ¼ cup chopped, cooked dried apricots into 2 cups sweetened whipped cream. Makes about 2 dozen.

HERMITS

1 c. butter or margarine
2 c. brown sugar, firmly packed
2 eggs
½ c. cool, brewed coffee
3½ c. sifted all-purpose flour
1 tsp. baking soda

½ tsp. salt
½ tsp. ground nutmeg
1½ tsp. ground cinnamon
2 c. raisins, chopped
1½ c. chopped walnuts

Heat oven to 400° F. Beat butter or margarine, sugar and eggs together until well-blended. Stir in coffee. Sift flour, soda, salt, nutmeg, and cinnamon together. Blend into shortening mixture. Stir in raisins and walnuts. Drop mixture by rounded teaspoonfuls, about 2 inches apart, onto greased cookie sheets. Bake 8 to 10 minutes or until cookie feels almost firm. Makes about 7½ dozen.

COCONUT MACAROONS

2 egg whites
⅛ tsp. salt
⅔ c. sugar
2 tbs. flour

1 can (3½ oz.) flaked coconut
¼ tsp. vanilla
½ tsp. almond extract

Heat oven to 325° F. Beat egg whites with salt until foamy. Add ⅓ cup sugar gradually. Continue beating until meringue forms stiff, glossy peaks. Blend remaining ⅓ cup sugar with flour and coconut; fold into meringue with vanilla and almond extract. Drop meringue mixture by rounded teaspoonfuls, about 2 inches apart, onto lightly greased cookie sheets. Bake 15 minutes or until lightly browned around edges. Transfer to wire racks; cool. Makes 1½ dozen.

PRESSED COOKIES

SPRITZ

1 c. soft butter or margarine
¾ c. sugar
3 egg yolks

1 tsp. vanilla or almond extract
2¾ c. sifted all-purpose flour

Heat oven to 400° F. Combine butter or margarine, sugar, egg yolks, and extract in bowl. Work in flour gradually. Press dough through cookie press, in design of your choice, about 1 inch apart, onto ungreased cookie sheets. Bake 7 to 10 minutes until just set, but not brown. Transfer to wire racks; cool. Decorate with candied cherries, if desired. Makes 5½ dozen.

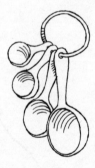

Double-Dip Nut Fingers

Prepare Spritz. Press dough through notched star tube of cookie press onto ungreased cookie sheets, making each cookie about 3 inches long. Bake; cool. Melt 1 package (6 ounces) semi-sweet chocolate pieces in top of double boiler, over hot, not boiling, water; blend in 2 tablespoons milk. Dip ends of cookies into chocolate, then into chocolate shot, nuts, colored sprinkles, or coconut. Place on wax paper until set. Makes 4 dozen.

Cinnamon Spritz

Prepare Spritz; add 1 teaspoon cinnamon with flour. Decorate as desired. Makes about 5½ dozen.

CHOCOLATE SPRITZ SANDWICHES

1 c. soft butter or margarine	1½ tsp. vanilla
2 sqs. unsweetened chocolate, melted and cooled	2⅓ c. sifted all-purpose flour
¾ c. sugar	1 can (13–14 oz.) vanilla frosting
3 egg yolks	Red or green food coloring

Heat oven to 400° F. Combine butter or margarine, chocolate, sugar, egg yolks, and vanilla in bowl; beat until fluffy. Blend in flour. Press dough through cookie press in design of your choice onto ungreased cookie sheets. Bake 7 to 10 minutes. Transfer to wire racks; cool. Sandwich cookies with prepared frosting tinted pink or green with food coloring. Makes about 3 dozen sandwiches.

ANISE COOKIES

1 c. soft butter or margarine	1½ tsp. anise extract
½ c. sifted confectioners' sugar	2½ c. sifted all-purpose flour
1 egg yolk	Confectioners' sugar

Heat oven to 350° F. Blend butter or margarine, ½ cup sugar, egg yolk, and extract together. Blend in flour slowly. Put mixture in pastry bag fitted with notched star tube. Press mixture onto ungreased baking sheets in tiny but tall swirls about 1 inch apart. Bake 8 minutes or until set but not brown. Do not overbake. Transfer cookies to wire rack; cool. When cool, shake a light cloud of confectioners' sugar over tops and decorate, if desired, with a tiny candied lilac floret. Makes about 3½ dozen.

3-WAY COOKIES

These cookies are versatile. They may be shaped easily and quickly as described in the recipe; they may be dropped by rounded teaspoonfuls onto cookie sheets when a soft cookie is desired; or they may be chilled and rolled out to be cut with fancy-shaped cookie cutters.

OLD-FASHIONED SUGAR COOKIES

3½ c. sifted all-purpose flour	1½ c. sugar
2½ tsp. baking powder	2 eggs
½ tsp. salt	3 tsp. vanilla
1 c. soft butter or margarine	Butter Sugar

Heat oven to 400° F. Sift flour, baking powder, and salt together. Beat butter or margarine, sugar, eggs, and vanilla in bowl until light and fluffy; add sifted dry ingredients gradually; blend thoroughly. Pinch off small pieces of dough; roll between palms of hands into balls about 1 inch in diameter; place about 2 inches apart on lightly greased cookie sheets. Butter bottom of water tumbler; dip in sugar; press balls of dough down carefully until they are about ⅛ inch

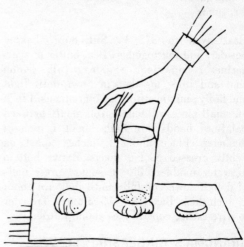

thick. Bake 10 to 12 minutes or until edges are golden. Transfer to wire racks; cool. Makes about 4 dozen.

Fresh Orange Cookies

Prepare dough as for Sugar Cookies, omitting vanilla. Add 1 tablespoon grated orange rind and 2 tablespoons orange juice. Shape into 1-inch balls; roll in granulated sugar; press down with tumbler. Bake and cool as directed. Decorate with Orange Frosting, if desired: Blend ¼ cup soft butter or margarine, 2 cups sifted confectioners' sugar, 2 tablespoons orange juice. and a few drops of yellow food coloring until of good spreading consistency.

Semisweets

Prepare dough as for Sugar Cookies. Chop 1 package (6 oz.) semi-sweet chocolate pieces finely; stir into dough. Shape and bake as directed. (If you wish to make these with only half the dough, use ½ package [½ cup] semi-sweet chocolate pieces, finely chopped.)

Other variations: Add 1 cup chopped nuts or ½ cup raisins and ½ cup chopped nuts to Sugar Cookie dough. Bake and cool as directed.

LEMON CRISPS

2½ c. sifted all-purpose flour	1 egg
½ tsp. baking powder	1 egg yolk
	1 tbs. grated lemon rind
¼ tsp. salt	3 tbs. lemon juice
¾ c. soft butter or margarine	Butter
	Sugar
1 c. sugar	

Heat oven to 375° F. Sift flour, baking powder, and salt together. Beat butter or margarine, 1 cup sugar, egg, egg yolk, lemon rind and juice together in bowl until light and fluffy; mix in sifted dry ingredients. Pinch off small pieces of dough; roll gently between palms of hands into balls about 1 inch in diameter. Place about 2 inches apart on lightly greased cookie sheets. Butter bottom of water tumbler; dip in sugar; press balls of dough down carefully until they are about ⅛ inch thick. Bake 12 to 15 minutes. Transfer to wire racks; cool. Makes about 3 dozen.

GRANDMA'S GINGERSNAP LEAVES

2½ c. sifted all-purpose flour	¾ c. sugar
2 tsp. ground ginger	1 egg
¼ tsp. ground cloves	½ c. molasses
¼ tsp. salt	2 tsp. baking soda
	1 tbs. hot water
⅓ c. soft butter or margarine	Sugar

Heat oven to 350° F. Sift flour, ginger, cloves, and salt together. Beat butter or margarine, ¾ cup sugar, egg, and molasses together in bowl until light and fluffy. Combine baking soda and water; stir into creamed mixture; mix in sifted dry ingredients. Pinch off small pieces of dough; roll between palms of hands into cylinders; taper one end to a point; dip in sugar to coat; place on greased cookie sheet. Press down carefully with spatula. Press wooden pick flat into cookie to make leaf veins. Cookies may also be shaped into 1-inch balls, pressed down, and baked. Bake 12 to 15 minutes. Transfer to wire racks; cool. Makes about 3 dozen.

MOLDED COOKIES

DOUBLE PEANUT CHUNKIES

1⅓ c. sifted all-purpose flour	⅔ c. cream-style peanut butter
½ tsp. baking powder	⅓ c. granulated sugar
¾ tsp. baking soda	½ c. brown sugar, firmly packed
¼ tsp. salt	1 egg
½ c. soft butter or margarine	1 c. finely chopped peanuts*

Heat oven to 375° F. Sift flour, baking powder, baking soda, and salt together. Beat butter or margarine, peanut butter, sugars, and egg in bowl until light and fluffy; mix in sifted dry ingredients. Pinch off small pieces of dough; roll gently into cylinders between palms of hands. Roll in chopped peanuts to coat well. Place about 2 inches apart on lightly greased cookie sheets; press down slightly with spatula. Bake 10 to 12 minutes. Transfer to wire racks; cool. Makes about 2 dozen.

* If peanuts are salted, wash with warm water and dry on paper towels.

CINNAMON-SUGAR COOKIES

2¾ c. sifted all- purpose flour	1½ c. sugar
2 tsp. cream of tartar	2 eggs 1 egg white, slightly beaten
1 tsp. baking soda	2 tbs. sugar
½ tsp. salt	1 tbs. cinnamon
1 c. butter or margarine	

Heat oven to 350° F. Sift flour, cream of tartar, baking soda, and salt together. Beat butter or margarine, 1½ cups sugar, and eggs together in bowl until light and fluffy. Add dry ingredients; blend. Shape dough into small balls; dip in egg white, then in mixture of 2 tablespoons sugar and cinnamon. Place about 2 inches apart on greased cookie sheets; press down centers with tines of fork. Bake 12 to 15 minutes or until lightly browned. Transfer to wire racks; cool. Makes about 5 dozen.

BIRDS' NESTS

2 c. sifted all- purpose flour	2 egg yolks 1 tsp. vanilla
¼ tsp. salt	2 egg whites, slightly beaten
1 c. soft butter or margarine	2 c. finely chopped nuts
½ c. brown sugar, firmly packed	Preserves or jellies

Heat oven to 350° F. Sift flour and salt together. Beat butter or margarine, sugar, egg yolks, and vanilla in bowl until light and fluffy. Work in sifted dry ingredients; mix until smooth. Pinch off small pieces of dough; roll gently between palms of hands to form balls about 1 inch in diameter. Dip in egg white, then in chopped nuts; place about 2 inches apart on ungreased cookie sheets. Flatten cookies slightly with palm of hand;

make indentation in center of each with thumb. Bake 12 to 15 minutes or until set. Transfer to wire racks; cool. Fill centers of cooled cookies with bright bits of preserves or jellies. Makes about 3½ dozen.

CHINESE ALMOND COOKIES

1 c. soft butter or margarine	3¼ c. sifted all- purpose flour
1 c. sugar	1½ tsp. baking soda
1 egg	1 c. whole,
¼ c. light corn syrup	blanched, shelled almonds
2 tbs. almond extract	1 egg 2 tbs. water

Heat oven to 350° F. Beat butter or margarine, sugar, and egg together until light and fluffy. Blend in corn syrup and almond extract. Combine flour and baking soda; blend into shortening mixture. Pinch off small pieces of dough about the size of a walnut; form into balls; place 2 inches apart on greased cookie sheets. Flatten each ball with palm of hand to ¼-inch thickness (cookies should be thick). Press a whole almond in center of each cookie. Beat egg with water; brush top of each cookie for a shiny glaze. Bake 12 to 15 minutes or until golden brown. Transfer to wire racks; cool. Makes 4 dozen.

SNOWDROPS

2 c. sifted all- purpose flour	½ c. sifted con- fectioners' sugar
¼ tsp. salt	1 tsp. vanilla
1 c. butter or margarine	Confectioners' sugar

Heat oven to 350° F. Sift flour and salt together. Beat butter or margarine, sugar, and vanilla in bowl until light and fluffy. Work in sifted dry ingredients gradually until mixture is smooth. Pinch off small pieces of dough; roll gently between palms of hands to form balls about 1 inch in diameter. Place about 1 inch apart on ungreased cookie sheets. Bake 12 to 15 minutes or until edges are light golden brown. Do not overbake or allow cookies to become brown. Transfer to wire racks; set rack on large piece of wax paper. Cool cookies slightly; sprinkle with confectioners' sugar. Let cookies cool completely; sprinkle generously with additional confectioners' sugar. Makes about 3½ dozen.

Almond Crescents

Prepare Snowdrops, stirring 1 cup ground almonds into creamed butter or margarine mixture; add flour mixture. Roll small pieces of dough gently into cylinders; shape into crescents. Bake and cool as directed.

SWEDISH BRANDY RINGS

3½ c. sifted all-purpose flour	1⅓ c. butter or margarine
1 c. sugar	⅓ c. chopped, blanched almonds
½ tsp. salt	
¼ c. brandy or lemon juice	

Sift flour, ¾ cup sugar, and salt into large bowl; add brandy or lemon juice. Cut in butter or margarine with pastry blender or two knives; mix with wooden spoon to form a smooth dough. Flour hands and pinch off small pieces of dough. Roll each piece into 6-inch-long strip; twist two strips together;

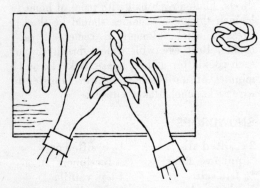

form into ring. Mix almonds and remaining ¼ cup sugar; spread on wax paper. Press rings down in sugar mixture; place, sugared side up, on greased cookie sheets. Bake at 400° F. for 8 to 10 minutes. Cookies should not be brown. Transfer to wire racks; cool. Makes about 3 dozen.

WREATHS (Berliner Kränze)

1 c. butter or margarine	½ tsp. almond extract
1 c. sifted confectioners' sugar	3 c. sifted all-purpose flour
2 egg yolks	1 egg white, slightly beaten
1 tbs. water	Green sugar
2 hard-cooked egg yolks, sieved	Candied cherries
½ tsp. vanilla	

Cream butter or margarine; gradually add confectioners' sugar. Add egg yolks, water, and sieved egg yolks. Add vanilla and almond extract. Add flour gradually; mix until blended. Chill 1 hour. Heat oven to 375° F. Roll a rounded teaspoonful of dough at a time on lightly floured board into a strip ¼ inch wide and 7 to 8 inches long. Loop ends to form a knot. Place on cookie sheet. Brush wreaths with egg white; sprinkle with green sugar. Bake 10 to 12 minutes or until very lightly browned. Transfer to wire racks; cool; garnish at knot with slivers of candied cherries. Makes 4 dozen.

SUGAR PRETZELS

½ c. butter or margarine	1¾ c. sifted all-purpose flour
½ c. sugar	½ tsp. baking soda
1 egg	½ tsp. salt
1 egg yolk	1 egg white
1½ tsp. orange extract	1 tbs. water
	1 c. finely chopped nuts

Beat butter or margarine, sugar, egg, egg yolk, and orange extract in bowl until light and fluffy. Sift flour, baking soda, and salt together; blend into butter-sugar mixture. Chill 2 hours in refrigerator or 20 minutes in freezer. Heat oven to 350° F. Break off small pieces of dough; roll on lightly floured board with palms of hands to pencil size, about 5 inches long and ¼ inch thick. Take single strand of dough; hold one end in each hand and quickly form loops; press ends down firmly. Brush cookies with egg white beaten slightly with water; sprinkle with chopped nuts. Place on lightly greased cookie sheets. Bake 12 to 15 minutes. Transfer to wire racks; cool. Makes about 3½ dozen.

CANDY CANES (Yulestav)

1⅓ c. butter or margarine	3 tbs. milk
¾ c. sugar	½ tsp. almond extract
3¾ c. sifted all-purpose flour	Red food coloring

Cream butter or margarine and sugar. Add flour alternately with milk and almond extract. Mix until blended. Divide dough in half, add enough food coloring to half the dough to tint deep pink. Chill dough 2 hours.

Heat oven to 350° F. Roll rounded teaspoon-ful of each color dough on lightly floured board to a strip ¼ inch wide and 6 inches long. Put a white strip and a pink strip side by side; twist together like rope. Place on un-greased cookie sheet. Curve top to form cane handle. Repeat to use all the dough. Bake 10 to 12 minutes or until delicately browned. Transfer to wire racks; cool. Decorate with Easy Confectioners' Sugar Glaze (*page 456*), if desired. Makes 2½ dozen.

PFEFFERNÜSSE

2¼ c. sifted all-purpose flour	¼ tsp. pepper
1 tsp. baking powder	2 eggs
2 tsp. ground cinnamon	1 c. sugar
½ tsp. ground cloves	1 tsp. grated lemon rind
½ tsp. ground mace	½ c. finely chopped candied citron
	Confectioners' sugar

Sift flour, baking powder, cinnamon, cloves, mace, and pepper together. Beat eggs until light; beat in sugar until very light and fluffy. Stir in dry ingredients. Mix in lemon rind and citron. Break off small pieces of dough; roll into 1-inch balls. Place cookies on greased cookie sheets about 1 inch apart. Cover with wax paper; let stand overnight. Bake at 350° F. for 20 minutes. Transfer to wire racks; cool. Roll in confectioners' sugar to coat. Store in tightly covered container for about a week to mellow. Makes about 4½ dozen.

POLYNÉES (Macaroon Tart)

6 tbs. butter or margarine	⅔ c. blanched almonds, or macadamia nuts, finely ground
3 tbs. sugar	
2 egg yolks	
1 c. sifted all-purpose flour	¾ c. sifted con-fectioners' sugar
	2 egg whites
	¼ tsp. almond extract

Cream butter or margarine until soft; add granulated sugar, creaming until mixture is light and fluffy. Add egg yolks and flour; blend until smooth. Chill 1 hour. While dough chills, make filling: Combine nuts, confectioners' sugar, egg whites, and almond extract in small bowl; beat until fluffy. Turn chilled dough out onto lightly floured board; shape into roll; pinch or cut off small pieces of dough. With floured hands, pat dough into thin layer to fit lightly buttered tiny, fluted tart pans or sandbakels. Fill three-quarters full with almond mixture; place on cookie sheet. Roll out remaining dough on well-floured board; cut in ½-inch-wide strips. Ar-range 2 strips in cross on top of each tart; crimp ends. Bake at 350° F. for 25 minutes or until golden brown. Let cool in tins; remove carefully from tins. Makes about 2 dozen tarts.

ROLLED COOKIES

NORWEGIAN PALETTES

1 egg	1 tsp. baking powder
½ c. sugar	½ tsp. salt
½ tsp. grated lemon rind	½ c. finely chopped almonds
½ c. butter or margarine	1 egg white, slightly beaten
1½ c. sifted all-purpose flour	Colored sugar or "shot" candies

Beat egg in large bowl; add sugar and lemon rind; continue beating until light and fluffy. Add butter or margarine; beat until butter is in pieces the size of small peas. *Secret: Leav-ing butter in small pices makes cookies flaky.* Sift flour, baking powder, and salt into egg mixture; mix until smooth; stir in almonds. Chill 1 hour. Roll chilled dough out on lightly floured board to ⅛-inch thickness; cut into rounds with floured 2½-inch cookie cutter. Cut hole in each cookie with floured thimble, slightly to one side of center, cookie will re-semble artist's palette. Brush cookies with beaten egg white; sprinkle with sugar or "shot"; transfer to greased cookie sheets with wide spatula. Bake at 350° F. for 8 to 10 min-utes. Watch carefully as these cookies brown readily. Transfer to wire racks; cool. Makes 2 dozen.

RAISIN-FILLED LEMON WAFERS

Raisin Filling

1 c. golden or dark raisins	2 tbs. flour
	Few grains of salt
½ c. brown sugar, firmly packed	2 tbs. lemon juice
	¼ c. water
	½ c. chopped nuts

Rinse raisins; drain; chop. Combine with brown sugar, flour, salt, lemon juice, and water in small saucepan. Cook over low heat, stirring constantly, until thick. Remove from heat; cool. Stir in nuts.

Dough

1¾ c. sifted all-purpose flour	1 pkg. (3 oz.) cream cheese
1 tsp. salt	⅔ c. sugar
⅛ tsp. baking soda	1 egg yolk
½ tsp. ground cinnamon	1 tsp. grated lemon rind
⅓ c. butter or margarine	1 tbs. lemon juice
¼ c. shredded process American cheese	Easy Confectioners' Sugar Glaze (*page 456*)

Sift flour, salt, baking soda, and cinnamon together. Cream butter or margarine in large bowl until soft; add cheeses and continue creaming. Add sugar gradually, creaming after each addition; continue creaming until light and fluffy. Stir in egg yolk, lemon rind and juice. Stir in sifted dry ingredients. Chill 1 hour. Roll out chilled dough on lightly floured board to ⅛-inch thickness; cut in rounds with floured 2-inch cutter. Place on greased cookie sheets. Bake at 375° F. for 6 to 8 minutes, or until edges are a delicate brown. Transfer to wire racks; cool. Put together with Raisin Filling. Decorate tops of cookies with Glaze. Top with candied cherries and angelica, if desired. Makes 3 dozen.

GINGERBREAD MEN

1 c. butter or margarine	2 tsp. baking soda
1 c. sugar	1 tsp. ground ginger
1 c. molasses	1 tsp. ground cinnamon
1 tbs. vinegar	
1 egg, beaten	¼ tsp. salt
4½ to 5 c. sifted all-purpose flour	Easy Confectioners' Sugar Glaze (*page 456*)

Put butter or margarine and sugar in large bowl. Heat molasses in saucepan to boiling; pour over butter or margarine and sugar; add vinegar; stir until well blended. Set aside to cool. When cool, add egg. Sift dry ingredients together; stir into molasses mixture; mix well. Chill overnight. Roll chilled dough out on well-floured board to ⅛-inch thickness; cut with floured, gingerbread-man shaped cookie cutter. Place on greased cookie sheets about 1 inch apart; brush with cold water. Bake at 350° F. for 8 to 10 minutes. Transfer to wire racks; cool. Decorate cooled cookies with glaze put through a pastry tube. Makes 3 dozen.

APRICOT NUT COOKIES

2 eggs	½ tsp. ground allspice
¾ c. butter or margarine	1 c. rolled oats
1 c. sugar	¾ c. finely chopped nuts
1½ c. sifted all-purpose flour	Sliced, blanched almonds
1 tsp. baking powder	Apricot preserves
1 tsp. ground cinnamon	Confectioners' sugar

Beat eggs lightly; reserve 2 tablespoons. Beat butter or margarine, sugar, and remaining beaten eggs until blended. Sift flour, baking powder, cinnamon, and allspice together; stir into creamed mixture. Add rolled oats and ¾ cup chopped nuts; chill several hours. Roll chilled dough out on floured board to ¼-inch thickness. Cut into rounds with scalloped or plain 2½-inch cookie cutter. Cut round centers out of half the cookies with ½-inch cookie cutter; brush these cookies with the reserved egg; sprinkle with sliced almonds. Place all cookies on greased cookie sheets, about 1 inch apart. Bake at 400° F. for 6 to 8 minutes. Transfer to wire racks; cool. When cool, spread solid rounds with thin layer of apricot preserves; top with cut-out rounds. Dust cookies with confectioners' sugar; spoon half teaspoon of preserves into center of each cookie. Makes 2 dozen.

LITTLE HATS (Zucker Hütchen)

1⅓ c. sifted all- purpose flour	½ c. sugar
¼ c. finely chopped citron	1 egg yolk
	2 tbs. milk
½ tsp. baking powder	1 egg white
	1½ c. sifted con- fectioners' sugar

⅓ c. butter or
   margarine
	½ c. finely chopped
	   almonds

Mix 4 tablespoons flour with citron. Combine remaining flour and baking powder. Cream butter or margarine and sugar; beat in egg yolk and milk. Add flour mixture gradually; stir in floured citron. Chill 2 hours. Heat oven to 350° F. Beat egg white until foamy. Add confectioners' sugar gradually; continue beating until meringue forms stiff, glossy peaks; fold in almonds. Roll out chilled dough on floured board to ⅛-inch thickness. Cut with floured 2-inch cookie cutter. Transfer cookies to lightly greased cookie sheets, placing them 1 inch apart. Put a spoonful of meringue in center of each cookie. Bake 10 to 12 minutes or until edges are very light brown. Transfer to wire racks; cool. Decorate with colored Decorator Frosting: Beat 1 egg white slightly; add 2 to 2½ cups sifted confectioners' sugar gradually; beat until stiff. Tint with few drops food coloring. Pipe around meringue. Makes 3½ dozen.

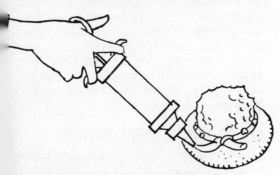

PISTACHIO DOUBLEDECKERS

½ c. butter or margarine	¼ tsp. salt
⅓ c. sugar	1 egg white
1 egg yolk	1 tbs. water
1 tsp. vanilla	1 c. chopped pistachio nuts
1⅔ c. sifted all- purpose flour	1 c. currant jelly

Blend butter or margarine, sugar, egg yolk, and vanilla in bowl. Sift flour and salt together; stir into butter-sugar mixture. Chill 2 hours. Heat oven to 375° F. Roll out small portions of chilled dough to ⅛-inch thickness. Cut out with scalloped or plain 2- or 2½-inch floured cookie cutter. Beat egg white and water slightly; brush on half the cookies. Sprinkle with nuts; leave remaining cookies plain. Place nutted and plain cookies on greased cookie sheets about 1 inch apart. Bake 10 to 12 minutes. Transfer to wire racks; cool. To assemble, spread plain cookies with thin layer of currant jelly. Press nutted top firmly on each. Makes 2½ dozen.

SCOTCH SHORTBREAD

2½ c. sifted all-
   purpose flour
	1 c. butter or
	   margarine

¾ c. sugar	

Sift flour and sugar together. Cut butter or margarine in small pieces into flour mixture. Mix in with fingers until stiff dough forms. Roll out on floured surface ½-inch thick; cut into small, fancy shapes. Place shortbread on lightly greased cookie sheets about 1 inch apart. Bake at 325° F. for 35 to 40 minutes or until golden brown. Transfer to wire racks; cool. Makes about 3 dozen.

SPRINGERLE

4 eggs	4 c. sifted all- purpose flour
2 c. sugar	¾ tsp. baking soda
1 tsp. anise extract	Anise seed

Beat eggs until light; add sugar; beat until mixture is very stiff and light, about 15 minutes at high speed on electric mixer. Add extract, flour, and soda; mix thoroughly. Roll out on lightly floured surface with regular rolling pin to ½-inch thickness. Roll with springerle rolling pin to ¼-inch thickness, pressing only once for clear imprint. Cut along dividing lines to separate cookies. Place carefully on lightly floured surface; cover with towel; let stand overnight to dry. Sprinkle greased cookie sheets with anise seed. Heat oven to 300° F. Lift cookies carefully; brush off excess flour; moisten bottom of each cookie with finger dipped in water. Place on prepared cookie sheets about 1 inch apart; bake 15 minutes or until dry but still pale and not brown. Moistened area on bottom of cookie will form characteristic "foot" of the springerle cookie. Transfer to wire racks; cool. Makes 5 to 6 dozen.

CHRISTMAS ORNAMENT COOKIES

3¾ c. sifted all- purpose flour	1 c. butter or margarine
1 tsp. baking powder	1½ c. sugar
½ tsp. salt	2 eggs
	2 tsp. vanilla

Sift flour, baking powder, and salt together; set aside. Beat butter or margarine, sugar, eggs, and vanilla in bowl until light and fluffy. Stir in sifted dry ingredients. Chill 2 hours. Heat oven to 400° F. Roll out small portions of chilled dough on lightly floured board to ¼-inch thickness. Cut out Christmas-ornament shapes (poinsettias, stars, hanging ornaments, horns, trees) with floured cookie cutters or by tracing with a sharp knife around a cardboard pattern you've made yourself. Place on greased cookie sheets about 1 inch apart. Bake 6 to 8 minutes. Transfer to wire racks; cool. Decorate as desired with packaged frosting, tinted as you wish; gumdrops; silver dragées; or other decorations. Makes about 3 dozen.

Painted Cookies: After baking and cooling Christmas Ornament Cookies, brush Christmas design of trees, stars, holly, and mistletoe with small brush and diluted food coloring.

CHRISTMAS GINGER COOKIES
(Pepparkakor)

3¾ c. sifted all- purpose flour	1 tsp. baking soda
1 tbs. ground ginger	1 c. butter or margarine
1 tbs. ground cinnamon	1 c. sugar
2 tsp. ground cloves	1 egg
	½ c. molasses

Sift flour, ginger, cinnamon, cloves, and baking soda together. Cream butter or margarine; add sugar gradually, beating until fluffy. Add egg and molasses; beat well. Add flour mixture gradually; beat until blended. Wrap in wax paper; chill overnight. Heat oven to 350° F. Roll out small portions of chilled dough on floured board. Cut out with floured, fancy cutters. Transfer to lightly greased cookie sheets; place about 1 inch apart. Bake 8 to 10 minutes or until lightly

browned. Transfer to wire racks; cool. Make design or outlines on cookies with white Decorator Frosting; see Little Hats (*page 471*). Makes 8 dozen.

LEBKUCHEN

⅔ c. honey	1 tsp. ground cloves
⅔ c. brown sugar, firmly packed	½ c. chopped candied citron
1 egg	½ c. chopped nuts
1 tsp. grated lemon rind	Candied cherries
1 tbs. lemon juice	Whole, blanched almonds
2⅔ c. sifted all- purpose flour	1 c. sugar
½ tsp. baking soda	½ c. water
1 tsp. ground cinnamon	¼ c. sifted con- fectioners' sugar
1 tsp. ground ginger	

Heat honey to boiling; cool. Add brown sugar, egg, lemon rind and juice, flour, soda, and spices; blend well. Stir in citron and ½ cup chopped nuts; chill dough several hours. Roll out chilled dough on floured board to ¼-inch thickness. Cut into rectangles 2x3 inches; place on greased cookie sheets, about 1 inch apart; decorate with cherries and almonds. Bake at 400° F. for 10 to 12 minutes. While cookies are baking, bring sugar and water to boiling in small saucepan; boil three minutes; stir in confectioners' sugar. Brush hot cookies with hot glaze; cool on wire racks. If glaze becomes stiff, add a few drops of water; heat until clear again. Store cookies in a tightly covered container to mellow. Makes about 3 dozen.

SPICED HONEY CAKES (Leckerli)

2¼ c. sifted all- purpose flour	½ tsp. grated lemon rind
2 tsp. ground cinnamon	1½ tbs. lemon juice
1 tsp. ground cloves	¼ c. brandy or kirsch
½ c. honey	⅓ c. mixed, finely chopped candied orange and lemon peel
½ c. sugar	
1 c. grated or finely ground almonds	1 c. water
	½ c. sugar

Sift flour, cinnamon, and cloves together. Simmer honey and ½ cup sugar until sugar dissolves. Remove from heat; add almonds, lemon rind and juice, and brandy or kirsch; mix well. Add flour mixture; mix until smooth. Stir in candied peel. Chill 1 hour. Roll out chilled dough on floured board ¼-inch thick to a rectangle 10x12 inches. Cut into 24 cookies. Place on well-floured board; cover; let stand overnight. Heat oven to 350° F. Combine water and ½ cup sugar in saucepan. Cook to 220° F. Remove from heat; reserve. Transfer cookies to greased cookie sheets; place about 1 inch apart. Bake 10 to 12 minutes or until very delicately browned. While cookies are baking, reheat glaze to boiling. Transfer cookies to wire racks. While hot, brush several times with glaze. Cool. Store cookies in airtight container 2 to 4 weeks to mellow. Makes 2 dozen.

DATE-NUT COOKIES

¾ c. soft butter or margarine	2 tsp. baking powder
1½ c. brown sugar, firmly packed	1 tsp. salt
1 egg	1 tsp. ground cinnamon
¼ c. milk	1 c. pitted dates, finely chopped
3 c. sifted all-purpose flour	1 c. nuts, finely chopped

Beat butter or margarine, brown sugar, egg, and milk in large bowl until well blended. Sift flour, baking powder, salt, and cinnamon into mixture; add dates and nuts. Mix thoroughly. Chill overnight. Roll chilled dough out on lightly floured board to ⅛-inch thickness; cut into rounds with floured 2-inch cutter. Place on ungreased cookie sheets, about 1 inch apart. Bake at 375° F. for 8 to 10 minutes or until lightly browned. Transfer to wire racks; cool. Makes about 5 dozen.

SPECIALTIES

KRUMKAKE

3 eggs	¼ tsp. ground cardamom
1 c. sugar	
1⅔ c. sifted all-purpose flour	¼ tsp. salt
	1 c. heavy cream

Beat eggs and sugar until very thick. Sift flour, cardamom, and salt together. Add alternately with cream to egg mixture. Heat krumkake iron to moderately hot on top of range. Do not allow to become too hot, as fragile cookies will burn. Drop a tablespoonful of batter on hot iron; bring cover down, but do not press hard. Cook over moderate heat about 30 seconds on each side. Peel cookie from iron; quickly roll around wooden dowel or cone-shaped form (whichever comes with your iron). Cookie will stiffen at once and may be removed from form as soon as you are ready to roll the next cookie. Serve as is or fill just before serving with whipped cream flavored with rum or brandy extract. Makes about 3 dozen.

MAZARINS (Nut-filled Tarts)

1 c. sifted all-purpose flour	2 eggs
¼ tsp. baking powder	1 c. sifted confectioners' sugar
5 tbs. butter or margarine	¼ tsp. almond extract
⅓ c. sifted confectioners' sugar	2 drops green food coloring
1 egg yolk	½ c. sifted confectioners' sugar
¾ c. blanched almonds, finely ground	1 tbs. water
	Chopped pistachio nuts

Sift flour and baking powder together. Cream butter or margarine in bowl until light; add ⅓ cup confectioners' sugar, creaming until mixture is light and fluffy. Stir in egg yolk and sifted flour mixture; blend until smooth. Chill 1 hour. While dough chills makes filling: Combine almonds, eggs, 1 cup confectioners' sugar, almond extract, and food coloring in medium-size bowl; blend well. Turn chilled dough out onto lightly floured board; shape into roll; pinch or cut off small pieces of dough. With floured hands, pat dough into thin layer to fit buttered tiny, fluted tart pans; fill three-quarters full with almond filling; place on cookie sheet. Bake at 350° F. for 20 minutes. Cool in tins; remove carefully. Mix confectioners' sugar and water until smooth and easy to spread. Frost tops; sprinkle with pistachio nuts. Makes 12 to 15 tarts.

ALMOND TARTS (Sandbakelser)

½ c. ground,
  blanched
  almonds
⅔ c. soft butter or
  margarine
⅔ c. sugar

1 egg white,
1 tsp. almond
  extract
1⅔ c. sifted all-
  purpose flour

Mix almonds, butter or margarine, sugar, egg white, and almond extract thoroughly in bowl. Blend in flour; chill thoroughly. Heat oven to 350° F. Press small amount of dough into tiny, fluted tart pans about 1¼ inches in diameter. Dough should form a thin shell about ¼ inch thick; do not fill pans solidly. Bake 8 to 10 minutes or until lightly browned. Cool 10 minutes; turn mold upside down; tap on table to loosen tarts. Cool thoroughly on wire racks. May be stored, covered tightly, for a week. Day of serving, serve plain, fill with slightly sweetened whipped cream, or turn over and dot top of fluted tart with bit of jelly or candied fruit, if desired. Makes about 6 dozen.

ALMOND FILLED PASTRY (Banketletter)

2 c. sifted all-
  purpose flour
1 tsp. salt
1 c. butter or
  margarine
5 tbs. ice water
2 cans (8 oz. ea.)
  almond paste

½ c. sugar
1 egg, beaten
½ tsp. lemon
  extract
1 egg white, slightly
  beaten
Sugar

Sift flour and salt together. Cut butter or margarine into flour until particles are the size of peas. Add water slowly, stirring with fork until dough forms. Wrap in wax paper; chill 1 hour. Combine almond paste, sugar, egg, and lemon extract. Form almond filling into four 12-inch rolls. Heat oven to 425° F. Roll chilled pastry on floured board into a rectangle 12½x16 inches. Cut pastry into 4 strips, each 12½x4 inches. Place a strip of pastry on wax paper. Place a roll of almond filling on edge of pastry. Lift wax paper and roll up pastry around filling; remove wax paper; press seam and ends to seal. Transfer to cookie sheet. Shape roll into a letter for a child's name or that of a party guest; use egg white to seal joined ends. Repeat with remain-

ing pastry and filling. Brush with egg white; sprinkle with sugar. Bake 25 to 30 minutes or until golden. Transfer carefully to wire racks; cool. Makes 4 letters.

FOLDING CHRISTMAS STARS (Julstjarnor)

1 lb. cold, unsalted
  butter or
  margarine
3⅓ c. sifted all-
  purpose flour

½ c. ice water
Tart red jelly
1 egg, beaten

Cut butter or margarine into flour until particles are the size of peas. Add ice water slowly while stirring with a fork until just blended. Wrap in wax paper; chill 30 minutes. Roll chilled dough out on floured board into a rectangle; fold in thirds; chill. Repeat rolling and folding 2 or 3 times. Heat oven to 475° F. Roll out half the dough on floured board ¼-inch thick. Cut into 4-inch squares. Place on cookie sheets, about 2 inches apart.

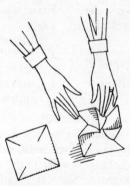

Place a spoonful of jelly in centers. Make 1½-inch cut from each corner toward center. Fold alternate corners in over center; seal with beaten egg. Chill 15 minutes. Brush with beaten egg. Bake 8 to 10 minutes or until well browned. Repeat with remaining dough. Transfer to wire racks; cool. Makes 16 stars.

KRANSEKAKE

This cake, known as pyramid cake, ring cake, or garland cake is a very special Scandinavian party cake used on the most festive occasions—Christmas, weddings, anniversaries. The rings—glazed and crunchy like macaroons—are set one on top of the other to build a pyramid and are then decorated to fit the occasion. When served, the rings are taken off, one by one, and broken into pieces.

4 egg whites
4 cans (8 oz. ea.)
    almond paste

3 c. sifted con-
    fectioners' sugar
Royal Frosting
    (*page 454*)
Food coloring

Beat egg whites until foamy in large bowl of mixer. Crumble in almond paste slowly. Beat mixture at low speed until all almond paste has been added and mixture is smooth. Add 3 cups sugar slowly until mixture is smooth and blended. Draw 12 circles on white bond paper or brown wrapping paper as guides, starting with the bottom and largest ring at 7½ inches and decreasing each circle by ½ inch until smallest measures 2 inches. Grease papers well. Spoon mixture into pastry bag without a tip but with an opening measuring about 1 inch in diameter. Squeeze almond mixture onto pattern circles following the

inside of the pencil mark. With remaining mixture, make 2 S-shaped curlicues and a star shape for decoration. Slide papers onto baking sheets; bake several rings at once, if possible. Bake at 300° F. for 25 to 30 minutes or until golden. Remove carefully from papers. Cool on wire racks. To assemble: Pipe Royal Frosting in wavy pattern over every other ring. Starting from bottom, assemble Kransekake in graduating circles. Press a little frosting on top to anchor star and S-shaped curlicues. Tint any remaining frosting with your choice of food coloring and decorate as desired.

TINY DOUGHNUTS

½ c. soft butter or
    margarine
1 c. sugar
4 eggs
3½ c. sifted all-
    purpose flour

½ tsp. hartshorn
    (ammonium car-
    bonate, a leav-
    ening available
    at your drug-
    store)
Fat or pure
    vegetable oil for
    frying

Beat butter or margarine and sugar together at medium speed on mixer. Add eggs, one at a time, beating well after each addition; continue to beat until mixture is light and fluffy. Combine flour and hartshorn; blend into butter-sugar mixture. Chill one to two hours or until easy to handle. Break off pieces of dough about size of a walnut; roll with hands on floured surface to pencil size about 6 inches long and ¼ inch thick. Form each piece into a ring, bringing one end up over other end; press ends firmly together. Put enough fat or oil into deep, heavy saucepan so it is two-thirds full when heated. Heat to 375° F. Fry doughnuts, a few at a time, until golden brown. Turn to brown second side. Drain well on paper towels. Dust with confectioners' sugar, if desired. Makes about 5½ dozen.

SWEDISH ROSETTES

½ c. sifted all-purpose flour	1 tbs. pure vegetable oil
1 tbs. sugar	½ tsp. vanilla
½ tsp. salt	Fat or pure vegetable oil for frying
1 egg	
½ c. milk	Confectioners' sugar

Sift flour, sugar, and salt together. Beat egg, milk, oil, and vanilla together until blended; stir into flour mixture. Heat fat or oil in electric skillet or heavy saucepan to 400° F. Heat rosette iron in fat for several minutes; shake off excess fat. Dip iron into batter just to top of iron; immerse quickly into hot fat; hold immersed until rosette begins to brown. Lift iron; shake off rosette; turn to brown the other side; drain on paper towels. When cool, dust lightly with confectioners' sugar. May be kept several weeks in a tightly covered container. Makes 3 dozen.

FILLED CHRISTMAS COOKIES
(Cucidata)

½ lb. dried figs	3 tbs. baking powder
½ lb. raisins	¼ tsp. salt
¼ c. candied orange peel	1½ c. butter or margarine
¼ lb. sweet chocolate, finely chopped	3 eggs
	1 c. milk
¼ c. honey	1½ tsp. vanilla
Dash of pepper	1½ tsp. anise extract
¼ tsp. ground cinnamon	3 c. sifted confectioners' sugar
¼ tsp. ground allspice	3 tbs. melted butter or margarine
¼ lb. mixed candied fruits, chopped	2 tsp. vanilla
	¼ c. lukewarm milk
8 c. sifted all-purpose flour	Multicolored sprinkles
1 c. sugar	

Heat oven to 375° F. Put figs, raisins, and orange peel through food grinder using medium blade. Mix in chocolate, honey, pepper, cinnamon, allspice, and candied fruits; mix well; reserve. Sift flour, sugar, baking powder, and salt together in bowl.

Cut in butter or margarine until mixture resembles cornmeal. Add eggs, 1 cup milk, 1½ teaspoons vanilla, and anise extract; mix until blended. Knead 5 minutes. Roll out part of dough at a time on floured board to ⅛-inch thickness. Cut with floured, fancy cookie cutters (be sure to cut 2 of each shape). Place a rounded teaspoonful of fruit-chocolate mixture on half the cookies; top with second cookie. Press edges together with tines of fork to seal. Make a small slit in top of each cookie. Transfer to lightly greased cookie sheets, place about 1 inch apart. Bake 15 to 18 minutes. While cookies bake prepare frosting: Mix together confectioners' sugar, melted butter or margarine, 2 teaspoons vanilla, and lukewarm milk. Transfer baked cookies to wire racks. Frost cookies while hot. Top with sprinkles. Cool. Makes about 8 dozen.

REFRIGERATOR COOKIES

VANILLA REFRIGERATOR COOKIES

½ c. butter or margarine	2 c. sifted all-purpose flour
1 c. sugar	½ tsp. baking soda
1 egg	¼ tsp salt
2 tsp. vanilla	

Beat butter or margarine, sugar, egg, and vanilla together until light and creamy. Sift flour, soda, and salt; blend into creamed mixture. Shape dough into a roll about 2 inches in diameter. Wrap in transparent plastic wrap or aluminum foil; chill several hours or overnight. Heat oven to 400° F. With sharp knife cut chilled dough into ⅛-inch slices. Place on ungreased cookie sheets, ½ inch apart. Bake 7 to 10 minutes or until lightly browned. Transfer to wire racks; cool. Makes about 6 dozen.

Butter Pecan Refrigerator Cookies

Prepare Vanilla Refrigerator Cookies, substituting 1 cup firmly packed brown sugar for 1 cup of granulated sugar. Add 1 cup finely chopped pecans.

Chocolate Refrigerator Cookies

Prepare Vanilla Refrigerator Cookies, blending 2 squares unsweetened chocolate, melted and cooled, into the creamed mixture.

Chapter Twenty-Five

Candies and Confections

Many a youngster's first cooking adventure is making a batch of fudge. It may not always be successful, but it's always lots of fun! Homemade candy is a delight to eat, to give, and to receive. And what is Christmas without the wonderful and traditional candies we think of as "sugarplums"? The art of candy making, easy to acquire with practice, is one of the most rewarding of the culinary arts.

Secrets for Making Candy

· Make candy on a cool, dry day for best results. Candy made on a damp or humid day may be sugary. If you must make candy on such a day, the *secret* is to cook it two degrees higher than the recipe directs. This should help produce a satisfactory product.
· Follow the recipe carefully and accurately.
· Use a saucepan large enough to allow the candy to boil freely without boiling over. If the recipe calls for covering the pan, be sure to select a pan with a tight-fitting cover.
· Watch candy carefully as it cooks. Temperature rises rapidly once it reaches 220° F.
· There are three ways to test candy when cooking it—*with a candy thermometer*, by the *cold water test*, or by *the thread test*.

The *thermometer test* is the most accurate and reliable:

Clip the thermometer on the side of the saucepan before starting to cook and leave it in the mixture all during the cooking. Be sure that the bulb is completely covered with syrup—not just the boiling foam—and that the thermometer does not rest on the bottom of the saucepan. To read the thermometer correctly, your eyes should be on a level with the mercury. When the candy has finished cooking, remove the thermometer and let it cool before washing.

The cold water test is the test to use if you don't have a candy thermometer. It takes practice to learn to feel and judge the proper state of the syrup in the cold water:

Use a small bowl freshly filled with cold water for each sample of syrup you test. Remove the saucepan from the heat while making the test to prevent overcooking in case the desired consistency has been reached by the time the test is started. Drop about one half teaspoon of syrup into the cold water. This will cool and harden the syrup. Shape it into a ball and test as follows:

Soft ball: Syrup stays in a mass which can be picked up into a ball which feels very soft and which flattens when removed from the water.

Firm ball: Syrup forms a firm ball in the cold water. It holds its shape and doesn't flatten when removed from the water.

Hard ball: Syrup forms a ball which is hard enough to hold its shape but is pliable.

Soft crack: Syrup separates into threads which are hard but not brittle.

Hard crack: Syrup separates into threads that are hard and brittle.

The thread test is an alternate test to the thermometer test in certain recipes which start with a simple sugar syrup. The cooked syrup is dropped from the tip of a spoon several times during cooking. When the syrup has reached proper temperature it will form a "thread" or filament of syrup which will increase in length as the temperature increases.

· If the recipe says to cool the candy, be patient. Don't beat or stir it until it has cooled to 110° F. or until bottom of pan is cool to palm of hand. If the candy is stirred while hot, it will become grainy because large sugar crystals will have formed.

· When ready to turn candy into pan, hold saucepan near the pan and pour quickly.

Storing Candy

Nearly all candy will keep longer and better if pieces are wrapped individually in wax paper or transparent plastic wrap, then placed in boxes, tins, or cartons.

Small hard candies are the exception. After they are completely cool, they can be stored without wrapping in airtight jars.

Never store candies that absorb moisture readily (caramels and hard candies) in the same container with those that lose moisture easily (fondants and fudge).

CHOCOLATE FUDGE

1⅓ c. milk	½ tsp. salt
4 sqs. unsweetened chocolate	3 tbs. butter or margarine
4 c. sugar	2 tsp. vanilla
3 tbs. light corn syrup	

Butter 8x8x2-inch pan lightly. Cook milk and chocolate in saucepan over low heat until chocolate is melted. Add sugar, corn syrup, and salt. Cook over low heat, stirring constantly, until sugar is dissolved. Cook until candy thermometer registers 234° F. (soft-ball stage). Move spoon across bottom of pan occasionally to prevent scorching, but do not stir. Remove from heat; add butter or margarine and vanilla; do not stir in. Let cool to 110° F. or until bottom of pan is comfortable to palm of hand. Beat until quite thick. Mixture will still be glossy.* Pour into buttered pan; cool; cut into rounds, squares, rectangles, or diamonds. Leave plain or decorate top with coconut, colored sprinkles, or pecan halves. Makes about 2 pounds.

*Note: If you overbeat and fudge becomes too stiff, turn it out and knead with hands until soft and pliable. It will be lighter in color and can be pressed into a pan and cut or shaped into a roll and sliced.

Variations: Prepare Chocolate Fudge. Cool to 110° F. Stir in one of the following:
  1 cup coarsely chopped walnuts or pecans
  1 cup miniature marshmallows
  1 cup halved candied cherries
Proceed with recipe as directed.

YUMMY MARSHMALLOW FUDGE

1½ c. sugar	1 jar (6½ to 7 oz.) marshmallow cream
⅔ c. evaporated milk (1 small can)	½ c. chopped nuts
2 tbs. butter or margarine	½ c. (4 oz. jar) candied cherries, halved
3 pkgs. (6 oz. ea.) semi-sweet chocolate pieces	

Butter 8x8x2-inch pan lightly. Combine sugar, milk, and butter or margarine in saucepan. Bring to boiling, stirring constantly to dissolve sugar. Regulate heat so mixture boils slowly. Boil 5 to 6 minutes or until candy thermometer registers 227° F. (soft-ball stage). Stir occasionally to prevent scorching. Remove from heat; add chocolate pieces and marshmallow cream at once. Beat vigorously until chocolate and marshmallow are dissolved and mixture is thick and glossy. Quickly beat in nuts and cherries. Pour into prepared pan. Cool; cut into squares. Makes about 3 pounds.

PENUCHE

3 c. light brown sugar, firmly packed	¾ c. milk
	¼ tsp. salt
¼ c. light or dark corn syrup	2 tbs. butter or margarine
	1 tsp. vanilla

Combine sugar, corn syrup, milk, salt, and butter or margarine in saucepan. Cook over medium heat, stirring constantly, until mixture comes to boiling. Continue cooking, stirring occasionally, until candy thermometer registers 238° F. (soft-ball stage). Remove from heat. Let cool to 110° F. or until bottom of pan is comfortable to palm of hand. Add vanilla. Beat until stiff and mixture loses its gloss. Pour into buttered pan. Cool. Cut into squares. Makes about 2 pounds.

DIVINITY

½ c. light corn syrup	¼ tsp. salt
2½ c. sugar	2 egg whites
½ c. water	1 tsp. vanilla

Combine corn syrup, sugar, water, and salt in saucepan. Cook over medium heat until candy thermometer registers 260° F. or syrup spins a 6-inch thread. When syrup is almost cooked, beat egg whites until stiff but not dry in bowl large enough to hold syrup mixture. Pour syrup slowly in thin stream over egg whites, beating at high speed until mixture holds shape and just begins to lose gloss. Beat in vanilla. Put through pastry bag using rosette tip, or drop from tip of teaspoon onto wax paper. Let stand until set. Decorate with candied cherry or angelica, if desired. Store in airtight container. Makes 1¼ pounds.

Fruited Divinity. Butter 8x8x2-inch pan lightly. Prepare Divinity as directed. Stir ½ cup mixed candied fruit, cut up, into mixture with vanilla. Spread evenly in prepared pan. Cool; cut in squares.

Seafoam Divinity. Prepare Divinity as directed, substituting 2½ cups brown sugar, firmly packed, for granulated sugar.

CREAMY PRALINES

1 pkg. (1 lb.) light brown sugar	1 tbs. butter or margarine
⅛ tsp. salt	2 c. (8 oz.) pecan halves
¾ c. evaporated milk	

Combine sugar, salt, evaporated milk, and butter or margarine in large saucepan. Cook, stirring constantly, until sugar is dissolved. Add pecans. Cook over medium heat, stirring constantly, until candy thermometer registers 234° F. (soft-ball stage). Remove from heat; cool 5 minutes. Stir rapidly until mixture begins to thicken and coat pecans lightly. Drop quickly from spoon onto buttered surface to form 3-inch patties. Let stand until cool and set. Makes about 20 pralines.

OLD-FASHIONED BUTTER CRUNCH

2 c. finely chopped almonds	2 tbs. water
	2 pkgs. (6 oz. ea.) semi-sweet chocolate pieces, melted
1 c. butter or margarine	
1¼ c. sugar	
2 tbs. light corn syrup	

Spread almonds in shallow pan; toast at 350° F. until golden. Melt butter or margarine in large heavy saucepan; add sugar, corn syrup, and water. Cook, stirring often, until candy thermometer registers 300° F. (hardcrack stage). Remove from heat; stir in 1 cup toasted almonds. Pour quickly into buttered 13x9x2-inch pan; cool completely. When set, turn out in one piece on wax paper. Spread half the melted chocolate over top; sprinkle with ½ cup almonds; let set. Turn candy over; spread with remaining chocolate; sprinkle with remaining almonds. Let stand until chocolate sets. Break into pieces. Makes 1 pound.

TWISTED KENTUCKY CREAMS

½ c. water	⅛ tsp. baking soda
2 c. sugar	½ c. heavy cream
¼ tsp. salt	

Butter 3 large cookie sheets or other large metal surfaces. Chill well. (This aids congealing of hot syrup.) Combine water, sugar, salt, and soda in saucepan. Cook until candy thermometer registers 250° F. or syrup spins a 3- to 4-inch thread. Add cream, a tablespoon at a time, so boiling does not stop. Lower heat; cook to 250° F. again. Mixture will be tan in color. Pour candy in thin ribbons onto cookie sheets. Let stand 5 minutes. Pick ribbons up; pull until pale ivory and quite stiff; twist into a rope. Cut into 1½-inch lengths on buttered sheets. Let stand until cold. Cover with wax paper. Let stand 3 to 4 hours. Candy will change from chewy to creamy. Store in airtight container. Makes about 1½ pounds.

FLOWER GARDEN MINTS

3 c. sifted confectioners' sugar	Red food coloring
2½ tbs. water	¼ tsp. wintergreen extract
2½ tbs. light corn syrup	Candied violets

Combine sugar, water, and corn syrup in top of double boiler. Heat over hot, not boiling, water until mixture becomes liquid enough to pour easily. Stir in red food coloring to tint a pastel pink and wintergreen extract. Drop from tip of teaspoon into circles onto wax paper. Top each with a candied violet. Let stand until set. Makes 3½ dozen.

Variations: For green mints, substitute green food coloring and ¼ teaspoon peppermint or spearmint extract for red food coloring and wintergreen extract in above recipe. For white mints, leave uncolored and add ¼ teaspoon peppermint extract.

VANILLA TAFFY

1 c. sugar	¼ tsp. cream of tartar
⅔ c. light corn syrup	1 tsp. vanilla
½ c. water	1 tbs. butter or margarine

Combine sugar, corn syrup, water, and cream of tartar in saucepan. Bring to boiling over medium heat, stirring constantly, until sugar is dissolved. Cook, without stirring, until candy thermometer registers 266° F. (hardball stage). Remove from heat; stir in vanilla and butter or margarine. Pour onto buttered platter or jelly-roll pan; let stand until cool enough to handle. Butter hands. Pull candy until it turns satiny and light in color. Pull into long strips; twist if desired; cut into 1-inch pieces with scissors. Wrap individually in transparent plastic wrap or aluminum foil. Makes ½ pound.

PEANUT BRITTLE

1 lb. shelled peanuts	3 tbs. butter or margarine
3 c. sugar	1 tsp. baking soda
1¼ c. water	1 tbs. water
½ c. light corn syrup	1½ tsp. vanilla

Butter one large cookie sheet or make your own by layering several thicknesses of foil. If peanuts are salted, wash in warm water; dry well with paper towels. Combine sugar, water, and corn syrup in saucepan. Cook over medium heat, stirring constantly, until sugar is dissolved and mixture comes to boiling. Boil without stirring until candy thermometer registers 270° F. (soft-crack stage). Add butter or margarine and peanuts. Continue cooking to 300° F. (hard-crack stage). Remove from heat. Mix soda with water. Add soda mixture and vanilla to hot candy. Allow bubbles to subside; pour out as thinly as possible on prepared pan. Cool; break into pieces. Makes about 2¾ pounds.

CANDY APPLES

8 large red apples	½ c. water
8 wooden skewers	1 tsp. cinnamon extract
3 c. sugar	1 tsp. red food coloring
½ c. light corn syrup	

Wash and dry apples; insert skewers in stem ends of apples. Combine sugar, corn syrup, and water in deep heavy saucepan. Bring to boiling over medium heat, stirring constantly. Cook without stirring until candy thermometer registers 285° F. (soft-crack stage). Remove from heat; add cinnamon extract and coloring; stir only enough to mix. Let mixture settle a few minutes. Hold each apple by skewer end; quickly twirl in syrup, tilting pan to cover apples with syrup. Allow excess to drip off; place on lightly buttered cookie sheet to cool. Store in cool place. Makes 8.

CARAMEL APPLES

1 pkg. (14 oz.) caramels	Wooden skewers
2 tbs. water	4 to 5 medium-size apples, washed and dried

Combine caramels and water in top of double boiler. Cook over hot, not boiling, water until caramels are melted and sauce is smooth, stirring occasionally. Insert wooden skewer into stem end of each apple. Dip into hot caramel sauce; twirl to coat. Scrape bottom of apple across rim of pan to remove excess caramel. Place coated apples, skewer end up, on buttered cookie sheet, platter, or wax paper. Chill until firm. Makes 4 to 5.

LOLLIPOPS

2 c. sugar	¼ tsp. lime extract
⅔ c. light corn syrup	½ tsp. green food coloring
1 c. water	3 doz. wooden skewers

Combine sugar, corn syrup, and water in saucepan. Cook over medium heat until candy thermometer registers 280° F. (soft-crack stage). Lower heat to keep syrup from darkening; cook to 300° F. (hard-crack stage). Remove from heat; let stand 1 minute. Add lime extract and green food coloring. Place skewers on buttered cookie sheet or bottom of large baking pan about 4 inches apart. Hold one end of stick firmly; pour syrup from tip of teaspoon allowing it to flow into circle at top of stick. Let cool; remove from cookie sheets. Makes about 3 dozen two-inch lollipops.

Red Lollipops. To make red lollipops, use ¼ teaspoon oil of cloves or cinnamon extract and ½ teaspoon red food coloring in place of lime extract and green food coloring in recipe.

Lollipop Stars. Prepare green or red lollipop syrup according to recipe. Allow bubbles to settle before starting to shape stars. Dip spoon into syrup. Shape free-form stars by letting syrup flow from spoon onto oiled surface. Several dips are necessary. Insert wooden skewers at once. Cool; remove from oiled surface. Makes about 3 dozen.

Lollipop Cones. Oil cornucopia molds or others metal molds (not glass or plastic). Place cornucopia tips in small jars to hold upright. Set other molds on a firm base. Prepare green or red lollipop syrup according to recipe. Pour hot syrup into molds. Insert wooden skewers when syrup is thick enough to support them. Remove cones from molds as soon as they are firm. Do not allow to set too long or they may be difficult to remove. It may be necessary to run molds quickly under hot water. Makes about 8 to 10.

POPCORN BALLS

1 c. light corn syrup	2 tbs. butter or margarine
1 c. sugar	1 tsp. vanilla
¼ c. water	8 c. popped popcorn (2 qts.)
1 tsp. vinegar	
Red or green food coloring	

Combine corn syrup, sugar, water, and vinegar in saucepan; add enough food coloring to tint bright pink or green. Cook over medium heat, stirring only until sugar is dissolved. Cook syrup until candy thermometer registers 260° F. (hard-ball stage). Add butter or margarine and vanilla. Pour over popcorn in large mixing bowl. Stir mixture quickly with spoon or fork so all little pieces of popcorn are coated with syrup. Butter hands; scoop up portions of mixture; press very lightly into balls. Drop on wax paper. Continue, working rapidly, until all mixture is used. Makes about 9 large or 18 small popcorn balls.

Popcorn Garlands

Make 18 small Popcorn Balls as directed. String balls on strong cord, using a heavy large-eyed needle. For more garlands and other colors, make recipe again.

Molasses Popcorn Balls

Prepare Popcorn Balls, substituting ½ cup molasses for ½ cup of the light corn syrup. Cook syrup mixture until candy thermometer registers 270° F. Proceed as recipe directs.

CANDIED ORANGE PEEL

4 large navel	¼ c. light corn
oranges	syrup
2 c. sugar	Yellow food
1 c. hot water	coloring
	Sugar

Remove peel from oranges in large pieces. Place in saucepan; cover with cold water. Bring to boiling; boil 2 minutes; drain. Repeat three times, discarding water each time. Cut peel into strips with scissors. Combine 2 cups sugar, water, corn syrup, and a few drops yellow food coloring in saucepan. Cook over medium heat, stirring until sugar is dissolved. Add peel; lower heat; cook slowly until peel is translucent and syrup is almost absorbed. Drain peel in colander. Roll, a few strips at a time, in sugar. Let stand in single layer on wire rack to dry sugar coating. Store in tightly covered container. Makes 1 pound.

Candied Grapefruit Peel

Substitute peel of 2 large grapefruit for orange peel. Cook in cold water 10 minutes each time in three changes of water. Proceed as above.

HEAVENLY HASH

3 pkgs. (6 oz. ea.)	3 tbs. butter or
semi-sweet choco-	margarine
late pieces	1 pkg. (6¼ oz.)
1 sq. unsweetened	miniature marsh-
chocolate	mallows
	1 c. chopped
	walnuts or pecans

Butter 8x8x2-inch pan lightly. Heat semi-sweet chocolate, unsweetened chocolate, and butter or margarine in top of double boiler over hot, not boiling, water until melted. Stir to blend. Add marshmallows and nuts; stir until

coated. Spread in pan. Candy may also be dropped by teaspoonfuls onto buttered cookie sheet. Chill until firm. Cut candy in pan into squares. Makes 1¾ pounds.

PEANUT-BUTTER PINWHEELS

½ c. cold mashed	1 tsp. vanilla
potatoes	¾ c. cream-style
5 to 6 c. sifted con-	peanut butter
fectioners' sugar	

Combine potatoes and enough confectioners' sugar to make mixture the consistency of pastry. Add vanilla; chill. Roll out between two pieces of wax paper to ¼-inch-thick rectangle. Remove top piece of wax paper. Spread evenly with peanut butter. Roll up from short end, jelly-roll fashion. Wrap in wax paper, transparent plastic wrap, or aluminum foil. Chill until firm. Cut in ¼-inch slices. Keep in cool place. Makes 4 to 5 dozen.

CHOCOLATE BALLS

½ c. butter or	3¼ c. sifted con-
margarine	fectioners' sugar
5 tbs. instant choco-	⅛ tsp. salt
late-flavored-	Chocolate shot or
drink mix	chopped pis-
	tachio nuts

Combine butter or margarine, chocolate-flavored mix, 2½ cups confectioners' sugar, and salt; beat until creamy. Knead or work in remaining ¾ cup sugar. Chill until firm. Shape into small balls; roll in chocolate shot or chopped pistachio nuts or in a combination of the two. Makes about 3 dozen.

FRUIT CONFECTION

½ c. dried apricots	½ c. walnuts
½ c. dried figs	1 tbs. lemon juice
1 c. raisins	Colored sugar

Put apricots, figs, raisins, and walnuts through food grinder, using medium blade. Add lemon juice. Shape into small balls, using about 1 tablespoon of mixture for each. Roll in colored sugar. Makes about 2 dozen.

MARZIPAN

2 cans (8 oz. ea.) almond paste	2 pkgs. (1 lb. ea.) confectioners'
1/3 c. light corn syrup	sugar, sifted
1 jar (6 1/2 to 7 oz.) marshmallow cream	1 tsp. ground cinnamon
	Food coloring
1 tsp. vanilla	Red sugar
	Artificial leaves

Mix almond paste, corn syrup, marshmallow cream, and vanilla in large bowl. Stir in sugar, 1 cup at a time, adding only enough so mixture holds its shape. Turn out onto board; knead until smooth. Cut or break off small pieces. Mold by hand into shapes of fruits and vegetables. Let stand several hours or overnight to form a crust before painting. For potatoes, leave marzipan unpainted and roll in cinnamon. Dilute food coloring. Paint fruits and vegetables with artist's brush to resemble actual ones. Roll strawberries in red sugar after painting. Apply leaves where appropriate while marzipan is still soft and pliable. Let dry. Makes 6 to 8 dozen.

GLAZED NUTS

1 1/2 c. sugar	2 c. walnuts
1/2 c. light corn syrup	3 tbs. melted butter or margarine
1/2 c. water	1 tsp. vanilla
1/4 tsp. salt	

Combine sugar, corn syrup, water, and salt in heavy saucepan. Cook over low heat, stirring constantly, until sugar is dissolved. Continue cooking over medium heat until candy thermometer registers 300° F. (hard-crack stage). Remove from heat. Add walnuts, butter or margarine, and vanilla. Spread quickly in shallow pan. Separate nuts with fork. Cool. Makes about 1 pound.

SPICY PECANS

1 egg white	2 tsp. ground cinnamon
2 tbs. water	
1 can (6 oz.) pecans	1/2 tsp. ground ginger
2/3 c. sugar	
	1/4 c. cornstarch

Heat oven to 250° F. Beat egg white and water slightly. Add pecans; stir until well moistened. Sift sugar, cinnamon, ginger, and cornstarch into shallow dish. Toss nuts in mixture until well coated. Spread on cookie sheet. Bake 1 1/2 hours, stirring often. Cool. Makes about 1/2 pound.

CREAM CENTERS

2 tbs. butter or margarine	4 tbs. chopped, drained maraschino cherries
2 c. sifted confectioners' sugar	2 tbs. chopped pistachio nuts
1/8 tsp. salt	4 to 5 sqs. semi-sweet chocolate
2 to 3 tsp. milk or cream	Candied rose leaves

Cream butter or margarine, 1 cup confectioners' sugar, and salt thoroughly. Add remaining 1 cup sugar and milk or cream alternately. Beat until smooth. Turn out onto board. Knead in cherries and pistachio nuts. Shape into small balls. Melt chocolate in top of small double boiler over hot, not boiling, water. Dip candies, one at a time, into chocolate; coat well. Set on wax paper; decorate with candied rose leaves; let harden. Makes about 1 1/2 dozen.

CHOCOLATE COATED PINEAPPLE

6 slices candied pineapple	5 sqs. semi-sweet chocolate

Cut each pineapple slice into quarters. Melt chocolate in top of small double boiler over hot, not boiling, water. Spear pineapple with two-tined fork. Dip in chocolate to coat. Set on wax paper. Let harden. Makes 2 dozen.

CHOCOLATE MARSHMALLOWS

5 sqs. semi-sweet chocolate	2 doz. marshmallows

Melt chocolate in top of small double boiler over hot, not boiling, water. Spear marshmallow with two-tined fork; dip into chocolate; coat about two thirds the way up sides. Place on wax paper, uncoated section on top. Decorate with pieces of red and green cherries, if desired. Makes about 2 dozen.

Chapter Twenty-Six

Freezing and Preserving

Whether it's bounty from your own garden you want to freeze or bushels of fresh fruits or vegetables purchased during the peak of harvest, or supermarket food bargains to be stashed away for future use, the freezer is a friend indeed.

There are some foods, too, you will want to pickle, or preserve. And what is more delicious than homemade jellies or jams from fruit plucked at the peak of ripeness?

Freezing

Home freezers have so completely changed our shopping and cooking habits, it's hard to imagine what we would do without them.

True freezers are those that maintain a zero temperature zone. The principal types are the *upright models, chest types,* and *two-door refrigerator-freezer* combinations. A freezing compartment of a refrigerator is not a true freezer. It is useful for ice-cube making and brief storage of ready-frozen foods, but it does not maintain the freezing zone necessary for long-term storage of frozen foods. Instructions for freezing on the following pages refer to the use of freezers with zero temperature zones, varying at most from $-5°$ F. to $+5°$ F., never higher.

Supermarket at Your Fingertips

By using your freezer wisely, you can save time and money and have a miniature super-

market in your kitchen. Buy foods at the peak of their season, when supplies are plentiful and prices low . . . cook ahead at leisure to have a well rounded selection of ready-to-heat dishes for family use and entertaining . . . keep emergency food "on ice" for spur-of-the-moment needs.

Most foods can be frozen, but a few change in texture; others freeze well but need to be used within a comparatively short time. *Not recommended for freezing:* bananas, lettuce, celery, cucumber, fresh tomatoes, mayonnaise, cooked egg white, cream (unless whipped), custards, cream pies or pie fillings, and gelatin salads.

Basic Rules of Freezing

· Freeze foods your family likes, in amounts you are likely to use within 6 months to a year.

• Choose only top quality foods—if properly packaged, quality of foods will be preserved by freezing, but never improved.

• Buy at peak of season or when real bargains are available.

• Prepare foods carefully; freeze immediately after picking or purchase. Store only at 0° F.

• Wrap in meal-size portions—the smaller the portion, the more quickly it thaws.

• Package carefully, using moisture-vapor-proof materials; seal tightly.

• Freeze a small quantity at a time. Keep foods waiting to be frozen in the refrigerator.

• Label each package or carton.

• Store so that foods can be found easily.

• Keep an up-to-date inventory. Devise a system listing foods in your freezer; check it from time to time; be sure to use frozen foods within the recommended maximum storage period.

Equipment and Packaging Materials

Nothing is more important than packaging foods properly. Only moisture-vaporproof packaging materials should be used, and the material should be odorless, tasteless, leakproof, and easy to handle, seal, and label.

Wrapping Papers

There's a large variety of these from which to choose. All are pliable to make a tight wrap. Fold in the way known as *drugstore wrap* whenever possible: place food in center of sheet (large enough to enclose the food); bring longest edges together and fold over 1 inch; fold again over and over until edges are flat and tight against the food. Push out all air pockets. Fold and tuck under the ends; heat-seal or tape with freezer tape to make secure and tight.

Aluminum foil is very flexible and can be easily self-sealed by folding over and crimping the edges. Heavy-duty aluminum foil is recommended for freezing.

Wax-coated laminated freezer papers are especially recommended for meat, though they do not mold as closely to the foods. Seal with freezer tape and tie securely with strong cord.

Transparent plastic sheet wrap is very flexible and air can be pushed out easily; some of the lighter-weight materials should be over-wrapped for extra protection. Seal fold and ends with freezer tape.

Transparent plastic bags have the same flexibility as plastic sheet wrap. Air can be pushed out easily and they can be fastened tightly with paper-covered wire twists.

Containers

Select containers that have tight-fitting lids and can be stacked easily on top of one another. When filling, always leave $\frac{1}{2}$ to 1 inch head space in the container to allow for expansion during freezing. Types include *aluminum foil* containers which can go from freezer to oven; *baking dishes* (some of these, too, can go direct from freezer to oven); *heavily waxed cartons,* ideal for stews, soups, liquids; *plastic containers;* and *glass jars,* especially recommended for fruit.

Sealing and Labeling Equipment

Use special freezer tape. To *heat-seal* plastic sheet wrapping, use an iron set at "warm," or an electric heat sealer designed for freezer use: just barely touch the overlapped edges of the plastic sheeting to seal.

A *china marking pencil or grease pencil* is useful for labeling and package identifications.

Overwrap materials for long-term storage include stockinette (loosely knitted tubular cotton fabric), butcher paper, or cheesecloth.

Storage of Commercially Frozen Foods

Even though commercially frozen foods are already packaged for freezer storage, it is important not to let them begin to thaw before they are put away in your home freezer.

• Select foods that are solidly frozen—if soft to the touch when purchased, they may already have thawed slightly.

• Make frozen foods the final items selected at the market.

• Keep frozen foods in insulated bags until you reach home; do not let them remain in a heated car or one parked in the summer sun for long periods.

• The moment you reach home, put the frozen foods in the freezer immediately; don't leave them on the kitchen counter.

MEATS

Guide to Freezing, Storing, and Thawing

Select only top-quality meat for freezing. Wrap carefully, pressing out all air, and seal securely. Wrap in meal-size portions, freeze small quantities at a time. As a general rule, thaw meat completely before cooking. Cook immediately after it thaws; do not refreeze. (For storage time chart see *page 137*.)

Roasts

To Freeze: Ask butcher to trim excess fat and bones. Large bones take up space in freezer, sharp ends may puncture wrapping paper. Cut freezer paper in sheets large enough to enclose meat. Wrap (*page 485*). Label with name of cut, weight, and date frozen.

To Cook: Thaw completely without unwrapping; cook as usual. Or, thaw until a meat thermometer can be inserted in center, cook to desired degree of doneness (check Meat Roasting Timetables in Chapter 11). If cooked frozen, meat will take longer to cook.

Steaks and Chops

To Freeze: Package in meal-size portions. Separate chops, individual steaks, or veal for scaloppine with double thickness of freezer wrap between them for easier separation when they are thawed. On label describe cut, number of portions, weight, and date frozen.

To Cook: Thaw completely without unwrapping. Cook as you would fresh meat. If cooked without thawing, double the usual cooking time. To test for doneness: cut a slit near the bone to check the degree of doneness.

Ground Meat

To Freeze: Shape ground meat into patties. Place double thickness of transparent plastic wrap, freezer paper, or aluminum foil between patties before wrapping. Meat-loaf mixture may also be formed into patties for quicker freezing and thawing. On label give number of serving portions, weight, and date frozen.

To Cook: Hamburger patties can be cooked without previous thawing; allow additional cooking time; make small slit in center to test for doneness. Or thaw completely and cook the usual way (*page 152*). To make meat loaf or meatballs from ground meat, thaw, season and reshape before cooking.

POULTRY

Guide to Freezing, Storing, and Thawing

Select top quality, strictly fresh poultry. It should be carefully dressed, with all pinfeathers removed, and the giblets wrapped separately.

Whole Birds: To freeze, tie wings and legs close to body to make package as compact as possible. Separately wrapped giblets may be slipped under wing or in cavity. Place bird on large sheet of freezer wrapping material; press material close to body; fold over in drugstore wrap. Or, place in large polyethylene bag; press out all air; seal with covered wire fasteners. *Do not stuff poultry before freezing.* Cover package with stockinette for added protection, if desired. Label with weight and date frozen.

To Cook: Thaw completely before cooking.

Split or Cut-up Birds: To freeze, place pieces together so they form an almost square package. Place in center of large sheet of freezer wrapping material; fold over in drugstore wrap; seal securely. On label give number of serving portions and date frozen.

To Cook: Thaw completely if it is to be broiled or fried; stewing chickens may be simmered without previous thawing.

Maximum storage time at 0° F.

Turkey	6 months
Chicken, smaller birds	6 months
Ducklings	4 months
Giblets (wrap separately)	1 to 2 months
Cooked chicken or turkey	3 months

FISH AND SHELLFISH

Guide to Freezing, Storing, and Thawing

Clean and scale all fresh-caught fish; wash and dry; wrap in freezer wrapping material; freeze immediately. Or, *ice-glaze:* dip fish in ice-cold water, freeze until film forms around fish, then wrap in freezer wrapping material. Seal and label, giving weight and date frozen.

If several small fish or several filets or steaks are being packaged together, separate with double thickness of freezer wrapping material. Thaw fish completely before cooking.

Shellfish should be frozen immediately after being caught. Cook while still frozen; avoid overcooking.

Maximum storage time at 0° F.

Lean whole fish, steaks, filets	3 to 6 months
Fatter fish (mackerel, salmon)	3 months
Commercially frozen fish	1 month
Shellfish (shrimp, lobster, crab, oysters, clams)	4 to 6 months
Cooked shellfish	1 to 2 months

VEGETABLES

Freeze only fresh, top-quality vegetables, still young and tender; freeze as soon as possible. Wash thoroughly in cold water; trim; cut off any bruised portions.

All vegetables except green peppers and chopped onions should be blanched or steam-scalded before freezing.

To Blanch: Place 1 gallon (4 quarts) water in large kettle; bring to full rolling boil. Place vegetables for freezing (no more than 1 pound at a time) in wire or perforated basket or cheesecloth bag; lower into boiling water. Shake several times during scalding period so all portions will be evenly heated. After specified length of time, remove from water immediately; plunge into ice water to cool rapidly and prevent further cooking. Chilling time is equal to blanching time. Drain thoroughly; pack at once.

To Steam-scald: Put 1-inch depth of water in large kettle. Place a rack or trivet in it high enough to keep food above water level. Bring water to full rolling boil. Add basket or cheesecloth bag holding vegetables; let vegetables rest on rack for designated scalding period; cover kettle; keep water boiling rapidly. (Or use a pressure cooker with rack, but do not put pet cock on cooker, do not clamp on lid tight.) After steaming, chill immediately as above; drain thoroughly. This method is excellent for all but leafy green vegetables.

To Pack: Pack vegetables in meal-size portions (2 cups make 3 or 4 servings).

The *loose-pack method* may be used for small vegetables such as peas, cut beans, diced carrots. Spread scalded, chilled, and drained vegetables on baking sheets or in large, shallow pans; place in freezer. They will be frozen in 1 to 2 hours, then can be scraped from tray and placed in containers. Label; return promptly to freezer.

Maximum storage time for vegetables at 0° F.

Commercially frozen	12 months
Home frozen	8 to 12 months
Cooked	1 to 2 months

Asparagus: Freeze as soon as possible. Break off tough ends; wash spears thoroughly; sort according to size. Blanch or steam-scald 3 to 3½ minutes; chill; drain. Pack in freezer containers.

Beans, green snap or wax: Use tender young beans. Cut in 2-inch pieces, slice lengthwise, or freeze whole. Blanch 2 minutes or steam-scald 3 minutes. Chill; drain. Pack in freezer containers.

Broccoli: Select dark green, compact heads; cut stalks or spears into uniform size, discarding woody stems. Grade stalks according to size. *Medium to large:* blanch 4 to 5 minutes or steam-scald 5 to 6 minutes. *Small stalks:* blanch 3 minutes or steam-scald 4 minutes. Chill; drain. Pack in freezer containers.

Brussels sprouts: Select compact, dark green sprouts; grade according to size. Wash. Blanch 4 minutes or steam-scald 5 minutes. Chill; drain. Pack in freezer containers.

Carrots: Wash and pare carrots; dice or slice. Baby carrots may be left whole. *Diced or sliced carrots:* Blanch 3 minutes or steam-scald 4 minutes. Chill; drain. Pack in freezer containers. *Whole baby carrots:* Blanch 5 minutes or steam-scald 6 minutes. Chill; drain. Pack in freezer containers.

Cauliflower: Wash; trim; separate into small flowerets. Blanch 3 minutes or steam-scald 4 minutes. Chill; drain. Pack in freezer containers.

Corn on the cob: Select young, tender but fully mature ears. Husk; remove all silks; grade according to size. *Small to medium:* blanch or steam-scald 7 to 9 minutes. *Large:* blanch or steam-scald 11 minutes. Drugstore wrap in transparent plastic wrap or aluminum foil or pack in freezer containers. *Cut corn:* Prepare as for corn on the cob. After processing cut off kernels with sharp knife. Chill thoroughly; pack in freezer containers.

Greens (spinach, kale, turnip greens, etc.): Wash thoroughly, taking care to remove all sand; remove heavy stems. Blanch spinach 2 minutes; kale, Swiss chard and turnip greens 2 minutes; collards 3 minutes. Pack in freezer containers.

Lima beans: Shell beans; wash; grade according to size; discard discolored or immature beans. *Large beans:* blanch 4 minutes or steam-scald 3 minutes. *Smaller beans:* blanch 2 minutes or steam-scald 2½ minutes. Chill; drain. Pack in freezer containers.

Onions: Frozen chopped onions are a great convenience. Chop in uniform pieces; pack in transparent plastic bags in measured amounts ranging from ½ to 2 cups, writing cup measure on outside of bag. Blanching or scalding not necessary.

Peas: Shell; sort, using only young, tender peas of uniform size. Blanch 1 minute or steam-scald 1½ minutes. Chill; drain. Pack in freezer containers.

Peppers (green): Wash; seed; cut into large pieces or chop, depending on how you wish to use them. Blanching or scalding not necessary. Pack in freezer containers. Peppers will not be crispy when thawed, but are fine for cooking.

Summer squash: Select young squash of uniform size with tender, unblemished skin. Cut in ½-inch slices or cubes. Blanch 3½ minutes or steam-scald 4½ minutes. Pack in plastic bags, waxed cartons, or drugstore wrap in transparent plastic wrap or aluminum foil.

Winter squash: Wash; cut in pieces; cook until tender. Mash pulp; chill. Pack in freezer containers.

FRUITS

Select fully ripe, perfect fruits, bright in color, of excellent flavor. If home grown, pick in cool of day, keep refrigerated until processed. If purchased, buy in quantity at peak of season, if possible direct from farm or grower.

Preparation: Wash a small quantity at a time; do not allow to stand in water. Drain in colander, then spread out on trays lined with paper towels. Cut out any bruised portions; stem berries; peel larger fruit.

Processing methods

Unsweetened pack is recommended for berries and rhubarb to be used in recipes calling for sugar or for special diets. Place in containers, leaving 1 inch head space; seal; freeze.

Dry sugar pack is best for fruits to be eaten uncooked. Place fruit in shallow pan; sprinkle evenly with sugar in specified amounts. Mix gently until juice is drawn out and sugar is dissolved.

Sugar syrup pack preserves color best but juices are diluted. Recommended for less-juicy types of fruit, or mixed fruit to be used in compotes. *Syrup:* combine sugar and water in saucepan. Cook over low heat, stirring until sugar is dissolved.

Syrup	Cups of Sugar	Cups of Water	Syrup Yield
Light	2	4	5
Medium	3	4	5½
Heavy	4¾	4	6½

Packaging for freezer: Use moisture-vapor-proof folding cartons with leakproof liners, square or round freezer containers with fitted lids, or sterilized wide-mouthed glass jars (especially recommended for syrup pack). Allow 1 inch head space.

Ascorbic acid (available at drugstores) or another anti-oxidant is recommended to preserve color for certain fruits, mainly apples, peaches, and sour cherries. Use ½ teaspoon ascorbic acid powder dissolved in 1 quart cooled sugar syrup. Add to fruit just before packing. Process and freeze small amounts at a time. Keep remaining fruit chilled in refrigerator. Label containers with name of fruit, date, amount, and amount of sweetening used.

Juices can be frozen with or without adding sugar. Ascorbic acid may be added (¼ teaspoon to each cup) if desired. Pack in glass containers; leave 1 inch head space for expansion.

Maximum storage time at 0° F.

Commercially frozen	12 months
Home frozen	8 to 12 months
Juices	8 to 12 months

Apples: Pare, core, and slice. Pack in light sugar syrup with ascorbic acid added to prevent darkening. Or for use in pies, steam-scald slices 1½ to 2 minutes; sprinkle with ½ cup sugar for each quart of sliced fruit.

Applesauce: Prepare as for serving fresh, sweetened to taste. Pack in freezer containers.

Blueberries: Remove leaves and stems; discard any bruised berries. Wash in cold water; drain, pat dry. Pack unsweetened or use 1 pound sugar to 3 quarts fruit for sugar pack; or use medium sugar syrup.

Cherries, red tart: Select ripe, firm cherries; discard overripe or discolored ones. Stem, wash, and pit. For pies, sugar-pack with 1 pound sugar to 3 or 5 pounds cherries (depending on desired sweetness). Add ½ teaspoon ascorbic acid for each cup sugar. Or cherries may be packed unsweetened.

Cherries, dark sweet: Select and prepare as for tart cherries. Sugar-pack with 1 part sugar to 4 parts fruit or pack unpitted cherries in medium sugar syrup with ascorbic acid.

Melon (*cantaloupe, honeydew, and watermelon*): Scoop out melon balls or cut into dice. Pack in natural juice, unsweetened or in medium sugar syrup.

Peaches: Immerse in boiling water ½ to 1 minute to loosen skins. Plunge into cold water to chill. Remove skins; pit, keeping under water as you work. Slice or cut into halves; drop immediately into medium sugar syrup with ascorbic acid added.

Raspberries: Use only fresh, unblemished fruit. Handle gently. Wash in ice water; drain on paper towel; sort for size. Sugar-pack with 1 pound sugar to each 3 to 5 quarts fruit or pack in medium sugar syrup.

Strawberries: Wash in ice water; hull; discard immature, overripe, or bruised berries. Whether sliced or whole, sugar-pack with 1 pound sugar to 3 to 5 quarts fruit. Whole berries may be packed in medium sugar syrup or may be packed unsweetened.

EGGS AND DAIRY PRODUCTS

Select fresh eggs and freeze when they are most abundant and low in price. Use waxed cartons, plastic containers, or glass jars in half pint or pint sizes with tight-fitting lids, allowing ½ inch head space.

Whole eggs: Break eggs into measuring cup. When planning to use for desserts, add 1 tablespoon sugar or light corn syrup for each cup of eggs. Add 1 teaspoon salt for use in main dishes. Stir to mix well. Pour into freezer containers. Label containers as to whether sweetened or salted; give both cup measure and number of eggs.

Egg yolks: Stir, do not beat, until smooth. For each cup of egg yolk, add 2 tablespoons sugar or corn syrup or 1 teaspoon salt. Label as for whole eggs.

Egg whites: No sugar or salt is needed when freezing.

Maximum storage time at 0° F.

Egg whites	9 months
Egg yolks or whole eggs	6 to 8 months

To Use: Thaw in refrigerator. 2½ tablespoons whole egg equals 1 fresh egg; 1 tablespoon yolk equals 1 fresh yolk; 1½ tablespoons whites equals 1 fresh egg white.

Cheese: Certain types of cheese can be frozen satisfactorily but will change in texture and consistency. Cream cheese should never be frozen. Semi-soft cheeses may be cut into cubes to be wrapped individually; these will be useful for cooking.

Whipped cream: Freezes well. Sweeten and flavor before freezing. For individual servings, make dollops of whipped cream on wax paper; freeze; then wrap individually in transparent plastic wrap; pack in containers. Use within 2 months.

Butter: If made from unsalted sweet pasteurized cream, butter can be stored up to 6 months.

Ice Cream: Store commercial ice cream in cartons in which it was purchased. Half gallon or gallon packages are economical if you consume a great deal of ice cream in your home, but remember, once a carton is opened quality begins to deteriorate. Cover any remaining ice cream with aluminum foil or transparent plastic wrap before replacing cover on carton. If you use only a pint at a time, it's better to purchase the ice cream in cartons of that size.

You can freeze ice cream for 2 to 3 months. For best flavor, allow ice cream to soften at room temperature 15 to 20 minutes before serving. Never refreeze after thawing.

BAKED GOODS

To Freeze Homemade Breads

· Make and bake as usual; cool completely. Wrap in plastic bags or sheet wrapping; seal tightly; label.
· Place rolls or coffee cakes on foil-covered cardboard or foil pie plate; wrap in plastic bag; seal tightly.
· Yeast breads or rolls can be frozen before baking, but they will rise better and have better texture if baked before freezing.

To Freeze Pies

Most pies freeze well with the exception of custard and cream pies.

Unbaked pies: For fruit pies, prepare according to recipe. Do not cut vents in top crust until ready to bake. Wrap; label; freeze. To bake, unwrap pie; make slits in top crust; place, unthawed, in preheated oven (temperature specified in recipe); bake, allowing 10 to 15 minutes longer than recipe time.

Baked pies: Prepare according to recipe. Cool completely. Wrap; label; freeze. Thaw and warm at 375° F. for 30 to 40 minutes.

Chiffon pies: Prepare according to recipe. Wrap; label; freeze.

Maximum storage time at 0° F.

Bakery bread (sliced)	
in original wrap	2 weeks
in freezer overwrap	4 weeks
Bakery brown n' serve rolls	2 to 3 months
Homemade yeast breads and coffee cakes	3 to 6 months
Bakery coffee cakes	3 months
Pies, unbaked,	6 months
baked	6 months
chiffon	2 months
Cakes, butter type	4 months
angel or sponge	6 to 8 months
Cookies, baked or unbaked	12 months

To Freeze Cakes

Cakes freeze well. To freeze unfrosted cakes: For layers, place each layer on foil-covered cardboard; wrap; label; freeze. For cupcakes, place side by side on foil-covered cardboard; wrap; label; freeze. Place loaf and pound cakes on foil-covered cardboard; wrap; label; freeze. Angel, sponge, chiffon, and fruitcakes are frozen the same way. To freeze frosted cakes: Place cake on foil-covered cardboard. Freeze until frosting is just firm. Wrap; label; freeze.

To Freeze Cookies

Freeze cookies baked or unbaked. Unbaked drop cookies may be frozen in two ways: Drop on cookie sheet by teaspoonfuls. Freeze and package the cookie balls. Or, pack cookie dough in cartons and freeze. Bar cookies should be baked before freezing. Cut in squares or bars and pack compactly in boxes or cartons. Rolled cookies may be baked and decorated before freezing. Arrange carefully in single layers on trays; wrap securely.

For Freezing Sandwiches, see page 76.

Thawing chart for baked goods	Time	Temperature
Bakery bread, sliced	3 to 4 minutes	place frozen in toaster
Commercial waffles	3 to 4 minutes	place frozen in toaster
Bakery or homemade yeast bread, unsliced	1–2 hours	room temperature
Rolls, coffeecakes, doughnuts	15 minutes	250 to 300° F. oven
Quick breads, loaf size	3 to 4 hours	room temperature
Cakes, not iced	1 hour	room temperature
iced 2-layer	3 hours	room temperature
angel or sponge tube cake	2 hours	room temperature
fruit cake, 1 pound	2 hours	room temperature
cupcakes	1 hour	room temperature
Cookies (unwrapped to thaw)	1 hour	room temperature
Pies, unbaked	1 hour 15 to 20 minutes	400° F. oven
baked	30 minutes	375° F. oven
chiffon	4 to 5 hours	refrigerator (38° F.)

COOKED FOODS

· Your home freezer can serve as a handy "savings bank" for leftovers, plan-aheads, and party foods. Casseroles and stews are especially suitable for freeze-now, cook-later meals. They can be stored in freezer-to-oven dishes or in meal-size portions wrapped in aluminum foil.

· Undercook rather than overcook any foods you plan to freeze; remember they will receive additional cooking when being reheated.

· Precooked foods have a shorter storage life than fresh meats and vegetables (see chart *page 492*).

· Be sure to write on the label the name of dish, number of servings, and date on which it was frozen.

· Freezing cooked meats and poultry: If it's to go into the freezer, put meat there as soon after cooking and cooling as possible, wrapping securely in freezer wrapping material.

· Leave cooked meat in large pieces; or remove fat and bone and slice, placing freezer paper between each slice. Or, cover meat in container with broth, sauce, or gravy. Reheat the frozen slices in gravy, broth, or sauce.

· Omit potatoes from stews before freezing. They will be much more flavorful if added fresh to the frozen stew when it is reheated.

· Sauces freeze beautifully. Pack in freezer containers with tight-fitting covers, leaving 1-inch head space for expansion.

· Soups that freeze well include vegetable, split pea, chicken noodle, onion soup, and chowders.

Maximum Storage Time at 0° F.

Macaroni and cheese	3 months
Chow mein	3 months
Baked beans	9 months
Spaghetti sauce	3 to 4 months
Stews and meat pies	6 months
Meat loaf	3 months
Sliced roast meat or poultry	2 months
Soups	6 months
Candied sweet potatoes	3 months
Commercial precooked foods	1 to 2 months

Pickling and Preserving

There is nothing lovelier than the fragrance of homemade chili sauce or chutney simmering away on the kitchen range. And what is more colorful on the holiday table than dishes of relishes and conserves?

VEGETABLES

To Sterilize Jars for Pickles and Preserves

Check jars for nicks, cracks, and sharp edges on sealing surfaces. Wash jars and lids in hot, soapy water. Rinse. Put jars and lids in large kettle. Cover with water. Bring to boiling; boil 10 minutes. Turn off heat. Leave jars and lids in water until ready to fill. Remove from hot water with tongs. Invert jars on paper towels to drain. Jars should be hot and dry when filled.

TOMATO CHUTNEY I

1 can (1 lb. 13 oz.) tomatoes, chopped	½ tsp. cumin seed
	¼ tsp. ground nutmeg
½ c. chopped onion (1 medium)	¼ tsp. mustard seeds
1 clove of garlic, minced	⅓ c. raisins, chopped
2 green apples, pared, cored, and chopped	½ tsp. salt
	½ to 1 c. light brown sugar, firmly packed
¼ tsp. crushed dried red pepper	1 c. vinegar
1 tsp. ground ginger	

Combine all ingredients in a large, heavy saucepan. Cook, uncovered, over medium heat, stirring occasionally, 20 to 30 minutes or until mixture is thick. To keep for future use, pour hot mixture into sterilized jars (*above*) and seal jars. If you are going to use it within a short time, cool the mixture and store it in the refrigerator. Makes about 3½ cups.

TOMATO CHUTNEY II

12 medium-size firm, ripe tomatoes	2 tsp. salt
	1 tsp. ground cinnamon
8 medium-size apples	1 tbs. ground ginger
4 medium-size red or green peppers	1 tsp. ground nutmeg
4 medium-size onions	3 c. brown sugar, firmly packed
1 pkg. (1 lb.) seedless raisins	¼ c. lime or lemon juice

Wash vegetables and apples. Scald, peel, core, and chop tomatoes. Pare, core, and chop apples; seed and chop peppers; peel and chop onions. Combine vegetables and apples with remaining ingredients in heavy kettle. Boil rapidly about 1¼ hours or until thickened. Pour at once into sterilized jars; seal. Label and store. Makes 12 half pints.

WATERMELON PICKLES

2 qts. prepared watermelon rind	1 lemon, thinly sliced
4 c. sugar	1 stick cinnamon (about 3 inches long)
2 c. vinegar	
2 c. water	1 tbs. whole cloves

To prepare watermelon rind: Remove all green from rind, peeling it about ¼ inch thick. Remove any pink melon left on rind. Cut rind into 1-inch cubes. Soak overnight in salt water to cover, using ¼ cup salt to each quart water. Drain; rinse rind in cold water. Put rind in a large kettle; cover with cold water; bring to boiling; simmer about 10 minutes or until barely tender. Drain well. Combine sugar, vinegar, 2 cups water, and lemon slices in kettle. Break cinnamon into pieces. Tie cinnamon pieces and cloves in small square of cheesecloth. Add to vinegar mixture. Bring to boiling, stirring until sugar is dissolved; simmer 10 minutes. Add rind; simmer until transparent. Ladle rind into hot, sterilized jars; pour syrup over; seal. Makes about 3 pints.

RED CHILI SAUCE

12 medium-size firm, ripe tomatoes	½ c. light brown sugar, firmly packed
4 medium-size onions	2 c. vinegar
6 large red peppers	1 tbs. mustard seed
2 large stalks celery	1 tbs. celery seed
1 tsp. salt	1 tbs. whole cloves
2 c. sugar	3 sticks whole cinnamon, broken
	1 tbs. whole allspice

Wash vegetables. Scald, peel, and core tomatoes; cut into quarters; chop very fine; pour into heavy kettle. Peel and quarter onions. Seed peppers; cut into strips. Cut celery into pieces. Grind onions, peppers, and celery, using coarsest blade of food grinder; discard juice. Mix vegetables with tomatoes; add salt, sugars, and vinegar. Tie spices loosely in cheesecloth bag (for easy removal later); add

to sauce. Boil mixture rapidly about 1½ hours or until as thick as desired, stirring occasionally. Stir often during last half hour to prevent sticking. Remove spice bag. Pour into hot, sterilized jars; seal. Label and store. Makes 6 half pints.

CORN RELISH

1 doz. large ears of corn	1 qt. diced celery
4 large green peppers, seeded and cut up	2 tsp. dry mustard
	½ tsp. celery seed
	1 tbs. mustard seed
4 large red peppers, seeded and cut up	½ tsp. turmeric
	1½ tbs. salt
5 large onions	2 c. sugar
	1 qt. vinegar

Boil corn 5 minutes. Cut kernels from ears of corn; there should be 2 quarts. Put green and red peppers and onions through food grinder using medium blade. Combine all ingredients in large kettle. Simmer 30 minutes, stirring often. Ladle into sterilized jars. Makes 8 pints.

MIXED MUSTARD PICKLES

1 medium-size head cauliflower	4 c. unpared large cucumber slices, ⅛ inch thick
3 green peppers	
1 lb. small white onions	1 c. salt
	6 c. water
2 lbs. green tomatoes	6 c. vinegar
	2 c. sugar
2 c. small cucumbers, 1½ inches long	2 tsp. celery seed
	¼ c. flour
	¾ tsp. turmeric
	¼ c. dry mustard

Wash cauliflower; remove outer green leaves. Break cauliflowerets apart. Cut peppers in half; remove seeds; slice in ¼-inch strips. Peel onions. Cut tomatoes in eighths. Combine all vegetables in a large bowl. Mix the salt and 4 cups water. Pour over vegetables; let stand at room temperature overnight. Bring vegetables in salt water to boiling. Combine vinegar, sugar, and celery seed in a saucepan. Blend flour, turmeric, and mustard with remaining 2 cups water. Stir mustard mixture into vinegar mixture. Cook, stirring constantly, until smooth and thickened. Drain salt water from vegetables. Stir in thickened vinegar sauce. Simmer 15 minutes, stirring gently from time to time. Fill sterilized jars. Makes about 7 pints.

JELLIES AND JAMS

Now you can make jellies and jams without even cooking them! With the aid of commercial pectin, garden-ripe fruits are easily turned into bright colored, fresh-flavored spreads. Or you can freeze the fruits right out of the garden and turn the frozen fruits into jellies or jams months later.

Commercial pectin comes in two forms, liquid and powdered. Recipe leaflets are included with each. Always follow directions for the particular pectin you are using—they are *not* interchangeable.

Cooked jams, jellies, and conserves have the advantage of being storable on a pantry shelf.

Uncooked jams and jellies should be stored in the freezer at 0° F. until needed. For use within 2 to 3 weeks, store in refrigerator.

For more information or additional recipes for jams or jellies, write General Foods Kitchens, General Foods Corporation, 250 North Street, White Plains, New York.

To Fill and Seal Glasses

To seal with paraffin: Remove jelly or jam from heat; skim off foam with metal spoon. Stir and skim, by turns, 5 minutes to cool slightly and prevent floating fruit in jam. Ladle quickly into glasses, leaving ½-inch space at top. Cover at once with ⅛-inch melted paraffin. Cool; cover glasses. Label; store in a cool place.

To seal without paraffin: Use jars with 2-piece metal lids. Remove jelly or jam from heat; quickly skim off foam with metal spoon. Ladle boiling hot jam into jars, leaving ⅛-inch space at top. Place lid on jar, screw band on tightly, and invert jar. Repeat with remaining jars. When all jars are filled, stand upright and cool. Shake gently after 30 minutes to prevent floating fruit. Label; store in a cool place.

COOKED GRAPE JELLY

3½ lbs. fully ripe	1 pkg. (1¾ oz.)
Concord grapes,	powdered pectin
washed	7 c. sugar
1½ c. water	

Prepare twelve 6-ounce jelly glasses and lids or covers (*page 492*). Crush grapes thoroughly; put in kettle. Add water. Simmer, covered, 10 minutes. Pour into jelly bag or a large square of cheesecloth several layers thick spread in a colander. Place in bowl. Bring corners of cloth together; twist bag; press with masher to extract juice. You should have 5 cups juice. If there is not quite enough juice, add small amount of water to jelly bag; squeeze again. Pour juice into 6- to 8-quart saucepan. Stir in pectin. Bring to boiling over high heat. Boil hard 1 minute. Add sugar. Bring to full, rolling boil (tumbling boil that cannot be stirred down). Boil hard 1 minute, stirring constantly. Remove from heat. See To Fill and Seal Glasses (*above*). Makes 12 glasses.

NO-COOK GRAPE JELLY

3 lbs. fully ripe	1 pkg. (1¾ oz.)
Concord grapes,	powdered pectin
washed	¾ c. water
5¾ c. sugar	

Prepare eight 6-ounce jelly glasses and lids or covers (*page 492*). Crush grapes thoroughly. Put in jelly bag or large square of cheesecloth several layers thick spread in a colander. Place in bowl. Bring corners of cloth together; twist bag; press with masher to extract juice. You should have 3 cups. If there is not quite enough juice, add small amount of water to jelly bag; squeeze again. Pour juice into large bowl; add sugar. Mix well. Mix pectin and water in small saucepan. Bring to boiling; boil 1 minute, stirring constantly. Stir into grape juice mixture. Continue stirring 3 minutes (a few sugar crystals will remain). Ladle quickly into prepared glasses. Cover at once with tight lids. Let set at room temperature (it may take 24 hours). Store in refrigerator. Plan to use within 3 weeks. Makes 8 glasses.

COOKED STRAWBERRY JAM

2 qts. fully ripe	1 pkg. (1¾ oz.)
strawberries,	powdered pectin
washed and	7 c. sugar
hulled	

Prepare eleven 6-ounce or eight 8-ounce jelly glasses and lids or covers (*page 492*). Crush strawberries, one layer at a time, so each berry is reduced to pulp. Measure, packing into cup; there should be 4½ cups. If there is not quite enough, add water to fill last fraction of cup needed. Put into 6- or 8-quart kettle. Mix in pectin. Stir over high heat until mixture boils hard. Stir in sugar. Bring to full rolling boil (tumbling boil that cannot be stirred down). Boil hard 1 minute, stirring constantly. Remove from heat. Follow directions in To Fill and Seal Glasses, *page 494*. Makes 11 or 8 glasses.

NO-COOK STRAWBERRY JAM

1 qt. fully ripe strawberries, washed and hulled	4 c. sugar 1 pkg. (1¾ oz.) powdered pectin ¾ c. water

Prepare six 8-ounce jelly glasses and lids or covers (*page 492*). Crush strawberries, one layer at a time, in large bowl. Stir in sugar. Mix pectin and water in small saucepan. Bring to boiling; boil 1 minute, stirring constantly. Stir into strawberry mixture. Continue stirring 3 minutes (a few sugar crystals will remain). Ladle quickly into prepared glasses. Cover at once with tight lids. Let set at room temperature (it may take 24 hours). Store in refrigerator. Plan to use within 3 weeks. Makes 6 glasses.

RED PEPPER AND ORANGE JAM

25 sweet red peppers 2 large oranges	2 c. vinegar 4 c. sugar 2 tsp. salt

Prepare six half-pint jars and covers (*page 492*). Wash and drain peppers; remove seeds and white membranes; cut peppers into strips. Cut oranges into eighths. Grind peppers, using coarsest blade of food chopper; drain well; discard juice. Grind oranges, add to drained peppers in kettle. Add vinegar, sugar, and salt; cook rapidly, stirring often, about 25 minutes or until jam is thick and clear. Remove from heat. Follow directions in To Fill and Seal Glasses (*page 492*). Makes 6 half pints.

MARMALADES, CONSERVES, AND BUTTER

CHINESE APPLE-GINGER MARMALADE

3 lbs. sugar	3 tbs. lemon juice
1¾ c. water	1 tbs. ground ginger
2 tbs. grated orange rind	3 lbs. cooking apples, peeled, cored, and diced
1 tbs. grated lemon rind	3 tbs. chopped candied ginger
⅓ c. orange juice	

Prepare twelve 8-ounce jelly glasses and lids or covers (*page 492*). Place sugar and water in 5- or 6-quart kettle. Add rinds, juices, and ginger; boil 5 minutes. Add apples and candied ginger; bring to boiling, stirring slowly. Let simmer gently 1 hour, stirring occasionally. Remove from heat. See To Fill and Seal Glasses (*page 494*). Makes 12 glasses.

SPICY TOMATO MARMALADE

12 medium-size firm, ripe, red or yellow tomatoes 2 large lemons	7 c. sugar ¼ c. chopped candied ginger

Prepare seven half-pint jars and covers (*page 492*). Scald, peel and core tomatoes; cut into eighths. Cut lemons in half lengthwise; slice paper thin. Combine tomatoes, lemons, and sugar in glass or pottery bowl; cover; refrigerate overnight. Next day drain off liquid, cook liquid and any undissolved sugar rapidly until syrup spins a thread from tip of spoon. Add tomatoes, lemons and ginger; cook over medium heat about 30 minutes or until tomatoes are transparent and marmalade is thickened. Stir occasionally; stir constantly during last few minutes of cooking. Remove from heat. Follow directions in To Fill and Seal Glasses (*page 494*). Makes 7 half pints.

APRICOT-PINEAPPLE CONSERVE

1 pkg. (8 oz.) dried apricots	½ c. finely chopped walnuts
1 can (1 lb. 4 oz.) crushed pine-apple	2 tbs. lemon juice
	4 c. sugar
⅔ c. seedless raisins	½ bottle liquid fruit pectin
	Melted paraffin

Prepare six 8-ounce jelly glasses and lids or covers (*page 492*). Combine apricots and enough water to just cover in small saucepan. Bring to boiling; simmer 5 minutes. Drain and chop; reserve ½ cup juice. Combine apricots, reserved juice, pineapple, raisins, nuts, and lemon juice in 4-quart saucepan. Add sugar; stir to blend well. Bring mixture to a full boil over high heat, stirring constantly. When conserve is bubbling rapidly over entire surface, boil hard 1 more minute, stirring. Remove from heat; stir in pectin. Ladle into prepared glasses. Cover at once with ⅛-inch layer of melted paraffin. Makes 6 glasses.

APPLE-TOMATO BUTTER

1 orange, quartered and seeded	1 can (about 1 lb.) tomatoes
5 medium-size apples, pared, quartered, and cored	1½ c. sugar
	2-in. cinnamon stick
	1 tbs. vinegar

Prepare five 6-ounce glasses and lids or covers (*page 492*). Put orange and apples through food grinder using medium blade. Combine with tomatoes in kettle. Cook, covered, over low heat 20 minutes or until fruit is soft. Press mixture through food mill or strainer. Return mixture to kettle. Add sugar, cinnamon, and vinegar. Bring to boiling; cook slowly, stirring occasionally, about 30 minutes or until thickened. Remove from heat. Follow directions in To Fill and Seal Glasses (*page 494*). Makes 5 glasses.

For additional recipes for pickling and preserving and information on home canning, write for the following publications:

Home Canning of Fruits and Vegetables (20¢ per copy)
USDA Bulletin #8
Division of Publications
Office of Information
US Department of Agriculture
Washington, D.C. 20250

Ball Blue Book (25¢ per copy)
Ball Brothers Co., Inc.
Muncie, Ind. 47303

Bernadine Home Canning Guide (25¢ per copy)
Bernadine, Inc.
P. O. Box 725
Evansville, Ind. 47706

Kerr Home Canning Book (25¢ per copy)
Kerr Glass Manufacturing Corp., Dept. 238
Sand Springs, Okla. 74063

Chapter Twenty-Seven

Barbecues and Outdoor Cooking

Come summer, the smoky fragrance of outdoor cooking floats from one suburban street to another, and those who aren't having barbecued spareribs probably are about to cut into juicy steaks or golden brown, spit roasted chickens.

We've come a long way since the barbecue craze first brought American families onto their patios for summer meals. Barbecuing isn't even restricted to summer any longer. So good is the special flavor of grilled hamburgers and marinated meats we're designing charcoal grills for indoors and using built-in gas-fired briquette grills and portable electric grills and rotisseries in our kitchens.

Patio barbecues range from the easiest kind of hamburgers or hot-dog meals to elegant gourmet feasts with wine.

Picnics travel in style today, more lazy and carefree than ever because most of the food is prepared ahead and transported in insulated cooler chests and jugs, or departmentalized wicker baskets roomy enough to hold an entire meal.

Pit cooking is becoming a popular way of preparing outdoor meals. Not that there's anything new about this method of cooking—the East Coast's clambake has been popular since the American Indians first taught us how, and Hawaii had its luaus long before the first missionaries came.

Also enjoyed by many are oyster roasts, campfire meals (with wood for fuel on rough stone fireplaces), and meals afloat in cabin cruisers or small yachts.

Barbecue Equipment

If you're in the market for a new grill, look the field over carefully to find one that gives you complete flexibility. If you belong to the every-other-Saturday outdoor cooking school, there's no sense in investing in anything more elaborate than a simple grill big enough for steaks, hamburgers, hot dogs, and cut-up chicken. On the other hand, if your family eats outdoors every nice summer night, those grills with hoods and motorized spits on which you can bake, broil, spit roast, smoke roast, and set a timer may be well worth the extra cost.

Principal Types of Charcoal Grills

Table and portable models

There are many of these: small square or bowl-shaped models with a single grid; hibachis made of cast iron set on wooden feet (these may or may not have adjustable grids); and the simple fold-up types which are intended primarily for traveling.

Free-Standing Models

Bowl-shaped braziers: They range from the simplest type with detachable legs and a one-position grid to elaborate models complete with hoods, motorized spits, and grids that can be adjusted to three or more heights. Things to look for: the metal of the bowl should be sturdy and thick so it won't burn out or rust easily; the mechanism which raises and lowers the grid should work easily and lock firmly in position; and the wire grid on which food cooks should be of sturdy material and hold steady on its center post.

Oblong grills: Some of these have tube-shaped fire boxes, others are rectangular. Many have adjustable dampers and most have half-hoods to shield food from the wind. Other features include bottom storage shelves, warming ovens in the hood, work counters at the side which can be folded down when not in use, and motorized spits.

Deluxe roll-around models: These have completely enclosed fireboxes, grids, and spits. If you're an ardent outdoor chef and cook most of your summer meals outdoors (or live in a climate where you can cook out all year), this is the type of grill for you. In addition to broiling and rotissing, you can roast, bake, and smoke on these. In fact, they'll cook your whole dinner. Just arrange the meat on the grid or spit, close the hood, and adjust the dampers. The heat from the fire circulates under the hood, reflects from the inner surfaces onto the meat, and allows the meat to cook in its own juices just as in your kitchen oven. The other foods are arranged on various attachments and bake right along with the meat. There are many styles available: rectangular, tube-shaped, or boxlike grills set on legs; upright boxlike grills that look like cabinets; deep bowl-shaped grills with bowl-shaped covers; and other, more unusual shapes. You'll find a wide variety of features to choose from: extra-large grids, oversized wheels, cutting boards, work counters, hood windows, temperature gauges, fire-starting devices, and storage cabinets.

Gas and Electric Grills

Gas-fired briquette grills. If you dislike the inconvenience of starting the fire and cleaning up the ashes, then you're sure to like the no-fuss, no-muss feature of these. Most may use either natural or LP gas as a fuel to heat permanent ceramic briquettes to a good cooking temperature. They may be permanent installations or portable units. Some are even designed for kitchen installation.

Portable electric grills and rotisseries. There are a variety of portable appliances to set up on your porch or patio or in the backyard which are a great boon to outdoor cookery.

Barbecue Utensils

Kitchen utensils belong in the kitchen. There are barbecue tools especially designed with long handles to avoid burns and spills, and many are designed to be hung conveniently near or on the grill. There are three basic types:

Tools for the fire—a safety must. To control the fire, you should have: 1) A rake to level the coals to a flat, even-cooking surface; 2) charcoal tongs to handle individual pieces of coal; 3) a poker to stoke the fire; 4) a scoop or shovel to add or remove coals. To help start the fire and ready it for cooking, an electric fire starter and a fire blower are great helps.

Tools for the food. These are some of the essentials: 1) A two-tined fork (great for getting food off skewers); 2) a basting brush; 3) tongs in two sizes—small or medium for efficient handling of steaks and chops, and large tongs for roasts; 4) one or more sharp knives; 5) a grill thermometer to indicate the exact heat of the coals. There are also gadgets for fun—a many-pronged hot dog roaster, handled barbecue skewers for kabobs, handled basket broilers.

Extras for cooking and serving. Foil baking pans to heat hors d'oeuvres, rolls, and other foods over the coals; cast iron cookware to cook a pot of stew or fry a batch of potatoes right on the grill; servers and trays that hold the food at just the right serving temperature; carts to transport fixin's from kitchen to patio.

Does Fuel Affect Flavor?

After many interviews and tests, here is what we found out. Fuel alone does *not* affect flavor. The way you use fuel does help determine which of these three flavors (charcoal, natural, or smoked) you'll end up with.

Charcoal flavor, that tantalizing taste we all associate with outdoor meat cookery, is not produced by a magic something in charcoal. Charcoal is flavorless and odorless. Charcoal flavor is actually produced when fats and other meat juices drip onto a hot fire, thus causing the fire to flame up and char the meat. The fire can be made of charcoal, charcoal briquettes, gas-fired briquettes, or wood.

Natural flavor is the flavor we normally associate with a particular food. You get a good, natural flavor from cooking on your kitchen range (but without the fun and drama of the outdoors). When barbecuing, you can produce this same natural flavor in these ways: 1) On a portable or electric grill; 2) on an open charcoal or gas-fired briquette grill when the meat is placed high enough above the fire so that there are no flare-ups; 3) in a closed, deluxe charcoal or gas-fired briquette grill over a low fire (in this case, you are actually roasting).

Smoked flavor can be achieved only by cooking over a fragrant wood fire or by tossing damp hickory chips or mesquite on a charcoal or gas-fired briquette fire. You'll discover that the smoked flavor is most pronounced when the cooking is done in a closed grill over a very slow fire.

Tips for Planning Outdoor Meals

• There's one cardinal rule always to keep in mind when planning an out-of-doors meal, whether it's a simple picnic or an elaborate party feast. Have an alternate plan ready in case of bad weather. It's not only rain that could wash out your party—often a sudden drop in temperature makes it too cool to dine in the open.
• While making up your menu, think in terms of transportation. A portable cart is a great help. It not only saves trips out to the barbecue, but is equally useful as a depository of used dishes and silver to be brought back.
• Make salads and desserts ahead.
• Place ice cubes around crisp vegetable relishes in serving bowls.
• Make sure the tall frosty pitchers holding chilled drinks tinkle with plenty of ice cubes.
• The go-withs are just as important as the main dish. Make sure hot weather menus include all essential food elements for a nourishing diet. And no matter how hot and humid

the weather, at least one hot food (besides the meat from the grill) should be included in every evening meal.

Building a Charcoal Fire

Charcoal comes in many forms, but most satisfactory are the compact briquettes made from hardwood. Keep them dry—if damp they take longer to ignite and create smoke.

Many different types of fire-starters are now on the market. The safest and surest are those of treated compressed paper. Liquid and jellied starters must be handled more carefully to avoid dangerous flare-ups. Briquettes may be soaked in liquid fire-starters in a metal container. Never add liquid to a fire already ignited, even if the briquettes look quite dead. Also, avoid any fire-starters which might impart unpleasant flavor to food. Electric fire-starters are quick, easy, and foolproof. Old-fashioned bellows are a help in whipping up a sluggish fire.

All fires need a draft. A fire box with adjustable dampers is the best kind. For units without such dampers, first line the box with aluminum foil, then place a thick layer of sand or coarse gravel over the foil. The foil collects dripping grease, makes clean-up easier: pick up foil, sand, and ashes and dump it all out at once.

The size of your fire is determined by the food to be grilled. Have the bed of charcoal a little wider all around than the area of the food to be cooked. Use a shallow fire for broiling; for roasting build a deeper fire at the rear of the grill, keep it replenished as briquettes burn down to soft ash.

How to judge the intensity of the fire. Charcoal grilling is always subject to guess. Certain kinds of charcoal give off more intense heat than others, weather makes a big difference (in cooler weather, food takes longer to cook), and breezes wafting over the food also slow down the process. There are grill thermometers available which will give the intensity of the heat inside the fire box.

Adjusting the temperature. When cooking over charcoal, it's easier to adjust the food to the heat than the heat to the food. This is why an adjustable grid is so important. For slower cooking raise the height of the grid, for faster cooking lower it.

But it may be so hot that even raising the grid is not enough. Then try spreading the briquettes farther apart; if still too hot, sprinkle briquettes lightly with water (but remove food temporarily—this will cause steam). If your fire is not hot enough, push the briquettes closer together, add a few fresh ones, placing the new briquettes under rather than over the coals. For spit roasting or any long cooking, you will need a deep bed of coals, several layers thick, and you may have to replenish the bed several times during cooking.

Safety measures. Beware of sparks flying when the fire is first started. If any flammable materials are nearby, these small sparks could quickly ignite them. Have a bottle of water with a sprinkler top handy. Sprinkle just enough water on any flare-ups to douse the flames, but don't soak the coals and ruin the fire.

Secrets for the Barbecue Chef

· As a general rule, all food should be at room temperature before cooking. If frozen, it should be completely thawed before placing on the grid unless recipe specifies otherwise; even refrigerated foods should be at room temperature from 1 to 2 hours before cooking. The one exception: thin steaks which you want to cook rare should be cold when placed on the grid.
· The grilling and spit roasting timetables on pages 502 and 503 are useful as an approximate guide.
· Most experts agree that meat should not be salted before grilling—that salt only draws out the juices and tends to toughen the meat. The best time to add salt is just before removing it from the grid, or after steak has been turned, sprinkle salt on the cooked side.
· Start the fire 30 minutes to 1 hour ahead (depending on the size of the grill and amount of fuel needed). Charcoal should be even gray in color with a ruddy glow before food is placed over it.

Definitions of Outdoor Cooking Methods

Grill: To cook on the open grids, directly above the heat.

Spit Roast: To fasten meat or poultry on a spit which will rotate steadily above or in front of the heat. *Rotisserie* cooking is the same thing but implies an electrically operated spit which may be used indoors or out, a separate unit, or an attachment for the gas or electric oven.

Skewer Cookery: Small pieces of meat, poultry, fish or vegetables are threaded on skewers and cooked directly over the heat. The skewers may be placed directly on the grid or may be used as attachments to motor-driven spits. Other terms for food so cooked: *En brochette* or *shish-kebab.*

Skillet Cookery: This is a favorite method with campers. Large, shallow, iron skillets are placed on the grid directly above the fire. It's the best method for frying or cooking any foods which require moist heat.

Foil-wrapped Foods: Many foods can be baked right in the ashes of the charcoal fire or on the grid if wrapped in aluminum foil. This is an especially good way to cook fresh or frozen vegetables.

Smoke Cooking: The food cooks very slowly in the heat of thick smoke induced by burning dampened hickory or other hardwood chips. An ancient Chinese method of cookery, it is used for fish, meat, and poultry. While the food is usually placed on hooks so that it hangs suspended in the smoke, smoke cooking is also possible in barbecue grills which have fitted hoods and adjustable dampers.

Pit Roasting: There are two methods of pit roasting—the open pit and the closed, or covered pit. Both require a pit lined with heated rocks and a layer of ferns, leaves, or corn husks. Open pit roasting now is usually done by professionals for large gatherings. One of the most popular examples of covered pit roasting is the Clambake (*page 507*).

MEAT

BEEF

Selecting Steaks

These are the steaks to buy for grilling: sirloin, porterhouse, T-bone, club, flank, and round (the last two may need tenderizing).

If buying club or T-bone steaks, allow one steak for each person; for other steaks figure ¾ to 1 pound of steak per person. Have steaks cut 1 to 2½ inches thick.

Score steak edges ½ to 1 inch apart to prevent curling. For steaks that need tenderizing, use instant meat tenderizer as label directs, or marinate them. (See marinade recipes, on *page 353*.)

When heat is ready, place steak on greased grill. For 1-inch steaks, meat should be 3 to 4 inches from coals; for thicker steaks, 6 to 7 inches from coals. Grill one side, turn with tongs (a fork lets juices escape), grill second side. Cut near bone to check doneness.

SALT STEAK

5 c. coarse kosher salt	Sirloin steak, 2½ inches thick
1½ c. water	

Mix salt and enough water to make a paste. Spread a layer half an inch thick on each side of steak. Place a wet paper towel on top of salt. Grill over hot coals about 25 minutes on each side for rare, longer for medium. Test by making a small cut in the center of the steak. Knock off salt crust and slice. Makes 5 or 6 servings. (Do not use a steak less than 2 inches thick or steak will be salty. Cook for about 20 minutes on each side for rare for a 2-inch steak.)

HAMBURGERS

Choose chuck, round, flank, or sirloin tip to be ground to order. Look for meat with a bright red color and some fat for flavor and juiciness. For lean meat (such as top round), when you have it ground to order, have 2 ounces of suet ground with each pound of meat. For juicy tender burgers, have your meat ground medium or coarse. A pound of ground beef makes 4 thick burgers or 8 thin ones.

Always handle ground beef lightly. Gentle handling keeps hamburgers tender, vigorous handling will toughen them. To shape hamburgers, divide ground beef into the number of portions desired. Pat each quickly and lightly into burger of desired thickness. Or shape meat into long cylinder and cut rounds of desired thickness.

Brush hamburgers with melted butter or margarine. Place on grill 3 to 4 inches from coals. When bottom is done, turn and grill the other side.

For hamburgers 1 inch thick cook each side 4 minutes for rare, 6 minutes for medium. Frozen hamburgers may be grilled without previous thawing: cook 6 minutes a side for rare, 8 minutes per side for medium.

Hamburger Go-Withs

Set out a selection of relishes, catsup, mustard, sliced onions, and assorted sauces. Or go international and top your burgers with one of the combinations on *page 152*.

HOT DOGS

Summer wouldn't be summer without those grilled frankfurters, known popularly as hot dogs. But we're all for some variations on a theme—to make these year-round favorites something extra special, try the ones on *pages 185-7*.

SPARERIBS

Fresh spareribs, which are readily available, are best for barbecuing.

Top-quality ribs have a good portion of meat between the rib bones and a thin covering over the bones. You may buy either regular ribs or loin ribs. The extra meatiness of the latter makes them excellent for barbecuing. "Country style spareribs" are cut with part of the backbone. Buy ¾ to 1 pound for each serving. Store them loosely wrapped in the refrigerator and plan to use within 2 days.

Spareribs may be grilled in one piece or cut between the ribs into serving-size pieces and then grilled. For threading on a spit, they are left in the single piece. Place ribs on grill 5 inches from coals. If they become as brown as you wish before they have finished cooking, wrap them in heavy-duty aluminum foil to complete cooking until tender.

Spareribs require long, slow cooking and must be thoroughly cooked with no pink visible. To cook over charcoal without any precooking requires 1 to 1½ hours. You can reduce the time by parboiling for 30 to 45 minutes or roasting in the oven at 350° F. for 45 minutes; this also has the advantage of melting off most of the excess fat. Then brush partially cooked ribs with basting sauce before placing over the coals. They should be turned and basted frequently. Cook until crisp, glazed, browned, and fork-tender.

Barbecue Sauce for Spareribs

1 c. chopped onion (1 large)	1 can (8 oz.) tomato sauce
¼ c. pure vegetable oil	2 tbs. butter or margarine
	2 tbs. vinegar

Sauté onion in oil until soft. Add remaining ingredients; simmer 10 minutes. Brush on ribs during grilling. Makes about 1½ cups.

Baste or Marinade for Ribs

2 tbs. soy sauce	½ c. pure vegetable oil
¼ c. wine vinegar	
1 clove of garlic, crushed	

Combine ingredients; brush on ribs while grilling. As marinade: double recipe; pour over ribs; let stand for several hours, turning often. Makes about 1 cup.

See Fruit Barbecue Baste for Spareribs, page 354.

GRILLED HAM SLICES

Ready-to-cook ham steak, 1 inch thick, should be grilled over low coals, 6 to 8 inches from heat for 5 to 7 minutes on each side. Baste as it cooks with:

Barbecue Sauce: Combine ½ cup catsup, ¼ cup vinegar, ¼ cup water and 1 teaspoon dry mustard. Simmer 5 minutes.

For Pineapple Baste for Ham Steaks, see page 354.

LAMB CHOPS, STEAKS, OR KABOBS

Trim excess fat from loin, shoulder, or rib chops and score edges to prevent curling. Try rubbing chops or steaks with herbs and olive oil before placing over fire—thyme and oregano or both are good with lamb. Lamb for kabobs may be cut from leg or shoulder.

Cook kabobs 4 to 5 inches above coals, turning frequently.

Another succulent way of grilling lamb is Leg O' Lamb Butterfly. Delicate in flavor, cut across the grain in tender pink slices, this makes a marvelous party offering.

LEG O' LAMB BUTTERFLY

5 to 6 lb. leg of lamb	1 pkg. Old-fashioned French dressing mix
	Seasoned salt

Have lamb boned and cut open butterfly fashion. Prepare French dressing according to package directions; pour over lamb in shallow pan and let stand about 1 hour; sprinkle generously with seasoned salt. Place the marinated lamb, fat side up, over medium-hot coals and broil 45 minutes to 1 hour, basting with marinade and turning to brown both sides. Cut in ¼-inch thick slices across the grain. Makes 6 to 8 servings.

For Marinades and Bastes for Lamb, see page 353.

GRILLING TIME-TEMPERATURE CHART

Meat	Cut	Size or Weight	Temperature (on grill thermometer)	Approximate Cooking Time (each side)		
				Rare	Medium	Well-done
Beef	Steak	1-inch thick	325–350° F.	4 to 6 min.	7 min.	10 to 12 min.
	Steak	1½ inches	325–350° F.	5 to 7	8 to 10	12 to 15
	Steak	2 inches	300–350° F.	8 to 12	15 to 18	20 to 25
	Steak	2½ inches	300–350° F.	12 to 15	18 to 23	25 to 30
	Flank Steak	whole	325–350° F.	4 to 5	5 to 7	——
	Hamburger	1-inch	300–325° F.	4	6	
	Kabobs	1½-inch cubes	325–350° F.	5 to 7	8 to 10	12 to 15
Lamb	Chops	1 to 1½ inches	300–325° F.	4 to 6	6 to 7	6 to 8
	Kabobs	1½ inches	300–325° F.	5 to 7	8 to 10	12 to 15
Ham	Slice	1 to 1½ inches	275–325° F.	—	—	15 to 18
Pork	Spareribs	4 pounds	200–225° F.	—	—	1½ hrs.
Frankfurters			350–375° F.	—	—	3 to 5 min.

Spit Roasting

· The *secret of success* in spit roasting is having the meat correctly balanced on the spit. If roast is off center, it will jerk and stop during cooking which interferes with the motor and results in uneven cooking. Secure the roast on the spit so it cannot slip around. Adjust and tighten holding forks carefully; use long skewers as an extra help if needed. Many grills have weight compensators to adjust the spit for balance during roasting.

Temperature should be lower than for broiling, but for charcoal cooking an even, deep fire bed must be maintained. If you have a spit thermometer, it should read from 250° to 300° F.

· The spit should turn away from the cook so fat drips into drip pan on the upward motion of spit with less danger of flare-ups. Build fire toward back; put drip pan in front, directly under meat.

· Cooking time will vary with the size and temperature of the meat, the temperature of the fire, and the breeze. It is best to use a meat thermometer. Insert tip in center of roast or inner thigh muscles of chicken or turkey. Be sure it touches no bone, fat, or metal of the spit. For rare, cook until meat thermometer registers 140° F.; medium to 150° F.; and for well-done, 160° F. to 170° F.

· Poultry, small and large birds, and all cuts of meat suitable for oven roasting may be spit roasted.

· For gas-fired grills and electric rotisseries, follow their specific directions for controlling temperature.

SPIT ROASTING TIME-TEMPERATURE CHART

Meat	Cut	Weight	Temperature (spit thermometer)	Approximate Cooking Time		
				Rare	Medium	Well-done
Beef	Standing rib	3 to 5 ribs	300° F.	2 hours (140° F.)	2½ to 3 hours (150° F.)	3½ to 4 hours (160° to 170° F.)
	Rolled rib	6 to 7 pounds	300° F.	2 hours (140° F.)	2½ to 3 hours (150° F.)	3½ to 4 hours (160–170° F.)
	Rump or Eye round	4 to 5 pounds	250° F.	2 hours	2½ to 3 hours	3½ to 4 hours
Lamb	Leg, bone in	7 to 8 pounds	300° F.	2¼ hours (140° F.)	3 to 3½ hours (150° F.)	4 hours (160–170° F.)
	Boned rolled leg	4 to 6 pounds	300° F.	1¾ to 2 hours	2¼ to 2½ hours	3 to 3½ hours
	Boned rolled shoulder	3 to 6 pounds	250° F.	2 to 2¼ hours	2½ to 3 hours	3½ to 4 hours
Pork	Loin	5 to 14 pounds	250° F.	———	———	2 to 4 hours (185° F.)
	Shoulder	3 to 6 pounds	250° F.	———	———	2 to 3½ hours (185° F.)
	Fresh Ham	10 to 16 pounds	250° F.	———	———	4 to 6 hours (185° F.)
	Spareribs	4 to 5 pounds	250° F.	———	———	1½ hours (185° F.)
Veal	Boned rolled shoulder	3 to 5 pounds	250° F.	———	———	1¾ to 2½ hours (170–180° F.)
	Boned rump	6 to 7 pounds	250° F.	———	———	3½ to 4 hours (170–180° F.)

POULTRY

Who can count the ways of barbecuing chicken? Place it cut up on the grill, cut in quarters or split in halves, spit roast it whole, use a different marinade or basting sauce each time. And have you tried barbecuing turkey? Or duckling? Whatever the bird, the sauce is important. Not only for adding luscious flavor, but keeping the tender flesh moist and succulent.

BARBECUING TIME-TEMPERATURE CHART

Bird	Size or Weight	Method of Cooking	Temperature of Fire	Approx. Cooking Time (Well-done 175° F.)
Chicken	Cut up	Grilling	300–325° F.	24 to 30 minutes
	Split	Grilling	300–325° F.	30 to 45 minutes
	Whole, 2 pounds	Spit roasting	300–325° F.	55 to 60 minutes
	Whole, 3 pounds	Spit roasting	275° F.	1 to 1½ hours
Cornish hens	Whole, 1 pound	Spit roasting	300° F.	45 to 60 minutes
Turkey	Cut up	Grilling	275° F.	45 to 55 minutes
	Split	Grilling	275° F.	1¼ to 1½ hours
	Whole, 4 to 6 pounds	Spit roasting	275° F.	1½ to 2 hours
	Whole, 6 to 8 pounds	Spit roasting	275° F.	2 to 2½ hours
	Whole, 8 to 10 pounds	Spit roasting	275° F.	2½ to 3 hours
	Whole, 10 to 12 pounds	Spit roasting	275° F.	3 to 3½ hours
	Frozen boned turkey roll—3 to 5 pounds	Spit roasting	275° F.	(Thaw before cooking) 2 to 2½ hours
Duckling	Split	Grilling	275° F.	45 to 60 minutes
	Whole	Spit roasting	275° F.	2 to 2½ hours

GRILLED CHICKEN

Wash chicken; drain and pat dry. Remove wings from quartered and halved chickens. (The wings do not require as long cooking as breast meat, and removal shortens cooking time of breast portion.) Season with salt, pepper, and poultry seasoning, if desired. Brush with melted butter or margarine.

Place chicken pieces on grill 6 to 8 inches above hot, glowing coals. The wings may be added 15 minutes after meatier pieces. Cook, turning occasionally, until meaty pieces are fork-tender, 30 to 55 minutes. Length of cooking time will depend upon size of chicken, heat of fire, and weather conditions. Chicken may be brushed with favorite barbecue sauce the last 15 minutes of cooking period, if desired.

SPIT ROASTED CHICKEN
(*Pictured opposite page 436*)

Wash chicken; drain and pat dry. Season body cavity with salt or poultry seasoning. Fasten neck skin to back with skewer. Flatten wings over breast, then tie cord around breast to hold wings securely. Tie drumsticks securely to tail.

Insert spit rod through center of bird from tail end toward front. Insert skewers firmly in place in bird and screw tightly. Test the balance. *Bird must balance on spit so it will rotate smoothly throughout the cooking period.*

Arrange hot charcoal briquettes at back of fire box. Place a foil drip pan in front of briquettes. Place spit in rotisserie and start motor as barbecue manufacturer directs.

Brush chicken with melted butter or margarine at beginning of cooking. Chicken may be brushed with Lemon Basting Sauce (*page 354*) or with bottled barbecue sauce the last 30 minutes of cooking time. Cook until thickest parts are fork-tender and drumstick feels soft when pressed between protected fingers, about 1½ to 2 hours. Cooking time will depend on size of chicken, heat of fire, weather conditions.

SPIT ROASTED ROCK CORNISH HENS

Thaw frozen birds completely before cooking. Follow directions on page 504 for Spit Roasted Chicken. Cook according to chart. If stuffed, allow an additional 20 minutes cooking time.

GRILLED TURKEY

Turkey may be cut up, quartered, or split in halves and cooked directly over the fire just like chicken. Because the pieces are larger, they require longer cooking and a slower fire (or the grid should be raised farther from the heat). Place pieces bone side or inside down first; turn several times during cooking. Brush with melted butter or margarine during first part of cooking; during last half hour baste with barbecue sauce. Or marinate the cut-up turkey pieces before cooking as in the following recipe for Barbecued Turkey. Remember, white meat cooks more quickly than dark; wings and pieces of breast may be finished before thighs or legs. To test for doneness, pierce leg with fork in thickest part. Turkey is done if meat is tender.

BARBECUED TURKEY

1 c. dry white wine	1 clove of garlic,
¼ c. pure vegetable	mashed
oil	1 tsp. salt
2 tbs. butter or	¼ tsp. pepper
margarine	½ tsp. leaf oregano,
½ c. finely chopped	crumbled
onion (1	½ tsp. leaf basil,
medium)	crumbled
⅓ c. chopped green	5 to 8 lb. turkey
pepper	

Combine wine, oil, butter or margarine, onion, green pepper, garlic, salt, pepper, oregano, and basil in saucepan. Simmer 10 minutes. Cut up turkey into 10 serving pieces (cut breast into 4 pieces); do not use back. Pour marinade over turkey in glass, pottery, or plastic bowl. Marinate 4 hours, turning occasionally. Remove turkey pieces; strain marinade. Place turkey on grill, bone side down. Grill about 25 minutes; baste with marinade while broiling. Turn; place a piece of foil loosely over top. Grill about 20 minutes. While grilling, sprinkle charcoal several times with a little water so turkey broils and steams and stays moist. Makes 5 or 6 servings.

SPIT ROASTED TURKEY

Turkeys of any size may be cooked on a rotisserie. Some rotisseries may be limited to a certain maximum-weight bird, so it is wise to check manufacturer's weight suggestions before buying a turkey for rotisserie cooking. For operation of rotisserie, follow manufacturer's directions.

Rub body cavity lightly with salt, if desired. Push drumsticks under band of skin at tail, or tie drumsticks securely to tail. Fasten neck skin to back with skewer. Flatten wings over breast, then tie cord around breast to hold wings securely.

Insert spit rod through center of bird from tail end toward front. Insert skewers firmly in place in bird and screw tightly. Test the balance. *Bird must balance on spit so it will rotate smoothly throughout the cooking period.* Place spit in rotisserie. Brush turkey with melted butter or margarine. Turkey may be brushed with Lemon Basting Sauce (*page 354*) or with bottled barbecue sauce, if desired, the last 30 to 45 minutes of cooking. Follow chart for rotisserie temperature setting and roast until done.

SPIT ROASTED BONELESS TURKEY ROLLS

Turkey rolls, sometimes called turkey roasts, are boneless white or dark meat or a combination of the two. They may be cooked in the oven or on the rotisserie. Leave rolls or roast in original wrapper and thaw in refrigerator from 1 to 2 days. Remove wrapper and leave string in place while cooking.

· Rinse roast with cold water; drain and pat dry. If roast is not preseasoned, rub lightly with salt and pepper.

· Insert spit rod through center of turkey roll. Insert skewers firmly in place in roast and screw tightly. Test the balance. *Roll must balance on spit so it will rotate smoothly throughout the cooking period.* Place spit in rotisserie. Insert meat thermometer so bulb rests in center of meat and does not touch spit. Brush roast with melted butter or margarine.

· Follow chart for rotisserie temperature setting and roast until done (170° to 175° F. on meat thermometer). No further basting is necessary.

· For best results in slicing, allow roast to stand 20 to 30 minutes to absorb the juices. Remove string; use a sharp knife or meat slicer and slice thinly across the roast.

DUCKLING

Barbecued duckling is a gourmet's delight. It can be split in halves and grilled directly over the fire, or spit roasted. Whichever way it is cooked, as much interior fat as possible should be removed before cooking, and a deep drip pan should be placed immediately beneath the duckling, with the fire banked to the back of the grill, for duck gives off considerable fat.

SPIT ROASTED DUCKLING

Season duckling cavity with salt, pepper, and one of the following: marjoram, poultry seasoning, or chopped garlic. If desired, place 1 orange or 1 apple, quartered, in cavity.

Skewer neck skin to back; tie cord crisscross fashion around duckling beginning at neck and ending with legs. Insert spit from tail through length of body, piercing neck. Insert skewers firmly at both ends and screw tightly.

Follow chart for rotisserie temperature setting and roast until done. Duckling is done when drumstick meat feels soft when pressed between protected fingers. A stuffed duckling requires about 3 hours.

FISH AND SHELLFISH

Grilled fresh salmon, roasted to a golden brown, dribbling with butter sauce, is one of the delights of summer. And what is a greater treat than fresh-caught brook trout gently sautéed in a heavy skillet?

For barbecuing over direct heat, steaks of such fish as salmon, halibut, and swordfish or small whole fish, such as porgies or yellow perch are most satisfactory. It's best to use a wire basket to hold the fish, or the grid may be well greased before the fish is placed on it. Most fish will be jucier and more flavorful if marinated in a seasoned oil mixture before cooking and sprinkled with lemon juice just after removing from the fire. (See recipe, Marinade for Fish, which follows.)

Filets, split small fish, and steaks should be sautéed or braised in a large skillet or shallow metal pan which has been seasoned with fat; turn with a pancake turner as soon as delicately browned on one side. Cook as briefly as possible: flesh should flake easily when

touched with a fork, or skin of whole fish should be firm when touched.

GRILLED FRESH SALMON

½ c. melted butter or margarine	1 large clove of garlic, sliced
⅓ c. lemon juice	5 to 7 lb. salmon, drawn

Combine butter or margarine, lemon juice, and garlic. Remove head, tail, and backbone of salmon. Cut salmon in half. Place salmon in oiled, flat, wire broiling basket with long handle. Brush flesh side with butter sauce. Grill flesh side about 10 minutes or until lightly brown, brushing with sauce occasionally. Turn salmon; brush side with sauce; place a piece of foil loosely on top. Continue broiling 10 to 15 minutes or until just done. Makes 6 to 8 servings.

BARBECUED FISH

Use 1- to 2-pound dressed fish (preferably fresh-water fish). Two hours prior to barbecuing, marinate fish in sauce (below). Place on grill over low charcoal fire and cook slowly about 15 to 20 minutes or just until fish flakes easily. Turn fish gently with greased pancake turner, basting with the marinade. (Cooking time may be less, depending on coals.) Serve 1 fish to each person.

Marinade for Fish

1 c. olive oil	2 tsp. leaf oregano, crumbled
⅔ c. lemon juice	
⅓ c. dry sherry	2 tsp. salt
½ tsp. hot-pepper sauce	2 tsp. pepper
	2 tsp. garlic powder
⅓ c. vinegar	1 tsp. soy sauce

Combine all ingredients. Makes about 2½ cups.

LOBSTER AND SHRIMP

The secret of tender lobster—and shrimp too—is quick cooking. Lobster needs to be cooked only until the shell is bright red and the white flesh opaque. Shrimp can be cooked on skewers over a moderate fire just until delicately pink and very lightly browned (marinate the shrimp in Marinade for Fish, *above*, before grilling).

Broiled Live Lobster. Split the lobster from end to end with a large knife, inserting the knife point at the head. (Or ask fish-market man to do this for you.) Place, shell side down, on grid 3 inches from heat. Brush the exposed flesh with a mixture of melted butter or margarine, lemon juice, minced parsley, salt, and pepper. Grill about 8 minutes or until shell is bright red; brush flesh a second time with butter mixture; turn; cook 6 minutes longer.

Barbecued Lobster Tails. Thaw lobster tails completely. Cut the underside membrane around edges and remove. Grasp tail in both hands and bend backwards until it cracks (to prevent curling). Or insert skewer to keep tail flat. Place shell side down on grill. Grill about 5 minutes. Brush flesh side with melted butter or Curry Butter *(page 350)*; turn and grill flesh side until meat is opaque and tender when pierced with a fork, about 3 to 5 minutes (depending on coals).

Grilled Lobster Tails in Foil. Thaw frozen lobster tails. Cut undershell around edge and remove. Place each lobster tail in a piece of foil 4 inches longer than the length of the tail, crimping edges so that foil stands up around the lobster. Place directly in ashes of charcoal fire for about 20 minutes or until shell is bright red and flesh opaque. Baste with melted butter or margarine or Curry Butter *(page 350)*.

CLAM BAKE

Dig a saucer-shaped hole about 2 feet deep and 4 feet wide. Line with large, flat stones fitted closely. Fill with wood and burn at least 3 hours. Brush embers aside, exposing surface of stones. Cover and ring with wire mesh. Top with layer of seaweed or corn sheaves. Load food.

First, put in a layer of clams, big ones in center. They provide the steam that prevents other food from charring. Then add corn, onions, potatoes, lobster, chicken, more seaweed or corn sheaves. Speed is needed to keep rocks hot.

Cover with heavy tarpaulin topped with 5- or 6-inch layer of sand to prevent steam from escaping. (Do not let sand sift into pit.) Locking steam in allows flavor of the various foods to mingle. Bake food 3 to 5 hours. Open pit. Sweep sand back carefully and scrape from tarpaulin. Roll back tarpaulin.

Clams should be eaten first. Place other foods on trays and cover with thick towels or tarpaulin to keep warm while you feast on the clams.

VEGETABLES

If your grill is large enough, you can cook vegetables along with the meat. Some can be foil-wrapped and baked in the glowing ashes of the fire while the meat cooks on the grill. Others can be threaded on skewers and cooked alongside the meat. And what tastes better than sweet corn roasted in its own husks?

POTATOES

Baked Whole in the Ashes: Scrub potatoes well. Prick well with fork. Place just as they are in the ashes or wrap each in aluminum foil. Allow a full hour's baking time, turning once unless potatoes are completely buried under ashes. When done, the skins should be crisp and a fork should easily penetrate the center of each. Cut a gash in the top of each potato and insert butter or margarine; serve with salt and pepper.

Foil-wrapped Potato Slices: These cook more quickly than the whole potatoes. Cut each potato lengthwise in 3 or 4 slices; place 1 cut potato in each sheet of aluminum foil; add butter or margarine and salt. Seal the edges of the foil by crimping; place each packet of potato in the ashes of the fire. Turn once so the heat reaches all sides. Allow 30 to 40 minutes, depending on fire. When packets are opened, potatos are ready to eat.

Sizzling French Fries: Heat frozen French fries in one of the following ways: 1) Place partially thawed frozen potatoes in a corn popper; heat directly over the coals, shaking occasionally. 2) Place in a skillet on the grill with a small pat of butter or margarine; shake occasionally so that melted fat is distributed through potatoes. 3) Wrap in aluminum foil; place packet of foil in the coals of the fire; allow 20 to 30 minutes cooking time, turning packet once. Open and sprinkle with salt to serve.

CORN

Roasted in the Husk: Soak ears of corn in salt water for ½ to 1 hour without disturbing the husks. Remove from water; shake off excess. Place on the grill, 4 or 5 inches above the coals (or the ears can be placed directly in the ashes of a moderate fire); turn occasionally. When husks have turned light brown on all sides, corn is ready. Pull back husks; the silk comes off with the husks. Serve with butter or margarine and salt.

Corn in Foil: Remove husks and silk from ears of corn; spread each ear with soft butter or margarine; wrap in aluminum foil. Lay ears on coals for 20 to 30 minutes, turning once.

Yankee Steamed Corn: Remove husks and silk from corn. Line large kettle with husks; cover bottom of kettle with water. Lay corn on husks; cover kettle. Bring to boiling on grill; steam 20 minutes.

SKEWERED VEGETABLES

Marinate any or all of these in bottled Italian-style dressing for ½ hour before cooking: green pepper strips, whole mushrooms, cherry tomatoes, cubes of eggplant, cubes of tender zucchini or yellow crookneck squash. Thread vegetables alternately on skewers. Broil until tender and lightly browned, 5 to 8 minutes, brushing occasionally with dressing.

GLAZED CARROTS

Pare and parboil 24 tender, young carrots or drain 1 can (about 1 pound) carrots. Place 4 carrots on each of 6 large squares aluminum foil. Add 1 tablespoon butter or margarine and 1 tablespoon maple-blended syrup to each. Bring edges of foil together; twist to close tightly. Grill 15 to 20 minutes. Makes 6 servings.

BAKED BANANAS

Peel bananas (allow 1 per person) and brush with butter or margarine. Spread with thin coating of orange marmalade and sprinkle with lemon juice. Wrap each in aluminum foil. Cook on grill 15 minutes.

SWEET POTATOES

Drain 2 cans sweet potatoes and divide among 6 squares of heavy foil. Brush potatoes with apricot preserves or orange marmalade. Drain 1 can (13½ oz.) pineapple chunks; top potatoes with pineapple. Bring edges of foil together; twist to close. Cook on grill 15 minutes. Makes 6 servings.

CHEESE TOMATOES

Cut 6 firm, ripe tomatoes in half. Season with salt and pepper. Mix 2 tablespoons each chopped green pepper, grated Cheddar cheese, and minced onion. Sprinkle on one half of tomato; top with second half; wrap in aluminum foil. Cook on grill 15 to 20 minutes, turning once or twice as they cook. Makes 6 servings.

QUICK GERMAN POTATO SALAD

Pare, dice, cook, and drain 2 pounds potatoes. Add ½ cup onion-flavored salad-dressing mix and ½ cup diced, cooked bacon. Toss well. Wrap in foil. Heat on grill 20 minutes. Makes 6 servings.

BREADS

Buns, rolls, or French bread can all be toasted over the charcoal grill. A quick way is to thread split buns or 1-inch thick slices of French bread on skewers and hold over the heat until lightly toasted. Or, butter the buns or sliced bread with plain or seasoned butter, wrap in aluminum foil, and heat on grill.

FIESTA BREAD

¼ c. soft butter or margarine	⅓ c. chopped green pepper
1 c. grated Cheddar cheese	⅓ c. chopped onion
½ c. catsup	1 large or 2 small loaves French bread
⅓ c. chopped ripe olives	

Mix butter or margarine, cheese, catsup, olives, green pepper, and onion thoroughly. Split bread lengthwise in half. Spread each half with butter mixture. Wrap each half in aluminum foil; heat in oven or on grill. Or, put halves together and wrap in foil before heating. Cut in slices to serve.

Chapter Twenty-Eight

Spice and Herb Guide

Are you one of those cooks who is afraid to use spices and herbs because you don't know how? But you've been sprinkling food with black pepper for years! And what about the nutmeg on the Christmas eggnog, the mustard you spread on hot dogs, and the sprig of mint you add to iced tea?

It's only the lesser-known herbs and spices that seem mysterious, and even these become familiar when we stop to think about the ways we've consumed them.

Take cardamom, for example. It sounds terribly exotic, doesn't it? "Grains of paradise," the Arabs used to call these big fragrant seeds. Yet it's cardamom that the Scandinavians use in their breads and pastries to produce that wonderfully aromatic sweetness.

Twenty-five years ago, oregano was virtually unknown—except among Italian-Americans. Today its special fragrance fills every pizzeria, and what American cook would think of trying to make spaghetti sauce without it?

Herbs, Spices, and Condiments

Herbs are the leaves of low-growing aromatic plants that grow in temperate zones. The ones we use most frequently are parsley, thyme, dill, oregano, bay leaves, and chives. But the various members of the onion family, including garlic, qualify as herbs, too. Celery too is an herb—especially the celery leaves.

Spices are usually parts of plants that grow in the tropics; they are the aromatic seeds, bark, roots, berries—almost everything but the leaves of plants. Some spices are sweet, some hot, some pungent.

Condiments is a generic term, including not only herbs and spices, but salt, monosodium glutamate, blended spice-and-herb mixtures such as curry powder and chili powder, liquid seasoners such as vanilla, Worcestershire, and hot-pepper sauce, and the concentrates such as beef-stock base, dehydrated horseradish, and dehydrated orange and lemon peel.

Secrets of Subtle Seasoning

· *Subtle* is the key word. Use herbs and spices with a light touch, underseasoning rather than taking a chance on permitting the seasoning to overpower the dish.
· Dried herbs are a marvelous help; they stay on the shelf ready to use whenever needed—but remember they have a limited shelf life. If a jar of herbs has been around some time, open it and sniff the aroma. If the aroma is very faint and reminiscent of straw, better replace it.
· There are several ways of releasing the flavor of dried herbs. One is to crumble the leaves in the palm of your hand by rubbing with the forefinger of your other hand. Another is to

add herbs and spices directly to the fat when sautéeing meat, fish, or poultry. Still another is to sprinkle the herb into liquid; bring to boiling; simmer gently at least 10 minutes. The more pungent herbs usually should not be added until the latter part of the cooking period; most of the sweeter ones may be added at the beginning.

· When making salad dressings or marinades, always add the condiments at the start. The longer they have to flavor the food, the better.

· If you buy fresh herbs store them in a tightly covered jar in your refrigerator or freeze them in small packets. (Instructions will be found on *page 517*.)

· It's a good rule to use only one or two herbs in the same recipe, unless the recipe specifically lists several, or unless you have learned certain especially good combinations.

Glossary of Herbs and Spices

Allspice. This spice, native to the Caribbean area and the only one produced exclusively in the area, resembles a blend of clove, cinnamon, and nutmeg in flavor. Available whole and ground.

Whole allspice
· add 3 to a pound of fish while poaching.
· add 8 to 10 to pot roast or a marinade for beef.
· use 3 to three cups pea soup.
Ground allspice
· add a dash to mashed sweet potatoes.
· sprinkle on tomato soup.
· use ⅛ teaspoon in stuffing for veal or lamb.
· use ⅛ teaspoon to a chocolate milk shake.
· use ¼ teaspoon in meat loaf.
· sprinkle lightly on fruit salad, fruit cup, or fruit compote.

Anise. The aromatic seed of a small fruit cultivated all through the temperate zone. It has a sweet licoricelike aroma and flavor. Available whole, it is used both whole and crushed.

Crushed anise seed
· use ¼ teaspoon for 4 servings.
· sprinkle over rolls before baking.
· add a pinch to green peas.
· use in court bouillon for fish or shellfish, ¼ teaspoon to a quart of liquid.
Whole anise seed
· use in sweet pickles.
· use for salad dressing.
· add to cookies.

Basil. This is a pungent herb cultivated extensively in California. It is available in leaf form and, in some areas, fresh.

Basil leaves
· add ½ teaspoon to 2 cups tomato or other liquid for sauce.
· combine ¼ teaspoon with ½ teaspoon leaf thyme, ¼ teaspoon leaf marjoram; tie in cheesecloth, add to soup or stock.
· add a pinch to baked scalloped tomatoes.
Fresh basil
· Crush ½ cup minced basil leaves in a mortar with 1 or 2 garlic cloves, ¼ teaspoon salt, and 1 or 2 tablespoons olive oil, to make a green paste which the Italians call Pesto Genovese. Great on spaghetti.

Bay Leaves. These are the dried leaves of the laurel or sweet bay tree. They have a distinct pungent flavor. Use sparingly!

Use whole leaf, 1 to approximately 6 cups liquid, in:
    fish chowders
    pickles
    court bouillon for poaching fish
Use crushed half or quarter leaf in:
    salad dressings
    marinades for beef and fish

Caraway Seeds. These come from a plant of the carrot family. The greatest supply comes from the Netherlands. The seeds may be used whole or crushed.

Crushed caraway seeds
· ½ teaspoon to a cup of cottage cheese.
· a pinch to salad dressings.
· ⅛ teaspoon to a cup of sliced cooked carrots.
· ¼ teaspoon to 8 small beets.
Whole caraway seeds
· 1 teaspoon to a pound of sauerkraut.
· 1 teaspoon to 3 cups shredded red cabbage.
· ½ teaspoon to 4 servings of noodles.
· 1 or 2 tablespoons sprinkled over tops of rolls or salt sticks before baking.

Cardamom. The pods of the cardamom are plump and cream colored and contain the aromatic dark brown seeds. They grow on a tall plant of the ginger family, but the taste and aroma is sweet, not hot, and marvelously fragrant. Available whole and ground.

Whole cardamom pods
· add to hot fruit punches, 1 or 2 to a quart.
· use in marinades for poultry or veal, 1 or

2 to a cup of sauce.
· add to mixed pickles.

Ground cardamom
· use in coffee cake, buns, Danish pastries, fruitcakes.
· blend ¼ teaspoon with ½ cup honey to sweeten fruits, especially peaches.
· add a pinch to meatballs.
· use ¼ to ½ teaspoon per cup of barbecue or basting sauces for chicken, duck, or fish.

Celery Seed, Salt, and Flakes. Celery seed is not related to the celery we know as a vegetable. It is a wild variety of celery commonly called smallage. It is available whole.

Whole celery seed (use sparingly)
· add ½ teaspoon to 4 cups coleslaw.
· sprinkle a few seeds over seafood salad.
· sprinkle over bread sticks before baking.
· add to pickles with other pickling spices.

Celery salt is a blend of ground celery seed and salt. Use it in recipes where you want a celery flavor, substituting it for part of the salt in the recipe.

Celery flakes are dried leaves and some stalk of the American celery plant.
· use 1 tablespoon in soups or stews.
· use 2 teaspoons to flavor tomato aspic.
· add 2 teaspoons to chicken or turkey giblets when making stock.

Chervil. This is one of the most delicately flavored of all herbs, related to the parsley family. Europe and California produce most of the crop. Available as dried leaves.

Crumbled leaves
· use 1 teaspoon to 2 cups cream sauce for fish.
· add 1 teaspoon to 2 cups broth for chicken or fish sauce.
· Add ¼ teaspoon to a cup of French dressing.
· Work ½ teaspoon into 2 tablespoons butter; place under skin of chicken.

Chives. Tiniest member of the onion family, the small green shoots are usually minced or chopped. Can be purchased freeze-dried, frozen, and fresh.

Sprinkle *minced chives* over:
Vichyssoise
tomato soups
tomato juice cocktail
cream sauces
baked or broiled fish

sour cream (for either a dip or as topping)
cottage cheese
scrambled eggs

Chili Powder. A blend of several ingredients, including cumin, oregano, hot, red pepper, and usually coriander. Manufacturer's blends differ; some are "hotter" than others.

Use by the tablespoon for:
hot barbecue sauces
Mexican-type stews
sparerib sauce

Use a pinch to add flavor interest to:
scrambled eggs
cheese dips
basting sauces and marinades
seafood sauces
kernel corn
baked dried kidney or lima beans

Cinnamon. Cinnamon is the aromatic bark of a Southeast Asian and Indonesian tree, stripped and rolled into quills. It is sold whole (sticks) or ground.

Whole cinnamon
· add a stick to beef stew.
· place a 1-inch piece in water with other seasonings for boiled meats.
· add a 3-inch piece to a quart of rhubarb or spiced peaches; a quart of hot cider, tea or coffee; to the water in cooking stewed fruits.
· use a stick in a cup of hot chocolate, tea, or hot wine drinks as a muddler.

Ground cinnamon
· sprinkle on fried bananas.
· add a dash to chicken or tomato soup.
· add 1 teaspoon to apple or peach pies.
· sprinkle on lamb chops while broiling or add ⅛ teaspoon to lamb stew.
· mix with sugar and sprinkle on fruit.
· add ¼ teaspoon to 2 cups tomatoes for sauce.

Cloves. Their name is said to come from the French word "clou" meaning nail. They are the unopened buds of the small evergreen clove tree. Their penetrating, pungent, almost hot flavor intensifies on standing. Use with care.

Whole cloves (remove before serving unless they are a garnish)
· add 2 or 3 studded in an onion to beef stew or stock for corned beef.
· use 6 to 8 in syrup while cooking fruit.

Ground cloves
· add a dash to mincemeat or fruit pies.
· use ¼ to ½ teaspoon to 2 quarts grape jelly or cherry jam.
· sprinkle on fish before baking.

Coriander. This pungent spice has a pleasing aromatic taste.

The seeds must be thoroughly dried before the fragrance develops. Morocco supplies most of the crop. Coriander is used extensively by sausage makers. Available whole and may be used whole or crushed.

Whole coriander
· add a few seeds to marinades for meats.
Crushed coriander
· sprinkle in small amounts over apples for pie.
· blend with curry powder, cumin and cinnamon for a less-hot, sweeter curry sauce.
· use in oriental rice dishes.
· add to Mexican sauces.
· add ⅛ to ¼ teaspoon to any standard gingerbread recipe.

Cumin (comino). Cumin seeds are gathered from a low-growing plant native to the Mediterranean. We are just beginning to use ground cumin in our kitchens, though we have been tasting this warm, pleasant spice for a long time as one of the ingredients in both curry powder and chili powder.

Whole cumin seed
· sprinkle over rye bread before baking.
· sprinkle on cheese-spread crackers, to be toasted under broiler.
· use in making chutneys, sweet pickles, or vegetable relishes.
Ground cumin
· sprinkle over scrambled eggs.
· add ¼ to ½ teaspoon to melted butter, margarine, or oil; brush over fish filets or chicken before broiling.
· blend with oregano, rub into lamb before roasting.
· add to meat and poultry sauces, in combination with small amounts of coriander and oregano or parsley.
· add to rice for a special gourmet touch.

Curry Powder. A blend of many spices and herbs, usually including cumin, coriander, fenugreek, turmeric, ginger, fennel, cardamom, cloves, and sometimes black pepper. Manufacturer's recipes vary considerably;

some curry powders are much hotter than others. Use sparingly unless you like very hot curry sauces.

For a *hot curry* sauce: use 1 tablespoon curry powder for each 2 cups liquid.

For a *mild curry* sauce: use ½ teaspoon powder for each 2 cups liquid.

For *a faint touch of curry*, sprinkle a pinch over:
   scrambled eggs
   salad dressings
   fish before broiling or baking
   chicken before broiling
· add to sour cream for a dip with onions or chives.
· add to tuna with sour cream or mayonnaise for a dip.
· combine with sour cream as a sauce for lima or green beans.

Dill. A member of the parsley family, this is a moderately aromatic herb. It is available as seed and leaves (called weed). Dill seed is more pungent than dill weed. It is also available, in some areas, fresh.

Dill seed
· ½ teaspoon to each 2 cups of liquid for fish stock.
· ¼ teaspoon, crushed, to 2 tablespoons butter for brushing on broiled fish or lamb chop.
· ¼ teaspoon to 1 cup cottage cheese for dip.
Dill weed
· ½ teaspoon in 2 cups tomato juice.
· ½ teaspoon in 1 cup cream sauce.
Fresh dill, minced
· sprinkle over cold soups.
· add to sliced cucumbers with vinegar and salt.
· add a teaspoon or so to scrambled eggs.
Frozen dill may be used like fresh dill; chop before thawing.

Fennel seed. Imported from India, it is the aromatic dried fruit or seed of a plant of the parsley family. It has a slight flavor of licorice. It is available whole.
· sprinkle a bit of crushed fennel over cooked green peas (⅛ teaspoon to 2 cups peas).
· add ½ teaspoon fennel seed to each 2 cups liquid for beef stew.
· sprinkle whole fennel seeds over fish before broiling or baking.

Filé Powder. Ground from dried sassafras leaves, it is an essential ingredient to a true New Orleans gumbo. Its peculiarity is that it must be added at the last moment, just before the dish is to be served, for it thickens the broth instantly. If reheated, the sauce may become gummy. Use 1 tablespoon to 2 quarts of liquid.

Garlic. Available year round in fresh form as well as in *garlic salt* and *garlic powder*. Its use is generally subject to the personal whim and individual taste of the cook. In using fresh garlic, remember that it's the juice of the garlic that contains most of the flavor. In making salads, crush the whole garlic clove in a garlic press, with a knife, or in a mortar and pestle.

Garlic powder is a dehydrated concentrate, contains no salt. *Garlic salt* is salt that has been flavored with fresh garlic, then the garlic itself is discarded. Use either according to taste.

Ginger. This is one of the few spices that grows below ground. It is available whole and ground. Rich and extremely pungent in flavor, its taste is hot and clean. Crystallized and preserved gingers are confections, not spices.

Whole ginger
· add a split 1-inch piece to marinade for chicken.
· use a 1- to 2-inch piece in cooking or canning fruits.
· in recipes calling for fresh ginger you may substitute whole ginger. Soak piece of whole ginger in cold water several hours; chop finely.

Ground ginger
· add a dash to bread pudding.
· add ¼ teaspoon to coconut before toasting.
· mix with butter or margarine and rub on chicken before roasting.
· ground ginger may be substituted for whole ginger in many recipes. Use 1 teaspoon ground ginger in place of ten ½-inch pieces.

Horseradish. Most familiar to us in jars, grated and blended with salt, ready to use.

Dehydrated horseradish is available. Reconstitute with water before using.

Prepared or reconstituted dried horseradish
· add 1 teaspoon to a cup of sour or sweet whipped cream as a sauce for boiled beef or poached fish.
· serve just as it is as a condiment for cherrystone clams or oysters on the half shell.
· combine 1 teaspoon to ¼ cup tomato catsup to make a cocktail sauce for seafood.

Juniper Berries. The berries of the small evergreen juniper bush are used much more in Europe than in this country, and are considered indispensable for game cookery. The Germans also use juniper berries in making sauerkraut. The flavor is delicate but unique.

Whole berries
· add 3 or 4 whole berries to 4 cups of liquid, in marinades and basting sauces for wild duck, pheasant, quail, venison, etc.

Lemon Peel. Not technically either an herb or spice, but used as a spice. It is usually grated and is available in dehydrated form. It is the dried, natural rind of the fresh fruit. Substitute equally for fresh, grated rind.

Grated or dried lemon peel
· use in veal stews.
· add to barbecue sauces for chicken or fish.
· use in marinades for veal, lamb, or pork.
· sprinkle on dessert sauces.
· mix into sponge cake batter.

Mace. Comes from the same plant as nutmeg. They are the only two spices to grow in the same fruit. It is similar though more delicate in flavor to nutmeg. Most readily available ground. Whole it appears as flat, branched, irregular pieces.

Whole mace
· add a blade of cooked fruits.
· add a blade to marinades or bastes for chicken, veal, or fish.

Ground mace
· add a dash to chocolate pudding.
· sprinkle on spinach while cooking.
· add a dash to a white sauce.
· sprinkle ⅛ teaspoon on custard.
· mix ¼ teaspoon in French dressing for fruit salad.
· traditional for pound cakes.

Marjoram. A cultivated cousin of oregano, but more delicate in flavor; both are members of the mint family. Available as dried leaves and ground.

Leaf marjoram
· add ¼ teaspoon to a 10-ounce package of frozen vegetables.
· add ½ teaspoon to stuffings.

Ground marjoram
· sprinkle over mushrooms or zucchini.
· rub on beef or veal before roasting.

Mint (spearmint). It is available fresh, or in dried flakes, and as extract.

Fresh mint sprigs may be served just as they are, in iced tea, pineapple punches, or wine punches.

Crushed fresh mint
· use in mint jelly, fruit salads, or fruit cocktails.
· add to peas or carrots.
· use in a sauce for lamb.

Mint flakes
Add to:
    lamb stews
    hot tea
    yogurt and thin-sliced cucumbers.

Mixed Pickling Spice. A ready-to-use mixture of peppercorns, mustard seed, coriander, dill, bay leaf, and hot-pepper pods. Used mainly for pickling but may be added to pot roasts, spiced fruits, and vegetables. Tie spices in cheesecloth for easy removal.

MSG or monosodium glutamate. The sodium salt of an amino acid present in almost all vegetable and animal protein. Its purpose is to enhance the flavor of foods rather than to add flavor of its own. Originally extracted from seaweed, the major sources are now sugar beets, corn, and wheat. The initials MSG are frequently used as an abbreviation. It is ideal with vegetables, seafood, poultry, and meats.
· add ½ teaspoon per cup of gravy or sauce.
· use ¼ teaspoon in water when cooking vegetables.
· add 1 teaspoon per pound when roasting or braising meat.
· use ½ teaspoon per pound when cooking fish.

Mustard. Available as mustard seed, dried mustard, and prepared mustards that range from very mild and delicate to wildly hot.

Most of the prepared mustards are blended from several varieties of mustard seeds.

Whole mustard seed
· use as a pickling spice for meats, shrimp, or vegetable relishes.

Dried mustard
· add ½ teaspoon to baked macaroni and cheese.
· use ¼ teaspoon in French dressing.
· add ¼ teaspoon to 2 cups cream sauce.

Nutmeg. The seed of an apricotlike fruit of the nutmeg tree, an evergreen which bears for more than fifty years. It is sweet in flavor and highly spicy and is sold whole or ground.

Whole Nutmeg must always be ground before using. Use a kitchen grater or a nutmeg grater. A whole nutmeg yields about 3 teaspoons ground. Use as you would ground nutmeg.

Ground Nutmeg
· sprinkle on milk shakes, eggnogs, hot chocolate.
· add a dash to apple pie filling or sprinkle on the crust.
· sprinkle on chicken or cream soups.
· add a dash to egg-milk mixture for French toast.
· use ¼ teaspoon in whipped cream.
· add ½ teaspoon to creamed chicken.
· sprinkle lightly on broiled chicken or fish.

Onion. Available as flakes, powder, salt, instant minced and chopped onion, shredded green onions (dehydrated) and onion juice.

Onion flakes. Use 1 tablespoon in 4 cups soup, or in 2 cups cream sauce or gravy.

Onion powder. Use 1 tablespoon in place of 1 medium-size onion. Blend with small amount of water and add to soup, stews, gravies, relishes, and salad dressings.

Onion salt. Use in place of all or part of salt called for in recipe.

Instant minced onions. One tablespoon soaked in 1 tablespoon water 3 to 5 minutes may be substituted for 1 medium-size chopped onion.

Instant chopped onions. Larger particles than minced onions. Use in the same manner.

Shredded green onions. These are milder in flavor than other onion products but may be used in place of them.

Onion juice. Onion juice is processed from juice squeezed from fresh onions. Use when mild onion flavor is desired.

Orange Peel. Like lemon peel, not technically an herb or spice, but used like one. It is the dried natural rind of the fresh fruit. One tablespoon of dried orange peel equals 1 tablespoon fresh grated rind.

Grated or *dried orange peel.* Use in:
  chicken or fish sauces
  veal stew
  fruit salads or compotes
  punches and fruit juice cups
  basting sauces for pork, ham, chicken or veal
  candied sweet potatoes, glazed carrots, or baked squash.

Oregano. One of the most commonly-used of all our dried herbs. The name means "joy of the mountain." It is imported from the Mediterranean countries and from Mexico. It is available ground and in leaf form.

Ground oregano
• use ¼ teaspoon to 1 pound ground beef.
• add to spaghetti and barbecue sauces.
Leaf oregano
• add ⅛ teaspoon to each cup of your favorite commercial tomato sauce.
• add ⅛ teaspoon for each 2 cups of stews and pot roasts.
• add to scrambled eggs.
• sprinkle over tomatoes before sautéeing.
• add to tossed salad greens.
• use in tuna dip with chopped pimientos, grated onion, and sour cream.

Paprika. The dried, stemless pod of a variety of red pepper, paprika is mild and sweet in flavor, slightly aromatic, and brilliant red. Add:
• 1 teaspoon to ½ cup butter or margarine for a baste for chicken.
• 1 teaspoon to seasoned flour to coat chicken.
• ¼ teaspoon to a cup of French dressing.
• 1 teaspoon to buttered crumbs for a casserole topping.
• sprinkle on creamed vegetables, soups, and baked potatoes.

Parsley. One of the most useful of all herbs, parsley is available fresh and as dried parsley flakes. They may be used interchangeably. To keep fresh parsley crisp, wash, shake dry, snip off the sprigs, and refrigerate in tightly-covered glass jars. It will keep fresh for 10 days.

Minced fresh parsley or *parsley flakes*
• use in almost any meat, chicken, fish or shellfish sauce.

• crush with garlic, use in marinades for lamb.
• combine with mayonnaise for a quick seafood sauce.
. add to cooked green beans, buttered carrots, or buttered parsnips.
• sprinkle over broiled or baked fish shortly before removing from oven.

Pepper. Without doubt the most well-known and most widely used spice. It is the berry of a vine of Indonesia, India, and Malaysia. Black pepper is picked when slightly underripe, then dried in the sun or over charcoal fires to attain its characteristic black, wrinkled appearance. White pepper is picked when it is fully ripe and dried. The black outer hull is removed, exposing the creamy, white core. White pepper is less pungent than black. Both are available whole and ground. Black pepper is also found as coarse ground pepper and cracked pepper.

Red Pepper. Included here are red pepper and cayenne, made from capsicum hot peppers. No relation to black and white pepper. Cayenne comes ground, red pepper crushed and ground, and there is a blend of the two. Each is hot and pungent—use with care.

Ground red pepper and ground cayenne
• add a dash to cream sauces, tomato sauce, Hollandaise, barbecue sauce.
• use a touch along with paprika to melted butter to sauce vegetables.
Crushed red pepper
• a good rule is to use a dash to ⅛ teaspoon in a 4-serving recipe and increase according to taste.

Poppy Seed. The little slate blue seeds we sprinkle over breads and use in salads and certain pastries do *not* come from the same variety of poppies as opium. It is imported mainly from the Netherlands. The flavor is delicate.
• sprinkle over yeast rolls, cake batter, or cookie dough before baking.
• add to cole slaw.
• great with scrambled eggs.
• add to buttered noodles, buttered carrots, or sprinkle over cooked celery root.

Rosemary. Another member of the mint family. California and Spain produce most of the crop. Rosemary leaves are available dried and, in some areas, fresh. The dried leaves look like miniature pine needles and are usually

crushed before using. This is a pungent herb.
· rub on lamb roast.
· add to chicken braised in a tomato sauce.
· crumble and sprinkle over salmon.
· use as a pickling spice.
· crumble and add to spiced fruit.

Saffron. This bright yellow spice is the world's most costly herb—it takes 225,000 stigmas from a particular kind of crocus to make a single pound. Fortunately, only a small amount needs to be used.

Whole leaf saffron is the more common form. This must be crushed before using or steeped in hot water before being added to other food.

Crushed saffron is still more costly and it has a shorter shelf life. Use a tiny, tiny pinch, steeped, to 2 cups of liquid.

Sage. An herb found in virtually all parts of the world, growing wild. It is native to southern Europe which produces most of the crop. It is available as dried leaves, ground, and crushed.
· add 1/8 teaspoon to a pound of ground pork to make spicy meatballs.
· use for bread stuffing for poultry, 1/4 teaspoon to 6 cups bread crumbs.
· add a pinch to fish chowders.
· sprinkle a few leaves over pork chops while sautéeing.
· blend with butter, serve as a sauce for baked or boiled fish.
· work a few leaves into grated Cheddar cheese for a dip.

Savory. There are both "winter" and "summer" varieties of savory, but summer savory is better known and more delicate in flavor. California is one of the main producers of the crop. Available in leaf form and ground.
· add to vinegar for salad dressings.
· add 1/4 teaspoon to 1 pound ground beef.
· add to green or dried beans.

Sesame seeds. This seed is also known as benne. The nutty flavor of sesame only comes out when these small white seeds are sautéed in butter or margarine, baked atop breads or rolls, or toasted for sprinkling on other foods. *To toast the seeds,* simply spread seeds in a shallow pan, place in a 350° F. oven until they turn delicately golden. Shake once or twice so they will toast evenly. May be used lavishly. Southwestern United States produces most of the crop.

· sprinkle over cheese dips.
· add to fish before broiling.
· use in salads.
· add to stuffing for roast chicken or turkey.
· add to cooked cabbage or noodles.

Tarragon. Known to the French as estragon, or "little dragon," because of the twisted shape of the roots. Like fennel and anise, the leaves of the tarragon plant have a licorice-like flavor, but tarragon is slightly sharper than the other two. California produces most of the crop. It is available as dried leaves and, in some areas, fresh.
· use *sprigs of fresh tarragon* in vinegar; place inside the cavities of small chickens before roasting.
· use *minced fresh tarragon* in salads; sprinkle over tomato slices.
Dried tarragon should be crumbled before using, or marinated in wine or vinegar, then strained.
Use 1/4 teaspoon for 4 servings in:
· chicken and seafood salads
· tartar or egg sauces
· omelets

Thyme. One of the most useful of herbs, it is a member of the mint family and is grown principally in California and France. It has a warm, aromatic, and slightly pungent flavor. Thyme is available both in leaf form and ground.
Leaf thyme
· use with fried tomatoes.
· sprinkle over lamb chops before grilling, rubbing well into the meat.
· add to bread stuffing with celery and onion for chicken or turkey.
· use with seafood of all kinds.
· add to onions and garlic as they simmer in butter for a particularly fragrant effect.
Ground thyme
· 1/4 teaspoon in clam chowders.
· 1/4 teaspoon in biscuit recipe.

Turmeric. Turmeric is the root of a plant of the ginger family, though it is very unlike aromatic ginger. It is somewhat medicinal in aroma with a slightly bitter taste. India produces most of the crop.
· add a dash to stuffed or scrambled eggs.
· add 1/4 teaspoon to bastes and marinades for chicken.
· use 1/2 teaspoon in dressing for seafood salads.

Vanilla Bean. The gourmet cook keeps on hand not only pure vanilla extract but also vanilla bean. Vanilla is the fruit of an orchid plant and is grown chiefly in the Malagasy Republic, Tahiti, and Mexico. The small black seeds inside the pod are used for flavoring ice cream and puddings. Bury a pod in your sugar canister for flavor. When steeped in hot liquid, this long, black, shrunken bean of the orchid family gives vanilla flavor at its finest. Two inches are sufficient to flavor a dish for four to six. You may like to open the bean and scrape out the inside to get a more pronounced flavor (only do this if the mixture would not be marred by the small black specks). You can reuse vanilla bean after steeping. Just rinse it quickly in hot water, dry and store for future use.

Vanilla Extract. This is the extract from crushed vanilla beans in a base of alcohol. A teaspoon of the extract is the usual amount called for in puddings, eggnogs, and fruit cakes.

Using the Blends, the Seasoned Salts, and Other Special Condiments

New special seasoning blends appear on the supermarket spice shelves all the time. There are barbecue spice mixtures, salad herbs, herbs for fish, spaghetti sauce herbs, blends called "bouquet garni" or "fines herbes" and seasoned salts in enormous variety. You'll find them convenient to use in many ways.

Drying and Freezing Fresh Herbs

Any herbs that you have grown yourself may be dried for winter use, or frozen in sealed packets in your freezer.

To dry your own herbs: Pick the young, tender shoots in the spring before they flower. Cut in the morning hours. Pick leaves from stems, spread in a single layer in a shallow pan, dry in 150° F. oven 1 to 2 hours or until crumbly. Or, tie in bunches and hang in a cool, dry place. When both leaves and stems are thoroughly dried, separate the leaves; pack loosely in airtight jars. Label jars.

To freeze: Wash carefully, shake dry, then pat gently on paper towel. When all excess moisture has been removed, place in small portions in small plastic bags, seal the bags with tape, freeze immediately.

Storing Purchased Dried Herbs and Spices

The attractive glass containers in which most herbs and spices and other dried condiments are sold these days make perfect containers for storage. Always keep tightly covered. You may have started your spice-shelf collection with a few jars that come with their own shelf. Such shelves are convenient, because they can be fastened to the wall near work centers, but ideally, both herbs and spices should be stored in a closed cabinet, not near any source of heat.

Place your favorite seasonings in the most convenient spot, for once you've learned the joy of subtle seasoning, you will be using herbs and spices more and more frequently to add a creative touch to all your cooking.

Chapter Twenty-Nine

Wines and Wine Cookery

The magic of wine is what it does for food. The simplest meal when served with wine become special. Somehow the lingering loveliness of wine heightens its flavor.

You don't have to be a connoisseur to enjoy wine. You should know a few simple facts, but there's no need to be confused about all the talk of vintages and grape varieties or to hesitate as to what wine is right for a certain food. There is only one way to learn about wine—*drink it!* The more frequently you serve wine with dinner, the more critical your taste buds will become.

A Brief Summary of the Basic Types of Wine and Foods to Accompany Them

There are no hard and fast rules about which wines should be served with which foods. Our list suggests wines and foods that complement each other, but you may find other combinations that you enjoy.

Appetizer or apéritif wines: These wines are fortified and they contain from 18 to 21% alcohol. They include dry or cocktail sherry and dry or sweet vermouth, and apéritif wines such as *Dubonnet* and *Byrrh*. They can be served chilled, at cool room temperature, or on the rocks. Serve them before dinner with canapés or hors d'oeuvres. The sweet varieties can be served with afternoon snacks.

Table wines: Basically table wines are what the name suggests—wine to serve at the table with meals. Their alcoholic content is low, ranging from 12 to 14%. Table wines include red, rosé, and white.

Red table wines: *Burgundy, Beaujolais, Claret,* and *Chianti* are good examples of this type. They should be served at cool room temperature and opened about a half hour before serving to allow the wine to "breathe." These wines are excellent with steaks, roasts, ham, chops, and other hearty foods.

Rosé wines: Rosé is a red wine with a delightful pink color. It is lighter than the other red wines, often sweeter than the dry red table wines. It complements almost all types of dishes and is especially nice with lighter foods—the same foods with which you'd serve white wine. Examples are *Rosé d'Anjou, Tavel,* and *Grenache Rosé*. It should be chilled as white wine.

White table wines: Examples of this group are Sauterne, Rhine wine, and Chablis or white Burgundy. Always serve a white dinner wine chilled. This group is at its best when served with poultry, lamb, veal, seafood, eggs, and lighter foods.

Dessert wines: These are mostly fortified wines. *Port, muscatel, sweet* or *cream sherry,* and *Tokay* are in this category. They may be served chilled or at cool room temperature and often accompany desserts and sweets. They can be served with or after dessert in the afternoon or after dinner.

Sparkling wines: *Champagne* and *Sparkling Burgundy* (a sweet, red wine) are the elegant, festive wines that comprise this group. They're perfect for any special occasion, may be served with or without food. If served at dinner, they may accompany any course or be served throughout.

Wine Terminology

Here are several terms anyone interested in wines will want to know:

Dry means the opposite of sweet. To the beginner, even a good dry wine may at first seem sour. It's a curious but undisputed fact that the more you drink wine the drier your palate becomes. This means that gradually you choose drier and drier wines until finally you will discover the semisweet wines that you preferred at first begin to seem too sweet.

Bouquet means the fragrance that drifts up from the wine. Each wine has its own bouquet, and as drinking wine is as much a matter of smell as taste, the way to appreciate a wine is to sniff it before taking a single sip. This is even truer with red wines than with white wines and it's the reason red wine is not chilled, for the volatile bouquet escapes more quickly from a wine served at room temperature.

Character describes the general impression of the wine. A good wine has *positive* character.

Full-bodied means the opposite of thin, and as you taste wines, you will begin to see the difference yourself. A thin wine seems almost watery, without character.

Tart means wine with pleasant acidity—not harsh or sour.

Vintage is a word which refers both to the harvesting of the grapes and the year in which the wine was produced. A "vintage wine" means one which was so outstanding when bottled that it becomes even better several years after remaining in the bottle. (And there are a few rare vintage wines which are superb twenty or even thirty years after

bottling—though wines of this rarity are worth their weight in gold.)

Not all wines that have a date on the label are rated as "vintage wines" by experts. In fact, the date can be a warning signal to the connoisseur who has learned that wines produced from a certain region in a certain year were inferior, or that a particular type of wine should not be purchased when it is more than three or four years old.

Vintage years matter more with French and German wines than with those produced in other countries. This is because of climate. When the growing season has been rainy or cold, the grapes will suffer and the wine will be of poorer quality. The farther north the vineyards, the fewer are the days of sunshine even in a good year. In California as well as in Spain and Italy, there is a longer growing season with more days of sunshine and consequently vintage years make less difference. However, a few California wines do carry an indication of vintage on their label.

Vin ordinaire in French means literally "ordinary wine," the table wine served at everyday family meals. It does not mean necessarily a poor or inferior wine—such wines simply have not been rated by the vintners as good enough to carry any special grades or labels, or to be sold according to the year of its vintage. Finding a good "vin ordinaire" is a matter of luck and few remain fresh and palatable for more than 3 or 4 years.

Fruity means a wine with an almost fruitlike taste (though by no means resembling grape juice).

Soft means the opposite of harsh. There are degrees of softness and harshness in all dry wines and when a wine is described as "soft" it means its lack of harshness is an outstanding characteristic.

Generic names refer to wine types such as apéritifs, rosé wine, sparkling wine.

Varietal names usually indicate the variety of grape with which the wine was made.

Regional varieties indicate the region or vineyard in which the wine was produced.

American and Imported Wines

In general, wines fall into two categories, American wines and imported ones. The

American-wine family consists of two branches: California wines and American wines. All wines produced outside of California are known as American, while those of California are, naturally, California wines. There is more to this than just state pride. The wines of California are produced entirely from European grape varieties while those of the other states are made from hybrid (crossbred) varieties. In New York State some very fine wines are being made from French hybrid varieties.

Our California and New York State wines are becoming better all the time, and impressing visitors from wine-growing countries, including France. Some other good wines are produced in the state of Ohio.

Fine French and German wines are the most expensive of the imported wines for two reasons. In both these countries, enormous care is taken in every step of wine production, and the best wines are treated as tenderly as premature infants. When a vintage is outstanding, the wine is put away to age, sometimes for several years, before it is placed on the market —a factor which in itself automatically increases the price. Also, in both these countries, labor costs are high.

In the Mediterranean countries, where wine is a beverage regarded much like water, and where labor costs are still quite low, very agreeable wines are produced abundantly and inexpensively.

Guide to American Table Wines

CALIFORNIA WINES

Grape varieties brought from Europe (many of them by the Spanish missionaries who founded the missions in California) are used to make California wines.

Red wines: *Burgundy*, which is velvety-soft, full-bodied, fruity, deep to dark red in color. Outstanding varietal names: Pinot Noir and Gamay. *Claret* is lighter in color, slightly more tart. Outstanding varietal names: Cabernet Sauvignon and Zinfandel.

White wines: *Sauterne*, which is moderately dry with medium body. Outstanding varietal names: Sauvignon Blanc and Semillon Blanc. (California's *Haut Sauterne* is a sweet wine, fruity and full-bodied.) *Rhine wine* is quite dry, light, and fruity. Riesling is the principal

varietal name. *Chablis* is the driest of the domestic white wines, quite tart, delicate. The outstanding varietal names: Pinot Blanc and Pinot Chardonnay.

Rosé wines: *Grenache Rosé* (varietal name) which is medium dry, light and pleasant; and *Gamay Rosé*, which has slightly more body.

NEW YORK STATE WINES

Native grape (hybrid) varieties are used in making most of the New York State wines. These are produced under some of the same generic names as the California and French wines.

Red wines: *Burgundy* is usually full-bodied and very flavorful. *Claret* is softer and has a lighter body.

White wines: *Chablis*, which is quite dry, with fair body. *Hock or Rhine Wine*—very dry, light body, fragrant. *Sauterne* is medium dry, with medium body. *Haut or Sweet Sauterne*, fairly sweet and with somewhat more body.

Rosé wines: These are usually quite fresh, fruity, spicy, and fairly light in body.

Guide to Imported Table Wines

We receive most of our imported wines from France, Italy, Germany, Spain, and Portugal. A few wines are also imported from Greece and Chile and other countries.

FRENCH WINES

France has four principal wine-producing regions, but the two most important are *Bordeaux* and *Burgundy*. White and red wines are produced in both these regions; the red wines are all dry wines, some of the white wines are very dry—others moderately sweet to very sweet.

Within these large wine-producing regions, there are individual wine areas, each of which is noted for certain outstanding wines. It is helpful to be familiar with some of these names so that when you shop for wine you will know what to look for and have a better understanding of what you are buying.

The red wines of Burgundy: *Beaujolais* is a wine area within the Burgundy wine region. Beaujolais is a pleasant, dry red wine, meant to be drunk while young (one to four years old). It is bright crimson in color, fruity, light- to medium-bodied. There are many other richer, fuller-bodied red Burgundy wines, such as *Pommard* and *Chambertin* which will always be more costly.

The white wines of Burgundy: The three most famous of the white Burgundies are *Pouilly-Fuissé*, a pale, greenish-gold white wine with flowery bouquet, which is extremely dry, light-bodied; *Chablis*, which is always dry and delicate; and *Montrachet* which may be dry to medium dry, a full-bodied wine, considered by many the greatest of the white Burgundies.

The red wines of Bordeaux: In general, the Bordeaux reds are a little more tart, a little more brisk than the red Burgundies. (These are the red wines the English call "clarets.") The most popular are *Mèdoc*, *Margaux*, *St. Julien*, and *St. Emilion*. They are dry, have deep color, rich bouquet, full body. Two very famous, very highly prized red Bordeaux wines are *Chateau Lafite-Rothschild* and *Chateau Haut-Brion*. Their prices are often astronomic, particularly if the wines are of outstanding vintage years.

The white wines of Bordeaux: The best known *dry* white bordeaux is *Graves*, which is usually fairly dry, pale in color, invigorating. It's in the Bordeaux region that *Sauternes* and *Haut Sauternes* are produced; Sauternes are always sweet, Haut Sauternes is the sweeter of the two. (French Sauternes is spelled with an s, even in the singular. It is never a dry wine. But American and California Sauterne, which drops the s, is usually dry.)

Wines of the Loire and Rhône Valleys: Both of these regions produce rosé wines. *Anjou rosé* from the Loire range from medium dry to semisweet. They are light and fruity, pleasant—usually inexpensive. The best known rosé of the Rhône valley is *Tavel*, which is very dry. All rosés should be drunk while young. The most famous red wine of the Rhône valley is *Chateauneuf-du-Pape*, which at its best is heady, rich, full-bodied, a robust wine with fine bouquet.

GERMAN WINES

Mostly white wines are exported from Germany, and they are some of the greatest white wines in the world.

The two best known regions are the Rhine and the Moselle—both named for the rivers which wind through the vineyard areas. The Moselle River is a tributary of the Rhine, but the wines of the Moselle are much lighter, drier, more tingling than those of the Rhine. Both Rhine and Moselle wines are produced from Riesling grapes, and many are also produced from Sylvaner grapes.

Each label on a German wine bottle gives the entire history of the wine: its region, the name of the vineyard, its type (when it was harvested), and the year of its vintage. *Liebfraumilch* is the best known Rhine wine name. Many wines from the Rhine now bear this label and there will be wide variations in price for them. Simply bear in mind that you will get what you pay for. Liebfraumilch will often be identified by a trade name as well. Well known examples are: *Liebfraumilch "Blue Nun Label," Liebfraumilch "Hanns Christof Wein," Liebfraumilch "Crown of Crowns," Liebfraumilch "Glockenspiel," Liebfraumilch "Madonna."*

OTHER IMPORTANT WINES

The best known of the Italian wines are the red Chiantis, most of which are put up in charming, straw-covered round bottles. When well aged, Chianti is tart, robust, with good bouquet. The younger Chiantis are very dry, much lighter in body, may be harsh.

The next most popular wines are Bardolino and Valpolicella, which come to us from poetic Verona. These wines are light-bodied, soft, well rounded. The Bardolinos, from grapes grown along the eastern shores of Lake Garda, tend to greater aroma, whereas the Valpolicellas have greater finesse.

The most famous sparkling wines of Italy are called Asti Spumante and Lachryma Christi. The former takes its name from the town of Asti in Piedmont. It is a delicious, fragrant muscat-flavored wine on the rich, sweet side. Lachryma Christi, also produced in Piedmont, is a more delicately flavored wine, medium dry.

Spain's best table wines come from the Rioja (pronounced Ree-o-ha) region which produces dry red, white, and rosé wines of very pleasant quality. (The famous Spanish sherries are produced in Jerez de la Frontera in southern Spain.)

Portugal's most delightful tables wines are the "green wines," which is another name for young—tart, light, they may be either red or white wines. Portugal also produces a number of rosés, some of which are very dry, others are moderately dry to semisweet.

CHAMPAGNE AND OTHER SPARKLING WINES

Technically, the only sparkling wine which can be called *champagne* is that produced in the Champagne district of France. But every other wine-producing country in the world has one or more wines some of which locally are called champagnes. They are not only white, but rosé ("pink champagne") and red, popularly known as Sparkling Burgundy.

Champagne is a wonderful wine for special occasions. The secret of its bubbles is natural carbonization: the wine is kept bottled during its second fermentation and the carbonic acid gas produced becomes a component part of the wine. This is why when a champagne cork is pulled, the cork comes out with a resounding pop and foam whooshes up, sometimes spilling over in a cascade. Champagne should be drunk immediately after the cork is pulled (once its bubbles have evaporated, it becomes flat).

Terminology classifying champagnes can be confusing. *Brut* or *Nature* mean very dry; *Extra Dry* or *Extra Sec* mean dry; *Dry* or *Sec* mean medium sweet.

Pink champagnes are usually crisply dry; sparkling burgundies are usually sweet.

How Cool is Chilled?

Chilled wine should have a temperature of about 45 to 50° F. It should not be ice-cold. Only white wines and rosé wines are chilled. Red wines are always (or nearly always) served at cool room temperature. In Europe, room temperature may be no more than 60 to 65° F., and for this reason, some wine experts hold that certain of the lighter red wines, too, can be briefly chilled.

To chill white or rosé wine, place the bottle in the refrigerator for 40 to 45 minutes before serving. Or chill it in a wine cooler: place the bottle (with cork or cap removed) in the cooler first, then surround with ice cubes and place a cloth napkin over the ice. Let the wine chill in the ice about half an hour. It

is not necessary to use the napkin when serving the wine; you may simply give the bottle a slight twist after pouring each glass so it will not drip. Or you may use a wine basket (holder) to serve with. Either way, you may leave the wine on the table (or in the cooler) between servings.

The Rituals of Wine Drinking

During the centuries, many rituals have developed connected with wine drinking, and these little ceremonies make the drinking of wine much more fun.

There is first of all the way it is poured and served. In fine restaurants, the waiter will always pour a very small bit of wine in the host's glass for him to taste and approve. When the host nods his head after the contemplative sip, indicating he finds the wine acceptable, the waiter will then fill the other glasses, and if he has been properly trained as a *sommelier* (wine steward), he will pour only enough wine in each glass to fill it one-third to one-half full.

With the first drink of wine, glasses are clicked to the accompaniment of a favorite toast—*à votre santé, bon appétit, skoal,* cheers, or whatever. (But *never* "bottoms up"!) Then it is proper to sniff the wine appreciatively for its bouquet, and finally to take a small sip. If it is a vintage wine, the first sip should be rolled around in the mouth so that its flavor may be fully appreciated. Only after this is it drunk like any other beverage.

Wineglasses

The reason for serving wine in stemmed glasses is that one should hold the glass by the stem, not cup it around the bowl of the glass. This is particularly true of white wine, which must not be warmed by the touch of the hands. Occasionally a fine vintage red wine is purposely held by the bowl of the glass rather than the stem to induce the volatile ethers of the bouquet—as a brandy glass is warmed by the hands.

The all-purpose, tulip-shaped wineglass may be used for all table wines. It ranges in size from 6 to 8 or 9 ounces. After you've learned to enjoy wines you may want to have special glasses for the different types, but this is not really necessary. Champagne is the only exception—its elegance deserves a special glass. It should be served in large-bowled or tulip-shaped champagne glasses so its sparkle and bubbles may be fully appreciated.

A serving of wine should be about four ounces, and a wine glass should never be more than half filled. The bouquet of the wine is just as important as the taste, and the tall sides of the glass direct that lovely aroma to the nostrils.

How to Buy and Store Wine

Once a bottle or jug of table wine has been opened and air is permitted to touch the wine, it begins to deteriorate. Few table wines will keep in drinkable condition more than two or three days after they have been opened —even if tightly corked again and stored in the refrigerator, their first fine zest begins to fade.

If you buy table wine in gallon containers, decant it into smaller bottles immediately after opening. Use within ten days to two weeks. To decant the wine, pour it into smaller bottles (quart, fifth, or pint size), cork tightly, and keep in a cool (but not cold) place. The same can be done with half gallons of wine.

The fortified wines, sherry, port, Madeira, muscatel, and Marsala, are not so fragile. Because of the brandy which has been added to them, they will keep in the bottle even after uncorking (or uncapping) for weeks or months without loss of flavor. These may be purchased by the gallon, though for ease in serving it is wise to decant them into smaller bottles; or they may be served from a carafe.

If you serve wine frequently, and like to have it on hand for cooking (see section which follows), it is sometimes a good idea to buy a type and brand you particularly like by the case. You can save on the price, but more important, the wine is on hand when you need it.

The best place to store wine (whether apéritif, table, or dessert types) is in a cool, dry place. This may be a cellar, or a closet which is not heated. Wine racks for holding the fifth- or quart-size bottles on their sides are inexpensive and make it possible to store an entire case on an ordinary closet shelf.

Or a wine rack is attractive as part of a room's decoration—display it on a shelf or wall. The reason for placing the bottle on its side is that the wine keeps the cork moist, and this in turn makes the cork swell to exclude all air.

Domestic wine bottles which have metal caps instead of corks will keep just as well in an upright position. However, when gallon-size bottles are decanted, it is better to stop up the bottle with a cork rather than a metal cap, for without a capping machine, the cap cannot be fastened on tightly enough to keep all air out.

Cooking With Wine

There are many cooks who shy away from cooking with wine. They are afraid of it or they think it is difficult and should remain in the province of a gourmet cook who specializes only in haute cuisine. First of all, cooking with wine is simple. It should be considered as an ingredient in the same way you think of onion, parsley, or your favorite seasonings.

Wine takes on a special personality as an ingredient. While the alcohol evaporates in the cooking, wine leaves a special touch that helps to complement the natural flavors inherent in most foods.

There is hardly a dish on any menu, from appetizers to desserts, that cannot be sparked to perfection with the careful use of wine. Just the right amount is important.

Wine should never overpower the taste of the food itself. Wine adds a zest to mild foods, such as veal or fish. When used to marinate meats, wine tenderizes and brings out flavor. When used to baste a roast, it makes a well-flavored sauce or gravy.

Generally speaking, you use a red table or dinner wine for red meats, game, and sharp cheese; the lighter-bodied red wines for ham, pork, lobster, roast duckling, variety meats, Italian food, and hearty veal or lamb dishes. Use a white table or dinner wine for mild cheeses and light meats such as veal and lamb, chicken, turkey, and for fish, oysters, clams, crab, lobster. Sherry and Madeira are excellent to flavor soups and sauces; slightly sweeter white wines enhance desserts and fruit salads.

Once you have mastered the art of cooking with wine with proven recipes you'll want to experiment on your own. It is not always necessary, for example, to use only red wines in dishes made with red meats and game and white wines in dishes made with light meat, seafoods, or poultry. Many good fish recipes use red wines (trout, for example) and, conversely, some white wines give just the right flavor to dishes made with red meats (beef à la mode). A good yardstick is to combine flavors that go well together. Just use your imagination and ingenuity. Become adventurous and experiment.

There are many recipes using wine throughout this book, and here are some tips to show other ways of using it in various dishes. The amounts listed are minimum—add more if you like. For red table wines use a Burgundy or claret. For white wines use sauterne, Rhine wine, or Chablis.

SOUPS

· *Cream soups:* Add 1 teaspoon sherry or dry white wine to each serving.
· *Meat and vegetable soups:* Add 1 teaspoon sherry or dry red wine to each serving.

SAUCES

· *Cream sauce and variations:* Add 1 tablespoon sherry or dry white wine for each cup of sauce.
· *Brown sauce and variations:* Add 1 tablespoon sherry or dry red wine per cup of sauce.
· *Tomato sauce:* Add 1 tablespoon sherry or dry red wine per cup of sauce.
· *Cheese sauce:* Add 1 tablespoon sherry or dry white wine for each cup of sauce.
· *Dessert sauces:* Add 1 tablespoon port or muscatel for each cup of sauce.
· *Spaghetti Sauce:* Add 1 cup dry red wine while sauce simmers.

MEATS

· *Pot roasts:* For beef, add ¼ cup red wine for each pound of meat; for veal and lamb, ¼ cup dry white wine per pound of meat.
· *Stews:* Add ¼ cup dry red wine per pound of meat to beef stews; ¼ cup dry white wine per pound of meat to veal or lamb stew.
· *Hamburgers:* Pour ¼ cup dry red wine for each pound of meat over hamburgers as they brown.

· *Gravies for roasts:* Add 2 tablespoons sherry, dry red, or dry white wine per cup of gravy.
· *Baked ham:* Baste a whole ham with 2 cups port or muscatel.
· *Boiled tongue:* Add ½ cup dry red wine per pound of meat.
· *Braised variety meats:* For kidneys, use ¼ cup sherry or dry red wine for each pound of meat; for liver use ¼ cup dry red or white wine for each pound of meat.

FISH

· *Broiled, baked, or poached:* Use ½ cup dry white wine for each pound.

POULTRY AND GAME

· *Chicken:* Baste with ¼ cup dry white or red wine per pound when broiling or sautéing. Add ¼ cup dry white wine per pound of chicken to fricassee.
· *Duck:* Baste wild or domesticated duck with dry red wine, allowing ¼ cup per pound of meat.
· *Venison:* For roast, pot roast, or stew, use ¼ cup dry red wine per pound of meat.
· *Pheasant:* Use ¼ cup sherry, dry red, or dry white wine per pound of meat when roasting or sautéing.
· *Gravy:* Add 2 tablespoons sherry, dry red, or dry white wine to each cup of turkey or chicken gravy.

FRUITS

· *Cups and compotes:* Add 1 tablespoon port, muscatel, sherry, rosé, dry red or white wine to each serving.
· *Strawberries:* Pour 2 tablespoons port or rosé over each serving of sugared strawberries.

CHEESE

· *Wine-Cheese Spread.* Blend dry sherry or port into a softened process cheese spread—3 tablespoons wine to a 6-ounce jar.

DESSERTS

· *Gelatin desserts:* Substitute dry red or white wine for half the water when making the gelatin.

Index

Enrich, defined, 346
Enriched flour, defined, 12
Entertaining. *See* Parties
Entrée, defined, 17
Escalopes de veau Provençal, 158
Escargots, 49
Escarole, 321-22
Espresso, 62
  royale, 62
Evaporated milk, defined, 10
Exotic Oriental lamb, 165

Fan-tan rolls, 112
Fan-tan shrimp with bacon, 53
Farina
  defined, 12
  gnocchi Parmesan, 282
Fats and oils. *See also* Shortening;
    specific fats
  dictionary of, 11
  in diet, 22
  polyunsaturated, 23
Favorite
  chocolate frosting, 453
  frankfurters, 186
  layer cake, 434
Feathered rice, 274
Fennel, 292
  buying, 292
  cooking, 292
  preparing, 292
  seed, 512
Feta cheese, defined, 268
Fettucini
  al burro Alfredo, 276-77
  Romano, 276
Fiesta bread, outdoors, 508
Fig(s), 312
  buying, 312
  fruit confection with, 482-83
  glazed fruit towers with, 358
  orange pudding, 376
  preparing, 312
  storing, 312
Filé powder, 513
Filet mignon. *See* Beef
Filets de poisson à la Normande,
    234
Filtered coffee, 61
"Find the letter" game, 41
Finnan haddie, 229
Finocchio (fennel), 292
  buying, 292
  cooking, 292
  preparing, 292
  seed, 512
Fish (and shellfish; seafood), 228-
    50. *See also specific kinds*
  appetizers, 47-48, 52-55
  in balanced diet, 21
  barbecued, 506
  bouillabaisse, 130
    defined, 17
  buying fresh, 229-20
  canned, 235-39
  chowder, New England, 129
  cioppino, 131
  cooking, 230-31
  drawn, defined, 229
  dressed, pan-dressed
    defined, 229
    how much to buy, 230
  filets
    defined, 230
    how much to buy, 230

Fish, filets *(Cont.)*
    Normandy style, 234
    oven-fried, 233
  freezing, 487
  fresh, 229-30
  frozen, 230
  gumbo, 132
    Creole, 131
  kinds of, 228-29
  Normandy style filets, 234
  oven-fried filets, 233
  paella, 206
  pie, 232
  puffs, Norwegian, 53
  salads, 334-36. *See also specific
      kinds*
    boutique, 334
    emerald, 334
  soufflé, 264
  steaks
    defined, 229
    how much to buy, 230
  sticks
    defined, 230
    how much to buy, 230
  storing
    fresh, 230
    frozen, 230, 487
  stuffings for, 254. *See also*
      Stuffings
  tempura, 58
  whole
    defined, 229
    how much to buy, 230
  wine cookery, 524
Fish-blow contest, 41
Fish house punch, 69
Fisherman's pie, 232
Flake, defined, 16
Flambé, defined, 18
Flame tokay grapes, 313
Floating island, 368
Flounder, 229
  filets Jacqueline, 234
  filets, Normandy style, 234
  pie, fisherman's, 232
  tempura, 58
Flour
  for breads, 102
  defined, 16
  dictionary of, 11-12
  measuring, 2
Flower garden mints, 480
Fluffy
  orange frosting, 454
  seven-minute frosting, 454
  sherried eggnog, 70
  spice cake, 438
Foamy sauce, 400
Foil. *See also specific foods
    wrapped in*
  freezing uses, 485
  for outdoor cooking, 500
Fold, defined, 16
Fold over, defined, 16
Folding Christmas stars, 474
Folic acid, 22
Fondant, defined, 18
Fondue
  Bourguignonne, defined, 18
  defined, 18
  easy cheese, 270
  ham and cheese, 270-71
  Swiss, 271
Fontina cheese, defined, 268

Foo Yung gravy, 265
Fork, carving, 194
Fortified milk, defined, 9
Franconia potatoes, 298
Frankfurters (hot dogs), 184-88
  barbecued
    grilled—temperature chart,
        502
    quick, 187
  and beans, 186
  Broadway, 186
  broiled, 184
  buying, 184
  con carne, 185
  cheese-stuffed, 86
  on chips, Creole, 187
  defined, 183
  favorite, 186
  glazed tangy, 186
  go-withs, 187
  grilled, 184
    temperature chart for outdoor,
        502
  heating, 184
  hoagie, 185
  and onions, 186
  pan- or griddle-broiled, 184
  pickled, 42
  and pineapple Oriental, 51
  pizza, 185
  pushcart, 186
  red and green, 186
  Scandinavian, 186
  simmered, 184
  stew, ranch-style, 188
  storing, 185
  sweet-sour, 185, 187
  teen club, 185
  Texas, 187
  woodsy, 186
  zippy, 185
Franz pancakes, 386
Frappés
  cranberry fruit, 394
  pineapple mint, 393
  strawberry, 393
  tropical, 394
Freezing, 484-92. *See also specific
      foods*
  basic rules, 484-85
  containers for, 485
  cooked foods, 491-92
  equipment, packaging materials,
      485
  kinds of freezers, 484
  sealing, labeling equipment, 485
  storage of commercially frozen
      foods, 485
  of various foods, 486-92
French (style)
  bread, 107
  chocolate, 66
  dressing, 342
    creamy, 343
    golden, 343
    tomato, 343
  hamburgers, 152
  -fried potatoes, 297
  frying (deep frying), 14,
      19
  ice cream, defined, 10
  market doughnuts, 122
  omelet, 258-61
    sweet, 261
  onion soup, 127

Mayonnaise, 344
dressing, chili, 49
Mazarins, 473
Meals, planning, 21-31
menus, 24-28
for overweight, 24, 27, 28-30
proteins, carbohydrates, fats
in, 22
special diets, 23
underweight and, 630-31
vitamins, minerals in, 22-23
Measuring, 2-3
Meatballs
appetizer, 50-51
Burgundy, 50-51
hot pot with, 154
Parisian, 51
spaghetti and, 277
for a crowd, 277
skillet, savory, 154
Swedish, 154
Meat loaf
Burgundy, 153
cheese-beef, 153
ham, glazed, 178
orange-, 178
home-style, 153
lamb
curried, 170
herb, 170
mixtures, defined, 152
supper, apple-glazed, 192
Meat sandwiches
basic, 77
for a crowd, 87
Meat sauce for pasta, 280-81
mushroom, 278
Meats, 135-98. *See also* Beef; *etc.*
in balanced diet, 21
braising, 136
broiling, 136
buying, 135
canned, 192-93
carving, 194-98
cooking methods, 136
dry heat, 136
moist heat, 136
freezing; frozen, 136-38, 486
cooked, 491-92
grilling, time-temperature chart
for, 502
luncheon. *See* Luncheon meats
outdoor cookery, 500-3
panbroiling, 136
panfrying, 136
roasting, 136
spit roasting, 503
storage time chart, 137
storing, handling, 136
tenderizers for, 138
variety, 189-91. *See also specific
meats*
wine in braised, 524
wine cookery, 524
Mediterranean salad, 332
Medium-gratin rice, 12, 272
Médoc wines, 521
Melba sauce, 401. *See also*
Peach(es): Melba
Melon(s), 314. *See also specific
kinds of melons*
Alaska
cantaloupe, 397
fruited, 396
appetizers, 45

Melon(s) *(Cont.)*
freezing, 489
fruit-filled watermelon, 314
fruits in Grand Marnier, 315
kinds of, 314
salads
cooler, 337
grape aspic, 337
serving, 314
storing, 314
en surprise, 357
Melt, defined, 16
Menus, 24-28
breakfast, 24-25
brunch party, 37
buffet, 36-37
children's party, 41ff
coffee party, 37-38
cookout, 37
dinner, 24, 26-27
party, 33, 34ff
luncheon, 25
party, 37
supper, 25, 27-28
tea party, 37-38
Meringue(s), 381-83, 462. *See also*
Baked Alaska
bars
apricot, 460
walnut, 460
cake, strawberry, 383
cherry, 462
defined, 18
jewels, 462
Melba nut, 382
mushrooms, 462-63
nut nests, 382
orange blossoms with, 394
pancakes, Hungarian, 385
peppermint, 462
pies
lemon, 421
lemon angel, 382
lime, 421
lime angel, 382
pineapple angel, 382-83
to prevent weeping, 402
-topped cream, 402
pistachio basket, 381
rice, apricot, 367
shells, 381
swan ice cream boats, 382
tarts, lime angel, 382
torte, schaum, 382
Merry cheese balls, 57
Mettwurst, defined, 183
Mexican (style)
chocolate chiffon cake, 446
hamburger, 152
Milk
in balanced diet, 21
dictionary of, 9-10
drinks, 73-74. *See also* Ice cream:
drinks; Overweight: beverages and
banana shake, 73
chocolate. *See* Chocolate:
beverages
coffee eggnog, 73
cranberry cow, 74
eggnog, 73
mocha frosted, 74
New Yorker special, 73
orange buttermilk, 74
raspberry shake, 73

Milk, drinks *(Cont.)*
strawberry eggnog, 74
strawberry shake, 74
tutti-frutti float, 73
Milk chocolate, defined, 7
Milk sherbet, lemon, 393
Mince (kind of chopping), defined,
16
Mince (meat) pie, 413
apple, glazed, 413
cranberry, 413
Minerals, 23
Mint(ed), 514. *See also* Peppermint
candies, flower garden, 480
chocolate sauce, quick, 399
sundae, 401
cooler, pineapple, 68
low-calorie, 75
cream rice, chocolate, 366-67
custard, stewed pears with, 356
frappé, pineapple, 393
fruit bowl, 316
stuffing, bass with, 231
Mix-chill-and-serve foods, 6
Mix-and-serve foods, 6
Mixed pickling spice, 514
Mocha
Bavarian cream, 365
coffee, 63
cream dessert, 398
cream puffs, 380-81
crunch angel pie, 424
frosted (beverage), 74
sauce, marshmallow, 401
torte, quick, 380
Mock Hollandaise sauce, 350
Molasses
cookies, soft, 460-61
defined, 13
gems (cupcakes), 442
popcorn balls, 482
Monosodium glutamate, 18, 514
Montrachet wine, 521
Moo goo gai pan, 211
Mornay sauce, 348
Mortadella, defined, 184
Moselle wines, 521
Mousse
cherry, parfait, 362
cucumber and crab, 340
defined, 18
salmon, 341
strawberry, frozen, 392
tomato-avocado, 338
Mousseline sauce, 349
Mozzarella cheese, defined, 268
Muffins, 90
apricot-date, 97
basic, 90
blueberry, 90
corn, 90
crunchy-topped, 90
jam, 90
jelly, 90
Mulled cider, 68
Multiplying recipes, 5
Münster cheese, defined, 268
Murghi curry, 203
Mushroom(s), 294
buying, 294
creamed, 294
and peppers Italiano, 294
pie, cheese, 270
pizza, 82
and potatoes, country-style, 299

559

To split cake layer: Mark all around layer, halfway between top and bottom, with wooden picks. Cut through, using picks as guide or pull heavy sewing thread back and forth through layer in a gentle sawing motion.

A sprinkling of parsley is often the perfect garnish, but to look its best the parsley must be dry. Chop it with a very sharp French knife, then squeeze it in a double thickness of paper towels to extract all the moisture and leave the parsley dry and nicely fluffed.

Use leftover pastry to make appetizer nibblers. Press the bits together and roll out ⅛-inch thick. Sprinkle with cinnamon and sugar or grated cheese; cut with pastry wheel, cookie cutter, or knife into strips and bake.